# Concise History of Western Music

Third Edition

# Concise History of Western Music

### Third Edition

Based on J. Peter Burkholder, Donald J. Grout, and Claude V. Palisca,
*A History of Western Music*, Seventh Edition

BARBARA RUSSANO HANNING

The City College of New York
The City University of New York

W. W. NORTON & COMPANY · NEW YORK · LONDON

W. W. Norton & Company has been independent since its founding in 1923, when William Warder Norton and Margaret D. Herter Norton first published lectures delivered at the People's Institute, the adult education division of New York City's Cooper Union. The Nortons soon expanded their program beyond the Institute, publishing books by celebrated academics from America and abroad. By mid-century, the two major pillars of Norton's publishing program—trade books and college texts—were firmly established. In the 1950s, the Norton family transferred control of the company to its employees, and today—with a staff of 400 and a comparable number of trade, college, and professional titles published each year—W. W. Norton & Company stands as the largest and oldest publishing house owned wholly by its employees.

Editor: Maribeth Payne
Manuscript Editor: Carol Flechner
Copy Editors: Carol Flechner, Alice Vigliani, and Michael Ochs
Project Editor: Allison Courtney Fitch
Managing Editor–College Books: Marian Johnson
Electronic Media Editor: Steve Hoge
Photograph Editors: Neil Ryder Hoos, Kelly Mitchell
Assistant Editor: Allison Courtney Fitch
Editorial Assistant: Graham Norwood
Designer: Chris Welch
Senior Production Manager: JoAnn Simony
Music Typesetter: David Budmen
Page Layout: Alice Bennett
Indexer: Marilyn Bliss
Composition by GGS Information Services, Inc.
Manufacturing by RR Donnelley, Willard, Ohio

ISBN-10: 0-393-92803-9
ISBN-13: 978-0-393-92803-7

W. W. Norton & Company, Inc., 500 Fifth Avenue, New York, N.Y. 10110
www.wwnorton.com

W. W. Norton & Company, Ltd., Castle House, 75/76 Wells Street, London W1T 3QT

3 4 5 6 7 8 9 0

# CONTENTS

*Maps*   ix

*Guide to Recordings*   xi

*Preface to the Third Edition*   xix


PART ONE

## The Ancient and Medieval Worlds

Introduction   3

1. **Music in Ancient Greece and Early Christian Rome**   18

   *Prelude*   18   •   *Music in Ancient Greek Life and Thought*   19   •   *Roman Music,*
   *200 B.C.E.–500 C.E.*   22   •   *The Early Christian Church: Musical Thought*   23   •
   *The Early Christian Church: Musical Practice*   25   •   *Postlude*   28

2. **Chant and Secular Song in the Middle Ages**   30

   *Prelude*   30   •   *Western Christian Chant and Liturgy*   31   •   *Genres and Forms of*
   *Chant*   35   •   *Medieval Music Theory and Practice*   44   •   *Medieval Song*   46   •
   *Postlude*   53

3. **Polyphony through the Thirteenth Century**   54

   *Prelude*   54   •   *Early Organum*   56   •   *Notre Dame Polyphony*   58   •   *The*
   *Motet*   64   •   *The Polyphonic Conductus*   67   •   *English Polyphony*   69   •
   *Postlude*   70

4. **French and Italian Music in the Fourteenth Century**   71

   *Prelude*   71   •   *The Ars nova in France*   72   •   *Italian Trecento Music*   80   •   *The*
   *Ars subtilior*   84   •   *Postlude*   85

PART TWO

The Age of the Renaissance

Introduction    89

5. England, France, and Burgundy in the Fifteenth Century: The Beginnings of an International Style    98

*Prelude*    98    ·    *English Music and Its Influence*    100    ·    *Music in Burgundian Lands*    102    ·    *Postlude*    110

6. Music of the Low Countries    112

*Prelude*    112    ·    *The Musical Culture of the Renaissance*    114    ·    *Northern Composers: The Generation after Du Fay*    117    ·    *The Next Generation: Josquin and His Contemporaries*    121    ·    *Postlude*    126

7. Secular Song and the Rise of National Styles in the Sixteenth Century    128

*Prelude*    128    ·    *The Rise of National Styles: Italy*    129    ·    *The Italian Madrigal*    130    ·    *The Rise of National Styles: Secular Song outside Italy*    137    ·    *The Rise of Instrumental Music*    141    ·    *Postlude*    144

8. Sacred Music in the Era of the Reformation    146

*Prelude*    146    ·    *The Music of the Reformation in Germany*    147    ·    *Reformation Church Music outside Germany*    149    ·    *The Counter-Reformation*    151    ·    *Postlude*    161

PART THREE

The Seventeenth Century

Introduction    163

9. Vocal Music of the Early Baroque    177

*Prelude*    177    ·    *General Characteristics of Baroque Music*    178    ·    *Early Opera*    183    ·    *Vocal Chamber Music*    194    ·    *Catholic Sacred Music*    199    ·    *Lutheran Church Music*    202    ·    *Postlude*    205

10. Instrumental Music Comes of Age    206

*Prelude*    206    ·    *Types of Instrumental Music*    207    ·    *Dance Music*    207    ·    *Variations*    210    ·    *Abstract Instrumental Works*    214    ·    *Postlude*    220

11. Opera and Vocal Music in the Late Seventeenth Century    222

*Prelude*    222    ·    *Italy*    222    ·    *France*    230    ·    *England*    235    ·    *Germany*    240    ·    *Postlude*    242

12. Instrumental Music in the Late Seventeenth Century    244

*Prelude*    244    ·    *Music for Organ*    245    ·    *Music for Harpsichord*    248    ·    *Ensemble Music*    253    ·    *Postlude*    265

PART FOUR

The Eighteenth Century

Introduction   267

13. Music in the Early Eighteenth Century   279

    *Prelude   279   •   Italy: Antonio Vivaldi   279   •   France: Couperin and
    Rameau   285   •   Germany: Johann Sebastian Bach   290   •   England: George Frideric
    Handel   305   •   Postlude   313*

14. The Early Classical Period: Opera and Instrumental Music in the Early and Mid-
    Eighteenth Century   315

    *Prelude   315   •   General Characteristics of the New Style   316   •   Opera buffa   319   •
    Opera seria   322   •   Opera Reform   325   •   Instrumental Music: Sonata, Symphony,
    and Concerto   329   •   The Empfindsamer Style   333   •   Postlude   338*

15. The Late Eighteenth Century: Haydn and Mozart   339

    *Prelude   339   •   (Franz) Joseph Haydn (1732–1809)   341   •   Haydn's Instrumental
    Music   342   •   Haydn's Vocal Works   351   •   Wolfgang Amadeus Mozart
    (1756–1791)   355   •   Mozart's Salzburg Years   355   •   Mozart's Vienna Years   357   •
    Postlude   372*

16. Ludwig van Beethoven (1770–1827)   374

    *Prelude   374   •   First Period   375   •   Second Period   379   •   Third
    Period   388   •   Postlude   395*

PART FIVE

The Nineteenth Century: The Age of Romanticism

Introduction   397

17. The Early Romantics   410

    *Prelude   410   •   Franz Schubert (1797–1828)   412   •   Hector Berlioz
    (1803–1869)   420   •   Felix Mendelssohn (1809–1847)   424   •   Robert Schumann
    (1810–1856)   429   •   Fryderyk Chopin (1810–1849)   432   •   Postlude   435*

18. The Later Romantics   438

    *Prelude   438   •   Franz Liszt (1811–1886)   439   •   Clara Schumann
    (1819–1896)   444   •   Johannes Brahms (1833–1897)   447   •   Piotr Il'yich Tchaikovsky
    (1840–1893)   453   •   Antonín Dvořák (1841–1904)   457   •   Postlude   459*

19. Opera and Music Drama in the Nineteenth Century   462

    *Prelude   462   •   French Grand (and Not So Grand) Opera   464   •   Italian
    Opera   469   •   German Romantic Opera   480   •   Church Music   489   •
    Postlude   492*

20. **The Final Bloom of Romanticism: European Music at the End of the Nineteenth Century**    493

   *Prelude*    493    ·    *The Austro-German Tradition*    494    ·    *National Trends*    504    ·
   *New Currents in France and Italy*    513    ·    *Postlude: The Beethoven Legacy*    518


PART SIX

The Twentieth Century and Today


Introduction    521

21. **The European Mainstream in the Early Twentieth Century**    536

   *Prelude*    536    ·    *The First Modern Generation*    536    ·    *Tonal and Post-Tonal Music*    546    ·    *Postlude*    559

22. **Music, Politics, and the People in the European Twentieth Century**    561

   *Prelude*    561    ·    *The Avant-Garde*    562    ·    *France*    564    ·    *Igor Stravinsky*    566    ·    *Béla Bartók*    577    ·    *Germany*    583    ·    *The Soviet Union*    587    ·    *Postlude*    592

23. **Music in America**    594

   *Prelude*    594    ·    *A Backward Glance: Music in the North American Colonies*    594    ·
   *Diverging Trends in Nineteenth- and Early Twentieth-Century America*    596    ·    *The Classical Tradition through Mid-Century*    605    ·    *Vernacular Styles*    613    ·
   *Postlude*    628

24. **The Changing World of Music since 1945**    630

   *Prelude*    630    ·    *Heirs to the Classical Tradition*    630    ·    *Serial and Nonserial Complexity*    636    ·    *New Sounds and Textures*    638    ·    *The Avant-Garde*    646    ·
   *The New Accessibility and Other Trends*    658    ·    *Postlude*    666

   *Further Reading*    A1
   *Glossary*    A7
   *Credits*    A27
   *Index*    A31

# MAPS

*Figure I.1*    The ancient Near East.    **4**

*Figure I.4*    The Roman Empire at the death of Augustus in 14 C.E.    **7**

*Figure I.6*    Europe in the mid-fourteenth century.    **9**

*Figure 2.1*    The diffusion of Christianity.    **31**

*Figure 2.7*    The Holy Roman Empire under Charlemagne around 800.    **36**

*Figure 2.16*    The linguistic boundary between Occitan (*langue d'oc*) in the south of France and Medieval French (*langue d'óïl*) in the north.    **48**

*Figure II.5*    Major centers for training musicians in the Renaissance.    **96**

*Figure 5.1*    The growth of Burgundian possessions, 1363–1477.    **99**

*Figure 6.1*    Western Europe, about 1500.    **113**

*Figure III.1*    Europe, about 1610.    **165**

*Figure 12.9*    Italy around 1650, showing the main centers for music and violin making.    **253**

*Figure 13.8*    Cities that figured in J. S. Bach's career.    **292**

*Figure 15.9*    Cities important in Mozart's life and career.    **356**

*Figure 15.13*  Vienna.    **360**

*Figure V.1*    Europe, 1815–1848.    **398**

*Figure 19.1*    European opera houses in the nineteenth century.    **463**

*Figure VI.1*    Europe during the Cold War (1945–1991).    **523**

*Figure 22.12*  Europe, 1900–1950.    **579**

# GUIDE TO RECORDINGS

| NAWM NO. | COMPOSER AND TITLE | TEXT PAGE | 12-CD SET (Vols. 1 & 2) | 6-CD SET (Concise) |
|---|---|---|---|---|
| **VOLUME 1** | | | | |
| 1 | *Epitaph of Seikilos* | 19 | 1/1 | 1/1 |
| 2 | Euripides: *Orestes* | 133 | 1/2 | — |
| 3 | Mass for Christmas Day, Gregorian chant Mass | 33 | | | |
| | a) Introit: *Puer natus est nobis* | 41 | 1/4 | — |
| | b) Kyrie | 42 | 1/8 | 1/2 |
| | c) Gloria | — | 1/12 | — |
| | d) Gradual: *Viderunt omnes* | 41/59 | 1/13 | — |
| | e) Alleluia: *Dies sanctificatus* | 41 | 1/15 | — |
| | f) Credo | — | 1/18 | — |
| | g) Offertory: *Tui sunt coeli* | 41 | 1/19 | — |
| | h) Sanctus | — | 1/20 | — |
| | i) Agnus Dei | — | 1/21 | 1/6 |
| | j) Communion: *Viderunt omnes* | 41 | 1/22 | — |
| | k) Ite, missa est | — | 1/23 | — |
| 4 | Chants from Vespers for Christmas Day | | | | |
| | a) First antiphon, *Tecum principium* | 39 | 1/24 | 1/7 |
| | b) Hymn, *Christe Redemptor omnium* | 38 | 1/28 | — |
| 5 | Ascribed to Wipo of Burgundy: *Victimae paschali laudes* | 43 | 1/29 | 1/11 |
| 6 | *Quem queritis in presepe* | 43 | 1/30 | — |
| 7 | Hildegard of Bingen: *In principio omnes* | 44 | 1/33 | 1/12 |
| 8 | Bernart de Ventadorn: *Can vei la lauzeta mover* | 49 | 1/36 | 1/15 |
| 9 | Comtessa de Dia: *A chantar* | 49 | 1/37 | — |
| 10 | Adam de la Halle: *Robins m'aime* | — | 1/38 | — |
| 11 | Walther von der Vogelweide: *Palästinalied* | 51 | 1/39 | — |
| 12 | Cantiga 159, *Non sofre Santa María* | 52 | 1/40 | 1/16 |

| NAWM NO. | COMPOSER AND TITLE | TEXT PAGE | 12-CD SET (Vols. 1 & 2) | 6-CD SET (Concise) |
|---|---|---|---|---|
| 13 | *La quarte estampie royal*, from *Le manuscrit du roi* | — | 1/41 | — |
| 14 | Organa from *Musica enchiriadis* | | | |
| | a) *Tu patris sempiternus es filius* | 56 | 1/48 | — |
| | b) *Sit gloria domini* | 56 | 1/49 | — |
| | c) *Rex caeli* | 56 | 1/50 | — |
| 15 | *Alleluia Justus ut palma* | 56 | 1/51 | 1/17 |
| 16 | *Jubilemus, exultemus* | 57 | 1/53 | — |
| 17 | Léonin: *Viderunt omnes* | 59 | 1/57 | — |
| 18 | Clausulae on *Dominus*, from *Viderunt omnes* | | | |
| | a) *Dominus*, clausula No. 26 | 62 | 1/66 | — |
| | b) *Dominus*, clausula No. 29 | 62 | 1/67 | — |
| 19 | Pérotin: *Viderunt omnes* | 63 | 2/1 | 1/19 |
| 20 | *Ave virgo virginum* | 67 | 2/13 | — |
| 21 | Motets on tenor *Dominus* | | | |
| | a) *Factum est salutare/Dominus* | 64 | 2/14 | — |
| | b) *Fole acostumance/Dominus* | 65 | 2/15 | 1/23 |
| | c) *Super te/Sed fulsit/Dominus* | 65 | 2/17 | — |
| 22 | Adam de la Halle: *De ma dame vient/Dieus, comment porroie/Omnes* | 66 | 2/18 | — |
| 23 | *Sumer is icumen in* | 70 | 2/21 | 1/25 |
| 24 | Philippe de Vitry: *In arboris/Tuba sacre fidei/Virgo sum* | 73 | 2/22 | — |
| 25 | Guillaume de Machaut: Kyrie, from *Messe de Nostre Dame* | 73 | 2/28 | 1/26 |
| 26 | Guillaume de Machaut: *Rose, liz, printemps, verdure* | 78 | 2/35 | 1/33 |
| 27 | Johannes Ciconia: *Sus une fontayne* | 79 | 2/39 | — |
| 28 | Jacopo da Bologna: *Fenice fù* | 81 | 2/42 | — |
| 29 | Gherardello da Firenze: *Tosto che l'alba* | 82 | 2/44 | — |
| 30 | Francesco Landini: *Non avrà ma' pietà* | 82 | 2/46 | 1/37 |
| 31 | *Alleluia, A nëwe work* | 100 | 2/49 | — |
| 32 | John Dunstable: *Quam pulchra es* | 101 | 2/52 | 1/40 |
| 33 | Binchois: *De plus en plus* | 103 | 2/54 | 1/42 |
| 34 | Guillaume Du Fay: *Resvellies vous* | 104 | 2/56 | — |
| 35 | Guillaume Du Fay: *Conditor alme siderum* | 104 | 2/59 | — |
| 36 | Guillaume Du Fay | | | |
| | a) *Se la face ay pale*, ballade | 104 | 2/61 | 1/44 |
| | b) Gloria, from *Missa Se la face ay pale* | 105 | 2/63 | 1/46 |
| 37 | Jean de Ockeghem: Agnus Dei, from *Missa De plus en plus* | 120 | 2/70 | — |
| 38 | Henricus Isaac: *Innsbruck, ich muss dich lassen* | 122 | 3/1 | — |
| 39 | Josquin des Prez: *Ave Maria . . . virgo serena* | 124 | 3/2 | 1/53 |
| 40 | Josquin des Prez | | | |
| | a) Kyrie, from *Missa Pange lingua* | 126 | 3/9 | 1/60 |
| | b) Credo (excerpt), from *Missa Pange lingua* | 126 | 3/12 | — |

| NAWM NO. | COMPOSER AND TITLE | TEXT PAGE | 12-CD SET (Vols. 1 & 2) | 6-CD SET (Concise) |
|---|---|---|---|---|
| 41 | Josquin des Prez: *Mille regretz* | 122 | 3/15 | — |
| 42 | Martin Luther: *Nun komm, der Heiden Heiland* and *Ein' feste Burg* | | | |
| | a) Attributed to St. Ambrose: *Veni redemptor gentium* | — | 3/16 | — |
| | b) Martin Luther: *Nun komm, der Heiden Heiland* | 300 | 3/17 | — |
| | c) Martin Luther: *Ein' feste Burg* | 147 | 3/18 | — |
| | d) Johann Walter: *Ein' feste Burg* | 148 | 3/19 | — |
| 43 | Loys Bourgeois: Psalm 134, *Or sus, serviteurs du Seigneur* | | | |
| | a) Psalm 134, *Or sus, serviteurs du Seigneur* | 149 | 3/20 | — |
| | b) William Kethe: Psalm 100, *All people that on earth do dwell* | 149 | 3/21 | — |
| 44 | William Byrd: *Sing joyfully unto God* | 152 | 3/22 | 1/63 |
| 45 | Giovanni Pierluigi da Palestrina | | | |
| | a) Credo, from *Pope Marcellus Mass* | 154 | 3/27 | — |
| | b) Agnus Dei I, from *Pope Marcellus Mass* | 154 | 3/35 | 1/68 |
| 46 | Tomás Luis de Victoria: *O magnum mysterium* | | | |
| | a) *O magnum mysterium*, motet | 158 | 3/36 | 1/69 |
| | b) Kyrie, from *Missa O magnum mysterium* | 158 | 3/40 | — |
| 47 | Orlando di Lasso: *Tristis est anima mea* | 159 | 3/43 | 2/1 |
| 48 | Juan del Encina: *Oy comamos y bebamos* | 141 | 3/46 | — |
| 49 | Marco Cara: *Io non compro più speranza* | 129 | 3/47 | — |
| 50 | Jacques Arcadelt: *Il bianco e dolce cigno* | 132 | 3/54 | 2/4 |
| 51 | Cipriano de Rore: *Da le belle contrade d'oriente* | 132 | 3/56 | 2/6 |
| 52 | Luca Marenzio: *Solo e pensoso* | 134 | 3/59 | — |
| 53 | Carlo Gesualdo: *"Io parto" e non più dissi* | 136 | 3/65 | 2/9 |
| 54 | Claudin de Sermisy: *Tant que vivray* | 137 | 3/68 | 2/12 |
| 55 | Claude le Jeune: *Revecy venir du printans* | — | 3/71 | — |
| 56 | Thomas Morley: *My bonny lass she smileth* | 139 | 3/79 | 2/15 |
| 57 | Thomas Weelkes: *As Vesta was* | 139 | 3/82 | 2/18 |
| 58 | John Dowland: *Flow, my tears* | 140 | 4/1 | 2/23 |
| 59 | Pierre Attaingnant (publisher): From *Danseries a 4 parties, second livre* | | | |
| | a) No. 1: Basse danse | 209 | 4/4 | 2/26 |
| | b) No. 36: Branle gay, *Que je chatoulle ta fossette* | 209 | 4/6 | 2/28 |
| 60 | Luis de Narváez: From *Los seys libros del Delphin* | | | |
| | a) *Cancion Mille regres* | — | 4/7 | — |
| | b) *Cuatro diferencias sobre "Guárdame las vacas"* | 196/212 | 4/8 | — |
| 61 | William Byrd: *Pavana Lachrymae* | 140/213 | 4/9 | 2/29 |
| 62 | Giovanni Gabrieli: *Canzon septimi toni a 8* | 199/217 | 4/15 | — |
| 63 | Claudio Monteverdi: *Cruda Amarilli* | 179 | 4/23 | 2/35 |
| 64 | Giulio Caccini: *Vedrò 'l mio sol* | 182/186 | 4/26 | 2/38 |
| 65 | Jacopo Peri: Le musiche sopra l'Euridice | | | |
| | a) Prologue: *Io, che d'alti sospir* | — | 4/28 | — |

| NAWM NO. | COMPOSER AND TITLE | TEXT PAGE | 12-CD SET (Vols. 1 & 2) | 6-CD SET (Concise) |
|---|---|---|---|---|
| | b) Aria: *Nel pur ardor* | — | 4/29 | — |
| | c) Dialogue in recitative: *Per quel vago boschetto* | 188 | 4/30 | — |
| 66 | Claudio Monteverdi: *L'Orfeo*, from Act II | | | |
| | a) Canzonetta: *Vi ricorda o boschi ombrosi* | 190 | 4/34 | 2/40 |
| | b) Recitative: *Mira, deh mira Orfeo* | — | 4/35 | — |
| | c) Dialogue in recitative: *Ahi, caso acerbo* | 191 | 4/36 | 2/41 |
| | d) Recitative: *Tu se' morta* | — | 4/40 | 2/45 |
| | e) Choral madrigal: *Ahi, caso acerbo* | — | 4/41 | 2/46 |
| 67 | Claudio Monteverdi: *L'incoronazione di Poppea*, Act I, scene 3 | 193 | 4/42 | 2/47 |
| 68 | Antonio Cesti: *Orontea*, from Act II | | | |
| | a) Scene 16, recitative: *E che si fa?* | — | 4/48 | — |
| | b) Scene 17, aria: *Intorno all' idol mio* | 194 | 4/49 | — |
| 69 | Barbara Strozzi: *Lagrime mie* | 197 | 4/51 | — |
| 70 | Alessandro Grandi: *O quam tu pulchra es* | 201 | 4/56 | — |
| 71 | Giacomo Carissimi: *Historia di Jephte* | | | |
| | a) Recitative: *Plorate colles* | 201 | 5/1 | 2/53 |
| | b) Chorus: *Plorate filii Israel* | 201 | 5/2 | — |
| 72 | Heinrich Schütz: *O lieber Herre Gott* | 204 | 5/4 | — |
| 73 | Heinrich Schütz: *Saul, was verfolgst du mich* | 204 | 5/7 | 2/54 |
| 74 | Girolamo Frescobaldi: Toccata No. 3 | 215 | 5/11 | 3/1 |
| 75 | Girolamo Frescobaldi: Ricercare after the Credo, in *Fiori musicali* | 216 | 5/13 | — |
| 76 | Biagio Marini: *Sonata IV per il violino per sonar con due corde* | 219 | 5/15 | — |
| 77 | Jean-Baptiste Lully: *Armide* | | | |
| | a) Overture | 229 | 5/23 | 2/58 |
| | b) Act II, scene 5: *Enfin il est en ma puissance* | 233 | 5/26 | 2/61 |
| 78 | Elisabeth-Claude Jacquet de la Guerre: Suite in A Minor | | | |
| | a) Prélude | 250 | 5/31 | 3/3 |
| | b) Allemande | 250 | 5/32 | 3/4 |
| | c) Courante I | 251 | 5/33 | 3/5 |
| | d) Sarabande | 251 | 5/34 | — |
| | e) Gigue | 251 | 5/35 | — |
| | f) Chaconne | — | 5/36 | — |
| | g) Gavotte | 251 | 5/37 | — |
| | h) Menuet | 251 | 5/38 | — |
| 79 | Henry Purcell: *Dido and Aeneas* | | | |
| | a) Recitative: *Thy hand, Belinda* | 238 | 5/39 | 3/6 |
| | b) Lament: *When I am laid in earth* | 237 | 5/40 | 3/7 |
| | c) Chorus: *With drooping wings* | 238 | 5/42 | — |
| 80 | Tomás de Torrejón y Velasco: *La púrpura de la rosa*, excerpt | — | 5/43 | — |
| 81 | Juan de Araujo: *Los coflades de la estleya* | — | 5/47 | — |
| 82 | Alessandro Scarlatti: *Clori vezzosa, e bella* | | | |
| | a) Recitative: *Vivo penando* | 226 | 5/56 | — |
| | b) Aria: *Sì, sì, ben mio* | 227 | 5/57 | — |
| 83 | Arcangelo Corelli: Trio Sonata, Op. 3, No. 2 | | | |
| | a) Grave | 256 | 6/1 | — |
| | b) Allegro | 256 | 6/2 | — |

| NAWM NO. | COMPOSER AND TITLE | TEXT PAGE | 12-CD SET (Vols. 1 & 2) | 6-CD SET (Concise) |
|---|---|---|---|---|
| | c) Adagio | 256 | 6/3 | 3/9 |
| | d) Allegro | 256 | 6/4 | 3/10 |
| 84 | Dieterich Buxtehude: Praeludium in E Major, BuxWV 141 | 245 | 6/6 | — |
| 85 | Antonio Vivaldi: Concerto for Violin and Orchestra in A Minor, Op. 3, No. 6, from *L'estro armonico* | | | |
| | a) Allegro | 284 | 6/13 | 3/12 |
| | b) Largo | 284 | 6/21 | — |
| | c) Presto | — | 6/22 | — |
| 86 | François Couperin: *Vingt-cinquième ordre* | | | |
| | a) *La visionaire* | 286 | 6/31 | 3/20 |
| | b) *La muse victorieuse* | 286 | 6/33 | 3/22 |
| 87 | Jean-Philippe Rameau: *Hippolyte et Aricie*, conclusion of Act IV | 289 | 6/35 | 3/24 |
| 88 | J. S. Bach: Prelude and Fugue in A Minor, BWV 543 | 293 | 6/38 | 3/27 |
| 89 | J. S. Bach: Chorale Prelude on *Durch Adams Fall* | 294 | 6/49 | — |
| 90 | J. S. Bach: *Nun komm, der Heiden Heiland*, BWV 62 | 300 | | |
| | a) Chorus: *Nun komm, der Heiden Heiland* | | 6/50 | 3/38 |
| | b) Aria: *Bewundert, o Menschen* | | 6/58 | — |
| | c) Recitative: *So geht aus Gottes Herrlichkeit* | | 6/60 | — |
| | d) Aria: *Streite, siege, starker Held!* | | 6/61 | — |
| | e) Recitative: *Wir ehren diese Herrlichkeit* | | 6/63 | — |
| | f) Chorale: *Lob sei Gott, dem Vater, ton* | | 6/64 | — |
| 91 | George Frideric Handel: *Giulio Cesare*, Act II, scenes 1 and 2 | | | |
| | a) *Eseguisti* | 308 | 6/65 | — |
| | b) *V'adoro pupille* | 308 | 6/68 | 3/46 |
| 92 | George Frideric Handel: *Saul*, Act II, scene I | | | |
| | a) Accompanied recitative: *The Time at length is come* | 310 | 6/71 | 3/49 |
| | b) Recitative: *Where is the Son of Jesse?* | 310 | 6/72 | 3/50 |
| | c) Chorus: *O fatal Consequence of Rage* | 310 | 6/73 | 3/51 |

VOLUME 2

| NAWM NO. | COMPOSER AND TITLE | TEXT PAGE | 12-CD SET (Vols. 1 & 2) | 6-CD SET (Concise) |
|---|---|---|---|---|
| 93 | Giovanni Battista Pergolesi: *La serva padrona* | | | |
| | a) Recitative: *Ah, quanto mi sta male* | 320 | 7/1 | 3/55 |
| | b) Aria: *Son imbrogliato io* | 320 | 7/3 | 3/57 |
| 94 | Johann Adolf Hasse: *Cleofide*, from Act II, scene 9, *Digli ch'io son fedele* | 325 | 7/7 | — |
| 95 | John Gay: *The Beggar's Opera*, from scene 13 | | | |
| | a) Aria XV: *My heart was so free* | 322 | 7/12 | — |
| | b) Aria XVI: *Were I laid on Greenland's coast* | 322 | 7/13 | — |
| 96 | Christoph Willibald Gluck: *Orfeo ed Euridice*, from Act II, scene 1 | 328 | 7/14 | — |
| 97 | William Billings: *Creation* | 595 | 7/20 | — |
| 98 | Domenico Scarlatti: Sonata in D Major, K. 119 | 330 | 7/22 | 3/61 |
| 99 | C. P. E. Bach: Sonata in A Major, H. 186, 2nd mvmt. | 334 | 7/26 | 3/65 |
| 100 | G. B. Sammartini: Symphony in F Major, No. 32, 1st mvmt. | 331 | 7/28 | — |

| NAWM NO. | COMPOSER AND TITLE | TEXT PAGE | 12-CD SET (Vols. 1 & 2) | 6-CD SET (Concise) |
|---|---|---|---|---|
| 101 | Johann Stamitz: Sinfonia No. 8 in E-flat Major, 1st mvmt. | 333 | 7/31 | — |
| 102 | J. C. Bach: Concerto for Harpsichord or Piano and Strings, Op. 7, No. 5, 1st mvmt. | 366 | 7/36 | — |
| 103 | Joseph Haydn: String Quartet in E-flat Major, Op. 33, No. 2 (*The Joke*), 4th mvmt. | 349 | 8/1 | 3/67 |
| 104 | Joseph Haydn: Symphony No. 92 in G Major (*Oxford*) | | | |
| | a) I. Adagio—Allegro spiritoso | 344 | 7/51 | 4/1 |
| | b) II. Adagio cantabile | 345 | 7/61 | — |
| | c) III. Menuetto: Allegretto | 345 | 7/65 | — |
| | d) IV. Presto | 345 | 7/70 | — |
| 105 | Wolfgang Amadeus Mozart: Piano Sonata in F Major, K. 332, 1st mvmt. | 361 | 7/79 | — |
| 106 | Wolfgang Amadeus Mozart: Piano Concerto in A Major, K. 488, 1st mvmt. | 366 | 8/6 | 4/11 |
| 107 | Wolfgang Amadeus Mozart: *Don Giovanni*, from Act I, scenes 1–2 | 369 | 8/24 | 4/29 |
| 108 | Ludwig van Beethoven: Piano Sonata in C Minor, Op. 13 (*Pathétique*), 3rd mvmt. | 376 | 8/29 | 4/34 |
| 109 | Ludwig van Beethoven: Symphony No. 3 in E-flat Major, Op. 55 (*Eroica*), 1st mvmt. | 380 | 8/36 | 4/41 |
| 110 | Ludwig van Beethoven: String Quartet in C-sharp Minor, Op. 131 | | | |
| | a) 1st mvmt. | 392 | 8/52 | 4/57 |
| | b) 2nd mvmt. | 392 | 8/54 | 4/59 |
| 111 | Franz Schubert: *Gretchen am Spinnrade* | 414 | 8/62 | 4/67 |
| 112 | Franz Schubert: *Der Lindenbaum*, from *Winterreise* | 414 | 8/68 | 4/73 |
| 113 | Robert Schumann: *Im wunderschönen Monat Mai* | 431 | 8/72 | — |
| 114 | Henry R. Bishop: *Home! Sweet Home!* | — | 8/73 | — |
| 115 | Stephen Foster: *Jeanie with the Light Brown Hair* | 597 | 8/75 | — |
| 116 | Robert Schumann: *Fantasiestücke*, Op. 12 | | | |
| | a) No. 2: *Aufschwung* | 429 | 8/76 | 4/77 |
| | b) No. 3: *Warum?* | 429 | 8/84 | — |
| 117 | Fryderyk Chopin: Mazurka in B-flat Major, Op. 7, No. 1 | 432 | 8/86 | — |
| 118 | Fryderyk Chopin: Nocturne in D-flat Major, Op. 27, No. 2 | 432 | 8/89 | 4/85 |
| 119 | Franz Liszt: *Trois études de concert*, No. 3: *Un sospiro* | 441 | 9/1 | 4/92 |
| 120 | Louis Moreau Gottschalk: *Souvenir de Porto Rico* | 600 | 9/7 | — |
| 121 | Hector Berlioz: *Symphonie fantastique*, 5th mvmt. "Dream of a Witches' Sabbath" | 422 | 9/16 | 5/1 |
| 122 | Felix Mendelssohn: Concerto for Violin and Orchestra in E Minor, Op. 64, 3rd mvmt.: Allegretto non troppo—Allegro molto vivace | 427 | 9/30 | 5/15 |
| 123 | Clara Schumann: Piano Trio in G Minor, Op. 17, 3rd mvmt.: Andante | 445 | 9/41 | 5/26 |
| 124 | Felix Mendelssohn: *Elijah*, Chorus: *And then shall your light break forth* | 427 | 9/45 | — |

| NAWM NO. | COMPOSER AND TITLE | TEXT PAGE | 12-CD SET (Vols. 1 & 2) | 6-CD SET (Concise) |
|---|---|---|---|---|
| 125 | Gioachino Rossini: *Il barbiere di Siviglia*, Act II, scene 5: Cavatina, *Una voce poco fa* | 471 | 9/48 | — |
| 126 | Carl Maria von Weber: *Der Freischütz*, Act II, finale: Wolf's Glen scene | 482 | 9/55 | — |
| 127 | Giuseppe Verdi: *La traviata*, Act III, scena and duet | 478 | 9/69 | 5/30 |
| 128 | Richard Wagner: *Tristan und Isolde*, from Act I, scene 5 | 487 | 9/78 | 5/39 |
| 129 | Georges Bizet: *Carmen*, from Act I, No. 10, seguidilla and duet | 469 | 10/1 | 5/47 |
| 130 | Modest Musorgsky: *Boris Godunov*, Coronation scene | 508 | 10/6 | — |
| 131 | Arthur Sullivan: *The Pirates of Penzance: When the foeman bares his steel* | 468 | 10/12 | — |
| 132 | Johannes Brahms: Symphony No. 4 in E Minor, 4th mvmt. | 453 | 10/18 | 5/52 |
| 133 | Richard Strauss: *Don Quixote*, themes and variations 1 and 2 | 502 | 10/25 | 5/59 |
| 134 | Amy Cheney Beach: Quintet for Piano and Strings in F-sharp Minor, Op. 67, 3rd mvmt. | 601 | 10/31 | — |
| 135 | John Philip Sousa: *The Stars and Stripes Forever* | 597 | 10/38 | — |
| 136 | Scott Joplin: *Maple Leaf Rag* | | | |
| | a) as played by Scott Joplin | 614 | 10/43 | — |
| | b) as played by Jelly Roll Morton | 619 | 10/47 | — |
| 137 | Gustav Mahler: *Kindertotenlieder* No. 1, *Nun will die Sonn' so hell aufgeh'n* | 499 | 10/51 | 5/65 |
| 138 | Claude Debussy: *Nuages*, from *Trois Nocturnes* | 540 | 10/59 | 5/73 |
| 139 | Sergei Rachmaninov: Prelude in G Minor, Op. 23, No. 5 | 546 | 10/67 | — |
| 140 | Alexander Scriabin: *Vers la flamme* | 546 | 10/72 | — |
| 141 | Arnold Schoenberg, *Pierrot lunaire*, Op. 21 | | | |
| | a) No. 8: *Nacht* | 551 | 11/1 | 6/1 |
| | b) No 13: *Enthauptung* | 551 | 11/4 | 6/4 |
| 142 | Arnold Schoenberg: Piano Suite, Op. 25 | | | |
| | a) Prelude | 552 | 11/8 | 6/8 |
| | b) Minuet and Trio | 552 | 11/9 | 6/9 |
| 143 | Alban Berg: *Wozzeck*, from Act III, scene 3 | 555 | 11/12 | 6/12 |
| 144 | Anton Webern: Symphony, Op. 21, 1st mvmt. | 558 | 11/15 | — |
| 145 | Igor Stravinsky: *The Rite of Spring* | | | |
| | a) *Danse des adolescentes* | 569 | 11/19 | 6/15 |
| | b) *Danse sacrale* | 570 | 11/23 | — |
| 146 | Igor Stravinsky: *Symphony of Psalms*, 1st mvmt. | 576 | 11/31 | — |
| 147 | Béla Bartók: *Music for Strings, Percussion and Celesta*, 3rd mvmt. | 580 | 11/36 | 6/19 |
| 148 | Charles Ives: *General William Booth Enters into Heaven* | 603 | 11/42 | 6/25 |
| 149 | Bessie Smith: *Back Water Blues* | 618 | 11/49 | — |
| 150 | King Oliver: *West End Blues* | 621 | 11/50 | — |
| 151 | George Gershwin: *I Got Rhythm*, from *Girl Crazy* | 624 | 11/55 | 6/32 |

| NAWM NO. | COMPOSER AND TITLE | TEXT PAGE | 12-CD SET (Vols. 1 & 2) | 6-CD SET (Concise) |
|---|---|---|---|---|
| 152 | Duke Ellington: *Cotton Tail* | 625 | 11/58 | 6/35 |
| 153 | Paul Hindemith: *Un cygne*, from *Six Chansons* | 586 | 11/64 | — |
| 154 | Dmitri Shostakovich: Symphony No. 5, Op. 47, 2nd mvmt. | 591 | 11/66 | — |
| 155 | Silvestre Revueltas: *Sensemayá* | 607 | 11/74 | 6/41 |
| 156 | Ruth Crawford Seeger: String Quartet 1931, 4th mvmt. | 610 | 11/83 | 6/50 |
| 157 | Aaron Copland: *Appalachian Spring*: Excerpt with Variations on "'Tis the Gift to Be Simple" | 611 | 11/86 | 6/53 |
| 158 | William Grant Still: *Afro-American Symphony*, 1st mvmt. | 612 | 12/1 | 6/63 |
| 159 | Charlie Parker and Dizzy Gillespie: *Anthropology* | 627 | 12/8 | 6/70 |
| 160 | Olivier Messiaen: *Quartet for the End of Time*, 1st mvmt. | 631 | 12/16 | 6/75 |
| 161 | Benjamin Britten: *Peter Grimes*, from Act III, scene 2 | 634 | 12/17 | — |
| 162 | Samuel Barber: *Hermit Songs*, No. 8: *The Monk and His Cat* | 635 | 12/23 | 6/76 |
| 163 | George Crumb: *Black Angels, Thirteen Images from the Dark Land* | | | |
| | a) Image 4: *Devil-Music* | 639 | 12/26 | — |
| | b) Image 5: *Danse macabre* | 639 | 12/27 | — |
| 164 | Milton Babbitt: *Philomel*, section I | 642 | 12/28 | 6/79 |
| 165 | Penderecki: *Threnody for the Victims of Hiroshima* | 644 | 12/33 | — |
| 166 | John Cage: *Music of Changes*, Book I | 647 | 12/40 | 6/84 |
| 167 | Karel Husa: *Music for Prague 1968*, 1st mvmt.: Introduction and fanfare: Adagio | — | 12/43 | — |
| 168 | John Adams: *Phrygian Gates* | 655 | 12/50 | — |
| 169 | Ellen Taaffe Zwilich: Symphony No. 1, 1st mvmt. | 659 | 12/59 | — |
| 170 | Arvo Pärt: *Seven Magnificat Antiphons* | | | |
| | a) No. 1: *O Weisheit* | 659 | 12/65 | — |
| | b) No. 6: *O König aller Völker* | 659 | 12/66 | — |
| 171 | Sofia Gubaidulina: *Rejoice!* Sonata for Violin and Violoncello, 5th mvmt. | 663 | 12/67 | — |
| 172 | Bright Sheng: *Seven Tunes Heard in China*, No. 1: Seasons | 658 | 12/75 | 6/87 |

# PREFACE TO THE THIRD EDITION

This new edition of *Concise History of Western Music* parallels the Seventh Edition of *A History of Western Music* (HWM) by J. Peter Burkholder, Donald J. Grout, and Claude V. Palisca, and matches the Fifth Edition of the two-volume *Norton Anthology of Western Music* (NAWM) by Burkholder and Palisca. However, while the new HWM has grown to thirty-five chapters, I have streamlined most of its contents into twenty-four chapters in *Concise*—two more chapters than the previous edition contained. These two chapters include a new treatment of instrumental music in the sixteenth and seventeenth centuries (constituting the new Chapter 10, which consolidates material that previously had been appended to other chapters) and a much expanded consideration of contemporary music (presented in the final chapter). As with the first and second editions of *Concise History of Western Music*, I have refrained from trying to tell too many stories at once. Thus, for example, music in the New World is not integrated into the chapters that deal primarily with developments in European music but is reserved for the last two chapters (23 and 24).

In other respects, however, *Concise* 3 reflects many of the changes that were made in HWM 7 and in the NAWM repertoire. These include a new attention to social history, cultural context, and performance practice, and an increase in the number and variety of musical excerpts from the nineteenth- and twentieth-century repertoires. The first is evident especially in the six essays introducing each historical period and in the "In Performance" sidebars occurring at intervals throughout the volume; the second accounts for the reorganization of the last two sections of the text into four chapters each on Romantic and modern music.

## Features

The following summary outlines the principal features of the text. Many of them are new, and all of them are designed to assist the readers in making their way through a narrative in which human choices and values play an important role.

- Expanded coverage of twentieth-century composers and genres, presented in four chapters (rather than the two of the previous edition), adjusts the balance between earlier and later periods of music history.
- Reorganization of nineteenth-century materials, now presented chronologically by individual composers rather than grouped according to genre, consolidates all the works of a particular composer in the same section of the text.
- New introductions to the main eras of music history provide overviews of the major political, artistic, and intellectual trends in each historical period.
- "Arts and Ideas" boxes present capsule accounts of some of the important figures in literature, science, philosophy, and the arts within each historical period.
- Six (new) "Innovations" essays briefly highlight specific musical, technological, or social innovations that significantly changed the dissemination, performance, or consumption of music.
- Ten (new) "In Performance" sidebars focus on practical issues of special importance and interest to performers and informed listeners.
- Preludes and Postludes at the beginning and end of each chapter provide overviews, summaries, retrospectives, or transitions that help to reinforce the material presented in the main narrative.
- Relevant "In Context" sidebars (formerly "windows") explore a variety of cultural issues that supplement and contextualize musical developments.
- Composer biographies (new) summarize the personal details and professional activities of the lives of many composers and list their major works.
- Occasional "Closer Look" boxes dwell on a particular work or event, in some cases offering a deeper analysis than the main narrative provides.
- Vivid, full-color illustrations and photographs throughout the volume replace the sporadic glossy plates of the earlier editions and serve to supplement and enhance important ideas, people, events, and related artistic trends presented in the text.
- "Vignettes" offer pithy and colorful excerpts from writings by or about the composers studied, illuminating their choices and providing insights into their works.
- Musical examples help to focus on specific features of the works studied.
- Timelines in almost every chapter set the musical events in a social and historical context, and promote a clearer view of their interrelationship.
- Detailed maps establish a location and context for musical events and works.
- Plentiful charts and diagrams summarize and clarify the forms of musical works and genres to help the reader grasp some of the essential historical structures of music.
- Marginal sideheads throughout identify key terms, composers, and works in the text, and focus attention on important concepts.
- A glossary at the end of the volume offers clear, concise definitions of musical terms.
- Cross-references to the scores and recordings intended to accompany this text are found throughout the volume. The scores are identified by their numbers in the *Norton Anthology of Western Music*, Fifth Edition. Boxed numbers in the margins refer to the corresponding CD tracks on the *Norton Recorded Anthology of Western Music*, coded in dark blue for the complete set (12 CDs) and light blue for the Concise set (6 CDs), respectively.
- "For Further Reading" provides an up-to-date bibliography corresponding to each historical period presented in the text.

## Accompanying Texts and Recordings

Although this book stands on its own as a narrative history, the reader's learning experience will be enriched by using it in tandem with the accompanying anthology, recordings, and study guide:

- The two-volume Norton Anthology of Western Music (NAWM), Fifth Edition, by J. Peter Burkholder and Claude V. Palisca (Volume 1: *Ancient to Baroque*; Volume 2: *Classic to Twentieth Century*), provides a comprehensive collection of 172 scores illustrating the most significant musical trends, genres, and national schools in the Western world from antiquity to the present. Among these are more than 75 new selections, including works from Spain and Latin America, more compositions by women and by twentieth-century composers, and examples of popular music and jazz through the mid-twentieth century. While almost every work appearing in the anthology is cited in the text of *Concise* 3, I have concentrated on the core repertoire recorded in the *Concise Norton Recorded Anthology of Western Music* (a set of 6 CDs, expanded from the 4 of the previous edition). My discussions of these works overlap with, but generally avoid repeating, the detailed musical essays that accompany them in the anthology volumes.
- The Norton Recorded Anthology of Western Music includes outstanding recordings of the entire NAWM repertory by some of the best ensembles performing today. It is available in both a complete set (12 CDs) and in a Concise set (6 CDs).
- The Study and Listening Guide by Jennifer L. King offers chapter outlines and objectives, study questions, review questions, key terms and names, and valuable guides to help the student listen more productively and retain essential material from the main text.

## Ancillary Materials

Like its predecessors, this new edition comes with a host of ancillary materials designed to help both student and teacher.

Electronic media are available to assist students in learning about the music and its history. (Details about the electronic media to accompany this edition can be found at www.wwnorton.com/musichistory.)

- The Electronic Listening Guide CD-ROM provides electronic listening guides for all of the selections in the *Norton Recorded Anthology of Western Music*, Concise Fifth Edition. The listening-guide software synchronizes historical overviews, commentary, and analysis with the music included in the *Recorded Anthology*.
- The Student Web site provides free access to Norton's Online Listening Lab, which presents over ten hours of listening in near-CD-quality streaming of historically significant works not included on the CD recordings as well as listening and factual quizzes to test key concepts and listening skills. The Online Tutor also offers
  
  listening quizzes for every work in the *Norton Recorded Anthology*;
  chapter outlines;
  FlashCards;
  a music glossary, hyperlinked to key terms for easy reference.

There are also three aides for the instructor:

- The Instructor's Manual by Roger Hickman provides instructors with lecture outlines, test questions, and suggestions for further reading as well as listening and other activities.
- The Norton Resource Library, available at www.wwnorton.com/nrl, includes a computerized version of the Test-Item file in the *Instructor's Manual* and convenient lecture outlines in PowerPoint. These are also available in Blackboard and WebCT course-management format.
- The Norton Media Library CD-ROM includes PowerPoint lecture outlines with eye-catching maps and illustrations from art sources.

# Acknowledgments

In preparing this Third Edition, I am indebted, first of all, to J. Peter Burkholder, whose broad knowledge and authoritative voice informs the Seventh Edition of *A History of Western Music* and from whose text I borrowed liberally for this revision. I have also profited enormously from comments about this new edition in all phases of its development by reviewers, some of whom spent a generous amount of time communicating their suggestions for improvement. The staff at W. W. Norton has been an unfailing source of ideas, enthusiasm, and support. I am particularly grateful to Maribeth Anderson Payne, music editor, who guided the book through its many stages, provided useful advice during all of them, and cheerfully tolerated my occasionally intransigent moods; to Carol Flechner, who meticulously edited the manuscript and offered some much appreciated perspective; and to assistant music editor and project editor Allison Courtney Fitch, who responded so promptly and patiently to my many cries for help. Others at Norton have also earned my admiration and gratitude for their invaluable assistance: Michael Ochs and Alice Vigliani, each of whom copyedited a section or two of the manuscript; Richard Wingell, who reviewed the entire text and made useful suggestions; JoAnn Simony, Neil Ryder Hoos, Chris Welch, and Alice Bennett, who are largely responsible for the book's beautiful appearance. I am also deeply grateful to Allison Benter for helping me assemble the Concise CD selections; David Budmen for setting the musical examples with such care; Benjamin Reynolds for proofreading the text; Marilyn Bliss for preparing the index; Graham Norwood for relaying messages; and Marian Johnson for coordinating all of the above. Those involved in the preparation and editing of the electronic media, especially Steve Hoge, also deserve my thanks.

In addition, I have incurred many debts to people outside of the Norton family: Juilliard graduate and CUNY doctoral student Ed Klorman, who generously shared his knowledge of performance practice with me; those colleagues and former colleagues at The City College of New York who willingly answered my questions about jazz and other areas of contemporary music; my students, who constantly keep me on my toes in the classroom; and former students and instructors around the country who have used the book in its previous incarnations and offered valuable suggestions. My acknowledgments would be incomplete were they not to express my heartfelt gratitude to my husband Robert W. Hanning, my mother Helen Russano, and other family members and friends for their patient support and endless encouragement. Finally, I dedicate this volume to my grandchildren Benjamin, Evan, and Noah, who will, I hope, continue to take great pleasure in music and be inspired to learn its secrets.

Barbara Russano Hanning
March 2006

ABBREVIATIONS

B.C.E.   Before Common Era (equivalent to B.C.)
C.E.     Common Era (equivalent to A.D.)

PITCH DESIGNATIONS

In this book, a note referred to without regard to its octave register is designated by a capital letter (A). A note in a particular octave is designated in italics, using the following system:

 *C* to *B*

 *c′* to *b′*

*c* to *b*

*c″* to *b″*

# WHY STUDY MUSIC HISTORY?

We study music history because in music, as in all other realms of human endeavor, the past influences and informs the present. Never in music history has this been more true than in our own time, when scholars have retrieved and restored so much music from the past, performers have brought it to life, and recordings, radio, television, and the Internet have disseminated it more widely than ever before. Generations ago, people had access only to music that was performed live by their parents, teachers, friends, and local entertainers. If they could read music and afford lessons, they might also have become acquainted with a few piano pieces by favorite composers or with the popular songs of Tin Pan Alley. In contrast, the technological revolution has made an overwhelming number of works available: ten centuries of written music as well as the (often unwritten) musical styles of cultures from around the globe.

Composers and musicians have always been influenced by the sounds around them, and today the possibilities are almost infinite. Accessible sounds range from the folk music of various cultures and ethnic groups to popular music broadcast over the airwaves or via the Internet, even to the raw sounds of nature (such as whale songs) harnessed by modern technology. These influences are absorbed almost unconsciously and are either unintentionally or purposely incorporated into new works. Other influences are also evident as throughout history composers of one generation have engaged in a conscious and determined struggle to define themselves in opposition to, or in sympathy with, the sounds and styles of previous generations. Like children growing away from their parents, composers sometimes rebel and strike out on their own, only later to acknowledge and embrace or transform the ways of their predecessors. We find this tension—between rejecting the immediate past and accepting or reinterpreting it—in every era of music history. In fact, it mirrors a pattern we recognize in all fields of learning and the arts since the beginning of recorded history. In modern times, however, the restoration of works from the more remote past has complicated the issue for creative artists by providing an awesome array of additional models and stylistic possibilities.

In itself, the influence of a rich past may not offer enough reason to study music history. But if we want to understand *why* the music we hear was composed to sound the way it does, we look to music history for explanations. And in the process of pursuing these explanations, not only will we become better listeners, but our deepened understanding will also increase the pleasure we derive from hearing and performing the music that we do. Beyond that, it is important to recognize music's emotional power and its role in society, which has always been a forceful one but which has grown in direct proportion to its increased presence in our lives. A heightened awareness of the place that music occupies in our society will be gained by examining the role it has played in past eras. Whether heard in the concert hall or in sports and political arenas, whether used as an important element of religious services or as a strategic device in consumer and marketing services, its significance bears on every facet of our culture, and our knowledge to a certain extent determines our responses to it at every level.

Dmin'

secus

ma re galile e

vidit du os fra

tres petrum et an

PART ONE

# The Ancient and Medieval Worlds

✻

PART CONTENTS

1. MUSIC IN ANCIENT GREECE AND EARLY
CHRISTIAN ROME  18

2. CHANT AND SECULAR SONG IN THE MIDDLE AGES  30

3. POLYPHONY THROUGH THE THIRTEENTH CENTURY  54

4. FRENCH AND ITALIAN MUSIC IN THE FOURTEENTH
CENTURY  71

From the beginning of human existence, singing has been a natural outlet for the expression of feelings. Probably even before the development of language, the utterances of the human voice gave vent to basic emotions—the wails of lament, the howls of pain, the giggles of joy, the quavering of fear. Once combined with language, singing became a powerful means of communicating not only generalized feelings, but also the most personal and subtle sentiments. By heightening and coloring the words, the singing voice can render their meaning with a force greater than they have when merely spoken.

In fact, vocal music dominates the first two parts of our history—antiquity through the Renaissance—but not because that is all there was. Rather, it constitutes most of what survives in written form. And that music, in turn, is a product almost exclusively of the elite and literate classes of society, and it is only a tiny fraction of all the music that was made through these centuries. Nevertheless, since the advent of recorded history, attitudes toward singing have reflected the cultural and intellectual concerns peculiar to a given time and place. For example, the ancient Greeks stressed vocal music at the expense of instrumental music because they expected from their arts a distinctive character (ethos) that only words could impart to music. All ancient Christian music was vocal, but during the Middle Ages some church leaders were troubled by the sensuality of the voice in the performance of religious plainsong (or chant) and expressed concern about the potential distractions of song as an aide to worship (see Saint Augustine on the dangers of music, page 23). In the court cultures of sixteenth-century Italy, the art of singing was particularly significant: not only was it a marker for grace and nobility, but it was also believed to be the link that connected us to the entire cosmos, putting the individual in touch with the harmony of the universe.

Archaeological remains, images, and early forms of writing all testify to the use of instrumental as well as vocal music in ancient Mesopotamia and Egypt in the Near East as far back as the fourth millennium B.C.E. (see Figure I.1). Physical and pictorial evidence exists of lyres and harps (Figures I.2 and I.3) as well as lutes, pipes, drums, cymbals, rattles, and bells. Written sources suggest that Babylonian musicians used seven-note diatonic scales and created the earliest known musical notation during the second millennium B.C.E. Even then, musicians probably did not depend on notation in order to play or sing, as modern performers do, but instead used it as a written record from which a tune could be reconstructed, as cooks use a recipe. Until the first semiaccurate symbols of pitch notation were invented in western Europe more than two thousand years later, most music was either played from memory or improvised. Despite the lack of surviving musical pieces, scholars believe that the repertories of ancient peoples were not very different from ours today: wedding songs, funeral dirges, military marches, work songs, nursery songs, dance music, tavern songs, banqueting music, devotional and ceremonial music, and

*Figure I.1. The ancient Near East.*

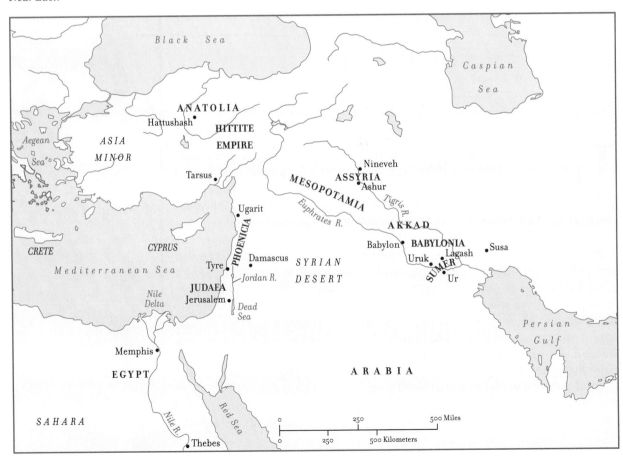

## TIMELINE The Ancient and Medieval Worlds

| MUSICAL EVENTS | HISTORICAL EVENTS |
|---|---|

### HISTORICAL EVENTS

**ca. 3500–3000 B.C.E.** Rise of Sumerian cities in Mesopotamia
**2500 B.C.E.** Royal tombs at Ur built

Babylonian writings about music **1800 B.C.E.**
Oldest nearly complete composition in **1400–1250 B.C.E.**
Babylonian notation

**800 B.C.E.** Rise of Greek city-states
**753 B.C.E.** Rome founded
**660 B.C.E.** Byzantium founded

Famous music-festival competition at Pythian games **582 B.C.E.**

**ca. 500 B.C.E.** Roman Republic begins

**ca. 380 B.C.E.** Plato, *Republic*
**ca. 330 B.C.E.** Aristotle, *Politics*

Musician with kithara

**ca. 33** Crucifixion of Jesus

**392** Christianity becomes official Roman religion
**400** Saint Augustine, *Confessions*

Boethius, *De institutione musica* **ca. 500**

**ca. 530** (Monastic) *Rule of Saint Benedict*
**590** Gregory I ("the Great") elected pope
**ca. 610–622** Founding of Islam by Muhammad

Earliest notated manuscripts of Gregorian chant **9th cent.**

**800** Charlemagne crowned emperor by pope
**800–821** *Rule of Saint Benedict* introduced in Frankish
lands

Illuminated manuscript

**ca. 1050** Watermills and windmills boost production
**1000–1300** European population triples
**ca. 1050** Romanesque style flourishes
**1066** Norman Conquest of England
**1095–1099** First Crusade
**1163** Cornerstone of Notre Dame of Paris laid; Gothic style
flourishes in northern Europe

Beginnings of Notre Dame polyphony **ca. 1180**

**1264–1274** Saint Thomas Aquinas, *Summa theologica*
**ca. 1266–1337** Giotto

**1309** Clement V moves papacy to Avignon
**1315–1322** Famine in northwestern Europe
**1337** Beginning of the Hundred Years' War
**1347–1350** Plague kills one-third of Europe
**1353** Boccaccio, *Decameron*
**1374** Death of Petrarch
**1378** Start of Great (papal) Schism
**1387–1400** Chaucer, *Canterbury Tales*

A rose window in the cathedral of Chartres

**1431** Joan of Arc burned at the stake

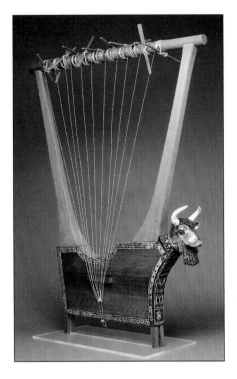

*Figure I.2 (left).  Reconstruction of a Sumerian bull lyre from the royal tombs at Ur, ca. 2500 b.c.e. The British Museum, London.*

*Figure I.3 (below).  Inlaid panel from Ur showing a bull lyre being played at a victory banquet, ca. 2600 b.c.e. The British Museum, London.*

stories sung to instrumental accompaniment—all functioning to comfort, edify, amuse, and celebrate. Although we can postulate a vibrant musical life in the ancient Near East, without actual music to perform, it remains almost entirely silent.

**Ancient Greece**

Ancient Greece is the earliest civilization that offers us enough evidence to construct a well-rounded view of musical culture. From the myth of Orpheus, who overturned the laws of nature with his singing, we understand the power with which music was invested. In real life, the Greeks used musical magic to heal the body as well as the soul. Carefully chosen melodies could banish illness and restore order in society. Not for nothing did Plato, in the fourth century B.C.E., recommend that the ideal state be founded on suitable types of music and warn against the unsettling effects of musical innovation. Citizens of Sparta were alarmed when the "modern" musician Timotheus performed with four additional strings on his lyre and the court ordered that they be snipped off. Lawlessness in art could lead to anarchy in society. Aristotle shared some of Plato's anxiety and stressed the importance of music in education (see vignette). However, he felt that sons of free citizens should not seek professional training on instruments or aspire to the virtuosity that performers demonstrated in competitions since it was menial and vulgar to play solely for the pleasure of others rather than for one's own improvement.

**Ancient Rome**

During the first millennium B.C.E., Rome rose from an insignificant settlement on the banks of the Tiber to perhaps the world's most successful empire. Around the time that Plato wrote his *Republic*, the actual republic of Rome, governed by a patrician or aristocratic class, was thriving on the Italian peninsula and absorbing many aspects of Greek culture. By the end of the first century C.E., Roman armies had conquered Greece and held sway over the entire Mediterranean world and western Europe, from Mesopotamia in the east to Spain in the west, and from Britain to Egypt (see Figure I.4). The musical culture they brought with them was basically that of the Greeks, which helps to explain why Greek theories became so pervasive and exerted so much influence on the various types of music and musical eras we study in this book.

**VIGNETTE**    Aristotle on the Doctrine of Imitation, Ethos, and Music in Education

*Music's importance in ancient Greek culture is shown by its appearance as a topic in books about society, such as Aristotle's* Politics. *Aristotle believed that music could imitate and thus directly affect character and behavior, and, therefore, should play a role in education.*

[Melodies] contain in themselves imitations of ethoses; and this is manifest, for even in the nature of the harmonial there are differences, so that people when hearing them are affected differently and have not the same feelings in regard to each of them, but listen to some in a more mournful and restrained state, for instance the so-called Mixolydian, and to others in a softer state of mind, for instance the relaxed harmoniai, but in a midway state and with the greatest composure to another, as the Dorian alone of the harmoniai seems to act, while the Phrygian makes men divinely suffused; for these things are well stated by those who have studied this form of education, as they derive the evidence for their theories from the actual facts of experience. And the same holds good about the rhythms also, for some have a more stable and others a more emotional ethos, and of the latter some are more vulgar in their emotional effects and others more liberal. From these considerations therefore it is plain that music has the power of producing a certain effect on the ethos of the soul, and if it has the power to do this, it is clear that the young must be directed to music and must be educated in it. Also education in music is well adapted to the youthful nature; for the young owing to their youth cannot endure anything not sweetened by pleasure, and music is by nature a thing that has a pleasant sweetness.

Aristotle, *Politics* 8.5, trans. Harris Rackham; in Oliver Strunk, ed., *Source Readings in Music Theory*, rev. ed. by Leo Treitler (New York: Norton, 1998), p. 29.

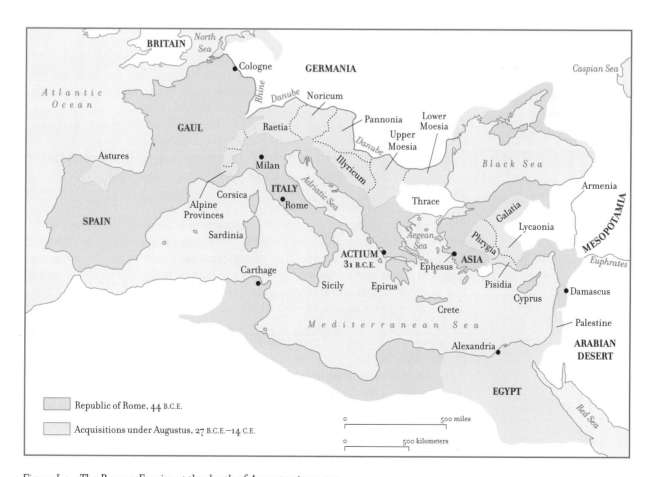

*Figure I.4.  The Roman Empire at the death of Augustus in 14 C.E.*

*Figure I.5.  Pope Leo III crowns Charlemagne emperor on Christmas day, 800, beginning a tradition of Germanic kings being crowned by the pope, one that would last until the fifteenth century.*

# The Early Middle Ages

To begin with, aspects of Greek musical thought influenced medieval church music and music theory, as it was transmitted to the West by Boethius (ca. 480–ca. 524; see Chapter 1), the most revered authority on music in the Middle Ages. This period in history, reckoned from the disintegration of the Roman Empire in the West during the fourth and fifth centuries to the middle of the fifteenth century, overlapping with the early Renaissance, saw the spread of the new religion, Christianity, and the establishment of many of the ideas and institutions of Western civilization, such as the university, trade guilds, and more. The term *Middle Ages* acknowledges the era's position in time between the ancient and modern worlds, or between the "classical" civilizations of Greece and Rome and the emergence of the new humanistic culture of the Renaissance. After the collapse of the Roman Empire, Christianity remained the most unifying force in medieval Europe. The papacy gradually gained secular authority; monastic communities, mostly following the Rule of Saint Benedict, had the effect of preserving classical learning; and missionaries, sent to convert the Germanic and other tribes, spread Latin civilization far and wide, including what became the first literate repertory of song—"Gregorian" chant (see Chapter 2).

**The Christian Church**    As in any age, medieval music was shaped by currents in the larger society. Its history is particularly interwined with the history of the Christian Church, the dominant social institution for most of the Middle Ages. Far from withdrawing from the world, the Church was very much a part of the world, and the relationship between "church" and "world" or between ecclesiastical and secular leadership advanced the cause of both sides. In the eighth century, Carolingian rulers made a concerted effort to create a new world order in which church and kingship worked together. This alliance was cemented in the year 800 when Charlemagne (742–814), ruler of the Frankish lands, went to Rome to be crowned emperor by the pope, thereby becoming the temporal ruler of the newly reconstituted Western Roman Empire anointed by the spritual ruler of Western Christendom (Figure I.5). One result of this political maneuver was the importation of Roman chant, along with Roman art and architecture as well as manuscript production and illumination, all brought across the Alps from Italy. Thus was Gregorian chant "imposed" on the Christian liturgy throughout Frankish lands, its repertory subsequently becoming stabilized and eventually singled out for preservation in written form.

Many aspects of Western music, from notation to polyphony, first developed within church music. Those who were educated at all were educated in schools established by the Church, and most composers and theorists were trained there. We can study medieval church music today only because, unlike some other repertories, it survived. And it survived—the product of a very small number of people of wealth, leisure, and literacy, in the largest monasteries and cathedrals—only because church musicians invented notation sometime during the ninth century, followed by a series of innovations in musical notation that enabled song to be written down with increasing accuracy.

**Church music**

In the political arena, three principal successors to the Roman Empire had emerged by the ninth century. The most direct successor was the Byzantine Empire in Asia Minor and southeastern Europe. The strongest and most vibrant was the Arab world, which, from the founding of Islam around 610 by Muhammad, rapidly expanded to dominate a vast territory from modern-day Pakistan through the Middle East, North Africa, and Spain. The weakest, poorest, and most fragmented of the three was western Europe. In this context, Charlemagne's coronation in 800 as emperor in Rome asserted to the world a

**Three empires**

*Figure I.6. Europe in the mid-fourteenth century.*

continuity with the Roman past, independence from the Byzantine East, and confidence in the future of civilization in western Europe.

European culture owes much to all three empires. The Byzantines preserved Greek and Roman science, architecture, and culture. Most writings that survive from ancient Greece exist only because Byzantine scribes recopied them. The Arabs extended Greek philosophy and science, fostered trade and industry, and contributed to medicine, chemistry, technology, and mathematics. Arab rulers were patrons of literature, architecture, and other arts. Charlemagne, as ruler of the Frankish kingdom and, after 800, Holy Roman emperor, also promoted learning and artistic achievement. He improved education, encouraging primary schools in monasteries and cathedral towns throughout his realm. By sponsoring scholarship and the arts, Charlemagne and his son Louis I the Pious (r. 814–843) made their courts into centers for intellectual and cultural life, setting a pattern for Western rulers that endured for a thousand years.

*Figure I.7. A fourteenth-century Italian depiction of the siege of Jerusalem during the first Crusade, during which thousands were massacred.*

# Political Change and Economic Development

After Louis's death, his empire was divided. Over the next few centuries the modern European nations began to emerge, although their boundaries changed frequently (see Figure I.6). The western part of the empire became France. Until about 1200, the French king was relatively weak, directly ruling only the area around Paris, while other regions were governed by nobles who owed nominal allegiance to the king but often acted independently. Their courts provided opportunities for poets and musicians, nurturing the troubadours and trouvères (see Chapter 2). In the eastern part of the empire, German kings claimed the title of emperor as Charlemagne's successors. Their realm, eventually known as the Holy Roman Empire, included non-German lands as well, from the Netherlands to northern Italy. The regional nobility in the empire competed for prestige by hiring the best singers, instrumentalists, and composers, which fueled the development of music until the nineteenth century. Outside the former Frankish lands, a centralized kingdom emerged in England in the late ninth century and continued after the Norman Conquest of England in 1066. Italy remained fragmented among several rulers, including the pope, and Spain was divided between Christian kingdoms in the north and Muslim lands in the south. The Crusades, a series of campaigns between 1095 and 1270 to retake Jerusalem from the Turks, ultimately failed but showed the growing confidence and military power of western Europe (Figure I.7).

These political developments went hand in hand with remarkable economic progress. Technological advances in agriculture and an expansion of cultivated lands led to great growth in production. An increasing food supply raised the standard of living and allowed the population to triple between 1000 and 1300. From about 1050 on, water-powered mills and windmills provided mechanical power for milling grain, manufacturing goods, and other uses, further boosting productivity. By 1300, western Europe had surpassed the Byzantine Empire and the Islamic world in economic strength.

The medieval economy was largely agricultural and the population mostly rural. Under feudalism, society was organized into three broad classes, as shown in Figure I.8: the nobility and knights, who controlled the land and fought the wars; priests, monks, and nuns, who studied and prayed; and peasants, the vast majority of the population, who worked the land and served the nobles. Peasants and serfs lived lives of oppression and drudgery, laboring from morning to night for the barest subsistence, which prompted occasional outbreaks of violent rebellion. By the twelfth century, trade in food and other products promoted the growth of markets, towns, and cities, although the largest centers were still small in modern terms: in 1300, Paris had about 200,000 residents, London about 70,000; Venice, Milan, and Florence about 100,000 each. Music was enjoyed at all levels of society, but the nobility particularly emphasized its importance and preservation as a symbol of wealth, leisure, and status.

*Figure I.8. Fourteenth-century French manuscript illumination from a Latin translation of Aristotle's Politics, illustrating the three estates, or classes of medieval society: the nobility, who governed and waged war; the clergy, who prayed; and the peasants, who worked the land controlled by the nobles. Royal Library of Belgium.*

## Learning and the Arts, 1050–1300

Prosperity provided resources for learning and the arts. Between the eleventh and thirteenth centuries, the European landscape became dotted with great cathedrals and abbeys (monastic churches), signaling a new sense of security

*Figure I.9 (right). The façade of the Romanesque church of Saint-Sernin, Toulouse, France (ca. 1080–1120).*

*Figure I.10 (below). The façade of the Gothic cathedral of Chartres, France.*

throughout Europe after centuries of Viking and other invasions. These were built first in the Romanesque style, modeled on the round arches of ancient Roman buildings (Figure I.9) and sometimes decorated with frescoes and sculptures. Then, in the mid-twelfth century, craftsmen created a new style of church architecture, later called Gothic, that was characterized by height and spaciousness frequently with soaring towers, pointed arches, shimmering light filtered through large stained-glass windows, and flying buttresses bracing the walls from outside (Figure I.10)—all resulting in a sense of lightness that sets it apart from the more grounded Romanesque style. Roughly parallel to this new architectural style is the intricate and graceful polyphony being written by composers at the Cathedral of Notre Dame in Paris in the early thirteenth century (see Chapter 3). Cathedral schools were established throughout western and central Europe, teaching future church officials Latin grammar, rhetoric, and music. After 1200, independent schools for laymen spread rapidly as well, fostering a more secular culture and a tremendous rise in literacy.

Beginning in the twelfth century, universities were founded in Bologna, Paris, Oxford, and other cities, and taught liberal arts, theology, law, and medicine. The study of Aristotle became more common and more popular as his works were translated from Greek and Arabic into Latin. But early in the thirteenth century, the teaching of Aristotle's books about natural science was forbidden at the University of Paris. In the 1240s, the scientist Roger Bacon, who wrote commentaries on several of Aristotle's books, became the first to lecture formally on the Greek philosopher's works at the university, defending and "correcting" them after they were condemned. As the concept of university education took hold, a new way of thinking known as Scholasticism tried to reconcile conflicting concepts of philosophy, religion, and science. Intellectuals within the church such as Saint Thomas Aquinas made new contributions to science and philosophy. Writers in vernacular languages produced a new literature of knighthood and chivalry in which courtly love was a major element. Courtly love presented a highly idealized image of love that contained elements common to all feudal relationships: the lover assumed a subordinate role to his beloved; he was her loyal "vassal" and, therefore, subject to her will. Much of the poetry of courtly love was sung, forming, along with chant, one of the two great monophonic repertories of medieval song.

## The Fourteenth Century

In the fourteenth century, western Europe's economy and population declined, ravaged by famine, war, and plague. Power struggles and scandals afflicted the Church, resulting in a series of French popes maintaining a

*Figure I.11. A fifteenth-century German tapestry depicting Joan of Arc arriving at the Château de Marçay, Chinon, in March 1428. She is dressed in knight's armor and is being greeted by King Charles VII. Centre Jeanne d'Arc, Orléans, France.*

## ARTS *and* IDEAS

One of the most influential philosophers in the history of Western civilization, **Plato** (ca. 427–347 B.C.E.) was convinced of the ultimately harmonious structure of the universe. The goal of his teachings was to show the rational relationship among the soul, the state, and the cosmos. His ideas about music, including its moral function in society, appear mainly in his dialogues, particularly *Republic, Laws,* and *Timaeus.*

The Greek philosopher **Aristotle** (384–322 B.C.E.), Plato's star pupil, relied on logic, analysis, and observation to discover what he thought were the universal truths about the world. His philosophy was often contrary to the religious doctrine of Christianity, prompting the development of Scholasticism, which tried to reconcile those ideas with religious beliefs. His views on music, expressed in the *Politics* and *Poetics,* formed the basis for later theories about emotional responses to music.

**Saint Augustine** (354–430 C.E.), still considered one of Christianity's most influential thinkers, was born in the Roman province of Numidia (modern-day Algeria) in north Africa and converted to Christianity in his early thirties. His *Confessions,* written when he was forty-five, tell of his spiritual journey from a worldly life to one devoted to religious thought (see Vignette, page 23).

The founder of monasticism in the West, **Saint Benedict** (ca. 480–ca. 543) withdrew from a life of privilege in Rome to a cave outside the city, where he lived in solitude for three years before forming his own monastic community (the Benedictines) on a mountaintop in Monte Cassino, a town in central Italy. His book, *The Rule of Saint Benedict,* outlined his views on monastic life, in which music occupied a place of enormous importance (see Chapter 2).

Born in Mecca on the Arabian peninsula, **Muhammad** (ca. 570–632) was the founder of Islam and the inspiration for a number of empires that dominated a large portion of the civilized world during the Middle Ages. Today there are more than 1 billion Muslims worldwide, fewer than one-fifth of whom are Arab. Muhammad's teachings were collected after his death as the Quran, the sacred text of Islam.

The English scientist **Roger Bacon** (1214–1292) probably studied at Oxford. He subsequently lectured on Aristotle at the University of Paris and introduced the study of light, integrating all known Greek and Islamic knowledge on the eye, vision, perspective, and optics. After joining the Franciscans, he came under suspicion by his superiors for the wealth of new ideas in his writings, the *Opus maius* (Major work), a vast encyclopedia of the arts and sciences, and of all the disciplines taught in universities at that time.

The works of **Saint Thomas Aquinas** (ca. 1225–1274) stand as the crowning achievement of medieval Scholas-

splendid court in Avignon, notorious for luxury and corruption. Along with French cardinals, who functioned truly as princes of the Church, they dispensed liberal patronage to musicians, artists, and scholars, among whom was the Italian poet Petrarch, whose lyrics were to inspire composers of polyphonic song two centuries after his death. The crisis of the papacy reached its climax in the Great Schism (1378–1417), during which there were two popes claiming legitimacy, one in Avignon and one in Rome (and, for a while, a third one in Pisa), with all of Europe being forced to take sides.

War      The Hundred Years' War (1337–1453), actually a series of intermittent sieges, raids, and battles, was part of the long and bitter rivalry between England and France that has surfaced periodically from the eleventh century until modern times. During its final phase, a French peasant girl who later became known as Joan of Arc, obeying "voices" she claimed to have heard, led an army of several thousand French forces to drive the English from French soil (Figure I.11). Although her expedition was successful, she was eventually captured, tried for heresy, and, still in her teens, burned at the stake in 1431.

tic philosophical theology. By drawing on Aristotelian thought, he elevated philosophy and theology in the minds of the learned for centuries. His greatest work, *Summa theologica* (a compendium of Christian doctrine), argued that reason and science are compatible with revelation and faith, then a radical position for a Christian theologian.

Italian sculptor and architect **Giovanni Pisano** (ca. 1250–1314), son of sculptor Nicola Pisano, apprenticed in his father's workshop. Together they initiated a new style of marble sculpture, culminating with Michelangelo in the Renaissance. Giovanni designed the façade of the cathedral in Siena and produced much of the sculptural decoration. Inspired by classical elements, his statuary is elegant and monumental as well as emotionally charged.

An Italian painter and designer, **Giotto** (1266–1337) was the first artist since antiquity whose fame extended beyond his lifetime and native region (Florence). He led painting in a new direction, away from the highly formal, stylized poses of Byzantine and northern European painting and toward a more lifelike depiction of movement and expression. His justly famous fresco cycles of the lives of Jesus, Saint Francis, and the Virgin Mary drew on classical principles of form, which humanized the figures in a way that became characteristic of Renaissance art.

**Petrarch** (Francesco Petrarca, 1304–1374) was raised in Avignon and studied law in France and at the University of Bologna. An avid collector of ancient manuscripts, he eventually replaced law with literary studies and composed works that influenced learning and literature long after his death. He is best known for his *Rime sparse*, a collection of sonnets and other lyric poems that set the standard for Italian vernacular verse for centuries.

Italian poet and storyteller **Giovanni Boccaccio** (1313–1375) was educated by his father for a career in commerce and law, but, drawn instead to literature, he became a Latin and Greek scholar as well as a prolific author. His classic secular work, the *Decameron*, is a collection of one hundred witty and occasionally bawdy tales set against the somber background of the plague in Florence.

**Geoffrey Chaucer** (ca. 1343–1400), the son of a prosperous London wine merchant, served two English kings (Edward III and Richard II) in a variety of governmental and civil service positions while creating a body of English poetry unequaled for its creative adaptation of French, Italian, and Latin sources. Its complex representation of interpersonal and societal relationships include *Troilus and Criseyde*, the magnificent story of a love affair tragically disrupted by the Trojan War, and *Canterbury Tales*, a collection of stories, varied in form, told by pilgrims on the road to Canterbury and featuring the celebrated and enigmatic "confessions" of the Wife of Bath and the Pardoner.

**Famine and plague**

The worst period of famine experienced in Europe during the Middle Ages occurred in the fourteenth century, from 1315 to 1317, when unusually heavy rains devastated crops and caused over 10 percent of the population to die of starvation. Later in the century, terrible epidemics of plague further decimated the population of cities like Florence so badly that they did not recover their numbers until the late nineteenth century. The desire to understand and control disease and nature also spurred advances in science and technology. Theories of light and vision (the chief sense for the acquisition of knowledge) were developed to a high degree of refinement, and theories of motion, explored at the universities of Paris and Oxford, provided the conceptual framework for Galileo's experiments three hundred years later.

**Science and technology**

An increasing interest in the natural world, the individual, and human nature led to a style in art and literature that was truer to life. During an outbreak of plague in Florence, Boccaccio wrote his *Decameron*, based on the premise that ten travelers escaping to the countryside amuse each other by telling stories. The pilgrims so imaginatively brought to life by Chaucer in his masterpiece, *Canterbury Tales*, engage in the same pastime on their way to the shrine of Saint

**Art and literature**

Thomas Becket, the martyred archbishop of Canterbury, who was assassinated in the cathedral there in 1170. Italian artists, like the sculptor Giovanni Pisano and the painter Giotto, anticipated the Renaissance in their works by incorporating classical elements and depicting the human form with greater realism (Figures I.12 and I.13).

Figure I.12 (left). Giovanni Pisano, Plato, ca. 1280. Duomo, Siena.

Figure I.13 (below). Giotto, The Nativity, detail, ca. 1305. Scrovegni Chapel, Padua, Italy.

Figure I.14. Andrea Orcagna (?), The Dream of Life, fresco, mid-fourteenth century. Campo Santo, Pisa.

The elite music of the late Middle Ages reflects many of these trends. A pre-occupation with structure and form in certain genres surfaced for the first time, perhaps partly as a response to the disorder in society (Chapter 4). Composers in France and Italy extended the repertory of courtly love lyrics in the vernacular to the polyphonic realm, and the elaborate textures and rhythmic complications characteristic of the repertory at the end of the fourteenth century are suggestive of the ostentatious pleasures of the court at Avignon. Polyphonic church music flourished—not only in the cathedrals—as princes and patrons in every country supported musicians to write and perform music for their private chapels, both to adorn the liturgy and to foster a sense of their own importance.

Music

# Music in Ancient Greece and Early Christian Rome

*Chapter Contents*

*Prelude* 18

Music in Ancient
Greek Life and
Thought 19

Roman Music, 200
B.C.E.–500 C.E. 22

The Early Christian
Church: Musical
Thought 23

The Early Christian
Church: Musical
Practice 25

*Postlude* 28

## PRELUDE

The history of western European music—that is, the art music of Europe and the Americas, as opposed to the musics of many Eastern and other cultures—begins with the ancient civilizations of the Near East and Mediterranean regions, particularly ancient Greece and Rome. Like many elements of European and American culture such as philosophy, literature, visual arts, and government, Western music has tangible connections to these early civilizations, links that go back more than three thousand years. We acknowledge these connections when we design our Supreme Court and other civic buildings to look like ancient Greek temples, when we talk about *platonic* love, and when we explain father-son conflicts in terms of the *Oedipus* complex.

Unlike the statues and architectural ruins of antiquity, however, the musical works themselves have vanished, except for about forty-five Greek songs and hymns (praise songs). But knowledge of Greco-Roman musical heritage was transmitted to modern civilization through written descriptions and through images that survived in painting or sculpture, on vases, buildings, tombs, and other artifacts from the ancient world. This evidence suggests that ancient Greek music has much in common with Western music. Then, as now, music was used in religious ceremonies, as popular entertainment, and as accompaniment to drama. Greek music theory—especially its ideas concerning pitch—was passed on to the ancient Romans and became the basis for Western music theory. During the first and second centuries, when the Roman Empire was in its heyday, cultivated people were supposed to be educated in music, just as they were expected to know Greek and Latin. Many of the emperors were patrons of music, and one—Nero—even aspired to personal fame as a musician.

With the decline of the Roman Empire, the intellectual musical heritage of ancient Greece and Rome was transmitted to the West, if incompletely and imperfectly, through the early Christian Church, specifically in the writings of the Church Fathers and other scholars who tried to understand and preserve this enormous body of information about music and other subjects. As the public rituals and musical practices of the early Church spread from Jerusalem to Asia Minor and westward into Africa and Europe, they picked up musical elements from different areas of the Mediterranean region. At first there was little standardization; but as the prestige of the Roman emperor declined, the importance of the Roman bishop (eventually, the pope) increased, and Christians began to acknowledge the authority of Rome in matters of faith and doctrine. This Roman dominance gradually led to the regulation and standardization of the Christian liturgy, or worship service, and eventually (in the seventh and eighth centuries) fostered the organization of a repertory of melodies for singing sacred texts now known as Gregorian chant.

# Music in Ancient Greek Life and Thought

In Greek mythology, music had a divine origin: its inventors and earliest practitioners were gods and demigods such as Apollo, Amphion, and Orpheus, and their music had magical powers. People thought it could heal sickness, purify the body and mind, and work miracles. In the Hebrew Scriptures, similar powers were attributed to music: we may recall the stories of David curing Saul's madness by playing the harp (1 Sam. 16:14–23) or of the trumpet blasts and shouting that toppled the walls of Jericho (Josh. 6:12–20).

Most of the approximately forty-five surviving examples of ancient Greek music come from relatively late periods. Among them we have the *Epitaph of Seikilos*, a brief song from about the first century C.E., inscribed on a tombstone (see Fig. 1.3 and its transcription in NAWM 1). From this and similar examples, and from what was written about Greek music, we may deduce some of its qualities, which reveal a close correspondence between theory and practice. It was primarily monophonic—that is, melody without harmony or counterpoint—but instruments often embellished the melody while a soloist or an ensemble sang it, thus creating heterophony (simultaneous performance of a melody in different ways by two or more parts). Greek music, moreover, was almost entirely improvised. Its melody and rhythm were intimately linked to the sound and meter of Greek poetry. Despite some similarities between Greek and early Christian musical practice, however, we have no evidence of any continuity in musical repertory from the earlier culture to the later one.

By contrast, Greek philosophy and theory profoundly affected musical thought in western Europe in the Middle Ages. From the ancient writers, we know much more about Greek musical thought than about the music itself. Philosophers such as Plato and Aristotle wrote about the nature of music, its place in the cosmos, its effects on people, and its proper uses in human society. In both the philosophy and the science of music, the Greeks achieved insights and established principles that have survived to this day. Here we will discuss only those that were most characteristic of, and important for, the later history of Western music. We will also discover that the word *music* had a much wider meaning to the Greeks than it has today.

The close union between music and poetry is one measure of the Greeks' broad conception of music. For them, the two were practically synonymous. Plato, for example, held that song (*melos*) was made up of speech, rhythm, and harmony (which he defined as an agreeable succession of pitches in a melody). "Lyric" poetry meant poetry sung to the lyre; the original Greek word for "tragedy" incorporates the noun *ōdē*, "the art of singing." Many other words that designated different kinds of poetry, such as *hymn*, were musical terms. In the *Epitaph of Seikilos* (NAWM 1), the musical rhythms of each line of the poem follow the text rhythms very closely. And if we knew the correct pronunciation of the ancient Greek verses, we might well discover that the contours of the melody match the rising and falling inflections of the words.

Extant Greek music

CD 1/1    CD 1/1

Greek theory

Music and poetry

---

**A CLOSER LOOK**    Ancient Greek Music: Kithara and Aulos

---

From earliest times, music was an inseparable part of religious ceremonies. The lyre was associated with the cult of Apollo, god of light, prophecy, and the arts, especially music and poetry. It was used to accompany dancing, singing, or recitation of epic poetry such as Homer's *Iliad* and *Odyssey*; to provide music for weddings; or to play for recreation. The lyre and its larger counterpart, the kithara (Fig. 1.1), had five to seven strings (later as many as eleven) that were plucked. The aulos was the characteristic instrument in the worship of Dionysus, god of fertility and wine; hence its presence in the drinking scene in Figure 1.2. A single- or double-reed instrument sometimes incorrectly identified as a flute, it often appears with twin pipes. It was also used in theatrical performances of the great Greek tragedies by Aeschylus, Sophocles, and Euripides created for the Dionysian festivals in Athens. These plays have choruses and other musical sections that combined or alternated with the sounds of the aulos.

From the sixth century B.C.E. or even earlier, both the lyre and the aulos were independent solo instruments. In fact, learning to play the lyre was a core element of the education of Athenian youth,

*Figure 1.1. A kitharode singing to his own accompaniment on the kithara. His left hand, which supports the instrument with a sling (not visible), is damping some of the strings, while his right hand has apparently just swept over all the strings with a plectrum. A professional musician like this one wore a long, flowing robe and a mantle. The Berlin Painter (?), detail from an Attic red-figured amphora, ca. 490 B.C.E. Metropolitan Museum of Art, New York.*

both male and female. Contests of kithara and aulos players as well as festivals of instrumental and vocal music became increasingly popular. When instrumental music grew more independent, the number of virtuosos multiplied and the music itself turned more complex. Alarmed by this trend, the philosopher Aristotle warned against too much professional training in general music education. A reaction against technical virtuosity and musical complexity set in, and by the beginning of the Christian era Greek music as well as its theory were simplified.

*Figure 1.2. Woman playing the double aulos in a drinking scene. Usually a single-reed but sometimes a double-reed instrument, the aulos was typically played in pairs. Here the player seems to finger identical notes on both pipes. Oltos (?), Attic red-figured drinking cup, 525–500 B.C.E. Museo Arqueológico Nacional, Madrid.*

*Figure 1.3. A tomb stele from Aydin, near Tralles, Asia Minor (now Turkey). It bears an epitaph, a kind of* scolion, *or drinking song, with pitch and rhythmic notation, identified in the first lines as being by Seikilos, probably first century C.E. See the transcription in NAWM 1. National Museum, Copenhagen.*

Greek philosophers believed that music could influence ethos, one's ethical character or way of being and behaving. Because of the Pythagorean view that the same mathematical laws governing music operate throughout the cosmos both in the visible and invisible world, even the human soul was seen as a composite whose parts were kept in harmony by numerical relationships. Music, then, could penetrate the soul and restore (or shatter) its inner harmony in the same way that *harmonia* determined the orderly motion of the planets. And the legendary musicians of mythology, it was believed, owed their ability to sway human beings as well as nature to this transforming power of music.

Closely related to the concept of ethos is Aristotle's theory of imitation, which explains how music affects behavior. Music, he writes in the *Politics* (ca. 330 B.C.E.), imitates (that is, represents) the passions or states of the soul, such as gentleness, anger, courage, temperance, and their opposites. Music that imitates a certain passion also arouses that passion in the listener and thereby influences a person's ethos. Habitual listening to music that stirs up ignoble passions, for example, may warp a person's character, whereas the right kind of music tends to fashion a person of good character. Aristotle argues, for example, that those being trained to govern should avoid melodies expressing softness and indolence and should listen instead to melodies that imitate courage and similar virtues.

Both Plato and Aristotle believed that a public system of education that stressed gymnastics to discipline the body and music to discipline the mind could create the "right" kind of person. In his *Republic*, written about 380 B.C.E., Plato insists that these two educational components must be balanced: too much music makes a man effeminate or neurotic while too much athletics makes him uncivilized, violent, and ignorant. Plato recommends the use of two modes (styles of melody)—Dorian and Phrygian—because they foster the passions of temperance and courage. He excludes other modes from his ideal republic and deplores current styles that rely on too many notes, on scales that are too complex, and on the mixing of incompatible genres, rhythms, and instruments. He disapproves of changing established musical conventions, saying that lawlessness in art and education inevitably leads to poor manners and anarchy in society. Aristotle is less restrictive than Plato about particular modes and rhythms. He holds that music can be used for amusement and intellectual enjoyment as well as for education. But he also believes that music is powerful enough, especially in combination with drama, to arouse certain emotions, like pity and fear,

Music and ethos

Theory of imitation

Music in education

in people and so relieve them of those same emotions through a process similar to medical catharsis.

In limiting the kinds of music they would allow in the ideal society, Plato and Aristotle showed their appreciation of the great power music held over people's intellectual and emotional well-being. In later centuries, the Church Fathers also warned regularly against certain kinds of music. Nor is the issue dead. In more recent times, guardians of morality have expressed concern about the kinds of music (and pictures, lyrics, and performances) to which young people are exposed, and ragtime, jazz, rock, punk, rap, and hip-hop have all been condemned for these very reasons.

Greek music theory

Our modern system of music theory and its vocabulary derives largely from ancient Greek musical thought. Greek theorists, from Pythagoras (ca. 580—ca. 500 B.C.E.) to Aristides Quintilianus nine hundred years later, not only discovered numerical relationships between pitches, but also developed systematic descriptions of the materials of music and the patterns of musical composition.

Music and number

For Pythagoras and his followers, numbers were the key to the universe, and music was inseparable from numbers. Rhythms were ordered by numbers, as was poetic meter, because each note or syllable was some multiple of a primary duration. Pythagoras was credited with discovering that the octave, fifth, and fourth, long recognized as consonances, are also generated by the simplest possible numeric ratios. For example, when a vibrating string is divided into segments one of which is twice as long as the other (expressed by the ratio 2:1), an octave results; 3:2 yields a fifth; and 4:3, a fourth.

Harmonics

The Greek discipline of harmonics, or the study of matters concerning pitch, laid the foundation for modern concepts such as notes, intervals, scales, and modes. These were first explored and defined by Greek writers, including Aristoxenus around 320 B.C.E. (*Harmonic Elements*) and Cleonides, who lived some five or six hundred years later. Intervals, such as tones, semitones, and ditones (thirds), were combined into scales. Certain intervals, such as the fourth, fifth, and octave, were recognized as consonant. The scale's principal building block

Tetrachords

was the tetrachord, made up of four notes spanning the interval of a fourth. Theorists recognized three kinds, or genera, of tetrachord: diatonic, chromatic, and enharmonic, the last involving intervals smaller than a semitone. Such variety allowed for a broad range of expression and many different nuances within melodies.

Because musical rhythms and sounds were ordered by numbers, they were thought to exemplify the general concept of *harmonia*, the unification of parts into an orderly whole. Through this concept—flexible enough to encompass mathematical proportions or the structure of society as well as musical intervals—Greek writers perceived music as a reflection of the order of the entire universe (see "Sounding and Silent Harmony," page 26).

Early Christian writers about music transmitted some of these Greek concepts to the Middle Ages in their original form. Other concepts were poorly understood and survived only after being adapted to the musical practice of Gregorian chant. Still others were forgotten altogether until their rediscovery by the great Renaissance humanist scholars of the fifteenth and sixteenth centuries (see Chapter 6).

## Roman Music, 200 B.C.E.—500 C.E.

The Romans took much of their musical culture from Greece, especially after the Greek islands became a Roman province in 146 B.C.E. (see Figure 1.4). As in

Saint Augustine on the Benefits and Dangers of Music

*Augustine is one of the most significant thinkers in the history of Christianity and Western philosophy. His* Confessions *are often considered the first modern autobiography. In the passage below, he expresses the tension between music's abilities to heighten devotion and to seduce with pleasure.*

When I recall the tears that I shed at the song of the Church in the first days of my recovered faith, and even now as I am moved not by the song but by the things which are sung—when chanted with fluent voice and completely appropriate melody—I acknowledge the great benefit of this practice. Thus I waver between the peril of pleasure and the benefit of my experience; but I am inclined, while not maintaining an irrevocable position, to endorse the custom of singing in church so that weaker souls might rise to a state of devotion by indulging their ears. Yet when it happens that I am moved more by the song than by what is sung, I confess sinning grievously, and I would prefer not to hear the singer at such times. See now my condition!

Saint Augustine, *Confessions* 10:33, trans. James W. McKinnon, in Oliver Strunk, ed., *Source Readings in Music History*, rev. ed. by Leo Treitler (New York: Norton, 1998), p. 133.

Greece, lyric poetry was often sung. Music was part of most public ceremonies and played an important role in religious rites, military events, theatrical performances, private entertainment, and education.

Rome's decline

During the great days of the Roman Empire in the first and second centuries C.E., art, architecture, music, philosophy, and other aspects of Greek culture were imported into Rome and other cities. Ancient writers tell of famous virtuosos, large choruses and orchestras, and grand music festivals and competitions. But with the economic decline of the empire in the third and fourth centuries, production of music on the large and expensive scale of earlier days ceased, leaving almost no traces on later European developments.

By the fifth century, the Roman Empire, which had for a time imposed peace on most of western Europe and on large parts of Africa and Asia as well, declined in wealth and strength. Unable to defend itself against invaders from the north and east, it was too large and weak to continue. The common civilization it had fostered throughout Europe splintered into fragments that would take many centuries to regroup and emerge as modern nations (compare maps, pages 36 and 113).

# The Early Christian Church: Musical Thought

As the Roman Empire declined, however, the Christian Church gained influence, becoming the main—and, often, the only—unifying force and channel of culture in Europe until the tenth century. With the help of the Church Fathers, highly influential Christian writers and scholars who interpreted the Bible and set down some guiding principles, the Church took over Rome's mission of civilizing and unifying the peoples under its sway. Writing in Greek (Clement of Alexandria, Origen, Saint Basil, and Saint John Chrysostom in the third and fourth centuries) or in Latin (Saint Ambrose, Saint Augustine, and Saint Jerome in the fourth and early fifth centuries), they saw in music the power to inspire divine thoughts and to influence, for good or evil, the character of its listeners (a version of the Greek concept of ethos). When the last Roman emperor finally

Church Fathers

**A CLOSER LOOK**    Boethius's *Fundamentals*

In the opening chapters of *De institutione musica*, the most original part of the treatise, Boethius divides music into three types. The first is the inaudible *musica mundana* (cosmic music), the numerical relations controlling the movement of the planets, the changing of the seasons, and the combination of elements. The second is *musica humana*, which harmonizes and unifies the body and soul and their parts. Last is *musica instrumentalis*, audible music produced by instruments and voices, which exemplifies the same principles of order as the other types of music, especially in the numerical ratios of its musical intervals.

Because music could influence character and morals, Boethius assigned it an important place in the education of the young, both in its own right and as an introduction to more advanced philosophical studies. In placing *musica instrumentalis*—the art of music as we commonly understand it now—in the third and presumably lowest category, Boethius indicated that, like his predecessors, he saw music primarily as a science, the discipline of examining the diversity of high and low sounds by means of reason and the senses, and only secondarily as a practice. Therefore, the true musician is not the singer or someone who makes up songs by instinct without understanding the nature of the medium, but rather the theorist and critic, who can use reason to make discoveries and judgments about the essence and the art of music.

*Figure 1.4. Fanciful portrayals of Boethius and Pythagoras, above, and Plato and Nicomachus, below. Boethius measures out notes on a monochord, a string stretched over a long wooden box with a movable bridge to vary the sounding length of the string. Pythagoras strikes the bells with hammers. The others were revered as authorities on music. An early twelfth-century drawing.*

left the throne in 476 C.E. after a terrible century of wars and invasions, the power of the papacy was already well established.

**Dangers of music**    Philosophers and Church leaders of the early Middle Ages disdained the idea that music might be enjoyed solely for its play of sounds, something we now take for granted. Without denying that the sound of music could be pleasurable, they held to the Platonic principle that beautiful things exist to remind us of divine and perfect beauty, not to inspire self-centered enjoyment or seduce our senses. This view forms the basis for many of the pronouncements against music made by some Church Fathers (and, later, by some theologians of the Protestant Reformation; see Chapter 8). Others, however, not only defended pagan art, literature, and music, but found themselves so deeply affected by them that they actually worried about taking pleasure in listening to music, even in church. Saint Augustine (354–430) expresses this concern in a well-known passage from his *Confessions* (see Vignette, page 23).

**Transmission of Greek music theory**    The music theory and philosophy of the ancient world—or whatever could still be found after the collapse of the Roman Empire and the invasions from the north—were gathered, summarized, modified, and transmitted to the West during the early Christian era, most notably by the writers Martianus Capella and Boethius.

    In his widely read treatise *The Marriage of Mercury and Philology* (early fifth century), Martianus described the seven liberal arts: grammar, dialectic (logic), rhetoric, geometry, arithmetic, astronomy, and harmonics (music). The first three, the verbal arts, came to be called the *trivium* (three paths), while the last four, the mathematical disciplines, were called the *quadrivium* (four paths) by Boethius.

    Boethius (ca. 480–ca. 524), depicted in Figure 1.4, was the most revered authority on music in the Middle Ages: his *De institutione musica* (The Fundamentals of Music), widely copied and cited for the next thousand years, treats music as part of the quadrivium. For Boethius, music is a science of numbers because numerical ratios and proportions determine intervals, consonances, scales, and tuning. Boethius compiled the book from Greek sources, mainly a long treatise by Nicomachus and the first book of Ptolemy's *Harmonics*. Although medieval readers may not have realized how much Boethius borrowed from other authors (a standard practice at the time), they understood that his statements were based on Greek mathematics and music theory.

*Martianus Capella*

*Boethius*

# The Early Christian Church: Musical Practice

During their first two or three centuries, Christian communities incorporated into their observances features of Greek music and the music of other cultures

*Greek legacy*

| TIMELINE  Greece and Rome | |
| --- | --- |
| **MUSICAL EVENTS** | **HISTORICAL EVENTS** |
| | **800 B.C.E.** Rise of Greek city-states |
| | **753 B.C.E.** Rome founded |
| | **ca. 700 B.C.E. or earlier** Homer's *Iliad* and *Odyssey* |
| | **660 B.C.E.** Byzantium founded |
| Famous music festival competition at Pythian games **582 B.C.E.** | |
| | **ca. 497 B.C.E.** Pythagoras dies |
| | **458 B.C.E.** Aeschylus, *Agamemnon* |
| | **414 B.C.E.** Euripides, *Iphigenia in Taurus* |
| | **ca. 380 B.C.E.** Plato, *Republic* |
| | **ca. 330 B.C.E.** Aristotle, *Politics* |
| Aristoxenus, *Harmonic Elements* **ca. 320 B.C.E.** | |
| | **46 B.C.E.** Julius Caesar becomes dictator |
| | **29–19 B.C.E.** Virgil, *Aeneid* |
| | **4 C.E.** Birth of Jesus |
| *Epitaph of Seikilos* **ca. 1st cent.** | **ca. 33** Crucifixion of Jesus |
| | **54** Nero becomes emperor of Rome |
| | **70** Temple at Jerusalem destroyed |

*Figure 1.5.* Venus Playing a Psaltery, *folio 42v of the fourteenth-century astrological treatise* Liber astrologiae. *Seated on an elaborate throne, the goddess is plucking a psaltery. On the left is a fiddle, on the right a cittern.*

For many thinkers of the ancient world, music was closely connected to astronomy because mathematics dominated the study of both subjects. In fact, Pythagoras (fl. 530 B.C.E.), who recognized the numerical relationships that govern musical intervals, is famous for his discovery of specific mathematical laws such as the familiar Pythagorean theorem. Ptolemy (second century C.E.), the most systematic of the ancient Greek theorists of music, was also the leading astronomer of antiquity. Numerical proportions were thought to underlie the systems both of musical intervals and of the heavenly bodies, and certain modes and notes were believed to correspond with particular planets, their distances from each other, and their movement in the heavens. Plato gave this idea poetic form in his myth of "the music of the spheres" (*Republic* 10.617), the unheard music produced by the harmonious relationships among the planets as they revolved around the earth.

In the Middle Ages, music was defined as the discipline that deals with numbers in their rela-tionship to sounds. Medieval Christian philosophers from Saint Augustine (354–430 C.E.) to Saint Thomas Aquinas (ca. 1225–1274) believed that a knowledge of proportion and number was essential to understanding God's universe. Seen as one of the seven liberal arts, music was grouped with the mathematical and speculative sciences in the quadrivium, the path of learning that led to the contemplation of philosophy. In this curriculum, music had a place of honor next to astronomy because, through numerical analogies and ratios, it could help explain connections between things perceived by the senses (such as sound), things knowable only through reason and speculation (such as the movement of heavenly bodies), and things that could never be known because they belonged to the realm of the divine (such as the mysteries of the human soul). So the numerical relationships that regulated both music and astronomy provided the foundation for knowledge about the order and system of the entire universe.

Pythagorean and Platonic ideas about cosmic harmony and music of the spheres continued until the end of the Renaissance and persist even into the modern era. Along the way, these ideas strongly influenced astronomers, physicians, architects, and poets, including Dante, Shakespeare, and Milton. In addition, astronomy and music had close ties to astrology, which has maintained considerable appeal since antiquity, despite arousing the suspicion of Christian philosophers and theologians through the ages and the derision of scientists and other rationalists today. Boethius's popular notions about *musica mundana* and *musica humana* (see page 24), which affirmed Greek theories about the relationship between the music of the spheres and music's influence on human character and morals, left the door wide open for astrology in the Middle Ages; then, as now, astrologers interpreted the influence of the heavenly bodies on human affairs. In astrological symbolism, the planets Venus and Mercury hold particular sway over the musical attributes of humans; for this reason, in medieval and Renaissance art depictions of Venus often include musical instruments.

bordering on the eastern Mediterranean Sea. However, for early Church leaders, music was the servant of religion, and they rejected the idea of cultivating music purely for enjoyment. They also disapproved of the forms and types of music connected with great public spectacles such as festivals, competitions, and dramatic performances, as well as the music of more intimate social occasions. It was not that they disliked music itself; but they wanted to wean converts away from anything associated with their pagan past. For this reason, the entire tradition of Christian music for over a thousand years was one of unaccompanied singing.

Christianity sprang from Jewish roots, and some elements of Christian observances derive from Jewish traditions, chiefly the chanting of Scripture and the singing of psalms, poems of praise from the Old Testament Book of Psalms. We find a parallel between the Jewish temple service and the Christian Mass of later centuries (described in Chapter 2) in the symbolic sacrifice in which worshippers and priests partake of the body and blood of Christ in the form of bread and wine. But the Mass also commemorates the Last Supper that Jesus shared with his disciples and thus imitates the festive Jewish Passover Seder, which was accompanied by psalm singing. Singing psalms assigned to certain days eventually became a central element in all Christian observances.

As the early Church spread from Jerusalem to Asia Minor, North Africa, and Europe, it absorbed other musical influences. For example, the monasteries and churches of Syria were important in the development of psalm singing and the use of strophic devotional songs, or hymns. The singing of devotional songs was the earliest recorded musical activity of Jesus and his followers (Matthew 26:30; Mark 14:26). Both psalms and other types of praise songs traveled from Syria by way of Byzantium (in Asia Minor) to Milan (Italy) and other Western centers.

In 395 C.E., the political unity of the ancient world was formally divided into Eastern and Western Empires, with capitals at Byzantium and Rome, followed eventually by a theological rift between Eastern and Western churches. The Western Church became the Roman Catholic Church and the bishop of Rome was known as the pope. The city of Byzantium (later Constantinople, now Istanbul), at the crossroads between Europe and Asia Minor, remained the capital of the Eastern Empire for more than a thousand years, until its capture by the Turks in 1453. During much of this time, Byzantium, located on the northern rim of the Mediterranean Sea, flourished as a cultural center that blended elements of Western, African, and Eastern civilizations. From the Byzantine Church, ancestor of the present-day Orthodox churches, missionaries took their Greek rites north to the Slavs, resulting in the establishment of the Russian and other Slavic Orthodox churches. But in the absence of a strong central authority, the various Christian churches of the Eastern Empire developed different liturgies. Byzantine musical practices left their mark on Western chant, particularly in the classification of the repertory into eight modes, or melody types, and in a number of hymns borrowed by the West between the sixth and ninth centuries.

In the West, the diffusion of the Latin liturgy and its music occurred in the fifth and sixth centuries, with the texts remaining more stable than the melodies. As in the East, local churches were relatively independent at first. Although they shared a large area of common practice, each Western region probably received the Roman heritage, including the Latin liturgy, in a somewhat different form. These original differences, combined with local variations, eventually produced several distinct Western liturgies and bodies of liturgical music between the fifth and eighth centuries. Peoples who inhabited what is now Italy, France, and Germany developed their own repertory of melodies for

Judaic heritage

Christian observances

Psalms and hymns

Eastern churches

Western churches

Chant dialects

singing sacred texts in Latin. We call these melodies chants, and the different regional styles may be called dialects by analogy to language. Gaul (approximately the same area as modern France) had the Gallican chant; southern Italy, the Beneventan; Rome, the Old Roman chant; Spain, the Visigothic, or Mozarabic; and the area around Milan, the Ambrosian. Eventually, most of the local versions either disappeared or were absorbed into the single uniform practice under the central authority of the Roman Catholic Church. From the thirteenth to the sixteenth centuries, the liturgy of the Western Church was increasingly Romanized.

*Rome's musical dominance*

*Gregorian chant*

How did the thousands of chant melodies associated with Christian worship survive over so many centuries? During the ninth century, Frankish monks and nuns—from modern-day Switzerland, France, and western Germany—played a crucial role in their preservation, not only by learning to sing them, but also by laboriously notating the texts and melodies by hand into manuscripts that were housed in monastic libraries (see Chapter 2, page 37). The repertory of melodies thus transmitted in writing, known as Gregorian chant, will be examined in the next chapter. Although its origins are still being unraveled by modern scholars, it remains one of the outstanding legacies of medieval civilization.

## POSTLUDE

Although many details are uncertain, we know that in the ancient world (1) music consisted essentially of a single melodic line; (2) vocal melody was intimately linked with the rhythm and meter of words; (3) musical performances were memorized or improvised (not read from notation), in keeping with accepted conventions; (4) philosophers believed that music was both an orderly system interlocked with nature and a force in human thought and conduct; (5) a scientifically based acoustical theory was in the making; (6) scales were built up from tetrachords; and (7) musical terminology was well developed. The last three elements of this heritage were specifically Greek; the others were common also among other cultures in the ancient world.

This heritage was transmitted to the West, if incompletely and imperfectly, through the Christian Church, the writings of the Church Fathers, and early medieval scholarly treatises that dealt with music and other subjects. The awesome powers attributed to music by the ancient Greeks were still convincing to Saint Augustine, who confessed his concern about the pleasure he experienced while listening to music. Boethius wrote an influential treatise based on the Greek view of music as a science of numerical ratios and an important educational force. In practice, early Christian Church music absorbed elements from many cultures, and local variants of the liturgy and its chant existed throughout the Byzantine and Western Roman Empires. Eventually, the practices of the Roman Church prevailed, and the body of melodies known as Gregorian chant became the established repertory in the West.

The church music we will be discussing in the next several chapters accounts for only a small part of the music making in the Middle Ages. Popular and folk traditions, from games and dances to work-related activities, learned aurally and passed on from memory, were all accompanied by instrumental or vocal music of which we have no knowledge. From the necessarily limited survey contained within the pages of this book, therefore, it might be easy to conclude that in the West sacred music came before secular music, or that vocal music preceded instrumental music, or that Christian worship music was the only kind of ritual music in existence in Europe for the first thousand years of the Common Era. But such conclusions would be inaccurate. It is simply that, thanks to notation, the chant repertory of Western Christian worship is available to us for study, unlike the many other musical repertories that have not been so preserved.

# Chant and Secular Song
# in the Middle Ages

*Chapter Contents*

*Prelude* 30

Western Christian
Chant and Liturgy 31

Genres and Forms of
Chant 35

Medieval Music Theory
and Practice 44

Medieval Song 46

*Postlude* 53

## PRELUDE

Two distinct bodies of song, one sacred (religious) and the other secular (worldly), flourished side by side during the Middle Ages—the thousand-year period that began with the fall of the Roman Empire in the fifth century. The sacred repertory, known as plainchant (eventually, Gregorian chant), was created for ceremonial use and served as a principal element in the communal *liturgy*, or worship service, of the Western Christian Church; it was essentially musical prayer (or, in the case of the psalms, praise), the devotional words heightened through melody and rhythm. Nonsacred songs—called *secular monody*—were of two types: courtly and elite or popular and traditional. Both types were intended mainly for entertainment or for communicating feelings. Like songs of any age, these gave voice to the celebration of heroes, the expression of protest, and, especially, the pain and pleasure of love. All three repertories—one sacred and two secular—were primarily monophonic, although for secular song instrumental accompaniments were probably improvised, especially for dancing, marching, exhorting to battle, and so on. All three originated in oral cultures, and their texts and melodies were initially performed from memory according to formulas handed down by older singers or invented by new poet-composers. Chants and courtly songs were transmitted this way for many centuries before they were eventually written down in a gradually evolving notation that developed in order to preserve the music, more or less accurately, for future generations. But for most people, music was purely aural, and most of the secular and nonliturgical music they heard, sang, and played has vanished. The second half of this chapter, then, of necessity focuses on the written repertory of courtly or aristocratic song that flourished in France in the late Middle Ages.

Christianity sprang from Jewish roots and spread westward from Jerusalem throughout the Roman Empire (see Figure 2.1). As the Western Christian liturgy was disseminated with its music, it changed and expanded over time; while the texts were relatively stable (they were written down hundreds of years before the melodies), the repertory of chant was more fluid, and the process of variation and expansion continued even after the advent of notation. Another important factor in the transmission and preservation of these melodies was their classification into church modes. Learned theorists who interpreted (and sometimes misinterpreted) Boethius, as well as teachers responsible for training student monks and nuns (who did not necessarily have any musical aptitude) to sing plainchant, created a system of medieval music theory and practice, at first based on practical considerations and then modified and elaborated from concepts inherited from the ancient Greek science of music. Other elements of this medieval system were newly invented—such as the syllables associated with sightsinging, which are still used in the classroom today.

Like plainchant, the repertory of medieval song outside the Church also comprised many different types and forms that had distinct functions and differing conventions. One kind was intended for performances of medieval drama (which included both religious and secular subjects), while another was epic or lyric in style. Among the most artful and refined were the songs of the twelfth- and thirteenth-century poet-composers—called troubadours and trouvères—who also wrote their own lyrics in either of the two principal French dialects of the time. Some features of these medieval lyrics are echoed in nineteenth-century art song (see Chapter 17) and even in modern rap: they all often deal openly with sensual subject matter, use coded language, and address some sort of coterie—a group of aristocrats at court, a closed circle of friends, or a commercial audience of fans.

# Western Christian Chant and Liturgy

The chants of the Christian Church rank among the great treasures of Western civilization. Like Romanesque architecture, they stand as a memorial to religious faith in the Middle Ages, embodying the sense of community and the aesthetic values of the time (see Figure 2.2). Not only does this body of plainchant include some of the noblest melodies to survive to modern times, it also served as the source and inspiration for later music in the Western art tradition, much of which bears its imprint. If we are to understand the various genres and forms of chant and how they were used in medieval ceremonial context, we need to

*Figure 2.1. The diffusion of Christianity.*

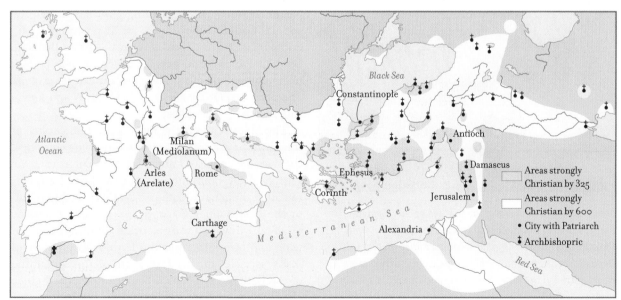

know the basic elements of the Western Christian liturgy, especially the daily Mass.

Because plainchant is a melody that projects the sacred and devotional words of ritual, its shape cannot be separated from its verbal message or from its place in the worship service. Musically, it can be as simple as a recitation on a single pitch or as elaborate as a long, winding melody that requires a highly trained soloist to perform it. The degree of musical elaboration depends on the function of the words in the ritual and on who is singing—a soloist, a trained choir, or the people. The position of the chant in the liturgy determines all this.

**Liturgy**    The body of texts and rites that make up a sacred service is known as the liturgy; its purpose is to glorify God and the saints, teach the Gospels—the life and works of Jesus—and exhort the worshippers along the path of salvation. At its core is a yearly cycle of readings from the Bible and a weekly cycle of readings from the Book of Psalms. The texts are prescibed according to the church calendar, a yearly cycle that determines which saints, events, and feast days are remembered in a given service, or which seasons of the church year (for example, the Advent season leading up to Christmas or the penitential Lenten season preparing for Easter) are being celebrated. Although much of each worship service is the same at every observance, other aspects change with the day or season.

These readings are at the core of the two principal types of service: the Office and the Mass. The Divine Office centers around the communal reading of the psalms. The Mass also includes readings and prayers, but is unique in its ritualistic commemoration of the Last Supper of Jesus and his disciples as recounted in the Gospels.

The Office, or Canonical Hours, first codified in the *Rule of Saint Benedict* (ca. 530), consists of a series of eight prayer services observed at specified times around the clock by the members of a religious community. By calling a group of monks or nuns to pray collectively every few hours (see Figure 2.3), the Office provides the ritual around which life in a monastery or convent is structured. It consists of prayers, recitation of scriptural passages, and songs.

Every Office liturgy includes several psalms, each with an antiphon, a chant sung before and after the psalm; lessons (Bible readings) with musical responses called responsories; hymns; canticles, poetic passages from elsewhere in the Bible than the Book of Psalms; and prayers. Over the course of a normal week, all 150 psalms are sung at least once. The principal Office services, liturgically and musically, are Matins and Vespers.

The Mass remains the most important service of the Catholic Church. In other Christian churches, the service is also known as the Eucharist, the Liturgy, Holy Communion, and the Lord's Supper, but all of them culminate in a symbolic reenactment of the Last Supper (Luke 22:19–20; 1 Corinthians 11:23–26) in which the celebrant blesses bread and wine and offers them to the faithful in memory of Jesus' sacrifice for the atonement of sin. An outline of the Catholic Mass, as it has been practiced since about 1200, appears in Figure 2.5, with letters pre-

*Figure 2.2. Interior view of the basilica of San Clemente, Rome, showing the choir stalls facing each other in front of the altar. As Christians grew in number, they met for worship in basilicas like this one, where sung words carried more clearly through the large, resonant space than did spoken words.*

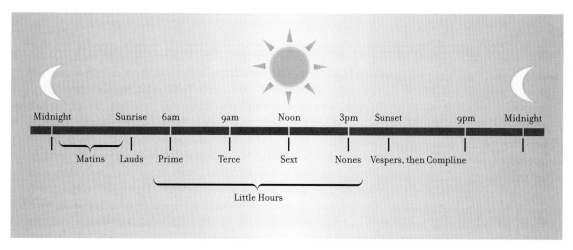

*Figure 2.3. The Office.*

ceding the important musical items to indicate their position in NAWM 3, the complete Mass for Christmas Day.

CD 1/4–23    CD 1/2–6

The liturgy of the Mass falls into three successive stages: introductory prayers; the instructional part, or Liturgy of the Word, during which the congregation listens to passages read or intoned from the Hebrew Scriptures and from the apostles and Gospel writers of the New Testament; and the Liturgy of the Eucharist, the unique part during which the bread and wine are consecrated and distributed. Within these three stages, some texts remain the same from one day to the next while others change according to the season or the particular occasion being celebrated. The variable texts, called the Proper of the Mass, include the Introit, Collects, Epistle, Gradual, Alleluia, Gospel, Offertory, Comunion, and others. The unchanging texts (each of which, however, may be sung to several different melodies throughout the year), called the Ordinary of the Mass, include the Kyrie, Gloria, Credo, Sanctus, Agnus Dei, and Ite, missa est.

Initially, chant melodies were learned by hearing others sing them, a process called oral transmission, leaving no written traces. How chant melodies were created and transmitted without writing from the fourth to the eighth century has been the subject of much study and controversy. Some scholars suggest that many chants were improvised within strict conventions based on formulas such as those used by epic singers and storytellers. We can find evidence for such oral composition in the chants themselves, many of which share the same melodic contour or feature characteristic cadential and other patterns. However, as long as this process depended on memory and learning by ear, melodies were subject to change and variation.

Oral transmission

Such variation was not suitable if the chants were to be performed in the same way each time in churches across a wide territory, as the pope and Frankish kings (Charlemagne and others) eventually came to require. In the late eighth and ninth centuries, therefore, rudimentary systems of musical notation were invented to standardize the performance of chant melodies. This coincided with a determined campaign by Frankish political leaders to promote a uniform liturgy and music in order to consolidate and increase their influence on worshippers throughout their lands. Trained "missionaries" traveled between Rome and the north to stabilize the repertory of tunes and suppress local variations. A persuasive tool of Frankish propaganda was the legend of Saint Gregory, who was reputed to have written down the chant melodies, guided by divine inspiration in the form of a dove singing in his ear (see Figure 2.8).

Notation of chant

**A CLOSER LOOK**    The Experience of the Mass

The Mass was the focal point of medieval religious life. For the illiterate populace, it was the main source of instruction about the central tenets of their faith. It was also—and most essentially—the ritual reenactment of the Last Supper in the Eucharist, a sacrament or sign that at once symbolized and encouraged the communal life of Christians. Ideally, these fundamental elements were meant to be presented in a way that would engage and inspire, gripping not only the mind but also the heart.

The building where Mass was celebrated was designed to evoke awe. Whether a simple rural church or a grand cathedral, it was likely to be the tallest structure most people would ever enter. The high ceiling and murals drew the eye upward in contemplation of the divine. Pillars and walls were adorned with sculptures, tapestries, or paintings depicting pious saints, the sufferings of Jesus, or the torments of hell, each image a visual sermon. In these resonant spaces, the spoken word was easily lost, but singing carried words clearly to all corners.

European Christians, especially in central and northern Europe, were not long removed from old pagan customs of propitiating the gods to ensure good crops or prevent misfortune, and they looked to Christian observances to serve the same role. Life for most was hard, and with the constant threat of disease, famine, and war, average life expectancy was under thirty years. Worship in a well-appointed church afforded not only an interlude of beauty, but also a way to please God and secure blessings in this life and the next.

In such a space, the Mass begins with the entrance procession of the priest and his assistants to the altar. The choir sings a psalm, the Introit (Latin for "he enters"), and continues with the Kyrie, whose threefold invocations symbolize the Trinity of Father, Son, and Holy Spirit. The Greek words and text repetitions reflect the Kyrie's origins in a Byzantine processional litany, a type of prayer consisting of a series of supplications with

*Figure 2.4.  The Last Supper (1492), a medieval wall painting by Canavesio from Notre-Dame des Fontaines, a tiny church in the mountain village of La Brigue, in southeastern France.*

Notation, then, was both a result of striving for uniformity and a means of perpetuating that uniformity.

Between the fifth and ninth centuries, the peoples of western and northern Europe converted to Christianity and adopted the doctrines and rites of the Roman Church. The official "Gregorian" chant was established in the Frankish Empire before the middle of the ninth century, and from then until nearly the close of the Middle Ages, all important developments in European music took place not in Rome, but north of the Alps. This shift in musical centers occurred partly because of political conditions. The Muslim conquests of Syria, North Africa, and especially Spain, completed by 719, left the southern Christian regions either in the hands of occupying forces or under constant threat of attack. Meanwhile, various cultural centers arose in western and central Europe. Between the sixth and eighth centuries, missionaries from Irish and Scottish monasteries established schools in their own lands and abroad, especially in what is now Germany and Switzerland. An English monk, Alcuin of York, helped Emperor Charlemagne in his project to revive education throughout the Frankish

| | Proper | Ordinary |
|---|---|---|
| Introductory Section | Introit (a)<br><br>Collect | Kyrie (b)<br>Gloria (c) |
| Liturgy of the Word | Epistle<br>Gradual (d)<br>Alleluia (or Tract) (e)<br>Sequence<br>(on major feasts)<br>Gospel<br>Sermon<br>(optional) | Credo (f) |
| Liturgy of the Eucharist | Offertory (g)<br><br>Secret<br>Preface<br><br><br><br>Communion (j)<br>Postcommunion | Prayers<br><br><br>Sanctus (h)<br>Canon<br>Pater noster<br>(Lord's Prayer)<br>Agnus Dei (i)<br><br>Ite, missa est (k) |

Blue: Sung by choir    Red: Intoned    Green: Spoken

*Figure 2.5. The Mass. The outline of the Mass with the most important musical parts indicated by letters corresponding to their position in NAWM 3, the complete Mass for Christmas Day.*

brief responses. There follows the Gloria, a song of praise, and a collective prayer (the Collect), intoned by the priest on behalf of all those present.

The Liturgy of the Word focuses on Bible readings (the Epistle and Gospel), florid chants (Gradual, Alleluia, and Sequence), church teachings (the Credo, or "I believe"), and meditation on their message (the sermon). In the Liturgy of the Eucharist, the priest turns from words to actions as he prepares, consecrates, and consumes the bread and wine. The main sung portions of this part of the Mass include the Offertory, a florid chant on a psalm verse, the Sanctus (Holy, holy, holy), and the Agnus Dei (Lamb of God), which, like the Kyrie, was adapted from a litany. After Communion is taken, the choir sings the Communion chant, based on a psalm. The priest concludes the service by singing Ite, missa est (Go, you are dismissed). From this phrase came the Latin name for the entire service, Missa, which became the English Mass.

Throughout the Mass, the music serves both to convey the words and engage the worshippers. As Saint Basil the Great (ca. 330–379), a father of the Eastern church, observed,

> When the Holy Spirit saw that mankind was ill-inclined toward virtue and that we were heedless of the righteous life because of our inclination to pleasure, what did he do? He blended the delight of melody with doctrine in order that through the pleasantness and softness of the sound we might unawares receive what was useful in the words.

Empire. One result of this eighth- and ninth-century renaissance was the development of important musical centers, including the famous monastery of Saint Gall in what is now Switzerland. Here, the northern, Frankish influence on plainchant is evident in melodic lines with more leaps, especially thirds, and in the introduction of both new melodies and new forms of chant such as tropes, sequences, and liturgical drama, all to be discussed below.

## Genres and Forms of Chant

Chants are classified in different, overlapping ways: (1) by their texts, which may be biblical or nonbiblical, prose or poetry; (2) by their manner of performance, which may be antiphonal (sung by alternating choirs), responsorial (with a choir responding to a soloist), or direct (simply by one choir); and (3) by their musical style, which may be syllabic (one note per syllable of text)

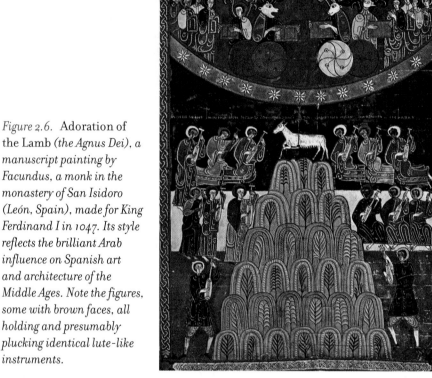

*Figure 2.6.* Adoration of the Lamb (*the Agnus Dei*), *a manuscript painting by Facundus, a monk in the monastery of San Isidoro (León, Spain), made for King Ferdinand I in 1047. Its style reflects the brilliant Arab influence on Spanish art and architecture of the Middle Ages. Note the figures, some with brown faces, all holding and presumably plucking identical lute-like instruments.*

*Figure 2.7. The Holy Roman Empire under Charlemagne around 800.*

or melismatic (many notes per syllable). This last distinction is not always clearcut since chants that are mostly melismatic usually include some syllabic sections or phrases, and many syllabic chants have occasional syllables with a prolonged melodic gesture of between two and seven notes each, passages that are sometimes called neumatic (from *neume*, or "pitch symbol" in chant).

Most parts of the Mass and Office are chanted to recitation formulas, simple melodic outlines that can be used with many different texts. Some parts of the

**IN CONTEXT**    In the Monastic Scriptorium

During the first millennium of Christianity, the preservation of liturgical texts and melodies in manuscripts—books laboriously written and copied by hand—became one of the great accomplishments of the monastic communities of the Middle Ages.

Manuscript production became a routine part of monastic life, and special places within the monastery were set aside as writing workshops, or scriptoria. The scriptorium also refers to the entire group of monks or nuns who were engaged in producing a manuscript, from those who prepared the ink and parchment or drew the lines on which the music was then notated, to the skilled workers who put the finishing touches on the book's covers. The bookmaking process extended beyond the scriptorium to the monks who toiled outside the monastery. An entire flock of sheep was needed to provide the parchment for a single book; and wild game such as deer and boar were hunted in order to furnish the leather used for binding the volumes.

But the copyist's job was central and involved both manual dexterity and intellectual fortitude. Trainees first had to learn how to make the letters and notes conform exactly to the style of writing that was in use at the time; there was little room for individuality. As a result, the scribes throughout northwestern Europe produced works of incredible regularity and perfect legibility.

Straightforward copying of text and music was only one stage of the manuscript's production.

*Figure 2.8. Saint Gregory writing with scribes. Franco-German school, ivory, ca. 850–875. Kunsthistorisches Museum, Vienna.*

Another was the exacting job of decorating the more important books with elaborate initials and capital letters in gold leaf or colored paints, and illustrating them with miniature scenes or brightening up the text's margins with illuminated designs. Finally came the binding, which could be more or less elaborate. The most important books were encased in ornamental covers made by specialized craftsmen and enriched with metals and gems.

All this labor helped to keep alive a widespread appreciation for music manuscripts, the creation of which represented so much effort and expense. And for the monks themselves, copying a book was regarded like prayer and fasting—as a way to keep one's unruly passions in check. But the monks also saw in their painstaking work a means of spreading the word of God. The abbot of one important Benedictine monastery in the twelfth century has this to say about the solitary monk who devotes his life to the scriptorium (as opposed to the garden or vineyards):

He cannot take to the plow? Then let him take up the pen; it is much more useful. In the furrows he traces on the parchment, he will sow the seeds of the divine words. . . . He will preach without opening his mouth; . . . and without leaving his cloister, he will journey far over land and sea.[1]

1. Peter the Venerable, abbot of Cluny, France, quoted by Jean LeClercq, *The Love of Learning and the Desire for God: A Study of Monastic Culture*, trans. Catharine Misrahi (New York: Fordham University Press, 1961), p. 128.

*Example 2.1: Antiphon:* Salve Regina

Sal - ve* Re - gi - na, ma-ter mi - se - ri - cor-di - ae:

Vi - ta, dul - ce - do, et spes nos - tra, sal - ve. Ad te

cla-ma - mus, ex-su-les, fi - li - i He - vae. Ad te sus-pi-ra -

mus, ge-men - tes et flen - tes in hac la - cri-ma - rum val - le.

*Hail, O Queen, Mother of mercy, our life, our sweetness and our hope! To thee do we cry, banished children of Eve; to thee do we send up our sighs, mourning and weeping in this vale of tears. . . .*

The asterisk indicates where the chant alternates between soloist and choir or between the two halves of the choir. Vertical lines indicate shorter or longer pauses at the ends of phrases and cadences. Notes are assumed to have equal duration, and a dot after a note doubles its value. For more on chant notation, see NAWM 3.

liturgy, however, are sung to fully formed melodies. The two are not entirely separate since even complex melodies may be elaborations of an underlying formula.

**Text setting**

Chant proclaims the text, sometimes straightforwardly and other times ornately. It follows that the musical contours of a chant generally reflect the way the Latin words were pronounced, with prominent syllables set to higher notes or to a melisma. But in florid chants, the word accent often takes a backseat to the melodic curve, resulting in long melismas on weak syllables, such as the final "a" of "alleluia" or "e" of "Kyrie." In such cases, the most important words or syllables of a phrase are emphasized with syllabic treatment that makes them stand out against the rich ornamentation of the unstressed syllables. Plainchant calls for word repetition only where it exists in the text of the prayer itself (such as the phrase "Kyrie eleison"; see page 42). Melodies usually conform to the rhythm of the text and to the liturgical function of the chant. Rarely does a melody realize emotional or pictorial effects.

**Melodic structure**

Every chant melody is divided into phrases and periods corresponding to the phrases and periods of the text. Many phrases follow the curve of an arch, beginning low, rising to a higher pitch, perhaps remaining there for a while, then descending at its conclusion. This simple and natural design occurs in a great variety of subtle combinations—extending over two or more phrases, for example, or including many smaller arches within its span. A less common melodic design, characteristic of phrases beginning with an especially important word, starts on a high note and descends gradually to the end.

**Chant forms**

We can distinguish three main forms in the chant repertory. One, exemplified in the psalm tone (one of eight melodies used for singing psalms), consists of two balanced phrases that correspond to the two halves of a typical psalm verse (see Example 2.2). In the second form—such as strophic form in hymns—the same melody is sung to several stanzas of text (as in NAWM 4b). A third is free form, which may be entirely original in its content or may incorporate a series of traditional melodic formulas into an otherwise original composition.

CD 1/28

*Figure 2.9.* *The Antiphon to the Blessed Virgin Mary,* Salve Regina mater misericordiae *(Hail, O Queen, Mother of mercy) as notated in a modern book of the most frequently used chants of the Mass and Office, the* Liber usualis.

We will now look at the important types of chants used in the Mass and Office, beginning with syllabic and proceeding to more melismatic styles.

## Chants of the Office

The formulas for chanting the psalms, called psalm tones, are among the oldest chants of the liturgy. These are designed so they can be adapted to fit the words of any psalm. There is one tone (formula) for each of the eight church modes (discussed below; see Example 2.3) and an extra one called the *tonus peregrinus,* or "wandering tone." In the Office, a psalm may be sung to any one of the tones, chosen to match the mode of its prescribed antiphon (see, for example, NAWM 4a).

A psalm tone consists of five separate melodic elements. It begins with an intonation (used only in the first verse of the psalm), which rises to a reciting tone, or tenor (a single, repeating note that is used for recitation), bends at the midpoint of the verse for a semicadence, or mediant, continues on the reciting tone (tenor) for the second half-verse, and concludes at the end of the verse by descending to a final cadence, or termination (see Example 2.2). This formula is repeated for each verse of the psalm. The final verse usually leads into the Lesser Doxology, an expression of praise to the Trinity, which is added to "christianize" the psalms, originally a body of Hebrew poetry inherited from the Jewish liturgy. The words of the Doxology, *Gloria Patri . . .* (Glory be to the Father . . . ), are fitted to the same psalm tone as the psalm verses (here shown as verses 9 and 10). Every psalm in the Office is framed by a different antiphon, attached to it solely for one particular day of the calendar year. So, although all 150 psalms are sung in the course of a week's cycle of Canonical Hours, each will have a new antiphon the following week and thereafter throughout the year. A model for the chanting of antiphon and psalm in the Office is outlined in

Psalm tones

CD 1/24    CD 1/7

Doxology

*Example 2.2: Outline of the psalmody of the Office*

| Antiphon | Psalm, 1st half-verse | | | Psalm, 2nd half-verse | | Antiphon |
|---|---|---|---|---|---|---|
| | Intonation Tenor | | Mediant | Tenor | Termination | |
| *Tecum . . .* | 1. Di-xit | Dominus | Do-mi-no me - o: | sede a | dex-tris me - is. | |
| | 2. | Donec ponam ini - | mi - cos tu - os, | scabellum pe - | dum tu - o - rum. | |
| | 3. | Virgam virtutis tuae emittet Domi-nus | ex Si - on: | dominare in medio inimico - rum tu - o - rum. | | |
| | 9. | Gloria | Pa-tri, et Fi-li-o, | et Spiri - | tu - i Sanc - to. | |
| | 10. | Sicut erat in principio, et | nunc et sem - per, | et in saecula saecu - | lo - rum. A - men. *Tecum . . .* | |

*Figure 2.10. A mid-fifteenth-century manuscript illumination showing monks singing an Office service. They are seated in front of the altar in two sets of choir stalls that face each other (compare with Figure 2.2). Two standing monks—presumably the cantor or leader and an assistant— lead the singing and probably perform the antiphons. The British Library, London.*

Example 2.2. (The full text of the antiphon *Tecum principium* [Thine shall be the dominion] and Psalm 109, *Dixit Dominus* [The Lord said], is found in NAWM 4.a.)

CD 1/24    CD 1/7

**Antiphonal psalmody**

This kind of psalmodic singing is called antiphonal (from the Greek for "sounding against") because the half verses alternate between two choirs or between a half choir and the full choir. The practice, believed to imitate ancient Syrian models, was adopted early in the history of the Christian Church.

In earliest times, the antiphon, a verse or sentence with its own melody, was probably repeated after every verse of a psalm, like the phrase "for his mercy endureth forever" in Latin Psalm 135 (English 136). Eventually, only the opening phrase of the antiphon was sung before the psalm, with the entire antiphon performed after the psalm.

**Antiphons**

Antiphons are more numerous than any other type of chant; about 1,250 appear in the modern chant books. However, many antiphons employ the same melody, using only slight variations to accommodate the text. Since antiphons were originally intended to be sung by a group rather than a soloist, the older ones are usually syllabic or only slightly florid, with stepwise melodic movement, comparatively simple rhythm, and a limited melodic range.

Early Christians often sang psalms responsorially, with a soloist performing each verse and the congregation or choir responding with a brief refrain. This practice is reflected in the Office responsories, chants that begin with a choral respond, proceed with a single psalm verse sung by a soloist, and close with a full or partial repetition of the respond.

## Chants of the Mass

**Introit**

Like the Office, the Mass included antiphonal and responsorial psalmody. Among the antiphonal chants are the Introit and Communion, belonging to the Proper of the Mass. The Introit was originally a complete psalm with its antiphon, the many verses of which were used to accompany the entrance procession. Over time, this opening part of the service was shortened so that today the Introit consists only of the original antiphon, a single psalm verse with the customary Doxology (*Gloria Patri*), sung to a more elaborate variant of a psalm tone, and a repetition of the antiphon (NAWM 3a). The Communion, coming near the end of the Mass as a counterpart to the Introit at the beginning, is a short chant, often consisting of only one scriptural verse (NAWM 3j). Some of the more elaborate antiphons developed into independent chants, retaining only a single psalm verse or none at all.

CD 1/4

CD 1/22

Musically, the most highly developed chants of the Mass are the Gradual (from Latin *gradus*, "step," with the gospel book being carried in procession from altar to lectern) and Alleluia, probably because they occur at moments in the service that are more contemplative, when no ritual action occurs. These are responsorial chants, intended for choir and soloist in alternation (NAWM 3d and 3e). Each has only one psalm verse, usually sung to a more elaborate melody than the verses of antiphonal chants and introduced—or, in the case of the Alleluia, framed—by a separate melody and text known as a respond.

Gradual and Alleluia

CD 1/13, 15

Graduals came to the Frankish churches (in what is now France) from Rome in a form that was already highly evolved. Their melodies and those of the Alleluia are very florid and have a similar structure (see the outline of an Alleluia, Figure 2.11 below). Certain melismatic formulas recur in different Graduals at similar points in the chant, such as intonations, internal cadences, and terminations. Some melodies consist almost entirely of such formulas, pointing to an earlier, prenotational time when singers had to rely on their memories; recurring patterns made performing that much easier. In the Alleluias, the respond text is always the single word "Alleluia" (from the Hebrew *Hallelujah*, "Praise God") with the final syllable "-ia" receiving an effusive melisma called a jubilus (see NAWM 3e). The responsorial performance of the Alleluia proceeds as follows: the soloist (or solo group) sings the word "Alleluia" up to the asterisk; the chorus repeats it and continues with the jubilus; the soloist then sings the psalm verse, with the chorus joining in at the last phrase; then the entire "Alleluia" is repeated by the soloist with the chorus joining in again at the jubilus.

CD 1/15

Responsorial performance

| Soloist | | Soloist | | |
|---------|-------------------------|-----------|--------------|----------|
| | Chorus | | Chorus | Chorus |
| Alleluia | *Allelu-ia...(jubilus)... | Ps. verse... | *Allelu-ia... | (jubilus) |

*Figure 2.11.*

Many Alleluias sound carefully planned and composed rather than improvised. For example, they often include what might be termed "musical rhyme," in which matching phrases occur at the ends of sections. Alleluias were created throughout the Middle Ages and spawned important new forms.

Offertories are as melismatic as Graduals but include the respond only (see NAWM 3g). In the Middle Ages, they were performed during the offering of bread and wine, with a choral respond and two or three very ornate verses sung by a soloist, each followed by the second half of the respond. When the ceremony was curtailed, the verses were dropped.

CD 1/19

## Later Developments of the Chant

The chants for the Mass Ordinary probably started out as simple syllabic melodies sung by the congregation. After the ninth century, these were replaced by more ornate settings for choral performance. The syllabic style was retained for the Gloria and Credo, which have the longest texts. The Kyrie, Sanctus, and

Chants of the Ordinary

*Figure 2.12.  The earliest surviving copy of the* Christmas dramatic trope Quem queritis in presepe, *in a manuscript collection from Saint-Martial de Limoges. For a transcription, see NAWM 6. Bibliothèque Nationale, Paris.*

Kyrie

Agnus Dei, because of the nature of their texts, have three-part sectional arrangements. The Kyrie, for example, suggests a setting in which the first and last sections are identical:

A   *Kyrie eleison, Kyrie eleison, Kyrie eleison*
B   *Christe eleison, Christe eleison, Christe eleison*
A   *Kyrie eleison, Kyrie eleison, Kyrie eleison*

CD 1/8     CD 1/2

The threefold repetition of each phrase of text may be reflected in a variety of musical forms, such as AAA BBB AAA′, AAA BBB CCC′ (as in NAWM 3b), or ABA CDC EFE′. The Kyrie is usually performed antiphonally, with half choirs alternating statements. The final Kyrie is often extended by the insertion of an additional phrase, allowing each half choir to sing a phrase before joining together for the last "eleison." (For the complete music and text for the Mass for Christmas Day, see NAWM 3.)

Many antiphons were composed for additional feasts introduced into the Church calendar between the ninth and thirteenth centuries. This same period produced a number of antiphons that were not attached to particular psalms, for use in processions and at special occasions. The four Marian antiphons—liturgically not antiphons at all, but independent compositions—are of comparatively late date (see, for example, the *Salve Regina*, Example 2.1).

Tropes

A trope expanded an existing chant in one of three ways: by adding (1) new words and music before the chant and often between phrases; (2) melody only, extending melismas or adding new ones; or (3) text only, set to existing melismas. The first type was by far the most common, used especially with Introits. All three types increased the solemnity of a chant by enlarging it, and all afforded musicians an outlet for creativity, paralleling the way medieval scribes embellished books with marginal decorations. Moreover, the added words provided a gloss, interpreting the chant text and linking it more closely to the occasion. For example, the Introit antiphon for Christmas day (NAWM 3a) used a text from the Hebrew Scriptures, a passage Christians view as a prophecy of Jesus' birth (Isaiah 9:6). Prefacing it with a trope text (here in italics) made this interpretation explicit:

CD 1/4

*God the Father today sent his Son into the world, for which we say,*
*rejoicing with the prophet: A child is born to us, and a Son is given. . . .*

Two other tropes to this same Introit appear in NAWM 6: a brief dialogue, *Quem queritis in presepe* (discussed below), and a textless melisma that embellishes the end of the antiphon.

CD 1/30

Trope composition flourished especially in monasteries during the tenth and eleventh centuries. We know the name of at least one composer, Tuotilo (d. 915), who was a monk at Saint Gall. Tropes were eventually banned by the Council of Trent (1545–1563; see Chapter 8) in the interest of simplifying and standardizing the liturgy. But they testify vividly to the desire of medieval church musicians to embellish the chant repertory. This same impulse played an important role in the development of polyphony, as we shall see in the next chapter.

Sequences began in the ninth century, probably as text additions to the jubilus in Alleluias, but they quickly became independent compositions. Notker Balbulus (his name means "The Stammerer"; ca. 840–912), another Frankish monk of Saint Gall, describes how he learned to write text syllables under long melismas to help him memorize them. The sequence was an important creative outlet from the tenth to the thirteenth centuries and later. Popular sequences were even imitated and adapted for secular genres, both vocal and instrumental, in the late Middle Ages. Like the tropes mentioned previously, most sequences were banned from the Catholic service by the liturgical reforms of the Council of Trent. The five that survive still hold vital places in the liturgy, such as the celebrated *Dies irae*, with its familiar melody, in the Requiem Mass (Mass for the Dead), and the Easter sequence *Victimae paschali laudes* (NAWM 5).

**Sequences**

CD 1/29   CD 1/11

## ✸ Hildegard of Bingen (1098–1179)

Born to a noble family in the Rhine region of Germany, Hildegard at age eight was consecrated to the church by her parents. Six years later she took vows at the Benedictine monastery of Disibodenberg, becoming prioress of the attached convent in 1136. Led by a vision, she founded her own convent around 1150 at Rupertsberg, near Bingen, where she was abbess.

Famous for her prophecies, Hildegard corresponded with emperors, kings, popes, and bishops and preached throughout Germany. Her many prose works include *Scivias* (Know the Ways, 1141–1151), an account of twenty-six visions, and books on science and healing.

Hildegard wrote religious poems as well as prose, and by the 1140s she began setting them to music. Her songs are preserved in two manuscripts organized in a liturgical cycle, with indications that many were sung in her convents and nearby monasteries and churches. Her *Ordo virtutum* (The Virtues, ca. 1151) is the earliest surviving music drama not attached to the liturgy.

*Figure 2.13. Hildegard of Bingen with Volmar, a monk who assisted her in recording her visions, in an illustration from Scivias.*

Hildegard exemplifies the flourishing musical culture of medieval women who, like their male counterparts, saw themselves as saving humanity through prayer.

**Major works:** *Ordo virtutum*, 43 antiphons, 18 responsories, 7 sequences, 4 hymns, 5 other chants

Liturgical drama

Liturgical drama also originated in troping. One of the earliest of these dramas, *Quem quaeritis in sepulchro* (Whom do you seek in the tomb?), took the form of a tenth-century dialogue—in effect, a trope—preceding the Introit for Easter Sunday Mass. In the dialogue, the three Marys come to the tomb of Jesus. The angel asks them, "Whom do you seek in the tomb?" They reply, "Jesus of Nazareth," to which the angel answers, "He is not here, He is risen as He said; go and proclaim that He has risen from the grave" (Mark 16:5–7). According to contemporary accounts, the dialogue was sung responsorially, and the scene was acted out. The Easter trope and a similar one for Christmas, *Quem queritis in presepe* (Whom do you seek in the manger? NAWM 6 and Figure 2.12), were performed all over Europe. Other plays survive from the twelfth century and later. The early thirteenth-century *Play of Daniel* from Beauvais and *The Play of Herod*, concerning the Slaughter of the Innocents, from Fleury, have now become staples in the repertories of early-music ensembles. The music for these plays consists of a number of chants strung together, with processions and actions that approach theatrical representation. A few manuscripts give evidence that the works were staged, with scenery, costumes, and actors drawn from the clergy.

CD 1/30

Hildegard of Bingen

Although most liturgical dramas from this period are anonymous, we have a unique, nonliturgical, but sacred music drama by Hildegard of Bingen (1098–1179; see biography and Figure 2.13). *Ordo virtutum* (The Virtues, ca. 1151) is Hildegard's most extended musical work, consisting of eighty-two songs for which she wrote both the melodies and the poetic verse (uncommon among authors of tropes and sequences). It is a morality play with allegorical characters such as the Prophets, the Virtues, the Happy Soul, the Unhappy Soul, and the Penitent Soul. All sing in plainchant except the Devil, who can only speak: the absence of music symbolizes his separation from God. The final chorus of the Virtues (NAWM 7) is typical of Hildegard's expansive melodic style.

CD 1/33    CD 1/12

Women were excluded from the priesthood, and as the choir took over the singing in services, they were also silenced in church. But in convents—separate communities of religious women (nuns)—they could hold positions of leadership and participate fully in singing the Office and Mass (which, however, was "said" by a priest). Here they also learned to read and write Latin and music, and had access to an intellectual life available to few outside convent walls. In this context, Hildegard achieved great success as prioress and abbess of her own convent and as a writer and composer. She claimed that her songs, like her prose writings, were divinely inspired. At a time when women were forbidden to instruct or supervise men, having a reputation for direct communication with God was one way she could be heard outside the convent. Her visions became famous, but her music was apparently known only locally. Although her writings were edited and published in the nineteenth century, her music was not rediscovered until the late twentieth century in the search to reclaim the history of music by women. She quickly became the most recorded and best-known composer of sacred monophony.

# Medieval Music Theory and Practice

Treatises in the age of Charlemagne and in the later Middle Ages reflected actual practice to a greater extent than the more speculative earlier writings. They always spoke of Boethius with reverence and passed along the mathematical fundamentals of scale building, intervals, and consonances that he transmitted from the Greeks. But reading Boethius did not help solve the immediate problems of how to sing intervals, memorize chants, and, later, read notes at sight. Theorists partially addressed these goals by establishing the system of eight modes, or *toni* ("tones"), as medieval writers called them.

The medieval modal system developed gradually, achieving its complete form by the eleventh century. It encompassed eight modes, each defined by the sequence of whole tones and semitones in a diatonic octave built on a *finalis*, or final. In practice, this note was usually the last note in the melody. The modes were identified by numbers and grouped in pairs; the odd-numbered modes were called authentic, and the even-numbered modes plagal (collateral). Each pair of modes shared the same final (identified as boxed whole notes in Example 2.3), but their melodies had different ranges: those belonging to the authentic modes rose above the final, and those in the plagal modes circled around or went farther below the final. The authentic modal scales may be thought of as analogous to white-key octave scales on a modern keyboard rising from the notes D (mode 1), E (mode 3), F (mode 5), and G (mode 7), with their corresponding plagals (modes 2, 4, 6, and 8) a fourth lower. These notes, of course, do not stand for specific "absolute" pitches—a concept foreign to plainchant and to the Middle Ages in general; they are simply a convenient way to distinguish the interval patterns, which are unique to each pair of modes, as partially shown in the example. In addition to the final, each mode has a second characteristic note, called the tenor or reciting tone (shown in Example 2.3 as whole notes), as in the psalm tones. Although the finals of the paired plagal and authentic modes are the same, their tenors are higher or lower in keeping with their ranges. The church modes also had Greek names (as shown in the example), although these were a misapplication of the ancient Greek scales. The modes became a primary means for classifying chants and arranging them in books for liturgical use. However, because many of the chants existed before the theory of modes evolved, their melodic characteristics do not always conform to modal theory.

*Example 2.3: The medieval church modes*

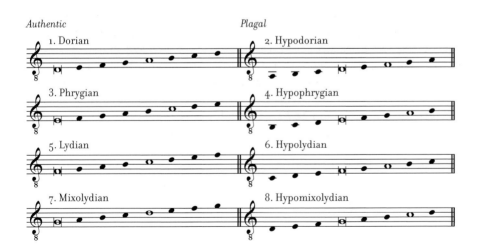

For teaching sightsinging, the eleventh-century monk Guido of Arezzo (ca. 991–after 1033) proposed a set of syllables—*ut, re, mi, fa, sol, la*—to help singers remember the pattern of whole tones and semitone in the six steps (known as hexachords) that begin on C, G, or F. (This became known as solmization.) In this pattern (for example, C–D–E–F–G–A), a semitone falls between the third and fourth steps, and all other steps are whole tones. The syllables (also known

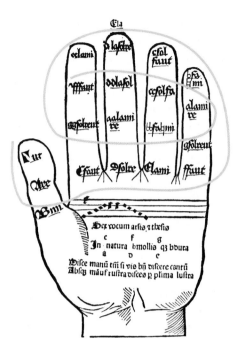

*Figure 2.14. The "Guidonian hand," a visual mnemonic device used for locating the pitches of the system of hexachords by pointing to the joints of the left hand. Although credited to Guido, the hand was probably a later application of his solmization syllables. The notes are laid out in a counterclockwise spiral, beginning with the lowest note (gamma ut) at the tip of the thumb, moving down the thumb, across the base of each finger, up the little finger, across the tips, down the index finger, and around the middle joints.*

as solfège or solfeggio) of solmization are still employed in teaching, except that in English we say *do* for *ut* and add a *ti* above *la.*

**The Guidonian hand**

Followers of Guido developed a pedagogical visual aid called the "Guidonian hand" (Figure 2.14). Pupils were taught to sing intervals as the teacher pointed with the index finger of the right hand to the different joints of the open left hand. Each joint stood for one of the twenty notes that made up the musical system of the time; any other note, such as F♯ or E♭, was considered "outside the hand." No late medieval or Renaissance music textbook was complete without a drawing of this hand.

**The staff**

In earlier stages of musical notation, scribes placed the note symbols, or neumes, above the text, sometimes at varying heights to indicate the relative size as well as direction of intervals (as in Figure 2.12). Eventually, one scribe conceived the idea of scratching a horizontal line in the parchment corresponding to a particular note and oriented the neumes around that line. This was a revolutionary idea: a musical sign that did not represent a sound, but clarified the meaning of other signs. In the eleventh century, Guido suggested an arrangement of lines and spaces from which evolved the modern staff. Guido's scheme not only enabled scribes to notate (relative) pitches precisely, but also freed music from its dependence on oral transmission. The achievement proved to be as crucial for the history of Western music as the invention of writing was for literature.

# Medieval Song

**Goliard songs**

Music outside the church spawned many different types and forms of song other than plainchant. A few of them will be described here. The oldest *written* specimens of secular music are songs with Latin texts, among them the goliard songs from the eleventh and twelfth centuries. Their poets and composers were students or clerics who exalted a libertine lifestyle, naming themselves after a fictitious and scurrilous patron, Bishop Goliath. The songs, preserved in numerous manuscript collections, celebrate three topics of interest to young men then, as now: wine, women, and satire. In most cases, however, the music does not survive in a notation precise enough to permit accurate modern transcriptions and performances.

The goliard songs, although written mostly in Latin, are early manifestations of literacy in the secular musical culture of western Europe. As the vernacular languages also gradually came to be written down, we begin to see glimpses of entire repertories—work songs, dance songs, lullabies, laments—that were lost over time. Among these are chansons de geste, praise songs, which celebrate the deeds of past warriors and present rulers, and love songs, which became popular at the increasingly powerful courts of western Europe.

The people who sang these and other secular songs in the Middle Ages were the jongleurs (from the same root as English *jugglers*), or minstrels (from the Latin *minister*, "servant"), who were either itinerants or in service to a particular lord, or sometimes both. Jongleurs traveled alone or in small groups from village to village and castle to castle, earning a precarious living by performing tricks, telling stories, and singing or playing instruments. Figure 2.15 shows a dancing bear accompanied by a jongleur playing a fiddle. Jongleurs especially were social outcasts, often denied the protection of the law and the sacraments of the Church. With the economic recovery of Europe in the eleventh and twelfth centuries, society became more stably organized, and towns sprang up. The minstrels' situation improved, though for a long time people continued to regard them with a mixture of fascination and revulsion. In the eleventh century, minstrels organized themselves into brotherhoods, which later developed into guilds of musicians offering professional training, much as a modern conservatory does.

Troubadours (male) or trobairitz (female, singular and plural) were poet-composers who flourished during the twelfth century in the south of France and spoke Provençal (also called the *langue d'oc or Occitan*). Trouvères were their equivalent in northern France (see Figure 2.16). One theory is that the art of the troubadours took its inspiration in part from the Arabic love poetry cultivated in Moorish Spain and then spread quickly northward. The trouvères, who were active throughout the thirteenth century, spoke the *langue d'oïl*, the medieval French dialect that became modern French (*oïl = oui*, "yes"; *oc* = "yes" in Occitan).

Neither troubadours nor trouvères constituted a well-defined group. They flourished in castles and courts throughout France. Some were kings: others came from families of merchants, craftsmen, or even jongleurs but were accepted into aristocratic circles because of their accomplishments. Many of the poet-composers not only created their songs but sang them as well; those who did not entrusted the performance to a minstrel. The songs are preserved in collections called *chansonniers* (songbooks). About 2,600 troubadour poems survive, only a tenth with melodies; by contrast, two-thirds of the 2,100 extant trouvère poems have music. No other surviving body of secular tunes and lyrics is as large.

The poetic and musical structures of the songs show great variety and ingenuity. Some are simple, others dramatic, suggesting two or more characters. Some of the dramatic ones were probably intended to be mimed; many obviously called for dancing. The dance songs may include a refrain sung by a chorus of dancers. An important structural feature of numerous trouvère

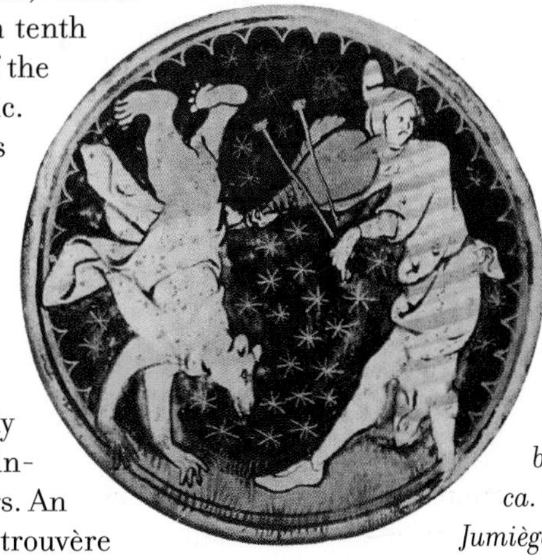

*Jongleurs*

*Troubadours and trouvères*

*Types of songs*

*Figure 2.15. Jongleur playing a fiddle while accompanying a dancing bear. French painting on glass, ca. 1350, from the abbey of Jumièges, Normandy.*

(as opposed to troubadour) songs, the refrain is a line or two of poetry that returns with its own music from one stanza to another. The troubadours especially wrote complaints about love, the subject par excellence of their poetry. But they also wrote songs on political and moral topics, songs that tell stories, and songs whose texts debate or argue esoteric points of chivalric or courtly love. Among these are several particular genres, such as the alba (dawn song), canso (love song), and tenson (debate song).

**Old Occitan lyrics**    Many old Occitan lyrics were openly sensual; others hid sensuality under a veil of *fine amour* or "refined love." The object of the passion they expressed was a real woman—usually another man's wife—but she was adored from a distance, with such discretion, respect, and humility that the lover is made to seem more like a worshipper content to suffer in the service of his ideal love. The lady herself is depicted as so lofty and unattainable that she would step out of character if she condescended to reward her faithful lover. By playing on common themes in fresh ways through artfully constructed lyrics, the poets demonstrate refinement and eloquence, two main requirements for success in aristocratic circles. Thus, the entire poetic genre was more fiction than fact, addressed as much to

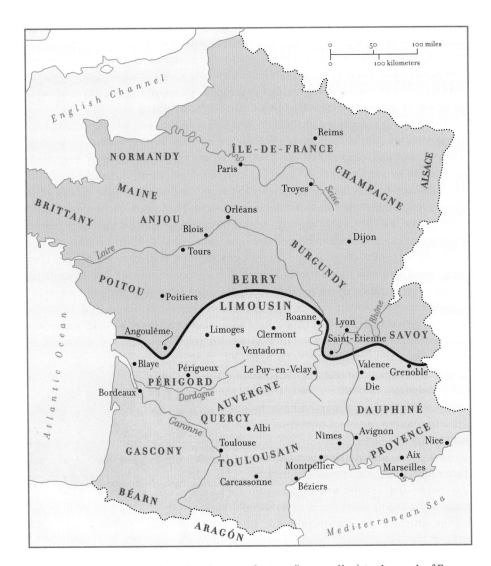

*Figure 2.16. The linguistic boundary between Occitan* (langue d'oc) *in the south of France and Medieval French* (langue d'oïl) *in the north.*

other men (patrons whose wives were being flattered) as to women, and rewarded not by love, but by social status.

Among the best preserved courtly songs is *Can vei la lauzeta mover* (When I see the lark beating, NAWM 8) by the troubadour Bernart de Ventadorn (ca. 1150–ca. 1180), one of the most popular poets of his time. Stories about his life assert that he was the son of a serf and baker in the castle of Ventadorn and rose to become the great lover of three noble ladies, including Eleanor of Aquitaine (see page 50). Of the eight stanzas of *Can vei la lauzeta mover*, the second typifies the lover's complaints that are the main subject of this repertory.[1]

CD 1/36   CD 1/15

**Bernart de Ventadorn**

| | |
|---|---|
| *Ai, las! tan cuidava saber* | *Alas! I thought I knew so much* |
| *d'amor, e tan petit en sai,* | *of love, and I know so little;* |
| *car eu d'amar no•m posc tener* | *for I cannot help loving a lady* |
| *celeis don ja pro non aurai.* | *from whom I shall never obtain any favor.* |
| *Tout m'a mo cor, e tout m'a me,* | *She has taken away my heart and myself,* |
| *e se mezeis e tot lo mon;* | *and herself and the whole world;* |
| *e can se•m tolc, no•m laisset re* | *and when she left me, I had nothing left* |
| *mas dezirer e cor volon.* | *but desire and a yearning heart.* |

Like Bernart's song, or canso, the typical troubadour and trouvère text is strophic, with all the stanzas sung to the same through-composed melody—that is, with new music for every line of poetry. The settings are generally syllabic with an occasional short melismatic figure near the end of a line. Such a simple melody invites improvised ornaments and other variants as the singer passes from one stanza to the next. The range is narrow—a sixth, perhaps, or an octave. Because the songs have finals on C, D, and F, the entire body of works displays a certain coherence. The notation yields no clue to the rhythm of the songs: they might have been sung in a free, unmeasured style, or in long and short notes corresponding to the accented and unaccented syllables of the words. Most scholars now prefer to transcribe them as they do plainchant—in neutral note values without bar lines.

**Typical song structure**

*Figure 2.17. Bernart de Ventadorn, as depicted in a thirteenth-century manuscript of troubadour songs. Bibliothèque Nationale, Paris.*

Each poetic line of a canso receives its own melodic phrase. While Bernart's song is essentially through-composed, a variety of formal patterns emerges through variation, contrast, and the repetition of short, distinctive musical phrases. Many of the troubadour and trouvère melodies repeat the opening phrases or section before proceeding in a free style—for example, AAB, or, in more detail, ab ab cdef. Phrases are modified on repetition, and elusive echoes of earlier phrases are heard; but the main impression is one of freedom, spontaneity, and simplicity, although in fact both the music and poetry are very skillfully crafted.

Some of these features are illustrated in another canso—the only song by a trobairitz to survive with music—composed by the Comtessa Beatriz de Día (d. ca. 1212). A *vida*, or biographical tale, written about a century later describes Beatriz as a "beautiful and good woman, the wife of Guillaume de Poitiers. And she was in love with Rambaud d'Orange and made about him many good and beautiful songs." In *A chantar* (To sing, NAWM 9) the countess berates her unfaithful lover and reminds him of her own worthy qualities. The song uses four distinct melodic phrases arranged in the form ab ab cdb.

**Beatriz de Día**

CD 1/37

---

1. Text and translation are from Hendrik van der Werf, *The Chansons of the Troubadours and Trouvères: A Study of the Melodies and Their Relation to the Poems* (Utrecht: A. Oosthoek, 1972), pp. 91–95, which presents versions of the melody from five different sources, showing surprising consistency of readings. The dot splitting two letters of a word, as in "no•m," stands for contraction.

Minnesinger

The troubadours served as the model for a German school of knightly poet-musicians, the Minnesinger, who flourished between the twelfth and fourteenth centuries. The love (*Minne*) of which they sang in their Minnelieder (love songs) was even more abstract than troubadour love and sometimes had a distinctly religious tinge. The music is correspondingly more sober. Some of the melodies are written in the church modes, while others sound like melodies built on major scales. Because of the rhythm of the texts, scholars think that the majority of the tunes were sung in triple meter. As in France, strophic songs were very common. Their tunes, however, were more tightly organized through melodic phrase repetition. A typical German poetic form called *bar* (AAB) inspired a common musical pattern: the melodic phrase A

## IN CONTEXT  Eleanor of Aquitaine and Her Courts of Love

The powerful Eleanor of Aquitaine (ca. 1122–1204) was born into an aristocratic family that presided over an immense realm in the south of France. Her grandfather was William IX, seventh count of Poitiers and ninth duke of Aquitaine, the first troubadour whose songs we have. Descended from a first-rate poet-composer (who is sometimes regarded as the originator of the courtly love lyric), Eleanor became a great patron of troubadours and trouvères, some of whom addressed her in their lyrics as the lofty lady of their heart's desire. Legend has it that she took Bernart de Ventadorn as her lover for a time (see page 49).

Eleanor was also married to two kings, Louis VII of France, whom she accompanied on the Second Crusade and later divorced, and Henry II (Plantagenet) of England, by whom she bore three daughters and five sons, two of whom also became kings of England: Richard I and John. When Richard, also called Coeur de Lion ("Lion Heart," 1157–1199), was taken prisoner on his return from the Third Crusade, she energetically collected the ransom to pay for his freedom. (Richard was also a trouvère, and the story of his imprisonment for two years in an Austrian dungeon is commemorated in moving lines from his song *Ja nus hons pris*, including "Never will a prisoner speak his mind fittingly unless he speaks in grief.")

Probably an educated musician herself, Eleanor was smart and strong-minded. Because of Henry's infidelities, her relations with him grew strained, and in 1170 she left London and established a court of her own in Poitiers, a geographic center of her native region, Aquitaine. She assisted her sons in an unsuccessful revolt against Henry in 1173 and was herself imprisoned by him for fourteen years,

*Figure 2.18. Likenesses of Eleanor of Aquitaine and her husband, Henry II of England, which were carved onto a Romanesque capital from a twelfth-century church in southern France.*

but her efforts eventually helped Richard secure the throne.

In the course of her long and tempestuous life, Eleanor attracted many artists, trouvères, and writers, some of whom—like Bernart—dedicated works to her. All sorts of artistic monuments to Eleanor still exist, ranging from a regal twelfth-century likeness of her head (supposedly paired with that of King Henry; see Figure 2.18) carved onto one of the capitals of a church near Bordeaux in Aquitaine and now in the Romanesque chapel of the Cloisters in New York, to the 1968 movie *The Lion in Winter*, for which Katharine Hepburn, in the role of Queen Eleanor, won an Oscar. There is also a popular biography by Marion Meade (1977).

(called the Stollen) is sung twice for the stanza's first two units of text, while the remainder, B (the Abgesang), containing new melodic material, is longer and sung only once.

The Middle High German texts include loving depictions of the glow and freshness of spring. There are also dawn songs, like the French alba, sung by the faithful friend who stands guard and warns the illicit lovers that dawn is approaching. A new genre is the Crusade song, recounting the experiences of those who renounced worldly comfort to join the Crusades (Christian military expeditions to recover the Holy Land from the Muslims). A famous example is the *Palästinalied* (Palestine song, NAWM 11) by Walther von der Vogelweide (ca. 1170?–ca. 1230?).

CD 1/39

## TIMELINE  The Middle Ages

| MUSICAL EVENTS | HISTORICAL EVENTS |
|---|---|
| | **313** Constantine I issues Edict of Milan |
| | **330** Constantinople becomes new capital of Roman Empire |
| Bishop Ambrose introduces **386** responsorial psalmody in Milan | |
| | **395** Separation of eastern and western Roman empires |
| | **413** Saint Augustine begins writing *The City of God* |
| Boethius, *De institutione musica* **ca. 500** | |
| | **ca. 530** (Monastic) *Rule of Saint Benedict*; Benedictine order founded |
| | **590** Gregory I ("the Great") elected pope |
| | **600s** Muslim conquests in Asia, North Africa, and southern Europe (completed by 719) |
| | **715** Gregory II elected pope |
| | **751** Pepin ("the Short") becomes king of the Franks |
| | **768** Charlemagne becomes king of the Franks with his brother |
| *Musica enchiriadis* **9th cent.** | **789** Charlemagne orders Roman rite used in empire |
| Earliest notated manuscripts of Gregorian chant **9th cent.** | **800** Charlemagne crowned emperor by pope |
| Monks at Saint Gall compose **10th cent.** tropes and sequences | **800–821** *Rule of Saint Benedict* introduced in Frankish lands |
| Guido of Arezzo, *Micrologus* **ca. 1025–1028** | |
| Gregorian chant replaces Hispanic **ca. 1071** (Mozarabic) chant in Spain | |
| Goliards flourish **11th cent.** | |
| | **1095–1099** First Crusade |
| | **ca. 1100** *Chanson de Roland* |
| | **1147–1149** Second Crusade |
| Hildegard of Bingen, *Ordo virtutum* **ca. 1151** | |
| Death of Bernart de Ventadorn **ca. 1180** | **1189–1192** Third Crusade |
| | **1204** Death of Eleanor of Aquitaine |
| Death of Beatriz de Día **ca. 1212** | |
| | **1347–1350** Plague devastates Europe |

*Figure 2.19. Troubadour Jaufré Rudel and the countess of Tripoli in a miniature from a French manuscript of the thirteenth century. Bibliothèque Nationale, Paris.*

**Cantigas**

CD 1/40    CD 1/16

*Figure 2.20. Walther von der Vogelweide as depicted in a fourteenth-century Swiss manuscript. Vogelweide means "bird-meadow," and his shield, shown in the upper left, includes a caged bird. Universitätsibibliothek, Universität Heidelberg.*

One of the treasures of medieval song is the *Cantigas de Santa María*, a collection of over four hundred cantigas (songs) in Galician-Portuguese in honor of the Virgin Mary. The collection was prepared about 1270–1290 under the direction of King Alfonso el Sabio ("the Wise") of Castile and León (northwest Spain) and is preserved in four beautifully illuminated manuscripts. Whether Alfonso wrote some of the poems and melodies is uncertain. Most songs in the collection relate stories of miracles performed by the Virgin, who was increasingly venerated from the twelfth century on. Cantiga 159, *Non sofre Santa María* (NAWM 12), tells of a cut of meat, stolen from some pilgrims, that Mary caused to jump about, revealing where it was hidden by the perpetrators. All the songs have refrains, perhaps performed by a group alternating with a soloist who sang the verses. Songs with refrains were often associated with dancing, a possibility reinforced by illustrations of dancers in the *Cantigas* manuscripts and by the dancelike rhythm of many of the songs.

*Figure 2.21. Illustrations from the* Cantigas de Santa María *(ca. 1250–1280) manuscript, showing musicians playing (clockwise from upper left) transverse flutes, shawms, pipes and tabors, and trumpets.*

## POSTLUDE

The spread and stabilization of the Roman rite through western Europe during the Middle Ages resulted in the creation of a repertory of Gregorian chant that survives to this day. This repertory includes many different types of chant, each with a distinct function within the liturgical celebrations of the Office and the Mass. It also contains many chronological layers, having evolved from early Christian times down to the sixteenth century, when some types of chant (new offices, liturgical dramas, hymns, and sequences) were still being written. Chants were classified into eight church modes and written down in a notation that gradually evolved as a means of teaching and standardizing its performance.

Secular songs also flourished. They were most sophisticated and virtuosic in the cultural centers and courts of the later Middle Ages. These songs, in a variety of strophic forms often including refrains, had many different uses, sometimes involving dance. Some were narrative or dramatic, others lyrical. The body of courtly love songs created by troubadours and trouvères as a monument to the sentiments and ideals of refined and courtly love remains unequaled for its sheer beauty and artfulness.

# Polyphony through the Thirteenth Century

*Chapter Contents*

*Prelude* 54

Early Organum 56

Notre Dame
Polyphony 58

The Motet 64

The Polyphonic
Conductus 67

English Polyphony 69

*Postlude* 70

## PRELUDE

A cultural revival in Europe during the eleventh and twelfth centuries sparked a period of intense activity in music. In this chapter, we will trace one outcome of this activity: the growth of polyphony in the church. By polyphony, we mean music in which voices sing together in independent parts. At first, polyphony was a style of performance, a manner of accompanying chant with one or more added voices. This heightened the grandeur of chant and, thus, of the liturgy itself, just as art and architectural decoration ornamented the church and, thus, the service. The added voices elaborated the authorized chants through a musical gloss or commentary, a process resembling that of troping; and, indeed, polyphony developed in the same regions and contexts as the monophonic tropes discussed in Chapter 2. Therefore, the kind of composed polyphony we associate with Notre Dame Cathedral in Paris has roots in a long prehistory of improvised polyphony, of which few written traces exist. We have good reason to believe that European musicians used polyphony in and outside of church long before it was first unmistakably described in a ninth-century treatise called *Musica enchiriadis* (Music Handbook).

When, in the ninth century, singers improvising on plainchant departed from simple parallel motion to give their parts some independence, they set the stage for counterpoint, the combination of multiple independent lines. The need for regulation of these simultaneous sounds led eventually to the precepts of harmony. As the parts were combined in more complex ways, refinements in notation permitted music to be written down and performed repeatedly. Written composition began to replace improvisation as a way of creating musical works, and notation began to replace memory as a means of preserving them. Music became more and more consciously structured and followed certain governing rules, such as those that applied to rhythm and consonance. Such precepts were eventually set down in learned treatises by writers known as theorists, and the four principles thus established—counterpoint, harmony, notation, and composition—have distinguished Western music ever since.

These changes came about gradually during the eleventh, twelfth, and thirteenth centuries; there was no sudden break with the past. Monophony remained the principal medium of both performance and new composition. Indeed, some of the finest monophonic chants, including antiphons, hymns, and sequences, were produced after 1200, some as late as the sixteenth century. Musicians continued to improvise as well, and many stylistic details of the newly composed polyphonic music grew out of improvisational practice.

After developments traceable from the ninth century, several types of polyphonic composition gained a secure place in the still small repertory of written musical composition in France by 1250 and in England soon afterward. We will study two of them in this chapter: organum and motet. Organum (pronounced *or'-ga-num*; Lat., pl. *or'-ga-na*) was, as we have suggested, a form of troping the chant. But now, instead of attaching a melodic trope to the beginning or end of an existing chant—a horizontal extension—organum offered the possibility of adding new layers of melody in a vertical dimesion. This polyphonic elaboration of plainchant reached its most sophisticated level in Paris at the cathedral of Notre Dame, a church built in the soaring, new Gothic style of the twelfth century (see Figure 3.4). By creating different rates of motion among the voice parts, composers of Notre Dame polyphony forced a breakthrough in rhythmic notation, which until then had been vague at best. They also began writing other polyphonic genres, the most enduring among them being the motet, which also had its origins in the process of troping, as we shall see. The motet eventually became the dominant genre of both sacred and secular polyphonic music.

The years 1050 to 1300 saw an increase in trading and commerce throughout western Europe, as its growing population began to build modern cities. The Normans (a warrior people originally from Scandinavia who had settled Normandy in northern France) crossed the English Channel to capture England, while Spain was seeking to liberate itself from Muslim conquerors. The First Crusade (1095–1099) united Christian ruling families from all over Europe in a successful campaign to drive the "infidel" Turks from Jerusalem. After centuries of political instability and limited literacy, Europe enjoyed a cultural revival, which included music and all the arts; we have seen some of its effects in the eloquent love songs of the troubadours and trouvères. Scholars translated important works from Greek antiquity and the Arab world into Latin, encouraging the development of music theory. Places of teaching and learning that eventually became universities sprang up in Paris, Oxford, and Bologna. Large Romanesque churches (see Figure 3.1), built on the architectural principle of the round arch of the Roman basilica, began to dominate the landscape, just as Gregorian chant and the Roman rite had prevailed in the liturgy. Pious donors funded hundreds of new monasteries and convents, filled by rising numbers of men, women, and children seeking a religious life. As scholars revived ancient learning, Saint Anselm, Saint Thomas Aquinas, and others associated with the intellectual movement called Scholasticism sought to reconcile classical philosophy with Christian doctrine through commentary on authoritative texts. The Romanesque style yielded to a new style of church architecture called Gothic, which emphasized height and spaciousness, with soaring vaults, pointed arches, slender columns, large stained-glass windows, and intricate carvings. Some of these developments found parallels in the art of written polyphony, which blossomed in certain

*Figure 3.1.  The church of San Martín de Frómista, Spain, which lies on the pilgrims' route to Santiago de Compostela, dates from about the middle of the eleventh century and is a fine example of the Romanesque style.*

regions of France and England in the twelfth and thirteenth centuries. (See "The Motet as Gothic Cathedral," page 68).

# Early Organum

The anonymous author of *Musica enchiriadis* examines and illustrates two distinct kinds of "singing together," both designated by the term organum. In one species of this early organum, a plainchant melody in the principal voice (Latin, *vox principalis*) is duplicated a fourth below by an organal voice (Latin, *vox organalis*). Either voice or both may be further duplicated at the octave to create an even richer sound (NAWM 14a and 14b). Of course, singing in parallel fourths sometimes produces a harsh tritone (such as occurs between f and b), and the adjustments needed to avoid it led to organum that was not strictly parallel (NAWM 14c). In this type, called oblique organum or organum with oblique motion, the added part became melodically differentiated from the plainchant, and a variety of wider intervals, including dissonances, came into use.

Contrary and oblique motion predominated over parallel motion in eleventh-century music, and, as a consequence, the polyphonic voices grew increasingly independent and more like equal partners. The organal voice shifted to a position above the chant (though the parts often cross), where it gained more rhythmic and melodic prominence, occasionally singing two notes against one of the principal voice. Consonant intervals—the unison, octave, fourth, and fifth—prevail, while others occur only incidentally (Example 3.1). The rhythm is identical to the unmeasured flow of plainchant, which forms the basis for all these pieces.

*Example 3.1: Eleventh-century organum*

In the eleventh century, polyphony was applied chiefly to the troped plainchant sections of the Mass Ordinary (such as the Kyrie and Gloria), to certain parts of the Proper (Tracts and Sequences), and to responsories of the Office and Mass (Graduals and Alleluias). Because polyphony demanded trained soloists who could follow rules of consonance while improvising or who could read the approximate notation, only the soloists' portions of the original chant were embellished polyphonically. In performance, then, polyphonic sections alternated with monophonic chant, which the full choir sang in unison. The solo sections from the *Alleluia Justus ut palma* (NAWM 15) are preserved in a set of instructions headed *Ad organum faciendum* (On making organum) and date from about 1100. The added voice proceeds mostly note against note above the chant, but toward the end of the opening "Alleluia," the performer sings a melismatic passage against a single note of the chant (Example 3.2). In this new style of organum, known today as free organum, the organal voice has more rhythmic and melodic independence.

*Example 3.2: Early twelfth-century organum*

[Soloists]

Organal voice
Principal voice

Al - le — lu — — — ia.

A more florid style of free organum appeared early in the twelfth century in Aquitaine, a region in southwestern France. In Aquitanian organum, the lower voice, usually an existing chant but sometimes composed anew, sustains long notes while the upper (solo) voice sings phrases of varying length. Pieces in this new style resulted in much longer organa, with a more prominent upper part that moved independently of the lower one. The chant, meanwhile, became elongated into a series of single-note "drones" that supported the melismatic elaborations above, thereby completely losing its character as a recognizable tune. The lower voice was called the tenor, from the Latin *tenere* ("to hold"), because it held the principal—that is, the first or original melody. For the next 250 years, the word *tenor* designated the lowest part of a polyphonic composition.

Writers in the early twelfth century began distinguishing between two kinds of organum. For the style just described, in which the lower voice sustains long notes while the upper voice moves more melismatically, they reserved the terms *organum, organum duplum,* or *organum purum* ("double organum" and "pure organum," respectively), all of which we now associate with organum that is free or florid in style. The other kind, in which the movement is primarily note against note, they called *discantus* (discant). When the Notre Dame composer Léonin was praised by a contemporary writer as *optimus organista*, he was not being called an "excellent organist" but "the best composer of organa" (see the biography, page 62). The same writer described Pérotin, Léonin's younger colleague, as the best *discantor*, or maker of discants.

We can see a good example of florid Aquitanian organum and discant in the two-voice *Jubilemus, exultemus,* illustrated in Figure 3.3 and transcribed in Example 3.3 (see NAWM 16 for the complete version). The section in Example 3.3a uses the florid style of organum, with melismas of three to fifteen notes in the upper part for most notes in the tenor. Example 3.3b shows a passage in discant style, with fewer notes in the upper part for every tenor note until the penultimate syllable, which typically has a longer melisma. In both excerpts, contrary motion is more common than parallel, and most note groups in the upper voice begin on a perfect consonance with the tenor, although dissonances generously pepper the melismas. In the discant section, as shown by the arrows, the composer seems to have chosen an occasional dissonance above the tenor note for variety and spice (as in "-ter-" of "eterna" and "-cu-" of "secula"). Phrases end on octaves or unisons, heightening the sense of closure.

When organum was written down (which ordinarily it was not), one part sat above the other, fairly well aligned as in a modern score, with the phrases marked off by short vertical strokes on the staff. Two singers, or one soloist and a small group, could not easily go astray. But when the rhythmic relation between the parts was complex, singers had to know exactly how long to hold each note. As we have seen, the late medieval notations of plainchant and of troubadour and trouvère songs did not indicate duration. Indeed, no one felt a need to specify it, for the rhythm was either free or was communicated orally. Uncertainty about note duration was not a serious concern in solo or monophonic singing but could cause chaos when two or more melodies were sung simultaneously. Composers in northern France solved this problem by devising a system

**Florid organum**

*Figure 3.2. Master of the Platerias Portal, King David bowing a rebec, ca. 1100. Granite. South portal, cathedral of Santiago de Compostela, Spain. The decorative folds of David's garment have their counterpart in the florid melismas of the more elaborate chants of the Mass and Office.*

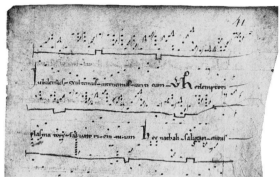

*Figure 3.3.  An example of two-voice Aquitanian organum,*
*also known as free or florid organum, which may have been*
*written as early as 1100. The solid lines separate the upper and*
*lower voices. (For a partial transcription, see below and NAWM*
*16.) Bibliothèque Nationale, Paris.*

*Example 3.3: Aquitanian florid organum and discant in* Jubilemus, exultemus

*a. Verse 2*

Re — demp - to — ri plas-ma - to — ri

sal - va — to - ri om — ni — um.

*To the redeemer, savior of all.*

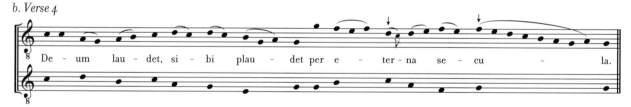

*b. Verse 4*

De — um    lau - det, si - bi    plau — det per e — ter - na   se - cu — la.

*Praise God and eternally applaud.*

of rhythmic notation involving patterns of long and short notes known today as
the rhythmic modes (see pages 60–61).

# Notre Dame Polyphony

Léonin

Musicians in Paris developed a still more ornate style of polyphony in the late
twelfth and early thirteenth centuries. Two composers associated with Notre
Dame Cathedral were Léonin (fl. 1150s–ca. 1201), who was a priest and poet-
musician, and Pérotin (fl. 1200–1230), who probably trained as a singer under
Léonin. Both composers may have studied at the University of Paris, which was
becoming a center of intellectual innovation; a typical classroom setting is
shown in Figure 3.7. Léonin compiled the first extensive repertory of composed

polyphony, the *Magnus liber organi* (Big Book of Organum). This collection contained two-voice settings of the solo portions of the responsorial chants (Graduals and Alleluias of the Mass, and Office responsories) for the major feasts of the church year, some or all of which he himself composed. For Léonin to undertake such a cycle shows a vision as grand as that of the builders of Notre Dame Cathedral. Some of the chants of the *Magnus liber* were elaborated not only by Léonin, but also by later composers, making them ideal for tracing the process of revision and substitution by which the repertory grew and the style evolved from one generation to the next. An ideal example is *Viderunt omnes*, the Gradual for Christmas Day.

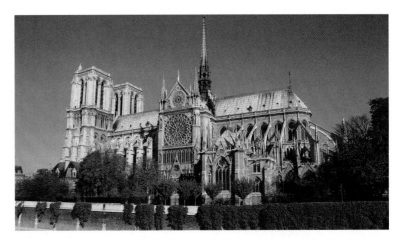

*Figure 3.4. The cathedral of Notre Dame in Paris, built about 1160–ca. 1345. Its great height, supported along its length and around its apse by flying buttresses, and its elaborate decoration have parallels in the unprecedented length, intricacy, and carefully worked-out structure of the music that composers wrote to sing in the cathedral.*

CD 1/57

If we compare Léonin's setting of *Viderunt omnes* (NAWM 17) with the original chant (NAWM 3d), we see that the composer provided polyphonic music only for the sections of the chant performed by soloists, while the choir was expected to sing the rest of the melody in unison, whether from memory or from another book. The responsorial chant by itself displays contrasts in form and sound in that some sections are syllabic and others are melismatic (see Figure 2.11 and 3.8). Léonin emphasizes these contrasts in his elaboration, which features two different styles of polyphony, organum and discant. In the opening section on "Viderunt," shown in Example 3.4, Léonin's organum extends the notes of the original melody into a series of drones, while his added voice spins expansive melismas above it. The original notation suggests a free, unmeasured rhythm; the fluid melody—loosely organized in a succession of unequal phrases often lingering on dissonances with the tenor—smacks of improvisational practice. Then, as the choir enters after the word "omnes," this lengthy soloistic beginning reverts to plainchant (see Figure 3.8).

*Example 3.4: Léonin, first section of* Viderunt omnes, *in organum duplum*

Léonin composed the next section of the Gradual in two styles, moving from organum to discant on the word "Dominus," where a long melisma had appeared in the original chant (see Example 3.5). Had he not quickened the pace of the tenor voice here, the result would have been a work of excessive length. But by writing occasional discant passages where the original chant was melismatic, and placing them alongside sections of plainchant and organum, Léonin created a piece of manageable size within the context of the liturgy and offered the worshippers a variety of pleasing textures without changing a word or note of

## A CLOSER LOOK   Modal Rhythm

The crystallization of the six rhythmic modes, which correspond roughly to the arrangements of long and short syllables and the quantitative principles of ancient Latin verse, highlights the dominant intellectual movement of Léonin's time—Scholasticism. Scholastic thought was based on established authorities and Fathers of the Church like Augustine and Boethius. In the emerging university curriculum of the twelfth century, music, included in the quadrivium, was studied along with arithmetic, astronomy, and geometry, and Boethius's *Fundamentals of Music* was still central to the discipline. Another famous textbook, Saint Augustine's *De musica*, written in the fourth century, analyzes the motion of poetic meters according to their "music" or "sounding numbers." Music, Augustine states, is "the art of measuring well."

1. LB
2. BL
3. LBB
4. BBL
5. LL
6. BBB

*Figure 3.5.*

Even though Latin poetry of the Middle Ages was no longer organized quantitatively—by the twelfth century, it was defined by stress rather than by syllable length—the theory of the rhythmic modes appears to have been adapted from the principles underlying the measurement of classical poetic meter. It posits that music, like poetry, can be ordered or measured by units of time that have an exact numerical relationship with one another, the long note being twice or three times the duration of the short note, or breve (L and B, respectively, in Figure 3.5). In this way, the new musical practice at Notre Dame, which may have originated in rhythmic patterns to aid in the memorization of organa's long melismas, was reconciled with the University of Paris curriculum that considered music a branch of mathematics—the science of numbers as they relate to sound. This revolutionary new application of old principles is what allowed Léonin to control and notate the simultaneous flow of melodies in his polyphonic works. And from this innovation, the development of musical notation in the West unfolds.

An innovator in his day, Léonin nevertheless adhered closely to convention by building his compositions on the traditional chants of the Mass and Office.

*Example 3.5: Léonin, discant clausula on "do-" of* Viderunt omnes

With his freshly composed layers of melody, made possible through the precise time measurement of the rhythmic modes, he amplified the holy words of the service and projected them into the vast Gothic spaces of the new cathedral in Paris (see Figure 3.4).

*Figure 3.6. This tympanum over the main portal of the Romanesque church of Saint-Pierre in Moissac, France (1125–1130), shows the medieval delight in small repetitive forms—in this case, the Twenty-four Elders of the Apocalypse. Each one holds an identical rebec or fiddle or perhaps a lutelike instrument (compare Figure 2.6) and has stopped playing to look up in astonishment at Christ, whose Second Coming is depicted above their heads.*

the original chant (see Figure 3.8), although he occasionally repeats a phrase to provide structural support for his discant elaboration.

A section in discant style was called a clausula (plural, clausulae), the Latin word for a clause or phrase in a sentence. Discant clausulae are characteristically more consonant than organa and have relatively short phrases and more lively pacing because both voices move in modal rhythm, creating contrast with the surrounding unmeasured sections of organa. Pérotin was credited with composing "very many better clausulae" (see the biography) as he and his contemporaries continued the work Léonin had begun, editing and updating the *Magnus liber.* Hundreds of separate clausulae appear in the same manuscripts as the organa themselves; and because some may have been designed to replace the original setting of the same segment of chant, they are sometimes called, collectively, *substitute clausulae.* One manuscript includes ten clausulae on the word "Dominus"

Clausula

Pérotin

Substitute clausulae

| Soloists | Chorus | Soloists | | | Chorus |
|---|---|---|---|---|---|
| Organum duplum | Plainchant | Organum duplum | Discant | Organum duplum | Plainchant |
| Viderunt omnes | fines terra... | ℣. Notum fecit | Do-[melisma] | minus salutare, etc. | justitiam suam |

*Figure 3.8.*

from *Viderunt omnes*, any one of which could have been used at Christmas Mass. The openings of two of them are shown in Example 3.6 (NAWM 18).

Both clausulae exhibit a common trait of discant in Pérotin's generation: the tenor repeats a rhythmic motive based on one of the rhythmic modes. Because these rhythmic patterns use shorter notes than Léonin's discant, the tenor melodies were often repeated, though over a longer span of time than the rhythmic pattern itself. The composer employs these repetitive musical means to create a sense of coherence for an extended passage, and both types of repetition

## Léonin (Leoninus) (fl. 1150–ca. 1201)
## Pérotin (Perotinus) (fl. late 12th and early 13th centuries)

*Figure 3.7. We have no images of Léonin or Pérotin. This illumination from an early fourteenth-century French manuscript shows a class at the University of Paris from their era. The British Library, London.*

Léonin served at the cathedral of Paris, in many capacities, beginning in the 1150s, before the current Notre Dame was begun. His title (Magister, or Master; see below) suggests that he earned a Master of Arts degree, presumably at the University of Paris, and eventually became a priest and then canon at Notre Dame. As a poet, he wrote a paraphrase, in verse, of the first eight books of the Bible as well as several shorter works.

Less is known about Pérotin. He, too, possibly, had a Master of Arts and must have held an important position at Notre Dame.

Virtually all we know about the musical activities of Léonin and Pérotin is contained in an anonymous treatise from about 1275. The writer makes a pointed comparison between the two composers:

> Note that Master Léonin, according to what was said, was the best composer of organa, who made the great book of organum [*magnus liber organi*] from the gradual and antiphonary to elaborate the divine service. And it was in use up to the time of Pérotin the Great, who edited it and made very many better clausulae or puncta, since he was the best composer of discant, and better than Léonin. But this is not to be said about the subtlety of the organum, etc.
>
> But Master Pérotin himself made excellent quadrupla [four-voice organa], like "Viderunt" and "Sederunt," with an abundance of colors of the harmonic art; and also several very noble tripla [three-voice organa], like "Alleluia posui adiutorium," "Nativitas," etc.[1]

Like the Scholastic theologians who commented on the Scriptures, adding their own layers of interpretation to those of previous scholars, Léonin and Pérotin expanded the musical dimensions of the liturgy.

1. Jeremy Yudkin, *The Music Treatise of Anonymous IV: A New Translation*, Musicological Studies and Documents 41 (Neuhausen-Stuttgart: American Institute of Musicology/ Hänssler-Verlag, 1985), p. 39.

*Example 3.6: Two substitute clausulae on "Dominus" from* Viderunt omnes

in the tenor—of rhythm and of melody—became very significant in the motet of the thirteenth and fourteenth centuries (see below and Chapter 4).

Pérotin "the Great" and his contemporaries expanded organum's dimensions by increasing the number of voice parts to three and (in two instances) to four. Since the second voice was called the duplum, by analogy the third was called the triplum and the fourth the quadruplum. These same terms also designated the composition as a whole: a three-voice organum came to be called an organum triplum, or simply triplum, and a four-voice organum a quadruplum. One of the two astonishing examples of four-voice organum—which stretches out the first word of the chant to extraordinary melismatic lengths—is Pérotin's setting of *Viderunt omnes* (NAWM 19). Like other works of its kind, it begins in a style of organum with patterned clusters of notes in modal rhythm in the upper voices above very long, unmeasured notes in the tenor (see Figure 3.9). As in Léonin's two-voice setting, such passages alternate with sections of discant, of which the longest is again on "Dominus" (not shown here).

**Triple and quadruple organum**

CD 2/1    CD 1/19

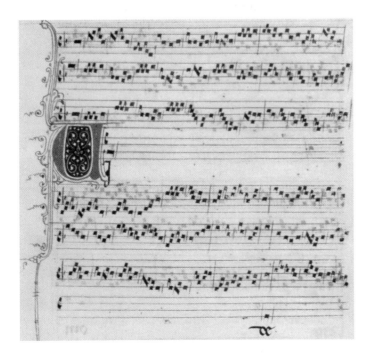

*Figure 3.9. Opening of Pérotin's setting of* Viderunt omnes *in organum quadruplum. The upper three voices are in modal rhythm over a sustained tenor note. (For a transcription, see NAWM 19.) Biblioteca Medicea Laurenziana, Florence.*

# The Motet

Origins

A clausula section of organum, cut loose from its larger setting, could enjoy a second life as a separate piece, an independent little composition in melismatic polyphony. When Latin or French words were added to the upper voice, a new type of work, originating like earlier genres in the familiar troping procedures, was created—the motet (from the French *mot*, meaning "word"). The Latin form, *motetus*, also designates the second voice—the original duplum, now sporting its own text. In three- and four-part motets, the third and fourth voices carry the same names—triplum and quadruplum, that they had in organum.

The motet originated, then, when composers at Notre Dame troped the clausulae of Pérotin and others. These clausulae, having earlier belonged to the genre of organum, themselves featured newly composed melodies layered above old chants. Thus, a defining characteristic of the motet was its use of borrowed chant material in the tenor. Such a tenor was known as the cantus firmus (Latin,

Cantus firmus

plain chant; plural, *cantus firmi*). Just as composers wrote new clausulae using the same favorite cantus firmi, so, too, did composers of motets throughout France and western Europe during the thirteenth century derive their works from a common stock of motet melodies—both tenors and upper parts—transforming them into new works.

Some motets were intended for nonliturgical use, and the upper voices could have vernacular texts while the tenor may have been played on instruments or vocalized wordlessly. After 1250, it was customary to use different but topically related texts in the two upper voices. These motets are identified by a compound title made up of the incipit (the first word or words) of each voice part, beginning with the highest, as in Example 3.7.

*Example 3.7:* Factum est salutare/Dominus

*Salvation was made known in the sight of the Gentiles.*

CD 2/14

Early motets

A typical early motet is *Factum est salutare/Dominus* (NAWM 21a), shown in Example 3.7 and based on one of the substitute clausulae from the *Magnus liber* (Example 3.6a). Like many early Latin motets based on clausulae, this text is a kind of trope on the original chant text, elaborating its meaning and drawing on its words or sounds. The poem ends with the word "Dominus" ("Lord") to which the tenor melody was originally sung, and incorporates several other words from the chant (underlined in the example), some of which are echoed in subsequent rhymes. The original discant clausula, a musical decoration of a word, is here embellished by the addition of words, like a gloss upon a gloss. The resulting motet is an ingenious composite artwork with multiple layers of borrowing and of meaning. In an eccesiastical culture that treasured commentary, allegory, and new ways of reworking traditional themes, such pieces must have been highly esteemed for their many allusions.

Musicians soon regarded the motet as a genre independent of church performance. In the process, the tenor lost its connection to a specific place in the

*Figures 3.10 and 3.11.
Details of the Twenty-four
Elders and their
instruments from the
Pórtico de la Gloria,
cathedral of Santiago de
Compostela, ca. 1158.*

liturgy and became raw material for new composition, a firm foundation for the upper voice or voices. This change in the role of motets raised new possibilities that encouraged composers to rework existing motets in several ways: (1) writing a different text for the duplum, in Latin or French, that was no longer necessarily linked to the chant text and was often on a secular topic; (2) adding a third voice to those already present; (3) giving the additional parts words of their own to create a double motet (one with two texts above the tenor). Composers also wrote motets from scratch, by laying out one of the tenor melodies from the Notre Dame clausula repertory in a new rhythmic pattern and adding new voices above it.

The two motets in Examples 3.8 and 3.9 illustrate some of these possibilities. *Fole acostumance/Dominus* (NAWM 21b) employs the same tenor as Example 3.7 but states it twice and substitutes a new, more quickly moving duplum for the original one. The doubled length and faster motion accommodate a much longer text, a secular French poem complaining that envy, hypocrisy, and deception have ruined France. The composer of *Super te Ierusalem/Sed fulsit virginitas/Dominus* (Example 3.9 and NAWM 21c) began with a portion of the same chant melisma on "Dominus" but imposed a different modal rhythmic pattern.

CD 2/15    CD 1/23

CD 2/17

*Figure 3.12.* The Last Supper *depicted under the tympanum arch of a mid-twelfth-century church in Charlieu, in the Loire district of France. The modular, multilayered structure of the arch's sculptural elements is typical of Romanesque and Gothic church portals and resembles the layered texture of a medieval motet.*

The two upper voices set the first and second halves respectively of a Latin poem on the birth of Jesus, thereby confirming its connection to the feast of Christmas on which the tenor melody was originally sung and making it appropriate to be performed during that season, either in private devotions or as an addition to the church service. As in most motets with more than two voices, the upper parts rarely rest together or with the tenor, so that the music moves forward in an unbroken stream.

*Example 3.8:* Fole acostumance/Dominus

*It is only a crazy habit that makes me sing.*

*Example 3.9:* Super te Ierusalem/Sed fulsit virginitas/Dominus

Triplum: *For you, Jerusalem, from a virgin mother, was born in [Bethlehem]...*
Duplum: *but her virginity glowed with the Spirit's breath. Therefore, pious...*

Franconian motet

In the earlier motets, all the upper parts were written in one melodic and rhythmic style. Later composers distinguished the upper voices from each other as well as from the tenor, achieving more rhythmic freedom and variety both between and within voices. In this new kind of motet, called Franconian (after Franco of Cologne, a composer and theorist who was active from about 1250 to 1280), the triplum bears a longer text than the motetus and features a faster-moving melody with many short notes. The result is the kind of layered texture seen, for example, in the motet by Adam de la Halle (ca. 1240–1288?), *De ma dame vient/Dieus, comment porroie/Omnes* (NAWM 22), illustrated in Example 3.11. Here, rhythmic differences between the voices reinforce the contrast of texts, the triplum voicing the complaints of a man separated from his sweetheart and the duplum (motetus) the woman's thoughts of him. Below them, the slowest-moving part, the tenor, repeats the melody for "omnes," from the Gradual *Viderunt omnes*, twelve times.

CD 2/18

The motet in France had an astonishing career in its first century. What began as a work of poetry more than a composition, fitting a new text to an existing piece of music, developed into the leading polyphonic genre, home to the most complex interplay of simultaneous and independent lines yet conceived. In their texts and structure, motets of the late thirteenth century mirrored both the cen-

*Example 3.10: A composite of Examples 3.7, 3.8, and 3.9, all on the same tenor or cantus firmus, "Dominus"*

*Example 3.11: Adam de la Halle,* De ma dame vient/Dieus, comment porroie/Omnes

Triplum: *From my lady comes the grievous pain which I bear and of which I will die if hope does not keep me alive . . .*

Duplum: *God, how can I find a way to go to him, whose [lover I am?]*

tury's intellectual delight in complication and its architectural triumph of the Gothic cathedral (see "The Motet as Gothic Cathedral," page 68).

## The Polyphonic Conductus

The Notre Dame composers and others in France, England, and elsewhere also wrote polyphonic conductus. These were settings for two to four voices of rhymed, metrical, strophic poems in Latin, rarely taken from the liturgy though usually on a sacred or serious topic. Typical is *Ave virgo virginum* (NAWM 20),

CD 2/13

**IN CONTEXT**  The Motet as Gothic Cathedral

*Figure 3.13. The nave of Notre Dame de Laon, looking west. This Gothic cathedral was built from about 1165 to 1215.*

A distinctive feature of music is its movement through time. But to understand time, we must be able to measure it. Composers of polyphony in the twelfth and thirteenth centuries devised a way of measuring musical time so that it could be manipulated and controlled. By the late thirteenth century, the motet, wholly a creation of French composers, illustrates this accomplishment better than any other genre of the era.

Each voice of a motet moves in its own rhythmic framework yet is perfectly compatible with every other voice. In the case of a three-voice motet, for example, the tenor measures the passage of time in long note values, while the middle voice superimposes its own rhythmic design, consisting of shorter values, on the support created by the tenor. Meanwhile, the highest voice relates to time differently from its two partners, usually in notes that move even more quickly than those of the middle voice and with phrases that coincide with (or sometimes overlap) the ends of the phrases below. The result is a three-tiered structure in which each level is independent of, yet completely coordinated with, the other two levels.

If we look at the interior space of a typical Gothic cathedral that was created by French architects during the very period in which the medieval motet flourished (see Figure 3.13), we see a formal design remarkably similar to the structure just described. Along either side of the nave, or central aisle of the church, are huge columns that have been placed at regular intervals to define the length of the cathedral and support its soaring height. Along the next higher story are the arches of the triforium, its space being measured by an arcade of shorter columns supporting bays of double arches. Superimposed atop this layer, just below the level at which walls give way to windows, is a third tier of still smaller, triple arches, ornamental rather than functional, independent of and yet perfectly harmonized with the lower levels.

The similarities described here are not accidental: the architects of the Gothic style codified their principles of design from the same mathematical laws that the creators of modal rhythm and the composers of motets used in establishing their theories of proportion and measure. The results of their efforts are, on the one hand, a glorious edifice in which we can "hear" a kind of silent music and, on the other, a genre of polyphonic composition that allows us to "see" the harmonious plan of its underlying structure.

Neo-Gothic churches are still being built in our day. The Gothic style, which many regarded with outright disdain for over three centuries, came back into favor about a hundred years ago, influenced by the completion of Germany's Cologne Cathedral in 1880. The chapel at West Point; Princeton University Chapel; Saint Thomas Church, Saint Patrick's Cathedral, and the huge cathedral of Saint John the Divine in New York City; the National Cathedral in Washington, D.C.; and Saint Paul's Anglican Church in Toronto; Montreal's Notre-Dame Cathedral; and more than a hundred other North American churches, not to mention the neo-Gothic churches in Mexico and South America—all testify to the inspiring grandeur of the Gothic style, which continues to strengthen the faith of believers and to fill even the most casual visitors with wonder. As Winston Churchill observed, "We fashion our buildings and then they fashion us."

which addresses the Virgin Mary and was perhaps used in special devotions and processions.

The conductus differs from other Notre Dame polyphony in musical features as well as text. First, the tenor was newly composed rather than taken from chant. Second, all voices sing the text together in essentially the same rhythm. The nearly homorhythmic quality of the conductus has been called *conductus style* when used for other genres. Third, the words are set syllabically for the most part, although (unlike *Ave virgo virginum*) many feature melismatic passages, called caudae ("tails") at the beginning, end, and before important cadences.

# English Polyphony

After the Norman Conquest of England in 1066, English culture and music were closely allied to those of France. English composers wrote in all the Notre Dame genres, although they preferred the more homorhythmic sonorities and fuller textures of conductus style to the more independent lines of sustained-tone organum. Most significant was their liking for imperfect consonances, often in parallel motion, which apparently reflects the influence of folk polyphony. These qualities may be seen in the most famous medieval canon or round, *Sumer*

| TIMELINE | The Ninth through the Thirteenth Centuries |
|---|---|

| MUSICAL EVENTS | HISTORICAL EVENTS |
|---|---|
| *Musica enchiriadis* **9th cent.** | |
| | **11th cent.** Romanesque churches and monasteries |
| | **1054** Final split between Roman and Byzantine churches |
| | **1066** Norman Conquest of England |
| | **1095–1099** First Crusade |
| | **1100** Cult of the Virgin Mary flourishes |
| Aquitanian polyphony **12th cent.** | **12th cent.** Universities of Bologna, Oxford, and Paris established |
| | **1147–1149** Second Crusade |
| Flourishing of Bernart de Ventadorn **ca. 1150–ca. 1180** | |
| Léonin at Notre Dame Cathedral, Paris **1163–1190** | **1163** Cornerstone laid for Gothic cathedral of Notre Dame, Paris |
| | **1189** Richard Coeur de Lion, king of England |
| | **1189–1192** Third Crusade |
| Pérotin at Notre Dame **ca. 1200–ca. 1238** | |
| | **1209** Saint Francis of Assisi founds Franciscan order |
| Death of Beatriz de Día **ca. 1212** | **1215** Magna Carta signed by King John of England |
| Early motets **early 13th cent.** | |
| *Sumer is icumen in* **ca. 1250** | |
| Franco of Cologne, *Ars cantus mensurabilis* **ca. 1280** | |

*Figure 3.14. A scene from the Bayeux tapestry (late eleventh century) depicting the funeral procession of King Edward I ("The Confessor") in 1066, whose death and succession was the immediate cause of the Norman invasion of England. Edward is being taken for burial to the newly completed Westminster Abbey in London, which has been extensively renovated since its founding by Edward. Note the two acolytes with bells below the bier.*

CD 2/21    CD 1/25

*is icumen in* (NAWM 23) from about 1250, also called a rota (from the Latin for "wheel") presumably because of the way the voices rotate through the texture.

The distinctive qualities of English polyphony, particularly the preference for imperfect consonances and for relatively simple, syllabic, and regular melodic phrases, exercised an important influence on fifteenth-century Continental composers and contributed to the development of an international Renaissance style (see Chapter 5).

## POSTLUDE

The history of polyphony in the Middle Ages parallels in many ways the development of monophonic song, including plainchant. Initially improvised, polyphony was eventually "composed" in notations devised to control its performance. The body of composition gradually expanded through the process of troping, whereby new melodies and/or texts were added to, or layered above, the original monophonic lines. By the late twelfth and early thirteenth centuries, organum and motet were well-established genres in which composers elaborated on chant tenors. Organum evolved from parallel types (where added voices merely duplicated the contour of the chant melody) to more florid pieces (where the added voices assumed greater melodic and rhythmic independence from the cantus firmus). Sections of discant-style organa, called clausulae, became separate works and, with added texts, gave rise to the motet, a new genre that dominated the polyphonic scene in France by the mid-thirteenth century.

These genres and conventions would soon be outmoded, however, because of newer motet styles. The rhythmic modes gradually became obsolete, and the chant tenor was relegated to a purely formal function, elevating the triplum to the status of a solo voice against the accompanying lower parts. The road was open to a new musical style, a new way of composing (Ars nova), in an age that would look back on the music of the latter half of the thirteenth century as the antique, outdated way (Ars antiqua).

# French and Italian Music in the Fourteenth Century

## PRELUDE

After the comparative stability of the thirteenth century, the fourteenth century experienced terror and turmoil. The Hundred Years' War (1337–1453) between France and England disrupted agriculture, manufacturing, and trade, and prolonged an economic decline initially caused by bad weather, famine, and floods. From 1348 to 1350, the Great Plague (also known as the Black Death) marched across Europe, wiping out a third of the population; almost everyone who became infected died in agony within days, while others fled the cities and towns to escape illness. Poverty, war, taxes, and political grievances combined to spark peasant and urban rebellions in France, England, Flanders (modern-day Belgium), Germany, Italy, and Spain.

The Church was also in crisis. In the thirteenth century, Europeans viewed the Church as the supreme authority not only in matters of faith, but also in intellectual and political affairs; now its authority, and especially the supremacy of the pope, was widely questioned. Early in the century, King Philip IV ("the Fair") of France had engineered the election of a French pope, who never went to Rome because of the hostility there to foreigners. Instead, from 1309 until 1378, the popes resided in Avignon, in southeastern France, under the virtual control of the French king. The papacy in Avignon was more like a princely court than a religious community, and it is not surprising that the surviving music from this period is almost entirely secular. The political situation became even more complicated when Italian factions elected their own pope and, between 1378 and 1417, there were two—and sometimes three—rival claimants to the papal throne. This state of affairs, compounded by the often corrupt life of the clergy, drew sharp criticism, expressed in polemical writings, in motet texts of the time, and in the rise of popular heretical movements. When the papacy finally moved back to Rome, it brought French music with it.

Europeans in the thirteenth century could generally reconcile revelation and reason, the divine and the human, the claims of the kingdom of God and those of the political powers of this world. But in the fourteenth century, people began to separate science from religion and to see different roles for church and state, notions still held today. Philosophers made a distinction between divine revelation and human reason, each prevailing only in its own sphere. In other words,

*Chapter Contents*

*Prelude* 71

The Ars nova
in France 72

Italian Trecento
Music 80

The Ars subtilior 84

*Postlude* 85

Figure 4.1.  Giotto (ca. 1266–1337), The Wedding Procession. This fresco (painting on wet plaster) is one of a series on the life of the Virgin Mary painted around 1305 in the Chapel of the Madonna della Carità de Arena, also known as the Scrovegni Chapel after the banker Enrico Scrovegni, who built the chapel on the site of a Roman amphitheater. Mary (with halo) leads a group of virgins, while a vielle player and two brass players provide music. The large-leaf branch jutting from the window is an allusion to the Virgin's pregnancy. Giotto created a sense of depth by placing the figures on different planes of the picture. Padua, Italy.

the church cared for people's souls while the state looked out for their earthly concerns. Without denying the claims of religion, this view spurred advances in science and technology; and an increasing interest in the world, the individual, and human nature made way for a growing secular culture.

The fourteenth century was also a period of remarkable creativity. The growth of literacy among the populace encouraged authors to write in the vernacular. Dante's Divine Comedy (1307), Boccaccio's Decameron (1353), and Chaucer's Canterbury Tales (1387–1400) are the great literary landmarks of the century, the latter two reflecting daily life and portraying people of all classes more realistically than earlier literature had done. The Florentine painter Giotto (ca. 1266–1337) broke away from the formalized Byzantine style and achieved more naturalistic representation, as seen in the facial expressions, posture, and garments of his figures (see Figure 4.1). Although there was no decline in the production of sacred music, the best-known composers of the time, Guillaume de Machaut and Francesco Landini, focused on secular music.

To Philippe de Vitry (1291–1361), French musician, poet, and bishop of Meaux, is attributed a treatise called Ars nova (The New Art; early 1320s). Modern scholars use the term Ars nova to denote the French musical style during his lifetime—that is, the first half of the fourteenth century. The stylistic and technical innovations of the Ars nova in France centered on rhythm and its notation, areas that became the playground of the fourteenth-century French composer (see Figure 4.11). Although the motet, in which many of these experiments occurred, continued to be a favorite French genre of composition, its topics had become less amorous and more political. It had also become structurally more complex than it had been in the thirteenth century, evident in the rhythmic and melodic patterning known as isorhythm, a new feature of the genre. Earlier advances in polyphony had generally been associated with sacred music; but the most important new genre of the fourteenth century was now the polyphonic art song. Indeed, the two musical giants of the era, Guillaume de Machaut in France and Francesco Landini in Italy, concentrated on writing love lyrics in the traditional refrain forms of the trouvères.

# The Ars nova in France

Roman de Fauvel

The flavor of the times is captured in the Roman de Fauvel, a narrative poem satirizing political corruption both secular and ecclesiastical, apparently written as a warning to the king of France and enjoyed in political circles and at court. Fauvel, a jackass who rises from the stable to a powerful position, symbolizes a world turned upside down. His name is an acrostic for the sins he personifies: Flattery, Avarice, Villainy (*U* and *V* were interchangeable), Variété ("Fickleness"), Envy, and Lâcheté ("Baseness"). He ultimately marries and produces little Fauvels, who destroy the world. A beautifully illuminated manuscript from around 1317 (see Figure 4.2) has 169 pieces of music interpolated within the poem. These constitute a veritable anthology of works from the thirteenth and early fourteenth centuries, some written for this collection, others chosen for their relevance to the poem's message. Most are monophonic, from Latin chants to secular songs. But 34 are motets, many with texts that denounce the lax morals of the clergy or refer to political events. Among these motets in the *Roman de Fauvel* are the first examples of the new style known as the Ars nova.

Philippe de Vitry, associated with the treatise by that name, may have written at least five of the motets in the *Roman de Fauvel*, and their tenors provide the earliest examples of a musically unifying device called isorhythm ("equal rhythm"). These tenors are laid out in segments of identical rhythm, which might recur as many as ten times in one piece, thus producing an isorhythmic motet. We have already seen this principle at work in the repertory that grew out of Notre Dame clausulae (see Example 3.9). But now, all this takes place on a much larger scale. The tenor is longer, the rhythms are more complex, and the whole line moves so slowly in comparison to the upper voices that it is heard less as a melody than as a foundation for the entire polyphonic structure. (An isorhythmic motet by Vitry from *Roman de Fauvel* may be seen in NAWM 24.)

Theorists of the time recognized two recurring elements in motet tenors, rhythmic and melodic. They called the repeating rhythmic unit the talea and the recurring segment of melody the color. The color and talea could be the same length, always beginning and ending together, but most often the color extended over two, three, or more taleae. In some motets, the endings of the color and talea do not coincide, so that repetitions of the color begin in the middle of a talea. Upper voices may also be organized isorhythmically, in whole or part, to emphasize the recurring rhythmic patterns in the tenor. Isorhythm was occasionally applied to compositions in other genres, as illustrated by the movement of Machaut's Mass (NAWM 25) discussed below.

**Isorhythmic motet**

CD 2/22

**Talea and color**

CD 2/28    CD 1/26

*Figure 4.2. A charivari, or noisy serenade, awakens Fauvel and Vaine Gloire after their wedding in the* Roman de Fauvel *(1310–1314), a poem by Gervais du Bus with many musical interpolations. Fauvel, an allegorical ass, embodies the sins represented by the letters of his name. Bibliothèque Nationale, Paris.*

What made the new musical style of the Ars nova possible was a set of innovations in notating rhythm, innovations that underlie our modern system of note values. The new notation required a rethinking of musical time. Composers of the Notre Dame school had conceived of musical rhythm in terms of repeating patterns of longs and shorts—the rhythmic modes (see Chapter 3). Their system was based on a unit of time that could be subdivided only in certain ways: long–breve (2:1), or breve–long (1:2), or breve–breve–breve (three shorts). The result was that any mode could be combined with any other, but the effect was a series of building blocks or modules that always implied triple groupings. As long as theorists conceived of musical time in this limited way—a succession of perfections, as the modules were called—many rhythms could not be written, including anything in duple meter.

As with the innovations at Notre Dame, it was again the French theorists and composers who created the new system of measured music (mensuration). Instead of relying on the limited modules of the old way (the Ars antiqua), they conceived of using a specific note form, the breve (■), as the basic building block of rhythm. This could be divided into either two or three notes of the next smaller value, the semibreve (♦), as shown in Figure 4.3; and semibreves, in turn, could be subdivided into two or three minims (♦), a new note form whose name means "least" in Latin. The division of the breve was called time (*tempus*) and that of the semibreve prolation (*pro-*

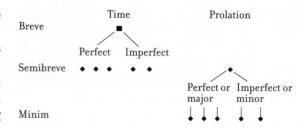

*Figure 4.3. The relationship of time and prolation.*

*latio*). Division was perfect or major ("greater") if triple, imperfect or minor (lesser) if duple.

The four possible combinations of time and prolation, shown in Figure 4.4, produce four different meters, comparable to four in use today. Later in the century, time and prolation were specified by mensuration signs that are the ancestors of modern time signatures. A circle indicated perfect time and an incomplete circle imperfect time; the presence or absence of a dot signaled major or minor prolation. The incomplete circle with no dot (◯) has come down to us as a signature for $\frac{4}{4}$ time (equivalent to imperfect time, minor prolation), showing the link between these four Ars Nova groupings and modern conceptions of meter.

Unlike the old system based on modules, the new system of notation indicated particular durations whose measurement or value resided in the note's shape and not in its relationship to the module or pattern of which it was a part. This made it possible for the first time to notate syncopation, a prominent feature in melodies by com-

## Guillaume de Machaut

The leading composer and poet of the Ars nova in France, Guillaume de Machaut (ca. 1300–1377), was fully involved in the political, intellectual, and ecclesiastical worlds of his time (see the biography). He composed in most of the genres then current, from motets to secular songs, and a survey of his music also serves to introduce the main types of Ars nova composition.

Motets

Most of Machaut's twenty-three motets date from relatively early in his career. They employ the traditional texture in which a borrowed tenor supports two upper voices with different texts. Like other motets of the time, Machaut's are longer and more rhythmically complex than earlier examples. Nineteen are isorhythmic, and in some cases the isorhythmic structure involves all three voices. Machaut frequently emphasized the talea's recurrences by the clever use of a technique called hocket, which also animates the polyphonic texture. In

Hocket

posers from the fourteenth century on. Indeed, one theorist wrote of the new system, "Whatever can be sung can be written down." That was certainly not true of rhythmic notation in the thirteenth century, when what could be written down greatly limited what could be composed.

The new notation of the Ars nova, then, accomplished several breakthroughs. It allowed for the notation of both triple and duple subdivisions of longer notes; it introduced new note shapes to indicate shorter durations than had previously been used; and it made possible a greater variety of rhythmic combinations and a more flexible flow of longer and shorter values, including syncopations.

Indeed, we see French composers exploring and exploiting all of these innovations, especially in the music of the latter part of the century. They also employed other notational devices, such as dotted and "colored" notes, for more complicated effects (see Figure 4.11, the Cordier heart). White notes, or open note-heads, replaced black notation about 1425; black was reserved for special usage. Renaissance composers added still shorter note values (the equivalent of our eighths and sixteenths). And with the addition of bar lines in the seventeenth century, rhythmic notation had evolved from its first manifestations to its modern form in little more than four hundred years.

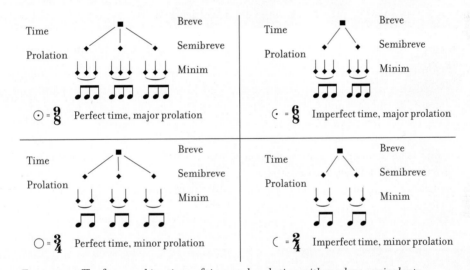

Figure 4.4.    The four combinations of time and prolation with modern equivalents.

hocket (French *hoquet*, "hiccup"), two voices alternate in rapid succession, one resting while the other sings. Although Machaut did not invent the technique, he used it to great effect.

Machaut's *Messe de Nostre Dame* (Mass of Our Lady) was probably the first polyphonic cycle of Mass Ordinary movements to be written by a single composer and conceived as a unit. Machaut likely intended it to be performed with one singer on each part, like most polyphony of the time. He apparently composed the work in the early 1360s for performance at a Mass for the Virgin Mary celebrated every Saturday at an altar of the cathedral in Reims. After his death, an oration for Machaut's soul was added to the service, and his Mass continued to be performed there well into the fifteenth century.

The six movements of Machaut's four-voice Mass are linked together by similarities of style and approach, and by some recurring motives and cadence tones. The Kyrie, Sanctus, Agnus Dei, and Ite, missa est are in motet style, each

Mass

CD 2/28    CD 1/26

using a different cantus firmus that is organized isorhythmically. The Gloria and Credo, having longer texts, are written in discant style—that is, essentially syllabic and largely homorhythmic, although both movements end with elaborate isorhythmic "Amens."

The Kyrie (NAWM 25) is typical of the isorhythmic movements. The tenor cantus firmus is the melody of a chant on the same Ordinary text, divided into taleae of different lengths for each section of the setting. A second supporting voice, called the contratenor ("against the tenor") and sharing the same range as the tenor, is also isorhythmic but has its own talea. Together they form the harmonic foundation of the four-part texture. Example 4.1 shows the opening of the Christe, including the first two statements of the seven-measure talea, marked by Roman numerals. The upper two voices move more rapidly, with syncopation typical of Machaut. They are also partly isorhythmic, which makes the recurring talea in the lower parts more evident, as does the placement of sustained notes on the first and fifth measures of each talea. In between these solid "pillars" of sound are lively rhythms that animate the texture, like the alternation of grounded columns and elaborately carved arches on the façade of a

## ✳ Guillaume de Machaut (ca. 1300–1377)

Machaut was the most important composer and poet in fourteenth-century France. His reputation as a poet exceeded that of Chaucer, on whom he exercised a profound influence, and his music has come to typify the French Ars nova.

Much of what we know of Machaut's life and career derives from his own narrative poems. He was born in the province of Champagne in northeastern France, probably to a middle-class family, was educated as a cleric, probably in Reims, and later took Holy Orders. Around 1323, he served John of

Figure 4.5.  In this miniature from the last manuscript of Guillaume de Machaut's works prepared during his lifetime (ca. 1372), the elderly Machaut is visited in his study by Love, who introduces his three children—Sweet Thoughts, Pleasure, and Hope. Bibliothèque Nationale, Paris.

Luxembourg, king of Bohemia, eventually becoming the king's secretary. In that role, he accompanied John on his travels and military campaigns across Europe, describing these exploits in his poetry. From 1340 until his death in 1377, Machaut resided in Reims as a canon of the cathedral, an office whose liturgical duties left ample time for poetry and composition. He had close ties to royalty all his life, always moving in courtly circles. Other patrons included John of Luxembourg's daughter Bonne, the kings of Navarre and France, and the dukes of Berry and Burgundy.

Machaut was the first composer to compile his complete works, a sign of his self-awareness as a creator. His patrons gave him the resources to supervise the preparation of several illuminated manuscripts containing his works, but the choice to do so seems to have been his own, inspired by a sense of his own worth as an artist and a desire to preserve his music and poetry for future generations.

**Major musical works:** Messe de Nostre Dame (Mass of Our Lady), Hoquetus David (hocket), 23 motets (19 isorhythmic), 42 ballades (1 monophonic), 22 rondeaux, 33 virelais (25 monophonic), 19 lais (15 monophonic), 1 complainte, and 1 chanson royale (both monophonic)

**Poetic works:** Remede de Fortune (Remedy of Fortune), Le livre du voir dit, numerous other narrative poems, over 280 lyric poems.

*Example 4.1: Guillaume de Machaut,* Messe de Nostre Dame, *beginning of Christe*

VIGNETTE   Jacques de Liège Rails against the Ars Nova

*Jacques de Liège (ca. 1260–after 1330) was probably a native of Liège, in modern Belgium, and studied at the University of Paris. His* Speculum musicae *(The Mirror of Music, ca. 1330) is the longest surviving medieval treatise on music. In the last of its seven books, he argued that the old style of the thirteenth century was more pleasing and "more perfect" than the new art of the younger generation.*

In a certain company in which some able singers and judicious laymen were assembled, and where new motets in the modern manner and some old ones were sung, I observed that even the laymen were better pleased with the ancient motets and the ancient manner than with the new. And even if the new manner pleased when it was a novelty, it does so no longer, but begins to displease many. So let the ancient music and the ancient manner of singing be brought back to their native land; let them come back into use; let the rational art flourish once more. It has been in exile, along with its manner of singing; they have been cast out from the fellowship of singers with near violence, but violence should not be perpetual.

Wherein does this lasciviousness in singing so greatly please, this excessive refinement, by which, as some think, the words are lost, the harmony of consonances is diminished, the value of the notes is changed, perfection is brought low, imperfection is exalted, and measure is confused?

Jacques de Liège, *Speculum musicae* 7.48, trans. Oliver Strunk and James McKinnon; in Oliver Strunk, ed., *Source Readings in Music History,* rev. ed. by Leo Treitler (New York: Norton, 1998), pp. 277–278.

Gothic cathedral (see Figure 4.6). To generate rhythmic activity, Machaut often relies on repeated figuration. For example, the descending figure in the second measure of the triplum, echoed later in both duplum and triplum, recurs frequently throughout the Mass, serving less as a unifying motive than as a way to create movement.

**Love songs**

Machaut was both the leading practitioner of the New Art in France and the last great poet-composer of monophonic courtly lyrics in the trouvère tradition. His songs were performed as entertainment in the courts and elite circles in which he moved. He wrote his monophonic pieces in the standard poetic forms cultivated by his predecessors, including the lai, a twelfth-century form akin to the sequence, and virelai, a type of song with refrain that had its heyday in the thirteenth and fourteenth centuries.

**Ars nova traits**

That Machaut also created polyphonic chansons (French for "songs") in the standard poetic refrain forms (*formes fixes*, especially rondeaux and ballades), is not surprising (see Chapter 2). His polyphonic settings reveal a new kind of lyricism, a treble-dominated style in which the upper voice (the treble or cantus) carries the text, supported by a slower-moving tenor without text. To this essential two-voice framework may be added one or two other untexted voices: a contratenor in the same range as the tenor or, less often, a fast-moving triplum in the treble range. This is the texture of his *Rose, liz, printemps, verdure* (Rose, lily, springtime, foliage, NAWM 26), composed in another of the "fixed forms," the rondeau—one that eventually surpassed the virelai in popularity and continued to be written well into the fifteenth century (see "The Fixed Forms of Fourteenth-Century Chansons," page 79, and "Instruments and Musica ficta in Fourteenth-Century Performance," pages 86–87). *Rose, liz* is unusual in its four-voice texture but is typical of Machaut's lyric style, with its long melismas, occupying as many as four measures, that enhance the appeal of the melody. These occur near the beginning and sometimes in the middle of poetic lines. Since they often fall on unimportant words or unaccented syllables, their function is formal and decorative rather than meaningful to the text. Also characteristic are the varied rhythms and supple syncopations made possible by the new notation of the period (see "Innovations: Writing Rhythm," pages 74–75). One hotly contested issue of the new style was whether a duple, or "imperfect," division of note values should be allowed along with the traditional triple, or "perfect," division. In this work, Machaut exploits them both simultaneously, as indicated by the double time signature of the NAWM transcription. Although Machaut's polyphonic chansons do indulge in the rhythmic sophistication of the Ars nova, they do not employ isorhythmic techniques; since the poetic forms determine their musical design in every case, no further structural organization was necessary. Like the other fixed forms, the rondeau has a strophic structure organized around a refrain; unlike the others, the refrain always has two sections, one of which returns halfway through the poem,

CD 2/35    CD 1/33

*Figure 4.6. Reims Cathedral, site of the coronation of French kings and of Machaut's activities as cleric, poet, and composer.*

| A CLOSER LOOK | The Fixed Forms of Fourteenth-Century Chansons |

All fourteenth-century chansons have two sections of music and a *refrain* (a phrase or section that repeats both words and music). What differs from one form to another is the arrangement of the two musical sections and the position of the refrain.

**Virelai**

Characteristic of the virelai is the form AbbaA in which A stands for the refrain, b for a musical phrase used twice at the beginning of each stanza, and a for the last part of the stanza, which uses the music of the refrain but with new words. The typical virelai has three stanzas, with the refrain linking them together: A bba A bba A bba A. The form of the virelai is represented below. (For an example, see the virelai given in NAWM 27.)

CD 2/39

| Refrain | | Stanza | | | | Refrain | |
|---|---|---|---|---|---|---|---|
| Lines of poetry: | 1 | 2 | 3 | 4 | 5 | 6 | 1 | 2 |
| Sections of music: | A | | b | b | a | | A | |

**Ballade**

The form of Machaut's ballades, inherited in part from the trouvères, consists of three or four stanzas, each sung to the same music and each ending with a refrain. Within each stanza, the first two lines (or pairs of lines) have the same music (a a), although often with different endings ($a^1$ $a^2$); the remaining lines and the refrain have a different melody, whose close might echo that of the first section. One possible scheme for the ballade, which matches Du Fay's *Resvellies vous* (NAWM 34), is represented below (where C stands for a refrain that reappears only in successive strophes):

CD 2/56

| Stanza | | | | | | | Refrain |
|---|---|---|---|---|---|---|---|
| Lines of poetry: | 1 | 2 | 3 | 4 | 5 | 6 | 7 | 8 |
| Sections of music: | a | | a | | b | | | C |

**Rondeau**

Like the virelai, the rondeau has only two musical sections, but in this case the refrain contains all of the music (A and B). Unlike any of the other *formes fixes*, however, the rondeau refrain partially returns midway through the piece. The form is ABaAabAB (again, capital letters indicate that both the music and the text of the refrain are sung). The following diagram matches Machaut's four-part rondeau, *Rose, liz* (NAWM 26):

CD 2/35

CD 1/33

| Refrain | | | Half Refrain | | Refrain | |
|---|---|---|---|---|---|---|
| Lines of poetry: | 1 2 3 | 4 5 | 6(1) 7(2) | 8 9 10 | 11(1) 12(2) 13(3) |
| Sections of music: | A | B a | A | a b | A B |

and the refrain in itself includes all the music for the rest of the piece (see diagram, above).

Judging by the number of chansons Machaut wrote in each of the *formes fixes*, his favorite was clearly the ballade, whose popularity, however, was to wane after 1400. Of the three types, the ballade was the most serious, appropriate for philosophical or historical themes or for celebrating a political event or person. It was also possibly the most challenging from a compositional point of view because it contained the least

*Figure 4.7. A miniature from the earliest manuscript of Machaut's collected works (ca. 1350), showing five couples dancing in a circle. The dancer farthest to the right is singing to accompany the dance. The singer resembles Machaut as pictured in the later manuscript in Figure 4.5, at a younger age. The music under the picture is a monophonic virelai by Machaut. Bibliothèque Nationale, Paris.*

amount of musical repetition relative to the text (see diagram, page 79). Machaut wrote more than forty ballades for two, three, and four parts; his typical settings were for high tenor solo with two lower parts. Those few ballades for two upper parts (as opposed to one), each having its own text, are called double ballades.

All of the *formes fixes* were derived from genres associated with dancing, as is evident by their use of refrains. Machaut's monophonic virelais could still be danced to; Figure 4.7 shows an illumination from a manuscript of his works in which a singer (perhaps Machaut himself) performs a monophonic virelai while he and several companions dance in a circle. But Machaut's polyphonic chansons were highly stylized and probably not intended for dancing. Often the repetitions of the refrain lines were invested with fresh meanings or given new contexts by the different words preceding them in each stanza, a subtlety that might be missed by inattentive listeners.

# Italian Trecento Music

The 1300s in Italy were known as the trecento (short for *mille trecento,* or "1300"). Where France had a monarchy with increasing power and stability, Italy was a collection of city-states, each with its own political, cultural, and linguistic traditions and alliances. From writings of the time, we learn how music accompanied nearly every aspect of Italian social life. In Boccaccio's *Decameron,* for example, a group of friends who have retreated to the country from plague-ridden Florence pass the time by telling stories, dancing, singing, and playing instruments (see the vignette, below). But most Italian music from the times was never written down. Even polyphony was still largely improvised in fourteenth-century Italian

*Giovanni Boccaccio (1313–1375) was one of the great fourteenth-century writers whose use of the local dialect of Tuscany, around Florence, made that dialect into the national literary language of Italy. His masterpiece is the* Decameron *(1348–1353), a collection of one hundred witty, sometimes ribald stories, told over a ten-day period by ten friends who have fled to the country to avoid the Black Death ravaging Florence. The evening before the first day of storytelling, they enjoy dinner, dancing, and music.*

The tables having been cleared away, the queen commanded that instruments be brought in, for all the ladies knew how to do the round dance, and the young men too, and some of them could play and sing very well. Upon her request, Dioneo took a lute and Fiammetta a viol, and began sweetly to play a dance. Then the queen together with other ladies and two young men chose a carol and struck up a round dance with a slow pace—while the servants were sent out to eat. When this was finished, they began to sing charming and merry songs. They continued in this way for a long time, until the queen thought it was time to go to sleep.

Giovanni Boccaccio, *Decameron,* Day One, Introduction.

*Figure 4.8. A page from the richly illustrated Squarcialupi Codex, an early fifteenth-century manuscript named for its fifteenth-century owner, Antonio Squarcialupi, showing Francesco Landini wearing a laurel crown and playing a portative organ. The portrait is set inside the initial letter M of Landini's madrigal* Musica son *(I am music). The decorative border depicts (counterclockwise from the upper left) a lute, vielle, cittern or citole, harp, psaltery, three recorders, a portative organ, and three shawms. Biblioteca Medicea Laurenziana, Florence.*

churches. At the courts, Italian *trovatori* of the thirteenth century followed in the footsteps of the troubadours, singing their songs from memory. The only music of the people to survive in manuscripts are the monophonic *laude*, or processional songs that were devotional in nature.

Composers of Italian trecento music cultivated the short, sensuously lyrical forms typical of Italy's native poets and musicians. The largest surviving body of polyphonic Italian music from the time is the repertory of secular songs written as refined entertainment for elite circles and wealthy patrons. The principal centers of trecento polyphony were cities in central and northern Italy, above all Florence, a particularly important cultural center from the fourteenth through the sixteenth centuries. Florence was the home of both Dante and Boccaccio as well as of Francesco Landini, the most famous Italian musician of the trecento.

Very few examples of Italian polyphony from before 1330 survive, but after that date there are several manuscripts. The most copious source is the magnificent Squarcialupi Codex, named for its former owner, the Florentine organist Antonio Squarcialupi (1416–1480). This is a retrospective anthology, copied about 1410–1415, which contains 354 pieces, mostly for two and three voices, by twelve composers of the trecento and early quattrocento (1400s). A miniature portrait of each composer appears at the beginning of the section containing his works, as shown in Figure 4.8. Three types of secular Italian composition are represented in the codex and in other manuscripts of the period: madrigal, caccia, and ballata.

Madrigals were idyllic, pastoral, satirical, or love poems usually set for two voices. Jacopo da Bologna's *Fenice fù* (A phoenix was I, NAWM 28) is a hauntingly beautiful example of this trecento form (see Figure 4.9). Its texture differs from a French chanson in that the two voices are relatively equal in melodic and

Squarcialupi Codex

Madrigal

CD 2/42

**Madrigal**

|                    | Stanza |   |   | Stanza |   |   | Ritornello |   |
|--------------------|--------|---|---|--------|---|---|------------|---|
| Sections of music: | a      |   |   | a      |   |   | b          |   |
| Lines of poetry:   | 1      | 2 | 3 | 4      | 5 | 6 | 7          | 8 |

**Ballata**

|                    | Ripresa |   |   | Stanza (2 piedi) |   |   |   | Volta |   |    | Ripresa |   |   |
|--------------------|---------|---|---|------------------|---|---|---|-------|---|----|---------|---|---|
| Sections of music: | A       |   |   | b                | b |   |   | a     |   |    | A       |   |   |
| Lines of poetry:   | 1       | 2 | 3 | 4                | 5 | 6 | 7 | 8     | 9 | 10 | 1       | 2 | 3 |

*Figure 4.9. Fourteenth-century Italian song forms.*

rhythmic style and occasionally echo one another. Typical of the Italian style are the long melismas carefully placed on the last accented syllable of each line of poetry; these are more florid in the upper voice but are entirely without the syncopations so characteristic of French music at this time.

Caccia

CD 2/44

The caccia parallels the French chace, in which a strict canon is set to lively, graphically descriptive words. The song's name in each language means "hunt," referring to the pursuit of one voice by another. In some cases, it also applies to the subject matter of the text, as in Ghirardello da Firenze's caccia (NAWM 29), which actually evokes a hunt. The musical imitations of calling the dogs and sounding the hunting horn are both high-spirited and comic, especially when treated in canon. Unlike its French and Spanish counterparts, the caccia usually has a free, untexted tenor in slower motion below.

Ballata

The polyphonic ballata, which became popular later than the madrigale and caccia, shows some influence from the treble-dominated French chanson. The word *ballata* (from *ballare*, "to dance") originally meant "a song to accompany dancing." Thirteenth-century ballate (of which no musical examples are known today) were monophonic dance songs with choral refrains, and in Boccaccio's *Decameron* the ballata was still associated with dancing. Although a few early fourteenth-century monophonic examples have survived, most of the ballate in the manuscripts are for two or three voices and date from after 1365. Their form, as outlined in Figure 4.9, resembles a single stanza of the French virelai (see the diagram on page 79).

## Francesco Landini

Francesco Landini

CD 2/46    CD 1/37

The leading composer of the trecento, Francesco Landini (ca. 1325–1397; see the biography and Figure 4.10) wrote 140 ballate, many of which are for two texted voices, like the earlier madrigale. Others, evidently later works, have three parts in a treble-dominated style, featuring solo voice with two untexted accompanying parts that were most likely sung, as in Machaut's chansons. Landini's ballata *Non avrà ma' pietà* (She will never have mercy, NAWM 30) typifies this genre's form and style. Melismatic passages decorate the ends and sometimes the beginnings of lines but never interrupt the middle of a verse, showing an early concern for text declamation—a characteristic feature of Italian music. The end of every line, and often a structurally important internal point as well, is marked by a cadence, which in the later works is usually of a type now known as the under-third or Landini cadence. Here, the progression from the major sixth to the octave is ornamented by a lower neighbor leaping up a third in the

Landini cadences

*Example 4.2: Francesco Landini, beginning of* Non avrà ma' pietà

She will never have mercy, this lady of mine . . . /Perhaps by her [the flames] would be extinguished . . .

Source: Leo Schrade, ed., *The Works of Francesco Landini*, Polyphonic Music of the Fourteenth Century 4 (Monaco: Éditions de l'Oiseau-Lyre, 1958), p. 144.

top voice (see measures 3–4, 5–6, and 10–11 of Example 4.2, which shows the first line of the refrain). A great appeal of Landini's music, in addition to its graceful vocal melody, lies in the sweetness of its harmonies. Sonorities containing both the intervals of the third and fifth or of the third and sixth are plentiful, though they never begin or end a section or piece.

Like their French counterparts, Italian composers of the trecento composed music in several genres, including settings of Mass Ordinary chants for two to four voices or for keyboard, along with some other liturgical settings and motets. In the late 1300s, the music of Italian composers began to lose its specific national characteristics and to absorb the contemporary French style. The trend was especially noticeable after the papal court moved from Avignon— where it had been for most of the century—back to Rome in 1377. Italians wrote songs to Fench texts in French genres, and their works recorded in late fourteenth-century manuscripts often appear in French notation. The influence was reciprocated in the fifteenth century, however, when composers from France and other northern countries took up positions in Italy and their music was unquestionably affected by what they heard and learned there.

English polyphony, sometimes called descant, was abundant in the fourteenth century, particularly in the sacred genres. It had a distinctive sound and other qualities that signaled its independence of musical trends on the Continent, not surprising considering England's cultural insularity. But its very distinctiveness was to have an enormous impact on Continental developments in the next century, as we shall discover in Chapter 5.

French influence

English music

## ✦ Francesco Landini (ca. 1325–1397)

Landini was born in northern Italy, probably in Florence or nearby Fiesole. The son of a painter, he was blinded by smallpox during childhood and turned to music, becoming an esteemed performer, composer, and poet. A master of many instruments, he was especially known for his skill at the organetto, a small portative organ.

Landini was organist at the monstery of Santa Trinità in 1361–1365, then became a chaplain at the church of San Lorenzo, where he remained until his death. Although he may have improvised organ music in church, he apparently wrote no sacred music and is best known for his ballate. Landini is a principal character in Giovanni da Prato's *Paradiso degli Alberti*, a narrative poem from around 1425 that records scenes and conversations in Florence from the year 1389. Giovanni includes a legendary incident that testifies to Landini's skill as a performer:

*Figure 4.10. The tombstone of Francesco Landini. The blind composer plays a portative organ, accompanied by two angel-musicians.*

> Now the sun rose higher and the heat of the day increased. The whole company remained in the pleasant shade, as a thousand birds sang among the verdant branches. Someone asked Francesco [Landini] to play the organ a little, to see whether the sound would make the birds increase or diminish their song. He did so at once, and a great wonder followed. When the sound began many of the birds fell silent and gathered around as if in amazement, listening for a long time. Then they resumed their song and redoubled it, showing inconceivable delight, and especially one nightingale, who came and perched above the organ on a branch over Francesco's head.

**Major works:** 140 ballate, 12 madrigals, 1 caccia, 1 virelai.

# The Ars subtilior

**Later fourteenth century**

French and Italian music of the late fourteenth century became ever more refined and complex, catering to the extravagant tastes of increasingly polished performers and the educated, courtly elite of society. In a paradox typical of the century, the papal court at Avignon was one of the main patrons of secular music. There and at other courts across southern France and northern Italy, a brilliant chivalric society allowed composers to flourish. Their music consisted chiefly of polyphonic ballades, rondeaux, and virelais, continuing the *formes fixes*. These chansons, mostly love songs, were intended for a highbrow audience—aristocrats and connoisseurs who esteemed this music because it developed every possibility of melody, rhythm, counterpoint, and notation. The composers' fascination with technique and their willingness to take a given procedure to new extremes have led music historians to term this repertory Ars subtilior ("the subtler art"). The refined and elevated style of these songs is matched by their sumptuous appearance in manuscripts, including fanciful decorations, intermingled red and black notes, ingenious notation, and occasional caprices that include a love song written in the shape of a heart (shown in Figure 4.11) or a canon in the shape of a circle.

Figure 4.11. The rondeau Belle, bonne, sage by Baude Cordier in a manuscript from ca. 1400. The texted cantus across the top is accompanied by textless tenor and contratenor lines. The red notation indicates changes of mensuration. The heart shape of the notation is a pun on the composer's name (cor is Latin for "heart"), and the word "heart" in the text is replaced with a red heart. Musée Condé, Chantilly, France.

Some songs from this period feature remarkable rhythmic complexities, reaching a level not seen again until the twentieth century. Voices move in contrasting meters and conflicting groupings; beats are subdivided in many different ways; phrases are broken by rests or suspended through chains of syncopations; and harmonies are purposely blurred through rhythmic disjunction. Whatever the notation allowed, someone would try. A virelai by Johannes Ciconia (ca. 1370–1412), *Sus une fontayne* (NAWM 27), nicely exemplifies the Ars subtilior.

Rhythmic complexity

CD 2/39

## POSTLUDE

The musical landscape of the fourteenth century presents a variety of new forms and practices. Ars nova musicians developed a sophisticated system for rhythmic notation that, in turn, allowed for greater freedom and flexibility of rhythmic play. At the same time, French composers created the structural device of

## IN PERFORMANCE    Instruments and Musica ficta in Fourteenth-Century Performance

*Figure 4.12. Tapestry from the Low Countries (ca. 1420), showing a man in courtly dress singing from a manuscript. He is accompanied by a woman playing a positive organ, which is portable but must be placed on a table to be played, rather than resting on a lap like the portative organ played by Landini in Figure 4.8. A boy stands behind the organ, pumping the bellows to force air through the pipes and produce the sounds. Musée des Tapisseries, Angers, France.*

The most common texture of a fourteenth- or fifteenth-century chanson was three parts, with only the cantus or uppermost part having the complete text for a stanza lined out under the notes. The supporting parts typically had only the first few words written at the opening of their music. We know from pictorial and literary sources of the time that polyphonic music was usually performed by a small vocal or instrumental ensemble or a combination of the two, with only one voice or instrument to a part. But there was—and still is—no uniform way of performing any particular piece. Some modern performing groups sing the text in all parts, assuming that the scribe meant the incipit, or opening words, as an abbreviation for the entire stanza and simply spared himself the effort of writing it out fully. Others assign instruments to the untexted lines, judging the lack of words to imply their use.

Recent scholarship suggests that Machaut and his contemporaries intended all the parts to be sung, with the lack of words in the supporting voices making the cantus stand out in relief. But in that case, might some or all of the parts have also been played on instruments? If the presence of a text does not mean that the part was always sung, or the absence of words that it was necessarily instrumental, we can say only that performances probably varied according to circumstances, depending on tastes and preferences and on the singers and players who happened to be on hand.

Manuscripts never specified instruments, leaving the choice of forces to the performers, guided by

## TIMELINE    Fourteenth-Century France and Italy

| MUSICAL EVENTS | HISTORICAL EVENTS |
|---|---|
| | **1304**  Birth of Francesco Petrarca |
| | **1305**  Giotto, frescoes, Scrovegni Chapel, Padua |
| | **1307**  Dante Alighieri, *Divine Comedy* |
| | **1309**  Pope Clement V moves the papacy to Avignon |
| *Roman de Fauvel* **1310–1314** | |
| | **1316–1334**  Reign of Pope John XXII |
| | **1337–1453**  Hundred Years' War between France and England |
| | **1348–1350**  Plague kills one-third of Europe |
| Jacopo da Bologna, *Fenice fù*  **ca. 1350s** | |
| | **1353**  Giovanni Boccaccio, *Decameron* |
| Machaut, *Messe de Nostre Dame*  **ca. 1360s** Death of Philippe de Vitry  **1361** | |
| | **1378–1417**  Great Schism of the papacy |
| | **1387–1400**  Geoffrey Chaucer, *Canterbury Tales* |
| Death of Francesco Landini  **1397** Johannes Ciconia, *Sus une fontayne*  **ca. 1400** | |

habit and tradition. One prevalent tradition had to do with sound quality. In the fourteenth through sixteenth centuries, instruments were grouped into two categories—haut (French for "high") and bas ("low")—based on their relative volume rather than pitch. The most common soft, or bas, instruments—bowed and plucked strings, woodwinds, portative organs—were used for indoor dancing and background music. The loud, or haut, instruments—shawms (ancestor of the oboe), trumpets, or trombones—were associated with outdoor and ceremonial music, and with dancing and processions (see Figure 4.1).

Just as the choice of instruments was normally left to the performers, so was the use of certain chromatic alterations known as *musica ficta* ("false music" or "feigned music"). This practice gave a special flavor to fourteenth-century French and Italian music and continued in use through much of the sixteenth century. Performers raised or lowered notes by a semitone (without benefit of written accidentals) to avoid the tritone F–B in a melody, to make a smoother melodic line, or to avoid sounding an augmented fourth or diminished fifth against the lowest note of the texture. Such alterations were also common at cadences, in order to make them sound sweeter and more emphatic (see Example 4.3). Cadences of the type shown in Example 4.3b would have both upper notes of the penultimate chord

*Example 4.3: Alteration at cadences*

a. Strict modal forms

b. Chromatically altered forms

c. Form with double leading tones

raised to avoid the tritone, resulting in a double leading-tone cadence (Example 4.3c), one of the most distinctive sonorities of the period.

Musica ficta would present no difficulty to modern performers if composers and scribes had written the sharps, flats, and naturals in the manuscript. But they often did not, or they did so inconsistently. In view of these factors, conscientious modern editors include only those accidentals found in the original sources and indicate in some way (usually above or below the staff) those that they believe should be additionally supplied by the performers.

isorhythm to control and organize their seemingly unlimited choices. Thus, the emphasis on structure and rhythmic play in fourteenth-century music was in part a response to the new freedom of Ars nova notation and in part, perhaps, a reaction to the forces of disorder and discontent in society at large.

The principal types of polyphonic composition in France were the polyphonic Mass Ordinary movement and cycle; the isorhythmic motet, which had an elusive structure and a complicated, layered texture; and the secular love songs in the fixed poetic forms inherited from the trouvères, which had very obvious structures involving refrains and simpler, songlike textures. These chanson types—chief among them the virelai, ballade, and rondeau—made use of a more ingratiating idiom as composers aimed for a sensuously appealing sound. New genres of composition (Mass, motet, and refrain song) emerged in Italy as well, some probably derived from popular musical practice. Italian smoothness of melody and clarity of declamation, and the growing use in both French and Italian traditions of prominent harmonic thirds and sixths all contributed to the new style of the fifteenth century.

Two very different composers of equally great renown dominated the scene in their respective countries: Machaut in France and Landini in Italy. By the year 1400, however, the French and Italian musical styles, formerly distinct, had started to merge and move toward an international style. As we will see in the following chapter, this new style became diversified in the next century by influences from other sources—chiefly England and the Low Countries.

PART TWO

# The Age of the Renaissance

PART CONTENTS

5. ENGLAND, FRANCE, AND BURGUNDY
IN THE FIFTEENTH CENTURY: THE BEGINNINGS
OF AN INTERNATIONAL STYLE 98

6. MUSIC OF THE LOW COUNTRIES 112

7. SECULAR SONG AND THE RISE OF NATIONAL STYLES
IN THE SIXTEENTH CENTURY 128

8. SACRED MUSIC IN THE ERA OF THE REFORMATION 146

The fifteenth and sixteenth centuries were a period of great change for European culture, literature, art, and music. To some, it seemed that the arts had been reborn after a period of stagnation. In his 1855 *Histoire de France*, Jules Michelet crystalized this notion by coining the term *Renaissance* (French for "rebirth") to designate the historical period after the Middle Ages. The idea of rebirth captures the aims of scholars and artists to restore the learning, ideals, and values of ancient Greece and Rome. But scholarship, literature, art, and music did far more than revive the old. Currents already strong in the late Middle Ages continued, and the introduction of new technologies, from oil painting to the printing press, brought radical changes. In many cases, classical antiquity provided the inspiration for something really new, including new ways to read and understand the Bible, literature in vernacular languages, and realism and perspective in painting.

The beginning of the Renaissance has been debated ever since the term *Renaissance* was introduced. No single event or generation inaugurated the Renaissance; it continued on political and economic paths established by the late

## TIMELINE  The Age of the Renaissance

| MUSICAL EVENTS | HISTORICAL EVENTS |
|---|---|

### MUSICAL EVENTS

Master of Female
Half-Lengths,
*The Lute Player*

Du Fay, *Missa Se la face ay pale*  **ca. 1450s**
Death of Dunstable  **1453**

*Idealized View of the City*, detail

Death of Du Fay  **1474**

Josquin, singer in Ducal Chapel, Milan  **ca. 1484–1489**

Death of Ockeghem  **1497**
Petrucci publishes *Odhecaton A*  **1501**

Death of Josquin  **1521**

Attaignant publishes first collection of chansons in Paris  **1528**

Arcadelt, first book of four-part madrigals  **1539**

Raphael, *Pope Julius II*

Zarlino, *Le istitutioni harmoniche*  **1558**

Palestrina's *Pope Marcellus Mass* published  **1567**

Yonge, *Musica transalpina*  **1588**

Dowland, *First Booke of Songes or Ayres*  **1597**

Death of Victoria  **1611**

### HISTORICAL EVENTS

**1415**  English under Henry V defeat French at Agincourt
**1417**  End of papal schism
**1419**  Philip III (the Good) begins his reign as
duke of Burgundy

**1431**  Joan of Arc executed

**ca. 1440**  Donatello, *David*

**1453**  End of Hundred Years' War (1337–1453);
Du Fay's *Lament on the Fall of Constantinople*
**1454**  Feast of the Oath of the Pheasant in Lille

**1467**  Charles the Bold of Burgundy succeeds Philip III
(the Good)

**1477**  Death of Charles the Bold; end of independent rule of
duchy of Burgundy

**1492**  First voyage of Columbus to America

**1504**  Michelangelo, *David*
**1509**  Henry VIII (d. 1547) becomes king of England
**1517**  Martin Luther, ninety-five theses
**1519–1556**  Charles V, Holy Roman emperor

**1527**  Sack of Rome
**1528**  Castiglione, *The Courtier*
**1532**  Henry VIII breaks with pope
**1535**  Execution of Sir Thomas More

**1543**  Copernicus, *On the Revolutions of the Heavenly Spheres*
**1545–1563**  Council of Trent
**1547–1553**  Reign of Edward VI
**1552**  Second Book of Common Prayer
**1553–1558**  Mary I restores Latin rite and link to Rome
**1558**  Elizabeth becomes queen of England and restores
Church of England

**1564**  Death of John Calvin

**1586**  El Greco, *Burial of the Count of Orgaz*
**1587**  Mary Stuart executed

**1594**  Shakespeare, *Romeo and Juliet*
**ca. 1595**  Caravaggio, *The Lute Player*

Middle Ages, rather than breaking with medieval traditions. Considering the Renaissance primarily as a movement in scholarship and the arts, some aspects are apparent already in the 1300s, while others emerged only in the 1500s, and many continued into the 1600s. In letters and the visual arts, the Renaissance began in Italy and spread north; in music, as we will see, northern composers played the leading role in the fifteenth century, Italians in the sixteenth. Here, we will define the span of the Renaissance as the fifteenth and sixteenth centuries, while recognizing that its characteristics developed over time.

In music, this period saw numerous developments as well. Since they did not all occur at once, the Renaissance is best understood as a time of continual and overlapping changes rather than as a unified style or movement. From the early fifteenth century on, musicians frequently held positions outside their native regions, especially in Italy. A new international sacred style emerged that drew on elements of French, Burgundian, Italian, and English traditions and on new rules for polyphony based on strict control of dissonance (see Chapter 5). The courts of Italy turned to the great choir schools of the north to recruit singers and composers. The late fifteenth century saw the emergence of two principal textures that would predominate in sixteenth-century music—imitative counterpoint and homophony. In the later fifteenth and sixteenth centuries, the revival of classical learning had many parallels in music, including a renewed interest in ancient Greek theory and ideals for music and a new focus on setting words with correct declamation while reflecting the meanings and emotions of the text (Chapter 6). The development of music printing in the early sixteenth century made notated music available to a wider public. Amateurs bought music to perform for their own entertainment, encouraging composers to produce new and more popular kinds of music, especially songs in vernacular languages and music for instruments (Chapter 7). The Reformation brought new forms of religious music for Protestant churches and, in reaction, new styles for Catholic music (Chapter 8). All of these changes have affected music in fundamental ways ever since.

> Repercussions in music

These developments will be taken up individually in the next four chapters. Here we will set the stage by placing the changes in music in the wider context of the Renaissance, showing some parallels with the other arts.

## Europe in the Renaissance

Several important political events occurred in the fifteenth and sixteenth centuries, including the end of the Hundred Years' War between the French and English in 1453; the fall of Constantinople to the Ottoman Turks that same year, ending the Byzantine Empire; and the rise of Europe as a world power. Larger ships, better navigational aids, and more powerful artillery helped Europeans expand their influence beyond the Mediterranean and northern Atlantic into the New World.

After the economic turmoil of the fourteenth century, the European economy stabilized around 1400 and began to grow. Regions specialized in different agricultural and manufactured products, and traded with each other across great distances. Towns and cities prospered from trade, and many city dwellers accumulated wealth through commerce, banking, and crafts. Merchants, artisans, doctors, and lawyers continued to increase in number, influence, and economic importance, seeking prosperity for their families, property and prestigious art for themselves, and education for their children. Rulers of small city-states sought to glorify themselves and their communities by erecting impressive

> Economy and society

*Figure II.1. Donatello,*
David, *ca. 1430. Bargello,*
*Florence. David, clad in*
*helmet and leg armor but*
*otherwise nude, stands*
*astride the head of the*
*slain Goliath. This bronze*
*statue was commissioned*
*by Cosimo de' Medici, ruler*
*of Florence. Showing the*
*beauty of the human*
*figure, as in the Greek and*
*Roman sculptures that*
*Donatello used as models,*
*it was the first free-*
*standing nude since*
*Roman times. Later in the*
*century, a Florentine*
*humanist compared the*
*composer Ockeghem to*
*Donatello, as each*
*"rediscovered" his*
*respective art.*

palaces and country houses decorated with new artworks, by hosting lavish entertainments, and by maintaining chapels of talented musicians. These conditions, strongest in Italy but gaining strength throughout western Europe during the fifteenth and sixteenth centuries, laid the economic and social foundations for the Renaissance.

Renaissance thinkers had broader access to the classics of Greek and Roman literature and philosophy than their medieval predecessors. Ottoman attacks on Constantinople beginning in 1396 led many Byzantine scholars to flee to Italy, taking with them numerous ancient Greek writings. They taught the Greek language to Italian scholars, some of whom also traveled to the East. Soon the Greek classics were translated into Latin, making most of Plato and the Greek plays accessible to Western Europeans for the first time. Scholars rediscovered complete copies of works on rhetoric by Cicero and Quintilian, and, later, other texts from Roman antiquity.

The increasing availability of ancient writings was complemented by new ways of using them. The strongest intellectual movement of the Renaissance was humanism, the study of the humanities and things pertaining to human knowledge. Humanists sought to revive ancient learning, emphasizing the study of grammar, rhetoric, poetry, history, and moral philosophy, centering on classical Latin and Greek writings. They believed these subjects developed the individual's mind, spirit, and ethics, and prepared students for lives of virtue and service. Humanists had faith in the dignity and nobility of humans and in our capacity to improve our condition through our own efforts. Gradually, humanistic studies replaced medieval Scholasticism, with its emphasis on logic and its reliance on authority as the center of intellectual life. The role of the Church was not diminished; rather, the Church borrowed from classical sources, sponsored classical studies, and supported thinkers, artists, and musicians.

## Renaissance Art and Architecture

Renaissance art shows striking contrasts with medieval art and several parallels with the new developments in scholarship and music.

The revival of classical antiquity in new guise is embodied in the bronze statue of *David* by Donatello (ca. 1386–1466), shown in Figure II.1, the first freestanding nude since Roman times. Nakedness in the Middle Ages implied shame, as in depictions of the Expulsion of Adam and Eve from the Garden of Eden. Here, nudity shows the beauty of the human figure, as in the Greek and Roman sculptures Donatello used as models. The work's naturalism—its attempt to reproduce nature realistically—is in tune with humanists' endeavor to see and understand the world as it really is.

The imitation of classical models and the naturalism Donatello exhibits here are typical of Renaissance art. These traits have parallels in music, as composers sought to please the ear with beautiful sonorities and seemingly natural melodies and rhythms. The lack of actual Greek and Roman music, however, caused composers to focus primarily on what was said about music in Greek writings.

Perspective

Italian painters had been pursuing greater realism since Giotto in the early fourteenth century (see Figure 4.1). But far more naturalistic representations were made possible in the early 1400s through the use of *perspective*, a method for representing three-dimensional space on a flat surface, creating a sense of depth. Figure II.2, a late fifteenth-century painting of an ideal city, shows the use of perspective, in which all parallel lines converge to a single vanishing point and objects of the same size appear smaller in exact proportion as they

*Figure II.2.* Idealized View of the City, *ca. 1840, by a painter from the school of Piero della Francesca, in the Ducal Palace in Urbino, northern Italy. The scene looks realistic because of attention paid to lighting and the use of perspective. All the lines that in three-dimensional reality would be parallel to each other, like the lines in the pavement or on the sides of buildings, converge toward a single vanishing point, just under the top of the doorway of the center building. Objects farther away from the viewer look smaller in exact mathematical proportion to their distance.*

grow more distant. This reflects what we might actually see, and creates the illusion of real space, in contrast to the fourteenth-century city-scape in Figure II.3, where the buildings seem heaped on top of one another, their distance from the viewer unclear.

The later picture is also more orderly, with clean lines, symmetry, and little clutter. This preference for clarity, typical of Renaissance architecture, contrasts markedly with Gothic decoration, such as the ornate carving on the façade of Reims cathedral in Figure 4.6. The use of columns with capitals on the center and leftmost buildings shows the Renaissance interest in imitating ancient architecture.

Another characteristic of humanism in general, and Renaissance art in particular, is a new interest in the individual. Faces, bodies, poses, and attire are rendered as though from nature, as lifelike as chisel or paintbrush will allow. Donatello's young David in Figure II.1 strikes a swaggering pose, fresh from his victory over Goliath; the unknown courtier in Figure 7.1 radiates a convincing air of self-importance. The many portraits painted in the Renaissance testify to the desire of patrons to be memorialized in art and the ability of artists to capture the personality of each subject.

*Clarity and classical models in architecture*

*Interest in individuals*

*Figure II.3.* Detail from The Effects of Good and Bad Government in the Town and in the Country *(1337–1391), a fresco by Ambrogio Lorenzetti painted in the Palazzo Pubblico (public palace) in Siena, a city in Tuscany in northern Italy. The subject of the painting illustrates the new humanist concern with government and civic virtues. Yet the technique is still medieval in many respects. While objects farther away are depicted as behind others and smaller than those closer to the viewer, there is no true perspective.*

## ARTS *and* IDEAS

The Florentine sculptor **Donatello** (ca. 1386–1466) was a pioneer in perspective, as is apparent in his bronze reliefs for the doors of the Florence Baptistery. His free-standing statues, many commissioned by his Medici patrons, are justly famous for their beautiful proportions and expressive details (see Figure II.1).

Called "the Maid of Orleans," **Joan of Arc** (ca. 1412–1431) was a French national heroine who raised an army to drive the English from French soil during the Hundred Years' War. More a spiritual than a military leader, she interpreted the "voices" she heard as direct inspiration from God. She was captured by the English, tried by French clerics for heresy and witchcraft, and burned at the stake in Rouen. She was elevated to sainthood only in 1920.

**Sandro Botticelli** (1445–1510), Florentine painter in the Medici orbit (see Figure II.6), combined sharp contours and sinuous line with a lyrical intensity that make his works seem like visual poetry (*La Primavera, Birth of Venus*).

The most wide-ranging genius of the age, **Leonardo da Vinci** (1452–1519) practiced all the arts of the Renaissance, including music, painting, sculpture, architecture, astronomy, optics, and mechanical engineering, as well as natural science. A native of Florence, he left to work for the Sforza dynasty in Milan and the French king Francis I. He ushered in the modern age of the individual, socially mobile artist and epitomized the artist's new role in society as not merely a craftsman but also a thinker and theorist.

A contemporary of Josquin, **Albrecht Dürer** (1471–1528) was the most important northern artist of the Renaissance. He raised the essentially northern medium of engraving to the status of high art by combining it with the techniques of late fifteenth-century Italian painting and a highly original and intense artistic vision.

The Polish astronomer **Nicolaus Copernicus** (1473–1543) articulated the first modern European theory of planetary motion around the sun, contradicting the ancient Ptolemaic system, which had placed the Earth at the center of the universe. His treatise *On the Revolutions of the Heavenly Spheres* was completed by 1530 but not published until he was on his deathbed.

In service to the Este family of his native Ferrara, **Ludovico Ariosto** (1474–1533) wrote the classic romantic epic *Orlando furioso* (1516), a fusion of French and English romance traditions centering around Charlemagne and King Arthur, with humanist echoes of the Latin and Italian poets Virgil and Petrarch. He was also a pioneer in Renaissance drama.

---

Musical parallels    Like the ideals of beauty and naturalism discussed above, clarity, depth, and interest in individuals also have parallels in music. Renaissance composers expanded the range of their pieces to include lower and higher pitches than before, and coordinated the separate lines of their polyphonic textures through points of imitation; in this way, their musical structures, especially in the sixteenth century, took on the clarity of line and function characteristic of Renaissance architecture and perspective in painting. Some composers set tunes that pay tribute to individuals, but even more important is the rising significance of composers as individual artists, as celebrated in their sphere as Donatello was in his.

# The Musical Renaissance

The broad intellectual and artistic currents of the Renaissance affected music deeply, yet in many respects music followed its own path. Without ancient music to draw on and without the ability of literature or art to depict reality naturalistically, musicians reflected humanism in other ways.

**Michelangelo Buonarroti** (1475–1564), Florentine sculptor and protégé of the Medici, was also a painter (Sistine chapel ceiling in Rome), architect (Medici tombs and the Laurentian Library), and poet (sonnets). More than any other Renaissance artist, his works illustrate the tension between classical and Christian subject matter, and reveal an awesome power that led him to be called "divine." Perhaps his most famous work is the huge figure of David (1504), the virtuous fighter for freedom against superior odds and a favorite hero of the Florentines.

An English statesman and author, **Sir (Saint) Thomas More** (1478–1535) described in his *Utopia* (1516) an ideal state founded entirely on reason. He opposed Henry VIII's divorce from Catherine of Aragon and refused to subscribe to the Act of Supremacy, which made the king head of the English Church. Imprisoned in the Tower of London in 1534, he was tried and beheaded for treason, and is celebrated as a martyr by the Roman Catholic Church.

**Baldassare Castiglione** (1478–1529) was a diplomat and author of *The Book of the Courtier* (see Chapter 7, page 129), both an idealized portrait of the court at Urbino and a skillful popularization of the ideas of humanist philosophers. His ruling precept, that all of the courtier's accomplishments in arms, letters, art, sport, music, or conversation should be marked by *sprezzatura*—an unforced quality of effortless superiority—became the trademark of the perfect gentleman in European society and remained so for centuries.

**Martin Luther** (1483–1546), the German leader of the Protestant Reformation, was ordained a priest in 1507, then became a professor at the University of Wittenberg. Shocked by the spiritual laxity in ecclesiastical Rome, he began his protest in 1517 by posting his historic ninety-five theses on the door of the castle church in Wittenberg.

**John Calvin** (1509–1564), the French Protestant theologian of the Reformation, preached the virtues of thrift, hard work, sobriety, and responsibility. Opposed to elaborate sacred polyphony, he condoned as service music only the congregational singing of the psalms. His influence spread throughout western Europe and, via his English followers, the Puritans, to North America.

Although originally from Greece, the painter **El Greco** (Domenicus Theotokopoulos; ca. 1541–1614) was active in Spain and Italy during the time of Victoria and Palestrina. Except for some portraits, two views of Toledo, and a mythological painting, his work—like theirs—deals almost exclusively with religious subjects. His highly subjective and dynamic style is suggestive of the religious fervor of the Counter-Reformation (see Figure 8.7).

The careers of musicians—their training, employment, and mobility—changed radically during this period. New musical institutions and enhanced support for musicians led to an unprecedented flowering of music. Rulers all over Europe established their own court chapels and hired musicians and clerics to staff them. Members of the chapel served as performers, composers, and scribes, furnishing music for church services as well as for secular entertainments. Figure II.4 shows the chapel of Philip the Good, duke of Burgundy, at Mass.

*Increased support for music*

Most fifteenth- and sixteenth-century composers were trained as choirboys and hired as singers, even though their reputations rested primarily on their compositions. In some cathedrals and chapels, choir schools taught not only singing, but also music theory, grammar, mathematics, and other subjects. Cities such as Cambrai, Bruges, Antwerp, Paris, Dijon, and Lyon, shown in Figure II.5, most renowned for their musical training in the fifteenth century, were later joined by Rome, Venice, and other Italian cities. This helps to explain why the most prominent composers of the fifteenth and early sixteenth centuries, such as Du Fay, Ockeghem, and Josquin, came from Flanders, the Netherlands, and northern France, while Italians became more prominent from the mid-sixteenth century on. Because only male children were admitted into choirs,

*Training of musicians*

*Figure II.4. Miniature by Jean le Tavernier, ca. 1457–1467. Royal Library of Belgium, Brussels. Philip the Good, duke of Burgundy, at Mass. Philip is in the center of the picture. The celebrant (the priest celebrating Mass) and deacon are at lower left, the singers in the chapel at lower right, and members of the court at the rear.*

women did not have this educational opportunity or the chance to make careers in public churches and princely courts. Nuns and novices in convents did receive musical instruction, and a few distinguished themselves as composers. Courts also employed instrumentalists, who typically were trained in the apprentice system and often were less musically literate than singers. Guilds protected the rights of instrumentalists; because they were secretive, we know much less about the training of instrumentalists than we do about the education of singers.

Many rulers avidly supported music and competed with each other for the best composers and performers. Like fine clothes and impressive pageantry, excellent music was both enjoyable in itself and valuable as a way of displaying wealth and power. The Medici, the leading family in Florence during most of this period, sponsored Franco-Flemish musicians such as Henricus (or Heinrich) Isaac (ca. 1450–1517) and Jacques Arcadelt (ca. 1507–1568) as well as native Italian painters and sculptors like Donatello, Botticelli (see Figure II.6), and Michelangelo. The Sforza, who ruled Milan from the 1450s, employed among their many singers Josquin des Prez (ca. 1450–1521), the leading composer of his generation, as well as Leonardo da Vinci, the leading artist. The court of Ferrara under the Este family hosted Josquin and his colleague Jacob Obrecht (1457/8–1505). Popes and cardinals were as committed as secular princes to a high standard of cultural activity and patronage. Some of the best musicians, artists, and scholars

*Figure II.5. Major centers for training musicians in the Renaissance.*

*Figure II.6.* Botticelli's Adoration of the Magi, *ca. 1475. In this treatment of the traditional religious subject, not only does the artist portray himself (standing apart on the extreme right, looking boldly out at the viewer), but he also replaces the three Magi (Wise Men) with several members of the Medici family—his patrons—dressed in elegant princely attire. Uffizi, Florence.*

of the Renaissance were sponsored by the pope and by cardinals from the Medici, Este, Sforza, and other families.

The presence at courts of musicians from many lands allowed composers and performers to learn styles and genres current in other regions. A large number of composers changed their place of service, exposing them to numerous types of music. The exchange of national traditions, genres, and ideas fostered the development of an international style in the fifteenth century, synthesizing elements from English, French, Burgundian, and Italian traditions. As new national styles of vernacular song emerged in the sixteenth century (see Chapter 7), the cosmopolitan careers of some composers prepared them to write songs in Italian, French, German, and Spanish with equal flair.

*Cosmopolitan musicians*

The Renaissance had a profound and enduring effect on music in subsequent centuries. In direct and indirect ways, developments in music paralleled those in other areas. The growing European economy, patronage for musicians, and the advent of music printing laid the economic foundation for an increase in musical activity that continued into later centuries. Humanism and the rediscovery of ancient texts fostered a reexamination of what music is and what it should do. Forged in this period were new musical styles that focused on consonance, clarity, direct appeal to the listener, natural declamation of words, and emotional expressivity. The musical language of the Renaissance lasted for generations and undergirds the treatment of dissonance, consonance, voice-leading, and text setting in most later styles.

*Legacy*

# England, France, and Burgundy in the Fifteenth Century: The Beginnings of an International Style

*Chapter Contents*

*Prelude* 98

English Music and Its
Influence 100

Music in Burgundian
Lands 102

*Postlude* 110

## PRELUDE

During the fifteenth century, music continued to move toward an international European style, retaining some characteristics of French and Italian music of the fourteenth century and incorporating new ingredients as well. English composers contributed decisively to this new style early in the century, but by 1500, Continental composers from northern France and the Low Countries had made it their own. These composers continued to cultivate secular genres, whose songlike texture (see page 103) even influenced settings of the Mass and the motet (which had itself become a fairly secular and ceremonial genre).

English victories during the Hundred Years' War, such as the Battle of Agincourt in 1415, left a strong English presence in France. The conquerors brought with them not only governmental and military personnel, but also composers and musicians to sing the Mass and provide secular entertainment. English music and its influence spread throughout the Continent, and a large number of British works were copied into Continental manuscripts during the first half of the fifteenth century. The music made quite an impression on the French, particularly the distinctive sound of its "lively consonances." A French poem of the early 1440s enthusiastically describes this new *contenance angloise* ("English quality"), citing especially the "marvelous pleasingness" that made English music so "joyous and remarkable" (see the vignette on page 101).

Toward the middle of the century, music in the Burgundian lands—the parts of France and the Low Countries ruled by the dukes of Burgundy—became the chief conduit for the new, international style that blended Italian, French, and English elements. Although the Burgundian dukes were nominally vassals of the kings of France, they virtually equaled them in power and influence. During the second half of the 1300s and the early 1400s, the ruling dukes acquired vast territories—adding to their original area of Burgundy, in east central France, most of the present-day Netherlands, Belgium, northeastern France, Luxembourg, and Lorraine—and presided over the whole until 1477 as though it were an independent kingdom (see Figure 5.1). Nearly all the leading composers active during the late fifteenth century came from these regions, and a number of them had some connection with the Burgundian court and chapel.

Chapels were musical establishments with salaried composers, singers, and sometimes instrumentalists who furnished music for church services. These ensembles might include as many as thirty professionals and members of the

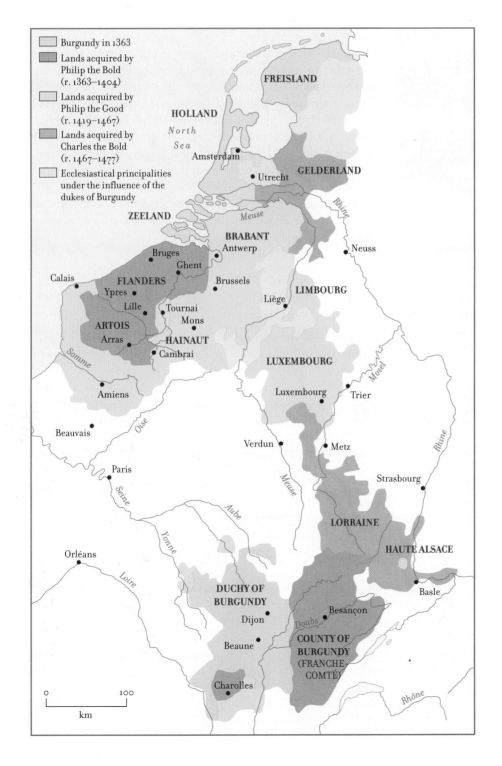

*Figure 5.1. The growth of Burgundian possessions, 1363–1477.*

court. The court and chapel of Philip the Good, duke of Burgundy (r. 1419–1467), and his successor, Charles the Bold (r. 1467–1477), were the most resplendent in fifteenth-century Europe (See Figure 5.2 and "The Feast of the Oath of the Pheasant," page 107). The majority of their musicians came from northern France, Flanders, and the Low Countries. In addition to his chapel, Philip the Good maintained a band of minstrels—trumpeters, drummers, viellists, lutenists, harpists, organists, and players of bagpipes and shawms—that included musicians from France, Italy, Germany, and Portugal.

The presence of many foreign musicians contributed to the cosmopolitan atmosphere of the Burgundian court. Also, members of the chapel themselves were continually moving from one court to another as better job opportunities arose. Inevitably, these circumstances fostered an international musical style. At the same time, the Burgundian court enjoyed such great prestige that its music influenced other European musical centers as well. A Flemish theorist writing about 1475 tells how the honor and riches offered to prominent musicians stimulated the growth of talent so much that music in his day seemed like "a new art, the source of which was among the English, with Dunstable at their head, and, contemporary with him in France, Du Fay and Binchois." These are the very composers who will be introduced in this chapter.

*Figure 5.2. An outdoor entertainment at the court of Philip the Good (1396–1467), duke of Burgundy. In the gardens of the Château de Hesdin, musicians play for the duke (center) and his company. In the foreground couples dance, while in the background hunters are chasing game. Detail from a sixteenth-century copy of an anonymous fifteenth-century painting,* The Garden of Love at the Court of Philippe le Bon. *Château de Versailles et de Trianon, Versailles, France.*

## English Music and Its Influence

From earliest times, England's sacred and secular art music, like northern Europe's generally, kept close connections with folk styles. It used homophonic discant style with all voices singing the same text rather than independent lines with different texts, and favored harmonic thirds and sixths as well as open fifths and octaves, eschewing the dissonances of the French motet. With its special penchant for these imperfect consonances, English discant has a fuller sound than music of the Continent and consequently seems more tonal than modal to modern ears. A good example is the *Sumer* canon introduced in Chapter 3 (NAWM 23). Then, too, English carols (songs in strophic forms with refrains) reveal a new stylistic feature: successions of simultaneous thirds and sixths in parallel motion (see NAWM 31). Such writing, which reflected the English taste for bright, harmonious textures, appeared as early as the thirteenth century and played an important role at this time, two hundred years later.

**Dunstable**  John Dunstable (also known as Dunstaple, ca. 1390–1453), named in Martin Le Franc's poem (see vignette, page 101), was the leading English composer of his time. He spent part of his career in France serving the English duke of Bedford, who was regent of France from 1422 to 1435 and commander of the English armies that Joan of Arc tried to drive off French land. Among Dunstable's sixty or so known compositions, we find examples of all the principal types and styles of polyphony that existed in his lifetime: isorhythmic motets, Mass Ordinary settings, secular songs, and three-part settings of miscellaneous liturgical texts. His twelve isorhythmic motets show that this old form was still in fashion. Some of the Mass sections, which make up about one-third of Dunstable's surviving

**Dunstable's motets**

CD 2/21 | CD 1/25

CD 2/49

works, also use isorhythm. We know of only a few secular songs attributed to Dunstable; several of these illustrate the expressive lyrical melodies and clear harmonic profile common to the English music of his time.

Historically, Dunstable's three-voice sacred pieces—settings of antiphons, hymns, Mass movements, and other liturgical or biblical texts—remain his most important works. Some use a cantus firmus in the tenor or an ornamented chant melody in the treble. Others have florid treble lines and borrowed melodies in the middle voice, with the tenor moving mostly in thirds and sixths below. Still others, like the antiphon *Quam pulchra es* (How beautiful you are, NAWM 32), are not based on an existing melody.

CD 2/52    CD 1/40

Other features of this work, however, are exceptional even in Dunstable's output. Its three voices are similar in character and nearly equal in importance. They move mostly in the same rhythm and usually pronounce the same syllables together in syllabic fashion. The brief melisma at the end of the word "Alleluia" animates the conclusion. The vertical sonorities are consonant, except for the brief suspensions at cadences, yet show considerable variety. Dunstable chose not to restrict himself to a cantus firmus or an isorhythmic scheme; instead, he allowed the accents and grouping of the words to determine the form of the

---

**VIGNETTE**    "The Contenance Angloise" (The English Quality)

*Martin Le Franc (ca. 1410–1461) was a poet, cleric, and secretary at the court of Savoy, where Guillaume Du Fay periodically worked as chapelmaster. At the wedding of the duke's son in 1434, both had occasion to meet Binchois, who was in the retinue of the visiting duke of Burgundy. In his poem* Le Champion des dames *(1440–1442), Le Franc praised the music of Du Fay and Binchois in terms that have shaped our view of fifteenth-century music history.*

∿

| | |
|---|---|
| *Tapissier, Carmen, Cesaris* | Tapissier, Carmen, Cesaris |
| *Na pas longtemps si bien chanterrent* | not long ago sang so well |
| *Quilz esbahirent tout paris* | that they astonished all Paris |
| *Et tous ceulx qui les frequenterrent;* | and all who came to hear them. |
| *Mais oncques jour ne deschanterrent* | But the day came when they did not discant |
| *En melodie de tels chois* | such finely wrought melody— |
| *Ce mont dit qui les hanterrent* | so those who heard them told me— |
| *Que G. Du Fay et Binchois.* | as G. Du Fay and Binchois. |
| *Car ilz ont nouvelle pratique* | For they have a new practice |
| *De faire frisque concordance* | of making lively consonance |
| *En haulte et en basse musique* | both in loud and soft music,[1] |
| *En fainte, en pause, et en muance* | in feigning,[2] in rests, and in mutations.[3] |
| *Et ont prins de la contenance* | They took on the guise |
| *Angloise et ensuy Dunstable* | of the English and follow Dunstable |
| *Pour quoy merveilleuse plaisance* | and thereby a marvelous pleasingness |
| *Rend leur chant joyeux et notable.* | makes their music joyous and remarkable. |

French text, trans. C. V. Palisca; in Charles van den Borren, *Guillaume Dufay: Son importance dans l'évolution de la musique au XVe siècle* (Brussels, 1926), pp. 53–54.

1. This distinction was explored in Chapter 4, pp. 86–87.
2. The word refers to the application of musica ficta; see Chapter 4, pp. 86–87.
3. A reference to shifting from one set of six scale steps (hexachord) to another in the solmization system devised by Guido; see Chapter 2, pp. 45–46.

*Figure 5.3. Among the painters who enjoyed the patronage of the dukes of Burgundy was Jan van Eyck (1390–1441), whose depiction of the angels' instruments in his Ghent Altarpiece is so vivid that modern instrument makers have used them as models for reconstruction. Shown here are a positive (or chamber) organ, a harp, and a vielle (or tenor fiddle), all belonging to the category of soft (bas) instruments, discussed on pages 86–87. Church of Saint Bavon, Ghent.*

music. Compared to the French-style motets of the time, this composition sounds astonishingly fresh, revealing even greater melodic and harmonic suavity than some of the secular songs of the day, and its attention to text declamation allies it to the Renaissance. Only the double-leading-tone cadences recall the medieval style.

*Quam pulchra es* is usually classified as a motet, even though it has no borrowed tenor. The term *motet,* coined in the thirteenth century for pieces that added text to the upper part of a discant clausula, gradually broadened its meaning to include any work with texted upper voices above a cantus firmus, regardless of whether the text was sacred or secular. By the early fifteenth century, the isorhythmic motet, which had been an Ars nova invention, was considered old fashioned, and by 1450 it disappeared. Meanwhile, the term was applied to settings of liturgical texts in the newer musical styles of the time, whether or not the settings were based on a chant melody. The term *motet* came to designate almost any polyphonic composition on a Latin text, including settings of texts from the Mass Proper and the Office. The erotic poetry of *Dunstable's Quam pulchra es* (Latin text and translation in NAWM 32) was nevertheless sacred, having been adapted by the Church from the Old Testament Song of Songs as an allegory of Christ's love for the individual soul. For a summary of the changing meanings of *motet,* see Figure 5.4.

# Music in Burgundian Lands

Most of the polyphonic compositions of the mid-fifteenth century were principally of four basic types: secular chansons with French texts, motets, Magnificats and hymn settings for the daily Offices, and settings of the Mass Ordinary. All but the Office music will be discussed in this chapter. Most pieces were for three voices, in a texture resembling the fourteenth-century French chanson or Italian ballata, with the cantus spanning up to a tenth, and the tenor and contratenor sharing a narrower range about a sixth below. As in some fourteenth-century secular songs, each line has a distinct role, with the main melody in the cantus, contrapuntal support in the tenor, and harmonic filler in the contratenor.

The foremost composers of music in the dominant, so-called Burgundian style of the fifteenth century were Guillaume Du Fay (also Dufay, ca. 1397–1474) and Gilles de Bins (more often called Binchois, ca. 1400–1460). The two are shown conversing in the miniature illuminating Martin le Franc's poem (see Figure 5.5). It may be significant that the painter depicted Du Fay standing next to an organ and Binchois holding a harp because, although both composers wrote in all the main genres of the day, Du Fay was particularly esteemed for his contributions to sacred music and Binchois for his secular songs or chansons.

Binchois flourished at the center of musical life in the Burgundian court, serving in the chapel of Duke Philip the Good from the 1420s until 1453. He did not travel widely and remained in this one post for three decades, which may help to explain the consistent quality of his style. But prior experience in the service of the earl of Suffolk, who was with the English forces occupying France, gave him direct knowledge of English musicians and made him a central figure in the creation of a Burgundian style that embraced the *contenance angloise.*

| **Motet** | |
|---|---|
| 1. early 1200s | Polyphonic piece derived from discant clausula, with words added to the upper voice |
| 2. 1200s–1300s | Polyphonic piece with one or more upper voices, each with sacred or secular text in Latin or French, above tenor from chant or other source |
| 3. 1400s on | Polyphonic setting of a Latin, especially liturgical, text other than the Mass Ordinary |
| 4. ca. 1310–1450 | Isorhythmic motet: a work with its tenor structured by isorhythm |
| 5. mid–1500s | Some polyphonic setting of a sacred text in other languages |

*Figure 5.4. The changing meanings of* motet.

Binchois composed more than fifty chansons, among them some of the greatest hits of the fifteenth century, when the term *chanson* denoted any polyphonic setting of a French secular poem. Chansons most often set stylized love poems in the courtly tradition of *fine amour* (see Chapter 2), and most followed the form of the rondeau (AB aA ab AB). Binchois's well-known rondeau *De plus en plus* (NAWM 33), from around 1425, illustrates his style and provides an example of a typical Burgundian chanson. One measure of its popularity is that a later composer, Jean de Ockeghem, used it as the basis for his setting of a Mass Ordinary (NAWM 37).

The opening of *De plus en plus* (More and more [renews again . . . my wish to see you]) reflects English influence in its upbeat opening, its relatively full, consonant harmonies, and its basically triadic melody (Example 5.1). Binchois continued the treble-dominated style of the fourteenth century, but his gracefully arched melodic contours and fluid, lilting rhythms enlivened by dotted figures and subtle syncopations are much less intricate than in chansons by Machaut or Ars subtilior composers. The end of the first phrase (Example 5.1, boxed notes) illustrates a newer version of the cadence formula used in the fourteenth century (compare Example 4.3). The major sixth between cantus and tenor still expands to an octave, often with the so-called "Landini" embellishment figure in the cantus, but the contratenor leaps up an octave to sound the fifth above the tenor's final note; the result sounds like a V–I cadence.

Binchois's chansons

CD 2/54    CD 1/42

CD 2/70

Cadences

*Figure 5.5.   Guillaume Du Fay next to a portative organ and Binchois holding a harp, in a miniature from Martin Le Franc's poem* Le Champion des dames *(1440–1442). Du Fay, Binchois, and Le Franc were together at Savoy in 1434 when Du Fay was in the service of the duke of Savoy, and the two composers may have met on other occasions as well. Paris, Bibliothèque Nationale, MS Fr. 12476, f. 98r.*

*Example 5.1: Binchois,* De plus en plus, *opening phrase*

*More and more renews again, . . .*

**Du Fay**

Guillaume Du Fay was the most famous composer of his time. His many travels (see biography) exposed him to a wide variety of music, from his French and Italian predecessors to his English and Burgundian contemporaries, and he absorbed many of their musical traits into his own works, sometimes combining contrasting styles in a single piece. His music represents well the international style of the mid-fifteenth century.

**Chansons**

Du Fay's blending of national traits can be traced in his chansons. While serving at the Malatesta court in Italy, he wrote *Resvellies vous* (Awake and be merry, NAWM 34) in 1423 to celebrate his patron's wedding. French characteristics are suggested by the ballade form itself (aabC), some rhythmic complications including persistent syncopation, and some dissonant ornamental notes. Italian elements are seen in the relatively smooth vocal melodies and virtuosic vocal melismas on the last accented syllable of each line of text. *Se la face ay pale* (If my face is pale, NAWM 36a), a chanson that Du Fay wrote about ten years later while at the court of Savoy, shows the strong influence of English music, with its short, tuneful, clearly marked phrases and its consonant harmonies.

CD 2/56

CD 2/61    CD 1/44

Du Fay wrote sacred music in a variety of styles. Many motets and Office pieces were in three voices with a texture resembling the chanson: the main melody in the cantus supported by tenor and contratenor. The cantus might be newly composed, but often it was an embellished version of a chant. Du Fay's setting of the hymn *Conditor alme siderum* (Bountiful creator of the stars, NAWM 35) paraphrases the chant in the treble part.

CD 2/59

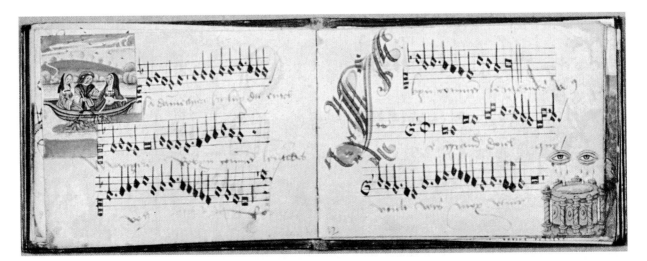

*Figure 5.6. Chansonnier of Tournai. Pages illustrated with miniatures. Note the eyes weeping tears into a bucket.*

In addition to motets in the modern chanson style, Du Fay and his contemporaries still wrote occasional isorhythmic motets for solemn public events, following the convention that a conservative musical style was more fitting for ceremonial and state occasions. Du Fay's magnificent *Nuper rosarum flores* (Roses recently [came]) was such a work; it was performed at the dedication of Filippo Brunelleschi's magnificent dome for the church of Santa Maria del Fiore (the "Duomo") in Florence in 1436 (see Figure 5.8). Du Fay's use of two isorhythmic tenors, both based on the same chant, may have been an allusion to Brunelleschi's use of two vaults to support the dome. Du Fay composed the motet while serving in the chapel of Pope Eugene IV, who presided over the ceremony. A writer who was in attendance described the bright-robed company of trumpeters, viellists, and other instrumentalists, and the singing choirs that struck the listeners with awe, so that the sound of music, the aroma of incense, and the sight of the beautiful pageant filled the spectators with wonder.

*Isorhythmic motets*

Like their English colleagues, composers on the Continent wrote polyphonic settings of Mass Ordinary texts in increasing numbers during the late fourteenth and early fifteenth centuries. Until about 1420, the various sections of the Ordinary were nearly always composed as separate pieces (Machaut's Mass

*Masses*

## Guillaume Du Fay (Dufay) (ca. 1397–1474)

Du Fay was addressed in a letter from the Florentine organist Antonio Squarcialupi as "the greatest ornament of our age." Surely the most cosmopolitan composer of his time, he excelled in every genre, and his music was known and sung throughout Europe.

The illegitimate son of an unknown father and a single woman, Du Fay was born in modern-day Belgium, near Brussels. He studied music and grammar in the cathedral school of Cambrai, in northeastern France, where he became a choirboy in 1409. As a young man, he worked as a singer and composer at various Italian courts and chapels, including the papal chapel, and in Savoy (a region that comprised parts of Italy, Switzerland, and France). At age thirty, probably while he was in Italy, he was ordained a priest. From at least 1439 until 1450, Du Fay's home base was his native Cambrai, by then under Burgundian control, where he served as an administrator at the cathedral and probably enjoyed an honorary appointment to the chapel of Duke Philip the Good. After another period as choirmaster in Savoy, he spent his last years at Cambrai as a canon of the cathedral, occupied with administrative tasks but still active as a composer, living in his own house and enjoying considerable wealth.

Du Fay's music survives in almost one hundred manuscripts copied between the 1420s and the

*Figure 5.7. Du Fay's funeral monument, showing the composer kneeling in prayer at the left.*

early sixteenth century in regions from Spain to Poland and from Italy to Scotland, attesting to his popularity and fame as a composer.

**Major works:** at least 6 Masses, 35 independent Mass movements, 4 Magnificats, 60 hymns and other chant settings, 24 motets (13 isorhythmic, 11 freely composed), 34 plainchant melodies, 60 rondeaux, 8 ballades, 13 other secular songs

*Figure 5.8. The cathedral of Santa Maria del Fiore, Florence. Du Fay wrote the isorhythmic motet* Nuper rosarum flores *for the consecration of the dome in 1436.*

and a few others excepted), although occasionally the compiler of a manuscript would group such separate items together. In the course of the fifteenth century, it became standard practice for composers to set the Ordinary as a musically unified whole, or a polyphonic Mass cycle. Writing a Mass became the supreme challenge to a composer's creative ingenuity, much as designing a chapel or painting an altarpiece was for an artist of the time. Just as those works were usually ordered and paid for by a particular institution or private patron, settings of the Mass Ordinary were sometimes commissioned for specific occasions or devotional services by individuals or families for whose benefit the Mass was then performed, as in Du Fay's *Missa Se la face ay pale* (see below), linked to his Savoy patrons. Similarly, the long tradition of composing Masses on the *L'Homme armé* tune (The Armed Man—a title with obvious military connotations) may be connected to the Order of the Golden Fleece, an association of noblemen from all over Europe instituted by Charles the Good of Burgundy, and to calls for a new Crusade (see page 107).

**Compositional techniques**

Composers in the fifteenth century devised a variety of means to link the separate sections of a Mass to each other. Some musical unity resulted simply from composing all five parts of the Ordinary in the same general style, whether freely composed, or based on paraphrased chants in the upper voice or on a cantus firmus in the tenor. Unity, then, initially derived from two factors: liturgical association—all movements were part of the cycle of prayers constituting the Mass Ordinary—and compositional procedure. Composers soon achieved a more perceptible and effective musical interconnection by using the same *thematic* material in all sections of the Mass. At first, this connection consisted only in beginning each movement with the same melodic motive, usually in the treble. Since the Ordinary sections do not follow one another in unbroken succession, a Mass that uses such a "head motive," or "motto," signals to the listener that a particular section belongs with the other sections of the Ordinary.

**Motto Mass**

**Cantus firmus or tenor Mass**

The motto technique was soon superseded by, or combined with, another: constructing each movement around the same borrowed melody or cantus firmus, normally placed in the tenor. The resulting cyclical form is known as a cantus firmus Mass, or tenor Mass. English composers wrote the earliest cantus firmus Masses; but the practice was soon adopted on the Continent, and by the second half of the fifteenth century it had become the principal type of Mass setting.

Placing the borrowed melody in the tenor followed the medieval-motet tradition but created compositional problems. The sound-ideal of the fifteenth century needed the lowest voice to function as a harmonic foundation, particularly at cadences. Letting the lowest voice carry a preexistent chant melody limited the composer's ability to provide such a foundation. The solution was to add

## IN CONTEXT  The Feast of the Oath of the Pheasant

When Constantinople, the last Christian stronghold in the East, fell to Turkish Muslims in 1453, reactions at the other end of Europe were immediate and profound. The leading composer of the time, Guillaume Du Fay, wrote a lament, a motet for which he chose a cantus firmus from a Latin chant with these words from the Lamentations of Jeremiah: "All her friends have dealt treacherously with her, among all her lovers she hath none to comfort her." Philip the Good, duke of Burgundy, was so troubled that he determined to launch a new Crusade to rescue the Eastern Church. Although the Crusade never materialized, Philip created quite a stir. As leader of the wealthiest and most cultured court of Europe, he assembled hundreds of noble lords and vassals and their ladies at a huge banquet, where they took a solemn oath to come to the aid of the captive Church.

The Feast of the Oath of the Pheasant, as it is known, took place in Lille on June 17, 1454. Court chroniclers described the event in ways that suggest that every detail was designed to enhance the theme. The tables were decorated with enormous constructions that came alive as people and animals emerged from them during interludes performed between courses. Music played a large role in the spectacle. During the first interlude, a church bell rang loudly, then three choirboys and a tenor sang a song. At other moments, minstrels sang and played on portative organs, bagpipes, lutes, krummhorns, flutes, fiddles, harps, and drums. There were pantomime tableaux, each punctuated by trumpet fanfares, involving knights on horseback, a falcon slaying a heron, and scenes from the adventures of Jason, heroic patron of the Knights of the Order of the Golden Fleece.

At the climax of the banquet, the interlude that symbolized the reason for the entire feast was staged. Into the huge hall a giant Arab led an elephant bearing on its back a miniature castle; within its tower was imprisoned a woman personifying Mother Church. After chanting a *complainte* bemoaning the fall of Constantinople, she begged the Burgundian nobles to take up her cause. At that point, the chronicles explain, it was the custom to present a live pheasant decorated with pearls and precious gems to the assembled noblemen "in order that they make useful and worthy vows." After the tables were taken out, the final episode was a joyous ballet.

The magnificence of the occasion reveals something about the extravagant lifestyle of the Burgundian court, where refinement mingled with vulgarity and chivalric ideals combined with religious sentiment. But it also shows that ceremonial music and theater were purposefully linked to meaningful action in life.

*Figure 5.9.* Philip the Good, *by Rogier van der Weyden (1400–1464). Philip wears the chain of the Order of the Golden Fleece, of which he was grand master.*

a part below the tenor, first called *contratenor bassus* ("low contratenor") and later simply *bassus*. A second contratenor called *contratenor altus* ("high contratenor"), later *altus*, sounded above the tenor. The highest part was the treble, called variously the *cantus* ("melody"), *discantus* ("discant"), or *superius* ("highest part"). These four voice parts became standard by the mid-1400s and remain so today.

**Four-voice texture**

The practice of writing the tenor cantus firmus in long notes was a holdover from the medieval motet. When the chosen melody was a plainchant, a rhythmic pattern was imposed on it and repeated, if the melody was repeated. When the borrowed melody was a secular tune, the song's original rhythm was retained; but in successive appearances, the pattern could be made faster or slower in relation to the other voices. As in the isorhythmic motet, the identity of the borrowed tune might, therefore, be thoroughly disguised, the more so now that it lay in an inner voice. Obscuring the cantus firmus in this way did not diminish its power to unify the five divisions of the Mass. Borrowed chant melodies came from the Proper or the Office, secular ones most often from the tenors of chansons; in neither case did they have any liturgical connection with the Ordinary. But the Mass usually owed its name to the borrowed melody, as in Du Fay's *Missa Ave regina caelorum*, based on the Marian antiphon; such a connection would also have made this particular setting suitable for performance at any Mass in honor of the Blessed Virgin.

*Missa Se la face ay pale*

CD 2/61    CD 1/44

One of the most celebrated tenor Masses is Du Fay's *Missa Se la face ay pale*, based on the tenor of his own ballade *Se la face ay pale* (If my face is pale [the cause is love], NAWM 36a). The practice of using one's own (presumably popular) love song as the basis for a liturgical composition may seem inappropriate to us today. But in the fifteenth century, when court and chapel composers were one and the same, it may have been motivated at least in part by pride of authorship—the desire of composers to mark works as their own and in a way that would be unmistakable to their employer and other listeners. Similarly, using a cantus firmus borrowed from another's song may have been a way of paying tribute to a colleague, as with Ockeghem's Mass based on Binchois's chanson *De plus en plus*, or, perhaps, of acknowledging the influence of a teacher. In any case, in the aesthetic of the time composers were prized for their ability to create something new from borrowed materials.

CD 2/63    CD 1/46

In the Kyrie, Sanctus, and Agnus Dei of Du Fay's *Missa Se la face ay pale*, the value of each note of the ballade's tenor melody is doubled. In the Gloria (NAWM 36b) and Credo, the cantus firmus is heard three times, first in notes that are triple their normal values, then in doubled note values, and finally at their original note values, so that the melody becomes easily recognizable only at the third hearing. In this way, Du Fay applied the principles of the isorhythmic motet on a larger scale. In Example 5.2a, we see the first phrase of the song in very long notes in the tenor at "Adoramus te," its first appearance in the Gloria. The next time this opening phrase occurs, at "Qui tollis peccata mundi" (Example 5.2b), the note values are smaller. The third time, at "Cum sancto spiritu" (Example 5.2c), the song is heard at its normal tempo. By speeding up the tenor's cantus firmus and imitating some of its motives in the other parts, Du Fay heightened the excitement of the closing "Amen."

**Layered texture in Du Fay's Masses**

The diverse character of the voices in Du Fay's Mass nearly overshadows the unity achieved by the threefold statement of the chanson melody in the tenor. As in the old-fashioned French motet, each voice exists as an independent layer, having its own melodic and rhythmic logic and function. The top two voices—the superius and the contratenor altus—maintain smooth melodic contours and occasionally exchange motives, while the contratenor bassus, more angular though still vocal, provides a harmonic foundation. This texture prevails in other Masses by Du Fay as well.

*Example 5.2: Guillaume Du Fay,* Missa Se la face ay pale, *Gloria*

*a. Cantus firmus at three times original duration*

*We adore thee. We glorify thee.*

*b. Cantus firmus at twice original duration*

*have mercy upon us. Thou who takest away the sins of the world.*

*c. Cantus firmus at original duration.*

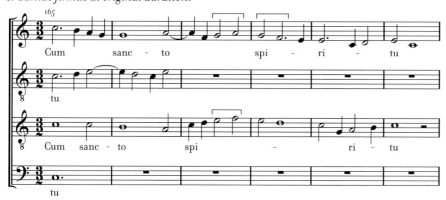

*With the Holy Spirit*

Consonance and dissonance are also carefully controlled rather than used haphazardly. The stronger dissonances appear as suspensions and resolve downward by step; this treatment of dissonance became standard and was considered "proper" practice in the sixteenth century. Other dissonances, mainly between beats, pass quickly. Otherwise, Du Fay favors thirds and sixths sounding with octaves, fifths, and fourths, producing many different qualities of triads on the beats.

Consonance and dissonance in Du Fay's Masses

Du Fay's four-part cantus firmus (or tenor) Masses are late works, dating for the most part after 1450. Their structural procedures distinguish them from the earlier chansons and chansonlike motets and Masses. As opposed to the pleasing qualities of the Burgundian chanson, some of their new features reflect an extremely artful or learned musical style, one that rose to prominence after the middle of the century.

## POSTLUDE

The English composer Dunstable and the Burgundian composers Binchois and Du Fay played a large role in forming and disseminating throughout Europe an international musical language, fused from French, Italian, and English elements. An overly simple description of the new style—but one that does not distort the truth entirely—might attribute its rhythmic suppleness to the French, its melodic suavity to the Italians, and its clear, bright harmonies to the English. The full consonant sound of sixths and thirds, sometimes in parallel succession, was adopted on the Continent. This new sound strongly influenced all types of composition and prompted composers to write homophonic or homorhythmic

---

**TIMELINE**  Fifteenth-Century England and Burgundy

| MUSICAL EVENTS | HISTORICAL EVENTS |
|---|---|
| | **1415** English under Henry V defeat French at Agincourt |
| | **1417** End of papal schism |
| | **1419** Philip III (the Good) begins his reign as duke of Burgundy |
| | **1431** Joan of Arc executed |
| Du Fay's motet *Nuper rosarum flores* **1436** written for dedication of Brunelleschi's dome of Santa Maria del Fiore, Florence | |
| Du Fay, *Missa Se la face ay pale* **ca. 1450s** | |
| Death of Dunstable **1453** | **1453** End of Hundred Years' War; fall of Constantinople |
| | **1454** Feast of the Oath of the Pheasant in Lille |
| Death of Binchois **1460** | |
| | **1467** Charles the Bold of Burgundy succeeds Philip III (the Good) |
| Death of Du Fay **1474** | |
| | **1477** Death of Charles the Bold; end of independent rule of duchy of Burgundy |

textures that emphasized the similarity among the parts rather than their differences. After about 1430, then, certain characteristic features of the new style emerged in the Burgundian orbit: predominantly consonant sonorities, including parallel $^6_3$ chords; control of dissonances; equal importance of the voices; greater melodic and rhythmic identity of lines; four-part textures; and occasional use of imitation. These features represented a departure from the musical style of the late Middle Ages and signaled the new age of the Renaissance.

# 6

# Music of the
# Low Countries

*Chapter Contents*

*Prelude* 112

The Musical Culture
of the Renaissance  114

Northern Composers:
The Generation after
Du Fay  117

The Next Generation:
Josquin and His
Contemporaries  121

*Postlude* 126

## PRELUDE

Music historians broadly apply the term *Renaissance*, meaning "rebirth," to the fifteenth and sixteenth centuries. During this period, important changes deeply affected the musical culture of western Europe—how people thought about music as well as the way music was composed, experienced, discussed, and disseminated. To be sure, although they could see and emulate the rediscovered architectural monuments, sculptures, plays, and poems, they could not actually hear ancient music. Although the revival of the arts and architecture of ancient Greece and Rome was in full swing by 1450, the music of antiquity could be understood only through the writings of classical philosophers, poets, essayists, and music theorists that were becoming available in translation. "Moderns" learned about the power of ancient music to move the listener and wondered why their own music did not have the same effect. For example, the influential religious leader Bernardino Cirillo (see page 115) expressed disappointment with the artful polyphonic music of his time. He urged musicians to follow the example of the other arts and to reclaim the power of classical musical styles and modes.

We may think of the musical Renaissance more as a general cultural movement and state of mind than as a specific set of musical techniques. Furthermore, music changed so rapidly during these centuries—though at different rates in different countries—that we cannot identify one uniform Renaissance style. Nevertheless, with the expansion of Burgundian territories and influence, the musical Renaissance spread chiefly from the Low Countries—regions of northeastern France, Belgium, and the Netherlands—to other areas of western Europe. In this chapter, we will explore the music of northern composers, who are referred to variously as French, Franco-Flemish, or Netherlandish, depending on where they were born. Each new generation built on the musical accomplishments of the previous one, and composers of the same generation competed with one another in writing Masses, motets, and chansons.

The chapter will close with a discussion of Josquin and his contemporaries. Of the large number of first-rank composers active around 1500, Josquin des

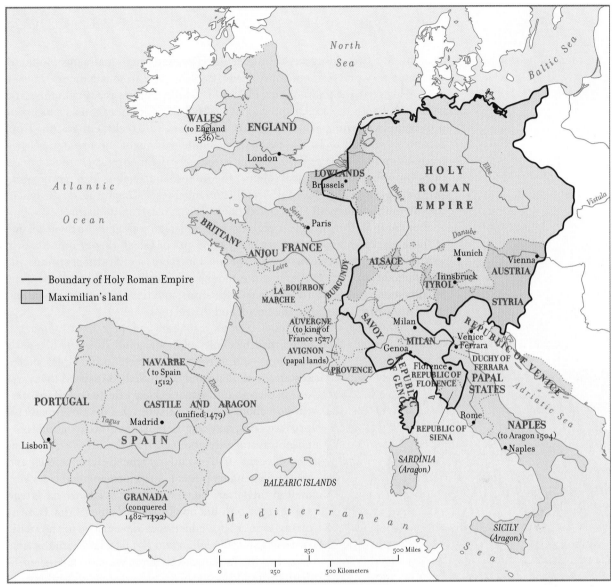

Figure 6.1. Western Europe about 1500. By this time, the Spanish rulers Isabella and Ferdinand had united Spain; the kings of France controlled several former quasi-independent fiefdoms within their borders, including Burgundy, Anjou, Brittany, and Provence; and Maximilian I, king of Germany and Holy Roman emperor, ruled directly over Austria, Alsace, and the Low Countries.

Prez (ca. 1450–1521) was surely the greatest.[1] Few musicians have enjoyed higher renown while they lived or exercised more profound and lasting influence. One of his contemporaries, Martin Luther, acknowledged Josquin's complete technical and expressive control of his art by calling him "master of the notes." Others hailed him as "the best of the composers of our time," the "father of musicians." Florentine diplomat and humanist Cosimo Bartoli wrote in 1567 that Josquin had been without peer in music, on a par with Michelangelo (1475–1564) in architecture, painting, and sculpture: "Both opened the eyes of all those who now take pleasure in these arts and shall find delight in the future."

1. Josquin's name, like that of many other composers of earlier times, is spelled in various ways: des Prez, Desprez, Despres; similarly, Du Fay's name is often seen as Dufay. Such flexibility resulted no doubt from the different pronunciations, alphabets, and customs in the many countries in which they worked and from the absence of standardized spelling, which came about only after the gradual increase in printing and literacy made it an issue.

# The Musical Culture of the Renaissance

**Musical humanism**

In addition to providing a new intellectual climate to the Renaissance, humanism had a very practical outcome: a rebirth of interest in music theory's Greek past. As early as 1424 at the court of Mantua, students were reading the musical treatise of Boethius (see Chapter 2) as a classical text rather than as a basis for professional training. Over the next half century, Greeks emigrating from Byzantium as well as Italian manuscript hunters brought the principal Greek treatises on music to the West. Among these were the theoretical works of Aristides Quintilianus, Claudius Ptolemy, Cleonides, and Euclid. Also newly available were passages by Plato and Aristotle on music (see Chapter 1). By the end of the fifteenth century, all of these treatises were translated into Latin.

**Gaffurio**

Franchino Gaffurio (1451–1522) was one musician-scholar who owned some of these works and incorporated many concepts of Greek theory into his own writings. His musical treatises were the most influential of his time, stimulating new thought on such matters as the modes, consonance and dissonance, the tonal system, tuning, word-music relationships, and the harmony of music and its relationship to the body, the mind, and the cosmos.

**Power of the ancient modes**

The rediscovery of the ancient Greek philosophers and their theory of musical modes—especially their belief that the choice of mode could affect the listener's emotions—led to renewed interest in the Greek modal system. Both Plato and Aristotle had insisted that various modes had different ethical effects (recall the discussion about ethos in Chapter 1). Like their medieval predecessors, however, Renaissance theorists and composers mistakenly assumed that the old Greek modes were identical to the similarly named church modes and that the legendary powers of the former could be attributed to the latter. The Swiss theorist Heinrich Glarean (1488–1563), in his book *Dodekachordon* (The Twelve-String Lyre, 1547), added four new modes to the traditional eight: the Aeolian and Hypoaeolian with the final on *A*, and the Ionian and Hypoionian with the final on *C*. With these additions, he tried to reconcile the theory of the modes with the practice of composers, who frequently employed tonal centers on *A* and *C*. In using something borrowed from ancient culture to modify his medieval heritage, Glarean was typical of his age.

The new emphasis on thirds and sixths posed a challenge to music theorists, who had defined only the octave, fifth, and fourth as consonant in the Middle Ages because these were generated by the simple ratios that Pythagoras had discovered. Moreover, although the imperfect consonances sounded rough to the ear and out of tune, fourths and fifths were perfectly consonant in the tuning system of the Middle Ages and were, therefore, along with the octave, the only permissible cadential sonorities. But by the beginning of the sixteenth century, music theorists began to yield to changing usage and adjusted tuning systems to make the thirds and sixths acceptable in theory and in practice. Accordingly, triads appeared more frequently in final cadences from the sixteenth century on.

*Figure 6.2. Music portrayed as a liberal art, probably from the 1470s by Justus of Ghent, a Netherlandish painter who was also active in Italy. The unidentified kneeling gentleman illustrates the new respect accorded the science of music in the Renaissance.*

**VIGNETTE**    Bernardino Cirillo on Reviving Ancient Music

*Bernardino Cirillo (1500–1575), rector of the famous shrine and pilgrimage destination the Santa Casa of Loreto, was a prominent churchman in mid-sixteenth-century Rome. Here, in a letter published during his lifetime (1549), he allies himself with the humanists by finding modern polyphony wanting in expression and urges a revival of the Greek doctrine of ethos and a restoration of the ancient modes.*

. . . Music among the ancients was the most splendid of all the fine arts. With it they created powerful effects that we nowadays cannot produce either with rhetoric or with oratory in moving the passions and affections of the soul. . . . By means of the power of song [using the correct modes], a slow and lazy man becomes lively and active; an angry man is calmed; . . . a miserable man becomes happy; and thus music governs human affections and has the power to alter them as need be. Now, where has this led?

. . .

I should like, in short, when a mass is to be sung in church, the music to be framed to the fundamental meaning of the words, in certain intervals and numbers apt to move our affections to religion and piety. . . . Each mode should be adapted to its subject, and when one has a lullaby to sing, or a plaintive song, one should do likewise. Thus the musicians of today should endeavor in their profession to do what the sculptors, painters, and architects of our time have done, who have recovered the art of the ancients; and the writers, who have reclaimed literature from the hell to which it was banished by corrupt ages; and as the sciences have been explained and given in their purity to our times. Thus the musicians should seek to recover the styles and modes, and the power of the Phrygian, Lydian, Dorian, and Mixolydian compositions, with which they would be able to do what they wish.

Bernardino Cirillo, letter to Ugolino Gualteruzzi, trans. Lewis Lockwood; in Oliver Strunk, ed., *Source Readings in Music History*, rev. ed. by Leo Treitler (New York, Norton, 1998), pp. 369–371.

**Consonance and dissonance**

As definitions of consonance and dissonance were reevaluated and distinctions between them sharpened, composers and theorists devised new rules for handling dissonance. Thus, from the practice of the fifteenth-century international style emerged a new style of counterpoint in which a work was composed note against note or melody against melody and which was based on a preference for consonance, including thirds and sixths, and on strict control of dissonance. This new approach to composition reflects the high value that musicians placed on beauty, order, and pleasing the senses, attitudes that closely parallel contemporary trends in art.

**Tinctoris**

The most up-to-date instruction book on counterpoint in the late fifteenth century was the *Liber de arte contrapuncti* (A Book on the Art of Counterpoint, 1477) by Johannes Tinctoris (ca. 1435–1511), a Flemish composer who settled at the court in Naples in the early 1470s. He deplored the works of the "older composers in which there were more dissonances than consonances" and proclaimed that nothing written before the 1430s was worth hearing. Tinctoris shows his sympathy with humanism by referring to numerous Greek and Roman writers; but lacking examples of ancient music, he claims only the composers of the last two generations, starting with Dunstable, as models worth imitating. Drawing on the practice of the composers he names, he devised strict rules for introducing dissonances, limiting them to passing and neighbor tones on unstressed beats and to syncopated passages (or what we call suspensions) at cadences. These rules were further refined in later treatises by Italian authors and finally synthesized in Gioseffo Zarlino's massive treatise *Le istitutioni harmoniche* (Harmonic Foundations) of 1558.

**Music and words**

In keeping with the ancient Greek view of music and poetry as virtually inseparable, humanists believed that music and words could derive added force from each other. The image of the ancient poet, singer, and accompanist united in a single person inspired both poets and composers of the Renaissance to seek a common expressive goal. Authors became more concerned with the sound of their verses, and composers with matching and projecting that sound. The grammatical structure of a text guided the composer in shaping its musical setting and in placing cadences (of greater or less finality) according to the text's punctuation. Inspired by the poet's message and images, composers tried new ways to express the content of the text. They were careful to follow the rhythm of speech and the natural accentuation of syllables, whether in Latin or the vernacular. Where singers had previously been responsible for matching syllables with the notated pitches and rhythms, composers now took greater care in aligning words with the music, although they had no control over copyists and rarely had the opportunity to correct proofs of their printed works.

**Music printing**

In fact, the development of the printing press in the mid-fifteenth century had a huge impact on the musical culture of the Renaissance—first, by producing books and treatises that helped spread the ideas of antiquity, and, in the next century, by putting music in the hands of a far greater number of people than the few who could afford to own even the simplest hand-copied *chansonnier* earlier. It is no exaggeration to say that the invention of music printing caused changes that were as revolutionary for musical culture in the Renaissance as the development of notation and music literacy had been for the Middle Ages or as the advent of sound recording was to be for music in our time.

**Why Italy?**

Why did the Renaissance begin in Italy? One reason was geography: Italy was close to, or even at the very source of, the learning and art that inspired the movement. Another reason was Italy's commercial dominance: its trade with Byzantium, its wealthy families (like the Medici, who were bankers), and its profusion of secular princes all spurred the growth of a worldly culture, as opposed to the ecclesiastical culture fostered by the great monasteries and cathedrals of northern Europe. The Italian peninsula in the fifteenth century was made up of a collection of city-states and small principalities that were often at war with each other. The rulers, many of whom had gained their positions by force, sought to glorify themselves and magnify their city's reputation. They did so in a variety of ways: by erecting impressive palaces and country houses decorated with newly commissioned artworks and recently unearthed artifacts from ancient civilizations; by maintaining chapels of talented singers and ensembles of gifted instrumentalists; and by lavishly entertaining neighboring potentates. Meanwhile, the citizenry—no longer in feudal service to a lord and free of military duties (wars were fought mostly by mercenaries)—accumulated wealth through commerce, banking, and crafts. Although they prayed and attended church, these people gave priority to earthly matters. They wanted prosperity for their families, property and prestigious art for themselves and their heirs, and education for their children along classical rather than religious lines. Personal fulfillment through learning, public service, and accomplishment motivated their individual lives as well as their social contacts and institutions.

**Patronage for music**

Just as the dukes of Burgundy had made their court a magnet for talented artists and musicians, the wealthy and powerful Italian dukes and princes recruited and attracted the most accomplished composers and musicians from France, Flanders, and the Netherlands to their cities. Thus, the Medici in Florence, the Este in Ferrara, the Sforza in Milan, and the Gonzaga in Mantua, to name only some of the Renaissance ruling families, became patrons to and employers of the learned singer-composers who had been trained in the magnificent cathedrals and chapels of the north.

# Northern Composers:
# The Generation after Du Fay

Although the migration of musical talent across the Alps to Italy had already begun in the fifteenth century (and was to continue for another three hundred years), Jean de Ockeghem (ca. 1420–1497) was one northern composer who was known in Italy only by reputation (see biography and Figure 6.6). More than half a century after his death, the Italian humanist Cosimo Bartoli paid him a tribute comparable to the one he gave to Josquin des Prez (quoted above, page 113): "I know well that Ockeghem was, so to speak, the first who in these times rediscovered music, which had almost entirely died out—not in other wise than Donatello, who in his time rediscovered sculpture."

*Ockeghem*

Most of Ockeghem's thirteen Masses resemble each other in their general sonority: four voices of essentially like character interact in a contrapuntal texture of independent melodic lines. He extended the bass, which before 1450 rarely moved below c, downward to G, F, and even C in special combinations of low voices. Ockeghem achieved a full, thick texture that gives his works a darker and more homogeneous sonority than we find, for example, in Du Fay's Masses.

*Masses*

---

## ❋ Jean de Ockeghem (Johannes Okeghem) (ca. 1420–1497)

Ockeghem was celebrated as a singer (he is said to have had a fine bass voice), as a composer, and as the model and perhaps mentor of many leading composers of the next generation, including Josquin, who wrote a moving lament on his death.

He was born and trained in the province of Hainaut in northeastern France, served briefly in Antwerp, and spent several years in France with the chapel of Charles I, duke of Bourbon. He is most closely identified with the French royal court, where he served three kings over a span of more than four decades. He was a member of the royal chapel from 1451 on, led the chapel as First Chaplain from 1454, and became master of the chapel in 1465. He was also treasurer at the royal church of Saint Martin of Tours from 1458 and became a priest around 1464. Both his career and his music are notably less cosmopolitan than those of Du Fay. He returned to his native region on occasion, where he was in touch with Du Fay, Binchois, and Busnoys, and traveled to Spain on a diplomatic mission for King Louis XI around 1470. But he seems never to have gone to Italy, and his music shows little Italian influence.

Ockeghem's known output was relatively small for a composer of this renown, although to be sure many of his works may have been lost or destroyed

*Figure 6.6. Relief portrait of Jean de Ockeghem, created by twentieth-century medalist Pierre Turin. (Photo courtesy of Arn Dekker, Cambridge, England.)*

by fire, war, or other devastations. Most of his works cannot be dated with any certainty. In some respects, his music continues in the style of previous generations; in others, it typifies his time; but in certain ways, it is unique, perhaps because his long service in one place encouraged the development of an individual idiom.

**Major works:** 13 Masses, Requiem Mass, at least 5 motets, 21 chansons

A great number of gentlemen and merchants of good account . . . [were entertained] by the exercise of music daily used in my house, and by furnishing them with [printed] books of that kind yearly sent me out of Italy and other places.

So wrote Nicholas Yonge, a London clerk with enough means and social position to support an active amateur musical life, in the dedication to his 1588 collection of madrigals, *Musica transalpina* (see Chapter 7). His words reveal how the music-printing and music-publishing business changed the way people used and enjoyed notated music during the Renaissance, allowing it to be cultivated not only in noble courts and churches, but also in ordinary households as recreation.

Printing from movable type, known in China for centuries and perfected in Europe by Johannes Gutenberg around 1450, was first used for music in the 1470s in liturgical books with chant notation. The application of movable type meant that notes could be assembled in any order, rearranged, and reused. This method proved much more practical than other procedures, such as carving music into wood blocks.

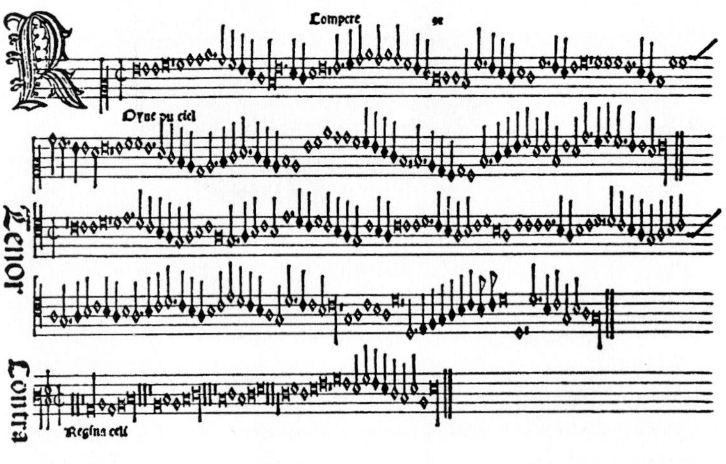

*Figure 6.3. Loyset Compère's chanson* Royne de ciel, *from* Harmonice musices odhecaton A, *published by Ottaviano Petrucci in 1501. The incipit of the text appears under the cantus part. The music uses the "white notation" of the Renaissance. The notes that look like diamond-shaped whole notes are semibreves; open notes with stems (akin to half notes) are minims; black notes with stems (like quarter notes) are semiminims; and flags are added to the semiminim to indicate shorter durations. The resemblance to common-practice notation is clear, except that no bar lines or ties are used.*

In 1501 in Venice, Ottaviano Petrucci (1466–1539) brought out the first collection of polyphonic music printed entirely from movable type, the *Harmonice musices odhecaton* (One hundred songs of harmonic music [polyphony]—it actually contained only ninety-six). Figure 6.3, a page from this collection, shows the elegance of his work. Petrucci used a triple-impression process in which each sheet went through the press three times: once to print the staff lines, another to print the words, and a third to print the notes and the florid initials. His method was time-consuming, labor-intensive, and costly, but his results were models of clarity and accuracy.

Petrucci was no less clever a businessman than he was a craftsman. Before setting up shop, he had procured a patent on his process and a "privilege" that effectively guaranteed a monopoly on music printing in Venice for twenty years. After sizing up the market, he decided to make his first volume (the *Odhecaton*) an anthology of secular song, including what he judged to be among the best tunes of his own and the preceding generations. These were short pieces for three or four parts that could easily be performed at home or in the company of friends. Two more song collections followed—*Canti B* in 1502 and *Canti C* in 1504—allowing Petrucci to corner the market for the most up-to-date and popular secular music of the day. By 1523, he had published fifty-nine volumes (including reprints) of vocal and instrumental music.

Printing from a single impression—using pieces of type that printed staff, notes, and text together in one operation—was apparently first practiced by John Rastell in London about 1520 and first applied on a large scale in 1528 by Pierre Attaingnant (ca. 1494–1551/2) in Paris. Although more efficient and less costly than Petrucci's triple-impression method, the process produced results that were much less elegant because the staff lines were no longer continuous but part of each piece of type; inevitably, the lines were imperfectly joined and, therefore, appeared broken or wavy on the page, as seen in Figure 6.4. Nevertheless, the practicality of the method ensured its commercial success. Attaingnant's proc-

*Figure 6.4. First portion of the superius part for the motet* Laudate Dominum *by Pierre de Manchicourt, as printed in Pierre Attaingnant's* Liber decimus quartus XIX musicas cantiones continet *(Paris, 1539). Attaingnant printed in a single impression, using type in which each note, rest, clef, or other sign includes the staff lines on which it sits.*

ess set the standard for all printed music until copperplate engraving became popular in the late seventeenth century.

Most ensemble music published in the sixteenth century was printed in the form of rectangular partbooks—each volume containing the music for a particular voice so that a complete set was needed to perform the piece. Partbooks were intended for use at home or in social gatherings (see Figure 6.5). Most church choirs continued to use the large handwritten choirbooks (see Fig. 6.7). Because there was not enough demand for these large books to make printing them economical, new ones were still being hand-copied in the sixteenth century even as printed collections began appearing.

In general, the existence of printed copies meant that both sacred and secular works would become known more widely and would be preserved for performance and study by later generations. This, in turn, made possible a heightened awareness of individual influence and achievement. Josquin des Prez was the first composer whose widespread renown and lasting impact was assured by the printing press since Petrucci devoted three volumes to the publication of Josquin's Masses during the composer's lifetime but no more than one volume to the works of any other composer.

The economics of supply and demand for printed music grew in ever widening circles: printing stimulated the desire for music books and increased their affordability, which, in turn, spurred the further development of music printing and competition among publishers. By the end of the sixteenth century, Rome, Nuremberg, Lyon, Louvain, Antwerp, and London had joined Venice and Paris as centers of music publishing, and printed music had become an indispensable part of musical life.

*Figure 6.5. A vocal quartet reading from partbooks. The rich costumes suggest that these are aristocratic amateurs performing for their own pleasure in the privacy of an idyllic island. Detail from an anonymous sixteenth-century painting. Musée de l'Hôtel Lallemant, Bourges, France.*

**Tenor Mass**

CD 2/70

CD 2/54 CD 1/42

**Cyclic Mass**

**Naming Masses**

Some of Ockeghem's Masses, like Du Fay's *Missa Se la face ay pale*, are tenor Masses, which are based on a single cantus firmus that is used as the basis for every movement. For example, the *Missa De plus en plus* (Agnus Dei in NAWM 37) takes as its cantus firmus the tenor part of the chanson by Binchois (NAWM 33), with whom Ockeghem may have studied. This work is among the type of Mass also called a cyclic Mass because its movements are unified musically: in this case, the Kyrie, Gloria, Credo, Sanctus, and Agnus Dei are all based on the same borrowed tenor line, which, though not as attractive and recognizable as the top voice, makes a firm foundation for the composition (see Example 6.1, giving the first phrase of Binchois's chanson and the beginning of Ockeghem's Agnus Dei, with the notes of the chanson numbered in the tenor). Yet unlike Du Fay's *Missa Se la face ay pale*, in which the chanson tenor appears in the original rhythm, here the cantus firmus is much more freely employed. To vary the sonority, Ockeghem followed the example of earlier fifteenth-century composers and scored whole sections for trios or duets. Sometimes he set one pair of voices against another pair, a device that later composers adopted enthusiastically for both sacred and secular music. He used imitation occasionally in his Masses, but this seldom involved all the voices.

In the fifteenth and sixteenth centuries, Masses without a cantus firmus sometimes took their titles from the mode in which they were written (for

*Example 6.1: Cantus firmus usage in Ockeghem's* Missa De plus en plus

*a. Binchois,* De plus en plus, *tenor*

*b. Jean de Ockeghem,* Missa De plus en plus, *Agnus Dei*

example, *Missa quinti toni*—Mass in mode 5). Ockeghem's *Missa mi-mi* derives its name from the first two notes of the bass voice, *e–A*, both of which in solmization were sung to the syllable *mi*. Some Masses, including Ockeghem's *Missa prolationum* and *Missa cuiusvis toni*, were named for a structural feature—in these cases, a canon. A Mass having neither a cantus firmus nor any other identifying peculiarity was often called a *Missa sine nomine* (Mass without a name—the musical equivalent of "Untitled" in modern art).

Although Ockeghem used imitation only sparingly, he did exploit a device known as canon, in which new parts are derived from an original one. In the method prevailing at the time, the composer wrote out two or more vocal parts and left instructions explaining how the singers should obtain additional voices from it. The written instruction itself was called canon, which means "rule" or "law." For example, the canon might tell the second voice to join in with the same melody starting a certain number of beats after the original and at the same or at a different pitch; it might direct the second voice to invert the first—that is, move by the same intervals but in the opposite direction; or it might require the second voice to join in with the melody sung backward—creating a type of canon called a retrograde or cancrizans ("crab") canon. Another possibility was to instruct the two voices to move at different rates of speed by giving each one a different time signature or mensuration sign. Thus, canons of this sort are called mensuration canons. Musicians valued such puzzle canons for the ingenuity and skill they displayed.

*Figure 6.7. This miniature, from a French manuscript of about 1530, shows a singer thought to be Ockeghem and eight other chapel musicians singing a Gloria in the usual fashion of the time—from a large manuscript choir book on a lectern. Paris, Bibliothèque Nationale, MS F.1587, fol. 58.*

In prestige and craft, writing secular music did not lag far behind Mass composition. Chansons from 1460 to 1480 show more and more use of imitative counterpoint, at first between the superius and tenor voices, later among all three parts. Most of Ockeghem's chansons, as well as those of his equally famous contemporary Antoine Busnoys (ca. 1430–1492), made use of the traditional *formes fixes* of courtly poetry. Of these, the rondeau's popularity endured until the end of the century, whereas that of the ballade and virelai declined. Certain chansons by Ockeghem, Busnoys, and their successors were enormous hits: some favorites appear again and again in manuscripts and prints from many different countries. Composers freely altered their own and others' chansons, rearranged them, and transcribed them for instruments. Above all, the chansons provided an inexhaustible supply of material for Masses, which might be based on either the superius or the tenor of the original songs.

Some medieval traits still common in the music of Ockeghem and Busnoys, such as the *formes fixes* and reliance on a tenor for structure, disappear in the next generation. Others, such as the use of a cantus firmus, continue but become less prominent. The newer elements, including greater equality of voices, more use of imitation, and expansion of range, were extended by their successors and became characteristic of sixteenth-century musical style.

Medieval and newer features

# The Next Generation:
# Josquin and His Contemporaries

Many of the next generation of Franco-Flemish composers modeled their works on those of Ockeghem. Among the most eminent figures were Jacob Obrecht (1457/8–1505), Henricus (Heinrich) Isaac (ca. 1450–1517), and Josquin des Prez (ca. 1450–1521). Each was born around the middle of the century, each

Ockeghem's pupils

Figure 6.8. Jacob Obrecht in a portrait from 1496 by an anonymous Flemish painter.

received his earliest musical training and experience in the Low Countries, and each traveled widely, working in various courts and churches in different parts of Europe, including Italy. Consequently, the careers of each illustrate the lively interchange in musical matters between northern and southern Europe—that is, between the Franco-Flemish centers and those of Italy and Spain. Obrecht, from the Dutch town of Bergen op Zoom, died in Italy of the plague while working as a member of the ducal chapel in Ferrara, where Josquin was also employed for a time. Isaac, Flemish by birth, also ended his years in Italy serving the Medici rulers of Florence. It is no surprise, then, that their music mixes, and even combines, northern and southern elements: the serious tone, formal structure, intricate polyphony, and subtly flowing rhythms of the north; the more spontaneous quality, simpler structure, homophonic texture, dancelike rhythms, and more clearly articulated phrases of the south. Isaac's tender song *Innsbruck, ich muss dich lassen* (Innsbruck, I must leave you, NAWM 38), with its appealing melody, sweet harmonies, and clear phrase structure, is a good example of the Italian style even though its text is in German.

CD 3/1

**Odhecaton**

The *Odhecaton*, the first printed anthology of chansons (see page 118), illustrates how deeply northern music penetrated into Italy. It contains works dating from about 1470 to 1500 by composers from the late Burgundian era to the generation of Obrecht, Isaac, and Josquin. In Petrucci's title *Harmonice musices odhecaton A*, the letter "A" indicates that it was planned as the first in a series. In fact, two more chanson volumes followed in short order. Over the next half century, Petrucci and other Italian music printers issued a great number of such anthologies by French and Franco-Flemish composers, attesting to the popularity and longevity of their songs.

**Chansons**

More than half of the chansons in the *Odhecaton* are for three voices, written primarily in the older styles. In the four-voice chansons, however, we see the genre developing toward a fuller texture, a more completely imitative counterpoint, clearer harmonic structure, and greater equality of voices. Duple meter replaced the more common triple meter of the Burgundian period. Many of these pieces, like the Masses of the time, were based either on a popular tune or on a single voice from some earlier chanson.

**Josquin's chansons**

By contrast with Ockeghem, Josquin des Prez virtually abandoned the *formes fixes*, choosing instead strophic texts and simple four- or five-line poems. The polyphonic fabric of his chansons is not formed from independent layers, like Ockeghem's, but is unified and interwoven with imitation, the most important new compositional device of the sixteenth century. Instead of the cantus-tenor voice pair providing the scaffolding of the texture, with the other voices filling in, all the parts are now structurally equal.

**Mille regretz**

*Mille regretz* (A thousand regrets, NAWM 41), a chanson attributed to Josquin though perhaps not by him, illustrates the style of about 1520. In contrast to the chansons of Du Fay and Ockeghem, the voices are more alike, yielding a homogeneous texture that alternates between homophony and imitation and between all four voices and ever-changing combinations of two or three voices.

CD 3/15

Each phrase of text receives its own treatment, a lesson that Josquin learned well from the Italian humanists.

Of all the composers we have studied since Du Fay, none enjoyed higher renown or exercised greater influence than Josquin (see biography and Figure 6.9). Composers from his own time through the late sixteenth century emulated and reworked his compositions. His music, privileged by Petrucci's printing press (see pages 118–119), continued to be recopied, published, and performed for almost a century after his death, a rare honor at a time when most music more than a few decades old was deemed unworthy of performance. His music was so esteemed and popular that publishers and copyists often attributed works by other composers to him; historians are still having difficulty sorting out which pieces are truly his.

*Josquin's influence*

The high proportion of motets in Josquin's output is noteworthy. In his day, the Mass was still the form that composers turned to in order to demonstrate mastery of their craft. But the Mass's liturgical formality, unvarying text, and established musical conventions left little room for experimentation. Motets, on the other hand, could be written on a wide range of relatively unfamiliar texts that offered interesting new possibilities for word-music relationships. For a Renaissance composer of Josquin's inclination, the motet became the most challenging and inviting genre of sacred composition.

*Motets*

---

**TIMELINE**   The Age of the Renaissance

| MUSICAL EVENTS | HISTORICAL EVENTS |
|---|---|
| Death of Du Fay **1474** | |
| Tinctoris, *Liber de arte contrapuncti* **1477** | |
| Josquin, singer in ducal chapel, Milan **ca. 1484–1489** | |
| | **1485–1603** Tudor dynasty in England |
| Obrecht, *Missa Fortunata desperata* **ca. 1490** | |
| | **1492** First voyage of Columbus to America |
| | **1495** Leonardo da Vinci, *The Last Supper* |
| Gaffurio, *Practica musice* **1496** | |
| Death of Ockeghem **1497** | |
| Petrucci publishes *Odhecaton A* **1501** | |
| | **1504** Michelangelo, *David* |
| | **1509** Henry VIII becomes king of England |
| | **1517** Martin Luther, ninety-five theses |
| | **1519–1556** Charles V, Holy Roman emperor |
| Death of Josquin **1521** | |
| | **1528** Castiglione, *The Courtier* |
| | **1543** Copernicus, *On the Revolutions of the Heavenly Spheres* |
| Glarean, *Dodekachordon* **1547** | |
| Zarlino, *Le istitutioni harmoniche* **1558** | |

Text and music

In keeping with humanist ideals, Josquin and his contemporaries tried to make the music communicate the meaning of the text. They carefully fit the musical stress to the accentuation of the words, whether Latin or vernacular, and wanted the words to be heard and understood. The highly florid lines of Ockeghem and other Franco-Flemish composers gave way to more direct syllabic settings in which a phrase of text was presented as an uninterrupted thought. Composers turned to the chanson and the Italian popular genres as models for their vocal writing.

*Ave Maria . . .*
*virgo serena*

CD 3/2    CD 1/53

We see Josquin's typical approach to motet writing in *Ave Maria . . . virgo serena* (Hail Mary . . . serene Virgin, NAWM 39), probably from about 1485, one of his best-known pieces. The music is perfectly crafted to fit the words. Josquin calls attention to the text by giving each segment a unique musical treatment and a concluding cadence on C. Although the texture varies, its main method of construction is imitation—that is, each voice takes up the same motivic idea, or "point of imitation," one after the other (Example 6.2). This serves to equalize and unify the voices, bringing the lines of the texture into a more congruous whole and creating an effect similar to that of perspective in painting. Before the last voice has finished its musical phrase, a different voice begins the next

## Josquin des Prez (Josquin Lebloitte, Dit Desprez) (ca. 1450–1521)

Josquin's motets, Masses, and songs were widely sung, praised, and emulated in his lifetime and for decades after his death. He was known by his given name because "des Prez" was a nickname.

Josquin's biography has been clarified by recent research, but there are still gaps. Historians only recently discovered his family name—Lebloitte—from a will leaving him a house and land in Condé-sur-l'Escaut in Hainaut, now in Belgium. His early life is undocumented, but he was probably born and trained in or near Saint-Quentin in northern France, about halfway between Paris and Brussels. He served in the chapel of René, duke of Anjou, at Aix-en-Provence in the late 1470s. After René's death in 1480, his singers transferred to the service of King Louis XI in Paris, and Josquin may have been among them.

Josquin spent much of his career in Italy, serving the Sforza family, rulers of Milan (ca. 1484–1489), and in the Sistine Chapel in Rome (1489–1495 or later). Josquin may have been in France at the court of King Louis XII from 1501 to 1503. He was appointed maestro di cappella to Duke Ercole I d'Este in Ferrara in 1503, commanding the highest salary in the history of that chapel. A recruiter for the duke had recommended Isaac instead, noting that although Josquin was a better composer, he demanded a higher salary and composed only when he wanted to and not when asked. The duke hired Josquin anyway, no doubt aware of the prestige to be gained by employing the best musician available. Josquin left after a year, apparently to escape the plague. From 1504 until his death in 1521, he resided at Condé-sur-l'Escaut, where he was provost at the church of Notre Dame.

IOSQVINVS PRATENSIS.

*Figure 6.9. Josquin des Prez, in a woodcut from Petrus Opmeer,* Opus chronographicum . . . *(Antwerp, 1611). Opmeer based his portrait on an oil painting that once stood in Saint Gudule Church in Brussels but was destroyed in the 1570s.*

**Major works:** about 18 Masses, over 55 motets and liturgical works, about 65 chansons (about 10 for instruments), and over 70 doubtful and misattributed works

phrase of text with a new subject. By having the voices overlap in this way, Josquin avoids a cadence until the first full grammatical stop at "serena," where all the parts sing together for the first time, building with increasing rhythmic activity to the first simultaneous cadence. The words are declaimed naturally, the accented syllables being given longer and higher notes in most cases, and their meaning is occasionally reinforced by a particularly suitable musical gesture. (A fuller discussion is given in NAWM.)

*Example 6.2: Josquin des Prez, motet:* Ave Maria . . . virgo serena

*Hail Mary, full of grace, the Lord is with you, serene Virgin.*

Not all of Josquin's work is so forward-looking. As we might expect, he employs conservative styles most conspicuously in his Masses, which abound in technical ingenuity. The majority uses a secular tune as a cantus firmus. *In Missa L'homme armé super voces musicales,* Josquin transposes the familiar tune,

*L'homme armé,* to successive degrees (or musical syllables—*voces musicales*) of the scale—C for the Kyrie, D for the Gloria, and so on—and includes a mensuration canon in the Agnus Dei.

He wrote *Missa Hercules dux Ferrariae* to honor Ercole (Hercules) I, who was duke of Ferrara from 1471 to 1505 and Josquin's employer at one point in his career. He used as a cantus firmus a *soggetto cavato dalle vocali,* a "subject drawn from the vowels" of a phrase, by letting each vowel indicate a corresponding scale syllable, thus:

**Parody Mass**

Josquin's *Missa Malheur me bat* illustrates the new approach of basing a Mass on an existing polyphonic work. Instead of using one voice as a cantus firmus, the composer borrows extensively from all voices of the model, reworking the latter's characteristic motives, points of imitation, and general structure in each movement of the Mass. This approach is especially successful when basing the Mass on a motet or chanson in the new, predominantly imitative or homophonic styles of the sixteenth century because in such works the tenor is not the main structural voice and no voice would function well as a cantus firmus. Typically, the resemblance to the model is strongest at the beginning and end of each movement, and the composer's skill is demonstrated by the new combinations and variations he can achieve within the borrowed material. A Mass composed in this manner is called a parody Mass because it reworks material from another polyphonic work. The parody Mass replaced the cantus firmus Mass as the dominant type around 1520.

**Paraphrase Mass**

CD 3/9–12    CD 1/60

*Missa Pange lingua* (excerpted in NAWM 40), one of the last that Josquin composed, represents another new type of work: the paraphrase Mass. It is based on the plainchant hymn *Pange lingua gloriosi* (Sing, tongue, of the glorious). But instead of using the hymn melody as a cantus firmus, Josquin paraphrases it in all four voices, in whole or in part, in each movement. Phrases from the hymn melody are adapted as motives that are treated in points of imitation, or occasionally in homophonic declamation. As with the parody Mass, the new technique still results in a cyclic Mass because the same basic material underlies each movement and, therefore, relates each movement to all the others.

Although composers continued to write cantus firmus Masses in the sixteenth century, they turned increasingly to parody and paraphrase techniques because they preferred these to the structurally confining cantus firmus technique, which came to be seen as archaic. It is likely that the source material was chosen for the same reasons as before: to suit a particular religious holiday or saint; to honor a patron; to convey meaning by alluding to the original words of the chanson or motet (which would not be heard, but perhaps remembered, by the listener); or, in the case of an imitation—that is, parody—Mass, to pay homage to another composer through emulation.

## POSTLUDE

The Renaissance was an era of rediscovery and rapid change that affected the way educated people lived and thought about their own times and culture. It had far-reaching consequences in all the arts and, with the help of the printing press, brought about new attitudes toward the creation, consumption, and reception of music. The international style that had begun to emerge from the variety of compositional techniques practiced in England and on the Continent during the 1400s now spread to Italy and throughout the Holy Roman Empire.

The Renaissance produced a number of specific musical styles and influenced many features of European art music. More and more, composers let the structure of the text determine the structure of the music. Polyphonic parts were unified through imitation and became nearly equal in importance. The quest by composers for full harmonies, singable melodies, and motivic relationships between the voices influenced the texture of sacred as well as secular pieces. Borrowed melodies, whether sacred or secular, were still used to unify large compositions, but the borrowed material was often distributed among the voices rather than confined to the tenor or superius. Although the tenor remained a key voice in the structure, the bass began to assume its modern role as the foundation of the harmony. Final cadences continued to close in perfect consonances, but elsewhere composers strove for full

*Figure 6.10. Kyrie of the* Missa Ave maris stella *by Josquin.*

triadic sonorities. Simplification and standardization of rhythm favored duple measure organized by the value of the breve (alla breve). The preferred sacred genres were the cyclical Mass and the motet. The chanson, breaking out of the *formes fixes*, was cast in new shapes, and its texture was gradually pervaded by imitation. Hidden and esoteric structural devices, such as isorhythm and mensuration canon, gave way to transparent textures, principally that of overlapping imitative sections, relieved occasionally by homophonic ones. These trends provided composers more compositional choices than they had had earlier and, aided by the success of music printing, more opportunity to communicate with a wider audience. Many of the trends discussed in this chapter continued throughout the sixteenth century.

# Secular Song and the Rise of National Styles in the Sixteenth Century

*Chapter Contents*

*Prelude* 128

The Rise of National
Styles: Italy 129

The Italian
Madrigal 130

The Rise of National
Styles: Secular Song
outside Italy 137

The Rise of
Instrumental
Music 141

*Postlude* 144

## PRELUDE

If fifteenth-century composers forged an international idiom, sixteenth-century musicians participated in a new flowering of national styles, especially in secular vocal music. Poets, writing in the vernacular, and composers in different regions naturally developed distinctive genres and forms. Music printing made possible the dissemination of music in the vernacular for amateurs to sing for their own pleasure, further encouraging the growth of national styles.

The development of music printing in 1501 (described in Chapter 6) also changed the economics of music. Prior to this, a musical composition was preeminently a performance—a service provided by musicians. Now for the first time in printed form, it could be sold as a commodity. The new supply of printed music dovetailed with a growing demand for notated music that amateurs could perform for their own enjoyment. People have always made music to entertain themselves and their friends, but for most of human history they did so without using notation. When notation was invented, it was used for church music and secular music of the aristocracy, as we have seen, leaving few written traces of the music making of the general populace. In the sixteenth century, first among the upper classes and then among the literate urban middle classes, the ability to read notation and to perform from printed music became an expected social grace. In Baldassare Castiglione's influential *Book of the Courtier* (1528), several speakers praise those who can sing and play from notation (see the vignette on page 129). Many paintings from the time, such as Figures 6.5 and 7.4, show singers or instrumentalists reading from published music, usually in the form of partbooks (described in Chapter 6). In such settings, music served as a kind of social glue, an activity that friends and family could enjoy together.

In vocal music, amateurs were most interested in singing in their own language, reinforcing an already evident trend toward diverse national genres and styles. Among the significant national genres of the sixteenth century were the

Spanish villancico, the Italian frottola, and a new kind of French chanson, all simple, strophic, mostly syllabic and homophonic, easily singable, and thus ideally suited for amateur performers. The genre that proved most significant in the long run was the Italian madrigal, in which Renaissance poets and composers brought to a peak their intense interests in humanism, in the individual, and in realizing in music the accents, images, and emotions of the text. Besides influencing later French chansons, madrigals gained fashion in England and were joined around the end of the century by the lute song. Through the madrigal, Italy and Italian composers became the leading forces in European music for the first time, a role they would maintain for much of the seventeenth century.

Although music with words continued to receive the most attention from composers and patrons, the rise of instrumental music in the sixteenth century initiated a process that led, centuries later, to its dominant position.

## The Rise of National Styles: Italy

In Italy, two types of native song prevailed when the northerners arrived, and other types developed during the sixteenth century. The two earlier types, the frottola and lauda (plural: frottole and laude), were both strophic, four-part homophonic songs with refrains, with the melody in the upper voice, simple diatonic harmonies, and words set syllabically to catchy rhythmic patterns that repeat from one line to the next. Frottole, composed and sung for entertainment in the sophisticated Italian courts of Ferrara and Mantua, were more highbrow versions of earthy, satirical street music. Laude, performed at semipublic gatherings of the faithful, were religious and devotional. Neither bore any resemblance to the intricate style of Franco-Flemish polyphony. Petrucci, the great Venetian music printer, published thirteen collections of these highly popular tunes (eleven of frottole and two of laude) within a span of ten years in the early sixteenth century (for an example of the frottola, see NAWM 49). The frottola may also have influenced the emerging new style of the French chanson (see page 137).

Later in the century, composers in Italy also cultivated other types of light secular song. The canzon villanesca (peasant song), or villanella for three

*Frottola and lauda*

CD 3/47

---

**VIGNETTE**   On Reading and Performing Music

*Baldassare Castiglione (1478–1529) was a courtier, ambassador, and poet. His most influential work was* The Book of the Courtier *(1528), a manual on proper behavior at court in the guise of conversations at the ducal palace in Urbino. The ability to sing and play from notation was expected.*

The Count began again: "Gentlemen, you must know that I am not satisfied with our Courtier unless he be also a musician, and unless, besides understanding and being able to read music, he can play various instruments. For, if we rightly consider, no rest from toil and no medicine for ailing spirits can be found more decorous or praiseworthy in time of leisure than this; and especially in courts where, besides the release from vexations which music gives to all, many things are done to please the ladies, whose tender and delicate spirits are readily penetrated with harmony and filled with sweetness. Hence, it is no wonder that in both ancient and modern times they have always been particularly fond of musicians, finding music a most welcome food for the spirit."

Baldesar Castiglione, *The Book of the Courtier*, trans. Charles S. Singleton (Garden City, N.Y.: Doubleday, 1959), p. 74.

*Figure 7.1. Bronzino (1503–1572), portrait of a courtier, 1530s. The subject radiates an air of self-importance and accomplishment (what Castiglione calls "sprezzatura"), and the portrait, along with many others by Renaissance artists, demonstrates a new interest in the individual. Metropolitan Museum of Art, New York.*

voices, was a lively little strophic piece in homophonic style. It flourished chiefly in the Neapolitan area and sometimes mimicked the more sophisticated madrigal. Two other important forms existed—the canzonetta (little song) and the balletto. The balletto, as the name suggests, was intended for dancing as well as singing or playing, and its typical "Fa-la-la" refrains later made their way into English songs of the period. In fact, German as well as English composers imitated both canzonette and balletti in the late sixteenth century.

Native Italian song was naturally and intimately bound up with native Italian poetry. Early in the century, a renewed appreciation for the great fourteenth-century Italian poet Petrarch (who had been crowned poet laureate in Rome in 1341) sparked a movement during which the poet's sonnets and other poems were analyzed, discussed, edited, and imitated. One admirer praised Petrarch for his combination of *piacevolezza* ("pleasingness") and *gravità* ("severity") and for his remarkable ability to match the sound qualities of his verses to the sense of their meaning. For example, harsh sentiments were expressed with words containing gruff consonants, while tender thoughts were couched in phrases that used soothing vowels and liquid consonants. The Petrarchan movement soon attracted the attention of composers, who found inspiration in the sound qualities of Petrarch's poetry. Many of the early madrigalists turned to Petrarch for their texts. So even though the madrigal arose in part from the merger of native and foreign musical styles, it owes its elevated tone and serious subject matter to the Petrarchan movement.

## The Italian Madrigal

The popularity of the Italian madrigal, which dominated secular music in the sixteenth century, allowed Italy to assume a leading role in European music for the first time. Unlike the trecento madrigal—which employed fixed patterns of poetic and musical repetition—the sixteenth-century madrigal was a through-composed setting of a short poem. The term *through-composed* says it all: every line of poetry received a different musical setting reflecting the rhythm and sense of the words. In contrast with the poetry of the frottola, madrigal poetry was more artful and elevated in tone, and borrowed its amorous situations from the pastoral genre, which was all the rage in the sixteenth century. Many madrigal texts were taken from works by major poets, including Ludovico Ariosto (1474–1533), Torquato Tasso (1544–1595), and Giovanni Battista Guarini (1538–1612); others were written in imitation of Petrarch. Their subject matter was either heroic or sentimental, and the poems became more and more sensual—even erotic—as the century progressed. Madrigal composers dealt attentively with the poetry, using a variety of homophonic and contrapuntal textures in a series of overlapping sections, each based on a single phrase of text, with all voices having essentially equal roles. In these respects, madrigals resemble motets of the same era. Most important, madrigalists aimed to match the seriousness or playfulness of the poetry with the elegance or wit of their music in order to communicate the poem's ideas, images, and emotions.

Madrigals were composed chiefly for the enjoyment of the singers themselves and were typically performed in mixed groups of women and men at social gatherings, after meals, and at meetings of academies (societies organized
to study and discuss literary, scientific, or artistic matters). The demand for
madrigals was great: counting reprints and new editions, some two thousand
collections were published between 1530 and 1600, and their popularity continued well into the seventeenth century. In addition to amateur performances,
by 1570 some princely patrons began to employ professional singers to perform
madrigals for audiences at court. The formation of virtuoso chamber ensembles
of professional singers encouraged composers to write more difficult music that
demanded the execution of florid runs, trills, and turns as well as the application of a variety of attacks, dynamics, and vocal color. In 1580, Alfonso d'Este,
duke of Ferrara, established the most famous of these ensembles—the *concerto
delle donne* (ensemble of ladies), a trio of trained singers (Laura Peverara, Anna
Guarini, and Livia d'Arco) appointed as ladies-in-waiting to his music-loving
wife, Margherita Gonzaga. Their performances at court, frequently together
with professional male singers, attracted so much attention and praise that the
Gonzaga of Mantua and the Medici of Florence formed ensembles to rival Ferrara's (see the vignette on page 135). The existence of these professional ensembles had other consequences, stemming from the separation between
performer and audience. Composers, instead of aiming their skills primarily at
the enjoyment of the singers themselves, increasingly addressed their works to
members of a listening audience—distinct from the performers—by dramatizing
and projecting the words through contrast and similar bold devices that were
readily perceived. In this way, they could hope to lead the listener more easily to
understand and delight in the poetry's overt as well as covert meanings, as the
performers had long been able to do.

The leading composers of the Italian madrigal, initially emigrants from the
north, also worked as church musicians and transferred their skills in sacred
polyphony to the writing of secular madrigals. The northerner Jacques Arcadelt
(ca. 1505–1568) sang in the pope's chapel for a time and later joined the royal

Social settings

*Concerto delle donne*

Arcadelt

*Figure 7.2. Cipriano de Rore in an
anonymous painting. Kunsthistorisches
Museum, Vienna.*

CD 3/54    CD 2/4

chapel in Paris. Arcadelt's madrigal *Il bianco e dolce cigno* (The white and sweet swan, NAWM 50), from about 1538, is justifiably among the most famous of the early madrigals. The poet cleverly contrasts the swan's literal death with his own figurative "death that in dying fills me with complete joy and desire," a metaphor for sexual climax, known in the sixteenth century as "the little death." The antitheses are further developed: the swan dies disconsolate, though singing—the traditionally mute creature supposedly emits a "swan song" just before its death—while the poet, though weeping, would be content to die "a thousand deaths a day." Arcadelt's setting plays with these poetic conceits in many ways, but principally it contrasts a sweet, homophonic texture that suggests contentment with the multiple imitative entrances of the phrase "a thousand deaths a day" (see Example 7.1).

*Example 7.1: Jacques Arcadelt,* Il bianco e dolce cigno, *measures 30–39*

*If when I die no other pain I feel,*
*with a thousand deaths a day I would be content.*

Rore

The madrigal achieved maturity at mid-century, particularly in the works of Cipriano de Rore (1516–1565), shown in Figure 7.2. Flemish by birth, Rore worked in Italy, chiefly in Ferrara and Parma, and briefly succeeded his teacher, Adrian Willaert, as music director at Saint Mark's in Venice. He became the madrigalist most admired by composers later in the century; Monteverdi in particular proudly claimed that he was following in Rore's footsteps (see Chapter 9).

In his madrigal *Da le belle contrade d'oriente* (From the fair regions of the East, NAWM 51) of about 1560–1565, Rore imbued every detail of the music with the sense and feeling of the poem, a sonnet modeled on Petrarch. The expanded

CD 3/56    CD 2/6

range of five voices suits this text particularly well since it allowed Rore to divide the ensemble into higher and lower groupings to distinguish subtly between the lovers' voices as they are about to part. Rore gives each line of text a distinct musical profile, choosing intervals associated with sadness especially for the woman's utterances, which also imitate natural speech inflections: rising semitones for "T'en vai" (You go); falling minor thirds, semitones, and minor seventh for "haimè!" (alas!); and falling minor thirds on "Adio!" (Farewell!). At the words "Sola mi lasci" (Alone you leave me), the lower voices drop out, leaving the soprano to sing a plaintive solo phrase, which ascends chromatically, A–B♭–B, to convey her anxiety and sadness.

As part of the humanistic revival of ancient Greek musical thought, theorists in the mid-sixteenth century embraced chromaticism, pointing to the chromatic and enharmonic tetrachords discussed by Greek writers (see Chapter 1 and NAWM 2). Zarlino, who devoted an entire chapter of his book *Le istitutioni harmoniche* (Harmonic Foundations, 1558) to instructing composers on how to set words to music, approved of direct chromatic motion ("movements which proceed through the semitone"), along with other uses of accidentals, as ways to express sorrow (see vignette, page 134). Rore frequently introduces notes outside the mode, sometimes to the point where all twelve notes of the chromatic scale appear in the course of just a few phrases, as in Example 7.2.

**Chromaticism**

CD 1/2

*Example 7.2: Cipriano de Rore*, Da le belle contrade d'oriente, *measures 28–36*

[Hope of my heart,] sweet desire,
*you go, alas! Alone you leave me! Farewell!*
*What will [become of me, gloomy and sad?]*

Other northerners

Among the many northern madrigal composers who wrote after the middle of the century, Orlando di Lasso, Philippe de Monte, and Giaches de Wert made important contributions to the genre. Orlando di Lasso (1532–1594) excelled as a church composer but was equally at home with the madrigal, the chanson, and the German part-song, or lied. Like Lasso, Philippe de Monte (1521–1603) was enormously productive in both sacred and secular domains. He began writing madrigals while a young man in Italy and continued uninterrupted throughout his many years of serving Philip II of Spain and the Hapsburg emperors in Vienna and Prague. He published thirty-two collections of secular madrigals and several books of *madrigali spirituali*. Giaches de Wert (1535–1596), born near Antwerp, spent nearly his entire life in Italy; he continued to develop the style of madrigal composition begun by Rore. His late style, full of bold leaps, speech-like declamation, and extravagant contrasts, exercised a marked influence on Monteverdi.

Marenzio

Toward the end of the century, the leading madrigalists were native Italians, not the northerners who first dominated the field. Luca Marenzio (1553–1599), who spent most of his career in Rome in the service of several cardinals, depicted contrasting ideas and images in his music with complete artistry and dazzling virtuosity. Like other madrigal composers of the late sixteenth century, Marenzio favored pastoral poetry, but he was by far the most prolific, publishing more than four hundred madrigals over a period of only two decades. One of his most celebrated is a setting of Petrarch's sonnet *Solo e pensoso* (Alone and pensive, NAWM 52). It is replete with examples of the typically clever "word painting" devices, later called madrigalisms, which evoke the meaning of individual

CD 3/59

---

**VIGNETTE** Suiting the Music to the Words

Le istitutioni harmoniche (*The Harmonic Foundations*) by Gioseffo Zarlino (1517–1590) was the most respected treatise of the mid-sixteenth century. His advice to composers on how to express emotions corresponds almost exactly to the practice of the prominent madrigal composers of his generation.

~~~

When a composer wishes to express harshness, bitterness, and similar things, he will do best to arrange the parts of the composition so that they proceed with movements that are without the semitone, such as those of the whole tone and ditone [major third]. He should allow the major sixth and major thirteenth, which by nature are somewhat harsh, to be heard above the lowest note of the concentus, and should use the suspension of the fourth or the eleventh above the lowest part, along with somewhat slow movements, among which the suspension of the seventh may also be used. But when a composer wishes to express effects of grief and sorrow, he should (observing the rules given) use movements which proceed through the semitone, the semiditone [minor third], and similar intervals, often using minor

sixths or minor thirteenths above the lowest note of the composition, these being by nature sweet and soft, especially when combined in the right way and with discretion and judgment.

It should be noted, however, that the cause of the various effects is attributed not only to the consonances named, used in the ways described above, but also the movements which the parts make in singing. These are two sorts, namely, natural and accidental. Natural movements are those made between the natural notes of a composition, where no sign or accidental note intervenes. Accidental movements are those made by means of the accidental notes, which are indicated by the signs ♯ and ♭. The natural movements have more virility than the accidental movements, which are somewhat languid. . . . For this reason the former movements can serve to express effects of harshness and bitterness, and the latter movements can serve for effects of grief and sorrow.

Gioseffo Zarlino, *Le istitutioni harmoniche* (1558) III.31, trans. Vered Cohen; in Gioseffo Zarlino, *On the Modes*, ed. Claude V. Palisca (New Haven: Yale University Press, 1983), p. 95.

*Vincenzo Giustiniani (1564–1637) was a well-to-do musical amateur who described contemporary musical life in* Discorso sopra la musica de' suoi tempi *(Discourse on the music of his times, 1628). His account of the women's vocal ensembles at Ferrara and Mantua in the 1570s reveals their manner of performance and some of the reasons they were so greatly esteemed.*

〰〰

These dukes [of Ferrara and Mantua] took the greatest delight in such music, especially in gathering many important gentlewomen and gentlemen to play and sing excellently. So great was their delight that they lingered sometimes for whole days in some little chambers they had ornately outfitted with pictures and tapestries for this sole purpose. There was a great rivalry between the women of Mantua and Ferrara, a competition not only in the timbre and disposition of their voices but also in ornamentation with exquisite runs joined opportunely and not excessively. . . . There was competition even more in moderating or enlarging the voice, loud or soft, attenuating it or fattening it as was called for, now drawing it out, now breaking it off with the accompaniment of a sweet interrupted sigh, now giving out long runs, distinct and well followed, now turns, now leaps, now long trills, now short ones, now sweet runs sung quietly, to which sometimes one suddenly heard an echo respond; and more still in the participation of the face, and of the looks and gestures that accompanied appropriately the music and conceits of the poetry; and above all, without any indecorous motions of body, mouth, or hands that might have diminished the effect of their songs, in enunciating the words so well that each one could be heard down to the last syllable and was not interrupted or overwhelmed by the runs and other ornaments. And many other particular artifices could be observed in these singers and recorded by one more expert than I. And in such noble situations these excellent singers strove with all their might to win grace from their masters, the princes, and also fame for them—wherein lay their usefulness.

Vincenzo Giustiniani, *Discorso sopra la musica de' suoi tempi* (1628), in Angelo Solerti, *Le origini del melodramma: Testimonianze dei contemporanei* (Turin: Fratelli Bocca, 1903), pp. 107–108; trans. Gary Tomlinson, in Oliver Strunk, ed., *Source Readings in Music History*, rev. ed. by Leo Treitler (New York: Norton, 1998), pp. 353–354.

words or phrases with a musical image: long note values for "deliberate and slow" steps (measures 15–24); quickly moving figures in close imitation for "flee" (measures 25–33); quarter notes alternating between two pitches a whole step apart for "footstep" (measures 33–41). Of these devices, Marenzio was an acknowledged master. But the opening of the madrigal goes well beyond word painting to create an extraordinary soundscape of loneliness and alienation, rendered by a painfully slow, ascending, chromatic scale in the soprano that rises through a ninth before reversing direction (at measure 16), moving all the while in stark rhythmic and melodic contrast to the other voices.

Ferrara, the city renowned as the home of the original *concerto delle donne*, also boasted several important madrigal composers, all Italians. Nicola Vicentino (1511–ca. 1576) explored chromatic passages in his madrigals, inspired by the chromatic and enharmonic types of Greek tetrachords. To promote his theories, Vicentino not only published a treatise, *L'antica musica ridotta alla moderna prattica* (Ancient Music Adapted to Modern Practice, 1555), but he also designed a specially constructed harpsichord and organ (an *arcicembalo* and *arciorgano*) that divided the scale into quarter tones on which to perform his experimental music. Vicentino was succeeded by the madrigalist Luzzasco Luzzaschi (ca. 1545–1607), who became a master at improvising on Vicentino's chromatic-enharmonic keyboards. Luzzaschi, in turn, influenced the madrigal composer most associated with chromaticism at the end of the century—Carlo Gesualdo, prince of Venosa (ca. 1561–1613).

*Figure 7.3. Don Carlo Gesualdo, prince of Venosa.*

Gesualdo

One of the most colorful figures in music history, Gesualdo was an aristocratic amateur who nevertheless sought publication for his music, unusual for nobility at the time. He was also a murderer: when he discovered his wife in bed with her lover, he killed them both on the spot—not so unusual among the nobility at the time. Gesualdo survived the scandal to marry Leonora d'Este, niece of Alfonso II, duke of Ferrara, in 1593.

CD 3/65     CD 2/9

In his madrigals, Gesualdo dramatizes and intensifies the antitheses in the poetry through sudden contrasts between diatonic and chromatic passages, dissonance and consonance, chordal and imitative textures, and slow- and fast-moving rhythmic motives. These contrasts may be seen in *"Io parto" e non più dissi* ("I depart." I said no more, NAWM 53), published in 1611 in his last book of madrigals. In the dialogue between the lovers, the woman's tearful pleas are conveyed by slow, chromatic, mostly chordal music touched with dissonance; and the man's return to life ("vivo son") after his symbolic, sexual death prompts a turn to faster, diatonic, imitative figures (Example 7.3). Although these devices tend to fragment the sense of the poetry, Gesualdo achieved continuity by avoiding conventional cadences; and despite the prevalent chromaticism in many of his madrigals, he also provided tonal coherence by emphasizing the main steps of the mode at important points.

*Example 7.3: Don Carlo Gesualdo, "Io parto" e non più dissi, measures 26–31*

*[". . . Ah, may I never*
*cease to pine away] in sad laments."*
*Dead I was, now I am alive, [for my spent spirits*
*returned to life at the sound of such pitiable accents.]*

Monteverdi

The madrigal had a special place in the career of Claudio Monteverdi (1567–1643), whose biography will be considered in Chapter 9, but whose compositions made a crucial stylistic transition in this genre—from the polyphonic vocal ensemble to the instrumentally accompanied song for duet or larger forces.

Of Monteverdi's eight books of madrigals, the first five, published between 1587 and 1605, are monuments in the history of the polyphonic madrigal. Without going to such extremes as Gesualdo, Monteverdi demonstrated remarkable expressive power through his smooth combination of homophonic and contrapuntal part writing, his sensitivity to the sound and meaning of the text, and his free use of chromaticism and dissonance. But certain features—only suggested in the music of his contemporaries—indicate that Monteverdi was moving swiftly and confidently toward a new idiom. For example, many of his musical motives are not melodic, but declamatory in the manner of the later style known as recitative; the texture often departs from the medium of five equal voices and becomes a duet over a harmonically supporting (vocal) bass; and ornamental dissonances and embellishments that previously would have occurred only in improvisation are written into the score.

*Cruda Amarilli* (Cruel Amaryllis, NAWM 63) exemplifies the flexible and lively style of Monteverdi's polyphonic madrigals. The sound is rich in musical invention, humorous yet weighty, and audacious yet perfectly logical in its harmonies (see the more detailed discussion in Chapter 9).

CD 4/23    CD 2/35

# The Rise of National Styles: Secular Song outside Italy

During the long reign of Francis I (1515–1547), composers in Paris associated with the royal court developed a new type of chanson that was light, fast, strongly rhythmic, and in four parts. Favored subjects were playful, amorous situations that allow for double meanings, although more serious texts were occasionally chosen. The text was set syllabically with many repeated notes, usually in duple meter. The principal melody was in the highest voice, the musical texture largely homophonic with occasional short points of imitation. Most pieces were divided into short sections that repeated in an easily grasped pattern, such as aabc or abca. The strophic, repetitive forms did not allow word painting, and composers focused on tuneful melodies and pleasing rhythms rather than profound expression of the text.

Such pieces were satisfying to sing and ideally suited for amateurs. Between 1528 and 1552, Pierre Attaingnant (ca. 1494–1551/2), the first French music printer, brought out more than fifty collections of such chansons—about 1,500 pieces altogether—and other publishers soon followed. The great number of chansons of this type printed in the sixteenth century, including hundreds of arrangements for voice and lute or for lute alone, testifies to their popularity.

The two principal composers in Attaingnant's early chanson collections were Claudin de Sermisy (ca. 1490–1562) and Clément Janequin (ca. 1485–ca. 1560). Sermisy's *Tant que vivray* (NAWM 54), shown in Example 7.4, is typical. The text is a lighthearted and optimistic love poem, far removed from the old tradition of courtly love. As in a frottola or villancico, the melody is in the top voice, and the harmony consists of thirds and fifths with only an occasional sixth above the bass. The voices mostly declaim the text together. One result is that accented dissonances appear where earlier chansons would have featured a syncopated suspension before a cadence, as on the third quarter note of measure 3 in the top voice. The opening long-short-short rhythm is common. The end of each line of text is marked by a relatively long note or repeated notes, emphasizing the form of the poetry.

Several of Sermisy's chansons were so popular that they were reprinted for decades and adapted into many new forms, from dance melodies to psalm tunes. Some even showed up in paintings, as in Figure 7.4.

Janequin wrote many kinds of chanson, including lyrical love songs, narrative songs, and bawdy songs. He was particularly celebrated for his descriptive chansons, which feature imitations of bird calls, hunting calls, street cries, and sounds of war. His most famous chanson was *La Guerre* (War), supposedly about

Sermisy

CD 3/68    CD 2/12

Janequin

*Example 7.4: Claudin de Sermisy,* Tant que vivray, *measures 1–8*

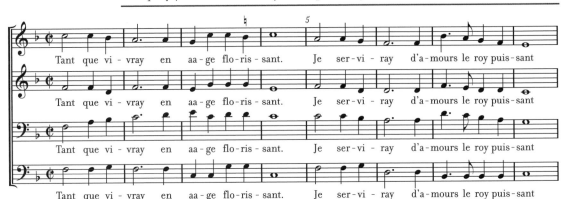

*As long as I am able-bodied,*
*I shall serve the potent king of love.*

the battle of Marignan (1515). *Le Chant des oiseaux* (The Song of the Birds) is filled with vocal warbles and chirping.

England    The late sixteenth century brought a fashion for Italian culture, art, and music to England. Many of Shakespeare's plays are set in Italy; and while everything from manners to clothing was affected, music was in the vanguard. Italian madrigals had begun to circulate in England in the 1560s, but the publication in 1588 of Nicholas Yonge's *Musica transalpina* (Music from across the Alps), a collection of Italian madrigals translated into English, accelerated the vogue for singing madrigals that was already under way. According to Yonge's preface, the pieces in the anthology were part of a repertory sung by gentlemen and merchants who met daily at his home (see "Music Printing," pages 118–119). The

*Figure 7.4.* Three Musicians (*or* The Concert), *by the Master of the Female Half-Lengths, shows the ways in which sixteenth-century part-songs could be performed. The music is Sermisy's Parisian chanson* Joyssance vous donneray. *The flutist reads from the soprano partbook, the singer performs the tenor part, and the lutenist adds the other voices from memory or perhaps improvises an accompaniment. The Harrach Collection, Schloss Rohrau, Vienna.*

*Figure 7.5. A copy (1600) of the lost* Coronation Portrait *of Elizabeth I (r. 1588–1603). National Portrait Gallery, London.*

popularity of this and other collections spurred native composers to cash in on the trend by writing their own compositions in the Italian manner. Leading English madrigal composers include Thomas Morley (1557/8–1602) and Thomas Weelkes (ca. 1573–1623).

Morley, the earliest and most prolific, wrote canzonets and balletts as well as madrigals, all based on Italian models. He composed his ballett *My bonny lass she smileth* (NAWM 56) in imitation of a specific balletto by Giovanni Giacomo Gastoldi, borrowing its dancelike meter and aspects of its text, rhythm, melody, and harmony. Like most balletts, it is strophic, with each stanza comprising two repeated sections of music (AABB). These are set homophonically with the melody in the top voice, and each concludes with a refrain, sung to the syllables "Fa-la-la," that is more contrapuntal, with some imitation between the parts. The distinctive rhythms, varied textures, and occasional contrapuntal challenges make Morley's "Fa-las" (as they are sometimes called) particularly satisfying to sing.

Morley

CD 3/79   CD 2/15

In 1601, Morley published a collection of twenty-five English madrigals by different composers modeled after a similar Italian anthology called *Il trionfo di Dori* (1592). He called his *The Triumphes of Oriana*, possibly in honor of Queen Elizabeth I (r. 1558–1603). Each madrigal in Morley's collection ends with the words "Long live fair Oriana," a name sometimes applied to Elizabeth.

*The Triumphes of Oriana*

One of the most famous madrigals in the collection is Weelkes's *As Vesta was* (NAWM 57), on his own poem. Elizabeth, who never married, was called the Virgin Queen, and the poem invokes both Diana, Roman goddess of virginity, and Vesta, Roman goddess of fire, hearth, and home and unmarried sister of Jupiter. Since word painting was a strong tradition in the madrigal, Weelkes as poet provided numerous opportunities for musical depiction, and Weelkes as composer capitalized on all of them. Most striking—and less conventional—is Weelkes's treatment of the final phrase. "Long live fair Oriana" is set to a motive that enters almost fifty times in all voices and all transpositions possible in the mode, suggesting the acclamation of a vast people. The effect is both virtuosic and meaningful, exemplifying the mixture of wit, wordplay, sentiment,

Weelkes

CD 3/82   CD 2/18

*Figure 7.6. John Dowland's song* What if I never speede *as printed in his* Third and Last Book of Songs or Ayres *(London, 1603). The song may be performed as a solo with lute accompaniment, reading from the left-hand page, or as a four-part vocal arrangement, with or without lute accompaniment, or by viols, with or without a singer. The altus, tenor, and bassus parts are arranged on the page to accommodate the performers' varying perspectives. British Library, London.*

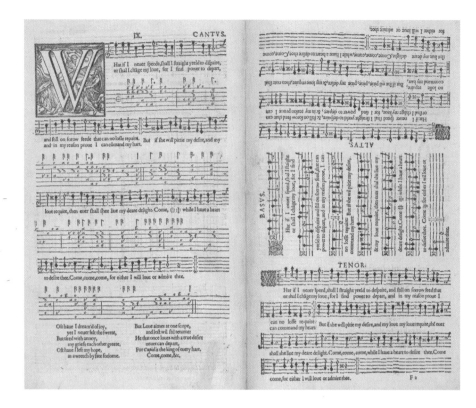

contrapuntal skill, melodiousness, and sheer pleasure for the singers that characterizes the best madrigals, English or Italian.

Madrigals, balletts, and canzonets were all written primarily for ensembles of unaccompanied solo voices, although many printed collections indicate on the title page that the music is "apt for voices and viol," presumably in any available combination. This flexibility made them ideal for amateurs. Ability to read a part, either vocally or instrumentally in such pieces, was expected of educated persons in Elizabethan England, as it was on the Continent.

Lute songs

In the early 1600s, the solo song with accompaniment became more prominent, especially the lute song (or air). The leading composers of lute songs were John Dowland (1563–1626) and Thomas Campion (1567–1620). The lute song was a more personal genre than the madrigal, with none of the latter's aura of social play. The music generally reflects the overall mood, with much less word painting than is typical of madrigals. The lute accompaniments, always subordinate to the vocal melody, have some rhythmic and melodic independence. Unlike madrigal collections, which were issued in partbooks, lute songs were printed in one book, with voice and lute part in vertical alignment on the same page. This format allowed singers to accompany themselves. In some collections, the songs appear both this way and in an alternative version, with three additional vocal parts so arranged on the page that performers sitting around a table could read all their parts from the same book (see Figure 7.6). The alternative four-part version, which sometimes resembled a madrigal, could be performed with either voices or instruments or both. The lute part is in tablature, a notational system that tells the player which strings to pluck and where to place the fingers on the strings, rather than indicating which pitches will result.

Dowland's remarkable *Flow, my tears* (NAWM 58)—perhaps Elizabethan England's best-known air—from his *Second Book of Ayres* (1600) spawned over two hundred variations and arrangements (see NAWM 61). It is in the form of a pavane, a sixteenth-century Italian processional dance, with three repeated

sections of music, or strains. A performer sings the first two stanzas of the poem to the first strain, the next two to the second, and the final stanza twice to the third strain, resulting in the musical pattern aabbCC. Even though the repeats prevent any concrete expression of individual words and phrases, Dowland's music matches the dark mood of the poetry.

In the late fifteenth century, during Ferdinand and Isabella's campaign to unify and invigorate Spain, Ferdinand and others at the Aragonese court encouraged the development of a traditional and uniquely Spanish music. They especially cultivated the villancico, which became the most important form of secular polyphonic song in Renaissance Spain. Although the name is a diminutive of *villano* ("peasant") and the texts are usually on rustic or popular subjects, villancicos were composed for the aristocracy. Short, strophic, syllabic, and mostly homophonic, they reflect a growing preference for simplicity and for what were considered more authentic representations of Spanish culture than the Spanish songs written in imitation of the polyphonic French chanson.

Juan del Encina (1468–1529), the first Spanish playwright, was a leading composer of villancicos. His *Oy comamos y bebamos* (Today let's eat and drink, NAWM 48) is typical of the genre. In language befitting the rustic nature of the play from which it comes, the text exhorts listeners to feast and be merry because tomorrow brings the first day of Lent, a season of fasting. The music, simple in melody, has focused harmonic progressions and dancelike rhythms marked by frequent metrical shifts between $\frac{3}{4}$ and $\frac{6}{8}$. For a complete discussion of the form of the villancico, see NAWM 48.

The Spanish villancico

CD 3/46

# The Rise of Instrumental Music

Why has our history so far been silent about instrumental music? From about 1450 to 1550, distinct styles, genres, and forms of instrumental music were emerging, and publications of instrumental works began to proliferate after about 1550. Yet, because almost all the composers we have studied were trained principally as singers (most were choirboys), they channeled their talents and made innovative contributions to the body of vocal music sung in churches and courts. As adults, even those who made their reputations as composers of secular music aspired to the position of chapel-master or, in modern terms, choir director—the most prestigious appointment any musician could have from about the twelfth century.

During the Middle Ages, distinct class and educational differences separated singers/composers from instrumentalists, who were less apt to be literate and often were expected to perform in situations in which improvisation was the norm—dancing, for instance, or ceremonial fanfare and the like. Since performers of instrumental music either improvised or played from memory, their music has not survived or has survived only in an approximate

*Figure 7.7. Detail from Albrecht Dürer's Jabach Altarpiece (ca. 1504), of two musicians—a shawm player and a drummer. Wallraf-Richartz Museum, Cologne.*

**IN PERFORMANCE**    Vocal Chamber Music or Accompanied Song?

*Figure 7.8.* The Lute Player *(1590s), one of several paintings on musical subjects by Michelangelo Merisi da Caravaggio (1571–1610). The youth is simultaneously playing and singing an Italian madrigal from the early sixteenth century, rendering it as a solo song with lute accompaniment. Solo singing became newly fashionable toward the end of the Renaissance, when Caravaggio was working in Rome. Private collection.*

The frottola, as well as French chansons and madrigals dating from about 1520 to 1550, was written for four voice parts; after the middle of the century, five voices became the rule for the madrigal, and settings for six or more voices were not unusual. The word *voices* should be taken literally: by definition, these were vocal chamber works with one singer to a part (see Figure 6.6). Throughout the sixteenth century, however, instruments sometimes doubled the voices or replaced some or all of the parts. This was particularly true of the frottola, which was presumably sung either a cappella (although Petrucci usually supplied the text only for the cantus) or as a song for solo voice with lute accompaniment, in which case the solo voice took the top part, the lutenist played the tenor and bass parts, and the alto was omitted altogether. Evidence for this practice exists in some arrangements published by lutenists early in the sixteenth century. Although we should be wary of taking iconographical evidence too literally—artists often imbued the theme of music with allegorical meaning—images like the one in Figure 7.4 suggest that French chansons were also subjected to similar arrangements or ad hoc instrumental performances.

Toward the end of the century, something similar took place in the madrigal repertory as well. Certain pieces published early in the century became so popular that they had a long afterlife in just such a performance tradition, one that allowed for spontaneous substitutions of instruments for voices or more formal transformations into instrumental transcriptions or variations. Vincenzo Giustiniani, a Roman nobleman and the same author who described the *concerto delle donne* in Ferrara (see page 135), also wrote about a new style of singing that appeared in the last quarter of the sixteenth century, "chiefly in the manner of one voice singing with accompaniment." We have independent testimony of this vogue in the painting by Caravaggio known as *The Lute Player* (see Figure 7.8), in which the youth is both playing and singing. Scholars have identified the open music book in the painting as the bass part of a madrigal by Jacques Arcadelt that had been published more than fifty years earlier. Indeed, the painting captures the yellowing condition of the book's pages. Although the style of Arcadelt's piece was by then old-fashioned compared to more recent examples of this rapidly changing genre, the fact that only the bass part is visible reflects the up-to-date performance practice of the end of the century: the performer would have sung the highest part and its text from memory, perhaps adding ornaments to enhance the melody's expressivity, while rendering on the lute a simple accompaniment improvised from the bass line. This type of performance was undoubtedly intended for more intimate settings in the privacy of one's own chamber or in the company of a few friends.

Caravaggio painted this work in the 1590s when, we may assume, the fashion of singing polyphonic madrigals as solo songs with instrumental accompaniment was in full swing. It was also the decade during which the composer Giulio Caccini was writing a new breed of madrigal expressly for solo voice with instrumental accompaniment (see Chapter 9) and forging the new "monodic" style of the early seventeenth century. The performance practice of decorative, accompanied singing, then, as practiced by the ladies in Ferrara and as depicted by Caravaggio's lute player was an important link between the Renaissance and the Baroque.

state. What seems like a greater emphasis on instrumental music after 1450 is, perhaps, an illusion: it may be only that more of it was written down once instrumentalists began performing polyphonic works that required coordination of parts. Even so, only a small portion of the instrumental music copied into manuscripts and printed in books during the Renaissance exists today.

A great deal of vocal music was often performed instrumentally, and instruments had participated with voices in polyphonic textures since the Middle

| TIMELINE | Secular Song in the Renaissance |
|---|---|

| MUSICAL EVENTS | HISTORICAL EVENTS |
|---|---|
| First edition of Encina's songbook *Cancionero*, **1496** including villancicos | |
| Petrucci issues thirteen frottola collections **1504–1514** | |
| | **1519–1556** Charles V, Holy Roman emperor |
| Death of Josquin **1521** | |
| | **1527** Sack of Rome |
| Attaingnant publishes first collection **1528** of chansons in Paris | **1528** Castiglione, *The Book of the Courtier* |
| Arcadelt, first book of four-part madrigals **1539** | |
| | **1543** Copernicus, *On the Revolutions of the Heavenly Spheres* |
| Zarlino, *Le istitutioni harmoniche* **1558** | **1558** Elizabeth I becomes queen of England |
| Rore, *Da le belle contrade d'oriente* **1566** (in *Fifth Book of Madrigals*) | |
| Concerto delle donne established in Ferrara **1580** | |
| Yonge, *Musica transalpina* **1588** | |
| | **1590** Spenser, *The Faerie Queene*, Books 1–3 |
| Morley, *The First Booke of Balletts* **1595** | **1594** Shakespeare, *Romeo and Juliet* **ca. 1595** Caravaggio, *The Lute Player* |
| Dowland, *First Booke of Songes or Ayres* **1597** | |
| Marenzio, *Solo e pensoso* (last book of madrigals) **1599** | |
| Morley issues *Triumphes of Oriana* **1601** | |
| Monteverdi, *Fifth Book of Madrigals* **1605** | |
| Gesualdo's last book of madrigals **1611** | |

Ages. Throughout the sixteenth century, much instrumental music remained closely associated, both in style and performance, with vocal music. Instruments sometimes doubled or replaced voices in secular and sacred polyphonic compositions. For example, the lowest parts of a madrigal or chanson were often reduced for lute or keyboard, becoming in effect an accompaniment to the melody performed by a solo voice (see "Vocal Chamber Music or Accompanied Song," page 142). Portions of a hymn or sections of the Mass (especially the Kyrie and Gloria) alternated with short organ pieces that substituted for the passages normally sung (such as one of the threefold Kyrie or Christe acclamations), incorporating some or all of the chant melody that they replaced. Composers also wrote organ pieces on liturgical or other cantus firmi as independent works, comparable to vocal motets.

Two different tendencies governed the rise of instrumental music in the Renaissance: (1) the exploitation of compositional styles and genres peculiar or idiomatic to the instruments themselves and functioning independently of vocal music; (2) the reliance on preexistent vocal genres, including mere substitution of instruments for voices, instrumental transcriptions and arrangements of vocal compositions, and newly composed instrumental works either based on or otherwise inspired by vocal models (see NAWM 61). These two tendencies will be explored, along with the genres that they fostered, in Chapter 10.

CD 4/9　　CD 2/29

# POSTLUDE

Developments in the sixteenth century included the emergence of new secular genres—madrigal, chanson, and villancico—as the sophisticated Franco-Flemish style encountered native traditions in Italy, France, and Spain. Among the composers in the generation after Josquin, Arcadelt and others in Italy were driven by the spirit of humanism to seek a close rapport between music and text. In both sacred and secular compositions, they shaped the music to follow the sound and syntax of the words and to represent musically the essence of a text's message. Yet they remained faithful to the Renaissance ideal of modal, diatonic counterpoint, equality and independence of voices, full harmony, controlled dissonance, and clarity of form.

Mid-century composers such as Rore sought an even closer bond between music and text, but they tilted the balance—at least in the madrigal—toward the expression of a poem's contrasting feelings and images, sacrificing a certain coherence and unity of style. At the same time, the madrigal became more extroverted and declamatory as composers attempted to project the sentiments of the text to a *listening* audience—that is, a social group other than the performers themselves. During the last decades of the century, composers found new ways to express intense passions and the clever conceits of modern poetry. Gesualdo and others explored chromaticism, while Monteverdi (as we shall see) experimented with dissonance, new textures, and speechlike rhythms that led him, in the first decade of the seventeenth century, to write opera. Because the Italian madrigal was the most forward-looking and innovative of the new sixteenth-century genres, these developments allowed Italian music to dominate the Baroque era and made Italy the leader in European music for the first time.

In France, chanson composers turned from writing serious motetlike polyphony to cultivating light, tuneful, homophonic songs. A number of English composers enthusiastically took up the new Italian trends, but the most characteristic genre to emerge from the widespread interest in vocal chamber music in the British Isles was the lute song, or air.

During this same period, instrumental music began to emerge from the long shadow cast by vocal music. By mid-sixteenth century, independent genres of written instrumental music could be distinguished by their functions and formal procedures—for example, dance, variations, and others (see Chapter 10). Around 1600, English lute and keyboard composers would take the lead in instrumental writing until a new generation of Italian composers emerged who devoted their attention completely to instrumental music.

# Sacred Music in the Era of the Reformation

## PRELUDE

*Chapter Contents*

*Prelude* 146

The Music of the
Reformation in
Germany 147

Reformation Church
Music outside
Germany 149

The Counter-
Reformation 151

*Postlude* 161

The Reformation began as a theological dispute that was set in motion by Martin Luther in 1517 and mushroomed into a rebellion against the authority of the Catholic Church and the spiritual leadership of Rome, the center of Western Christianity. The liturgical changes that eventually ensued naturally brought about musical changes, which differed from country to country according to the degree of reform advocated by the various Protestant leaders: Luther in Germany; Calvin and his followers in France, the Low Countries, and Switzerland; and Henry VIII in England.

At first, the music of the Reformation in Germany, written by Lutheran composers, remained very close to the traditional Catholic sources and styles of plainsong and polyphony. Some music retained the original Latin texts, other works used German translations, and still others had new German texts fitted to the old melodies (this work was called a contrafactum). The Lutheran Church's most distinctive and important musical innovation became the strophic hymn—called Choral or Kirchenlied (church song) in German and chorale in English—intended for congregational singing in unison. Just as plainchant was the basis for musical expansion and elaboration for Catholic composers, so, too, the repertory of chorales became the starting point for a great deal of Lutheran church music from the sixteenth century until the time of Johann Sebastian Bach (1685–1750) and beyond.

Reformation church music outside Germany developed along similar lines, except that Calvin and leaders of other Protestant sects opposed certain elements of Catholic ceremony much more strongly than Luther had. They distrusted the allure of art in places of worship and in services, and prohibited singing of texts not found in the Bible. As a result, the only notable contributions to music from the Calvinist churches were their Psalters—rhymed metrical translations of the Book of Psalms set to newly composed melodies or, in many cases, to tunes of popular origin or from plainchant. Since the Calvinists discouraged musical elaboration, they seldom expanded the Psalter tunes into larger vocal or instrumental forms. In England, under Henry VIII, the Anglican Church's separation from Rome in 1534 occurred more for political than for religious reasons; so English church music was less affected and remained closer to Catholic musical traditions (except that the English language replaced Latin in the liturgy).

The Catholic Church met the defection of the Protestant reformers by starting its own program of internal reform known as the Catholic Reformation. This movement not only resulted in many liturgical reforms, it also reaffirmed the power of music to affect the hearts and minds of the faithful through an appropriate style of sacred polyphony. At the same time, a broader movement, known as the Counter-Reformation, attempted to win back those who had left the Catholic Church, appealing to their senses through the sheer beauty of its liturgy, religious art, and ceremonial music. Among all the Catholic composers of sacred music to succeed in this strategy, the Roman Giovanni Pierluigi da Palestrina (1525/6–1594) was the most important. Not only did he capture the essence of the musical Counter-Reformation, but his style also became a model for church-music composition—one that has served teachers and students of counterpoint to this day.

## The Music of the Reformation in Germany

The central position of music in the Lutheran Church reflects Luther's own convictions. He was a singer, a composer of some skill, and a great admirer of Franco-Flemish polyphony, especially the works of Josquin des Prez. He believed strongly in the educational and ethical power of music and wanted the entire congregation to participate in the music of the services. Although he altered the words of the liturgy to conform to his own views on certain theological points, he kept much of the Catholic liturgy, some in German translation and some in Latin, a language he considered valuable for educating the young.

*Lutheran church music*

In applying Luther's beliefs to local conditions, congregations all over Germany developed a number of usages. Large churches with trained choirs generally kept much of the Latin liturgy and its polyphonic music. Smaller congregations adopted a German Mass (*Deudsche Messe*), published by Luther in 1526, which followed the main outlines of the Roman Mass but differed from it in many details and replaced most elements of the Proper and Ordinary with German hymns or chorales.

*German Mass*

Just as most Catholic church music developed from plainsong enriched by harmony and counterpoint and reworked into larger musical forms, so Lutheran church music largely grew out of the chorale. As in plainsong, the chorale originally consisted essentially of only two elements—a text and a tune. The congregation learned the tenets of their faith and celebrated the yearly cycle of religious holidays by singing these easily memorized hymns, comprised of simple, metrical tunes and rhyming verses. A large number of chorales were newly composed; Luther himself wrote many texts and some melodies. The best known is *Ein' feste Burg ist unser Gott* (A sturdy fortress is our God, 1529, NAWM 42c), shown in Example 8.1, which became the anthem of the Reformation. Adaptations of secular and devotional songs or Latin chants supplied an even larger number of chorale tunes. Thus, the Easter sequence *Victimae paschali laudes* (NAWM 5) provided the model for *Christ lag in Todesbanden* (Christ lay in the bonds of death).

*Chorale*

CD 3/18

CD 1/29 | CD 1/11

Luther and his colleagues used many well-known secular tunes for chorales, substituting religious words. The resulting compositions, called contrafacta (Latin for "counterfeits"), often had wholly new texts but sometimes included clever reworkings of the existing poems. The most famous contrafactum (but not by Luther) is *O Welt, ich muss dich lassen* (O world, I must leave you), based on the lied *Innsbruck, ich muss dich lassen* (NAWM 38).

CD 3/1

*Example 8.1: Martin Luther,* Ein' feste Burg

Ein' fe - ste Burg ist un — ser Gott, ein gu - te Wehr und Waf — fen.
Er hilft uns frei aus al - ler Not, die uns jetzt hat be - trof — fen.

Der alt bö - se Feind, mit Ernst ers jetzt meint; gross Macht und

viel List sein grau - sam Rü - stung ist; auf Erd ist nicht seins Glei — chen.

*A sturdy fortress is our God, a good defense and weapon.*
*He helps us free from all afflictions that have now befallen us.*
*The old, evil enemy now means to deal with us seriously;*
*great power and much cunning are his cruel armaments;*
*on Earth is not his equal.*

**Polyphonic chorale settings**

**CD 3/19**

Lutheran composers soon began to write polyphonic settings of chorales, using a variety of approaches borrowed from existing genres. Some composers used the older technique of the German lied, placing the unaltered chorale tune in long notes in the tenor and surrounding it with three or more free-flowing parts, as in the setting by Luther's collaborator Johann Walter (1496–1570; see NAWM 42d). Others developed each phrase of the chorale imitatively in all voices in the manner of Franco-Flemish motets. Still others wrote in a simple, almost chordal style, with the tune in the soprano instead of the tenor; this became the preferred arrangement.

*Figure 8.1. The Calvinist Temple at Lyon in a 1564 painting that shows the austerity of Calvinist churches. The preacher wears no elaborate vestments, there is no choir or altar, the focus is on the pulpit, and the only decorations are coats of arms in the windows and above the pulpit. Bibliothèque Publique et Universaire, Geneva.*

The choir, sometimes doubled by instruments, commonly alternated chorale stanzas sung in four parts with the congregation, which sang in unison without accompaniment. After 1600, it became customary to have all the parts played on the organ, while the congregation sang all the verses of the tune. This style of harmonization and performance has continued to the present and is evident in almost all Protestant hymnbooks. More elaborate treatments of the chorale—for example, for organ solo or for trained choir—also became part of the Lutheran church-music repertory in Germany. By the end of the sixteenth century, some Protestant composers, following the example of Orlando di Lasso (see pages 158 ff.) among others, created chorale motets or free polyphonic compositions around the traditional melodies, incorporating personal interpretations and pictorial details in the manner of the Latin motet. Others used chorale tunes as the basis for organ improvisations. Both traditions culminated more than a hundred years later in the keyboard chorale preludes and vocal chorale fantasias of J. S. Bach.

# Reformation Church Music
# outside Germany

The Reformation influenced musical developments in France, the Low Countries, and Switzerland quite differently than in Germany. John Calvin (1509–1564) fervently rejected the Catholic liturgy and its trappings, believing with the English Puritans that the distraction of the senses, however innocent, might lead people astray (see "Music as a Symbol for Human Frailty," page 150). Seeking to focus worship on God alone, Calvin stripped churches and services of all ornament, including paintings, musical instruments, and elaborate polyphony. Consequently, the only music heard in the Calvinists' worship service was the singing of psalms to monophonic tunes published in collections called Psalters. The principal French Psalter was published in 1562, with all 150 psalm texts translated into strophic, rhyming, and metrical verse, and set to melodies selected or composed by Loys Bourgeois (ca. 1510–ca. 1561). The melodies move mostly by step, giving them an austere simplicity. The best known is the tune for Psalm 134 (NAWM 43a) shown in Example 8.2. Because it was used in English Psalters for Psalm 100, it became known as "Old Hundredth."

French Psalter

CD 3/20

*Example 8.2: Original melody from the French Psalter of 1562, with a later adaptation*

Psalm 134

Or sus, ser - vi - teurs du Sei - gneur, Vous qui de nuit en Son hon - neur

*Arise, you servants of the Lord, you who by night in his honor . . .*

Presbyterian hymnal

All peo - ple that on earth do dwell, Sing to the Lord with cheer - ful voice

Like Lutherans, Calvinists originally sang psalms only in unaccompanied unison at church services. For devotional use at home, they availed themselves of settings in four or more parts, with the tune either in the tenor or the soprano, sometimes in simple chordal style and sometimes in fairly elaborate motetlike arrangements.

The most prominent French composers of psalm settings were Claude Goudimel (ca. 1520–1572) and Claude Le Jeune (ca. 1528–1600); the leading Netherlandish composer was Jan Pieterszoon Sweelinck (1562–1621). Translations of the French Psalter appeared in Germany, Holland, England, and Scotland, and the Reformed Churches in those countries took over many of the French tunes. The Germans adapted Psalter melodies for use as chorales. The French model also influenced the most important English Psalter of the sixteenth century; and the Psalter brought by the Pilgrims to New England in 1620 was a combination of the English and the French-Dutch traditions.

Even though English composers were aware of developments in Continental music, they worked in relative isolation. No Franco-Flemish musicians came to England until after 1510, and English composers only gradually adopted the prevailing international style of imitative counterpoint. Meanwhile, native production of secular music continued. Manuscripts from the time of Henry VII and Henry VIII (r. 1509–1547) contain a variety of songs and instrumental

England

pieces in three- and four-part settings, reflecting many facets of court life, including popular elements.

Most of the surviving English polyphonic music from this period is sacred—Masses, Magnificats, and devotional antiphons or motets in honor of the Blessed Virgin Mary. Even after the break with Rome, Latin motets and Masses continued to be written because the tradition of Latin sacred polyphony was valued for its links to the past and its musical splendors. Many works illustrate the

## IN CONTEXT  Music as a Symbol for Human Frailty

Paintings that incorporate musical subjects often help us understand the way people thought and felt about music in their society. The great reformers Luther and Calvin regarded music as God's gift, whose highest and only purpose was to honor God. But while Luther considered music on earth to be a preview of the heavenly choir, Calvin warned of its dangers as a source of temptation.

This picture illustrates an entire class of sober still lifes that became very popular in northern countries after the Reformation. Known as *vanitas* (vanity) paintings, they testify to the transience and sometimes the distractions of art and of all earthly pleasures and possessions. Musical instruments, because of their rapidly decaying sound, were well-known *vanitas* symbols and served as favorite props along with other objects, as in *Vanitas: Still Life with a Violin* (1629) by Pieter Claeszoon, a Dutch painter who specialized in this theme.

The term *vanitas* as used in this title comes from the opening of the Book of Ecclesiastes (in its Latin translation from the Hebrew): "Vanitas vani-

tatum, omnia vanitas." (Vanity of vanities! All things are vanity! What profit has man from all the labor which he toils at under the sun? One generation passes and another comes, but the world forever stays.) Literature as well as painting of the time frequently expressed this idea, with its compelling reminder of human mortality.

Every object in Claeszoon's painting contains a symbolic meaning that contributes to the *vanitas* message. The human skull obviously signifies death, and the smoking oil lamp, recently extinguished, reminds us that life inevitably comes to an end. What good will our accumulated wealth—represented by the ornate empty goblet on the left and the gilded beaker on the right as well as by the rare and exotic shells—be to us then? Even our learning, gathered from books or inscribed with the quill pen, will not help us after death. That our time on earth runs out is suggested by the watch, whose mechanism lies exposed in its case. The violin and bow, lying at the center of the painting but partly hidden behind the skull, function as emblems of temporality, of the impermanence of music and all the arts, and of the tenuous pleasures associated with them.

The impact of these paintings (and there were many made for middle-class consumers) may be compared to that of contemporary commercial art. However, the message was a negative one: worldly goods are a hindrance to leading a virtuous life; music and other pleasures are frivolous; and learning is ephemeral. The visual effect, all the more convincing because of its shocking realism, was no doubt as persuasive for a seventeenth-century Dutch citizen as the symbol of skull-and-crossbones on a package of cigarettes would be for us today.

*Figure 8.2. Pieter Claeszoon,* Vanitas: Still Life with a Violin, *1629. Hoogsteder & Hoogsteder, The Hague, the Netherlands.*

English preference for full textures, display a strong feeling for the harmonic dimension of music, and achieve textural variety through the use of contrasting voice groups. Long melismas executed simultaneously in all voices often resulted in passages of extraordinary beauty and expressiveness.

Toward the middle of the century, the leading English composer was Thomas Tallis (ca. 1505–1585), whose career reflects the religious upheavals and bewildering political changes that influenced English church music in this period. Under Henry VIII, Tallis wrote Latin Masses (including one parody Mass) and motets. Under Edward VI (r. 1547–1553), he composed music for the Anglican service and motets to English texts. During the reign of Catholic Queen Mary, he wrote a number of Latin hymns, and his large seven-voice Mass *Puer nobis* probably also dates to those years. Under Queen Elizabeth, Tallis composed music to both Latin and English words. His late works include two sets of Lamentations, among the most eloquent settings of these verses from the Hebrew Scriptures used as responsories in the Office of Holy Week. One remarkable feature of all his compositions (and of much sixteenth-century English music) is the obvious vocal quality of the melodies. They strike the listener not as an interplay of abstract musical lines, but as a profusion of human voices—so closely is the melodic curve wedded to the natural inflection of speech and so imaginatively does it project the content of the words.

*Tallis*

# The Counter-Reformation

In the wake of the Protestant Reformation and the capture and sack of Rome (1527), advocates of internal reform came to power in the Catholic Church. Their main tool of change was the Council of Trent, which met intermittently in Trent (a city in northern Italy) between 1545 and 1563 to find ways to purge the Church of abuses and laxities. In the discussions of liturgical reform, church music took up only a small part of the council's time, but it was the subject of serious complaints. Some contended that the Mass was profaned when its music was based on secular cantus firmi or chansons. Others argued that complicated polyphony made it impossible to understand the words, even if they were pronounced correctly—and often they were not. Musicians were accused of using instruments inappropriately, of being careless in their duties, and of having an irreverent attitude. Despite these charges, the Council of Trent's final pronouncement on church music was extremely general. Neither polyphony nor the imitation of secular models was specifically forbidden. The council merely banished from the Church everything "lascivious or impure" and left the task of implementing the directive to the local bishops.

Meanwhile, in those countries that remained Catholic, music was changed relatively little by the religious turbulence of the sixteenth century and even less by the Council of Trent. The Renaissance was still in full swing, and Flemish composers remained in prominent positions all over Europe. Among the best known was Adrian Willaert (ca. 1490–1562; see Figure 8.3), whose career took him to Rome, Ferrara, Milan, and finally Venice, where he was director of music at the principal church, Saint Mark's, for thirty-five years. There he trained many eminent Italian musicians, including the theorist Gioseffo Zarlino (see Chapter 6) and the composers Cipriano de Rore and Nicola Vicentino (see Chapter 7). With his long career in Italy, Willaert was most affected by the humanist movement and the attention it paid to the relationship between music

*Figure 8.3. Woodcut portrait of the aged composer Adrian Willaert, published as the frontispiece to the collection of his motets and madrigals,* Musica Nova, *issued in 1559.*

**A CLOSER LOOK** Anglican Church Music

The Church in England formally separated from the Roman Catholic Communion in 1534 under Henry VIII. English gradually replaced Latin in the church service, and in 1549 the Act of Uniformity made the English Book of Common Prayer the only prayer book permitted for public use. A brief return of Roman Catholicism occurred under Mary Tudor (r. 1553–1558); but Elizabeth I restored the English rites, and during her reign (1558–1603) the Church of England was established essentially in its present-day form, which includes the Episcopal Church in the United States.

The subsequent changes in language and liturgy finally gave rise to a new body of church music in English. Thomas Tallis (see page 151), whose major efforts went into Latin church composition, also contributed some English works. William Byrd (see page 160), a Roman Catholic composer of Latin motets and Masses, also wrote five services and about sixty anthems (motetlike compositions on English texts) for Anglican use. Orlando Gibbons (1583–1625), often called the father of Anglican church music, composed works that are thoroughly English in spirit, even though their technique derives from the Latin tradition. Thomas Weelkes (ca. 1576–1623) and Thomas Tomkins (1572–1656) also produced English church music of lasting quality.

The principal forms of Anglican music are the service and the anthem. A complete service consists of the music for fixed portions of Morning and Evening Prayer (corresponding to the Catholic Matins and Vespers) and for Holy Communion (which corresponds to the Roman Mass). Music for a Great Service is contrapuntal and melismatic, for a Short Service, chordal and syllabic—but there is no difference in content between the two. One of the finest examples of Anglican church music remains the Great Service of William Byrd.

The English anthem corresponds to the Latin motet. Byrd's energetic *Sing joyfully unto God* (NAWM 44) illustrates one type (full anthem), written in contrapuntal style for unaccompanied chorus throughout. Another type of anthem (verse anthem) employs one or more solo voices with organ or viol accompaniment and has brief alternating passages for chorus. This type, which developed from the consort song, was highly popular in England during the seventeenth century.

CD 3/22

CD 1/63

*Figure 8.4. Henry VIII, in a portrait by Hans Holbein the Younger.*

and words. Like the Italian madrigalists who followed in his footsteps, he carefully molded his music to the pronunciation of the words by matching long notes to accented syllables, and planned his compositions to suit the structure and meaning of the text in every detail. For example, he never allowed a rest to interrupt a word or thought within a phrase and brought the voices to a cadence only at the end of a unit of text. Willaert was also one of the first composers to insist that his printer place the syllables exactly under their correct notes rather than spread them anywhere within the phrase.

## Palestrina

Although the concern for the intelligibility of words in polyphonic music was long-standing among humanists and churchmen alike (see "Cirillo on Reviving Ancient Music," page 115), it became linked to Giovanni Pierluigi da Palestrina (1525/6–1594; see biography and Figure 8.5), the premier Italian composer of

### ✸ Giovanni Pierluigi da Palestrina (1525/6–1594)

Palestrina's name is legendary among church musicians for his almost exclusive concentration on sacred music and his lifelong loyalty to Rome and the goals of the Counter-Reformation. As a result, the "Palestrina style" became the standard for polyphonic church music in later ages.

Born near Rome in the small town of Palestrina, he served as a choirboy and received his musical education at the church of Santa Maria Maggiore in Rome. After seven years as organist and choirmaster in Palestrina (1544–1551), he returned to Rome under the patronage of Pope Julius III and became choirmaster of the Julian Chapel at Saint Peter's (1551–1555). In 1555, he was briefly a singer in the Sistine Chapel choir but had to relinquish the honor because he was married. He spent the remaining forty years of his career in Rome as choirmaster at two important churches: Saint John Lateran (1555–1560) and Santa Maria Maggiore (1561–1566). He also taught music at the new Jesuit seminary and eventually returned to his position at the Julian Chapel (1571–1594).

Palestrina composed more Masses than any other composer. His main secular works are madrigals. Late in life, he confessed that he "blushed and grieved" to have written music for love poems.

After the Council of Trent ordered changes in the liturgy, Palestrina and a colleague were commissioned to revise the official chant books to conform to the new liturgy and purge the chants of "barbarisms, obscurities, contrarieties, and su-

Figure 8.5. Giovanni Pierluigi da Palestrina in a contemporary painting, 1594. Istituto dei Padri dell'Oratorio, Rome.

perfluities." The revised edition, which arbitrarily eliminated melismatic passages, was completed by others after Palestrina's death and published in 1614. It remained in use until the early twentieth century, when Benedictine monks produced new editions based on surviving early manuscripts.

Palestrina married Lucrezia Gori in 1547, and they had three sons. After he lost two of them in the 1570s to the plague, followed by Lucrezia in 1580, Palestrina considered becoming a priest. Instead, in 1581 he married Virginia Dormoli, an affluent widow whose financial resources allowed him to publish his own music. His reputation as a composer, already high in his lifetime, grew exponentially after his death, and he eventually became known as "the Prince of Music."

**Major works:** 104 Masses, over 300 motets, 35 Magnificats, about 70 hymns, many other liturgical compositions, about 50 spiritual madrigals with Italian texts, and 94 secular madrigals

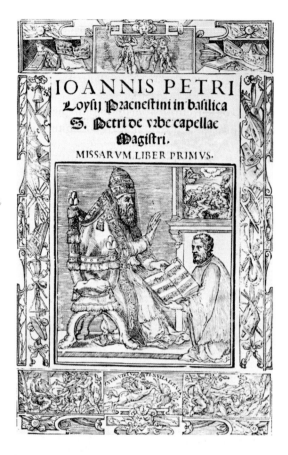

*Figure 8.6. Title page of the first published collection of works by Palestrina (Rome: Valerio and Luigi Dorico, 1554). The composer is shown presenting his music to Pope Julius III.*

CD 3/27

CD 3/35    CD 1/68

church music in the sixteenth century. According to a legend already circulating soon after his death, Palestrina saved polyphony from being condemned by the Council of Trent by composing a six-voice Mass that was both reverent in spirit and attentive to the words. The work in question was the *Missa Papae Marcelli* (Pope Marcellus Mass; Credo and Agnus Dei I in NAWM 45a and 45b), published in Palestrina's *Second Book of Masses* in 1567. While the legend is probably inaccurate, Palestrina did note in his dedication to the collection that the Masses it contained were written "in a new manner," no doubt responding to the desire of some for greater clarity in presenting the text.

Palestrina style

Palestrina's style was the first in the history of Western music to have been consciously preserved, isolated, and imitated as a model for sacred polyphony. Few composers before Bach are as well known today, and perhaps no other composer's technique has received closer scrutiny. Better than any of his contemporaries, he captured the essence of the sober, conservative, yet elegantly expressive style of the Counter-Reformation.

Masses

Palestrina studied the works of the Franco-Flemish composers and completely mastered their craft. Half of his Masses are parody Masses, many based on polyphonic models by leading contrapuntists of previous generations or on his own motets. Palestrina used the old-fashioned cantus-firmus method for a few of his Masses (including the first of two he wrote on the traditional *L'homme armé* melody), but generally he preferred to paraphrase the chant in all the parts rather than confine it to the tenor voice. Also reminiscent of the older Flemish tradition are a small number of canonic Masses. Six Masses, including the *Pope Marcellus Mass*, are free, using neither canons nor borrowed material.

Pope Marcellus Mass

Palestrina's melodies share qualities with plainchant: their curve often describes an arch, and the motion is mostly stepwise with few repeated notes. In the first Agnus Dei from the famous *Pope Marcellus Mass* (Example 8.3 and

NAWM 45b), for example, we observe long, gracefully shaped phrases, easily singable and staying for the most part within the range of a ninth. The few leaps greater than a third are immediately filled in by notes that reverse the direction of the skip and smooth the contour. The rhythmic units vary in length without ever creating extreme contrasts of motion. The flowing melodies remain in the diatonic modes; Palestrina studiously avoided chromaticism, admitting only those alterations demanded by the conventions of musica ficta (see Chapter 4).

This same Agnus Dei also illustrates how Palestrina unifies a composition by purely musical means. Each phrase of the text has its own musical motive, and the contrapuntal development of each motive through imitation overlaps at a cadence with the next phrase. But there is more connection between motives than mere succession; Palestrina also achieves organic unity through systematic repetition of phrases and by carefully placing cadences only on those scale degrees that define the mode.

Form

*Example 8.3: Giovanni Pierluigi da Palestrina*, Pope Marcellus Mass: *Agnus Dei I*

## TIMELINE    The Era of the Reformation

| MUSICAL EVENTS | HISTORICAL EVENTS |
|---|---|
| | **1532** Henry VIII breaks with pope |
| | **1534** Formal separation of Church of England and Rome |
| | **1539** English Bible adopted |
| | |
| | **1545–1563** Council of Trent |
| | **1547–1553** Reign of Edward VI |
| | |
| | **1552** Second Book of Common Prayer |
| | **1553–1558** Mary I restores Latin rite and link to Rome |
| Palestrina issues first book of Masses **1554** | |
| | **1558–1603** Reign of Elizabeth I; restores Church of England |
| French Psalter published **1562** | |
| | **1564** Death of John Calvin |
| Palestrina's *Pope Marcellus Mass* published **1567** | |
| | |
| Death of Tallis **1585** | |
| | **1586** El Greco, *Burial of the Count of Orgaz* |
| | **1587** Mary Stuart executed |
| Death of Palestrina and Lasso **1594** | |
| | **1603–1625** Reign of James I (Jacobean period) |
| Monteverdi publishes fifth book of madrigals **1605** | |
| Death of Victoria **1611** | |
| Monteverdi appointed director of music, **1613** Saint Mark's, Venice | |
| | **1620** Pilgrims arrive in Massachusetts |
| Death of William Byrd **1623** | |
| | **1625–1648** Reign of Charles I |

*Text declamation*

CD 3/27

Palestrina composed the *Pope Marcellus Mass* in the 1560s, when the Council of Trent was urging in the *Canon on Music to Be Used in the Mass* that "the words be clearly understood by all." His attention to text setting is particularly evident in the Credo (NAWM 45a), where the voices often pronounce a given phrase simultaneously rather than in the staggered manner of imitative polyphony. To achieve variety, Palestrina divided the six-voice choir into various smaller groups, each with its particular sonorous color, and reserved the full six voices for climactic or particularly significant words, such as "Et incarnatus est" (and [He] was made incarnate [flesh]).

## Palestrina's Contemporaries

After Palestrina, the most illustrious composers of sacred music at the end of the sixteenth century were the Spanish priest Tomás Luis de Victoria (1548–1611), the cosmopolitan Orlando di Lasso (1532–1594; see also Chapter 7), and the Englishman William Byrd (ca. 1540–1623), who remained a lifelong Catholic even though he worked for the Anglican Church and monarchy. Their compositions—all products of the international musical language of the late Renaissance—share characteristics of Palestrina's polished style, yet each composer is different enough to warrant separate attention here.

Throughout the sixteenth century, a close connection existed between Spanish and Roman composers. Victoria spent two decades in Rome, where he almost certainly knew Palestrina and may have studied with him. Returning to

Victoria

---

**A CLOSER LOOK**   Palestrina's Counterpoint

$P$alestrina's counterpoint conforms in most details with the precepts of Willaert's style as transmitted by Zarlino in *Le istitutioni harmoniche*. The music is written almost entirely in the alla breve measure of ¢, which in the original editions (as in Example 8.4) consists of a downbeat and upbeat of one semibreve each (two half-notes in the transcription of Example 8.3). The independent lines are expected to meet in a full triad on each beat. This convention is broken for suspensions—a contrapuntal device in which a voice, consonant with the other parts on the upbeat, is held through the downbeat while one or more of the other parts forms a dissonance against it; then the suspended voice resolves into a consonance by moving downward by step. This alternation of tension and relaxation—strong dissonance on the downbeat and sweet consonance on the upbeat—more than the recurrence of accented syllables, endows the music with a pendulum-like pulse. Dissonances between beats may occur if the voice that is moving does so in stepwise fashion. Palestrina's only exception to this rule is his use of the cambiata, in which a voice leaps a third down from a dissonance to a consonance instead of approaching it by step. (The term *cambiata* means "exchanged"—that is, a dissonance is exchanged for a consonance.)

*Example 8.4: Contrapuntal analysis of Example 8.3, measures 10–15, Tenors I, II, Basses I, II*

The alternation of consonance and dissonance is clearly evident in Example 8.4, which gives the lowest four voices of Example 8.3, measures 10–15, in their original values. P stands for passing note, S for suspension, and C for cambiata; numbers indicate the dissonant intervals and their resolutions; arrows mark the down- and upbeats.

The smooth diatonic lines and the discreet handling of dissonance give Palestrina's music a consistent serenity and transparency. Another positive quality of his counterpoint lies in the vertical combination of voices. Because the voice groupings and spacings are so varied, the same harmony produces a large number of subtly different shadings and sonorities.

CD 3/40

CD 3/36    CD 1/69

Spain about 1587, he became chaplain to the Empress Maria, for whose funeral services he wrote a famous Requiem Mass in 1603. In the spirit of the Counter-Reformation, he composed sacred music exclusively. Although his style resembles Palestrina's, Victoria infused his music with greater expressive intensity, and he utilized more notes outside the diatonic modes. For example, in his Mass *O magnum mysterium* (O great mystery, NAWM 46b), which is in transposed first mode, the sixth degree is often lowered and the seventh raised, as in the later minor mode.

Like most of Victoria's Masses, this one is a parody Mass based on his own motet, *O magnum mysterium* (Example 8.5 and NAWM 46a), in which the opening motive, with its stark falling and rising fifth imitated downward throughout the entire musical space, conveys the magnitude, wonder, and mystery of Christ's birth. Although this is a more dramatic gesture than any Palestrina would have used, Victoria achieved the same melodic and rhythmic smoothness and suave triadic harmonies as his Roman contemporary.

Lasso

Orlando di Lasso was the last in the long line of sixteenth-century Franco-Flemish composers and perhaps the most international in terms of his career and his compositions. Unlike Palestrina and Victoria, he wrote many secular

*Figure 8.7. El Greco, Burial of the Count of Orgaz, 1586–1588. A contemporary of Victoria, El Greco (1541–1614) was also active in Italy and Spain in the late sixteenth century. His religious paintings are associated with an intensely expressive and visionary style, as in this large canvas, where the burial scene below, with its relatively naturalistic array of contemporary citizens of Toledo, is crowned by a fantastic one, filled with divine elements. Santo Tomé, Toledo.*

*Example 8.5: Tomás Luis de Victoria, motet:* O magnum mysterium

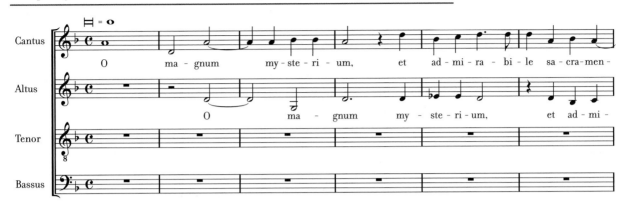

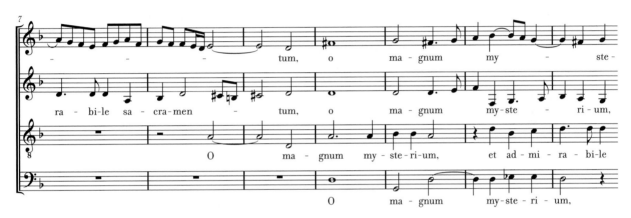

works. By the age of twenty-four, Lasso had already published books of madrigals, chansons, and motets, and his total production eventually amounted to
over two thousand works. Yet he ranks with Palestrina as one of the great composers of sacred music in the late sixteenth century. Whereas Palestrina became
a model of the restrained church style and of strict counterpoint, Lasso was
equally influential as an advocate of emotional and pictorial text expression,
even in sacred music.

Lasso's *Tristis est anima mea* (1565; Sad is my soul, NAWM 47), one of his
most deeply moving and vivid settings, illustrates this approach. The text is
based on the words of Jesus before he was crucified as reported by Matthew
(26:38) and Mark (14:34). The motet's opening (Example 8.6) is a masterful

*Example 8.6: Orlando di Lasso, motet:* Tristis est anima mea

*Figure 8.8.  Orlando di Lasso at the keyboard (a virginal) leading his chamber ensemble in Saint George's Hall at the Munich court of Albrecht V, duke of Bavaria. Shown are three choirboys (in the middle of the group by the virginal, to Lasso's left), about twenty singers, and fifteen instrumentalists. Miniature by Hans Mielich, in a manuscript of Lasso's* Penitential Psalms. *Bayerische StaatsBibliothek, Munich.*

sound image of sadness, expressed by a descending-semitone motive sung to the word "Tristis" (sad), which dominates the first nine measures along with carefully drawn-out suspensions. This use of the suspension to achieve emotional tension rather than to prepare a cadence was common in the madrigal but still rare in sacred music. Later in the motet, there is a lively contrapuntal section to represent the watchful vigilance Jesus demanded of his disciples. At the words "you will take flight," Lasso presents eleven entrances of a running subject to portray the eleven disciples fleeing when Jesus is attacked by the twelfth disciple, Judas, and the mob. The words of the text prompt not only the rhythms, accents, and contours of the motives, but the music's every gesture: harmonic effects, textures, suspensions, points of imitation, and the weight and placement of cadences.

More fully than any other sixteenth-century composer, Lasso synthesized the achievement of an epoch. He was so versatile that we cannot properly speak of a "Lasso style." He was a master of Flemish, French, Italian, and German styles and of every genre from lofty church music to the bawdy secular song. His motets were especially influential, particularly on German Protestant composers. Lasso's creative use of musical devices to convey the emotions and depict the images of his texts led to a strong tradition of such expressive and pictorial motives among German composers, as we will see with Heinrich Schütz (Chapter 9) and Johann Sebastian Bach (Chapter 13).

William Byrd, the most important English composer between Dunstable in the fifteenth century and Henry Purcell in the seventeenth, probably studied music under Thomas Tallis in the royal chapel and was appointed organist of Lincoln Cathedral in 1563. About ten years later he moved to London to take up duties as a member of the royal chapel, a post he held for the rest of his life even while maintaining his allegiance to Rome. In 1575, he and Tallis were granted a monopoly for music printing in England, which he continued to control after Tallis's death in 1585.

In view of the religious situation in England at the time, he understandably wrote only three Masses (one each for three, four, and five voices); yet these are considered the finest Masses by any English composer.

Byrd probably intended his earlier Latin motets for private devotional gatherings of secret Catholics, or recusants, but he designed the later ones, published in two collections (*Gradualia* 1605, 1607), for liturgical use. In the dedication of the first collection, he praised the power of scriptural texts to inspire a composer's imagination:

> I have found there is such a power hidden away and stored up in those words [of Scripture] that—I know not how—to one who meditates on divine

things, pondering them with detailed concentration, all the most fitting melodies come as it were of themselves, and freely present themselves when the mind is alert and eager.

This passage also serves as an eloquent reminder that many Renaissance composers relied on the text as their starting point for musical invention.

# POSTLUDE

*Renaissance, Reformation, Counter-Reformation*—these terms have been used to suggest different aspects of sixteenth-century musical styles and practices. Yet their meanings overlap, and more than one term may be applicable to the same composer. Certainly, their qualities outlived the chronological boundary of the year 1600, which is the convenient but artificial limit usually assigned at least to the Renaissance period. Although our discussion of Renaissance music officially ends with this chapter, the musical characteristics connoted by the word *Renaissance* persisted well into the next century, when Palestrina's style continued to be revered by some as the "absolute perfection" of church music. In retrospect, Palestrina's style became known as the *stile antico*, the "old style," shared by Victoria, Lasso, Byrd, and earlier Renaissance composers such as Josquin and Willaert.

The new musical practices of the Reformation—especially those involving the chorale—had far-reaching consequences for music history: ultimately, they resulted in, among other things, Bach's glorious church cantatas and in his superb harmonizations of the chorales, which still serve as a bible for students of harmony. Finally, the goal of the Counter-Reformation—which had idealized sacred polyphony as a vehicle for drawing "the hearts of the listeners . . . to desire of heavenly harmonies"[1]—was to reconquer the minds and souls of the faithful, bringing them back into the papal fold. This Counter-Reformation attitude, intent on manipulating the senses and the emotions, influenced the new Baroque musical aesthetic, which we will explore next.

1. From a draft of the Council of Trent's recommendation on chuch music.

# PART THREE

# The Seventeenth Century

## PART CONTENTS

**9. VOCAL MUSIC OF THE EARLY BAROQUE 177**

**10. INSTRUMENTAL MUSIC COMES OF AGE 206**

**11. OPERA AND VOCAL MUSIC IN THE LATE SEVENTEENTH CENTURY 222**

**12. INSTRUMENTAL MUSIC IN THE LATE SEVENTEENTH CENTURY 244**

In music history, we invoke the term *Baroque* to describe the period between 1600 and 1750. While the word is sometimes still used in its original, negative sense—"abnormal," "bizarre," "exaggerated," "grotesque"—art critics of the nineteenth century gave it a more positive spin. For them, *Baroque* summed up the delightfully flamboyant, theatrical, and expressive tendencies of seventeenth-century art and architecture. Eventually, the word also embraced poetry and drama, and, finally, music historians followed suit and adopted it in the twentieth century to describe the music of the age. Although we now recognize that a single adjective cannot adequately suggest the many different musical styles in use during these years, there are certainly traits that early seventeenth-century composers share with those in the first half of the eighteenth century. In the following chapters (9 through 12), we will discover the common elements in the music of Monteverdi and Corelli, who flourished at the beginning and end of the period, respectively, as well as in the music of the generations of composers who lived between them. (Bach, arguably the greatest of the Baroque composers, will be examined in Chapter 13.)

# Europe in the Seventeenth Century

**The scientific revolution**

Around the year 1600, Europe was in the midst of a scientific revolution, led by a new breed of investigators who relied on mathematics, observation, and practical experiments, not on received opinion. Johannes Kepler showed in 1609 that the planets, including the earth, move around the sun in elliptical orbits at speeds that vary according to their distance from the sun. During the following decade, Galileo Galilei demonstrated the laws that control motion and used the newly invented telescope to discover sunspots and moons orbiting Jupiter. Sir Francis Bacon argued for an empirical approach to science, relying on direct observation rather than on ancient authorities. Balancing Bacon's inductive method, René Descartes posited a deductive approach that explained the world through mathematics, logic, and reasoning from first principles. These two strands joined in the work of Sir Isaac Newton, whose law of gravitation, developed in the 1660s, combined acute observation with mathematical elegance and set the pattern for scientific methods for centuries to come. The same interest in what is useful and effective, rather than what is hallowed by tradition, is apparent in seventeenth-century music and lay at the heart of the new styles in art and music around 1600, including the second practice (described below) and opera.

**Politics, religion, and war**

The seventeenth century also saw new thinking about politics, ranging from those who advocated democracy in England to those who supported absolute monarchy in France and the divine right of kings like Louis XIV to rule an all-powerful sovereign state. Religious debates sometimes broke out into war; while some long-standing conflicts were resolved, new ones were ignited. In France, Henry IV issued the Edict of Nantes in 1598 guaranteeing some freedom to Protestants while confirming Catholicism as the state religion. Protestant England and Catholic Spain ended decades of war in 1604, and the Calvinist Netherlands gained independence from Spain in 1609 and became a republic. But religious strife between German Protestants and Catholics precipitated the Thirty Years' War (1618–1648), which later included political rivalries among France, Sweden, and Denmark on the one hand, and the Holy Roman Empire and Spain on the other (see Figure III.1). Actually a series of wars, this conflict devastated Germany, reducing the population in some areas by more than half. The English Civil War (1642–1649), primarily a battle for power between the king and Parliament, also had religious aspects. It culminated in the execution of King Charles I (r. 1625–1649) during the Puritan Revolution, led by Oliver Cromwell (1599–1658), who in effect presided over a military dictatorship until the monarchy was restored with the coronation of Charles II in 1660. Italy remained entirely Catholic and thus was spared religious wars, although southern Italians staged an unsuccessful revolt against Spanish domination in mid-century.

**Colonialism**

Meanwhile, Europeans were expanding overseas. During the seventeenth century, the British, French, and Dutch established colonies in North America, the Caribbean, Africa, and Asia in competition with Spain and Portugal. Especially lucrative imports were sugar and tobacco, new luxury items for Europe, grown on plantations in the Americas. These crops required intensive labor provided by the cruel trade in human life that brought Africans to the New World as slaves. Europeans who settled in the Western Hemisphere brought their traditions with them, including Catholic service music and villancicos to the Spanish colonies and Protestant psalm and hymn singing to British North America (see Chapter 23).

**Capitalism**

Britain, the Netherlands, and northern Italy prospered from capitalism, a system in which individuals invested their own money (capital) in businesses

*Figure III.1.   Europe, about 1610.*

designed to return a profit. An important innovation was the joint stock company, which pooled the wealth of many individuals while limiting their risk. These companies were formed to finance opera houses in Hamburg, London, and other cities. By putting money in the hands of individuals to invest or spend locally, capitalism boosted the economy. Among the effects on music were the rise of public opera and public concerts as well as an increased demand from the upper and middle classes for published music, musical instruments, and music lessons. In consequence, instrumental music came of age during the seventeenth century (see Chapters 10 and 12), and new genres of vocal and instrumental chamber music flourished.

Musicians continued to depend on patronage from court, church, or city, and the types of music that won support varied from region to region. Musicians were best off in Italy, which was wealthy from trade yet still dominated by a

Patronage

combination of princely courts: the Spanish presence in the south, Papal States around Rome, and independent states in the north (see Figure III.1 and Figure 12.13). Rulers, cities, and leading families supported music and the arts as a way of competing for prestige. Aristocrats in Florence sponsored a brilliant series of musical and theatrical innovations around 1600, spawning similar efforts by the dukes of Mantua, churchmen in Rome, and the government and citizens of Venice (see Chapter 9). Their support continued Italy's reign as the dominant influence in European music through the mid-eighteenth century.

In France, power and wealth were increasingly concentrated in the monarchy. Louis XIV (r. 1643–1715) controlled the arts, including music, and used them to assert his glory. During the seventeenth century, France replaced Spain as the predominant power on the Continent; partly as a result, French music was widely imitated, while the music of Spain had little presence beyond its borders. Civil war and parliamentary prerogative limited the wealth of the English royalty, but their patronage strongly influenced national tastes. The calamity of the Thirty Years' War sapped treasuries throughout the Holy Roman Empire, but after mid-century, German courts and free city-states built up their musical establishments, drawing on influences from both Italy and France. The Church continued to support music, although its role was less important than it had been in previous centuries.

Along with aristocratic, civic, and ecclesiastical patronage, many cities had "academies," private associations that, among other functions, sponsored musical activities. Public opera houses were established in many cities, beginning in Venice in 1637. Public concerts to which one subscribed or paid admission first occurred in England in 1672, but the practice did not become widespread in Europe until the later 1700s.

## From Renaissance to Baroque

*Figure III.2. Saint Peter's Square and Basilica at the Vatican in Rome, designed by Gian Lorenzo Bernini in 1657.*

The seventeenth century was the Golden Age of European drama, beginning with William Shakespeare (1564–1616) and ending with the great French tragedian Jean Racine (1639–1699). But it was also an age in which the collaboration of theater with painting and music culminated in the invention of opera, a new theatrical genre that became the art form par excellence of Baroque Europe. At the same time, painting and sculpture became intensely and explicitly theatrical in their own right; along with music, they shared in the theater's immediacy, attempting to function as a kind of show, a *rappresentazione*, designed to move and impress an audience. Even the literature of the time often had theatrical qualities (see vignette on page 168), and vivid images in the poems of Giambattista Marino and John Donne, as well as dramatic scenes in the epic *Paradise Lost* by John Milton and the novel *Don Quixote* by the Spaniard Miguel de Cervantes at times suggest the power of a staged performance.

In art and architecture, as in music, the Baroque began in Italy. Rome provided the stage for Gian Lorenzo Bernini, the outstanding

## TIMELINE  The Seventeenth Century

| MUSICAL EVENTS | HISTORICAL EVENTS |
|---|---|
| | **1590** Guarini's pastoral drama *Il pastor fido* |
| | **1598** Henri IV issues Edict of Nantes |
| Artusi attacks Monteverdi in print; **1600** first surviving opera performed in Florence | |
| | **1602** Dutch East India Company chartered |
| Monteverdi, *Fifth Book of Madrigals*, with *Cruda Amarilli* **1605** | |
| | **1607** First English colony in Virginia at Jamestown |
| | **1609** Kepler sets forth his astronomical laws |
| | **1610** Galileo publishes *Starry Messenger,* with observations of Jupiter's moons |

Galileo's telescope

Gesualdo's last book of madrigals **1611**

| | **1616** Death of Shakespeare |
| | **1618–1648** Thirty Years' War |
| | **1620** Artemisia Gentileschi, *Judith Slaying Holofernes;* Bacon, *New Instruments* |
| | **1623** Bernini, *David* |
| | **1632** Galileo charged with heresy for claiming the Earth revolves around the sun |

Gentileschi, *Young Woman with a Violin*

First public opera house opens in Venice **1637**    **1637** Descartes, *Discourse on Method*

**1642–1649** English Civil War
**1643–1715** Reign of Louis XIV in France
**1645–1652** Bernini, *Ecstasy of Saint Teresa*

Bernini, *Ecstasy of Saint Theresa*

**1667** Milton, *Paradise Lost*
**1669** Death of Rembrandt

**1677** Racine, *Phèdre*

Hamburg opera house opens **1678**
Scarlatti's first opera in Rome **1679**

Lully, *Armide* **1686**

**1687** Newton, *Principia mathematica*

Rembrandt, self-portrait with turban

Purcell, *Dido and Aeneas* **1689**

sculptor of the century. In addition to Saint Peter's Basilica (Figure III.2) and fountains, piazzas, and sculpture all over the city, he designed a stunning chapel for one of his Roman patrons, for which he fashioned a sculptural group of Saint Teresa in Ecstasy (see Figure 9.11), positioning it as though it were a theatrical performance (see page 200). Contrasting Michelangelo's famous statue of David from the early sixteenth century (Figure III.3) with Bernini's *David* of about 1620 (Figure III.4) shows the difference between Renaissance and Baroque artistic goals. Michelangelo evoked ancient Greek statuary with his standing nude, celebrated the nobility and beauty of the human figure through balance and proportion, and portrayed his hero as contemplative and still, with only a furrowed brow to suggest the coming battle with Goliath. Bernini captures David as he winds up to sling the stone, his body expressing dynamic action, his muscles taut, his lips and face tense with exertion. The effect is dramatic, making the viewer respond emotionally rather than with detached admiration.

The affections

Expressing emotion was at the core of the Baroque aesthetic, and emotion was a function of motion. The dynamic movement so characteristic of the art of the seventeenth century and the active bass lines so typical of its music are closely linked to the theory of the affections, a concept that empowered all the arts of this period. The affections—emotions such as sorrow, joy, anger, love, fear, excitement, or wonder—were believed to be relatively stable states of the soul, each caused by a certain combination of spirits, or "humors," in the body. According to Descartes, once these spirits were set in motion by external stimuli via the senses, they then conveyed their motions to the soul, thus bringing about specific emotions. His treatise *The Passions of the Soul* (1645–1646), an attempt to analyze and catalogue the affections, posited a simple mechanical theory to explain their cause: for every action in the physical universe there is an equal and opposite reaction, and for every motion stimulating the senses there

---

**VIGNETTE** The Dramatization of Poetry

Baroque theatricality infused poetry as well as art and music. The poem below uses the image of the poet as a fortified city attacked by the enemy, Love. Written by Giulio Strozzi (1583–1652) and set by Claudio Monteverdi in his Eighth Book of Madrigals (1638), the poem is witty in its theatricality: as the crisis grows more intense, the protagonist shouts (at the end of each verse) to his imagined companions.

〜

The insidious enemy, Love, circles
The fortress of my heart.
Hurry up, for he is not far away.
Arm yourselves!

We must not let him approach, so he can scale
Our weak walls,
But let us make a brave sally out to meet him.
Throw on the saddles!

His weapons are no fakes, he draws nearer
With his whole army.
Hurry up, for he is not far from here.
Everyone to his post!

He intends to attack the stronghold of my eyes
With a vigorous assault.
Hurry up, for he is here without any doubt.
Everyone to his horse!

There's no more time, alas, for all of a sudden he
Has made himself the master of my heart.
Take to your heels, save yourselves if you can.
Run!

My heart, you flee in vain, you are dead.
And I hear the arrogant tyrant,
The victor, who is already inside the fortress,
Crying "Fire, slaughter!"

Giulio Strozzi, *Gira il nemico insidioso*.

*Figure III.3 (left).* **Michelangelo's** David *(1501–1504), which evokes ancient Greek statuary and illustrates the ideals of Renaissance human-ism, including nobility, balance, and calm.*

*Figure III.4 (right).* **Bernini's** David *(ca. 1620), embodying the dramatic and Baroque qualities of motion and emotion. Galleria Borghese, Rome.*

is a specific emotion evoked in the soul. Action and reaction, motion and emo-tion—these concepts underlie the basic imperative of the sister arts in this pe-riod and help to explain their goal: to move the emotions and conjure the passions, or affections, in the soul.

In an essay on expression in painting, French painter and designer Charles Le Brun (1619–1690) portrayed and labeled an entire gallery of emotions and their corresponding facial gestures to serve as examples for artists (Figure III.5). In similar fashion, composers of opera displayed a musical gallery of emotions in writing a series of arias in every act, each for a particular character

*Figure III.5. Charles Le Brun (1619–1690), who dominated seventeenth-century French painting as head of the Royal Academy of Painting and Sculpture, drew these facial expressions illustrating various emotional reactions such as alarm, fear, anger, hope, sorrow, and so forth. They were published at the end of the century as "Method for Learning How to Draw the Passions" in his* Conférence . . . sur l'expression générale et particulière *(Amsterdam and Paris, 1698). Writers about music made similar attempts to isolate and catalogue the passions.*

# ARTS *and* IDEAS

## Science and Philosphy

**Francis Bacon** (1561–1626), English philosopher, statesman, and essayist, wished to be known as a "second Aristotle." His most important writings (*The Advancement of Learning* and *New Instruments,* 1620, published in Latin) opposed Scholastic thinking and reasoning from authority, arguing instead for clarity of observation and firsthand scientific experiment and philosophic investigation.

German astronomer **Johannes Kepler** (1571–1630) helped to establish the validity of the sun-centered Copernican system by his application of the laws of physics to the motion of heavenly bodies. His *Commentaries on the Motion of Mars* and *Harmony of the Worlds* were published in 1609 and 1619, respectively.

**Galileo Galilei** (1564–1642), the Italian astronomer, physicist, and philosopher known simply as Galileo, was the son of humanist musician and theorist Vincenzo Galilei (see Chapter 9), whose interest in the mathematics of tuning systems helped to inspire his son's career. A staunch advocate of Copernicus, Galileo was harassed and denounced by the Church after publishing his *Dialogue on the Great World Systems* (the first scientific treatise written in Italian, 1632), although he was acclaimed and revered in other circles, as much for his accomplishments in physics and mathematics as for his astronomical theories.

**René Descartes** (1590–1650), French mathematician and philosopher, divided the universe into mutually exclusive but interacting spirit and matter, the spirit being subject to reason and the matter being subject to mechanical laws. His treatise *The Passions of the Soul* (1650) helps to explain the Baroque theory of the affections (see below). In *Discourse on Method* (1639), he subjected all received opinions to his challenge of "methodical doubt," arguing from the principle *Cogito, ergo sum* ("I think, therefore I am"), which he held to be a model of certainty. (See Figure 12.14.)

The "Einstein of his day," **Isaac Newton** (1642–1727) was an English mathematician and natural philosopher whose accomplishments include laying the foundation for modern calculus, discovering the composition of light, and developing the law of universal gravitation. His major work, *Principia mathematica* (1687), which presented his method of reasoning from physical events, signified the beginning of a new era of scientific investigation.

## Literature

Italian author **Giambattista Guarini** (1538–1612) was the poet most responsible for the pastoral vogue that swept Europe in the seventeenth century. His famous verse play *Il pastor fido* (The Faithful Shepherd) inaugurated the hybrid literary genre of tragicomedy. Its lyrics provided the text for hundreds of madrigal settings, and its dramatic action took the first steps toward opera.

As a soldier, Spanish author **Miguel de Cervantes** (1547–1616) fought in several battles, was captured by Turks, and was ransomed from slavery in Algiers. His taste for adventure informs his greatest work, *Don Quixote* (in two parts, 1605 and 1615), in which he portrays the interaction between the visionary idealist (the title character) and the undisguised realist (the squire Sancho Panza), and details their fantastic misadventures. Overflowing with vitality, the work won immediate success in Spain and was quickly translated into English, French, and Italian, which helps explain its enormous influence on the modern novel.

**Giambattista Marino** (also Marini, 1569–1625) wrote the epic romance *L'Adone* (1623) on the loves of Venus and Adonis. His rich, sensuous, imagistic language substitutes excitement and wonder for the more moderate styles of Renaissance poets. His delight in bizarre subjects and ostentatious virtuosity, which aims to overwhelm the reader, set the tone for the literary Baroque.

The English Metaphysical poet **John Donne** (1572–1631) early in his career wrote love poetry characterized by a highly personal tone and, later, religious poems of great intellectual power and deep learning that are obsessed with death and a yearning for immortality (examples are the sonnets "Death Be Not Proud" and "Batter My Heart"). His interest in the theme of the paradoxical human union of spirit and matter marks him as a writer of the Baroque age.

Creator of the classic French farce, **Molière** (Jean-Baptiste Poquelin, 1622–1673) established and starred in his own acting troupe, which became a favorite at court. His plays—among them *The Bourgeois Gentleman, The Wise Women, The Phony Doctor,* and *The Hypochondriac* (a role he was playing, ironically, when he died)—wittily satirize human behavior and often feature conflict between the sexes or social classes and rivalry between young and old. (See Figure 11.8.)

**John Milton** (1608–1674), English poet, writer, and supporter of the Puritan cause against the monarchy, as well as a humanist and lover of music and literature (author of the masque *Comus*), is one of the most respected figures in English literature. His masterpiece *Paradise Lost* (1667), a national epic in twelve books, followed by *Paradise Regained* (1671), explores themes of temptation and sin.

French dramatist **Jean Racine** (1639–1699) specialized in tragedies of passion in which his characters, many of whom became subjects of opera, are portrayed with unrivaled psychological depth. His plays (including *Iphigénie, Phèdre,* and *Athalie*) adhere to classical values and explore moral issues with subjects such as revenge, jealousy, the agony of guilt, and the renunciation of love for duty.

## Art

The foremost Flemish painter of the seventeenth century, **Peter Paul Rubens** (1577–1640) spent his apprentice years in Italy, where he learned the newest techniques of color, light, and shade. Back in Antwerp, his reputation flourished, and he received commissions from the French court as well as from British and Spanish royalty. He mastered all genres, including portrait, landscape, religious, history, and allegory, and his work was championed by the "moderns" in part because of its use of the visual to appeal to the emotions. (See Figure III.9.)

**Artemisia Gentileschi** (1593–ca. 1653), Tuscan painter and pupil of her father, Orazio, was the first Italian woman whose accomplishments not only were praised by her contemporaries but also influenced other artists. She worked in Rome, Florence, Genoa, and Naples, and refused to limit herself to the genres of portraiture and devotional pictures deemed suitable for women, also tackling powerful historical subjects. (See Figure III.6.)

Considered by his contemporaries the greatest of living painters, **Nicolas Poussin** (1594–1665), although French, spent most of his time in Rome surrounded by ancient art, which he emulated in his own work. His methods became the basis of French classical art and were taught at the French Academy of Painting and Sculpture, established in Paris in 1648. His work was intended to appeal to reason and intellect, rather than arousing a response through the senses. (See Figures III.8 and 12.7.)

Appointed architect of Saint Peter's church in 1629, **Gian Lorenzo Bernini** (1598–1680) left his mark especially on modern Rome by virtue of the commissions he received from cardinals and popes to design churches, chapels, fountains, monuments, tombs, and statues. The astonishing virtuosity of his marble works, characterized by their semblance of exuberant motion and dramatic action, makes him the dominant figure of the Italian Baroque. (See Figures III.2 and III.4 as well as Figure 9.11.)

**Diego Velázquez** (1599–1660), the most celebrated Spanish painter of the seventeenth century, enjoyed the close friendship of King Philip IV, who appointed him to positions at court—including administrator of the royal galleries—that often interfered with his freedom to paint. His subtle portraits of the royal family and other members of the court combine a deep psychological intensity with a serene sense of dignity, and his treatment of more ordinary subjects illustrates his interest in naturalism. (See Figure III.7.)

The greatest master among Dutch artists of the time, **Rembrandt van Rijn** (1606–1669) was renowned as the painter, etcher, and draftsman of a prodigious number of works. His use of dramatic contrasts of light and shade, and the warm brown and gold hues of his canvases reveal the influence of Italian painters. But the greatest appeal of his work lies in its profound humanity, notable in his frequent portraits of the old and the poor.

**Jan Vermeer** (1632–1675), a Dutch genre and landscape painter, was unusual among Baroque artists in making stillness an expressive virtue. He never left his native Delft and enjoyed only slight recognition during his short life. What distinguished him from contemporaries was his mastery of shimmering colors and textures, and his representation of reflected light, as well as his meticulous attention to detail. (See Figure 12.8.)

and situation on stage, seeking to render a psychological portrait of that character aroused by a certain emotion. By imitating the emotion in musical gestures—melodic and rhythmic motives—the composer expected to cause the listener to experience the corresponding affection.

**Importance of the senses**

Such theories were reinforced by the scientific discoveries of the era. Galileo's observations through the telescope and his experiments with the laws of motion had demonstrated that the senses as well as reason were instruments of learning. Placed in the service of human knowledge, then, the eyes and ears could be conduits through which to influence emotions and behavior. Giambattista Marino, perhaps the most influential poet of the early seventeenth century, eloquently described the new roles of painting and poetry in this way: "[Painting] imitates chiefly the external, that is, the features of the body, [poetry] the internal, that is, the affections of the soul; one causes us almost to understand with the senses, the other to feel with the intellect." This new respect for the senses helps to explain the reason for the seemingly trivial debates that raged in the seventeenth century over such matters as whether design or color in painting was the more important element in representing a subject convincingly, or whether composers were justified in using dissonance more freely than their predecessors in order to express the words more forcefully (see below). These were meaningful issues if the goal of stirring the affections was to be achieved.

**Action and reaction, motion and emotion**

Like the sculptor Bernini, painters of the period frequently concentrated on subjects involving physical action and psychological reaction. For example, Artemisia Gentileschi's powerful work *Judith Slaying Holofernes* (ca. 1620, Figure III.6) depicts the biblical heroine *in the act* of decapitating her victim at the same time as she recoils in disgust from his gushing blood. The first operas were also tellingly about a single significant action—often merely narrated—and the reaction it prompted, such as Orpheus's response to the death of Eurydice.

*Figure III.6. Artemisia Gentileschi,* Judith Slaying Holofernes, *ca. 1620. The painting, a depiction of both violent action and psychological reaction, reveals the essential theatricality of Baroque art. Galeria degli Uffizi, Florence.*

*Figure III.7.   Diego Velázquez (1599–1660), Three Musicians, ca. 1618, from among his works that portray a world of subheroic characters—in this case, a boy holding a guitar, a blind vihuela player, and a violinist. Note the monkey behind the boy's back—a symbol of baseness or ignorance.*

In music, a motion intended to represent and ultimately stimulate an emotion could be encoded in many ways, the most obvious being by means of rhythm. This was the principle behind Monteverdi's *concitato genere* ("excited style"; see page 195) and the relentless motion of a Baroque ostinato bass pattern, such as the doleful descending tetrachord that eloquently imitates the drooping gesture of sorrow (see below, pages 196–197, and the laments presented in NAWM 58, 69, 71b and 79b).

In seeking to move the affections, painting in the Baroque period did not always aspire to be beautiful. Among the many artists influenced by the kind of naturalism characteristic of Bernini and Gentileschi was the court painter Diego Velázquez. He not only produced intimate portraits of the Spanish royal family but also, like some of his Dutch contemporaries, chronicled a subheroic world of vernacular experience, of humble subjects pursuing ordinary activities (Figure III.7). Many of the paintings by the Dutch master Jan Vermeer include musical instruments, perhaps as a sign of affluence and leisure or as an allusion to love and courtship, or perhaps merely to represent the power of the sense of hearing (see Figure 12.8). In the seventeenth century, Dutch painting also experienced a golden age; and for the sheer power of his naturalistic detail, Rembrandt stands out among his peers. Just as in music Monteverdi broke the rules of counterpoint in order to make certain dissonances acceptable for expressive purposes, disturbing the smooth surface of the texture with crude "imperfections" (see below), so, too, Rembrandt—by choosing models from among the most ordinary and coarse specimens of humanity and daring to show them as they were, sometimes marred by warts and wrinkles (as in his own self-portraits)—made physical imperfection acceptable in art.

CD 4/1    CD 2/23

CD 4/51

CD 5/2

CD 5/40    CD 3/7

Naturalism

# The Musical Baroque

Along with painting and poetry, music became one of the sister arts when it allied itself inseparably with words during the Renaissance. As a sister art, then, it participated in both theory and practice in the various aesthetic dialogues or debates that characterize the seventeenth century. Chief among these was the quarrel between the "ancients" and the "moderns," or between conservatives and innovators. For example, in painting, particularly in France, the traditionalists upheld the superiority of design (or drawing) over color and championed the artist Nicolas Poussin, who modeled the figures in his canvases after antique sculpture (Figure III.8) The partisans of color, the modernists, rallied around Peter Paul Rubens, questioning the supremacy of ancient sculpture and arguing that color, light, and shade could produce a more compelling imitation of nature than could drawing alone (Figure III.9).

At the heart of the debate between the conservatives and moderns in music was the subject of text expression. With the publication of Claudio Monteverdi's *Fifth Book of Madrigals* in 1605, the composer distinguished between a *prima pratica* and a *seconda pratica*, or a first and second "practice," or compositional method. By the first, he meant the received rules of counterpoint, the style of vocal polyphony codified by Zarlino in the mid-sixteenth century and cultivated by Palestrina. By the second, Monteverdi meant the adventurous style of the modern Italians such as Rore, Marenzio, and himself. In the first practice, according to Monteverdi, the musical values prevailed over the words, while in the second practice the text dominated and dictated its musical setting. Just as the advocates of color over design in painting thought they could achieve a more convincing representation of nature, Monteverdi believed that his modern (second) practice—with its use of unorthodox dissonances and unexpected harmonic progressions (see Chapter 9)—would make his music more affecting.

**Classifications**

The 1600s was a century of classifications—of naming and ordering everything from the passions of the soul (as in Descartes' treatise, discussed above)

*Figure III.8. Nicolas Poussin (1594–1665), The Rape of the Sabine Women, ca. 1635–1640. An advocate of drawing and formal design, and, therefore, a believer in the primacy of line over color, Poussin went so far as to fashion miniature statues in clay, arranging them in three-dimensional dioramas in preparation for painting his history canvases. Musée du Louvre, Paris.*

to the various musical styles and functions that emerged early in the century. Although not a theorist, Monteverdi enumerated a staggering array of options available to the composer: first and second practices (roughly equivalent to *stile antico* and *stile moderno*, or old and new compositional methods); distinct musical languages appropriate to music's differing functions—church, chamber, theater, and dance; styles implying categories or types of affections—relaxed, moderate, or excited; and more. The century witnessed similar tendencies in instrumental music, too: the ordering of dances into suites and suites into tonal cycles; the symmetrical arrangement of movements (slow–fast–slow–fast) into sonatas and the grouping of sonatas into collections for church or chamber (see Arcangelo Corelli's works in Chapter 12). There were centripetal forces that held pieces together, such as ostinato basses, underlying harmonic patterns, recurring tutti sections; and centrifugal forces that pushed them apart, such as the improvisational impulse behind a stream of fantasy-like sections of a toccata or the expansion of such divergent sections into separate, contrasting movements. Eventually, these became codified into pairs of contrasting pieces: prelude and fugue, allemande and courante, recitative and aria.

The tension between order and disorder, control and freedom, is also mirrored in the architectural forms of the century. On the one hand, in the façade and formal gardens of the royal palace of Versailles may be seen the rhythm and order of classicism, with its symmetrically positioned forms and repetitive, fixed modules (see Figure III.10). On the other hand, the plan of one of the Baroque churches (see Figure III.11) designed by Bernini's colleague in Rome, the architect Francesco Borromini (1599–1667), is a complex structure of asymmetrical, irregular shapes that are neither cross, octagon, oval, nor rectangle. This duality between control and freedom also appeared in England, where the playwright Ben Jonson wrote both court masques and antimasques. The masques were musical plays that portrayed a world of ideal abstractions, whereas antimasques were antic or grotesque interludes that introduced disintegrating forces and resorted to comedy and satire. Antimasque elements continued to influence the English stage, as the witches in Henry Purcell's opera

Order and disorder

*Figure III.9.  Detail from Peter Paul Rubens (1577–1640),* The Rape of the Sabine Women, *ca. 1635–1640. Of Flemish origin, Rubens achieved enormous success as both painter and diplomat at the courts of Italy, the Netherlands, England, and Spain. The followers of Rubens challenged the supremacy of ancient sculpture and argued in favor of color, light, and shade, which they believed could produce a more convincing imitation of nature than could drawing alone. National Gallery, London.*

*Figure III.10. Garden façade of the palace of Versailles, built 1661–1690. The columns and arches echo classical architecture, and the mythological statuary throughout the building and grounds reinforce the links that Louis XIV sought to make between his reign and Greek and Roman civilization.*

*Dido and Aeneas* (1689) attest (see Chapter 11). Indeed, in most Baroque music there is a constant creative tension between control and freedom or between composition and improvisation.

It was in the very nature of Baroque expression to place the arts on an equal footing as valid interpreters of human experience and to foster their association in seventeenth-century Europe. Their combined powers—such as the sculpture, architecture, and lighting brought together in Bernini's chapel (Figure 9.11), or the music, poetry, and theater synthesized in a Monteverdi opera (see Chapter 9)—immeasurably enhanced their individual effect. All the arts in the seventeenth century sought to move the affections, and that goal licensed painters, sculptors, poets, and musicians to transcend previously established limits in order to imitate and penetrate the invisible realm of the soul.

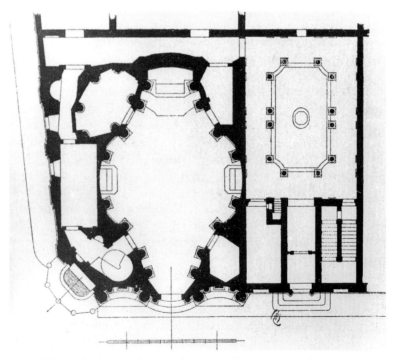

*Figure III.11. Francesco Borromini's plan for San Carlo alle Quattro Fontane, Rome, begun 1638, revealing the basic irregularity of Baroque design.*

# Vocal Music of the
# Early Baroque

*Chapter Contents*

*Prelude* 177

General
Characteristics of
Baroque Music 178

Early Opera 183

Vocal Chamber
Music 194

Catholic Sacred
Music 199

Lutheran Church
Music 202

*Postlude* 205

## PRELUDE

As with other epochs, boundary dates for the Baroque period are only approximations. Many general characteristics of Baroque music appeared before 1600, and many were declining by the 1730s. But within the chronological limits of 1600 to 1750, composers accepted an innovative set of conventions for organizing music and adopted certain ideas about how music should sound. Most important, they believed that music, by acting on the emotions, should move the listener.

Italian musicians living around 1600 knew they were inventing new ways of making music. They devised new idioms, such as basso continuo, monody, and recitative; new styles, marked by unprepared dissonance, greater focus on the solo voice or instrument directed by a supporting bass line; and new genres, including opera. This generation saw the most deliberate cultivation of the new in music since the Ars nova in the early 1300s (see Chapter 4).

Italian trends continued to dominate musical fashions during the seventeenth and early eighteenth centuries, and by 1750 the international language of European music had acquired a distinct Italian accent. Despite its political fragmentation, Italy remained the most influential region of Europe in musical matters during this period. Several Italian cities loomed disproportionately larger on the musical map than their real size or political power suggested. Florence, for example, hosted a brilliant period of musico-theatrical innovation at the dawn of the seventeenth century that led to the flowering of early opera. Rome continued to influence sacred music and for a time became an important center of opera, several types of vocal chamber music, and instrumental music. Venice, a leading musical city throughout the seventeenth century, nurtured the development of opera, as did Naples in the eighteenth century. Generations of composers centered at Saint Mark's church in Venice wielded a mighty influence on Baroque choral and instrumental music as well.

The religious differences that had separated northern Protestant Europe from the Catholic south in the sixteenth century continued to echo in seventeenth-century music. Several new genres of sacred music emerged, such as the sacred vocal concerto and the oratorio; these were cultivated both in southern Europe, where Catholic sacred music flourished, and in northern Europe,

**VIGNETTE** Monteverdi's Reply to Artusi, 1605

*In his* Fifth Book of Madrigals *(1605), Monteverdi included a brief preface asserting that there is a "different way" of treating consonance and dissonance in his modern second practice. Here the composer sought to defend his work against the criticisms of Artusi, who championed the older, or first, contrapuntal practice. In response to Artusi, Monteverdi deliberately gave the offending work,* Cruda Amarilli *(NAWM 63), primacy of place in the collection. Two years later, his brother Giulio Cesare further explained that in the second practice the music serves the expression of the text rather than following its own rules as taught by Zarlino in the first practice. The text was the "mistress of the harmony," the dominant factor in the partnership of words and music, and, therefore, the one that called the tune.*

~~~

Don't be surprised that I am giving these madrigals to the press without first replying to the objections that Artusi made against some very minute portions of them. Being in the service of His Serene Highness of Mantua, I am not master of the time I would require. Nevertheless I wrote a reply to let it be known that I do not do things by chance, and as soon as it is rewritten it will see the light under the title, *Seconda pratica overo Perfettione della moderna musica* [Second Practice, or the Perfection of Modern Music]. Some will wonder at this, not believing that there is any other practice than that taught by Zarlino. But let them be assured concerning consonances and dissonances that there is a different way of considering them from that already determined, which defends the modern manner of composition with the assent of the reason and the senses. I wanted to say this both so that the expression *seconda pratica* would not be appropriated by others and so that men of intellect might meanwhile consider other second thoughts concerning harmony. And have faith that the modern composer builds on foundations of truth.

Live happily.

C. V. Palisca, "The Artusi-Monteverdi Controversy," in *The New Monteverdi Companion*, ed. Denis Arnold and Nigel Fortune (London: Faber & Faber, 1985), pp. 151–152.

where Lutheran church music spread through German-speaking lands and Scandinavia. Throughout Europe, instrumental music found its place in both religious and secular circles, expanding on genres that had their beginnings in the sixteenth century. This development will be explored in the next chapter, although many of the general characteristics of Baroque music discussed here pertain to instrumental music as well.

The changes occurring in intellectual and artistic realms profoundly influenced the course of music history. While seventeenth-century thinkers discarded outmoded ways of viewing the world and proposed new explanations, musicians expanded their vocabulary to meet new expressive needs. As scientists such as Galileo and Newton developed new ideas within the framework of older methods, so composers—such as Claudio Monteverdi in his madrigals and Heinrich Schütz in his motets—poured more intense and more varied emotions into the musical genres they inherited from the Renaissance. Much early seventeenth-century music was truly experimental; but by the middle of the century, the new resources of harmony, tone color, and form had created a common language with a clear vocabulary, grammar, and syntax.

## General Characteristics of Baroque Music

Baroque composers were united in a common goal: to express or represent a wide range of feelings vividly and vigorously, continuing the efforts begun in the late sixteenth-century madrigal. They sought musical means to express or arouse the affections. Rather than express their personal feelings, composers, like painters, wanted to represent human emotions in a generic sense.

The second practice

One tool for expression was the use of dissonance, for which there were established rules. As we have mentioned, Claudio Monteverdi (1567–1643; see biography and Figure 9.5) referred to these as part of the first practice, the compositional method that prevailed in the sixteenth century. By deliberately breaking the rules governing the handling of dissonance, as he did in some of the madrigals in his *Fifth Book*, Monteverdi sought to express the text more forcefully, inaugurating what he later called a new, second practice, better suited to moving the affections. The madrigal *Cruda Amarilli* (Cruel Amaryllis, NAWM 63) is a good example. To dramatize the harsh sound and meaning of the opening words, Monteverdi "incorrectly" introduced and resolved dissonances in measures 2 and 6, both in the bass and the upper voices (see Example 9.1, where the offending notes are marked with an asterisk). Similarly, at "ahi lasso" (alas), the canto sings a descending phrase, imitative of a sigh, in which two successive notes create unprepared dissonances with the bass.

CD 4/23   CD 2/35

*Example 9.1: Claudio Monteverdi,* Cruda Amarilli

*Cruel Amaryllis, who with your very name*
*[teach bitterly] of love, alas . . .*

*Figure 9.1. A theorbo, a type of lute with long, unstopped bass strings, often used to accompany singers. The alternate Italian name, chitarrone (large kithara), reflects Italians' interest in ancient Greek music. The instrument's first known appearance was in the Florentine intermedi of 1589 (see page 183), whose theme was the power of Greek music; the theorbo may have been invented for the occasion. Detail from* The Five Senses *by Theodoor Rombouts, ca. 1630. Museum voor Schone Kunsten, Ghent.*

Basso continuo

Although *Cruda Amarilli* was not printed until 1605, the year of publication of Monteverdi's *Fifth Book of Madrigals*, it must already have been in circulation before 1600. In that year, Giovanni Maria Artusi published his scathing commentary, *L'Artusi overo delle imperfettioni della moderna musica* (The Artusi; or, Concerning the Imperfections of Modern Music), which vehemently criticized Monteverdi for the grating dissonances and contrapuntal liberties in this and other madrigals in the *Fifth Book*. Monteverdi defended himself in a brief response (see vignette, page 178), justifying his new practice on the grounds that expressing the text through striking musical means was more important than following the traditionl rules of counterpoint.

In contrast to the rhythmically unvaried flow of Renaissance polyphony, music during the Baroque period was either very free or very metric. Composers used flexible, speechlike rhythms for vocal recitative (see below) and for improvisatory solo instrumental pieces like toccatas and preludes (see Chapter 10). For other music they deployed regular rhythms, such as those found in dances, that were conventional ways to arouse a particular affection. Bar lines became common for the first time (see Figure 9.3) and eventually indicated recurring patterns of strong and weak beats. Along with the active bass lines and propulsive harmonic motion of much Baroque music, the pervasiveness of these rhythmic patterns parallels the dynamic movement so characteristic of the painting and sculpture of the seventeenth century. The two types of rhythm, flexible and metric, were often used in succession to provide contrast, as we will discover in the pairing of recitative and aria or toccata and fugue.

The prevailing texture of Renaissance music is a polyphony of independent voices, all similar in motion and nearly equal in importance. By contrast, the new texture of seventeenth-century music is homophonic, typically consisting of a firm bass and a florid treble, held together by unobtrusive harmonies. A single melody line supported by accompanying parts was not in itself new—something like it appears in earlier vocal genres and was frequently used, for example, in the performance of sixteenth-century chansons and madrigals (see Chapter 7, "In Performance," page 142). What was new around 1600 was the contrast between bass and treble that emphasized the two essential lines of the texture and subordinated the inner parts. Significantly, when three voices were used, a second treble line was introduced, further highlighting the contrast between top and bottom.

Related to this polarity between treble and bass was the system of notation called *thorough bass* or *basso continuo* (Italian for "continuous bass"). In this system, the composer wrote only the melody and bass, leaving it to the performers to fill in the appropriate chords or inner parts. Moreover, the notation appeared in score format rather than in parts, which gave music an entirely new look on the page, as shown in Figure 9.3. The bass and chords were played on one or more continuo instruments, typically harpsichord, organ, lute, or theorbo—a large lute with extra bass strings, also called a chitarrone (see Figure 9.1). By the later seventeenth century, the bass line was frequently reinforced by a viola da gamba, cello, bassoon, or other bass instrument that could sustain tones. When the chords to be played were other than common triads in root position, or if nonchord tones (such as suspensions) or accidentals were needed, the composer usually added figures—numbers or flat or sharp signs—above or below the bass notes to indicate the precise pitches required, as in Figure 9.3. Such a bass line is called a *figured bass*. The realization—the actual playing—of such an accompaniment varied according to the type of piece and the skill and taste of the player, who had considerable room for improvisation (see "In Performance," page 182).

Not all pieces used basso continuo; because its purpose was accompaniment, it was unnecessary in solo lute and keyboard music. Then too, old-style unaccompanied motets and madrigals were sometimes published with a continuo part, to conform with the new practice.

Another reason the texture of Baroque music sounds different from that of the Renaissance is that seventeenth-century composers frequently combined voices with instruments, assigning different roles to each, in contrast to the sixteenth-century preference for homogeneous ensembles. The result was the concertato medium (from Italian *concertare*, "to reach agreement"). In a musical concerto, contrasting forces are brought together in a harmonious ensemble. Today we think of concertos as pieces for soloists and orchestra, but the meaning was broader in the seventeenth century, embracing such genres as the concerted madrigal for one or more voices and continuo, and the sacred concerto, a sacred vocal work with instruments.

Basso-continuo composition led naturally to thinking of consonant sounds as vertical entities or chords rather than as discrete intervals over the bass. This notion, in turn, allowed a dissonance to be viewed less as an interval between two voices than as a note that does not fit into a chord. As a result, a greater variety of intervals was tolerated. Many remained ornamental and experimental, but by the mid-seventeenth century, conventions governed how they could be introduced and resolved. Chromaticism followed a similar development, from experimentation around the turn of the century to freedom within an orderly scheme by mid-century. Chromaticism was used especially to express intense emotions in vocal works, to suggest harmonic exploration in instrumental pieces, and to create distinctive subjects for treatment in imitative counterpoint.

While the features described above tend to characterize the entire Baroque period, one aspect of music that did change is harmonic organization. Musicians in the early seventeenth century still thought of themselves as working within the system of church modes, but they considered these to belong to one of two large affective areas, known as *cantus mollis* and *cantus durus* (literally, "soft song" and "hard song"). The first was indicated by a key signature of one flat and used chords belonging to the flatter regions of the tonal spectrum; it was deemed appropriate for the expression of subdued and pleasant emotions. The other had a key signature of no sharps or flats, and its harmonies explored the sharper regions (using accidentals where necessary); its language was reserved for harsher and more strident emotions. By the last third of the century, however, Corelli, Lully, and other composers were writing music that today we would unhesitatingly call tonal, operating within the system of major and minor keys familiar from music of the eighteenth and nineteenth centuries. But it wasn't until 1722 that Rameau's *Treatise on Harmony* offered the first complete theoretical formulation of the new system, which by then had existed in practice for over half a century.

Like the Renaissance version of the modal system, then, tonality evolved gradually. The long-standing use of certain techniques—standard cadential progressions, bass movement by a fourth or fifth, conventional bass patterns, the use of suspensions and other dissonances to create forward motion— eventually bred a consistent set of procedures that could be codified in a theory. Although early Baroque works often point toward a tonal center, the mere

The concertato medium

Chords and dissonance

Chromaticism

Cantus mollis and durus

Tonality

presence of such techniques did not yet mean that the works were tonal. Still, the figured bass was important in the development of tonality because its notation drew attention to the succession of chords. Indeed, figured bass became the link between counterpoint and homophony, bridging the gap between a linear-melodic concept of musical structure and a chordal-harmonic one.

---

**IN PERFORMANCE**    Realizing the Basso Continuo

---

The ability to realize a figured bass at sight is expected of any accompanist of Baroque music and requires considerable skill in improvisation. The performer might play only chords or add passing tones or melodic motives that echo ideas appearing in the treble or bass parts. Example 9.2 shows two possible realizations of the opening phrase of Caccini's madrigal for solo voice presented in Figure 9.3. The first merely adds the chords implied by the intervals between bass and treble, as well as those that are specified by the figures. The second is more active, using moving parts—with passing and neighbor tones and an embellished suspension—to fill out the texture. Whether one or another style is more appropriate in improvising a given performance would depend on a number of factors: the number and sustaining power of the accompanying instruments, the tempo chosen for the song, the size of the room and its audience. The written music remains the same; its realization varies from one performance to another. Modern editions of works with continuo may print an editor's realization in smaller notes to distinguish them from what the composer actually provided (compare Figure 9.3 with its realization in NAWM 64), but even those are only the editor's recommendations to the performer.

In choosing how to realize the bass, the continuo player (or players—some early seventeenth-century scores call for a miniature band of performers) had to be sensitive to the interpretation and style of the soloist, much as the rhythm-section players in a jazz combo interact with a singer or lead melody instrument. Many instruction manuals were published throughout the seventeenth and eighteenth centuries to guide organists and other keyboard players in the art of continuo playing. In addition to teaching the basic principles of chord realization, some suggest that the player should add passage work, especially when the singer holds or repeats a note; but others warn against a realization that is too "ornamental" and apt to detract from the song's expressivity. The author of one text distinguishes between those who play with "invention and variety, now with gentle strokes and repeating notes/chords, now with generous passage-work" and those with "technical facility but little learning" who play endless and unmusical runs (Agostino Agazzari, *Del sonare sopra il basso* [On Playing above the Bass], 1609).

Such performance practices varied from nation to nation and from one generation to another. But what remained constant in Baroque music is the centrality of the performer and performance, not the composer and the work.

*Example 9.2: Two possible continuo realizations for the opening of* Vedrò 'l mio sol

*a. Chordal style*

*b. With figuration*

*I'll see my sun.*

*Figure 9.3. Giulio Caccini's madrigal* Vedrò 'l mio sol *as printed in* Le nuove musiche *(Florence: Marescotti, 1601–1602). In this early example of thorough-bass notation, the bass is figured with the exact intervals to be sounded in the chords above it—for example, the dissonant eleventh resolving to the tenth in the first measure.*

# Early Opera

An opera is a drama sung to continuous or nearly continuous music and staged with scenery, costumes, and action. It is composed to a libretto (Italian for "little book"), a play usually written in rhymed and unrhymed verse. The quintessential art form of the age, combining as it did action and reaction, drama and spectacle, poetry, music, and the visual arts, opera was to become the most common path to fame and even, occasionally, fortune for many Baroque composers and performers.

## Forerunners

Although the earliest operas date from the very end of the sixteenth century, the association of music with drama goes back to ancient times. The choruses and principal lyric speeches in the plays of Euripides and Sophocles were sung (see NAWM 2), as were medieval liturgical dramas (see NAWM 6). Some Renaissance plays incorporated songs or sung choruses; others presented musical interludes, known as intermedi, between their acts. On important occasions at the Italian courts, such as the 1589 wedding in Florence of Grand Duke Ferdinand de' Medici and Christine of Lorraine, these intermedi became elaborate musical productions, with choruses, soloists, large instrumental ensembles, and spectacular costumes and stage effects (see Figure 9.2, page 184). The production of the 1589 Florentine intermedi called for the collaboration of artists, poets, composers, musicians, singers, and choreographers, many of whom were later involved in the earliest operas. The intermedi, therefore, exercised a direct influence on the beginnings of opera.

Another source for early opera was the pastoral drama, a play in verse with incidental music. In a tradition derived from ancient Greece and Rome, pastoral

CD 1/2 | CD 1/30

Florentine intermedi

Pastoral drama

*Figure 9.2. Detail from costume designs for the 1589 Florentine intermedi, probably by Bernardo Buontalenti, who also designed the sets and stage machinery for this elaborate production in celebration of a Medici wedding.*

poetry told of idyllic love in an imaginary world of fields, woods, and fountains, peopled by simple rustic youths and maidens as well as mythological characters. In this idealized setting, song seemed the natural mode of discourse. By the end of the sixteenth, century pastoral plays were very much in vogue at Italian courts. The most popular was by the Ferrarese court poet Giovanni Battista (or Giambattista) Guarini; his *Il pastor fido* (The Faithful Shepherd, 1590) was not only performed as a theater piece, but also supplied lyrics for hundreds of madrigal settings, including Monteverdi's *Cruda Amarilli* (NAWM 63). The first operas, then, also drew on the poetic and musical traditions of the pastoral.

Greek tragedy as
a model

Despite these musical and theatrical precedents, opera might never have emerged without the interest of humanist scholars, poets, musicians, and patrons in ancient Greek tragedy. They hoped to revive the legendary ethical powers attributed to ancient tragedy, which some believed was entirely sung, by creating modern works that were equally forceful in performance. In this respect, opera fulfilled a profoundly humanist agenda, providing a parallel in dramatic music to the emulation of ancient Greek sculpture and architecture in art.

Girolamo Mei

The prime mover behind the idea that the entire text of a Greek tragedy was performed in song was Girolamo Mei (1519–1594), a Florentine scholar who edited several Greek dramas. While working in Rome as a cardinal's secretary, Mei conducted a great deal of research on Greek music, particularly its role in the theater. After reading in Greek almost every treatise on music that survived from the ancient world, he concluded that Greek music had consisted of a single melodic line, sung by a soloist or chorus, with or without accompaniment. Such a direct delivery of the text could evoke powerful emotional effects in the listener through the natural expressiveness of the voice via the register, rhythms, and contours of its utterance.

The Florentine
Camerata

Mei communicated his ideas to colleagues in Florence, notably Count Giovanni de' Bardi (1534–1612) and Vincenzo Galilei (ca. 1520s–1591), a lute player, singer, composer, theorist, and father of the astronomer Galileo. From the early 1570s, Bardi hosted an informal academy at his palace in Florence, where scholars discussed literature, science, and the arts, and musicians performed new music. Bardi's young protégé, the singer-composer Giulio Caccini (1551–1618), later referred to this gathering as Bardi's "Camerata" (circle or coterie). Mei's letters about Greek music often appeared on the agenda.

If Mei was the elder statesman of Bardi's Camerata, Galilei was its advance man. In his *Dialogo della musica antica et della moderna* (Dialogue on Ancient and Modern Music, 1581), Galilei used Mei's ideas to criticize the theory and practice of vocal counterpoint and proposed a revival of the Greek ideal of the union of music and poetry through monody, the ancient style of solo singing (or *monodia*, from the Greek *monos*, "alone"). Like Mei, Galilei argued that the semantic and emotional message of the text was impaired by counterpoint: if, as in the fashionable madrigals and motets of the time, some voices were low and others high in register, some rose while simultaneously others descended, some moved in slow notes together with others in faster rhythms, then not only were the words distorted and the music's emotional message neutralized, but the resulting web of contradictory impressions confused the listener and served merely to show off the cleverness of the composer and the skillfulness of the performers.

The term *monody* is used by modern historians to embrace all the styles of accompanied solo singing practiced in the late sixteenth and early seventeenth centuries (as distinct from *monophony*, which is unaccompanied melody). Solo singing was not new in Florence at the turn of the century. Italian Renaissance culture had a long and venerable tradition of improvised solo singing on melodic formulas (known as *arie*, or "airs"), used to recite epic and other strophic poems over a light accompaniment. Among many other musicians renowned in their day, the painter Leonardo da Vinci (1452–1519) was famous for improvising songs and accompanying himself on the lira viol, a bowed string instrument. The special significance of the art of singing in the elite music making of the time arose from the conviction that the individual was connected to the entire universe through harmony and that the best way to express this connection was by giving voice to song. At the end of the Renaissance, by reaffirming that solo singing had the ability to express psychological and moral reality, the Camerata's discussions of Greek music led several members down new paths.

The debate over the relative merits of old and new implied in the title of Galilei's *Dialogo* conforms to one of the central concerns of seventeenth-century aesthetics, as we have seen. Like his contemporaries in the arts, Galilei equated "ancient" and "modern" with "old" (in the sense of "antique" or "classical" rather than "conservative") and "new" (in the sense of "au courant" or "fashionably modern"), and he championed the qualities of the old as worthy of adoption by new or modern composers, whose works he thought did not measure up to the ideals of Greek music. In this way, Galilei's and Bardi's generation was privileging the "ancient" style over the "modern," perhaps for the first time in music history, just as Renaissance artists and sculptors had done when they emulated the marble statues and architectural remains of antiquity. After the turn of the century, however, the "new" or modern style of music was redefined to include those composers who put into practice the reforms advocated by the older generation, either by modifying the rules of counterpoint to allow for a more expressive "second practice," as Monteverdi did, or by rejecting counterpoint altogether, as the composers of monody did. Although it had roots in the oral tradition of improvised solo singing—which, by its very nature, focused on the performer—composed monody became the newest of the new musics.

*Le nuove musiche* (The New Music; more correctly, Musical Works in a New Style) was in fact the title of Giulio Caccini's path-breaking 1602 collection of solo songs with basso continuo. The songs divide into two distinct formal types

Vincenzo Galilei

Monody

Oral traditions

Ancient versus modern

Caccini's *New Music*

*Figure 9.4. A sketch of Jacopo Peri, costumed as the legendary singer Arion, a role he played in the Florentine intermedi of 1589. Arion, returning from concerts in Corinth, sings an elaborate aria just before he plunges into the sea to escape his mutinous crew. The music was by Jacopo Peri and Christofano Malvezzi, the costume by Bernardo Buontalenti.*

in use by the fashionable poets of the day: madrigal and air. Those with strophic settings (many stanzas sung to the same music) he called arias (Italian for "airs"), which at this time could mean any written setting or improvised oral performance of strophic poetry. The others he called madrigals, which were through-composed like the polyphonic madrigals. In his foreword, Caccini boasted that his madrigal *Vedrò 'l mio sol* (I'll see my sun, NAWM 64 and Figure 9.3) was greeted in Bardi's Camerata "with affectionate applause." Caccini set each line of poetry as a separate phrase ending in a cadence, shaping his melody according to the natural accentuation of the text. Although singers were expected to add embellishments in performance, Caccini occasionally wrote his own, new ornaments into the music, hoping to teach his pupils how to execute them and where to place them so that they didn't distort the words. Faithful to the goals of the Camerata, he insisted that ornaments should be used sparingly and then only to enhance the message of the text, not merely to display vocal virtuosity. His foreword to *Le nuove musiche* includes descriptions of the vocal ornaments then in use and instructions about their execution, providing a valuable resource for scholars and singers. In his day, Caccini was much in demand as a teacher of the new style of solo singing and trained many of the singers who performed at court, where some participated in the first operas. In many ways this collection, with its lengthy and meticulous preface about the art of singing, was a monument to his deceased mentors as well as a legacy to his students, among whom were many members of his own family.

CD 4/26    CD 2/38

## The First Operas

After Bardi moved to Rome in 1592, discussions about ancient and modern music continued under the sponsorship of another nobleman and musician,

Jacopo Corsi (1561–1602), who was a member of another Florentine circle, the Accademia degli Alterati. Among the participants were two veterans of the 1589 intermedi, poet Ottavio Rinuccini (1562–1621) and composer Jacopo Peri (1561–1633), shown in Figure 9.4. Convinced that Greek tragedies were sung in their entirety, they set out to re-create the ancient genre in modern form. They first experimented with Rinuccini's pastoral poem *Dafne,* performed privately for invited guests in Corsi's palace in Florence in 1598. Although only fragments of the music survive, this was the first opera: a staged drama, modeled on Greek plays set entirely to music, with a new kind of singing designed specifically for theatrical delivery. It was followed in October 1600 by Rinuccini's more ambitious drama *L'Euridice,* set to music by Peri and Caccini, and performed during the court festivities celebrating the marriage of Maria de' Medici to Henry IV of France. Because Caccini, who wanted to protect his position at court, would not allow his singers to perform Peri's music, the first performance consisted of a combination of both composers' settings. In their rivalry to claim credit for writing the "first" opera, both composers published their scores a few months later (though Caccini's work appeared slightly earlier than Peri's), and the status of the new theatrical genre was assured.

*L'Euridice* elaborated the well-known myth of Orpheus and Eurydice, giving it a happy ending to suit the joyous occasion. The story demonstrates music's power to move the emotions: through his singing, Orfeo (Orpheus) persuades the gods of the underworld to restore his bride, Euridice, to life. Peri and

*L'Euridice*

---

**VIGNETTE**  Peri's Description of His Recitative Style

*In the preface to his opera* L'Euridice, *published in 1601, Jacopo Peri described his search for a new kind of musico-theatrical delivery partly adapted from his understanding of ancient Greek drama and partly based on his own analysis of the oral patterns of speech. This new style, known as recitative, became an essential component of the new genre of opera.*

∿

Putting aside every other manner of singing heard up to now, I dedicated myself wholly to seeking the kind of imitation necessary for these poems. And I reflected that the sort of voice assigned by the ancients to singing, which they called diastematic (as if to say sustained and suspended), could at times be hastened and made to take an intermediate course between the slow sustained movements of song and the fluent and rapid ones of speech, and that it could be adapted to my purpose (just as the ancients, too, adapted the voice to reading poetry and heroic verses), and made to approach that other kind of speech, which they called continuous and which our moderns (though perhaps for another purpose) also used in their music.

I recognized likewise that in our speech some sounds are pronounced in such a way that a har-

mony can be built upon them, and that in the course of speaking we pass through many others that are not so intoned, until we reach another that will support a progression to a new consonance. Keeping in mind those inflections and accents that serve us in our grief, in our joy and in similar states, I made the bass move in time to these, now more, now less [frequently], according to the affections. I held [the bass] firm through both dissonances and consonances until the voice of the speaker, having run through various notes, arrived at a syllable that, being intoned in ordinary speech, opened the way to a new harmony. I did this not only so that the flow of discourse might not offend the ear (as though stumbling over the repeated notes it encountered with more frequent consonant chords), but also so that the voice would not seem to dance to the movement of the bass, particularly in sad or solemn subjects, granted that other more joyful subjects would require more frequent movements [changes of harmony].

Jacopo Peri, *Le musiche sopra l'Euridice* (Florence, 1600), trans. in C. V. Palisca, *Humanism in Italian Renaissance Musical Thought* (New Haven: Yale University Press, 1985), pp. 428–432; amended by B. R. Hanning.

**A CLOSER LOOK** Peri's Recitative

The speech in which Dafne (the Messenger) tells of Euridice's death (NAWM 65c) exemplifies the new recitative style, and Example 9.3 shows how Peri followed his own prescription for composing recitative (see below, and the vignette on page 187). The vertical boxes identify the syllables that are sustained or accented in speech and support a consonant harmony; the horizontal boxes contain the syllables that are passed over quickly in speech and may be set by either dissonances (marked by asterisks) or consonances against the bass and its implied chords. The manner in which the dissonances are introduced and then left often violates the rules of counterpoint, as in measures 3, 4, and 5; the attempt to imitate speech exempts these notes from normal musical conventions. This combination of speechlike freedom and songlike, harmonized, accented syllables realized Peri's idea of a dramatic delivery halfway between speech and song.

*Example 9.3: Jacopo Peri,* L'Euridice

*But the lovely Eurydice*
*dancingly moved her feet on the green grass*
*when—O bitter, angry fate!—*
*a snake, cruel and merciless,*
*that lay hidden among flowers and grass*
*bit her foot . . .*

Caccini, both singers by profession, had similar approaches to theatrical music. But Caccini's setting is more melodious and lyrical, resembling the songs of *Le nuove musiche*, whereas Peri's is better suited to the drama because he found a new way to imitate speech and varied his musical style according to the situation.

Why was the imitation of speech so important to Peri and his librettist, Rinuccini? Galilei and other humanists had reinforced the teaching of the Greek philosophers that "how one speaks" the words reveals their underlying emotion. For a songwriter, it became a question of how to set the words musically to disclose their innate significance, allowing the melody hidden in the tonal and rhythmic shapes of the words themselves to suggest the contours, rhythms, and accents of the melody. If the composer succeeded in doing that, the meaning inherent in the words would be revealed and would, in turn, disclose the emotional state of the performer and ultimately influence or move the listeners to experience a similar state.

So Peri invented a new style of singing, soon known as recitative, for the dialogue portions of *L'Euridice*, and he wrote a detailed explanation of his procedure in the preface to the published score (see vignette, page 187). There Peri reviewed the distinction made by the ancient Greeks between the "continuous" fluctuation or sliding pitches of speech and the intervallic, or "diastematic," motion of song. He sought a kind of speech-song that was halfway between them, similar to the style scholars thought the Greeks used for reciting heroic poems. On the one hand, by writing long notes in the bass line and allowing the voice part's shorter notes to pass through both consonances and dissonances—thereby imitating the continuous, sliding pronunciation of syllables—he freed the voice from the harmony enough so that it sounded like the pitchless declamation of speech. On the other hand, where a syllable of text was stressed in speaking—in Peri's words, "intoned"—he formed a consonance with the bass. Thus, Peri conceived of recitative as a spontaneous-sounding, speechlike medium for imitating, expressing, and arousing the emotions, following the natural rhythmic patterns and pitch inflections of the voice.

Recitative, then, was an extreme form of monody and opera's most radical innovation because it sought not merely to imitate speech but to eradicate completely the distinction between speaking and singing, or between words and music. It did so by fusing the two elements into an inseparable whole, creating a new language that was more than speech but less than song—as Peri described it: a language able to communicate simultaneously to both the intellect and the emotions. Although Peri and his associates knew they had not brought back Greek music, they believed they had created a speech-song that not only resembled what had been used in the ancient theater but was also compatible with modern musical practice.

The performance and publication of the *Euridice* operas attracted a lot of attention in the musical world, and within the decade Claudio Monteverdi tried his hand at the new genre—so successfully that his *Orfeo* (1607) became the first opera to achieve a permanent place in the repertory. Monteverdi patterned *Orfeo*, in its subject matter and its variety of styles, on the earlier works; but his concept of recitative, especially, is clearly derived from Peri's score, a copy of which he must have studied. Already an experienced composer of madrigals and church music (see biography, page 190), Monteverdi drew on a rich palette of vocal and instrumental resources. Through careful tonal organization, his recitative achieves more continuity and a longer line than that of his predecessor although, like Peri's, it becomes intensely expressive at significantly dramatic moments. Furthermore, Monteverdi and his librettist, Alessandro Striggio, interspersed many solo airs, duets, madrigalesque ensembles, and

Imitation of speech

Recitative

Monteverdi's Orfeo

CD 4/28–30

CD 4/34

CD 3/47

dances, which, taken together, make up a larger proportion of the work than in Peri's opera and furnish a welcome contrast to the recitative. The ritornellos—recurring instrumental sections—and choruses help organize the scenes into schemes of almost ceremonial formality.

Many passages from *L'Orfeo* parallel those from the *Euridice* (NAWM 65), but it becomes clear immediately that the proportions are very much expanded. The ritornello to the Prologue is carefully scored, and although the Prologue itself, like Peri's, is patterned on the air for singing poetry that derived from oral tradition, Monteverdi wrote out each strophe, varying the melody while leaving the harmony intact. Orfeo's strophic canzonet, *Vi ricorda, o boschi ombrosi* (Do you remember, O shady woods, NAWM 66a), is a simple dance song in which the bridegroom recalls how his unhappiness turned to joy as he won Euridice. Again, the musical idiom is a traditional one: the hemiola rhythm is the same as in many frottole written a hundred years earlier (see NAWM 49, for example), and the harmonization with root-position chords is also similar.

## ✳ Claudio Monteverdi (1567–1643)

*Figure 9.5. Claudio Monteverdi, in a 1640 portrait by Bernardo Strozzi. Landesmuseum Ferdinandeum, Innsbruck.*

Monteverdi stood out among his contemporaries as the most innovative and imaginative composer of his day, a distinction that caused his music to be attacked in public as too radical. His genius lay in creating vocal works—madrigals, operas, and sacred pieces—that brought music's expressive partnership with words to new heights.

Monteverdi was born in Cremona, in northern Italy, and was trained there by the cathedral's music director. He was a prodigy as a composer and had already published two collections each of madrigals and sacred music when, at age twenty-three, he took a position as a string player at the court of Vincenzo Gonzaga, duke of Mantua. He married a court singer, Claudia Cattaneo, and in 1601 was appointed court music director by the duke.

The Gonzagas commissioned Monteverdi's first operas, *L'Orfeo* (1607) and *L'Arianna* (1608; only the heroine's much-praised lament survives). Between the two premieres, Claudia died, leaving

Monteverdi with two young sons. Overworked and poorly paid, Monteverdi suffered ill health, but he remained in Mantua under slightly better conditions until a new duke dismissed him in 1612. The following year he became maestro di cappella at Saint Mark's in Venice, the most prestigious musical post in Italy, where he remained until his death thirty years later. He wrote a great deal of sacred music for Saint Mark's and decided to join the priesthood in 1632.

Throughout his career, however, Monteverdi reserved a special place in his work for the madrigal, publishing no fewer than 250 in nine collections over five decades. He transformed the genre from the witty, polyphonic, a cappella part-songs of the late Renaissance to powerful explorations of the concertato medium and updated its language with emotionally charged dissonances and declamatory melodies in the new, dramatic, Baroque style.

His last works, two operas written in his seventies for the Venetian stage, were remarkably "modern" in style and technique. After his death in 1643, he was lauded in both poetry and music, and his influence, though not long-lived, spread via the circulation of his published works and the operas of his younger contemporaries.

**Major works:** 3 surviving operas—*L'Orfeo, Il ritorno d'Ulisse,* and *L'incoronazione di Poppea*; 9 books of madrigals; 3 other volumes of secular songs; *Vespro della Beata Vergine*; 3 Masses; 4 collections of sacred music.

Like Peri, Monteverdi reserves the most modern style for dramatic dialogue and impassioned speeches. The Messenger's narrative relating how Euridice perished from a snakebite, in NAWM 66c, beginning *In un fiorito prato* (In a flowered meadow) on page 409, imitates the characteristics of Peri's recitative, but the harmonic movement and melodic contour are more broadly conceived. Orfeo's lament (Example 9.4) displays a new expressive force that leaves the first monodic experiments far behind. In the passage that begins "Tu se' morta" (You are dead), each phrase of music, like each phrase of text, builds on the preceding one and intensifies it through pitch and rhythm. The dissonances against sustained chords, marked with asterisks, enhance the illusion of Orfeo's halting speech, and the rests, syncopations, and word repetitions in the melody suggest his state of shock. The raw passage from an E-major chord to a G-minor chord (measures 3–4) emphasizes his poignant question, Why must I continue to live, when my bride—my "life"—is dead? The progress of the melody parallels Orfeo's changing mood—from his initial despair to his resolution to follow and rescue Euridice from the realm of death.

CD 4/36

*Example 9.4: Claudio Monteverdi, L'Orfeo, Tu se' morta*

*You are dead, my life, and I still breathe?*
*You have departed from me . . .*

Despite the interest aroused by the first operas, only a few more were written and performed during the next thirty years. The Florentine court continued to prefer ballets, masques, and intermedi for glamorizing state weddings and other events. When a Polish prince visited Florence in 1625, the court staged a combination of ballet and musical scenes—*La liberazione di Ruggiero dall'isola d'Alcina* (The Liberation of Ruggiero from the Island of Alcina) written by Francesca Caccini (1587–ca. 1645). Billed as a ballet, the work had all the trappings of opera: opening sinfonia, prologue, recitatives, arias, choruses, instrumental ritornellos, and elaborate staging (see Figure 9.6). Commissioned by the archduchess, *La liberazione* explores the theme of women and power, with two sorceresses—one good and one evil—delineated by contrasting musical styles, contending over the young knight Ruggiero.

Francesca Caccini

*Figure 9.6. Stage design by Giulio Parigi for the second change of scene in Francesca Caccini's* La liberazione di Ruggiero, *produced in 1625 at the Medici villa of Poggio Imperiale. The setting is the enchanted island of the sorceress Alcina, who holds the pagan knight Ruggiero captive there. The plot is based on an episode in Ludovico Ariosto's epic* Orlando furioso *(1532). Engraving by Alfonso Parigi.*

ISOLA D'ALCINA SECONDA MVTA DELLE SCENE

Francesca Caccini had a brilliant career as a singer, teacher, and composer, becoming the highest-paid musician employed by the grand duke of Tuscany. The daughter of Giulio Caccini, she performed frequently with her sister Settimia and stepmother, Margherita, in a *concerto delle donne* that rivaled the famous ensemble at Ferrara (see Chapter 7). She composed music for at least fourteen dramatic entertainments, making her among the most prolific composers of theater music at the time.

## Opera in Rome and Venice

Rome

In the 1620s, the center for new developments in opera shifted to Rome, where wealthy prelates vied with each other in offering lavish entertainments. Subjects expanded from pastoral and mythological plots to include episodes from the epics of Torquato Tasso, Ludovico Ariosto, and Giambattista Marino; the lives of saints; and the first comic operas. The most prolific librettist was Giulio Rospigliosi (later Pope Clement IX), who helped establish libretto writing as an independent craft. His most famous libretto, *Il Sant'Alessio* (1632), based on the life of the fifth-century Saint Alexius, was set to music by Stefano Landi (1587–1639). Because Baroque theater relied on the concept of *la meraviglia* (Italian for "wonderment") to arouse astonishment and inspire awe in audiences, operas often emphasized spectacular stage effects—showing the devils and demons in *Sant'Alessio* being consumed in flames, for example.

In Roman opera, solo singing increasingly fell into two clearly defined types—recitative and aria. The recitatives were more speechlike than Peri's or Monteverdi's, and the arias were melodious and mainly strophic. Because women were prohibited from the stage in Rome, female roles there were given to castrati (sing., castrato), males who were castrated before puberty to preserve their high vocal range. Later in the seventeenth and in the eighteenth centuries, castrati also sang in operas outside Rome but almost always in male rather than female roles (see Chapter 13). Since women were also generally banned from

Castrati

singing in church, boys and castrati performed the higher parts in sacred polyphony throughout Italy.

A decisive step in the history of opera occurred in 1637 with the opening in Venice of the first public opera house, Teatro San Cassiano. Until then, musical theater had been supported by wealthy aristocratic patrons for courtly and elite audiences, but now it was presented for and attended by a paying public, with financial backing from wealthy and prominent families who rented boxes for the season (see Figure 9.7). Venice was ideal for public opera. Although small in size, its reputation for freedom from religious and social restraints attracted thousands of visitors each year for carnival, which ran for several weeks between the day after Christmas and the day before Lent (a penitential period leading to Easter during which public entertainments were banned). By the end of the century, there were nine theatrical stages competing for audiences, and more than 150 operas had been produced.

*Venetian opera*

After Monteverdi moved to Venice in 1613 and became maestro di cappella at Saint Mark's church, he continued to write operas and other dramatic works in addition to composing church and vocal chamber music (discussed below). In his seventies but still very much up on the latest musical trends, he composed three operas for the Venetian stage. Two survive: *Il ritorno d'Ulisse* (The Return of Ulysses, 1640), based on the last part of Homer's *Odyssey*, and *L'incoronazione di Poppea* (The Coronation of Poppea, 1642), a historical opera on the Roman emperor Nero's illicit affair with the ambitious Poppea, whom he eventually married. *Poppea*, often considered Monteverdi's masterpiece, lacks the varied instrumentation and stage effects of *Orfeo* because it was written for a commercial theater instead of a wealthy court presentation, but it surpasses *Orfeo* in its depiction of human character and passions. The love scene between Nero and Poppea in Act I, scene 3 (NAWM 67), demonstrates Monteverdi's nuanced language as he changes styles to reflect the character's shifting feelings: expressive recitative inflected with dissonance and chromaticism as Poppea pleads with Nero not to leave her bedchamber; calmer or more excited recitation for dialogue, as the situation warrants; aria styles with ritornellos, often in triple meter, for declarations of love; and passages that lie somewhere between recitative and aria style, often called arioso. Content more than poetic form, and heightened emotional expression rather than the wish to charm or dazzle, determine the shifts from one level of musical expression to another. Thus the stylistic variety in *Poppea*, though even greater than in *Orfeo*, serves the same dramatic goals.

*Monteverdi's L'incoronazione di Poppea*

CD 4/42    CD 2/47

Among Monteverdi's successors in Venice were his pupil Pier Francesco Cavalli (1602–1676) and Antonio Cesti (1623–1669). Cavalli was a leading figure on the Venetian musical scene, composing for the theater during most of his working life. The most celebrated of his more than thirty operas was *Giasone* (Jason, 1649), which incorporates most of the conventions of the period, including complicated

*Figure 9.7. A view of the Teatro San Giovanni Grisostomo, one of the first public opera houses in Venice, showing the stage with sets in place, the orchestra in front of the stage, and several tiers of boxes, which offered both a better view and greater prestige for audience members than seating on the main floor. Engraving from 1709. Museo Correr, Venice.*

dramatic intrigue that mixes serious and comic elements, and a formal separation of recitative and aria based on dramatic function. Cesti was Cavalli's most serious competitor but spent much of his career abroad. His *Orontea*, written for Innsbruck in 1656, was one of the most frequently performed operas in the seventeenth century, appearing on stages all over Italy as well as in Austria. Typical for mid-century opera, most of the action unfolds in simple recitative, and a new lyrical idiom reigns in the arias, which are mainly in strophic form and crystallize the affective moments of the plot. The melody of *Intorno all' idol mio* (Around my idol, NAWM 68b), in which Orontea confesses her love for Alidoro, reveals smooth, mainly diatonic lines and flowing triple meter, characteristics gratifying to the singer and audience alike. The two violins, no longer restricted to ritornellos before and after the singer's strophes, play throughout the aria.

CD 4/49

Italian opera at mid-century

By the middle of the seventeenth century, Italian opera had acquired the main features it would maintain without significant change essentially for the next two hundred years: (1) concentration on solo singing rather than ensembles and instrumental music; (2) the separation of recitative and aria; and (3) the introduction of distinctive styles and forms for the arias, which attracted most of the attention from composers and audiences. The Florentine view of music as the servant of the poetry and drama had by now been reversed: the Venetians and their imitators saw the drama and poetry as scaffolding for the musical structures, but their interest centered on the visual elements of scenery, costumes, and special effects and, most of all, on the arias and the stars who sang them (see Chapter 11).

# Vocal Chamber Music

Although opera by mid-century had become the focus of musical life in Venice, elsewhere it was still an uncommon event. Chamber music for mixed voices and instruments remained the standard fare for private music making (see Figure 9.8). The concertato medium, whether monody or other textures with basso continuo, permeated all genres of chamber and church music. Composers found new ways of organizing their works—including ritornellos, strophic variations, repeating bass patterns, and contrasting styles and textures—to create large-scale forms and enrich the expressive resources of their music.

Strophic aria

From the beginning of the century, Italian composers turned out thousands of pieces for solo voice or small vocal ensemble with basso continuo. Following Caccini's *Le nuove musiche*, these pieces were published in numerous collections of madrigals, arias, dialogues, and duets, and some were more widely known than any of the operas. Several of the formal types that became crucial to opera were first perfected in solo song. An example is the strophic aria that permitted a composer to repeat the same melody, perhaps with minor rhythmic modifications, for each stanza of poetry; write a new melody over the same bass line for successive stanzas; or keep the same harmonic and melodic plan for all the stanzas, but vary the surface musical details. The last two procedures, known as strophic variations, were favorite techniques for instrumental as well as vocal composition (see Chapter 10).

Concerted madrigals

The importance of the concertato medium—competing or contrasting forces—can be gauged by its impact on the madrigal. We can trace the change from the unaccompanied polyphonic madrigal to the concerted madrigal with instrumental accompaniment in Monteverdi's fifth through eighth books of madrigals. Beginning with the last six madrigals of his *Fifth Book* (1605), Monteverdi includes a basso continuo and sometimes calls for other instruments as

*Figure 9.8.* Le concert, *a painting by Nicholas Tournier from the early seventeenth century, illustrates the new concertato style of mixed voices and instruments—in this case, solo voice with bass viol, spinet, violin, and lute. Musée du Louvre, Paris.*

well. Solos, duets, and trios are set off against the full vocal ensemble, and there are instrumental introductions and recurring instrumental interludes (ritornellos). Monteverdi entitled his seventh book *Concerto* (1619) and described it as containing "madrigals and other kinds of songs," without specifying that it includes strophic variations and canzonettas as well as through-composed madrigals.

Monteverdi's eighth book, entitled *Madrigali guerrieri et amorosi* (Madrigals of War and Love, 1638), features a remarkable variety of concertato forms and types, including madrigals for five voices with continuo; solos, duets, and trios with continuo; and large works for chorus, soloists, and orchestra. The eighth book also contains two sung *balli* (dances or ballet) and the *Combattimento di Tancredi e Clorinda* (The Combat of Tancredi and Clorinda), a work blending mime and music that was first performed in 1624. Here Monteverdi set the portion of Tasso's *Gierusalemme liberata* (Jerusalem Delivered) that describes the armed confrontation between the crusader knight Tancredi and the pagan heroine Clorinda, ending with her death (see Figure 9.9). Monteverdi assigns the narrative text to a tenor, who delivers it in recitative. The brief dialogue between Tancredi and Clorinda is sung by characters who also mime the actions during the narrative. The instruments (strings with continuo) accompany the voices and play interludes that suggest the action—the galloping of horses, the clashing of swords, the excitement of combat. To convey anger and warlike affections and actions, Monteverdi devised what he called in the book's preface the *concitato genere* ("excited style"), characterized by rapid reiteration of a single note, whether on quickly spoken syllables or in a measured string tremolo. Other composers imitated this device, which became a widely used convention.

Many works used basso ostinato (Italian for "obstinate" or "persistent bass"; often called "ground bass" in English), a short pattern in the bass that repeats while the melody above it changes or, in some cases, elaborates a matching melodic outline. Most ostinato basses were in triple or compound meter, usually two, four, or eight measures long. There was a well-established tradition in

*Madrigals of War and Love*

Ostinato basses

*Figure 9.9. The scene from Torquato Tasso's epic poem* Gierusalemme liberata *(1590), in which Tancredi, after mortally wounding an enemy warrior in the Crusades, discovers on removing the Saracen's armor that it is his beloved, Clorinda. Monteverdi set their speeches to music in his* Combattimento di Tancredi e Clorinda. *Accompanied by two violins, a viola da braccio, and basso continuo, Clorinda sings, "The heavens open; I go in peace." Beinecke Rare Book and Manuscript Library, New Haven.*

CD 4/8

Spain and Italy of singing or playing popular songs and dances, composed or extemporized, to familiar ostinato basses such as *Guárdame las vacas* (see NAWM 60b), its close relative the romanesca, and the *Ruggiero*. (Ruggiero was one of the heroes of Ariosto's epic, so the name betrays the pattern's origins in the Renaissance oral tradition of singing the stanzas of epic poetry to a repeating melodic formula with a standard harmonization that eventually became a bass pattern.) Such patterns, which provided a ready-made, logical structure for composing or improvising a lengthy song or dance, underlie many vocal and instrumental works of the early seventeenth century (see Chapter 10).

Certain patterns, such as the descending tetrachord (a stepwise descent spanning a fourth), became associated with particular affections. Monteverdi used a minor descending tetrachord ostinato in his *Lamento della ninfa* (Lament of the Nymph) from his eighth book of madrigals, *Madrigali guerrieri et amorosi*. Its falling contour and relentless repetition are perfectly suited to convey a sense of inescapable sorrow. In the passage in Example 9.5, the recurring instrumental bass line establishes a tonal center and regular phrases, while the vocal melody suggests the nymph's distress through strong dissonances (marked with an **x**) and irregular phrases that seem to struggle against the restrictive four-measure groupings of the pattern. Three male singers, who form the inner voices of the five-part concerted texture, introduce and comment on her lament, turning this madrigal into a miniature unstaged drama. Throughout the Baroque period, especially in opera, composers used various forms of the descending tetrachord ostinato, which became emblematic of sorrowful affections.

*Example 9.5: Monteverdi,* Lamento della ninfa, *with descending tetrachord bass*

[Spoken to Love:] *Make my love return as he once was, or kill me yourself so that I will not torment myself any longer.*

A new genre of vocal chamber music developed from the strophic aria, on the one hand, and the extended, quasi-dramatic madrigal, such as Monteverdi's Lament of the Nymph, on the other—that is, the cantata, meaning simply a piece that was "sung." By mid-century, the genre had established itself in Italy as a piece for voice and continuo on an intimate poetic text having several sections that included recitatives and arias as well as arioso passages. Among leading cantata composers of the mid-seventeenth century were Luigi Rossi (1597–1653) and Giacomo Carissimi (1605–1674) in Rome—the first an opera composer, the second remembered chiefly for his oratorios (see below)—and Barbara Strozzi (1619–1677) in Venice (see biography).

Strozzi's *Lagrime mie* (NAWM 69), published in her *Diporti di Euterpe* (Pleasures of Euterpe, 1659), is representative of the solo chamber cantata in presenting successive sections of recitative, arioso, and aria, and of Strozzi in its emotional focus on unrequited love. The first section, which invokes the distraught lover's tears, begins with a stunningly doleful cry, which bursts upon the ear at the top of the vocal register and makes its way downward over a stationary harmony, faltering in its syncopated rhythms and prolonging the dissonances D♯, A, and F♯ to imitate the lover's wailing and lamentation (see Example 9.6). The passage recurs several times like a refrain, helping to unify the rather loose poetic and musical structure of the rest of the work. The opening section has the rhythmic flexibility and harmonic language of the most expressive recitative; yet it is also marked by the word repetition and intervallic motion associated with aria. Throughout the cantata, Strozzi changes style and figuration frequently to capture the successive moods and images of the text with a fluidity that recalls Monteverdi's late operas. And several times in the bass line she subtly alludes to the slowly descending tetrachord to underline phrases like "lumi dolenti, non

Cantata

CD 4/51

Strozzi's chamber cantata

piangete" (pained eyes, do not weep!). The overall effect, combining contrasting musical elements and shifting emotions, is typical of the concerted chamber style at mid-century.

*Example 9.6: Barbara Strozzi, Lagrime mie*

*Tears of mine, [what holds you back] . . . ?*

## Barbara Strozzi (1619–1677)

*Figure 9.10. Female musician with viola da gamba, almost certainly a portrait of Barbara Strozzi around 1637, painted by Bernardo Strozzi (perhaps a relative). Her seductive costume, the flowers in her hair, and the musical attributes (instruments and songbook) suggest that the subject is a personification of La Musica, allegorized as an invitation to sensual love. Gemäldegalerie Staatliche Kunstsammlungen, Dresden.*

Strozzi was a rarity among Baroque composers in that she achieved notoriety as a singer and composer despite not having access, as a woman, to the realms of opera and church music. She sang her own music, the bulk of which was intended for in-timate, private gatherings, and consequently became the central figure in an academy created in part to showcase her talents.

She was born in Venice, the adopted (and perhaps natural) daughter of poet and librettist Giulio Strozzi. Her father nurtured her ambitions as a composer and introduced her to the intellectual elite of Venice. From her teens, she sang at the Strozzi home for gatherings of poets and other writers, formalized in 1637 as the Academy of the Unisoni. She studied with Pier Francesco Cavalli, the leading Venetian opera composer and a student of Monteverdi's. She was supported financially by her father, by the noble patrons to whom she dedicated her publications, and probably by Giovanni Paolo Vidman, the apparent father of at least three of her four children.

Between 1644 and 1664, Strozzi published eight collections of music (one is now lost). Her publications contain over one hundred madrigals, arias, cantatas, and motets, placing her among the most prolific composers of vocal chamber music of the century. Indeed, she published more cantatas than any other composer of the time. Her choice to publish her music was unusual for women musicians in the seventeenth century and may reflect the feminist sympathies of her father and his circle.

**Major works:** 3 collections of cantatas and arias, 2 of arias, and 1 each of madrigals and motets.

# Catholic Sacred Music

Just as Bernini used theatrical effects for his religious sculpture and architecture (see "The Ecstasy of Saint Teresa," page 200 and Figure 9.11), so Catholic composers adopted the theatrical style for church music, setting religious texts as sacred concertos that made use of basso continuo, the concertato medium, monody, and operatic styles from recitative to aria. The goal was the same in both cases: to convey the Church's message in the most dramatically effective and, thus, persuasive way.

Yet sacred music did not abandon polyphony altogether. Composers were routinely trained to write in the old contrapuntal style associated with Palestrina (Chapter 8) and known as the *stile antico* ("old style"), which coexisted alongside the *stile moderno* ("modern style"). A composer might deploy both styles, sometimes in a single piece. Over time, the *stile antico* was modernized as composers added a basso continuo and dependence on church modes gradually gave way to major-minor tonality. At the end of the Baroque period, Johann Joseph Fux codified this quasi-Palestrinian counterpoint in his famous treatise *Gradus ad Parnassum* (Steps to Parnassus, 1725), which remained the most influential textbook on counterpoint for the next two centuries.

*Stile antico*

At the heart and soul of daily musical life in Venice was the great eleventh-century church of Saint Mark, with its Byzantine domes, bright gold mosaics, and spacious interior (see Figure 10.11). Most of the city's ceremonial occasions took place in this church, which was adjacent to the palace of the Doges (the governing magistrates of the republic), and in its vast piazza (see Figure 9.13). Venetian sacred music glorified the majesty of state and church for solemn and festive celebrations in magnificent displays of sound and pageantry. It was characteristically full and rich in texture, homophonic rather than contrapuntal, varied and colorful in sonority. Massive chordal harmonies, better suited to the church's acoustics and to outdoor performance, replaced the intricate polyphonic lines of the Franco-Flemish composers.

Venice

From before the time of Willaert (Chapter 8), composers in the Venetian region often wrote for two choruses that sometimes echoed one another in antiphony, a style particularly suited to psalm settings. The medium of divided choirs (*cori spezzati*), which encouraged homophonic choral writing and spacious rhythmic organization, did not originate in Venice but found a congenial home there. In the polychoral music of Giovanni Gabrieli (ca. 1553–1612)—who served as organist and composer of ceremonial music at Saint Mark's (see biography in Chapter 10)—the performance forces grew to grandly large-scale proportions (hence the modern term *grand concerto*). Two, three, four, even five choruses, each with a different combination of high and low voices, mingled with instruments of diverse timbres, answered one another antiphonally, alternated with solo voices, and joined together in massive sonorous climaxes. Sometimes the choirs were separated spatially, with groups in the two organ lofts, one on each side of the altar, and another on the floor. Gabrieli's concerted motets and innovative instrumental works (see Chapter 10 and NAWM 62) explored these new resources.

Large-scale sacred concerto

CD 4/15

The Venetian school exercised broad influence during the late sixteenth and early seventeenth centuries. Gabrieli's students and admirers spread his style throughout northern Italy, Germany, Austria, and Scandinavia. His most famous pupil was Heinrich Schütz, the greatest German composer of the mid-seventeenth century (see pages 202–205).

Venetian influence

The small sacred concerto for few voices, in which one, two, or three solo voices sang to the accompaniment of an organ continuo, was much more familiar

Small sacred concerto

By the mid-seventeenth century, the dramatic gestures and attitudes of the stage permeated the style of sacred works, too, as we shall see in the music of Schütz and Carissimi. Nowhere is this more evident than in the church of Santa Maria della Vittoria in Rome, where Gian Lorenzo Bernini's marble sculpture *The Ecstasy of Saint Teresa* dominates the Cornaro Chapel. The Cornaro family commissioned Bernini, working in Rome, to design a side chapel within the church as their final resting place. The commission gave Bernini the opportunity not only to create a sculptural group for the chapel's altarpiece, but also to plan and decorate its entire setting. Perhaps at the family's request, he chose as his subject the popular Saint Teresa of Ávila (see Figure 9.11).

*Figure 9.12. Bernini, Cornaro Chapel, marble relief on side wall.*

*Figure 9.11.* The Ecstasy of Saint Teresa, *sculpted by Giovanni Bernini (1598–1680) for the Cornaro Chapel in the church of Santa Maria della Vittoria in Rome.*

Saint Teresa (1515–1582), a Spanish nun, was one of the greatest mystics of the Catholic Church. In her autobiography, she describes how, in one of her many visions, an angel repeatedly pierces her heart with a golden arrow, her pain made bearable by the sweet sensation of her soul being caressed by God. With consummate skill, Bernini transformed Saint Teresa's words into action and reaction: the angel is frozen *in the act* of plunging the arrow into the saint's breast, bringing about her mystical union with Christ, the heavenly bridegroom. Saint Teresa *reacts* by swooning in an ecstatic trance, her limbs dangling, her head tipped back, her eyes half closed, and her mouth forming an almost audible moan. The pair is bathed in a warm and mysterious glow coming through the chapel's hidden window of yellow glass, architecturally contrived to throw a spotlight on the scene.

Bernini reinforces the theatricality of it all by his stunning treatment of the chapel's side walls: there, in pews that resemble theater boxes, he depicts the members of the Cornaro family in almost three-dimensional relief, as though they are witnessing the enactment of this dramatic mystery (see Figure 9.12). Because Bernini created the illusion of the Cornaro family sitting in the same space in which we are moving, we feel as if they are alive. In this way, we, too, are drawn in, both physically and emotionally, to the Baroque world of Saint Teresa's vision; we become the audience at a command performance of this silent, sacred opera.

Discussion about the chapel and its sculpture is based on Rudolf Wittkower, *Gian Lorenzo Bernini: The Sculptor of the Roman Baroque*, 2nd ed. (London: Phaidon, 1966), pp. 24–26.

to the average churchgoer than the large-scale concerto. One of the first com- posers to exploit this medium for church music was Lodovico Viadana (1560–1627), who in 1602 published a collection, *Cento concerti ecclesiastici* (One Hundred Sacred Concertos). These were intended for performance during Mass, replacing the older-style motet during the Offertory or Communion.

Where resources permitted, the grand concerto was combined with the con- certo for few voices, as in Monteverdi's pioneering *Vespers* of 1610, which in- clude all varieties of solo, choral, and instrumental groupings. In these settings for the liturgical Office, Monteverdi also incorporated the traditional psalm tones while exploiting the new musical resources of the time—recitative, aria, and concerto.

Alessandro Grandi (1586–1630), Monteverdi's deputy at Saint Mark's in Venice in the 1620s, composed many solo motets that used the new styles of monody. His *O quam tu pulchra es* (NAWM 70), published in 1625, blends ele- ments from recitative, solo madrigal, and lyric aria. The changing styles reflect the moods of the text, drawn from the Song of Songs, a book in the Hebrew Scriptures whose dialogue between two lovers was taken as a metaphor for God's love for the church.

CD 4/56

In Rome, the dramatic impulse found an outlet in sacred dialogues, which com- bined elements of narrative, dialogue, and commentary. Toward mid-century, such works began to be called oratorios because they were most often performed during the Lenten season (the period of penitence before Easter) in the oratory, the part of a church where groups of the faithful met to hear sermons and sing devotional songs, in keeping with the reforming spirit of the Council of Trent (see Chapter 8).

Oratorio

Like operas, oratorios used recitatives, arias, duets, and instrumental pre- ludes and ritornellos. But oratorios differed from operas in several ways: their subject matter was religious; they were seldom, if ever, staged; action was de- scribed or suggested rather than mimed; there was often a narrator, called a *storicus* ("storyteller") or *testo* ("text"); and the chorus—usually an ensemble of several voices singing one to a part—could take various roles, from participating in the dramatic dialogue to meditating on or narrating events. Oratorio librettos were in Latin or Italian.

Oratorio versus opera

The leading composer of Latin oratorios was Giacomo Carissimi, one of sev- eral composers in Rome associated with the circle of Queen Christina of Sweden (see Chapter 12). A synopsis of Carissimi's *Jephte* exemplifies the mid-century oratorio. The Latin libretto comes from the Book of Judges 11:29–40, with some paraphrasing and added material to emphasize the Lenten themes of obedience and suffering. The narrator introduces the story in recitative. Jephtha, leader of the Israelites, vows that if the Lord gives him victory over the Ammonites in the impending battle, he will sacrifice the first thing he sees on his return home. That turns out to be his beloved only daughter, who, along with her friends, wel- comes Jephtha with songs of rejoicing (solo arias, duets, choruses). After a sec- tion of dialogue, in recitative, between father and daughter in which she learns of her father's vow and accepts her fate, the chorus relates how the daughter, still a virgin, goes away to the mountains with her companions to bewail her ap- proaching untimely death. She then sings a lament, to which the chorus re- sponds, as in a Greek tragedy (this final scene is in NAWM 71). The lament is a long, affecting recitative, sweetened, as was customary in sacred music, with moments of florid song and with arioso passages built on sequences. Two sopra- nos, representing the daughter's companions, echo some of her cadential phrases. The choral response, a moving six-voice lamentation, employs both polychoral and madrigalistic effects, including a descending tetrachord in the opening measures of the basso continuo.

Carissimi's *Jephte*

CD 5/1–2    CD 2/53

# Lutheran Church Music

In German-speaking regions, composers in both the Catholic and Lutheran churches soon took up the new monodic and concertato techniques. Sacred music in Austria and Catholic southern Germany remained under strong Italian influence, with Italian composers particularly active in Munich, Salzburg, Prague, and Vienna. Composers in the Lutheran central and northern regions gradually began to employ the new media, sometimes using chorale tunes as melodic material. Alongside compositions in *stile moderno*, Lutheran composers continued to write polyphonic chorale motets as well as motets on biblical texts that did not use chorale melodies. Many were in the large-scale concerto medium, showing German musicians' admiration for the Venetian fashion.

Heinrich Schütz

The pioneering German composer Heinrich Schütz (1585–1672), like many of his countrymen for centuries to come, completed his musical education in Italy. He studied in Venice with Giovanni Gabrieli from 1609 to 1612 and renewed his acquaintance with Italian music in 1628, when he found it much changed under Monteverdi's tenure at Saint Mark's (see biography and Figure 9.14).

Sacred concertos

Consequently, Venetian magnificence and color appear frequently in Schütz's music. His sacred works were published in a series of collections that show a remarkable variety. The first, *Psalmen Davids* (Psalms of David, 1619), combines sensitive treatment of German texts with the magnificence of the Venetian large-scale concerto for two or more choruses, soloists, and instruments, following the model of Gabrieli. The first book of *Symphoniae sacrae* (Sacred Symphonies, 1629) presents concerted Latin motets for various small combinations of voices and instruments. Published in Venice during Schütz's second sojourn there, it shows the strong influence of Monteverdi and Grandi, combining recitative, aria, and concerted madrigal styles.

*Figure 9.13.*   Procession in Piazza San Marco (1496) by Gentile Bellini, which includes singers and instruments, with Saint Mark's church in the background. Galleria dell'Accademia, Venice.

## TIMELINE  The Early Baroque Period

| MUSICAL EVENTS | HISTORICAL EVENTS |
|---|---|
| Meetings of Giovanni de' Bardi's Camerata **ca. 1573–1587** | |
| V. Galilei, *Dialogo della musica antica et* **1581** *della moderna* | |
| Intermedi for Medici wedding, Florence **1589** | |
| | **1590** Guarini, *Il pastor fido* |
| Death of Palestrina and Lasso **1594** | |
| Peri, *Dafne* **1598** | |
| Artusi attacks Monteverdi in print; *L'Euridice,* by **1600** Peri and G. Caccini, performed in Florence | |
| G. Caccini, *Le nuove musiche* **1602** | |
| | **1604** Shakespeare, *Othello* |
| Monteverdi, *Fifth Book of Madrigals* **1605** | **1605** Bacon, *On the Advancement of Learning* |
| Monteverdi, *Orfeo,* in Mantua **1607** | |
| | **1609** Kepler sets forth his astronomical laws |
| Gesualdo's last book of madrigals **1611** | |
| Monteverdi appointed director of music, **1613** Saint Mark's, Venice | |
| Gabrieli, *Symphoniae sacrae II* **1615** | |
| | **1618–1648** Thirty Years' War in Germany |
| Schütz, *Psalmen Davids* **1619** | |
| | **1620** *Mayflower* brings first English colonists to New England |
| F. Caccini, *La liberazione di Ruggiero* **1625** | |
| Schütz, *Symphoniae sacrae I* **1629** | |
| | **1632** Galileo charged with heresy for claiming Earth revolves around the sun |
| First public opera house opens in Venice **1637** | **1637** Descartes, *Discourse on Method* |
| Monteverdi, *Madrigali guerrieri et amorosi* **1638** | |
| Monteverdi, *L'incoronazione di Poppea,* in Venice **1642** | |
| | **1645–1652** Bernini, *The Ecstasy of Saint Teresa* |
| Schütz, *Symphoniae sacrae III*; Carissimi, *Jephte* **1650** | |
| Barbara Strozzi, *Diporte di Euterpe* **1659** | |

CD 5/4

In 1636 and 1639, when the Thirty Years' War had reduced the number of musicians in the Dresden court chapel, Schütz published his *Kleine geistliche Konzerte* (Small Sacred Concertos), motets for one to five solo voices with continuo that are perfect microcosms of his style. *O lieber Herre Gott* (NAWM 72) from the 1636 collection illustrates how Schütz matched music to text and used elements of Italian monody.

CD 5/7 | CD 2/54

Two more books of *Symphoniae sacrae*, featuring sacred concertos in German, appeared in 1647 and 1650. The last installment, published after the Thirty Years' War, used the full musical resources of the Dresden chapel, now again available. Many of its pieces are laid out as dramatically conceived "scenes." One of the most stunning is the large-scale concerto *Saul, was verfolgst du mich* (NAWM 73),

## Heinrich Schütz (1585–1672)

The first German composer of international stature, Schütz is known especially for his church music and for his intellectual and emotional depth in conveying the meaning of words.

The son of an innkeeper, Schütz showed an early talent for music. Although his family did not want him to pursue music as a career, his singing at age twelve so impressed Moritz, landgrave of Hesse, that the nobleman insisted on bringing Schütz to Kassel and sponsoring his education in music and other subjects.

Moritz persuaded him to go to Venice in 1609 and study composition with Giovanni Gabrieli.

*Figure 9.14. Heinrich Schütz at about age seventy (ca. 1655), in a portrait by Christoph Spetner. Bibliothek der Leipzig Universität.*

After Gabrieli died in 1612, Schütz returned to Kassel as court organist, but the elector of Saxony pressured Moritz first to lend and ultimately to grant him the young musician, showing not only that Schütz was greatly esteemed as a musician but that musicians were essentially servants, not entirely free to decide their own destinies.

From 1615 to his death in 1672, Schütz was chapel master for the elector's court in Dresden, although he took leaves to visit Italy, where he made Monteverdi's acquaintance, and to work briefly at other courts. Schütz wrote music for all major ceremonies at court, secular and sacred. The former included the first German opera (1627), several ballets, and other stage works, although almost none of this music survives. He apparently did not write independent instrumental music. What remains is a great quantity and variety of concerted church music. Some had personal resonance: his first sacred collection, *Psalmen Davids*, was published shortly before his 1619 wedding to Magdalena Wildeck, and her death in 1625 prompted simple four-part settings of a German Psalter (published 1628). His *Musikalische Exequien* (1636) was funeral music for a friend and patron. But most was simply service music, each piece perfectly suited to the text at hand and the musicians at his disposal.

**Major works:** *Psalmen Davids* (polychoral psalm settings in German), *Cantiones sacrae* (Latin motets), *Symphoniae sacrae* (sacred symphonies, 3 volumes), *Musikalische Exequien* (funeral music), *Kleine geistliche Konzerte* (small sacred concertos, 2 volumes), *The Seven Last Words of Christ*, *Christmas Story*, 3 Passions.

which calls for two choirs doubled by instruments, six solo voices, two violins, and continuo, and combines the polychoral style of Gabrieli with the dissonant rhetoric of Monteverdi. It brings to life the moment when Saul, a Jew on the way to Damascus to round up Christian prisoners, is stopped by a blinding flash of light and the voice of Christ calling to him: "Saul, why do you persecute me?" The experience leads to his conversion and to his new career as the Apostle Paul, spreading the Gospel. Paired solo voices rising from the depths of the basses through the tenors to the sopranos and violins represent the flash of light and the voice leaping from the desert. Christ's question "Why do you persecute me?" is a mesh of dissonant anticipations and suspensions. Then the polychoral style takes over as the choruses and soloists together reverberate with echoes, suggesting the effect of Christ's voice bouncing off rocky peaks in the desert. This large-scale sacred concerto shows how well Schütz assimilated the bold dissonance practices and coloristic techniques of the Venetians.

During his lifetime, Schütz's music was known mainly in Lutheran areas of Germany, and after his death it faded from the repertory until it was revived in the nineteenth and twentieth centuries. Yet he helped to establish Germany as a central part of the European tradition rather than as a peripheral region. His synthesis of German and Italian elements was essential in laying the foundation for later German composers, from Bach through Brahms.

Legacy

# POSTLUDE

During the period 1600 to 1750, called by music historians the Baroque era and dominated largely by Italian tastes and fashions, composers shared a penchant for dramatic expression; collectively, they devised a music vocabulary that aimed at representing human passions and moving the affections, whether their music was intended for theater, church, or chamber. The extraordinary burst of innovation in the early seventeenth century is as apparent in the chamber and church music of the time as in opera. Yet they all drew deeply on sixteenth-century traditions as well, redefining existing genres and approaches by combining them with new styles and techniques. Monody and madrigal were combined; form was achieved via the organization of the bass and the harmonies it supported, and through the systematic introduction of ritornellos, ostinato patterns, and variation techniques; and the typical basso-continuo texture—a florid treble supported by a firm bass—was varied by the use of the contrasts inherent in the concertato medium. By these means, composers enlarged and enriched the representational and emotional resources of music.

New types of composition—solo song, opera, oratorio, sacred vocal concerto, cantata—incorporated novel styles of writing such as recitative and aria. Choral textures also assimilated the new dramatic aesthetic. In both Catholic and Lutheran church music, composers availed themselves of a wide range of styles of both secular and religious origins to convey an intended message to their listeners. One especially noteworthy development of the period was the recognition that different styles were appropriate for different purposes. Thus, the older *stile antico* was preserved and practiced alongside newer styles; because of its associations with sacred music and with pedagogy, it was often deployed to evoke the solemnity and authority of tradition. Nevertheless, because the primacy of the text and the persuasive delivery of its message were central to any vocal work of the period, rhetorical effectiveness was prized far above stylistic purity.

# Instrumental Music
# Comes of Age

*Chapter Contents*

*Prelude*  206

Types of Instrumental
Music  207

Dance Music  207

Variations  210

Abstract Instrumental
Works  214

*Postlude*  220

## PRELUDE

O ur story so far has focused on vocal music since the great majority of pieces that survive from earlier periods are for voices, alone or with instruments. While not designed for instruments, much of this vocal music was performed on instruments. Of course, dances, fanfares, and other pieces intended for instruments were played throughout the Middle Ages and Renaissance. But since performers played from memory or improvised, little of this music survived in notation. Instrumental music was functional: people welcomed it to accompany dancing or dining but seldom listened to it or played it for its own sake, and thus it was valued less highly than vocal music. This limitation began to fade during the sixteenth century, when churches, patrons, and musical amateurs increasingly cultivated instrumental music and artists celebrated the rich variety among types of instruments, such as those shown in Figure 10.1. The growth in music for instruments is partly an illusion; it simply means more was being written down. But that change in itself shows that music without voices was now more often deemed worthy of preservation and dissemination in writing.

The rise of instrumental music during the Renaissance and its coming of age in the Baroque era is evident in the cultivation of new instruments, new roles for instrumental music, new genres, and new styles, as well as in the growing supply of written music for instruments alone, including many published collections. By the end of the seventeenth century, instrumental music had moved out of the long shadow cast by vocal music to gain independence and become the latter's equal in both quantity and quality.

At the same time, instrumental composers borrowed many elements typical of the new vocal idioms, including employment of the basso continuo, interest in moving the affections, focus on the soloist, and use of virtuosic embellishment and stylistic contrast. Even specific styles such as recitative and aria made their mark on instrumental music, especially on works for violin, which rose to prominence in the seventeenth century partly because it was able to mimic the expressive qualities of the solo voice.

# Types of Instrumental Music

Within the newly flourishing instrumental repertoire, certain basic compositional procedures may be identified that divide the works into five broad categories. To some extent, these classifications are artificial because elements of one category often appear in works of another. But while the types listed here are neither exhaustive nor mutually exclusive, they are useful as an introduction to the main genres that arose during the sixteenth century and prevailed throughout the Baroque era.

- dances and other pieces in stylized dance rhythms, whether independent, paired, or linked together in a suite
- pieces that vary a given melody (variations, partita), chorale (chorale variations, chorale partita), or bass line (partita, chaconne, passacaglia)
- keyboard or lute pieces in improvisatory style, called toccatas, fantasias, or preludes (see "Improvisatory Genres," page 214)
- fugal pieces in continuous imitative counterpoint, called ricercari, fantasias, fancies, capriccios, or fugues (see "Continuous Genres," page 216)
- pieces with contrasting sections, often in imitative counterpoint, called canzonas or sonatas (see "Sectional Genres," page 217)

# Dance Music

Social dancing was widespread and highly valued beginning in the Renaissance, and well-bred people were expected to be accomplished dancers (see "Social Dance," page 208). Performers frequently improvised dance music or played dance tunes from memory, as in earlier times. But with the advent of music printing, many dance pieces were published in collections issued by Petrucci, Attaingnant, and other publishers, for ensemble, lute, or keyboard.

*Figure 10.1.* Apollo and the Muses *was painted by Maerten de Vos (1532–1603) on the underside of a harpsichord lid, a common practice at the time that served to individualize the instrument and enhance its value. In fact, the spinet or virginal within this painting has just such an elaborate scene painted on its lid. Apollo, crowned in laurel, plays a kithara; two of the Muses sing from partbooks while one of them holds a trumpet; others play lutes, virginal, fiddle, tambourine, cornett, and harp. Musées royaux des Beaux-Arts de Belgique, Brussels.*

Dancing is essential in a well-ordered society, because it allows males and females to mingle and observe one another. How else does a lady decide whom to marry? Through dancing, she can tell whether someone is shapely and fit or unattractive and lame, whether he is in good health or has unpleasant breath, and whether he is graceful and attentive or clumsy and awkward.

So writes the dancing master Thoinot Arbeau (pen name for the astronomer Jehan Tabourot) in his *Orchésographie* (1589), the best-known dance treatise of the Renaissance. He offers these views to a young man who has just returned home from a big city where he devoted many years to studying law but where, as he confesses with some regret, he did not make time to learn to dance. Belatedly, the young man has realized that, far from being a frivolous pastime, dancing is a pleasant and profitable activity, one that confers and preserves health provided it is practiced in moderation at suitable times and in appropriate places. It is especially recommended for those who lead sedentary lives, such as students intent upon their books and young women who spend long hours at knitting and needlework.

Most dances of the sixteenth and seventeenth centuries were performed by couples who arranged themselves in rows or circles. Some dances, like the pavane, were elegant and dignified, involving a series of gliding steps as in a stately procession. Others, like the various branles, were executed with sideways or swaying motions. Still others, like the galliard, required such nimble steps and leaps that sometimes the man had to hoist his partner in the air. (With the ladies dressed in the elaborate costumes that we see in Figure 10.2, it is no wonder the women needed help getting off the ground.)

As the dancing master went on to suggest to his new pupil, dancing is also a kind of mute rhetoric by which persons, through movement, can make themselves understood and persuade onlookers that they are gallant or comely and worthy to be acclaimed, admired, and loved. Such attitudes help to explain the importance of social dance in the musical culture of the past. And although the steps may be different, the social value of dance in society today remains remarkably unchanged.

*Figure 10.2.  Detail from* Dancing Party, *ca. 1639, by Pieter Codde (1599–1678), a Dutch painter active in Amsterdam. The dancing man, whose face is hidden behind a mask, wears a theatrical costume and holds his hat in his hand. His female partner lifts the hem of her skirt to execute the steps of what appears to be a galliard. The dancers are accompanied by a lutenist, who may also be singing. Private collection.*

Figure 10.3. *Title page of Silvestro Ganassi's instruction book on recorder playing,* Opera intítula Fontegara *(1535). A recorder consort and two singers perform from printed partbooks. In the foreground are two cornetti, and on the wall hang three viols and a lute.*

Functional and stylized dance music

These published dances show that dance music served two very different purposes in the Renaissance. Dances for ensemble were functional music, suitable for accompanying dancers. In these pieces, the principal melody is typically in the uppermost part, sometimes highly ornamented, but often left plain, allowing the performer to add embellishments. The other parts are mostly homophonic, with little or no contrapuntal interplay. Most dance pieces for solo lute or keyboard, on the other hand, are stylized, intended for the enjoyment of the player or listeners rather than for dancing; these often include more elaborate counterpoint or written-out decoration. This type of dance music was probably the earliest to gain independence from vocal music because it drew attention to the instrument itself and its characteristics. The use of social dance music for solitary music making is interesting; perhaps the pleasure of solo performance was enhanced by incorporating the familiar rhythms of dance, which carried associations with social interaction or with the physical motions of dancing. Whatever the reason, from the Renaissance to the present, many instrumental works are stylized dances.

Each dance follows a particular meter, tempo, rhythmic pattern, and form, all of which are reflected in pieces composed for it. This particularity of rhythm and form distinguishes each type of dance from the others and gives all dance music a character unlike that of other kinds of music. Dance pieces feature distinct sections, usually repeated, with two, three, or more sections depending on the dance. Usually the phrase structure is clear and predictable, often in four-measure groups, so that dancers can follow it easily.

These features may be seen in Attaingnant's *Danseries à 4 parties* (Dances for Four Players, 1547, NAWM 59), which opens with a *basse danse* ("low dance"), a stately couples dance marked by gracefully raising and lowering the body. The music consists of two sections, each repeated. This structure, called binary form, became standard for dances in the seventeenth and eighteenth centuries.

CD 4/4    CD 2/26

Attaingnant's prints do not specify which instruments should play which parts; the choice was up to the performers. Not until the seventeenth century, when instrumental music began to develop characteristic idioms peculiar to one type of instrument or another, did composers name instruments in their scores. Most wind and string instruments were built in sets or families, covering the

*Figure 10.4. Musicians, a painting by Reinhold Timm, dated ca. 1620, portrays four musicians playing bass viol, harp, lute, and transverse flute. These instruments are listed in the inventory of the royal chapel of Denmark, where King Christian IV employed a number of English virtuosos, two of whom ran away from the court, taking the instruments with them.*

entire range from soprano to bass, so that any of the *Danseries* could theoretically be played entirely by recorders or viols, for example. In England, an ensemble comprised of members of the same family of instruments was known as a consort (see Figure 10.3). More common later in the sixteenth century were mixed ensembles, called in English "broken" consorts, that used instruments from different families (see Figure 10.4). With the advent of the new concertato medium, however, uniform timbres gave way to basso-continuo textures, and combinations of contrasting sounds became the rule in instrumental as well as in vocal music.

Performers often grouped dances in pairs or threes. A favorite combination was a slow dance in duple meter followed by a fast one in triple meter on the same tune, the music of the second dance being a variation of the first. One such pair, the pavane (or pavan) and galliard, was a favorite in sixteenth-century France and England. The pavane was a stately dance in three repeated strains (AABBCC), and the more lively galliard followed the same form with a variant of the same melody. Figure 10.5 shows three couples dancing a pavane, clearly more reserved and less vigorous than the galliard shown in Figure 10.6. A similar pairing of dances in slow duple and fast triple meter was the passamezzo and saltarello, popular in Italy and elsewhere.

The idea of linking together two or three dances, such as the pavane and galliard was extended in the seventeenth century to create a suite of several dances, used either for dancing or as chamber music. Johann Hermann Schein's *Banchetto musicale* (Musical Banquet, 1617) contains twenty suites for five instruments with continuo, each having the sequence padouana (pavane), gagliarda (galliard), courante, allemande, and tripla, the last a triple-meter variation of the allemande. Some of the suites build on one melodic idea that recurs in varied form in every dance, and others are linked by more subtle melodic similarity. The keyboard suite will be explored in Chapter 12.

In the Baroque era, dances continued to be composed for social dancing, for theatrical spectacles, and in stylized form for chamber music for lute, keyboard, or ensemble. In fact, dance music was so central to musical life that dance rhythms permeated other instrumental and vocal music, secular and sacred alike. For example, slow dance types, such as the saraband and, later, the minuet, were often used in arias to convey certain affections; and some sonatas, even those intended for performance during church services, often included dance movements.

## Variations

Improvising on a tune to accompany dancing has ancient roots, but the form known as variation form is a sixteenth-century invention, used for independent instrumental pieces rather than as dance accompaniment. Variations combine change with repetition, taking a given theme—an existing or newly composed tune, bass line, harmonic plan, melody with accompaniment, or other musical subject—and presenting an uninterrupted series of variants on that theme. The goal was to showcase the variety that could be achieved in embellishing a basic idea and, often, to provide a technical challenge as the figuration becomes increasingly complex, but the result was a very practical solution to the problem of how to achieve length and coherence in a piece without words. For this reason, perhaps, it became the formal type most favored by composers of instrumental music in the early seventeenth century.

Some of the earliest books of printed music included variations on dance tunes written specifically for the lute. Pavane variations, for example, featured either a varied repetition of each strain (AA′BB′CC′) or several variations of a single strain. The lute, shown in Figures 10.2 and 10.4, was the most popular household instrument in the sixteenth century and continued to be a mainstay of the basso-continuo ensemble in the seventeenth century. The standard lute had a pear-shaped body with a rounded back, and a long neck with a flat fingerboard at the end of which a pegbox (where the strings attached to tuning pegs) turned back at a right angle. It had one single and five double strings, usually tuned G–c–f–a–d′–g′, which were plucked with the fingers. Frets, made of strips of leather wound around the neck, marked where the player stopped the string with the fingers of the left hand to raise the pitch one or more semitones. A skilled player could produce a great variety of effects, from melodies, runs, and ornaments of all kinds to chords and counterpoint. The instrument was capable of a variety of roles: lutenists accompanied singing, played in ensembles, and performed solos.

The lute, introduced by the Arabs into Spain, had been known in Europe for almost five hundred years. Its very name was derived from the Arabic *al-ʿud*.

*Lute music*

*Figure 10.5 (left). Three couples dance a stately pavane at a party in the court of Duke Albrecht IV in Munich. The dancers are accompanied by a flute and drum visible in the left balcony, while the right balcony holds a kettledrum player and two trumpeters, whose instruments are hung up. In the background, the duke and a lady play cards. Engraving by Matthäus Zasinger, ca. 1500. Kupferstichkabinett, Dresden.*

*Figure 10.6 (right). A couple dancing a galliard, accompanied by pipe and drum, fiddle, and what appears to be a viol. Woodcut by Hans Hofer, ca. 1540.*

Figure 10.7.  Title page of Parthenia; or,
The Maydenhead, a collection of music
for virginal by William Byrd and other
English keyboard composers presented to
Princess Elizabeth on her wedding in 1613.
Parthenia were Greek maidens' choral
dances, so both the title and subtitle
allude whimsically to the bride, the
keyboard instrument's name, and the fact
that this was the first such collection ever
printed.

Perhaps because of its non-European origins, much of the lute's solo repertory
developed independently of mainstream vocal music and became the first to
harbor a style that was idiomatic to the instrument; what sounded and felt "natural" on the lute could not easily be played or imitated on another instrument
and was certainly out of the realm of the voice. This is evident even from its special type of notation known as tablature, which indicates not the pitch of each
sound (as in vocal music) but its position on the instrument's fingerboard (see
Figure 7.6). Closely related to the lute was the Spanish vihuela, which had a flat
back and guitar-shaped body.

   Lute performers and composers also created sets of variations on standard
airs for singing poetry, such as the Italian romanesca and Ruggiero, or the
Spanish tune *Guárdame las vacas* (see Example 10.1), which feature a spare
melodic outline over a standard bass progression. The 1538 collection of works
for vihuela by Spanish composer Luys de Narváez (fl. 1526–1549), *Los seys libros
del Delphin* (The Six Books of the Dauphin), contains the first published sets of
variations (called *diferencias* in Spanish), including *Guárdame las vacas* (NAWM
60b). In the first examples of the genre, ideas that would characterize variation
form for the next five centuries are already in place: each variation preserves the
phrase structure, harmonic plan, and cadences of the theme, while recasting the
melody with a new figuration that distinguishes it from the other variations.

CD 4/8

Example 10.1: Luys de Narváez, "Guárdame las vacas," *structural outline of melody
and bass*

*Figure 10.8. Engraving after Hendrik Goltzius (1558–1617) of Saint Cecilia playing the organ in the company of two singing angels. The association between young women and keyboard playing was affirmed by images of the newly popular Saint Cecilia, a fifth-century virgin martyr who became the patron saint of music. Depictions such as this engraving, which obviously inspired the title page of* Parthenia *(Figure 10.7), proliferated during the seventeenth century as both the saint's stature and the status of instrumental music grew. (See also Figure 12.7, a later painting by Poussin.)*

English virginalists

The variation enjoyed an extraordinary flowering in the late sixteenth and early seventeenth centuries among a group of English keyboard composers known as the English virginalists, after the name of their instrument, which was a member of the harpsichord family. (As such, its robust sound was produced by using the keys to activate quills that plucked the strings.) Works by the leading English composer William Byrd (see Chapter 8) appear in the first published collection of music for virginal, *Parthenia* (1613), shown in Figure 10.7. (See also Figure 10.8.) The English virginalists typically used dances or familiar songs of the time as themes for variation. Their interest in varying melodies distinguishes the English from earlier Spanish and Italian composers, who focused more on bass patterns and bare melodic outlines. The songs used were generally short, simple, and regular in phrasing. The melody may be presented intact throughout an entire set of variations, passing at times from one voice to another; more often, it is broken up by decorative figuration, so that its original profile is only suggested. Each variation typically uses one type of figuration. In most variation sets, the rhythmic animation increases as the work progresses, though often ending with a slower final variation.

An example of English variation technique is Byrd's *Pavana Lachrymae* (NAWM 61), based on Dowland's lute song *Flow, my tears* (NAWM 58). The song already has the typical form of a pavane (AABBCC), with three strains, each repeated. Byrd varied each strain and then added a second, more active variation for the repetition, producing the form AA'BB'CC'. He retained the outline of the vocal melody in the right hand while adding short accompanying motives or decorative turns, figurations, and scale patterns that are imitated between the hands.

The variation principle permeated many of the instrumental genres of the seventeenth century, although the term *variation* did not always appear in the title. Composers of the early seventeenth century often used the term *partite* ("divisions" or "parts") for sets of variations; later it was applied to dance suites as well.

| CD 4/9 | CD 2/29 |
| CD 4/1 | CD 2/23 |

New subjects for variation forms emerged in the seventeenth century and became "standards." Among these, the most popular were the chaconne and passacaglia, the first deriving from the chacona, a lively dance-song imported from Latin America, and the second from the Spanish passacalle, a ritornello improvised over a simple cadential progression. Both were essentially bass or harmonic progressions rather than melodies. Although the earliest known keyboard variations on these forms are by an Italian composer, Girolamo Frescobaldi (see biography on page 215), the terms soon appeared in France, Germany, and elsewhere, and always to designate variations over a ground bass. Whether traditional or newly composed, these repeated progressions were usually four measures long, in triple meter and slow tempo.

# Abstract Instrumental Works

## Improvisatory Genres

The instrumental genres we have seen so far are all based on dance patterns or derived from song, the two traditional wellsprings of music. But the other genres outlined at the beginning of this chapter may be viewed as abstract because they cultivated several types of music that were truly independent of dance rhythms or borrowed tunes. Most of these developed from habits of improvisation on polyphonic instruments such as lute or keyboard, while others drew on imitative textures derived from vocal music. Such pieces could be played or listened to for their own sake, and improvisers and composers frequently employed unusual or highly expressive effects to attract listeners' attention.

*Introductory and improvisatory pieces*

Performers on keyboard and lute often had reason to improvise: to introduce a song, to fill time during a church service, to establish the mode of a subsequent chant or hymn, to test the tuning of a lute, or to entertain themselves or an audience. Compositions that resemble such improvisations rank among the earliest examples of solo instrumental music and became mainstays of the repertoire for solo players. Such pieces were given a variety of names, including prelude, fantasia, or ricercare. Not based on any preexisting melody, they unfold freely, with varying textures and musical ideas. They served the same function as an introduction to a speech, preparing the listener and establishing the tonality for what followed.

The toccata, from the Italian *toccare* ("to touch"), was the principal genre of lute and keyboard music in improvisatory style. Established in the sixteenth

*Figure 10.9. Church musicians depicted on a carved lectern from Biecz, Poland, 1633. The organ, played by one person while another works the bellows, is mounted on lions' feet. A mustached singer reads from a partbook on the lower left, while a pair of string players complete the concertato ensemble. Compare this organ, which has no pedal rank, with the instruments shown in Figures 12.1 and 12.3.*

## ✳ Girolamo Frescobaldi (1583–1643)

As one of the first composers of international stature to focus primarily on instrumental music, Frescobaldi helped to raise it to a par with vocal music. He cultivated every keyboard genre of his era and wrote vocal works and ensemble canzonas.

Born in Ferrara, Italy, Frescobaldi was trained there in organ and composition. In 1608, he became organist at Saint Peter's in Rome. He supplemented his income by serving noble patrons and teaching keyboard, which gave him an outlet for harpsichord and other chamber music. He published collections of keyboard works with dedications to various patrons. In 1628, he became organist to the grand duke of Tuscany in Florence, then returned to Rome and Saint Peter's in 1634

Figure 10.10. Girolamo Frescobaldi in his forties, in a chalk drawing by Claude Mellan.

under the patronage of the Barberini family, nephews of the pope. By then, his music was celebrated in France, Flanders, and Germany.

After his death, Frescobaldi remained widely admired across Europe. His keyboard music was a model for composers as late as J. S. and C. P. E. Bach, particularly his toccatas because of their bold harmonies and technical difficulty, and his ricercari and other imitative works because of their learned counterpoint.

**Major works:** keyboard toccatas, fantasias, ricercari, canzonas, and partitas; *Fiori musicali*, with 3 organ Masses; ensemble canzonas; madrigals, chamber arias, motets, and 2 Masses.

century as a kind of "warm-up" piece, full of scalar and other florid passages that burst forth from the player's fingers at irregular intervals, the toccata continued to thrive in the seventeenth century. Toccatas could be played on the harpsichord (as chamber music) or the organ (as church music; see Figure 10.9).

The most important composer of toccatas was Girolamo Frescobaldi (1583–1643; see biography and Figure 10.10), organist at Saint Peter's in Rome. Toccata no. 3 from his first book of toccatas for harpsichord (1615; NAWM 74) is typical in featuring a succession of brief sections, each focused on a particular figure that is subtly varied. Some sections display virtuoso passage work, while others pass ideas between the hands. Each section ends with a cadence, weakened harmonically, rhythmically, or through continued movement in order to sustain momentum until the very end. According to the composer's preface, the various sections of these toccatas may be played separately, and the player may end the piece at any appropriate cadence, reminding us that in the Baroque era written music was a platform for performance, not a fixed text. Frescobaldi indicated that the tempo is not subject to a regular beat but may be modified according to the sense of the music, especially by slowing at cadences.

> Frescobaldi's toccatas
>
> CD 5/11    CD 3/1

The role of the toccata as service music is illustrated by those in Frescobaldi's *Fiori musicali* (Musical Flowers, 1635), a set of three organ Masses, each containing all the music an organist would play at Mass. All three include a toccata before Mass and another at the Elevation of the Host before Communion, and two add another toccata before a ricercare. These toccatas are shorter than his ones for harpsichord but just as sectional, and they feature the sustained tones and harmonic surprises often found in organ toccatas.

> *Fiori musicali*

Frescobaldi's most famous student was Johann Jacob Froberger (1616–1667), organist at the imperial court in Vienna. Froberger's toccatas tend to alternate improvisatory passages with sections in imitative counterpoint. His pieces were the model for the later merging of toccata and fugue, as in the

> Johann Jacob Froberger

CD 6/6

CD 6/38    CD 3/27

works of Buxtehude (see NAWM 84), or their coupling, as in Bach's toccatas or preludes and fugues (see NAWM 88).

## Continuous Genres

**Ricercare and fugue**

CD 5/13

The seventeenth-century ricercare was typically a serious composition for organ or harpsichord in which one subject, or theme, is continuously developed in imitation. The Ricercare after the Credo from Frescobaldi's *Mass for the Madonna* in *Fiori musicali* (NAWM 75) is remarkable for the skillful handling of chromatic lines and the subtle use of shifting harmonies and dissonance, revealing a quiet intensity that characterizes much of Frescobaldi's organ music. As shown in Example 10.2, the subject has a strong profile marked by leaps and a slow chromatic ascent, making it easy to hear the subject on each entrance, while the faster diatonic countersubject offers contrast.

*Example 10.2: Girolamo Frescobaldi, Ricercare after the Credo, from* Mass for the Madonna, *in* Fiori musicali

In the early seventeenth century, some composers, especially in Germany, began to apply the term *fugue* (from the Italian *fuga*, "flight"), formerly used for the technique of imitation itself, to a genre of serious pieces that treat one theme in continuous imitation. As we will see in Chapters 12 and 13, fugues became increasingly important in the late seventeenth and early eighteenth centuries.

**Fantasia**

The keyboard fantasia, an imitative work on a larger scale than the ricercare, had a more complex formal organization. The leading fantasia composers in this period were the Dutch organist Jan Pieterszoon Sweelinck (1562–1621) and his German pupil Samuel Scheidt (1587–1654). In Sweelinck's fantasias, a fugal exposition usually leads to successive sections with different countersubjects, sometimes treating the subject in rhythmic augmentation or diminution. Scheidt's *Tabulatura nova* (New Tablature, 1624) includes several monumental fantasias. He called it new because instead of using tablature notation, like most German organ music of the time, Scheidt adopted the modern Italian practice of writing out each part on a separate staff in the pitch notation used for vocal and ensemble music. The works of Scheidt, and his influence as a teacher, were the foundation of a remarkable development of north German organ music in the Baroque era.

**English consort fantasias**

In England, music for viol consort was a mainstay of social music making in the home. The leading genre was the imitative fantasia, often called *fancy*, which would treat one or more subjects in a fugal fashion. Structurally, it functioned just like the solo keyboard fugues or ricercari, but it was intended for ensemble performance. Popular composers included Alfonso Ferrabosco the Younger (ca. 1575–1628), son of an Italian musician active at Queen Elizabeth's court, and John Coprario (ca. 1575–1626), whose Italianized name (he was born Cooper) exemplifies the English fashion for things Italian.

## Sectional Genres

The canzona was an imitative piece for keyboard or ensemble in several contrasting sections, played either as chamber music or in church. Canzonas featured markedly rhythmic themes and a more lively character than ricercari. The most celebrated composer of ensemble canzonas was Giovanni Gabrieli (ca. 1555–1612; see biography and Figure 10.11, below), organist and supervisor of instrumental music at Saint Mark's church in Venice (see Figure 10.12). His splendid polychoral motets, with their *cori spezzati* ("divided choirs"), and his innovative instrumental works, both genres shaped by the rich musical environment of Venice (see Chapter 9), employed all the resources available at the church, which had a long tradition of organ music and a permanent ensemble of first-rate instrumentalists. These were mostly brass and wind players, whose instruments sounded at the core of the processional and ceremonial music heard in Piazza San Marco (see Figure 9.13), but the roster also included violinists and bassoon players. Additional players were hired on major feast days, when as many as two dozen instrumentalists performed alone or together with the choir of twenty to thirty voices.

Gabrieli and other Venetian composers applied the idea of divided choirs to their instrumental works. The *Canzon septimi toni a 8* (Canzona in Mode 7 in Eight Parts, NAWM 62) from Gabrieli's *Sacrae symphoniae* (Sacred Symphonies, 1597)

Canzona

Ensemble canzonas

CD 4/15

---

### ✷ Giovanni Gabrieli (ca. 1555–1612)

Gabrieli was one of the leading composers of the late Renaissance and early Baroque periods, associated particularly with the opulent style of instrumental and concerted sacred music in Venice.

Little is known about Gabrieli's early life and training. In his teens and early twenties, he was in the service of Duke Albrecht V in Munich, where he studied with Orlando di Lasso. In 1585, he won appointment as second organist at Saint Mark's, serving alongside his uncle Andrea Gabrieli until the latter's death that August. That same year, the younger Gabrieli also was elected organist to the Scuola Grande di San Rocco, one of the most prominent of the *scuole* ("schools"), or charitable confraternities, of Venice. The *scuole* sponsored religious observances and performances, participated in civic celebrations, and strove to outdo each other in pageantry and music, giving Gabrieli ample opportunity to compose lavish music for large forces. At Saint Mark's, he was the main composer of ceremonial music, producing about a hundred motets, most for multiple choirs. As second organist, Gabrieli supervised the instrumentalists, and his ensemble canzonas and sonatas were no doubt written for them. He served both Saint Mark's and San Rocco until his death in 1612.

*Figure 10.11. Giovanni Gabrieli, 1602, by Annibale Carracci (1560–1609), whose work focused on more natural portraits and rejected the mannered style of the day.*

**Major works:** about 100 motets, over 30 madrigals, 37 ensemble canzonas, 7 sonatas, and about 35 organ works, including ricercari, canzonas, toccatas, and *intonazioni*.

*Figure 10.12. Interior of the eleventh-century church of Saint Mark (architecturally known as a basilica), where Venetian composers cultivated a style of composition and performance involving multiple antiphonal choirs (cori spezzati) of voices, instruments, or a combination of the two.*

Ensemble sonatas

resembles a double-chorus motet for two groups of four instruments, with basso continuo accompaniment specified for organ. Like other canzonas, it presents a series of contrasting sections, some imitative, others more homophonic. The two instrumental groups alternate long passages, engage in more rapid dialogue, and sometimes play together, especially at the end. The canzona had no standard form; in this case, its form is defined by a refrain that appears three times.

The Venetian sonata (Italian for "sounded") was a close relative of the canzona, consisting of a series of sections each based on a different subject or on variants of a single subject. Both canzonas and sonatas were used at Mass or Vespers as introductions or postludes, or to accompany significant rituals. The *Sonata pian' e forte* from Gabrieli's *Sacrae symphoniae* has earned a prominent place in music history because it is among the first instrumental ensemble pieces to designate specific instruments in the printed parts: in the first choir, cornett (a wooden wind instrument resembling a straight or curved trumpet— see Figure 10.3) and three sackbuts (early trombones); in the second, a violin and three sackbuts. Another innovation in the printed music was indicating passages as *pian* (*piano*, meaning "soft") or *forte* ("loud"), one of the earliest instances of dynamic markings in music. Through contrasts of one instrumental choir against the other, single choir with both together, loud versus soft, and slow homophonic passages with faster motion and points of imitation, Gabrieli created a purely instrumental work with as much interest, variety, and depth of content as a madrigal or motet.

Elsewhere in Italy, the term *sonata* was used early in the seventeenth century to refer broadly to any piece for instruments. It gradually came to designate a composition that resembled a canzona in form but had special characteristics. Sonatas were often scored for one or two melody instruments, usually violins, with basso continuo, while the ensemble canzona was written in four or more parts and could be played without continuo. Sonatas often exploited the idiomatic possibilities offered by a particular instrument and imitated the modern expressive vocal style, while the typical canzona displayed more of the formal, abstract quality of Renaissance polyphony.

One of the earliest composers of sonatas for solo violin and continuo was Biagio Marini (1594–1663). Marini served for a time as violinist at Saint Mark's under Monteverdi and then held various posts in Italy and Germany. His *Sonata IV per il violino per sonar con due corde*, from Op. 8 (NAWM 76), published in 1629, is an early example of what may be called "instrumental monody." Like the canzona, it has contrasting sections, but almost every one features idiomatic violin gestures, including large leaps, double stops, runs, trills, and embellishments (see Example 10.3b). Marini's sonata opens with an expressive melody, shown in Example 10.3a, that is reminiscent of a solo madrigal, even adopting Caccini's vocabulary of *affetti*, or ornaments, before turning almost immediately to idiomatic sequential figures. Rhapsodic and metrical sections alternate, resembling the contrasts between recitative and aria styles that were developing about this time.

Biagio Marini

CD 5/15

*Example 10.3: Biagio Marini, Sonata*

a.

b.

**TIMELINE**  Instrumental Music Comes of Age

| MUSICAL EVENTS | | HISTORICAL EVENTS |
|---|---|---|
| First publication of instrumental music: lute tablature issued by Petrucci | **1507** | |
| | | **1517**  Reformation begins |
| Attaingnant's first instrumental publication, for lute | **1529** | |
| Narváez, *Los seys libros del Delphin* | **1538** | |
| | | **1545–63**  Council of Trent |
| | | **1558–1603**  Reign of Elizabeth I of England |
| Gabrieli at Saint Mark's, Venice | **1585–1612** | |
| Arbeau, *Orchésographie* | **1589** | |
| Gabrieli, *Sacrae symphoniae* | **1597** | |
| First surviving opera, *L'Euridice*, performed in Florence | **1600** | |
| | | **1601**  Shakespeare, *Hamlet* |
| Caccini, *Le nuove musiche* | **1602** | |
| | | **1610**  Galileo publishes *Starry Messenger* |
| *Parthenia*, collection of works for virginal, published | **1613** | |
| | | **1618–1648**  Thirty Years' War |
| Schütz, *Symphoniae sacrae I* published; Marini, Sonatas for Violin and Continuo, Op. 8, published | **1629** | |
| Frescobaldi, *Fiori musicali* published | **1635** | |
| | | **1645–1652**  Bernini, *The Ecstasy of Saint Teresa* |

By the middle of the seventeenth century, the canzona and sonata had merged, and the term sonata came to stand for both. However, styles for voice and for each family of instruments gradually diverged, eventually becoming so distinct that composers could purposefully borrow vocal idioms in instrumental writing and vice versa.

# POSTLUDE

The extraordinary burst of innovation associated with opera and vocal music in the early seventeenth century is equally apparent in the instrumental music of the time, whether for soloist or ensemble, church or chamber. Yet, like opera, instrumental music also drew deeply on sixteenth-century traditions, redefining existing genres and approaches by combining them with new styles and techniques, and by assimilating the new dramatic aesthetic of the Baroque era.

The sixteenth century saw the rise of instrumental music cultivated for its own sake, whether derived from dance music, related to vocal music, or conceived as abstract music independent of dance or song. Some genres of instrumental music continued into the Baroque era and beyond, including stylized dances, variations of sacred and secular tunes, and preludes or toccatas and fugues. Whereas composers of Renaissance polyphony had not differentiated between instrumental and vocal writing, to the point where almost any combination of voices and instruments was interchangeable, even the earliest music for solo lute, organ, or harpsichord manifested a quality peculiar, or idiomatic, to the instrument. The pursuit of such idioms fostered the increasing separation and independence of instrumental from vocal music. Then, too, the more prominent role of the soloist in the Baroque era—whether singer, violinist, or wind player—enticed composers to adapt their writing in order to take advantage of the particular attributes of one medium or the other. Famous teachers and practitioners of the art of singing promoted new standards of virtuosity and new expressive devices for moving the emotions that were then adapted to instruments. Once instrumental and vocal styles had sufficiently diverged and achieved their distinct idioms, composers could transfer these styles from vocal to instrumental works and vice versa, writing a violin melody that sighed like a voice or a vocal melody that blared like a trumpet.

Instrumental music continued to gain independence until, by the late eighteenth century, it reached a level of prestige higher than that of most vocal music. Moreover, the tradition of playing instrumental music for one's own pleasure, alone or with friends, was well established by the early seventeenth century and has endured to this day.

# Opera and Vocal Music in the Late Seventeenth Century

*Chapter Contents*

*Prelude* 222

Italy 222

France 230

England 235

Germany 240

*Postlude* 242

## PRELUDE

Opera spread throughout Italy as well as to other countries during the second half of the seventeenth century. The principal Italian center remained Venice, whose opera houses were famous all over Europe. Germany imported Venetian opera, which then fused with native styles into a national German opera. France resisted Italian influence and eventually developed its own operatic idiom—one that was largely determined by the court's penchant for ballet and the tastes of Louis XIV, who acquired his nickname le Roi Soleil ("the Sun King") after dancing in a court ballet costumed as Apollo (see Figure 11.5). The reception of opera in England, however, was different: there King Charles I was beheaded in 1649, and during the ensuing Commonwealth period the puritanical climate was hardly friendly to the cultivation of such an extravagant art form. Even after the restoration of the English king in 1660, the monarchy was too weak and its treasury too depleted to support opera on the grand scale of the French or the Italians.

Vocal music for chamber and church also flourished during this period. The Italian chamber cantata, as well as French, English, and German song and concerted church music, were all influenced by the language of opera—especially recitative and aria—and by its musical vocabulary of the affections. Despite borrowings across borders, however, distinctive national styles developed that were shaped in part by the politics and culture of their respective countries.

## Italy

The birthplace of opera, Italy continued to be the stylistic source for composers of opera and chamber cantata all over Europe. And what these two genres had in common were recitative and aria, which developed a set of conventions that remained relatively unchanged throughout the century.

# Opera

As opera spread across Italy and outward to other countries, the principal Italian center remained Venice, whose public opera houses were famous all over Europe. Venetian theaters continued to vie with one another in luring audiences to their opera productions. More than the drama or spectacle, it was the singers and arias that attracted the public (see the vignette below). By offering high fees, impresarios competed for the most popular singers, who sometimes earned more than twice as much as composers (see "Innovations: Singer Power and Singer Worship—the Diva," page 224).

*Singers*

The singers' vehicle was the aria. While it was common in mid-century for an opera to include twenty-four arias, sixty became the norm by the 1670s. The favorite form at that time was the strophic song, in which several stanzas were performed to the same music. Also common were ground-bass arias, short two-part arias in AB form, and three-part arias in ABB′ and ABA or ABA′ forms. Many had refrains.

*Aria types*

By the end of the century, the most prevalent form was the da capo aria, essentially a large ABA structure (see diagram on page 227). Any repetition gave

---

**VIGNETTE**    A Frenchman's Account of Venetian Opera, ca. 1672

*An aristocratic Frenchman, having spent two years in Venice, published his impressions of the city and its inhabitants. Particularly interesting is this account of his experiences at the opera, where members of the audience were vociferous in expressing their enjoyment of the singers.*

~~~

At Venice they act in several operas at a time. The theaters are large and stately, the decorations noble and the alterations of them good. But they are very badly illuminated. . . . The ballets or dancing between the acts are generally so pittiful, that they would be much better omitted; for one would imagine these dancers wore lead in their shoes. Yet the assembly bestow their applauses on them, which is merely for want of having seen better. . . .

They that compose the musick of the opera endeavour to conclude the scenes of *the principal* actors with airs that charm and elevate, that so they may acquire the applause of the audience, which succeeds so well to their intentions, that one hears nothing but a thousand "Benissimos" together. Yet nothing is so remarkable as the pleasant benedictions and the ridiculous wishes of the gondoliers in the pit to the women singers, who cry aloud to them, *Sia tu benedetta, benedetto il padre che te gen-*

*erò* ["Bless you, and bless the father who conceived you"]. But these acclamations are not always within the bounds of modesty, for those impudent fellows say whatever they please, as being assur'd to make the assembly rather laugh than angry.

Some gentlemen have shewn themselves so transported and out of all bounds by the charming voices of these girls, as to bend themselves out of their boxes crying, *Ah cara! mi butto, mi butto* ["Ah dear one! I shall jump, I shall jump"], expressing after this manner the raptures of pleasure which these divine voices cause to them. . . . Nevertheless all things pass with more decency at the opera than at the comedy [i.e., the spoken theater], as being most commonly frequented by the better sort of people. One pays four livres at the door, and two more for a chair in the pitt, which amounts to three shillings and sixpence English, without reckoning the opera-book [libretto] and the wax-candle every one buys; for without them even those of the country would hardly comprehend any thing of the history [the plot] or the subject matter of the composition.

Alexandre-Toussaint Limojon, Sieur de Saint-Didier, *La Ville et la république de Venise* (1680), in Fra. Terne, *The City and Republick of Venice*, trans. Fra. Terne, 3 vols. in 1 (London, 1699).

From its very beginnings, opera was a complicated, costly, even extravagant affair requiring
the collaboration of the librettist, the composer
(who held a decidedly lower status than the author of
the words), and the artists whose performances engaged the audience directly. In addition, it demanded
the services of a vast array of craftspeople and
providers who worked behind the scenes. Among
these silent and unseen participants—including stage
managers, carpenters, painters, costume designers,
tailors, hairdressers, and copyists—none was more
crucial than the impresario, who was roughly equivalent to the modern producer. (Transferred into English from the Italian, the word *impresario* acquired
its distinctive meaning with the rise of Venetian
opera.) The theater's owner, head of one of the noble
families of Venice, entrusted the impresario with
managing the theater successfully for one season at a
time, which meant bringing in a profit after all the
production expenses and artists' fees were paid. Naturally, the economic outcome depended in good

*Figure 11.1b. Giuseppe Torelli's design for the final scene of
Carlo Caproli's "Le nozze di Peleo e di Theti." Engraving by
Israel Silvestre after François Francart, 1654.*

measure on the impresario's decisions about how
many and which operas were to be performed in a
given season. Competition was fierce, so the impresario also had to consider the financial risks involved
in mounting spectacular scenic effects (Figures 11.1a
and 11.1b) or hiring the most highly paid singers, and
measure these costs against the potential gains of attracting larger audiences.

This volatile commercial atmosphere fostered,
among other things, the phenomenon of the operatic
diva (or star). Impresarios went to great lengths and
expense to secure effective performers because they
realized that a singer could make or break an entire
opera season no matter what work was being produced. Although singer power had been a theme in
opera from its beginnings—think of Orfeo, whose
legendary song persuaded supernatural forces to return his spouse to life—that power now resided with
the singers themselves rather than the characters
they portrayed. Sopranos, especially those who were
able to win favor through virtuosic ornamentation
and persuasive interpretation, quickly achieved
stardom. Once having made it to the top, a diva could
demand that composers and librettists alter roles to
suit her particular vocal talents and range. In doing
so, she not only exercised her star power but actually
influenced the development of opera in ways that
eventually affected its dramatic structure as well as
its musical values.

The career of Anna Renzi (see Figure 11.2), leading lady of the Venetian operatic stage in the 1640s,
is a case in point and illustrates the rise in stature of

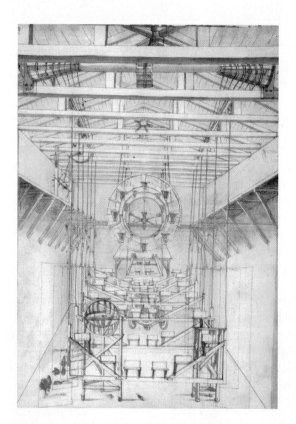

*Figure 11.1a. Stage designers of Baroque opera specialized
in rapidly moving scenery for their most dazzling effects.
Shown here is the machinery for one such set; a drawing of
the intended realization appears as Figure 11.b.*

the female singer. Renzi was only about twenty years old when her teacher brought her from Rome to Venice to perform the title role in the work that was scheduled to open the newest public opera house in that city—the Teatro Novissimo. The composer, Francesco Sacrati, undoubtedly tailored the role specifically to her in order to capitalize on her particular talents. That she played a woman pretending to be afflicted with madness on that occasion and then, a few years later, created the role of Nero's spurned empress Ottavia in Monteverdi's *Incoronazione di Poppea* speaks to her capabilities as an actress, one who could impart a certain dramatic intensity to her characters. Although her powers as a performer were by all accounts splendid, her meteoric ascent was at least in part a product of media hype. The librettist of her first Venetian opera, Giulio Strozzi, anxious to prove that public opera employed singers as divine as those of the wealthiest courts, published a special volume of adulatory poetry in her honor in 1644. The engraving of her likeness seen in Figure 11.2 comes from that volume.

In an introductory essay, Strozzi describes Renzi's stage presence and vocal qualities, stressing the apparently spontaneous nature of her movements and gestures: "Our Signora Anna is endowed with such lifelike expression that her responses and speeches seem not memorized but born at the very moment. In sum, she transforms herself completely into the person she represents." He goes on to praise her diction and vocal delivery, extolling her "fluent tongue, smooth pronunciation, not affected, not rapid, a full, sonorous voice, not harsh, not hoarse." He also remarks on her stamina and resilience, her ability to "bear the full weight of an opera no fewer than twenty-six times, repeating it virtually every evening . . . in the most perfect voice." Finally, Strozzi approaches Renzi's offstage attributes and portrays her as a person of "great intellect, much imagination, and a good memory . . . ; of melancholy temperament by nature [she] is a

Figure 11.2. *The famous opera singer Anna Renzi, in an engraving from Giulio Strozzi's adulatory book* The Glories of Signora Anna Renzi the Roman. *The elegiac couplet in Latin below her oval portrait reads: "When Anna merely pretends to sing, she delights the inmost heart; but when she truly sings, little by little she ravishes the very soul."*

woman of few words, but those are appropriate, sensible, and worthy."[1] Although she did not have what might be called a "classic beauty," Renzi's qualities essentially set the standard for the prima donna (Italian for "first lady," the lead soprano in an opera).

Divas became larger-than-life heroines with lucrative international careers. Following her memorable Venetian years, Renzi performed roles in other Italian cities and in Innsbruck, where Queen Christina of Sweden, who was then visiting the Austrian court, acknowledged her stunning skills by making her a present of her own medal and chain. Other prima donnas (and leading male singers) enjoyed similarly close relationships with patrons, composers, librettists, and impresarios in whose homes they sometimes lived when they were on the road. It is no surprise that they frequently exploited these ties by insinuating themselves into the creative process, exerting their influence on such matters as the selection of a plot, the number and length of arias written for their parts, and the casting of supporting roles. Occasionally a singer even refused to participate in a production unless a particular composer was commissioned to write the music.

Singer power and singer worship, then, ultimately played a big part in the direction that opera took in the seventeenth century. But the story does not end there. After taking hold of the Venetian imagination, the glamorous world of opera and its stars went on to captivate all of Europe and eventually the Americas. Even today, the powerful personalities of divas and their equivalents outside of opera—rock stars and film icons—are the driving force behind much of the entertainment industry.

1. Quotations from Giulio Strozzi are taken from Ellen Rosand, *Opera in Seventeenth-Century Venice: The Creation of a Genre* (Berkeley: University of California Press, 1991), pp. 228–235.

the singer a chance to ornament the melody with new embellishments and impressive vocal display.

Arias typically reflected the meaning of the text through musical motives in the melody or accompaniment. For example, a composer might imitate trumpet figures or a march to portray martial or vehement affections, or use a lively gigue, a sultry sarabande, or other dance rhythm to suggest feelings or actions conventionally associated with that dance.

## Chamber Cantata

The cantata had become the leading form of vocal chamber music in Italy, and the center of cantata composition was Rome. There, wealthy aristocrats and diplomats sponsored regular private parties for the elite, where the entertainment often included a cantata written expressly for the occasion. Because cantatas were meant for performance before a small, discriminating audience in a room without a stage, scenery, or costumes, they invited elegance, refinement, and wit that would be lost in a spacious opera house. Moreover, the demand for a new cantata at frequent intervals offered poets and composers regular work and chances to experiment.

CD 4/51

Cantatas around 1650 featured many short, contrasting sections, as we saw in Barbara Strozzi's *Lagrime mie* (NAWM 69). By the 1660s, poets and composers settled on a pattern of separate and alternating recitatives and arias, normally two or three of each, making for a much longer work. Most cantatas were written for solo voice with continuo, although some featured two or more voices. The text, usually pastoral love poetry, took the form of a dramatic narrative or soliloquy.

Scarlatti cantatas

The more than six hundred cantatas of Alessandro Scarlatti (1660–1725) mark a high point in this repertory. Scarlatti, shown in Figure 11.3, was also a leading opera composer whose works held sway in Rome and Naples (see Chapter 12, page 261). His artful and varied use of recitative and da capo aria pairs helped to ensure their reigning position in vocal music well into the eighteenth century. Scarlatti's chamber cantata *Clori vezzosa, e bella* (Charming and pretty Clori), consisting of two recitative-aria pairs, is typical of the solo cantata around 1690–1710. The second recitative (NAWM 82a) exemplifies Scarlatti's mature style in using a wide harmonic range, chromaticism, and diminished-seventh chords, rare for the time, to convey strong emotions or add bite to a cadence.

CD 5/56

*Figure 11.3. Alessandro Scarlatti, in an oil painting by an unknown artist. Liceo Musicale, Bologna.*

The most common form of aria in Scarlatti's operas and cantatas is the da capo aria. The form takes its name from the words "Da capo" ("from the head") placed at the close of the second section, instructing the performers to return to the beginning of the aria and repeat the first section, producing an ABA form. Typically, the A section is itself a small two-part form, with two different settings of the same text, each introduced by a brief instrumental ritornello. In Scarlatti's hands, the da capo aria was the perfect vehicle for sustaining a lyrical moment through a musical design that expressed a single sentiment, often joined with a related or opposing one in the contrasting middle section.

Both arias in *Clori vezzosa, e bella* are da capo arias. The second, *Sì, sì ben mio* (NAWM 82b), has this structure:

CD 5/57

| Section: | 1 | | | | 2 | 1 repeats |
|---|---|---|---|---|---|---|
| | Ritornello | A1 | Rit | A2 | B | |
| Key: | Dm | Dm→Gm | Gm | Gm→ Dm | FM→ V of Dm | |

In some da capo arias, the first section closes with another ritornello, or the opening ritornello is omitted when the first section repeats.

Example 11.1 shows the first half of this aria's first section. The spritely gigue rhythm contrasts ironically with the lover's request for "more torments for my heart." The opening ritornello introduces motives that the voice takes up and develops. The first vocal statement closes in the subdominant, the continuo states the second measure of the ritornello in that key, and the voice reenters with the second setting of the same text. The B section offers contrast in turning to a major key and more hopeful sentiments as the voice sings a new but related melody.

*Example 11.1: Alessandro Scarlatti,* Clori vezzosa, e bella, *opening of aria* Sì, sì, ben mio

*Yes, yes, my love, yes, yes,*
*I would like, through you, still more torments for my heart.*

The da capo aria became the standard aria form in the eighteenth century for opera and cantata alike because it offered great flexibility in expression. The music of the B section could be as similar or contrasting as the poetry required,

Embellishment and Improvisation in the Baroque

Baroque music is centered on the performer and the performance, not on the composer and the work. Baroque musicians regarded written scores merely as a basis for performance rather than as an unalterable text. Performers were expected to add to what the composer had notated not only in order to complete or supplement the original ideas, as when they realized a basso continuo, but also and especially in order to enhance the music's expressive powers, as when they ornamented a melody while performing. Performance practices relating to improvisation and embellishment varied from nation to nation and from one generation to another, but they were always an essential part of the performer's training and skill. Although the task is complex and controversial, modern players and scholars try to reconstruct these practices based on written treatises, descriptive accounts, and transcribed improvisations.

The word *ornamentation* now connotes something superficial, an added decoration that has no intrinsic merit; but for the Baroque musician it was the chief

*Example 11.2: Claudio Monteverdi*, Possente spirto, *from* L'Orfeo, *Act III*

*[wherever there is] so much beauty as hers is paradise.*

way of moving the affections. At the beginning of the Baroque era, Giulio Caccini even coined the Italian term *affetti* to indicate collectively the ornaments he taught with his new style of solo singing (see Chapter 9). Eventually, both vocalists and instrumentalists recognized two principal ways of ornamenting a melodic line. First, brief formulas called *ornaments*—such as trills, turns, appoggiaturas, and mordents—were added to certain notes to emphasize accents, cadences, and other significant points in the melody. Special signs sometimes—though not always—indicated their placement (see Chapter 12). The French were especially artful in specifying the exact placement and precise execution of ornaments. Second, more extended embellishments—such as scale and arpeggio passages (*passaggi*), and other types of flourishes—were added to create a free and elaborate paraphrase of the written line. This process—sometimes called division, diminution, or figuration—was especially appropriate to melodies in slow tempo. Example 11.2 is an excerpt from the aria in Monteverdi's opera *L'Orfeo* (see Chapter 9). Orfeo sings the aria at a point in the drama in which his powers as a musician are crucial to his success in retrieving Euridice—the more moving his song, the better his chances—demonstrating how closely the concept of ornamentation was linked to persuasive expression. The aria was published with the original tenor melody on the top staff and, below it, an embellished version that represents the kind of ornamentation added by a singer in one performance.

Performers were free not only to embellish a written score but also to change it in other ways. Singers often added cadenzas—elaborate passages decorating important cadences—to arias, and later these became a feature of solo instrumental works as well. Sections of variation sets and movements of suites were omitted or rearranged as desired. Title pages of ensemble collections encouraged players to choose which instruments and even how many to use for a performance. In every respect, the written music—whether published or not—was regarded as a script that could be adapted to suit the convenience and the varying tastes and habits of the performers. French musicians, for example, placed more emphasis on rhythmic freedom than on the kind of melodic ornamentation characteristic of Italian opera. Thus, some seventeenth- and eighteenth-century French writers on music advocated certain rhythmic modifications that were to be applied to the written notes in particular situations. For example, passages notated in equal values were typically played unequally, lengthening the first of every pair of eighth notes in a series, and shortening the second, resulting in a string of uneven, triplet like rhythms called *notes inégales* ("unequal notes"). A related French practice is overdotting, in which a dotted note is prolonged beyond its notated value—according to the performer's taste—while the following note is necessarily shortened. These changes, which may be heard in the NAWM recording of Lully's opera overture (77a), for example, serve to emphasize the beats and sharpen the rhythmic profile of the passages to which they are applied. But more important, they were thought to impart a certain stylish elegance to the performance, not unlike the "swing" effect in jazz.

CD 5/23

CD 2/58

while the form guaranteed a contrast of key, a sense of departure and return, and harmonic and thematic closure. Singers typically introduced new embellishments on the repetition of the A section, providing the perfect opportunity to display their artistry.

# France

Deferring to the country's strong cultural traditions of dance and spoken theater, French composers were slow to adopt Italian vocal styles. And when they did, the sound of the French language, with its different rhythms and accents from Italian, required adjustments to the pace and flow of the music that produced results and practices very distinct from the Italian styles.

## Opera

By around 1700, Italian opera was flourishing in every corner of western Europe except France. Having long opposed Italian opera on political and artistic grounds, the French finally established a national opera in the 1670s under the royal patronage of Louis XIV (r. 1643–1715, see Figure 11.4). Two powerful traditions influenced French opera: the sumptuous and colorful ballet, which had flourished at the royal court ever since the late sixteenth century; and the classical French tragedy, represented best by the works of Pierre Corneille (1606–1684) and Jean Racine (1639–1699). France's literary and theatrical culture insisted that poetry and drama be given priority on the stage. The king's love of, and participation in, the art of dancing ensured that the ballet also continued to have a prominent place in French opera (see Figures 11.5 and 11.6). The composer who succeeded in reconciling the demands of drama, music, and ballet was Jean-Baptiste Lully (1632–1687; see biography). His

*Figure 11.4. Louis XIV in his sixties, in a portrait by Hyacinthe Riguad from around 1700. The king is surrounded by images that convey his grandeur: a red velvet curtain, multicolor stone column, impressive wig, and enormous ermine robe covered on one side with gold fleurs-de-lis, the symbol of French royalty. His crown is by his side, shadowed and partially obscured, as if he did not need to emphasize the sign of his power, even while his hand and staff draw the eye to it. His elongated, upright stature and exposed, perfectly shaped legs proclaim his physical strength and remind the viewer of his renown as a dancer. Musée du Louvre, Paris.*

*Figures 11.5 and 11.6. (Left) Eventually earning a reputation as a brilliant dancer, Louis XIV got his nickname le Roi Soleil (the Sun King) after having danced in a court ballet dressed in the golden-rayed costume of Apollo, shown here. (Right) At the end of the century, his reign in decline, the helios symbol appeared in this Protestant caricature, which depicts Louis as a persecuting Inquisitor.*

new synthesis, *tragédie en musique*, later renamed *tragédie lyrique*, persisted for a century.

When Jean-Baptiste Lully, an Italian musician, came to Paris as an adolescent, he soon attracted the attention of the French king and proceeded to spend the rest of his adult life in France. From 1653, as director of the smaller of the king's two string orchestras and eventually of the larger ensemble as well (see below), he composed instrumental music and dance pieces for Italian operas produced at court. He also provided overtures, dances, and vocal numbers for court ballets, and he collaborated with comic playwright Molière to create a series of successful comédies-ballets that blended elements of ballet and opera (see Figure 11.8). Then, in 1672, with Louis XIV's support, he purchased a royal privilege granting him the exclusive right to produce sung drama in France and established the Académie Royale de Musique. The exercise of this monopoly not only made him a rich man but also made him the virtual dictator of music and

Lully

## Jean-Baptiste Lully (1632–1687)

Lully was the most powerful force in French music in the seventeenth century, creating a French type of opera, pioneering the French overture, and fostering the modern orchestra.

Born in Florence, Lully came to Paris at age fourteen as Italian tutor to a cousin of Louis XIV. In Paris, he completed his musical training and studied dance. His dancing so impressed Louis that in 1653 he appointed Lully court composer of instrumental music and director of the Petits Violons. In 1661, Lully became Superintendent of Music for the King's Chamber, taking over the Vingt-quatre Violons du Roi as well as the Petits Violons, and became a French citizen. His marriage the next summer to Madeline Lambert, daughter of composer Michel Lambert, was witnessed by the king and queen, showing how high Lully had risen at court.

Lully composed music for numerous court ballets and sacred music for the royal chapel. He turned to comédies-ballets in 1664, then in 1672 to opera, where he gained his greatest fame.

The discipline Lully imposed on his orchestra, enforcing uniform bowing and coordinated use of ornaments, won admiration, was widely imitated, and became the foundation for modern orchestral practice. Although Lully conducted with a long staff or cane instead of a baton, the tradition of dictatorial leadership that he introduced, modeled on the king's own absolute power, has been continued by later conductors.

Lully's close relationship with Louis XIV was clouded by scandal in 1685, when the king learned that Lully had seduced a young page in his service.

*Figure 11.7. Jean-Baptiste Lully, in a bronze bust by Antoine Coyzevox placed on Lully's tomb in the church of Notre-Dame-des-Victoires, Paris.*

Lully remained rich and powerful but had to rely on other patrons. He died in 1687 after he hit his foot with his staff while conducting and the injury turned gangrenous.

**Major works:** *Alceste, Armide*, and 13 other operas; 14 comédies-ballets; 29 ballets (most in collaboration with other composers); numerous motets and other liturgical music.

*Figure 11.8. An engraving representing the production of Molière's comedy* Le Malade imaginaire *before Louis XIV at Versailles in 1673. Most of Molière's theatrical entertainments were presented at Louis's court.*

musical taste in France as long as he lived and even perpetuated his influence for decades after his death.

**Quinalt's librettos**

Lully's librettist, the esteemed playwright Jean-Philippe Quinault, provided the composer with five-act dramas combining serious plots from ancient mythology or chivalric tales with frequent divertissements ("diversions"), long interludes of dancing and choral singing. He cleverly intermingled episodes of romance and adventure with adulation of the king, glorification of France, and moral reflection. His texts were overtly and covertly propagandistic, in tune with Louis's use of the arts. Each opera included a prologue, often singing the king's praises literally or through allegory. The plots depicted a well-ordered, disciplined society, and the mythological characters and settings reinforced the parallels Louis sought to draw between his regime and ancient Greece and Rome. The librettos also provided opportunities for spectacles to entertain the audience, as illustrated in Figure 11.9.

Lully's music projected the formal splendor of Louis's court. Each opera began with an *ouverture* (French for "opening"), marking the entry of the king (when he was present) and welcoming him and the audience to the performance. Lully's French overtures, as they are now called, were appropriately grand and followed a format that he had already used in his ballets. There are two sections, each played twice. The first is homophonic and majestic, marked by dotted rhythms and anacrustic (upbeat) figures rushing toward the downbeats. The second section is faster and begins with a flurry of fugal imitation,

*Figure 11.9. Design for Lully's opera* Armide *(1686), in an ink wash by Jean Bérain. It shows the burning of Armide's palace, which she ordered in a fury over her failure to murder Renaud and over his escape from her power. In the foreground, Renaud, in armor, bids farewell to Armide. Bibliothèque Nationale, Paris.*

sometimes returning at the end to the tempo and figuration of the first section. The overture to Lully's opera *Armide* (1686; NAWM 77a) exemplifies the genre.

CD 5/23    CD 2/58

A divertissement usually appeared at the center or end of every act, but its connection to the surrounding plot was often tenuous. These extended episodes, which directly continued the French ballet tradition, offered opportunities for spectacular choruses and a string of dances, each with colorful costumes and elaborate choreography. The divertissements were especially appealing to the public. Dances from Lully's ballets and operas became so popular that they were arranged in independent instrumental suites, and many new suites were composed imitating his divertissements.

To project the dramatic dialogue, Lully adapted Italian recitative to French language and poetry. This was no simple task since the style of recitative typical in Italian opera of the time was not suited to the rhythms and accents of French. Lully is said to have solved the problem by listening to celebrated French actors and closely imitating their declamation. Certainly the timing, pauses, and inflections often resemble stage speech, although Lully did not aspire to create the illusion of speech as in a recitative by Peri (Chapter 9). Also, the bass is often more rhythmic and the melody more songful than in Italian recitative.

*Adapting recitative to French*

In what would later be called *récitatif simple* ("simple recitative"), Lully followed the general contours of spoken French while shifting the metric notation between duple and triple to allow the most natural declamation of the words. This style was frequently interrupted by a more songlike, uniformly measured style, *récitatif mesuré* ("measured recitative"), which had more deliberate motion in the accompaniment. More lyrical moments were cast as airs—songs with a rhyming text and regular meter and phrasing, often featuring the meter and form of a dance. Far less elaborate and effusive than arias in Italian operas, airs were typically syllabic or nearly so, with a tuneful melody, little text repetition, and no virtuosic display.

*Récitatif simple, récitatif mesuré, and air*

Armide's monologue in Act II, scene 5, of *Armide* (NAWM 77b) illustrates this mixture of styles. The scene begins with a tense orchestral prelude suffused with dotted rhythms. The sorceress, dagger in hand, stands over her captive, the sleeping warrior Renaud. In simple recitative, she speaks of her determination to kill him as revenge for freeing her captives, but she is prevented from acting because she has fallen in love with him. Measures of four, three, and two beats are intermixed, permitting the two accented syllables in each poetic line to fall on downbeats. Rests follow each line and are also used dramatically, as when Armide vacillates between hesitation and resolve in the excerpt shown in Example 11.3a. When she finally decides to use sorcery to make him love her, her new determination is reflected in measured recitative, in Example 11.3b. This leads to an air with the meter, rhythm, and character of a minuet (see Chapter 12), a dance associated with the surrender to love. It is accompanied only by continuo, as are most of Lully's airs, but is introduced by an orchestral statement of the entire air, which would perhaps have been choreographed.

CD 5/26    CD 2/61

Lully's influence extended beyond the arena of opera and ballet. Elsewhere in France and in Germany, composers and musicians both admired the discipline with which he conducted his players and imitated his methods of scoring. The first large ensembles of the violin family, Lully's bands became the model for the modern orchestra—an ensemble whose core consists of strings with more than one player performing each part. Louis's predecessor had established the Vingt-quatre Violons du Roi (Twenty-four Violins of the King), which typically played music in a five-part texture: six soprano violins, tuned like the modern violin, on the melody; twelve alto and tenor violins tuned like the modern viola, divided among three inner parts; and six bass violins, tuned a whole tone lower than the modern cello, on the bass line. In 1648, the Petits Violons

String orchestras

*Example 11.3: Jean-Baptiste Lully*, monologue Enfin il est en ma puissance, *from* Armide

*a. Simple recitative*

What makes me hesitate? What in his favor does pity want to tell me? Let us strike . . . Heavens! Who can stop me? Let us go on with it . . . I tremble! Let us avenge . . . I sigh!

*b. Measured recitative*

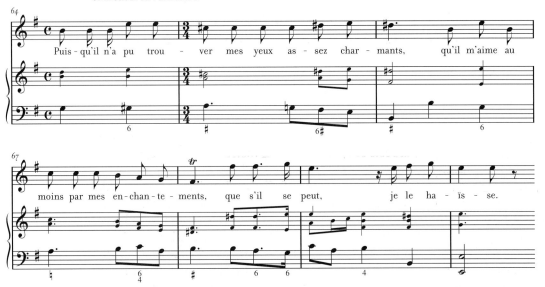

*Since he could not find my eyes charming enough, let him love me at least through my sorcery, so that, if it's possible, I may hate him.*

(Small String Ensemble), with eighteen strings, was created for Louis XIV's personal use. These two groups accompanied ballets, balls, the king's supper, and other court entertainments. By the 1670s, the term *orchestra* was used for such ensembles, after the area in front of the stage in a theater where the musicians were usually placed for opera and other entertainments.

## Church Music

Until about 1650, French church music was dominated by the old style of Renaissance counterpoint. In the second half of the century, in sacred as in secular vocal music, French composers borrowed genres invented in Italy—notably the sacred concerto and oratorio—but wrote in distinctively French styles.

Composers in the royal chapel produced numerous motets on Latin texts. These were of two main types: the *petit motet* ("small motet"), a sacred concerto for few voices with continuo, and the *grand motet* ("large motet") for soloists, double chorus, and orchestra, corresponding to the large-scale concertos of Gabrieli and Schütz. *Grands motets* featured several sections in different meters and tempos, encompassing preludes, vocal solos, ensembles, and choruses. Lully and Marc-Antoine Charpentier (1634–1704), a pupil of Carissimi, wrote outstanding *grands motets*. Louis XIV's favorite sacred composer was Michel-Richard de Lalande (1657–1726), whose more than seventy motets reveal a masterly command of the resources of the *grand motet*: syllabic solos, homophonic and fugal choruses, and operatic airs and duets, with frequent contrasts of texture and mood.

*Petit motet and grand motet*

Charpentier introduced the Latin oratorio into France, drawing on the model of Carissimi but combining Italian and French styles of recitative and air. He usually assigned a prominent role to the chorus, often a double chorus, and his thirty-four oratorios are full of dramatic contrasts and vivid text setting.

*Marc-Antoine Charpentier*

## England

English music drew inspiration from both Italy and France, in combination with native traditions. Royal patronage exercised a major influence, as in France, but music for the public grew increasingly important. Despite attempts to introduce opera, the English monarchy, aristocracy, and public preferred native genres of dramatic and ceremonial vocal music.

## Musical Theater

A favorite court entertainment since the time of Henry VIII was the masque. Masques shared many aspects of opera, including instrumental music, dancing, songs, choruses, costumes, scenery, and stage machinery, but they were long collaborative spectacles akin to French court ballets rather than unified dramas with music by a single composer. One such work was *The Triumph of Peace* (1634) by William Lawes (1602–1645) and others. This highly elaborate masque began with a procession of all the principal characters on horseback through the streets of London, featured multiple changes of scenery, and included several antimasques, or scenes of low comedy (see page 175). The genre was appealing to all segments of society, both as public spectacle and as private entertainment, and shorter masques were produced not only in aristocratic ballrooms but also in theaters and private schools.

*Masques*

Mixed genres

After the English Civil War (1642–1649), Cromwell's Puritan government prohibited stage plays but not concerts or private musical entertainments. This policy allowed the production of the first English "operas"—not operas in the Italian sense, but mixtures of elements from spoken drama and the masque, including dances, songs, recitatives, and choruses. After the Restoration in 1660, audiences eagerly returned to the theaters, where plays often included masques or similar musical episodes. Charles II had spent his exile in France, and French music and court ballet became increasingly influential in England after his return. But an attempt to introduce French opera in the 1670s failed, and there was little interest in dramas set to continuous music. Only two dramas sung throughout met any success, both composed for private audiences rather than for the public: John Blow's *Venus and Adonis* (ca. 1680) and Henry Purcell's *Dido and Aeneas* (1689).

*Dido and Aeneas*

Henry Purcell (1659–1695), England's leading composer and a royal favorite (see biography below), composed *Dido and Aeneas* in 1689. The first known performance took place at an exclusive girl's boarding school in Chelsea, but the work may previously have been staged at court. Purcell's score is a masterpiece of opera in miniature: there are only four principal roles, and the three acts take only about an hour to perform. Indebted in many ways to Blow's *Venus and Adonis*, the work masterfully incorporates elements of the English masque and of French and Italian opera.

French and Italian elements

The overture and homophonic choruses in dance rhythms resemble those of Lully, and the typical scene structure also follows Lully's example, with solo singing and a chorus leading to a dance. The most notable Italian element is the presence of several arias, rare in French opera or English masque. Three arias are built entirely over ground basses, an important type in Italian opera. The last of these, and one of the most moving arias in all opera, is Dido's lament,

# Henry Purcell (1659–1695)

Celebrated after his death as "the British Orpheus," Purcell was favored by royal patronage throughout his career. His father, a member of the Chapel Royal, died just before his son's fifth birthday. Purcell joined the Chapel Royal as a choirboy and proved to be a gifted prodigy as a composer, publishing his first song at the age of eight. When his voice broke, he was apprenticed to the keeper of the king's keyboard and wind instruments. In 1677, he became composer for the violins at court, and in 1679 he succeeded John Blow as organist of Westminster Abbey, a post he retained for the rest of his brief life. He died at the young age of thirty-six, and his funeral was held in the hallowed Westminster Abbey, where he was also buried.

One of the greatest of all English composers, Purcell wrote enormous amounts of music in almost all genres. His primary focus was vocal music: he composed songs for home performance, choral music for Anglican services and royal cere-

*Figure 11.10. Henry Purcell in 1695, in a portrait by John Closterman. National Portrait Gallery, London.*

monies, and music for the theater. Purcell's greatest accomplishment was in consciously fashioning a viable English song that sounded at once natural and expressive.

**Major works:** *Dido and Aeneas* (opera), 5 semi-operas, incidental music for 43 plays, 65 anthems, 6 services, numerous odes, songs, and catches, and chamber and keyboard music.

When I am laid in earth (NAWM 79b), which follows the Italian tradition of setting laments over a descending tetrachord (see Chapter 9), here altered chromatically. As shown in Example 11.4, Purcell creates great tension by rearticulating suspended notes on strong beats, intensifying the dissonance.

CD 5/40    CD 3/7

*Example 11.4: Henry Purcell,* Dido and Aeneas, *Act III, Scene 2, Dido's lament*

Amid these foreign influences, the English traits are still strong. The use of dance for dramatic purposes owes less to Lully than to the masque tradition. Many solos and choruses use the style of the English air: tuneful, diatonic, in the

English elements

*Figure 11.11. In a painting by Andrea Sacchi (1599–1661) dating from the 1630s, the abandoned queen Dido, lamenting, holds to her breast her lover's sword, which is to be the instrument of her suicide. Musée des Beaux-Arts de Caen.*

CD 5/42

English recitatives

CD 5/39    CD 3/6

Semi-operas

Occasional music

major mode, with simple, catchy rhythms. Others, like the closing chorus *With drooping wings* (NAWM 79c), convey a profound sense of sorrow. Descending minor-scale figures portray the "drooping wings" of cupids, and arresting pauses mark the words "never part."

In the recitatives, Purcell draws on precedents to fashion melodies flexibly molded to the accents, pace, and emotions of the English text. Dido's final recitative, *Thy hand, Belinda* (NAWM 79a), is a miniature masterpiece that portrays the dying Dido through a slow, stepwise, meandering descent tinged with chromaticism (see Figure 11.11).

*Dido and Aeneas* had no successors because the English strongly preferred spoken drama. For public theaters, Purcell wrote incidental music for almost fifty plays, most in the last five years of his life. During this period, he also wrote the music for five works in the mixed genre called dramatic opera or semi-opera—a spoken play with an overture and four or more masques or substantial musical episodes—including *The Fairy Queen* (1692), based on Shakespeare's *A Midsummer Night's Dream*.

England did not develop a native tradition of full-fledged opera until the late nineteenth century. Although Purcell died young, there is no sign that he would have inaugurated one had he lived. Without support for it from the monarchy, as in France, or from the public, as in Venice and other cities, there was no role for opera in English.

## Ceremonial and Domestic Music for Voice

Vocal music outside the theater owed relatively little to foreign models. The royal family often commissioned large works for chorus, soloists, and orchestra for ceremonial or state occasions, such as royal birthdays, the king's return to London, or holidays. Purcell's magnificent *Ode for St. Cecilia's Day* (1692), with its elaborate choruses and declamatory solos—one of which was sung by the composer himself "with incredible graces"—was a direct ancestor of Handel's English oratorios (see Chapter 13). In addition to hundreds of theater songs, Purcell wrote a large number of vocal solos, duets, and trios, all published for home performance. A specialty of Purcell and other English composers in this period was the catch, a round or canon with a humorous, often ribald text. Catches were sung unaccompanied by a convivial group of gentlemen as a musical parallel to the bawdy songs and coarse jokes of other all-male gatherings.

Anthems and services remained the principal genres of Anglican church music after the Restoration. Since Charles II favored solo singing and orchestral accompaniments, Blow, Purcell, and their contemporaries produced many verse anthems for soloists with chorus (see "A Closer Look: Anglican Church Music," page 152). Coronation ceremonies inspired especially elaborate works. Purcell also set nonliturgical sacred texts for one or more voices with continuo, evidently for private devotional use.

Perhaps more important in the long run than the music composed in seventeenth-century England was an institution pioneered there: the public concert. Until the 1670s, concerts were private affairs, given for an invited audience by amateurs, by performers employed by a patron, or by learned academies. Then, in London, several trends came together: a middle class interested in listening

Church music

The public concert

---

**VIGNETTE**   The First Public Concerts

*Concerts that anyone can attend for the price of a ticket are so much a part of modern musical life that it is hard to imagine they are only three centuries old. The public concert is an English invention, inspired by the presence in London of excellent musicians with inadequate salaries and of middle-class audiences eager to hear music but without means to employ their own musicians. The first concert series was advertised in the London Gazette in December 1672:*

These are to give notice, That at Mr. *John Banisters* House (now called the Music-School) over against the *George Tavern* in *White Fryers*, this present Monday, will be Music performed by excellent Masters, beginning precisely at 4 of the clock in the afternoon, and every afternoon for the future, precisely at the same hour.

~

*Roger North, a writer and critic, recalled the concerts:*

But how and by what steps Music shot up into such request, as to crowd out from the stage even comedy itself, and to sit down in her place and become of such mighty value and price as we now know it to be, is worth inquiring after. The first attempt was

low: a project of old Banister, who was a good violin, and a theatrical composer. He opened an obscure room in a public house in Whitefriars, filled it with tables and seats, and made a side box with curtains for the music. 1$^S$ [one shilling] apiece, call for what [food and drink] you please, pay the reckoning [the bill], and *Welcome gentlemen.*

~

*Elsewhere, North noted that Banister was "one of the [King's] band of violins" whose "course of life was such as kept him poor" and who started the concert series "by way of project to get a little money." The performers, "the best hands in town," were*

the mercenary teachers, chiefly foreigners, who attended for a *sportula* [a gift or share of the proceeds] at the time. Sometimes consort, sometimes solos, of the violin, flageolet (one of Banister's perfections), bass viol, lute, and song *all'Italiana*, and such varieties diverted the company, who paid at coming in.

John Wilson, ed., *Roger North on Music, Being a Selection from His Essays Written during the Years c. 1698–1728* (London: Novello, 1959), pp. 302–303, 352 (spelling and punctuation modernized).

to music, a large number of excellent musicians in the service of the royal court and the London theaters, and the inability of the king to pay his musicians well, which encouraged them to find means of supplementing their income. Impresarios rented rooms in or attached to taverns, charged an entrance fee, and paid the performers out of the proceeds (see vignette on page 240). Soon the first commercial concert halls were built, and modern concert life began. Public concerts gradually spread to the Continent, reaching Paris in 1725 and major German cities by the 1740s.

# Germany

In German-speaking lands, composers blended elements from both French and Italian styles with native traditions. In opera, this resulted mostly in eclectic works; but in the case of sacred vocal music, German composers achieved a unique and enduring synthesis in the genre of sacred concerto, which blossomed into the chorale cantata in the eighteenth century.

## Opera

Italian composers were welcomed at Austrian and German courts, where opera in Italian became central to musical life. In addition to Italian composers who made opera careers in Germany, native composers also took up the genre. In the eighteenth century, several of the most successful composers of Italian opera were German, from Handel and Hasse to Gluck and Mozart (see Chapters 13, 14, and 15).

Opera in German

After scattered experiments, opera in German found a home in Hamburg with the opening in 1678 of the first public opera house in Germany. In this prosperous commercial center, the opera house was a business venture designed to turn a profit through year-round productions of works that would appeal to the middle class. Local poets translated or adapted librettos from Venetian operas and wrote new ones that were similar in subject matter and general plan. Composers adopted the recitative style of Italian opera but were eclectic in their arias. In addition to Italianate arias, they occasionally wrote airs in the French style and in the rhythms of French dances. Also common in early German opera, especially for lower-class or comic characters, are short strophic songs in the popular style of northern Germany, displaying brisk, forthright melodies and rhythms. The foremost and most prolific of the early German opera composers was Reinhard Keiser (1674–1739), who wrote almost sixty works for the Hamburg stage. A slightly younger composer who directed the Hamburg Opera between 1722 until it closed in 1738, Georg Philipp Telemann (1681–1767), also wrote numerous works for it.

Telemann

Although opera was only a tiny fraction of his output, Telemann was regarded by his contemporaries as one of the best composers of his era. He was also the most prolific, with over 3,000 vocal and instrumental works to his credit, in every genre and style of the time. The flexibility that allowed him to draw elements from various traditions and adapt or synthesize them to suit any purpose or audience—such as the German nobles for whom Telemann wrote his suites in French style—gave his music broad appeal. Indeed, he was much more typical, more widely published, and more popular in his day than J. S. Bach, who got an important position in Leipzig only after Telemann had turned it down, having used the offer to leverage a raise as director of the Hamburg Opera.

## Lutheran Vocal Music

After the ravages of the Thirty Years' War, churches in the Lutheran territories of Germany quickly restored their musical forces. However, two conflicting tendencies arising within the Church inevitably affected the music. Orthodox Lutherans, holding to established doctrine and public forms of worship, favored using all available resources of choral instrumental music in their services. In contrast, Pietists, or those who emphasized private devotions and Bible readings, distrusted formality and high art in worship, and preferred simple music and poetry that expressed the emotions of the individual believer. The resulting conflict gave rise to two distinct genres: elaborate works for public worship and devotional songs intended for private use.

Lutherans possessed a common heritage in the chorale, which formed the foundation for both private and public worship (see Chapter 8). New poems and

Chorales

### TIMELINE  Vocal Music in the Later Seventeenth Century

| MUSICAL EVENTS | HISTORICAL EVENTS |
|---|---|
| Anna Renzi is leading lady in Venetian opera **1640s** | |
| | **1642–1649** English Civil War |
| | **1643–1715** Reign of Louis XIV in France |
| Lully first comes to Paris **1644** | **1644** Bernini, *The Ecstasy of Saint Teresa* |
| Crüger, *Praxis pietatis melica* **1647** | |
| | **1648** Treaty of Westphalia ends Thirty Years' War; Commonwealth in England |
| | **1649** Charles I executed |
| Carissimi, *Jephte* **1650** | |
| | **1653** Cromwell dissolves Parliament |
| Barbara Strozzi, *Lagrime mie* **1659** | |
| | **1660–1685** Reign of Charles II in England |
| | **1661** Louis XIV assumes power |
| Royal Academy of Music founded in Paris **1669** | |
| Lully begins producing operas; **1672** first public concert series in London | |
| Buxtehude inaugurates Abendmusiken series **1673** | **1673** Molière, *Le Malade imaginaire* |
| | **1677** Racine, *Phèdre* |
| Hamburg opera house opens **1678** | |
| Scarlatti's first opera in Rome **1679** | |
| | **1685** James II of England crowned |
| Lully, *Armide* **1686** | |
| | **1687** Newton, *Principia mathematica* |
| Purcell, *Dido and Aeneas* **1689** | |
| | **1690** Locke, *An Essay Concerning Human Understanding* |

melodies continued to be composed, many of them intended not for congregational singing but for use in private devotions at home. The most influential Lutheran songbook of the time was Johann Crüger's *Praxis pietatis melica* (Practice of Piety in Song), issued in 1647 and reprinted in over forty editions during the next half century. Crüger set the melodies over figured bass and added accidentals to the old modal chorale melodies to make them fit emerging conventions of triadic harmony.

*Concerted church music*

At the same time, orthodox Lutheran centers provided a favorable environment for developing the sacred concerto for public worship. The backbone was the concerted vocal ensemble on a biblical text, as established by Schütz and others in the early and mid-seventeenth century. Of more recent vintage was the solo aria, normally in Italian style, on a strophic, nonbiblical text. The chorale was the most traditional and characteristically German ingredient, set either in the concertato style or in simple harmonies. Composers often drew on these elements in various combinations to create multimovement works. Today such works are usually referred to as cantatas, but their composers called them concertos, sacred concertos, or simply "the music" for a service.

*Buxtehude*

Dieterich Buxtehude (ca. 1637–1707) and Johann Pachelbel (1653–1706) followed in Schütz's footsteps by writing sacred concertos for chorus, solo voices, and orchestra, with or without the use of chorale texts and melodies. The most famous of a long line of composers working in or near Nuremberg, Pachelbel frequently wrote for double chorus, like many composers in southern Germany, where Venetian influence remained powerful.

Buxtehude, a northerner rooted in the native Lutheran tradition, was organist at the Marienkirche in Lübeck, where he composed and played much of his church music for the Abendmusiken, public concerts following the afternoon church services in Lübeck during the Advent season. These concerts were long, varied, quasi-dramatic affairs, on the order of loosely organized oratorios, incorporating recitatives, strophic arias, chorale settings, and polyphonic choruses, as well as organ and orchestral music. Among the vocal works composed for these concerts is a setting of *Wachet auf*, a sacred concerto consisting of a series of variations on the chorale. The Abendmusiken attracted musicians from all over Germany, including the twenty-year-old J. S. Bach, who made a kind of pilgrimage during the autumn of 1705 to Lübeck, traveling a distance of more than two hundred miles on foot, to hear the elderly Buxtehude play. In addition to his sacred choral works, Buxtehude was justly famous for his organ music, which will be discussed in the next chapter.

# POSTLUDE

Recitative and aria became the most characteristic styles of vocal music in the seventeenth century in all European nations. While Italian recitative spawned several different varieties, French recitative took another path, responding to the sonic patterns of the French language. Among the aria types common in this period—strophic, ostinato, and da capo—perhaps the most important, and certainly the most ubiquitous, was the da capo aria. Its function was to epitomize and explore a particular affection, to portray and project a psychological state, in much the same way a film director is sometimes compelled to dwell on the close-up or slow-motion camera shot in order to convey the emotional values of a particular scene. Not confined to amorous or heroic sentiments, the da capo aria was also suited to the expression of religious piety or fervor and so was eventually adopted by composers of church music such as oratorios or any work having dramatic elements.

Whereas Alessandro Scarlatti, among a host of competing Italian composers, represented the most forward-looking trends in Italy, Lully exercised a virtual monopoly over the musical stage in France. His *tragédies lyriques* were stylistically conservative and continued to be performed unchanged even after the death of Louis XIV in 1715. Across the Channel, Purcell synthesized French and Italian elements with native styles into a unique English operatic style that, however, did not survive into the eighteenth century.

In German-speaking lands, composers drew deeply on both French and Italian styles, remaking the foreign elements to suit local tastes and blending them with homegrown traditions such as the Lutheran chorale. In doing so, they laid the foundations for the extraordinary developments of the eighteenth century, when German and Austrian composers would play key roles in forging a new international musical language.

# Instrumental Music in the Late Seventeenth Century

*Chapter Contents*

*Prelude* 244

Music for Organ 245

Music for Harpsichord 248

Ensemble Music 253

*Postlude* 265

## PRELUDE

3  $Sy^u$  36 57 24 25

Once instrumental music had come into its own, composers had to make decisions about what instruments to use rather than simply what kind of piece to write. During the second half of the seventeenth century, the possibilities offered by modern organs, by double-manual harpsichords (instruments with two keyboards, each with a distinct sound), by improved wind instruments (see "The Music of la Grande Écurie, or the Great Stable," on page 264) and particularly by the violin family inspired new idioms, genres, and formal structures. A sixth instrumental category, the concerto, was added to the five discussed in Chapter 10. Because of the new importance composers accorded the sound and distinct characteristics of instruments, this chapter is organized around the two most prevalent types of instrumentation: music for solo keyboard, which includes organ and harpsichord music; and ensemble music, which includes chamber and orchestral music for a variety of instrumental combinations, all employing the ever-present keyboard as a supporting, or continuo, instrument.

The principal genres associated with each of these categories are

*For keyboard:* toccata (or prelude, fantasia) and fugue; arrangements of Lutheran chorales or other liturgical material (chorale prelude, chorale partita, etc.); variations; passacaglia and chaconne; suite; and sonata (after 1700). Taken together, the genres listed here represent all five categories discussed in Chapter 10.

*For ensemble:* sonata, sinfonia, and suite which grew out of dance and the abstract sectional genres discussed in Chapter 10; and concerto, a new category that belongs exclusively to this group.

Among the keyboard instruments, the so-called Baroque organ (see Figure 12.1) is familiar to us from the many copies of instruments that exist today, modeled especially on those originally constructed by the skilled German organ builders of the late seventeenth and early eighteenth centuries. They emulated the full French organ sound, with its colorful ranks of pipes, used to play solos and contrapuntal lines.

While organs were constructed mainly in churches, the keyboard instrument of choice for princely chambers and household use was the harpsichord, called clavecin in French (see Figure 12.4), which was easily adapted to solo or ensemble playing. Although the most prominent harpsichord makers were Flemish, like the Ruckers firm in Antwerp (see Figure 12.8), the most eminent composers for the instrument during the seventeenth century were French.

By about 1700, the French clavecinists and the north German organists had established distinct styles. But in the realm of instrumental chamber music, as in opera and cantata, Italians reigned as the undisputed masters and teachers. The seventeenth and early eighteenth centuries constituted the age of the great violin makers of Cremona—Nicolò Amati (1596–1684), Antonio Stradivari (1644–1737; see below), and Bartolomeo Giuseppe Guarneri (1698–1744). It was also the age of great string music in Italy, as we will discover.

## Music for Organ

Organ music enjoyed a golden age in the Lutheran areas of Germany between about 1650 and 1750. Dieterich Buxtehude (ca. 1637–1707), one of the best-known Lutheran composers of the late seventeenth century (see Figure 12.2), continued the tradition established by the Flemish composer Sweelinck and had a powerful influence on J. S. Bach, whose keyboard music will be discussed in the next chapter. Buxtehude was organist at Saint Mary's Church in Lübeck, one of the most important and lucrative musical posts in northern Germany. He composed organ pieces as well as sacred concerted music, and he played organ solos as preludes to chorales and other parts of the service. Buxtehude was famed for his Abendmusiken, a series of free public concerts during the Advent season that attracted listeners from all over Germany.

Most organ music written for Protestant churches served as a prelude to something else—a chorale, a scriptural reading, or a larger work. Such pieces were often chorale settings, or they were toccatas or preludes that contained fugues or culminated in them.

Buxtehude's toccatas typify those of seventeenth-century German composers in presenting a series of short sections in free style that alternate with longer ones in imitative counterpoint. Filled with motion and climaxes, the toccatas display a great variety of figuration and take full advantage of the organ's idiomatic qualities. Their capricious, exuberant character made them ideal vehicles for virtuosic display at the keyboard and on the pedals.

The free sections simulate improvisation by contrasting irregular rhythm with an unceasing stream of sixteenth notes, by using phrases that are deliberately irregular or have inconclusive endings, and by featuring abrupt changes of texture, harmony, or melodic direction. Example 12.1 shows a passage that is typical of toccata style, from Buxtehude's Praeludium in E Major (NAWM 84). The virtuoso part for the pedals (the lowest staff in the score) includes long trills; when the pedal sustains a tone, the two hands erupt in rapid passage work with many unpredictable changes of speed, direction, and figuration. At the opposite extreme is a later, slow-paced free section marked by suspensions and many passing key changes.

*Figure 12.1. Organ built in 1695 for Saint John's church in Hamburg, now in a church at Kassel. The elaborate carving of the chest encasing the pipes and the decorative angels are typical of the Baroque organ. The tall pipes in the center and around the sides of the upper half of the instrument produce the deepest notes, played by the pedals. Compare this instrument to the more modest one pictured in Figure 10.9.*

CD 6/6

*Example 12.1: Dieterich Buxtehude, Praeludium in E Major, toccata section*

In the Praeludium in E, five such sections in toccata style frame four fugal sections, each featuring imitative counterpoint on a different "subject" and in a different meter or tempo. All four blend into the free sections that follow them.

Fugue

CD 6/38    CD 3/27

In the eighteenth century, the two types of section, fugal and free, grew in length and became separate movements, so that the typical structure consisted of a long toccata or prelude in free style followed by a fugue (see NAWM 88).

*Figure 12.2.  A painting by Johannes Voorhout (1647–1723) belonging to the genre known as a "Music Company" (ca. 1674) that shows a group of friends making music. It includes the only known portrait of composer Dieterich Buxtehude, pictured with his hand to his head in front of a sheet of music. The instruments being played, probably by friends in Buxtehude's circle, are viola da gamba, harpsichord, and lute, although the elegantly dressed lutenist may represent an allegory of the pleasures of friendship and music. The man standing on the left in the feathered hat is the painter himself. Museum für Hamburgische Geschichte.*

Figure 12.3. A singer accompanied by a positive organ. Engraving by Martin Engelbrecht (1684–1765). "The Organ," a poem inscribed below the illustration, reads in translation: "The organ may be called the foundation of music, because through its ranks of pipes much wisdom may be imparted. All voices must conform to its sound and cadence. One need only pull the stops, and it resonates strong, dulcet, low, or mild. It leads a variety of instruments in sweet harmonies and lets itself be heard most delightfully in churches to praise the Supreme One."

Composers wrote fugues both as independent pieces and as sections within preludes or toccatas. Fugue subjects usually have a clearly defined melodic character and a lively rhythm. As in other contrapuntal genres, independent voices enter with the theme in turn. In a fugue, a set of these entries is called the exposition. Normally, the subject is stated by one voice in the tonic and answered by another in the dominant. The voices continue to alternate subject and answer throughout the exposition. Short episodes (passages in which the subject does not appear), characterized by lighter texture or sequences, usually separate the first and later full or partial expositions. These episodes may modulate to various keys before the final statement of the subject returns in the tonic. The return is often intensified by devices such as pedal point, stretto (in which statements of the subject pile up in quick succession), or augmentation (in which the rhythmic values of the subject are doubled).

While toccatas, preludes, and fugues remained independent of vocal music, organ compositions based on chorales used the melodies in a number of different ways. In the organ chorale, the tune was enhanced by harmony and counterpoint. In the chorale variation, also called chorale partita, the chorale tune served as the theme for a set of variations. In a chorale fantasia, the composer fragmented the chorale melody and developed the resultant motives through virtuoso finger work, echoes, imitative counterpoint, and ornamentation.

Chorale compositions

The last type is a chorale prelude, a term often applied to any chorale-based organ work but used here to denote a short piece in which the entire melody is presented just once in readily recognizable form. This type of chorale setting did not appear until the 1650s. The name suggests an earlier liturgical practice

Chorale prelude

*Figure 12.4. Double-manual harpsichord built by Michel Richard, Paris, 1688. Collection of Musical Instruments, Yale University, New Haven.*

in which the organist played through the tune, improvising the accompaniment and ornaments, as a prelude to the congregation's or choir's singing of the chorale. Later, when they were written down, such pieces were called chorale preludes even if they did not serve the original purpose. In effect, the work was a single variation on a chorale, and it consistently pursued any one of a number of different variation techniques from beginning to end.

# Music for Harpsichord

Because of its popularity at court, lute music flourished in France during the early seventeenth century and left a permanent mark on French keyboard style. The leading lute composer was Denis Gaultier (1603–1672), whose two published collections instructed amateurs on how to play the lute. During the seventeenth century, the clavecin, shown in Figure 12.4, displaced the lute as the main solo instrument, while harpsichord music absorbed many characteristics of lute style. Important harpsichord composers, or clavecinists, include Jacques Champion de Chambonnières (1601/2–1672), Jean-Henry D'Anglebert (1629–1691), Élisabeth-Claude Jacquet de La Guerre (1665–1729; see biography below), and François Couperin (1668–1733; see Chapter 13). All of them served Louis XIV in various capacities but are best known today for their printed collections of harpsichord music, marketed to a growing public of well-to-do amateur performers.

Agréments

Lutenists systematically developed the use of agréments, ornaments designed to emphasize important notes and give the melody shape and character. Agréments became a fundamental element of all French music, and the proper use of ornaments was a sign of refined taste. Agréments were often left to the discretion of the player, especially in other countries, but French composers worked out precise ways of notating them. Figure 12.6 shows the table of agréments in D'Anglebert's *Pièces de clavecin* (Harpsichord Pieces, 1689), the most comprehensive of many such tables published in collections of harpsichord music. Some of these ornaments are discussed in "Baroque Ornamentation" later in this chapter.

Style brisé

Lute style also strongly influenced the texture of harpsichord music. Since lutenists often struck only one note at a time, they sketched in the melody, bass, and harmony by sounding the appropriate tones—now in one register, now in another—and relying on the listener's imagination to supply the continuity of the various lines. This technique, sometimes described by the French phrase *style brisé* ("broken style"), was imitated by harpsichord composers and became an intrinsic part of French harpsichord style, as seen in Example 12.2 below.

## Dance Music

Dances formed the core of the lute and keyboard repertory, reflecting their importance in French life. Composers arranged ballet music for lute or harpsichord and composed original music in dance meters and forms. Most dance

---

### ✳ Élisabeth-Claude Jacquet de La Guerre (1665–1729)

Women continued to play an active role in the music of the seventeenth century, from singers and composers to patrons of art, as well as hostesses at private gatherings where music was actively cultivated. One such extraordinary woman was the French composer Élisabeth-Claude Jacquet de La Guerre, born into a family of musicians and instrument makers. Trained by her father, she was the original child prodigy in music. From the age of five, she sang and played the harpsichord at Louis XIV's court and was a favorite of the king's mistress. In 1677, the Paris journal *Mercure galant* gushed:

> There is a prodigy who has appeared here for the last four years. She sings at sight the most difficult music. She accompanies herself, and others who wish to sing, on the harpsichord, which she plays in an inimitable manner. She composes pieces and plays them in any key one suggests.

Some years later, the same writer called her "the marvel of our century."

In 1684, she married the organist Marin de La Guerre and moved permanently to Paris. There she taught harpsichord and gave concerts that won her wide renown. She enjoyed the patronage of Louis XIV and dedicated most of her works to him, including the first ballet (1691, now lost) and first opera (*Céphale et Procris*, 1694) written by a Frenchwoman.

Jacquet de La Guerre is best known for her two published collections of harpsichord pieces (1687 and 1707) and three books of cantatas. Her violin and trio sonatas show an interest in the Italian in-

*Figure 12.5. A portrait by François de Troy (1645–1730) of Élisabeth-Claude Jacquet de La Guerre seated at a harpsichord and holding a quill pen and sheet of (music) paper, all attributes of her talents as a musician. Private collection, London.*

strumental style. Her output was small but encompassed a wide variety of genres, and she was recognized by her contemporaries as one of the great talents of her time.

**Major works:** *Céphale et Procris* (opera), 3 books of cantatas, 2 books of *Pièces de clavecin*, 8 violin sonatas, 4 trio sonatas.

*Figure 12.6. Table of ornaments from* Pièces de clavecin *(1689) by Jean-Henry D'Anglebert, showing for each ornament its notation, name, and manner of performance. (See "In Performance: Baroque Ornamentation," pages 258–259.)*

music for lute or keyboard was stylized, probably intended not for dancing but for the entertainment of the player or a small audience. Paired two- and four-measure phrases occur frequently in dance music, matching the patterns of many dance steps.

Earlier dances had assumed a variety of forms, such as the three repeated sections of the pavane or the repeating bass of the passamezzo. Most seventeenth-century dances were in binary form: two roughly equal sections, each repeated, the first leading harmonically from the tonic to close on the dominant (sometimes the relative major), the second returning to the tonic. This form was widely used for dance music and other instrumental genres over the next two centuries.

French composers often grouped a series of stylized dances into a suite, as did their

CD 5/31–38    CD 3/3–5

German counterparts (see Chapter 10). The tempo and rhythm contributed to the character of each dance. A look at excerpts from Jacquet de La Guerre's Suite No. 3 in A Minor from her *Pièces de clavecin* (1687, NAWM 78), shown in Example 12.2, illustrates both the structure of a typical suite and the most common types of dance. All but two movements, the prelude and a chaconne, are in binary form. Although none of the movements would have been used for dancing, the steps and associations of the dances were known to the listeners and influenced the rhythm and style of the music.

*Example 12.2: Elizabeth-Claude Jacquet de la Guerre,* Pièces de clavecin, *movements from Suite No. 3 in A Minor*

a. *Prelude*

b. *Allemande*

c. *Courante*

d. *Sarabande*

e. *Gigue*

f. *Gavotte*

g. *Minuet*

Many suites begin with a prelude in the style of a toccata or other abstract work. Here it is an unmeasured prelude, a distinctively French genre whose nonmetric notation allows great rhythmic freedom, as if improvising. In Example 12.2a, the whole notes indicate arpeggiated chords, the black notes show melodic passages, and the slurs show groupings or sustained notes.

The allemande (French for "German"), no longer danced in the seventeenth century and thus highly stylized, was usually in a moderately fast $\frac{4}{4}$ beginning with an upbeat. As shown in Example 12.2b, all voices participate in almost continuous movement, and agréments appear often. Signs of the style brisé include the opening arpeggiation of the tonic chord in the bass and staggered rhythms between the voices. The courante (French for "running" or "flowing"), in Example 12.2c, also begins with an upbeat but is in a moderate triple or compound

*Figure 12.7. Nicolas Poussin (1594–1665),* Saint Cecilia *seated at a harpsichord in the company of angels (1627–1628). Images of the patron saint of music playing the harpsichord (rather than the organ, her original attribute) affirmed its suitability for young women and its popularity for domestic music making. See also Figures 10.7 and 10.8. Prado, Madrid.*

meter ($\frac{3}{2}$ or $\frac{6}{4}$) or shifts between the two. The steps were dignified, with a bend of the knees on the upbeat and a rise on the beat, often followed by a glide or step. The sarabande was originally a quick, lascivious dance song from Latin America. When it came to France through Spain and Italy, it was transformed into a slow, dignified dance in triple meter with an emphasis on the second beat, as in Example 12.2d. The melodic rhythm in the first measure is especially common. The

*Figure 12.8. Jan Vermeer (1632–1675),* The Music Lesson. *This work, painted by the prominent Dutch master around 1665, belongs to a genre associating music with courtship that not only was popular during the seventeenth century but also emphasized the link between the harpsichord and domestic music making, particularly by women. The meticulously rendered keyboard instrument at which the woman stands, her back to us, is exactly like the virginals made by the famous Ruckers firm in Antwerp. Its open lid reveals the inscription* Musica letitiae comes . . . medicina dolorum *("Music is the companion of joy and the cure for sorrow"). The viol and the empty chair in the foreground imply the possibility of a duet. The Royal Collection, London.*

giga (Italian for "jig"; French, *gigue*) originated in the British Isles as a fast solo dance with rapid footwork. It became stylized as a movement in fast compound meter such as $\frac{6}{4}$ or $\frac{12}{8}$, with wide melodic leaps and continuous lively triplets. Sections often begin with fugal or quasi-fugal imitation, as in Example 12.2e.

Numerous other dances could appear in suites. Jacquet de La Guerre's suite also includes a gavotte, a duple-time dance with a half-measure upbeat, as in Example 12.2f. It concludes with a minuet, an elegant couple dance in moderate triple meter, shown in Example 12.2g, that remained fashionable well into the eighteenth century.

## Ensemble Music

In the realm of instrumental chamber music, as in opera and cantata, Italians remained the undisputed masters and teachers. The late seventeenth century and early eighteenth century were not only renowned for their violin makers in Italy, but also for their great string music, of which the leading genres were the sonata and the instrumental concerto (see Figure 12.9).

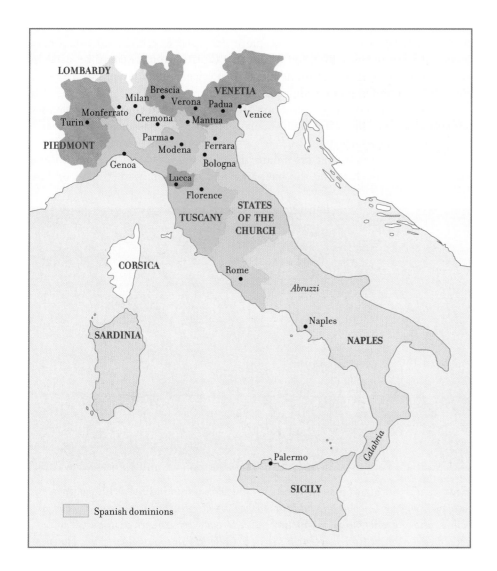

*Figure 12.9. Italy around 1650, showing the main centers for music and violin making.*

## Chamber Music: The Sonata

The word *sonata* appears regularly on Italian title pages throughout the seventeenth century. In the earlier decades of the century, the term (like the parallel word *sinfonia*) chiefly denoted a prelude or interlude in a predominantly vocal work. After 1630, the two terms were used more and more often to designate separate instrumental compositions.

Sonatas in the first half of the seventeenth century consisted of a number of small sections differentiated by musical material, texture, mood, character, and sometimes meter and tempo, as in the Marini sonata briefly discussed in Chapter 10 (NAWM 76). As composers developed the genre, these sections gradually became longer and more self-contained. Finally, composers separated the sections into distinct movements, so that in time the sonata became a multimovement work with contrasts between movements. These contrasts were in sympathy with the theory of the affections (see Chapter 9), which held that music stimulated the bodily humors and could keep them in balance by offering a diversity of moods. While some composers still maintained thematic similarities between movements, thematic independence of movements increasingly became the rule.

By about 1660, two main types of sonata had emerged. The sonata da camera, or chamber sonata, featured a series of stylized dances, often beginning with a prelude. The sonata da chiesa, or church sonata, contained mostly abstract movements, often including one or more that used dance rhythms or binary form but were not usually titled as dances. Church sonatas could be used in church, substituting for certain items of the service, and both types were played for entertainment in private concerts.

The most common instrumentation after 1670 for both church and chamber sonatas was two treble instruments, usually violins, with basso continuo. Such a work is called a trio sonata because of its three-part texture; but a performance can feature four or more players if more than one is used for the basso continuo, such as a cello performing the bass line and a harpsichord, organ, or lute

*Development of the sonata*

*CD 5/15*

*Trio sonatas*

*Figure 12.10.  Portrait of the string band of Grand Duke Ferdinand de' Medici, ca. 1685, by Antonio Domenico Gabbiani. In addition to the harpsichord, the instruments depicted are violins, alto and tenor violas, mandolin, and cello. An ensemble such as this could have performed the concerti grossi of Corelli's Opus 6. Galleria Palatina, Palazzo Pitti, Florence.*

Just as Italian composers excelled in writing songs and arias for the solo voice from the beginning of the seventeenth century, so, too, it was the Italians who created new instrumental genres—solo sonata, trio sonata, and concerto—that called on the violin to imitate the subtlety, expressivity, and virtuosity of the singing voice. Thus, it is no surprise that it was also the Italians—specifically, a few families of instrument builders in Cremona—who developed the art of violin making to a peak that has never been surpassed. During their heyday, the violin became the new agent of that artistic power which had previously resided only in the voice.

Antonio Stradivari (ca. 1644–1737) was the most prominent member of his universally renowed family of instrument makers in the area of northern Italy famed for violin construction. He was possibly a pupil of Nicolò Amati, founder of another dynasty of violin makers. During his long life, Stradivari made or supervised the production of more than 1,100 instruments—including harps, guitars, violas, and cellos—about half of which survive and are still being used today by some of the world's leading string players. Figure 12.11 shows one of the few Stradivari violins that has been restored to its original form, with a shorter fingerboard and the neck angled back only slightly from the body. Thousands of violins were made in tribute to Stradivari and modeled on his superior construction design; with no intention to deceive, these instruments bear the label "Stradivarius," although they were produced neither by the master nor by his workshop, which, by the mid-eighteenth century, was engaged in a healthy rivalry with that of the Guarneri family.

*Figure 12.11. Violin, 1693, by Antonio Stradivari, restored to its original Baroque form. The Metropolitan Museum of Art, New York.*

What was involved in making a "Strad," and why are these instruments so highly prized? To begin with, Stradivari selected woods of the highest possible quality—pine for the front and sides, and maple for the back of the instrument. Then he proceeded to carve the pieces, taking care to get just the right degree of arching because the body of the instrument is not flat but slightly rounded, and arrive at just the right amount of thickness because even the tiniest variation in the thickness of the wood will affect the instrument's resonance. Next he cut the elegantly shaped f-holes into the front piece to optimize the vibrations and maximize the sound. Finally, he applied the varnish to protect the instrument from dirt and to stop it from absorbing moisture. In addition to its practical function, the varnish itself added greatly to the beauty of the instrument by giving it a radiant, orange-brown sheen and highlighting the grain patterns on the wood's surface. In an effort to explain the extraordinarily rich and powerful tone of a Stradivarius violin, a popular theory held that its varnish had some sort of magic ingredient. However, historical research has shown that the varnish is no different from that used by ordinary furniture makers when Stradivari was alive. Other theories have advanced the idea that the wood was first soaked in water and then specially seasoned before being carved, or that the grain of the wood used is tighter than that of modern woods. But so far, scientists have been unable to ascertain any measurable qualities that set these instruments apart. Even if such properties are discovered, the intrinsic superiority of a Stradivarius remains a matter not only of science but also of a long-lost art.

doubling the bass and filling in the chords. The texture we find in the trio sonata, with two high melody lines over basso continuo, was popular from the mid-seventeenth century and served many other types of solo music, both vocal and instrumental.

Solo sonatas, for violin or other instrument with continuo, were at first less numerous than trio sonatas but gained in popularity after 1700. Composers also wrote sonatas for larger groups, up to eight instrumental parts with continuo, as well as a few for unaccompanied string or wind instruments.

Solo and ensemble sonatas

## Arcangelo Corelli's Sonatas

Unlike most of his countrymen, Arcangelo Corelli (1653–1713; see biography, below) composed no vocal music; instead, he sang through the violin, the instrument that most nearly approaches the lyric quality of the human voice. Although fewer than ninety pieces of his survive, they served as models of form and style that composers followed for the next half century.

Trio sonatas

In his trio sonatas, Corelli emphasized lyricism over virtuosity. He rarely used extremely high or low notes, fast runs, or difficult double stops. The two violins, treated exactly alike, frequently cross and exchange music, interlocking in suspensions that give his works a decisive forward momentum. Example 12.3 shows a passage from the first movement of his Trio Sonata in D Major, op. 3, no. 2 (NAWM 83), that features several typical traits of Corelli's style: a walking bass, with a steadily moving pattern of eighth notes, under free imitation between the violins; a chain of suspensions in the violins above a descending sequence in the bass; and a dialogue between the violins as they leapfrog over each other to progressively higher peaks.

CD 6/1–4    CD 3/9–10

Church sonatas

Most of Corelli's church trio sonatas consist of four movements, often in two pairs, in the order slow-fast-slow-fast. Although there are many exceptions to this pattern, it gradually became a norm for Corelli and later composers. The first slow movement typically has a contrapuntal texture and a majestic, solemn character. The Allegro that follows normally features fugal imitation, with the

### ✳ Arcangelo Corelli (1653–1713)

*Figure 12.12. Portrait of Arcangelo Corelli, ca. 1700, by Hugh Howard. Oxford University, England.*

Renowned as violinist, teacher, and composer, Corelli had an unparalleled influence on performers and composers alike. His solo and trio sonatas for one or two violins with continuo represent the crowning achievement in Italian chamber music of the late seventeenth century.

Born into a well-to-do family in a small town in northern Italy, he studied violin and composition in Bologna beginning in 1666. By 1675, Corelli was living in Rome, where he quickly became a leading violinist and composer, enjoying the support of Queen Christina of Sweden and other patrons.

As a violinist, teacher, and ensemble director, he helped to raise performance standards to a new level. His teaching was the foundation of most eighteenth-century schools of violin playing. Others may have surpassed him in bravura, but his playing was full of expression, as is suggested in this account from 1702: "His eyes will sometimes turn red as fire, his countenance will be distorted, his eyeballs roll as in agony, and he gives in so much to what he is doing that he does not look like the same man."

Beginning in 1681, Corelli published a series of collections of trio sonatas, violin sonatas, and concerti grossi that were disseminated across Europe, bringing him international fame.

**Major works:** 6 published collections known by opus (work) number—Op. 1 (1681), 12 trio sonatas (sonate da chiesa); Op. 2 (1685), 12 trio sonate da camera (one is a chaccone); Op. 3 (1689), 12 trio sonate da chiesa; Op. 4 (1695), 12 trio sonate da camera; Op. 5 (1700), 12 solo violin sonatas; Op. 6 (1714), 12 concerti grossi—6 other trio sonatas and 3 quartets, for the three instruments and basso continuo.

*Example 12.3: From Corelli, Trio Sonata, Op. 3, No. 2, first movement*

bass line being a full participant. This movement is the musical center of gravity for the church sonata, and it retains elements of the canzona in its use of imitation, of a subject with a marked rhythmic character, and of variation at later entrances of the subject. The subsequent slow movement most often resembles a lyric, operatic duet in triple meter. The fast final movement usually features dancelike rhythms and often is in binary form. All of these traits are true of Op. 3, No. 2. We have seen in Example 12.3 the contrapuntal web of suspensions and imitations in the first movement. The opening of the second movement features exact imitation between first violin and bass; the third movement, in the relative minor, is songlike with some imitation; and the finale is an imitative gigue in binary form whose subject often appears in inversion.

Corelli's chamber sonatas usually begin with a prelude, after which two or three dances may follow, as in the French suite. Often the first two movements resemble those of a church sonata, with a slow introduction and fugal Allegro. Some of the introductions feature dotted rhythms, recalling the French overture. The dance movements are almost always in binary form, with each section repeated, the first section closing on the dominant or relative major and the second making its way back to the tonic. Rather than sharing an almost equal role as in the church sonatas, the bass line in the chamber sonatas is almost pure accompaniment.

Corelli's solo violin sonatas are also divided between church and chamber sonatas, following similar patterns of movements but allowing considerably more virtuosity. In the Allegro movements, the solo violin sometimes employs double and triple stops to simulate the rich three-part sonority of the trio sonata and the interplay of voices in a fugue. There are fast runs, arpeggios, extended perpetual-motion passages, and cadenzas—elaborate solo embellishments at a cadence, either notated or improvised. The slow movements were notated simply but were meant to be ornamented freely and profusely (see "In Performance: Baroque Ornamentation").

In Corelli's sonatas, movements are thematically independent from each other (with rare exceptions) and tend to be based on a single subject stated at the outset. The music unfolds in a continuous expansion of the opening subject, with variations, sequences, brief modulations to nearby keys, and fascinating

Chamber sonatas

Solo sonatas

Thematic organization

**IN PERFORMANCE**   Baroque Ornamentation

Linked to the desire to stir the emotions, ornaments originated in improvisation—that is, they were applied spontaneously to make a performance more expressive and, in the case of certain dissonant ornaments, to add a touch of spice that the notated music lacked. Even though they might be written out later or at least indicated by special symbols (as in Example 12.2 and Figure 12.6), ornaments still retained a degree of spontaneity.

In playing both keyboard and ensemble music of the Baroque era, the performer had to learn how to interpret the variety of different signs indicating characteristic ornaments, or agréments, in the scores. More important, if their placement was not given, the player needed to decide independently where and what kind of ornaments to introduce tastefully. A number of "tutors," or practical treatises, were published in the seventeenth and eighteenth centuries to guide performers in the application and interpretation of ornaments. Most were written for a specific instrument and tailored to the tastes of a certain country, for practices varied from region to region. One of the most important treatises in France was *L'Art de toucher le clavecin* (The Art of Playing the Harpsichord, 1716) by François Couperin. Both an admired performer and a renowned composer (see Chapter 13), Couperin gave precise and detailed instructions for fingering and executing the agréments, discussing other aspects of harpsichord playing as well.

Sometimes composers, particularly in France, included instructions about decoding their symbols right in their published works. Figure 12.6, the table of agréments in D'Anglebert's *Pièces de clavecin* (Harpsichord Pieces, 1689), illustrates this practice. Abbreviations or signs for the most common ornaments are named and their proper execution suggested on the staff below each series of ornaments. For example, the mordent (*pincé*, or "pinched" in French) appears at the beginning of the second row, followed by another *(autre)*, longer version. Next comes a trill (*tremblement*, or "trembling") combined with a mordent. Ascending and descending appoggiaturas follow. In the top row, starting from the middle, D'Anglebert depicts a series of turn figures (~), some in combination with other ornaments.

Skilled performers were expected to add even more extensive embellishments, especially to the slow movement of a work, which was often notated simply but meant to be ornamented elaborately and freely. In 1710, the Amsterdam publisher Estienne Roger reissued Corelli's solo sonatas, showing for the slow movements both the original solo parts and embellished versions that, Roger claimed, represented the way the composer himself played the sonatas, as in Figure 12.13. Although Corelli lived until 1713, he never publicly affirmed or denied that the embellishments were his. But they surely reflect the practice of his time and are believed by modern scholars to be authentic.

One of Corelli's students, Francesco Geminiani (1687–1762), published an important violin method, *The Art of Playing on the Violin* (1751), which, like Couperin's treatise for harpsichord, elucidates the performance practices of the age. Geminiani compares the performer to an orator, an idea that was widely held and often repeated in the

subtleties of phrasing. This steady spinning out of a single theme, in which the original idea seems to generate a spontaneous flow of musical thoughts, is highly characteristic of the late Baroque from about the 1680s on.

Tonal organization    Corelli's music is fully tonal, marked with the sense of direction or progression that, more than any other quality, distinguishes tonal music from modally influenced music. Example 12.3, for instance, features several series of chords whose roots move down the circle of fifths, falling by a fifth or rising by a fourth (see measures 8–10 and 10–14). This is the normal direction for chord progressions in tonal music, whereas earlier music may move up the circle of fifths as easily as down. The increasing use, over the course of the seventeenth century, of directed progressions like Corelli's demonstrated the importance of the new functional harmony we call tonality.

Corelli often relied on chains of suspensions and on sequences to achieve the sense of forward harmonic motion on which tonality depends: measures 10–12

*Figure 12.13.  The Adagio of Corelli's Sonata op. 5, no. 3, in the edition printed about 1711 for John Walsh, London, and based on a 1710 edition by Estienne Roger, Amsterdam. The violin part is given both as originally published and in an embellished version said to represent the way Corelli himself performed it. Yale University Music Library, New Haven.*

Baroque, one that helps to explain the central role of ornamenation: "The intention of musick is not only to please the ear but to express the sentiments, strike the imagination, affect the mind, and command the passions." He continues by urging the violinist to use his instrument in a manner that rivals "the most perfect human voice" by imitating those qualities that result in eloquent speech.

Both Couperin's and Geminiani's treatises, as well as many others from the period, have been reprinted for modern performers. Geminiani spent many years in Ireland and England and published his work in English (London, 1751); Couperin's *Art de toucher* is available in English translation.

in Example 12.3 display both suspensions in the violins and a sequence in the bass, resulting in a progression down the circle of fifths. Corelli's music is almost completely diatonic; beyond secondary dominants (as in measures 8 and 12 in Example 12.3), we find only a rare diminished-seventh chord or Neapolitan sixth at a cadence. His modulations within a movement—most often to the dominant and the relative minor or major—are always logical and straightforward. He either kept all movements of a sonata in the same key or, in major-key sonatas, cast the second slow movement in the relative minor.

Composers all over Europe, especially Henry Purcell in England (see Chapter 11) and François Couperin in France (see Chapter 13), were greatly influenced by Italian trio sonatas, which were synonymous with the works of Corelli, and freely imitated or adapted them. The motivic techniques and principles of tonal architecture that Corelli helped to develop were extended by Vivaldi, Handel, Bach, and other composers of the next generation. He has been called the first

Influence and reputation

major composer whose reputation rests exclusively on instrumental music and the first to create instrumental works that became classics, continuing to be played and reprinted long after his death.

## The Concerto

**Music for orchestra**

Toward the end of the seventeenth century, musicians began to distinguish between music for chamber ensemble, with only one instrument for each melodic line, and music for orchestra, in which each string part was performed by two or more players. We have seen that the French court had a string ensemble, essentially the first orchestra, with four to six players per part. By the 1670s, similar ensembles were formed in Rome and Bologna, followed by others in Venice, Milan, and elsewhere. For special occasions in Rome, Corelli often led a pick-up orchestra of forty or more, gathered from players employed by patrons throughout the city (see "Queen Christina of Sweden and Her Circle"). While some pieces, such as the overtures, dances, and interludes of Lully's operas, were clearly intended for orchestra, and others, such as Corelli's solo violin sonatas, could be played only as chamber music, a good deal of seventeenth- and early eighteenth-century music could be performed either way. For instance, on a festive occasion or in a large hall, each line of a trio sonata might be played by several performers.

**Instrumental concerto**

In the 1680s and 1690s, composers created a new kind of orchestral composition that soon became the most important type of Baroque instrumental music and helped to establish the orchestra as the leading instrumental ensemble. In the long-standing tradition of adapting old terms to new uses, the new genre was called concerto. Like the vocal concerto, it united two contrasting forces into a harmonious whole in an instrumental version of the concertato medium. It combined this texture with other traits favored at the time: florid melody over a firm bass; musical organization based on tonality; and multiple movements with contrasting tempos, moods, and figuration. Concertos were closely related to sonatas and served many of the same roles: they were played at public ceremonies, entertainments, and private musical gatherings, and they could substitute for elements of the Mass.

**Types of concerto**

By 1700, composers were writing three kinds of concertos. The first two types—concerto grosso and solo concerto—were more numerous and, in retrospect, more important. Both systematically played on the contrast in sonority between many instruments and one or only a few. The concerto grosso set a small ensemble (concertino) of solo instruments against a large ensemble (concerto grosso). In the solo concerto a single instrument, most often a violin, contrasted with the large ensemble. The large group was almost always a string orchestra, usually divided into first and second violins, violas, and cellos, with basso continuo and bass viol either doubling the cellos or separate. In a concerto grosso, the concertino normally comprised two violins, accompanied by cello and continuo, the same forces needed to play a trio sonata, although other solo string or wind instruments might be added or substituted. In both solo concerto and concerto grosso, the full orchestra was designated tutti ("all") or ripieno ("full"). The third type, the orchestral concerto, was a work in several movements that emphasized the first-violin part and the bass, distinguishing the concerto from the more contrapuntal texture characteristic of the sonata.

**Corelli's concertos**

Since Roman orchestras were typically divided between concertino and ripieno, Roman composers favored the concerto grosso. Corelli's *Concerti grossi* Op. 6, written in the 1680s and published in revised form in 1714, are essentially trio sonatas, divided between soli and tutti. The larger group echoes the smaller, fortifies cadential passages, or otherwise punctuates the structure through doublings. Corelli's approach was widely imitated by later composers in Italy, England, and Germany.

While Roman practice treated the orchestra as an expansion of the concertino, in northern Italy the soloists were adjuncts to the orchestra. Composers

Giuseppe Torelli

---

**IN CONTEXT**   Queen Christina of Sweden and Her Circle

In 1681, Arcangelo Corelli dedicated his first opus, twelve trio sonatas (da chiesa), to Queen Christina of Sweden (1626–1689):

> If Your Majesty will have the generosity, as I hope, to both receive with favor and support these first fruits of my studies, it will renew my strength to continue with my other works, which are already in draft; and to make known to the world that perhaps I am not wrong to aspire to the glorious position of Your Majesty's servant. . . .

Who was this eminence whom Corelli hoped would become his patron?

Nearly thirty years earlier, Christina had abdicated her throne, left Sweden dressed as a man, converted to Catholicism, and in 1655 established her court-in-exile in Rome, where, until her death in 1689, she presided as an independent thinker, avid book collector, and beneficent patron. In Rome, Christina founded at least two academies that attracted scholars and poets, theologians and philosophers, librettists and composers, as well as members of the Roman aristocracy. She encouraged open discussion of ethical and scientific questions at a time when Galileo's theories were still taboo. She supported theatrical and operatic performances around the city, right under the nose of the reigning pope Innocent XI, who was oppressively hostile to the stage. And she regularly sponsored concerts at her palace, which became an important center in the city's musical life. Among others, Alessandro Scarlatti, who had just begun his long career as a composer of operas and cantatas (see page 226), was employed by Christina. He described himself in 1680 as her maestro di capella, a position he held until his departure for Naples in 1684.

One of the foremost violinists in Rome, Arcangelo Corelli also became a protégé of Christina, as he had hoped in the dedication to his Opus 1, quoted above. After entering her service as a

*Figure 12.14. This detail, from a seventeenth-century painting by Pierre Dumesnil, shows a youthful Queen Christina of Sweden (seated to the left of the table) presiding in the company of scholars, clerics, and others in her circle. Standing opposite her is René Descartes. Château de Versailles et de Trianon.*

chamber musician, he attracted her attention by composing and performing sonatas for her academy. When Christina organized a huge concert at her palace in honor of the new English ambassador to the Holy See, she asked Corelli to conduct an orchestra of 150 string players and an ensemble of more than 100 singers and soloists lent by the pope. On this magnificent occasion, there were seats for 150 ladies, and the number of gentlemen who were left standing was even greater. In 1689, Corelli again directed a large group of performers in two solemn Masses to celebrate Christina's apparent recovery from illness. Unfortunately, she died one month later.

Christina was among the most prominent intellectuals of her day, as suggested by the painting in which, surrounded by scholars and clerics, she engages the philosopher René Descartes (1596–1650) in animated discussion (see Figure 12.14).

| Tutti | Soli | Tutti | Soli | Tutti |
|---|---|---|---|---|
| Ritornello I | Solo I | Ritornello II | Solo II | Ritornello III |

| | | | | | | | | |
|---|---|---|---|---|---|---|---|---|
| Motives: | a | b | | a | b | | a | b |
| Key: | i | i | v | III | | iv | V$_7$ i | i |

*Figure 12.15.  Master plan of a Corelli concerto*

there focused first on the orchestral concerto, then on the solo concerto and concerto grosso. Giuseppe Torelli (1658–1709), a leading figure in the Bologna school, composed all three types, including the first concertos ever published (his Op. 5; 1692). In his concertos, we can see a new notion of the concerto develop. He wrote trumpet concertos for services in San Petronio, and his Op. 6 (1698) includes two solo violin concertos, perhaps the first by any composer. Six more violin concertos and six concerti grossi appeared as his Op. 8 (1709). Most of these works follow a three-movement plan in the order fast-slow-fast, taken over from the Italian opera overture. This schema, introduced to the concerto by Venetian composer Tomaso Albinoni (1671–1750) in his Op. 2 (1700), became the standard pattern for concertos.

**Framing ritornellos**

In the fast movements of his violin concertos, Torelli often used a form that resembles and may have been modeled on the structure of the A section of a da capo aria (see Chapter 11 and Figure 12.15). There are two extended passages for the soloist, framed by a ritornello that appears at the beginning and end of the movement and recurs, in abbreviated form and in a different key, between the two solo passages. The solos present entirely new material, often exploiting the virtuosity of the soloist, and modulate to closely related keys, providing contrast and variety. The return of the ritornello then offers stability and resolution. Torelli's approach was developed by Antonio Vivaldi into ritornello form, the standard pattern for eighteenth-century concertos, as we will see in the next chapter.

## Larger Ensembles

**Orchestral music**

Toward the end of the seventeenth century, a generally recognized distinction arose between chamber music—ensemble music with only one instrument to a part—and orchestral music. Prior to that, composers did not express their preferences, and the choice depended on circumstances. For instance, an orchestral ensemble might play a trio sonata da chiesa scored for two solo violins if the size of the auditorium made it desirable or if the occasion were festive. But neither the designation "sinfonia" or "concerto" nor the presence of three, four, or more melodic parts above the bass necessarily called for an orchestra rather than a chamber group of players.

Beyond the use of basso continuo and the predominance of stringed instruments, no common standard regulated either the makeup of an ensemble or the number of instruments to a part. Opera houses, of course, maintained orchestras, so opera overtures in both Italy and France, as well as the numerous dances that formed an indispensable part of French opera, were always written specifically for orchestral performance. In addition, the French king kept a whole stable (literally) of wind, brass, and timpani players, who performed at military and outdoor ceremonies and sometimes joined the chapel, chamber, or opera ensembles, adding instrumental color (see "The Music of La Grande Écurie, or the Great Stable," page 264).

The ensemble sonata and particularly the instrumental suite had a long life in Germany, where musical traditions frequently became part of everyday life (see Figure 12.17). German composers preferred relatively large ensembles and liked the sound of wind instruments as well as strings. Collegia musica, or associations of performers, in many German towns offered citizens the opportunity to play and sing together for their own pleasure. Town bands (*Stadtpfeifer*) and, in Lutheran regions, church musicians enriched the ordinary lives of the people. In some places, chorales or sonatas called *Turmsonaten* ("tower sonatas") were played daily on wind instruments from the tower of a Rathaus ("town hall") or church.

Ensemble music in Germany

**TIMELINE**   Instrumental Music in the Late Seventeenth Century

| MUSICAL EVENTS | HISTORICAL EVENTS |
|---|---|
| | **1658–1705** Leopold I reigns as Holy Roman emperor |
| Buxtehude appointed organist at Lübeck **1668** | |
| Lully begins producing operas; **1672** first public concert series in London | |
| Buxtehude inaugurates Abendmusiken series **1673** | |
| | **1677** Racine, *Phèdre* |
| Corelli, Op. I trio sonatas **1681** | |
| | **1683** First coffeehouse opens in Vienna |
| Birth of J. S. Bach and Handel **1685** | |
| Death of Lully; Jacquet de La Guerre, *Pièces de clavecin* **1687** | **1687** Newton, *Principia mathematica* |
| | **1688** Louis XIV invades Holy Roman Empire |
| | **1689** Death of Queen Christina |
| Torelli publishes first concertos **1692** | **1692** Salem witchcraft trials in Massachusetts |
| Death of Purcell **1695** | |
| Corelli, Op. 5 violin sonatas **1700** | |
| J. S. Bach hears Buxtehude's Abendmusiken **1705** | |
| Death of Buxtehude **1707** | |
| | **1715** Death of Louis XIV |
| Couperin, *The Art of Playing the Harpsichord* **1716** | |
| Death of Scarlatti **1725** | |
| Death of Stradivari **1737** | |

The orchestral suite

Lully's German disciples introduced French standards of playing, along with the French musical style, into their own country. One result was a new type of orchestral suite that flourished in Germany from about 1690 to 1740. The dances of these suites, patterned after those from Lully's ballets and operas, did not appear in any standard number or order. Because they were always introduced by a pair of movements in the form of a French overture, the word *ouverture* soon came to designate the suite itself. Among the early collections of orchestral suites was Georg Muffat's *Florilegium* (1695 and 1698), which includes an essay with musical examples about the French system of bowing, the

## IN CONTEXT The Music of la Grande Écurie, or the Great Stable

*Figure 12.16. Perspective view from the Château of Versailles of the Place d'Armes and the Stables, 1688 (oil on canvas) by Jean-Baptiste Martin (1659–1735). The musicians of the Grand Écurie (Great Stable) provided music for the pomp and ceremony of all manner of events under Louis XIV. Château du Grand Trianon, Versailles.*

Louis XIV's musicians of the Great Stable played at all manner of events that took place outdoors: processions occasioned by royal weddings and funerals, fireworks displays commemorating royal births, visits by foreign dignitaries, military reviews, hunts, and other types of games and pageants. Like the uniformed trumpeters who always preceded the king's coach when he rode out from his palace, stable musicians often mounted horses on these occasions, which helps to explain their association with what we now think of as an undignified place of lodging (see Figure 12.16). In fact, the stable musicians were Louis XIV's best wind and brass players. They performed ceremonial music on instruments such as fifes and drums, oboes and bassoons, cornetts and trumpets, all of which could easily be heard in the open air. Stable musicians were relatively well paid and sometimes enjoyed privileges that exempted them from taxa-

tion or permitted them to pass their position on to their sons.

Because employment as a stable musician offered status and job security, the institution of the Great Stable became a proving ground for several important families of wind players. A member of one such family, Jean Hotteterre (ca. 1610–ca. 1692), not only had the opportunity to perfect his playing technique but also experimented with the construction of several kinds of wind instruments. Fashioning them out of wood, he sometimes included elegant ornamental details in ivory and ebony, signs that his instruments were highly prized and appreciated at court. Lully's inclusion of woodwinds in his opera orchestra also became a factor in their improvement since his interest in writing music for these instruments stimulated their makers and players to strive for a sweeter, more refined sound—one that merited a place alongside the Vingt-quatre Violons du Roi (Twenty-Four Violins of the King; see Chapter 11).

Wind players and instrument makers at the French court are generally believed to have been responsible for creating the Baroque oboe. This instrument differed from its predecessor, the shawm, in having a fully freestanding reed (rather than a partially enclosed one) that allowed for greater control of intonation and tone quality. Instead of being constructed out of a single piece of wood, the instrument had three sections that were fitted together in such a way as to facilitate the most delicate adjustments in tuning. It also had an expanded, two-octave range, and its improved design and smaller finger holes allowed the player to produce more accurate chromatic pitches. Flutes were treated to similar modifications and improvements. Thus, despite its unpromising name, the Great Stable actually initiated the rise to prominence of woodwind instruments in today's orchestras.

*Figure 12.17. Detail of an anonymous painting depicting an evening concert by the collegium musicum in the university town of Jena, Germany (1744). Assembled in the town square around a harpsichord, the musicians play strings and winds, trumpets and kettledrums (which are suspended in a platform resembling a table) and are joined by a few singers. Notice the long music stands and the ring of torchbearers, who are lighting the occasion. Museum für Kunst und Gewerbe, Hamburg.*

playing of agréments, and similar matters. A host of other German composers, including Telemann and J. S. Bach, wrote overture suites (see Chapter 13).

## POSTLUDE

Two types of instrumental music became prominent during the second half of the seventeenth century: (1) solo keyboard music, especially that written for the harpsichord in France and the great Baroque organs built in Germany; and (2) ensemble music, dominated by the violin, whose famous Italian makers flourished during this period. Important genres of keyboard music included toccata and fugue, a variety of chorale-based compositions cultivated by Lutheran composers, stylized dance suites, and all sorts of variations, especially the chaconne and passacaglia. Influential composers were Dieterich Buxtehude in Germany and Élisabeth-Claude Jacquet de La Guerre in France. Ensemble forms—sonatas for church and chamber, and concertos—emerged in Italian centers such as Bologna and Rome, and from there spread throughout Europe. Pioneers in these genres were Arcangelo Corelli and Giuseppe Torelli. Although chamber and trio textures predominated, orchestral music began to have a life of its own in the opera overture and concerto, while soloists refined the art of ornamentation for expressive purposes as well as for virtuosic display.

Even though instrumental music explored and exploited the independent idioms of organ, harpsichord, and violin, composers still aimed to move the affections. How was this possible in the absence of words? They borrowed and adapted the already rich harmonic, melodic, and rhythmic vocabulary of vocal music, dance, and theatrical music, with all of its affective associations. With this essentially international, Baroque language, Corelli on the violin could lament as effectively as any operatic heroine; Jacquet de La Guerre on the harpsichord could charm her listeners as elegantly as any ballet dancer; and Buxtehude on the organ could inspire awe as convincingly as a massive church choir.

# PART FOUR

# The Eighteenth Century

**PART CONTENTS**

**13. MUSIC IN THE EARLY EIGHTEENTH CENTURY 279**

**14. THE EARLY CLASSICAL PERIOD: OPERA
AND INSTRUMENTAL MUSIC IN THE EARLY
AND MID-EIGHTEENTH CENTURY 315**

**15. THE LATE EIGHTEENTH CENTURY: HAYDN
AND MOZART 339**

**16. LUDWIG VAN BEETHOVEN (1770-1827) 374**

Continuities between the seventeenth and eighteenth centuries are greater than any differences. Certainly there was not the kind of sudden stylistic revolution in the arts, fueled by aesthetic debates and controversy, that had occurred at the beginning of the Baroque age. Rather, the history of this century's music can be seen as a long, leisurely, albeit lively, argument about older and newer tastes and styles that was carried on in newspapers, journals, salons (gatherings held in private homes and usually hosted by aristocratic women), and coffeehouses. The "older" eighteenth century manifested itself in the late-Baroque styles of Bach, Handel, and their contemporaries, all of whom are discussed in Chapter 13. The "newer" eighteenth century, often called the Age of Reason or the Enlightenment, is also known in music history as the Classical era and is covered in Chapters 14 through 16.

The word *Classical* is applied to the mature styles of later eighteenth-century composers such as Haydn, Mozart, and Beethoven. Their music is classic—an adjective that also refers to the ancient Greeks and Romans—because it shares many attributes of the art and architecture of antiquity. At its best, Classical music reached a consistently high standard and possessed the qualities of noble

*Figure IV.1. Matthäus Daniel Pöppelmann's Glockenspiel (Carillon) Pavilion at Zwinger Palace in Dresden, Germany (1711–1728), with its curves and carved ornaments, is a good example of the rococo style in architecture.*

simplicity, balance, perfection of form, diversity within unity, seriousness of purpose, and restrained use of ornamentation. However, many different personal and regional styles thrived for generations before the three composers just named reached their peak, and all shared some of these qualities to a greater or lesser extent. Thus, although a wealth of stylistic diversity existed among the various musical genres such as opera and church music, it is convenient and appropriate to call the years from approximately 1730 to 1815 the Classical era even though its boundaries overlap the preceding Baroque and subsequent Romantic periods. For example, interest in music of the early eighteenth century has long centered on Vivaldi, Couperin, Rameau, J. S. Bach, and Handel, each of whom established an individual style by combining elements from the mature Baroque tradition in new ways. Chapter 13 will focus on these composers as the last representatives of the Baroque age. But even during their lifetimes, Baroque musical styles were giving way to more modern ones, especially in Italy, as we will note in Chapter 14.

Other terms have also been coined to characterize the early phases of Classical style in the eighteenth century, among them *rococo*, *galant*, and *empfindsam*. *Rococo* originally described a style of architectural decoration that softened the angular forms of earlier French design with curved arabesques (*rocaille*, or "rockwork"), at the end of the seventeenth century (see Figure IV.1). We might view the highly ornamented pieces of François Couperin in the early eighteenth century as musical counterparts to the architectural movement, but a broader application of the term has lost favor among historians. The French word *galant* was widely used during the eighteenth century to describe literature that was elegant and courtly and paintings in which the subject matter was light and flirtatious, as shown in Figure IV.2. It was a catchword for everything that was considered modern, smart, chic, smooth, easy, and sophisticated. Contemporary music theorists distinguished between the learned or strict style of contrapuntal writing and the freer, more chordal, galant style, the latter marked by an emphasis on "naturalness"—simple melody with light accompaniment—which became stylish in the 1730s.

**Empfindsamer style** The German word *Empfindsamkeit* (noun) or *empfindsam* (adjective) derives from the verb *empfinden*, "to feel." *Empfindsamkeit*, which means "sentimentality" or "sensibility," is a quality associated with the intimate, sensitive, and subjective tendencies of some eighteenth-century literature and art (see below). We will see how it is relevant to certain musical works during the Classical era—for example, some keyboard sonatas by C. P. E. Bach—in Chapter 14.

## Europe in the Eighteenth Century

**Realignment** In political and social terms, as in music, the eighteenth century moved from continuity with the past, through new currents, to radical change. When the century began, a balance of power was emerging in Europe among several strong, centralized states, each supported by a professional military and government bureaucracy. France had the biggest army, but the lavish domestic and foreign expenditures of Louis XIV (r. 1643–1715) and, later, Louis XV (r. 1715–1774) depleted the treasury even before their expansionist ambitions were checked by other nations. England had the most powerful navy and used it to wrest India, Canada, and several Caribbean islands from France during the

Seven Years' War (1756–1763). Austria took Hungary back from the Turks, and now, as the Austro-Hungarian Empire, its increasing influence was reflected by the emergence of its capital, Vienna, as the leading musical city in Europe. A new power arose when Prussia became a kingdom in 1701 and developed one of the Continent's largest and best-trained armies. Late in the century, Poland fell victim to the centralized states around it; Prussia, Russia, and Austria divided Poland's territories among themselves and erased it from the map for over a century. By then, the French Revolution was generating the winds of change that would remake the political culture of Europe.

The population of Europe expanded rapidly, especially after 1750. New methods of agriculture and new crops like the potato, introduced from the New World, met the growing demand for food. Although roads were still bad—it took four days to travel a hundred miles—manufacturing and trade increased. The poor increasingly suffered dislocation from the land and overcrowding in the cities, becoming victims of the very progress that helped the well-born and the lucky. The middle class grew in size and economic clout, while the landed aristocracy became less important even though they still occupied the top rung of the social ladder. As the continent became more urbanized, nature was increasingly idealized. Antoine Watteau inaugurated a new genre of painting, the *fête galante*, which perfectly captured the nostalgia for an idyllic rural life (Figure IV.2), while the squalor of lower-class city life and the mores of high society were satirized in the paintings and engravings of William Hogarth.

Many new schools were founded, both for the elite—teaching the traditional Greek and Latin—and for the middle classes—providing more practical education. Frederick the Great of Prussia (r. 1740–1786; see Figure 14.11) and Empress Maria Theresa of Austria (r. 1740–1780; see Figure IV.3) sought to require primary school for every child. By 1800, half the male population of England and France was literate, and women, usually home-taught, were catching up. Daily newspapers began in London in 1702 and quickly spread to other cities. More and more books were published, purchased, read, and circulated. At public coffeehouses, meetings of learned societies, and salons, people avidly discussed current events, ideas, literature, and music. Amid this broadening

Education and learning

*Figure IV.2. Antoine Watteau,* The Music Party *(ca. 1717–1718), one of his many* fêtes galantes, *a genre noted for flirtatious interaction. The central figure is a theorbist tuning his instrument, perhaps a metaphor for initiating gallant conversation. Watteau's style is distinguished by its restrained use of gesture and emotion, a quality associated with Classicism. Wallace Collection, London.*

## TIMELINE The Eighteenth Century

| MUSICAL EVENTS | HISTORICAL EVENTS |
|---|---|

Eighteenth-century organ

**1702** First daily newspaper in England
**1707** England and Scotland officially unite to form Great Britain

**1715–1774** Reign of Louis XV

**1717–1718** Watteau, *The Music Party*

J. S. Bach becomes cantor in Leipzig **1723**

**1723** Joshua Reynolds born

Concert spirituel series begins in Paris **1725**

**1727–1760** Reign of George II of England

Haydn born **1732**

**1740–1786** Reign of Frederick the Great of Prussia; Maria Theresa crowned Holy Roman Empress

Handel, *Messiah* **1742**

**1748** Pompeii excavated
**1749** Fielding, *Tom Jones*

Death of J. S. Bach **1750**

**1751–1780** Publication of Diderot's *Encyclopédie*

Death of Handel **1759**

**1759** Voltaire, *Candide*
**1760–1820** Reign of George III of England
**1762** Rousseau, *The Social Contract*
**1764** Winckelmann, *A History of Ancient Art*
**1765** Joseph II becomes Holy Roman emperor and co-ruler with Maria Theresa; Greuze; *Girl with a Dead Canary*
**1768** Royal Academy of Art founded in London

Beethoven born **1770**

**1770** Gainsborough, *Blue Boy*
**1774–1792** Reign of Louis XVI of France
**1775** Beaumarchais, *Barber of Seville;* outbreak of the American Revolution

Gainsborough, *Blue Boy*

Burney, *A General History of Music* **1776–1789**
C. P. E. Bach, *Clavier Sonatas for Connoisseurs* **1779**
*and Amateurs*

**1776** American Declaration of Independence

**1781** Kant, *Critique of Pure Reason*
**1784** Beaumarchais, *The Marriage of Figaro*
**1788** Gibbon, *The History of the Decline and Fall of the Roman Empire*
**1789–1792** The French Revolution

Haydn receives honorary degree in **1791**
Oxford; death of Mozart

**1792–1794** Reign of Terror in France
**1793** Whitney invents cotton gin; Louis XVI and Marie Antoinette beheaded after French Republic begins

**1799** Napoleon becomes First Consul of the French Republic

Beethoven, *Eroica* Symphony **1803**

**1804** Bonaparte crowns himself Emperor Napoleon
**1805–1809** Napoleon's forces occupy Vienna
**1806** Holy Roman Empire dissolved

Death of Haydn **1809**

Jane Austen

**1813** Wellington defeats Napoleon at Waterloo; Austen, *Pride and Prejudice*
**1814–1815** Congress of Vienna

interest in learning, thinkers such as Voltaire and Jean-Jacques Rousseau sought to analyze social and political issues through reason and science, spawning the Enlightenment, the most vibrant intellectual movement of the century.

The Enlightenment embraced rationalism—the view that reason, combined with experience and knowledge, could solve problems, including scientific ones. The emphasis on reasoning from experience and from careful observation assigned greater importance to the examination of the human mind, the emotions, social relations, and established institutions. In Germany, Immanuel Kant's insight into the nature of knowledge initiated what he called a "Copernican revolution in philosophy," which held that objective reality can be understood only through empirical experience—that is, defining the world through the senses. In France, the methodology of reason in accumulating and codifying knowledge led to the monumental *Encyclopédie* (1751–1765), edited by Denis Diderot and Jean le Rond d'Alembert. In the sphere of religion, the movement valued individual faith and practical morality more than the supernatural and the Church. In social behavior, naturalness was preferred to formality and to conventions that were seen as artificial.

The French leaders of the Enlightenment, known as philosophes, were social reformers more than philosophers. In response to the inequalities between the condition of the common people and that of the privileged classes, they developed doctrines about individual human rights, some of which were incorporated into the American Declaration of Independence and by the framers of the Constitution of the United States. Their sharp social criticism also helped set the stage for the French Revolution and the downfall of the old political order.

Enlightened rulers such as Frederick the Great of Prussia, Catherine the Great of Russia, and Holy Roman Emperor Joseph II (Maria Theresa's son, shown in Figure IV.3) not only patronized the arts and letters, but also promoted social change and improved the lives of their subjects. Some even subscribed to the teachings of the secret fraternal order of Masons, whose tenets were based on humanitarianism and the idea of universal brotherhood. Founded in London in

**The Enlightenment**

**The philosophes**

**Humanitarianism**

*Figure IV.3.  Friedrich Heinrich Füger (1751–1818),* Maria Theresa of Austria Surrounded by Her Children. *At the right is Joseph II, who ruled jointly with Maria Theresa from 1765 until her death, whereupon he became the sole ruler until he died in 1790. Österreichische Galerie Belvedere, Vienna.*

*Figure IV.4. An early nineteenth-century sketch by Massimo Gauci of the character of Figaro, as portrayed in a performance of Beaumarchais's* Marriage of Figaro *at the King's Theatre in London in 1823. City of Westminster Archive Centre, London.*

the early eighteenth century, Freemasonry spread rapidly and numbered among its adherents statesmen (George Washington), poets (Johann Wolfgang von Goethe), and composers (Haydn and Mozart) as well as kings. Among other works, Mozart's opera *Die Zauberflöte* (The Magic Flute) and Schiller's *Ode to Joy* (set by Beethoven in the finale of his Ninth Symphony) reflect the eighteenth-century humanitarian movement.

The promise of a new political and economic order, in which the industrial revolution and middle-class entrepreneurship would eventually overtake the entrenched wealth of the landed aristocracy, was naturally echoed in the arts. The emergence of the novel—a genre that celebrates the lives of ordinary people—such as Henry Fielding's *Tom Jones* (1749) and Samuel Richardson's *Pamela* (1740–1741), went hand in hand with the new concern for the individual. Similarly, some think that the symphony, which became an important focus for Classical composers and the chief vehicle for Haydn's enormous popularity insofar as it depended upon the precise collaboration of orchestral forces, was an expression of communal sentiment and a reflection of new, democratic ideals.

The fictional character who best symbolizes the challenge to the old order is Figaro, the rascally servant and protagonist of two French comedies by Beaumarchais: *The Barber of Seville* (1775) and *The Marriage of Figaro* (1784). It is no accident that both plays were almost immediately turned into operas, the latter in a brilliant setting by Mozart. Beaumarchais was briefly imprisoned for his audacious criticism of the ruling classes, illustrated by a remark Figaro addresses

*Figure IV.5. Contemporary oil painting of the fall of the Bastille, July 14, 1789. The citizens of Paris stormed the old fortress, a symbol of royal authority, to obtain the guns and ammunition stored there and to protect the new municipal government from attack by the king's forces. The action cost almost one hundred lives but demonstrated the popular will for revolutionary change. The anniversary is now celebrated as Bastille Day, a French national holiday. Châteaux de Versailles et de Trianon, Versailles.*

*Figure IV.6. Jacques-Louis David,* Napoleon's Consecration as Emperor and the Crowning of Josephine as Empress, *1806–1807. The event occurred at Notre Dame Cathedral in Paris in 1804. Musée du Louvre, Paris.*

to the audience in one of his provocative monologues: "What have you [the nobility] done to deserve such wealth? You took the trouble to be born, and nothing else." An unsophisticated barber and jack-of-all-trades, Figaro is a clever and resourceful schemer who not only outwits his aristocratic master in romance, but makes him look ridiculous into the bargain. In short, he was the spokesperson and hero of the new age (Figure IV.4).

### The French Revolution

While the French Revolution was inspired in part by the ideas of the Enlightenment, it also had other causes. The first phase of the Revolution (1789–1792) was reformist. Stimulated by King Louis XVI's ruinous fiscal policies and supported by popular uprisings like the assault on the Bastille, shown in Figure IV.5, a National Assembly of well-to-do citizens forced the king to accept a new constitution for France and set up elected local governments. But after Austria and Prussia attacked France in 1792, seeking to restore the old regime, a more radical group came to power, declared France a republic, and executed the king and his queen (Marie Antoinette). In this second phase (1792–1794), as French armies fought off attacks, the government maintained control by putting tens of thousands of political opponents to death during the Reign of Terror. In the third phase, the government adopted a more moderate constitution and sought to restore order, but opposition and economic hardship continued.

### Napoleon Bonaparte

In 1799, Napoleon Bonaparte, an army general and war hero, became First Consul of the Republic. Ignoring the elected legislature, Bonaparte consolidated power and in 1804 crowned himself emperor in Notre Dame Cathedral (see Figure IV.6). Through a series of military victories, he overran nearby countries, expanded French territories, ended the 840-year-old Holy Roman Empire, and created client states in Spain, Switzerland, and most of Germany and Italy, installing his own siblings as rulers. He introduced reform that made government more efficient, the legal system more uniform, and taxation less burdensome, carrying out some of the goals of the Revolution. But a disastrous military

# ARTS *and* IDEAS

## Philosophy and Literature

**Voltaire** (pen name of François-Marie Arouet, 1694–1778) was a French satirist, philosopher, historian, prolific writer, and irreverent wit whose unorthodox ideas were a constant source of irritation to the political and religious authorities of his time. His most famous work, *Candide* (1759), is a brilliant satire on the Age of Reason; it gives literary expression to his outrage against all forms of religion and privilege.

Swiss-born French philosopher **Jean-Jacques Rousseau** (1712–1778) was also a political theorist, writer, and composer. His essays and novels celebrate the "natural man"—one whose behavior is guided by human nature rather than by society's mores—oppose inequality and oppression, and reject the idea that progress in the sciences and arts increases one's happiness. His most influential work, *The Social Contract* (1762), is a treatise on government and the rights of citizens.

The philosophe **Denis Diderot** (1713–1784) compiled, coedited, and contributed to the monumental (28 volume) *Encyclopédie, ou Dictionnaire raisonné . . .* (1751–1780). His writings include novels, satire, art criticism, and philosophy in which he presents insights into the physical, moral, and social universe, including studies on how people who are blind or are deaf and mute learn.

**Johann Joachim Winckelmann** (1717–1768) was a German art historian whose writings on the sculpture of ancient Greece and Rome provided a theoretical basis for eighteenth-century Classicism. His *History of Ancient Art* (1764) considers how the political freedom of the ancient Greek city-states is one of the conditions that led to the flowering of its art, and his descriptions of the marbles were widely quoted in travel books and art treatises. His work had a major impact on the discipline of art history.

In his *Critique of Pure Reason* (1781), the German philosopher and university professor **Immanuel Kant** (1724–1804) attempted to define the function and limits of rational understanding. He maintained that while reason can understand a thing considered as an object, reason cannot understand the thing in itself. Thus, he challenged the Enlightenment's faith in the unlimited scope of reason.

**Beaumarchais** (the pen name of Pierre Augustin Caron, 1732–1799) was a French dramatist, courtier, and watchmaker to Louis XV. He is best known for creating one of the world's cleverest servants, Figaro, and presenting Figaro's exploits in two comic masterpieces, *The Barber of Seville* (1775) and *The Marriage of Figaro* (1784). Both plays were transformed into operas, the latter composed by Mozart on a libretto by Lorenzo Da Ponte (see Figure 15.16) and the former by Gioachino Rossini, among others (see Chapter 19 and also Figure IV.4).

English historian **Edward Gibbon** (1737–1794) wrote *The History of the Decline and Fall of the Roman Empire* (1776–1788), which ranges over thirteen centuries. His controversial point of view blamed Christianity for Rome's decline and fall, which he deemed "the greatest, perhaps, and most awful scene in the history of mankind."

---

campaign against Russia led to Napoleon's defeat and abdication in 1814. As a congress of the major European powers met in Vienna to finalize the peace treaty, Napoleon escaped from exile and briefly resumed power, only to suffer final defeat in 1815 at Waterloo in Belgium. Although the Revolution and Napoleon's wars of conquest ultimately failed, they changed European society utterly, giving rise to new cultural and political agendas in the nineteenth and early twentieth centuries.

## From Baroque to Classical

Aim of Classicism

If the aim of the Baroque arts was to move the emotions, the aim of Classicism was to construct an ideal vision of life and nature in tune with Enlightenment

English novelist **Jane Austen** (1775–1817) was the seventh child of a country parson and spent her life almost entirely within her family circle, having no contact with London literary life. Out of the materials of such a narrow world she completed six novels, among them *Emma, Mansfield Park, Pride and Prejudice,* and *Sense and Sensibility.* (See "Music and Social Custom in British Society," pages 318–319.)

## Art

The French painter **Antoine Watteau** (1684–1721) created a distinctive pictorial world in which elegantly attired people are depicted in conversation or making music in a secluded, often bucolic setting. Known as *fêtes galantes,* these works are associated with the "superficial" rococo style, but their subjects are subtle and ambiguous, suggesting both psychological interaction and theatrical fantasy (see Figure IV.2).

**William Hogarth** (1697–1764), the influential founder of an English school of painting, is best remembered for his satirical engravings of low-life scenes of the period. By publishing engravings after his own paintings, he demonstrated that artists could become independent of wealthy patrons (see Figure 14.3).

The foremost portrait painter in eighteenth-century England, Sir **Joshua Reynolds** (1723–1792) executed more than 2,000 portraits of people whose poses were intended to invoke Classical values and enhance their subjects' dignity. His influential *Discourses on Art,* propounding a rationalist view of the ideal of beauty, were delivered to the students and members of the Royal Academy between 1769 and 1790, and earned him a wide reputation as a man of letters.

Standing apart from the Classical style of his contemporaries is the work of French painter **Jean-Baptiste Greuze** (1725–1805), who became famous for his genre scenes of family life and his expressive heads (see Figure IV.10). A keen observer of detail in the tradition of seventeenth-century Dutch masters, he combined faithful realism with sentimental drama, often suggesting an underlying moral.

The English painter **Thomas Gainsborough** (1727–1788) was the contemporary and rival of Sir Joshua Reynolds. Known for his virtuosic landscapes and portraits, especially *Blue Boy* (1770), he was also an accomplished musician and sophisticated intellectual. Rather than following an academic ideal of art, he grounded his style in the imagery of contemporary life (see Figures 14.1 and 14.14).

**Jacques-Louis David** (1748–1825), the foremost painter of the Napoleonic era, directed the Classical revival in French art. Like Beethoven, he adopted the ideals of Republicanism and placed his hopes in Napoleon. His grandly heroic paintings became a political manifesto about returning to the patriotic and moral values associated with republican Rome (see Figures IV.6, IV.8, and V.6).

goals of realism, restraint, harmony, and order. Renewed study of the Classical past was spurred by the writings of such figures as Johann Joachim Winckelmann and stimulated by the architectural discoveries of the ancient Roman ruins at Herculaneum (1738) and Pompeii (1748; see Figure IV.7). The culture of that earlier age was perceived as a worthy and achievable ideal, and attempts to recapture its style and subject matter were directed at the moral improvement of the viewer, giving art a socially beneficial role. Thus, the Enlightenment desire to foster progress seemed well served by the contemporary understanding of Classical art as one that promoted greater seriousness and moral commitment than the frivolous rococo style, which some saw as an extravagant and superficial extension of the ornamental Baroque. Winckelmann's assertion in 1755 that "there is only one way for moderns to become great and, perhaps, unequalled: by imitating the Ancients" set the artistic agenda for the second half of the century.

*Figure IV.7. A Roman courtyard in the excavated city of Pompeii on the Bay of Naples in southern Italy. It was buried along with Herculaneum by an eruption of nearby Mount Vesuvius in the year 79 C.E. and was rediscovered in the mid-eighteenth century.*

Realizations in the arts

*Figure IV.8. David's portrait of Napoleon I in imperial dress, 1805. Musée des Beaux-Arts, Lille.*

In keeping with these goals, the painter Jacques-Louis David perfected a new type of history painting that featured morally uplifting themes from antiquity. Actively involved in Revolutionary politics, David also portrayed Napoleon as a larger-than-life hero in the tradition of the Roman Caesars (see Figure IV.8). Contemporary sculpture followed Winckelmann's precepts of noble simplicity and calm grandeur. The semicircular plans and tiered seating of Greek and Roman amphitheaters were adapted for political assemblies and lecture halls (see Figure IV.9), promoting the educational aspirations of the era. In England, the influential portraitist Sir Joshua Reynolds became the first president of the newly founded Royal Academy in London (1768); his series of classicizing discourses on art, delivered annually to the Academy, had the important secondary effect of raising the status of the arts and artists in Britain to a new peak. On the Continent, Beethoven's so-called heroic, post-Revolutionary style actualized these Classical ideals in music, thereby changing society's concept of music and of composers, and earning him universal acclaim (Chapter 16).

Strong as it was, the influence of rationalism in the eighteenth century was tempered by a deep vein of sentimentality that surfaced both in literature and in the arts. The word *sensibilité* ("sensibility") entered the vocabulary of criticism for the first time, along with the belief that sentiment or feeling is more important than reason in the apprehension of truth. For example, notwithstanding his involvement in the *Encyclopédie*, Rousseau celebrated nature and the emotions over culture and progress in his writings. His objections to the rules of Classical art on the grounds that they constrained creative liberty, and his championing of

Figure IV.9. The Sheldonian Theatre, Oxford University. Designed by Christopher Wren in the 1660s, the building has the Neoclassical shape of an amphitheater and is still used for concerts and ceremonial occasions. Haydn's Symphony No. 92 was performed there in 1791 as part of a three-day festival commemorating his receiving an honorary Doctor of Music degree.

the importance of educating the senses, allied him to the nineteenth-century Romantic movement. Rousseau's ideas about music were similarly anti-establishment—he promoted the notion that music and all artistic activity should be part of everyday life rather than the exclusive province of professionals.

These ideas found an echo in the new respect accorded the medium of genre painting, represented principally by Jean-Baptiste Greuze. The philosophe Diderot heaped praise upon Greuze's genre scenes, many of which concentrated on themes of ordinary family life, undoubtedly because the critic saw in them the visual equivalent of his own sentimental dramas. Greuze also frequently depicted moral or pathetic subjects, as illustrated by the idealized *Girl with a Dead Canary* (Figure IV.10). The world he created on canvas may find its musical equivalent in the *empfindsamer* style of composers like C. P. E. Bach, to be discussed in Chapter 14; but its literary parallel is surely found in the novels of Jane Austen, whose complex and subtle view of human nature elevated a narrow world of unremarkable domestic relationships into a revealing microcosm of middle-class society. In fact, it is worth noting that the protagonists of *Sense and Sensibility*—two marriageable sisters of opposite personalities, representing "sense" and "sensibility," respectively—embody the two characteristic intellectual currents of the age: reason and sentiment.

Figure IV.10. Jean-Baptiste Greuze, Girl with a Dead Canary, ca. 1765. Although Diderot analyzed the painting as symbolizing the loss of virginity, the superficial subject and its treatment are typical of the painter's sentimental style. National Gallery of Scotland, Edinburgh.

## The Place of Music in the Classical Era

As the pursuit of learning and the love of art became more widespread, particularly among the expanding middle class, a growing interest in hearing and making music spurred composers and publishers to address a general public beyond the select group of experts and connoisseurs. Amateur musicians bought music that they could understand and play, and music publishers catered especially to them. Most of the published music for keyboard, chamber ensemble, or voice and keyboard was designed for amateurs to perform at home for their own pleasure. The growing enthusiasm for music also fostered the development of connoisseurs, informed listeners who cultivated a taste for the best in music. Thus, C. P. E. Bach's keyboard works published in 1779 were entitled *Sonatas for Connoisseurs and Amateurs*; and Mozart aimed at pleasing his Viennese audiences with a musical style that combined sophisticated art with appealing entertainment (Chapter 15).

*A topic of interest*

Popular treatises were written with an eye to bringing culture within the reach of all, while what might be called "the Figaro factor"—depicting everyday people with everyday emotions—had far-reaching effects in the world of opera: comic opera or opera buffa encroached on and satirized the more staid opera seria, eventually setting a course for opera reform, both musically and dramatically (Chapter 14). As the musical public broadened, more people became interested in reading about music and discussing it. By mid-century, magazines devoted to musical news, reviews, and criticism began to appear, catering to both amateurs and connoisseurs. The public's curiosity about music extended to its origins and past styles, addressed in the first universal histories of music, among which was Charles Burney's *A General History of Music* (1776–1789).

*Public concerts*

As wealth was redistributed because of the new economy, private patronage declined and a modern audience for music emerged among the more affluent citizens of Europe (see "Music and Social Custom in British Society," page 318). Public concerts competed with the older-style private concerts and academies. In Paris, the Concert spirituel series was founded in 1725, and other concert series began in cities all over Europe (see "The Public Concert," pages 358–359). This increased concert activity created a favorable climate for instrumental music, which eventually rivaled opera in popularity by the end of the century. Chamber or solo sonatas, symphonies, and concertos for pianoforte and other instruments became the new vehicles to fame for composers of the Classical period. The ceaseless demand for new music accounts for the vast output of many eighteenth-century composers and the phenomenal speed at which they worked.

*Musical tastes and styles*

Many musical styles coexisted in the eighteenth century, each supported by strong adherents and criticized by detractors. Every country had distinctive traditions and developed a national form of opera. Works in new styles, such as the operas of Pergolesi and Hasse, were written at the same time as Rameau's operas, Handel's oratorios, and J. S. Bach's fugues, all representative of the late Baroque and all discussed in Chapter 13. But despite the array of styles, leading writers in the middle and late eighteenth century articulated the prevailing view of what was most valued in music. Instead of the contrapuntal complexity and spun-out instrumental melody of Baroque music, audiences and critics preferred music that featured a vocally conceived melody in short phrases over spare accompaniment. Writers held that the language of music should be universal rather than limited by national boundaries and should appeal to all tastes at once, from the sophisticated to the untutored. The best music should be noble as well as entertaining, expressive within the limits of decorum, and "natural"—free of technical complications and capable of immediately pleasing any sensitive listener. The composers we will encounter in Chapters 14, 15, and 16 shared most of these values. The best among them created works unprecedented in their individuality, dramatic power, wide appeal, and depth of interest.

# Music in the Early Eighteenth Century

## PRELUDE

The early eighteenth century—particularly between 1720 and 1750—was a period of stylistic change in music. The newer, galant style was emerging to compete with the older, Baroque styles. This newer music sounded more songful and less contrapuntal, more natural and less artificial, more sentimental and less intensely emotional than its Baroque counterpart. We will explore the galant style, an early stage of the Classical era, in the next chapter, but its influence is already apparent in some of the later works by Vivaldi, Rameau, J. S. Bach, and Handel, the four masterful composers discussed in this chapter. Together with Couperin, Rameau's older contemporary, these composers summarize and, to some extent, synthesize the Baroque musical qualities and trends we have studied so far in Italy, France, Germany, and England. All of these figures were successful and eminent during their own time. All were aware of new currents in musical thought, each finding his own solution to the conflicts between contrapuntal and homophonic, older and more recent styles. All worked within the established genres of the late Baroque. Vivaldi excelled as a composer of concertos and operas. Couperin wrote stylish music, especially for keyboard, and advocated a synthesis of French and Italian styles. Rameau wrote opera and instrumental music in France and developed new ideas about harmony and tonality in his theoretical writings, some aspects of which were incorporated into later theory. J. S. Bach, somewhat isolated in Germany from the main European cultural centers, brought to consummation all forms of late Baroque music except opera. And Handel, who also excelled in composing Italian opera, recognized the social changes in England that created the perfect climate for a new kind of oratorio, one that long outlived the audiences for which it was intended.

*Chapter Contents*

*Prelude* 279

Italy: Antonio
Vivaldi 279

France: Couperin
and Rameau 285

Germany: Johann
Sebastian Bach 290

England: George
Frideric Handel 304

*Postlude* 313

## Italy: Antonio Vivaldi

At the beginning of the eighteenth century, Venice, though declining in political power and headed for economic ruin, still remained the most glamorous city in Europe. It was full of tourists, tradespeople, intellectuals, prostitutes, artists,

*Figure 13.1. Women singers and string players (upper left), thought to be from the Pio Ospedale della Pietà, give a concert in Venice honoring Archduke Paul and Maria Feodorovna of Russia. Painting of 1782 by Francesco Guardi (1712– 1793). Alte Pinakothek, Munich.*

and musicians—all attracted to its colorful and exciting diversity. Musicians sang on the streets and canals; gondoliers had their own repertory of songs; amateurs played and sang in private academies; and opera impresarios competed for the best singers and composers.

Venice

Public festivals, more numerous in Venice than elsewhere, remained occasions of musical splendor, and the musical establishment of Saint Mark's was still famous. The city had always taken pride in its musical greatness—as a center of music printing, of church music, of instrumental composition, and of opera. Even in the eighteenth century, Venice never had fewer than six opera companies, which together played thirty-four weeks of the year. Between 1700 and 1750, the Venetian public heard ten new operas annually, and the count was even higher in the second half of the century.

In addition to these musical establishments, Venice nurtured a unique group of institutions that were actually state-run shelters for chronically ill, poor, and homeless children, including many who were illegitimate, orphaned, or otherwise abandoned. The Pio Ospedale della Pietà was one of four such "hospitals" that provided quality music education for women outside the convent and that became famous as musical centers. Already in the seventeenth century, some were accepting nonresident girls and boarders who paid for their tuition. Educating the girls in music served several purposes: it occupied their time; it enhanced their prospects for marriage or prepared them for convent life; and it earned donations for the hospitals through regular performances, such as the concert pictured in Figure 13.1. Careers as instrumentalists or church musicians were not open to women, and, before the girls were allowed to leave, they had to promise never again to perform in public. For this among other reasons, services with music at the Pietà and other places of worship in Venice attracted large audiences. Travelers wrote of these occasions with enthusiasm and even amusement at the unusual sight of a choir and orchestra comprised mainly of teenage girls (see vignette, page 282). Thus, like their counterparts, the boys' conservatories in Naples, the Venetian ospedali had a notable impact on the musical life of the entire peninsula, serving as premier laboratories for composers associated with them.

The best-known Italian composer of the early eighteenth century was Antonio Vivaldi (1678–1741), a native Venetian who spent most of his career there (see his biography, below). A virtuoso violinist, master teacher, and popular composer of opera, cantatas, and sacred music, he is known today primarily for his concertos, which number around five hundred. From 1703 to 1740, Vivaldi's main position was that of conductor, composer, teacher, and superintendent of musical instruments at the Pio Ospedale della Pietà. His job required him to maintain the string instruments, teach his students to play, and meet the public's demand for new music—there were no "classics" and few works of any kind survived more than two or three seasons. Such relentless pressure accounts both for the vast output of many eighteenth-century composers and for the phenomenal speed at which they worked. Vivaldi was expected to furnish new oratorios and concertos for every church holiday at the Pietà. Concertos were especially well suited for players of varying abilities because the best performers could show off their skill in the solo parts while those of lesser ability could play in the orchestra.

Vivaldi's concertos have a freshness of melody, rhythmic verve, skillful treatment of solo and orchestral color, and clarity of form that have made them

Concertos

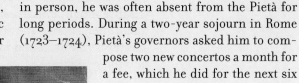

## Antonio Vivaldi (1678–1741)

Internationally renowned as a virtuoso violinist, Vivaldi was one of the most original and prolific composers of his time, and his influence on later composers was profound. Born in Venice, the eldest of nine children of a violinist at Saint Mark's, Vivaldi trained for both music and the priesthood, a combination that was not unusual at the time. His bright red hair earned him the nickname of *il Prete Rosso* (the Red Priest).

In 1703, the year he was ordained, he became a music teacher at the Pio Ospedale della Pietà, a Venetian orphanage and school for girls. He was later appointed director of concerts, a position of greater responsibility, and he remained at the Pietà until 1740, with some breaks in service.

*Figure 13.2. Antonio Vivaldi, in an engraving by François Morellon La Cave from around 1725.*

Like most of his contemporaries, Vivaldi composed every work for a definite occasion and for particular performers. For the Pietà, he composed oratorios, sacred music, and especially concertos. He also fulfilled forty-nine opera commissions, most for Venice and a few for elsewhere. Between 1713 and 1719, the theaters of Venice staged more works by him than by any other composer. Since he usually supervised the production of his operas

in person, he was often absent from the Pietà for long periods. During a two-year sojourn in Rome (1723–1724), Pietà's governors asked him to compose two new concertos a month for a fee, which he did for the next six years; this arrangement is one of the most direct signs of Vivaldi's value to them as a composer, distinct from his roles as teacher and performer.

In the 1720s, Vivaldi took the contralto Anna Girò as his singing pupil (and, some gossiped, his mistress, although he denied it). In 1737, he was censured for conduct unbecoming a priest. By then, his popularity with the Venetian public had dwindled, and he increasingly sought commissions elsewhere, traveling to Amsterdam in 1738 and Vienna in 1740. He earned enormous sums of money from his music but spent almost all of it, and when he died in Vienna in 1741, he was given a pauper's funeral.

**Major works:** About 500 concertos (including *The Four Seasons*), 16 sinfonias, 64 solo sonatas, 27 trio sonatas, 21 surviving operas, 38 cantatas, and about 60 sacred vocal works.

perennial favorites. Working at the Pietà, having skilled performers at his disposal, and being required to produce music at a prodigious rate provided Vivaldi with a workshop for experimenting with the concerto. The secret of Vivaldi's success and of the profound influence he exercised on other composers was a simple but flexible recipe that allowed him to achieve extraordinary variety through ever-changing combinations of a few basic elements.

Vivaldi achieved a remarkable range of colors and sonorities through different groupings of solo and orchestral instruments. His orchestra at the Pietà probably consisted of twenty to twenty-five string instruments, with harpsichord or organ for the continuo. The strings were divided in what was becoming the standard arrangement: violins I and II, violas, cellos, and bass viols (usually doubling the cellos). This was always the core group, although in many concertos Vivaldi also called for flutes, oboes, bassoons, or horns, any of which might be used as solo instruments or in the ensemble. He also used special coloristic effects, like pizzicato and muted strings.

**Instrumentation of the concertos**

About 350 of Vivaldi's concertos are for orchestra and one solo instrument—mostly for violin, but many also for bassoon, cello, oboe, flute, viola d'amore, recorder, or mandolin. The concertos for two violins give the soloists equal prominence, producing the texture of a duet for two high voices. The concertos that call for several solo instruments feature the same opposition between virtuoso soloists and orchestra that is found in Vivaldi's solo concertos.

**Three-movement structure**

With occasional exceptions, Vivaldi followed a three-movement plan: an opening fast movement; a slow movement in the same or a closely related key (relative minor, dominant, or subdominant); and a final fast movement in the tonic, often shorter and sprightlier than the first. By using this format so consistently, Vivaldi helped establish it as the master plan for concertos over the next three centuries.

## VIGNETTE  Concerts at the Pio Ospedale della Pietà

*The Frenchman Charles de Brosses toured Italy in 1739–1740 and wrote his impressions in letters to friends, later collected for publication. His account of concerts at the Pio Ospedale della Pietà, where Vivaldi had long overseen instrumental music, gives us a sense of the institution and of the concerts performed by its residents, although de Brosses was mistaken when he called them nuns.*

A transcending music here is that of the hospitals [orphanages]. There are four, all made up of illegitimate or orphaned girls or girls whose parents are not in a condition to raise them. They are reared at public expense and trained solely to excel in music. So they sing like angels and play the violin, the flute, the organ, the violoncello, the bassoon. In short no instrument is large enough to frighten them. They are cloistered in the manner of nuns. They alone perform, and each concert is given by about forty girls. I swear to you that there is nothing so charming as to see a young and pretty nun in her white robe, with a bouquet of pomegranate flowers over her ear, leading the orchestra and beating time with all the grace and precision imaginable. Their voices are adorable for their quality and lightness, because here they don't know about roundness or a sound drawn out like a thread in the French manner. . . .

The hospital I go to most often is that of the Pietà, where one is best entertained. It is also first for the perfection of the symphonies. What an upright performance! It is only there that you hear the first stroke of the bow [*le premier coup d'archet*]—the first chord of a piece attacked as one by the strings, of which the Opéra in Paris falsely boasts.

Charles de Brosses, *L'Italie il y a cent ans; ou, Lettres écrites d'Italie à quelques amis en 1739 et 1740*, ed. M. R. Colomb, 2 vols. (Paris: Alphonse Levavasseur, 1836), I, pp. 213–214.

*Figure 13.3.  A page from one of Vivaldi's manuscripts—a tutti section from the finale of the Concerto in A for solo violin and four-part string ensemble.*

Ritornello form

We saw in Chapter 12 that Torelli structured the fast movements of his concertos like the A section of a da capo aria, with a ritornello at the beginning, middle, and end framing two long episodes for the soloist. Vivaldi's concertos expand on this pattern, producing what is now known as ritornello form. This is less a formal mold than it is an approach or a set of guidelines, one that allows a great deal of variety:

- Ritornellos for the full orchestra alternate with episodes for the soloist or soloists.
- The opening ritornello is composed of several small units typically two to four measures in length, some of which may be repeated or varied. These segments can be separated from each other or combined in new ways without losing their identity as the ritornello.
- Later statements of the ritornello are usually partial, comprising only one or some of the units, sometimes varied.
- The ritornellos are signposts to the tonal structure of the music, confirming the keys to which the music modulates. The first and last statements are in the tonic, at least one (usually the first in a new key) is in the dominant, and others may be in closely related keys.
- The solo episodes are characterized by virtuosic, idiomatic playing, sometimes repeating or varying elements from the ritornello but often presenting scales, arpeggiations, or other figuration. Many episodes modulate to a new key, which is then confirmed by the following ritornello. Sometimes the soloist interrupts or plays some part of the closing ritornello.

All these points are illustrated by the two fast movements in Vivaldi's Concerto for Violin and Orchestra in A Minor, Op. 3, No. 6 (NAWM 85). Example 13.1 shows the opening ritornello of the first movement. Each of the segments, denoted by letter, has a strongly etched, individual character that makes it easy to remember. Each is a distinct harmonic unit, enabling Vivaldi to separate and

CD 6/13–22    CD 3/12

recombine the segments later on. In both movements, later statements of the ritornello are only partial, and some vary motives from the original ritornello, as do some of the solo episodes. New figurations are introduced in the episodes, as shown in Example 13.2, providing even more variety within a clearly understood structure; one passage—Example 13.2c—exploits the open strings of the violin (tuned g–d′–a′–e″) for impressive leaps.

Typical of Vivaldi is that each movement has some little aberration that makes it unique in form, yet the overall strategy is clearly the same. Far from following a textbook plan, Vivaldi's ritornello structures show almost infinite variety in form and content.

*Example 13.1: Antonio Vivaldi, Concerto in A Minor, Op. 3, No. 6, opening ritornello*

*Example 13.2: Antonio Vivaldi, Concerto in A Minor, Op. 3, No. 6, first movement, examples of figuration in solo episodes*

Vivaldi was the first concerto composer to make the slow movement as important as the fast ones. His slow movement is typically a long-breathed, expressive, cantabile melody, like an adagio operatic aria or arioso, to whose already rich figuration the performer was expected to add embellishments. Some slow movements are through-composed, and others use a simplified ritornello or two-part form. The slow movement in Op. 3, No. 6, is unusual in that the bass instruments and continuo are silent, and the soloist is accompanied only by the upper strings, which play sustained tones.

Vivaldi once said he could compose a concerto faster than a copyist could write out the parts. One reason was that ritornello form allowed him to spin out relatively long movements from a small amount of material that he repeated, transposed, varied, and recombined. In both fast and slow movements, he frequently used sequences, generating several measures from a short motive while dramatizing a strong chord progression, as in the second segment (B) of Example 13.1.

Despite his reliance on formulas, what is most striking about Vivaldi's concertos is their variety and range of expression. His works were known for their spontaneity of musical ideas, clear formal structures, assured harmonies, varied textures, and forceful rhythms. He established a dramatic tension between solo and tutti, not only giving the soloist contrasting figuration, as Torelli had already done, but also letting the soloist prevail as a dominating musical personality.

In addition to composing many of his concertos for the Pietà, Vivaldi also wrote on commission and earned money through publications. Nine collections of his concertos (Opp. 3–4 and Opp. 6–12) were published in Amsterdam, the last seven apparently printed at the publisher's expense instead of being subsidized by the composer or a patron, as was common. This shows Vivaldi's value to his publisher and reflects the immense popularity of his concertos, especially in northern Europe. Several of these collections were given fanciful titles, in part to attract buyers: Op. 3, *L'estro armonico* (Harmonic Inspiration, 1711); Op. 4, *La stravaganza* (Extravagance, 1716); Op. 8, *Il cimento dell'armonia e dell'inventione* (The Test of Harmony and Invention, 1725); and Op. 9, *La cetra* (The Kithara, 1727), evoking ancient Greece. Some individual concertos were also given titles and even programs. Most famous are the first four concertos in Op. 8, known as *The Four Seasons*. Each of these is accompanied by a sonnet, perhaps written by Vivaldi himself, that describes the season, and the concertos cleverly depict the images in the poetry, taking advantage of the variety possible in ritornello forms.

*Figure 13.4.  Antonio Vivaldi (1678–1741), "the Red Priest," drawn in Rome in 1723 by P. L. Ghezzi. It is the only authenticated portrait of the composer.*

Vivaldi's music reflects the stylistic changes of the first half of the eighteenth century. At the conservative extreme are his trio and solo sonatas, which emulate the style of Corelli. Most of his concertos were part of the stylistic mainstream, responding to and often creating contemporary trends. At the progressive extreme are the solo concerto finales, the orchestral concertos, and most of the sixteen sinfonias—works that establish Vivaldi as a founder of the Classical symphony (see Chapter 14).

Range of styles

# France: Couperin and Rameau

While Italy had many cultural centers, France had only one, Paris, the capital and by far the largest city. Musicians in the provinces dreamed of careers in

Paris, where patrons, publishers, and an eager public waited to hear and see the latest music. Only there could a composer achieve true success and a national reputation. Although other cities had concert series in which amateurs could perform, Paris was home to the most prestigious concert organizations like the Concert spirituel, a public concert series founded in 1725. The royal court of Louis XV (r. 1715–1774) continued to support musicians, but no longer dominated musical life, as had the court of his great-grandfather, Louis XIV. In its place, a wider range of patrons and institutions supported musicians and composers.

Reconciling French
and Italian styles

Since the seventeenth century, Italian music in France was viewed as a foreign influence, welcomed by some and resisted by others. The latest Italian music could be heard in Paris, particularly the sonatas and concertos of Corelli, Vivaldi, and others, and the relative merits of French and Italian styles were discussed constantly in salons and in print. Many French composers sought to blend the two musical styles, especially in genres pioneered in Italy.

## François Couperin

Among the most active proponents of blending French and Italian tastes was François Couperin (1668–1733). His career reflects the growing diffusion of patronage in France: he was organist to the king and at the church of Saint Gervais in Paris, but earned much of his money teaching harpsichord to members of the aristocracy and publishing his own music. His harpsichord *ordres*, or suites, published between 1713 and 1730, were loose aggregations of miniature pieces, most in dance rhythms and in binary form but highly stylized and refined, intended as recreation for amateur performers. Thoroughly French yet individual in style, most of these pieces carry evocative titles. Couperin's *Vingt-cinquième ordre* (Twenty-fifth Suite, 1730; excerpts in NAWM 86), for example, contains *La Visionaire* (The Dreamer), a whimsical French overture; *La Mistérieuse* (The Mysterious One), an allemande; *La Montflambert*, a tender gigue probably named after the wife of the king's wine merchant; *La Muse victorieuse* (The Victorious Muse), a fast dance in triple time; and others. Couperin's book *L'Art de toucher le clavecin* (The Art of Playing the Harpsichord, 1716) is one of the most important sources for performance practice of the French Baroque.

CD 6/31    CD 3/20

CD 6/33    CD 3/22

Chamber works

In his chamber music, Couperin synthesized French with Italian styles. By means of the titles, prefaces, and choice of contents for his published collections, he proclaimed that the perfect music would be a union of the two national styles. He admired the music of both Lully and Corelli, and celebrated them in suites for two violins and harpsichord: *Parnassus; or, The Apotheosis of Corelli* (1724) and *The Apotheosis of Lully* (1725). In the second work, Lully is represented as joining Corelli on Mount Parnassus to perform a French overture and then a trio sonata. Couperin was the first and most important French composer of trio sonatas, beginning in 1692. His collection *Les Nations* (The Nations, 1726) contains four *ordres*, each consisting of a sonata da chiesa in several movements followed by a suite of dances, thus combining the most characteristic genres of France and Italy in a single set. He also wrote twelve suites that he called "concerts" for harpsichord and various combinations of instruments, each consisting of a prelude and several dance movements. He entitled the first four *Concerts royaux* (Royal Concerts, published 1722) because they were played before Louis XIV. Couperin published the last eight in a collection entitled *Les Goûts-réunis* (The Reunited Tastes, 1724), signifying that they combined French and Italian styles.

# Jean-Philippe Rameau

Jean-Philippe Rameau (1683–1764) had an unusual career, spending two decades as an organist in the provinces, winning recognition as a music theorist around the age of forty, and achieving fame as a composer in his fifties (see his biography, below). Attacked then as a radical, he was assailed twenty years later as a reactionary. His writings founded the theory of tonal music, and his operas established him as Lully's most important successor.

## ✹ Jean-Philippe Rameau (1683–1764)

Possessing a strong intellect, Rameau emerged late in life as the most significant music theorist of his era. Practically unknown before the age of forty, he also became the leading composer in France because of the operas and ballets he turned out in his fifties and sixties.

Rameau was born in Dijon, in Burgundy (east-central France), the seventh of eleven children. From his father, an organist, Rameau received his first and, as far as we know, only formal musical instruction. He attended a Jesuit school and was sent to study in Italy briefly as a teenager. After two decades holding positions as organist in various provincial French towns, he settled in Paris in 1722, seeking better opportunities. His pathbreaking *Traité de l'harmonie* (Treatise on Harmony), published that year, quickly won him renown as a theorist. He made a living teaching harmony and playing continuo but could not find a position as organist until 1732. In 1726, at age forty-two, he married a nineteen-year-old singer and harpsichordist, Marie-Louise Mangot, and over the next two decades they had four children.

Success as a composer came gradually and late. He published some cantatas and two books of harpsichord pieces in the 1720s. He found patrons who helped to support him, particularly Alexandre-Jean-Joseph le Riche de la Pouplinière. His first opera, *Hippolyte et Aricie* (1733), helped build his reputation as a composer, followed by four other operas and opera-ballets in the next six years. Rameau served la Pouplinière as organist and in various capacities until 1753, and members of his patron's circle became enthusiastic backers as well. In 1745, the king of France granted him an annual pension. The next few years were his most productive and successful, with eleven dramatic works by 1749. Given his late start, it is remarkable that over twenty-five of his ballets and operas were staged, more than those by any other French composer of the eighteenth century.

Polemical writings and theoretical essays occupied Rameau's closing years. He died in Paris in 1764 at the age of eighty-one. Feisty to the end, he found strength even on his deathbed to reproach the priest administering the last rites for chanting poorly.

**Major works:** 4 *tragédies en musique* (*Hippolyte et Aricie, Castor et Pollux, Dardanus,* and *Zoroastre*); 6 other operas, *Les Indes galantes,* and 6 other opera-ballets; 7 ballets, harpsichord pieces, trio sonatas, cantatas, and motets.

*Figure 13.5. Jean-Philippe Rameau, in a copy by Jacques Aved of a portrait by Jean-Baptiste-Siméon Chardin. Musée des Beaux-Arts de Dijon.*

When he settled in Paris in 1722, Rameau's prospects as a composer were poor: he had neither money nor influential friends nor the disposition to curry favor at court. Although he aspired to become a composer of operas—indeed, it was the only road to real fame—the monopoly of the Académie Royale de Musique thwarted that ambition. Seeking better opportunities, he wrote airs and dances for a few musical comedies, pieces with spoken dialogue performed at the popular theaters. He published some cantatas and several books of keyboard pieces. Meanwhile his reputation as a teacher and organist began to attract students. Finally, Rameau's luck changed when, in 1732, he was appointed organist, conductor, and composer-in-residence to the wealthy tax collector Alexandre-Jean-Joseph le Riche de la Pouplinière (1693–1762), who supported an orchestra, sponsored concerts for the wealthy, and took pleasure in promoting the careers of obscure musicians. He maintained several residences in Paris as well as houses in the country nearby. His salon attracted a diverse company of aristocrats, writers (Voltaire and Rousseau), painters (Van Loo—see Figure 13.15—and La Tour), adventurers (Casanova), and above all, musicians.

**Operas**

La Pouplinière helped Rameau make his name as an opera composer. He funded a production of *Hippolyte et Aricie*, which was performed privately in 1733 before being produced in Paris later that same year, winning both admiration and scorn. A string of successes followed, including the opera-ballet *Les Indes galantes* (The Gallant Indies, 1735) and the opera *Castor et Pollux* (1737), generally considered his masterpiece. After a relatively fallow period in the early 1740s came his most productive years—from the comedy *Platée* (1745) to the tragic opera *Zoroastre* (1749), the most important of Rameau's later works.

**Lullistes versus Ramistes**

From the first, Rameau's operas stirred up a storm of critical controversy. The Paris intelligentsia divided into two noisy camps, one supporting Rameau and the other attacking him as a subverter of the good old French opera tradition of Lully. The Lullistes found Rameau's music difficult, forced, grotesque, thick, mechanical, and unnatural—in a word, Baroque. Rameau protested, in a foreword to his opera-ballet *Les Indes galantes*, that he had "sought to imitate Lully, not as a servile copyist but in taking, like him, nature herself—so beautiful and so simple—as a model."

**Comparison with Lully**

Rameau's theater works resemble Lully's in several ways: both composers exhibit realistic declamation and precise rhythmic notation in the recitatives; both mix recitative with more tuneful, formally organized airs, choruses, and instrumental interludes; and both include long divertissements. But within this general framework, Rameau introduced many changes.

**Melodic and harmonic style**

The melodic lines offer one notable contrast. Rameau the composer constantly practiced the doctrine of Rameau the theorist—that all melody is rooted in harmony (see "A Closer Look: Rameau's Theories," page 289). Many of his melodic phrases are plainly triadic and make clear the harmonic progressions that must support them. Orderly relationships within the tonal system of dominants, subdominants, and modulations govern the harmony. Rameau drew from a rich palette of chords and progressions, including chromatic ones, diversifying his style much more than Lully's and achieving dramatic force through expressive, highly charged dissonances that propel the harmony forward.

**Instrumental music**

Rameau made his most original contribution in the instrumental sections of his operas—overtures, dances, and descriptive symphonies that accompany the stage action. The French valued music for its powers of depiction, and Rameau was their champion tone painter. His musical pictures range from graceful miniatures to broad representations of thunder (*Hippolyte et Aricie*, Act I) or earthquake (*Les Indes galantes*, Act II). The depiction is often enhanced by novel orchestration, especially independent woodwind parts.

| A CLOSER LOOK | Rameau's Theories |

Theory—or the "science" of music, as it was called at the time—engaged Rameau throughout his life as he tried to derive the basic principles of harmony from the laws of acoustics. In his numerous writings, Rameau not only clarified the musical practice of his time but also influenced music theory for the next two hundred years. A synopsis of his most important ideas about tonal harmony follows:

1. A chord is the primal element in music. The major triad is generated naturally when a string is divided into two, three, four, and five equal parts, which produces the octave, the fifth above it, the double octave, and the major third above that. (Rameau later became aware that the overtone series supports this theory.)

*Figure 13.6. Jean-Philippe Rameau, seated near his harpsichord with pen and music paper in hand, occupies himself with writing, an activity suggestive of his status as a thinker.*

2. Chords are built up by thirds over a fundamental tone (root), so that triads can be expanded to seventh chords and, beyond the octave, to ninth and eleventh chords.

3. In a series of chords, the succession of fundamental tones becomes the *basse fondamentale*, or fundamental bass, the underlying or determining bass line of the progression. Rameau also asserted the identity of a chord through all its inversions.

4. He coined the terms *tonic*, *dominant*, and *subdominant* and established these three chords as the pillars of tonality. By clarifying the relationship of other chords to the primary triads, Rameau formulated the hierarchies of functional harmony.

5. Modulation results from the change in function of a chord (in modern terminology, a pivot chord).

In comparison to Italian composers, Rameau, like Lully and other French composers, minimized the contrast between recitative and air. He often moved smoothly between styles to suit the dramatic situation. Frequently, the most powerful effects are achieved by the joint use of solo and chorus. Choruses remained prominent in French operas long after they were no longer used in Italy, and they are numerous throughout Rameau's works.

Airs and choruses

The closing minutes of Act IV of *Hippolyte et Aricie* (NAWM 87) illustrate the high drama that Rameau could achieve by combining all these elements. A divertissement of hunters and huntresses is suddenly followed by tragedy, so fast that the audience has little time to adjust. Throbbing strings depict a rough sea, while rushing scales in the flute and violins evoke high winds. A monster appears, and the chorus, singing over the orchestra, begs for aid from the goddess Diana. Hippolyte steps up to fight the monster as his beloved Aricie trembles in

CD 6/35    CD 3/24

*Hippolyte et Aricie*

fear; they, too, sing over the orchestra, the texture of the accompanied recitative borrowed from contemporary Italian opera. The monster breathes flame and smoke, then disappears and the orchestra stops abruptly. When the smoke clears, Aricie mournfully sees that Hippolyte is gone, and the chorus comments on the tragedy in stirring, richly dissonant homophony. The rapid juxtaposition of styles continues as Phèdre, Hippolyte's stepmother, enters, hears the news from the chorus, and laments his death, for which she feels responsible. Although no full-fledged air appears—indeed, one would be inappropriate—short segments of airlike melody are intermixed with measured and unmeasured recitative, with and without the orchestra, over varying styles of accompaniment, each element perfectly placed for maximum dramatic effect.

*Rameau as theorist*

Rameau's influence as a music theorist trumps his importance as a composer. Inspired by the works of Descartes and Newton, he approached music as a subject to be studied empirically and explained according to rational principles. In the music of his contemporaries—especially Corelli—Rameau observed harmonic practices that he described and codified into universal laws. He recorded his methods in *Traité de l'harmonie* (Treatise on Harmony, 1722), one of the most influential theoretical works ever written. By the late eighteenth century, his concepts about music theory became the principal basis for teaching harmony (see: A Closer Look: Rameau's Theories," page 289).

# Germany: Johann Sebastian Bach

Toward the middle of the eighteenth century, for the first time in history, the leading composers in Europe came from German-speaking lands. Telemann, Handel, members of the Bach family, Haydn, and Mozart all rose to prominence not by inventing new genres, as the Italians had done in the two previous centuries, but by synthesizing elements from Italian, French, German, and other national traditions in new, rich ways. The German secret was a balance of tastes between native trends and foreign influences. No one exemplifies this better than Johann Sebastian Bach (1685–1750; see the biography and Figure 13.7).

*German patrons*

In the eighteenth century, German-speaking central Europe continued to be divided among hundreds of political entities, from the large states of Austria, Saxony, and Brandenburg-Prussia to tiny principalities and independent cities. Each of these supported music. Some rulers followed Louis XIV's example of displaying their power and wealth through patronage of the arts, as did the Holy Roman emperors in Vienna and King Frederick II (the Great) of Prussia (r. 1740–1786) in Berlin. City governments were also significant employers of musicians, especially in Lutheran areas, where the town council was often responsible for hiring music directors for the churches.

Compared to Vienna and Berlin or the exciting cosmopolitan centers of Venice and Paris, however, an eighteenth-century traveler would have found the world of Lutheran Germany—where Bach spent his entire career—very ordinary indeed. For example, one of its principal cities, Leipzig, had several prominent churches and one of Europe's oldest universities, but not one opera house after 1729 nor any princes or bishops in residence. For the last twenty-five years of his life, Bach lived and worked in Leipzig, where he was forced to confront apathy and to engage in petty disputes with town and university officials. Although he enjoyed a reputation in Protestant Germany as an organ virtuoso and skilled composer of contrapuntal works, he remained unknown in wider circles. Unlike Vivaldi, who traveled and was recognized throughout Europe, or Rameau, who rubbed shoulders with Parisian high society, Bach, though enormously learned, was essentially a working musician who composed in order to satisfy his superiors, to please and edify his fellow citizens, and to glorify God.

Bach composed in all the genres of his time with the exception of opera. He wrote primarily to meet the demands of the positions he held, and his works may be grouped accordingly. Thus, at Arnstadt (1703–1707), Mühlhausen (1707–1708), and the court and chapel of the duke of Weimar (1708–1717), where he was employed as an organist, he composed mostly for organ. At

## Johann Sebastian Bach (1685–1750)

Now considered one of the greatest composers ever, Bach regarded himself more modestly—as a conscientious craftsman doing his job to the best of his ability. He was a virtuoso organist and keyboard player, a skilled violinist, and a prolific composer in almost every genre then current except opera.

Bach came from a large family of musicians from Thuringia, in central Germany. So synonymous was the family name with "musician" that in 1693 the local count urgently called for "a Bach" to fill a vacancy in his orchestra. But at that point, Johann Sebastian was still attending the Latin school in his birthplace, Eisenach, where he received a solid grounding in theology and humanistic studies. He must have learned violin from his father, a court and town musician who died when Bach was just ten years old. Johann Sebastian then lived and studied music with his older brother Johann Christoph Bach, organist in Ohrdruf. Bach spent the years 1700 to 1702 in school at Lüneburg, where he encountered the organist Georg Böhm and experienced the French repertoire and style of the local orchestra. (For cities important in Bach's career, see Figure 13.8.)

Bach's first positions were as a church organist, beginning at Arnstadt in 1703, when he was eighteen, and then at Mühlhausen in 1707. That year he married Maria Barbara Bach, his second cousin, with whom he had seven children before her death in 1720. His second wife, Anna Magdelena Wilcke, a court singer from a family of musicians, whom he married a year later, bore him thirteen children, seven of whom died in infancy. From his

Figure 13.7. *Johann Sebastian Bach. Detail from the Bach monument at Leipzig.*

time at Mühlhausen to the end of his life, Bach tutored private students in performance and composition, including several of his own sons, and served as an organ-building consultant.

In 1708, Bach became a court musician for the duke of Weimar, first as organist and later as concertmaster. He was appointed Kapellmeister (music director) at the court of Prince Leopold of Anhalt in Cöthen in 1717. After a stay of six years, Bach moved to Leipzig, a center of Lutheran church music, to become cantor of the Saint Thomas School and civic music director, one of the most prestigious positions in Germany.

After a lifetime of prodigious activity as a composer and performer, Bach's last two years were marked by disease (probably diabetes), vision problems, and severe eye pain. At his death after a stroke, he left a small estate, split among his nine surviving children and his wife, who died in poverty ten years later.

Bach's works are identified by their number in Wolfgang Schmieder's catalogue of his compositions, abbreviated BWV for Bach-Werke-Verzeichnis (Bach Works Catalogue).

**Major works:** *Saint Matthew Passion, Saint John Passion,* Mass in B Minor, about 200 church cantatas and 30 secular cantatas, about 200 organ chorales and 70 other works for organ. *Brandenburg Concertos, Well-Tempered Clavier, Clavierübung, A Musical Offering, The Art of Fugue,* and numerous other keyboard, ensemble, orchestral, and sacred compositions.

Figure 13.8.  Cities that figured in J. S. Bach's career are indicated in red on this map of modern Germany. In Bach's time, Germany comprised a number of duchies, bishoprics, principalities, and electorates of the Holy Roman Empire. For example, Leipzig and Dresden were in the electorate of Saxony, Lüneburg in that of Hanover, Berlin in that of Brandenburg. Hamburg and Lübeck belonged to the duchy of Holstein, and Anhalt-Cöthen and Weimar were themselves tiny dukedoms.

Cöthen (1717–1723), where he worked as music director for a princely court, he composed mostly works for keyboard or instrumental ensembles as well as music for instruction and for domestic or court entertainment. He produced most of his cantatas and other church music during his years in Leipzig (1723–1750), where his final position as cantor of Saint Thomas's School and music director at Saint Thomas's and Saint Nicholas's churches carried considerable prestige in the Lutheran world. Some of his most important mature compositions for organ or harpsichord also date from the Leipzig period, including teaching pieces for his many private students. Consequently, our survey of Bach's compositions follows the order that corresponds approximately to his places of employment.

## Bach at Arnstadt, Mühlhausen, and Weimar: The Organ Works

Bach was trained as a violinist and organist, but it was organ music that first attracted his interest as a composer. As a youth, he visited Hamburg to hear the organists there; and, while working in Arnstadt, he made a journey on foot to

Lübeck—a distance of about 225 miles—to hear the famous Buxtehude, who was then almost seventy. There, the music of the older composer so fascinated him that he overstayed his leave and got into trouble with his employers.

As a church organist, Bach focused on the genres employed in Lutheran services: chorale settings, played before each chorale and sometimes to accompany the congregation; toccatas, fantasias, preludes, and fugues, featured as introductions or interludes at other points in the service and also suitable for recitals (see the vignette on page 299 for the place of "preluding" in a Lutheran service).

One of the favorite larger musical structures in this period was the combination of prelude (or toccata or fantasia) and fugue. Most of Bach's important compositions in this form are idiomatic for the organ and technically difficult, although they never parade empty virtuosity, and their well-defined fugue subjects show remarkable inventiveness. His well-known Toccata in D Minor, BWV 565 (before 1708?), recalls both the form established by Buxtehude, in which a prelude alternates sections of free fantasia with fugues, and the exuberant spirit and length of the earlier work (see NAWM 84).

**Preludes and fugues**

**CD 6/6**

While at Weimar, Bach became fascinated by the music of Vivaldi. He arranged several Vivaldi concertos for organ or harpsichord solo, writing out the ornaments and occasionally reinforcing the counterpoint or adding inner voices. As a consequence, Bach's own style began to change. From Vivaldi, he learned to write concise themes, to clarify the harmonic scheme, and to develop subjects into grandly proportioned formal structures based on the ritornello idea.

Vivaldi's influence is evident in Bach's preludes and fugues composed at Weimar, such as the Prelude and Fugue in A Minor, BWV 543 (NAWM 88). In the prelude, violinistic figuration resembling that of concerto solos, as in Example 13.3a, alternates with toccata sections. Contrasting textures, sequences, circle-of-fifth progressions, clear tonal structure, and returns of the opening material in new keys all recall Vivaldi's typical procedures. The fugue subject, shown in Example 13.3b, is also violinistic, featuring the rapid oscillation between a repeated note and a moving line that on a violin is accomplished by alternating strings. Typical of Bach fugues, the form closely resembles a concerto fast movement. The fugue subject functions like a ritornello, returning in related keys as well as the tonic. Between these statements are episodes that have the character of solo sections, often marked by lighter texture, sequences, or a change of key.

**Vivaldi's influence**

**CD 6/38**    **CD 3/27**

*Example 13.3: J. S. Bach, Prelude and Fugue in A Minor, BWV 543, opening and fugue subject*

*a. Opening of prelude*

*b. Fugue subject*

Bach wrote over two hundred chorale settings for organ, encompassing all known types in a constant search for variety. At Weimar, he compiled a manuscript collection, the *Orgelbüchlein* (Little Organ Book), containing forty-five

**Chorale settings**

short chorale preludes. These served in church as introductions before the congregation sang the chorale. But Bach also had a pedagogical aim, as is true for several of his other collections. The title page reads: "Little Organ Book, in which a beginning organist is given guidance in all sorts of ways of developing a chorale, as well as improving his pedal technique, since in these chorales the pedal is treated as completely obbligato [essential, not optional]." He added the words "To honor the Most High God alone, and for the instruction of my fellow men." In each prelude, the chorale tune is heard once through, but otherwise the settings vary greatly. The melody may be treated in canon, elaborately ornamented, or accompanied in any number of styles. Some preludes symbolize the visual images or underlying ideas of the chorale text through musical figures in a tradition extending back through Schütz to the Italian madrigalists. In *Durch Adams Fall* (Through Adam's fall), BWV 637 (NAWM 89), shown in Example 13.4, while the top line carries the chorale tune, jagged descending leaps in the bass depict Adam's fall from grace. Meanwhile, the twisting chromatic line in the alto portrays the sinuous writhing of the serpent in the Garden of Eden, and the downward sliding tenor combines with both to suggest the pull of temptation and the sorrow of sin.

CD 6/49

*Example 13.4: J. S. Bach, chorale prelude on* Durch Adams Fall, *BWV 705*

Bach conceived his later organ chorales in grander proportions. The settings are less intimate and subjective, replacing the vivid expressive details of the earlier works with a purely musical development of ideas.

## Bach at Cöthen and Leipzig: The Harpsichord Music

Bach's music for harpsichord includes masterpieces in every current genre: preludes, fantasies, and toccatas; fugues and other pieces in fugal style; suites; and sets of variations. In addition, there are early sonatas and capriccios, miscellaneous short works (including many teaching pieces), and concertos with orchestra. The harpsichord compositions, which were not bound to a local German tradition or liturgy as organ works were, reveal the international features of Bach's style—the intermingling of Italian, French, and German characteristics—to an even greater extent than the pieces for organ do.

*The Well-Tempered Clavier*

Undoubtedly, Bach's best-known works for keyboard are the double cycle of preludes and fugues that he entitled *Das wohltemperirte Clavier* (The Well-Tempered Clavier—also called The Well-Tempered Keyboard—Books I and II, 1722 and ca. 1740, respectively). Each book consists of twenty-four preludes and fugues, one pair in each of the twelve major and minor keys, arranged in rising chromatic order from C to B. Book I is more unified in style and purpose than Book II, which includes compositions from many different periods of Bach's life. Both sets were designed to demonstrate the possibilities of playing in all

**A CLOSER LOOK**    The Well-Tempered Clavier

The title of Bach's *Well-Tempered Clavier,* his collection of forty-eight preludes and fugues in all the major and minor keys, requires some explanation. By using the generic term "clavier," Bach signaled that these pieces could be played on different types of keyboard instruments, leaving the decision to the performer's preference and common sense. A brilliant, toccata-like prelude, while playable on any keyboard instrument, might sound best on the sparkling harpsichord. The clavichord—whose sweet and intimate sound made the instrument a special favorite of Bach—seems more suitable for some of the gentler and more lyrical preludes (see Figure 13.9). And because of its greater sustaining power, the organ might be ideal for certain of the fugues in the cycle. Since Bach never intended the collection to be performed as a single work, it follows that no single instrument can do justice to all the pieces in both books. However, there are some pieces in the collection that would sound equally good whether plucked (harpsichord), struck (clavichord), or blown on the organ.

"Well-tempered" refers to the keyboard's tuning. Unlike the lute, where frets marked off twelve equal semitones in the octave, keyboard octaves in the sixteenth and seventeenth centuries were not usually so equally divided. In practice this meant, for example, that B♭ was not the same as A♯, even though they shared the same key. Unequal half steps thus made it impossible to play in tune in every key or to modulate through the entire circle of fifths. But when all semitones are equalized, even though they are fractionally out of tune, it becomes possible to move into and out of more distant keys without hearing passages that sound "bad." Equal or near-equal temperament (tuning) was the system advocated (though not invented) by Bach in this work and the system that remains in use on keyboard instruments today.

*Figure 13.9. A plate from Michael Praetorius's* Syntagma musicum *(1619) showing (1) a clavicytherium, or upright harpsichord and (2, 3, and 4) several types of clavichord. The small size of the latter instrument is partly owing to the fact that it is fretted and has fewer strings than keys. Thus, different pitches are produced when keys strike a string at different points along its complete length. The instrument's popularity continued well into the eighteenth century, when Bach's son Carl Philipp Emanuel conceived some of his newly expressive keyboard music largely in terms of the sweet and delicate sound of the clavichord.*

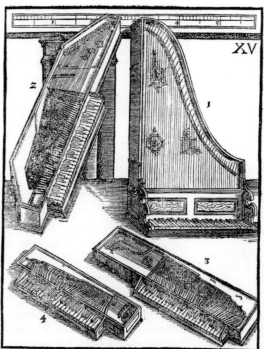

1. Clavicytherium.    2. Clavichordium, Italianischer Mensur.
2. Gemein Clavichord.    4. Octav Clavichordium.

keys on an instrument tuned in near-equal temperament, then still novel for keyboards (see "A Closer Look: *The Well-Tempered Clavier*," page 295).

But Bach had pedagogical aims as well. The typical prelude (see Figure 13.10) assigns the player a specific technical task, so that the piece functions as an étude. In addition, the preludes illustrate different types of keyboard performance conventions and compositional practices. For example, Nos. 2 and 21 of Book I are toccatas, No. 8 a sonata slow movement, No. 17 a concerto fast movement, and No. 24 a trio sonata. The fugues constitute a compendium of fugal writing, from two to five voices and from an archaic ricercare (Book I, No. 4, in C♯ minor) to techniques of inversion, canon, and augmentation (Book I, No. 8, in D♯ minor). As in the organ fugues, each subject has a clearly defined musical personality that unfolds throughout the entire fugue.

Suites

Bach's harpsichord suites show the influence of French and Italian as well as German models. He wrote three sets of six: the "English" suites, the "French" suites, and the six partitas. The designations "French" and "English" for the suites are not Bach's own, and both collections blend French and Italian qualities in a highly personal style. In line with German tradition, each suite contains the standard four dance movements—allemande, courante, sarabande, and

Measures 21 (2nd half)–24 (1st half), in Bach's autograph

Measures 21–26, in Carl Czerny's edition

Measures 22–24, in Hans Bischoff's edition

*Figure 13.10. A passage from the first prelude in Part I of* The Well-Tempered Clavier *is shown in Bach's autograph manuscript and in two publications. Carl Czerny's edition (first published in the 1830s), evidently based on a copy made after Bach's death, incorporates an inauthentic extra measure after measure 22; elsewhere, Czerny adds phrasings, tempo markings, and dynamics not present in Bach's manuscript (for instance, the "dimin" in measure 21). In his edition of 1883, Hans Bischoff tries to present as accurate a reproduction of the source as possible. This aim, while not without its problems in practice, is generally adopted by modern scholars.*

*Figure 13.11. A collegium musicum gathering (in a coffeehouse?), with performers assembled around a harpsichord. Such gatherings were a feature of musical life in Germany from the sixteenth century on. Bach led a collegium in Leipzig in the 1730s. Anonymous eighteenth-century painting. Germanisches Nationalmuseum, Nuremberg.*

gigue—with additional short movements following the sarabande. Each of the "English" suites opens with a prelude in which Bach transferred Italian ensemble idioms to the keyboard. The prelude of the third "English" suite, for example, simulates a concerto allegro movement with alternating tutti and solo. The dances in the "English" suites are based on French models and include several examples of the *double*, or ornamented repetition of a movement.

Bach raised the keyboard theme-and-variations genre to a new high in the *Goldberg Variations* (1741). All thirty variations preserve the bass and the harmonic structure of the theme, a sarabande in two balanced sections. Every third variation is a canon, the first at the interval of a unison, the second at a second, and so on through the ninth. For the thirtieth and last variation, Bach wrote a quodlibet, combining two popular song melodies in counterpoint above the bass of the theme. The noncanonic variations take many different forms, including fugue, French overture, slow aria, and, at regular intervals, a sparkling bravura piece for two manuals. The result is a unique work that draws on many existing types, like a summation of the music of his time.

*Goldberg Variations*

## Bach at the Princely Court of Cöthen: Solo and Ensemble Music

At Cöthen, Bach wrote sonatas, partitas, and suites for unaccompanied violin, cello, and flute in which he created the illusion of a harmonic and contrapuntal texture. By requiring the string player to stop several strings at once and by writing solo melody lines that leap from one register to another and back, he suggested an interplay of independent voices. The incomparable chaconne from Bach's unaccompanied Violin Partita in D Minor illustrates this technique. Bach's chief compositions for chamber ensemble are his sonatas for violin, viola da gamba, or flute and harpsichord. Most of these works have four movements in slow-fast-slow-fast order, like the sonata da chiesa. Indeed, most of them are virtual trio sonatas since the right-hand harpsichord part is often written as a melodic line in counterpoint with the other instrument.

Bach's best-known orchestral works are the six *Brandenburg Concertos*, dedicated in 1721 to Christian Ludwig, margrave of Brandenburg—who had requested

*Brandenburg Concertos*

some pieces—but composed during the previous ten or so years. For all but the first, Bach adopted the three-movement, fast-slow-fast order of the Italian concerto as well as its triadic themes, steady driving rhythms, ritornello forms, and overall style. The third and sixth are orchestral concertos without featured soloists: the others pit solo instruments in various combinations against the body of strings and continuo, and, hence, are concerti grossi. As is typical for him, Bach also expanded on his model, introducing more ritornello material into the episodes, featuring dialogue between soloists and orchestra within episodes, and enlarging the form with devices such as the astonishing long cadenza for the harpsichord (normally a continuo instrument) in the Fifth Concerto.

**Collegium musicum**

Most of Bach's other orchestral music was written in the 1730s, when he directed the Leipzig collegium musicum, which was made up mostly of university students. By the early eighteenth century, such organizations often presented public concerts, like the outdoor concert shown in Figure 12.17. Leipzig's collegium had done so since its founding by Telemann in 1704. Bach apparently wrote his two violin concertos and Concerto in D Minor for Two Violins for such concerts. He was one of the first to write—or arrange—concertos for one or more harpsichords and orchestra, which he no doubt led in performance from the keyboard. The concerto for four harpsichords and orchestra is an arrangement of a Vivaldi concerto for four violins, and most or all of the others are arrangements of concertos by Bach or perhaps by other composers. Bach also wrote four orchestral suites, once again balancing Italian influences with French ones.

**Other instrumental works**

Two of Bach's late instrumental works form a class in themselves. *Musikalisches Opfer* (A Musical Offering) is a collection of various kinds of pieces, all based on a theme proposed by Frederick the Great of Prussia (see Example 13.5). Bach had improvised on the theme while visiting the monarch at Potsdam in 1747, subsequently writing out the improvisations and later revising them. He then added a trio sonata in four movements for flute (King Frederick's instrument), violin, and continuo in which the theme also appears, had the set printed, and dedicated it to the king. *Die Kunst der Fuge* (The Art of Fugue), composed in the final decade of Bach's life and apparently left unfinished at his death, systematically demonstrates all types of fugal writing. It consists of eighteen canons and fugues in the strictest style, all based on the same subject or one of its transformations and arranged in a general order of increasing complexity.

*Example 13.5: J. S. Bach, theme from* A Musical Offering, *BWV 1079*

## Bach at Leipzig: The Vocal Music

In 1723, when Bach was appointed cantor of Saint Thomas's School and Leipzig's director of music, he was not the first choice of the city councilmembers, who had hopes of hiring a more "modern" musician—Georg Philipp Telemann (1681–1767), who was then regarded as the greatest living composer besides Handel. (Telemann turned the job down after using the offer to wangle a raise from his employer in Hamburg.) Saint Thomas's School was a long-established institution that took in both day and boarding pupils. It provided fifty-five scholarships for boys and young men chosen on the basis of their musical and general scholastic abilities. In return, they sang or played in the services of four

Leipzig churches and fulfilled other musical duties. As cantor of Saint Thomas's School, Bach was obliged to teach four hours each day (Latin as well as music) and also to prepare music for the services at Saint Thomas and Saint Nicholas. In addition, he had to promise to lead an exemplary Christian life and not to leave town without permission from the mayor. He and his family lived in an apartment in one wing of the school, where his study was separated by a thin partition from the homeroom of the second-year schoolboys.

The citizens of Leipzig spent a great deal of time in church—at daily services, special celebrations on festival days, and regular Sunday programs beginning at seven in the morning and lasting until about noon. At the Sunday services, the choir (comprised of a minimum of twelve singers) sang a motet, a Lutheran Mass (Kyrie and Gloria only), hymns, and a multimovement cantata. Bach carefully wrote down the order of events on the back of one of his cantata scores (see the vignette below).

The sacred cantata figured prominently in the Lutheran liturgy of Leipzig. The subject matter was often linked to the content of the Gospel reading, which immediately preceded it. This suggests that Bach's role was like that of a musical preacher whose responsibility was to interpret and comment on the Gospel reading in the cantata and to bring its message forcefully home to the congregation. Singers and instrumentalists, however inadequate they may have been at times, were always at his disposal. Altogether, the Leipzig churches required fifty-eight cantatas each year, in addition to Passion music for Good Friday, Magnificats at Vespers for three festivals, an annual cantata for the installation of the city council, and occasional music such as funeral motets and wedding cantatas. Between 1723 and 1729, Bach composed four complete annual cycles, each with about sixty cantatas. He apparently composed a fifth cycle during the 1730s and early 1740s, but many of these cantatas and many of those from the fourth cycle have not survived, leaving only three cycles extant in their entirety.

*Church cantatas*

---

**VIGNETTE**   Music in Lutheran Church Services

*In his first year as cantor and music director in Leipzig, Bach wrote out the order of events, particularly the musical ones, for the main morning service on the first Sunday in Advent. The main musical item was the cantata, which Bach refers to here as "the principal composition." The subject for the cantata was usually linked to the Gospel reading that immediately preceded it, and the sermon would often be on a similar theme. The choir also sang a motet and the Kyrie, the congregation sang chorales, and the organist (probably Bach himself) performed a prelude, often improvised, before each choral work.*

〜

1. Preluding
2. Motet
3. Preluding on the Kyrie, which is performed throughout in concerted manner
4. Intoning before the altar
5. Reading of the Epistle
6. Singing of the Litany

7. Preluding on [and singing of] the Chorale
8. Reading of the Gospel
9. Preluding on [and performance of] the principal music [cantata]
10. Singing of the Creed [Luther's Credo hymn]
11. The Sermon
12. After the Sermon, as usual, singing of several verses of a hymn
13. Words of Institution [of the Sacrament]
14. Preluding on [and performance of] the music [probably the second part of the cantata].

After the same, alternate preluding and singing of chorales until the end of the Communion, *et sic porrò* [and so on].

From Hans T. David and Arthur Mendel, eds., *The New Bach Reader: A Life of Johann Sebastian Bach in Letters and Documents*, rev. and expanded by Christoph Wolff (New York: Norton, 1999), p. 113, no. 113.

We have in existence, then, approximately two hundred cantatas by Bach, some newly written for Leipzig, others refashioned from earlier works. Under tremendous time pressure to produce this repertory. Bach sometimes reworked movements from his chamber and orchestral compositions and inserted them into his Leipzig cantatas. For example, a movement from one of the Brandenburg Concertos and no fewer than five movements from the solo harpsichord concertos found a niche in the cantatas. But given Bach's religious outlook, which offered even his secular art "to the glory of God," there is nothing incongruous or surprising about this accommodation. In the early cantatas, the composer responded to the changing affections and images of the text with music of intense dramatic expression and unexpectedly varied forms. By comparison, the later Leipzig cantatas are less subjective in feeling and more regular in structure but still powerfully effective.

**Chorale cantatas**

CD 6/50–64    CD 3/38

Although no single example can suggest the breadth and variety of Bach's cantatas, *Nun komm, der Heiden Heiland*, BWV 62 (NAWM 90), composed in 1724 for the first Sunday in Advent, illustrates some of his typical procedures. This work was part of his second cycle for Leipzig, which consisted of cantatas whose words and music were based on chorales. The unknown poet who wrote the texts of these cantatas used the first and last stanzas of a chorale for the opening and closing choruses, and paraphrased the middle stanzas in poetry suitable for recitatives and arias. Bach then based the opening chorus on the chorale melody, ended the work with a simple four-part harmonization of the chorale for its closing stanza, and set the middle movements as recitatives and arias in operatic style for the soloists, with few, if any, references to the chorale melody. For this cantata, Bach and the librettist used Luther's Advent chorale *Nun komm, der Heiden Heiland* (Now come, Savior of the heathens; see NAWM 42b).

CD 3/17

**Opening chorus**

As we often find in Bach's choral works, the opening chorus displays an ingenious mixture of genres—here, concerto and chorale motet. The orchestra begins with a sprightly ritornello that would be at home in a Vivaldi concerto, yet features the chorale as a cantus firmus in the bass. Repeated rising figures evoke the sense of welcome and anticipation in the chorale's text, which heralds the coming of the Savior. As in a concerto, this ritornello serves as a frame for the movement, recurring three times in shortened or transposed form before its full reprise in the tonic at the end. But instead of episodes, Bach presents the four phrases of the chorale in the chorus, set in cantus firmus style: the sopranos, doubled by the horns, sing each phrase in long notes above imitative counterpoint in the other three parts, while the orchestra continues to develop motives from the ritornello. The first and fourth phrases are preceded by the lower voices in a point of imitation based on the chorale. Example 13.6 shows the fore-imitation and subsequent soprano entrance for the first chorale phrase. The mixture of secular and sacred models and of old-style counterpoint and cantus firmus with modern Italianate style is characteristic of Bach, creating a depth of meanings through references to many familiar types of music.

The four solo movements set sacred texts in operatic idioms. A da capo aria for tenor muses on the mystery of the Incarnation. As if to show Jesus's humanity, Bach wrote the aria in minuet style with predominantly four-measure phrasing, evoking the physical body through dance. Next are a recitative and aria for bass, praising the Savior as a hero who conquers evil. The recitative includes word painting, such as a run on "laufen" (to run). The aria follows the operatic conventions for heroic or martial arias, with the orchestra playing in octaves throughout and the figuration emphasizing rapid motions, large leaps, and jumping arpeggios. The soprano and alto join in an accompanied recitative, moving in sweet parallel thirds and sixths as they express awe at the nativity

*Example 13.6: J. S. Bach*, Nun komm, der Heiden Heiland, *BWV 62, entrance of the first phrase of the chorale*

*a. Fore-imitation in other parts*

*b. Cantus firmus in soprano*

*Now come, Savior of the heathens*

*Figure 13.12. Johann Sebastian Bach in a portrait by Elias Gottlob Haussmann (a 1748 copy of a 1746 original). Shown in Bach's hand is the manuscript of his triple canon for six voices, BWV 1076.*

Mass in B Minor

scene. The closing chorale verse is a doxology, praising Father, Son, and Holy Spirit.

For performance in Leipzig at Vespers on Good Friday, Bach wrote five Passions, two of which survive; they tell the story of Jesus's crucifixion. Both the *Saint John Passion* (1724; later revised), based on John 18–19, and the *Saint Matthew Passion* (1727; revised 1736), based on Matthew 26–27, employ recitatives, arias, ensembles, choruses, chorales sung by the chorus, and orchestral accompaniment. This type of setting, drawing on elements from opera, cantata, and oratorios, had replaced the older type composed by Schütz and others, which combined plainsong narration with polyphony (see Chapter 9). In both Passions, a tenor narrates the biblical story in recitative, soloists play the parts of Jesus and other figures, and the chorus sings the words of the disciples, the crowd, and other groups. At other times, the chorus comments on events, like the chorus in a Greek drama, and also sings the huge opening and closing numbers. The interpolated recitatives, ariosos, and arias serve a similar purpose, reflecting on the story and relating its meaning to the individual worshipper.

Although now performed as works for large choir and orchestra, recent research on the performance parts suggests that Bach's Passions were intended for just four solo and four ripieno singers, who divided the roles among them and joined together for the choral movements.

Bach assembled the Mass in B Minor, his only complete setting of the Catholic Mass Ordinary, between 1747 and 1749. He drew most of it from music he had composed much earlier. He had already presented the Kyrie and Gloria in 1733 to the Catholic elector of Saxony in hopes of getting an honorary appointment to the electoral chapel, which he did receive three years later. The Sanctus was first performed on Christmas Day 1724. He adapted some of the other sections from cantata movements composed between 1714 and 1735, replacing the German text with the Latin words of the Mass and reworking the music. Of the newly composed sections, the opening of the Credo and the *Confiteor* (a later passage of the Credo) are in *stile antico*, the *Et incarnatus* (also in the Credo) and *Benedictus* (from the Sanctus) in modern styles.

Throughout the work, Bach juxtaposed contrasting styles, making the Mass in B Minor a monumental compendium of approaches to church music. Since the Mass was never performed as a whole during Bach's lifetime and is too long to function well as service music, he may have intended it as an anthology of movements, each a model of its type, that could be performed separately. As a collection of exemplary works, the Mass in B Minor stands with the *Well-Tempered Clavier, Art of Fugue,* and *Musical Offering* as witness to Bach's desire to create comprehensive cycles that explore the furthest potential of a medium or genre.

## Reception History

The history of Bach's music tells a story of burial and resurrection. Only a few pieces were published in his lifetime, almost all for keyboard; the rest remained only in handwritten copies. Bach's sons Carl Philipp Emanuel and Johann Christian were influenced by him but went their own ways, and for a time their fame eclipsed his.

Musical tastes changed radically in the middle of the eighteenth century. The new style that emerged from the opera houses of Italy and invaded Germany and the rest of Europe made Bach's music sound old-fashioned. The composer-critic Johann Adolph Scheibe (1708–1776) considered Bach unsurpassable as an organist and keyboard composer, but he found the rest of Bach's music overly elaborate and confused (see the vignette, below), preferring the more tuneful and straightforward style of younger German composers such as Johann Adolf Hasse (1699–1783; see Chapter 14).

Bach's obscurity in the mid-eighteenth century was not total. In the second half of the century, some of the preludes and fugues from *The Well-Tempered Clavier* appeared in print, and the whole collection circulated in innumerable manuscript copies. Haydn owned a copy of the Mass in B Minor; Mozart knew *The Art of Fugue* and studied the motets on a visit to Leipzig in 1789. Citations from Bach's works appeared frequently in the musical literature of the time, and the important periodical, the *Allgemeine musikalische Zeitung*, opened its first issue (1798) with a Bach portrait. A fuller discovery of Bach began in the nineteenth century, with the publication of a biography by Johann Nikolaus Forkel in 1802. The revival of the *Saint Matthew Passion* by composer-conductor Carl Friedrich Zelter (1758–1832) and its 1829 performance at Berlin under Felix Mendelssohn's direction did much to inspire interest in Bach's music.

The establishment of the Bach-Gesellschaft (Bach Society), founded by Robert Schumann and others in 1850 to mark the centenary of Bach's death, led to the publication of the first collected edition of Bach's works, completed in sixty-one volumes by 1900. Today, there is a second complete edition (the Neue Bach-Ausgabe), and almost all of Bach's works have been recorded at least once. We realize the central position that Bach occupies in the history of Western music when we consider that, of the eight recordings of European classical music placed on *Voyager 1* and *2*, the first man-made objects to leave the solar system, three were by Johann Sebastian Bach.

## VIGNETTE   A Critique of Bach's Style

*The composer and critic Johann Adolph Scheibe (1708–1776) considered Bach unsurpassable as an organist and keyboard composer. However, he found much of the rest of Bach's music overly elaborate and confused, preferring the more tuneful and straightforward styles of younger composers such as Johann Adolph Hasse (see Chapter 14). Scheibe's critique is only one volley in the long argument between advocates of Baroque style and partisans of the new galant style.*

~

This great man would be the admiration of whole nations if he had more amenity, if he did not take away the natural element in his pieces by giving them a turgid and confused style, and if he did not darken their beauty by an excess of art. Since he judges according to his own fingers, his pieces are extremely difficult to play; for he demands that singers and instrumentalists should be able to do with their throats and instruments whatever he can play on the clavier. But this is impossible.

Every ornament, every little grace, and everything that one thinks of as belonging to the method of playing, he expresses completely in notes; and this not only takes away from his pieces the beauty of harmony but completely covers the melody throughout. All the voices must work with each other and be of equal difficulty, and none of them can be recognized as the principal voice. In short, he is in music what Mr. von Lohenstein was in poetry. Turgidity has led them both from the natural to the artificial, and from the lofty to the somber; and in both one admires the onerous labor and uncommon effort—which, however, are vainly employed, since they conflict with Nature.

From "An able traveling musician," letter, in Johann Adolph Scheibe, *Der critische Musikus* (May 14, 1737); trans. in Hans T. David and Arthur Mendel, eds., *The New Bach Reader: A Life of Johann Sebastian Bach in Letters and Documents*, rev. and expanded by Christoph Wolff (New York: Norton, 1998), p. 338, no. 343.

## George Frideric Handel [Georg Friedrich Händel] (1685–1759)

*Figure 13.13. George Frideric Handel at his composing desk, in a portrait by Philippe Mercier.*

Handel, recognized since his own time as the dominant figure in eighteenth-century English music, was a master of all types of vocal and instrumental composition. He is best known for his English oratorios, a genre he invented, and for his Italian operas.

Handel was born in Halle, Germany, the son of a barber-surgeon at the local court. His father wanted him to study law, but he practiced music secretly. His organ playing at the age of nine impressed the duke, who persuaded Handel's father to let him study with Friedrich Wilhelm Zachow, composer, organist, and church music director in Halle. Under Zachow, Handel became an accomplished organist and harpsichordist, studied violin and oboe, mastered counterpoint, and learned the music of German and Italian composers by copying their scores. He entered the University of Halle in 1702 and was appointed cathedral organist. The following year, he abandoned both and moved to Hamburg, the center of German opera. There he played violin in the opera-house orchestra and wrote his own first opera, *Almira*, performed with great success in 1705, when he was just twenty.

The following year, Handel traveled to the homeland of opera at the invitation of Prince Ferdinand de' Medici. Winning recognition as a promising young composer, he associated with the leading patrons and musicians of Florence, Rome, Naples, and Venice, and made the acquaintance of Corelli and Scarlatti, whose influence stamped his work. While in Italy, Handel wrote a large number of Italian cantatas, two oratorios, and the operas *Rodrigo* (1707) for Florence and *Agrippina* (1709) for Venice.

Following a brief period at the court in Hanover, Germany, Handel spent the rest of his life in London, where he served numerous aristocratic patrons and enjoyed the lifelong support of the British royal family. In the 1730s, after three decades of writing Italian operas for the London theaters, Handel turned to oratorios in English, mostly on sacred subjects. He also published a considerable amount of instrumental music, from solo and trio sonatas to concertos and orchestral suites, including *Water Music* and *Royal Fireworks*.

Handel never married. In Italy and London, he lived with various patrons until 1723, when he leased a house in an upper-class neighborhood, where he stayed the rest of his life. There were rumors of brief affairs with sopranos, but none has been substantiated. Recently, scholars have noted that several of his patrons moved in social circles where same-sex desire was common and that the texts of the cantatas Handel wrote for these patrons often allude—in coded terms—to love between men. Whether Handel himself had intimate relationships with anyone of either sex remains open to question.

Handel's imperious, independent nature and cosmopolitan tastes made him a formidable presence, but the rougher sides of his personality were balanced by a sense of humor and redeemed by a generous and honorable approach to life. Experiencing both successes and failures, criticism as well as praise, Handel suffered physical ailments as he aged, notably a paralytic stroke in 1737 (from which he recovered) and blinding cataracts in his final years. By the end of his life, he ranked among the most revered figures in London, and some three thousand people attended his funeral at Westminster Abbey, where he is buried alongside kings and princes.

**Major works:** *Messiah, Saul, Samson, Israel in Egypt*, and about 20 other oratorios; *Giulio Cesare* and about 40 other Italian operas; numerous odes, anthems, and other sacred vocal music; about 100 Italian cantatas; about 45 concertos, 20 trio sonatas, 20 solo sonatas, numerous keyboard pieces, and orchestral suites.

# England: George Frideric Handel

Compared to Vivaldi, Rameau, and Bach, each thoroughly rooted in his own country, George Frideric Handel (1685–1759) moved comfortably among German-, Italian-, and English-speaking cities (see the biography and Figure 13.13). His German music teacher gave him a thorough education in organ, harpsichord, counterpoint, and current German and Italian idioms. As a young man, three years at the Hamburg opera house and four years in Italy helped to lay the foundations of his style. He matured as a composer in England, the country then most hospitable to foreign composers. Moreover, England provided the choral tradition that made Handel's oratorios possible. Vivaldi's influence on the musical world was immediate, although he died almost totally forgotten; Rameau's was felt more slowly and then mainly in the fields of opera and music theory; and Bach's work lay in comparative obscurity until the nineteenth century. But Handel won international renown during his lifetime, and his music has been heard ever since, making him the first composer whose music has never ceased to be performed.

Handel's music was enormously popular. When his *Music for the Royal Fireworks* was given a public rehearsal in 1749, it attracted an audience of over 12,000 people and stopped traffic in London for three hours. How could a composer gain such popularity, and why should it be Handel? The answer to the first question is that for virtually the first time, a composer was working for the public—not just for a church, a court, or a town council—and it is the public that bestows popularity. And why Handel? He was supremely adaptable, able to measure and serve the taste of the public because of his cosmopolitan and eclectic style, which drew on German, Italian, French, and English music.

Although Handel achieved his greatest fame writing music for public performance, he was no freelancer. From his early years in Italy to the end of his life, he enjoyed the generous support of patrons. Their wishes often determined what he composed, yet their support also allowed him freedom to write operas and oratorios for the public. Handel's most important patrons were the British monarchs. In 1713, Queen Anne granted Handel a pension of £200 a year (roughly twice what Bach made in Leipzig). After she died in 1714 and the elector of Hanover (Handel's former employer) was crowned King George I, he doubled Handel's pension to £400, and thereafter it was raised again. But while he was closely identified with the royal house, most of his activities were in the public sphere, writing and producing operas and, later, oratorios, and composing for publication.

Popularity

Patrons

## The Operas

Handel devoted thirty-six years to composing and directing operas, which contain much of his best music. In an age when opera was the main concern of ambitious musicians, Handel excelled among his contemporaries.

Handel's blending of national styles is evident from his first opera, *Almira* (1705), written for Hamburg when he was nineteen. He kept to the local fashion of setting the arias in Italian and the recitatives in German so the audience could follow the plot. Imitating Reinhard Keiser, the dominant opera composer in Hamburg, Handel patterned the overture and dance music after French models, composed most of the arias in the Italian manner, and incorporated German elements in the counterpoint and orchestration. In Italy, he learned from Scarlatti's cantatas and operas how to create supple, long-breathed, rhythmically varied melodies that seem naturally suited for the voice, amply demonstrated in

International style

Handel's *Agrippina* (Venice, 1709). Ever after, his operatic style was uniquely international, combining French overtures and dances, Italianate arias and recitatives, and German traits, notably the tendency to double the vocal line with one or more instruments.

London operas

Handel's *Rinaldo* (1711) was the first Italian opera composed for London. Its brilliant music and elaborate stage effects made it a sensation and helped establish Handel's public reputation in England. The arias were published by John Walsh, bringing Handel additional revenue. He wrote four more operas in the 1710s, and, with revivals of *Rinaldo*, a Handel opera was staged almost every season.

Royal Academy of Music

In 1718–1719, about sixty wealthy gentlemen, with the support of the king, established a joint stock company—called the Royal Academy of Music—for producing Italian operas. The operas were staged at the King's Theatre in the Haymarket, and Handel was engaged as the music director. He traveled to Germany to recruit singers, mostly Italians performing in Dresden and other courts. Perhaps his biggest catch was the arrogant but widely celebrated castrato Senesino. Giovanni Bononcini (1670–1747) was brought from Rome to compose operas and to play in the orchestra. Later, the eminent sopranos Francesca Cuzzoni (1696–1778) and Faustina Bordoni (1697–1781) joined the group (see Chapter 14). For this company, which flourished from 1720 to 1728, Handel composed some of his best operas, including *Radamisto* (1720), *Ottone* (1723). *Giulio Cesare* (Julius Caesar, 1724), *Rodelinda* (1725), and *Admeto* (1727). The subjects of Handel's operas were the usual ones of the time: episodes from the lives of Roman heroes freely adapted to include the maximum number of intense dramatic situations, or tales of magic and marvelous adventure revolving around the Crusades.

Recitative styles

The action was developed through dialogue rendered in the two distinct types of recitative that emerged in Italian opera in the early eighteenth century. One type, accompanied only by basso continuo, set stretches of dialogue or monologue in as speechlike a fashion as possible (as in the Scarlatti recitative in Example 11.1). It would later be called *recitativo semplice*, or "simple recitative,"

*Figure 13.14. A painting (by Antonio Longhi?) of a Baroque opera performance. The leading man (perhaps a castrato) seems to be comforting the prima donna while a third character, holding a sword, looks on. Offstage, people are seated or standing in various states of inattentiveness, which does not necessarily mean that they were not listening; portraying the audience in attitudes of conversation may have been the artist's way of suggesting that opera was often a topic for lively discussion.*

*Figure 13.15. Charles André (Carle) Van Loo (1705–1765) painted* The Grand Turk Giving a Concert for His Consort, *1727, as one among many pictures that borrowed exotic subjects, usually with Turkish or Spanish backgrounds. The presence of Turkish embassies throughout Europe and the eighteenth century's fascination with Turkish music and culture make this scene more realistic than would appear at first glance (see "In Context," Chapter 19, pages 466–467). A further touch of realism is provided by the legible music on the harpsichord: a fidelity-affirming aria from Handel's newest opera* Admeto *(1727), beginning "Si caro, si" (Yes, dear, yes). The aria also suggests a possible interpretation of the painting, as does the dog lying in the foreground, an age-old symbol of faithfulness. The painter's own wife was the model for the woman seated at the harpsichord and presumably the one singing these words, which adds another layer of meaning to Van Loo's painting. The two violins and harpsichord form a typical concertato accompaniment for a Baroque aria. Wallace Collection, London.*

and eventually *recitativo secco,* or "dry recitative." The other type, called *recitativo obbligato* and later *recitativo accompagnato,* or "accompanied recitative," used stirring and impressive orchestral outbursts to dramatize tense situations. These interjections reinforced the rapid changes of emotion in the dialogue and punctuated the singer's phrases.

Solo da capo arias allowed the characters to respond lyrically to their situations. Each aria represented a single specific mood or affection, or sometimes two contrasting but related affections in the A and B sections. At the singers' insistence, the arias had to be allocated according to the importance of each member of the cast and had to display the scope of each singer's vocal and dramatic powers. Thus, the prima donna ("first lady"), the soprano singing the leading female role, normally demanded the most and the best arias (hence the modern meaning of that term). In addition, Handel wrote for specific singers, seeking to show off their abilities to best advantage.

Handel's scores are remarkable for the wide variety of aria types. They range from brilliant displays of florid ornamentation, known as coloratura, to sustained, sublimely expressive pathetic songs, such as *Se pietà* in *Giulio Cesare.* Arias of regal grandeur with rich contrapuntal and concertato accompaniments contrast with arias containing simple, folklike melodies or arias in which the

Arias

The castrato voice resulted from the same impulse that motivates today's athletes to take hormones and steroids: the desire to control and manipulate nature in order to enhance a performer's abilities. The ever-increasing demand by opera audiences for virtuosic superstars and the rise of certain castrato soloists to fame and fortune in turn stimulated the production of castrati throughout Italy, especially among poor families who saw it as a possible way of improving their miserable circumstances. However, although thousands aspired to stardom, only a few ever achieved the fame of a Farinelli, whose career took him from triumph to triumph in all the operatic capitals of Europe. His voice was legendary for its range, spanning more than three octaves, and for its breath control, which enabled him to sustain a note for a full minute before having to inhale. Charles Burney, the keen eighteenth-century observer and author, helps us understand why Farinelli and other castrati were adored by audiences, swarmed by fans, coddled by composers, paid huge sums by producers—in short, treated very much like modern athletes.

He was seventeen when he left [Naples] to go to Rome, where, during the run of an opera, there

was a struggle every night between him and a famous player on the trumpet, in a song accompanied by that instrument. . . . The audience began to interest themselves in the contest, and to take different sides: after severally swelling out a note, in which each manifested the power of his lungs, and tried to rival the other in brilliancy and force, they had both a swell and a shake [a crescendo and a trill] together, by thirds, which was continued so long, while the audience eagerly awaited the event, that both seemed to be exhausted, and, in fact, the trumpeter, wholly spent, gave it up, thinking, however, his antagonist as much tired as himself, and that it would be [considered a draw]; when Farinelli with a smile on his countenance, shewing he had only been sporting with him all this time, broke out all at once in the same breath, and with fresh vigour, and not only swelled and shook the note, but ran the most rapid and difficult divisions [passage-work], and was at last silenced only by the acclamations of the audience. From this period may be dated that superiority which he ever maintained over all his contemporaries.[1]

The painting shown here depicts Farinelli (Carlo Broschi, 1705–1782) as he appeared in 1734, the year

strings play in unison with the voice throughout. The pastoral scenes are noteworthy examples of eighteenth-century nature painting. Some arias feature the tone color of a particular instrument to set the mood, as the French horn does in Caesar's aria *Va tacito e nascosto* ([The clever hunter] moves stealthily and hidden) from *Giulio Cesare* in which both voice and instrument imitate a hunting horn.

*Scene complexes*

One or both types of recitative are sometimes freely combined with arias, ariosos, and orchestral passages to make larger scene complexes that recall the freedom of Monteverdi's operas and foreshadow the methods of later composers such as Gluck (see Chapter 14). Instead of presenting the plot in recitative and then the aria with orchestral ritornello as a static moment, Handel interleaves these elements so that the plot continues to move forward. In *Giulio Cesare*, Act II, Scenes 1–2 (NAWM 91), after dialogue in simple recitative, Cleopatra's da capo aria *V'adoro pupille* is interwoven with other elements. Caesar has been brought to a grove, where he overhears Cleopatra singing. An orchestral sinfonia, essentially the opening ritornello, introduces the aria's principal motive. From his hiding place, Caesar unexpectedly breaks in, expressing awe in a brief recitative. Cleopatra sings the first and middle sections of the aria, then stops, transfixed. Caesar again comments in recitative, wondering at the beauty of the song. Only then does Cleopatra take up the repetition of the A section, now not just a conventional formal device but something more profound since we know of Caesar's entrancement.

CD 6/65–68    CD 3/46

of his debut in London with the Opera of the Nobility—the company that rivaled Handel's own (see
below)—led by Nicola Porpora, who had been
Farinelli's teacher in Naples. The portrait gives us a
good idea of the physical characteristics typical of
castrati: somewhat effeminate facial features, including a smallish head and a smooth pale skin with
no beard; a large chest; well-rounded hips; and narrow shoulders. Contemporary writers also commented on their fairly tall stature, which was unusual
in the eighteenth century, and their tendency to obe-
sity. In addition to illustrating these general characteristics, the portrait presents Farinelli, the singular
virtuoso, as a commanding presence, exquisitely
outfitted in brocade, fur-trimmed velvet, and lace,
his right hand leaning on a harpsichord as if acknowledging what must have been the principal tool
of his training. We may assume from his authoritative, even arrogant, pose that he had already reached
the height of his powers. In fact, he retired from the
stage only three years later, at age thirty-two, having
been invited to Madrid, where he spent the next two
decades in the service of the Spanish kings.

[1]Charles Burney, *The Present State of Music in France and
Italy*, vol. 1 of Percy A. Scholes, ed., *Dr. Burney's Musical Tours in
Europe* (London: Oxford University Press, 1959), pp. 153–155.

*Figure 13.16. Portrait in oils of Farinelli (Carlo Broschi),
1734, by Bartolommeo Nazari. Royal College of Music,
London.*

Throughout the opera, Handel's characteristic combination of national elements is apparent. Cleopatra's aria is in French sarabande rhythm, arousing the
associations that dance carried with dignity, love, and seduction. Yet the da capo
form of the aria is Italian, the voice is doubled by instruments in the German
manner, and the orchestra is divided as in an Italian concerto grosso, with
soloists (the concertino) accompanying the voice and the full orchestra offering
punctuation.

Stressed by rising salaries for the singers and a scandalous dispute between
the two sopranos Cuzzoni and Bordoni, the Royal Academy dissolved in 1729.
Although the collapse has sometimes been linked to the popular success in 1728
of *The Beggar's Opera*, John Gay's English ballad opera (see Chapter 14), which
satirized opera and the Academy, the main causes were financial. Handel and a
partner took over the theater, formed a new company, and had several great
successes with Senesino in the major roles. But Senesino found Handel dictatorial; he left in 1733 and soon joined a competing company, the Opera of the Nobility, which featured the Neapolitan composer Nicola Porpora (1686–1768)
and the highest-priced singers in Europe, including Farinelli (see above). The
two companies spent so much on singers and staging, and so completely divided
the London public, that by 1737 both were nearly bankrupt, and the Opera of the
Nobility closed that summer. Although Handel continued to write and produce
operas until 1741, none matched his earlier successes.

Handel as impresario

*Figure 13.17. An oratorio performance, rendered in the satirical style of the English painter and engraver William Hogarth (1697–1764), a contemporary of Handel who was a keen observer and critic of social customs.*

## The Oratorios

In the 1730s, Handel devised a new genre that would reward him as richly as opera had and bring his greatest popularity: the oratorio. The Italian oratorio was essentially an opera on a sacred subject, presented in concert, usually in a religious building rather than onstage.

Handel's most important innovation in the oratorios was his use of the chorus. Italian oratorios had at most a few ensembles. Handel's experience with choral music led him to give the chorus much more prominence. His early training had made him familiar with Lutheran choral music and with the south German combination of chorus with orchestra and soloists. He was especially influenced by the strong English choral tradition, which had existed for centuries. Thus, in his oratorios, the chorus makes a crucial contribution. It plays a variety of roles, participating in the action, narrating the story, or commenting on events like the chorus in Greek drama. The grand character of his choral style, drawn from the English tradition, fits the oratorio's emphasis on communal rather than individual expression.

In his choruses, Handel was a dramatist, a master of effects. He wrote for chorus in a style simpler and less consistently contrapuntal than Bach's. He alternated passages in fugal texture with solid blocks of harmony and often set a melodic line in sustained notes against one in quicker rhythm. Everything lies well for the voices, and the orchestra usually reinforces the vocal parts, making his choral music a pleasure to sing—one factor in its enduring popularity.

Handel's first oratorio in English was *Esther*, revised from a masque of about 1718. Like his operas but unlike oratorios in Italy, Handel's oratorios were usually performed in theaters. *Esther*, which premiered at the King's Theatre in 1732, was the first in a series of oratorios that Handel put on in almost every subsequent Lenten season as a way to extend his earnings from opera, which could not be staged during Lent. But the decisive move from opera to oratorio began when subscriptions to the 1738–1739 opera season were insufficient; so, *Saul* instead of a new opera, Handel composed the oratorio *Saul* for a three-month season of choral works in early 1739.

The closing scene of Act II (NAWM 92) illustrates the blending of genres in Handel's oratorios. Saul, king of Israel, sees the young military hero David as a rival. In an accompanied recitative in martial style (NAWM 92a) Saul resolves to have David killed. Dialogue between Saul and his son Jonathan, David's beloved friend, is rendered in simple recitative (NAWM 92b). After these two numbers in styles borrowed from opera, Handel presents not an aria, but a chorus that reflects on the morality of the situation: *O fatal Consequence of Rage* (NAWM 92c). It comprises a series of three fugues, each ending with a majestic homorhythmic passage. In typical Handelian style, the chorus is filled with musical gestures that convey the meaning of the text. Here the falling tritone to express sorrow in the opening fugue subject and the use of rapid repeated notes to express rage both recall techniques first introduced by Monteverdi (see Chapter 9).

*Messiah*     A new oratorio that premiered in Dublin, Ireland, *Messiah* (1741) would become Handel's most famous work. Its libretto is unusual: instead of telling a story, it unfolds as a series of contemplations on the Christian idea of

CD 6/71    CD 3/49

CD 6/72    CD 3/50

CD 6/73    CD 3/51

redemption using texts drawn from the Bible, beginning with Old Testament prophecies and going through the life of Christ to his Resurrection. However, the music of *Messiah* is typical of Handel, full of his characteristic charm, immediate appeal, and mixture of traditions—from the French overture to the Italianate recitatives and da capo arias, the Germanic choral fugues, and the English choral anthem style.

Handel and a collaborator leased a theater in London to present oratorios every year during Lent. As an added attraction at these performances, the composer played an organ concerto or improvised at the organ during intermissions. Figure 13.17 shows a contemporary sketch of an oratorio performance, with a chorus and orchestra each numbering about twenty. Since oratorios needed no staging or costumes and could use English singers, who were a good deal less expensive than Italian ones, it was much easier to turn a profit. Oratorios also appealed to a potentially large middle-class public that had never felt at home with the aristocratic entertainment of opera in Italian.

*Performing oratorios*

Stories from the Hebrew Bible and Apocryphal books were well known to middle-class Protestant listeners, much more so than the historical or mythological plots of Italian opera. Therefore, most of Handel's oratorios were based on the Scriptures. Moreover, such subjects as *Saul, Israel in Egypt* (1739), *Judas Maccabaeus* (1747), and *Joshua* (1748) had an appeal that derived from something beyond familiarity with the ancient sacred narratives: in an era of prosperity and expanding empire, English audiences felt a kinship with what they saw as the chosen people, whose heroes triumphed with the special blessing of God. The English public's enthusiastic response to these works laid the foundation for the immense popularity that made Handel's music the prevailing influence in British musical life for more than a century.

*Librettos*

We have seen that Bach often borrowed and reworked his own or other composers' music. Although this practice was common at the time, Handel borrowed more than most. Three duets and eleven of the twenty-eight choruses of *Israel in Egypt*, for example, were taken in whole or in part from the music of others, while four choruses were arrangements from earlier works by Handel himself. When such instances of borrowing were discovered in the nineteenth century, Handel was charged with plagiarism because audiences and critics at that time valued originality and demanded original themes. In Handel's time, simply presenting another composer's work as one's own was condemned, but borrowing, transcribing, adapting, rearranging, and parodying were universal and accepted practices. A contemporary theorist and composer, Johann Mattheson, suggested that when Handel borrowed, he more often than not "repaid with interest," finding new potential in the borrowed material.

*Figure 13.18. Handel memorial in Westminster Abbey, London, sculpted in 1760 by Louis-François Roubiliac. The music shows the soprano aria* I know that my Redeemer liveth *from* Messiah.

GEORGE FREDERICK HANDEL Efq.
born February XXIII. MDCLXXXIV.
died April XIV. MDCCLIX.
L.F.Roubiliac inv.'et sc.'

## Instrumental Works

Although Handel made his reputation with vocal works, he wrote a great deal of instrumental music. Much of it was published by John Walsh in London, earning Handel extra income and keeping his name before a public that performed music at home. His keyboard works include two collections of harpsichord suites that contain not only the usual dance movements but also examples of most keyboard genres

Figure 13.19. Johann Zoffany, The Sharp Family's Boating Party on the Thames, ca. 1781. On their barge, named the Apollo, the Sharps regularly gave outdoor concerts in which Handel's music was prominently featured. National Portrait Gallery, London.

current at the time. Handel composed some twenty solo sonatas and almost as many trio sonatas for various instruments. Corelli's influence can be heard in these works, but the sophisticated harmonies and vivacious fast movements reflect a later Italian style.

**Ensemble suites**    Handel's most popular instrumental works are his two suites for orchestra or winds, both composed for the king and intended for outdoor performance. *Water Music* (1717) contains three suites for winds and strings, played for the king from a boat during a royal procession on the river Thames. *Music for the Royal Fireworks* (1749), for winds (although Handel originally included strings), was composed to accompany fireworks set off in a London park to celebrate the Peace of Aix-la-Chapelle.

**Concertos**    Handel's concertos mix tradition and innovation but tend toward a retrospective style. His six Concerti Grossi, Op. 3 (published 1734), feature woodwind and string soloists in novel combinations. He invented the concerto for organ and orchestra, which he performed during the intermissions of his oratorios and published in three sets (1738, 1740, and 1761). His most significant concertos are the Twelve Grand Concertos, op. 6, composed during one month in 1739 and published the next year. Instead of following Vivaldi's model, Handel adopted Corelli's conception of a sonata da chiesa for full orchestra (see Chapter 12), although he often added a movement or two to the conventional slow-fast-slow-fast pattern. The serious, dignified bearing and the prevailing full contrapuntal texture of these concertos hark back to the early part of the century, when Handel was forming his style in Italy.

**Handel's reputation**    The English came to regard Handel as a national institution—and with good reason. He passed all his mature life in London, becoming a naturalized British citizen in 1727, and wrote all his major works for British audiences. He was the most imposing figure in English music during his lifetime, and the English public nourished his genius and remained loyal to his memory.

# POSTLUDE

In this chapter, we have studied the lives and works of the eighteenth-century composers who represent, in many respects, both the radiant peak and the afterglow of the musical Baroque in Italy, France, Germany, and England. Each made lasting contributions.

Although Vivaldi was a complete master of opera, he is best remembered for his influence on instrumental music of the middle and later eighteenth century.

| TIMELINE The Early Eighteenth Century | |
|---|---|
| MUSICAL EVENTS | HISTORICAL EVENTS |
| J. S. Bach Studies in Lüneburg **1700** | |
| | **1702** First daily newspaper in England |
| Handel in Hamburg; Vivaldi appointed to the Pietà **1703** | |
| J. S. Bach travels to Lübeck to hear Buxtehude **1705** | |
| | **1707** Naples comes under Austrian control |
| J. S. Bach becomes court organist in Weimar **1708** | |
| Handel, *Rinaldo*, in London **1711** | **1711** Charles VI crowned Holy Roman emperor |
| Vivaldi, Concertos, Op. 3 **1712** | |
| | **1714** Elector of Hanover crowned George I of England |
| | **1715–1774** Reign of Louis XV |
| J. S. Bach appointed Kapellmeister in Cöthen **1717** | **1717** Watteau, *The Music Party* |
| Rameau, *Traité de l'harmonie*; J. S. Bach, **1722** *The Well-Tempered Clavier*, Book I | |
| J. S. Bach becomes cantor in Leipzig **1723** | |
| Handel, *Giulio Cesare*; Couperin, *Apotheosis of Corelli* **1724** | |
| Vivaldi, *The Four Seasons*; Concert spirituel **1725** series begins in Paris | |
| J. S. Bach, *Saint Matthew Passion* **1727** | **1727–1760** Reign of George II of England |
| Gay, *Beggar's Opera* **1728** | |
| Rameau, *Hippolyte et Aricie* **1733** | |
| | **1734** Voltaire, *Philosophical Letters* |
| | **1740** Frederick the Great of Prussia crowned; Maria Theresa of Austria crowned Holy Roman empress |
| Handel, *Messiah* **1742** | |
| J. S. Bach, *Musical Offering* **1747** | |
| | **1749** Henry Fielding, *Tom Jones* |

His impact equaled that of Corelli a generation earlier, and his codification of ritornello form provided a model for later concerto composers. His successors admired and emulated his concise themes, clarity of form, rhythmic vitality, and logical flow of musical ideas. Among those who learned from Vivaldi was J. S. Bach, who made keyboard arrangements of at least nine of Vivaldi's concertos, including five from Op. 3. Later in the eighteenth century, concerto composers adopted and developed Vivaldi's dramatic conception of the soloist's role.

Couperin's harpsichord music was well known in his lifetime, in England and Germany as well as France, then slowly fell out of fashion. Rameau's work, dominated by his operas (which are especially noteworthy for their novel instrumental music), is characterized by the French traits of clarity, grace, moderation, elegance, and interest in pictorialism. In these respects, he may be compared to his contemporary, the painter Watteau (see Figure IV.2). Equally typical of his countrymen, Rameau thought of himself as a philosophe as well as a composer, an analyst as well as a creator. In short, he was one of the most complex and productive musical personalities of the eighteenth century.

Bach was an encyclopedic composer: he absorbed into his works all the genres, styles, and forms of his time and developed their potential to a degree never even imagined by others. In his music, the often conflicting demands of harmony and counterpoint, of melody and polyphony reached a tense but satisfying balance. The continuing vitality of his compositions cannot be explained in a few words, but among the qualities that stand out are his concentrated and distinctive themes, his ingenious counterpoint, his copious musical invention, the majestic formal proportions of his works, his imaginative musical representation of pictorial and symbolic ideas, and the careful attention paid to every detail. A composer who spent most of his life teaching, Bach wrote challenging and rewarding pieces for students at every level, from beginning to advanced. He worked in positions that constantly demanded new music for immediate performance, embraced a wide variety of genres and approaches, and aspired to explore all the possibilities of every kind of music he encountered. It is no wonder that Bach achieved the central position he now occupies in the Western musical tradition.

Handel's greatness and historical significance rest largely on the fact that his compositions, especially the choral works, still command an eager audience. His music aged well because he embraced devices that became important in the new style of the mid-eighteenth century. Handel's emphasis on melody and harmony, as compared to the more strictly contrapuntal procedures of Bach, allied him with the fashions of his time. As a choral composer in the grand style he had no peer. He was a consummate master of contrast, not only in choral music but also in all types of composition. And in the oratorios, he deliberately appealed to a middle-class audience, recognizing social changes that had far-reaching effects on music.

# The Early Classical Period: Opera and Instrumental Music in the Early and Mid-Eighteenth Century

## PRELUDE

**M**usical life in the early Classical period reflected the international culture that spread throughout Europe during the Enlightenment. German symphony composers were active in Paris; Italian opera composers and singers worked in what are now Austria and Germany, as well as in Spain, England, Russia, and France. In a climate where shared humanity mattered more than national and linguistic differences, the flutist Johann Joachim Quantz (1697–1773), writing from Berlin in 1752, proposed that the ideal musical style was made up of the best features of music from all nations (see the vignette, page 316).

This universality of the new Classical style in part depended on its similarity to the logic of intelligible speech, which proceeds in any language through a series of words arranged to follow one another, with some repetitions, stops, and starts, forming units that make the ideas readily understood. Music was thought to be more or less "natural" to the extent that it emulated the flow of speech. According to leading critics of the time, educated people wanted music to communicate expression without artifice—that is, in a manner free of any complication that would hinder music's enjoyment and appeal. Writers distinguished between the learned or strict style of contrapuntal writing—associated particularly with the German Baroque—and the freer, more tuneful, homophonic writing that was becoming fashionable, particularly in Italy. Known at the time as the galant style, its values became the foundation for the musical idiom of the mid- to late eighteenth century that we call the Classical style.

This chapter will focus on developments in the early Classical period, roughly to 1770. We find the new characteristics enumerated below most evident in the music of Gluck, presented here, and Haydn and Mozart, who will be discussed in the next chapter.

*Chapter Contents*

*Prelude* 315

General Characteristics of the New Style 316

Opera buffa 319

Opera seria 322

Opera Reform 325

Instrumental Music: Sonata, Symphony, and Concerto 329

The *Empfindsamer* Style 333

*Postlude* 338

315

# General Characteristics of the New Style

Melody    The focus on melody in the new eighteenth-century style led to a more linear construction that contrasted sharply with the motivic variation and thorough-bass accompaniment characteristic of earlier styles. J. S. Bach, for example, would announce the musical idea of a movement—a melodic-rhythmic subject embodying the basic affection—at the outset. He would then spin out his material with relatively infrequent and inconspicuous cadences, and with sequential repetition of phrases as a principal constructive device, the result being either a highly integrated movement without sharp contrasts or (as in many Vivaldi concertos) a formal pattern of contrasts between thematic tutti and nonthematic solo sections. In either case, the phrase structure was usually so indistinct as to be elusive.

In the new styles, however, the melodic flow is divided by predictable resting points into smaller units or phrases. Instead of spinning out an unbroken string of musical ideas, the composer articulates them through a series of distinct, regular phrases typically two or four measures in length (but sometimes three, five, or six measures). By analogy with verbal composition, two or more phrases (sometimes called antecedent and consequent), relating to each other like subject and predicate parts of a sentence, form a period—that is, a complete musical thought concluded by a cadence. Moreover, the symmetrical phrases that constitute a period are usually marked by the repetition of small motivic units that serve to balance and integrate the structure. We use the adjective *periodic* to describe a composition comprised of a succession of such periods; or we may say
Melodic periodicity    that a composition has the quality of *periodicity*. The terminology of phrases and periods was borrowed from rhetoric, the art of oration or speech. Eighteenth-century theorists frequently compared a melody to a sentence or a musical composition to a speech. In this view, the composer is like a skilled orator who

---

**VIGNETTE   The Merging of National Styles**

*Throughout the seventeenth and early eighteenth centuries, Italy and France were the leading musical nations, and their distinctive styles were admired and imitated in other countries. But by the mid-eighteenth century, musicians, audiences, and critics increasingly preferred music that mixed national characteristics. Flutist and composer Johann Joachim Quantz (1697–1773), writing in his* Essay on a Method for Playing the Transverse Flute *(1752), argued that the ideal music blended the best elements of many nations and appealed to the widest audience. He noted that this mixed taste was typical of German composers, and, indeed, many of the best-known composers of the era were German.*

In a style that consists, like the present German one, of a mix of the styles of different peoples, every nation finds something familiar and unfailingly pleasing. Considering all that has been discussed about the differences among styles, we must vote for the pure Italian style over the pure French. The first is no longer as solidly grounded as it used to be, having become brash and bizarre, and the second has remained too simple. Everyone will therefore agree that a style blending the good elements of both will certainly be more universal and more pleasing. For a music that is accepted and favored by many peoples, and not just by a single land, a single province, or a particular nation, must be the very best, provided it is founded on sound judgment and a healthy attitude.

From Johann Joachim Quantz, *Versuch einer Anweisung, die Flöte traversiere zu spielen* (Berlin: Voss, 1752), ch. 18, sec. 89.

**VIGNETTE**  Forkel on Oratory and Music

*Johann Nikolaus Forkel (1749–1818) was a German music historian, theorist, organist, university professor, and author of the biography of J. S. Bach that sparked that composer's revival in the nineteenth century. In his* General History of Music, *Forkel draws this revealing parallel between oratory and composition, one that echoes earlier eighteenth-century theorists in its insistence on communicating ideas in a logical and hierarchical order.*

〰

An orator would behave unnaturally and contrary to the goals of edifying, persuading, and moving [an audience] by giving a speech without first determining what is to be the main idea [*Hauptsatz*], the secondary ideas [*Nebensätze*], the objections and refutations of the same, and the proofs. . . . As musical works of any substantial length are nothing other than speeches by which one seeks to move the listener to a certain empathy and to certain emotions, the rules for the ordering and arrangement of ideas are the same as in an actual oration. And so one has, in both, a main idea, supporting secondary ideas, dissections of the main idea, refutations, doubts, proofs, and reiterations. Similar means to our end (in the musical sense) must be used. This order and sequence of the individual sections is called the aesthetic ordering of the ideas. A musical work in which this ordering is so arranged that all thoughts mutually support and reinforce one another in the most advantageous way possible, is well ordered.

Johann Joachim Forkel, *Allgemeine Geschichte der Musik*, 2 vols. (Leipzig: Schwickert, 1788–1801), I, p. 50; adapted from the translation in Mark Evan Bonds, *Wordless Rhetoric: Musical Form and the Metaphor of the Oration* (Cambridge, Mass.: Harvard University Press, 1991), p. 123.

develops a subject, reinforcing it with repetition and new arguments, and who carefully arranges his thoughts to make them intelligible, persuasive, and moving (see the vignette, above).

The division of the melody into phrases and periods is supported by harmony marked by frequent half and full cadences. Thus, the continuous harmonic motion typical of older styles was also broken into a series of smaller units that repeatedly stop and go, more or less strongly, depending on whether the cadence marks off a phrase, a period, or the end of a larger section. Because the harmony articulates the phrases, rather than driving the music forward, it tends to change less frequently than in the older Baroque style. To compensate for the slower harmonic rhythm, composers often animated the musical texture by pulsing chords or other rhythmic means. One of the most widely used devices in keyboard music was the Alberti bass, shown in Example 14.1. Named for the Italian composer Domenico Alberti (ca. 1710–1746), who used it frequently to accompany his galant-style melodies, this device broke each of the underlying chords into a simple repeating pattern of short notes that produced a discreet chordal background, thereby setting off the melody to advantage.

*Harmonic periodicity*

*Alberti bass*

*Example 14.1: Domenico Alberti*, VIII sonate per cembalo, *Op. 1 (London, 1748), Sonata III, Allegro ma non tanto*

Unlike Italy, France, and Germany, Britain did not produce any prominent composers during the eighteenth and nineteenth centuries. Handel, who was of German birth, dominated the musical scene in Britain for most of the eighteenth century, but no other composer became similarly associated with that country until Sir Arthur Sullivan (half of the Gilbert-and-Sullivan team) composed his operettas in the late nineteenth century. This is a curious phenomenon, especially considering the impressive works of literature (novels by Jane Austen, for example) and art (paintings by Thomas Gainsborough, among others) from this period. We know from these works, however, that amateur music making was an important part of English life, but that the serious pursuit of music and its cultivation at a professional level were shunned by ladies and gentlemen of British society.

The novels of Jane Austen (1775–1817), herself an accomplished amateur pianist, provide insight into the proper role of music among the leisure classes in England. Austen's heroines bear the primary responsibility of providing entertainment at home and so are able to demonstrate, by their pleasant singing voices and keyboard skills, that they have used their leisure well. At the same time, they must give the impression of not practicing very much, because to attain any degree of virtuosity would imply neglect of more important pursuits. If Elizabeth in *Pride and Prejudice* played too well—that is, well enough to perform in public—

she would have reached a level of proficiency deemed vulgar for the future wife of the refined and gallant Mr. Darcy.

In real life, very few young women performed in public or earned a living through music. The Linley sisters of Bath, depicted in a 1772 portrait by Thomas Gainsborough (1727–1788), were rare exceptions (see Figure 14.1). Elizabeth and Mary Linley were taught music by their father, Thomas Linley, a minor composer who produced public concerts in Bath and London that helped to showcase his unusually talented daughters as singers. At thirteen, Elizabeth made her London debut in a masque performed at Covent Garden and thereafter appeared regularly in oratorios and other works until her marriage (at age nineteen) to the famous playwright Richard Brinsley Sheridan. Although Sheridan did not permit his wife to continue a singing career, she did help him and her father to manage London's Drury Lane Theatre, of which they were co-directors. Mary, who was four years younger than Elizabeth, eventually appeared in performances with her sister as well as alone until she, too, married and withdrew from public life.

Gainsborough, who was also an accomplished amateur musician, befriended and painted many musicians, among them Johann Christian Bach (see Figure 14.14) and Thomas Linley. His images (the most famous being *The Blue Boy*) are admired for their grace and naturalness of expression, qualities we associate with the new Classical style

Emotional contrasts     Composers of the new eighteenth-century style still constructed a movement based on related keys but abandoned the older idea of expressing just one basic affection. Instead, they began to introduce contrasts between the various parts of a movement or even within the themes themselves. At the same time, natural philosophers also changed their perceptions about the emotional life of an individual. No longer believing that a person once aroused to a certain state of mind—anger or fear, for instance—remained in that affection until moved by some stimulus to a different state, they now observed that feelings were in a constant state of flux, jostled by associations that might take unpredictable turns. Daniel Webb wrote of the pleasure a person experiences "not, as some have imagined, the result of any fixed or permanent condition of the nerves and spirits, but from a succession of impressions, and greatly augmented by sudden or gradual transitions from one kind of strain of vibrations to another."[1] Composers no longer tried to transport listeners into a state of religious fervor or

1. Daniel Webb, *Observations on the Correspondence between Poetry and Music* (London: Dodsley, 1769), p. 47.

in music. Although Thomas Linley never achieved an international reputation as a composer, the following statement by an anonymous contemporary (published in his obituary in the *Gentleman's Mag-* *azine* in 1795) could describe equally well most of Gainsborough's paintings: "His compositions always soothe and charm by delicacy, simplicity, and tenderness."

*Figure 14.1. In this 1772 double portrait of the Linley Sisters—both were still in their teens with already established singing careers—Thomas Gainsborough sets the young women in a spring woodland of blooming primroses. Elizabeth, the elder, wears cool blue and looks away as though preoccupied; in fact, she would elope with the playwright Richard Brinsley Sheridan before the portrait was finished. Mary, holding some sheet music on her lap, is dressed in a warm, golden-brown gown; in contrast to her sister, she directly engages the viewer by her lively expression. From an unusually talented musical family, the sisters defied the conventions of eighteenth-century British society by singing in public until their marriages put an end to their professional careers.*

sympathetic identification with a character onstage. Instead, they now expected listeners to follow a series of musical thoughts like verbal discourse and understand their logic. Listening to a piece of music could thus be a daring exploration of different related or even opposed feelings.

## Opera buffa

Many of the stylistic traits associated with the Classical period had their origins in the first decades of the eighteenth century in Italian musical theater. Because tradition weighed less heavily on comic opera than on opera seria, it was more hospitable to innovations. An Italian opera buffa at this time was a full-length work with six or more singing characters and, unlike comic opera in other countries, was sung throughout. It served a moral purpose by caricaturing the foibles of both aristocrats and commoners, vain ladies, miserly old men, awkward and clever servants, deceitful husbands and wives, pedantic lawyers and

*Figure 14.2. Painting of a performance of an intermezzo, a short comic work given between the acts of an opera seria. Venetian school, eighteenth century. Museo Teatrale alla Scala, Milan.*

*La serva padrona*

CD 7/1, 3    CD 3/55, 57

notaries, bungling physicians, and pompous military commanders. These figures generally resemble the stock characters of the commedia dell'arte, the improvised comedy popular in Italy since the sixteenth century. The comic characters often spoke or sang in dialect, as they did in some of the Venetian comedies, or the entire play might be in the local dialect, as in Naples. The comic cast was usually complemented by a number of serious characters who interacted with the comic characters, particularly in amorous intrigues, and were central to the main plot. The dialogue was set in rapidly delivered recitative and accompanied by keyboard only. The arias presented short tuneful phrases, often repeated, accompanied by simple harmonies and organized into tidy periods.

Another important type of Italian comic opera, the intermezzo, developed out of the custom of presenting short comic musical interludes between the acts of a serious opera or play. These intermezzi contrasted sharply with the grand and heroic manners of the principal drama, sometimes even parodying its excesses. The plots were mostly situation comedies involving a few ordinary people who sang, as in serious opera, recitatives and arias.

Giovanni Battista Pergolesi (1710–1736) was an early master of the comic intermezzo. One of the most original composers in the early Classical style, he wrote *La serva padrona* (The Maid as Mistress) as an interlude to one of his own serious operas in 1733 in Naples. Its performance in Paris twenty years later set off the *querelle des bouffons* (see page 328).

In two brief acts, *La serva padrona* is lightly scored (for strings and continuo) and uses only two singing characters, soprano and bass, as well as a third character who is mute. A scene in which Serpina, the maid, warns her grumpy boss and would-be lover, Uberto, that she is about to marry the mute character, Vespone, displays the extraordinary aptness and nimbleness of Pergolesi's music (see NAWM 93). Serpina delivers the news in simple recitative, to which Uberto reacts first in an agitated obbligato recitative, then in a da capo aria. Neither the main nor the middle section develops a single musical motive; rather, there are as many melodic ideas as there are thoughts and moods in the text. The first line, in which Uberto exclaims in patter style how confused he is, repeats the same music three times, reinforcing it for the listener but also suggesting Uberto's mental paralysis (Example 14.2a). Then Uberto, realizing that something mysterious is stirring his heart (measure 15), waxes lyrical as he asks himself whether he is in love. But a sober voice within checks his ardor—he should think of himself, guard his interests and independence—and now the melody shifts to deliberate, brooding, drawn-out notes (Example 14.2b). The middle section, instead of presenting contrasting music, develops earlier material, converting some of the musical motives of the first section into the minor mode. The stopping and starting in the musical flow of ideas and the abrupt shifting between motives also suggests the comic actor's physical gestures and actions on stage, all mimicking his indecision and confusion.

Unlike opera seria, which maintained its character across national boundaries, comic opera took different forms in different countries. It usually

*Example 14.2: Giovanni Battista Pergolesi*, Son imbrogliato già, *from* La serva padrona

*I am all mixed up. I have a certain something in my heart. Truly, I cannot tell [whether it's love or pity].*

*[I hear a voice that tells me:] Uberto, think of yourself.*

represented everyday people in familiar situations and required relatively modest performing resources. Although traveling Italian troupes of opera buffa players were much in demand and performed in Italian, home-grown comic opera librettos were always written in the national tongue, and the music itself tended to accentuate the national musical idiom. From humble beginnings the comic opera grew steadily in importance after 1760, and before the end of the century many of its characteristic features were absorbed into the mainstream of operatic composition. The historical significance of comic opera was twofold: it responded to the widespread demand for naturalness during the latter half of the eighteenth century, and it anticipated the trend toward musical nationalism, which became prominent during the nineteenth century.

The French counterpart of opera buffa, known as opéra comique, began around 1710 as a lowly form of popular entertainment performed at parish fairs. Until the middle of the century, the music consisted almost entirely of popular tunes (vaudevilles) or simple melodies imitating such tunes. The visit of an Italian comic opera troupe to Paris in 1752 stimulated the production of comic operas in which original airs (called ariettes) in a mixed Italian-French style were introduced along with the old vaudevilles. Ariettes gradually replaced the vaudevilles until, by the end of the 1760s, they, too, were completely discarded and all the music was freshly composed. Christoph Willibald Gluck (see below), one of the composers exposed to the French opéra comique during this transitional decade, arranged and composed a number of such works for the entertainment of the Vienna court. The French philosopher Jean-Jacques Rousseau (1712–1778) wrote a charming little comic opera in 1752, *Le Devin du village* (The Village Soothsayer).

*French opéra comique*

The French opéra comique, like all the national variants of light opera except the Italian, used spoken dialogue instead of recitative. Following the European trend in the second half of the century, opéra comique dealt boldly with the social issues that were agitating France during the pre-Revolutionary years. The leading French opera composer of the time was Belgian-born André-Ernest- Modeste Grétry (1741–1813), whose masterpiece is *Richard Coeur-de-Lion* (1784).

Ballad opera rose to popularity in England after the extraordinary success of *The Beggar's Opera* in 1728. This piece broadly satirizes fashionable Italian opera; its music, like that of the early opéra comique, consists for the most part of

*English ballad opera*

*Figure 14.3. A ticket for a performance of* The Beggar's Opera *at the Theatre Royal at Covent Garden in London. The evening's receipts were to be paid to Thomas Walker, the actor playing the central character, the notorious thief and murderer Macheath. In the engraving by renowned satirist William Hogarth (1697–1764), Polly and Lucy, both in love with Macheath, plead for his release from prison.*

CD 7/12, 13

popular tunes—ballads—set to new words and a few numbers that parody familiar operatic airs (see excerpts in NAWM 95). The immense popularity of ballad operas in the 1730s signaled a general reaction in England against foreign opera—that "exotic and irrational entertainment," as Dr. Samuel Johnson called it. As we have already seen (page 309), that reaction was one reason Handel turned his energies from opera to oratorio in the latter part of his life, partly in response to the success of ballad opera.

German singspiel

Although singspiel had existed in Germany since the sixteenth century, the success of the ballad opera in the eighteenth century inspired its revival. At first, librettists adapted English ballad operas, but they soon turned to translating or arranging French comic operas, for which the German composers provided new music in a familiar and appealing melodic vein. Many of the eighteenth-century singspiel tunes found their way into German song collections and, in the course of time, have virtually become folk songs. The principal composer of singspiel music during this period was Johann Adam Hiller (1728–1804) of Leipzig. In northern Germany, the singspiel eventually merged with early nineteenth-century native opera. In Bavaria and Austria, and particularly in Vienna, farcical subjects and treatment became fashionable, with lively music in a popular vein influenced by Italian comic opera.

## Opera seria

The light and charming style of opera buffa soon invaded serious opera. Opera seria was based on Italian librettos that treated serious subjects and were purged of comic scenes and characters. Its standard form came from the Italian

Metastasio

poet Pietro Metastasio (1698–1782), whose dramas many eighteenth-century composers set to music hundreds of times. Metastasio's success with librettos for Naples, Rome, and Venice—most notably *Didone abbandonata* (Dido Abandoned) in 1724—led to his appointment in 1729 as court poet in Vienna. He remained in Vienna for the rest of his life, turning out a profusion of Italian librettos and many works for special occasions at the imperial court. His heroic operas, based on ancient Greek or Latin tales, present a conflict of human passions, often pitting love against duty. They were intended to promote moral-ity through entertainment and to present models of merciful and enlightened rulers. The magnanimous tyrant—for example, Alexander the Great in *Alessan-dro nell'Indie* or Titus in *La clemenza di Tito*—is a favorite character. The librettos conventionally present two pairs of lovers and several subordinate personages. The action provides opportunities for introducing varied scenes—pastoral or martial episodes, solemn ceremonies, and the like. The resolution of the drama, which rarely has a tragic ending, often turns on a heroic deed or a sublime ges-ture of renunciation by one of the principal characters.

The three acts of an opera seria almost invariably consist of alternating recitatives and arias: recitatives promote the action through dialogue, while each aria is a virtual dramatic soliloquy in which a principal actor gives vent to an overriding emotion or reaction to the preceding scene. Although occasional duets or larger ensembles do occur—and the rare chorus in a simple style—the main musical focus of the Italian opera seria is on the aria, which eighteenth-century composers created in astounding profusion and variety.

---

**A CLOSER LOOK**    The Da Capo Aria

The most frequently used form for vocal music in the first half of the century was the da capo aria, a basic scheme that permitted enormous variation in detail. Metastasio's two-stanza aria texts set the standard for the full-blown da capo aria from the 1720s through the 1740s. The form, originally presented in Chap-ter 11, is now somewhat expanded and may be represented by the following out-line (in which the keys, indicated by Roman numerals, are hypothetical).

| | | | | | | | | Fine | | Da capo al fine |
|---|---|---|---|---|---|---|---|---|---|---|
| Music: | Ritornello | A1 | | Rit. | A2 | | Rit. | | B | |
| Text: | | lines 1–4 (stanza 1) | | | lines 1–4 developed | | | | lines 5–8 (stanza 2) | |
| Key: | I | I | V | V | V or I | I | I | | vi | |

*Figure 14.4. Structure of the da capo aria.*

Often two keys are contrasted in the first main period (the A1 section); then the material in the second key is brought back in the tonic at the close of the sec-ond main period (the A2 section). The ritornello structure is comparable to that of a Baroque concerto, but its expanded harmonic scheme and formal methods are closer to instrumental works of the Classical period. (For an example and discussion of an aria that conforms to this outline, see NAWM 94 and page 326.)

After about the middle of the century, composers explored ways to shorten the repetitious and long-winded A sections with their full da capo repetition. They invented various schemes that abbreviated the return of the ritornello and the primary section, often by altering the instruction "da capo" (from the begin-ning) to "dal segno" (from the sign), indicating that only a portion of the A sec-tion is repeated, or writing out an abridged return (see the aria by Pergolesi, NAWM 93, for an example).

CD 7/7

CD 7/3

CD 3/57

Reign of the singers

Turning the aria into the primary significant musical ingredient in opera opened the way to abuses. Singers, including the famed Italian castrati, made arbitrary demands on the poets and composers, compelling them to alter, add, and substitute arias without respect for dramatic or musical appropriateness. Moreover, the melodic embellishments and cadenzas that singers added at will were often mere displays of vocal acrobatics (see "In Performance: Vocal Embellishments," page 326). Some of the excesses were enumerated in *Il teatro alla moda* (The Fashionable Theater), a famous satire on the opera and everything connected with it, published anonymously in 1720 by the composer Benedetto Marcello.

New features of
da capo arias

Despite these criticisms, the da capo aria continued to grow and evolve. Arias written in the first decades of the century had usually projected only one affection through the development of a single motive. Now composers started to express a succession of moods, using a variety of musical material that ranged from lighthearted to tragic. The aria's ritornello may introduce all the material sung later, thus resembling the orchestral exposition of a concerto (see below). In this way, vocal music began incorporating structural features of instrumental

---

**IN CONTEXT** An Eighteenth-Century Diva, Faustina Bordoni

The career of Faustina Bordoni (1700–1781), leading lady of the operatic stage in the first half of the century, illustrates the commanding stature of the diva. Bordoni established her reputation in Venice while still in her teens and went on to have a lucrative international career that lasted into her fifties. She created several roles in Handel's London operas and enjoyed great successes in Munich and Vienna, where she became a favorite of the empress and sang duets with the empress's daughter Maria Theresa. Burney praised her fluent articulation, trills, improvised embellishments, and expressive power. He also emphasized her exceptional breath control, which allowed her to sustain a note longer, "in the opinion of the public," than any other singer. Universally admired as one of the great singer-actresses of her age, Bordoni married the composer Johann Adolf Hasse in 1730 and from then on was associated chiefly with his music. The next year they were hired by the Saxon court at Dresden, where she was a big hit in the title role of his *Cleofide* (see NAWM 94). She was paid 1,000 ducats as prima donna; he received only 500 as the composer. Hasse remained as Kapellmeister in Dresden for more than thirty years, and Faustina sang in at least fifteen of his many opere serie before retiring from the stage. On one notorious occasion, egged on by her fans, she actually exchanged blows on stage with another great soprano, Francesca Cuzzoni, during a performance of an opera in which they were both appearing. She is shown here as Attilia in Hasse's *Attilio Regolo* in a costume designed for the original production at the Dresden court theater, January 12, 1750.

*Figure 14.5. Faustina Bordoni (1700–1781), universally admired as one of the great singer-actresses of her age. Sächsische Landesbibliothek, Dresden.*

music—the sonata and concerto—something that remained true throughout the eighteenth century. But the vocal melody still dominated the music and carried it forward, and the orchestra provided harmonic support to the singer, rather than adding independent contrapuntal lines. The melodies were usually presented in four-measure units, consisting of two-measure antecedent and consequent phrases. When a composer deviated from this formula, it was usually for a deliberately unbalancing effect. Handel employed this new idiom in his late operas such as *Alcina* (1735) and *Serse* (1738), as did Pergolesi (see page 320) and a German, Johann Adolph Hasse (1699–1783).

*Figure 14.6.  Johann Adolf Hasse, in a pastel portrait by Felicitas Hoffmann. Dresden Gallery, Dresden.*

Hasse (shown in Figure 14.6) was acknowledged by most of his contemporaries as the great master of the opera seria. For most of his life, he directed music and opera at the court of the elector of Saxony in Dresden, but he spent many years in Italy, married the celebrated Italian soprano Faustina Bordoni, and became so thoroughly Italian in his musical style that the Italians nicknamed him "il caro Sassone" (the dear Saxon). His music is the perfect complement to Metastasio's poetry: the great majority of his eighty operas use Metastasio librettos, some of which he set two and even three times. Hasse was the most popular and successful opera composer in Europe around the middle of the century, and the contemporary English music historian Charles Burney reveals the qualities that endeared him to the connoisseurs:

> . . . the most natural, elegant, and judicious composer of vocal music . . . now alive; equally a friend to poetry and the voice, he discovers as much judgment as genius, in expressing words, as well as in accompanying those sweet and tender melodies, which he gives to the singer.[2]

The famous da capo aria *Digli ch'io son fedele* (Tell him that I am faithful; NAWM 94) from Hasse's *Cleofide* (1731), his first opera for Dresden, illustrates the qualities that Burney admired (see "In Performance: Vocal Embellishments," and Example 14.3).

CD 7/7

## Opera Reform

Certain Italian composers wanted to bring opera into harmony with the changing ideals of music and drama. They sought to make the entire design more "natural"—that is, more flexible in structure, more deeply expressive, less laden with coloratura, and more varied in other musical resources. They did not abandon the da capo aria but modified it and introduced other forms as well; they employed arias and recitatives less predictably in order to move the action forward more rapidly and realistically; they made greater use of obbligato recitative and ensembles, such as trios; they made the orchestra more important, both for its own sake and for adding harmonic depth to accompaniments; they reinstated choruses, long absent in Italian opera; and they stiffened their resistance to the arbitrary demands of the solo singers.

Two of the most important figures in the movement of reform were Nicolò Jommelli (1714–1774) and Tommaso Traetta (1727–1779). That both these Italian composers worked at courts where French taste predominated—Jommelli in Stuttgart and Traetta in Parma—naturally led them to create a cosmopolitan type

---

2. Charles Burney, *The Present State of Music in Germany . . .* , 2nd ed., 2 vols. (London, 1775), I, pp. 238–239.

## IN PERFORMANCE    Vocal Embellishment

An elaborated version of Hasse's da capo aria from *Cleofide* (NAWM 94) survives in the hand of amateur flutist and composer Frederick II, king of Prussia (r. 1740–1786), as sung by the castrato Antonio Uberi, known as Porporino. This version, written out above Hasse's melody in Example 14.3, is ablaze with trills (a), mordents (b), rapid turns (c), appoggiaturas (d), scales, triplets, and arpeggios. Scholars believe that such embellishments were added especially in the da capo repetition, where, after concentrating on the words and their dramatic message the first time through, the performer was expected to embroider the melody so as to enhance the aria's expression and display an impressive vocal technique. Indeed, the execution of such ornamentation required extraordinary vocal flexibility and dexterity, perfect intonation, careful breath control, and precise articulation. And, whether or not the singer was improvising the ornaments anew at every performance, the ability to remember the outline of the original melody was important, as were the training and imagination to know how to vary it tastefully. One of the great castrati of the age, Pier Francesco Tosi (ca. 1653–1732), wrote a singing treatise that reflects these practices (translated into English as *Observations on the Florid Song*).

*Example 14.3: J. A. Hasse,* Cleofide, *Act II, Scene 9,* Digli ch'io son fedele

*Tell him that I am faithful,*
*tell him that he's my darling;*
*to love me; that I adore him;*
*that he not yet despair.*

of opera. As the composer of some one hundred stage works, Jommelli enjoyed great popularity; his arias permeate the many collections of Italian vocal music that circulated in manuscripts copied during the second half of the eighteenth century. Traetta aimed to combine the best of French *tragédie lyrique* and Italian opera seria in his *Ippolito ed Aricia* (1759), adapted from the same libretto that Rameau had set. He even utilized some of Rameau's dance music and descriptive symphonies, and, unusual for this time in Italy, included a number of choruses. For the solo roles, Traetta relied on the conventional genres of recitative and aria. In his own way, Traetta reconciled the two types of music drama—Italian and French—years before Gluck set out to do so.

Christoph Willibald Gluck (1714–1787; shown in Figure 14.7) achieved a synthesis of French and Italian opera that made him the man of the hour. Born in what is now Bavaria of Bohemian parents, Gluck studied with Sammartini in Italy (see page 331), visited London, toured in Germany as conductor of an opera troupe, became court composer to the emperor Charles VI at Vienna, and triumphed in Paris under the patronage of Marie Antoinette. Initially, he composed operas in the conventional Italian style but was strongly affected by the reform movement in the 1750s. Spurred on by the forward-looking impresario Giacomo Durazzo, he collaborated with the poet Raniero de Calzabigi (1714–1795) to produce at Vienna *Orfeo ed Euridice* (1762) and *Alceste* (1767). In a dedicatory preface to *Alceste*, Gluck expressed his resolve to remove the abuses that had deformed Italian opera (see the vignette below) and to confine music to its proper function—to serve the poetry and advance the plot—this to be accomplished without regard to either the outworn conventions of the da capo aria or the desire of singers to show off their skill in ornamental variation. He further aimed to make the overture an integral part of the opera, to adapt the orchestra to dramatic requirements, and to lessen the contrast between aria and recitative in order to foster musical continuity.

*Figure 14.7. Christoph Willibald Gluck, in a 1775 portrait by Joseph-Siffred Duplessis. Kunsthistorisches Museum, Vienna.*

---

**VIGNETTE**  Gluck on the Reform of Opera

*In his manifesto on operatic reform, published in Italian in the dedication of his score of* Alceste *(1769), Christoph Willibald Gluck expounded ideals that were characteristic of the early Classical period.*

~~~

I sought to confine music to its true function of serving the poetry by expressing feelings and the situations of the story without interrupting and cooling off the action through useless and superfluous ornaments. I believed that music should join to poetry what the vividness of colors and well disposed lights and shadows contribute to a correct and well composed design, animating the figures without altering their contours.

I further believed that the greater part of my task was to seek a beautiful simplicity, and I have avoided a display of difficulty at the expense of clarity. I assigned no value to the discovery of some novelty, unless it were naturally suggested by the situation and the expression. And there is no rule that I did not willingly consider sacrificing for the sake of an effect.

From Christoph Willibald Gluck, *Alceste* (Vienna, 1769), dedication.

---

**A CLOSER LOOK** The Rivalry between French and Italian Opera

The musical atmosphere of the French capital was so charged that Gluck's *Iphigénie en Aulide* awakened extraordinary interest. Long-simmering critical opposition to the old-fashioned, state-subsidized French opera had erupted in 1752 in a pamphlet war known as the *querelle des bouffons* ("quarrel of the comic actors"). The immediate occasion for the dispute was the presence in Paris of an Italian opera company that for two seasons had enjoyed sensational success with its performances of Italian comic operas and intermezzi, particularly Pergolesi's *La serva padrona*. Practically every intellectual and would-be intellectual in France took part in the debate—partisans of Italian opera on one side and friends of French opera on the other. Jean-Jacques Rousseau, one of the leaders of the "Italian" faction, vehemently attacked the aristocratic opera of the late Baroque era for its artificial plots and complicated music. He published an article in which he praised Ital-

ian composers' emphasis on "natural" melody and argued that the French language was inherently unsuitable for singing. Rousseau and his friends represented enlightened opinion in Paris. As a result of their campaign, the traditional French opera of Lully and Rameau soon lost favor. But nothing appeared to take its place until Gluck arrived on the scene. Gluck cleverly represented himself—or was represented by his supporters—as wanting to prove that a good opera could be written to French words: he claimed to want Rousseau's help in creating "a noble, sensitive, and natural melody . . . music suited to all nations, so as to abolish these ridiculous distinctions of national styles."[1] He thus appealed at the same time to the patriotism and to the curiosity of the French public.

1. Christoph Willibald Gluck, Letter to the Editor, *Mercure de France* (Feb. 1773).

---

Gluck aspired to "a beautiful simplicity," which he realized in the celebrated aria *Che farò senza Euridice?* (What shall I do without Euridice?) from *Orfeo* and in other airs, choruses, and dances from the same work. *Alceste* is more dramatic and monumental in contrast to the prevailingly pastoral and elegiac tone of *Orfeo*. In both, Gluck molded the music to the drama, intermingling recitatives, arias, and choruses in large unified scenes. He also assigned an important role to the chorus, as is illustrated by the chorus of Furies in Act II (NAWM 96), which is integrated into the action. In this scene, Orfeo, accompanied by harp and strings to imitate the sound of his lyre, pleads for the liberation of Euridice, which the Furies resist, provoking and challenging Orfeo.

CD 7/14

Gluck achieved his mature style in *Orfeo* and *Alceste*, amalgamating Italian melodic grace, German seriousness, and the stately magnificence of the French *tragédie lyrique*. After the success of those two works, he was ready for the climax of his career, the Paris production of *Iphigénie en Aulide* (Iphigenia in Aulis) in 1774. With a libretto adapted from Racine's tragedy, this work, too, was a tremendous success. Revised versions of *Orfeo* and *Alceste* (both with French texts) swiftly followed, along with a new setting of Quinault's *Armide* (1777) to the same libretto that Lully had used in 1686. Gluck's next masterpiece, *Iphigénie en Tauride* (Iphigenia in Tauris, 1779), is a work of large proportions that displays an excellent balance of dramatic and musical interest, and utilizes all the resources of opera—orchestra, ballet, solo and choral singing—to produce a total effect of classical tragic grandeur.

Influence

Gluck's operas became models for the works of his immediate followers in Paris. His influence on the form and spirit of opera was transmitted to the nineteenth century through composers such as Niccolò Piccinni (1728–1800), Luigi Cherubini (1760–1842), and Hector Berlioz (1803–1869).

# Instrumental Music: Sonata, Symphony, and Concerto

Many of the characteristic genres of Baroque instrumental music fell out of fashion in the Classical period, including preludes, toccatas, fugues, chorale settings, and dance suites. Composers continued to write variations, fantasias, and individual dances for keyboard, but the major genres became multimovement works such as the sonata, symphony, and concerto.

## Sonata

In the Baroque era, *sonata* generally meant a multimovement work for a small group of instruments, most often in trio texture. In the Classical period, the word had different meanings for different composers, two of whom we will study here—Domenico Scarlatti and C. P. E. Bach. It also connoted a compositional procedure or form, first articulated by the German theorist Heinrich Christoph Koch (1749–1816).

Alessandro Scarlatti's son Domenico Scarlatti (1685–1757; shown in Figure 14.8), who was born the same year as Bach and Handel, was the chief Italian keyboard composer of the eighteenth century and a remarkably original creative artist. He left Italy in 1720 or 1721 to work as a musician for the king of Portugal. When his pupil, the infanta of Portugal, was married to Prince Ferdinand of Spain in 1729, Scarlatti followed her to Madrid, where he remained for the rest of his life in the service of the Spanish court. Being thus removed from the musical mainstream of Europe—Italy—he became a remarkably original performer-composer and seems to have created his own keyboard idiom virtually without models. He published his first collection of harpsichord sonatas (called on the title page *essercizi,* "exercises") in 1738, but most of his 555 sonatas are known to us through scribal copies from his time.

Scarlatti's sonatas are organized by means of tonal relationships in the standard late Baroque and early Classical binary pattern used for dance pieces and other types of composition. They have two sections, each repeated, the first closing in the dominant or relative major (rarely some other key), the second modulating further afield and then returning to the tonic. This basic scheme underlies much instrumental and solo vocal music in the eighteenth century. In Scarlatti's sonatas, the closing part of the first section invariably returns at the end of the second section, but in the tonic key. (This is sometimes referred to as a partial recapitulation.) What is new and different is Scarlatti's way of stringing together short, repetitious phrases, each of which has a unique place in the compositional design. Some phrases function as openers—for example, by defining the key with an arpeggiated fanfare; others are unstable and introduce accidentals outside the key, serving as transitions; still others are cadential formulas. Although each phrase introduces a well-defined, sometimes contrasting motivic idea, not all are equally important, and some have a clearer role to play in the piece's structure than others. Nevertheless, Scarlatti's compositional method of inventing discrete and differentiated phrases has more in common with Classical than with Baroque procedures.

Domenico Scarlatti

*Figure 14.8. Domenico Scarlatti, in a portrait from about 1740 by Domingo Antonio de Velasco.*

*Figure 14.9. First page of the original edition of* Essercizi per gravicembalo *(1758) by Domenico Scarlatti.*

CD 7/22    CD 3/61

The one-movement sonata written around 1749 identified as K. 119 or Longo 4.15[3] (NAWM 98) illustrates Scarlatti's style and exhibits many of the genre's traits. It has two sections, each repeated. After a brilliant opening, several ideas are announced, each immediately restated. The first, a broken-chord motive spanning two octaves, is introductory. The next bold theme (Example 14.4a), immediately repeated, never returns. The third (Example 14.4b) is purely

*Example 14.4: Domenico Scarlatti, Sonata K. 119, motives*

3.  The sonatas are identified by K. numbers in Ralph Kirkpatrick's index of the sonatas or by a different set of numbers in A. Longo's complete edition of the sonatas.

cadential; the fourth (Example 14.4c), imitating the rhythm and effect of castanets, has a modulatory function here but comes back again to close each half of the sonata. Then the central idea arrives in the dominant minor (Example 14.4d). It is inspired by Spanish guitar music, with an almost constant a′ sounding like an open string being strummed alongside those being fingered. This thematic element is developed throughout the piece: in the second section, it rises to a vigorous climax in which all the notes of the key but one are sounded together (Example 14.4e).

The majority of Scarlatti's sonatas after 1745 appear as pairs in the manuscripts, each pair comprising, in effect, a sonata of two movements, always in the same key (though one may be major and the other minor), sometimes similar in mood, sometimes contrasted. Many eighteenth-century composers, from Alberti to Mozart, wrote sonatas in two movements, possibly under Italian influence, although there is no evidence that they took the idea from Scarlatti. In fact, just as Scarlatti seems to have had no predecessors, so, too, he had no successors, with the exception of a few Iberian composers, notably the Catalan Antonio Soler (1729–1783).

## Symphony

Keyboard sonatas and orchestral compositions of similar form during the early part of the eighteenth century took on the shape of the Italian opera overture or sinfonia. About 1700, the overture had assumed a three-movement structure in the order fast-slow-fast: an Allegro, a short lyrical Andante, and a finale in a dance rhythm such as a minuet or a gigue. Such overtures, as a rule, had no musical connection with the operas they introduced and were played as independent pieces in concerts. It was a natural step, then, for Italian composers to begin writing concert symphonies using the general plan of opera overtures. The earliest of these, dating from around 1730, are equally indebted to the tradition of the late Baroque concerto and of the trio sonata in details of structure, texture, and thematic style. One of the early works in this genre, the Symphony in F Major (ca. 1744) by Giovanni Battista Sammartini (1701–1775) of Milan, is scored for two violins, viola, and bass. The opening Presto (NAWM 100) presents a variety of ideas in rapid succession, much like a Scarlatti keyboard sonata. The binary form, with full (rather than partial) recapitulation of the opening tonic and closing dominant sections, however, fits the scheme of the new, Classical sonata-form movement as described below.

Most instrumental music from the Classical period, whether or not the work was called sonata, trio, string quartet, or symphony, comprises three or four movements of contrasting mood and tempo. The first movement is usually in what is now known as sonata form, also called first-movement form. Since the nineteenth century, this form has been viewed mainly in terms of primary and secondary themes arranged in a three-part structure (see, for example, in the vignette on page 317 Forkel's ideas on composition); but eighteenth-century writers understood it as a two-part or binary form expanded into three large periods or sections and organized by phrase structure and harmony. The two views are compared in Figure 14.10.

In addition, nineteenth-century writers developed a new vocabulary to describe the form, which is still the accepted way of talking about it.

1. An exposition (usually repeated), incorporating a first theme or group of themes in the tonic (P); a transitional or bridge passage (T) leading to a second, often more lyrical theme or group (S) in the dominant or the

*Early symphonies*

*Sammartini*

CD 7/28

*Sonata form*

**EIGHTEENTH-CENTURY VIEW; EXPANDED BINARY FORM**

| FIRST SECTION | | SECOND SECTION | |
|---|---|---|---|
| One Main Period | | First Main Period | Second Main Period |
| Key: ‖: I  -  V  :‖ | | ‖: V  -  on V | I  -  I  :‖ |

**NINETEENTH-CENTURY VIEW; TERNARY FORM (ABA')**

| EXPOSITION | DEVELOPMENT | RECAPITULATION |
|---|---|---|
| Key: ‖: I  -  V  :‖ | X      on V | I  -  I  ‖ |
| Themes: P  T  S  K | | P  T  S  K |

*Figure 14.10. Views of first-movement form. In this diagram, P = primary theme, S = secondary theme, T = transitional material, and K = closing material.*

relative major (if the movement is in a minor key); and a closing theme or cadential reinforcement (K) in the same key. An introduction often precedes the exposition.

2. A development section, which modulates to new keys, possibly even remote ones, in which motives or themes from the exposition are presented in new aspects or combinations.

3. A recapitulation, in which the material of the exposition is restated in the original order but with all themes in the tonic; following the recapitulation, there may be a coda.

This description of sonata form is obviously an abstraction, dwelling particularly on the key scheme and the melodic-thematic ideas. So understood, it fits a good many sonata movements of the late Classical period and the nineteenth century. Many composers, however, departed from it in creative ways—by introducing tonal deflections or secondary developments, or by reordering the themes in the recapitulation—while still adhering to the relatively stable structures outlined above.

Mannheim and Stamitz

Mannheim, Vienna, and Berlin were the principal German centers of symphonic composition after 1740. Under the leadership of Johann Stamitz (1717–1757), the Mannheim orchestra became renowned all over Europe for its virtuosity

*Figure 14.11. Frederick the Great playing the flute, accompanied by a small orchestra, with C. P. E. Bach at the harpsichord. Painting by Adolph von Menzel, 1852. Nationalgalerie, Berlin.*

(Burney called it "an army of generals"), for its astonishing and novel dynamic range—from the softest *pianissimo* to the loudest *fortissimo*—and for the thrilling sound of its crescendo, though many of the striking dynamic effects and the dramatic contrasts were adapted from the Italian opera overture. An example of the first movement of a Stamitz symphony, which includes many dynamic indications, is NAWM 101.

CD 7/31

Another center of symphonic writing in the 1740s was Vienna, home to Georg Matthias Monn (1717–1750) and Georg Christoph Wagenseil (1715–1777). In Wagenseil's music, we find the pleasant, typically Viennese lyricism and good humor that is such an important feature of Mozart's work. The Viennese composers, for the most part, favored contrasting theme groups in their sonata-form movements.

Vienna

The principal symphonists of the Berlin, or north German, school clustered around Frederick the Great, who was himself a composer (see Figure 14.11); Johann Gottlieb Graun (1702/3–1771) and Carl Philipp Emanuel Bach (1714–1788) were two of its chief members. The north Germans were conservative, as is evident in their holding to the three-movement structure for the symphony and in their reluctance to introduce sharp thematic contrasts within a movement. But they were also forward-looking, often utilizing thematic development within a dynamic, organically unified, serious, and quasi-dramatic style, as well as enriching the symphonic texture with contrapuntal elements.

Berlin

## The Empfindsamer Style

Berlin was also a center of the *empfindsamer,* or sentimental, style of composition (see page 268), which German composers began introducing into their instrumental music toward the middle of the century. Two of J. S. Bach's sons are important in this connection. The eldest, Wilhelm Friedemann (1710–1784), was a gifted organist and composer whose life ended in disappointment and poverty because he could not adjust to the requirements for a successful musical career. Carl Philipp Emanuel (see Figure 14.12) was one of the most influential composers of his generation. Trained in music by his father, he served at the court of Frederick the Great in Berlin from 1740 to 1768 and then became music director of the five principal churches in Hamburg. His compositions include oratorios, songs, symphonies, concertos, and chamber music; but most numerous and important are his works for keyboard. In 1742, he published a set of six sonatas (the *Prussian* Sonatas) and, in 1744, another set of six (the *Württemberg* Sonatas). These sonatas were new in style and exerted a strong influence on later composers. His favorite keyboard instrument was not the harpsichord but the softer, more intimate clavichord, which had a capacity for delicate dynamic shadings. The clavichord enjoyed a spell of renewed popularity in Germany around the middle of the eighteenth century before both it and the harpsichord were gradually supplanted by the pianoforte. The last five sets of C. P. E. Bach's sonatas (1780–1787) were evidently written with the pianoforte chiefly in mind, as were many of the later keyboard pieces of W. F. Bach. This instrument, ancestor of the modern piano and now commonly called the "fortepiano," permitted the player to vary the loudness from *piano* to *forte* by striking the keys with lesser or greater force.

*Figure 14.12. Carl Philipp Emanuel Bach, in a pastel portrait by his distant cousin Gottlieb Friedrich Bach, court organist and painter in Meiningen.*

The main characteristics of *empfindsamer* style, of which C. P. E. Bach was a leading exponent, are apparent in the second movement, Poco Adagio (NAWM 99), of the fourth sonata of his *Sonaten für Kenner und Liebhaber* (Sonatas for Connoisseurs and Amateurs; composed in 1765 but not published until 1779). It begins with a kind of melodic sigh, a singing motive ending in an appoggiatura that resolves on a weak beat, followed by a rest (Example 14.5). This opening is decorated with a turn, Scotch snaps (the short-long dotted rhythms on beat 2), and a trill. The great variety of constantly changing rhythmic patterns—short dotted figures, triplets, asymmetrical flourishes of five and thirteen notes—gives the music a restless, nervous quality. The abundant ornaments serve expressive rather than merely decorative ends.

*Example 14.5: C. P. E. Bach, Sonata, Poco adagio*

The *empfindsamer* style of C. P. E. Bach and his contemporaries often exploited the element of surprise, with abrupt shifts of harmony, strange modulations, unusual turns of melody, suspenseful pauses, changes of texture, sudden *sforzando* accents, and the like. The subjective, emotional qualities of this *Empfindsamkeit* reached a climax during the 1760s and 1770s. The trend is sometimes described by the expression *Sturm und Drang*—"storm and stress"—a

Sturm und Drang

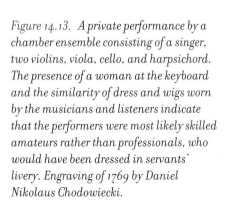

*Figure 14.13. A private performance by a chamber ensemble consisting of a singer, two violins, viola, cello, and harpsichord. The presence of a woman at the keyboard and the similarity of dress and wigs worn by the musicians and listeners indicate that the performers were most likely skilled amateurs rather than professionals, who would have been dressed in servants' livery. Engraving of 1769 by Daniel Nikolaus Chodowiecki.*

movement in German literature that relished tormented, gloomy, terrified, irrational feelings. Later, composers moderated this emotionalism, but its characteristics resurfaced in some instrumental music to be discussed in the next chapter.

## Concerto

Johann Christian Bach (1735–1782; shown in Figure 14.14), J. S. Bach's youngest son, among the first to compose piano concertos, was also an important composer of symphonies as well as chamber music, keyboard music, and operas. After being trained in music by his father and his elder brother C. P. E. Bach, Johann Christian made his way to Milan at the age of twenty. He studied with the celebrated theorist, teacher, and composer Padre Giovanni Battista Martini (1706–1784) of Bologna. Bach was appointed organist of the cathedral at Milan in 1760, by which time he had converted to the Roman Catholic faith. Two years later, after two of his operas had been successfully produced in Naples, he moved to London, where he enjoyed a long career as composer, performer, teacher, and impresario. He had great success there with some forty keyboard concertos, written between 1763 and 1777. The title of his Op. 7 (ca. 1770), *Sei concerti per il cembalo o piano e forte* (Six Concertos for Harpsichord or Pianoforte), bears witness to his early adoption of the pianoforte for public performance. The eight-year-old Mozart spent a year in London

*Figure 14.14.   English painter Thomas Gainsborough's portrait of Johann Christian Bach, J. S. Bach's youngest son, who settled in London. Among the many other musicians whose vibrant portraits were executed by Gainsborough are the Linley sisters (see Figure 14.1). National Portrait Gallery, London.*

---

**A CLOSER LOOK**   Symphony Orchestras

Orchestras in the eighteenth century had three main fields of activity: church, theater, and chamber or concert room. The Italians, who had perfected the violin and other string instruments, were largely interested in church and theater music, where the orchestra served mainly as support for the vocal medium and consisted essentially of strings, as in Sammartini's symphony (NAWM 100). The French, who had added many technical improvements to instruments of the wind family, were especially passionate about opera and ballet, and Lully and Rameau had played an important role in the development of orchestral instruments and ensembles in France. As these composers and their counterparts elsewhere in Europe responded to the enhanced qualities and variety of instruments in every category, they began to devote increasing attention in their compositions to tone color. The result was the establishment of symphony orchestras as ensembles in their own right, independent of their function in church or theater. For the first time, orchestral music was distinguished from chamber music and became more forceful and varied in sound. By the middle of the eighteenth century, although all the essential musical material was still assigned to the strings, more attention was paid to the wind instruments (flutes, oboes, and bassoons) and the brass (horns and occasionally trumpets), which were regularly used for doubling the strings, reinforcing and coloring the melodic ideas, and filling out the harmonies. Court orchestras rose to special prominence in France and Germany. But, as German composers took the lead in developing purely instrumental forms such as symphony and concerto, it was in German lands that some of the most renowned orchestras in Europe came into being.

CD 7/28

(1764–1765), during which time he met Bach and was very much impressed with Bach's music. Mozart later converted three of Bach's keyboard sonatas into concertos (K. 107/21b) and must have had Bach's models in mind when he wrote his first piano concerto, K. 175, in 1773. The first movement of Bach's Concerto for Harpsichord or Piano and Strings in E, Op. 7, No. 5 (102), illustrates many features typical of the concerto at this time. It retains elements of the ritornello structure and textural contrasts of the Baroque period but is imbued with the contrasts of key and thematic material characteristic of the sonata.

To demonstrate these parallels, Figure 14.15 aligns the elements of ritornello form and sonata form with the first movement of Bach's concerto, outlined in

---

**TIMELINE**  The Early Classical Period

| MUSICAL EVENTS | HISTORICAL EVENTS |
|---|---|
| | **1717** Watteau, *The Music Party* |
| Concert spirituel begins in Paris **1725** | |
| *The Beggar's Opera* in London **1728** | |
| | **1729** Metastasio appointed court poet in Vienna |
| Hasse, *Cleofide* in Dresden **1731** | |
| Pergolesi, *La serva padrona* in Naples; **1733** Rameau, *Hippolyte et Aricie* in Paris | |
| D. Scarlatti, first collection of harpsichord sonatas **1738** | |
| Sammartini, Symphony in F Major, no. 32 **ca. 1740** | **1740–1786** Reign of Frederick the Great of Prussia <br> **1740** Maria Theresa of Austria crowned Holy Roman empress |
| C. P. E. Bach, *Prussian* Sonatas for keyboard; **1742** Handel, *Messiah* | |
| Death of J. S. Bach **1750** | |
| | **1751** First volume of French *Encyclopédie* published |
| Pergolesi, *La serva padrona* in Paris; **1752** *Querelle des bouffons* | |
| | **1759** Voltaire, *Candide* <br> **1760–1820** Reign of George III of England |
| Gluck, *Orfeo ed Euridice* in Vienna **1762** | **1762** Rousseau, *The Social Contract* <br> **1765** Joseph II becomes Holy Roman emperor and co-ruler with Maria Theresa |
| J. C. Bach, *Keyboard Concertos*, Op. 7 **ca. 1770** | **1770** Gainsborough, *Blue Boy* |
| | **1774–1792** Reign of Louis XVI, king of France <br> **1775–1783** American Revolution |
| Hawkins, *A General History of the Science* **1776** *and Practice of Music*; Burney, *A General History of Music* (through 1789) | **1776** Declaration of Independence |
| C. P. E. Bach, *Clavier Sonatas for Connoisseurs* **1779** *and Amateurs* | |
| | **1780** Death of Maria Theresa; Joseph II sole Hapsburg ruler <br> **1781** Kant, *Critique of Pure Reason* |
| | **1788** Gibbon, *Decline and Fall of the Roman Empire* |

| Ritornello Form | | Sonata Form | | Form of J. C. Bach Movement | |
|---|---|---|---|---|---|
| SECTION | KEY | SECTION | KEY | SECTION | KEY |
| Ritornello | I | | | Ritornello ("Orchestral Exposition") | |
| | | | | First theme | I |
| | | | | Transition | I |
| | | | | Second theme | I |
| | | | | Closing theme | I |
| Episode | | Exposition | | Solo ("Solo Exposition") | |
| | | First theme | I | First theme | I |
| | | Transition | mod | Transition, extended with new ideas | mod |
| | | Second theme | V | Second theme | V |
| | | Closing theme | V | Closing theme varied | V |
| Ritornello | V | | | Ritornello | |
| | | | | Closing theme abbreviated | V |
| Episode | | Development | mod | Solo ("Development") | mod |
| Ritornello | X | | | (Ritornello) | |
| | | | | Brief orchestral cadence | on V |
| Episode | | Recapitulation | | Solo ("Recapitulation") | |
| | | First theme | I | First theme | I |
| | | Transition | mod | Transition, altered | I |
| | | Second theme | I | Second theme | I |
| | | Closing theme | I | Closing theme varied | I |
| | | | | Cadenza | |
| Ritornello | I | | | Ritornello | |
| | | | | Closing theme | I |

*Figure 14.15. Concerto first-movement form in J. C. Bach's Op. 7, No. 5, compared with ritornello and sonata forms.*

the right-hand column. The Baroque plan of alternating ritornellos and episodes is clearly reflected in Bach's concerto, yet the three solo "episodes," in which the soloist takes the lead and the orchestra provides accompaniment and punctuation, have the shape of an exposition, development, and recapitulation of a sonata. The only long ritornello is the first, which introduces most of the movement's material in the tonic: in some modern views of concerto first-movement form, this is called the "orchestral exposition," followed by the "solo exposition." The later ritornellos can use any element from the first one, and here Bach mostly uses the closing theme. As is often the case, both the transition and the development introduce new ideas.

By Bach's time, it had become a tradition for the soloist to play a cadenza, usually improvised, just before the final orchestral ritornello. The cadenza had developed from the trills and runs that singers inserted, particularly before the return of the opening section in the da capo aria. By convention, concerto cadenzas are typically introduced by a weighty $^6_4$ chord, and the soloist signals the orchestra to reenter by playing a long trill over a dominant chord.

Cadenza

The parallels between this movement and Mozart's K. 488 (see Chapter 15) are striking though not surprising since, by 1770, the main outlines of the first-movement form for the solo concerto were well established.

## POSTLUDE

The early Classical period explored a wealth of new genres, forms, and expressive means. Much of the innovation originated in opera, particularly comic opera. There, the urge to entertain and reach a wider audience led to a simplification of means and a striving for naturalness of expression. From the Italian theaters, the new styles spread through the cosmopolitan network of musicians, composers, and directors to centers such as Paris, Mannheim, and Vienna. Many practices spilled out of the theaters into the concert halls and private chambers. The new interest in naturalism purged Italian opera of its excesses and resulted in a spare, transparent, logical—almost proselike—flow of musical ideas that could be grasped on first hearing. Instrumental music in particular—sonata, symphony, and concerto—profited from these developments because it was now intelligible even without a text or a title. These changes laid the foundation for the increasing importance of instrumental music in the Classical period.

# The Late Eighteenth Century: Haydn and Mozart

Classicism, having been nurtured by the Enlightenment, reached its peak in the late eighteenth century. This was also the age of "enlightened" rulers like Joseph II (r. 1765–1790), who fostered the liberal atmosphere in cosmopolitan Vienna that continued to attract artists and musicians from all over Europe, among them (Franz) Joseph Haydn (1732–1809) and Wolfgang Amadeus Mozart (1756–1791), the two most remarkable composers of the late eighteenth century. Both men experienced the currents that led up to the French Revolution and, in Haydn's case, lived to see the changes that began to unfold in its wake. They also had many other things in common even though Haydn was the elder by twenty-four years. They were personal friends; each admired and was influenced by the music of the other. They were both practicing musicians—Mozart a virtuoso pianist and highly efficient string player, Haydn a fine violinist who also conducted from the harpsichord—and they both composed prolifically, paying the utmost attention to detail.

Their lives and careers also differed in many ways, which helps to explain some significant differences in their respective compositional styles and output. Haydn, born during J. S. Bach's lifetime, lived to the ripe old age of seventy-seven. Mozart, born in 1756, died in the prime of his life, at the age of thirty-five. Haydn's growth to artistic maturity was much slower than that of Mozart, a child prodigy whose star rose quickly and burned brightly for only a few decades. Haydn worked loyally during most of his career in the service of a noble Hungarian family. Mozart, craving the celebrity and adulation he had earned as a boy, gave up a steady job in his hometown of Salzburg to become a free agent in Vienna. Most importantly, Mozart traveled a great deal in his early years—to England, Italy, Germany, and France—and absorbed the many styles and practices current in these countries, whereas Haydn found his models within local traditions around Vienna.

Because Haydn remained in the same job for so long, his career does not easily divide itself into distinct periods. We will, therefore, discuss his works according to genre: first Haydn's instrumental music, where he made his most original contribution, and then Haydn's vocal works, which include operas, oratorios, and Masses. By contrast, Mozart moved around a lot, and each new

*Chapter Contents*

*Prelude* 339

(Franz) Joseph Haydn (1732–1809) 341

Haydn's Instrumental Music 342

Haydn's Vocal Works 351

Wolfgang Amadeus Mozart (1756–1791) 354

Mozart's Salzburg Years 355

Mozart's Vienna Years 357

*Postlude* 373

# ✹ (Franz) Joseph Haydn (1732–1809)

*HAYDN! Great Sovereign of the tuneful art:*
*Thy works alone supply an ample chart*
*Of all the mountains, seas, and fertile plains*
*Within the compass of its wide domains.—*

So wrote the celebrated music historian Charles Burney in 1791 on Haydn's arrival in England. Indeed, Haydn was hailed in his time as the greatest composer alive. In public life, he exemplified the Enlightenment ideals of good character, piety, and kindness. He was also an ambitious entrepreneur and skillful businessman, capable of both seriousness and humor, and he devoted his enormous talent to satisfying his patrons and pleasing his audiences.

Born in Rohrau, a village about thirty miles southeast of Vienna, Haydn became a choirboy at Saint Stephen's Cathedral in Vienna, where he acquired practical experience in music and learned singing, harpsichord, and violin. Dismissed at seventeen when his voice changed, Haydn barely

*Figure 15.1.  (Franz) Joseph Haydn, in an oil portrait by Thomas Hardy, painted in 1791–1792 during Haydn's first sojourn in London. Royal College of Music, London.*

supported himself as a freelance musician, composer, and teacher. He mastered counterpoint using Fux's *Gradus ad Parnassum*, studied the music of other composers, and took composition lessons from Nicola Porpora, a famous Italian composer and singing teacher who had been Handel's rival in London.

Haydn became music director for Count Morzin in about 1757 and probably wrote his first symphonies for the count's orchestra. Three years later, he married a wigmaker's daughter, Maria Anna Keller, although he was really in love with her sister, who became a nun; his long marriage was unhappy, childless, and marked by extramarital affairs on both sides.

In 1761, Haydn entered the service of a Hungarian prince, Paul Anton Esterházy, and continued in the family's service for the rest of his life. For years, Haydn was responsible for composing on demand, presenting concerts or operas weekly, and assisting with almost daily chamber music. While the position forced him to compose at a prodigious rate, it also allowed him to hear his music in excellent performances and to experiment with new ideas. During visits to Vienna, Haydn took part in the city's intellectual and musical life. It was there around 1784 that he met Mozart, and their mutual admiration blossomed.

The publication of Haydn's music brought him praise and fame throughout Europe and generated commissions from many other patrons. Between 1790 and 1795, he made two extended trips to London, where he had long been famous, to compose, give concerts, and teach. His triumphs in London raised his reputation at home, and he was invited to return to Vienna as court music director for Prince Nikolaus Esterházy II with minimal duties. During his last decade, his health declined and he composed very little; but when he died in 1809, he was universally admired.

**Major works:** 104 symphonies, 20 concertos, 68 string quartets, 29 keyboard trios, 126 baryton trios, 47 keyboard sonatas, 15 operas, 12 Masses, *The Creation, The Seasons,* numerous other ensemble, keyboard, and vocal works.

*Figure 15.2. In this hall in the Eszterháza Palace, near Eisenstadt, where the Viennese court spent the summer, Haydn (from around 1768) conducted his symphonies while playing the first violin.*

location brought new opportunities for composition. Therefore, we will discuss his works chronologically according to place, grouping them generally into his years in Salzburg and then Vienna, even though he did not confine his activities solely to these cities.

# (Franz) Joseph Haydn (1732–1809)

Haydn (see the biography and Figure 15.1) spent nearly thirty years at the court of Prince Paul Anton Eszterházy and his brother Miklós under circumstances that were ideal for his development as a composer. Although in later years he filled commissions from others and traveled extensively, his years at Eszterháza had a formative influence on his career.

The remote country estate of Eszterháza, near Eisenstadt (see Figure 15.13), was designed to rival the splendor of the French court at Versailles; the palace and grounds boasted two theaters, one for opera and one for puppet plays, as well as two large and sumptuously appointed music rooms in the palace itself (see Figure 15.2). Haydn was required to compose whatever music the prince demanded, to conduct the performances, to train and supervise all the musical personnel, and to keep the instruments in repair (see "Haydn's Contract," page 345). He built up the orchestra to about twenty-five players. Operas and concerts became weekly events, and almost every day in the prince's private apartments chamber music was heard. The prince himself usually played the baryton, an instrument resembling a large viola da gamba with an extra set of resonating metal strings that could be plucked like a harp (see Figure 15.3). Haydn wrote some 165 pieces for the baryton, mostly trios with viola and cello.

Although Eszterháza was isolated, Haydn kept abreast of current developments in the world of music through the constant stream of distinguished guests

Music at Eszterháza

*Figure 15.3. This baryton, shown leaning against its case, was owned by Prince Nikolaus Esterházy; it was made in Vienna by Johann Joseph Stalmann in 1750. The instrument, a favorite of the prince's, resembled a bass viol but had a set of sympathetic strings that could be plucked, and that added to its resonance. Haydn created a baryton repertory of some 165 pieces so that the prince could participate in chamber music. Hungarian National Museum, Budapest.*

and artists, and through occasional trips to Vienna. He had the double advantage of a devoted, highly skilled troupe of singers and players and an intelligent patron, whose requirements may have been burdensome but whose understanding and enthusiasm were inspiring. As Haydn once wrote, "My prince was pleased with all my work, I received applause, and as conductor of an orchestra I could make experiments, observe what strengthened and what weakened an effect and thus improve, substitute, make cuts, and take risks; I was isolated from the world; no one in my vicinity could make me lose confidence in myself or bother me, and so I had to become original."[1]

## Haydn's Instrumental Music

Although Haydn's long career as a composer reflected the changing tastes of the times and his works explored a variety of genres, certain enduring traits stand out in his music, especially in the symphonies.

Overview of the symphonies

Of Haydn's more than 104 symphonies, at least 92 were completed by 1789, most of them for Prince Esterházy's orchestra. Beginning about 1768, they were performed in the palatial concert room shown in Figure 15.2, with Haydn leading the orchestra while playing the violin. During the 1780s, he composed six symphonies (Nos. 82–87), now known as the *Paris* Symphonies, on commission for a concert series in the French capital. His last twelve, the *London* symphonies (Nos. 93–104), were written during the 1790s for a concert series organized by impresario and violinist Johann Peter Salomon in that city. Many of his symphonies (as well as many of the quartets) have acquired nicknames for one reason or another, few of them given by the composer himself.

1. Trans, Elaine Sisman, in "Haydn, Shakespeare, and the Rules of Originality," in Elaine Sisman, ed., *Haydn and His World* (Princeton: Princeton University Press, 1997), p. 3.

## Symphonic Form

Haydn's earliest symphonies were typically three-movement works—fast, slow, fast—a form derived from the Italian opera overture (sinfonia). Other symphonies from the early period are in four movements, all in the same key, recalling the slow-fast-slow-fast sequence of the sonata da chiesa. During the late 1760s, however, Haydn established the four-movement pattern described here as the standard for the Classical era: I—Allegro; II—Andante moderato; III—Minuet and Trio; IV—Allegro.

The Classical symphony generally demanded the most attention from its audience in its first movement. The first-movement form described here is only an abstract design that more or less matches any specific symphonic first movement by Haydn. Its procedures may be observed in the opening movement of Symphony No. 92 in G Major, the *Oxford* Symphony, so called because Haydn presented it to Oxford University when he went there to receive an honorary doctoral degree in 1791 (see NAWM 104 and the accompanying commentary; see also the diagram of the basic sonata-form structure on page 332). Although the

CD 7/51–70    CD 4/1

---

**VIGNETTE  Haydn's Contract**

*When he entered the service of Prince Paul Anton Esterházy, Haydn was named Vice-Kapellmeister, allowing the elderly Kapellmeister to retain his title but giving Haydn sole direction of orchestral, chamber, and dramatic music. His contract, excerpted below, spells out his duties and his social standing as a house officer, higher than that of a servant yet still required to wear the court uniform. On the death of the Kapellmeister in 1766, Haydn succeeded to the title. The limits in clause 4 on circulating his music to others were later relaxed, and he earned both fame and money through performances and publications elsewhere.*

2. The said Joseph Heyden [sic] shall be considered and treated as a member of the household. Therefore his Serene Highness is graciously pleased to place confidence in his conducting himself as becomes an honorable official of a princely house. He must be temperate, not showing himself overbearing toward his musicians, but mild and lenient, straightforward and composed. It is especially to be observed that when the orchestra shall be summoned to perform before company, the Vice-Capellmeister [namely, Haydn] and all the musicians shall appear in uniform, and the said Joseph Heyden shall take care that he and all the members of his orchestra follow the instructions given, and appear in white stockings, white linen, powdered, and with either a pigtail or a tiewig. . . .

4. The said Vice-Capellmeister shall be under obligation to compose such music as his Serene Highness may command, and neither to communicate such compositions to any other person, nor to allow them to be copied, but he shall retain them for the absolute use of his Highness, and not compose for any other person without the knowledge and permission of his Highness.

5. The said Joseph Heyden shall appear daily in the antechamber before and after midday, and inquire whether his Highness is pleased to order a performance of the orchestra. On receipt of his orders he shall communicate them to the other musicians, and take care to be punctual at the appointed time, and to ensure punctuality in his subordinates. . . .

7. The said Vice-Capellmeister shall take careful charge of all music and musical instruments, and be responsible for any injury that may occur to them from carelessness or neglect.

8. The said Joseph Heyden shall be obliged to instruct the female vocalists, in order that they may not forget in the country what they have been taught with much trouble and expense in Vienna, and, as the said Vice-Capellmeister is proficient on various instruments, he shall take care himself to practice on all that he is acquainted with.

Trans. in Karl Geiringer, *Haydn: A Creative Life in Music* (New York: Norton, 1946), pp. 52–53.

*Oxford* Symphony is a late work, it is being used here to illustrate the principles being discussed because it is exemplary.

First-movement form

A typical first-movement Allegro alternates stable and unstable periods. The stable periods—the statements of the primary, secondary, and closing material—are usually presented in balanced four-measure phrases and are clearly set off by cadences, at least in the early symphonies. A combination of string and wind ensembles presents the thematic ideas. The unstable passages, mainly transitions and developments, are often scored for full orchestra and are characterized by bustling rhythmic energy, sequences, modulatory twists and turns, overlapping phrases, and avoidance of cadences. Slow introductions, when they occur, are usually unstable from the outset (see NAWM 104a).

CD 7/51    CD 4/1

Exposition

In a typical Allegro movement, Haydn reiterates the opening statement immediately but with some destabilizing turns of harmony or rhythm that steer the music in a new direction. A transition or bridge passage to the dominant or relative major or minor follows. The transition is usually a loud passage with dramatic, rushing figures, a perfect foil for the second thematic section, which is more lightly scored, melodically distinctive, and harmonically stable. In most of the symphonies of the 1770s and 1780s, Haydn clearly contrasted the secondary material with the opening idea. But in some, as in the *Oxford* and the later *London* symphonies, Haydn built the second thematic section on the opening material, albeit sometimes with significant alteration. The exposition usually ends with a closing section for full orchestra based on a cadential, repetitive, vigorous figure, sometimes harking back to the opening but usually distinct from the primary and secondary subjects. In some of the movements, the section in the secondary key is devoted entirely to the closing material.

Development

Haydn rarely introduced new thematic ideas after the exposition's closing double bar. The development often begins with a restatement of the opening subject, or sometimes with transitional material or with one of the other subjects. Motives from the exposition are combined, superimposed, extended, and manipulated in many other ways. Abrupt changes of subject, digressions, and sudden silences are particularly characteristic of Haydn's developments. He also often enriched them through the use of counterpoint, which brought the older learned style into works of the more modern galant style. In the course of his career, Haydn increased the length and artfulness of the development section until it roughly equaled the other sections of the sonata form, providing an appropriate counterweight to them.

Recapitulation

We are usually well prepared for the recapitulation, often because it is preceded by an extended dominant pedal, but Haydn sometimes disguises or plays down its arrival so that we may not recognize that it has begun until after the fact. Frequently, the opening statement is rescored or extended in new ways. In the first movement of the *Oxford* Symphony, both the first and second phrases of the principal theme are now imitated in the flute, introducing counterpoint where there was none in the exposition; this makes it sound at first as if the development is continuing. The recapitulation section reprises all of the material from the exposition in the tonic, although sometimes a theme originally in the major mode may return in the minor or vice versa. Also, instead of curtailing the transition because he does not need to modulate, Haydn likes to intensify and animate it by simulating a modulation. He does so in this movement, where motives from the closing theme unexpectedly show up in the transitions. Haydn sometimes gives more emphasis to the secondary and closing themes in his recapitulations. For example, after the closing subject in this movement, Haydn continues to develop material from all three thematic areas and to recombine it in unexpected ways.

Second movement

The second movement of a Haydn symphony almost always offers an oasis of calm and gentle melody after the contrasts, drama, and complexity of the first movement. Many of the slow movements are in sonata form without repeats, and in later works Haydn often used theme and variations. In the *Oxford* Symphony (NAWM 104b), the slow movement is in ternary form, with a songlike theme, a dramatic middle section in the tonic minor, an abbreviated reprise, and a quiet, introspective coda that features woodwind instruments and employs colorful chromatic harmonies. Such contrasting minor sections and quiet codas are common in Haydn's later symphonies.

CD 7/61

The third movement, a Minuet and Trio in most Classical symphonies, provides another type of contrast since it is shorter than either of the first two movements, it is in a more popular style, and its form is easy for listeners to follow. The Minuet itself is always in a two-part (binary or rounded binary) form—‖:a:‖:b(a′):‖. The Trio is built along similar lines; it is usually in the same key as the Minuet (possibly with a change of mode), but it is shorter with lighter orchestration, sometimes reduced to a three-part texture, and has its own thematic content—‖:c:‖:d(c′):‖. After the Trio, the Minuet returns da capo, resulting in a three-section ABA form for the movement as a whole. The very directness of the form, however, allowed Haydn to introduce interest and humor. In the *Oxford* Symphony, for example (NAWM 104c), the Minuet has phrases of six measures rather than the usual four; unexpected harmonies, syncopations, pauses, and changes of dynamic level keep the listener off-balance. Haydn's Minuet and Trio movements contain some of his most charming music and are remarkable for their wealth of musical ideas, harmonic invention, and instrumental color—all happy traits in such a modest form.

Minuet and Trio

CD 7/65

After the easygoing Minuet, the fourth and final movement closes the symphony with a new buildup of tension that moves to climax and then release. The finale is typically faster and shorter than the first movement, overflowing with high spirits and nimble gaiety, and full of impish surprises. The finale of the *Oxford* Symphony (NAWM 104d), like many of Haydn's finales, is in sonata form. The playful first theme also appears in the dominant to open the secondary thematic section. It returns again at the end of the exposition and predominates in the development, thereby illustrating the economy of means so characteristic of Haydn's late symphonies. In other symphonies from the 1770s on, Haydn favored rondo finales, a form in which the main theme, usually itself a small complete binary form, alternates with several contrasting thematic sections, often in the pattern ABACABA. Some are sonata-rondos, in which the A and B sections resemble the primary and secondary theme groups in a sonata-form exposition, C is a modulatory development passage, and B returns near the end in the tonic.

Finale

CD 7/70

## The Symphonies

The symphonies of 1768–1772 show Haydn as a composer with a mature technique and fertile imagination. No longer viewing the symphony as light entertainment or as a delightful overture to an opera, Haydn now regarded it as a serious work that demanded close listening. The deeply emotional and agitated character of some of these symphonies, particularly those in minor keys, has been associated with the literary movement known as Sturm und Drang ("storm and stress"). Many are longer, more rhythmically complex, more contrapuntal, and more dramatic than his earlier symphonies. They are marked by abrupt constrasts between loud and soft, with more crescendos and *sforzati*, all used to startling effect. The harmonic palette is richer than in the early symphonies, and modulations range more widely.

The symphonies of 1768–1772

According to a well-known story, Haydn wrote the *Farewell* Symphony in F♯ Minor (No. 45, 1772) as a hint to Prince Esterházy that it was time to move

*Farewell* Symphony

back into town from his summer palace and give the musicians a chance to see their families again. The final Presto unexpectedly leads to an Adagio, in the course of which one section of the orchestra after another concludes its part and the players get up and leave; only two first violins remain to play the closing measures.

The symphonies of 1773–1788

In the next group of symphonies, beginning around 1773, Haydn turned from minor keys and passionate accents to a more cheerful style, influenced by his comic operas. However, since audiences expected symphonies to be not only appealing and easy to understand but also serious, ambitious, stirring, and impressive, reflecting the esteem with which the genre was regarded in the 1770s, Haydn met these expectations with works like his Symphony No. 56 in C Major (1774), which is festive and brilliant, and others in this key that use high trumpets and timpani but that also encompass a broader emotional range: the agitation characteristic of the Sturm und Drang style now serves to contrast with more stable, songlike phrases.

*Paris* symphonies

In the 1780s, Haydn increasingly composed for the public, selling his symphonies to patrons or publishers abroad. The six *Paris* symphonies of 1785–1786, his grandest so far, were commissioned for the large orchestra of the Concerts de la Loge Olympique, consisting of flute, two oboes, two bassoons, two horns, and strings, occasionally augmented by trumpets and timpani. Queen Marie Antoinette, who would be executed under the guillotine within the decade, is said to have loved especially Symphony No. 85, subsequently called *La Reine* (The Queen). After all six (Nos. 82–87) were performed again in 1787, this time at the Concert spirituel, a reviewer noted how "this great genius could draw such rich and varied developments from a single subject, so different from the sterile composers who pass continually from one idea to another."

Symphonies Nos. 88–92

Symphonies Nos. 88 to 92, written in 1787 and 1788, were also composed on commission; the last of this group, No. 92 (discussed above), accompanied Haydn to Oxford University a few years later, when he was awarded an honorary degree. Like the *Paris* Symphonies, they offer deep expression combined with masterful technique, and a mixture of popular and learned styles that gave them wide, immediate, and lasting appeal.

*London* symphonies

The invitation from Johann Peter Salomon in 1790 to compose and conduct six—and, later, six more—symphonies for the cosmopolitan and exacting audiences of London spurred Haydn to supreme efforts. Hailed by the British as "the greatest composer in the world," he was determined to live up to what was expected of him, and the *London* Symphonies (Nos. 93–104) are indeed his crowning achievements. Everything he had learned in forty years went into them. While he did not depart radically from his previous works, he brought all the elements together on a grander scale, with more brilliant orchestration (now including clarinets), more daring harmonic conceptions, more intense rhythmic drive, and, especially, more memorable thematic inventions.

Harmony

Harmonic imagination plays an important part in the slow introductions of the *London* Symphonies. These opening sections have a portentous quality, a deliberately dramatic suspense that grips the listener awaiting the Allegro. They are either set in the tonic minor of the Allegro (as in Symphonies Nos. 101 and 104) or they gravitate toward the minor mode as a foil for the major mode of the ensuing fast movement (as in No. 94).

Movement forms

As much as the *London* Symphonies achieve a new brilliance and spaciousness, they are also characterized by a certain thematic compactness and economy of means. The movements in sonata form tend to revolve around the primary subject. This subject often pervades the section in the dominant, which in Haydn's earlier work usually presented a light, graceful contrast to the dynamic opening. The slow movements take either the form of a theme and variations (Nos. 94, 95, 97, 103) or a free adaptation of sonata form. One feature common to both is a contrasting minor section. The minuets, no longer courtly dances, are Allegro movements in Minuet and Trio pattern. Like the corresponding movements of the late quartets (see below), they are already scherzos in everything but name and tempo. Some of the finales are in sonata form, but Haydn's favored pattern is the rondo or sonata-rondo, a form in which an opening A section returns following each of several contrasting sections—typically, ABACABA.

Haydn's shrewd appraisal of London's musical tastes is evident. The sudden *fortissimo* crash on a weak beat in the slow movement of Symphony No. 94 has given this work its nickname, *Surprise;* it was put there because, as Haydn later acknowledged, he wanted something novel and startling to take people's minds off the rival concerts of his former pupil Ignaz Pleyel (1757–1831). The greater tunefulness may also have been prompted by this competition since Pleyel's strong suit was melody. Haydn turned to Slovenian, Croatian, and other peasant tunes that he remembered from his youth. Symphony No. 103 displays characteristic instances of folklike melodies, and the finale of Symphony No. 104, with its imitation of the bagpipe, is particularly suggestive of a peasant dance (Example 15.1). Similar allusions are the "Turkish"-band effect (triangle, cymbals, bass drum) and the trumpet fanfare in the Allegretto of the *Military* Symphony (No. 100), and the ticking accompaniment in the Andante of Symphony No. 101 (the *Clock*). Haydn always aimed to please the casual music lover as well as the expert, and it is a measure of his greatness that he succeeded in delighting both.

*Special effects*

*Example 15.1: Joseph Haydn, Symphony No. 104, Finale, Allegro spiritoso*

## The String Quartets

By the time Haydn was forty, his reputation as the first great master of the string quartet was assured. Unlike symphonies, which were often performed by professionals for a paying or invited audience, string quartets were primarily for amateurs to play for their own pleasure. Haydn's mature quartets are very much addressed to the players, who all share in the conversation among the instruments: the first violin plays the leading role, but the cello and inner parts often carry the melody or engage in dialogue. The evolution of his sixty-eight quartets parallels that of the symphonies in many respects—from early mastery, through increasing length and emotional depth, to completely individual late works.

Haydn tended to compose and publish his quartets in groups of six, which was common in published collections of the eighteenth century. Opp. 9 (ca. 1770), 17 (1771), and 20 (1772) established for the quartet the same four-movement pattern as is found in the symphony, but with the Minuet often before instead of after the slow movement. In the sonata-form movements, Haydn adopted strategies unique to his quartets. After the principal theme—almost always dominated by the first violin—he usually chose a looser texture in which

*Opp. 9, 17, and 20*

*Example 15.2: Joseph Haydn, String Quartet in G Major, Op. 33, No. 5, Scherzo*

the main motives pass from one instrument to another. In place of the passages for full orchestra that highlight the transitions in the symphonies, Haydn favored loud unisons or stark modulatory gestures. The development sections of the Op. 20 quartets are nearly equal in length to the exposition and recapitulation. Moreover, motives first presented in the exposition are developed over the entire movement, a procedure that Haydn followed throughout his career. Haydn systematically included at least one quartet in a minor key in each set of six, just as he exploited minor keys in the contemporary Sturm und Drang symphonies. Furthermore, three quartets from Op. 20 end with fugues, which suggests that Haydn was attempting to raise this genre from the lighter, more galant style of writing for string quartet that had been fashionable in Paris during the 1760s.

*Example 15.3: Joseph Haydn, String Quartet, Op. 33, No. 2, Presto, closing passage*

Ten years went by before Haydn composed the six quartets of Op. 33 (1781) and advertised to potential subscribers that the works were written in a "quite new and special way." They are lighthearted, witty, and tuneful, perhaps influenced by Mozart's six quartets K. 168–173, which were published a few years earlier. One new feature is that the Minuets, here entitled "Scherzo" (Italian for "joke" or "trick"), literally do play tricks on the courtly dance by breaking the normal metrical pattern, as shown in Example 15.2.

*Humor in Op. 33*

Even apart from the Scherzos, Op. 33 contains some of Haydn's happiest strokes of wit and humor. One of three rondo finales in Op. 33 is the Presto of No. 2 (NAWM 103), nicknamed *The Joke* because of enigmatic rests in the coda that "refuses" to end (see Example 15.3). But humor pervades the whole movement, as Haydn mischievously plays with the listener's expectations throughout. Not only are Haydn's themes playful in themselves, but the sparkling dialogue between players must have added merriment to the amateur-quartet evenings that were held in cities such as London, Paris, and Vienna, in country estates of the nobility, and even in monasteries.

CD 8/1   CD 3/67

In his remaining years at Eszterháza, Haydn composed another thirty-four quartets, of which the six of Op. 76 (1797) display his experimentation with new forms and techniques as well as his overall broadening of the genre. As in his later symphonies, Haydn frequently began the second thematic area by repeating the first theme in the new key and used the closing section to inject contrast. He also expanded the harmonic frontiers of Classicism, foreshadowing Romantic harmony in his use of chromatic progressions and chords, enharmonic changes, and fanciful tonal shifts. The Minuets of Op. 76, while less playful than those of Op. 33, are full of offbeat accents, "extra" measures, exaggerated leaps, and other satirical features such as the incongruous canon of No. 2 (Example 15.4), with its clumsy five- and six-bar phrases, that completely contradicts the graceful essence of this dignified dance. In contrast to such moments of

*Later quartets*

*Example 15.4: Joseph Haydn, String Quartet Op. 76, No. 2, Menuetto*

*Figure 15.4. Table for playing string quartets, from about 1790. With the tabletop (in the background) removed and the music racks raised (as shown here), the four players face one another, ideally positioned to listen to each other and engage in the "conversation" that string-quartet playing was thought to embody. Kunsthistorisches Museum, Vienna.*

drollery, however, is the beautiful theme and variations that constitute the slow movement of Op. 76, No. 3. Haydn composed the melody as a birthday tribute for Kaiser Franz (Example 15.5), but its memorable phrases later became the national anthem of the Austro-Hungarian Empire and serve to this day as the German national anthem. Like his late symphonies, then, Haydn's late quartets marvelously juxtapose the serious with the jocular, the artful with the folksy, and the complex with the simple.

*Example 15.5: Joseph Haydn,* Gott erhalte Franz den Kaiser *(hymn)*

*May God preserve Franz, the Kaiser/Our good Kaiser Franz!/Long may he live/in fortune's bright light!/The climbing laurel blooms for him/Bestowing him with wreaths of honor wherever he goes./May God preserve Franz, the Kaiser/Our good Kaiser Franz!*

## Keyboard Sonatas

Haydn's early keyboard sonatas can be performed on a harpsichord, which allows for only certain changes in dynamics. His later sonatas, however, call for the performer to realize dynamic markings such as *sforzando* and *crescendo*, sudden accents, and other variations of touch that require a pianoforte. Haydn used a clavichord in his early years, but by 1780 he had a piano available. The author-

*Figure 15.5.* George, Earl of Cowper, with the Family of Charles Gore, *1775, by Johann Zoffany, showing a square piano and a cello. Such pianos were the main domestic musical instrument from the 1760s through the mid-nineteenth century. Yale Center for British Art, Paul Mellon Collection, New Haven.*

ized contemporary printed editions of the sonatas after 1780 give "fortepiano" or "pianoforte" as the first option, along with "clavicembalo" (usually meaning harpsichord). Haydn's piano sonatas follow the same lines of development observed in the symphonies and quartets.

His last sonatas demonstrate how much in touch he was with the latest musical fashions and developments. Among them, Sonata No. 52 in E♭ merits special attention. Long a favorite of recitalists, it was written in 1794 for virtuoso Therese Jansen Bartolozzi and published in England around 1800 as a "Grand Sonata for the Piano Forte"—and grand it is in every way. The sonata begins in the manner of the French overture, with full chords in dotted rhythm, and thoroughly exploits the power and scope of the new pianos.

## Haydn's Vocal Works

In a modest autobiographical sketch of 1776 written for an Austrian encyclopedia, Haydn named his most successful works: three operas, an Italian oratorio, and his setting of the *Stabat Mater* (1767)—a work well known in Europe in the 1780s. He made no mention of the sixty-odd symphonies that he had written by then and referred to his chamber music only to complain that the Berlin critics dealt with it too harshly. Haydn may have been reticent about the symphonies because they were little known outside Eszterháza. Also, as a child of the Baroque, he believed that vocal music was more important than instrumental music. It was not until his symphonies and string quartets were so enthusiastically received in Paris and London during the 1780s and 1790s that he realized how highly regarded they were. By the early nineteenth century, Haydn's reputation rested primarily on his instrumental works.

Eszterháza was an international center for opera, despite its remote location, and Haydn spent a lot of his time and energy on opera while he worked there. Between 1769 and 1790, he arranged, prepared, and conducted some seventy-five operas by other composers. Of his own fifteen or more Italian operas, most were comic, with music abounding in humor and high spirits. He also composed three serious operas, of which the most famous was the "heroic drama" *Armida*

Operas

(1784), remarkable for its dramatic accompanied recitatives and arias on a grand scale. Although successful in their day, Haydn's operas are rarely produced now, having been eclipsed by the enduring appeal of his instrumental music and his oratorios (see below).

**Masses**

Among Haydn's best-known vocal works are his Masses, especially the last six, which he composed for an Esterházy princess between 1796 and 1802. These are large-scale, festive works for chorus, full orchestra (including trumpets and timpani), and four vocal soloists, written in a style that blends traditional elements, such as choral fugues at the end of the Gloria and Credo movements, with modern elements from the opera and symphony. Haydn wrote his *Missa in tempore belli* (Mass in Time of War, 1796) and *Missa in angustiis* (Mass for Troubled Times, 1798), also known as the *Lord Nelson Mass*, during the Napoleonic Wars. Like the Masses of his contemporaries, Haydn's have a flamboyance that matches the ornate architecture of the Austrian Baroque churches in which they were performed. After learning that some critics thought his sacred music was too cheerful, Haydn responded by saying that at the thought of God, his heart "leaped for joy," and he doubted that God would scold him for praising the Lord "with a cheerful heart."

**Oratorios**

During his stay in London, Haydn became acquainted with Handel's oratorios. At Westminster Abbey in 1791, he was so deeply moved by the Hallelujah Chorus in a performance of *Messiah* that he burst into tears and exclaimed: "He is the master of us all." Haydn's appreciation for Handel inspired the choral parts of his late Masses and especially his oratorios *The Creation* (completed 1798) and *The Seasons* (completed 1801). *The Creation* text was based on the biblical narrative and Milton's *Paradise Lost; The Seasons* was loosely adapted from a much earlier poem by James Thomson. Although the German texts of both oratorios were written by Baron Gottfried van Swieten, the imperial court librarian in Vienna and a busy musical amateur, they were issued simultaneously in German and English as a gesture both to Handel's influence and to the English public's delight in choral music.

The popularity of both works rests largely on their naïve and loving depiction of nature and of innocent joy in the simple life. Haydn's instrumental introduc-

*Figure 15.6. Eighteenth-century opera performance, perhaps at the Eszterháza opera house. Theater-Museum, Munich.*

*Figure 15.7. Performance of Haydn's* The Creation *on March 27, 1808, in the banquet hall of the University of Vienna. Engraving after the watercolor by Balthasar Wigand. Historisches Museum der Stadt Wien.*

tions and interludes are among the finest examples of tone painting in music at the time. His "Depiction of Chaos" at the beginning of *The Creation* introduces confusing and disturbingly dissonant harmonies. The transition in the following recitative and chorus, with its awesome choral outburst on the C-major chord at the words "and there was Light" made a profound impression on audiences and was extolled by contemporary writers as the supreme example of the sublime in music (Example 15.6).

*Example 15.6: Joseph Haydn,* Die Schöpfung (The Creation), *Part I, Und Gott sprach*

## ✳ Wolfgang Amadeus Mozart (1756–1791)

*Figure 15.8. Wolfgang Amadeus Mozart, in an unfinished portrait from about 1789 by his brother in-law Joseph Lange.*

Mozart composed prolifically from the age of six until his premature death at thirty-five. A master of every medium, he is widely considered one of the greatest musicians of the Western classical tradition. His mature works, mainstays of the repertory, epitomize the Classical style.

Mozart was born in Salzburg, an independent Austrian city ruled by a despotic archbishop. His father, Leopold, was a violinist and composer in the archbishop's service. When Wolfgang and his older sister Nannerl showed remarkable musical talent at an early age, Leopold trained them and took them throughout Europe, exhibiting their skills as child prodigies. Wolfgang was a phenomenon: by the age of three, he had developed perfect pitch; at five, he was an accomplished harpsichord player; at six, he was composing; at seven, he could read at sight, harmonize melodies on first hearing, and improvise variations on any tune handed to him. Although they were arduous, these trips exposed Mozart to an enormous range of musical styles. He also composed at a stupendous rate, turning out thirty-four symphonies, sixteen quartets, five operas, and over one hundred other works before his eighteenth birthday. At age sixteen, he was appointed third concertmaster in Salzburg, where his duties included composing church music.

Much more interested in opera and instrumental music, Mozart left the archbishop's service in 1781, over his father's objections, and settled in Vienna, convinced that he could make a living as a freelance musician. Indeed, he quickly became the darling of the Viennese public, establishing himself as a pianist and scoring a success with his singspiel *Die Entführung aus dem Serail*. With Leopold's grudging consent, he married Constanze Weber, a singer, in the summer of 1782. Their marriage was happy and affectionate. Four children died in infancy, but two sons lived into adulthood, the younger becoming a composer.

Composing at a prodigious pace, teaching private students, performing in public and private concerts, and selling his works to publishers brought Mozart a good income and impressed his father. At a quartet party in Mozart's home, Haydn told Leopold, "Before God and as an honest man I tell you that your son is the greatest composer known to me. . . . He has taste and, what is more, the most profound knowledge of composition." By the late 1780s, there were money troubles, apparently due more to rising family expenses than to declining income. Mozart's death at the prime of his life prompted a variety of false rumors, including that he was poisoned, but it seems to have resulted from a sudden high fever. Unprepared for such an unexpected end, Constanze hastily arranged for Mozart to be buried in a pauper's grave, the actual position of which remains unknown to this day.

Mozart's almost six hundred compositions are listed and numbered chronologically in a thematic catalogue begun by the composer himself (see Figure 15.14), then compiled by Ludwig von Köchel in 1862, whose "K" numbers are universally used to identify Mozart's compositions.

**Major works:** *Die Entführung aus dem Serail, Le nozze di Figaro, Don Giovanni, Così fan tutte, Die Zauberflöte*, 15 other operas and singspiels, 17 Masses, Requiem, 55 symphonies, 23 piano concertos, 15 other concertos, 26 string quartets, 19 piano sonatas, numerous songs, arias, serenades, divertimenti, and dances. (The traditional numbering of some Mozart works, such as symphonies 1 through 41 and Piano Concertos 1 through 27, assigned by publishers, exclude some works and include some dubious others.)

# Wolfgang Amadeus Mozart
# (1756–1791)

Wolfgang Amadeus Mozart was born in Salzburg, then a Bavarian city with a long musical tradition. A lively provincial center of the arts, it was the seat of an archbishop and one of the numerous quasi-independent political units within what was to become the German Empire. Mozart's father, Leopold, served in the archbishop's chapel and eventually became its assistant director. From this position, he was ideally placed to provide his two children, Wolfgang and his older sister, Marianne, or Nannerl, with a thorough musical education.

During his apprentice years until around 1773, Mozart was completely under the tutelage of his father in practical affairs and in most musical matters as well (see the biography and Figure 15.8). Leopold was a composer of some ability and reputation, and the author of a celebrated treatise on violin playing. Thanks to his father's excellent teaching and to his own performing in dozens of cities during his formative years, as shown in Figure 15.9, young Mozart was exposed to every kind of music written or heard in contemporary western Europe. In Paris, he became interested in the keyboard works of Johann Schobert (ca. 1735–1767). In London, he met J. C. Bach, whose music had a lasting influence on him. In Italy, he assimilated the traditions of opera seria, was influenced by Sammartini and other Italian symphonists, and studied counterpoint with Padre Giovanni Battista Martini. And in Vienna, he came into contact with Haydn's music, which became increasingly important in the young composer's creative life. He absorbed it all with uncanny aptitude, imitating others' works while improving on them. The ideas that influenced him not only echoed in his youthful compositions but also continued to grow in his mind, sometimes bearing fruit many years later. In this way, his work became a synthesis of national styles, a mirror that reflected the music of an entire age, all illuminated by his own genius.

*Mozart's teachers*

## Mozart's Salzburg Years

After touring Europe as a child prodigy with his father, Mozart lived chiefly in Salzburg, complaining frequently about the narrow provincial life and the lack of opportunities. In an effort to improve his situation, he undertook another journey in September 1777, this time with his mother, to Munich, Augsburg, Mannheim, and Paris. But all his hopes for a good position in Germany or France came to nothing. And, sadly, his mother took ill in Paris and died there in July 1778. He returned to Salzburg early the following year, more disconsolate and restless than ever. Nevertheless, he was steadily growing in stature as a composer and received a commission to compose an opera seria for Munich. He spent months there composing and supervising the production of *Idomeneo* (1781). The music for *Idomeneo* is dramatic and pictorial; in its numerous accompanied recitatives, its conspicuous use of the chorus, and its inclusion of the spectacular, the opera reveals the influence of Gluck and the French *tragédie lyrique*.

*Idomeneo*

Among the other important works of this period are thirteen piano sonatas and several sets of variations for piano, including those on the French air *Ah, vous dirais-je maman*, K. 265 (300e), better known as *Twinkle, twinkle, little star.* The variations were probably intended for pupils, but the sonatas were part of

*Piano sonatas*

Mozart's concert repertory. Before that time, he had improvised such pieces as needed, so that few solo piano compositions from the early years have survived.

The sonatas K. 279 through K. 284 were undoubtedly meant to be published together: there is one in each of the major tonalities in the circle of fifths from D down to E♭; and the six works show a wide variety of form and content. Köchel 310 (300d), Mozart's first minor-key sonata, betrays the influence of Schobert (see above) in its full chordal accompaniments and stringlike tremolos (Example 15.7).

*Figure 15.9. The cities that were most important in Mozart's career are indicated in red. But his travels, particularly during his younger years, include all those in black as well.*

*Example 15.7: Wolfgang Amadeus Mozart, Piano Sonata K. 310 (300d), Allegro maestoso*

Sonata K. 331 (300i) is notable among the sonatas from the early 1780s for its first movement, which is in variation form, and for its finale. The latter, marked "Rondo alla turca," imitates the Janissary music of the Turkish military bands—then popular in Vienna—with their cymbals and triangles and exaggerated first beats. (Mozart also included "Turkish music" in his comic singspiel *Die Entführung aus dem Serail*, The Abduction from the Harem; see page 367.)

Mozart also composed serenades and divertimenti in the 1770s and early 1780s for garden parties or actual outdoor performances, for weddings and birthdays, and for concerts at the homes of friends and patrons. The most familiar of Mozart's serenades is *Eine kleine Nachtmusik* (A Little Night Music, K. 525; 1787), a work in four movements for string quintet but now usually played by a small string ensemble. Among the most notable compositions of Mozart's Salzburg period are the Violin Concertos K. 216, 218, and 219, in G, D, and A, respectively (all 1775), and the Piano Concerto in E♭ Major, K. 271 (1777), with its romantic slow movement in C minor. The three violin concertos are the last of Mozart's compositions in this genre. Piano Concerto K. 271, however, is but the first of a long series of great works that he wrote in hopes of captivating the Viennese public.

Other instrumental music

## Mozart's Vienna Years

By the middle of the eighteenth century, the largest and fastest-growing German-speaking city was Vienna (see "Cosmopolitan Vienna," page 360). When Mozart moved there in 1781, he convinced his father that, by taking a few pupils and playing in concerts, he could earn vastly more money than as a court musician in his hometown. He was right in thinking that no other city could give him so many opportunities; in the next five years, Mozart appeared as a soloist in at least seventy-one concerts, both private and public, which took place in the palaces of the nobility as well as in the city's theaters, restaurants, and public gardens. Leopold Mozart wrote approvingly to his daughter after hearing Mozart perform one of his own piano concertos in public: "A great many members of the aristocracy were present. Each person pays a gold sovereign or three ducats for these concerts. . . . Your brother . . . pays only half a gold sovereign each time he uses the hall."

Indeed, his first years in the imperial capital went well. His singspiel *Die Entführung aus dem Serail* (The Abduction from the Harem, 1782), was performed repeatedly. He had all the distinguished pupils he

*Figure 15.10. Three Mozarts making music: Leopold, violin; Amadeus, age seven, piano; and Marianne (Nannerl), age eleven, singing from a score. Engraving by Jean-Baptiste Delafosse, based on a watercolor of about 1764 by Louis Carrogis de Carmontelle. Musée Condé, Chantilly.*

During the eighteenth century, public concerts and concert series arose in many cities alongside the private concerts and academies that had long been presented by wealthy individual patrons and clubs. Private concerts were by invitation only, and the aristocratic patrons who sponsored them normally assumed all the costs. Public concerts, by contrast, were usually moneymaking ventures for which tickets were sold. Tickets were offered for an individual event or by subscription to a series, and anyone who could pay the price could attend. But ticket prices were not affordable for most people, so the audience for public concerts came mostly from the upper middle and wealthy leisure classes.

Concert halls and concert societies flourished in London starting in 1672 and especially after 1720. At pleasure gardens such as Vauxhall, shown in Figure 15.11, the public paid an entrance fee to enjoy music and other entertainment outdoors. A remarkable institution for the day was the Academy of Ancient Music, devoted to the performance of sixteenth- and seventeenth-century sacred music, madrigals, and other music of earlier times; its founding in 1726 inaugurated concerts of music from the past, which became increasingly popular over the next two centuries. By the second half of the eighteenth century, musical life in London centered around public concerts, including the annual subscription series put on from 1765 to 1781 by Johann Christian Bach and Carl Friedrich Abel.

Paris had a very rich concert life throughout the eighteenth century. As in England, occasional outdoor celebrations drew a wider public, but it was not until after the French Revolution that entertainment for the masses developed in any significant way. In 1725, the composer and oboist Anne Danican Philidor founded the Concert spirituel series, which lasted until 1790 and became the century's most famous concert institution. The repertoire encompassed new music from France and other nations, with performers from across the Continent. The presentation of sonatas and concertos by Vivaldi and other Italians fostered a growing taste for Italian music in France, and from mid-century on, performances of symphonies by German and Austrian composers spurred French composers to cultivate the genre. Haydn's symphonies were heard beginning in 1777, and the following year Mozart's Symphony No. 31, K. 297 (300a), received its premiere at the Concert spirituel and is known for this reason as his *Paris* Symphony. Mozart's account of the event in a letter to his father reveals something of the audience's reaction and how much it meant to him:

> I had heard that final Allegros, here, must begin . . . [with] all the instruments playing together, mostly in unison. I began mine with nothing but the first and second violins playing softly for eight bars—then there is a sudden *forte*. Conse-

*Figure 15.11. Concert at Vauxhall Pleasure Gardens, where for a fee the public could enjoy music and other entertainment outdoors. Here, Mrs. Weischel sings from the "Moorish-Gothick" temple, accompanied by the orchestra behind her, while the writer Samuel Johnson and his companions eat in the supper box below. Watercolor, ca. 1784, by Thomas Rowlandson. Print Collection, New York Public Library.*

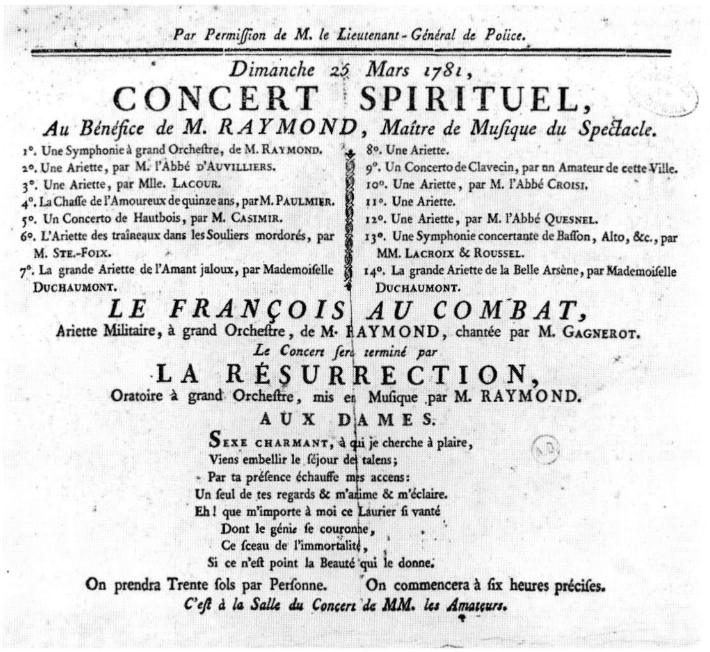

*Par Permiſſion de M. le Lieutenant-Général de Police.*

*Dimanche 25 Mars 1781,*

**CONCERT SPIRITUEL,**

*Au Bénéfice de M. RAYMOND, Maître de Muſique du Spectacle.*

1°. Une Symphonie à grand Orcheſtre, de M. RAYMOND.
2°. Une Ariette, par M. l'Abbé D'AUVILLIERS.
3°. Une Ariette, par Mlle. LACOUR.
4°. La Chaſſe de l'Amoureux de quinze ans, par M. PAULMIER.
5°. Un Concerto de Hautbois, par M. CASIMIR.
6°. L'Ariette des traîneaux dans les Souliers mordorés, par M. STE.-FOIX.
7°. La grande Ariette de l'Amant jaloux, par Mademoiſelle DUCHAUMONT.
8°. Une Ariette.
9°. Un Concerto de Clavecin, par un Amateur de cette Ville.
10°. Une Ariette, par M. l'Abbé CROISI.
11°. Une Ariette.
12°. Une Ariette, par M. l'Abbé QUESNEL.
13°. Une Symphonie concertante de Baſſon, Alto, &c., par MM. LACROIX & ROUSSEL.
14°. La grande Ariette de la Belle Arsène, par Mademoiſelle DUCHAUMONT.

***LE FRANÇOIS AU COMBAT,***

Ariette Militaire, à grand Orcheſtre, de M. RAYMOND, chantée par M. GAGNEROT.

*Le Concert ſera terminé par*

**LA RÉSURRECTION,**

Oratoire à grand Orcheſtre, mis en Muſique par M. RAYMOND.

AUX DAMES.

SEXE CHARMANT, à qui je cherche à plaire,
Viens embellir le ſéjour des talens;
Par ta préſence échauffe mes accens:
Un ſeul de tes regards & m'anime & m'éclaire.
Eh! que m'importe à moi ce Laurier ſi vanté
Dont le génie ſe couronne,
Ce ſceau de l'immortalité,
Si ce n'eſt point la Beauté qui le donne.

On prendra Trente ſols par Perſonne. On commencera à ſix heures préciſes.

*C'eſt à la Salle du Concert de MM. les Amateurs.*

*Figure 15.12. Poster advertising a Concert spirituel to be given on March 25, 1781.*

quently, the listeners (just as I had anticipated) all went "Sh!" in the soft passage—then came the sudden *forte*—and no sooner did they hear the *forte* than they all clapped their hands. I was so glad, that, the minute the Symphony was finished, I went to the Palais Royal, ordered a good ice cream, said my Rosary as I had vowed to do, and went home.

The movement toward public concerts spread to German lands as well. Approximately a decade after Bach's death, J. A. Hiller began a concert series in Leipzig, which continued after 1781 in the new concert hall at the Gewandhaus (Clothiers' Exchange); the Gewandhaus Orchestra still exists and has become one of the most famous orchestras in the world. Similar concert organizations were founded in Vienna (1771) and in Berlin (1790).

Public concerts were advertised by word of mouth and through handbills, posters, notices in newspapers, and other printed media. Figure 15.12 shows a poster for a 1781 concert by the Concert spirituel in Paris, to begin "precisely at six o'clock." To judge from the announced program, it lasted about three hours, which was typical at the time. It included a variety of vocal and instrumental genres, rather than being made up entirely of a single genre such as orchestral works, piano music, or songs, as are today's concerts. Only one composer is named, a Mr. Raymond, who directed the concert and received the profits. In some cases, the name given for a piece was that of the featured performer, which was of greater concern to the public than the composer. Listed ninth is "A Harpsichord Concerto, [performed] by an Amateur of this City." The unnamed amateur who played the keyboard was probably a woman and, therefore, not yet acceptable as a professional instrumentalist.

An eighteenth-century concert was a social occasion as well as an opportunity to hear music. Audience members could stroll around and converse, paying attention only to those pieces that interested them; the silent, motionless audience was an invention of the nineteenth century. The presence of women in the right social class was essential for making the event a social success, so Raymond made sure they felt welcome by including a poem at the bottom of the poster:

*TO THE LADIES,*
*Charming sex, whom I seek to please,*
*Come embellish the abode of our talents;*
*By your presence warm up my accents:*
*Just one of your glances enlivens and enlightens me.*
*Oh, what does it matter to me, this much-vaunted Laurel*
*With which genius is crowned,*
*This seal of immortality,*
*If it is not Beauty who bestows it.*

Eighteenth-century Vienna is a striking example of a cosmopolitan cultural center where conditions seem to have been ideal for music. Geographically, Vienna stood at the crossroads of four musical nations—Germany, Bohemia (now the Czech Republic), Hungary, and Italy—and, being the capital of the powerful Hapsburg Empire, it was also central in political terms. Between 1745 and 1765, the emperor was a Frenchman, Francis Stephen of Lorraine. The imperial court poet was the Italian Metastasio. A German, Johann Adolf Hasse, composed operas in Italian set to Metastasio's librettos, sometimes for state occasions. The manager of the court theaters was Count Giacomo Durazzo, a diplomat from Italy. An imported French company mounted a regular season of French comic operas. French-style ballets were also popular, though the music tended to be by local composers, among them Gluck, whose partner in operatic reform was Raniero de Calzabigi, another Italian. The most influential musician in Vienna during the last quarter of the century was Antonio Salieri (1750–1825), who had been brought there from Venice at the age of fifteen. He eventually succeeded Florian Gassmann as imperial court composer and conductor of Italian opera, a post he held for thirty-six years. This mix of cultures underlay the phenomenon that has been called, not altogether appropriately, the "Viennese" Classical style.

Its most notable representatives were not actually Viennese but came there from other, smaller centers: Haydn from Rohrau, a village near Eisenstadt on the Hungarian border; Mozart from Salzburg, a town with a distinct Italian flavor, it being a hundred miles to the west and that much closer to the Italian peninsula; and Beethoven (see Chapter 16) from Bonn, in north central Germany, not far from where the Bach family had originated.

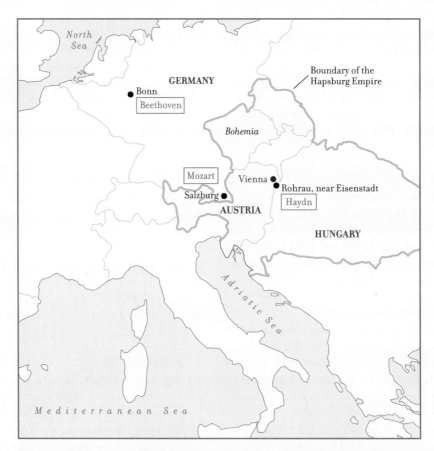

*Figure 15.13. Vienna—the capital of Austria and geographically at the crossroads of Germany, Bohemia, Hungary, and Italy—was the magnet that drew Haydn, Mozart, and Beethoven.*

was willing to take, he was idolized by the Viennese public both as pianist and composer, and he led the bustling life of a successful freelance musician. But after four or five seasons, the fickle public deserted him, his pupils dropped in number, commissions were few, family expenses mounted, and his health declined. Worst of all, no permanent position with a steady income came his way except for an appointment in 1787 as chamber-music composer to the emperor at less than half the salary that Gluck, his predecessor, had received. Perhaps because he had a poor head for business, he was chronically short of money. The most pathetic pages in Mozart's correspondence are the begging letters written between 1788 and 1791 to a merchant friend and brother Freemason, who always responded generously.

Most of the works that immortalized Mozart's name he composed in Vienna between the ages of twenty-five and thirty-five, when the promise of his childhood and early youth came to fulfillment. In every kind of composition, he achieved a seemingly perfect synthesis of form and content, of the galant and learned styles, of polished charm and emotional depth. The principal influences on Mozart during these last ten years of his life came from his continuing study of the works of Haydn and his discovery of those of J. S. Bach and Handel. He was introduced to Bach's music by Baron Gottfried van Swieten, who during his years as Austrian ambassador to Berlin (1771–1778) had become an enthusiast for the music of north German composers. (He later wrote the librettos of Haydn's last two oratorios.) In weekly reading sessions at van Swieten's home during 1782, Mozart became acquainted with Bach's *Art of Fugue, Well-Tempered Keyboard,* and other works. Bach's influence was deep and lasting, and may be seen in the increased contrapuntal texture of Mozart's later works (for example, his last piano sonata, K. 576). It was probably also through van Swieten that Mozart became interested in Handel, whose *Messiah* Mozart reorchestrated in 1788–1790.

Mozart's style at the beginning of his Vienna period is exemplified by the first movement of the Sonata in F Major, K. 332 (NAWM 105), one of three sonatas composed in 1781–1783 and published as a set in 1784 (K. 330–332). Especially characteristic of Mozart are his themes and his combination of heterogeneous styles. (See the full discussion in NAWM.)

Among the other solo-piano compositions of the Vienna period, the most important are the Fantasia and Sonata in C Minor (K. 475 and 457). The fantasia foreshadows Schubert's piano sonatas in its melodies and modulations, while the sonata would serve as the model for Beethoven's *Sonate pathétique.*

In 1785, Mozart published six string quartets dedicated to Joseph Haydn as a token of his gratitude for all that he had learned from the older composer. These quartets (K. 387, 421, 428, 458, 464, and 465) were, as Mozart said in his dedicatory letter, "the fruit of a long and laborious effort"; indeed, the manuscripts show what for Mozart was an unusually large number of corrections and revisions. As we have seen, Haydn's Op. 33 quartets (1781) had fully established the technique of pervasive thematic development with near equality of the four instruments.

In Mozart's *Haydn* Quartets, although the themes remain characteristically Mozartean in their Italianate tunefulness, they are subjected to much more intensive motivic development than before. A greater emphasis on detail and a faster rate of change in texture and dynamics also betray Haydn's influence. Thus, Mozart shows his capacity to absorb the essence of Haydn's achievement without becoming a mere imitator.

The String Quartet in D minor (K. 421) stands out because of its tragic mood. The old descending tetrachord of the Baroque lament appears in the bass under the opening theme; a few measures later, although the piece has barely begun,

Baron van Swieten

Solo piano works

CD 7/79

The *Haydn* Quartets

the first violin reaches for the highest note heard in the entire movement (Example 15.8). When, following the contrasting secondary and closing groups in F major, the theme returns in E♭ major after the double bar, the same descending bass line immediately darkens the optimistic reawakening.

*Example 15.8: Wolfgang Amadeus Mozart, String Quartet K. 421, Allegro moderato*

**Quintets**

For all the excellence of his quartets, Mozart's quintets for two violins, two violas, and cello have been praised in even stronger terms. The String Quintets in C Major (K. 515) and in G Minor (K. 516), composed in the spring of 1787, are comparable to the last two symphonies in the same keys. Another masterpiece, the Clarinet Quintet in A Major (K. 581), was composed at about the same time as the opera buffa *Così fan tutte* and captures some of its comic spirit.

## Symphonies

Like Haydn, Mozart approached the symphony in his maturity with great seriousness. He wrote only six in the last ten years of his life—having earlier produced nearly sixty—and devoted much time and thought to their composition.[2] The symphonies written before 1782 served most often as concert or theatrical

2. In the nineteenth century, the publisher Breitkopf & Härtel numbered forty-one Mozart symphonies. This count, which is still in occasional use, omits some two dozen early symphonic works while including three that are not by Mozart: "No. 2," by Leopold Mozart; "No. 3," by Carl Friedrich Abel; and "No. 37," a symphony by Michael Haydn for which Mozart supplied an introduction.

"curtain raisers"; those composed after he settled in Vienna constituted the main feature on concert programs or at least shared billing with concertos and arias. The *Haffner* Symphony, K. 385, written in 1782 for the elevation to nobility of Mozart's childhood friend Sigmund Haffner, and the *Linz* Symphony, K. 425, written in 1783 for a performance in that city, typify the late symphonies in their ambitious dimensions, greater demands on performers (particularly wind players), harmonic and contrapuntal complexity and chromaticism, and final movements that are climactic rather than light. These symphonies are in every way as artful as the *London* symphonies of Haydn, and some may indeed have served as models for the older composer. The others of this group—recognized as his greatest—are the *Prague* Symphony in D Major (K. 504) and the Symphonies in E♭ Major (K. 543), G Minor (K. 550), and C Major (K. 551, named the *Jupiter* by an English publisher). The last three were composed within a six-week period during the summer of 1788.

Each of the six symphonies is a masterpiece with its own special character, in some cases influenced by other music that Mozart was working on at the time. The opening gesture of each leaves an indelible impression. Both the *Haffner*

*Example 15.9: Wolfgang Amadeus Mozart, Haffner Symphony, K. 385, Allegro con spirito*

*Wolfgang Amadeus Mozart, Jupiter Symphony, K. 551, Allegro vivace*

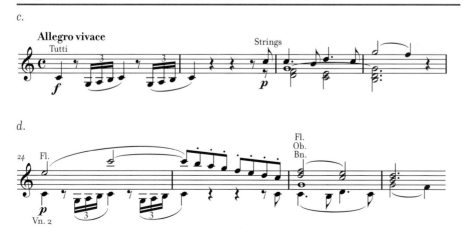

and the *Jupiter* begin with loud, forceful unison statements followed by delicate ensemble responses (Example 15.9a, c). In both works, the disparate elements of the theme are immediately wedded through counterpoint (Example 15.9b, d).

Most unusual is the beginning of the Symphony in G Minor, which opens *piano*, rare in symphonies before this one, with a soft, undulating melody suffused with sighing gestures. Some of Mozart's symphonies are imbued with the spirit of his operas—for example, the comical element in the otherwise heroic *Jupiter* Symphony. For the closing section of the first movement, Mozart borrowed the melody of a comic aria he had written (Example 15.10). The repeated cadences in the symphony that follow this quotation are also from the world of comic opera.

*Example 15.10: Wolfgang Amadeus Mozart,* Un bacio di mano, *K. 541 (comic aria)*

*You are a simpleton, my dear Pompeo,/You'd better go study the ways of the world.*

**Introductions**

The slow introductions to Symphonies K. 425, 504, and 543 are animated by the energy of the French overture, with its majestic double-dotted rhythms, intense harmony, and anacrusis figures. Rather than intimating subtly what is to come, as Haydn sometimes did, Mozart created suspense, tantalizingly wandering away from the key and making its return an important event.

**Finales**

As in Haydn's late symphonies, the finales do more than send an audience away in a cheerful frame of mind. They balance the serious and important opening movement with a highly crafted counterweight, fashioned with wit and humor. In the Allegro assai of the G-Minor Symphony, the acrobatic transformation of the main theme at once startles and pokes fun, with its wild leaps and pregnant silences (Example 15.11). There is also a touch of bravura in the finale of the *Jupiter* Symphony, which combines its four-note fugue subject in counterpoint with five other motives: a countersubject, two ideas from the transition, and both motives from the second subject of the sonata form. The coda weaves all these together in an unsurpassed triumph of Ars combinatoria, the art of combination and permutation derived from mathematics that eighteenth-century music theorists taught as a means of achieving melodic variety in composition (see Example 15.12 in which P, S, and T stand, respectively, for primary theme, secondary theme, and transitional motives).

*Example 15.11: Wolfgang Amadeus Mozart, Symphony in G Minor, K. 550, Allegro assai*

*Example 15.12: Wolfgang Amadeus Mozart, Jupiter Symphony, K. 551, Allegro molto*

## Piano Concertos

Seventeen concertos for piano occupy a central place in Mozart's output during the Vienna years. He wrote them primarily as vehicles for his own concerts, and we can gauge the rise and fall of his popularity in Vienna by the number he composed each year: three in 1782–1783, four in each of the next two seasons, three again in 1785–1786, and only one for each of the next two seasons; after that no more until the last year of his life, when he wrote K. 595 to play at a local concert. The first three Vienna concertos—K. 414, 413, and 415—as Mozart wrote to his father,

> strike a happy medium between what is too easy and too difficult . . . very brilliant, pleasing to the ear, and natural, without being vapid. There are passages here and there from which connoisseurs alone can derive satisfaction; but these passages are written in such a way that the less learned cannot fail to be pleased, though without knowing why.[3]

It is clear from this passage that Mozart was hoping to seduce his Viennese audiences by offering them a combination of art and entertainment, thereby pleas-

---

3. Wolfgang Amadeus Mozart, letter to Leopold Mozart, Dec. 23, 1782, trans. in Emily Anderson, ed., *The Letters of Mozart and His Family* (New York: Norton, 1989), p. 1242.

*Figure 15.14. Page from the catalogue of his own works, which Mozart began in 1784, listing four of his piano concertos and a piano quintet. The list became the basis of the Köchel catalogue by which we number and classify Mozart's works today. British Library, London.*

ing a wide range of listeners. The remaining concertos include works in a great variety of moods, ranging from K. 488 in A Major, which is in a comparatively light vein (see NAWM 106), to K. 491 in C minor, one of Mozart's great tragic creations.

**Concerto form**

CD 8/6   CD 4/11
         CD 7/36

Mozart's concertos follow the traditional three-movement pattern in the sequence fast-slow-fast. The first movement blends elements of ritornello and sonata form, as do the concertos of J. C. Bach, Mozart's primary model for these keyboard works. Comparing the first movement of Mozart's Piano Concerto in A Major, K. 488 (NAWM 106), composed in 1786, to the J. C. Bach concerto (NAWM 102) outlined on page 337, we see the same general features:

- The solo sections resemble the exposition, development, and recapitulation of a sonata form, with the soloist accompanied by, and sometimes in dialogue with, the orchestra.
- The opening orchestral ritornello (the "orchestral exposition") introduces the movement's primary theme, transitional material, secondary theme, and closing theme, but remains in the tonic.
- The ritornello returns, greatly abbreviated, to mark the end of the first solo and the end of the movement.

These features accord well with the form of a concerto's first Allegro, as described by the contemporary theorist Heinrich Christoph Koch: "three main periods performed by the soloist, which are enclosed by four subsidiary periods performed by the orchestra as ritornellos."[4] Furthermore, like his predecessors, Mozart typically punctuates the main themes with passages for full orchestra (tutti) that function as transitions or closing passages (TT and KT in the diagram below); these elements also reappear, like partial or mini-ritornellos, in various keys throughout the movement. A diagram of the entire opening ritornello ("orchestral exposition") and first solo section ("solo exposition") of Mozart's K. 488 is shown in Figure 15.15. Notice that the modulation to the new

4. Heinrich Christoph Koch, *Introductory Essay on Composition . . .*, trans. Nancy Kovaleff Baker (New Haven: Yale University Press, 1983), p. 210.

| Section: | Exposition | | | | | | | | |
|---|---|---|---|---|---|---|---|---|---|
| Tonal center: | Tonic | | | | Dominant | | | | |
| Instruments: | Orchestra | | | | Solo with Orchestra | | | | |
| Themes: | P | T T | S | KT | P | T T | S | K | T T |
| Measure: | 1 | 18 | 30 | 46 | 67 | 82 | 98 | 114 | 137 |

In this diagram, P = primary group; S = secondary group; KT = closing tutti; TT = transitional tutti; K = closing group.

*Figure 15.15. The exposition (sometimes called a "double exposition") of the first movement of Mozart's Piano Concerto in A Major, K. 488.*

key is not accomplished until the solo section gets under way. Therefore, in the opening orchestral ritornello, the passage (TT at measure 18) between the first and second themes (P and S) merely serves as a connection between themes rather than as a real transition between keys (which is how it functions at measure 82).

Like Bach, Mozart includes a cadenza for the soloist, but his cadenza usually interrupts the final ritornello, as it does here. Both composers introduce new material at the beginning of the development, which becomes the focus of that section. The differences are in the details that make each first movement unique. The resulting form follows convention in most respects yet may surprise the listener with several individual features. This movement by Mozart is suffused with his characteristic wealth of melodic invention, diversity of figuration, and elegance.

The second movement of a Mozart concerto resembles a lyrical aria. It is in the subdominant of the principal key or, less often, in the dominant or relative minor. Its form may vary but is most often a sonata form without development, a set of variations, or a rondo. The finale is typically a rondo or sonata-rondo on themes with a popular character. These are treated in scintillating virtuoso style with opportunities for one or more cadenzas.

That Mozart put substance before fireworks may be seen in the cadenzas that he sketched or fully notated for his concertos. The cadenza had developed from the trills and runs that singers inserted, particularly before the return of the opening section in the da capo aria. Mozart's early cadenzas similarly consisted of flourishes without thematic links to the movement, but after the 1780s they served to balance the longer modulatory or development sections. These cadenzas—almost second development sections—cast new light on familiar material in daring flights of technical wizardry.

Although the concertos were showpieces intended to dazzle an audience, Mozart never allowed display to gain the upper hand. He always maintained a healthy balance of musical interest between the orchestral and solo portions, and his infallible ear regulated the myriad combinations of colors and textures that he drew from the interplay between the piano and orchestral instruments, especially the winds. Moreover, the goal of composing for an immediate public response did not keep him from expressing the most profound musical ideas.

*Cadenzas*

## Operas

Opera was still the most prestigious of the musical genres, and Mozart eagerly sought opportunities to compose for the stage. Once in Vienna, his fame was established by *Die Entführung aus dem Serail* (1782), with which he brought German singspiel into the realm of great art without altering its established features. This work tells a romantic-comic story of adventure and rescue, and is set in a Turkish harem. Such "oriental" settings and plots were popular, in part

*Die Entführung aus dem Serail*

*Figure 15.16. Lorenzo Da Ponte, in a portrait by an unknown American artist. Best known as the librettist of Mozart's* Marriage of Figaro, Don Giovanni, *and* Così fan tutte, *Da Ponte went to London in the 1790s and to America in 1805, where he was at various times a grocer, private teacher, bookdealer, translator, and eventually professor of Italian at Columbia University. He became an American citizen and sought to bring Italian culture to his new nation.*

because they provided a taste of the exotic while making the Turks, long-standing enemies of Austria-Hungary, seem less threatening. Depicting the Turkish characters as humane and fully rounded, Mozart aimed to capture their temperaments and feelings in his music (see "Mozart's Depiction of Character and Mood," page 369).

**Da Ponte operas**    Mozart's next operas were three Italian comic operas: *Le nozze di Figaro* (The Marriage of Figaro, 1786), *Don Giovanni* (Don Juan, 1787), and *Così fan tutte* (All Women Are Like That, 1790). All were set to librettos by Lorenzo Da Ponte (1749–1838), poet for the imperial court theater who later came to America and became a professor of Italian in New York (see Figure 15.16). Although *Fi-*

**Le nozze di Figaro**    *garo* followed the conventions of opera buffa (see Chapter 14), Da Ponte's libretto raised it to a higher level, giving greater depth to the characters, intensifying the social tensions between classes, and introducing moral issues. Mozart's psychological penetration and his genius for musical characterization similarly lent a greater seriousness to the genre. Character portrayal occurs not only in solo arias, but especially in duets, trios, and larger ensembles. The ensemble finales allow these characters to clash, combining realism with ongoing dramatic action and superbly unified musical form. Mozart's orchestration—

*Figure 15.17. Saint Michael's Square in Vienna. In the foreground is the Burgtheater, where Mozart performed several of his piano concertos in the mid-1780s and where the premieres of* The Marriage of Figaro *and* Così fan tutte *took place.*

particularly his use of winds—played an important role in defining the characters and situations.

*Figaro* enjoyed only moderate success in Vienna, but its enthusiastic reception in Prague led to the commission for *Don Giovanni*, which was performed there the following year. The medieval legend of Don Juan, on which the plot is based, had been treated often in literature and music since the early seventeenth century. But Mozart, for the first time in opera, took the character of Don Juan seriously—not as an incongruous mixture of farcical figure and horrible blasphemer, but as a romantic hero, a rebel against authority, a scorner of common morality, and a supreme individualist, bold and unrepentant to the last (see In Context: "Mozart and His Father," page 370). It was Mozart's music rather than Da Ponte's libretto that raised the Don to this stature, while parading his gluttony and selfishness. The Romantic musical imagination of the nineteenth century relished the demonic quality of the opening measures of the overture, a quality intensified by the sound of the trombones in the cemetery scene and accompanying the apparition of the statue in the finale. Some of the other characters, even though they are subtly ridiculed, must also be taken seriously: the tragic Donna Elvira, jilted by the Don but still attempting to reform him, and Leporello, more than a commedia dell'arte servant-buffoon, revealing deep sensitivity and intuition.

*Don Giovanni*

That *Don Giovanni* incorporates opera-seria characters, situations, and styles into the comic opera, effectively merging the two genres, is illustrated by the very first scene (NAWM 107). Alone on stage and waiting for his master to emerge from a nocturnal rendezvous, Leporello complains of his treatment by Don Giovanni in an opera buffa–style aria, with a touch of aristocratic horn

CD 8/24    CD 4/29

**VIGNETTE**    Mozart's Depiction of Character and Mood

*In his operas, Mozart portrays the personalities of the characters and conveys their feelings so perfectly through his music that listeners can immediately understand them—sometimes better than the characters understand their own predicament. In a letter to his father, written while composing* Die Entführung aus dem Serail, *Mozart described how he made the music of two arias fit the characters, the situation, and the singers who would premiere the roles.*

Osmin's rage will be rendered comical by the use of Turkish music. In composing the aria, I made [the singer] Fischer's beautiful deep tones really glisten. . . . The passage *Therefore, by the beard of the Prophet*, etc., is, to be sure, in the same tempo, but with quick notes—and as his anger increases more and more, the Allegro assai [a faster tempo]—which comes just when one thinks the aria is over—will produce an excellent Effect because it is in a different tempo and in a different key. A person who gets into such a violent rage transgresses every order, moderation, and limit; he no longer knows himself, in the same way the Music must no longer know it-self. But because passions, violent or not, must never be expressed to the point of disgust, and Music must never offend the ear, even in most horrendous situations, but must always be pleasing, in other words always remain Music, I have not chosen a key foreign to F, the key of the aria, but one that is friendly to it, not however its nearest relative in D minor, but the more remote A minor. Now about Bellmont's aria in A Major. "Oh how anxious, oh how passionate!" Do you know how I expressed it?—even expressing the loving, throbbing heart? With two violins playing in octaves. This is the favorite aria of everyone who has heard it—it's mine too. And it was written entirely for Adamberger's voice. One can see the trembling—faltering—one can see his heaving breast—which is expressed by a crescendo—one can hear the whispering and the sighing—which is expressed by the first violins with mutes and one flute playing in unison.

Wolfgang Amadeus Mozart, letter to Leopold Mozart, Sept. 26, 1781, in Robert Spaethling, ed. and trans., *Mozart's Letters, Mozart's Life* (New York: Norton, 2000), p. 286. Punctuation and spelling have been modernized.

*Figure 15.18.  The Mozart family, painted by J. N. della Croce in the winter of 1780–1781. Mozart's mother is represented by her portrait hanging on the wall. She had died in Paris a few years earlier (1778), while accompanying Mozart on his first trip without his father. Mozart Museum, Salzburg.*

The relationship between Leopold Mozart and his son was interesting and complex. Leopold recognized and respected the boy's genius; he worked very hard to further young Wolfgang's career, trying—vainly, as it turned out—to secure him a worthy permanent position. Leopold was his son's devoted mentor and friend who saved Wolfgang's every jotting for posterity and remained, by most accounts, free from selfish motives. Yet, as happens in most father-son relationships at some point, a strain developed between them—in this case, one that worsened over the years and (according to one of Mozart's biographers)[1] profoundly influenced the composer's emotional life and creativity.

As a child prodigy, Mozart seemed happy to please his parents. But difficulties began to appear when he reached adolescence and felt that his father was attempting to undermine his independence. After Mozart left Salzburg for Vienna and married Constanze Weber in 1782—a union that Leopold opposed—the rupture between them became permanent. Leopold rejected Wolfgang and Constanze's children, and the bitterness between father and son contributed to Mozart's estrange-

ment from his only sibling, the sister with whom he had been close as a child. When Leopold died in 1787, he was proud of Wolfgang's achievements as a composer but apparently still resentful and unforgiving about what he considered to be his son's irresponsible career choices and dissolute lifestyle. Mozart, in turn, after his father's death, fell into increasing financial and emotional difficulty and gradually succumbed to the depression and anxiety that plagued him during the years before his own untimely death at the age of thirty-five.

The year 1787 also saw the completion of Mozart's *Don Giovanni* (see page 369), which received its premiere five months after Leopold's funeral and may bear the marks of Mozart's tortured relationship with his father. There is no doubt that his music reinforces some troubling aspects of Da Ponte's libretto: on the one hand, we admire Don Giovanni for his grace, charm, and bravery; on the other hand, we deplore his depraved behavior toward women and his thoughtless murder of Donna Anna's father, the Commendatore, at the beginning of the opera. When the Commendatore's ghostly statue reappears in the finale to claim his revenge, we are torn between hoping that Don Giovanni repents his ways and saves himself, and wanting him to accept his fate and be punished. In the most powerful, terror-inspiring moments of the opera, Mozart's music makes us understand that through the Don's refusal to repent, he seals his own doom while freely choosing his fate. Could it be that in those moments Mozart was playing out his own family drama by accepting his father's poor appraisal of his character, blaming himself for not living up to his father's expectations, and, therefore, identifying with Don Giovanni's simultaneous resistance to authority and surrender to punishment?

1. Maynard Solomon, *Mozart: A Life* (New York: Harper-Collins, 1995).

calls when he confesses his desire to live like a gentleman rather than a servant. He is interrupted by a clamor as Don Giovanni and Donna Anna emerge from her house, where he has tried to seduce her and perhaps succeeded. In furious pursuit, she sings in dramatic opera-seria style, and the Don replies in kind, while Leporello comments on the situation in buffo style from his hiding place. Donna Anna's father, the Commendatore, rushes onto the stage and challenges Don Giovanni to fight. They do, and the Commendatore is mortally wounded—a shocking turn of events for a comedy. In a powerful trio, as the orchestra ticks away his last moments, the Commendatore pants out his dying words while the others comment, each in characteristic fashion. In the following recitative, master and servant instantly revert to the comic banter of opera buffa.

Throughout the opera, three different types of characters, each representing a distinct social class, interact: Donna Anna and other nobles, who emote in the elevated, dramatic tone of opera seria; Leporello and his peers, mostly lower-class, marked by the buffoonery of opera buffa (although they show both cleverness and wisdom); and Don Giovanni, who, as an opportunistic libertine, passes easily from one world to the other. All these levels come together in the finale of Act I, where Mozart masterfully coordinates three onstage dance bands playing simultaneously: an elegant minuet for the nobles, a lively contredanse for Don Giovanni, and a rustic waltz for Leporello.

*Così fan tutte* is an opera buffa in the best Italian tradition, with a brilliant libretto glorified by some of Mozart's most melodious music. It is also a very moving drama about human frailty, exploring the themes of temptation, betrayal, and reconciliation.

Mozart wrote *Die Zauberflöte* (The Magic Flute, 1791) in the last year of his life. Although outwardly a singspiel—with spoken dialogue instead of recitative and with some characters and scenes appropriate to popular comedy—its action is filled with symbolic meaning and its music is so rich and profound that it ranks as the first great German opera. The largely solemn mood of the score reflects the relationship between the opera and the teachings and ceremonies of Freemasonry. We know that Mozart valued his Masonic affiliation, not only from allusions in his letters but especially from the serious quality of the music he wrote for Masonic ceremonies in 1785 and for a Masonic cantata he composed in 1791 (K. 623), his last completed work. In *The Magic Flute*, Mozart interwove the threads of many eighteenth-century musical styles and traditions: the vocal opulence of Italian opera seria; the folk humor of the German singspiel; the solo aria; the buffo ensemble, which is given new musical meaning; a novel kind of accompanied recitative applicable to German words; solemn choral scenes; and even (in the duet of the two armed men in Act II) a revival of the Baroque chorale-prelude technique, with contrapuntal accompaniment. The reconciliation of older and newer styles is summed up in the delicious overture, which combines sonata form with fugue.

*Figure 15.19.  Don Giovanni about to meet his punishment at the hands of the Commendatore, or stone guest, whom the Don had boldly invited to dinner, in the final scene of* Don Giovanni. *This is from the title page of an early edition (1801). Breitkopf & Härtel, Leipzig.*

## Church Music

Requiem

Since Mozart's father worked as a musician for the archbishop of Salzburg and Mozart himself served there as concertmaster and organist, it was natural for Mozart to compose church music from an early age. However, with notable exceptions—principally the Requiem—his settings of sacred texts are not counted among his major works. The Requiem, K. 626, was Mozart's last work, and the circumstances of its anonymous commission in July 1791, under conditions of absolute secrecy, are bizarre. It seems that a Viennese nobleman wished to pass the work off as his own. But Mozart, unaware of this fact and being ill and depressed, superstitiously conceived the idea that he was writing his own Requiem. Left unfinished at his death, it was completed by his pupil and collaborator Franz Xaver Süssmayr (1766–1803), who added some instrumental parts to Mozart's draft and set the Sanctus, Benedictus, and Agnus Dei, in part repeating music that Mozart had composed for an earlier section.

---

**TIMELINE** The Late Eighteenth Century

| MUSICAL EVENTS | HISTORICAL EVENTS |
|---|---|
| Death of J. S. Bach **1750** | |
| Pergolesi, *La serva padrona* in Paris **1752** | |
| | **1760–1820** Reign of George III of England |
| Haydn hired by Prince Esterházy **1761** | |
| Gluck, *Orfeo ed Euridice* in Vienna **1762** | |
| Mozart tours as child prodigy **1762–1773** | **1765–1780** Maria Theresa and Joseph II rule Austria |
| Mozart concertmaster at Salzburg **1772** | |
| Gluck, *Orphée et Euridice* in Paris **1774** | **1774–1792** Reign of Louis XVI of France |
| | **1775** Beaumarchais, *Barber of Seville* |
| | **1776** American Declaration of Independence |
| | **1780** Death of Maria Theresa; Joseph II sole Hapsburg ruler (until 1790) |
| Haydn, Op. 33 quartets; Mozart freelances in Vienna **1781** | |
| | **1784** Beaumarchais, *Marriage of Figaro* |
| Mozart, *Haydn* Quartets **1785** | |
| Mozart, *Don Giovanni* in Prague **1787** | |
| Haydn, *Oxford* Symphony **1789** | **1789–1794** French Revolution |
| Death of Mozart; Haydn, first *London* Symphonies **1791** | |
| Haydn, *The Creation* **1798** | |

# POSTLUDE

This chapter about Haydn and Mozart does not presume to cover the music of the late eighteenth century, for these two composers shared the stage with a host of others. Some of their names may be familiar from the pages of this book—for example, the opera composers Gluck and Salieri. To those may be added dozens more, active in instrumental music as well as opera, each of whom contributed something unique to the period and each of whom deserves further study. But the music of Haydn and Mozart not only met with great success during the composers' lifetime, it also continued to be known and performed after their death. It provided models for Beethoven and many other composers of their own and succeeding generations. By the early nineteenth century, some of their compositions had become classics, part of the core group of works that cultured people were expected to know. Eventually, their music was dubbed "Classical," which, in turn, became the adjective most often applied to any work of the late eighteenth century. Still, Haydn and Mozart composed such complex and varied music, ranging over all the genres current in their day and maintaining that precarious balance between wide and deep appeal, that only they managed to achieve such widespread and enduring fame. Simply put, their music represents the best that the period produced.

# Ludwig van Beethoven
## (1770–1827)

*Chapter Contents*

*Prelude* 374

First Period 375

Second Period 379

Third Period 388

*Postlude* 395

PRELUDE

In 1792, George Washington was president of the United States; Louis XVI and Marie Antoinette were imprisoned by the leaders of the new French Republic; Viennese life, not yet under Napoleonic rule, presented an atmosphere of frivolous gaiety, at least on the surface; Haydn was at the height of his fame; and Mozart had been dead since the previous December. Early in November 1792, the ambitious twenty-one-year-old composer and pianist Ludwig van Beethoven traveled from the city of Bonn on the Rhine to Vienna, a five-hundred-mile journey that took a week by stagecoach. He ran short of money and for a while kept a detailed account of his finances. After he reached Vienna, one of the entries in his notebook records an expenditure of 25 groschen (pennies) for "coffee for Haidn and me."

The big city suited Beethoven perfectly. He soon established himself with the help of the contacts he maintained among members of the Austrian, Bohemian, and Hungarian aristocracy, who encouraged and supported him. The revolutions in France and America had brought far-reaching, even cataclysmic, changes to their world. The industrial revolution, which was well under way throughout Europe by this time, forging advances in medicine, science, and industry, was also leaving its mark on nineteenth-century society, which soon came to regard invention and progress as the norm. Rather than placing their faith in authority and having respect only for the past, people of the new industrial age believed in progress and cultivated an unprecedented enthusiasm for the future. Thus, Beethoven is said to have responded confidently to an uncomprehending critic of his works, "Oh, I have not written them for you, but for a later age."

Beethoven's total number of works is small by comparison to the output of Haydn and Mozart: 9 symphonies, for example, to Haydn's 100-plus or Mozart's 50-plus. A partial explanation is that Beethoven's symphonies are longer and grander. But another reason is that Beethoven had not the facility or speed of Haydn and Mozart: he apparently wrote music with great deliberation and sometimes only after periods of intense struggle. We can see this struggle in his sketchbooks, which document the progress of a musical idea through various stages until it reached its final form (see the commentary, NAWM 108). The sketches for the String Quartet in C♯ Minor, Op. 131, for example, are three times as long as the finished work.

Another glimpse into Beethoven's working habits reveals the extent to which he was guided by what the Romantics called "inspiration." A young composer he befriended recalled Beethoven saying:

> You will ask me whence I take my ideas? That I cannot say with any degree of certainty: they come to me uninvited, directly or indirectly. I could almost grasp them in my hands, out in Nature's open, in the woods, during my promenades, in the silence of the night, at the earliest dawn. They are roused by moods which in the poet's case are transmuted into words, and in mine into tones, that sound, roar and storm until at last they take shape for me as notes.[1]

Scholars have customarily divided Beethoven's works into three periods on the basis of style and chronology. During the first period, to about 1802, Beethoven was assimilating the musical language of his time and finding his own voice as a composer. He wrote the six String Quartets Op. 18, the first ten piano sonatas (through Op. 14), the first three piano concertos, and the first two symphonies. The second period, in which his rugged individualism asserted itself, runs to about 1816 and includes the Symphonies Nos. 3 to 8, the incidental music to Goethe's drama *Egmont*, the *Coriolan* overture, the opera *Fidelio*, the last two piano concertos, the Violin Concerto, the String Quartets Opp. 59 (the *Rasumovsky* Quartets), 74, and 95, and the Piano Sonatas through Op. 90. The third period, in which Beethoven's music generally became more reflective and introspective, includes the last five piano sonatas, the *Diabelli Variations* for piano, the *Missa solemnis*, the Ninth Symphony, and the last great quartets.

## First Period

Beethoven's first decade in Vienna, where he quickly established himself as a pianist and composer, was relatively trouble-free. For a while, he had rooms in a house owned by Prince Karl von Lichnowsky, with whom he traveled to Prague for concerts in 1796 and who sponsored concerts in his palace in Vienna. Another patron, Prince Lobkowitz, kept a private orchestra that played in Vienna and at his Bohemian country estates; he bought rights to first performances of some of Beethoven's works. Lobkowitz, Prince Kinsky, and Archduke Rudolph—youngest brother of the reigning emperor Francis II and Beethoven's piano and composition student—joined in setting up an annuity for the composer so that he would stay in Austria when he got an attractive offer from Jérôme Bonaparte, king of Westphalia. Many of Beethoven's works of this and later periods are dedicated to these patrons. With their help and by selling a number of important works to a Leipzig publisher, performing as a pianist in concerts that he or others organized, and giving piano lessons, Beethoven became the first composer who managed to make a living as an independent musician and composer.

Like Mozart, Beethoven's success as a pianist depended in part on his writing works that showcased his talents, while at the same time appealing to the amateur market. Indeed, the largest group of compositions written during his first decade in Vienna were sonatas, variations, and shorter works for piano.

*Patrons*

---

1. Alexander Wheelock Thayer, *Thayer's Life of Beethoven*, rev. and ed. Elliot Forbes, 2 vols. (Princeton: Princeton University Press, 1967), II, p. 873.

## Ludwig van Beethoven (1770–1827)

As the composer whose career and music best reflect the tumultuous changes in the decades around 1800, Beethoven became the most familiar cultural icon of Western art music. His symphonies, concertos, string quartets, and piano sonatas are central to the repertory of classical music, and later composers could not escape his influence.

Beethoven was born into a musical family in Bonn, a town on the Rhine in northwestern Germany. His father, Johann, was a court musician employed by the elector of Cologne, just downriver. He taught Ludwig piano and violin, and had every intention of turning the boy, who was small for his age, into a child prodigy. He took Ludwig out of school at age eleven so that Ludwig could concentrate exclusively on music and placed his training in the hands of a reputable local composer, Christian Gottlob Neefe (1748–1798), an organist in the Baroque tradition of counterpoint and improvisation.

Beethoven visited Vienna in 1787 and met Mozart, who prophesied a bright future for him. After returning to Bonn, he also made the acquaintance of Haydn, who stopped there on his way to London in December 1790. On Haydn's recommendation, Beethoven went to Vienna for further study and settled there permanently in 1792. His lessons with Haydn began late that year and continued until the older composer left in 1794 on his second visit to London.

Unlike Mozart, Beethoven did not seek a court appointment in Vienna. He was able to live comfortably on commissions, sales of music (hand-copied as well as printed), public concerts, and support from aristocratic sponsors. Confident in his own worth as an artist, he treated his patrons with independence and even occasional rudeness. His presumption of social equality led him repeatedly to fall in love with women of noble rank, whom he, as a commoner, could not marry (and some of whom were already married; see "The Immortal Beloved," page 390). Beethoven's lifestyle appeared poorer than it actually was. Moving from one apartment to another after arguments with his landlords, and his social and professional life constantly in jeopardy after the onset of his deafness, he never succeeded in establishing a permanent home.

Around 1802, his gradual loss of hearing provoked a personal crisis, including thoughts of suicide, which he voiced in a letter called the Heiligenstadt Testament (see page 378). But he emerged from his despair with new resolve and proceeded to compose works of unprecedented

**Piano sonatas**

Beethoven dedicated his first three piano sonatas to Haydn; in them, he reveals his debt to the older composer's style by creating themes from brief motives that are then extensively developed. But these sonatas all have four movements, as in a symphony, instead of the usual three, and in the last two he replaced the Minuet with a more dynamic Scherzo. Again, like Mozart, Beethoven often used strong contrasts of style or topic to delineate the form and broaden the expressive range.

*Sonate pathétique*

The title of Beethoven's eighth piano sonata, *Sonate pathétique* ("with pathos," a term used in rhetoric), Op. 13 (1799), indicates the composer's intention to evoke feelings of pity or compassion. In C minor, the outer movements have a stormy, passionate character that Beethoven's predecessors associated with that key. The *Grave* introduction sets a mood of drama and high seriousness, while its dense textures lend the work a symphonic breadth. The opening measures of the introduction are recalled at symmetrically placed landmarks—namely, the beginning of the development section and after the end of the recapitulation. The powerful Allegro that follows whips up a storm of excitement not heard before in Beethoven's or any other composer's piano sonatas. While the middle movement is a profoundly serene and songful Adagio in A♭ major, the sonata-rondo finale (NAWM 108) reverts to the serious intensity of the first movement, not at all like the typically lighthearted rondos of

scope and depth. The music of the next dozen years established him as the most popular and critically acclaimed composer alive. Through sales to publishers and support from patrons, notably a permanent stipend set up for him in 1809, he was able to devote himself entirely to composition and write at his own, very deliberate pace.

On his brother Caspar's death in 1815, Beethoven became guardian for his nephew Karl, giving Beethoven the family he had long desired but also bringing years of conflict with Karl's mother, Johanna. Growing deafness, bouts of illness, political upheavals, and the death or departure of many friends and patrons led to his increasing withdrawal from society. His music became more intense, concentrated, and difficult.

After years of ill health, Beethoven died at age fifty-six. Analysis of a lock of hair clipped after his death showed massive amounts of lead, suggesting that his illnesses were caused or aggravated by lead poisoning from his dishes or wine flasks. His funeral procession was witnessed by over 10,000 people, and his popularity and influence have continued unabated ever since.

*Figure 16.1.   Beethoven with a lyre, in a portrait from around 1804 by his friend Willibrord Joseph Mähler, an amateur painter. The composer kept this painting, suggestive of his status as a modern Orpheus, on his wall all his life. Historisches Museum der Stadt Wien.*

**Major works:** 9 symphonies, 11 overtures, 5 piano concertos, 1 violin concerto, 16 string quartets, 9 piano trios, 10 violin sonatas, 5 cello sonatas, 32 large piano sonatas, many piano variations, the opera *Fidelio*, the *Missa solemnis* and Mass in C Major, as well as arias, songs, and numerous other works.

Haydn and Mozart. Its theme recalls the second theme of the opening movement, and the key of its central episode echoes the A♭ of the slow movement, creating the sort of intermovement connections that mark many of Beethoven's later works.

Beethoven waited until he was well established in Vienna and confident in his craft before composing his first string quartets and symphonies. He knew that these were genres for which Haydn, then regarded as the greatest living composer, was famous, so that writing the same sorts of pieces would invite people to compare him with his former teacher. For that very reason, they offered Beethoven a chance to prove himself as a composer.

Beethoven's first six quartets, published in 1800 as Op. 18, are indebted to both Haydn and Mozart but are no mere imitations. Beethoven's individuality shines through in the character of his themes, frequent unexpected turns of phrase, unconventional modulations, and subtleties of form. Almost every movement is unique. The slow movement of No. 1, which Beethoven reportedly said was inspired by the tomb scene in *Romeo and Juliet*, is especially striking and perhaps the most dramatic—even operatic—movement yet written for string quartet. The hilarious scherzo of No. 6 emphasizes offbeats so convincingly that the listener is continually befuddled about the meter. The rondo finale has a long, intense, slow introduction labeled *La malinconia* (Melancholy), which is

Op. 18 string quartets

*Figure 16.2. Beethoven-Haus, the house in Bonn where Beethoven was born in 1770. It now contains a museum of Beethoven memorabilia and is open to the public.*

recalled later in the movement. By simultaneously following and subverting tradition in these quartets and creating stark juxtapositions of contrasting emotions and styles, Beethoven charts a new course for his later works.

First Symphony    Beethoven's Symphony No. 1 in C Major, Op. 21, was premiered in 1800 at a concert that offered, typically for its time, a potpourri of miscellaneous works (see "The Public Concert," page 358), including a septet and a piano concerto, also by Beethoven; a symphony by Mozart; an aria and duet from Haydn's oratorio *The Creation*; and improvisations at the piano by Beethoven himself. The four movements of the First Symphony reveal that Beethoven adhered to the Haydn-

---

**A CLOSER LOOK**    The Heiligenstadt Testament

The impression that Beethoven gave of being moody and unsociable had much to do with his increasing deafness. He began to lose his hearing around 1796, and by 1820 he was almost completely deaf. In the autumn of 1802, Beethoven wrote a letter, now known as the Heiligenstadt Testament, intended to be read by his brothers after his death. In it, he describes in moving terms how he suffered when he realized that his malady was incurable.

I must live almost alone like one who has been banished, I can mix with society only as much as true necessity demands. If I approach near to people a hot terror seizes upon me and I fear being exposed to the danger that my condition might be noticed. Thus it has been during the last six months which I have spent in the country. . . . What a humiliation for me when someone standing next to me heard a flute in the distance and *I heard nothing*, or someone heard a *shepherd singing* and again I heard nothing. Such incidents drove me almost to despair, a little more of that and I would have ended my life—it was only *my art* that held me back. Ah, it seemed to me impossible to leave the world until I had brought forth all that I felt was within me. . . . Oh Providence—grant me at last but one day of *pure joy*—it is so long since real joy echoed in my heart. . . .[1]

1. Alexander Wheelock Thayer, *Thayer's Life of Beethoven*, rev. and ed. Elliot Forbes, 2 vols. (Princeton: Princeton University Press, 1967), I, pp. 304–306.

VIGNETTE    Beethoven's Playing and Improvising at the Piano

*When, for several weeks in 1791, Beethoven's Bonn employer, the elector of Cologne, presided over a meeting of the Teutonic Order at Mergentheim in southern Germany, he took his musicians along. Carl Ludwig Junker, a composer and writer on music and art, came to hear them and published a glowing account of Beethoven's playing.*

I have also heard one of the greatest of pianists—the dear, good Bethofen. . . . I heard him extemporize in private; yes, I was even invited to propose a theme for him to vary. The greatness of this amiable, light-hearted man as a virtuoso may, in my opinion, be safely judged from his almost inexhaustible wealth of ideas, the highly characteristic expressiveness of his playing, and the skill he displays in performance. I do not know that he lacks anything for the making of a great artist. I have often heard Vogler play by the hour on the pianoforte—of his organ playing I cannot speak, not having heard him on that instrument—and never failed to wonder at his astonishing ability. But Bethofen, in addition to skill, has greater clarity and profundity of ideas, and more expression—in short, he speaks to the heart. He is equally great at an *adagio* as at an *allegro*. Even the members of this remarkable orchestra are, without exception, his admirers, and are all ears when he plays. Yet he is exceedingly modest and free from all pretension. He, however, acknowledged to me that, upon the journeys which the Elector had enabled him to make, he had seldom found in the playing of the most distinguished virtuosi that excellence which he supposed he had a right to expect. His manner of treating his instrument is so different from the usual that he gives the impression of having attained his present supremacy through a path that he discovered himself.

From Heinrich Philipp Carl Bossler, *Musikalische Correspondenz* (Nov. 23, 1791), adapted from trans. by Henry Edward Krehbiel; in Alexander Wheelock Thayer, *Thayer's Life of Beethoven*, rev. and ed. Elliot Forbes, 2 vols. (Princeton: Princeton University Press, 1967), I, p. 105.

Mozart model. Yet he sought to distinguish himself in certain details: the unusual prominence given to the woodwinds, the frequent and carefully placed dynamic markings (one of the most essential traits of his early style), the scherzo-like character of the third movement, and the long and important codas of the other movements.

## Second Period

Within a dozen years after coming to Vienna, Beethoven was acknowledged throughout Europe as the foremost pianist and composer for piano of his time and a symphonist on a par with Haydn and Mozart. His innovations were recognized, although they were sometimes dismissed as eccentricities. He was befriended by the most prominent families of Vienna and attracted devoted and generous patrons. He drove hard bargains with his publishers, getting them to bid against each other, and followed Haydn's lead in publishing works in several countries at once to preserve his rights and maximize his returns. Although he wrote on commission, he often dodged deadlines. He could afford, as he said, to "think and think," to revise and polish a work until it suited him.

In part because of his growing deafness, Beethoven carried around notebooks in which he scribbled bits of conversation. He also kept sketchbooks in which he notated themes and plans for compositions, worked out the continuity of each piece, and gradually filled in details. Figure 16.3 shows a page from the sketchbook for Beethoven's Third Symphony. Thanks to these sketchbooks, we can follow the progress of his ideas through various stages until they reached

Notebooks and sketchbooks

final form (see the commentary in NAWM 109). By composing in this deliberate way, Beethoven created music in which the relation of each part to the whole was painstakingly crafted, a trait much admired in the nineteenth century.

**Personal crisis**

When Beethoven realized that his hearing loss was getting worse and that it would become permanent, he suffered a psychological crisis that he describes in a letter written from Heiligenstadt, a town outside Vienna where he was vacationing (see "The Heiligenstadt Testament," page 378). After considering suicide, he emerged from his despair with a new resolve to continue composing, which may have translated into his music as a determination to say something new with each new piece. In fact, some have interpreted his compositions after 1802 as narratives or dramas reflecting the struggle of his own life. Often their thematic material is compared to a protagonist who struggles against great odds and eventually triumphs.

**Eroica Symphony**

The Symphony No. 3 in E♭ Major, Op. 55 (1803–1804), which Beethoven eventually named *Sinfonia Eroica* (Heroic Symphony), exemplifies his new approach. In fact, it marks a radical departure in Beethoven's symphonic writing because, beyond presenting conventional moods and abstract topics, as his first symphony had done, it has a subject—the celebration of a hero—and expresses in music the ideal of heroic greatness. It is also longer and more complex than any previous symphony, which made it difficult for audiences to grasp at first, although it was soon recognized as an important work.

**First movement**

CD 8/36    CD 4/41

Following the analogy drawn above, we may think of the first movement (NAWM 109)—a very large sonata form—as a story about challenge, struggle, and final victory, with its first theme as the main character. After two introductory chords, the theme shown in Example 16.1a emerges in the triadic shape of a fanfare, implying a heroic character, but sinks down suddenly to introduce an un-

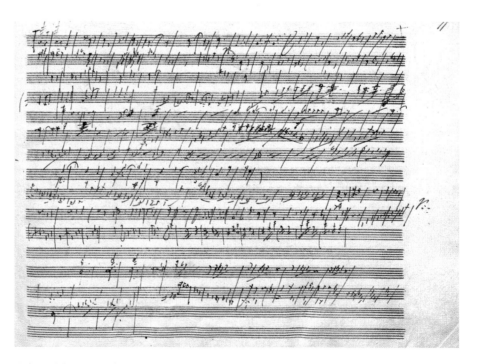

*Figure 16.3. A page from the sketchbook that Beethoven used while composing his Symphony No. 3 in E♭ Major (Eroica). For a partial transcription, see NAWM 109. Kraków, Biblioteka Jagiellónska, MS Landsberg 6, p. 11.*

expected C♯, suggesting some inner conflict or flaw. Over the course of the movement, the theme is subjected to a variety of adventures in the form of diverse musical treatments; it is portrayed as striving, being opposed and subdued, but eventually triumphing. These are described in some detail in the NAWM discussion. The most striking event is the recurrence of the syncopations first heard near the beginning, which culminate in the crashing, offbeat, dissonant chords of the terrifying climax of the development section (Example 16.1b).

*Example 16.1: Ludwig van Beethoven, Symphony No. 3 in E♭ Major, first movement*

*a. Opening theme*

*b. Rhythmic climax near the end of the exposition*

One of the most suggestive reappearances of the main theme is in the horn, just before the suspenseful dominant preparation for the recapitulation. The harmonic shock of the dominant-tonic conflict created by the premature return of the main theme in the horn convinced some early listeners that the horn player had mistakenly entered too soon. Carl Czerny, Beethoven's pupil, proposed this entrance be eliminated; the French composer and Beethoven-admirer Hector Berlioz even thought it was a copyist's mistake. But the sketches show that Beethoven contemplated this clever ploy from the very first draft.

There is evidence that Beethoven intended to dedicate this symphony to Napoleon, the enlightened hero who had promised to lead humanity into the new age of liberty, equality, and fraternity. According to the pianist Ferdinand Ries, however, when Beethoven heard that Napoleon had proclaimed himself emperor (in May 1804), he angrily tore up the title page containing the dedication, disappointed that his idol proved to be an ambitious ruler on the way to becoming a tyrant. The story is an exaggeration: the title page of Beethoven's own score, which survives, originally read "Sinfonia grande intitolata Bonaparte" (Grand Symphony entitled Bonaparte), later corrected to read "Geschrieben auf Bonaparte" (composed on Bonaparte). On August 26, 1804, months after this alleged incident, Beethoven wrote to his publisher Breitkopf & Härtel: "The title of the symphony is really Bonaparte. . . .[2] When the symphony was first published in Vienna two years later, it bore the title "Sinfonia Eroica . . . composta per festeggiare il sovvenire di un grand Uomo" (Heroic Symphony . . . composed to celebrate the memory of a great man). Whatever his feelings toward Napoleon, Beethoven conducted the symphony in Vienna in 1809 at a concert that Bonaparte was to have attended.

Dedication to Napoleon

2. Emily Anderson, ed. and trans., *Letters of Beethoven*, 3 vols. (London: Macmillan, 1961), letter no. 96.

*Funeral March*        It is the second movement—the *Funeral March*—more than anything else in the symphony that links the work with France, the republican experiment there, and Napoleon. The customary slow movement is replaced by a march in C minor, full of tragic grandeur and pathos, and a contrasting "trio" in C major, brimming with fanfares and celebratory lyricism, after which the march returns, broken up with rests suggestive of sighs at the end. At the opening of the *Funeral March*, the thirty-second notes of the strings imitate the sound of muffled drums used in the Revolutionary processions that accompanied French heroes to their final resting place (Example 16.2).

*Example 16.2: Ludwig van Beethoven, Symphony No. 3 in E♭ Major, Funeral March*

*Fidelio*        Beethoven began work on his only opera, *Fidelio*, almost immediately after finishing the Third Symphony, and the two works share the Revolutionary atmosphere. Not only was the rescue plot popular at the turn of the century, but also the libretto itself was borrowed from a French Revolutionary-era opera, *Léonore; ou, L'Amour conjugal* (Leonore; or, Conjugal Love), in which Leonore, disguised as a man, rescues her husband from prison. Beethoven's music transforms this conventional material, making the chief character, Leonore, an idealized figure of sublime courage and self-denial. The whole last part of the opera glorifies Leonore's heroism and the great humanitarian ideals of the Revolution.

        Composing this opera gave Beethoven even more trouble than he had had with his other works. The first performances of the original three-act version, called *Leonore*, took place in November 1805, just after the French armies had

*Figure 16.4. An anonymous portrait of the Malfatti family, who originally came from Lucca, Italy. Giovanni, standing behind the piano with music in hand, moved to Vienna in 1795 and eventually became one of Beethoven's doctors. His niece, Therese, seated at the piano, inspired deep affection in Beethoven, who was profoundly hurt when the family refused his proposal of marriage in 1810.*

marched into Vienna. Rearranged and shortened to two acts, the opera was brought out again the following March but immediately withdrawn. Finally, after still more extensive revisions, in 1814 a third version proved successful. In the course of all these changes, Beethoven wrote no fewer than four different overtures for the opera.

The chamber music of the middle period abounds in fresh explorations of each genre. Examples are the three string quartets of Op. 59, which are dedicated to the musical amateur Count Rasumovsky, the Russian ambassador to Vienna, who played second violin in a quartet that was said to be the finest in Europe. As a compliment to the count, Beethoven introduced a Russian melody as the principal theme for the finale of the first quartet and another in the third movement of the second quartet. These two quartets, composed in the summer and autumn of 1806, had such a new style that musicians were slow to accept them. When Count Rasumovsky's players first read through the Quartet No. 1 in F Major, they were convinced that Beethoven was playing a joke on them. The first movement is particularly peculiar in its use of single, double, and triple pedal points, frequent changes of texture—the melody accompanied sometimes by double stops or harmonically tense homorhythmic episodes—imitations of horns, unmelodious passages exploiting the extreme ranges of the instruments, fugues cropping up out of nowhere, and startling unison passages.

The Fourth, Fifth, and Sixth Symphonies were all composed between 1806 and 1808, a time of exceptional productivity. Beethoven worked on the Fourth and Fifth Symphonies at the same time; the first two movements of the Fifth, in fact, were already done before the Fourth was completed. The two works are very different, as though Beethoven wished to express polar feelings at the same time. Joviality and humor mark the Fourth Symphony in B♭ Major, Op. 60, while the Fifth, Op. 67, in C Minor, has always been considered the musical projection of Beethoven's struggle with fate. The outcome of the struggle is suggested by the transition from C minor to C major just before the triumphant finale,

*Rasumovsky* Quartets

Middle symphonies

Fifth Symphony

---

**IN PERFORMANCE** Beethoven's Tempo

Written music was traditionally viewed as a vehicle for the performer, who was at liberty to alter it in performance—for instance, by adding embellishments. But beginning with Beethoven, the idea of strict adherence to the composer's score, as if it were a sacred text to be re-created with devotion and restraint, became a hallmark of the Classical performance tradition. This meant (as it does even today) that, rather than put forward their own personalities, interpreters must subordinate their understanding of the work to the composer's vision and dedicate their skill to bringing that vision into existence with each piece. For their part, composers began to assert more and more control over the performance by using frequent dynamic markings and other notational symbols, such as specifications for phrasing and articulation.

One particularly problematic area to pin down with any precision was tempo—or how fast a piece should be played. According to eighteenth-century convention, the correct tempo of any meter could be understood by studying courtly dance pieces. The assumption was that each dance had a certain fixed tempo, determined both by its meter and the note values chosen by the composer, who also assigned the piece an appropriate Italian tempo term (Adagio, Andante, Allegro, and so forth) to match those characteristics. When transferred to a context other than dance, then, the same combination of tempo term, meter, and note values was seen to imply a particular tempo. But the dances in question did not survive the disintegration of the aristocratic social order that prevailed in Europe before the French Revolution and the Napoleonic Wars; as the minuet, gavotte, and similar dances gradually disappeared from the repertory, so did the yardstick by which tempo had been measured.

The early decades of the nineteenth century saw significant changes in the way composers specified the tempo of their pieces. For one thing, they recognized the imprecise and subjective nature of conventional designations and began to insist on a precise tempo, recognizing that a well-chosen tempo is vital to the effective realization of a piece of music. For another, they worried that the enormous expansion of the amateur market for music publishing meant that their music would come into the hands of people with little or no knowledge of this difficult subject. In keeping with their efforts to exercise increasing control over the performance of their works, then, many nineteenth-century composers turned to the metronome, newly patented by Johann Nepomuk Maelzel around 1815, as a method for designating exact tempos (see Figure 16.5).

Beethoven took great care in assigning metronome marks to his music, even when it meant adding them to works he had composed earlier, before the widespread adoption of the device. Until the 1980s however, many a conductor or virtuoso turned a blind eye to Beethoven's indications, claiming that they were faulty or problematic, or ignoring them in favor of their own aesthetic preferences; and some musicians still regard it as their inalienable right to select their own tempo in performing Beethoven's and other composers' works. In Beethoven's case, discrepancies occur particularly where the composer seems to have aimed for the fastest tempo at which a piece could be played without loss of essential

---

likened to a grand expansion of the move from chaos to light that he found in Haydn's *Creation*. The first movement is dominated by one of the best-known themes in all of Western music: the four-note anacrustic motive ( ♪♪♪𝅗𝅥 ) that is emphatically announced at the outset. The same rhythmic idea recurs in various forms in the other three movements. The transition from minor to major takes place in an inspired passage that begins with the timpani softy recalling the rhythmic motive and leading without a break from the Scherzo into the finale. Here, the entrance of the full orchestra with trombones on the C-major chord has an electrifying effect. The finale of the Fifth Symphony adds a piccolo and a contrabassoon as well as trombones to the normal complement of strings, woodwinds, brass, and timpani.

detail. Indeed, Beethoven's apparent liking for extremely rapid tempos in certain types of movements caused consternation even among his contemporaries, and it is possible that he sometimes overestimated the capacity of mere mortal musicians. More recent scholarship,[1] however, and especially recordings by groups using period instruments—that is, those that approximate the qualities of the eighteenth and early nineteenth centuries, such as instruments with gut strings or valveless brass instruments—have vindicated many of Beethoven's supposedly problematic metronome marks. At the same time, sensitive musicians agree that historically appropriate tempos should not be rigidly bound to a single, immutable metronome mark, but should also take into account such factors as the varying physical and acoustic conditions in which a performance takes place.

1. See Clive Brown, *Classical and Romantic Performing Practice 1750–1900* (New York: Oxford University Press, 1999).

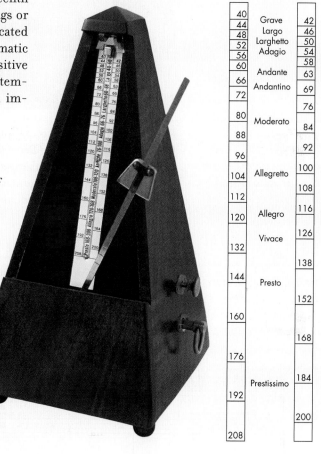

*Figure 16.5. The metronome consists of a mounted steel pendulum that produces an audible measure of the passage of time, like the ticking of a clock; but, unlike a clock, its speed can be set between 40 and 200 beats per minute, depending on the position of the small weight attached to the pendulum. The inventor, Johann Nepomuk Maelzel, also published a metronome scale, linking tempo terms with specific speeds. The scale has two sets of numbers, indicating a certain flexibility. For example, Andante could be anywhere in the range of 60 to 63 beats per minute and Presto between 144 and 152 beats per minute. Beethoven and others set the metronome marking by designating a particular note value and indicating how many times per minute it should be heard.*

*Pastoral* Symphony

The Sixth (*Pastoral*) Symphony in F Major, Op. 68, was composed immediately after the Fifth, and the two were premiered on the same program in December 1808 at the Theater an der Wien, shown in Figure 16.6. Each of the *Pastoral*'s five movements bears a subtitle that suggests a scene from life in the country. Beethoven adapted his descriptive program to the normal sequence of movements, inserting an extra movement (*Storm*) that serves to introduce the finale (*Thankful Feelings after the Storm*). In the coda of the Andante movement (*Scene by the Brook*), flute, oboe, and clarinet join harmoniously in imitating birdcalls—the nightingale, the quail, and the cuckoo (Example 16.3). All these programmatic effects—which the composer himself warned against taking literally, calling the subtitles "expressions of feeling

*Figure 16.6. An anonymous 1825 engraving of the Theater an der Wien. Beethoven's famous four-hour concert of December 22, 1808, took place in this bitterly cold hall. The program included the first public performances of the Fifth and Sixth Symphonies; the first Vienna performance of the Fourth Piano Concerto, with the composer as soloist, and, following some other pieces, the Choral Fantasy, Op. 80. Historisches Museum der Stadt Wien.*

rather than depiction"—are subordinate to the expansive, leisurely form of the symphony as a whole.

*Example 16.3: Ludwig van Beethoven, Symphony No. 6 in F Major, Scene by the Brook*

**Symphonies Nos. 7 and 8**

Symphonies No. 7 in A Major, Op. 92, and No. 8 in F Major, Op. 93, were both completed in 1812. Once again, Beethoven explored the diverse capabilities of a single genre by producing a pair of opposites: the Seventh is on a large scale, the Eighth greatly condensed. They were well received at their premieres in late 1813 and early 1814, respectively, but even more thunderous applause greeted another work performed at both concerts: *Wellington's Victory* (1813), a "program" symphony (see Chapter 17) that depicted the English defeat of Napoleon at Vittoria that summer, complete with the sound of 188 cannon shots provided by the bass drum and precisely written into the score.

**Overtures**

Beethoven's orchestral overtures are related in style to the symphonies, usually taking the form of a symphonic first movement. Besides the *Leonore* Overtures, written for *Fidelio,* his most important works in this genre are *Coriolan*

(1807), inspired by a tragic drama that was performed occasionally in Vienna, and *Egmont*, composed with songs and incidental music for an 1810 perform- ance of Goethe's play.

Beethoven composed ten piano sonatas between 1800 and 1805. Among them are Op. 26 in A♭, with another funeral march, and Op. 27, Nos. 1 and 2, each designated "quasi una fantasia"—the second is popularly known as the *Moonlight* Sonata. In Op. 31, No. 2, in D minor, the whole opening section of the first movement, with its rushing passages and abrupt punctuation, has the char- acter of an instrumental recitative, anticipating the opening of the first move- ment of the Ninth Symphony. The introductory *largo* arpeggio returns at the start of the development section and again at the beginning of the recapitula- tion, each time in expanded form and with new links to the surrounding music, its last appearance leading into an expressive recitative (see Example 16.4). The finale of this sonata is an exciting *moto perpetuo* in rondo form.

Piano sonatas

*Example 16.4: Ludwig van Beethoven, Piano Sonata in D Minor, Op. 31, No. 2*

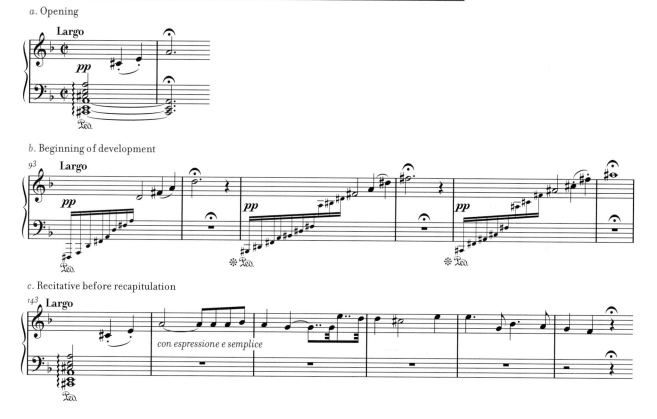

a. Opening

b. Beginning of development

c. Recitative before recapitulation

Outstanding among the sonatas of this middle period are Op. 53 in C major (1804), called the *Waldstein* Sonata after the patron to whom it is dedicated, and Op. 57 in F minor (1805), known simply as the *Appassionata* (Impassioned [Sonata]). In the first movement of the *Waldstein*, Beethoven managed to make the key of C major sound dark and brooding by means of the obstinate thunder- ing of thick, low chords, to which a figure high in the right hand answers like a flash of lightning (Example 16.5a). Then the storm clears, and a bright, chordally accompanied melody in E major glistens where a theme in the domi- nant is expected (Example 16.5b). The "normal" arrival of the dominant in the second part of the exposition is delayed until near the double bar, just in time to bring back the opening. In the recapitulation, the second theme is first heard in A major, and its restatement in C major is reserved for the coda. Similarly,

*Waldstein* and *Appassionata* sonatas

Beethoven poses a problem of key relationships in the *Appassionata* and solves it over the course of the entire movement. Through such means, together with unusual and evocative thematic ideas, Beethoven turned his sonatas into dramas of contrast, conflict, and resolution.

*Example 16.5: Ludwig van Beethoven, Piano Sonata in C Major, Op. 53, Allegro con brio*

a.

b.

**Piano concertos**

During his first decade in Vienna, Beethoven composed three piano concertos to play at his own concerts, following the custom of Mozart a decade earlier. But the concertos of his middle period are, like the symphonies, written on a grander scale. In the Piano Concerto No. 5 in E♭ Major, Op. 73 (the *Emperor*; 1809), and the Violin Concerto in D Major, Op. 61 (1806), Beethoven greatly expanded the music's expressive range and dimensions. At times, the soloist seems pitted against the orchestra, as if playing the part of a lone hero contending with opposing forces. In the first movement of the *Emperor* Concerto, for example, the soloist enters with a (written-out) cadenza-like passage even before the orchestra's exposition begins. Such contrast between soloist and orchestra, rather than cooperation (as in the original meaning of *concerto*), was to become a frequent feature of nineteenth-century concertos.

## Third Period

The years up to 1815 were, on the whole, peaceful and prosperous for Beethoven. His music was played regularly in Vienna, and he was celebrated both at home and abroad. Thanks to the generosity of patrons and the steady demand from publishers for new works, his financial affairs were in good order. But his deafness posed a more and more serious challenge. Since it caused him to lose contact with others, he retreated into himself, becoming morose, irascible, and morbidly suspicious even of his friends. Family problems, ill health, and unfounded apprehensions of poverty also plagued

Beethoven during his last decade, and it was only by a supreme effort of will that he continued composing. He wrote his last five piano sonatas between 1816 and 1821. He completed the *Missa solemnis* in 1822, the *Diabelli* Variations in 1823, and the Ninth Symphony in 1824, each after long years of labor. The final quartets, Beethoven's musical testament, followed in 1825 and 1826. At his death in 1827, he had plans for a tenth symphony and many other new works.

By 1816, Beethoven had resigned himself to living in a soundless world of tones that reverberated only in his mind. More and more his compositions acquired a meditative character, the urgent sense of communication replaced by a feeling of assured tranquillity, passionate outpouring by calm affirmation. The language became more concentrated, more abstract. Extremes met: the sublime and the grotesque in the Mass and the Ninth Symphony, the profound and the apparently naïve in the last quartets. Classical forms remained, like the features of a landscape after a geological upheaval—recognizable here and there under distorted contours, lying at strange angles beneath the new surface.

*Characteristics of late style*

In his late compositions, Beethoven seems to have wanted to extract every bit of meaning latent in his themes and motives. As had always been the case with his development sections, it became especially true of his variation technique during this late period. Variations appear within the slow movements of the Piano Sonata No. 29 in B♭ Major, Op. 106, the String Quartet in A Minor, Op. 132, and in the finale of the Ninth Symphony (after the introduction), to mention a few examples. Although he composed only one independent set for piano during this period—the *Thirty-three Variations on a Waltz by Diabelli*, Op. 120, completed in 1823—it surpasses anything in this genre since Bach's *Goldberg Variations*. Rather than altering the theme in a fairly straightforward manner, Beethoven transformed the very character of the theme, thus setting these variations apart from earlier ones. Diabelli's commonplace little waltz expands surprisingly into a world of variegated moods—solemn, brilliant, capricious, mysterious—ordered with due regard for contrast, grouping, and climax. Each

*Variations*

---

**VIGNETTE** Beethoven's Appearance

*Sir Julius Benedict (1804–1885), a German-born composer and conductor in England, first saw Beethoven when he accompanied his teacher, Carl Maria von Weber (see Chapter 19) to Vienna in 1823. Beethoven was in his fifty-third year.*

If I am not mistaken, on the morning that I saw Beethoven for the first time, Blahetka, the father of the pianist, directed my attention to a stout, short man with a very red face, small, piercing eyes, and bushy eyebrows, dressed in a very long overcoat which reached nearly to his ankles, who entered the shop [the music store of Steiner and Haslinger] about 12 o'clock. Blahetka asked me: "Who do you think that is?" and I at once exclaimed: "It must be Beethoven!" because, notwithstanding the high color of his cheeks and his general untidiness, there was in those small piercing eyes an expression which no painter could render. It was a feeling of sublimity and melancholy combined.

Alexander Wheelock Thayer, *Thayer's Life of Beethoven*, rev. and ed. Elliot Forbes, 2 vols. (Princeton: Princeton University Press, 1967), II, p. 873.

*Figure 16.7. A contemporary caricature of Beethoven striding around Vienna, seemingly oblivious to his surroundings.*

My angel, my all, my very self—Only a few words today and at that with pencil (with yours)—Not till tomorrow will my lodgings be definitely determined upon—what a useless waste of time—Why this deep sorrow when necessity speaks—can our love endure except through sacrifices, through not demanding everything from one another; can you change the fact that you are not wholly mine, I not wholly thine. . . .

In the summer of 1812, Beethoven wrote this impassioned letter to a woman whom he addressed as the Immortal Beloved, and whose identity posed a baffling riddle for generations of Beethoven biographers. Whether the letter was ever delivered was also a matter of speculation; dated July 6 but with no year, it was found among the composer's effects after his death. Although Beethoven had several close friendships with women, he never married; in fact, even his most serious romantic attachments were short-lived. Who, then, was his secret, undying love?

In a biography published 150 years after the composer's death, Maynard Solomon convincingly unravels the mystery of Beethoven's Immortal Beloved by re-creating a powerful web of circumstantial evidence from contemporaneous documents. He proposes that the woman was Antonie Brentano, a beautiful Viennese matron with four children whom Beethoven met in 1810, when she was thirty. (See her miniature portrait, painted on ivory, also found among Beethoven's possessions when he died—Figure 16.8.) Her husband was Franz Brentano, a merchant from Frankfurt who had obtained her father's permission to marry her when she was only eighteen years old. The couple resided far from Vienna in his native city, where Antonie missed her family and suffered periods of depression and mysterious physical ailments. During her father's illness and death in 1809, they moved back to Vienna and lived in her family's mansion. She persuaded her husband to open a branch of his business there and remained in Vienna for three

Figure 16.8. An unsigned miniature on ivory of Antonie Brentano, ca. 1812.

years while she settled her father's affairs and disposed of his estate.

During this period (1810–1812), Beethoven was a regular visitor to the Brentano household, where he attended the quartet concerts that were performed there and often played the piano himself. He dedicated several compositions to Antonie and, during her periods of gloomy withdrawal when she would admit no one else to her company, consoled her with his piano improvisations. At some point, their attachment transformed itself into love, despite the looming prospect of Antonie's fated return to Frankfurt with her husband.

It is probably no accident, then, that the letter to the Immortal Beloved—which eventually raises the issue of their living together—was written shortly after the final auction of her father's possessions.

If Antonie was willing to leave her husband and remain in Vienna rather than return to Frankfurt, Beethoven was unprepared for such a commitment. Ultimately, he renounced the possibility of a union so heavily weighted with conflicting ethical and emotional implications. But his anguish and ambivalence are apparent in this letter, written while en route to Karlsbad, where he was expecting to have a reunion with Antonie during the Brentanos' vacation that summer. Whatever happened during their meeting,[1] the two separated in the fall, the Brentanos went back to Frankfurt, and Beethoven remained in Vienna. Although they kept in touch, they probably never saw each other again.

1. The planned climactic meeting in Karlsbad was at the center of the 1994 film *Immortal Beloved*, in which the event was aborted by fate. The film, however, so distorted the facts as we know them that the encounter, had it taken place, would have reunited Beethoven with his sister-in-law (widow of his deceased brother), whom the script outrageously hypothesized as Beethoven's true Immortal Beloved. Despite such liberties, the film's portrayal of Beethoven (played by Gary Oldman) and his music is very moving.

For further information, see Maynard Solomon, *Beethoven*, 2nd rev. ed. (New York: Schirmer, 1998), esp. ch. 15, pp. 207–246.

variation is built on motives derived from some part of the theme but altered in rhythm, tempo, dynamics, or context so as to produce a new design. In straying so far from its originally unpromising theme, the *Diabelli Variations* became the model for Schumann's *Symphonic Études*, Brahms's *Variations on a Theme of Handel*, and many other nineteenth-century works in this genre.

Another feature of Beethoven's late style is an emphasis on continuity. Within movements, he achieves continuity by intentionally blurring divisions between phrases or placing cadences on weak beats. Long harmonic arches and leisurely paced melodies communicate a feeling of vastness in movements such as the Adagio of the String Quartet in E♭ Major, Op. 127 (1824–1825) or the *Benedictus* of the *Missa solemnis*. Beethoven also emphasized continuity between movements, sometimes indicating that successive movements should be played without a pause. For example, in the first movement of the Ninth Symphony, the Introduction is in the same tempo as the Allegro and flows directly into it.

The improvisatory character of some passages in his earlier piano sonatas (as in Example 16.4) may give us some idea of Beethoven's actual improvisations that so impressed his listeners (see "Beethoven's Playing and Improvising at the Piano," page 379). In his later piano sonatas, this compositional style becomes more prominent as Beethoven lingers over a phrase musingly—for example, in the slow movement of the Piano Sonata No. 28 in A Major, Op. 101—or seems to lose himself in a detail—such as the trill that goes on for pages in the last movement of Piano Sonata No. 30 in E Major, Op. 109. Sometimes these reflective passages culminate in moments of instrumental recitative, as in the Adagio of Piano Sonata No. 31 in A♭ Major, Op. 110, and in various transitions within his late chamber and orchestral music as well, such as the passage preceding the finale of the Ninth Symphony.

Beethoven's search for new expressive means in his late works gave rise to new sonorities, such as the widely spaced intervals at the end of the Piano Sonata Op. 110, the simultaneous use in all four instruments of *pizzicato* or *sul ponticello* effects (playing on the bridge to produce a thin sound) in the Scherzo of the C♯-Minor String Quartet, Op. 131 (see below), and the extraordinary dark coloring of the orchestra and chorus at the first appearance of the words "Ihr stürzt nieder" (Prostrate yourselves) in the Ninth Symphony finale. Some moments almost require a miracle to make them "sound" in performance; the ideas seem too big for human capabilities to express. For this reason, early critics believed that, perhaps because of his deafness, Beethoven's musical conceptions demanded too much of the players. But we have no reason to believe that even a Beethoven with perfect hearing would have altered a single note, either to spare tender ears or to make life easier for performers. Such insistence on the composer's vision at the expense of the performer's freedom and the audience's comfort was to develop into an important strain in nineteenth- and, especially, twentieth-century music, with Beethoven becoming the model for later composers.

Beethoven's late style takes on a timeless quality through the prominent use of imitation and fugal texture. His attraction to these techniques undoubtedly came from a number of sources: his lifelong reverence for the music of J. S. Bach and Handel; his familiarity with works by Haydn and Mozart. But it was also perhaps a by-product of the meditative quality of his late style. We find numerous canonic imitations and learned contrapuntal devices in all the late works, particularly in the fugatos that play a central role in development sections, such

Continuity

Improvisatory passages

New sonorities

*Figure 16.9. Beethoven at age forty-eight. Chalk drawing by August von Klöber, 1818. Beethoven-Haus Bonn.*

CD 8/52    CD 4/57

Form

Quartet Op. 131

CD 8/52–54
CD 4/57–59

as in the finale of the Piano Sonata Op. 101. Many movements are predominantly fugal—for example, the finales of the Piano Sonatas Opp. 106 and 110; the first movement of the String Quartet in C♯ Minor, Op. 131 (NAWM 110a); the gigantic *Grosse Fuge* for String Quartet Op. 133; and the two double fugues in the finale of the Ninth Symphony.

As with texture and sonority, so too with form in the instrumental works of Beethoven's third period: on a larger scale, his quest for new means of expression led him to reconceive the number and arrangement of movements. Each of the last five piano sonatas has a unique succession of movement types and tempos, often linked without pause. Two of the late quartets have four movements, but the others have five, six, and—in the case of the String Quartet in C♯ Minor, Op. 131—seven movements, played without breaks between them (the first two are in NAWM 110). The arrangement of forms, keys, and tempos in this quartet illustrates how Beethoven simultaneously follows and departs from tradition in his late works:

| Mvt. | Form | Key | Tempo | Time Sig. |
|---|---|---|---|---|
| 1 | Fugue | C♯ minor | Adagio ma non troppo e molto espressivo | ¢ |
| 2 | Sonata-rondo | D major | Allegretto molto vivace | 6/8 |
| 3 | Brief recitative and transition | B minor to V of A major | Allegro moderato— Adagio | c |
| 4 | Variations | A major | Andante | 2/4 |
| 5 | Scherzo | E major | Presto | ¢ |
| 6 | Brief rounded binary | G♯ minor | Adagio quasi un poco andante | 3/4 |
| 7 | Sonata form | C♯ minor | Allegro | ¢ |

All this can only be forcibly reconciled with the Classical sonata scheme by imagining (1) and (2) as an introduction and first movement, (3) and (4) as an introduction and slow movement, (5) as a traditionally placed Scherzo, and (6) and (7) as an introduction and finale. Beethoven's concern for integrating the movements is clearly paramount; therefore, in addition to blurring the divisions between them, he also unifies them through subtle motivic and key relationships. For example, the most prominent notes in the fugue subject (marked with asterisks in Example 16.6) forecast the keys of the principal movements of the rest of the work; and two motives from the first theme group of the finale (only one is shown in Example 16.6) also echo the fugue subject.

*Example 16.6: Ludwig van Beethoven, String Quartet in C♯ Minor, Op. 131, Allegro molto vivace, fugue subject compared to the finale motive*

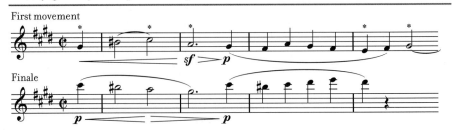

* = prominent notes that appear as the tonic of a later movement.

Like all of Beethoven's late sonatas and quartets, Op. 131 is a piece for connoisseurs. Although it appeals to listeners on many levels—it is dramatic, emotionally rich, even funny in the Scherzo—only those "in the know" about music are likely to notice the clever combination of tradition and innovation or appreciate the complex relationships between the whole and the individual parts.

The most imposing public works of the last period are the *Missa solemnis* and the Ninth Symphony; and, like his late sonatas and quartets, both reexamine the traditions of their respective genres. Beethoven regarded the Mass as his great-

*Missa solemnis*

---

**TIMELINE**    The Beethoven Years

| MUSICAL EVENTS | HISTORICAL EVENTS |
|---|---|
| Beethoven born in Bonn **1770** | |
| Gluck, *Orphée et Euridice* in Paris **1774** | |
| | **1776**  American Declaration of Independence |
| | **1781**  Kant, *Critique of Pure Reason* |
| Mozart, *Don Giovanni* in Prague **1787** | |
| | **1789–1794**  French Revolution |
| Death of Mozart **1791** | |
| Beethoven moves to Vienna **1792** | |
| | **1793**  Whitney invents cotton gin; Louis XVI and Marie Antoinette beheaded after French Republic begins |
| Beethoven, *Sonate pathétique* **1797–1798** | |
| Haydn, *The Creation* **1798** | |
| | **1799**  Napoleon becomes First Consul of French Republic |
| Beethoven, Heiligenstadt Testament **1802** | |
| Beethoven, *Eroica* Symphony **1803** | |
| | **1804**  Napoleon crowns himself emperor |
| Beethoven, *Fidelio* performed unsuccessfully **1805** | **1805–1818**  Napoleon's forces occupy Vienna |
| | **1806**  Holy Roman Empire dissolved; Francis continues as emperor of Austria |
| Premiere of Beethoven's Fifth and Sixth Symphonies **1808** | **1808**  Goethe, *Faust,* Part I |
| Death of Haydn; Beethoven given lifetime annuity **1809** | |
| Beethoven, letter to the Immortal Beloved **1812** | |
| | **1813**  Wellington defeats Napoleon at Waterloo; Jane Austen, *Pride and Prejudice* |
| Beethoven's *Fidelio* performed successfully **1814** | **1814–1815**  Congress of Vienna |
| Invention of the metronome **1815** | |
| Beethoven, Ninth Symphony **1823** | |
| Beethoven, late string quartets **1824–1826** | |
| Death of Beethoven **1827** | |

est work—a deeply personal yet universal confession of faith—full of erudite musical references and liturgical symbols. Originally intended to celebrate the elevation of Archduke Rudolph to archbishop of Olmütz in 1820, the work grew too long and elaborate for liturgical use; instead, like Bach's B-Minor Mass, it became an encyclopedic, idealized treatment of a well-loved text.

The choral writing owes something to Handel, whose music Beethoven revered. But a Handel oratorio was a string of independent numbers, whereas Beethoven shaped his setting of the Kyrie, Gloria, Credo, Sanctus, and Agnus Dei as a unified five-movement symphony with voices. As in the late Masses of Haydn, choruses and solo ensembles freely combine and alternate within each movement. Beethoven's attention to musical form led him to take liberties with the liturgical text, such as the rondo-like recurrences of the word "Credo," with its musical motive in the third movement.

Ninth Symphony

The Ninth Symphony was first performed on May 7, 1824, on a program with one of Beethoven's overtures and three movements of his Mass. Beethoven, though deaf, was conducting. The large and distinguished audience applauded vociferously after a portion of the symphony. Beethoven did not turn around to acknowledge the applause because he could not hear it: one of the soloists tugged at his sleeve and directed his attention to the clapping hands and the waving hats and handkerchiefs, whereupon he finally realized the audience's reaction and bowed. The receipts at the concert were large, but so little remained after expenses that Beethoven accused his friends who had managed the affair of cheating him. A repetition two weeks later before a half-full house resulted in a deficit. Thus was the Ninth Symphony launched into the world.

The work's most striking innovation remains its use of chorus and solo voices in the finale. Beethoven had thought as early as 1792 of setting Schiller's *Ode to Joy*, but more than thirty years went by before he decided to work this text in to his Ninth Symphony. Consistent with his ethical ideals and religious faith, he selected stanzas that emphasize universal fellowship through joy and its basis in the love of an eternal heavenly Father. Beethoven must have been concerned about the apparent incongruity of introducing voices at the climax of a long instrumental symphony (the whole takes more than an hour), and his solution to this aesthetic problem no doubt determined the unusual form of the last movement:

- tumultuous introduction, inspired by the operatic genre of accompanied recitative
- review and rejection (by instrumental recitatives) of the themes of the preceding movements; proposal and joyful acceptance of the "joy" theme
- orchestral exposition of the theme in four stanzas
- return of the tumultuous opening
- bass recitative: "O Freunde, nicht diese Töne! sodern lasst uns angenehmere anstimmen und freudenvollere" (O friends, not these tones! Rather let us sing more pleasant and joyful ones)
- choral-orchestral exposition of the joy theme, *Freude, schöner Gotterfunken* (Beautiful joy, divine spark), in four stanzas, varied (including a "Turkish" march), and a long orchestral interlude (double fugue) followed by a repetition of the first stanza
- new theme, for orchestra and chorus: *Seid umschlungen, Millionen!* (Be embraced, O millions!)
- double fugue on the two themes
- brilliant *prestissimo* choral coda, bringing back the Turkish percussion, in which the joy theme is repeated in strains of matchless sublimity

Everything here builds on tradition, but the whole is unprecedented. Beethoven's combination of innovation with respect for the past, of disparate styles, and of supreme compositional control with profound emotional expression is characteristic of his last period and has been seen as a measure of his greatness.

Figure 16.10.  Beethoven's signature, from a letter written in French to piano manufacturer Thomas Broadwood, ca. 1817.

## POSTLUDE

When Beethoven died, his funeral procession drew over 10,000 mourners. Having celebrated heroism in his music, he had himself become a cultural hero, one whose reputation grew throughout the nineteenth century. His life story helped to define the Romantic view of the creative artist as a social outsider who suffers courageously to bring humanity a glimpse of the divine through art.

Only a few of Beethoven's contemporaries understood his late works, which in any event were so personal that they could hardly be imitated. His influence on later composers resulted mostly from the works of the middle period, especially the *Rasumovsky* Quartets, the Fifth, Sixth, and Seventh Symphonies, and the piano sonatas. Even in these works, it was not the Classical element in Beethoven's style, but the Revolutionary element—the free, impulsive, mysterious, demonic spirit, the underlying conception of music as a mode of self-expression—that fascinated the Romantic generation. As E. T. A. Hoffmann wrote: "Beethoven's music sets in motion the lever of fear, of awe, of horror, of suffering, and awakens just that infinite longing which is the essence of romanticism. He is accordingly a completely romantic composer. . . ."[3] But since Hoffmann also realized the importance of structure and control in Beethoven's music and in the works of Haydn and Mozart, whom he called "romantic" as well, perhaps he used the word as a general term of commendation. Romantic or not, Beethoven was one of the great disruptive forces in the history of music in that no subsequent composer could view the symphony—or, indeed, any instrumental genre—the way it had been seen before.

---

3. E. T. A. Hoffmann, "Beethoven's Instrumental Music" (1813), trans. Oliver Strunk; in Oliver Strunk, ed., *Source Readings in Music History*, rev. ed. by Leo Treitler, vol. VI: *The Nineteenth Century*, ed. Ruth A. Solie (New York: Norton, 1997), p. 153.

PART FIVE

# The Nineteenth Century: The Age of Romanticism

PART CONTENTS

**17. THE EARLY ROMANTICS 410**

**18. THE LATER ROMANTICS 438**

**19. OPERA AND MUSIC DRAMA IN THE NINETEENTH CENTURY 462**

**20. THE FINAL BLOOM OF ROMANTICISM: EUROPEAN MUSIC AT THE END OF THE NINETEENTH CENTURY 493**

The word *romantic* derived from the medieval romance, a narrative in verse or prose about the adventures of heroic figures such as King Arthur or his knights, which often took place in mysterious or exotic settings. It connoted something distant, legendary, and fantastic, an imaginary or ideal world far from everyday reality. In the nineteenth century, especially in German-speaking lands, the term was applied first to literature, then to music and art. In contrast to classic poetry, which was deemed objectively beautiful, limited in scope and theme, and universally valid, Romantic poetry transgressed rules and limits, expressing insatiable longing and the richness of nature. Like the political liberalism espoused by such authors as Charles Dickens and Victor Hugo or the idealist philosophy of Friedrich Nietzsche, Romantic art focused on the individual and on expression of the self. By the mid-nineteenth century, the works of Haydn and Mozart were seen as Classical—that is, elegant, natural, simple, clear, formally closed, and universally appealing—while Romantic music was identified with a search for the original, interesting, evocative, expressive, or extreme. But the two designations were not necessarily mutually exclusive. Consequently, employing the terms *Classical* and *Romantic* to describe opposite qualities can be misleading because the continuity between these two style periods is more essential than the contrast between them; while Romantic traits are found in some eighteenth-century music, many Classical characteristics persisted throughout the nineteenth century. The music of Beethoven was regarded as possessing all the qualities of both worlds, and to the extent that composers emulated his works, they saw themselves as guardians of classical traditions as well as innovators.

# Europe in the Nineteenth Century

**The new order**

The upheavals of 1789–1815 changed the European political landscape. The French Revolution made peasants and workers into citizens instead of subjects. Napoleon's wars swept away old political boundaries and spread the Revolutionary ideals of liberty, equality, and fraternity or brotherhood—the last being an idea that lay behind national identity—giving rise to cultural and political

*Figure V.1. Map of Europe, 1815–1848.*

**TIMELINE** The Nineteenth Century

## MUSICAL EVENTS

Lord Byron

Death of Beethoven **1827**

Berlioz, *Symphonie fantastique* **1830**

Liszt tours Europe and Russia as a virtuoso pianist **1839–1847**

Schumann, *Dichterliebe* **1840**

London firm of Broadwood **1850**
making 2,000 pianos a year

Liszt, *Faust* Symphony **1854**

Queen Victoria

Wagner writes the music drama *Tristan und Isolde* **1859**

Premiere of Schubert's *Unfinished* Symphony **1867**

Verdi writes Requiem in memory of Manzoni; **1874**
Musorgsky, *Pictures at an Exhibition*

Yuon, *Cupolas and Swallows*

Death of Brahms **1897**

## HISTORICAL EVENTS

**1804** Napoleon crowns himself emperor of France

**1812–1818** Byron, *Childe Harold*
**1814** Goya, *The Third of May 1808*
**1815** Napoleon defeated at Waterloo; Congress of Vienna
redefines European boundaries
**1819** Schopenhauer, *The World as Will and Representation*

**1825** First railway begins operating in England
**1827** Delacroix, *Death of Sardanapalus*

**1831** Goethe, *Faust,* Part II

**1837** Victoria crowned queen of England; reigns until 1901

**1844** Turner, *Rain, Steam, and Speed: The Great Western
Railway*
**1848** Marx and Engels, *Manifesto of the Communist Party;*
Seneca Falls Convention, beginning of women's suffrage
movement
**1848–1849** Unsuccessful revolutions throughout Europe

**1852–1870** Second French Empire under Napoleon III

**1859** Darwin, *On the Origin of Species by Natural Selection*
**1859–1861** Garibaldi overthrows Bourbon monarchy; Victor
Emmanuel II becomes king of a united Italy
**1860s** Bismarck unites Prussia with other states to forge German
Empire
**1861** Serfdom abolished in Russia
**1862** Hugo, *Les Misérables*

**1867** Austrian Empire reorganized as Austro-Hungarian
monarchy
**1869** Opening of the Suez Canal; Tolstoy, *War and Peace*
**1870–1871** Franco-Prussian War; France defeated and
Germany unified

**1877** Edison invents the phonograph

**1888** Pasteur Institute founded in Paris

*Figure V.2. In* Rain, Steam and Speed: The Great Western Railway *(1844), J. M. W. Turner explores light and color in depicting the effects of nature. He also ironically suggests the limits of technology by including a hare running ahead of the train. National Gallery, London.*

trends that gained force throughout the nineteenth century (see "In Context," page 507). In 1814–1815, the Congress of Vienna drew a new map for the European continent, shown in Figure V.1, made up of far fewer states than the Continent had previously claimed. Although Italy and German-speaking lands were still partitioned, the inhabitants of each felt an increasing sense of a nation united by language and culture. So did the people in lands that had recently lost independence, such as Poland, or that had long endured foreign domination, such as Hungary and Bohemia: to them, the independent nation-state seemed an ideal worth fighting for. But repression held aspirations for freedom in check, until the stirring but largely unsuccessful revolutions of 1848–1849.

Social upheaval

Along with political revolution came social upheaval. The transfer of power from the landholding hereditary aristocracy to the urban middle class spawned new ideological movements, such as socialism and Marxism, which challenged the established order. In the new society, the economically productive forces—the bourgeois, capitalist class—replaced the unproductive feudal nobility in a new industrial order. Based as it was on economic determinism and capitalist free enterprise, the new order emphasized the individual as never before. This is reflected in the writings of philosopher Arthur Schopenhauer, who attributed new powers to the impelling will, which he believed controls the intellect and consciousness and, therefore, drives one's existence. At the same time, individual wills come into conflict, causing continual strife and frustration in the world and producing desires that, according to Schopenhauer, can be eased only by philosophy and the arts. Thus, the artist became the new visionary of the Romantic movement; and, among the arts, music was accorded a new respect, taken more seriously than ever before.

Meanwhile, new technologies had transformed the economy from chiefly rural and agricultural, with most goods made by hand, to an urban economy based on manufacturing by machine. This gradual change, known as the industrial revolution, began in Britain during the late eighteenth century and spread across Europe and North America over the next hundred years. It started in the textile industry with inventions such as the cotton gin (1793), leading to mass production of cloth in large factories powered by water mills or by the new steam engine (invented 1769). Other industries followed suit, including instrument-making firms (see pages 418–419). Mass production lowered costs and thus prices, driving out competitors who worked by hand. Despite long hours and often bad working conditions, men, women, and even children came to work in the factories and the coal and iron mines that kept them running. Therefore, the industrial revolution brought unprecedented prosperity and leisure for the urban middle and merchant classes at the expense of the landholding aristocracy on the one hand and the poor and working classes on the other. In many ways, the redistribution of power among the classes and the confounding of their traditional relationships were as disruptive to nineteenth-century society as the French Revolution and Napoleonic Wars had been.

At the same time, scientific and technological innovations brought about profound changes in people's daily lives. Scientists like Edward Jenner and Louis Pasteur introduced vaccines, pasteurization, and other advances in the health sciences that contributed to an enormous increase in the population of the world's industrialized countries. Railroads fundamentally altered travel and commerce. The invention of the telegraph and telephone revolutionized communication. And other new technologies, such as Thomas Edison's lightbulb and phonograph, not only enhanced people's leisure time but also created repercussions for the music industry that are playing out even today (see Chapter 22). But science also raised disturbing new questions about mankind's origins and place in the universe. Charles Darwin's biological theory of evolution by natural selection caused shock waves that are still being felt in schools and churches, just as it raised societal issues about "the survival of the fittest," with implications that continue to be debated today among politicians and other leaders.

The changed economic and political order in Europe dramatically affected musicians in several ways. As the aristocracy was impoverished by war and inflation and over one hundred small states were eliminated, the number of courts supporting the arts was drastically reduced. The typical musician no

Decline of patronage

*Figure V.3.* Family Concert in Basle (1849) by Sebastian Gutzwiller shows a typical domestic scene of music making: a woman performs on a square piano while various other family members play violin and flute or engage in different activities. Öffentliche Kunstsammlung Kunstmuseum Basel.

longer served a prince or church, but made a living as a free agent through public performance, teaching, composing on commission, or creating music for publication. While patrons had expected their employees to play several instruments and, like Bach and Haydn, to compose in most genres, musicians were now competing in an open market and often made their reputations through specialization. Among the most prominent musicians of the age were virtuosos—performers such as violinist Niccolò Paganini and pianist Franz Liszt (see Chapter 18) who specialized in one instrument and dazzled audiences with displays of technical wizardry. Many composers also specialized in one medium, such as Fryderyk Chopin in piano music and Giuseppe Verdi in opera.

**Middle-class music making**

As the aristocracy declined, the urban middle class grew in size and influence. Since people had the money and leisure to purchase instruments and learn to play them, amateur music making became an important outlet for the middle classes. In many homes, evenings were a time for making music with family and friends, singing or playing the piano, violin, flute, guitar, harp, or other instruments, as shown in Figure V.3. All these amateurs needed music to play, creating a boom in music publishing. In the 1770s, the largest publishers in London, Paris, and Leipzig had listed hundreds of items in their catalogues; in the 1820s, they listed tens of thousands of pieces. Technology again proved crucial: lithography, invented around 1796, enabled publishers to print music cheaply with elaborate illustrations that helped it sell. In an effort to make their music appealing and accessible to amateur performers, composers wrote tuneful melodies with attractive accompaniments, familiar chord progressions with intermittent dramatic or colorful harmonic contrasts, simple songlike forms, little counterpoint, strong musical and extramusical associations, and evocative titles. The most successful music offered something novel and individual that made it stand out from the crowd. However, originality was now marked not by how one treated conventional material, as in the Classical era, but by the innovative qualities of the material itself. Furthermore, as interest in national culture grew, composers incorporated national traits in song, instrumental music, and opera. The eighteenth-century cosmopolitan ideal was gradually replaced by the expectation that composers would write music true to their national identity. The new idioms, born of the con-

*Figure V.4. Henry Fuseli's* The Nightmare *(ca. 1781), a chronologically pre-Romantic work, exemplifies the kind of fantastic scene—exploiting terror, violence, eroticism, and the macabre—that attracted some nineteenth-century artists. Freies Deutsches Hochstift, Frankfurt-am-Main.*

stellation of factors described above and focused on melody, emotion, novelty, individuality, and in some instances ethnicity, paralleled Romanticism in literature and art and came to be called *Romantic*.

## From Classical to Romantic

Perhaps the best way to understand Romanticism is as a reaction—or, more precisely, a multitude of reactions—to the rationalist ideals of the eighteenth-century Enlightenment. The belief in the perfectability of society on logical principles received a devastating blow from the events of the late eighteenth century: first a terrible reign of terror in the aftermath of the French Revolution, and then a period of war all over Europe that ended only in 1815. Some people, their confidence in the power of reason thus undermined, reacted by turning away from civilization to contemplation of the natural world, leading to the great outburst of nature poetry that reached its peak in the lyrics of Lord Byron, Shelley, and Keats; or to the ambitious landscape paintings of John Constable and J. M. W. Turner (see Figure V.2). Others favored retreat into the *supernatural* worlds of spiritualism, mysticism, or even fantasy, as can be seen in the more visionary works of Henry Fuseli and Francisco Goya (see Figures V.4 and V.5). Another form of retreat was to be found in the revival of past traditions, such as the Middle Ages, by artists like Edward Burne-Jones and his circle, evident in Figure V.6, and in the music dramas of Richard Wagner (see Chapter 19). Still another was the exploration of unknown and exotic worlds, either real or imagined, by writers like E. T. A. Hoffmann and artists such as Eugène Delacroix, whose painting *The Death of Sardanapalus*, based on a tragedy by Lord Byron, is discussed below.

Among the most telling visual signs of Romantic style is color, which was explored for its optical effects as well as for its symbolic associations. Many artists associated with the movement (Delacroix and Turner, among others) were interested in color theory, and even Goethe, known today mainly for his literary

Interest in color

*Figure V.5. Francisco Goya's* The Third of May 1808 *(1814) depicts the execution of Spanish insurgents by French soldiers during the invasion of Spain. Goya's decidedly graphic and emotional representation of the horrors of war demonstrates the Romantic notion of a visionary and political role for art. Museo del Prado, Madrid.*

works, wrote a book about it. The concern with color led most Romantic theorists to view painting, as opposed to sculpture, as the quintessential visual art of the period. Sculpture, they argued, with its emphasis on form, was essentially Classical, whereas painting, with its emphasis on color and illusion, was essentially Romantic.

**Classicism in painting**

In fact, Romanticism first appeared in painting as a way of opposing academic and classical tendencies. Classicism was cultivated during a period of Neoclassical revival at the end of the eighteenth century in France, where Jacques-Louis David emerged as the leading painter. Years of study in Rome visiting its ruins and ancient monuments prompted David to adopt a "classical" style and to use subject matter derived from antiquity, as seen in Figure V.7. In *The Loves of Paris and Helen,* David represents the fabled pair of lovers from Greek legend as the perfection of manhood and the epitome of womanly beauty. Like Renaissance statues that have been suddenly brought to life, these figures appear relaxed (albeit restrained) in their architecturally austere love nest, far from the fray of the Trojan War that resulted when Paris abducted Helen. This same classicizing tendency underlies the heroic scale and epic quality of much Romantic music, including not only many symphonies but also, for example, Hector Berlioz's monumental five-act opera *Les Troyens* (The Trojans; see page 468).

**Romanticism in painting**

Challenges to this restrained, predominantly Classical style in painting arose in France as well, among Romantic artists who employed a colorful, painterly style that contrasted with the severity of the Classical mode. In general, they treated two types of subjects: modern life, often at its most harrowing; and exotic historical themes, sometimes bordering on the fantastic. (Again, Berlioz provides a revealing musical parallel in his quasi-autobiographical *Symphonie fantastique*; see Chapter 17). A good example of the first type is *The Raft of the "Medusa"* by Théodore Géricault, shown in Figure V.8. The subject, which represents a contemporary occurrence in the exalted language of monumental art, was taken from an event that had caused a huge stir in France. It shows the victims of a catastrophic shipwreck, having been shamefully abandoned by the crew and left to drift for weeks, caught in the dramatic moment between hope

*Figure V.6. Edward Burne-Jones painted* Le Chant d'amour *(1868–1877) on a subject that borrowed themes from medieval tapestry design and early Renaissance painting, demonstrating the interest shared by many Romantic artists in a "simpler" past. Metropolitan Museum of Art, New York.*

*Figure V.7. Jacques-Louis David,* The Loves of Paris and Helen *(1788). An older contemporary of Beethoven, David was the most important European painter during the French Revolutionary period and a leader of the French Neoclassical style. Musée du Louvre, Paris.*

and despair as they attempt to signal their rescuers. The sensational story involved outbreaks of mutiny and cannibalism on the raft, and Géricault exploits the pessimistic and tense narrative with muted colors and dramatic gestures, suggesting the antiheroic and desperate plight of man's struggle against the forces of nature.

The second type of subject that appealed to Romantic painters is illustrated by Delacroix's *Death of Sardanapalus* (see Figure V.9), which became as important a manifesto for Romantic painting as Victor Hugo's works were for literature. Sardanapalus was a legendary Assyrian monarch who lived in great luxury but who died, after having set fire to his palace, in a conflagration that consumed his entire court. Delacroix's treatment combines Byronic exoticism with the use of vivid color as a means of conveying sensation. The same painterly application of color is also evident in his subdued but nonetheless intense portrait of Fryderyk Chopin (see Figure 17.14).

As the impact of French Romantic history painting spread throughout Europe from the late 1820s, other genres competed to attain a comparable status. Chief among them were landscape painting, portraiture, and especially genre painting (scenes of everyday life), whose popularity increased in proportion to the growing power of the bourgeoisie. At the same time, many of the forces and qualities that characterized Romanticism in art and literature were also influencing developments in music.

## Romanticism in Music

In music, Romanticism is not so much a collection of style traits as a state of mind that enabled composers to seek individual paths for expressing intense feelings—for example, melancholy, yearning, or joy. Composers respected the

# ARTS *and* IDEAS

## Science and Philosophy

German philosopher **Arthur Schopenhauer** (1788–1860) wrote *The World as Will and Representation* (1819), which held, among other things, that music was unique among the arts because it could express the will directly. His emphasis on the will as a motivating force influenced Nietzsche and the psychology of Freud; his impact on Wagner is discussed in Chapter 19.

English naturalist and author **Charles Darwin** (1809–1882) developed the theory that the origin of species derives by descent through the natural selection of those best adapted to survive in the struggle for existence. His monumental *On the Origin of Species* was published in 1859.

German economist, philosopher, and socialist **Karl Marx** (1818–1883), along with Friedrich Engels, promoted the idea that the state throughout history has been a device for the exploitation of the masses by a dominant class; that class struggle has been the main agency of historical change; and that the capitalist system, containing the seeds of its own decay, will be superseded by a socialist order and a classless society. His major works are the *Manifesto of the Communist Party* (1848), written for the Communist League, and *Das Kapital.*

**Louis Pasteur** (1822–1895) was a French chemist and microbiologist whose work demonstrated that many diseases are caused by microorganisms. He developed some vaccines as well as a technique for killing harmful bacteria in fluids such as milk by heating the liquid for a specific amount of time. He was the first director of the Pasteur Institute, founded in Paris in 1888 to continue his research on virulent and contagious diseases.

**Friedrich Wilhelm Nietzsche** (1844–1900), German philosopher, emphasized the "will to power" as the chief motivating force of both the individual and society. He rejected Western bourgeois civilization and looked to the "superman" to create a new heroic morality that would exist beyond the conventional standards of good and evil. Among his works are *The Birth of Tragedy* (1872) and *Thus Spake Zarathustra* (1883–1891), which inspired a tone poem by Richard Strauss.

U.S. inventor **Thomas Alva Edison** (1847–1931) patented more than a thousand devices, including the phonograph and the incandescent lightbulb.

## Literature

**Johann Wolfgang von Goethe** (1749–1832), German poet, dramatist, and prose writer, was a modern Renaissance man. Influenced by Greco-Roman civilization, Homer, and Shakespeare, he was a classical humanist with romantic leanings whose works, particularly *Faust* (1790–1832), were tremendously admired throughout the nineteenth century and inspired many musical treatments.

**E. T. A. Hoffmann** (1776–1822), German author of novels, short stories, and criticism, was also an opera composer and set designer. His sometimes bizarre fiction helped to establish the grotesque vein that became popular in some nineteenth-century literature and art.

Italian novelist and poet **Alessandro Manzoni** (1785–1873) believed in a united Italy. He became famous through his historical novel about Milan under Spanish rule in the seventeenth century, *I promessi sposi* (The Betrothed), which is among the greatest works of Italian literature in modern times. Verdi composed his Requiem as a memorial to Manzoni.

English poet **George Gordon, Lord Byron** (1788–1824) became famous throughout Europe as the embodiment of Romanticism with his quasi-autobiographical *Childe Harold,* which he dubbed a "romance" (meaning a narrative of adventure). The work introduced the century's "Byronic hero"—alienated, gloomy, passionate, mysterious—a figure who had countless descendants in life and art. Byron's legendary status was aided by his good looks, lameness (he had a club foot), flamboyant lifestyle, and exile from England.

**Heinrich Heine** (1797–1856) was the most popular German poet of his day, whose lyrics inspired settings by Schubert, Schumann, and others. By choosing in 1831 to settle in Paris, he became a noted literary man of exile, a counterpart of Chopin, and a leader of Parisian cosmopolitan society.

**Alexander Sergeyevich Pushkin** (1799–1837) was a Russian poet and dramatist whose works inspired operas by Glinka, Musorgsky, Tchaikovsky, and others. Under the influence of Shakespeare and Byron, Pushkin blended Western and Russian culture and had an enormous impact on subsequent Russian literature, despite his death at a young age after being wounded in a duel over his wife.

French poet, playwright, and novelist **Victor Hugo** (1802–1885) was a leader of the Romantic movement in Paris. He is best known for the humanity and compassion of his novels *Les Misérables* and *Notre-Dame de Paris*. Several of his plays served as the basis for librettos of operas by Verdi and others, including the modern musical *Les Misérables,* which has been translated into twenty-one languages and performed in 38 countries.

The prolific English novelist **Charles Dickens** (1812–1870) depicted life at all levels of society in Victorian England, attacked injustice and social hypocrisy, and created a host of characters with such vividness that their names became household words (for example, Ebenezer Scrooge). His novels include *A Christmas Carol, David Copperfield, Bleak House, Great Expectations,* and *A Tale of Two Cities.*

The sisters **Charlotte Brontë** (1816–1855) and **Emily Brontë** (1818–1848) wrote, respectively, the classic English novels *Jane Eyre* and *Wuthering Heights*. Among other Romantic themes such as the supernatural and the lure of the exotic, they articulated in their works the need of women for both love and independence.

Russian writer Count **Leo Tolstoy** (1828–1910) set his titanic novel *War and Peace* (1862–1869) against the backdrop of the Napoleonic invasion of Russia in 1812. The novel views history as a force marching to its own ends in which human characters play only an accidental role. His popular work *Anna Karenina* concerns the tragedy of a woman's blind faith in romantic love.

## Art

The works of Anglo-Swiss painter **Henry Fuseli** (1741–1825) reveal his Romantic fascination with terrifying and weird subjects. He was a great stimulus to a younger generation of artists who adopted the Romantic concept of the artist as prophet and visionary.

The Spaniard **Francisco Goya** (1746–1828), in addition to being a court painter of elegant and realistic portraits, produced highly individualistic and emotional works that depicted the horrors of war in the aftermath of the Napoleonic invasion of Spain in 1808.

The English painter **Joseph Turner** (1775–1851) took Romantic landscape painting to its height, mastering both dramatic scenes of disasters and quiet moments of intense lyricism. He explored the effects of nature in his paintings, in which he achieved transcendent, almost abstract effects with color.

**Théodore Géricault** (1791–1824), arguably the greatest painter of the first half of the nineteenth century despite his premature death, began his career by celebrating the heroism of Napoleonic France but turned to representing antiheroic subjects, such as the monumental *Raft of the "Medusa,"* which combines the uplifting qualities of history painting with a theme of utter despair.

**Eugène Delacroix** (1798–1863), a close friend of Fryderyk Chopin and George Sand, had a tremendous influence on the later Romantics as a colorist. He favored turbulent scenes inspired by mythology, literature (especially Byron and Shakespeare), and history, and he was recognized as the leader of the opposition to the Neoclassical school of Jacques-Louis David.

English painter and decorative artist Sir **Edward Burne-Jones** (1833–1898) was a leading figure in the Pre-Raphaelite movement, which took its inspiration from the early Renaissance. His paintings of subjects from medieval legend and classical mythology vividly illustrate the late nineteenth-century fantasy of a medieval Golden Age that so attracted Wagner.

*Figure V.8.* The Raft of the "Medusa" *by Théodore Géricault (1819) dramatically portrays a sensational contemporary tragedy, underlining the realist and antiheroic qualities of some Romantic art. Musée du Louvre, Paris.*

conventions of form and tonal relations up to a point, but their imaginations drove them to trespass limits that once seemed reasonable and to explore new realms of sound.

Some nineteenth-century writers (Schopenhauer and Liszt, for example) considered instrumental music the ideal Romantic art because, being independent of words, it could perfectly communicate pure emotion. An aria is limited by its text and can only express feelings that develop from a dramatic situation. Although the composer conjures up the emotion, it resides outside the creator in the character represented by the singer. But instrumental music can express the composer's own feelings; without being limited to particular emotions, like love or jealousy, its content may simply be turbulence or indeterminate longing, or even a certain restless "vacuum of the passions" (*vague des passions*)—a full, young heart seeking an object, such as Berlioz aimed to portray in the first movement of his *Symphonie fantastique* (see Chapter 17).

Although composers held instrumental music in the highest regard, poetry and literature occupied a central place in their thoughts and careers. A number of these composers were also extraordinarily articulate in the literary field. Berlioz, Schumann, and, later, Liszt wrote distinguished essays on music. Schubert and Schumann attained a new and intimate union between music and poetry in their art songs, and the lyrical spirit of the lied even imbued their instrumental music. Similarly, leading Romantic novelists and poets wrote about music with deep love and insight or involved themselves in music more directly; the writer E. T. A. Hoffmann, for example, was a successful composer of operas.

The ideal of instrumental music as the premier mode of expression and the strong literary orientation of nineteenth-century composers converged in the concept of *program music*. The term referred to instrumental music associated with poetic, descriptive, or narrative subject matter and came to be viewed as the opposite of *absolute music*, which purportedly had no such extramusical associations. Whether the program was outlined in detail or merely suggested, the music usually transcended its subject and could be understood and appreciated on its own. The program did not necessarily inspire or even precede the music; sometimes it was imposed as an afterthought.

*Figure V.9. Eugène Delacroix's* Death of Sardanapalus *(1827) illustrates the Romantic use of color to suggest emotion, as well as the attraction to sensational and exotic subjects. Musée du Louvre, Paris.*

Romantic composers also seemed intent on testing the limits of musical expression, which meant pushing to extremes such elements as dynamic shadings, harmonic logic, formal boundaries, even the physical capabilities of performers. One pair of opposites they explored with equal enthusiasm was the monumental and the miniature; at the same time as orchestras became larger and more colorful, matching the grandeur and boldness of some French history paintings, nineteenth-century composers cultivated many intimate genres for solo piano, solo voice, and chamber ensemble. In addition to writing hundreds of imposing works for orchestra, they produced thousands of pieces on a smaller scale—for piano solo, various chamber combinations, and voice—among which are the characteristic miniatures that portray a mood or communicate a sentiment in a matter of minutes.

The next four chapters are devoted to the music of Beethoven's successors in the nineteenth century. The extent to which these composers shared traits of Classicism or Romanticism, cultivated absolute or program music, and composed large-scale or miniature works varies with each individual and remains to be explored. Chapters 17 and 18 present representative composers and their works from the first half and second half of the century. Chapter 19 gives an overview of opera and related genres throughout the century and, therefore, covers the same chronological period as the first two chapters together, this time concentrating on developments in musical theater. Finally, Chapter 20 traces the last bloom of Romanticism in the closing decades of the nineteenth and the beginning of the twentieth centuries, and it paves the way for understanding the manifestations of musical modernism.

# The Early Romantics

## PRELUDE

*Chapter Contents*

*Prelude* 410

Franz Schubert
(1797–1828) 412

Hector Berlioz
(1803–1869) 420

Felix Mendelssohn
(1809–1847) 424

Robert Schumann
(1810–1856) 429

Fryderyk Chopin
(1810–1849) 432

*Postlude* 435

The first generation of Romantic composers found new ways to engage the established musical genres of the eighteenth century: orchestral music and other large-scale works such as concerto and oratorio; song; solo piano music; chamber music; and opera. As we survey representative composers to about 1850, we shall examine their contributions where relevant to the first four genres, postponing a discussion of opera until Chapter 19.

A principal tenet of Romanticism was that instrumental music could communicate pure emotion without using words. So the orchestra, with its infinite variety of colors and textures, became the medium par excellence of Romantic music. Most nineteenth-century composers we will study had to master the orchestra and prove themselves in the area of symphonic composition. Moreover, they had to come to terms with how the towering figure of Beethoven had transformed the symphony.

Central to public concert life was the orchestra, and the audience in the nineteenth century was increasingly made up of the middle class. The court orchestras of Mannheim, Vienna, Berlin, and other cities in the eighteenth century had played to mixed audiences of nobility and city people, a pattern that continued into the nineteenth century. But now, public concerts—such as those organized by choral and other societies, benefit concerts arranged for various causes, and subscription concerts sponsored by individual entrepreneurs—became more popular. The experience of hearing a symphony orchestra was still a relatively rare event for a music lover of any class. Among the composers who conducted orchestral concerts, partly of their own music, were Berlioz, Mendelssohn, and Schumann. Although the prominence given to the symphony in this book is out of proportion to the place symphonic music actually occupied in the activities of composers, musicians, and the public in this period, such prominence reflects the importance accorded it by audiences, critics, and the composers themselves, who increasingly used it as a means of communication with a new middle-class public.

Song—particularly the German art song, or lied (plural: lieder)—became a favorite outlet for intense personal feelings. In the works of Franz Schubert, for example, the lied was the perfect foil to the "heavenly length" of his symphonies. At once the most suitable medium for the literary and lyrical tendencies of Romanticism, the lied enjoyed a brilliant efflorescence in the nineteenth century—one that has never been matched.

A new type of song, the ballad, appeared toward the end of the eighteenth century. As a poetic genre, it was cultivated in Germany in imitation of the traditional ballads in the folk cultures of England and Scotland. Most ballads were fairly long poems, alternating narrative and dialogue in a tale filled with romantic adventures and supernatural incidents. Romantic ballads demanded a musical treatment quite different from the short, lyric, strophic lied of the eighteenth century. Their greater length necessitated a greater variety of themes and textures, which, in turn, required some means of unifying the whole. Moreover, the music needed to capture and enhance the contrasting moods and movements of the story. The ballad, then, expanded on the lied both in its form and in the range and force of its emotional content. The piano, instead of mere accompaniment, became an equal partner with the voice in illustrating and intensifying the meaning of the poetry.

Lieder composers often grouped their songs into collections with a unifying characteristic, such as texts by a single poet or a focus on a common theme. Such a collection is called a song cycle, in which all the songs are to be performed in order as movements of a multimovement vocal work. This format opened the possibility of telling a story through a succession of songs, combining the narrative emphasis of ballads with the focused expressivity of the lyric poem. The song cycle became especially typical of the nineteenth century, providing a balance between small and large forms, lyric and narrative content, and unity and variety, qualities strongly valued at the time.

The piano, much enlarged and strengthened since Mozart's day (see "Innovations," pages 418–419), became the perfect instrument for conveying repertory from either end of the spectrum: concertos of grandiose proportions or brief statements of fleeting impressions. It was capable of producing a full, firm tone at any dynamic level and of responding in every way to demands for both expressiveness and virtuosity. Composers developed new ways of writing for the instrument, such as splitting the accompaniment between two hands, reinforcing the melody by simulating the orchestral technique of doubling, and calling for extended legato effects with the help of the pedal. For all these reasons, many Romantic composers of orchestral music—Schubert, Mendelssohn, and Robert Schumann, whom we will meet in this chapter, Liszt and Brahms in the next—also devoted their energy to writing solo music for piano, while others—like Chopin—made it the sole focus of their creative activity.

The medium of chamber music was not as congenial to many Romantic composers. It lacked the improvisational spontaneity and virtuosic glamour of the solo piano or the solo voice on the one hand, and the glowing colors and powerful sound of the orchestra on the other. It is, therefore, not surprising that the arch-Romantics Berlioz, Liszt, and Wagner contributed almost nothing to the repertory of chamber music nor that the best nineteenth-century chamber works came from those composers who felt closest to the Classical tradition—Schubert, Brahms, and, to a lesser degree, Mendelssohn and Schumann.

In this chapter, we will survey five of the most important composers of the first Romantic generation in the order in which they were born: Franz Schubert, Hector Berlioz, Felix Mendelssohn, Robert Schumann, and Fryderyk Chopin. The contributions that each one made to the characteristic musical genres just outlined will be discussed in the order of the prominence they command within each composer's output.

# Franz Schubert (1797–1828)

A prolific composer in every genre, Schubert used virtually all the musical languages of his time. His contributions to song, symphonic, solo-piano, and chamber-music repertoires are substantial and remain significant (see biography and Figure 17.1).

## Lieder

*Melody*

**CD 8/68**  **CD 4/73**

If the new Romantic style focused on melody, the songs of Franz Schubert surely set the tone for the century. Few composers have possessed so fully Schubert's gift for creating beautiful melodies. Many of his songs have the simple, artless quality of folk song and the ability to suggest uncomplicated feelings (for example, *Heidenröslein* [see Example 17.1a] and *Der Lindenbaum* [NAWM 112]). Others are suffused with sweetness and melancholy (*Am Meer; Der Wanderer*). Still others are declamatory, intense, and dramatic (*Aufenthalt; Der Atlas* [see Example 17.1b]). Every mood or nuance of feeling finds expression in Schubert's apparently effortless stream of melody, which flows equally well in his songs and instrumental works.

*Example 17.1a: Franz Schubert,* Heidenröslein, *measures 1–4*

*A boy saw a rosebud standing, a rosebud on the heath*

*Example 17.1b: Franz Schubert,* Der Atlas, *measures 5–12*

*I, the unlucky Atlas! A world, the whole world of pain must I bear.*

Along with a genius for melody, Schubert possessed a strong feeling for harmonic color. His complex modulations, sometimes embodying long passages in
which the tonality is kept in suspense, powerfully underline the dramatic qualities of his song texts. Striking examples of harmonic boldness may be found in
*Gruppe aus dem Tartarus* and *Das Heimweh*, a song that also illustrates Schubert's
trademark device of alternating between the major and minor forms of the
triad. Masterly use of chromatic coloring within a prevailing diatonic sound is
another Schubert characteristic (*Am Meer; Lob der Thränen*). His modulations
typically move from the tonic toward flat keys, and the mediant or submediant is
a favorite destination.

Harmony

## Franz Schubert (1797–1828)

Homely, humble, and hidden in Beethoven's
shadow, Franz Schubert was nevertheless the first
great song writer of the Romantics and an as-
toundingly prolific composer of all kinds of music.
In addition to composing more than 600 lieder, he
made important contributions to the piano, chamber, and symphonic repertories.

The son of a schoolteacher, Schubert grew up in
cosmopolitan Vienna. After studying theory and
performance, and taking composition lessons
from court music director Antonio Salieri, he displayed sufficient musical talent to win a free first-
class education at a prestigious Vienna boarding
school. Educated to follow his father's profession,
he actually worked as a schoolteacher for three
years before devoting himself entirely to writing
music. He composed with astonishing speed and
fluency; in 1815 alone (having just turned eighteen
and even while teaching) he wrote 144 songs. By
1821, Schubert's music was being widely performed in Vienna and he was earning substantial
sums from publishers.

Although Schubert never married, he had a
large circle of friends in Vienna. Not physically
handsome, he was nicknamed *Schwammerl*, which
means "mushroom" but probably connoted something like "Fatso." His close friendships with men
and veiled references made by his friends have
suggested to some scholars that he was homosexual, although others dispute this conclusion. He
apparently contracted syphilis by January 1823,
and the last years of his life were clouded by illness. When he died at the age of thirty-one, his
tombstone was inscribed "Music has here buried a
rich treasure but still fairer hopes." Given the
brevity of Schubert's career, his output of almost
one thousand separate works is truly amazing.

*Figure 17.1. Franz Schubert, in a watercolor portrait from
1825 by Wilhelm August Rieder. Gesellschaft der
Musikfreunde, Vienna.*

**Major works:** two song cycles, *Die schöne Müllerin*
and *Winterreise*, as well as hundreds of individual
songs; 9 symphonies, notably No. 8 in B Minor
(*Unfinished*) and No. 9 in C Major (*The Great*);
about 35 chamber works, including Piano Quintet
in A Major (*The Trout*), String Quartet in D Minor
(*Death and the Maiden*), and String Quintet in C
Major; 22 piano sonatas; many short piano pieces;
17 operas and singspiels; 6 Masses; and 200 other
choral works.

Texts

Schubert set poetry by many writers, often dwelling on a single poet for a time. From Goethe alone he took fifty-nine poems, setting some of them more than once. Some of Schubert's finest lieder are found in his two song cycles on poems by Wilhelm Müller, *Die schöne Müllerin* (The Pretty Miller-Maid, 1823) and *Winterreise* (A Winter's Journey, 1827). The *Schwanengesang* (Swan Song, 1828), not intended as a cycle but published as such posthumously, includes six songs on poems by Heinrich Heine.

Form

The form always suits the shape and meaning of the text. When a poem sustains a single image or mood, Schubert typically uses strophic form, with the same music for each stanza, as in *Heidenröslein* (Little Heath Rose, 1815) and *Das Wandern* (Wandering), the first song in *Die schöne Müllerin*. Contrast or change is often depicted in modified strophic form, in which some strophes repeat the same music but others vary it or use new music; an example is *Der Lindenbaum* (The Linden Tree) from *Winterreise*, described below. Some songs are in ternary form (ABA or ABA'), as in *Der Atlas* (Atlas), or bar form (AAB), as in *Ständchen* (Serenade), both from *Schwanengesang*. Longer narrative songs may be through-composed, with new music for each stanza, like the ballad *Erlkönig* (The Erlking, 1815), or combine declamatory and arioso styles as in an operatic scene, like *Der Wanderer* (The Wanderer, 1816); in either case, recurring themes and a carefully planned tonal scheme lend unity.

Accompaniments

Often the piano accompaniment matches some pictorial image in the text, as in *Wohin?* (Whither?) or *Auf dem Wasser zu singen* (Singing on the Water). Schubert designed such pictorial features not only to illustrate but also to enhance the mood of the song. So the accompaniment of *Gretchen am Spinnrade* (Gretchen at the Spinning Wheel, NAWM 111)—one of the earliest (1814) and most famous of the lieder—suggests not only the whir of the spinning wheel by a constant sixteenth-note figure in the right hand and the perpetual motion of the treadle by the left hand, but also the agitation of Gretchen's thoughts as she sings of her beloved in Goethe's epic poem *Faust*. Similarly, in *Erlkönig* (The Erlking), one of Schubert's relatively few ballads—also on a Goethe text—the pounding octave triplets in the accompaniment depict at once the galloping of the horse and the frantic anxiety of the father as he rides "through night and wind" with his sick, frightened child clasped in his arms. The delirious boy imagines that he sees the legendary Erlking, enticing him to a land where he will be comforted by the swaying, dancing, and singing of the Erlking's daughters. Schubert has characterized in an unforgettable manner the three actors in the drama: the concerned father, the bewitching Erlking, and the increasingly terrified child.

CD 8/62    CD 4/67

*Erlkönig*

*Winterreise*

*Winterreise* (Winter's Journey) consists of twenty-four poems by Müller that express the nostalgia of a lover revisiting in winter the haunts of a failed summer romance. In one of the songs from this cycle, *Der Lindenbaum* (The Linden Tree, NAWM 112), the poet dwells on the memory of the tree under which he used to lie dreaming of his love. Now, as he passes it, the chilly wind rustles the branches, which seem to call him back to find rest—or death.

CD 8/68    CD 4/73

The modified strophic form marks the progress of the story: the first strophe, remembering summer love, is in major; the second changes to minor to suggest the chill of winter; the third heralds the cold wind with a new, declamatory melody; and the fourth returns to the major mode and the original melody, now sounding more threatening than comforting. The subtle ways in which the music interprets the poem and the musical elements change in response to the progress of the poem demonstrate how well Schubert conveys meanings through music that deepens our experience of the text.

Schubert's ability to capture the mood and character of a poem and make the music its equal in emotive and descriptive power, along with the sheer beauty of

*Figure 17.2. Schubert at the piano accompanying a singer in the home of Joseph von Spaun. The sepia drawing by Moritz von Schwind (1868) conveys the intensely emotional engagement with music that was characteristic of the age. Historisches Museum der Stadt Wien.*

his music and the pleasure it gives to those who perform it, have endeared Schubert's songs to his contemporaries and to generations of singers, pianists, and listeners. His songs set the standard that later song composers strove to match (see Figure 17.2).

## Orchestral Music

Schubert's *Unfinished* (No. 8, in only two movements) has been called the first truly Romantic symphony by virtue of its lyricism, its adventurous harmonic excursions, and its enchanting colors. Originally planned as a four-movement work, it was his first attempt at a large-scale symphony. We are struck immediately by its haunting opening in B minor. After this brief but unusual introduction, the first theme begins with a quietly stirring figure in the low strings that then combines with a soaring melody, played pianissimo first by the oboes and clarinets and later joined by other woodwinds that help build to a fortissimo climax. After an extremely brief transition (only four measures) that modulates to the surprising key of G major, Schubert presents the relaxed second theme in the cellos, accompanied by syncopated figures in the violas and clarinets over the pizzicato of the double basses. Instead of centering the development section and coda on these two themes, as Haydn or Beethoven might have done, Schubert focuses on the introductory subject. In this way, Schubert met his listeners' expectations for symphonic development while devoting the main thematic areas to the presentation of memorable, seductive melodies like those of his songs. Unfortunately, no one heard this example of Schubert's stunning orchestral voice until many years after his death because the symphony, written in 1822, was not performed until 1865.

    Schubert's "Great" Symphony in C Major (No. 9, composed in 1828—the last year of his life—and first performed in 1839) received that nickname because of its "heavenly length," much admired by Robert Schumann (see vignette, page 417). Schumann appreciated Schubert's expansion of the form to accommodate his appealing melodies and orchestral effects and, after having avoided writing a symphony himself, was inspired to follow Schubert's example (see below). In fact, Schubert's Symphony in C Major provided an important model for younger composers by showing how Beethovenian development could be

*Unfinished* Symphony

"Great" Symphony in C Major

integrated, along with the new Romantic emphasis on songlike melodies, striking harmonies, and evocative orchestral colors, into the Classical form of the symphony.

## Solo Music for Piano

During the nineteenth century, the piano emerged as the quintessential instrument of the salon or living room, creating a steady demand for music that amateurs and professionals could play in a domestic setting. This was particularly important to freelance composers like Schubert and Chopin. Among Schubert's works suitable for amateurs are dozens of marches, waltzes, and other dances, as well as several short pieces that became for piano literature what his lieder are to the vocal repertory. These include six *Moments musicaux* (D. 789)[1] and eight Impromptus (D. 899, 935), each of which creates a distinctive mood. These works set a standard for every subsequent Romantic composer of intimate piano pieces. Schubert's most important larger works for the piano are his eleven completed sonatas and the *Wanderer Fantasie* (D. 760). More than many of his compositions for piano, the fantasy makes virtuosic demands on the player's technique. Its four movements, which are linked together, center around the Adagio second movement, a series of variations on his song *Der Wanderer*. The remaining movements use motives from the song as well.

Sonatas    In his piano sonatas, Schubert departs in subtle ways from the standard Classical patterns, often introducing three keys in his expositions (for example, tonic, mediant, and dominant) instead of two. Schubert's expansive melodies, even though they are not themes that lend themselves to motivic development, recur in different environments that give them new meaning each time. While composing his last three piano sonatas (all in 1828), Schubert was obviously aware of Beethoven's works, as witness the stormy first movement of the Sonata in C Minor (D. 958) and the finale of the Sonata in B (D. 960), which begins like the finale of Beethoven's Quartet Op. 130. But these are superficial similarities; Schubert is nowhere more independent, more the melodist than in these sonatas. The last of them, in B♭, perhaps his greatest work for the piano, opens with a long singing melody, doubled at the lower octave, which returns throughout the movement in various guises, major and minor, complete and fragmented.

## Chamber Music

Schubert modeled his first quartets on works by Mozart and Haydn, and wrote them primarily for his friends to enjoy. The most popular work from his earlier period is the *Trout* Quintet for piano, violin, viola, cello, and bass (1819), so called because of the Andantino variations, inserted between the scherzo and the finale, on his own song *Die Forelle* (The Trout). The quintet's slow movement is a masterpiece of serene, simple beauty. Schubert's mature period in chamber music—when he grappled wtih Beethoven's influence—begins in 1820 with an Allegro in C Minor, D. 703, commonly called the *Quartettsatz*, intended as the first movement of a string quartet that he never completed. Three important

---

1. Schubert's works are best identified by the number assigned to them in *Schubert: Thematic Catalogue of All His Works in Chronological Order*, originally by Otto Erich Deutsch and Donald R. Wakeling (New York: Norton, 1951) and subsequently corrected and enlarged by others. Thus, the letter D preceding the number of a Schubert work stands for "Deutsch," the name of their first cataloguer.

works followed, his last in the genre—the Quartets in A Minor, D. 804 (1824); in D Minor, D. 810 (1824–1826, nicknamed "Death and the Maiden"); and in G Major, D. 887 (1826).

The Quartet in A Minor begins with a long singing melody that calls out for words, while the lower strings provide harmony and rhythmic ostinatos for thirty-one measures. Then, out of the first few notes of the melody, Schubert builds exciting transitional episodes, the second theme, and most of the development section with a variety of textures, returning from time to time to the opening texture. The two inner movements have quotations of melodies from Schubert's own works—in one case a song, showing how readily Schubert incorporated his lieder melodies into an instrumental context. The finale, a cheerful Allegro in Hungarian style, contrasts with the dark mood of the preceding three movements.

**Last three quartets**

The grimly serious Quartet in D Minor distributes its main ideas among the four instruments. Its central movement is a set of variations on Schubert's gripping song *Der Tod und das Mädchen* (D. 531, Death and the Maiden). The Quartet in G Major, on a larger scale than the other two, exhibits Schubert's habit of alternating major and minor forms of the triad, reversed and differently colored at the recapitulation.

Schubert wrote his masterpiece of chamber music, the String Quintet in C Major, D. 956, during the last two months of his life. The added instrument is a second cello, providing an unusually deep range that was particularly appealing in its lushness. Schubert obtained exquisite effects from this combination. The ideas are set forth and developed in the first movement in a truly symphonic

**String Quintet**

---

**VIGNETTE**   Schumann on Schubert's Symphony in C Major

*When he visited Schubert's brother Ferdinand in 1839, Robert Schumann discovered the manuscript of Schubert's "Great" Symphony in C Major, which had never been performed in public. Through Schumann's intercession, it was performed that same year at the Gewandhaus Concerts in Leipzig under the direction of Mendelssohn. In a review of the piece the following year, Schumann praised it as revealing both an unknown aspect of Schubert and a new approach to the symphony.*

~~~

I must say at once that anyone who is not yet acquainted with this symphony knows very little about Schubert. When we consider all that he has given to art, this praise may strike many as exaggerated, partly, no doubt, because composers have so often been advised, to their chagrin, that it is better for them—after Beethoven—"to abstain from the symphonic form." . . .

On hearing Schubert's symphony and its bright, flowery, romantic life, the city [of Vienna] crystallizes before me, and I realize how such works could

be born in these very surroundings. . . . Everyone must acknowledge that the outer world—sparkling today, gloomy tomorrow—often deeply stirs the feeling of the poet or the musician; and all must recognize, while listening to this symphony, that it reveals to us something more than mere beautiful song, mere joy and sorrow, such as music has ever expressed in a hundred ways, leading us into regions that, to our best recollection, we had never before explored. To understand this, one must hear this symphony. Here we find . . . a suffusing romanticism that other works by Franz Schubert have already made known to us.

And then the heavenly length of the symphony, like that of a thick novel in four volumes. . . . How this refreshes, this feeling of abundance, so contrary to our experience with others when we always dread to be disillusioned at the end and are often saddened through disappointment.

From *Neue Zeitschrift für Musik* 12 (1840): 82–83, after the translation, by Paul Rosenfeld, in Robert Schumann, *On Music and Musicians*, ed. Konrad Wolff (New York: Norton, 1946), pp. 108–111.

The industrial revolution was not a single event, but a series of inventions and applications that together radically changed the way goods were manufactured. Items that had been made by hand for centuries—the word *manufacture* itself originally denoted handcrafting—could now be mass-produced by machine, allowing them to be much more widely available and less costly. In addition, existing products were improved, and new ones developed in a continuous stream of innovation.

Music-instrument manufacture was one of the many industries that became revolutionized. One profound change was in the sheer quantity of instruments that could be produced. In the 1770s, the output of even the largest piano-making firms in Europe was only about 20 pianos a year because every piece of each instrument needed to be made by hand. Around 1800, John Broadwood & Sons of London was manufacturing about 400 pianos a year by employing a large and specialized workforce. However, by 1850 the firm was using steam power and mass-production techniques to make over 2,000 pianos a year, turning out each one a hundred times faster than before. Many were grand pianos, but most were the smaller square pianos (see Figures 17.3 and 17.12) more suitable for a domestic setting. Because they were produced in such quantity, pianos became inexpensive enough for middle-class families to afford.

The design of the piano was also improved during the late eighteenth and nineteenth centuries through a number of innovations. The damper pedal, by raising all the dampers off the strings, let tones continue to sound even after the keys were released, allowing greater resonance, closer imitation of orchestral sound, and new pianistic effects. The metal

*Figure 17.3.* The Duet *by George Goodwin Kilburne, a painting from the late nineteenth century showing domestic music making with performers playing harp and square piano. Haynes Fine Art Gallery, Worcester, England.*

*Figure 17.4. Boehm-system flute (1856) by Theobald Boehm. Bate Collection, Oxford, England.*

frame, introduced in England during the 1820s, resulted in instruments with higher string tension and thus greater volume, wider dynamic range, longer sustain, and better legato. By 1850, the piano's range was extended to seven octaves (from the six of Beethoven's day) and a double-escapement action permitted a more rapid repetition of notes that in turn enabled a new level of virtuosity. All of these new capabilities were exploited by performers and composers, and the piano became the indispensable instrument for home music making as well as for public concerts. The growth of domestic music making stimulated composers to write some pieces of a less technically demanding nature and required publishers to make printed music more readily available, which in turn spurred the proliferation of amateur musical societies and concert organizations, which then attracted larger audiences, and so on, in ever-widening circles of increasingly affordable production and consumption.

Other instruments benefited from the same spirit of innovation. Paris had been the center of the harp industry at the close of the eighteenth century largely because Queen Marie Antoinette, herself a harpist, popularized the instrument for domestic use. Just before the French Revolution, Paris had as many as fifty-eight harp teachers and a great many harp makers, including Sébastien Érard, who moved his firm to London after the Revolution and registered the first British patent ever granted for a harp. Érard's firm, which also produced pianos, was important in overcoming the technical problems of the single-action pedal harp, such as its instability of pitch, frequent breaking of strings, and limited modulation. His most remarkable improvement was a new fork mechanism, operated by a set of pedals that allowed the strings to be temporarily shortened, raising the pitch by one half-step. Eventually, Érard patented a harp that could be played in any key because each string could be adjusted almost instantaneously to produce any of three semitones. By 1820, the firm had sold 3,500 of these instruments, whose principles are still in use by modern pedal-harp makers.

Still other instruments profited from a combination of new technologies, enterprising innovators, and improved methods of manufacture. For exam-

ple, Theobald Boehm, a goldsmith and musician with experience in the steel industry, established a successful flute factory in Munich in 1828. He experimented with a number of designs for mechanisms that would achieve a uniform tone production, superior sound volume, and better control of tuning. By 1849, he had created the modern "Boehm-system flute," an all-metal instrument with large holes that were closed not by the bare fingers but by padded keys, linked with each other by a series of rods and axles to facilitate accuracy and speed (see Figure 17.4). Others applied Boehm's ideas to the clarinet and the saxophone, a new wind instrument invented by Adolphe Sax about 1840.

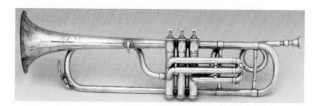

*Figure 17.5. Trumpet with piston valves (ca. 1865) by Antoine Courtois of Paris. Metropolitan Museum of Art, New York.*

Brass instrument makers applied the valve technology of the steam engine—in which valves controlled the flow of steam, water, or air—to the manufacture of trumpets and horns, finally enabling these instruments to produce all the notes of the chromatic scale. The valves allow a player to open one or more lengths of pipe to extend the sounding length of the air column and thus lower the pitch by one or more semitones (see Figure 17.5). Many new brass instruments were created as well, including the tuba, which became the bass of the orchestral brass section.

Similar mechanical innovations brought about by the industrial revolution—such as interlocking rods, gears, and screws—also improved the construction and tuning of the timpani in the early nineteenth century. By the late nineteenth century, the piano, the harp, and the wind, brass, and percussion instruments of the orchestra had almost reached their modern form, thanks to the inventors and industrialists who applied the century's new technology to music.

way. The beautiful E♭-major melody of the second theme, shown in Example 17.2, appears first in the cellos in parallel thirds before it reaches the first violin. Its recapitulation in A♭, a third down from the tonic (just as E♭ is a third up), completes a tonal scheme that was characteristic in the nineteenth century. The finale, with its playful themes and abrupt modulations, is in a lighter style, relaxing the tension built up by the first three movements. The quintet has the profound lyricism, unobtrusive contrapuntal mastery, long melodic lines (for example, the first fifteen measures of the Adagio), and wealth of harmonic invention that characterize Schubert's late piano sonatas.

*Example 17.2: Franz Schubert, String Quintet in C Major, D. 956, first movement, second theme*

# Hector Berlioz (1803–1869)

*Symphonie fantastique*

If Hector Berlioz had been a character in a Romantic novel, we would surely describe him as a Byronic hero (see biography and Figure 17.6). Because his imagination tended to run in parallel literary and musical channels, Berlioz subtitled his first and most famous work, *Symphonie fantastique*, "Episode in the Life of an Artist" and provided it with an autobiographical program (see NAWM 121, pages 425–426). Composed in 1830, only three years after Beethoven's death, the work is "fantastic" in the sense that it is a psychological fantasy, a product of the imagination—in this case, a musical drama without words. As Berlioz wrote, "The program should be regarded in the same way as the spoken words of an opera, serving to introduce the musical numbers by describing the situation that evokes the particular mood and expressive character of each." The literary influences in the program are too numerous to detail, although Goethe's *Faust* is conspicuous among them, and the fantasized situations are depicted in the passionate prose of a young and sensitive artist.

*Idée fixe*

Berlioz brings back the opening theme of the first Allegro, shown in Example 17.3—the idée fixe, or the obsessive image of the hero's beloved, according to the program—in all the other movements. The first movement, *Rêveries et passions*, consists of a slow introduction followed by an Allegro in modified sonata form; the second is a waltz, replacing the Classical scherzo; the third is a pastorale, an Adagio in a large, two-part form; the fourth movement is a macabre and descriptive orchestral tour de force; and the finale, an introduction and

# ✳ Hector Berlioz (1803–1869)

*Figure 17.6. Hector Berlioz in a portrait by Émile Signol painted in 1832 during Berlioz's stay in Rome. Villa Medici, Rome.*

Hector Berlioz was something new in music: not only a radically original composer but also a well-known music critic and one of the first people to have a career as an orchestral conductor. He is especially remembered for his achievement in writing symphonies, operas, and choral works, which was remarkable for the time considering that he was neither a concert pianist nor a ranking performer on any instrument.

Berlioz was born in southeastern France near the Alps, the son of a well-to-do doctor and a pious mother. Well educated and well read in the classics, he developed a fascination with music, taught himself harmony from textbooks (including Rameau's *Traité de l'harmonie*), and began to compose in his teens. When Berlioz was seventeen, his parents sent him to medical school in Paris, but his interest in music frequently lured him to the opera, where he heard works by Gluck and Rossini, among others. He studied composition at the Conservatory and eventually abandoned medicine to make his mark as the first important French composer since Rameau.

By the time Berlioz produced his first major work, he had become enchanted by Beethoven's symphonies, Shakespeare's plays, and the English actress Harriet Smithson, whose performance in the role of Hamlet's Ophelia led him to pursue her obsessively. When she rejected his advances, he began to sketch out his extraordinary *Symphonie fantastique*, which served as a kind of musical auto-

biography to monumentalize his feelings. After a rocky courtship, they finally married and had a son, to whom Berlioz remained devoted even after his infatuation for Smithson faded and the couple split up. After she died in 1864, he married the singer Marie Recio, with whom he had long had an affair. In his final years, Berlioz grew ill and disillusioned about the failure of his music to gain acceptance, especially in France. He died at age sixty-five, having outlived two wives, his son, and most of his family and friends.

Berlioz was one of the most literary of composers; not only did he write music criticism, his own memoirs, and the first modern treatise on orchestration, but he emulated the authors he most admired—Virgil, Shakespeare, and Goethe—in his own musical compositions: the opera *Les Troyens* (The Trojans), adapted from the *Aeneid* (discussed in Chapter 19); *Beatrice and Benedict*, an opera based on Shakespeare's *Much Ado about Nothing*; his dramatic symphonies, *Romeo and Juliet* and *The Damnation of Faust*, the latter inspired by Goethe's epic poem. Even his very first opera, which includes the *Roman Carnival* scene that gave rise to his popular overture, was based on the memoirs of the Italian sculptor Benvenuto Cellini. He also wrote the *Grande messe des morts* (a huge Requiem), an orchestral song cycle *Les Nuits d'été* (Summer Nights), and other songs with orchestra or piano accompaniment.

*Figure 17.7. Berlioz's wife, Harriet Smithson, as Ophelia in Shakespeare's* Hamlet.

CD 9/16    CD 5/1

Allegro entitled "Dream of a Witches' Sabbath" (NAWM 121), uses a transformation of the idée fixe and two other themes—one of them the chant sequence *Dies irae*—first singly, then in combination.

*Example 17.3: Hector Berlioz,* Symphonie fantastique, *Op. 14, first movement, Allegro agitato e appassionato assai*

The *Symphonie fantastique* is original not only because it represents a transformation of the symphony to serve narrative and autobiographical purposes but also because it presents a dazzling musical vocabulary. It is partly a matter of details—melodies, harmonies, rhythms, phrase structures—and partly Berlioz's astounding ability to express the many shifting moods and the essential emotional content of his drama in music that has great communicative power. His vivid imagination and his inventive orchestral sonorities shine through in nearly every measure. Berlioz achieved unity in the symphony as a whole—the kind of unity Beethoven forged in his Third and Fifth Symphonies—by introducing a recurring theme and by developing the dramatic idea through all of the five movements.

*Harold en Italie*

Berlioz's second symphony, *Harold en Italie* (1834; title suggested by Lord Byron's *Childe Harold*), is a set of four scenes inspired by the composer's recollections of an Italian sojourn. Each movement is connected by a recurrent theme, played by solo viola. The instrument is featured throughout, though less prominently than in solo concertos; for this reason, the great violinist Niccolò Paganini (1782–1840), who commissioned the work from Berlioz, refused to play it. In each movement, the viola melody combines contrapuntally with the other themes, and the solo instrument continually blends with different orchestral groups in a ravishing display of sonorities. The finale explicitly sums up the themes of the preceding movements.

*Roméo et Juliette*

Five years after *Harold en Italie*, Berlioz produced his "dramatic symphony" in seven movements, *Roméo et Juliette*, for orchestra, soloists, and chorus. In adding choral parts to the orchestra, he was following Beethoven's example; but in this work the voices enter in the prologue and are used in three of the symphonic movements as well. Although the Classical order of movements can still be traced, the series of independent scenes approaches an unstaged opera or

| A CLOSER LOOK | The Symphony Orchestra |

In the 1780s, Haydn's orchestra at Eszterháza consisted of fewer than 25 instruments: a core of strings (10 violins, 2 violas, 2 cellos, and 2 basses) plus 2 oboes, 2 bassoons, 2 horns, and keyboard. Sometimes a performer would double on another instrument; for example, the first oboist might be called upon to play flute in one movement. The court orchestra in Mozart's Vienna was marginally bigger: it used a few more strings and 2 flutes in addition to the other winds. But only forty years later, Beethoven's Ninth Symphony was premiered in Vienna by a force of 61 players plus a large chorus. In addition to the strings (without keyboard, which was no longer necessary as a foundation for the orchestra), it called for a pair each of flutes, oboes, clarinets, bassoons, horns, trumpets, and trombones. By the 1830s, orchestras in Paris, too, had grown enormously and typically employed between 70 and 80 players, including some 50 strings (usually 24, 8, 10, 8). Berlioz scored his *Symphonie fantastique* for piccolo, 2 flutes, 2 oboes, English horn, 2 clarinets, bass clarinet, 4 bassoons, 4 horns, 2 cornets, 2 trumpets, 3 trombones, and 2 ophicleides (large, keyed brass instruments, eventually replaced by tubas), as well as a variety of percussion instruments (including bells) and 2 harps.

*Figure 17.9.* Musicians in the Orchestra, *painted in 1868 by Edgar Degas, shows a few members of the woodwind section crowded against the string players. Musée d'Orsay, Paris.*

In addition to the increase in numbers, changes in the construction of instruments greatly enhanced the power of the strings and the efficiency of the winds (see "Innovations," pages 418–419). At the same time, the expansion in the orchestra's size created a need for a permanent, baton-wielding conductor as well as larger concert halls, many of which were built in the late 1800s in such cities as Vienna, London, New York, and Boston.

As orchestras became fuller and richer in texture and timbre, audiences at first condemned their "noisiness"; listeners complained that Beethoven's symphonies, for example, had too many notes. But when nineteenth-century ears became accustomed to the new complexity and volume of orchestral sound, Mozart's scores were considered too empty! The Romantic taste for monumentality and expressivity demanded still more volume, more brilliance, more color, and more variety. By the end of the nineteenth century, the Vienna Philharmonic regularly had more than one hundred players, and many composers were still aiming to keep them all occupied.

The question arises: did the developing orchestra, like some gigantic machine, drive the composers to write bigger scores, or was it the composers themselves who pioneered the increasingly massive sonority of the symphony orchestra?

*Figure 17.8. Court musicians from the eighteenth century. The anonymous painter suggests that the conductor is a menacing tyrant who will not tolerate any wrong notes.*

what the composer later called a "dramatic legend"—a genre he perfected in *La Damnation de Faust* (1864). Nonetheless, *Roméo et Juliette* is essentially a symphonic work.

Berlioz's first three symphonies, especially the *Symphonie fantastique*, made him the first leader of the Romantic movement's radical wing. All subsequent composers of program music—including Strauss (see Chapter 20) and Debussy (see Chapter 21)—were indebted to him. Berlioz's orchestration initiated a new era: he enriched orchestral music with new resources of harmony, color, expression, and form; and his use of a recurrent theme in different movements (as in the *Symphonie fantastique* and *Harold en Italie*) was an important impulse toward the development of the cyclical symphonic forms of the later nineteenth century. By example and precept, he was also the founder of modern orchestration and conducting. (See "A Closer Look," page 423.)

# Felix Mendelssohn (1809–1847)

Unlike Berlioz, who exploited originality and innovation, Mendelssohn studied and imitated Classical models. His mastery of form, counterpoint, and fugue, which blended influences from Bach, Handel, Mozart, Beethoven, and his Romantic contemporaries, helped to determine his personal style. Although he composed in a variety of genres, this discussion will concentrate on his larger, orchestrally based pieces and on his piano works.

## Orchestral Works

Mendelssohn's symphonies, overtures, and violin concerto all follow Classical models, with departures that show the strong impact of Romanticism. For example, his two most important symphonies carry geographical subtitles—the *Italian* (No. 4, 1833) and the *Scottish* (No. 3, 1842). They preserve impressions

*Figure 17.10. Watercolor by Felix Mendelssohn, entitled* Amalfi in May 1831, *a view of the Gulf of Salerno from Amalfi, near Naples, in southern Italy. Mendelssohn sketched, drew, and painted throughout his journeys in Italy and Britain. Bodleian Library, Oxford University.*

## ✺ Felix Mendelssohn (1809–1847)

As a child prodigy, Mendelssohn equaled or even surpassed Mozart's precocious musical talent. A renowned pianist, organist, conductor, and one of the most prominent composers of his generation, Mendelssohn wrote music that combines Romantic expressivity with Classical forms and techniques.

Felix was the grandson of Moses Mendelssohn (1729–1786), the leading Jewish philosopher of the Enlightenment in Germany. Although Jews were slowly gaining legal rights, his family converted to Protestantism when Mendelssohn was a child. (He later acknowledged his Lutheran faith in his *Reformation Symphony* [1840], in which he quotes one of Luther's hymns.) His family was at the center of Berlin's intellectual life. His father, a wealthy banker, and his mother, an amateur pianist, encouraged their children's musical interests, and both Felix and his sister, Fanny, were trained from an early age by excellent teachers. A good amateur artist, he painted lovely watercolors and sketched many of the places he visited when, after his schooldays were over, his father topped off his education by sending him away to travel.

As a boy, Mendelssohn showed astounding musical talent, composing a strikingly polished octet for strings at the age of sixteen and, in the following year, a brilliant concert overture for orchestra, inspired by his reading of Shakespeare's *A Midsummer Night's Dream*. At age twenty, he conducted a performance of the *Saint Matthew Passion* in Berlin that helped spark a revival of interest in Bach's music. He composed at an astonishing rate throughout his life, marked by frequent travel, concert tours as pianist and conductor, and positions as music director in Düsseldorf, music director and conductor of the Gewandhaus Orchestra in Leipzig (1835–1840 and 1845–1847), and in various capacities in Berlin (1840–1844). In 1843,

*Figure 17.11.  Felix Mendelssohn at age twenty. Watercolor portrait by Warren Childe (1829). Staatsbibliothek zu Berlin.*

he founded the Leipzig Conservatory, whose faculty included Robert Schumann. Mendelssohn was also a great favorite in England, where his popularity took him often, prompting the composition of his oratorio *Elijah*, in the tradition of Handel. Queen Victoria, who graciously consented to receive the dedication of the *Scottish* Symphony, loved to pass musical afternoons in his company (see Figure 17.12). He died in November 1847 after suffering a series of strokes.

**Major works:** 5 symphonies, a violin concerto, 2 piano concertos, 4 overtures, incidental music to *A Midsummer Night's Dream*, 2 oratorios, numerous chamber works, pieces for piano or organ, choral works, and songs.

he gained of sounds and landscapes on trips to Italy and the British Isles, which he also recorded in drawings and paintings like the one in Figure 17.10.

The *Italian* Symphony celebrates the south—sunny and vibrant. The slow movement suggests a procession of chanting pilgrims trudging along the road. In the finale, we can imagine people in the city squares dancing the spirited saltarello. The first movement opens with an expansive melody, shown in Example 17.4, whose sighing lurches, many sequences, and repeated postponement of closure are inspired by Italian opera, although its character is instrumental rather than vocal. The second theme is similarly constructed,

*Italian* Symphony

giving both thematic areas more the quality of well-shaped tunes than of material for future development. As a consequence, the development section dwells on a new melodic idea, a motive that gradually builds to a new theme in combination with the opening figure of the first theme. All three themes are recalled in the recapitulation, binding the movement together. In this way, Mendelssohn neatly accommodates his broad, tuneful themes within the developmental structure of sonata form.

*Example 17.4: Felix Mendelssohn, Symphony No. 4 in A Major* (Italian), *Op. 90, Allegro vivace*

*Scottish* Symphony

The four movements of the *Scottish* Symphony are played without pause, suggesting a seamless flow of reminiscence. Mendelssohn creates a Scottish flavor through several devices: the ornamental tones of bagpipe music are represented by grace notes, the theme of the second movement includes a "Scotch snap" (a short-long rhythmic figure, with the short note on the beat), and several of the themes use pentatonic (five-note) scales found in the folk music of the Hebrides islands. In Example 17.5, some of the principal melodic ideas are transposed to A minor/C major for easy comparison. The use of folk idioms illustrates the Romantic interest in faraway places, native music, and local color. It also shows how strongly the melodies, particularly the tunes used as themes, determine the expressive character of symphonic music in this period.

Overtures

Mendelssohn's affinity for depicting musical landscapes is evident in his overtures The *Hebrides* (also called *Fingal's Cave*, 1832), on another Scottish topic, and *Meerestille und glückliche Fahrt* (Becalmed Sea and Prosperous Voyage, 1828–1832). His masterpiece in the genre is the *Midsummer Night's Dream Overture*, written in 1826 when he was seventeen, which set the standard for all subsequent concert overtures. A picture of the fairies in Shakespeare's famous play, it is a brilliant example of perpetual motion for a full orchestra trained to tiptoe like a chamber ensemble. The Classical overture structure of sonata form without repeats is perfectly clear, but the listener's attention is drawn to Mendelssohn's imaginative use of musical figuration and orchestral color to evoke everything from fairy dust to the braying of Bottom after his head is magically transformed into that of a jackass. Seventeen years later, Mendelssohn wrote additional incidental music for a production of the play, including the famous *Wedding March*.

Violin concerto

Like Mozart and Beethoven before him, Mendelssohn was a virtuoso pianist and wrote several concertos for his own performances. Yet, for Mendelssohn as for Beethoven, a concerto was more an expression of the composer than a mere vehicle

*Example 17.5: Felix Mendelssohn, Symphony No. 3 in A Minor (Scottish), Op. 56, some principal melodic ideas*

for the soloist. The Violin Concerto in E Minor (1844, finale in NAWM 122) is widely regarded as one of Mendelssohn's best works and one of the greatest violin concertos by any composer. The three movements are linked through thematic content and connecting passages; a transition leads from the opening Allegro molto appassionato to the lyrical Andante, and an introduction to the last movement alludes to the first movement's opening theme. The middle movement, in ABA′ form, is a romance for violin and orchestra driven by a slowly unfolding melody. The sonata-rondo finale has the elfin qualities of a scherzo. Although there are plenty of opportunities for the soloist to show off, the concerto always seems motivated by a greater expressive purpose, making this piece a consummate example of the concerto's conversion from virtuoso showpiece to classical genre. The balance between violin and orchestra is especially clear in the finale, as the leading melodies move seamlessly from soloist to orchestra and back.

CD 9/30    CD 5/15

Mendelssohn's involvement with music of the past prompted him to write two successful oratorios, *St. Paul* (1836) and *Elijah* (1846), which have become standards of the choral repertory. Both were composed for choral festivals, treated biblical subjects, and received great acclaim. The final chorus of *Elijah* (NAWM 124) is Handelian in spirit, with a powerful homorhythmic opening, a vigorous fugue with a culminating statement in chordal harmony, and a contrapuntal Amen. At the same time, Mendelssohn drew on more recent styles by playing with contrasts between major and minor and using touches of chromaticism.

Oratorios

CD 9/45

## Piano Works

Mendelssohn's best-known piano works are his *Lieder ohne Worte* (Songs without Words), forty-eight short pieces grouped in eight books. In the first "song" (1830), shown in Example 17.6, the similarity to the lied is immediately

*Songs without Words*

*Figure 17.12. Mendelssohn playing for Queen Victoria, who acquired a Broadwood square piano for Buckingham Palace in 1840. Jewish Chronicle Archives, London.*

apparent. It could be written on three staves—the bass and sixteenth-note arpeggiations for the pianist's left and right hands, and the melody for a singer. Having to cover all three lines with two hands produces interesting pianistic problems—how to bring out the melody and bass in a smooth legato while using mainly the weaker fourth and fifth fingers, and how to divide the sixteenth-note figuration evenly between the two hands. The piece exploits the piano's ability to respond to the player's varying touch, louder for the melody and bass and softer for the accompaniment, even when they are played by fingers of the same hand.

*Example 17.6: Felix Mendelssohn,* Songs without Words, *Book 1, Op. 19, No. 1*

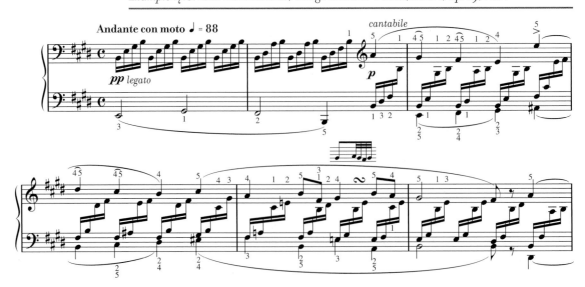

The influence of Mendelssohn's study of Bach is apparent in the perpetual motion, recalling several preludes from *The Well-Tempered Clavier*. Beyond these technical matters, the piece appeals to the player or listener for the same reasons that a well-crafted song does: an engaging melody and interesting accompaniment that convey a distinct mood. The *Songs without Words* contain many distinguished examples of the Romantic miniature and exemplify Mendelssohn's belief that music is capable of expressing feelings or thoughts that are inexpressible in words, reflecting the idealist philosophy that underpins Romantic thought.

# Robert Schumann (1810–1856)

Robert Schumann (see biography and Figure 17.13), like Schubert and Mendelssohn, also composed in all the major genres of the nineteenth century, but he concentrated on one at a time—piano music until 1840, then songs in that year, symphonies in 1841, chamber music in 1842–1843, and dramatic music in 1847–1848.

## Piano Music

Schumann was a master of the miniature form, as his contributions to piano and song literature testify. The bulk of his piano compositions are short character pieces, often grouped into colorfully named sets: *Papillons* (Butterflies); *Carnaval*; *Fantasiestücke* (Fantasy Pieces; see NAWM 116), *Kinderscenen* (Scenes from Childhood); and *Nachtstücke* (Night Pieces). Charming little pieces for children are gathered in the *Album für die Jugend* (Album for the Young). The titles that Schumann gave to the collections and to separate pieces suggest that he wanted listeners to associate them with extramusical poetic fancies. This attitude is typical of the period, although he usually wrote the music before thinking up the title. He instilled in his music the depths, contradictions, and tensions of his own personality; it is by turns ardent and dreamy, vehement and visionary, whimsical and learned. Both in his literary writings and in a piano work entitled *Davidsbundlertänze* (Dances of the David League), the different facets of Schumann's nature are personified in the figures of Florestan, Eusebius, and Raro, members of an imaginary league called the *Davidsbund* that took its name from the biblical David and campaigned against musical Philistines. Florestan was the impulsive revolutionary; Eusebius, the youthful dreamer; and Raro, the wise, mature master; but they all converged in Schumann the composer.

Schumann gave each of the *Fantasiestücke* (Fantasy Pieces) a whimsical title; what binds them together is their flights of fantasy. The second piece in the set, entitled *Aufschwung* (Soaring, NAWM 116a), reveals the Florestan side of Schumann's personality. It features four strongly contrasting ideas arranged in a complex ternary form with transition (ABA′ CDC Trans AB′ A″), coordinating essentially independent blocks of music in a logical form. The impulsive A theme pounds out a dramatic motive, then soars up through four rising octaves and down in a syncopated melody; the tonic F minor is indicated by a repeated half cadence but never appears until the very end of the piece. The B theme soars in a different way, the melody climbing chromatically, supported by rushing figuration and an inner voice paralleling the melody.

The third piece in the set, *Warum?* (Why?, NAWM 116b), evokes Schumann's Eusebius side, contemplating an enigmatic motive through changes of register,

Character pieces

CD 8/76, 84   CD 4/77

Fantasiestücke

CD 8/76   CD 4/77

CD 8/84

# ✴ Robert Schumann (1810–1856)

Robert Schumann's story reflects the quintessential Romantic composer's tendency to combine literary pursuits with musical ones. An outstanding composer, especially of piano music, songs, and symphonies, he was also one of the most prolific and influential music critics of his times.

Schumann studied piano from age seven and soon began to compose. After pursuing a law degree at the university, he dedicated himself to becoming a concert pianist, studying with Friedrich Wieck in Leipzig. An injury to his right hand, caused or aggravated by a finger-strengthening device, cut short his career. As the son of a writer and book dealer, Schumann had always had an intense interest in literature. So, while he continued to compose, he also founded a magazine in Leipzig, the *Neue Zeitschrift für Musik* (New Journal of Music); with him as editor from 1834 to 1844, it quickly became the most important journal of its kind and is still published today. His essays and reviews provided strong leadership for the Romantic movement: he opposed empty virtuosity, urged the study of older music, and was among the first to praise Berlioz's *Symphonie fantastique*, to advocate the music of Chopin

and Brahms when they were still virtually unknown, and to champion the instrumental music of Schubert (see vignette, page 417).

Schumann had fallen in love with Clara Wieck, his piano teacher's daughter, who at age twenty was already one of the leading pianists in Europe (see Chapter 18). But Clara's father opposed the relationship, and only after a period of hardship and adversity, which included a lawsuit against Wieck the father, were they finally married in 1840. The years that followed were the happiest in the composer's life.

Most of Schumann's important piano compositions were written before 1840. In that year—the year of his engagement and marriage—he devoted his energies exclusively to songwriting; not until the following year, 1841, did he begin composing symphonies and then chamber music. He and Clara concertized throughout Europe, with Robert conducting and Clara at the piano. In 1850, he became municipal music director in Düsseldorf, his only salaried position as a musician, but increasing signs of mental instability forced him to resign in 1853. His last years were troubled by depression and melancholy; he suffered hallucinations and tried to commit suicide early in 1854. He spent the remaining two years of his life in a private asylum near Bonn.

**Major works:** more than 300 piano pieces, including *Papillons* (Op. 2), *Carnaval* (Op. 9), *Fantasiestücke* (Op. 12), *Kreisleriana* (Op. 16), and *Album for the Young* (Op. 68); about 300 songs, including two cycles: *Dichterliebe* (A Poet's Love) and *Frauenliebe und -leben* (A Woman's Love and Life); one opera (*Genoveva*); several oratorios; 4 symphonies; a piano concerto; and various works of chamber music.

*Figure 17.13. Robert and Clara Schumann in 1850. Daguerreotype (early photograph) by Johann Anton Vollner. Musée d'Orsay, Paris.*

harmony, and shape as if weighing a question that cannot be resolved. Even at the end, as the motive appears three times in the tonic, it somehow sounds unanswered.

## Songs

Among lied composers, Schumann was the first important successor to Schubert, although their styles are very different: whereas Schubert's songs nearly always maintain a certain Classical serenity and poise, Schumann's are restless and intense. After some years of publishing only piano music, Schumann wrote more than 120 songs in 1840, which he called his "year of song." He concentrated on love songs, including the song cycles *Dichterliebe* (A Poet's Love) and *Frauenliebe und -leben* (A Woman's Love and Life). He was inspired in part by his impending marriage to Clara Wieck, a renowned pianist and composer (see Chapter 18). Schumann turned to song to express the passions and frustrations of love, to make money from a lucrative genre, and to synthesize his two great interests—music and poetry.

Schumann believed that music should capture a poem's essence in its own terms and that voice and piano should be equal partners in this effort. His specialty was to give the piano a relatively long commentary at the beginning or, more frequently, at the end of a song, proving that it is no mere accompaniment. Like Schubert, he typically uses a single figuration throughout to convey the central emotion or idea of the poem. For his cycle *Dichterliebe*, Schumann chose sixteen poems from Heinrich Heine's *Lyrical Intermezzo* (1823) and arranged them to suggest the various stages of a relationship—from longing to initial fulfillment, abandonment, dreams of reconciliation, and, finally, resignation.

In the first song, *Im wunderschönen Monat Mai* (In the marvelous month of May, NAWM 113), the poet confesses a newborn love. The tonal ambiguity of the opening and the tension between voice and piano express his tentative feelings and reflect the pessimistic outlook of the cycle as a whole. The appoggiaturas and suspensions that begin almost every other measure underline the poet's longing and desire; and the music's refusal to settle into a key, ending the song on a dominant seventh, betrays his bittersweet anxiety about whether his love will be returned. In the seventh song, *Ich grolle nicht* (I bear no grudge), the poet's defiant attitude after the lover has left him demands a more declamatory, less tuneful setting. He vows he is not resentful, although his heart is breaking. But pounding octaves in the bass and accented pulsating chords in the right hand suggest his anger, dissonances at "Herz" (heart) and "verlor'nes" (lost) show his pain, and thus the music makes his words ring hollow, revealing the wounded pride beneath his bravado. These added layers of meaning demonstrate Schumann's success in making the piano accompaniment as important as the vocal melody, the music as significant as the words, and the composer an equal partner with the poet.

Music and poetry

*Dichterliebe*

CD 8/72

## Symphony and Chamber Music

The prestigious status that Beethoven had conferred on the symphony made it a rite of passage to full recognition for any composer. Thus, in 1841, Schumann embarked on his "symphony year." After several starts, the composer completed his First Symphony in B♭ Major and drafted another that was to become his fourth. In addition to Beethoven, his primary orchestral models were Schubert's "Great" Symphony in C Major and the symphonies and concertos of

Symphonies

Mendelssohn, which showed how songlike themes could be integrated into developmental forms.

Two of Schumann's four symphonies bear descriptive titles: No. 1, *The Spring,* a hymn to nature; and No. 3, *The Rhenish,* which dwells on the majesty of the Rhineland countryside, including the grand cathedral at Cologne. The four movements of Symphony No. 4 in D Minor are joined by harmonic links and played without pause, like those of Mendelssohn's *Scottish* Symphony; the symphony also has a transitional passage leading to the finale, as in Beethoven's Fifth Symphony. Moreover, each movement contains themes derived from the slow introduction, making the entire work an integrated cycle.

*Chamber works*    Schumann followed his "lieder year" and his "symphony year" with a "chamber-music year" in 1842–1843. After studying the quartets of Haydn and Mozart, he composed three string quartets (Op. 41), a piano quartet, and a piano quintet in rapid succession. In his critical writings, he had argued that string quartets should resemble a four-way conversation, and he took care to meet this ideal by spreading the material among all the parts. In 1847, after studying Bach, Schumann introduced a new, more polyphonic approach to chamber music with his Piano Trios No. 1 in D Minor, Op. 63, and No. 2 in F Major, Op. 80. These were his most influential chamber works, especially on Brahms and other German composers.

# Fryderyk Chopin (1810–1849)

Unlike his contemporaries who wrote in all the standard genres of the early nineteenth century, Fryderyk Chopin concentrated almost exclusively on works for solo piano, and he composed some 200 pieces in this genre (see biography and Figure 17.14; also see "In Context," page 436). These are enjoyed by connoisseurs and amateurs alike because his idiomatic writing and his genius for exploiting the sonorous possibilities of the piano make them as pleasing to play as they are to hear.

*Dance forms*    Among the solo works, the dance forms stand out for their sheer beauty and sensuality. His waltzes evoke the ballrooms of Vienna, but his polonaises and mazurkas are suffused with the spirit of Poland. Polonaises (the word means "Polish" in French) are dances in $\frac{3}{4}$ meter often marked by a rhythmic figure of an eighth and two sixteenths on the first beat. Chopin's go beyond the stylized polonaise of Bach's time to assert a vigorous, sometimes militaristic, national identity. The mazurka was originally a Polish folk dance that became popular in the ballrooms of high society. Its stately triple meter with an accented second or third beat, frequent dotted rhythms, and unusual ornaments and modal effects make it sound rather like an exotic minuet—sometimes playful, sometimes brooding. The Mazurka in B♭ Major, Op. 7, No. 1 (NAWM 117), illustrates the genre. (See also "In Performance: *Tempo Rubato*," page 434.)

CD 8/86

*Nocturnes*    The nocturnes, impromptus, and preludes are Chopin's most soulful and introspective works. He got both the name and the general idea of the nocturnes—descriptive pieces that evoke the quiet and/or fretful dreaminess of night—from the Irish pianist and composer John Field (1782–1837), whose nocturnes parallel Chopin's in a number of ways. Although Field anticipated some of Chopin's mannerisms, he could not match the rich harmonic imagination that so powerfully supports Chopin's lyrical lines, as in the D♭ Nocturne, Op. 27, No. 2 (NAWM 118).

CD 8/89    CD 4/85

*Preludes*    Chopin composed his preludes at a time when he was deeply immersed in the music of Bach. Like the preludes in *The Well-Tempered Clavier,* these brief, sharply defined mood pictures utilize all the major and minor keys, although

## Fryderyk Chopin (1810–1849)

Chopin was the Romantic composer most closely identified with the piano. His solo piano music won him enormous popularity during his lifetime and, through its enduring appeal, has occupied a central place in the repertory ever since.

Chopin was born near Warsaw to a French father and a Polish mother in a country that was then under Russian domination. After he received early training at the Warsaw Conservatory, his talent as a pianist, improviser, and composer of music that was unmistakably Polish in character assured him a strong following in his native country. In search of an international reputation, however, he left there in 1830 to tour Vienna and Germany, where Schumann called the public's attention to him with the words "Hats off, gentlemen, a genius!" When Chopin learned of the disastrous Polish revolt against Russia in November, instead of returning to Poland he journeyed to Paris, where he settled in 1831. He never again saw his homeland, but his abiding affection for it colors much of his music and shines through particularly in dances such as his polonaises and mazurkas.

In Paris, Chopin soon gained entry into the most elite social circles, where he met artists, writers, and other musicians, including Berlioz, Rossini, and Liszt. He became the most fashionable piano teacher for wealthy students, whose fees meant that he could give up concertizing, although he still played at private concerts and in salons. He also earned considerable sums from his publications. He never married but had a long liaison with the novelist George Sand (see "In Context," page 436). During their stay in Majorca, he was diagnosed with tuberculosis. He suffered with it for ten years and finally succumbed while he was on a grueling performance tour of England and Scotland. He was buried in Paris, but his heart was sent to Warsaw and was interred there.

All of Chopin's works are either for solo piano or piano with other forces: 110 dances (mazurkas, waltzes, and polonaises), 4 ballades, 4 scherzos, 10 nocturnes, 27 études, 25 preludes, 2 piano concertos, 3 sonatas, 5 chamber works, and 20 songs. Among the chamber works is a late cello sonata, which hints at directions Chopin might have explored had he lived longer than his thirty-nine years.

*Figure 17.14. Portrait of Fryderyk Chopin by Eugène Delacroix (1838). Musée du Louvre, Paris.*

the circle of fifths determines their succession—C major, A minor, G major, E minor, and so on—whereas Bach's were arranged in rising chromatic steps—C major, C minor, C♯ major, C♯ minor, and so on. Chopin's rich chromatic harmonies and modulations influenced many later composers, as did the enormously varied textures of his piano writing.

Chopin projected his ideas onto a larger canvas in the ballades and scherzos. He was one of the first to have used the name *ballade* for an instrumental piece. His works in this genre—especially Op. 23 in G Minor and Op. 52 in F Minor— capture the mood swings of the narrative ballads by contemporary poets (see page 411), which are filled with romantic adventures and supernatural incidents. The principal scherzos are his Op. 20 in B minor and Op. 39 in C♯ minor. Although these pieces are not joking or playful like their Classical counterparts, they are tricky and quirky (which the term *scherzo* also implies),

Ballades and scherzos

**IN PERFORMANCE**    Tempo Rubato

Most of Chopin's pieces are introspective and, within clearly defined formal outlines, suggest the quality of improvisation, or of a spontaneous flow of ideas. In this respect, a certain apparent (though controlled) freedom of delivery is appropriate in performance, as with recitative, which imitates the flexibility of speech rhythms. Such freedom is inherent in the tempo marking *rubato*, an effect most strongly associated with Chopin's mazurkas. (Some 75 percent of the written appearances of the term in Chopin's work occur in his mazurkas, where it is used as a tempo marking that governs the entire piece. In other types of pieces, it might be indicated as an expression mark intended to obtain for only a few measures.) In Italian, *tempo rubato* means "stolen time," or time extended, slowed down, or stretched beyond its literal duration, implying some distortion of the strict tempo that may be applied to a few notes or to entire phrases. Chopin described it as a slight pushing or holding back of the right-hand melody while the accompaniment continues in strict time, although he is also known to have used this expressive device in both hands at once. A glossary of Italian musical terms published in a French magazine (*Le pianiste*, 1834) names Chopin as the composer most closely identified with *tempo rubato*.

Chopin himself was not theatrically overwhelming as a pianist (as Liszt was, for example), and other virtuosos have emphasized the heroic side of his music more than he himself could or would have. According to one critic, he had a small sound, though his playing was "elegant, relaxed, and graceful; . . . marked by both brilliance and clarity." But his own rhythmically inflected manner of performing was unique and nearly impossible to reproduce—perhaps even completely impossible if one had not heard him play. Contemporary critics recognized that, since no arrangement of known note values can accurately express rubato, it was elusive at best and the undoing of amateurs at worst. Indeed, the need to apply rubato still renders even the simplest mazurkas somewhat treacherous to play.

Like the damper pedal, rubato can also be used in places where it is not marked, and nineteenth-century performers availed themselves of both devices freely for expressive purposes. Although Chopin's works are certainly gratifying to perform, many of them demand of the pianist not only a flawless technique and a sensitive touch but also an imaginative use of the pedals and a subtle execution of *tempo rubato*.

*Figure 17.15. Autograph score of a mazurka dated Paris 1834 and signed by Chopin.*

particularly in their thematic material and rhythm. They are also serious, vigorous, and passionate works, organized—as are the ballades—in forms that grow organically from the musical ideas.

Chopin's études—twelve in each of Opp. 10 and 25, and three without opus number—are important landmarks in defining the piano idiom. Because études are intended primarily to develop technique, each one as a rule is devoted to a specific technical skill pursued through repetition of a single figure. Among the technical challenges in Opus 25 are parallel diatonic and chromatic thirds in the right hand (No. 6), parallel sixths in the right hand (No. 8), and chromatic octaves in both hands (No. 10). In No. 11, a brilliant yet highly evocative étude, the right hand spins out a perpetual filigree of sixteenth notes against a vigorous march theme in the left hand (see Example 17.7). Through much of the piece, the right hand's passage work alternates between chromatic appoggiaturas or passing notes and chord tones. Chopin's études are not only intensely concentrated technical studies but also transcendent poetic statements, successfully combining virtuosity with significant artistic content. In this respect, Liszt and Brahms followed Chopin's lead.

*Études*

*Example 17.7: Fryderyk Chopin, Étude, Op. 25, No. 11*

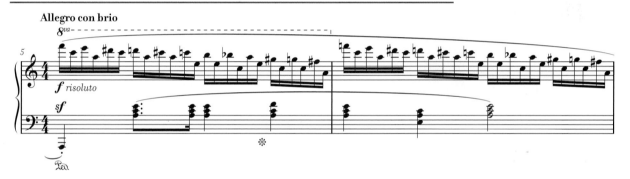

POSTLUDE

The first Romantic composers explored new realms of expression in all mediums—orchestral, chamber, and solo music—giving particular prominence in the smaller forms to voice and piano. They reveled in pushing sounds to extreme limits, moving in the space of a few measures from the most bombastic fortissimo to the most delicate pianissimo, from the greatest possible dramatic turbulence to the simplest lyric serenity, from calculated chaos to cool calm. They indulged equally in luxurious length and tantalizing brevity, making symphonies longer and miniature forms shorter. They accomplished these effects by manipulating instrumentation, harmony, dynamics, and other elements in original ways, inventing new tempo markings to articulate their urgent moods, and new narrative strategies to achieve greater formal freedom as well as greater coherence.

Looking back from approximately mid-century, where this chapter ends and the next begins, we may profitably review some of the highlights of the early Romantic generations. The 1820s saw the first performance of Beethoven's Ninth Symphony, the centennial performance of Bach's *Saint Matthew Passion*, the composition of Mendelssohn's *Midsummer Night's Dream Overture*, and all of Schubert's mature music, including his song cycles *Die schöne Müllerin* and *Winterreise*. By 1830, the year of the first performance of the *Symphonie fantastique*, both Beethoven and Schubert were dead and Berlioz and Chopin were rising stars in the musical firmament. The youthful Franz Liszt and the child prodigy

Clara Wieck (both of whom we shall discuss in the next chapter), along with the violin virtuoso Niccolò Paganini, were stunning concert audiences with their prodigious talents. During the next decade, the 1830s, Mendelssohn wrote his *Italian* Symphony and Schumann composed all of his important piano music. In 1840, the year of Schumann's *Dichterliebe*, he and Clara Wieck were married.

**IN CONTEXT** A Ballad of Love

*Figure 17.16. Anonymous nineteenth-century portrait of George Sand. Frederic Chopin Museum, Warsaw.*

The novelist George Sand (Aurore Dudevant, 1804–1876) adopted her male pseudonym after she left her husband and moved to Paris, where she eventually met Fryderyk Chopin. She was forward and freethinking; he was fastidious and frail. She was a single mother who smoked cigars and wore men's clothing; he suffered from tuberculosis and required solitude and mothering, although he enjoyed the company of aristocratic friends. Despite their differences in age and experience—she was six years older than he and immensely more worldly— they developed a romantic relationship that coincided with his most productive years as a composer.

A prolific correspondent and diarist, Sand described Chopin's creative process as a combination of effortless improvisation and painstaking revisions:

His musical composition was spontaneous and miraculous. [Ideas] would come to him unexpectedly and without effort. They simply burst forth out of his piano, sublime and complete. . . .

But then began the most heartbreaking labor I have ever seen, consisting of a succession of struggles, uncertainties, and impatience to recapture certain details of the theme he had heard. What he had conceived as a whole he analyzed too much in trying to write down, and his dismay at not being able to capture it exactly again threw him into a kind of despair. He would shut himself up in his room for whole days at a time, weeping, pacing back and forth, smashing his pens, repeating or changing one measure a hundred times. . . . He sometimes spent six weeks on one page, only to finish by writing it exactly as he had sketched it at the first draft.[1]

As Chopin's manuscripts show no sign of such extraordinary efforts, Sand may have exaggerated— indeed, romanticized—his creative process under the assumption that genius was always accompanied by only the most titanic labors.

The couple's liaison lasted nine years, during which time they lived partly in Parisian society and partly at Nohant, the quiet country estate that Sand had inherited. Their holiday escape to Majorca during the winter of 1838–1839 turned into a terrible ordeal. Although Chopin managed to complete his Twenty-four Preludes (Op. 28) there, his health was permanently damaged by the bad weather and primitive living conditions. Nevertheless, they spent several more peaceful and productive years together after returning to France. Then, overwhelmed by intrigues involving a rivalry between Sand's two grown children, the lovers' affection for one another gradually dwindled, and by 1847 they were separated. Alone and physically ailing, Chopin lost all interest in composing and died two years later at the age of thirty-nine.

1. George Sand, *Histoire de ma vie . . .* , 20 vols. (1854); repr. in 4 vols. (Paris: Calmann-Lévy, 1928–1932?), IV, p. 470; adapted from the translation by William G. Atwood, *The Lioness and the Little One: The Liaison of George Sand and Frédéric Chopin* (New York: Columbia University Press, 1980), pp. 136–137.

By 1850, when the Bach Society was founded, Mendelssohn (who had been an important figure in the revival of Bach's music) and Chopin were already dead. Liszt's concert career was over, and he had begun writing his earliest symphonic poems, a genre that would occupy him for the next decade (see Chapter 18). Political upheavals in Europe created the first great waves of migration to the New World, while the industrial revolution had begun to change the ways in which people experienced music. In the next chapter, we will discuss the impact of these events as well as the continued influence of Beethoven on the music of the later Romantics during the second half of the nineteenth century.

# The Later Romantics

## PRELUDE

*Chapter Contents*

*Prelude* 438

Franz Liszt
(1811–1886) 439

Clara Schumann
(1819–1896) 444

Johannes Brahms
(1833–1897) 447

Piotr Il'yich
Tchaikovsky
(1840–1893) 453

Antonín Dvořák
(1841–1904) 457

*Postlude: The Beethoven
Legacy* 459

The industrial revolution, which was well under way by the time Beethoven composed his first symphony, brought far-reaching—some would say cataclysmic—changes to the nineteenth century, as we have noted. Advances in medicine, science, technology, and industry all left permanent marks on society, which soon came to regard invention and progress as the norm. Rather than placing their faith in authority and respecting the past exclusively, people of the new industrial age maintained a belief in progress and cultivated an unprecedented enthusiasm for the future. Even Beethoven, the most admired composer of his time, is said to have responded confidently to an uncomprehending critic of his music that his works were written not for his contemporaries but "for a later age."

At the same time that people valued novelty and innovation, interest in music of the past intensified. The new discipline of musicology was established, and scholars unearthed, published, and studied music by Palestrina and Lasso, Schütz and Bach—whose complete works were issued, many for the first time, between 1851 and 1899—Handel and Mozart, and, of course, Beethoven, whose sketches provided a whole new field for scholars to mine. Since many of these composers were German, it was only natural that German scholars and publishers brought out their editions, linking the revival of past music to nationalism (see Chapter 20). The mixture of old and new music had wide-ranging consequences for programming; by the later nineteenth century, performers and audiences had available a variety of musical styles such as had never before been present simultaneously in the performing tradition.

The continuing exposure to past music posed new problems for living composers. How were they to appeal to audiences who were primarily accustomed to hearing only works already familiar to them, most of which were composed a generation or more ago? The composers that we will encounter in this and the next two chapters responded in varying ways. Some, like Brahms, competed with the Classical masters on their own ground, writing symphonies and chamber works worthy of comparison with Beethoven's, and songs and piano pieces that rival the achievements of Schubert and Chopin. Others, like Wagner and Liszt, thought the legacy of Beethoven pointed in a different direction, toward new genres such as music drama and symphonic poem. In German-speaking lands, these differing aesthetic attitudes polarized around Brahms and Wagner and around the dichotomies between absolute music and program music, and between tradition and innovation. Advocates of absolute music—music understood on its own terms, as an abstract play of sound and form—sided with the critic Eduard Hanslick (1825–1904), whose essay *On the Beautiful in Music* (1854) appeared in response to the writings of Wagner (see vignette, page 483) and Liszt (see vignette, below). Hanslick challenged the principles of program music and the whole late Romantic notion that music's expressive value was enhanced by its association with the other arts, and he championed Brahms as upholder of the great tradition of German Classical instrumental music (see vignette, page 451).

The composers presented in this chapter, in order of their birth, include some of the most successful of the later Romantic generations: Franz Liszt, Clara Wieck Schumann, Johannes Brahms, Piotr Il'yich Tchaikovsky, and Antonín Dvořák. They have been chosen in part because, among them, they adopted a wide range of strategies for meeting the challenges of their time.

# Franz Liszt (1811–1886)

Style

The cosmopolitan career of Franz Liszt was matched by his eclectic style, the result of many factors and influences (see biography and Figures 18.1 and 18.2). His Hungarian roots show in his compositions based on or inspired by national melodies and perhaps also informed his colorful, extroverted personality. Superimposed on his ethnicity were his early Viennese training and a strong strain of French literary Romanticism, with its ideal of program music as represented by the works of Berlioz (many of Liszt's pieces have explicit programmatic titles). He modeled his piano style after several impressive Viennese and Parisian virtuosos, adding his own vocabulary of stunning effects

---

**VIGNETTE**   Liszt on Music as Direct Expression

*In an essay defending Berlioz's "instrumental poem"* Harold in Italy, *Liszt explained that in his view the work's content took shape precisely because it could not be expressed in words, images, and ideas. But he went on to say that in some cases a composer was justified in using a program to clarify his intentions.*

~~~

Music embodies feeling without forcing it to contend and combine with thought, as it is forced in most arts and especially in the art of words. If music has one advantage over the other media through which a person can represent the impressions of the soul, it owes this to its supreme capacity to make each inner impulse audible without the assistance of reason. Reason, after all, is restricted in the diversity of its means and is capable only of confirming or describing our affections, not of communicating them directly in their full intensity. To accomplish this even approximately, reason must search for images and comparisons. Music, on the other hand, presents at once the intensity and the expression of feeling. It is the embodied and intelligible essence of feeling, capable of being apprehended by our senses. It permeates them like a dart, like a ray, like a mist, like a spirit, and fills our soul.

From Franz Liszt and Princess Caroline von Wittgenstein, *Berlioz and His "Harold" Symphony* (1855), adapted from the translation in *Vignettes in Music History: The Romantic Era* (New York: Norton, 1965), p. 109.

# ✳ Franz Liszt (1811–1886)

Liszt stands out among his peers as an arch-Romantic, a tone poet who reconceived the language of music as an independent system of communication and claimed for it a world of its own. His accomplishments were exceedingly broad and far-reaching: as a conductor he championed the music of the future while simultaneously honoring that of the past; as a performer he devised new playing techniques and transported his audiences to new heights; and as a composer he made the piano sound like an orchestra and strove to make the orchestra simulate poetry.

One of the most intriguing musical personalities of his day, Liszt was born in Hungary, the son of an official in the service of Prince Miklos Esterházy. He studied piano with Carl Czerny in Vienna and theory and counterpoint with Antonio Salieri. At the age of eleven, Liszt played several public concerts, inaugurating a dazzling career as a virtuoso. The family subsequently moved to Paris, where Liszt studied theory and composition with private teachers and, after his father's death in 1827, earned a regular income by teaching piano to wealthy pupils and as a traveling virtuoso. He left the concert stage in 1848 and devoted the rest of his career to composing, conducting, and teaching.

From 1848 to 1861, Liszt was court music director at Weimar, where he encouraged new music by conducting performances of many important works, among them the premiere of Wagner's opera *Lohengrin* in 1850. Several well-publicized love affairs with women of elevated social status as well as honors showered upon him all over Europe added glamour to his fame as pianist, conductor, and composer. His relationship with the countess Marie d'Agoult resulted in three children, one of whom, Cosima, married Richard Wagner. A man of enormous contradictions, Liszt abandoned his life of pleasure and moved to Rome in 1861 where, in his mid-fifties, he took minor orders in the Catholic Church and became known as Abbé Liszt (see Figure 18.2).

**Major works:** 13 symphonic or tone poems for orchestra (*Les Préludes*, *Orpheus*, *Hamlet*), 2 symphonies (*Faust* and *Dante*); hundreds of large- and small-scale pieces for piano (Sonata in B Minor, *Années de pélerinage*, *Transcendental Études*, 19 Hungarian rhapsodies, transcriptions of orchestral and operatic works and of Paganini's violin pieces), 3 piano concertos and other works for piano and orchestra (*Totentanz* [Dance of Death], *Fantasia on Hungarian Folk Melodies*), 4 Masses and other choral works, organ pieces, chamber music, and songs.

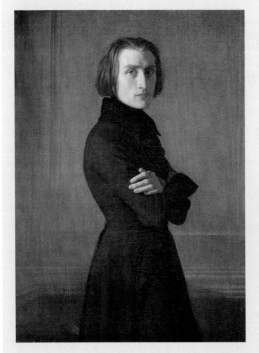

*Figure 18.1 (left). Franz Liszt in a portrait by Henri Charles Lehmann, painted in 1838. Note how Liszt's long, tapered fingers are highlighted against his black sleeve. Musée Carnavalet, Paris.*

*Figure 18.2 (right). Liszt-L'Abbé in a caricature by Spy (English artist Leslie Ward) that appeared in Vanity Fair a few months before Liszt's death in 1886.*

to theirs. He adopted as well the lyricism of Chopin's melodic line, his rubato rhythmic license, and his harmonic innovations, again amplifying and enhancing them.

In Paris, Liszt came under the spell of the great Italian violinist Niccolò Paganini (1782–1840), one of the most hypnotic artists of the nineteenth century (see Figure 18.3). Stimulated by Paganini's fabulous technical virtuosity, Liszt resolved to accomplish similar miracles on the piano and succeeded in becoming the greatest pianist of his time. He pushed the instrument to its furthest limits both in his own playing and in his compositions, which are technically beyond the ability of most amateurs. He directly imitated the master in his six *Études d'exécution transcendante d'après Paganini* (Transcendental Technical Studies Based on Paganini, 1851), transcribing four of Paganini's solo violin Caprices, Op. 1, and his *La Campanella* (The Bell) from the Violin Concerto No. 2 in B Minor.

As a young man Liszt cut a dashing figure, but as a performer he was absolutely galvanizing, "subjugating his hearers with a power that none could withstand. For him there were no difficulties of execution, the most incredible seeming child's play under his fingers."[1] In fact, Liszt's unusually long and tapered fingers gave him an enormous reach and allowed him to play rapid consecutive tenths as easily as most pianists could play octaves. He was as showy as Chopin was understated and used his virtuosity very purposefully to cultivate a following. In fact, he is credited not only with having invented the modern piano recital—an entire program executed by one artist rather than by a variety of soloists offering a potpourri of selections—but also with the idea of placing the piano sideways on the stage so as to display his elegant profile and imposing hands to the audience. He was for his time the high priest of the piano (see Figure 18.4 and vignette, page 442).

*Figure 18.3. Contemporary satirical print showing Niccolò Paganini playing the violin as astonished musicians look on. Bibliothèque Nationale de l'Opéra, Paris.*

## Piano Music

Liszt aimed his *Trois études de concert* (Three Concert Études, 1849) at particular technical problems. In *Un sospiro* (A Sigh, NAWM 119), for example, a slower-moving melody must be projected outside or within rapid broken-chord figurations. The pedal makes this possible by sustaining harmonies while the two hands brave treacherous leaps over each other to pick out a floating pentatonic tune and then a tonally anchored answer.

Much of Liszt's piano music consists of arrangements: transcriptions of Schubert songs, Berlioz and Beethoven symphonies, Bach organ fugues, excerpts from Wagner's music dramas, and fantasies on operatic arias. These pieces were useful in their day for bringing important works to a wide audience

*Un sospiro*

| CD 9/1 | CD 4/92 |

Transcriptions

---

1. Charles Hallé, *Life and Letters of Sir Charles Hallé*, ed. C. E. Hallé and M. Hallé (London, 1896). Hallé, an accomplished pianist, first heard Liszt perform in Paris in 1836.

*Figure 18.4. Liszt piano recital in Berlin, as depicted in an 1842 book by Adolph Brennglas on the city. The adulation of the audience, suggested by the excited gestures of the onlookers—one woman actually faints—is supported by many contemporary accounts. But another aspect of the picture is misleading: Liszt normally played from memory, an innovative custom that became standard practice.*

unacquainted with the originals. Also, by transferring orchestral idioms to the piano, Liszt demonstrated new possibilities for that instrument. He also wrote piano music that makes free use of national elements. Chief among these are the nineteen *Hungarian Rhapsodies*, based on traditional Hungarian melodies and ornamentation styles.

In Liszt's Sonata in B Minor (1853)—one of the outstanding piano compositions of the nineteenth century—four themes are worked out in one unbroken movement that is subdivided into three sections, analogous to the three movements of a Classical sonata. The themes are transformed and combined in a free rhapsodic order, but one that is perfectly suited to the thematic material. In this work, Liszt successfully adapted a unifying strategy that he had worked out for his symphonic pieces—the technique of thematic transformation, in which a central motive is used throughout a work but systematically reworked to reflect rapidly shifting moods or programmatic ideas (see below).

In some of his late works, Liszt experimented with harmonies that surprisingly anticipate late nineteenth- and twentieth-century developments. He was one of the first composers to make extensive use of augmented triads (see Example 18.2), which are prominent in the Sonata in B Minor and in the late piano piece *Nuages gris* (Gray Clouds, 1881), along with other unconventional harmonies. Liszt also rewrote many of his songs in this late period, adopting the more ambiguous harmonic vocabulary that he used in the late piano works.

## Orchestral Music

The foremost composer of program music after Berlioz, Liszt wrote twelve symphonic poems between 1848 and 1858 and a thirteenth in 1881–1882. Liszt's term *symphonic poem* is significant: he did not call these works symphonies,

*Liszt's first concert in Vienna as a mature artist (1838) created a sensation comparable to the one Paganini had made a decade earlier. The review by the correspondent from Germany's leading music journal, the* Allgemeine musikalische Zeitung, *ended with this extravagant description.*

∼

After the concert, he stands there like a conqueror on the field of battle, like a hero in the lists; vanquished pianos lie about him, broken strings flutter as trophies and flags of truce, frightened instruments flee in their terror into distant corners, the hearers look at each other in mute astonishment as after a storm from a clear sky, as after

thunder and lightning mingled with a shower of blossoms and buds and dazzling rainbows; and he the Prometheus, who creates a form from every note, a magnetizer who conjures the electric fluid from every key, a gnome, an amiable monster, who now treats his beloved, the piano, tenderly, then tyrannically; . . . he stands there, bowing his head, leaning languidly on a chair, with a strange smile, like an exclamation mark after the outburst of universal admiration: this is Franz Liszt!

From Piero Weiss and Richard Taruskin, eds., *Music in the Western World: A History in Documents* (New York: Schirmer, 1984), p. 365.

presumably because they were relatively short and were not divided into separate movements in a conventional order. Instead, each presents a continuous form with sections contrasting in character and tempo; a few themes are developed, repeated, varied, or transformed. These works are "poems" by analogy to literary poems. Not a drama, narrative, or prose exposition, the symphonic poem is an imaginative structure free of the conventions of traditional genres. The content and form may be suggested by a picture, statue, play, poem, scene, personality, or something else, but the subject is converted into music without specific reference to the details of the original. The title and, usually, a program, which may or may not have been written by the composer, identify the subject. So, for example, Liszt's *Hunnenschlacht* (The Battle of the Huns) is related to a mural painting, *Mazeppa* to a poem, *Hamlet* to Shakespeare's hero, *Prometheus* to the myth and also to a poem by Herder, and so on.

Two of Liszt's best symphonic poems, *Orpheus* and *Hamlet*, are concise musical portraits that originated as introductions to theatrical performances. The first, for Gluck's opera, was inspired by an Etruscan vase in the Louvre depicting Orpheus singing to the accompaniment of a lyre; the second, an overture for Shakespeare's play, is a penetrating psychological study. Liszt's programs, like those of Berlioz, do not relate stories told in music, but run parallel with them. The music evokes the ideas and states of feeling expressed in the different medium of the original subject (see vignette, page [5.45]).

Several of the symphonic poems are one-movement symphonies that contain lingering vestiges of sonata form and of the contrasts in mood and tempo found in the standard four-movement sequence. Liszt devised a method of unifying a composition by transforming a single motive to reflect the diverse moods needed to portray a programmatic subject. We call this method *thematic transformation*. In *Les Préludes* (1854; based on a poem of the same title by Alphonse-Marie-Louis de Lamartine [1790–1869]), he applied this method with notable artistic success. A three-note motive that has both a rhythmic and a melodic shape (Example 18.1a) is modified and expanded to take on different characters: amorphous, like a prelude (Example 18.1b); resolute (c); lyrical (d and e); stormy (f and g); excited (h); and martial (i). A more distant metamorphosis (e) serves as a contrasting theme and is itself subjected to transformations. (Asterisks in Example 18.1e show its relationship to the basic three-note motive.)

Thematic
transformation

*Example 18.1: Franz Liszt,* Les Préludes, *thematic transformation*

Liszt used a similar method in his Piano Concerto in B♭ Major, composed at about the same time.

*Faust* Symphony

The works that Liszt called symphonies are also programmatic. He dedicated his masterpiece, the *Faust* Symphony (1854), to Berlioz. It consists of three movements, labeled *Faust, Gretchen,* and *Mephistopheles,* with a finale (added later) for tenor soloist and men's chorus, setting the *chorus mysticus* that closes Goethe's drama. The first three movements correspond to the Classical plan: introduction and Allegro (in a loose sonata form), Andante (three-part form), and Scherzo (three-part form, followed by a long additional development and coda). The first theme of the *Faust* movement uses one of Liszt's favorite chords—the augmented triad, here transposed sequentially downward through four chromatic steps so as to comprise all twelve notes of the chromatic scale (see Example 18.2). Themes are interchanged among the movements and transformed in accordance with the program. The *Mephistopheles* movement, for example, is made up largely of sinister caricatures of the *Faust* themes (Berlioz similarly caricatured the idée fixe in the *Symphonie fantastique*), and the *Gretchen* melody is used as the principal theme of the finale. Liszt in this symphony most successfully combined a grandiose and momentous program with music of great inspiration, substance, and passion, in a form whose huge dimensions are justified by the scope and power of the generating ideas.

*Example 18.2: Franz Liszt,* Faust *Symphony, Introduction*

Liszt's influence

Liszt's influence was far-reaching. Composers such as Bedřich Smetana (*Má vlast*), César Franck (*Psyché*), Camille Saint-Saëns (*Le Rouet d'Omphale, Danse macabre*), and Piotr Il'yich Tchaikovsky (*Francesca da Rimini*) appropriated the genre of the symphonic poem. Liszt's bold chords and chromatic harmonies helped form Wagner's style after 1854; and Liszt's manipulation of small sets of intervals and pitches, as well as the experimental harmonies of his late works, enjoyed unexpected resonance in the twentieth century.

# Clara Schumann (1819–1896)

Clara Wieck Schumann had a remarkably long career as a pianist, composer, and teacher (see biography and Figure 18.5). Women were discouraged from composing large-scale works like symphonies; but, since the piano was the centerpiece of domestic music making, it was acceptable for women composers to write smaller-scale works involving piano (see Figure 18.6). As a prominent pianist, Clara showcased her husband's works as well as her own, which include polonaises, waltzes, variations, preludes and fugues, a sonata, and character pieces. She also wrote several collections of lieder, including one coauthored with Robert Schumann. They had a similar approach to

# Clara Schumann (1819–1896)

One of the foremost pianists of her time, Clara Wieck Schumann was also a distinguished composer and teacher. Although her career was in some ways closely tied to that of her husband, Robert Schumann, in her day she was more famous as a virtuoso than he was as a composer.

From an early age, Clara was trained to become a concert pianist by her father, Friedrich Wieck. Recognized as a child prodigy from her first public appearance in Leipzig at age nine, she toured throughout Europe and earned the praise of Goethe, Mendelssohn, Chopin, Paganini, and, of course, Schumann, who had also been a pupil of her father's. By the age of twenty, already one of the leading pianists in Europe, she was studying composition with Schumann and had several published works to her credit.

The couple's courtship was thwarted by Wieck, who did not want his daughter to marry a composer and journalist of such limited financial means. No doubt he also feared that marriage and motherhood would curtail her public appearances and, therefore, her earning power. Although Clara did limit her touring after marrying Robert and while raising their eight children, she continued to perform and compose, encouraged by her husband. After his death in 1856, Clara stopped composing; but she went on performing and teaching for another forty years, promoting Robert's music. Later in life she edited the first complete edition of his works with the help of Johannes Brahms, who had become a devoted friend. Her interpretations of the sonatas and concertos of Beethoven and of works by Bach, Chopin, and others attracted critics for their poetic sensitivity and masterful technique with none of the ostentatious display associated with other virtuosi. Because of her reputation and longevity as a solemn "priestess" of her art, she had a great influence on pianism and concert life in the nineteenth century.

**Major works:** Piano Trio, Op. 17, other chamber music, two piano concertos, many pieces for solo piano, and several collections of lieder.

*Figure 18.5. Clara Wieck at the piano, as she looked before her marriage to Robert Schumann in 1840. Color lithograph by F. Giere.*

song setting, which involved capturing each poem's mood in long preludes and postludes, maintaining a particular figuration throughout each song, and making the voice and piano equal partners in conveying the images and feelings of the poem.

Clara Schumann regarded her Piano Trio in G Minor, Op. 17 (1846), as her best work; indeed, it may have inspired her husband's trios that were composed in the following year. The sonata-form first and last movements combine traits from Baroque, Classical, and Romantic models: memorable songlike themes; rich polyphonic treatment; development through motivic fragmentation and imitation; fugue; and rousing codas. The second movement is in minuet tempo but is labeled "Scherzo" to highlight its subtle rhythmic tricks. The slow movement (NAWM 123) is outwardly simple in

Piano Trio

CD 9/41   CD 5/26

form—a modified ABA with a melancholy first section resembling a nocturne and a more animated B section. But the effect is enriched by constantly changing textures. As we see in Example 18.3, for example, the opening melody appears three times, each time in a different instrument (piano, violin, and cello, respectively) and with ever more complex accompanying figuration.

The music of Clara Schumann disappeared for more than a hundred years until it was revived in the late twentieth century, when musicians sought out deserving pieces by women composers.

*Example 18.3: Clara Schumann, Piano Trio in G Minor, Op. 17, third movement*

*a. Opening melody in piano*

*b. Restatement in violin*

*c. Reprise in cello*

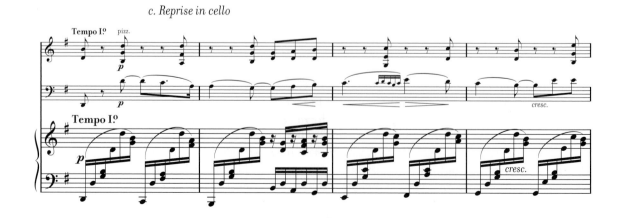

Figure 18.6.  *Clara Schumann performing with her close friend, the violinist Joseph Joachim. Print after a chalk drawing (1854) by Adolph von Menzel. Robert-Schumann-Haus, Zwickau.*

# Johannes Brahms (1833–1897)

Johannes Brahms matured as a composer just as the classical repertoire came to dominate concert life (see biography and Figure 18.7). Therefore, he fully understood what it meant to compose for audiences whose tastes were formed by the classical masterpieces of previous centuries: his own music had to embrace the past yet be different enough to offer something new and appealing. In practice, that meant applying the principles of sonata form more conscientiously than almost any other composer of his generation and adhering to the traditional genres of instrumental music (sonata, string quartet, symphony, concerto, and so on) while at the same time manipulating their formal conventions in the spirit of Haydn and Beethoven. Nevertheless, Brahms's erudition was balanced by a deeply Romantic sensibility, so that his music appealed at once to casual listeners drawn to its lyrical beauty and sincere expressivity as well as to connoisseurs who admired its integrity and elegant craft.

## Piano Music

Like every other self-respecting composer since J. S. Bach, Brahms was trained as a keyboard player. As a young man in 1852–1853, he wrote virtuoso music for his own use, including three large sonatas in the tradition of Beethoven. These works also incorporate the chromatic harmony of Chopin and Liszt and the songlike style of Schumann's character pieces. In his twenties, Brahms focused on variation form, culminating in the *Variations and*

## ✸ Johannes Brahms (1833–1897)

Brahms was the leading German composer of his time in every field but opera, and he was the true successor of Beethoven in many ways. Through his concept of developing variation, he was also an important influence on twentieth-century music.

Like Beethoven, Brahms was from a northern German city (Hamburg) but chose, as Beethoven had done, to spend his adult life in Vienna. He was highly regarded as a keyboard player and, as a young man, formed a traveling duo with a Hungar-

*Figure 18.7. Portrait of Johannes Brahms in middle age, by Léo B. Eichhorn (1872–ca. 1940). Private collection.*

ian violinist; he retained a lifelong taste for Hungarian popular music, which he cultivated in many compositions. He also developed a love for music of the great composers of the past and was involved in editing works by C. P. E. Bach, François Couperin, and others.

Brahms first met the Schumanns when he was twenty years old, and the couple quickly became his strongest supporters. Schumann praised Brahms in print, launching his career, and helped him secure a publisher. After Schumann's suicide attempt and during his confinement for mental illness, Brahms remained close to the family while Clara returned to her life as a performer. Whether or not she reciprocated his romantic feelings after Schumann died in 1856, they became devoted friends for life and Brahms remained a bachelor.

Brahms made his living by concertizing as a pianist and conductor and by selling his music to publishers. From 1872 to 1875, he directed the chorus and orchestra of the Gesellschaft der Musikfreunde (Society of the Friends of Music) and programmed mostly German works from the sixteenth century through his own day. In his last two decades, he traveled widely as a conductor, performing mainly his own works, and was awarded numerous honors. He died of liver cancer less than one year after Clara Schumann's death and was buried in Vienna's Central Cemetery near Beethoven and Schubert.

**Major works:** 4 symphonies, 2 piano concertos, a violin concerto, 2 overtures, 2 serenades, 3 string quartets, 21 other chamber works, 3 piano sonatas, numerous piano pieces (rhapsodies, intermezzi, variation sets), *A German Requiem*, works for chorus and other vocal ensembles, and about 200 lieder.

*Fugue on a Theme of Handel*, Op. 24 (1861), and the difficult, étude-like *Variations on a Theme of Paganini*, Op. 35 (1863). While his models included Bach's *Goldberg Variations* and Beethoven's *Diabelli Variations*, his twenty-five variations on Handel's theme are actually a series of short character pieces, without titles, but evoking by turns Chopin and Mozart, a Hungarian rhapsody, an Italian siciliana, a French musette, a scherzo, a march, a fugue, and so on. In this way, he succeeded in breathing new life into one of the oldest instrumental genres.

In his last two decades, Brahms issued six collections of shorter pieces that are perhaps his greatest contribution to keyboard literature. They rival the pianism of Chopin, Schumann, and Liszt; but again, they avoid descriptive or programmatic titles in favor of generic names such as *intermezzo, cappriccio,* and *rhapsody.* Most are in ABA′ form and have songlike melodies, resembling character pieces but without reference to extramusical associations. The varied textures, surprising harmonies, and deft counterpoint in these pieces show Brahms's familiarity with keyboard music from Bach to his own time, while the full sonorities, frequent doubling of the melody, and persistent use of cross-rhythms and contrasting meters in different lines are central to Brahms's style.

**Short piano works**

## Chamber Music

Some critics have suggested that Brahms's musical personality was best expressed in his chamber music, much of which includes piano. He first concentrated on this medium in his thirties; but, knowing that his string quartets especially would elicit direct comparisons to Beethoven, Brahms waited until he turned forty to issue his first set of two (Op. 51, 1873). Meanwhile, he produced several works for piano and strings, including his popular Quintet in F Minor, Op. 34 (1864; see Figure 18.8). And he continued to cultivate chamber music in his later years; his famous Quintet for Clarinet and Strings, Op. 115, and the Sonatas for Clarinet and Piano, Op. 120, date from the 1890s. Not only are the quantity and quality of his production impressive—twenty-four works in all—but the variety of combinations is interesting: string quartets, quintets, and sextets; piano trios and quartets for various ensembles, including strings with waldhorn (a natural horn, without valves) or clarinet. The latter works stand out in a century when few major composers wrote chamber works featuring wind instruments, as

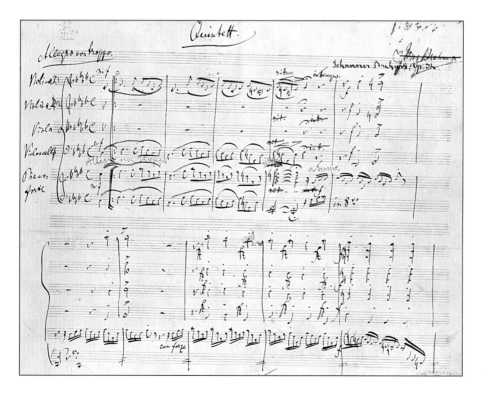

*Figure 18.8. The opening of the Brahms Piano Quintet, Op. 34, autograph in the composer's hand. Library of Congress, Washington, D.C.*

opposed to orchestral works in which the winds and brass often merely supplied color.

**Piano Quintet**

Opus 34 (1864) in F Minor, stunningly successful as a piano quintet, is the third metamorphosis of this work. Brahms originally composed it as a string quintet with two cellos; he later arranged it effectively for two pianos; and then Clara Schumann advised him to combine the string and piano sonorities for the final version. The first movement is a powerful, closely knit Allegro in sonata form. Brahms's treatment of the opening idea (see Example 18.4a) during the exposition aptly illustrates the technique associated with Brahms known as

**Developing variation**

*developing variation.* In diminution, the theme becomes a piano figure against string chords (b); a lyrical melody in the first violin (c); then, with note values doubled and the figure transformed, it is subjected to close imitation in the two violins (d). The key relationships are remote: the second theme group, in C♯ minor, is recapitulated in F♯ minor; the slow movement, in A♭, has a middle section in E major.

*Example 18.4: Johannes Brahms, Piano Quintet in F Minor, Op. 34, first movement*

The spirit and even the themes of the quintet's third movement, a scherzo, recall Beethoven's Fifth Symphony, which is also in C minor. Both composers' trios are in C major, but Beethoven invented truly contrasting material and textures, whereas Brahms developed the same ideas as in the Scherzo. The robust rhythms and the fleeting hints of a hurdy-gurdy in its persistent pedal points give the entire Brahms movement a rustic quality that captures one facet of the Beethovenian tradition.

## Symphonies

Brahms's concern to position his music alongside the classical masterworks is apparent in his treatment of the symphony. He approached the composition of a symphony with great care and deliberation, knowing that it would have to withstand comparison with those of Beethoven; ultimately, he wrote only four of them.

Already in his forties, Brahms finished his Symphony No. 1 in C Minor, Op. 68, in 1876, after laboring over it on and off for more than twenty years. It has the conventional sequence of movements—fast, slow, a light movement, and fast—the first and last having slow introductions. Yet the third movement is not a scherzo, as was typical of Beethoven, but a lyrical intermezzo, a substitution that Brahms repeats in his other symphonies. The key scheme of the symphony—C minor; E major; A♭ major and B major; and C minor and major—is characteristic of the Romantic era in its use of the major-third relation and the shifts between minor and major. As in Beethoven's Fifth, the initial C minor gives way to a triumphant major at the end of the last movement.

*First Symphony*

The main theme of the finale is a hymnlike melody (see Example 18.5) that suggests a parallel to the finale of Beethoven's Ninth Symphony. Yet there are no voices, as if to say that for Brahms, Beethoven's recourse to words is not necessary. Although the symphony fully absorbed Beethoven's influence—the conductor Hans von Bülow dubbed it "Beethoven's Tenth"—it also draws from other models and includes much that is original, as Eduard Hanslick recognized (see vignette, below).

---

**VIGNETTE**   Hanslick's Review of Brahms's First Symphony

*The most articulate proponent of absolute music was Eduard Hanslick (1825–1904), the dean of Viennese music criticism, who believed that music should be understood and appreciated on its own terms rather than for its ties to anything outside music. Here he praises Brahms's long-awaited First Symphony, implying that its emulation of Beethoven's Ninth in the finale, without having recourse to voices, steered music's course back to its proper realm—that of pure instrumental music—and away from the ill-advised direction that Beethoven's Romantic followers (Liszt and Wagner) had taken toward symphonic poem and music drama (see Chapter 19).*

Even the layman will immediately recognize it as as one of the most individual and magnificent works of the symphonic literature. In the first movement, the listener is held by fervent emotional expression, by Faustian conflicts, and by a contrapuntal art as rich as it is severe. The Andante softens this mood with a long-drawn-out, noble song, which experiences surprising interruptions in the course of the movement. The Scherzo strikes me as inferior to the other movements. The theme is wanting in melodic and rhythmic charm, the whole in animation. The abrupt close is utterly inappropriate. The fourth movement begins most significantly with an Adagio in C minor; from darkening clouds the sound of the woodland horn rises clear and sweet above the tremolo of the violins. All hearts tremble with the fiddles in anticipation. The entrance of the Allegro with its simple, beautiful theme, reminiscent of the "Ode to Joy" in the Ninth Symphony, is overpowering as it rises onward and upward, right to the end.

. . . And so, having relieved myself of these minor reservations, I can continue in the jubilant manner in which I began. The new symphony of Brahms is a possession of which the nation may be proud, an inexhaustible fountain of sincere pleasure and fruitful study.

From Henry Pleasant, ed. and trans., *Hanslick's Music Criticisms* (Baltimore: Pelican, 1963), pp. 125–128; quoted in Piero Weiss and Richard Taruskin, *Music in the Western World: A History in Documents* (New York: Schirmer, 1984), pp. 404–405.

*Example 18.5: Johannes Brahms, Symphony No. 1 in C Minor, Op. 68, Finale, opening theme*

Second Symphony

The success of the First Symphony prompted Brahms immediately to write another, No. 2 in D Major, Op. 73 (1877). In contrast to the First, it has a peaceful, pastoral character. Symphony No. 3 in F Major, Op. 90, came some years later (1883). The opening measures, shown in Example 18.6, illustrate three frequent characteristics in Brahms's music: wide melodic spans; cross relations between major and minor forms of the tonic triad; and metric ambiguity between duple ($^6_4$) and triple ($^3_2$) divisions of the bar (the indicated duple meter is seemingly contradicted by Brahms's rhythmic motive, which invites hearing the theme in $^3_2$).

*Example 18.6: Johannes Brahms, Symphony No. 3 in F Major, Op. 90, first-movement theme*

The conflict between major and minor recurs in the last movement, which begins in F minor and settles in F major only in the coda. The finale's second theme features another Brahmsian trademark: the clash between two different simultaneous meters, with the accompaniment in four and the melody in six (see Example 18.7).

*Example 18.7: Johannes Brahms, Symphony No. 3 in F Major, Op. 90, fourth movement, Allegro*

Brahms began his Symphony No. 4 in E Minor, Op. 98 (1885), by setting out a chain of thirds in which all the notes of the harmonic minor scale are used serially before any is repeated (see Example 18.8). The thematic statement in the first violins continues with a similar series, this time rising from the keynote E to C, completing an eight-measure phrase. Another series of thirds accompanies the melodious second subject, and at the start of the recapitulation Brahms unfolds the initial series of thirds in augmentation.

*Example 18.8: Johannes Brahms, Symphony No. 4 in E Minor, Op. 98, first movement, Allegro non troppo*

The finale of this work (NAWM 132) is a chaconne, a form indicative of Brahms's fascination with Baroque music. It is at once a set of variations on a basso ostinato and on a harmonic pattern. Brahms drew the rising bass figure from the final chorus of Bach's Cantata 150, adding a crucial chromatic note, but he may have had other models in mind as well, such as Buxtehude's Ciacona in E Minor. The use of a variation movement to end a symphony recalls Beethoven's *Eroica*, one of the few symphonies to feature such a finale; and, like Beethoven, Brahms first presents his bass line as a melody in the upper register and works it into the bass only after several variations. All three variation finales (by Bach, Beethoven, and Brahms) are laid out in a broad three-part form with a contrasting middle section.

Brahms's critics labeled him a conservative, but one of the most radical composers of the twentieth century, Arnold Schoenberg (who coined the phrase *developing variation* in connection with Brahms—see page 450), hailed him as a progressive. Although neither classification is accurate by itself, both are true to some degree. Brahms was among the first to view the entire range of music of the past and present as material to draw upon in composing his own new and highly individual music—a stance that we will see repeatedly in composers of the twentieth century. By introducing new elements into traditional forms and trying to meet the master composers on their own ground, he was arguably pursuing a more difficult course than those who simply made their mark through innovation.

# Piotr Il'yich Tchaikovsky (1840–1893)

The classical repertoire of instrumental music centered on works by German and Austrian composers from Bach to Brahms. But some composers from eastern Europe active in the later nineteenth century found a secure place within it. Inevitably, they brought something different to the European musical landscape, flavored as much by their cultural heritage as by their individual character. Of these new voices, the Russian Piotr Il'yich Tchaikovsky (1840–1893) and the Bohemian Antonín Dvořák (1841–1904) were by far the most successful.

Culturally, nineteenth-century Russia often looked to the West for models, particularly to France and the Austro-Hungarian Empire. So it is not surprising

Ballets

that Tchaikovsky (see biography and Figure 18.9) was drawn to writing for the ballet, a particularly French genre, or that he made the waltz, a dance associated with Viennese ballrooms as seen in Figure 18.10, the cornerstone of his ballet scores and elevated it to a new status in symphonic music. Tchaikovsky's three ballets—*Swan Lake* (1876), *The Sleeping Beauty* (1889), and *The Nutcracker* (1892)—include more than twenty waltz scenes, most of them strung together in a chain of several waltzes, to which he gave an entirely new range of character. Tchaikovsky won spectacular success with his ballets, outdoing the French on their own turf; they are still perhaps the most famous and frequently performed works in the ballet repertory. For them, he created a style that combined memo-

## ✳ Piotr Il'yich Tchaikovsky (1840–1893)

The most prominent Russian composer of the nineteenth century, Tchaikovsky was a depressive who attempted suicide more than once. His works, however, are, for the most part, cheerful and colorful, and their appeal has endured to the present time.

He was born in a distant province of Russia but moved with his family to Saint Petersburg, where he graduated from law school at age nineteen, destined for a career in government. After four years as a civil servant, Tchaikovsky enrolled as a student at the newly founded Saint Petersburg Conserva-

*Figure 18.9. Photograph of Tchaikovsky in 1893, the last year of his life.*

tory, where he studied with the composer Anton Rubinstein and was among the first students to graduate. He quickly found a teaching position at the new Moscow Conservatory, where he remained for twelve years.

While Tchaikovsky's professional career was successful, his personal life was in disarray. Bouts of depression aside, he was troubled by the growing confirmation of his homosexuality. In 1877, he tried to escape into a hasty and disastrous marriage, after which, on the verge of a complete breakdown, he fled back to Saint Petersburg. Enthralled by his music, a wealthy widow, Nadezhda von Meck, became his financial supporter and intellectual correspondent, though the two took care never to meet. Her patronage enabled him to resign his teaching position in 1878 and devote himself entirely to composition.

Tchaikovsky traveled throughout Europe as a conductor and even made a brief tour of the United States, where, in 1891, he was invited to take part in the ceremonies inaugurating New York's Carnegie Hall. Although he embraced his Russian musical heritage, he sought to reconcile it with such European styles as Italian opera, French ballet, and German symphony and song. Perhaps for this reason, he was the first Russian whose music appealed to Western tastes. He died of cholera at the age of fifty-three.

**Major works:** 8 operas, including *Eugene Onegin* (1879) and *Pique Dame* (The Queen of Spades, 1890); 3 ballets: *Swan Lake* (1876), *The Sleeping Beauty* (1889), and *The Nutcracker* (1892); 6 symphonies; 3 piano concertos; a violin concerto; symphonic poems and overtures, including *Romeo and Juliet* (1870) and the *1812 Overture* (1880); and some chamber music and songs.

*Figure 18.10.* The Viennese Ball, *a painting by Wilhelm Gause (1853–1916). Historisches Museum der Stadt Wien.*

rable tunes, some of which are suggestive of Russian folk melodies and rhythms, with wonderfully colorful orchestration perfectly suited to the fairy-tale atmosphere of the stories and to the gestures of classical ballet (see Figure 18.11).

Among Tchaikovsky's other works for the stage are a number of operas, two of which he based on works by the Russian author Alexander Pushkin (1799–1837).

Operas

*Figure 18.11. A nineteenth-century photograph of members of the cast of the first performance of Tchaikovsky's ballet* Swan Lake.

*Eugene Onegin* (1879) is notable for penetrating the passions of its characters and for the way numerous themes are generated from a germ motive first announced in the orchestral prelude. In *The Queen of Spades* (1890), Tchaikovsky matched the ghoulish atmosphere of Pushkin's story and re-created the spirit of the eighteenth-century Russia of Catherine the Great by borrowing musical ideas from that period.

Fifth Symphony    Although Tchaikovsky's six completed symphonies broke no new formal ground, they are noteworthy for their lyricism, orchestration, and dramatic quality. Symphony No. 5 in E Minor (1888) builds on the cyclic method of some of his predecessors. The brooding motto announced in the introduction (see Example 18.9) recurs in all four movements: in the first movement's development section; before the coda of the lyrical Andante; as a coda to the third movement; and, greatly recast, as an introduction to the finale. The work as a whole demonstrates Tchaikovsky's mastery of orchestration, particularly in the sweeping effects he achieves in setting instrumental choirs against each other; in the Più mosso sections of the Andante, for example, we hear throbbing syncopations in the strings against a soaring melody in the winds. The usual scherzo is replaced by a waltz, a dance for which Tchaikovsky had great affinity, as we have noted.

*Example 18.9: Piotr Il'yich Tchaikovsky, Symphony No. 5 in E Minor, Op. 64, first movement, motto theme*

*Pathétique* Symphony    He used a waltz again in the second movement of his last symphony, No. 6 in B Minor, the *Pathétique* (1893), but this time he changed the Viennese $\frac{3}{4}$ into a Russian $\frac{5}{4}$, as seen in Example 18.10. The order of movements is novel; the dance comes second, then a vivacious rondo in march character, and finally an extraordinarily somber slow movement that fades away at the end over a low pulse in the strings, like the beating of a dying heart. The darkly passionate character of the first movement (which quotes the Russian Orthodox Requiem), together with the tragic tone of the finale, led Tchaikovsky's brother to nickname the symphony *Pathétique*. The composer died suddenly within a few weeks of conducting its first perfomance in Saint Petersburg.

*Example 18.10: Piotr Il'yich Tchaikovsky, Symphony No. 6 in B Minor* (Pathétique), *Op. 29, second movement, waltzlike theme in $\frac{5}{4}$ meter, scored for cellos*

| MUSICAL EVENTS | HISTORICAL EVENTS |
|---|---|
| Mendelssohn, *Midsummer Night's Dream* Overture **1826** | |
| Death of Beethoven **1827** | |
| Death of Schubert **1828** | |
| Berlioz, *Symphonie fantastique* **1830** | |
| | **1831** Goethe, *Faust*, Part II |
| | **1837** Victoria becomes queen of England; reigns until 1901 |
| New York Philharmonic Society founded **1842** | |
| | **1848** Marx and Engels, *Manifesto of the Communist Party* |
| Bach-Gesellschaft (Society) founded **1850** | |
| Liszt, *Les Préludes* **1854** | |
| | **1859** Darwin, *On the Origin of Species by Natural Selection* |
| | **1859–1861** Garibaldi overthrows Bourbon monarchy; Victor Emmanuel II becomes king of a united Italy |
| | **1860s** Bismarck unites Prussia with other states to forge German Empire |
| | **1864** Tolstoy, *War and Peace* |
| Premiere of Schubert's *Unfinished* Symphony **1865** | **1865** Lincoln assassinated |
| Brahms, First Symphony **1876** | |
| | **1877** Edison invents the phonograph |
| Death of Wagner **1883** | |
| Dvořák, *New World* Symphony **1893** | |
| Death of Brahms **1897** | |

# Antonín Dvořák (1841–1904)

Sometimes called "the Bohemian Brahms," Antonín Dvořák (see biography and Figure 18.12) was one of the first composers from a "peripheral" country to gain an international reputation. He accomplished this largely by emulating Beethoven and Brahms in his cultivation of the symphony. Beethoven had removed that genre from the realm of abstract ideas and forms, and had transformed it into a medium capable of expressing individual heroism and communal feeling. As such, the symphony was the perfect vehicle for composers wishing to integrate nationalistic elements into their music.

## ✳ Antonín Dvořák (1841–1904)

Dvořák was an advocate of nationalism in music and a leader in bringing the musical traditions of his native Bohemia (now the Czech Republic) into the European mainstream.

He came from a peasant background (his father was an innkeeper) and, unlike some of his compatriots, resisted the idea of giving up the Czech countryside for life in Prague or Vienna. As a young man, he took a job playing viola in the Czech National Theater and eventually became a professor of composition at the Conservatory of Prague. Inspired by the older Czech composer Bedřich Smetana, he combined native folk and national elements with the Classical symphonic tradition in his instrumental music, drawing on dance rhythms and melodic inflections of rustic popular music. He also composed operas based on Bohemian village life, Bohemian fairy tales, and Slavic history. His instrumental music was strongly influenced by Brahms, who persuaded his own publisher to accept Dvořák's works and urged the younger composer to leave Prague behind and come to "the big city"—Vienna. But although Dvořák was intellectually an international composer in the Viennese symphonic tradition, as many of his works demonstrate, his emotional allegiance remained with his native land.

Dvořák traveled frequently to England, where his choral works were very popular, and through his friendship with Tchaikovsky he paid a visit to Russia. But his most famous voyage was to America, when he was invited to become the artistic director of a new musical academy in New York (1892–1895). He was hired with the expectation that he would show the way to a new national style of art music for the United States. Although his sojourn provided inspiration for his own compositions (the *New World* Symphony, the *American* Quartet, and others), he could not be persuaded to stay long enough to establish a native school of composition. But in a magazine article written in 1895, a few months before he returned to Europe, Dvořák sounded this mildly encouraging note:

> Undoubtedly the germs for the best in music lie hidden among all the races that are commingled in this great country. The music of the people is like a rare flower growing amidst encroaching weeds. Thousands pass it, while others trample it under foot, and thus the chances are that it will perish before it is seen by the one discriminating spirit who will prize it above all else. The fact that no one has yet arisen to make the most of it does not prove that nothing is there. . . . The music of the people, sooner or later, will command attention and creep into the books of composers.[1]

**Major works:** 9 symphonies (No. 9, *From the New World*, 1893); four concertos (notably the Cello Concerto in B Minor, 1894–1895); symphonic poems and other works for orchestra such as *Slavonic Rhapsodies* (1878) and *Slavonic Dances* (orchestrated 1886); 12 operas, including *Rusalka* (1900); many chamber works, piano pieces, songs, and choral works.

*Figure 18.12.   Antonín Dvořák conducting at the 1893 World's Columbian Exposition in Chicago, in a painting by V. E. Nádherný.*

1. Antonín Dvořák, "Music in America," *Harper's* 90 (February 1895), as excerpted in Josiah Fisk, ed., *Composers on Music: Eight Centuries of Writings*, 2nd ed. (Boston: Northeastern University Press, 1997), p. 163.

incident is brought to life intensely and on a heroic scale. *Les Troyens* represents the Romantic consummation of the French opera tradition descended from Lully, Rameau, and Gluck.

A landmark in the history of French opera was *Carmen* by Georges Bizet (1838–1875), first performed at Paris in 1875. Like the original version of *Faust*, *Carmen* was classified as an opéra comique simply for technical reasons—it contained spoken dialogue (later set in recitative by another composer)—and despite the stark realism of its drama, which ends with a tragic murder. Bizet's rejection of a sentimental or mythological plot signaled a narrow but important move toward realism. In its Spanish setting and Spanish rhythms and tunes, however, *Carmen* typifies exoticism, a vein running through the entire nineteenth century and evident in some other French operas and ballets of the period (see "In Context," pages 466–467).

The Spanish flavor was embodied especially in the character of Carmen, a seductive Gypsy who works in a cigarette factory. Her suggestive costume, behavior, words, and music all serve to portray her as an outsider, both forbidding and enticing. Bizet borrowed three authentic Spanish melodies, including Carmen's famous habanera *L'Amour est un oiseau rebelle* (Love is a rebellious bird) and a folk song she sings in Act I. But most of the Spanish-sounding music is Bizet's own invention, blending elements associated with Gypsy or Spanish music with the modern French style; the result is an opera of extraordinary rhythmic and melodic vitality. Chromatic harmony, sudden tonal shifts, ninth chords—the vocabulary of Chopin and Liszt that Bizet surely absorbed as a virtuoso concert pianist in his youth—enrich the score even further. The Fate motive shown in Example 19.1 emphasizes augmented seconds, considered a trademark of Gypsy music, and a variant of the same motive accompanies Carmen's first entrance. She seduces Don José, an upright army corporal, by singing a seguidilla (NAWM 129), a type of Spanish song in fast triple time. The accompaniment pattern imitates the strumming of a flamenco guitar, the vocal melody features melismas and grace notes, and the harmony suggests the Phrygian mode—all features conventionally linked to Spanish music. The exoticized Spanish atmosphere conveyed to the French audience a sense of sexual allure and danger (see Figure 19.5). The opera provoked outrage among some at the premiere, and its composer never lived to see its gradual acceptance and eventual success as one of the most popular operas of all time—Bizet died three months after the premiere.

*Example 19.1: Georges Bizet,* Carmen, *augmented-second motive associated with Carmen's fate*

# Italian Opera

If asked who was the most famous and important living composer, many people in Europe around 1825 would have answered not Beethoven but rather Gioachino Rossini (see biography). He is best known today for his comic masterpiece *Il barbiere di Siviglia*, generally ranked among the supreme examples of Italian comic opera. Yet Rossini's reputation during his lifetime rested as much

Bizet's *Carmen*

CD 10/1    CD 5/47

Rossini

## ✳ Gioachino Rossini (1792–1868)

Rossini had a meteoric career as an opera composer: beginning at the age of eighteen, he wrote almost forty operas in half as many years and then, at the height of his fame and fortune, far short of his fortieth birthday, he suddenly and mysteriously stopped. Although he wrote grand operas as well as serious operas, his fame today rests especially on his comic operas, which include some of the most popular ever written.

Born in Pesaro on the Adriatic coast of Italy to musical parents, he enrolled in the Bologna Conservatory, where his studies of counterpoint and the music of Haydn and Mozart deepened his craft. An able singer himself, Rossini perfectly understood the singing voice. He wrote his first opera for Venice but earned an international reputation by the age of twenty-one. Like Mozart, whose musical style was similar, he apparently composed with incredible facility (sometimes writing an opera in a month or less), though often borrowing or transforming overtures and arias from his own previous works. Rossini scored his greatest success with *Il barbiere di Siviglia* (The Barber of Seville), composed and produced in Naples in 1816 (a decade before Beethoven's death). In 1822, he married the soprano Isabella Colbran, with whom he had worked as musical director of the

Figure 19.6.  *Gioachino Rossini around 1816, the year he composed* Il barbiere di Siviglia. *Painting by Vincenzo Camuccini. Museo Teatrale alla Scala, Milan.*

Teatro San Carlo in Naples. Eventually they traveled to London and then settled in Paris, where he became director of the Théâtre Italien. His last and greatest opera, *Guillaume Tell* (William Tell, 1829), written in French for Parisian audiences, combines Italian lyricism with French grand opera (see page 465).

The remaining forty years of his life were marred by illness—some say hypochondria, others bipolar disorder—but he was financially comfortable, entertaining in his villa outside Paris, composing some sacred music and witty piano pieces and songs, eating to excess, and inventing recipes that he exchanged with some of the most famous chefs in Europe. He died in 1868, known best for music written four decades earlier.

**Major works:** 39 operas, including *Tancredi*, Venice, 1813; *L'Italiana in Algeri* (The Italian Woman in Algiers), Venice, 1813; *Il barbiere di Siviglia* (The Barber of Seville), Rome, 1816; *Otello*, Naples, 1816; *La Cenerentola* (Cinderella), Rome, 1817; *Mosè in Egitto* (Moses in Egypt), Naples, 1818; *Semiramide*, Venice, 1823; *Guillaume Tell* (William Tell), Paris, 1829. Additional works include Stabat Mater, *Petite Messe solennelle*, and other sacred works; and smaller vocal and instrumental pieces collected in *Soirées musicales* and *Péchés de vieillesse* (Sins of Old Age).

Figure 19.7.  *Spanish soprano Isabella Colbran (Rossini's wife) holding a lyre, an emblem of her Orphic status as a singer.*

on his serious operas such as *Otello* and *Guillaume Tell.* Rossini was the most popular and influential opera composer of his generation, in part because he blended aspects of opera buffa and opera seria into both his comic and serious operas, making them all more varied, more appealing, and more true to human character. The new conventions that he established for Italian opera were to endure for over half a century.

Rossini helped create a style of Italian opera known as *bel canto*—literally, "beautiful song." The term refers to the glorification of beautiful singing in an elegant style characterized by lyrical lines, seemingly effortless technique, and florid delivery. In bel canto operas, the most important element is the voice—even more important than the story, the orchestra, and the staging. Rosina's entrance aria from *Il barbiere, Una voce poco fa* (A voice a short while ago [resounded here in my heart]), seems to acknowledge that fact, not only with its music but also with its opening words as she confesses to having been swept off her feet by Lindoro's tuneful serenade (see NAWM 125 and discussion below). Yet some of the most amusing and captivating moments in Rossini's comic operas are not bel canto, but in the style typical of the patter arias of buffo characters such as Figaro himself (the "barber" of the title, and the same character as in Beaumarchais's play and Mozart's opera). These numbers are characterized by rapidly delivered clever lines, sometimes mixed with nonsense syllables, that are repeated often and must be sung with incredible speed and precision. (An early example of the type is Uberto's aria from Pergolesi's *Serva padrona,* NAWM 93.)

A combination of beautiful melody (bel canto) and comic patter appears in the justly famous *Una voce poco fa* (NAWM 125) from *Il barbiere di Siviglia.* In this witty two-section or "double" aria (called a *cavatina* in this case because it is Rosina's entrance aria), Rossini achieves the illusion of action by changing tempo and style; the various sections also serve to portray Rosina's complicated situation—wooed by her guardian, who wants her money, but in love with a poor soldier—and the different facets of her character—part docile lady, part scheming vixen (as suggested by the caricature shown in Figure 19.8). In typical fashion, he juxtaposes two separate lyrical sections—an opening *cantabile* and a

Bel canto

CD 9/48

Patter arias

CD 7/1, 3    CD 3/55, 57

Rosina's aria

CD 9/48

*Figure 19.8. Caricature of Italian soprano Adelina Patti (1843–1919) in the role of Rosina from Rossini's* Il barbiere di Siviglia. Opera News *(March 2005).*

*Example 19.2: Gioachino Rossini,* Il barbiere di Siviglia, *changes of style in* Una voce poco fa

*a. Quasi-recitative*

*A voice a short while ago here in my heart resounded.*

*b. Patter song*

*The guardian I shall refuse, I shall sharpen my wits.*

faster, more brilliant conclusion, called a *cabaletta*. These are further divided through changes of style, as shown in Example 19.2.

The first section of the cantabile—as Rosina narrates being serenaded by and falling in love with Lindoro—is broken into small phrases punctuated by orchestral chords, a style that recalls accompanied recitative (Example 19.2a). When she swears to outwit her guardian, the style briefly changes to a comic patter song (Example 19.2b). Similarly, Rossini uses the cabaletta to reveal both sides of Rosina's personality: loving and obedient, singing a bel canto melody (Example 19.2c); but also a viper and trickster, showing off her sudden vocal leaps and rapid passage work in buffo style (Example 19.2d). The whole monologue reveals her control of the situation in Rossini's masterful combination of bel canto melody, wit, and comic description.

Rossini's style    As illustrated by this double aria, Rossini's style combines an irrepressible melody with animated rhythms, clear phrase structure, and well-shaped though sometimes unconventional musical periods. His spare texture and orchestration support rather than compete with the voice, while featuring individual

*c. Cabaletta, lyrical opening*

*I am docile, I am respectful . . .*

*d. Cabaletta, contrasting comic style*

*But if they touch my weaker side, I can be a viper . . .*

instruments, especially winds, for color. His harmonic schemes are not complex but often are original, and he shares with other early nineteenth-century composers a fondness for bringing the mediant keys into close proximity with the tonic. Another important aspect of comic opera is the quickly paced ensemble scene, and Rossini manages this feature with sparkle and gusto. Here and elsewhere he frequently uses a simple but effective device, the crescendo—building up excitement by repeating a phrase, louder each time and often at a higher pitch, sometimes giving the impression of a world about to spin out of control. The crescendo, also a prominent feature of many of Rossini's popular overtures, became his trademark.

Vincenzo Bellini (1801–1835) was a younger contemporary of Rossini who came to prominence after Rossini had retired from opera composition. Bellini preferred dramas of passion with fast, gripping action. Of his ten operas, all serious, the most important are *La Sonnambula* (The Sleepwalker, 1831), *Norma* (1831), and *I Puritani* (The Puritans, 1835). Bellini is known for long, sweeping, highly embellished, intensely expressive melodies that have a breadth, a

Bellini

*Figure 19.9.  Swedish soprano Jenny Lind (1820–1887) in the title role of Donizetti's* La Fille du régiment, *performed at Her Majesty's Theatre in London, 1847. Private collection.*

flexibility of form, and a tinge of sadness that we associate with the nocturnes of Chopin (who was, incidentally, a great fan of Bellini's operas).

**Donizetti**

One of the most prolific Italian composers of the second quarter of the century was Gaetano Donizetti (1797–1848), who turned out some seventy operas as well as hundreds of works in other genres. His most enduring operas are *Anna Bolena* (1830) and *Lucia di Lammermoor* (1835); the opéra comique *La Fille du régiment* (The Daughter of the Regiment; Paris, 1840—see Figure 19.9); and the buffo operas *L'elisir d'amore* (The Elixir of Love; 1832) and *Don Pasquale* (1843). Donizetti had some of Rossini's instinct for the theater and talent for melody, and in *Don Pasquale* he created a work that is in a class with *Il barbiere*. As a composer of serious opera, Donizetti was the immediate historical forerunner of Verdi: both were attuned to the taste and judgment of the Italian public, and their work is deeply rooted in the life of the people.

## Giuseppe Verdi (1813–1901)

For fifty years after Donizetti, Giuseppe Verdi (see biography and Figure 19.11) was the ruling presence in Italian music, which continued to be dominated by the stage. The first of his twenty-six operas was produced in 1839, when he was twenty-six years old, the last in 1893, when he was eighty. While his approach to dramatic structure and musical style evolved during these years, he enjoyed many successes at each stage of his career. Hence, the name *Verdi* is practically synonymous with Italian music of the second half of the nineteenth century.

**Opera and nationalism**

In contrast to developments farther north, where opera competed with other genres and where native and foreign composers vied with each other for the public's approval, Italy had a long, indigenous operatic tradition that was unchallenged by, for example, the symphony. Italians loved opera first and foremost. The Romantic issue that most affected their music at this time was nationalism (see "In Context," page 507), and here Verdi was uncompromising: he firmly believed that each nation should cultivate its own native music. He deplored the influence of foreign (especially German) ideas in the work of his younger compatriots and cultivated a personal musical style that remained resolutely independent. However, except for his loyalty to the traditions of Italian opera, Verdi's work is rarely overtly nationalistic. Yet he supported and became identified with the Risorgimento ("resurgence"), a movement that aimed to liberate Italy from foreign rule, reunite its various regions, and reclaim the leading role it had played in Roman antiquity and the Renaissance. Some of his early operas contain choruses that were politically inflammatory, such as the eloquent hymn in *Nabucco* that is sung by the Hebrew slaves exiled in Babylon—a thinly disguised reference to the Italians longing for freedom from their own oppressors. To patriotic Italians, the letters *V-E-R-D-I* eventually came to represent an acronym for their popular figurehead, Vittorio Emmanuele, Rè d'Italia; so Verdi's name became a symbol of the revolution and "Viva VERDI!" (meaning "Long live Victor Emanuel, King of Italy!") a patriotic rallying cry.

Approach

Verdi's treatment of opera as human drama (in contrast to the Germans' emphasis on romanticized nature and mythology, as we will see) linked him to his Italian predecessors. He usually chose the opera's story himself, stating his preference for "subjects that are novel, big, beautiful, varied and bold—as bold as can be." That suggests that he wanted librettos with fast action, striking contrasts, unusual characters, and strong emotional situations—and, indeed, those qualities describe most of his operas. Collaborating closely with his librettist, Verdi planned the sequence of musical forms to make sure each singer had plenty of opportunities for arias, dramatic duets, and larger ensembles. Once the libretto was complete, he wrote out a draft with the vocal melodies and essential accompaniment, then a skeleton score with more of the elements filled in. The final step was the orchestration, usually completed after the rehearsals had begun and he could hear how the singers sounded in the theater. Verdi's

*Figure 19.10. Teatro alla Scala (La Scala) in Milan, where many of Verdi's operas were first produced. It was built in the late eighteenth century by the Empress Maria Theresa.*

## ✸ Giuseppe Verdi (1813–1901)

*Figure 19.11.   Giuseppe Verdi at age seventy-two, based on a pastel portrait by Giovanni Boldoni (1886). Galleria Nazionale d'Arte Moderna, Rome.*

Verdi's long career dominates the history of Italian music in the second half of the nineteenth century. Today his operas remain among the most frequently performed works on the international stage.

"My youth was hard," Verdi recalled. His father was a tavern keeper and grocer in a hamlet near Busseto in northern Italy, an area that was oppressed alternately by the French and the Austrians. As a child, Verdi played the organ in church and studied music locally. When he took the entrance exam for the Milan Conservatory, he was evaluated as a promising composer with "genuine imagination" but was refused admission for lack of accomplishment in counterpoint. Rejected and humiliated, Verdi returned to Busseto to become the town's *maestro di musica*. In 1836, he married Margherita Barezzi, the daughter of a local merchant and patron who had sponsored his early musical education, and they had two children, both of whom died before their first birthday. When, in 1840, his wife also died, Verdi was left alone and despondent in Milan, where he had brought his family in hopes of having a career as an opera composer; he was then not even twenty-seven years old.

After several discouraging years writing for Milan's opera house, La Scala (see Figure 19.10), Verdi's luck began to change. He scored a huge success with his biblical opera *Nabucco* (Nebuchadnezzar, 1842), initiating a time of enormous productivity that the composer later referred to as "my galley-slave period": nineteen operas in fifteen years for theaters in Milan, Venice, Rome, Naples, Florence, London, Paris, and Trieste. His greatest hits among these works are still his most popular: *Rigoletto* (1851), *Il trovatore* (1853), and *La traviata* (1853).

Verdi met the highly intelligent soprano Giuseppina Strepponi (see Figure 19.12) when she, as the leading female role in *Nabucco*, helped to launch his career. She provided the tempering, stabilizing influence he needed, and the two formed a lifelong partnership; they lived together openly as lovers for many years before marrying in 1859. Their relationship was the object of much gossip, about which Verdi rebuked his former father-in-law in a letter: "I have nothing to hide. In my house there lives a lady, free, independent, a lover of solitude, as I am. . . . Neither I nor she

involvement even extended to his rehearsing, directing, and sometimes conducting the opera's premiere. He could afford to take more time than his predecessors had done because he was better paid for each new opera and, thanks to improved copyright laws, could count on income from royalties and from sales of the published scores. Although he used that time to calculate the most effective setting and work out the details of performance, his overriding concern was not for the singers or even for the music, but rather for the opera's dramatic impact on the audience. Everything else was subordinate to that. Verdi maintained that just as there was no greater crime than boredom in the theater, there was also no greater compliment than an audience that was so taken with a performance it would come back for more. His strategy worked: although he wrote far

owes to anyone at all any account of our actions. . . . I demand liberty of action for myself . . . since my nature rebels against conformity."[1]

After *La traviata*, Verdi took more time with each opera, writing only six in the sixteen years from *Les Vêpres siciliennes* (1855) to *Aida* (1871). Then he retired from the stage, focusing on the farm he had purchased near his birthplace and living off royalties from his music for another fifteen years. Eventually his publisher, Giulio Ricordi, persuaded him to write two last operas. In his seventies and after much deliberation, Verdi produced his crowning achievements: *Otello* (1887) and *Falstaff* (1893), one a tragedy, the other a comedy, both on Shakespearean subjects.

Verdi supported the Risorgimento (see page 475) and, though having little tolerance for political machinations, became a reluctant deputy in the first Italian Parliament (1861–1865). But his lack of participation was unimportant; he had already served the cause of Italian unification through his operas, some of which were subtle appeals against foreign domination. When he died at eighty-eight, he had become a national institution. Escorted by a procession of nearly 300,000 mourners, his remains—along with Strepponi's—were interred in Milan at the home for retired musicians he had helped to found and which he had called "my last and best work." The funeral itself, in keeping with his wishes, was a very quiet affair, "without music or singing."

1. From a letter Verdi wrote to his father-in-law and one-time patron, Antonio Barezzi; quoted by Andrew Porter, "Verdi," in *The New Grove Dictionary of Music and Musicians*, ed. Stanley Sadie, 20 vols. (London and New York: Macmillan, 1980), XIX, p. 650.

*Figure 19.12. Italian soprano Giuseppina Strepponi (1815–1897), who later became Verdi's second wife, in a portrait from around the time they first met.*

**Major works:** 26 operas, including *Nabucco* (1842), *Rigoletto* (1851), *Il trovatore* (1853), *La traviata* (1853), *Les Vêpres siciliennes* (1855), *Simon Boccanegra* (1857), *Il ballo in maschera* (1859), *La forza del destino* (1862), *Don Carlos* (1867), *Aida* (1871), *Otello* (1887), *Falstaff* (1893); Requiem and other Latin sacred works.

fewer operas than Rossini or Donizetti, Verdi's have been far more frequently performed than theirs ever since.

**Style**

To produce the dramatic impact that he sought, Verdi's primary medium was vocal melody (in contrast to the orchestral and choral luxuriance of French grand opera). The secret of his popularity was his ability to capture character, feeling, and situation in memorable melodies that sound both fresh and familiar. Many use a simple form that makes them easy to follow, and they combine regular phrasing and plain harmony with an intriguing rhythmic and melodic motive that catches the listener's attention. So aware was Verdi of the appeal of his melodies that he strove to keep a new opera's best tunes from being leaked to the public before the premiere. But his craft did not stop at melody. He had a wide knowledge of the music of his predecessors and revered Beethoven above all. He respected the conventions of Rossini's musical scene structure (see below), adopted some of the refinements of Donizetti and the emotional intensity of Bellini, and learned much from the harmony and orchestration of Meyerbeer. But after absorbing any stylistic influence, he fully assimilated it and made it part of his own language.

**Early operas**

Verdi's creative life falls roughly into three periods, the first culminating in 1853 with *Il trovatore* and *La traviata*. During the early period, many of his operas told intimate stories of personal tragedy, such as *Luisa Miller*, and were influenced by French culture. *Rigoletto* and *La traviata* were adapted from plays by Victor Hugo (*Le Roi s'amuse*, The King Enjoys Himself) and Alexandre Dumas the Younger (*La Dame aux camélias*, The Lady of the Camellias), respectively.

**La traviata**

Many features of Verdi's early mature works are summed up in *La traviata*, an opera about love and death or, as Verdi put it, "a subject of the times." Although the opera was written in great haste, the resources at his command are plainly evident in the scene of the final act in which Violetta, the "fallen woman" of the title, and her lover, Alfredo, reconcile after their separation, to which she had agreed out of consideration for his family's reputation (NAWM 127). The scene follows the structure that Rossini had standardized for duets (see "A Closer Look," page 479), yet it features a new kind of melody—more tuneful than recitative in some sections and more declamatory than outright song in others— a style that Verdi developed still further in his late operas. After the *scena* between Violetta and her maid, Alfredo's entrance launches the *tempo d'attacco*, or first movement, a tuneful song in which they alternate phrases. The following slow movement (Andante mosso), in which Alfredo and Violetta look forward to life together as she recovers her health in Paris, is almost as simple and direct as a popular song. The *tempo di mezzo* offers a series of startling changes in mood and style as Violetta collapses, insists nothing is wrong, and ultimately despairs that her illness will prevent their union. These emotions intensify in the cabaletta; it brings the scene to a rousing conclusion following a common form for Verdi—AABA' with coda—which allows him to introduce contrast and end on an emotional climax. Throughout the scene, Verdi takes every opportunity to exploit stark contrasts, strong emotions, and catchy melodies while keeping the action moving in an almost perfect marriage of drama and music.

CD 9/69    CD 5/30

**Middle period**

Ventures into grand opera—*Les Vêpres siciliennes* and *Don Carlos*, both premiered in Paris—characterize Verdi's middle period, ending with *Aida* (1871). Operas appeared less frequently now, as Verdi engaged in a certain amount of musical experimentation. In these operas, the action is more continuous; solos, ensembles, and choruses are more freely combined; harmonies become more daring, and the orchestra is treated with great originality. He introduced comic roles in *Un ballo in maschera* and *La forza del destino*. At crucial points in both these operas, Verdi brought back distinctive themes or motives introduced earlier in the score. Such reminiscence motives, already common in the works of other composers and used previously in his *Rigoletto*, help unify the work both dramatically and musically. All the advances of the second period are gathered up in *Aida*, which unites the heroic quality of grand opera with solid dramatic structure, vivid character delineation, pathos, and a wealth of melodic, harmonic, and orchestral color. Commissioned for the Cairo opera, *Aida* takes place in Egypt, giving Verdi the chance to introduce exotic color and spectacle.

**Reminiscence motives**

**Late works**

A decade had elapsed since the premiere of *Aida*, when Verdi's publisher, Giulio Ricordi, coaxed him out of retirement with the proposal that he set a new libretto based on *Othello*, a play by his favorite dramatist, Shakespeare. During that decade, a number of important works had joined the musical canon—among them Verdi's Requiem (1874, in memory of Alessandro Manzoni), Bizet's *Carmen*, all four of Brahms's symphonies, and Wagner's huge cycle of operas on the *Ring* (see "A Closer Look," page 486)—and Ricordi was eager to see Verdi give Italian opera a boost. The poet and composer Arrigo Boito (1842–1918) wrote the libretto, which presents a powerful human drama that the music intensifies at every turn.

---

**A CLOSER LOOK**    Typical Scene Structure of Nineteenth-Century Italian Opera

In earlier operas, the dramatic action was confined to dry recitative passages (*recitativo secco*), and the emotional reactions were explored in static arias, sung with little or no change of mood or tempo. In the early nineteenth century, Rossini and his librettists established a very specific structure for an extended aria or duet that accommodated new developments in the story line and reflected the changing moods of the characters. This formula might be thought of as an expansion of the double-aria structure illustrated by Rossini's *Una voce poco fa* (NAWM 125).

CD 9/48

**I. Aria (so-called double aria)**

| Scena recitative | | 1. *Primo tempo:* 1st mvmt. slow, cantabile, andante, etc. | 2. *Tempo di mezzo:* mid. mvmt. ensemble, chorus, transition | 3. *Cabaletta* often fast |
|---|---|---|---|---|

**II. Duet**

| Scena recitative | 1. *Tempo d'attacco* opening mvmt. | 2. Slow mvmt. | 3. *Tempo di mezzo* | 4. *Cabaletta* often fast |
|---|---|---|---|---|
| | action | stasis | action | stasis |

*Figure 19.13.*

A typical Rossinian scene structure begins with an orchestral introduction and recitative section (called *scena*) that sets the scene. Thereafter, the sections or movements differ, as does the terminology, depending on whether the piece is a solo aria (indicated as I in Figure 19.13) or an ensemble such as a duet (indicated as II). The latter is more complex and allows for at least the possibility of more contrasts in tempo and mood as the situation develops. In an aria, after the introduction, the character launches into a formal song known as the *primo tempo*, or first movement (I.1). In a duet, there are two movements in the first phase of the number: the somewhat dialogue-like *tempo d'attacco* (II.1) and then a more formal song that the two characters sing—either in alternating phrases or simultaneously in harmony. (See the excerpt from Verdi's *La traviata*, NAWM 127). After I.1 (or, in a duet, II.2), an interlude usually follows—a *tempo di mezzo*, or middle movement (hence I.2 or II.3), which may be a transition or interruption by an ensemble or chorus, and in which something happens to provoke a change in the situation or mood. This section leads to the final movement, or cabaletta (I.3 or II.4), a lively and brilliant solo or duet in the same key, part or all of which is literally repeated, though perhaps with improvised embellishments. The successive parts of a typical Rossinian scene complex, then, allowed lyrical highpoints (or moments of stasis) to coexist with dramatic action. The structure also gave the singers a chance, usually during the repeat of the cabaletta, to show off their virtuosity and bring the scene to a rousing conclusion. Verdi adapted this scene structure for many of the solos, duets, and ensembles in his operas (see NAWM 127 and discussion on page 478).

CD 9/69

CD 5/30

CD 9/69

CD 5/30

*Otello*

Another seven years passed before *Otello* was finally produced in Milan in 1887. The time and care Verdi took in creating the new opera clearly reflected his response to the evolving musical situation; despite his deliberate isolation, he was responsive to new trends. Like Donizetti before him, Verdi strove for continuity in music and action: "If only in opera there could be no cavatinas, no duets, no trios, no choruses, no finales, etc., and if only the whole opera could be, so to speak, all one number, I should find that sensible and right."[1] In his late operas, he realized this ideal most completely, by using unifying motives in the orchestra and by not breaking the flow of music within each act. The traditional scheme of declamatory and lyrical solos, duets, ensembles, and choruses is often present, but Verdi arranges these units in larger scene complexes that flow into one another so that the lyrical highpoints are connected by long transitions rather than abruptly set off as separate pieces. Instead of the number opera typical of the eighteenth century or the "scene opera" of Verdi's earlier style, we can now speak about "act opera," in which the musical units are neither individual arias nor separate scenes, but entire acts. Each act has a musical continuity that reinforces the inexorable sweep of its dramatic content. We find ourselves holding our collective breath (and our applause) until the curtain comes down at the end of the act; only then may we exhale and express (or withhold) our approval. The fourth act of *Otello*, set in Desdemona's bedroom and ending in her murder by an Otello crazed with jealousy, is an excellent example of this musical continuity (see "A Closer Look," next page).

*Falstaff*

Two years after the premiere of *Otello*, Boito suggested an opera on scenes from Shakespeare's *The Merry Wives of Windsor* and *Henry IV* involving the character Falstaff. If *Otello* was the consummation of Italian tragic opera, *Falstaff* holds a parallel place in comic opera: as *Otello* reshaped dramatic lyrical melody, so *Falstaff* transformed the characteristic element of opera buffa—the ensemble. Carried along over a nimble, endlessly varied orchestral background, the comedy speeds to its climaxes in the great finales of the second and third acts. At times, Verdi seems to be satirizing the entire Romantic century, himself included. The last scene culminates in a fugue on the words "Tutto nel mondo è burla. / L'uom è nato burlone" (All the world's a joke. We are all born fools).

# German Romantic Opera

*Figure 19.14. Carl Maria von Weber, in a portrait by Caroline Bardua.*

German Romantic opera began with *Der Freischütz* (The Accursed Marksman) by Carl Maria von Weber (1786–1826; see Figure 19.14), first performed in Berlin in 1821. Written and premiered while Beethoven was still alive, Weber's work set the pace for German opera for the rest of the century. Its unusual harmonies and orchestral effects are especially forward-looking. The libretto characteristically involves ordinary folk caught up in supernatural events against a background of wilderness and mystery. This and other plots often resemble fairy tales: mortals act not merely as individuals, but as agents of superhuman forces, whether good or evil. In giving such great importance to folklore, nature, and supernatural elements, German opera differs sharply from contemporary French and Italian opera. But its musical styles and forms draw directly from those other countries, although the use of simple folklike melodies introduces a distinctly national element. German opera also displays increasingly chromatic

---

1. From a letter Verdi wrote to his librettist for *Il trovatore*; quoted by Andrew Porter, "Verdi," in *The New Grove Dictionary of Music and Musicians*, ed. Stanley Sadie, 20 vols. (London and New York: Macmillan, 1980), XIX, p. 642.

**A CLOSER LOOK**   Verdi's *Otello*, Act IV

The act opens with a brief prelude, scored only for winds. The absence of strings lends an eerie quality that keeps us suspended in operatic time, between past and future. When the curtain rises, Desdemona and her confidante, Emilia, talk about Otello's strange behavior; Desdemona apprehensively gets ready for bed. Passages marked "recitativo," with sparse chords in the orchestra, alternate with melodious outpourings that pick up motives from the prelude. Desdemona sings a sad song she learned from her mother's maid about a woman, abandoned by her lover, who asks that her funeral garland be cut from a willow tree. The melody of the first line of this "Willow Song," *Piangea cantando* (She wept as she sang), was already heard in the prelude. Between the strophes, she "speaks" instructions to Emilia and even realistically interrupts her song with comments. After Desdemona bids Emilia good night, an instrumental epilogue dwells on a motive from the prelude played against an ominous chromatic descending tremolo marked *ppppp*.

In the second scene, which flows imperceptibly out of the first, Desdemona recites her nightly *Ave Maria* (Hail Mary) kneeling before an image of the Virgin. She sings at first on a monotone, then breaks into a hymnlike aria. The third scene again follows without pause: Desdemona has barely fallen asleep when several soft motives are developed in the lower strings as Otello makes his stealthy entrance; he places a scimitar on the table, extinguishes a candle, opens the bed-curtains, and kisses her three times before slaying her. The most prominent of these motives are a staccato turn-figure in the violas punctuated by a muffled bass drum (Example 19.3a) and a recall of the love duet of Act I. This reminiscence motive (Example 19.3b), originally sung to the words "un bacio" (a kiss), here accompanies the gestures implied by the final couplet in Shakespeare's play as Otello, after having been apprehended and made to realize Desdemona's innocence, stabs himself and then drags himself back to her bedside to expire beside her:

*Figure 19.15.* A poster from around 1900 advertising a production of Shakespeare's play.

I kissed thee ere I killed thee. No way but this,
Killing myself, to die upon a kiss.

*Example 19.3: Giuseppe Verdi,* Otello, *Act IV, Scene 3, motives*

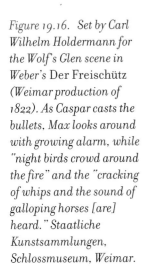

*Figure 19.16. Set by Carl Wilhelm Holdermann for the Wolf's Glen scene in Weber's* Der Freischütz *(Weimar production of 1822). As Caspar casts the bullets, Max looks around with growing alarm, while "night birds crowd around the fire" and the "cracking of whips and the sound of galloping horses [are] heard." Staatliche Kunstsammlungen, Schlossmuseum, Weimar.*

harmony, the use of orchestral color for dramatic expression, and an emphasis on the inner voices of the texture, in contrast to the Italian stress on melody.

*Der Freischütz*

CD 9/55

In *Der Freischütz*, rustic choruses, marches, dances, and airs mingle in the score with multisectional arias in the Italian style. The finale of Act II, the Wolf's Glen scene (see discussion in NAWM 126), illustrates how Weber ingeniously exploited the orchestra to depict the scene's eerie natural setting (see Figure 19.16). It also incorporates elements of the melodrama, a genre of musical theater that combined spoken dialogue with background music. The immense popular success of *Der Freischütz*, based both on its appeal to national sentiment and on the beauty of its music, was not matched either by Weber's later works or by those of his immediate followers. One of Weber's younger contemporaries, the great melodist Franz Schubert, also wrote German Romantic opera. Although these works contain some excellent music, they never reached the stage during his lifetime and, largely overshadowed by Wagner's music dramas, have remained in obscurity ever since.

## Richard Wagner and the Music Drama

Goals

For Richard Wagner (see biography), the outstanding composer of German opera and one of the most influential artistic personalities of his day, music's purpose was to serve the goals of dramatic expression. Consequently, all of his important compositions are for theater. Furthermore, during the course of his long career, he single-handedly transformed the contemporary concept of opera into a new sort of union between music and dramatic text that resulted in what he dubbed *music drama.* Wagner believed in the absolute oneness of drama and music—that the two are organically connected expressions of a single dramatic idea. His reformist ideal differed from conventional opera, in which song predominates and the libretto serves mainly as a framework for the music; but it was also not unlike the vision of the earliest opera composers, who took as their model ancient Greek drama, in which the words had been declaimed throughout in a singing style similar to what they called recitative. For Wagner, the union of music and poetry came naturally, since he wrote the text as well as the music; and both these elements joined forces with scenic design, staging, and acting to form what he dubbed a *Gesamtkunstwerk* (*Gesamt*, meaning "total" or "unified"; *Kunst*, meaning "art"; *Werk*, meaning "work"; thus, a "unified work of art").

*Gesamtkunstwerk*

Wagner's mature music dramas, beginning in the 1850s with *Tristan und Isolde*, were influenced by the Romantic philosophy of Arthur Schopenhauer (1788–1860), whose views about music had also impressed Liszt and other Romantic composers. Schopenhauer believed that music was the one art that embodied the deepest reality of all human experience—our emotions and drives—and could, therefore, give immediate expression to these universal feelings and impulses in concrete, definite form without the intervention of words. Words and ideas were the product of reason, which governed only "Appearance," whereas emotions resided in the "Will," which Schopenhauer deemed the dominant and ultimate reality. Wagner described his having read Schopenhauer's *The World as Will and Representation* in 1854 as the most important event of his life. He subsequently considered the action of his music dramas to exist on two levels, projecting both an inner and an outer aspect. While the orchestra communicates the interior drama, the sung words articulate its outer aspect—the events and situations that cause the plot to evolve. It follows, then, that the orchestra in Wagner's scores is the driving force of the emotional drama, the true engine that propels the work toward its conclusion; the vocal lines—unlike Italian arias with orchestral accompaniment—are only part of the complete

Schopenhauer's influence

## VIGNETTE    The Artwork of the Future

*In* The Artwork of the Future *(1850), Richard Wagner argued that Beethoven strove to discover the full potential of music and found it in his Ninth Symphony by rooting his music in the* word. *Thus, for Wagner, purely instrumental music after Beethoven was sterile ("the* last *symphony had already been* written"), *and only the artwork that combined all the arts was worthwhile.*

∿

This last *symphony* of Beethoven's is the redemption of music out of its own element as a *universal art.* It is the *human* gospel of the art of the future. Beyond it there can be no *progress,* for there can follow on it immediately only the completed artwork of the future, *the universal drama,* to which Beethoven has forged for us the artistic key.

*Thus from within itself music accomplished what no one of the other arts was capable of in isolation . . .* to offer to its sister arts a redeeming hand. . . .

Man as artist can be fully satisfied only in the union of all the art varieties in the *collective* artwork [*Gesamtkunstwerk*]; in every *individualization*

of his artistic capacities he is *unfree,* not wholly that which he can be; in the collective artwork he is *free,* wholly that which he can be.

. . . The highest collective artwork is the *drama;* it is present in its *ultimate completeness* only when *each art variety, in its ultimate completeness,* is present in it.

True drama can be conceived only as resulting from the *collective impulse of all the arts* to communicate in the most immediate way with a *collective public;* each individual art variety can reveal itself as *fully understandable* to this collective public only through collective communication, together with the other art varieties, in the drama, for the aim of each individual art variety is fully attained only in the mutually understanding and understandable cooperation of all the art varieties.

From Richard Wagner, *Das Kunstwerk der Zukunft: Sämtliche Schriften und Dichtungen,* 6th ed., 12 vols. (Leipzig, 1912–1914); trans. Oliver Strunk, in Oliver Strunk, ed., *Source Readings in Music History,* rev. ed. by Leo Treitler (New York: Norton, 1998), pp. 1108–1109 and 1112.

Richard Wagner (1813–1883)

Wagner was a crusader for reform in opera and created a visionary ideal for musical theater—a *Gesamtkunstwerk*—which he saw as a ritual, with himself as high priest or chief wizard controlling all of its elements. His emphasis on music as the driving force of the drama, his use of leitmotifs as an organizing principle, and his creative manipulation of chromatic harmony had a profound and far-reaching impact on many later composers. He was, in effect, the Beethoven of his age.

Wagner was born in Leipzig, the ninth child of a police clerk who died shortly after his son's birth. Wagner's stepfather was an actor, a poet, and a portrait painter who evidently cultivated Richard's intellectual gifts. His early passions were theater and music, and he was particularly inspired by Weber's operas and Beethoven's symphonies. By the age of twenty he was writing librettos, composing operas, and working as a conductor for various regional opera companies. After he married the soprano Minna Planer in 1836, the couple spent several unhappy years in Paris, where Wagner worked as a music journalist while trying, unsuccessfully, to get his works performed. Having returned to Germany, his first triumph came in 1842 with *Rienzi*, a five-act grand opera, followed by *Der fliegende Holländer*, in the early Romantic style of Weber. Their success led in 1843 to his appointment as second Kapellmeister for the king of Saxony in Dresden, directing the opera, conducting the orchestra, and composing for court occasions.

Wagner supported the 1848–1849 insurrection and had to flee Germany after a warrant was issued for his arrest. He escaped to Switzerland, where, during his dozen years in exile, he found the leisure to formulate his theories about opera and to publish them in a series of essays, the most important of which are *Das Kunstwerk der Zukunft* (The Artwork of the Future, 1850; see vignette, page 483) and *Oper und Drama* (Opera and Drama, 1851, revised 1868). There he also composed *Das Rheingold*, the first of his massive cycle of four music dramas about a cursed golden ring, *Der Ring des Nibelungen*. But with no regular income he complained, "I too am plagued by the need for gold!" Eventually, he found a patron in the young King Ludwig II of Bavaria, who became a fanatical fan, paid his debts (Wagner was a habitual gambler), granted him an annual pension, and sponsored the production of *Tristan und Isolde*, *Die Meistersinger*, and the first two operas in the *Ring* cycle.

Wagner's personal life was beset by stormy relationships—with King Ludwig and other patrons—and he channeled the energy from his disastrous

musical web. Wagner condemned as superficial and degenerate the French and Italian variety of opera, in which arias and other artificial set pieces unjustifiably impeded the action and reduced the libretto to a perfunctory role. In Wagner's music dramas, by contrast, the orchestra plays such an important role that these works are essentially symphonies with words, joining symphonic development with literary content.

Continuity    Especially in *Tristan*, the music is seamless throughout each act—not formally divided into recitatives, arias, or separate scenes—thus accelerating a growing tendency toward continuity in nineteenth-century opera, as we have seen with Verdi. (However, broad divisions and more traditional musical forms are sometimes still distinguishable, especially in Wagner's last few music dramas.) Wagner achieved coherence within the continuity of the action and seamless music

Leitmotifs    by means of the *leitmotif* (guiding, or leading, motive), a musical idea associated with a particular person, thing, emotion, or symbol in the drama. The association is established by sounding the leitmotif (usually in the orchestra) at the first appearance on stage or mention of the subject, and by its repetition at subsequent appearances or citations. Often the significance of a leitmotif can be derived from the words to which it is first sung. But the leitmotif is more than a musical label, for it accumulates significance as it recurs in new contexts: it may recall an object in situations where the object itself is not present; it may be

love affair with Mathilde Wesendonck, the wife of one of his patrons, into his sensuous opera about Tristan and Isolde, legendary victims of a forbidden love that could not be consummated in life. His second love affair was with Cosima, by whom he had three children out of wedlock. The daughter of Franz Liszt through his liaison with Countess Marie d'Agoult, Cosima was the wife of the conductor Hans von Bülow, another of Wagner's ardent admirers and promoters of his work. Wagner finally married Cosima in 1870, a month after her divorce.

Wagner dreamed of a permanent festival of his operas in his specially designed theater in Bayreuth, Germany (see Figure 19.20), begun in 1872. The first festival was held there in 1876, during which the complete *Ring* cycle was launched (see page 486 and Figures 19.19 and 19.20), and the second in 1882, with performances of his last opera, *Parsifal.* The following year Wagner died of a heart attack. His grave lies in the garden at Bayreuth, where his operas are still performed.

*Figure 19.17. Richard Wagner, in a portrait by Franz von Lenbach.*

**Major works:** 13 operas, including *Rienzi* (1842), *Der fliegender Holländer* (1843), *Tannhäuser* (1845), *Lohengrin* (1850), *Tristan und Isolde* (1859), *Die Meistersinger von Nürnberg* (1868), *Das Rheingold* (1869), *Die Walküre* (1870), *Siegfried* (1874), *Götterdämmerung* (1876), *Parsifal* (1882).

varied, developed, or transformed as the plot develops; similar motifs may suggest a connection between the objects to which they refer; motifs may be contrapuntally combined; and, by their repetition, motifs may help unify a scene or an opera as recurrent themes unify a symphony. Finally, by presenting and developing leitmotifs, Wagner's orchestra guides the listener through the drama.

*Tristan und Isolde*

Wagner's idea of music drama and his use of leitmotifs are illustrated effectively in *Tristan und Isolde.* The libretto, written by Wagner himself, is derived from a medieval romance by Gottfried von Strassburg about a secret, illicit, and overpowering passion that leads to the lovers' death. In Act I, as Tristan delivers Isolde to marry King Mark of Cornwall, the doomed pair fall in love by accidentally drinking a love potion. From that moment, they are caught up in a drama that presents sexual love as the dominant force in life (the Will), a force that transcends duty, loyalty, and family ties (all aspects of Appearance). The scene demonstrates the effective intertwining of action, scenery, and musical forces: as the sailors aboard ship drop anchor and prepare to greet King Mark, a castle comes into view atop a nearby cliff; but Tristan and Isolde, having drunk the potion, remain lost in mutual contemplation, unaware of what is taking place around them. The leitmotifs signal the interior drama as the couple gradually realize the import of their action and recognize the feelings that begin to overwhelm them.

**A CLOSER LOOK**   Wagner's Ring Cycle

Wagner's tetralogy *Der Ring des Nibelungen*, which ranks as the composer's most colossal achievement, is a four-opera cycle woven out of stories from medieval Norse legends featuring giants and dwarfs, gods and mortals. Nearly thirty years in the making, it consists of about nineteen hours of music that Wagner intended to be performed over four consecutive evenings, although it is possible—in fact, even usual—to attend a production of only one of the four in a given season. All are linked by a common set of characters and musical motives, or leitmotifs. The "ring" of the title refers to a ring that the gnome Alberich fashioned out of the gold he stole from the river Rhine, where it was guarded by Rhine maidens. Wagner's stunning evocation of the watery riverbed at the opening of the first opera, *Das Rheingold*—by prolonging the tonic chord for 136 measures—is but one of the brilliant special effects of his orchestral palette and was matched by the watery stage effects shown in Figure 19.18. Wotan, ruler of the gods (see Figure 19.19), tricks Alberich into giving up the ring

*Figure 19.19. Wotan, ruler of the gods.*

and also captures a hoard of gold, which he uses to pay the giants for building his new castle, Valhalla. But Alberich has put a curse on the ring that will bring its wearer misery and death. In the course of the mega-opera, the prophecy of the curse is fulfilled: Wotan's doomed empire comes to a fiery end, with more special effects, in the last drama of the cycle, *Götterdämmerung* (The Twilight of the Gods); and the Rhine maidens reclaim the ring. Despite its fantastical setting, the *Ring's* themes—greed, power, innocence, passion, and betrayal, to name a few—are as universally relevant now as then.

*Figure 19.18. Photograph of singers portraying the Rhine maidens in the 1876 Bayreuth premiere of the* Ring *cycle. They were enclosed in a special contraption that gave the illusion that they were swimming beneath the Rhine.*

Example 19.4 shows several leitmotifs in the order they appear in this, the climactic scene of Act I (NAWM 128). The text sung at each leitmotif's most characteristic appearance is given along with the motive. They are, for the most part, short, concentrated, and intended to represent their object at various levels of meaning. The motive in Example 19.4c, for example, is identified with the intense longing that Tristan and Isolde feel for each other after drinking the love potion. The cause-and-effect relationship may be seen by comparing the

CD 9/78    CD 5/39

*Example 19.4: Richard Wagner,* Tristan und Isolde, *leitmotifs*

first chord of this example (4c), symbolizing longing and desire, with the last chord of Example 19.4b, the motive associated with the love potion. The rising chromatic line characterizes their yearning, particularly as it ends on its highest pitch over an unresolved dominant-seventh chord in A minor. Later in the scene, however, Wagner expands and intensifies the motive over the same dominant-seventh chord (19.4d), but this time the progression resolves deceptively to the chord on the sixth degree, symbolizing that the longing is destined to remain unfulfilled. The mutability of Wagner's leitmotifs is one quality that distinguishes them from the reminiscence motives appearing in operas by Verdi and Weber and in Wagner's own earlier works. Another and more important difference, of course, is that Wagner's leitmotifs form the basic musical substance of the score; he uses them not once in a while but constantly, in close alliance with every step of the action. (See NAWM 128 for a detailed discussion of the scene, illustrating how the motives and harmonic progressions acquire meaning and symbolize the dramatic situation.)

*Endless melody*

Wagner's leitmotifs also serve as material for forming his "endless melodies," which are not the foursquare phrases set off by the rests and cadences of earlier composers. The leitmotifs, their development, their restatements and variants, and the connective tissue linking them form the stuff of musical prose with which Wagner wanted to replace the poetic rhythms of symmetrical phrases. The impression we have of endless melody results from the ongoing continuity of line, unbroken by the stops and restarts of Classical musical syntax. At the same time, Wagner's harmony contributes to the sensation of ceaseless motion. He achieves this by means of complex chromatic alterations of chords (note the half-diminished-seventh chord on F at the close of motive 19.4b), the constant shifting of key, the avoidance of resolutions, and the blurring of progressions with suspensions and other nonchord tones. All of these techniques combine in *Tristan* to produce a novel, ambiguous kind of tonality that expresses yearning and frustrated desire by evoking yet evading traditional harmonic expectations—a perfect match of style to substance.

*Wagner's influence*

Few works in the history of Western music have so deeply impacted succeeding generations of composers as *Tristan und Isolde*. Especially in its harmony, we see the culmination of a personal style that, influenced by the chromatic idiom of Liszt's symphonic poems, went on to forge a new vocabulary—one that

*Figure 19.20. The Bayreuth Festival Theater, designed by Otto Brückwald, incorporated Wagner's ideals for the production of music drama. The illustration— actually an advertisement for Liebig's meat extract— shows Wagner at the theater's inauguration, shaking hands with Kaiser Wilhelm I; Liszt is at his side.*

The reception of Wagner's work in the twentieth century was affected by political, ethnic, and religious policies and issues. Moreover, as a published writer, Wagner made his views known not only about music but also about literature, drama, and even political and moral topics. The National Socialist (Nazi) movement in Germany appropriated his music as a symbol of the best of Aryan and German culture. The anti-Semitism expressed in his essay *Das Judentum in der Musik* (Judaism in Music), which appeared under a pseudonym in 1850 and under Wagner's name in 1869, has alienated some listeners and musicians from his music dramas.

What drove Wagner to write this, he explained to Liszt, was his dislike of Meyerbeer, whose music he once admired and from whom he had sought help to get his early works performed. When critics noted the obvious influence of Meyerbeer on Wagner's music, his feelings turned against the composer, perhaps because he took offense at the implications of this suggestion. In his essay, Wagner attributed the "weakness" of Meyerbeer's music to the fact that he was Jewish and cosmopolitan (having left his native Germany for Italy and then Paris)—and, therefore, lacked national roots, without which a composer could not have an authentic style. Wagner's essay added strength to an anti-Semitic undercurrent in German culture.[1]

1. For a well-documented review of this issue, see Jacob Katz, *The Darker Side of Genius: Richard Wagner's Anti-Semitism* (Hanover, N.H.: University Press of New England, 1986).

stretched traditional tonal language almost to the breaking point. Some composers after Wagner, particularly those of German origin, understandably wondered whether tonal music had anything left to say. Others, especially among the French, rejected what they perceived as Wagner's overbearing orchestral rhetoric. In fact, more has been written about Wagner—both pro and con—than about any other musician. His own collected writings span sixteen volumes (excluding letters), and these, together with his music dramas, regained for dramatic and representational music the prestige that some had argued belonged to absolute music alone. His extraordinary vision of opera as a *Gesamtkunstwerk* affected virtually all later composers of opera, not to say modern filmmakers, whose works necessarily involve the synthesis of disparate elements such as scenography, acting, special effects, and, in a sense, a hidden orchestra playing leitmotifs. Also, as one of the first great conductors and a master of orchestration, Wagner left an example that inspired composers for several generations to come.

## Church Music

The tension between Romantic musical energy, at times so flamboyant, and sacred themes was a problem for composers of church music in the nineteenth century. A case in point is Berlioz, whose magnificent religious works—the *Grande Messe des morts* (Requiem, 1837) and the *Te Deum* (1855)—were intended for special occasions. They are dramatic symphonies for orchestra and voices using poetically inspiring texts that happen to be liturgical. They do not belong to an ecclesiastical but to a secular and patriotic tradition inspired by the great musical festivals of the French Revolution. Both works are of huge dimensions, not only in length and in the number of performers they require but also in grandeur of conception. For example, Berlioz's Requiem calls for a massive choir and an orchestra of 140 players, including 4

Berlioz

brass choirs, 4 tam-tams, 10 pairs of cymbals, and 16 kettledrums to accompany the chorus at "Tuba mirum" in the *Dies irae*. Moreover, Berlioz obtains many brilliant musical effects in his control of these forces, revealing his complete mastery of orchestration.

Liszt    The big sacred scores of Liszt, like those of Berlioz, were also created for special occasions: the Festival Mass (1855) for the consecration of a cathedral in Hungary, and the Mass for the coronation of the king of Hungary in 1867. Their scale and style correspond to Liszt's own ideal of Romantic sacred music, which he outlined in 1834, but which he never quite welded into a consistent style in his church music:

> For want of a better term we may call the new music "humanitarian." It must be devotional, strong, and drastic, uniting on a colossal scale the theatre and the church, at once dramatic and sacred, splendid and simple, ceremonial and serious, fiery and free, stormy and calm, translucent and emotional.[2]

Cecilian movement    Toward the middle of the century, an agitation for musical reform arose within the Roman Catholic Church. The Cecilian movement, named after Saint Cecilia, the patron saint of music (see Figures 10.8 and 12.7), was stimulated in part by a Romantic interest in music of the past. This helped bring about a revival of the sixteenth-century a cappella style and the restoration of Gregorian chant to what was thought to be its pristine form.

Bruckner    Anton Bruckner (1824–1896) succeeded as no one before him in uniting the spiritual and technical resources of the nineteenth-century symphony with a reverent and liturgical approach to the sacred texts. His Masses and symphonies have many qualities and even some musical themes in common. A solitary, simple, profoundly religious person, who was thoroughly schooled in counterpoint, Bruckner served as organist of the cathedral at Linz and from 1867 as court organist in Vienna. Bruckner composed his D-Minor Mass in 1864 and a larger one in F minor in 1867; like all his works, they were subjected to numerous revisions. The influence of the Cecilian movement is apparent in some of Bruckner's motets—for example, the strictly modal Gradual *Os justi* (1879) for unaccompanied chorus, or *Virga Jesse*, written in a modernized diatonic style.

Rossini    Two Italian opera composers, Gioachino Rossini and Giuseppe Verdi, made important contributions to church music. The operatic style of Rossini's *Stabat Mater* (1832, 1841) was expressly forbidden in 1903 by Pope Pius X's famous encyclical *Motu proprio*. But the style of the questionable operatic arias was not intended by the composer nor perceived by his public to be flippant or inappropriate.

Verdi    Verdi composed his Requiem (1874) in memory of Alessandro Manzoni, author of *I promessi sposi*, the most famous Italian novel of the nineteenth century. The Requiem adapts the sacred texts—somewhat rearranged—to the vocal and instrumental resources of his operas and adds some powerful choruses.

The Romantic oratorio    The main strength of the nineteenth-century oratorio lay in its use of the chorus, and there its descent from Handel is obvious. Mendelssohn, Brahms, and Bruckner wrote compellingly for chorus. Brahms's *Ein deutsches Requiem* (A German Requiem, 1868), for soprano and baritone soloists, chorus, and orchestra, has for its text not the liturgical words of the Latin Requiem Mass but Old Testament passages of meditation and solace in German, chosen by the composer himself. Brahms's music, like that of Schütz and Bach, is inspired by

2. Reprinted in Franz Liszt, *Gesammelte Schriften*, 6 vols. (Leipzig, 1881), II, pp. 55–57.

a deep concern with mortality and by the hope for salvation. In the German Requiem, these solemn thoughts are expressed with intense feeling and clothed with the opulent colors of nineteenth-century harmony, regulated always by spacious formal architecture and guided by Brahms's unerring judgment for choral and orchestral effect.

## TIMELINE  Nineteenth-Century Opera

| MUSICAL EVENTS | HISTORICAL EVENTS |
|---|---|
| Rossini, *Il barbiere di Siviglia* **1816** | |
| | **1819** Schopenhauer, *The World as Will and Representation* |
| Weber, *Der Freischütz* **1821** | |
| Bellini, *Norma* **1831** | |
| Meyerbeer, *Les Huguenots* **1836** | |
| Verdi, *Nabucco*; Wagner, *Rienzi* **1842** | |
| Wagner, *Der fliegende Holländer* **1843** | |
| Wagner, *Tannhäuser* **1845** | |
| | **1848** Marx and Engels, *Manifesto of the Communist Party*; revolutions in Europe |
| Wagner, *Lohengrin* **1850** | |
| Verdi, *Rigoletto* **1851** | |
| Verdi, *Il trovatore* and *La traviata* **1853** | |
| Berlioz, *Les Troyens* **1858** | |
| Verdi, *Il ballo in maschera*; Wagner, *Tristan und Isolde* **1859** | **1859** Darwin, *On the Origin of Species by Natural Selection* |
| | **1861** Victor Emmanuel crowned king of Italy |
| Verdi, *La forza del destino* **1862** | **1862** Hugo, *Les Misérables* |
| Verdi, *Don Carlos* **1867** | |
| Wagner, *Die Meistersinger von Nürnberg* **1868** | |
| Wagner, *Das Rheingold* and *Die Walküre* **1869** | **1869** Opening of the Suez Canal; Tolstoy, *War and Peace* |
| Verdi, *Aida* **1871** | |
| Musorgsky, *Boris Godunov* **1874** | |
| Bizet, *Carmen* **1875** | |
| Premiere of Wagner's *Der Ring des Nibelungen*, Bayreuth **1876** | |
| Gilbert and Sullivan, *The Pirates of Penzance* **1879** | **1879** Edison invents the electric lightbulb |
| Wagner, *Parsifal* **1882** | |
| Death of Wagner; Metropolitan Opera opens in New York **1883** | |
| Verdi, *Otello* **1887** | |
| | **1889** L'Exposition Universelle in Paris |
| Verdi, *Falstaff* **1893** | |

# POSTLUDE

Although French composers contributed significantly to opera in the Romantic century, and some works such as Gounod's *Faust* and Bizet's *Carmen* entered the permanent repertory, the two giants of nineteenth-century opera were Verdi and Wagner. Although worlds apart in their compositional styles, together they transformed opera once more into drama. Having absorbed the innovations of French grand opera, each went on to cultivate his own national style and to represent the quintessential expression of opera in his respective country.

Verdi's relation to the Romantic movement was complex. Contrary to the prevailing winds, which exalted instrumental music over vocal, he concentrated on the expression of human emotion through the voice. Furthermore, his attitude toward nature was rather neutral for a Romantic composer: while he respected nature, he did not sentimentalize or mystify it in his music, as did Wagner and other German composers. Instead he depicted natural settings and phenomena—the storm music in *Rigoletto* and *Otello*, for example, or the exotic atmosphere in *Aida*—in a concise, though convincing, way. And though he remained a Classicist in many ways, adhering to traditional forms of arias, ensembles, and set pieces, he also tried to surpass these old conventions so that an act from a drama might become a piece of unbroken music.

Wagner's signficance is threefold: he brought German Romantic opera to its consummation; by fusing operatic and symphonic idioms, he created a new genre, the music drama, in which all elements contributed meaningfully to the unified work of art (*Gesamtkunstwerk*); and, by so thoroughly exploiting harmony and chromaticism for expressive purposes, particularly in *Tristan*, he forged a hyperextended tonal idiom that hastened the dissolution of tonality. Composers after Wagner found there was no turning back. His music remains overwhelmingly powerful and arouses in its listeners that all-embracing state of ecstasy, at once sensuous and mystical, toward which all Romantic art had been striving.

Finally, church music from this period was characterized by the monumentality of large choral and orchestral forces and the colorful dramatic treatments typical of opera on the one hand, and by the retrospective and more sober goals of the Cecilian movement on the other.

# 20

# The Final Bloom of Romanticism: European Music at the End of the Nineteenth Century

## PRELUDE

In the eighteenth century, composers had aspired to styles fashionable in other countries as well as their own. Handel, for example, wrote in a mixture of Italian, French, German, and English styles, depending on the genre and the destination of the music. The Viennese composers of the Classical period reflected the tastes of the Hapsburg rulers and the society around the imperial court, which included a fondness for Italian opera, French theater and ballet, Italian and German orchestral music, and the dance and popular music of Hungary, Poland, Bohemia, and Croatia. All this changed in the nineteenth century, when the movement known as nationalism began to encourage an emphasis on native literary and linguistic traditions, an interest in folklore, an enthusiasm for patriotism, and a craving for independent identity. A sense of pride in language and native literature formed part of the national consciousness that led to German and Italian unification (see "In Context," page 507). How much national consciousness affected music—what and how composers wrote—has already been implied in previous chapters. In this chapter, we will discover that the rise of national trends prompted some composers to search for an independent, native voice, especially in Russia and the countries of eastern Europe, where the dominance of German music was felt as a threat to national cultural identity.

New currents in France, too, were at least in part sparked by nationalism, although these took many different paths. Finally, new trends also emerged in Italian opera in the late nineteenth century, involving more realistic librettos and greater naturalism.

*Chapter Contents*

*Prelude* 493

The Austro-German Tradition 494

National Trends 504

New Currents in France and Italy 513

*Postlude* 518

# The Austro-German Tradition

Wagner held an enormous fascination for European musicians in the last quarter of the nineteenth century. Many composers came under his spell, even as most struggled to find their own styles while making use of his innovations in harmony and orchestration. Composers in the Austro-German tradition continued to cultivate the solo song with piano accompaniment, the symphony and symphonic poem, and opera.

## Anton Bruckner

*Figure 20.1. Oil painting of Anton Bruckner (1896), based on a photograph by A. Huber. Gesellschaft der Musikfreunde, Vienna.*

Whereas Liszt showed how to compose purely orchestral music in a Wagnerian spirit, Anton Bruckner (1824–1896), shown in Figure 20.1, tried the more daunting tasks of absorbing Wagner's style into the traditional symphony and of writing church music that united the technical resources of nineteenth-century music with a reverent, liturgical approach to the sacred texts. Profoundly religious, Bruckner was thoroughly schooled in counterpoint and served as organist of the cathedral in Linz, Austria, and as court organist in Vienna from 1867 to his death. (His church music is discussed on page 490.)

Bruckner wrote nine numbered symphonies and two early unnumbered ones. He looked to Beethoven's Ninth Symphony as a model for procedure, purpose, grandiose proportions, and religious spirit. His symphonies typically begin, like Beethoven's Ninth, with a vague agitation in the strings out of which a theme gradually condenses and then builds up in a crescendo, conveying a sense of coming into being. Although we can view many of these movements in terms of sonata form, the continuous development of musical ideas, characteristic of Beethoven and Wagner, gives Bruckner's symphonies a monumental dimension.

Finales

The hymn of the finale of Beethoven's Ninth served as a model for the chorale-like themes in most of Bruckner's finales, although he never used voices. Structurally, too, Bruckner imitated Beethoven's Ninth in having his finales often echo subjects from earlier movements. At the same time, Bruckner's debt to Wagner is evident in large-scale structures, the great length of the symphonies, lush harmonies, sequential repetition of entire passages, and the huge orchestra.

## Hugo Wolf

Lieder

Hugo Wolf (1860–1903) is best known for adapting Wagner's methods to the German lied. Wolf produced most of his 250 lieder in short periods of intense creative activity between 1887 and 1897, when he was incapacitated by a mental breakdown. He published five principal collections of lieder, each devoted to a single poet or group: Eduard Mörike (1889), Joseph Freiherr von Eichendorff (1889), Goethe (1890), and German translations of Spanish poems (1891) and Italian poems (1892 and 1896). By concentrating on one poet or group at a time and placing the poet's name above his own in the titles of his collections, Wolf indicated a new ideal of equality between words and music, derived from Wagner's music dramas. Wolf had little use for the folk-song type of melody and strophic structures characteristic of Brahms. Instead, he judiciously applied to the lied Wagner's notion of a collective artwork, achieving a fusion of poetry and music, and of voice and piano, without subordinating either to the other.

A good illustration of Wolf's approach is *Lebe wohl!* (Farewell) from the Mörike songbook, shown in Example 20.1. The vocal line adapts Wagner's arioso style, presenting a speechlike rhythm and pitch contour. As in Wagner's operas, continuity is sustained by the instrumental part rather than the voice, which often parallels melodies in the piano. The chromatic voice-leading, appoggiaturas, anticipations, and wandering tonality are clearly inspired by the idiom of *Tristan und Isolde* (compare NAWM 128). The music is a perfect reflection of the text in declamation and in emotion, aptly conveying the desperation of a rejected lover.

CD 9/78   CD 5/39

*Example 20.1: Hugo Wolf,* Lebe wohl!, *measures 1–4*

*"Farewell!" You are not aware of what it means, this word of pain;*

## Gustav Mahler

The two most successful German composers of their generation, Gustav Mahler (1860–1911) and Richard Strauss (1864–1949), both found ways to intensify elements from their heritage and create music at once familiar and radically new. Mahler (see biography and Figure 20.2) was the leading Austro-German composer of symphonies after Brahms and Bruckner, and one of the great masters of the song for voice and orchestra. Influenced by the Romantic composers Berlioz, Schumann, Liszt, and Wagner, as well as by the Viennese composers from Haydn through Bruckner, Mahler, in turn, influenced Schoenberg, Berg, Webern, and others.

Mahler extended Beethoven's concept of the symphony as a bold personal statement. He once observed that to write a symphony was to "construct a

Symphony as world

# Gustav Mahler (1860–1911)

Better known during his lifetime as a conductor than as a composer, Mahler devoted his mature compositional energies to only two genres, symphony and song. The two were closely connected in his mind—symphony became his personal creative world and his songs provided a link to it.

Born to Jewish parents in a remote Bohemian village, Mahler always felt like an outcast, even after he settled in Vienna and converted to Catholicism. He showed musical talent from the age of four, and when he was fifteen his father, a tradesman, allowed him to enroll at the Conservatory in Vienna, where he divided his attention between music and literature. In addition to studying piano, harmony, and composition, he wrote poetry and became a passionate, lifelong reader.

Mahler's dynamism, precision, and expressivity—traits that are exaggerated in the caricature shown in Figure 20.2—earned him an international reputation as an opera conductor. He was just thirty-seven when, after conducting at numerous opera houses, including Prague, Leipzig, Budapest, and Hamburg, he attained the coveted position of artistic director of the Vienna Opera, where he was granted unprecedented powers. He went on to conduct the Metropolitan Opera in New York from 1907 to 1910 and the New York Philharmonic from 1909 to 1911.

In 1902, Mahler married the famous Viennese beauty Alma Schindler (1879–1964), an artist's daughter and herself a talented student of composition. The marriage survived the difference in their ages and attitudes, and they had two daughters, one of whom died of scarlet fever in 1907, an event that drastically changed Mahler's attitude toward life and art. Subsequently, his American concert programs contained a large number of new works, which, in turn, led to a renewed interest in the music of the past.

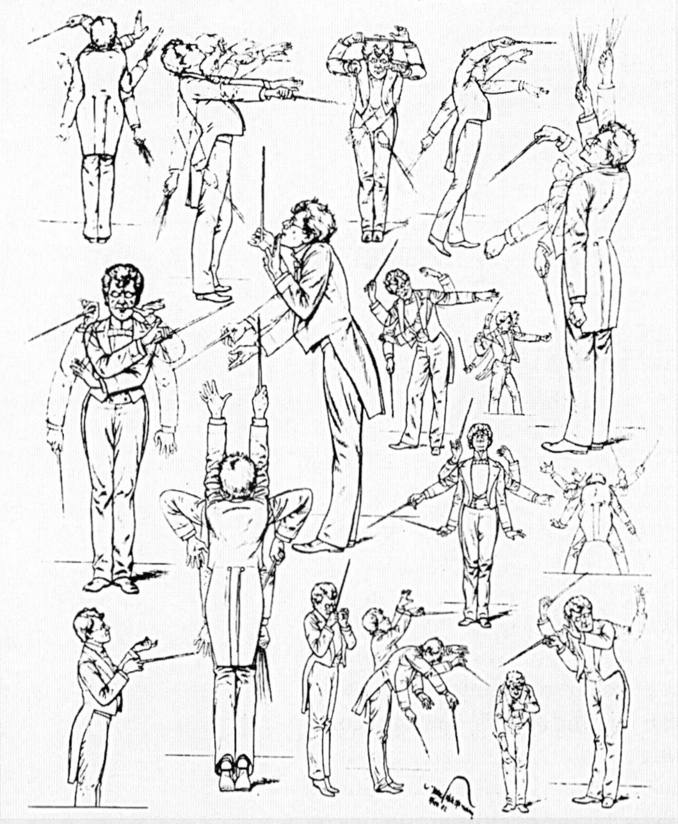

As a composer, Mahler inherited the Romantic traditions of his forerunners, especially the Classical and Romantic legacy of the Viennese composers from Beethoven to Bruckner. But most of all he revered Wagner, whose ideas about art as a kind of religion resonated with his own philosophy. Composing mainly in the summers between busy seasons of conducting, he completed five orchestral song cycles and nine symphonies, leaving a tenth unfinished. The symphonies, all programmatic in concept, have an astonishing variety of movements, including many with voices. He revised most of his works repeatedly, especially the first seven symphonies.

Mahler died, after contracting a bacterial infection, a few weeks short of his fifty-first birthday.

**Major works:** Five orchestral song cycles, including *Lieder einer fahrenden Gesellen* (on his own poetry), *Des Knaben Wunderhorn*, *Kindertotenlieder*, and *Das Lied von der Erde*; and ten symphonies (the last unfinished).

*Figure 20.2. Caricature of Gustav Mahler as conductor, by Hans Schliessmann, published in 1901. The face, glasses, haircut, stature, and gestures are all those of Mahler. Gesellschaft der Musikfreunde, Vienna.*

*Figure 20.3.* Music (*1895*), *by Gustav Klimt (1862–1918), a leader of the Secessionist group of artists in Vienna who challenged the narrow realism supported by the art establishment. This painting, for the music room of a wealthy industrialist, combines allusions to the classical past—notably the ancient Greek kithara (see Figure 1.1)—with a sensuous modern style influenced by symbolism. Neue Pinakothek, Munich.*

world," and his symphonies often convey a sense of life experience, as if telling a story or depicting a scene. For example, in the slow introduction to his First Symphony, the strings softly sustain the note A in seven octaves, producing an effect of vast space, filled in at times by ideas in other instruments—a melody in the winds, clarinets with hunting-horn calls, a trumpet fanfare, a cuckoo call, a Romantic horn theme in parallel thirds—like the sounds of humans and nature heard across a great landscape. In this and other works, he often drew on the styles and rhythms of Austrian folk songs and dances, using them at times to suggest his urban audience's nostalgia for rural scenes and simpler times.

In accord with Mahler's interest in presenting a world, his symphonies often imply a program. For the first four symphonies, he wrote detailed programs in the manner of Berlioz and Liszt but later suppressed them. No such clues exist for the Fifth, Sixth, and Seventh Symphonies (composed between 1901 and 1905), yet the presence of pictorial details, material borrowed from his own songs, and the overall plan of each work combine to suggest that the composer had extramusical ideas in mind like those ascribed to Beethoven's Third and Fifth Symphonies. Thus, Mahler's Fifth moves from a funereal opening march to triumph in the scherzo and a joyous finale. The Sixth is his "tragic" symphony, culminating in a colossal finale in which heroic struggle seems to end in defeat and death. The Ninth, Mahler's last completed symphony (1908–1909), conjures up a mood of resignation mixed with bitter satire, a strange and sad farewell to life.

Mahler the symphonist cannot be separated from Mahler the song composer. Themes from his *Lieder eines fahrenden Gesellen* (Songs of a Wayfarer, 1883–1885, revised 1891–1896) appear in the opening and closing movements of the First Symphony (1884–1888, revised 1893–1896 and 1906). Following the examples of Beethoven, Berlioz, and Liszt, Mahler used voices in four of his symphonies, most extensively in the Second (first performed in 1895) and Eighth (1906–1907). The Second, Third, and Fourth incorporate melodies and texts from his cycle of twelve songs, written between 1892 and 1898, on folk poems

*Programmatic content*

*Songs in the symphonies*

A CLOSER LOOK    Mahler's Fourth Symphony

The Fourth Symphony (1892–1900), one of Mahler's most popular, illustrates several of his compositional techniques and hints at his programmatic thinking. Because each movement strongly differs from the others, it exaggerates the contrasts in a traditional four-movement symphony, as if to suggest the world's variety (see pages 495–497). The work begins in one key (G major) and ends in another (E major), implying that life's adventures do not always bring us back home.

The first movement contrasts Romantic styles with the late eighteenth-century symphony through references to Haydn's and Mozart's styles and by using sonata-form conventions. The exposition has clearly articulated themes, shown in Example 20.2: a principal theme in the tonic G major (20.2a), a lyrical second theme on the dominant (20.2b), and a playful closing theme (20.2c). In the first theme, Mahler follows Mozart in using contrasting rhythmic and melodic figures (compare Example 15.9) but outdoes him in the number and variety of motives. There are surprises and deceptions that recall Classical-era wit: unexpected sforzandos, dynamic changes, and harmonic twists; portions of the theme used to accompany or interrupt other portions; and figures expanded to the point of pomposity (like the dotted figure in measure 6 as extended in measures 8–9), played upside down (that same figure in measure 12, in contrary motion with itself in the cellos), or varied in other surprising ways.

By contrast to these Classical-era elements, the second theme resembles a Romantic song and is introduced in the cellos and later joined by the horn, two quintessentially Romantic instruments. The development is fantasy-like and tonally daring, a Romantic outburst in a Classical frame, as Mahler shows how the two idioms can be blended in a single movement. When motives from the themes are reassigned to different instruments and recombined in new ways, they sound ironic and self-parodying, suggesting a feverish dream in which remembered images pop up from the subconscious in strange and distorted guises. The recapitulation restores lucidity and logic, but there is no going back to the innocence of the opening; the movement achieves balance by embracing all the possibilities it includes rather than trying to resolve all the potential conflicts, in a musical metaphor for the compromises required of us by the complexities and contradictions of modern life. This movement's interweaving of Classical references, Romantic fantasy, and modern style has a close counterpart in the paintings of Mahler's friend and fellow Viennese Gustav Klimt, whose painting *Music* appears in Figure 20.3.

The second movment, in $\frac{3}{8}$, is a musical representation of the Dance of Death, a favorite subject in old German paintings. A solo violin—the strings retuned a

from the early nineteenth-century collection *Des Knaben Wunderhorn* (The Boy's Magic Horn). For a closer look at Mahler's Fourth Symphony, see above.

Instrumentation and sound

Mahler's instrumentation is highly unusual. His works typically require an enormous number of performers. The Second Symphony calls for a huge string section, 17 woodwinds, 25 brasses, 6 timpani and other percussion, 4 harps, organ, soprano and alto soloists, and a large chorus; the Eighth demands an even larger array of players and singers, earning its nickname "Symphony of a Thousand." But the size of the orchestra tells only part of the story. Mahler showed great imagination in combining instruments, achieving effects ranging from the most delicate to the gigantic. Often only a few instruments are playing

*Example 20.2: Gustav Mahler, Symphony No. 4 in G Major, first movement, themes*

*a. First theme*

*b. Second theme*

*c. Closing theme*

whole tone higher than normal—suggests the medieval fiddle of a certain grisly folklore demon. After this grim scherzo, the slow movement is down-to-earth in its mournful and, at times, impassioned lyricism.

The last movement, composed years before the others, is a song for soprano voice on a text from the early nineteenth-century folk collection *Des Knaben Wunderhorn* (The Boy's Magic Horn) that presents a child's vision of Heaven.

as he selects different chamber-orchestra groupings from his vast palette of sounds. Mahler was one of the first composers to envision music as an art not just of notes but of sound itself, an approach that became more common over the course of the twentieth century.

Irony haunts the *Kindertotenlieder* (Songs on the Death of Children, 1901–1904), an orchestral song cycle on poems of Friedrich Rückert. The first song, *Nun will die Sonn' so hell aufgeh'n* (NAWM 137), achieves the transparency of chamber music through its spare use of instruments. Mahler's characteristic post-Wagnerian harmony intensifies the emotion through stark contrasts of dissonance with consonance and of chromaticism with diatonicism. Thin

*Kindertotenlieder*

CD 10/51    CD 5/65

textures and simple melodies and rhythms produce an effect of understated restraint, ironic for a song about the death of one's child. The irony is heightened at times by an emotional mismatch between text and music: the opening line, "Now will the sun so brightly rise again," is sung to a woeful, descending, D-minor melody, while the next phrase rises chromatically to a sunny D major on the words "as if no misfortune occurred during the night."

*Das Lied von der Erde*

*Das Lied von der Erde* (The Song of the Earth, 1908) rivals the Ninth Symphony as the high point of Mahler's late works. It is a song cycle for tenor and alto soloists with orchestra based on poems translated from the Chinese. The texts alternate between frenzied grasping at the dreamlike whirl of life and sad resignation at having to part from all its joys and beauties. Just as Mahler called on the human voice in his symphonies to complete his musical thought with words, here he calls on the orchestra to sustain and supplement the singers, both in accompaniment and in extensive connecting interludes. The exotic atmosphere of the words is lightly suggested by instrumental color and the use of the pentatonic scale. In no other work did Mahler so perfectly define and balance the two sides of his personality, ecstatic pleasure and deadly foreboding—a dualism that also characterizes the autumnal mood of the late nineteenth century.

## Richard Strauss

Richard Strauss (see biography and Figure 20.4) was a dominant figure in German musical life for most of his long career. Like Mahler, he mastered the medium of the orchestra and made his reputation as both a conductor and a composer. But unlike Mahler, who held essentially to the traditional, multimovement symphony even while imbuing it with programmatic elements, Strauss attached himself to the more radical Romantic genre of the symphonic poem, which he preferred to call a *tone poem.*

*Models*

Strauss's chief models were the programmatic works of Berlioz and Liszt, whose colorful orchestration, transformation of themes, and programs he emulated in his own symphonic poems. Like theirs, some of Strauss's works are based on literature, including *Don Juan* (1888–1889), *Macbeth* (1888; revised 1891), *Also sprach Zarathustra* (Thus Spoke Zoroaster, 1896), and *Don Quixote* (1897). Others draw on his personal experience: *Tod und Verklärung* (Death and Transfiguration, 1888–1889) was inspired by Strauss's recovery from a life-threatening illness, and *Ein Heldenleben* (A Hero's Life, 1897–1898) is openly autobiographical, caricaturing his critics in cacophonous passages while glorifying his triumphs with citations from his early works.

*Types of symphonic programs*

The program of a symphonic poem may be descriptive or philosophical in nature. Whereas the orchestral music of a work based on a descriptive program aims to represent a series of specific events, as in Berlioz's *Symphonie fantastique*, a work based on a philosophical program typically evokes only generalized ideas and emotions, as in Liszt's *Les Préludes.* Strauss's symphonic poems are of both types, although they often include descriptive elements in the philosophical type and vice versa.

*Don Juan*

*Don Juan* is Strauss's first completely mature work, and its success established his reputation while he was still in his twenties. Most of the piece evokes general moods of activity, boldness, and romance, rather than following a specific plot. Even more than *Don Juan*, *Till Eulenspiegels lustige Streiche* (Till Eulenspiegel's Merry Pranks, 1894–1895) is vividly representational, telling the comic tale of a trickster's exploits. The realistic details of Till's adventures are specified by marginal notes the composer added to the printed score. Two themes for Till are used and developed like leitmotifs, changing to suggest his

*Till Eulenspiegels lustige Streiche*

activities and situation. Yet the specific events are so thoroughly blended into the musical flow that the work could be heard simply as a character sketch of a particularly appealing rascal, or just as a piece of musical humor. This illustrates an important point about program music in the nineteenth and early twentieth centuries: as in opera, the suggestion of events and ideas outside music allows and explains the use of novel musical sounds, gestures, and forms, but in most

## ✳ Richard Strauss (1864–1949)

Strauss's long career, spanning eighty-five years across two centuries, belongs equally to two different musical eras: looking backward to the nineteenth century, he was the obvious heir to Liszt and Wagner, and the last of the orchestral tone poets; looking forward to the twentieth century, especially with the notoriety achieved by his operas written just after the turn of the century, he became the first in a long line of modernists who made Vienna their home.

The son of a horn player at the conservative Bavarian court in Munich, Strauss grew up in a musical environment. He was given private instruction in piano, theory, violin, and instrumentation, and he had written quite a number of pieces by the time he enrolled, albeit briefly, at the university. While still in his teens, he came to the attention of the noted German conductor Hans von Bülow, who programmed one of his works, commissioned another, and then invited him to conduct it. Strauss went on to have a long and prosperous conducting career, holding positions in the opera houses of Munich, Weimar, Berlin, and Vienna, and leading most of the world's great orchestras as guest conductor of his own works.

In 1894, Strauss married the soprano Pauline de Ahna, and during the ensuing five years he was exceptionally prolific as a composer. By 1900, he had won fame with a series of symphonic poems for orchestra. Most of them portrayed the adventures of literary characters or his own life in realistic psychological detail, and they were written in a progressive, post-Wagnerian musical language.

After 1900, Strauss concentrated for a while on writing operas, not the least of which are *Salome* and *Elektra*, two of the many dramatic female roles that he created. The musical world was shocked by the violence of their librettos and the anarchy of their scores; and although both operas were vilified as lurid and blasphemous art, that verdict generated enough publicity to ensure their subsequent success. With the royalties from frequent

*Figure 20.4. A 1914 color lithograph of Richard Strauss, taken from an 1890s portrait painted at the peak of Strauss's career as a composer of symphonic poems. Private collection.*

productions, Strauss built the villa in which he and his wife spent their remaining years, save for a brief period of voluntary exile in Switzerland after World War II.

Although Strauss continued to compose until the end of his life, when he succumbed to a weakened heart at age eighty-five, the brilliant German musical life of which he had been a leader for half a century had already ceased to exist.

**Major works:** many orchestral works, including the symphonic poems *Don Juan*, *Macbeth*, *Till Eulenspiegels lustige Streiche*, *Tod und Verklärung*, *Also Sprach Zarathustra*, *Don Quixote*, and *Ein Heldenleben*; more than a dozen operas, including *Salome*, *Elektra*, and *Der Rosenkavalier*; and about 200 lieder.

*Figure 20.5. Page from the German translation of Miguel de Cervantes's* Don Quixote, *first published in 1837 and reprinted in the 1890s, showing Don Quixote (right), who imagines himself to be a knight, with his servant, Sancho Panza, acting as his squire. British Library, London.*

cases the music still makes sense on its own terms, presenting, developing, and recalling themes and motives in ways that both parallel and diverge from the processes and forms of earlier music. Strauss indicated that the piece is "in rondo form." It is not a rondo in the Classical sense, but rondo-like because the two Till themes keep recurring in a variety of guises, enlivened by shrewd touches of instrumentation. Rondo is an appropriate form for Till, who remains the same fool after each prank.

*Also sprach Zarathustra* is a musical commentary on Nietzsche's long prose poem, which proclaimed that the Christian ethic should be replaced by the ideal of a superman who is above good and evil. Although the general course of the program is philosophical, moments are directly representational. Zoroaster's address to the rising sun in the prologue inspired the splendid opening, with a deep C in the organ pedal and contrabassoon, a rising brass fanfare, opposing C-minor and C-major triads, thumping timpani, and triumphant orchestral culmination for full orchestra. The passage became one of Strauss's most famous when it was used in the soundtrack of the film *2001: A Space Odyssey* (1968) to accompany both the sunrise and a scene meant to suggest the birth of human reason.

**Also sprach Zarathustra**

As the rondo suits *Till Eulenspiegel*, so variation form fits the adventures of the knight Don Quixote and his squire, Sancho Panza, shown in Figure 20.5, whose personalities are shaped by their frustrating experiences. We are no longer in a world of merry pranks but in one of split personalities and double meanings. The wry humor and cleverness in *Don Quixote* (see excerpt in NAWM 133) lie not so much in the apt depiction of real things as in the play with musical ideas. Much of this work has a chamber-music sound because it is conceived in contrapuntal lines, and its themes attach to particular solo instruments, notably the cello for Don Quixote and bass clarinet, tenor tuba, and viola for Sancho Panza. "Variations" here does not mean preserving a melody or harmonic progression and its form through a number of statements. Rather, the themes of the two main characters are transformed, building on Liszt's technique of thematic transformation, so that the beginnings of the themes (shown in Example 20.3a and b) sprout new melodic continuations.

**Don Quixote**

CD 10/25    CD 5/59

*Example 20.3: Richard Strauss, Don Quixote, Op. 35, themes*

*a. Don Quixote, the Knight of the Sorrowful Countenance*

*b. Sancho Panza*

Having established himself in the 1880s and 1890s as the leading composer of symphonic poems after Liszt, Strauss turned to opera, seeking to inherit Wagner's mantle. In 1905, he scored a triumph with *Salome,* and from then on he lavished the powers of depiction and characterization that he had honed in his symphonic poems almost exclusively on opera. His primary models were Wagner and Mozart, composers from the Austro-German tradition whose operas he enjoyed conducting most of all and who—despite the great differences between them—were both adept at using contrasting styles to capture their characters' personalities, articulate their emotions, and convey the dramatic situation. But he dealt with subjects, actions, and emotions stranger than any attempted before in opera. These stimulated him to forge harmonically complex and dissonant musical idioms that greatly influenced two later developments: the growth of musical expressionism (see Chapter 21) and the complete dissolution of tonality in German music.

*Salome,* a setting of a one-act play by Oscar Wilde in German translation, is a case in point. In this decadent version of the biblical story, Salome, by performing her famous Dance of the Seven Veils, entices Herod to deliver the head of John the Baptist on a silver platter so that she can kiss his cold lips. In some passages, Strauss achieves a blistering level of dissonance by superimposing ideas, using all twelve chromatic notes in quick succession and harmonies with up to seven notes. At times, the music seems to be in two keys at once. With these and similar devices, Strauss captures the macabre tone and atmosphere of the drama with great expressive force. Yet some passages in this opera sound as sweetly diatonic, consonant, and clearly key-centered as others are chromatic, dissonant, and ambiguous. The intense effect Strauss achieves here is predicated on our expectations that the dissonances will resolve. For his purposes of musical dramatization, Strauss needed the polarities inherent in tonal music between dissonance and consonance, chromaticism and diatonicism, instability and stability, tension and resolution.

With *Elektra* (1906–1908), Strauss began a long and fruitful collaboration with the Viennese playwright Hugo von Hofmannsthal (1874–1929) that would result in seven operas. Adapted from a play by Sophocles, *Elektra* dwells on the

*Operas*

*Salome*

*Elektra*

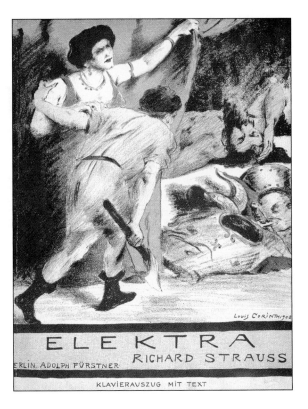

*Figure 20.6. A 1908 cover design by Louis Corinth for the piano score of Strauss's* Elektra, *showing the vengeful heroine prompting her dutiful brother to murder their mother's lover after having already killed their mother,* Clytemnestra. *British Library, London.*

emotions of insane hatred and revenge (see Figure 20.6). Accordingly, Strauss intensified the chromaticism, dissonance, and tonal instability at times even beyond *Salome*, offset at other times by serene, diatonic, and tonally stable passages. Like Wagner, Strauss heightened both musical coherence and dramatic power through the use of leitmotifs and the association of certain keys with particular characters.

*Der Rosenkavalier*    *Der Rosenkavalier* (The Knight of the Rose, 1909–1910) takes us into a sunnier world of elegant, stylized eroticism and tender feeling in the aristocratic, powdered-wig milieu of eighteenth-century Vienna (see Figure 20.7). Here, deceptively simple diatonic music dominates while chromaticism, novel harmonic twists, unpredictably curving melodies, and magical orchestral colors suggest sensuality and enchantment. The whole score, with its mingling of sentiment and comedy, overflows with the lighthearted rhythms and melodies of Viennese waltzes—a witty anachronism, since the waltz craze did not begin until the early nineteenth century, and an ironic comment on Strauss's own culture in which the waltz had become merely a sentimental, bourgeois remnant of the Austro-Hungarian Empire.

Style and effect    Strauss's operas, different as they are from one another, all betray his cunning use of musical styles and his intensification of the polarities inherent in tonality to depict characters and convey the drama. Ultimately, his is a rhetorical art that seeks to engage the audience's emotions directly, as a film composer might do, and he needed just as wide a range of style and effect.

## National Trends

The search for an independent, native voice—one important aspect of nationalism (see "In Context," page 507)—was most pressing in Russia, France, England, Scandinavia, and the countries of eastern Europe whose composers

*Figure 20.7. Watercolor by Pierre Laprade (1875–1931) illustrating Strauss's* Der Rosenkavalier, *which premiered in Dresden in 1911. Private collection.*

wanted to be recognized as equals of their Austro-German counterparts. Employing native literature, folk songs, and dances, or imitating their musical character were among the several strategies composers explored for developing a style that had ethnic identity. Individual composers in these countries differed in their level of interest in a nationalist agenda. Thus, composers who were marginal nationalists will be included here alongside those who were more active nationalists.

## Russia

When nationalism began to affect Russian artists, opera proved valuable as a genre in which a distinctive Russian identity could be proclaimed through subject matter, set design, costumes, and music. Ironically, while nationalism was a force for unification in Germany and Italy and for liberation struggles in Austria-Hungary, in Russia it was primarily a tool of propaganda for the absolutist government under the czar.

The first Russian composer recognized both by Russians and internationally as an equal of his Western contemporaries was Mikhail Glinka (1804–1857), who established his reputation in 1836 with the patriotic, pro-government historical drama *A Life for the Czar*, the first Russian opera sung throughout. Some of the recitative and melodic writing has a distinctive Russian character, attributable to modal scales, quotation or paraphrasing of folk songs, and a folklike idiom. Glinka based his second opera, *Ruslan and Lyudmila* (1842), on a poem by Russia's leading poet, Alexander Pushkin (1799–1837). It contains many imaginative uses of the whole-tone scale (see page 511), chromaticism, dissonance, and variation technique applied to folk songs. Glinka is valued in the West for the Russian flavor of these operas, which satisfied Western tastes for both the national and the exotic. But he was more important to his countrymen as the first to claim a

Mikhail Glinka

**VIGNETTE**  The Mighty Handful

*In a 1909 memoir, critic and composer César Cui recalled the gatherings almost fifty years earlier when the circle around Mily Balakirev met to pore over scores and argue about music. They opposed academic correctness, prized the most progressive composers of western Europe, and saw themselves as part of that international current.*

～

We formed a close-knit circle of young composers. And since there was nowhere to study (the conservatory didn't exist) our *self-education* began. It consisted of playing through everything that had been written by all the greatest composers, and all works were subjected to criticism and analysis in all their technical and creative aspects. We were young and our judgments were harsh. We were very disrespectful in our attitude toward Mozart and Mendelssohn; to the latter we opposed Schumann, who was then ignored by everyone. We were very enthusiastic about Liszt and Berlioz. We worshipped Chopin and Glinka. We carried on heated debates (in the course of which we would down as many as four or five glasses of tea with jam), we discussed musical form, program music, vocal music, and especially operatic form.

From César Cui, "Pervye kompozitorskie shagi Ts. A. Kiui," in *Izbrannye stat'I* (Leningrad: Muzgiz, 1952), p. 544; trans. Richard Taruskin in Richard Taruskin, *Defining Russia Musically: Historical and Hermeneutical Essays* (Princeton: Princeton University Press, 1997), p. xv.

place for Russia in the international musical world. This paradox pervades the reception of Russian music: foreign audiences and critics often prize what is recognizably national in it above all other characteristics, which is often not what the composers themselves or their compatriots most esteemed.

Looking westward

When Czar Alexander II emancipated the serfs in 1861, he did so as part of a broader effort to modernize Russia and catch up to Western Europe. For some, modernization included westernizing Russia's technology and education. All who composed operas, ballets, symphonies, or sonatas adopted Western genres and approaches, whatever their style. But, while some pursued professional training in the Western mode, others opposed academic study as a threat to their originality.

Conservatories

A key figure was Anton Rubinstein (1829–1894), virtuoso pianist and prolific composer who founded the Saint Petersburg Conservatory in 1862 with a program of training on the Western model. His pianist brother Nikolay Rubinstein (1835–1881) founded the Moscow Conservatory in 1866 along similar lines. Their work raised the standards of musicianship all over Russia and led to a strong tradition of Russian pianists, violinists, composers, and others that continues today.

The Mighty Handful

Tchaikovsky was the most prominent Russian composer of his time (see Chapter 18), but others also found a place in the repertoire. Standing against the professionalism of the conservatories were five composers dubbed *moguchaya kuchka*, or the Mighty Handful (or Mighty Five): Mily Balakirev (1837–1910), Aleksander Borodin (1833–1887), César Cui (1835–1918), Modest Musorgsky (1839–1881), and Nikolay Rimsky-Korsakov (1844–1908). Of these, Musorgsky and Rimsky-Korsakov are discussed below. Only Balakirev, who was their leader and informal teacher, had conventional training in music, but it would be wrong to call the others amateurs. They admired Western music but studied it on their own (see vignette, above), outside the academic musical establishment, whose exercises and prizes they scorned. It was because of their enthusiasm for Schumann, Chopin, Liszt, Berlioz, and other progressive composers in the West that they sought a fresh approach in their own music. As part of that new approach, they incorporated aspects of Russian folk song, modal and exotic scales, and folk polyphony, but they also adopted traits from the Western composers they most admired.

## IN CONTEXT  Music and Nationalism

Although Germany and Italy had been politically fragmented since the Middle Ages, the steady rise of nationalist sentiment during the second half of the nineteenth century supported the unification of both regions. In the 1860s, under the leadership of Prime Minister Otto von Bismarck, Prussia combined with Saxony, Bavaria, Hesse, and other German states to forge the German Empire. In Italy, the 1848 revolts against foreign rule inspired the Risorgimento ("resurgence"), a movement that sought to unite Italy and reclaim the leading role it had played in Roman antiquity and during the Renaissance. In 1859–1861, after the armies of Sardinia expelled Austrian rulers from northern Italy and conquered most of the Papal States, revolutionaries under Giuseppe Garibaldi overthrew the Bourbon monarchy in Sicily and southern Italy, and then acknowledged the ruler of Sardinia, Victor Emmanuel II, as king of a united Italy. But both new nations had identity problems. How could people who all their lives had considered themselves Saxons or Bavarians, Venetians or Sicilians suddenly become Germans and Italians? The motivation for their acknowledging a national rather than merely a local identity derived, at least in part, from the realization that the populations within each group had a common language and cultural heritage, including shared literary and artistic traditions.

In music, nationalism meant that some composers deliberately cultivated melodic, rhythmic, and harmonic styles or chose subjects that carried associations with their own ethnic group. Sometimes this involved using genuine native folk songs and dances or imitating their musical characteristics. Certain composers, particularly those from the marginalized countries in eastern Europe and Russia, urgently felt the need to resist the then-current cosmopolitan musical language that was so dominated, in their view, by Austro-German instrumental music. They were determined to invent an independent national style that could embody the spirit of their respective homelands. By the end of the nineteenth century, Dvořák, himself a Czech, writing from New York about music in America, could express his pleasure at the creation of various nationalist idioms in Europe (see biography, page 458).

For others, exploiting a national style seemed not to have been a conscious decision but rather the inevitable consequence of being a native. For example, Grieg, in seeking to identify himself as a supporter of the nationalist cause for Norway's independence from Sweden, insisted that "the spirit of my native land, which has long found a voice in the traditional songs of its people, is a living presence in all I give forth."[1] By seeking only to bring out the "spirit" of his native land, Grieg was free to use or ignore actual folk sounds and rhythms. Chopin was part of a massive exodus from Poland after the 1830 revolt against Russian domination was defeated. Since the majority of these émigrés settled in France, the center of Polish political, intellectual, and cultural life in the 1830s and 1840s lay in Paris, where Chopin quite naturally gave voice to their yearnings for home through his mazurkas and other pieces imbued with the spirit of his native land. Other composers also became identified with a national ethos largely because their music was a source of admiration and pride for their compatriots. For example, among Italians living anywhere in the peninsula and even among those who migrated to America, Verdi was revered as a symbol of national unity and patriotism. Even though he seldom chose Italian subjects for his operas and rarely incorporated Italian folk styles, his name was, nevertheless, synonymous with Italian reunification, and his career virtually defined Italian music during his long lifetime (see Chapter 19).

1. Quoted from Bjarne Kortsen, ed., *Grieg the Writer*, 2 vols. (Bergen: Kortsen, 1972), I, p. 36.

## Modest Musorgsky

Widely considered the most original of the Mighty Handful, Musorgsky earned a living as a clerk in the civil service and received most of his musical training from Balakirev. His principal works were the operas *Boris Godunov* (1868–1869; revised 1871–1874), based on Pushkin's historical drama about the czar of Russia from 1598 to 1605 (see Figure 20.8); and *Khovanshchina* (The Khovansky Affair, 1872–1880, completed by Rimsky-Korsakov after Musorgsky's death). The realism so prominent in nineteenth-century Russian literature echoes especially in *Boris Godunov* in the way Musorgsky imitates Russian speech, in his life-like musical depiction of gestures, and, in the choral scenes, the sound and stir of the crowds. The painter Ilya Repin similarly captured both realism and nationalism in a last portrait of the composer, shown in Figure 20.9.

*Melodic style*

CD 10/6

Musorgsky's individuality shines through every aspect of his music, as illustrated by the famous Coronation Scene from *Boris Godunov* (NAWM 130). Example 20.4 shows Boris's first statement in the scene, after he is hailed as the new czar. The vocal melody exemplifies Musorgsky's approach. He set words naturalistically, following the rhythm and pacing of speech as closely as possible—almost always syllabic, with accented syllables on strong beats, often higher and louder than the surrounding notes. As a result, his vocal music tends to lack lyrical melodic lines and symmetrical phrasing, but at the same time he avoided the conventions of recitative. He sought a melodic profile closer to Russian folk songs, which typically move in a relatively narrow range, rise at the beginning of phrases and sink to cadences, and often repeat one or two melodic or rhythmic motives. All these characteristics are apparent here, as witness the free melodic and rhythmic repetition of measures 3–4 in measures 5–6 of Example 20.4, for instance.

*Harmony*

Musorgsky's harmony is essentially tonal, projecting a clear sense of the key, but in many respects it is highly original, even revolutionary. He often juxtaposes distantly related or coloristic harmonies, usually joined by a com-

*Figure 20.8. Anonymous seventeenth-century portrait of Boris Godunov, the protagonist of Musorgsky's opera, based on Pushkin's play, in which Boris is suspected of murdering the young heir apparent to the throne in order to gain the crown for himself. Museum of History, Moscow.*

*Example 20.4: Modest Musorgsky*, Boris Godunov, *Coronation Scene, opening of Boris's speech*

*My soul suffers. Some kind of involuntary fear has stifled my heart with ominous premonitions.*

mon tone. One such progression is the chord sequence of C minor, A♭ minor, and G major (measures 3–4) in Example 20.4, which includes two chord pairings that became staples of eerie or gloomy movie music in the twentieth century. Those chord pairings are: two minor triads whose roots are a major third apart (C and A♭ minor, which share E♭), and a minor and a major triad with a common third degree (A♭ minor and G major share C♭/B). These types of chord progressions are not the result of naïve experimentation, as some have imputed to Musorgsky, but show his intellectual approach to composition and his familiarity with Liszt, Glinka, and other composers who had used such progressions.

Another trait that is characteristic of Musorgsky and of much Russian music is composition by the repetition and accumulation of large blocks of material rather than by continuously developed action. *Boris Godunov* is a series of episodes or tableaux held together by an epic thread and the central figure of the czar. Its dramatic structure is, therefore, enhanced by the score, which juxtaposes successive sections, each relatively consistent in style and figuration but strongly contrasting with one another. The opening section of the Coronation Scene (NAWM 130), for example, elaborates on two chords with roots a tritone apart (A♭ and D). After twice building to a peak of intensity, this section yields to a new one (at measure 40), a kaleidoscope of different ideas culminating in the chorus singing a folk song in C major, accompanied by the first traditional harmony in the scene. Musorgsky rarely uses actual folk melodies; this tune adds an element of realism, as do the bells that ring constantly up to this point, like the church bells of Moscow.

*Figure 20.9. Portrait of Modest Musorgsky by Ilya Repin, painted in early March 1881, only two weeks before the composer's death from complications of alcoholism. Artist and composer shared a devotion to nationalism, reflected in the peasant shirt Musorgsky wears, and to realism, evident in the unblinking depiction of his unkempt hair, watery eyes, and red nose. State Tretyakov Gallery, Moscow.*

CD 10/6

*Figure 20.10. Design for the City Gate of Kiev, from a memorial exhibition held in Moscow in 1874 of Viktor Hartmann's works. The closing movement of Musorgsky's* Pictures at an Exhibition, *a majestic rondo, is called* The Great Gate of Kiev *and is based on Hartmann's design—a massive stone structure that was never built.*

**Instrumental music**

Musorgsky's principal nonoperatic works are a symphonic fantasy, *Night on Bald Mountain* (1867); a set of piano pieces, *Pictures at an Exhibition* (1874; later orchestrated by Ravel); and song cycles. *Pictures at an Exhibition* is a suite of ten pieces inspired by an exhibition Musorgsky saw of over four hundred sketches, paintings, and designs by his late friend Viktor Hartmann, who shared with the composer an interest in finding a new artistic language that was uniquely Russian. Several of the paintings are rendered in character pieces, stiched together by interludes that vary a theme meant to represent the viewer walking through the gallery. Figure 20.10 shows Hartmann's design for a commemorative gate to be built at Kiev that combined classical columns, capitals, and arches with decoration modeled on Russian folk art. In Example 20.5, Musorgsky translates this image into a grand processional hymn that similarly combines Western and Russian elements, blending Classical procedures (rondo form) with a melody that resembles a Russian folk song and harmonies that suggest the modality and parallel motion of folk polyphony.

*Example 20.5: Modest Musorgsky,* Pictures at an Exhibition, The Great Gate of Kiev, *measures 1–8*

# Nikolay Rimsky-Korsakov

Another of the Mighty Handful, Nikolay Rimsky-Korsakov studied music with private teachers and with Balakirev while pursuing a career in the Russian navy. In 1871, he became a professor at the Saint Petersburg Conservatory, abandoning the anti-academic stance of the Balakirev circle. Ironically, Rimsky-Korsakov's professionalism guaranteed the continuation of a distinctively Russian school. As a conductor, he championed Russian music; as an academic, he arranged and edited two collections of Russian folk songs (1875–1882) and wrote the harmony text most frequently used in Russia as well as a widely known manual on orchestration, a skill at which he was an acknowledged master; and as a composer, he incorporated folk tunes and their melodic characteristics into his own compositions, as well as completing and orchestrating works by Glinka, Musorgsky, and others, thus helping to ensure their survival. He also taught some of the most important composers of the next generation, including Aleksander Glazunov and Igor Stravinsky.

Rimsky-Korsakov is best known for his programmatic orchestral works, although he also wrote symphonies, chamber music, choruses, and songs, as well as operas. The symphonic suite *Sheherazade* (1888) displays his genius for orchestration and musical characterization. Based on tales from the *Arabian Nights*, it typifies the quality of exoticism. Its four movements, each on a different story, are woven together by the themes of the Sultan and his wife Sheherazade, the storyteller, portrayed by a solo violin.

*Orchestral works*

It was through his operas that Rimsky-Korsakov proved his abiding interest in nationalism. Several of his fifteen operas draw on Russian history, plays, epics, or folktales. In many, including *The Golden Cockerel* (1906–1907), he alternates a diatonic, often modal style used for the everyday world with a lightly chromatic, "fantastic" style that suggests the world of supernatural beings and magical occurrences.

*Operas*

A key element of the fantastic style was the use of scales or pitch collections in which the same sequence of intervals occurs several times, so that there is more than one possible tone center. The simplest such scale is the whole-tone scale (or whole-tone collection), consisting solely of whole steps; another is the octatonic scale (or octatonic collection), which alternates whole and half steps. Both are shown in Example 20.6. While each of the twelve major scales contains a unique collection of seven notes, there are only two whole-tone collections and three octatonic collections, as shown in Examples 20.6a and 20.6b; any other transposition of these scales will simply reproduce the same series of pitches. Because they lack the strong gravitation toward a tonic that is characteristic of diatonic scales, the whole-tone and octatonic scales create a sense of floating or otherworldliness.

*Whole-tone and octatonic scales*

Tchaikovsky and the Mighty Five developed musical styles that were strongly individual, markedly national, yet suffused with elements from the West. In turn, they influenced Western composers of the very late nineteenth and early

*Russian influence*

*Example 20.6: Scales based on equal divisions of the octave*

*a. Whole-tone scales*

*b. Octatonic scales*

twentieth centuries, who were especially drawn to the Russians' block construction, orchestral colors, use of modality, and new scales. In less than a century, Russian music went from being peripheral to being a major current in Western music.

## National Trends in Other Countries

Bohemia

Among the lands of central Europe, Bohemia (now part of the Czech Republic) had for centuries been politically attached to Austria and so, unlike Russia, had always been in the mainstream of European music. The two principal Bohemian or Czech composers of the nineteenth century were Bedřich Smetana (1824–1884) and Antonin Dvořák (see Chapter 18, page 457). Although they leaned toward nationalistic subjects in their program music and operas, their musical language was basically European. Like the Russians, Smetana and Dvořák are better known outside their native land for their instrumental music than for their operas.

Smetana

Smetana sought to create a national music in his String Quartet No. 1, *From My Life* (1876), and in his cycle of six symphonic poems collectively entitled *Má vlast* (My Country, ca. 1872–1879). Of the latter, the best known is *The Moldau*, a picture of the river that winds through the Czech countryside on its way to Prague. But the most stirring is *Tábor*, named after the city where followers of radical religious reformer Jan Hus (ca. 1369–1415) built a fortress that became a symbol of Czech resistance to outside oppression. *Tábor* falls into two sections that resemble the slow introduction and Allegro of a symphonic first movement. In each half, fragments of a Hussite chorale are presented and developed until the entire chorale theme appears in full for the first time at the end. Smetana uses this process to embody the legend that the Hussite warriors will gather strength and emerge from their stronghold in the Czech people's time of need.

Grieg in Norway

At the same time that the Mighty Five were forging a distinct Russian idiom, Edvard Grieg (1843–1907) was writing a series of songs, short piano pieces, and orchestral suites that incorporated the modal melodies and harmonies as well as the dance rhythms of his native Norway. An ethnic character emerges most clearly in his songs on Norwegian texts, in some numbers within his two *Peer Gynt* Suites (1888 and 1891), and especially in the *Slåtter*, Norwegian peasant dances that Grieg arranged for the piano from transcripts of country fiddle playing. His piano style, with its delicate grace notes and mordents, owes something to Chopin as well as to the Germanic tradition of Mendelssohn and Schumann, whose music was the stuff of his education in Leipzig. The Norwegian influence in his music is drawn from Norwegian folk songs and dances, and is reflected in his modal turns of melody and harmony (Lydian raised fourth, Aeolian lowered seventh, alternative major-minor third); frequent drones in the bass or middle register (suggested by the drone strings on Norwegian stringed instruments); and the fascinating combination of $\frac{3}{4}$ and $\frac{6}{8}$ rhythm in the *Slåtter*. Not all Grieg's music was nationalist; among his best-known pieces is the Piano Concerto in A Minor (1868; revised 1907), a bravura work that remains a favorite.

Elgar in England

Edward Elgar (1857–1934) was the first English composer in more than two hundred years to enjoy wide international recognition. The English in the late nineteenth century did not strive for a distinctive national style, preferring to adopt what seemed the universal language of the Classical tradition. Accordingly, Elgar's music is untouched by folk songs or any other noticeable national tradition. He derived his harmonic style from Brahms and Wagner, and drew from Wagner the system of leitmotifs in his oratorios. The oratorio *The Dream of*

*Gerontius* (1900), on a poem by Catholic convert John Henry Newman and influenced by Wagner's *Parsifal*, gives the orchestra an expressive role as important as that of the chorus. His symphonic output includes the *Enigma Variations* (1899), the cello concerto, and two symphonies.

# New Currents in France and Italy

In concert music as in opera, Paris was the center of French musical life once it recovered from the Revolution of 1789. In keeping with a tradition that stretched back to royal control of music in the seventeenth century (see Chapter 11), French music remained linked to politics. Concert series, composers, and even musical styles were often associated with political movements or events. An enduring product of the Revolutionary era was the Paris Conservatoire, the first modern conservatory, founded by the government in 1795 as part of the new national system of education. It became the model for national and regional conservatories all over Europe and has been a dominant force in French musical life ever since. Another product of political events, the Société Nationale de Musique (National Society of Music) was founded in 1871, when the government and the Parisian elite sought to reassert the vibrancy of French culture after the embarrassing defeat of the Franco-Prussian War. The society gave performances of works by French composers and set about reviving the great French music of the past through editions and performances of Rameau, Gluck, and sixteenth-century composers.

The growth in concert activity, proliferation of music schools, revival of past traditions, and encouragement of new music created a stimulating climate that helped Paris regain a leading position in music. Two main strands in composition can be identified before the emergence of impressionism (discussed in Chapter 21): a cosmopolitan tradition, transmitted through César Franck (1822–1890) and his pupils, and a more specifically French tradition, embodied in the music of Gabriel Fauré (1845–1924) and passed on to countless twentieth-century composers through his students, especially the famous pedagogue Nadia Boulanger (1887–1979).

## Cosmopolitan Tradition in France

César Franck was born in Belgium, came to Paris to study at the Conservatoire, and became a professor of organ there in 1871. Working mainly in instrumental genres and oratorio, he achieved a distinctive style by blending traditional counterpoint and classical forms with Liszt's thematic transformation, Wagner's harmony, and the Romantic idea of cyclic unification through thematic return. Typical of Franck's approach is the *Prelude, Chorale, and Fugue* (1884) for piano, which emulates a Baroque toccata in the prelude, introduces a chorale-like melody in distant keys, presents a fugue on a chromatic subject that has been foreshadowed in both previous sections, and closes by combining the opening toccata texture with the chorale melody and fugue subject in counterpoint. It is a piece that could only have been written by someone who had absorbed the thematic and harmonic methods of Liszt and Wagner and also the organ music of Bach and the French Baroque.

*Franck*

Franck has been called the founder of modern French chamber music. His chief chamber works are a Piano Quintet in F Minor (1879), a String Quartet in D Major (1889), and the Violin Sonata in A Major (1886). All are cyclic, featur-

ing themes that recur or are transformed in two or more movements. His Symphony in D Minor (1888), a model of cyclic form, is perhaps the most popular French symphony after Berlioz.

## The French Tradition

The other tendency in French music drew primarily on earlier French composers from Couperin to Gounod and approached music with order and restraint, treating it more as sonorous form than as expression. Instead of emotional displays and musical or programmatic depiction, we hear subtle patterns of tones, rhythms, and colors. The music sounds more lyric or dance-like than epic or dramatic. It is economical, simple, and reserved rather than profuse, complex, or expansive.

The refined music of Gabriel Fauré, who is shown in Figure 20.11, embodies the qualities of the French tradition. He studied under Saint-Saëns, held various posts

*Figure 20.11. Gabriel Fauré in a portrait by John Singer Sargent (1889). Bibliothèque du Conservatoire Nationale Supérieure de Musique et de Danse, Paris.*

as an organist, and was a founder of the National Society for French Music. He became professor of composition at the Paris Conservatoire in 1896 and was its director from 1905 to 1920, when he resigned because of a hearing loss. Fauré wrote some music in larger forms, including his best-known work, the Requiem (1887), and two operas. But he was primarily a composer of songs, of piano music—chiefly preludes, impromptus, nocturnes, and barcarolles—and of chamber music.

Songs

Fauré began by composing songs in the manner of Gounod, and lyrical melody, with no display of virtuosity, remained the basis of his style. But in his

*Example 20.7: Gabriel Fauré, Avant que tu ne t'en ailles, excerpt*

*What joy in the fields of ripe wheat.*

maturity, from about 1885, he developed a new style in which melodic lines are fragmented and harmony becomes much less directional. *Avant que tu ne t'en ailles* (Before you depart), from the song cycle *La bonne chanson* (The Good Song, 1892), illustrates these characteristics. Each phrase of melody is a declamatory fragment in its own tonal world, joined to the others only by subtle motivic echoes. In the passage shown in Example 20.7, the chords consist mainly of dominant sevenths and ninths, as in Wagner's chromatic music, but the tension melts as one chord fades into another because Fauré links chords through common tones. In each of the first three measures, for example, the dominant-seventh chord on G♯ is succeeded by an E♯-major triad, which neutralizes the leading-tone tendency of the B♯ in the vocal line; instead of moving to C♯, the B♯ becomes the fifth of the new chord (E♯ major). The F♯, the seventh of the first chord in the piano part, is treated as an appoggiatura. Such harmonic successions dilute the need for resolution and undermine the pull of the tonic, creating a sense of repose or even stasis that is the opposite of the emotional unrest in Wagner's music. Here the chromaticism that is the lifeblood of so much expressive music in the nineteenth century becomes instead a means to achieve equilibrium and restraint, attributes that have long been esteemed in French music.

## New Currents in Italian Opera

By the late nineteenth century, Verdi was such a central figure that later Italian opera composers struggled to escape his shadow. As opera houses increasingly performed works already in the repertory rather than new ones, few operas by composers after Verdi found a permanent place there. Two operas that did enter the repertory are *Cavalleria rusticana* (Rustic Chivalry, 1890) by Pietro Mascagni (1863–1945) and *I pagliacci* (The Clowns, 1892) by Ruggero Leoncavallo (1858–1919), often paired with each other in performance. Both are examples of verismo (from Italian *vero*, "true"), an operatic parallel to realism in literature. Instead of treating historical figures or faraway places, verismo presents everyday

Verismo

*Figure 20.12. Photograph of Giacomo Puccini at Torre del Lago in 1909. Private collection.*

*Figure 20.13.  Theatrical poster by Adolfo Hohenstein for Puccini's* Tosca, *which premiered in Rome in 1900. Illustrated is the highly dramatic scene at the end of Act II in which Tosca, having killed the villainous chief of police, Scarpia, places lighted candles beside his head and a crucifix on his chest. Museo Teatrale alla Scala, Milan.*

people, especially the lower classes, in familiar situations, often depicting events that are brutal or sordid. Though short-lived, verismo had parallels or repercussions in France and Germany, and today the veristic impulse lives on in television's reality shows and movie dramas.

Puccini            The most successful Italian opera composer after Verdi was Giacomo Puccini (1858–1924), shown in Figure 20.12. The son of a church organist and composer, he was slated to follow in his father's footsteps but chose instead to focus on opera. After studying at the conservatory in Milan, Puccini attracted attention with his first opera in 1884. His third opera, *Manon Lescaut* (1893), catapulted him to international fame and established him as one of the rising stars of his generation.

Style            Puccini created a highly individual personal style by blending Verdi's focus on vocal melody with elements of Wagner's approach—notably the use of recurring melodies or leitmotifs, less reliance on conventional operatic forms, and a greater role for the orchestra in creating musical continuity. Puccini often juxtaposed different styles and harmonic worlds in order to suggest his diverse characters, such as impoverished artists and other residents of the Parisian Latin Quarter in *La Bohème* (1896); the idealistic singer Tosca and the evil Scarpia in *Tosca* (1900; see Figure 20.13); a Japanese woman and her American lover in *Madama Butterfly* (1904); or various levels of ancient Chinese society in *Turandot* (1926).

In Puccini's operas, the arias, choruses, and ensembles are usually part of a continuous flow rather than set off as independent numbers. The standard scene structure pioneered by Rossini and observed in most of Verdi's operas is replaced by a fluid succession of sections in different tempos and characters. Musical ideas grow out of the dramatic action, blurring the distinction between recitative and aria. Example 20.8 shows a pivotal moment in *La Bohème*, after the poet Rodolfo, having just met Mimi, touches her hand for the first time. The melody begins on a single note, as if in recitative, then blossoms in a series of short phrases, each initiated by a large upward leap; simple and understated, it conveys Rodolfo's surging emotions under a placid exterior. The accompaniment is also simple, with a violin melody above offbeat pulsations (see the piano part in measures 2 ff.); yet the harmony never entirely comes to rest, as each tonic chord (Db-F-Ab) is colored either by an added sixth on Bb (measures 2, 5, and 9) or by a bass note (Ab), the fifth of the chord (measures 2 and 6). The lyrical melody becomes a recurring theme, yet it does not stand apart as a separate aria. Through these very simple means, Puccini responds directly to the text and the situation. His melody-centered, colorful, and emotionally direct style has won his operas a permanent place in the repertory and has exercised a strong influence on scoring for film and television today.

*La Bohème*

*Example 20.8: Giacomo Puccini,* La Bohème, *Act I, measures 1–9*

*What a frozen little hand! Let me warm it up. What's the use of searching [for your key]? We won't find it in the dark.*

This sampling of a few composers can give only a taste of the variety of national and individual styles in Europe in the second half of the nineteenth century. Composers often first found a niche for their music within a local, regional, or national performing tradition. A lucky few won a broader audience, often by capitalizing on their national identity, especially when that nation was not yet represented in the international repertory. This remained true for composers in the early twentieth century, as we will see in the next chapter.

POSTLUDE

By the end of the nineteenth century, what seemed to have been the mainstream of musical development in the late eighteenth century had broken into many smaller currents. Foremost among the Austro-Germans were Mahler and Strauss. Mahler inherited the Romantic tradition of Berlioz, Liszt, Wagner, and their Viennese counterparts—Beethoven, Schubert, Brahms, and Bruckner. A restless experimenter with wide-ranging interests, Mahler expanded the symphony and the orchestral lied; at the same time, he cleared a path to a new age by influencing the Viennese composers of the next generation—Schoenberg, Berg, and Webern (see Chapter 21). Whereas Mahler essentially adhered to the tradi-

**TIMELINE**  Late Romanticism

| MUSICAL EVENTS | HISTORICAL EVENTS |
|---|---|
| Glinka, *A Life for the Czar* **1836** | |
| | **1848** Revolutions in Europe |
| Liszt, *Faust Symphony* and *Les Préludes* **1854** | **1855–1881** Reign of Alexander II of Russia |
| Wagner composes *Tristan und Isolde* **1857–1859** | **1859** Darwin, *On the Origin of Species by Natural Selection* |
| | **1861** Victor Emmanuel II crowned king of Italy |
| | **1862** Hugo, *Les Misérables* |
| | **1870–1871** Franco-Prussian War: France defeated and Germany unified |
| Smetana, *Má vlast* **1872–1879** | |
| Musorgsky, premiere of *Boris Godunov* **1874** | **1875** Third French Republic |
| Wagner, premiere of complete *Ring* cycle **1876** | **1877** Edison invents the phonograph |
| Tchaikovsky, *Eugene Onegin* **1879** | |
| Franck, Symphony in D Minor **1884** | |
| Brahms, Fourth Symphony **1885** | |
| Verdi, premiere of *Otello* **1887** | |
| Rimsky-Korsakov, *Sheherezade* **1888** | |
| Wolf, *Mörike Lieder* **1889** | **1889** Eiffel Tower erected |
| Dvořák, *New World* Symphony **1893** | |
| Puccini, *La Bohème* **1896** | |
| Strauss, *Don Quixote* **1897** | |
| Mahler, *Fourth Symphony* **1900** | |
| Strauss, *Salome* **1905** | |
| Mahler directs opera in New York **1907–1910** | |

tional symphony and its musical architecture, even while admitting many programmatic and operatic elements, Strauss attached himself to the more radical
Romantic genre of the symphonic poem and eventually even dared to write operas in the wake of Wagner's domination of that genre.

The rise of nationalism stimulated new bursts of native musical creativity in
many countries, Russia and France being among the most significant for later
musical developments. In Russia, Musorgsky emerged as the most original and
influential of the group of five composers known as the Mighty Handful; but national flavor also helped composers of other lands to gain a niche in the permanent repertoire. In France, a revival nurtured by several factors and traditions,
not least an awareness of the importance of its own musical past, produced a
number of fine composers, including César Franck and Gabriel Fauré. France's
musical renewal also deposited on the doorstep of the twentieth century a composer of the first rank—Claude Debussy—who, as we shall discover, enabled
composers of all nationalities to create new styles that turned away from the influence of Wagner and the Romantics.

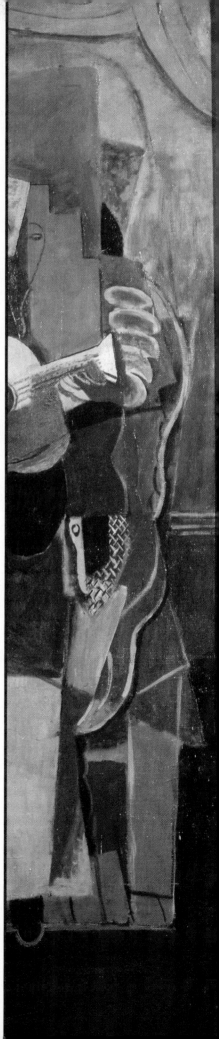

PART SIX

# The Twentieth Century and Today

PART CONTENTS

**21. THE EUROPEAN MAINSTREAM IN THE EARLY TWENTIETH CENTURY 536**

**22. MUSIC, POLITICS, AND THE PEOPLE IN THE EUROPEAN TWENTIETH CENTURY 561**

**23. MUSIC IN AMERICA 594**

**24. THE CHANGING WORLD OF MUSIC SINCE 1945 630**

## Modern Times

Few eras have been as self-consciously "modern" as the early twentieth century. The pace of technological and social change was more rapid than in any previous era, prompting both an optimistic sense of progress and nostalgia for a simpler past.

The growth of industry continued to foster an expanding economy. As in the nineteenth century, people migrated from rural areas to cities, although not without regret; popular songs and Mahler symphonies alike expressed a yearning for home and the countryside. Economic inequalities prompted workers to organize in labor unions to fight for better conditions, inspired social reformers to work with the poor, and aroused revolutionary movements in Russia and elsewhere. International trade continued to increase. European nations grew rich importing raw materials and then marketing manufactured goods to the world. The great powers—Britain, France, and the German, Austro-Hungarian, Russian, and Ottoman empires—competed for dominance, while the peoples of eastern Europe, from the Balkans to Finland, agitated for their own freedom.

Increasing tensions and complex political issues culminated in World War I (1914–1918).

United States

During these years, the United States emerged as a world power. American industries and overseas trade expanded rapidly, growing to rival the industrial powerhouses of Britain and Germany. The United States' entrance into World War I in April 1917 on the side of Britain and France tipped the scales against Germany and Austria-Hungary, and President Woodrow Wilson played a leading role in negotiating the peace. After the war, while the nations of Europe were faced with war debt, crippling inflation, and a shattered infrastructure, the United States and Canada, which had suffered far fewer casualties, enjoyed a financial boom. But as in Europe, rapid economic development brought social conflict. Immigrants continued to stream into the United States, now increasingly from southern and eastern Europe, and their presence in cities caused strains with earlier immigrant groups. Looking for new opportunities, African Americans from the South moved to the large northern cities but, because of racist attitudes, settled into segregated neighborhoods, giving rise to a black urban culture in which music was a major cultural force.

New nations and ideologies

World War I brought an end to the large European empires and yielded independence to Finland, Estonia, Poland, Czechoslovakia, and Hungary. In Russia the Bolsheviks—radical Marxist revolutionaries—seized power in late 1917 and set up a dictatorship, forming the Soviet Union. In several other nations, democratic governments gave way to totalitarian rule. Benito Mussolini and the fascists took over the Italian government in 1922, and the Spanish Civil War (1936–1939) brought Francisco Franco to power. In Germany, the democracy formed after World War I, known as the Weimar Republic for the city where the constitution was drafted, proved too weak to deal with mounting economic problems. After the National Socialists (Nazis) won an electoral plurality, their leader, Adolf Hitler, was appointed chancellor in 1933 and soon established a dictatorship. In a fierce anti-Semitic campaign, the Nazis passed laws to deprive Gypsies, homosexuals, and especially people of Jewish background of their citizenship and all other rights, driving into exile countless writers, artists, composers, and scholars, many of whom settled in the United States.

Economic depression

In America, increased prosperity and leisure time helped make the post–World War I years a golden age for music, both popular and classical. American culture and music, especially jazz, profoundly influenced Europeans during the 1920s. But in October 1929, the New York stock market crashed, sparking a worldwide depression. Unemployment approached 50 percent in some areas, producing unprecedented turmoil. In response, governments in Europe and the Americas undertook relief in public-works programs such as the New Deal in the United States.

World War II and after

The economies in most nations were still recovering when Germany invaded Poland in September 1939, thereby beginning World War II, the most global and destructive war the world had ever seen. Germany, Italy, and, in the eastern theater, Japan were defeated by the Allies, but at great cost. Millions were dead: soldiers killed in action, civilians in bombing raids, and Jews and other victims in Nazi death camps. Much of Europe and the Far East lay in ruins, and many of the buildings, cultural institutions, and works of art created over the centuries were destroyed. The atrocities of the Holocaust and the use of nuclear weapons to end the war provoked a wide range of cultural reactions, from the French existentialist literature of Jean-Paul Sartre and Albert Camus to a growing fashion for horror and science-fiction films.

At war's end, the Soviet Union occupied most of eastern Europe. By 1948, it reabsorbed some countries that had been independent between the wars, such as Estonia, and installed communist regimes under its control in others, such as

*Figure VI.1. Europe during the Cold War (1945–1991).*

The Cold War

Poland, Czechoslovakia, and Hungary. Communist governments also took power in Yugoslavia, Albania, and China. Western nations responded with attempts to contain the expansion of communism. International relations for the next two generations were framed by the political conflict, known as the Cold War, between the United States and its allies on the one hand and the Soviet Union and communist nations on the other. Figure VI.1 shows a map of postwar Europe, divided between the North Atlantic Treaty Organization (NATO)—an alliance of the United States, Canada, and European democracies—and the Soviet Union's parallel organization, the Warsaw Pact. Symbolic of this political conflict was the metaphor of the "Iron Curtain," and the reality of the division between a democratic, pro-Western government in West Germany and a communist government in East Germany was confirmed by the erection in 1961 of the Berlin Wall.

New international institutions such as the United Nations, founded in 1945, furthered cooperation but could not defuse all tensions. At times, the Cold War heated up, as in the Korean War (1950–1953), the Cuban missile crisis (1962), and the Vietnam War (1964–1975). It also played out in scientific competition, such as the race into space, won by the United States with the first moon landing in 1969. Both sides engaged in cultural competition as well, involving Olympic sports, chess matches, and music performance and composition.

The United States, least damaged among the combatant nations in World War II, again enjoyed a postwar period of rapid economic growth. Technological innovations and stepped-up productivity resulted in historically high incomes for

Economic expansion

## TIMELINE   The Twentieth Century and Today

| MUSICAL EVENTS | HISTORICAL EVENTS |
|---|---|

**HISTORICAL EVENTS**

**1872** Monet, *Impression: Soleil levant*
**1876** Mallarmé, *L'Après-midi d'un faune*
**1893** Munch, *The Scream*

Debussy, *Prélude à L'Après-midi d'un faune* **1894**
Joplin, *Maple Leaf Rag* **1899**

Renoir, *Dance in the City*

**1900** Freud, *The Interpretation of Dreams*
**1903** The Wright brothers fly first successful airplane
**1906** Cézanne, *Mont Sainte-Victoire*
**1907** Braque and Picasso paint first cubist pictures
**1908** Ford designs the Model-T automobile
**1911** Schoenberg, *Self-Portrait*

Stravinsky, premiere of *The Rite of Spring* **1913**

**1913** Publication of volume 1 of Proust's *Remembrance of Things Past*
**1914–1918** World War I
**1914–1921** Joyce, *Ulysses*
**1916** Einstein proposes general theory of relativity
**1917** Russian Revolution; U.S. enters World War I
**1918–1919** Britain and U.S. give women the right to vote
**1922** Eliot, *The Waste Land;* first sponsored radio broadcast in the United States; Fascists take over government in Italy

Albert Einstein

Electric microphones introduced **1925**
Duke Ellington's band plays **1927–1931**
the Cotton Club in Harlem
Brecht and Weill, *The Threepenny Opera* **1928**

**1929** Woolf, *A Room of One's Own;* New York stock market crash begins Great Depression

BBC Symphony Orchestra **1930**
founded in London
Steiner, film score for *King Kong* **1933**

Picasso, *Weeping Woman*

**1933** World's Fair in Chicago; murals of Benton
**1934** Doctrine of socialist realism adopted in Soviet Union
**1936–1939** Spanish Civil War
**1937** Picasso, *Guernica*
**1939** Steinbeck, *The Grapes of Wrath*
**1939–1945** World War II; conflict ends with defeat of Italy, Germany, and Japan

Stravinsky and Bartók emigrate to the United States **1940**
Messiaen, *Quartet for the End of Time* **1941**

**1945** Cold War between Soviet Union and United States begins
**1950–1953** Korean conflict
**1952** Matisse, *Tristesse du roi* (Sadness of the King)

Penderecki, *Threnody: To the Victims of Hiroshima* **1960**

**1961** Berlin Wall erected
**1963** President Kennedy assassinated
**1964–1975** Vietnam conflict

Babbitt, *Philomel* **1964**
Moog and Buchla synthesizers introduced **1966**

Rocket Launch

**1968** Student riots in Paris; antiwar protests in United States; Reverend Martin Luther King, Jr. assassinated
**1969** First humans set foot on the moon
**1972** President Nixon visits China
**1980** Solidarity strikes in Poland
**1982** New disease described, later called AIDS

Zwilich, Symphony No. 1 **1983**
Adams, *Nixon in China* (opera) **1987**

**1989** Berlin Wall torn down
**1991** Soviet Union dissolves, ending Cold War

Bright Sheng, **1995**
*Seven Tunes Heard in China*

**2001** Terrorist attacks on World Trade Center (New York) and Pentagon

Adams, *Doctor Atomic* **2005**

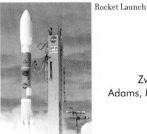

factory and office workers that lifted most Americans into the middle class. Western European countries and Japan underwent similar economic growth, aided by investments from the United States. Cooperation through the Common Market and NATO wove Western Europe together, making old nationalist tensions increasingly obsolete.

Starting with British India in 1947, European colonies throughout Asia and Africa won independence and emerged as new nations. The growing political and economic significance of Asia and Africa encouraged cultural exchanges that generated a rising interest in music of the non-Western world, both in the West and in American popular music throughout the world. The nonviolent strategies Mohandas Gandhi developed to win independence for India were adopted by Martin Luther King, Jr. and others in the effort to win equal civil rights for African Americans, a movement in which music played a significant role as unifier and inspiration. The civil rights movement in turn emboldened others in the 1960s and 1970s, from student organizations and protests against the Vietnam War to the women's and gay liberation movements.

The late 1960s and 1970s brought a series of political and economic shocks to Western nations. Student protests symbolized a growing gulf between younger and older generations. In the United States, urban riots, growing discord over the Vietnam War, and the assassinations of Martin Luther King, Jr. and Robert F. Kennedy marked increasing social strife. The Organization of Petroleum Exporting Countries cut oil production in 1973 to force up prices, leading to economic disruptions and inflation for the next decade.

Meanwhile, Cold War tensions began to ease during the 1970s. Under the policy of détente, the United States and the Soviet Union sought greater cultural contacts and signed treaties to reduce nuclear arms. European leaders reached across the East-West divide, while President Nixon initiated diplomatic relations with the communist government in China after years without formal contact.

Increasing communication with the West and the election of a Polish pope, the first from a communist country, helped to inspire movements for change in Eastern Europe. Beginning with the 1980 strike by the Solidarity movement in Poland and climaxing with the fall of the Berlin Wall in 1989 and the political reunion of East and West Germany the following year, the people of central and Eastern Europe freed themselves from Soviet domination with remarkably little bloodshed. In the Soviet Union itself, Mikhail Gorbachev's policies of *glasnost* ("openness") and *perestroika* ("restructuring") encouraged freer expression and a more entrepreneurial economy. Although Gorbachev was seeking to reform the Soviet Union, the ultimate result was its dissolution in 1991. Its fifteen constituent republics, from massive Russia to tiny Armenia, became independent nations with governments ranging from democratic to authoritarian.

The Soviet Union's collapse ended the Cold War that had defined the postwar world. It did not end the fear of a nuclear attack, however, because of the spread of knowledge and technology for manufacturing nuclear weapons. In the post-Soviet era, regional conflicts from the Middle East to the Korean peninsula became more urgent, and civil wars proliferated, from the Balkans and Africa to the Philippines. Extremists increasingly turned to terror as a tactic, whether directed at their own government, as in the 1995 Oklahoma City bombing, or other lands, as in al-Qaeda's attack on the World Trade Center in New York City and the Pentagon in Washington, D.C., on September 11, 2001.

In the economic realm, the end of the Cold War encouraged a trend toward integration across national boundaries. The Common Market became the European Union, absorbing new members from Eastern Europe and pursuing a unified European economic system, symbolized by the euro, a new international currency introduced in 2002. Asian countries enjoyed rapid growth, sustained

Independence and civil rights

Détente and democracy

Collapse of European communism

New conflicts

Global economy

by increasing trade with the rest of the world. Reductions in trade barriers and new technologies led to rising productivity in the Western democracies, producing an economic boom in the 1990s. By then, almost every country was part of an interwoven global economy.

# The Arts and the Modern Human Condition

New views on the human mind

In the wake of the industrial revolution, psychologists raised new questions about what it meant to be human. Sigmund Freud developed psychoanalysis, theorizing that human behavior springs from unconscious desires that are repressed by cultural restraints and that dreams are windows into a person's internal conflicts. Ivan Pavlov showed that dogs accustomed to being fed after a bell was rung would salivate at the sound of the bell even if no food was present and that humans could likewise be conditioned to respond to stimuli in predictable ways. These approaches challenged the Romantic view of individuals as protagonists of their own dramas, seeming instead to portray humans as subject to internal and social forces of which they were only dimly aware. Such changing views of human nature played a strong role in literature and the other arts.

*Figure VI.2. Claude Monet,* Impression: Soleil levant (Sunrise; 1872). *Monet entered this work and eight others in an exhibition he helped to organize in 1874. A disapproving critic headlined his mocking review "Exhibition of the Impressionists," picking up on Monet's title and coining a term that would define an entire artistic movement. Instead of mixing his colors on a palette, Monet juxtaposed them on the canvas to capture impressions of the early light of day. He and other impressionist painters popularized outdoor painting and specialized in representing sunlight and water, two of the most formless yet luminous aspects of nature. Musée Marmottan, Paris.*

*Figure VI.3.  Paul Cézanne,* Mont Sainte-Victoire *(1906). Cézanne painted many versions of this scene, which was visible from his house in Aix-en-Provence in southern France, rendering the massive mountain and the details of the town nestled in the countryside as blocks of color placed side by side in geometrical arrangements. Kunstmuseum, Basel.*

Sustained by Romantic notions of art as a window on the divine and of the artist as an enlightened visionary, artists increasingly regarded their work as an end in itself to be appreciated for its own sake. Success was measured not by wide popular appeal but by the esteem of intellectuals and fellow artists. Many artists searched for new and unusual content or techniques. Symbolist poets such as Paul Verlaine, Stéphane Mallarmé, Paul Valéry, and Stefan George, for example, used intense imagery, symbols, and disrupted syntax to evoke an indefinite, dreamlike state and to suggest feelings and experiences rather than describing them directly. Similarly, modernist novelists such as James Joyce and Marcel Proust broke with the Victorian aim of telling a story or expounding a moral; instead they aspired to discovering what Proust called "a different self" through the exploration of a sensibility based on the interaction of conscious and subconscious thought.

In the late nineteenth century, French painters known as impressionists—named after Claude Monet's painting *Impression: Soleil levant* (1872), shown in Figure VI.2—inaugurated the first in a series of artistic movements that utterly changed styles and attitudes toward art. Rather than depicting things realistically, the impressionists sought to capture atmosphere and sensuous impressions from nature, adopting a stance of detached observation rather than direct emotional engagement. In Monet's paintings, objects and people are suggested by a few brush strokes, often of starkly contrasting colors, leaving it to the viewer's eyes and mind to blend the colors and fill in the missing details. The effect of light on an object is often as much the subject of a painting as is the

Impressionism

*Figure VI.4. Pablo Picasso,* The Treble Clef *(1912). This cubist painting includes a violin on the right, broken into its various components and planes, and a clarinet on the left, stylized as gray, blue, and brown bands, some with finger holes, and concentric circles with a cone to represent the instrument's bell. Private collection.*

object itself. Although impressionist paintings are widely popular today, they were at first poorly received, derided as lacking in artistic skill and opposed to traditional aesthetics. Such reactions would also greet other modern styles of painting and music.

Each impressionist painter had a highly individual style, and later artists extended their ideas in unique ways. Paul Cézanne depicted natural scenes and figures as orderly arrangements of geometrical forms and planes of color, as in his painting of Mont Sainte-Victoire (1906) in Figure VI.3. Pablo Picasso and Georges Braque further abstracted this idea in cubism, a style in which three-dimensional objects are represented on a flat plane by breaking them down into geometrical shapes such as cubes and cones, and juxtaposing or overlapping them in an active, colorful design. Figure VI.4 shows an example, one of a series Picasso painted in 1912 that used two musical instruments as a subject.

The revolution begun by impressionism stimulated new ways of making, seeing, and thinking about paintings, giving birth to movements such as expressionism (discussed in Chapter 21), surrealism, and abstract art. In most of these new movements, artists and their approving critics no longer placed a high value on beauty or on pleasing the viewer, as had painters from the Renaissance to the Romantic era. Instead, they valued originality and substance, demanding that the viewer work to understand and interpret the image. Surrealist painters like Salvador Dalí and René Magritte explored the dreamlike world of the unconscious opened up by Freud; and artists associated with the expressionist movement, like the Norwegian Edvard Munch, whose work is shown in Figure VI.5, and the composer Arnold Schoenberg, one of whose self-portraits is shown in Figure VI.6, gave vent to feelings of anxiety and alienation that seemed

Cubism

*Figure VI.5. Edvard Munch,* The Scream *(1893). Munch's work was especially concerned with the expressive representation of emotions, particularly anguish, despair, fear, and melancholy. Here, the swirling colors, eerie shapes, and featureless face all combine to symbolize a dreamlike, soundless scream. Munch Museum, Oslo.*

to pervade modern society. Other artists sought to objectify the horrors of warfare, as Picasso did in *Guernica*, painted after the bombing of civilians during the Spanish Civil War.

Disillusionment with modern society also showed itself in literature: T. S. Eliot's *The Waste Land*, with its many references to literature of the past; James Joyce's stream-of-consciousness novel *Ulysses*; Marcel Proust's multivolume novel of time and memory, *Remembrance of Things Past*; the politically engaged plays of Bertolt Brecht; and the feminist novels and essays of Virginia Woolf. Impelled by the worldwide depression of the 1930s, many artists reexamined their role and sought to make their work relevant to the economic and social problems of the time. John Steinbeck, in his novel *The Grapes of Wrath*, wrote about farmers impoverished by the dust bowl in the American Plains and exploited in California. Artists such as Diego Rivera in Mexico (see Figure 23.17), and Thomas Hart Benton in the United States pictured social conditions in simple, direct, yet modern styles that could be understood by everyone, as shown in Figure VI.7. Many classical composers likewise sought to write music that was accessible to all, hoping to catch the imagination of ordinary working people.

*Figure VI.6. Arnold Schoenberg,* Self-Portrait *(ca. 1911). By depicting the subject walking away, his back to the viewer, the painting suggests the alienation of the artist from society and its conventions. Arnold Schönberg Center, Vienna.*

*Figure VI.7.* Electric Power, Motor-Cars, Steel *is the title of this panel from the murals by American painter Thomas Hart Benton for the Indiana Hall at the 1933 World's Fair in Chicago. It shows workers and designers in the steel mills of northwest Indiana, electric-power generation, and the automobile industry, thus celebrating the industries that helped lift the country out of the Great Depression of the 1930s. Indiana University Archives, Bloomington.*

# The Technological Revolution

One symbol of progress in the modern age was the electrification of industry, businesses, and homes. Electric lighting increasingly replaced gas lighting, and electrical appliances were produced for the home market. Another symbol was the internal combustion engine fueled by petroleum, which gradually replaced coal engines in steamships and factories (see Figure VI.7). By streamlining production and distribution, Henry Ford made his Model T the first widely affordable automobile, launching the modern world's love affair with the car. Wilbur and Orville Wright flew the first working airplane in 1903, and by the end of the next decade airplanes were used for both military and commercial purposes. New products, improved transportation, and new marketing techniques combined to expand the mass market for manufactured goods.

**The rise of a music industry**

The rapid growth of diverse musical styles between the world wars was also due in part to new technologies (see Innovations, pages 574–575). Recordings, radio broadcasting, and the introduction of sound to motion pictures enabled the preservation and rapid distribution of music in performance, not just in score. Now a musical performance, formerly as impermanent as a moment in time, could be preserved, admired, and replayed many times. This change created a new mass market and new commercial possibilities; it also allowed performers to share in the benefits of mass distribution and vaulted some performers—whether of classical, jazz, or popular music—to international stardom.

**Recordings and radio**

From the 1890s through the 1910s the popular music industry had revolved around sheet music, but after the war publishers realized that recordings offered a market of potentially unlimited size. Songwriters and bandleaders also turned to recordings, often tailoring their pieces to fit the three- to four-minute limit of a 78-rpm record side. Musicians also profited from exposure via radio broadcasting since music proved to be a good way of filling large periods of airtime. Radio caught on quickly; by 1924 there were over 1,400 radio stations around North America, and during the 1920s national broadcasting systems were developed in all the major European nations. Recordings were still too poor in quality to be played successfully over the radio, so stations relied primarily on live performers in their own studios and on regional or national transmissions of live shows. Stations in Europe and the Americas sponsored orchestras, such as the BBC Symphony Orchestra (founded 1930) in London and the NBC Symphony Orchestra (1937) in New York. Dance bands, such as the one led by Benny Goodman, also made use of the new medium to gain wider exposure.

In the years following the Second World War, television and home stereo systems that played radio stations and long-playing records (LPs) increasingly brought entertainment and music into the home. The invention of the transistor led to miniature portable radios that could be taken anywhere, bringing broadcast music into cars and the outdoors. Disc jockeys played recordings of popular songs on the radio, replacing most of the live music shows of previous decades. Tape recorders, invented during the 1930s and widely available from the 1950s on made it possible for individuals to preserve and manipulate sounds, thereby enabling the entire field of electronic music.

Greater access
to music

By the end of the century, news, entertainment, and the arts had become global. The spread of communications satellites and cable television, and the advent in the 1980s and 1990s of personal computers, fax machines, cell phones, and the Internet put people around the world in immediate touch with one another. Many issues, from the environment to drug trade to terrorism, crossed national boundaries, requiring countries to work together. With easy travel, diseases such as influenza and AIDS spread rapidly across the globe, prompting international cooperation in response. The new global culture was symbolized by New Year's Day in 2000, when television showed celebrations of the new millennium all over the world, as midnight moved across time zones from New Zealand to Alaska.

Globalization

Improved communications and travel also fostered a global market for the arts. Many forms of entertainment—from Hollywood movies to touring groups of traditional artists such as the Bulgarian Women's Choir and Tuvan throat-singers from Outer Mongolia—now reach audiences all over the world. Asians, including Japanese-born Seiji Ozawa (formerly long-time conductor of the Boston Symphony Orchestra) and Chinese-born musician Tan Dun (composer of the Oscar-winning film score *Crouching Tiger, Hidden Dragon*), have become prominent as musicians in the Western classical tradition. At the same time, some Americans and Europeans have become proficient performers of Indian, Javanese, and other Asian musics. Music from around the world is now easily accessible through recordings, the Internet, and live performances. The diversity of the world's music has brought a growing awareness in Europe and the Americas that each musician's work is but one strand in a global tapestry.

Global arts

## The Changing World of Music

We will see all these trends reflected in music in the next several chapters. Music was directly affected by the expanding economy, new technologies, the devastation of World War I, the emergence of the United States on the world stage, the role of African American urban culture as a breeding ground for new musical styles, new thinking about human nature, and the new artistic movements, with particularly close parallels to symbolism, impressionism, expressionism, and cubism.

In the years just before and after World War I, a younger group of composers carried out a more radical break from the musical language of the past than their

Modernism

**ARTS** *and* **IDEAS**

## Science and Technology

Russian physiologist and experimental psychologist **Ivan Pavlov** (1849–1930) received the Nobel Prize in medicine in 1904 for his work on digestion. He also developed a mechanistic theory of human behavior, explained in his chief work, *Conditioned Reflexes* (1926).

**Sigmund Freud** (1856–1939), Austrian psychiatrist and founder of modern psychoanalysis, inspired one of the great intellectual movements of the twentieth century. His writings instigated, among many other things, the transformation of modern culture's attitudes toward human sexuality, religion, and childhood development and sparked the recognition of the unconscious and its influence on behavior. *The Interpretation of Dreams* (1900), *The Ego and the Id* (1923), and *Civilization and Its Discontents* (1930) are among his major works.

American industrialist **Henry Ford** (1863–1947) was a pioneer manufacturer of automobiles. Originally a machinist and engineer with the Edison Company, he launched his own firm in Detroit, Michigan, in the first decade of the century. By cutting production costs, adapting conveyor-belt and assembly-line methods to car manufacturing, and featuring an inexpensive, standardized car, he outdistanced his competitors and became the largest automobile producer in the world, regarded by many as the apostle of mass production.

**Wilbur Wright** (1867–1912) and **Orville Wright** (1871–1948), American airplane inventors and brothers, experimented with aircraft design and achieved the first controlled and sustained flight in 1903.

Scottish biologist Sir **Alexander Fleming** (1881–1955) first observed the antagonistic effect of penicillin mold on bacteria in 1928, although it was not until after the Second World War that antibiotics were widely used to cure disease, thereby markedly increasing life expectancy.

## Literature

**Stéphane Mallarmé** (1842–1898) anticipated the French Symbolists in his belief that poetry should evoke thoughts through suggestion rather than description and affirmed that it should approach the abstraction of music. One of his best-known poems, *L'Après-midi d'un faune* (1876; The Afternoon of a Faun), inspired a symphonic poem by Debussy, which in turn was choreographed as a sensuous ballet by Vaslav Nijinsky (see page 572 and Figure 21.2).

French author **Marcel Proust** (1871–1922) transformed the genre of the novel with his monumental work *À la recherche du temps perdu* (Remembrance of Things Past; originally in 16 volumes, 1913–1927), a semiautobiographical cycle that is less a story than an interior monologue. His vision and technique were vital to the development of modernism in that he raised artistic endeavor almost to the status of a religion.

**James Joyce** (1882–1941), Irish writer of novels, short stories, and poems, is known for his revolutionary innovations in narrative techniques, making extensive use of the interior monologue or stream of consciousness. His unique and inventive use of the English language at first caused his books (*Ulysses*, 1914–1921; *Finnegans Wake*, 1912–1939) to be banned by censors, misunderstood by the public, and denounced by critics as unintelligible, nonsensical, and obscene. In that respect, they embody a frequent theme of the modernist novel—the difficulty of communicating.

English author **Virginia Woolf** (1882–1941) advocated cultural and intellectual independence for women in her novels (*To the Lighthouse*, 1927; *Orlando*, 1928) and essays (*A Room of One's Own*, 1929). Her works are noted for their psychological penetration, sensitive style, and evocation of place and mood. Depressed by the war and fearful of recurring mental breakdowns, she committed suicide.

predecessors or contemporaries did, while maintaining strong links to tradition. These composers, known as modernists, reassessed inherited conventions as profoundly as the modernists in art who pioneered expressionism, cubism, and abstract art. Modernists in both art and music did not aim to please viewers or listeners at first sight or upon first hearing, an attribute that had been considered essential in the eighteenth and nineteenth centuries. Instead, they sought to

**T. S. Eliot** (1888–1965), a Harvard-educated American poet and critic who migrated to England, won the 1948 Nobel Prize in literature. His most famous poem, *The Waste Land* (1922), broke with nineteenth-century poetic tradition by employing complex allusions and dense imagery, influenced by the French Symbolists. In his hands, modernist poetry became a particularly exalted and sophisticated form of cultural criticism.

**John Steinbeck** (1902–1968), awarded the Nobel Prize in literature in 1962, is best remembered for his strong sociological novel *The Grapes of Wrath* (1939), one of the great American novels of the twentieth century. A realistic and naturalistic portrayal of life among the depressed economic classes of the United States, it reveals the author's proletarian sympathies and also presents a universal picture of disaster victims.

French existential philosopher, playwright, and novelist **Jean-Paul Sartre** (1905–1980) subscribed to a radical individualism that saw humans as responsible but lonely beings who must continually struggle against an unfavorable environment in order to achieve any degree of authenticity. His philosophy was partly a response to the Second World War and to the struggle of the Free French against Nazism, as was his monumental work *Being and Nothingness* (1943).

## Art

The forerunner of modernism in painting, **Paul Cézanne** (1839–1906) articulated revolutionary principles that became fundamental to twentieth-century art. Among them was the idea that art is a harmony not derived from nature but existing in and for itself. His belief that a painting "should represent nothing but color" is evident in his many versions of *Mont Sainte-Victoire* (Figure VI.3).

**Claude Monet** (1840–1926), one of the foremost painters of landscape in the history of art, was a founder of impressionism. His work explores the constantly changing quality of light and color in different atmospheric conditions and at various times of the day, as illustrated in his *Impressions: Soleil levant* (Sunrise, 1872), shown in Figure VI.2, the work that gave the French movement its name.

Norwegian artist **Edvard Munch** (1863–1944) took the lead among artists in exploring the borders between the conscious and unconscious, thereby paving the way for German expressionism. "Inside us are worlds," he wrote. His most famous work, *The Scream* (1893), shown in Figure VI.5, exemplifies his emotionally charged style.

Spanish-born **Pablo Picasso** (1881–1973) was a painter, sculptor, printmaker, decorative artist, and writer. Although he was active mainly in France, he dominated twentieth-century European art, initiating or impacting most of the artistic dialogues that took place during his long lifetime. Together with Georges Braque, he was responsible for cubism, one of the most radical definitions of how a work of art constructs its meaning (see Figure VI.4). Because of his enormous versatility, technical virtuosity, prolific output, and unquestionable originality, he became the very image of the modern artist.

Mexican painter **Diego Rivera** (1886–1957) won international acclaim for his vast public murals, in which he created a new style based on socialist ideals and on the native and popular heritage of Mexican culture. His images use symbols drawn from Christian and Aztec cultures, exalt the peasant and working classes, and had a worldwide influence on public art. (See Figure 23.7.)

Painter and lithographer **Thomas Hart Benton** (1889–1975) was the best-known American muralist of the 1930s and 1940s. Noted for his dramatization of American themes in a graphic style using strong colors, he executed murals for The New School for Social Research in New York, the Missouri statehouse in Jefferson City, and the Postal Service and Department of Justice buildings in Washington, D.C., among others. (See Figure VI.7.)

challenge our perceptions and capacities, providing an experience that would be impossible through traditional means. Modernists offered an implicit critique of mass culture and easily digested art, and their writings often show it. These composers saw no contradiction in claiming the masters of the past as models. In fact, they saw their own work as continuing what the pathbreaking classical composers had started, not as overthrowing that tradition. The paradox of all modern classical music—that it must partake of the tradition yet offer something new—is especially acute in the work of modernist composers, who are often most radical in the ways they interpret and remake the past.

**Stylistic diversification**

The period between World Wars I and II saw remarkable changes in musical life and continued diversification in musical styles. Recordings and radio made new kinds of music available to more listeners than ever before, no matter what their level of musical training. These technologies brought about widespread dissemination of the classical repertory from Bach to Bartók as well as less well-known music from the remote past to the present. Classical concert music and opera remained the most prestigious musical traditions, but the varieties of popular music were better known and usually more lucrative. Especially prominent were trends from the United States, notably jazz. Music, always an accompaniment to "silent" movies, became an integral part of sound films, and many composers of opera, classical concert music, musicals, and popular songs found a place in the movie industry. Styles of classical music grew ever more varied as composers responded in individual ways to musical trends from modernism to the avant-garde and to political and economic conditions in their respective nations.

The victory over Fascism, the economic boom, new technologies, and the winds of freedom helped to inspire a period of unprecedented experimentation in music. Composers of art music went in numerous directions, sharing less common ground as they explored new possibilities. A few composers, such as Igor Stravinsky and Aaron Copland, were able to support themselves with commissions, royalties, and income from conducting or performances. Other composers sought patronage, but without the kings and aristocracy of earlier times, it had to come from new sources. In Europe, composers were supported by the state, through radio stations, annual subsidies, grants, arts agencies, and educational institutions.

**New forms of patronage**

In the United States and Canada, many composers found employment as teaching faculty in universities, colleges, and conservatories, giving themselves time to compose, a ready audience, and access to performing organizations, including ensembles created specifically to present new music. Since colleges and universities prize academic freedom, the music coming from academic composers has been diverse, varying from traditional styles to avant-garde and experimental. Indeed, the safety of tenure and the ivory tower tended to isolate composers from the public and make them independent of its support. To a great extent, the type of music encouraged at a school varied with the composers who taught there. Among many refugees from Europe, Arnold Schoenberg taught at the University of California at Los Angeles, Darius Milhaud at Mills College in Oakland, California, and Paul Hindemith at Yale, to name but a few. In addition to colleges and universities, urban centers and mass media allowed musicians to find small but devoted audiences that would support specialized types of music, creating niche markets in which everything from early-music groups to avant-garde rock bands could thrive.

Of the dizzying number and variety of trends in this century, we will explore some of the most important and distinctive. Chapter 21 surveys the first modern generation of composers in Europe, among them Claude Debussy in France and Arnold Schoenberg and his followers in Germany and Austria; we will also examine the variety of tonal, atonal, and post-tonal approaches that they devised. Other composers, especially those who identified with a particular national heritage, are also represented. In Chapter 22, we look at avant-garde and futurist trends in Europe, and at the effects of political disruptions and government policies on music, particularly in Nazi Germany and the Soviet Union. We also note how composers like Stravinsky and Bartók responded to their individual ethnic backgrounds and, at the same time, left footprints on the international musical landscape. Chapter 23 concentrates on the American twentieth century and discusses its various vernacular styles—such as those manifested in band music, popular song, musical theater, and film—as well as its jazz and classical music. The influence of European immigration and of African American musical culture on both traditional and art music in the Americas is also studied. In the final chapter, we identify many of the myriad trends in European and American classical music since the Second World War, linking individual composers with one or more of the styles that most closely define their music. Many other composers and styles remain to be explored, from a perspective that will undoubtedly look very different to the next generation of teachers and students.

# The European Mainstream in the Early Twentieth Century

## PRELUDE

*Chapter Contents*

*Prelude* 536

The First Modern
Generation 536

Tonal and Post-Tonal
Music 546

*Postlude* 559

Modern composers in the classical tradition all faced a common challenge—how to secure a place in an increasingly crowded concert repertory by writing works that performers, audiences, and critics deemed worthy of performance alongside the classics of the past. To succeed, their music had to meet the criteria established by the classics: to be works of high quality that participated in the tradition of serious art music; to be works of lasting value, rewarding both performers and listeners through many rehearings and close study; and to be works that proclaimed a distinctive musical personality by offering a unique style and perspective that balanced tradition and novel elements. Faced with these common problems, modern composers created highly individual solutions, differing in what they valued most in their nationalist traditions, in what they discarded, and in what innovations they introduced. Most continued to use tonality, but many wrote music that diverged from the common-practice tonal language in use since the time of Bach, resulting in the atonal and post-tonal practices we will survey in this chapter. As a result of these different solutions, music became increasingly diverse in style and approach, a process that accelerated throughout the twentieth century.

## The First Modern Generation

We have already seen how the careers and music of Mahler and Strauss exemplify the search by those in the first generation of modern composers for a personal style that absorbed what was useful from the past, and was true to their national identity, yet was distinctive and individual. We will continue to note the interplay between tradition and innovation and between national identity and personal style as we survey a number of major composers from nations across Europe, beginning with Claude Debussy, the premier modernist in France.

## Claude Debussy

While Mahler and Strauss extended Wagnerian harmony to new levels of rhetorical intensity, their French contemporary Claude Debussy (1862–1918; see biography) took it in a different direction: toward rhetorical understatement. His admiration for Wagner's works, especially *Tristan* and *Parsifal*, was coupled with revulsion against Wagner's bombast and his attempts to expound philosophy in music. Debussy drew from the French tradition a preference for indirect, tasteful, and restrained expression, admiring particularly his older contemporary

### ✸ Claude Debussy (1862–1918)

Claimed by some as a major source of modern music, Debussy's evocative style introduced a new aesthetic of suggestive sounds and delicate colors. Not surprisingly, he was a composer who numbered among his friends as many poets and painters as musicians.

Born in a suburb of Paris to a middle-class family, Debussy began studying at the Conservatoire in Paris at the age of ten, first piano and then composition. In the early 1880s, he worked for Tchaikovsky's patron Nadezhda von Meck and twice traveled to Russia, where he heard the recent works of Rimsky-Korsakov and others that deeply influenced his style and orchestration. In 1884, he won the coveted Prix de Rome and spent two years in Italy. Returning to Paris in 1887, he cultivated friendships with several Symbolist poets and other artists. Although he dutifully made the pilgrimage to Bayreuth to hear Wagner's operas in 1888 and 1889, he came away having recognized both the power of the music and his own need to avoid being overly influenced by it.

In the 1890s, Debussy lived with his lover, Gabrielle Dupont, in Montmartre, the bohemian neighborhood in Paris that had become a center for the new artistic movements. He found his own voice in composing a series of songs, his early piano music, his *Prelude to "The Afternoon of a Faun,"* and, especially, his opera *Pelléas et Mélisande*, whose 1902 premiere made him a star overnight. He made a living through his work as a music critic and through an income from his publisher.

After Gabrielle left him in 1898, Debussy married Lilly Texier. But in 1903, he fell in love with Emma Bardac, with whom he had a child in 1905 and whom he married in 1908. By then, he was well established as France's leading modern composer, producing orchestral works like *La Mer* and *Images* and piano pieces that soon entered the standard repertory. Although depressed by World War I and a diagnosis of cancer in 1914, he soon regained his productivity and composed his Études and three chamber sonatas before his death in 1918.

**Major works:** *Pelléas et Mélisande* (opera); *Prelude to "The Afternoon of a Faun," Nocturnes, La Mer, Images, Jeux*, and other orchestral works; Preludes, Études, *Images, Children's Corner*, and many other piano pieces; string quartet, sonatas, and other chamber works.

*Figure 21.1. Portrait of Claude Debussy by Jacques-Émile Blanche, completed in 1902. Musée d'Art et d'Histoire, Saint-Germain-en-Laye.*

Emmanuel Chabrier (1841–1894). He found new ideas in Russian composers, especially Balakirev, Rimsky-Korsakov, and Musorgsky; in medieval music, notably parallel organum; and in music from Asia. Blending these and other influences, he produced works of striking individuality that had a profound impact on almost all later composers.

*Style*    Although Debussy's music is often called impressionist by analogy to the impressionist painters (see pages 527–528), it also shares qualities with the Symbolist poets by evoking a mood through suggestion, connotation, and indirection. This stylistic connection was reinforced by his friendships with Symbolist poets and his use of their texts for songs and dramatic works. As in their poetry, the normal syntax is often disrupted, and our attention is drawn instead to individual images that carry the work's structure and meaning. He creates musical images through motives, harmony, exotic scales (such as the whole-tone, octatonic, and pentatonic scales), instrumental timbre, and other elements, which he then juxtaposes. Motives need not develop but may repeat with small changes, like an object viewed from different perspectives; dissonances need not resolve; sonorities may move in parallel motion; contrasts of scale type underlie the articulation of phrases and sections; and instrumental timbres are intrinsic to the musical content rather than being simply coloration.

*Piano music*    These traits are evident in Debussy's piano music. In the passage from *L'Isle joyeuse* (The Joyous Isle, 1903–1904) in Example 21.1, each motive is associated with a particular figuration, chord or series of chords, scale type, dynamic level, and range on the piano, producing a succession of images that remain distinct from one another even as each flows into the next: (a) a rising major-third

*Example 21.1: Claude Debussy,* L'Isle joyeuse, *measures 23–29*

motive in a whole-tone environment; (b) an upward sweep in the B Dorian diatonic scale; (c) a partially chromatic motive based on undulating thirds; (d) a pentatonic filigree; and (e) chromatic lines in contrary motion over an A pedal, combined with motive (c). In the motion from one segment to the next, some notes remain the same and some change, producing the effect of a leisurely harmonic progression.

The harmonic styles of Wagner and Liszt influenced Debussy's use of chromatic and whole-tone chords, but our desire to hear resolution is absent. Instead, we are content to enjoy each moment as it comes. Debussy usually maintained a tonal focus—a kind of key center, here A—but he defied the conventional tonal relationships between chords and allowed each chord a degree of independence. This changed attitude toward harmony, inviting us to take pleasure in each event rather than await a resolution, gives his music a feeling of detached observation. Debussy once said of his music, "There is no theory. You merely have to listen. Pleasure is the law." Of course, pleasure can lead to joy or even ecstasy, as it does in the climactic conclusion of this piece, so it should not be imagined that Debussy's music is without emotion.

Many of Debussy's other piano pieces also have evocative titles, often suggesting a visual image, like *Estampes* (Engravings, or Prints, 1903) and the two sets of *Images* (1901–1905 and 1907). *Children's Corner* (1906–1908) depicts a child's world, including a sly poke at Czerny's piano exercises in *Dr. Gradus ad Parnassum* and a salute to American ragtime (with a satirical quotation from Wagner's *Tristan*) in *Golliwogg's Cake-Walk*. The twenty-four Preludes (two books, 1909–1910 and 1911–1913) are character pieces whose picturesque titles are placed at the end rather than the beginning of each piece to allow performers and listeners to form their own images. Other works are relatively abstract, although unmistakably in Debussy's style: *Suite bergamasque* (ca. 1890) and *Pour le piano* (1894–1901) update the French tradition of the keyboard suite, and the late Études (1915) explore pianistic timbre as well as technique in the tradition of Chopin.

Debussy's orchestral music shows the same characteristics as his piano works, with the added element of instrumental timbre. Often a particular instrument is associated with a certain motive, and different musical layers are separated through tone color. His works require a large orchestra, which is seldom used to make a loud sound but instead offers a great variety of tone colors and textures. Even more than Mahler, Debussy treated music as an art of sound and reveled in the wide range of sounds available in the orchestra.

Debussy based his celebrated *Prélude à "L'Après-midi d'un faune"* (Prelude to "The Afternoon of a Faun," 1891–1894) on a Symbolist poem by Mallarmé, and he treats the subject with the same detachment and delicacy that French Symbolist poets did (see Figure 21.2). At the same time, he shared the impressionist painters' fascination with atmosphere, color, and light—qualities that are evident in his masterful orchestral technique. The variety of his orchestral palette is well represented in the three *Nocturnes* (1897–1899): we find subdued, imagist instrumentation in *Nuages* (Clouds), the brilliance of the full ensemble in *Fêtes* (Festivals), and the blending of orchestra with a wordless female chorus in *Sirènes* (the Sirens of Greek mythology). And in *La Mer* (The Sea,

Harmony

*Figure 21.2.  Costume sketch for the faun by Léon Bakst (1866–1924), who also designed the stage set for Sergei Diaghilev's ballet (1912) based on Debussy's* Prélude. *Wadsworth Athenaeum, Hartford.*

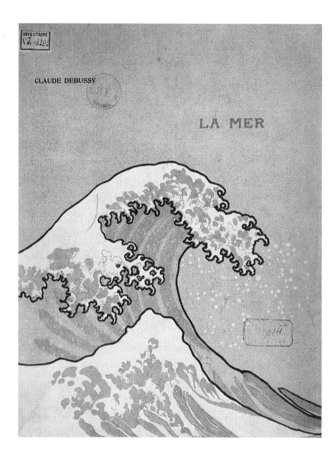

*Figure 21.3. Original cover for Debussy's orchestral score of* La Mer, *first published in 1905. The design, based on a popular print by the Japanese artist Katsushika Hokusai (1760–1849) from his renowned series* Thirty-six Views of Mount Fuji, *reflects the nineteenth-century French enthusiasm for the arts of East Asia. Bibliothèque Nationale, Paris.*

1903–1905), subtitled "three symphonic sketches," the orchestra captures the movements of the sea through rapidly changing musical images (see Figure 21.3).

*Nuages* (NAWM 138) from *Nocturnes* exemplifies the interaction of timbre with motive, scale type, and other elements to create a musical image. There are three sections in modified ABA′ form. The piece begins with an oscillating pattern of fifths and thirds—adapted from a Musorgsky song—that conveys an impression of movement but no harmonic direction, an apt analogy for slowly moving clouds. Each time the pattern appears in the A section, it features different tone colors or pitches or both, sometimes changing into a series of parallel triads or ninth chords. In the abbreviated A′ section, the pattern practically disappears, giving the impression of dispersing clouds. Contrasting with this figure's inconstancy is one that changes little: an English-horn motive that quickly rises and slowly falls through a segment of the octatonic scale. The English horn sometimes omits or repeats some of its final notes, but the motive is never developed, transposed, or given to another instrument, and the English horn never plays anything else; there is a complete identification between timbre and motive. It is not clear what, if anything, these musical images represent: they are themselves, lending coherence to the music and helping to convey a sense of stillness and contemplation.

Debussy's lifelong engagement with texts—he was also a music critic—made him particularly interested in the written word. Notable among his songs are settings of several major French poets, including Charles Baudelaire, Paul Verlaine, and the ballades of fifteenth-century poet François Villon. He repeatedly sought out dramatic projects, such as incidental music for Gabriele D'Annunzio's mystery play *The Martyrdom of Saint Sebastian* (1910–1911) and the ballet *Jeux* (1912–1913), and several unfinished works. His only completed opera,

**Nuages**

CD 10/59  |  CD 5/73

**Songs and stage music**

*Pelléas et Mélisande* (1893–1902), which was his response to Wagner's *Tristan und Isolde,* made his reputation when it premiered at the Paris Opéra-Comique. The veiled allusions and images of the text—a Symbolist play by Maurice Maeterlinck—are matched by the strange, often modal harmonies, subdued colors, and restrained expressiveness of the music. The voices, set in fluent recitative that matches the flow of the French language, are supported but never dominated by a continuous orchestral background, while the instrumental interludes connecting the scenes carry on the mysterious inner drama.

The changes that Debussy introduced in harmonic and orchestral usage became one of the seminal forces in the history of music. The composers who at one time or another came under his influence include nearly every distinguished composer of the early and middle twentieth century, from Ravel, Messiaen, and Boulez in France to Puccini, Janáček, Strauss, Scriabin, Ives, Falla, Bartók, Stravinsky, Berg, and others from many national traditions, as well as American jazz and popular musicians. His emphasis on sound itself as an element of music opened doors to new possibilities later explored by Varèse, Cage, and many other composers.

*Influence*

## Maurice Ravel

Maurice Ravel (1875–1937) is often grouped with Debussy as an impressionist. Although some of his works seem to fit the label, he might better be called an assimilationist because his music encompasses a variety of influences. At the same time, it carries his distinctive stamp, which is marked by consummate craftsmanship, traditional forms, diatonic melodies, and complex harmonies within an essentially tonal language.

The impressionist side of Ravel, and some differences from Debussy, are illustrated in the piano piece *Jeux d'eau* (Water Games, 1901; see Figure 21.4).

*Distinctive traits*

*Figure 21.4. Georges d'Espagnat,* Reunion de Musicens chez les Godebski *(Reunion of Musicians at the House of Cipa Godebski)(1910). From left to right: Florent Schmidt, Deodat de Severac, Michel Calvocoressi, Cipa Godebski (seated), Albert Roussel, Ricardo Viñes (at the piano), and Maurice Ravel. Bibliotheque de L'Opera, Paris.*

Here, Ravel drew on Liszt's pianistic techniques and in turn gave Debussy some ideas for his own watery music. The passage in Example 21.2 includes many innovative textures, such as parallel dissonant chords under rushing scales, and chords and arpeggiated figures that emphasize open fifths and fourths. This passage juxtaposes whole-tone with diatonic music, as in *L'Isle joyeuse,* shown above in Example 21.1. Unlike Debussy, though, Ravel treats his whole-tone sonorities as dissonant harmonies that must resolve, culminating in a complex reworking of the traditional ii–V–I tonal cadence (outlined by a box in the example): a progression from an F♯ ninth chord (drawn from one whole-tone scale) through an F–A–B–D♯ augmented sixth chord (drawn from the other whole-tone scale) to a resolution on the tonic E major. Also characteristic of Ravel are the prominent major sevenths he attaches to the tonic and subdominant chords in measure 7, creating a spiky dissonant sound that Debussy normally avoided.

*Example 21.2: Maurice Ravel,* Jeux d'eau, *measures 6–7*

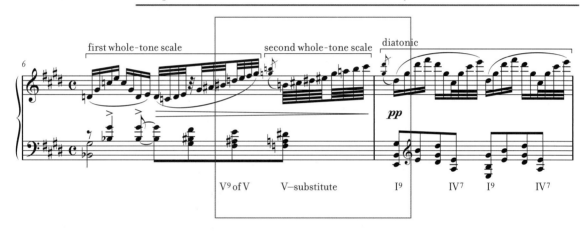

Varied influences

The descriptive piano pieces in the sets *Miroirs* (Mirrors, 1904–1905) and *Gaspard de la nuit* (Gaspard of the Night, 1908), the orchestral suite *Rapsodie espagnole* (Spanish Rhapsody, 1907–1908), and the ballet *Daphnis et Chloé* (1909–1912) likewise invoke impressionism in their strong musical imagery, brilliant instrumental technique, and colorful harmonies. But Ravel also absorbed ideas from older French music and from the Classical era. He borrowed from the French Baroque tradition of stylized dances and suites in his piano pieces *Menuet antique* (1895), *Pavane pour une infante défunte* (Pavane for a Dead Princess, 1899), and *Le Tombeau de Couperin* (Memorial for Couperin, 1914–1917), all of which he later orchestrated. His songs draw on French art and popular traditions, ranging in subject from humorous and realistic characterizations of animal life in *Histoires naturelles* (1906) to three Symbolist poems by Stéphane Mallarmé for voice and chamber ensemble (1913). His interest in Classical forms is clear in works such as the String Quartet in F (1902–1903) and the Violin Sonata (1923–1927). Ravel also looked to popular traditions outside France, using Viennese waltz rhythms in the orchestral poem *La Valse* (1919–1920); Gypsy style in *Tzigane* for violin and piano or orchestra (1924); blues in the Violin Sonata; and jazz elements in the Piano Concerto for the Left Hand (1929–1930), composed for pianist Paul Wittgenstein, who had lost his right arm in World War I. Many works feature Spanish idioms, including Ravel's famous *Bolero* (1928), an orchestral rumination on a single theme that is varied by changes of instrumentation and a gradual crescendo. Working in a classical tradition that esteemed originality, Ravel avoided repeating himself by drawing on a wide range of sources and giving each piece its individual stamp.

## Spain: Manuel de Falla

French, Russian, and other composers had often used Spanish elements to create an exotic atmosphere. In the early twentieth century, Spanish composers sought to reclaim their national tradition, using authentic native materials in order to appeal to their own people and to gain a foothold in the international repertoire. The principal Spanish composer of the time, Manuel de Falla (1876–1946), developed a nationalism that resisted the merely exotic. He collected and arranged national folk songs, introducing a wider public to the variety in the folk tradition. His earlier works—such as the opera *La Vida breve* (Life Is Short, 1904–1913) and the ballets *El Amor brujo* (Love, the Sorcerer, 1915) and *El Sombrero de tres picos* (The Three-Cornered Hat, 1916–1919)—are imbued with the melodic and rhythmic qualities of Spanish popular music. His finest mature works are *El Retablo de maese Pedro* (Master Pedro's Puppet Show, 1919–1923), based on an episode from the great Spanish novel *Don Quixote,* and the Concerto for Harpsichord with Five Solo Instruments (1923–1926), which harks back to the Spanish Baroque. Both pieces combine specific national elements with the Neoclassical approach that was popular after World War I to produce music that is both nationalist and more broadly modern.

## England: Ralph Vaughan Williams

The English musical renaissance begun by Elgar (see Chapter 20) took a nationalist turn in the twentieth century, when composers sought a distinctive voice for English art music after centuries of domination by foreign styles. Cecil Sharp (1859–1924), Ralph Vaughan Williams (1872–1958), and others collected and published hundreds of folk songs, leading to the use of these melodies in compositions such as Vaughan Williams's *Norfolk Rhapsodies* (1905–1906) and *Five Variants of "Dives and Lazarus"* (1939). Along with Gustav Holst (1874–1934), his close friend and classmate at the Royal Conservatory of Music, Vaughan Williams became a leader of the new English school (see Figure 21.5).

*Figure 21.5. Photo portrait of Ralph Vaughan Williams, ca. 1951, by Norman Parkinson.*

Vaughan Williams cultivated a national style in his works, which include nine symphonies and other orchestral pieces, film scores, works for band, songs, operas, and many choral pieces. He drew inspiration not only from folk song but also from English hymnody and the music of earlier English composers such as Thomas Tallis and Henry Purcell. He also studied with Ravel and was strongly influenced by Debussy, Bach, and Handel. Vaughan Williams exemplified a trait common to several modern English composers: he wrote both art music and practical, or utilitarian, music, using elements from each tradition in the other. He gained a profound knowledge of hymnody as musical editor of the new *English Hymnal* in 1904–1906, writing later that "two years of close association with some of the best (as well as some of the worst) tunes in the world was a better musical education than any amount of sonatas and fugues." Throughout his long career, he conducted local amateur singers and players, for whom he wrote a number of pieces. Such links with amateur music-making kept Vaughan Williams

LEOŠ JANÁČEK

*Figure 21.6. Cover of Leoš Janáček's* Moravian Folk Songs, *illustrated by Karel Svolinský and published in Prague in 1947. British Library, London.*

and other English composers from cultivating an esoteric style addressed only to elite listeners.

The national quality of Vaughan Williams's music comes from his incorporation or imitation of British folk tunes and his assimilation of the modal harmony of sixteenth-century English composers. One of his most popular works, *Fantasia on a Theme of Thomas Tallis* (1910) for double string orchestra and string quartet, is based on a Tallis hymn in the Phrygian mode that Vaughan Williams had revived for the *English Hymnal.* The piece introduces fragments of the tune, states it simply once, and develops motives from it in a free fantasy, using antiphonal sonorities and triads in parallel motion in a modal framework. Like his teacher Ravel, Vaughan Williams found ways to write varied music that was at the same time national and recognizably individual in style.

## Czech Nationalism: Leoš Janáček

Spain and Britain were independent nations for whom nationalism was primarily a cultural issue. But for the peoples of Eastern Europe under the Austro-Hungarian and Russian empires, it was also an urgent political concern. Music that reflected a people's language and traditions was valuable at home as an assertion of an independent national identity and abroad as an appeal for international recognition as a nation.

The leading twentieth-century Czech composer, Leoš Janáček (1854–1928), cultivated genres of Western art music, especially opera, but sought a specifically national style. Beginning in the 1880s, he collected and edited folk music from his native region of Moravia (see Figure 21.6), studied the rhythms and inflections of peasant speech and song, and devised a highly personal idiom based on them. He asserted his independence from Austria not only in melodic style but also in his characteristic procedures. His music relies on contrasting sonorities, harmonies, motives, and tone colors, and it proceeds primarily by repeating and juxtaposing ideas in a manner akin to Musorgsky or Debussy rather than by developing them, as in the Germanic tradition.

Operas

After winning local renown for his folk song and dance collections, Janáček gained wider prominence in his sixties, when his opera *Jenůfa*, based on a Moravian subject and premiered at Brno in 1904, was performed in Prague twelve years later and again in Vienna in 1918, the year that Czechoslovakia gained independence after the dissolution of Austria-Hungary. With new confidence from both personal and political triumphs, in his last decade Janáček produced a string of operas that dominated the Czech stage between the world wars and later became part of the international repertory, including *Kát'a Kabanová* (1921), *The Cunning Little Vixen* (1924), *The Makropulos Affair* (1925), and *From the House of the Dead* (1928). In his operas, strongly contrasting ideas are used to delineate diverse characters and situations. His instrumental works, such as the flashy orchestral *Sinfonietta* (1926) and two late string quartets (1923 and 1928), depend on similar contrasts.

## Finland: Jean Sibelius

Much like his peer Janáček, Finnish composer Jean Sibelius (1865–1957) was deeply moved by the spirit of nationalism. Sibelius sought expression for his fervent patriotic sentiments by incorporating themes of national identity into his compositions, even after Finland achieved its independence from Russia following the Revolution of 1917. He became fascinated with the Finnish national epic, the *Kalevala*, which he mined for texts to set in his vocal works and for subjects to treat in his instrumental music.

Sibelius established his reputation as Finland's leading composer in the 1890s with a series of symphonic poems, including *Kullervo* (in five movements with soloists and chorus), *The Swan of Tuonela*, and his most famous (and political), *Finlandia*. From 1897 to the end of his life, he was supported by the Finnish government as a national artist. He then turned to the international audience around 1900 with publication and performances of his symphonic poems and with his first two symphonies (1899 and 1901–1902) and Violin Concerto (1903–1904), followed by five more symphonies through 1924. Sibelius devised a personal style marked by modal melodies, uncomplicated rhythms, insistent repetition of brief motives, pedal points, and strong contrasts of orchestral timbres and textures, all designed to create a distinctive sound and musical discourse far removed from the nineteenth-century academic tradition in which he had been trained. Sibelius's search to reconcile his status as an outsider with the classical heritage, to blend nationalism with international appeal, and to balance innovative with traditional elements reveals many of the fault lines in twentieth-century music.

## Russia: Sergei Rachmaninov and Alexander Scriabin

The works of Rachmaninov and Scriabin illustrate the wide variety of personal styles in this period. Classmates at the Moscow Conservatory, neither was interested in folk music or overt nationalism. Rather, each developed an individual idiom that drew both on Russian traditions and on the cosmopolitan heritage of the virtuoso pianist-composer.

*Figure 21.7. Sergei Rachmaninov in a 1940 portrait by Boris Chaliapin.*

Sergei Rachmaninov (1873–1943), shown in Figure 21.7, made his living primarily as a pianist, especially after leaving Russia in 1917 in the wake of the Russian Revolution and making his home in the United States. His notable works include three symphonies, the symphonic poem *The Isle of the Dead* (1907), and the choral symphony *The Bells* (1913). But his most characteristic music is for piano, especially the twenty-four preludes (1892–1910) and two sets of *Études-Tableaux* (1911 and 1916–1917) for piano solo, the four piano concertos, and *Rhapsody on a Theme of Paganini* for piano and orchestra (1934), a salute from one great virtuoso to another.

Rachmaninov, like Tchaikovsky, cultivated a passionate, melodious idiom. Some have dismissed his music as old-fashioned; but, like other composers in the first modern generation, he sought a way to appeal to listeners enamored of the classics by offering something new and individual yet steeped in tradition. Rather than following Strauss, Debussy, and Scriabin by introducing innovations in harmony—thereby violating both his temperament and the demands of the audience for touring virtuosos—he focused on other elements of the Romantic tradition, creating melodies and textures that sound both fresh and familiar. Like others who wrote the best popular music or who adhered to venerable traditions such as Italian opera, Rachmaninov made his mark by using conventions in a way no one had done before.

**Prelude in G Minor**

**CD 10/67**

Rachmaninov's Prelude for Piano in G Minor, Op. 23, No. 5 (1903, NAWM 139), illustrates the composer's ability to create innovative textures and melodies within traditional harmonies and ABA′ form. At the opening of this work, Rachmaninov immediately commands our attention by elaborating a simple G-minor triad in a new and distinctive way, using a pattern of energetic, marchlike rhythms and alternating registers that continues with variation throughout the A section.

**Scriabin**

Alexander Scriabin (1872–1915), shown in Figure 21.8, traveled a different path. He began by writing nocturnes, preludes, études, and mazurkas in the manner of Chopin, then gradually absorbed the chromaticism of Liszt and Wagner; the octatonic scale and other exotic elements from Rimsky-Korsakov; and the juxtapositions of texture, scale, and figuration from Debussy and from fellow Russian composers. He gradually evolved a complex harmonic vocabulary all his own. Besides piano music, he wrote symphonies and other orchestral works, notably *Poem of Ecstasy* (1908) and *Prometheus* (1910). During performances of *Prometheus*, the composer asked for the concert hall to be flooded with changing colored light. His own sense perceptions caused him to link particular pitches to colors, and he aspired to a synthesis of all the arts with the aim of inducing states of mystic rapture.

*Figure 21.8. Caricature of Alexander Scriabin by John Minnion.*

The changes in Scriabin's musical language can be followed in his ten piano sonatas, of which the last five, composed between 1912 and 1913, dispense with key signatures and tonality. He replaced conventional tonal harmony by choosing for each work a complex chord that serves as a kind of tonic and as the source of a work's melodic and harmonic material. The referential chord typically contains one or two tritones and is usually part of an octatonic scale, sometimes with one added note. These chords resemble Wagner's *Tristan* chord (see Chapter 19), yet they are treated as static objects and do not produce a yearning toward resolution; instead of the desire Wagner sought to invoke, they suggest a transcendence of desire, which can be read as erotic or mystic, depending on the context. Scriabin creates a sense of harmonic progression by transposing and altering the referential chord, enlivening the texture with vigorous figuration, until the chord returns at the end, sometimes with alterations. Such pieces cannot be described as tonal, but the novel harmony serves most of the functions of tonality, establishing a home tonal region, departing from it, and returning. Scriabin's *Vers la flamme* (Toward the Flame), Op. 72 (1914, NAWM 140), a one-movement "poem" for piano, illustrates this process. The predominant figuration changes from section to section, producing an effect of static blocks of sound that are juxtaposed, as in Musorgsky's and Debussy's music.

**Vers la flamme**

**CD 10/72**

## Tonal and Post-Tonal Music

Of all the composers in the classical tradition that we have surveyed here, Scriabin traveled the furthest from common-practice tonal harmony, Rachmaninov the least far. The others can be placed at different points along a spectrum between these extremes. Tonality, for all composers of the time, was an unavoidable issue: the demand for originality made conventional chord progressions seem stale; yet composers who strayed too far might lose their audience.

That it was still possible to compose tonal music in the twentieth century is clear from the careers of Strauss (Chapter 20), Ravel, Vaughan Williams,

Rachmaninov, and many younger composers active through the 1930s and beyond, who found new flavors and possibilities within tonality but never abandoned it. Yet other composers, including Debussy, Falla, Janáček, and Scriabin, moved beyond tonal practice in the early 1900s as each developed a personal musical language that followed its own rules. Even when a tonal center can be identified in one of their works, whether a single pitch as in Debussy's *L'Isle joyeuse* or a chord complex as in Scriabin's *Vers la flamme,* it no longer makes sense to describe the music as tonal, because the harmonic language diverges too far from common practice. The most general term for such music is *post-tonal,* which embraces all the new ways composers found to organize pitch, from atonality to neotonality (see Chapter 24). The new possibilities of post-tonal idioms were part of the marvelous diversity of twentieth-century music in the classical tradition, as were the individual approaches to tonality.

## Arnold Schoenberg

Arnold Schoenberg (1874–1951; see biography and Figure 21.9) was committed to continuing the German classical tradition, and for that reason felt compelled to move beyond tonality to *atonality*—a term for music that avoids establishing a tonal center—and then to the twelve-tone method, a form of atonality based on systematic orderings of the twelve notes of the chromatic scale. His innovations made him famous in some quarters and—because the resulting music was both dissonant and difficult to follow—notorious in others.

Like other modernists of his generation, Schoenberg began by writing tonal music in late Romantic style. The chromatic idiom of his first important work, a

Tonal works

---

**VIGNETTE** New Music and Tradition

*Arnold Schoenberg saw no contradiction between tradition and innovation. For him, the tradition of classical music was a legacy of innovation, and it was his job as a composer to weave threads from the past and the present into something truly new. He returned to this theme constantly in his writings.*

In higher art, only that is worth being presented which has never before been presented. There is no great work of art which does not convey a new message to humanity; there is no great artist who fails in this respect. This is the code of honor of all the great in art, and consequently in all great works of the great we will find that newness which never perishes, whether it be of Josquin des Prez, of Bach or Haydn, or of any other great master.

Because: Art means New Art.

My teachers were primarily Bach and Mozart, and secondarily Beethoven, Brahms, and Wagner. . . .

I also learned much from Schubert and Mahler, Strauss and Reger too. I shut myself off from no one, and so I could say of myself:

My originality comes from this: I immediately imitated everything I saw that was good, even when I had not first seen it in someone else's work.

And I may say: often enough I saw it first in myself. For if I saw something I did not leave it at that; I acquired it, in order to possess it; I worked on it and extended it, and it led me to something new.

I am convinced that eventually people will recognize how immediately this "something new" is linked to the loftiest models that have been granted us. I venture to credit myself with having written truly new music which, being based on tradition, is destined to become tradition.

From Arnold Schoenberg, "New Music, Outmoded Music, Style and Idea" and "National Music (2)," in *Style and Idea: Selected Writings of Arnold Schoenberg,* ed. Leonard Stein, trans. Leo Black (London: Faber, 1975), pp. 114–115 and 173–174, respectively.

tone poem for string sextet entitled *Verklärte Nacht* (Transfigured Night, 1899), derived from that of Wagner's *Tristan und Isolde*, while the symphonic poem *Pelleas und Melisande* (1902–1903) draws on Mahler and Strauss. The huge cantata *Gurrelieder* (Songs of Gurre, 1900–1901, orchestration completed 1911) outdoes Wagner in emotional fervor, and Mahler and Strauss in the complexity of its scoring.

*Developing variation*    Schoenberg soon turned away from late Romantic gigantism and toward chamber music. He found in Brahms the principle of developing variation (see Chapter 18) and applied it in his own works, such as the String Quartet No. 1 in D Minor, Op. 7. All the themes in that composition and most of the subsidiary

## ✳ Arnold Schoenberg (1874–1951)

Perhaps the most self-consciously modern composer of his generation, Arnold Schoenberg was a product of Europe's musical hothouse—the Vienna of Brahms and Mahler. He emerged from that intense environment to become one of the truly influential composers of the twentieth century, best known for his atonal and twelve-tone music.

Schoenberg came by his musical heritage honestly. He was born in Vienna, the son of a Jewish shopkeeper. He began violin lessons at age eight, then taught himself to compose by imitating the music he played. When his father died in 1891, Schoenberg had to leave school and work as a bank clerk. His instruction in theory and composition was minimal, although the composer Alexander von Zemlinsky served for a time as sounding board and teacher.

Schoenberg married Zemlinsky's sister, Mathilde, in 1901, and they moved to Berlin, where he worked at a cabaret until Richard Strauss got him a job teaching composition. Two years later he returned to Vienna and taught privately, attracting his two most famous students, Alban Berg and Anton von Webern. He had the support of Mahler and other progressive musicians, but his works met with resistance, especially after he adopted atonality in 1908. He took up painting in an expressionist style (see "Expressionism," on page 550) and developed friendships with several expressionist painters (one of whom had an affair with Mathilde, who

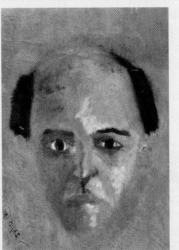

*Figure 21.9.  Arnold Schoenberg, Self-Portrait (1910), showing his interest in expressionism in painting. Arnold Schönberg Center, Vienna.*

briefly left Schoenberg before returning for the sake of their two children).

After World War I, Schoenberg founded and directed the Society for Private Musical Performances in Vienna, which between 1919 and 1921 gave about 350 performances of music by himself and his students and colleagues. After a creative impasse, he formulated the twelve-tone method used in the Piano Suite (1921–1923) and most of his later works.

After Mathilde died in 1923, Schoenberg married Gertrud Kolisch, with whom he had three more children. When the Nazis came to power in 1933 and announced their intention to remove all Jewish instructors from faculty appointments, he moved his family to France. He then traveled on to the United States, finally arriving in Los Angeles in 1934. He was appointed to a professorship at UCLA and retired in 1944 at age seventy. He died in Los Angeles in 1951 on July 13, having always feared the number 13.

**Major works:** 4 operas: *Erwartung, Die glückliche Hand, Von Heute auf Morgen,* and *Moses und Aron*; *Pierrot lunaire, Gurrelieder,* and numerous songs and choral works; 2 chamber symphonies, Five Orchestral Pieces, Variations for Orchestra, and other orchestral works; 5 string quartets, *Verklärte Nacht,* Wind Quintet, and other chamber works; Piano Suite and several sets of piano pieces.

voices evolve from a few germinal motives through variation and combination. A one-movement work, combining an enlarged sonata form with the four standard movements of a quartet, it owes much to Liszt's Piano Sonata in B Minor (Chapter 18), demonstrating Schoenberg's willingness to blend influences in order to create something new.

The quartet exemplifies Schoenberg's twin goals for his music: to continue the tradition and to say something that had never been said before (see vignette). He asked of each work that it not simply repeat but build on the past. Remarkably, he required the same *within* each piece: except for marked repeats in binary forms, nothing should repeat exactly. As he wrote, "With me, variation almost completely takes the place of repetition." This principle of nonrepetition between and within pieces helps explain the evolution of Schoenberg's style.

Nonrepetition

In 1908, Schoenberg began to compose pieces that avoided establishing any note as a tonal center. Others called such music *atonal*, although Schoenberg disliked the term. He felt compelled to abandon tonality in part because the heightened chromaticism, distant modulations, and prolonged dissonances of music since *Tristan* had weakened the pull of the tonic, making its declaration at the end of a piece seem increasingly arbitrary. Schoenberg had emulated Strauss and others in devising novel progressions and avoiding conventional cadences, as the principle of nonrepetition demanded; but it became harder and harder to find new ways to resolve complex chromatic chords and arrive at the tonic convincingly. The ambiguities led Schoenberg to what he called "the emancipation of the dissonance"—freeing dissonance from its need to resolve to consonance, so that any combination of tones could serve as a stable chord that did not require resolution.

Atonal music

Without a tonal backbone, how was music to be organized? Schoenberg relied on three methods: developing variation, the integration of harmony and melody, and chromatic saturation. All had been used in tonal music, but now he drew on them more fully to provide structure. In addition, he often used gestures from tonal music, forging links to tradition and making his music easier to follow. One of Schoenberg's first entirely atonal pieces, dating from March 1908, is *The Book of the Hanging Gardens*, a cycle of fifteen songs on texts by Symbolist poet Stefan George (Op. 15, 1908–1909). The sense of floating in tonal space created by music that does not gravitate to a tonic is perfectly suited to the vague eroticism of the poetry, which expresses, through outward symbols, the inner dynamics of a love affair.

Coherence in atonal music

Schoenberg integrated melody and harmony through a process he called "composing with the tones of a motive," which springs directly from developing variation. In this process, he manipulated the notes and intervals of a motive to create chords and new melodies. One way this worked was to treat the notes of a motive containing three or more pitches just as we might a triad or other tonal chord: as a collection of pitches that could be transposed, inverted, and arranged in any order and register to generate melodies and harmonies. Theorists later termed such a collection a *set* or, more formally, *pitch-class set*, using *pitch-class* to mean one of the twelve notes of the chromatic scale and its enharmonic equivalents in any octave. Using a limited number of sets gives the music a consistent sound. Schoenberg tended to use sets that formed strong dissonances because those sets are most distinctive and, therefore, easier to follow as the music unfolds. This integration of melody and harmony harks back to music of earlier eras.

Compositional process

Pitch-class sets

Atonal music can also be shaped through what is called *chromatic saturation*, the appearance of all twelve pitch-classes within a segment of music. We saw this method at work in Example 20.1, a song of Hugo Wolf that is highly chromatic but still tonal, in which all twelve chromatic notes are stated in the first phrase and again in the next two measures. In an atonal context, the appearance

Chromatic saturation

In the early twentieth century, several groups of German and Austrian painters embraced an international movement called *expressionism*, which also extended to literature, music, dance, theater, and architecture. Expressionism developed from the subjectivity of Romanticism but differed from it in the introspective experience that it aimed to portray and how it chose to portray it.

Expressionist painters such as Ernst Ludwig Kirchner and Richard Gerstl rejected traditional Western aesthetic values by representing real objects or people in grossly distorted ways, characterized by an intensely expressive use of pure colors and dynamic brushstrokes, as in Gerstl's portrait of the Schoenberg family (Figure 21.10). These artists and others drew on contemporary themes involving the dark side of city life, in which people lived under extreme psychological pressure, as well as bright scenes from the circus and music halls that masked a more gloomy reality. They aspired to represent inner experience, to explore the hidden world of the psyche, and to render visible the stressful, emotional life of the modern person—isolated, helpless in the grip of poorly understood forces, prey to inner conflict, tension, anxiety, and fear, and tormented by ele-

mental, irrational drives, including an eroticism that often had morbid overtones. That is also how the Viennese doctor Sigmund Freud, founder of psychoanalysis, described the deepest level of memory and emotional activity in his *Interpretation of Dreams* (1900). In short, expressionism sought to capture the human condition as it was perceived in the early twentieth century.

Arnold Schoenberg and his pupil Alban Berg were two leading exponents of expressionism in music, which paralleled expressionist art by adopting a similarly desperate and revolutionary style. Its characteristics are evident in Schoenberg's *Erwartung*, an opera in which a lone protagonist—emblematic of the artist's alienation from society and its conventions—gives voice to what the composer described as a dream of Angst, an overwhelming feeling of dread or anxiety. Its distorted melodies and fragmented rhythms, violently graphic musical images, and discordant harmonies create the quasi-hysterical atmosphere typical of the style. In none of Schoenberg's expressionist pieces nor in Berg's opera *Wozzeck* did these composers try to create music that is pretty or naturalistic (as the impressionists did); rather, they deployed the most direct—even drastic—means, no matter how unappealing, to convey extreme and irrational states of mind.

Schoenberg was also an amateur painter and took lessons from Gerstl, one of the foremost expressionist artists in Austria. Schoenberg's most striking pictures, a series of "gazes" in the form of faces, not only emphasize the act of looking but also suggest the same feelings of claustrophobia and angst as those portrayed in *Erwartung*. With other Viennese expressionists, Schoenberg also shared an interest in producing self-portraits (see Figure 21.9 and Figure VI.6 on page 529). They indicate, perhaps, his constant questioning, both of his own identity and of his place among the modernists.

*Figure 21.10. Portrait of the Schoenberg family by Richard Gerstl. Österreichische Galerie im Belvedere, Vienna.*

of a note that has not recently been sounded can give a sense of moving forward harmonically. Additionally, once the twelfth chromatic note has appeared, there can be a sense of fullness and completion, which Schoenberg used to reinforce the feeling of completing a phrase. Through these means, Schoenberg sought to write atonal music that was as logical as tonal music.

In addition to *The Book of the Hanging Gardens*, Schoenberg's works from this period include Three Piano Pieces, Op. 11; Five Orchestral Pieces, Op. 16; and *Erwartung* (Expectation), Op. 17, a one-character opera for soprano. In the works with orchestra, he followed Mahler in treating instruments soloistically and in swiftly alternating timbres to produce a great variety of colors. *Erwartung*, the height of expressionism in music, uses exaggerated gestures, angular melodies, and unrelenting dissonance to convey the tortured emotions of the protagonist (see "Expressionism," page 550). In this opera, Schoenberg pushed nonrepetition to an extreme: the work is not only atonal, it has no themes or motives that return and lacks any reference to traditional forms. The fluid, constantly changing music suits the nightmare-like text.

Another expressionist work that incorporates some of these devices combined with a return to a more traditional use of motives, themes, and long-range repetition is *Pierrot lunaire* (Moonstruck Pierrot, 1912), a cycle of twenty-one songs drawn from a larger poetic cycle by the Belgian Symbolist poet Albert Giraud. Schoenberg scored the text, translated into German, for a woman's voice with a chamber ensemble of five performers who play nine different instruments. In keeping with the principle of nonrepetition, the combination of instruments in each movement is unique. The voice declaims the text in *Sprechstimme* ("speaking voice"), also called *Sprechgesang* ("speech-song"), approximating the written pitches in the gliding tones of speech, while following the notated rhythm exactly—an innovative idea that blends the traditional notions of song and melodrama. The inexact pitches evoke an eerie atmosphere for the Symbolist text, in which the clown Pierrot suffers gruesome visions provoked by a moonbeam that takes many shapes.

Expressionist features of the work aside, Schoenberg highlights many traditional elements. Each poem has a refrain, and Schoenberg typically sets the repeated lines of text with a variant of their original music at the original pitch level, thereby creating a sense of departure and return, as in tonal music. We find varied repetition at all levels, from motives and chords to themes, sections, and one entire song: No. 7, *Der kranke Mond* ("The Sick Moon") is recast as an instrumental epilogue heard at the end of No. 13, *Enthauptung* (Beheading, in NAWM 141b). The cycle includes several traditional forms and genres, including a waltz, a serenade, a barcarole (a boating song of Venetian gondoliers), and an aria over a walking bass, reminiscent of Bach. Schoenberg called No. 8, *Nacht* (Night, NAWM 141a), a passacaglia because the unifying motive—a rising minor third followed by a descending major third—is constantly repeated, with some rhythmic variation, in all parts and is often treated in canon. The omnipresence of this motive, whose notated contour in original and inverted forms resembles wings, fittingly illustrates Pierrot's obsession with the giant moths that enclose him in a frightening trap and shut out the sun. Even *Enthauptung*, which appears to abandon thematic development for anarchic improvisation, unfolds by constantly varying the initial ideas to capture the images and feelings in the text.

Schoenberg still faced a problem: using his atonal methods, he could not match the formal coherence of tonal music and had to rely on a text to sustain pieces of any length. He formulated a solution in his twelve-tone method, which he described as a "method of composing with twelve tones that are related only to one another" (rather than to a tonic) in the early 1920s, after several years during

Atonal works

*Pierrot lunaire*

| CD 11/4 | CD 6/4 |

| CD 11/1 | CD 6/1 |

Twelve-tone method

**A CLOSER LOOK**    Schoenberg's Piano Suite, Op. 25

CD 11/8–9

CD 6/8–9

The Piano Suite (excerpted in NAWM 142) illustrates some of Schoenberg's methods. Throughout the work, the row appears in only eight forms (shown in Example 21.3a): the untransposed prime form (P-0); the prime transposed up six semitones (P-6); the inversion in the same two transpositions (I-0 and I-6); and their retrogrades (R-0, R-6, RI-0, and RI-6). Schoenberg designed the row so that each of these begins on either E or B♭ and ends on the other pitch, and all the primes and inversions have G and D♭ as the second pair of notes (see the box in Example 21.3a). The recurrence of E, B♭, G, and D♭ in the same places creates a consistency that Schoenberg saw as an analogue to staying in a single key throughout, the normal practice in a Baroque keyboard suite, although it is much more difficult for a listener to hear. The first four notes of R-0 give a nod to Schoenberg's model, J. S. Bach, by spelling his name: B♭-A-C-B♮ (B-A-C-H, in German nomenclature).

CD 11/8

CD 6/8

Example 21.3b shows the rows deployed at the beginning of the Prelude (NAWM 142a). P-0 is in the right hand as melody, divided into motives of four notes each (in brown, blue, and aqua circles respectively). Twelve-tone theo-

*Example 21.3: Arnold Schoenberg, Piano Suite Op. 25*

*a. Row forms*

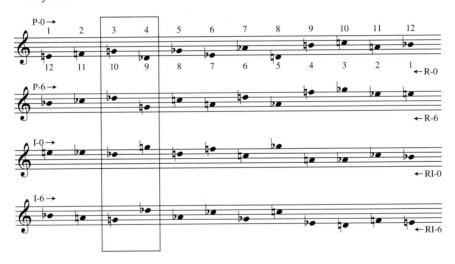

which he published no music. The basis of a twelve-tone composition is called a *row*, or *series*, which consists of the twelve pitch-classes arranged in an order chosen by the composer and produces a particular sequence of intervals. The tones of the series may be used both successively, as melody, and simultaneously, as harmony or counterpoint, in any octave and with any desired rhythm. The row may be used not only in its original, or *prime*, form but also in *inversion*, in *retrograde* order (backward), and in *retrograde inversion*, and may appear in all twelve possible transpositions of any of the four forms (see Figure 21.11). The twelve-note series is often broken into segments of three to six notes, which are then used as sets to create melodic motives and chords. As a rule, the composer states all twelve pitches of the series before going on to use the series in any of its forms again (unless two or more statements occur simultaneously). In this way,

rists call such groups of four consecutive notes from the row *tetrachords*, using the ancient Greek term in a new sense (see Chapter 1). In the left hand, as accompaniment, we find P-6, using the same division into tetrachords and presenting the last two simultaneously. Each tetrachord is a different type of set, containing different intervals, so in featuring them Schoenberg continued his earlier practice of composing with sets. There is also a canon between the pitches of each hand, recalling Bach's contrapuntal practice. At the end of measure 3, I-6 begins, presenting all three tetrachords simultaneously, each in its own rhythm. The last two notes of its first tetrachord overlap the statement of R-6 in measure 5; that is, pitches 3 and 4 of I-6 (in the brown circle) are the same as pitches 9 and 10 of R-6 (in the next brown circle). The row-form R-6 also presents the tetrachords simultaneously, but here the texture is less contrapuntal and more chordal than it was in the preceding measure.

Typical for a piece in this style, all the movements use the same eight row forms, which was, in Schoenberg's mind, comparable to establishing unity through tonality.

*b. Prelude*

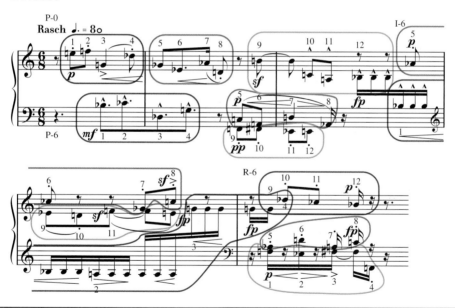

Schoenberg simulated the structural functions of tonality, using the transposition of his rows as an analogue to modulation in tonal music.

After focusing on vocal works in his atonal period, Schoenberg turned to traditional instrumental forms, as if to demonstrate the power of his method to reconstitute tonal forms in a new musical language. Among these works, composed between 1921 and 1949, are the Piano Suite Op. 25, modeled on the keyboard suites of Bach; Variations for Orchestra Op. 31; Third and Fourth String Quartets, Opp. 30 and 37; Violin Concerto Op. 36; and Piano Concerto Op. 42. In these pieces, motives and themes are presented and developed, using the tonal forms and genres of Classical and Romantic music, but twelve-tone rows stand in for the keys. For a closer look at a movement from Schoenberg's Piano Suite Op. 25, see page 552 and the discussion in NAWM 142.

Return to form

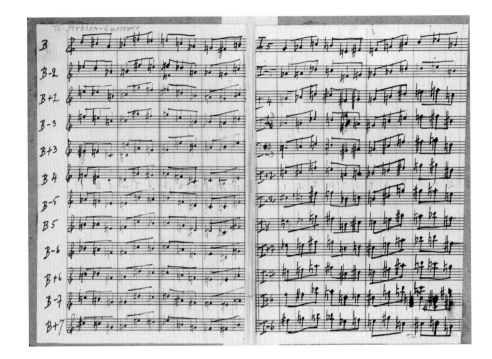

*Figure 21.11. Schoenberg's tone-row chart from his Fourth String Quartet (1937), illustrating the various transpositions and inversions of the work's basic series of tones. Arnold Schönberg Center, Vienna.*

Schoenberg as modernist

We have discussed Schoenberg's music at some length not only because of its complexity and its enormous influence on others, but also because the problems he chose to address as a modern composer and the way he faced them did much to shape the course of musical practice in the twentieth century. His desire to match the achievements of his forebears pressed him both backward—to reclaim the genres, forms, procedures, and gestures of the past—and forward toward a new musical language.

The Second Viennese school

Schoenberg attracted many devoted students. The two most notable, Alban Berg and Anton von Webern, were both natives of Vienna and are often grouped with Schoenberg as members of the second Viennese school, drawing an implicit connection to the first Viennese threesome, Haydn, Mozart, and Beethoven.

## Alban Berg

Alban Berg (1885–1935), shown in Figure 21.13, below, began studies with Schoenberg in 1904 at age nineteen. Although he adopted his teacher's atonal and twelve-tone methods, listeners found his music more approachable. He achieved much greater popular success than his teacher, especially with his opera *Wozzeck*, which premiered in 1925. His secret lay in infusing his posttonal idiom not only with the forms and procedures of tonal music, as Schoenberg had done, but also with its expressive gestures, characteristic styles, and other elements that quickly conveyed meanings and feelings to his hearers. In this respect he was a direct heir of Mahler and Strauss.

Wozzeck

*Wozzeck* is the outstanding example of expressionist opera. The libretto, arranged by Berg from a fragmentary play by Georg Büchner (1813–1837), presents the soldier Wozzeck as a hapless victim of his environment, despised by his fellow men, forced by poverty to submit to a doctor's experiments, betrayed in love, and driven finally to murder and suicide (see Figure 21.12). The music is atonal, not twelve-tone, and includes *Sprechstimme* in some scenes. Each of the three acts has continuous music, with the changing scenes (five in each act) linked by orchestral interludes.

*Figure 21.12. Scene from Alban Berg's* Wozzeck, *showing the Captain and Wozzeck in one of their bizarre interactions.*

Berg highlights the drama and organizes the music through the use of leitmotives, pitch-class sets identified with the main characters, and traditional forms that wryly comment on the characters and situation. The first act includes a Baroque suite, suggesting the formality of Wozzeck's captain; a rhapsody, suiting Wozzeck's fantastic visions; a march and lullaby for a scene with his mistress, Marie, and their child; a passacaglia for the doctor's constant prattling about his theory; and a rondo for Marie's seduction by a rival suitor, who tries repeatedly until she gives in. The second act, the heart of the drama, is a symphony in five movements, including a sonata form, a fantasia and fugue, a ternary slow movement, a scherzo, and a rondo. The third act presents six inventions, reflecting Wozzeck's growing obsession: on a theme (seven variations and a fugue); on a note (B); on a rhythm; on a chord; on a key; and on a duration (the eighth note).

The invention on a rhythm in Act III, Scene 3 (NAWM 143), illustrates Berg's approach. Just after murdering Marie, Wozzeck sits in a tavern drinking and singing, then dances briefly with Marie's friend Margret; she sits on his lap and sings a song, but when she spies blood on his hand, Wozzeck becomes agitated and rushes out. The scene begins with an onstage, out-of-tune tavern piano that is playing a wild polka, shown in Example 21.4. The music is atonal—the notes in the first two measures comprise the set associated with Wozzeck—but it instantly conveys the impression of a popular dance tune, through triadic accompaniment under a melody that moves by step and by skip. Just as the singers on stage are acting their parts, so, too, the atonal music is acting the part of tonal music, and its meaning is immediately clear. The melody lays out the rhythmic theme for the scene, which is then obsessively reiterated at various levels of augmentation and diminution, so that it is almost always present. By constantly repeating the rhythm, Berg unifies the scene through developing variation and also reveals Wozzeck's preoccupation with his guilt, which he cannot escape. When Wozzeck sings a folk song and Margret a popular song with piano accompaniment, Berg imitates recognizable tonal styles in an atonal idiom. The almost constant references to tonality and to familiar styles and genres help to keep listeners engaged, while the atonality heightens the dramatic impact.

CD 11/12    CD 6/12

Example 21.4: Berg, Wozzeck, Act III, Scene 3, tavern piano with rhythmic pattern and Wozzeck's set

**Twelve-tone works**

Soon after *Wozzeck* was premiered, Berg adopted twelve-tone methods, turning them to his own ends. He often chose rows that allowed for tonal-sounding chords and chord progressions, connecting the new style with the past and investing his music with immediate emotional impact. His chief twelve-tone works are his *Lyric Suite* for string quartet (1925–1926), his Violin Concerto (1935), and a second opera, *Lulu* (1928–1935), whose orchestration was not quite complete when he died.

## TIMELINE The European Mainstream in the Early Twentieth Century

| MUSICAL EVENTS | HISTORICAL EVENTS |
|---|---|
| | **1872** Monet, *Impression: Soleil levant* |
| Debussy, *Nocturnes* **1897–1899** | |
| Rachmaninov, Piano Concerto No. 2 in C Minor **1900–1901** | **1900** Freud, *The Interpretation of Dreams* |
| Ravel, *Jeux d'eau* **1901** | |
| | **1903** Wright brothers fly first successful airplane |
| Premiere of Strauss's opera *Salome* **1905** | **1905** Einstein's first paper on the theory of relativity |
| | **1906** Cézanne, *Mont Sainte-Victoire* |
| | **1907** Braque and Picasso paint first cubist pictures |
| Schoenberg writes first atonal pieces **1908** | **1908** Ford designs the Model T automobile |
| Vaughan Williams, *Fantasia on a Theme of Thomas Tallis* **1910** | |
| Sibelius, Fourth Symphony **1910–1911** | |
| Schoenberg, *Pierrot lunaire* **1912** | |
| Scriabin, *Vers la flamme* **1914** | **1914–1918** World War I |
| Falla, *El amor brujo* **1915** | |
| First Prague performance of Janáček's opera *Jenůfa* **1916** | **1916** Einstein proposes general theory of relativity |
| Berg, *Wozzeck* **1917–1921** | **1917** Russian Revolution brings Bolsheviks to power |
| Schoenberg writes first twelve-tone work, **1921–1923** Piano Suite Op. 25 | |
| Webern, Symphony Op. 21 **1927–1928** | |
| | **1929** New York stock market crash begins Great Depression |
| Schoenberg flees Germany, emigrates to **1933** the United States | **1933** Hitler comes to power in Germany |
| | **1938** Germany absorbs Austria |
| | **1939–1945** World War II |

Berg designed the row of the Violin Concerto with four interlocking minor and major triads, marked with square brackets in Example 21.5a, which permits frequent references to tonal chords while using twelve-tone procedures. The piece includes evocations of a violin tuning its open strings (using notes 1, 3, 5, and 7 of the row), tonal chord progressions, Viennese waltzes, a folk song, and a Bach chorale. The last of these, *Es ist genug!* (It is enough!) alludes to the death of the young woman to whose memory Berg dedicated the concerto. As shown in Example 21.5b, the chorale melody begins with three rising whole steps, like the last four notes of Berg's row, and Bach's harmonization contains chords that may be seen as sets from which Berg may have derived the row. Thus the quotation of the chorale is not something foreign, but stems directly from the row itself.

*Violin concerto*

*Example 21.5: Row from Berg's Violin Concerto and Bach's* Es ist genug!

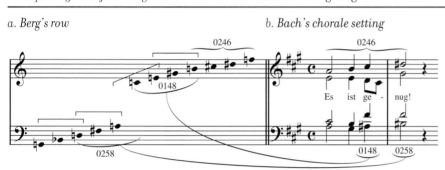

*a. Berg's row*    *b. Bach's chorale setting*

Berg's concerto can be understood on first hearing by anyone familiar with tonal music, yet its structure is wholly determined by twelve-tone procedures. Thus his music accommodates innovation with tradition, its inner structure transformed just as radically as in Schoenberg's music, but with more familiar sounds kept on the surface.

## Anton von Webern

Anton von Webern (1883–1945), shown in Figure 21.13, began lessons with Schoenberg in 1904, at the same time as Berg. He was already studying musicology under Guido Adler at the University of Vienna, where he received a Ph.D. in 1906 and absorbed ideas about music history that influenced his own (and perhaps also Schoenberg's) development.

Webern believed that music involves the presentation of ideas that can be expressed in no other way; that it operates according to rules of order based on natural law rather than taste; that great art does what is necessary, not arbitrary; that evolution in art is also necessary; and that history—and thus musical idioms and practices—can move only forward, not backward. After Schoenberg had formulated, and Webern and Berg had adopted, the twelve-tone method, Webern argued in a series of lectures published posthumously as *The Path to the New Music* that twelve-tone music was the inevitable result of music's evolution because it combined the most advanced approaches to pitch (using all twelve chromatic notes), musical space (integrating the melodic and harmonic dimensions), and the presentation of musical ideas (combining Classical forms with polyphonic procedures and unity with variety, deriving every element from the

*View of music history*

*Figure 21.13. Anton von Webern with Alban Berg in 1912.*

thematic material). With his view of history, Webern regarded each step along the way from tonality to atonality to twelve-tone music as an act of discovery, not invention. This gave him—and Schoenberg—total confidence in their own work, despite the incomprehension and opposition they encountered from performers and listeners. Webern's concept of the composer as an artist expressing new ideas, yet also as a researcher making new discoveries, sprang from his training in musicology; it became enormously influential in the mid- to late-twentieth century.

Webern's style     Webern, like Schoenberg and Berg, passed through the stages of late Romantic chromaticism, atonality, and twelve-tone organization, the last beginning in 1925 with the three songs of Op. 17. His works, about equally divided between instrumental and vocal, are mostly for small chamber ensembles.

Economy of means     Webern was at heart a Romantic who sought to write deeply expressive music. Yet because he believed great art should do only what is necessary, his music is extremely concentrated. When writing his Six Bagatelles for String Quartet Op. 9 (1911–1913), he remarked that once he had incorporated all twelve notes, he often felt that the piece was finished. Another atonal work, No. 4 of his Five Pieces for Orchestra Op. 10, runs to only six measures, and the last of his Three Little Pieces for Cello and Piano Op. 11, to just twenty notes. Even larger works, like the Symphony Op. 21 (1927–1928) and the String Quartet Op. 28 (1936–1938), are only eight or nine minutes long, and his entire mature output takes less than four hours to play. The dynamics are understated as well; specified down to the finest gradations, they seldom rise above *forte.* Perhaps influenced by his musicological studies—for his dissertation he edited a volume of sixteenth-century Mass movements by Heinrich Isaac—he often used techniques of Renaissance polyphony, including canons in inversion or retrograde. Unlike Berg, he avoided using sets or rows with tonal implications.

CD 11/15     The first movement of the Symphony Op. 21 (NAWM 144) illustrates Webern's use of twelve-tone procedures, canons, instrumentation, and form. The entire movement is a double canon in inversion. Example 21.6 shows the beginning, with canon 1 in the upper two staves and canon 2 on the bottom. Instead of separating the canonic lines by making each a continuous melody with a distinctive timbre and range, Webern deliberately integrates them. Each line is filled with rests, changes timbre frequently, and weaves back and forth through the same three-octave range. The succession of timbres is as much part of the melody as are the pitches and rhythms, a concept known as *Klangfarbenmelodie* ("tone-color melody"), in which changes of tone color are perceived as parallel to changing pitches in a melody.

*Klangfarbenmelodie*

*Example 21.6: Anton von Webern, Symphony Op. 21, double canon at the opening*

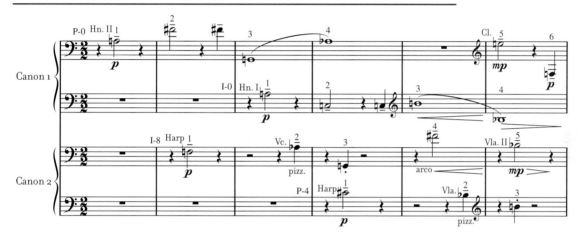

Although Webern received little acclaim during his lifetime and has never gained wide popularity, recognition of his work among scholars and composers grew steadily in the years after World War II. His music had an abiding influence on some composers in Italy, Germany, France, and the United States, especially in the first two decades after the war.

Influence

# POSTLUDE

The music of the early twentieth century was remarkably diverse, making it difficult to classify. Some music historians have treated Debussy as a late Romantic figure; others regard him as a seminal force in modern music. Similarly, composers like Mahler and Strauss have been grouped with the late Romantics, as in Chapter 20 of this text, while other writers have positioned them among the moderns. In truth, all the composers of this generation have aspects of both eras, combining nineteenth-century elements with twentieth-century sensibilities. Perhaps that is why much of their music—especially that of Mahler, Strauss, Debussy, Ravel, Sibelius, and Rachmaninov—has proven extremely popular with listeners. By contrast, Schoenberg's music won him both a central place in the modernist tradition as well as an enduring unpopularity with most listeners and a great many performers, who valued the familiar musical language and conventions that he felt compelled to abandon. The disconnection between audiences and connoisseurs in their evaluation of music, evident already in the reception of Beethoven's late quartets, reached a new intensity with Schoenberg and many other modernists, and became a principal theme of twentieth-century music.

However, tastes change over time, and critical disputes about what is most valuable in music have altered the reputations of certain composers dramatically, sometimes more than once. For example, when critics and scholars increasingly came to view tonality as old-fashioned, appreciation of Strauss and Sibelius declined, only to be revived later in the century when their innovations became better understood and when increasing numbers of living composers reclaimed the sounds and methods of tonal music. Nevertheless, although some music by composers surveyed in this chapter may sound late Romantic in spirit or technique, what makes all of it modern is the composer's overwhelming sense of measuring oneself against the past.

# 22

# Music, Politics, and the People in the European Twentieth Century

## PRELUDE

*Chapter Contents*

*Prelude*  561

The Avant-Garde  562

France  564

Igor Stravinsky  566

Béla Bartók  577

Germany  583

The Soviet Union  587

*Postlude*  592

**M**usic has been linked to politics since the days of Plato and Aristotle, who wrote about its place in the ideal society (see Chapter 1). But in the nineteenth century, some writers claimed that classical music was an autonomous art that transcended politics and should be composed, performed, experienced, and admired for its own sake, separate from political or social concerns. The new "science" of musicology that emerged during the nineteenth century reinforced this view, focusing more on the styles and procedures of past music than on its social functions. To some extent, treating music on its own terms was an admirable ideal, allowing many listeners to enjoy music for its own sake and as a respite from the concerns of the day. But in other respects, from its cultivation by the economic and social elite to its association with nationalism, classical music never fully escaped politics.

The modern era brought new links between music and politics. Economic troubles and political conflicts led many composers to believe that art which set itself apart from social needs was in danger of becoming irrelevant to society at large. As the gap widened between the unfamiliar sounds of modernist music and the ability of listeners to understand it, composers tried to bring contemporary music closer to the general public by crafting widely accessible concert works or by writing music for films, theater, and dance. Convinced that music performed by amateurs and school groups was as important as art music, some composers wrote works that were within the capabilities of amateurs and rewarding to perform yet modern in style. Others used music, especially musical theater, to engage current social, political, and economic issues. Nationalism continued as a strong force in most countries, exemplified in the musical styles of individual composers and in efforts to edit, publish, and perform music of the nation, including both folk music and the written music of earlier times.

Most governments sponsored musical activities directly, and public schools increasingly included music in the curriculum. Throughout most of Europe, radio was controlled by the government and was a major employer of composers and performers. Totalitarian governments insisted that music under their regimes support the state and its ideologies. Although musical styles were often identified with particular ideologies, these links were contingent on the unique political situation in each nation; the same style, even the same piece, could be seen as progressive or socialist in one place and conservative or fascistic in another.

While modern composers were devising ways to say something new within the classical tradition, the years before World War I also brought the first stirrings of a movement that directly challenged that tradition and would grow in importance over the course of the century: the avant-garde. Originally a French military term, it described an advance group that prepared the way for the main army. The term was then adopted as early as the mid-nineteenth century for and by French artists who saw themselves as a vanguard exploring new territory. In music, the term gained currency around the time of the First World War.

This chapter will begin by surveying some avant-garde composers and then move to a discussion of how several important modern composers in Europe dealt with various political movements, the disruptions caused by two world wars, and the ideological forces for change in twentieth-century music.

# The Avant-Garde

Although the term *avant-garde* is sometimes applied to anyone who departs from convention or to modernists such as Schoenberg, it is most helpful when used more narrowly for art that is iconoclastic, irreverent, antagonistic, and nihilistic—for art that seeks to overthrow accepted aesthetics and start afresh. Rather than attempt to write music suited for the classical repertoire, avant-garde composers have challenged the very concept of deathless classics, asking their listeners to focus instead on what is happening in the present. Their movement is marked not by shared elements of style but by shared attitudes, particularly an unrelenting opposition to the status quo.

## Erik Satie

One aspect of the avant-garde is exemplified by the music of the French composer Erik Satie (1866–1925), which wittily upends conventional ideas. His three *Gymnopédies* (1888) for piano, for example, challenged the Romantic notions of expressivity and individuality. Instead of offering variety, as expected in a set of pieces, they are all ostentatiously plain and unemotional, using the same slow tempo, the same accompanimental pattern, virtually the same melodic rhythm, and similar modal harmonies and puzzling dynamics. Satie's use of modal and unresolved chords opened new possibilities for Debussy and Ravel, who turned them to different uses but did not follow his avant-garde tendencies.

Between 1900 and 1915, Satie wrote several sets of piano pieces with surrealistic titles like *Three Pieces in the Form of a Pear* (1903, which actually has seven pieces) and *Automatic Descriptions* (1913). Most had running commentary and tongue-in-cheek directions to the player, such as "withdraw your hand and put it in your pocket," "that's wonderful!" or "heavy as a sow." These phrases satirized the titles and directions of Debussy and other composers of descriptive and programmatic music (see Figure 22.1). Moreover, by printing the commentary on the music rather than in a program so that only the player was aware of it, Satie critiqued the idea of concert music and reclaimed the fading tradi-

*Figure 22.1. Costume for a ballet on Erik Satie's* Trois morceaux en forme du poire *(Three Pieces in the Form of a Pear, 1890–1903), actually seven pieces for piano for four hands. Archives de la Fondation Erik Satie, Paris.*

tion of music for the player's own enjoyment. But the comic and critical spirit resides also in the music itself, which is spare, dry, capricious, brief, repetitive, parodistic, and witty in the highest degree. The classical masterworks are a particular target: the three *Dessicated Embryos* (1913) poke fun at the musical language of Beethoven, Schubert, and Chopin, among others. Clearly, Satie was not out to create masterpieces that would take their place in the great tradition; rather, he was challenging the very bases of that tradition.

In his larger pieces, Satie sought to create music that would fix our attention on the present. His "realistic ballet" *Parade* (1916–1917), featuring a scenario by the writer Jean Cocteau, choreography by Léonide Massine, and scenery and costumes by Picasso, introduced cubism (see page 528) to the stage, as illustrated in Figure 22.2. In the cubist spirit of including fragments of everyday life, Satie's score incorporated jazz elements, a whistle, a siren, and a typewriter. It caused a scandal, as did his later ballet with film, *Relâche* (No Show Tonight, 1924). His biting, antisentimental spirit, economical textures, and severe harmony and melody influenced the music of his younger compatriots Milhaud and Poulenc, among others, and he was a significant inspiration for the American avant-garde, notably Virgil Thomson and John Cage.

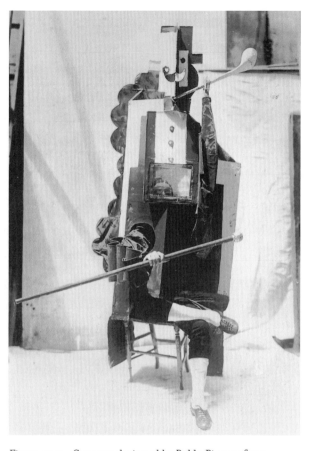

*Figure 22.2. Costume designed by Pablo Picasso for a character in the first production of Satie's ballet* Parade *(1917). Picasso's designs for the sets and costumes of this ballet brought his cubist style to the stage. Bibliothèque Nationale, Paris.*

## Futurism

Although Satie questioned traditional assumptions about expressivity, individuality, seriousness, masterworks, and the very purpose of music, he used traditional instruments and musical pitches. Italians calling themselves *futurists* rejected even those. In *The Art of Noises: Futurist Manifesto* (1913; see vignette, page 564), the futurist painter Luigi Russolo earnestly argued that musical sounds had become stale and that the modern world of machines required a new kind of music based on noise. He and his colleagues built new instruments called *intonarumori* (noisemakers), each capable of producing a particular kind of noise over a range of at least an octave and a half. The composers wrote pieces for these instruments, alone or with traditional instruments, and presented them in concert between 1913 and 1921 in Italy, London, and Paris.

In opposition to the constant recycling of classics in the concert halls, futurist music was impermanent, perhaps deliberately so; only one fragment of Russolo's music survives, and the instruments were destroyed during World War II. But the movement continued in various forms in Italy, France, and Russia during the 1920s and 1930s, and it anticipated or stimulated many later developments, including electronic music, microtonal composition, and the pursuit of new instrumental timbres. As different as futurist music was from Satie's, both focused on the experience of listening in the present moment and on an iconoclastic rejection of the music and aesthetics of the past, attributes that remained central to avant-garde music throughout the twentieth century.

# France

Notions of classicism

During and after World War I, nationalists asserted that French music was intrinsically classical, as opposed to the Romanticism of the Germans. Thus Neoclassicism—the use of classical genres and forms, tonal centers, and common-practice or neotonal harmonies, allied with emotional restraint and a rejection of Romantic excess (see below, pages 565 and 573)—became the prevailing trend in France after the war, one associated with patriotism. But exactly how to define *classicism* was a point of contention. Conservatives identified it with balance, order, discipline, and tradition, in contrast to the irrationality and individualism of Romanticism. More progressive composers, like Ravel (see Chapter 21), saw the classic as encompassing the universal and not merely the national. His music included elements from Viennese waltzes

---

**VIGNETTE** The Art of Noises

*Futurism began in 1909 as a literary and artistic movement in Italy celebrating the dynamism, speed, machines, and violence of the twentieth century. Luigi Russolo (1885–1947) was a futurist painter who turned his attention to music in 1913. In* The Art of Noises: A Futurist Manifesto, *Russolo laid out his argument for music based on noise rather than musical pitches.*

The art of music at first sought and achieved purity and sweetness of sound; later, it blended diverse sounds, but always with intent to caress the ear with suave harmonics. Today, growing ever more complicated, it seeks those combinations of sounds that fall most dissonantly, strangely, and harshly upon the ear. We thus approach nearer and nearer to the *music of noise.*

This musical evolution parallels the growing multiplicity of machines, which everywhere are assisting mankind. Not only amid the clamor of great cities but even in the countryside, which until yesterday was ordinarily quiet, the machine today has created so many varieties and combinations of noise that pure musical sound—with its poverty and monotony—no longer awakens any emotion in the hearer. . . .

We must break out of this narrow circle of pure musical sounds, and conquer the infinite variety of noise-sounds.

Everyone will recognize that every musical sound carries with it an incrustation of familiar and stale sense associations, which predispose the hearer to boredom, despite all the efforts of innovating musicians. We futurists have all deeply loved the music of the great composers. Beethoven and Wagner for many years wrung our hearts. But now we are satiated with them and derive much greater pleasure from ideally combining the noises of street-cars, internal-combustion engines, automobiles, and busy crowds than from rehearing, for example, the "Eroica" or the "Pastorale." . . .

Every manifestation of life is accompanied by noise. Noise is therefore familiar to our ears and has the power to remind us immediately of life itself. Musical sound, a thing extraneous to life and independent of it, an occasional and unnecessary adjunct, has become for our ears what a too familiar face is to our eyes. Noise, on the other hand, which comes to us confused and irregular as life itself, never reveals itself wholly but reserves for us innumerable surprises. We are convinced, therefore, that by selecting, co-ordinating, and controlling noises we shall enrich mankind with a new and unsuspected source of pleasure. Despite the fact that it is characteristic of sound to remind us brutally of life, the Art of Noises must not limit itself to reproductive imitation. It will reach its greatest emotional power through the purely acoustic enjoyment which the inspiration of the artist will contrive to evoke from combinations of noises.

From Luigi Russolo, *The Art of Noises: A Futurist Manifesto,* translated by Stephen Somervell, in Nicolas Slonimsky, *Music since 1900,* 4th ed. (New York: Scribner, 1971), pp. 1299–1301; repr. in Oliver Strunk, ed., *Source Readings in Music History,* rev. ed. by Leo Treitler (New York: Norton, 1998), pp. 1330–1332.

(*La Valse*), Spain (*Bolero*), Gypsy style (*Tzigane*), blues (Violin Sonata), and jazz (Concerto for the Left Hand), all rejected by the conservative nationalists.

## Les Six

A younger group of composers absorbed the strong influence of Neoclassicism but sought to escape the old political dichotomies. Arthur Honegger (1892–1955), Darius Milhaud (1892–1974), Francis Poulenc (1899–1963), Germaine Tailleferre (1892–1983), Georges Auric (1899–1983), and Louis Durey (1888–1979) were dubbed "Les Six" (The Six), in a parallel to the Mighty Five in Russia (see Chapter 20), by a French journalist who saw them as seeking to free French music from foreign domination. They drew inspiration from Satie and were hailed by writer Jean Cocteau, who called for new music that would be fully French and anti-Romantic in its clarity, accessibility, and emotional restraint.

The group, pictured in Figure 22.3, collaborated in joint concerts and other projects but did not remain together long. Instead of conforming to Cocteau's program, they each wrote highly individual works that drew on a wide range of influences, including but not limited to Neoclassicism. Tailleferre was the most in tune with Neoclassical ideals, drawing on Couperin and Rameau (see Chapter 13) in her Piano Concerto (1923–1924) and other works. Auric was the most taken with Satie's avant-garde approach. But the most individual were Honegger, Milhaud, and Poulenc, who achieved success independent of the group and found ways to make their music distinctive within the broad outlines of Neoclassicism.

Arthur Honegger excelled in music of dynamic action and graphic gesture, expressed in short-breathed melodies, strong ostinato rhythms, bold colors, and dissonant harmonies. His symphonic movement *Pacific 231* (1923), a translation into music of the visual and physical impression of a speeding locomotive, was hailed as a sensational piece of modernist descriptive music. Honegger won an international reputation in 1923 with his oratorio *King David*, which combined the tradition of music for amateur chorus with allusions to styles from Gregorian chant to Baroque polyphony to jazz. The evocations of pre-Romantic styles, use of traditional forms and procedures, and prevailing diatonic language all reveal the impact of neoclassicism.

Darius Milhaud produced an immense quantity of music, including piano pieces, chamber music (notably, eighteen string quartets), suites, sonatas, symphonies, film music, ballets, songs, cantatas, operas, and music for children. His works are diverse in style and approach, ranging from the comic frivolity of the ballet *Le Boeuf sur le toit* (The Ox on the Roof, 1919) to the earnestness of the opera-oratorio *Christophe Colomb* (1928) and the religious devotion of the *Sacred Service* (1947), which reflects Milhaud's Jewish heritage. He was especially open to sounds and styles from the Americas. Saxophones, ragtime syncopations, and the blues (see Chapter 23) find their way into his ballet *La Création du monde* (The Creation of the World, 1923). Brazilian folk melodies and rhythms appear in *Le Boeuf sur le toit* and in the orchestral dances *Saudades do Brasil* (Souvenirs

Darius Milhaud

*Figure 22.3. Jacques-Émile Blanche,* Les Six (Hommage à Satie) *(The Group of Six [Homage to Satie]) (1922–1923). This group portrait, from about 1921, shows five of the six composers and three of their collaborators. Clockwise from the bottom left are Germaine Tailleferre, Darius Milhaud, Arthur Honegger, conductor Jean Wiener, pianist Marcelle Mayer, Francis Poulenc, writer Jean Cocteau, and Georges Auric. Musée des Beaux-Arts, Rouen.*

of Brazil, 1920–1921). In addition to the syncopated rhythms and diatonic melodies of Brazilian dance, the latter uses polytonality, in which two lines of melody and planes of harmony, each in a distinct and different key, sound simultaneously, illustrated in Example 22.1. This procedure would become associated with Milhaud, although many used it before and since. In all his music, Milhaud blended ingenuity, freshness, and variety with the clarity and logical form he had absorbed from Neoclassicism. Yet his openness to foreign influences, from jazz to Schoenberg, was a far cry from the program of nationalist classical purity initially adopted by Les Six.

*Example 22.1: Darius Milhaud*, Saudados do Brasil, *I, No. 4*, Copacabaña

**Francis Poulenc**    Francis Poulenc drew especially on the Parisian popular chanson tradition sustained in cabarets and revues. This too, violated the strictures of Neoclassicism, which rejected influence from "lower" forms of music. Poulenc's compositions revel in an ingratiating harmonic idiom, draw grace and wit from popular styles, and combine sharp satire with pleasing melody, as in his surrealist comic opera *Les Mamelles de Tirésias* (The Breasts of Tiresias, 1940). The *Concert champêtre* (Pastoral Concerto) for harpsichord or piano and small orchestra (1928) evokes the spirit of Rameau and Domenico Scarlatti, and his sonatas and chamber works for various groups of instruments bring an expressive, song-influenced melodic idiom and fresh, mildly dissonant harmonies into classical genres and forms. Among his other compositions are a Mass in G for a cappella chorus (1937), several motets, other choral works, and numerous songs. His three-act opera *Dialogues of the Carmelites* (1956) is an affecting meditation on the execution of Carmelite nuns during the French Revolution, raising issues of religion, politics, allegiance, and personal choice that had deep resonances in French political life.

# Igor Stravinsky

The composer whose music caused the greatest stir in France was not French at all, but rather the Russian émigré Igor Stravinsky (1882–1971; see biography). Stravinsky began his musical career as a Russian nationalist and then became a cosmopolitan—and arguably the most important composer of his time. He created an individual voice by developing several style traits, most derived from Russian traditions, into his distinctive trademarks: undermining meter through unpredictable accents and rests or through rapid changes of meter; frequent ostinatos; layering and juxtaposition of static blocks of sound; discontinuity and interruption; dissonance based on diatonic, octatonic, and other collections of notes; and dry, antilyrical, but colorful use of instruments. He forged these traits during his "Russian" period (to about 1918) and used them again in his later works. Through Stravinsky, elements of Russian music became part of a common international modernist practice.

# Igor Stravinsky (1882–1971)

Like Picasso in the field of art, Stravinsky was the very icon of the twentieth-century composer, with his multiple stylistic transformations reflecting in some ways the cataclysmic upheavals of two world wars. Like Picasso, too, he was active in the foreground of every major stylistic trend of the century, spearheading some but participating in all.

Stravinsky was born in Orianienbaum, near Saint Petersburg in Russia, to a well-to-do musical family. He began piano lessons at age nine and studied music theory in his later teens but never attended the Conservatory. His most important teacher was Rimsky-Korsakov, with whom he studied composition and orchestration privately. Stravinsky's marriage in 1906 to his cousin Catherine Nosenko resulted in four children.

Stravinsky demonstrated his command of his teacher's rich, colorful style in *Scherzo fantastique* and *Fireworks*. After hearing these two pieces in 1909, the impresario Sergei Diaghilev commissioned Stravinsky to compose for the Ballets Russes (Russian Ballet), which reigned in Paris from 1909 to 1929. For Diaghilev, Stravinsky wrote the ballets that made him famous and that are still his most popular works: *The Firebird*, *Petrushka*, and *The Rite of Spring*. He collaborated on them with choreographers Mikhail Fokine, founder of the modern ballet style, and Vaslav Nijinsky, one of the greatest dancers of the early twentieth century.

Stravinsky moved to Paris in 1911, spent the war years in Switzerland, and, having realized that the Bolshevik Revolution meant permanent exile from Russia, returned and settled in France in 1920. By then, he had already begun to compose in the Neoclassical idiom that would characterize his music for the next three decades. The commotion at the *Rite of Spring* premiere had bestowed on him a delicious notoriety; and because he performed tirelessly, first as a pianist and then as a conductor, Stravinsky was well known in 1920s Europe and America. He continued to work with the Ballets Russes, where one of his favorite collaborators was the choreographer George Balanchine.

Catherine died in March 1939, after which he moved to the United States, arriving within weeks of the outbreak of World War II. In March 1940, he married Vera Sudeikin, with whom he had been having an affair since the early 1920s. He settled in Hollywood, not far from Schoenberg and Rachmaninov, and wrote several pieces that referred to American styles, such as the *Ebony Concerto* for the jazz clarinetist Woody Herman and his band. His last major Neoclassical work was the opera *The Rake's Progress*, which premiered in Venice in 1951.

In 1948, Stravinsky met Robert Craft, who, as Stravinsky's assistant, imparted his enthusiasm for the twelve-tone music of Schoenberg and Webern. By the mid-1950s, Stravinsky had absorbed twelve-tone methods into his own idiom. Most of his late works are serial, and many are religious, from *Canticum sacrum* in 1955 through the *Requiem Canticles* in 1965–1966. Stravinsky and his wife moved to New York in 1969, where he died two years later. At his widow's suggestion, he was buried in Venice, not far from Diaghilev's grave.

**Major works:** *The Firebird, Petrushka, The Rite of Spring, L'Histoire du soldat, Symphonies of Wind Instruments, Les Noces*, Octet for wind instruments, *Oedipus rex, Symphony of Psalms*, Symphony in C, Symphony in Three Movements, *The Rake's Progress, Agon, Requiem Canticles.*

*Figure 22.4. Photograph of Igor Stravinsky in Paris in May 1913, the month of the premiere of* The Rite of Spring.

## Russian Period

*The Firebird*

Stravinsky wrote his most popular works early in his career: the ballets *The Fire-bird* (1910), *Petrushka* (1910–1911), and *The Rite of Spring* (*Le Sacre du printemps*, 1911–1913), all commissioned by Russian choreographer and impresario Sergei Diaghilev for the Ballets Russes in Paris. *The Firebird*, based on Russian folk-tales, stems from the Russian nationalist tradition and especially from the exoticism of Rimsky-Korsakov. Throughout, humans are characterized by dia-tonic music, while supernatural creatures and places are cast in octatonic or chromatic realms, following Rimsky's standard practice.

*Petrushka*

In *Petrushka*, Stravinsky introduced several of the stylistic traits that became closely identified with him. The opening scene of the ballet depicts a fair in Saint Petersburg during the final week of carnival season. Here, we find Stravinsky's characteristic blocks of static harmony with repetitive melodic and rhythmic patterns as well as abrupt shifts from one block to another. Each group of dancers receives its distinctive music: a band of tipsy revelers, an organ grinder with a dancer, a music-box player with another dancer, the puppet the-ater where Petrushka stars. Seemingly unconnected musical events interrupt each other without transition and then just as suddenly reappear, creating a kaleidoscope of diverse textures that has been compared to the cubism of Pablo Picasso (see page 528 and Figures 22.2 and VI.4). The juxtaposition of contrast-ing blocks, which Stravinsky absorbed from the Russian practice of Musorgsky and Rimsky-Korsakov, is here linked to the discrete visual tableaux of ballet.

Stravinsky enhanced the Russian elements and popular carnival atmosphere throughout the ballet by borrowing and elaborating several Russian folk tunes, a popular French song, and Viennese waltzes. Rather than integrating these bor-rowings, Stravinsky preserved their contexts, heightening the differences be-tween their styles to make each block of sound as distinctive as possible. The passage in Example 22.2, which accompanies the drunken merrymakers, is based on a folk song from Rimsky-Korsakov's 1877 collection of traditional songs. But Stravinsky avoids the dominant-tonic harmony of Rimsky's version; instead, he places the melody in the bass and simulates folk harmony, in which voices sing in parallel fifths and octaves, often against drones. In contrast to the diatonic folk songs, Stravinsky uses music based on octatonic scales for the su-pernatural elements, but the harmony is now more biting than in *The Firebird*.

*Example 22.2: Igor Stravinsky,* Petrushka, *passage based on Russian folk song*

*Example 22.3: "Petrushka" chord, with octatonic scale from which it derives*

*Figure 22.5a (left).* *"Painted maiden" costume designed by Nicholas Roerich for the original production of Stravinsky's ballet,* The Rite of Spring, *1913. Compare Stravinsky's description of the adolescent girls as "knock-kneed and long-braided Lolitas" (see vignette, page 571, and "A Closer Look," page 572). Ballets Russes, Paris.*

*Figure 22.5b (right).* *Photograph of the actual costume, re-created for a 2003 production of* The Rite of Spring *at the Royal Opera House in Covent Garden and worn by an artist of the Kirov Ballet Company.*

The puppet Petrushka, who has been brought to life by a magician, is characterized in the famous "Petrushka chord" that combines F♯-major and C-major triads, both part of the same octatonic scale, as shown in Example 22.3.

Stravinsky's distinctive style crystallized in *The Rite of Spring*. The subject was still Russian, but now it was an imagined fertility ritual set in prehistoric Russia, during which an adolescent girl is chosen for sacrifice and must dance herself to death. Stravinsky again borrowed folk melodies, while the scenario, choreography, and music are marked by primitivism—a deliberate representation of the elemental, crude, and uncultured—and cast aside the sophistication and stylishness of modern life and trained artistry. Figure 22.5 illustrates (a) a costume from the original production and (b) its modern re-creation. The audience at the premiere was utterly shocked, and some showed their disapproval by provoking a notorious riot (see vignette, page 571 and "Stravinsky's Notorious Ballet," page 572). Later, the piece became one of the most frequently performed and universally appreciated compositions of its time.

The characteristics of Stravinsky's mature idiom can be heard in the first scene, *Danse des adolescentes* (Dance of the Adolescent Girls, NAWM 145a), whose opening measures are shown in Example 22.4. Despite the regular barring, each pulse in the first two measures is played with the same strength, negating the hierarchy

*The Rite of Spring*

CD 11/19 | CD 6/15

of strong and weak beats that is essential to meter. Then, accented chords, doubled by eight horns, create an unpredictable pattern of stresses that destroys any feeling of metrical regularity. Yet, while the listener is utterly disoriented metrically and rhythmically, the music is cleverly conceived for ballet; the passage makes an eight-measure period, and the dancers can count four-measure phrases. This reduction of meter to mere pulsation was the element that most strongly conveyed a sense of primitivism in the music and the results were electrifying. In the final dance of the ballet, the *Danse sacrale* (Sacrificial Dance, NAWM 145b), Stravinsky adopted two additional strategies that reduce meter to pulse: rapidly changing meters and unpredictable alternation of notes with rests.

CD 11/23

**Ostinatos and juxtaposed blocks**

The entire passage in Example 22.4 is built from ostinatos, including pounded or arpeggiated chords and the melodic ostinato in the English horn. Stravinsky uses these repeating figures to create static blocks of sound, which he places next to one another without transition. Here, one block is replaced by another, then returns. Within each block—and indeed, throughout the piece—there is no development of motives or themes as traditionally understood, but rather repetition and unpredictable variation.

**Layering**

Often Stravinsky builds up textures by layering two or more independent strands of music on top of one another. The material at measure 9 is composed

*Example 22.4: Igor Stravinsky,* The Rite of Spring, *opening of* Danse des adolescentes

*The first performance of Igor Stravinsky's* The Rite of Spring *on May 29, 1913, was greeted by a riot. As he told the story almost half a century later, he was as shocked by the audience's reaction as some listeners were by the spectacle. Apparently, it was the choreography, more than the music, that provoked the audience, and ever since the piece has usually been performed in concert rather than as a ballet.*

That the first performance of *Le Sacre du printemps* was attended by a scandal must be known to everybody. Strange as it may seem, however, I was unprepared for the explosion myself. The reactions of the musicians who came to the orchestra rehearsals were without intimation of it and the stage spectacle did not appear likely to precipitate a riot. . . .

Mild protests against the music could be heard from the very beginning of the performance. Then, when the curtain opened on the group of knock-kneed and long-braided Lolitas jumping up and down [*Danses des adolescentes*], the storm broke. Cries of "Ta gueule" ["Shut up!"] came from behind me. I heard Florent Schmitt shout "Taisez-vous garces du seizième" ["Be quiet, you bitches of the sixteenth"]; the "garces" of the sixteenth arrondissement [the most fashionable residential district of Paris] were, of course, the most elegant ladies in Paris. The uproar continued, however, and a few minutes later I left the hall in a rage; I was sitting on the right near the orchestra, and I remember slamming the door. I have never again been that angry. The music was so familiar to me; I loved it, and I could not understand why people who had not yet heard it wanted to protest in advance. I arrived in a fury backstage, where I saw Diaghilev flicking the house lights in a last effort to quiet the hall. For the rest of the performance I stood in the wings behind Nijinsky holding the tails of his *frac*, while he stood on a chair shouting numbers to the dancers, like a coxswain.

From Igor Stravinsky and Robert Craft, *Expositions and Developments* (Garden City, N.Y.: Doubleday, 1962), pp. 159–164.

of three layers distinguished by timbre (English horn, bassoons, and pizzicato cellos) and motivic figuration, with the top line also set off by register and pitch collection because the notes of the English horn are the only ones heard in the treble and their pitches are unique to that layer.

In typical Stravinsky fashion, the patterns within successive blocks contrast markedly with each other, creating discontinuity. Yet the collection of pitches being used in each differs by only one note (C), lending a strong sense of continuity. Stravinsky offsets the obvious surface discontinuities of his music with more subtle connections.

Most dissonance in Stravinsky's music is based on the scales used in Russian classical music, such as the diatonic and octatonic collections. Here the dissonant chords in measures 1–8 combine an F♭-major triad in the lower strings with a first-inversion dominant-seventh chord on E♭ in the upper strings to produce a sonority that has all seven notes of the A♭ harmonic-minor scale.

Stravinsky often identified a musical idea with a particular timbre. Here, the pounding chords are always in the strings with horn reinforcements, and the English-horn ostinato recurs only in that instrument throughout the first half of the dance. In the second half, it migrates through several other instruments. In music without motivic development, such changes of timbre are one way to provide variety, a technique Stravinsky learned from Glinka and Rimsky-Korsakov. His preference for dry rather than lush or resonant timbres is reflected in his use of instruments. This sound is evident in the staccato string chords, which are all played with a down-bow to create even emphasis and natural separations; in the pizzicato cellos; and in the staccato English horn and

Discontinuity and connection

Dissonance

Timbre and orchestration

*Small-ensemble works*

bassoons. Having developed these techniques, Stravinsky continued to use them throughout his career.

During World War I, the wartime economy forced Stravinsky to turn away from the large orchestra of his early ballets toward small combinations of instruments to accompany stage works. For *L'Histoire du soldat* (The Soldier's Tale, 1918), he called for six solo instruments in pairs (violin and double bass, clarinet and bassoon, cornet and trombone) and one percussionist to play interludes in a spoken narration and dialogue. In the marches, tango, waltz, and ragtime movements of *L'Histoire*, and in *Ragtime* (1917–1918), shown in Figure 22.7, Stravinsky discovered ways to imitate familiar styles while using the devices that had become his trademarks. Stranded in western Europe by the war and then by the Bolshevik Revolution in his home country, he began to move away from Russian topics while retaining the distinctive traits that stemmed largely from his Russian training.

---

**A CLOSER LOOK**   Stravinsky's Notorious Ballet

A handsome Russian dancer and choreographer, Vaslav Nijinksy (1888–1950), in collaboration with Diaghilev and Stravinsky, burst colorfully upon the sedate, pastel world of classical ballet in Paris during the second decade of the twentieth century. In 1912, the year before the notorious premiere of Stravinsky's *Le Sacre du printemps* (The Rite of Spring), audiences had been scandalized by Nijinsky's first choreographed ballet, set to Debussy's symphonic poem *Prélude à "L'Après-midi d'un faune"* (see page 539 and Figure 21.2). In that work, Nijinsky himself danced the role of the faun, a mythological creature half man, half goat. The ballet was shockingly original in its sensuous atmosphere and sexually suggestive movements, portraying the faun's visions of ethereal nymphs.

The next year, encouraged by Diaghilev and intent on pursuing his own unique course, Nijinsky created the perfect counterpart on stage to Stravinsky's galvanizing score of *Le Sacre*. According to an account by one of the dancers, Nijinsky was bent on reproducing every note of the music in his choreography, thereby emphasizing the jarring impact of the orchestra's explosive rhythms and unpredictable harmonies. The effect was further enhanced by the set and costume designs of the Russian-born painter Nicholas Roerich, who transformed his ideas about the prehistory of his native land and its primitive cultures into bold colors and exotic forms (see Figure 22.6). The costumes were loose-fitting garments and headbands, hand-painted with geometric shapes that were repeated in the steps and angular movements of the dancers. Nijinsky's choreography was similarly bold and unorthodox, completely defying the audience's expectations and the graceful poses of classical ballet. As Stravinsky himself revealed in his graphic description of the first performance (see vignette and Figures 22.5a and b), not only did the dancers representing the "Lolitas" or tribal maidens wear long pigtails, but they also were intentionally awkward, moving in "knock-kneed" fashion with their toes turned in. At one point, according to an account by one of the dancers, they stalked across the stage in such exaggerated frontal poses that their silhouettes resembled a row of clumsy storks!

*Figure 22.6. Tableau with dancers. Painting by Nicholas Roerich of one of his set designs for the original production of Stravinsky's* The Rite of Spring. *State Russian Museum, Saint Petersburg.*

## Neoclassical Period

In 1919, Diaghilev asked Stravinsky to orchestrate pieces by the eighteenth-century composer Pergolesi (including music erroneously attributed to him) to accompany a new ballet, *Pulcinella*. Stravinsky applied his distinctive stylistic traits to the music, reworking a number of pieces so that they retained the original music faithfully yet sounded more like Stravinsky than Pergolesi. He later spoke of this experience as his "discovery of the past, the epiphany through which the whole of my late work became possible." In the same year of 1920, he completed the *Symphonies of Wind Instruments*, which applied the methods distilled in *The Rite of Spring* to an entirely abstract composition.

Thus was launched the Neoclassical stage of Stravinsky's career. Although the term *Neoclassicism* (first discussed in connection with Les Six on page 565) has many shades of meaning, it has come to represent a broad movement from the 1910s to the 1950s in which composers revived, imitated, or evoked the styles, genres, and forms of pre-Romantic music, especially that of the eighteenth century, then called Classical (*Baroque* as a term for seventeenth- and early eighteenth-century music became widely used only after 1940). Neoclassicism grew in part from a rejection of Romanticism, whose associations with intense emotions, irrationality, yearning, individualism, and nationalism were all suspect in the wake of the wanton destruction of World War I. Stravinsky was widely recognized as the leader of the Neoclassical movement. His Neoclassical period, from 1919 to 1951, marks a turn away from Russian folk music and toward earlier Western art music as a source for imitation, quotation, or allusion.

*Figure 22.7. Title page designed by Picasso for Stravinsky's piano arrangement of* Ragtime, *published by J. & W. Chester Ltd., London, 1919.*

This step was useful to Stravinsky because the fashion in the West for Russian nationalism was beginning to fade, in part because the political and cultural ties between France and Russia had dissolved after the Bolshevik Revolution. In technical terms, imitating and alluding to music in the classical tradition was hardly different from what he had been doing in making use of folk and popular materials; so Neoclassicism in effect gave him new subject matter without requiring him to retool completely. Neoclassicism also addressed the dilemma of establishing a place in the crowded classical repertoire. Stravinsky had already solved the problem of creating an individual style. He now used his distinctive idiom, forged in the Russian traditions, to establish fresh links to the Western classical tradition, just as Schoenberg used his modernist twelve-tone procedures to resurrect the forms and genres of the classical past. Yet even as Stravinsky became thoroughly cosmopolitan, he always remained something of an outsider in Western Europe, and instead of Schoenberg's agonized expressionism, we find in Stravinsky's music an emotional detachment. Thus his Neoclassical style adopts an anti-Romantic tone, reflecting a preference for balance, coolness, objectivity, and absolute (as opposed to program) music.

**Uses of Neoclassicism**

Stravinsky's Neoclassicism and its continuity with his earlier style are both evident in his *Symphony of Psalms* (1930) for mixed chorus and orchestra, based on psalms from the Latin Vulgate Bible. Stravinsky said he used Latin because the ritualistic language left him free to concentrate on its phonetic qualities, but its use also refers back to the long tradition of Latin texts in Western church music. Baroque features include almost perpetual motion, frequent ostinatos (also a Stravinsky trademark), and a fully developed fugue in the second movement.

*Symphony of Psalms*

The advent of recording technology had the most significant impact on musical culture of any innovation since the printing press. It completely revolutionized the way we experience and share music as listeners, performers, or composers. When Thomas Edison made the first sound recording in his laboratory in Menlo Park, New Jersey, in 1877, using his tinfoil cylinder phonograph shown in Figures 22.8 and 22.9, he intended his new device as a dictation machine for offices. He had no idea that his invention would catapult some musicians to fame and fortune, deliver their product to huge audiences, and spawn a multibillion-dollar industry.

Edison's phonograph recorded sound by a mechanical process. The sound waves were transmitted to a needle, which cut a groove into the cylinder as the latter was being turned by a hand crank. The impressions in the groove corresponded to the sound waves. To play back the record, the process was reversed: as the crank turned the cylinder, the shape of the groove made the needle move, which in turn transmitted the recorded sounds through the air.

Edison soon replaced his fragile tinfoil cylinders with wax cylinders, which could be mass-produced by a molding process. Adding a motor to the machine made it possible to maintain a steady speed of rotation, necessary for recording music. Members of John Philip Sousa's band and other artists made recordings that were sold commercially, but quantities were limited because each cylinder had to be recorded separately. In 1887, Emile Berliner developed a more practical system that recorded on a flat shellac disc, which could be used as a mold to make any number of duplicates. Record players like the one in Figure 22.10 became available in the 1890s, and 10-inch discs with a capacity for four minutes of music were sold for a dollar each, the equivalent of about twenty dollars today. (Edison switched to shellac cylinders, which kept pace with discs for some twenty-five years.)

The early discs featured famous artists, such as the great Italian tenor Enrico Caruso (1873–1921), who made his first recording in 1902 and whose many records encouraged the medium's acceptance as suitable for opera. Because he became one of the recording industry's earliest superstars, it has been said that "Caruso made the phonograph and it made him." His recordings also preserved his performances beyond the grave. The new technology allowed performers to achieve for the first time the kind of immortality previously available only to composers.

Mechanical recording was well suited for voices, but the limited range of frequencies that it could reproduce made orchestra music sound tinny. For years, the only symphony available was Beethoven's Fifth, recorded in 1913 by the Berlin Philharmonic for His Master's Voice. Because it was such a long piece, the company had to issue it on eight discs gathered in an "album," which became the standard format for longer works. In the 1920s, new methods of recording and reproduction using electricity—including the electric microphone—allowed a great increase in frequency range, dynamic variation, and fidelity, making the medium still more attractive to musicians and music lovers. Falling prices and continuing improvement of the recording process stimulated a growing market for recordings, from popular songs and dance numbers to the classical repertoire. Record companies competed to record the most popular performers, and by the late 1940s most of the better-known orchestral works had been recorded more than ten times each.

*Figure 22.8. The design of Thomas Alva Edison's first "talking machine," a cylinder phonograph built in 1877. To record, a person spoke into the mouthpiece while cranking the handle. Edison Birthplace Museum, Milan, Ohio.*

Encouraged by competition, companies continued to develop further improvements. In 1946, Columbia Records introduced the long-playing record, or LP, which rotated at 33⅓ revolutions per minute instead of 78, used smaller grooves, and thus allowed thirty-two minutes of music per side instead of four. Music lovers bought the LPs by the millions and got rid of their old 78s. High-fidelity and stereophonic records were introduced in the 1950s, which also saw the debut of an entirely new recording technology: magnetic tape. Philips introduced cassette tapes in 1963, and by the 1970s cassette sales were rivaling those of records. Then in 1983, Philips and Sony unveiled the compact disc, or CD, which stored recorded sound in digital code etched onto a 4-inch plastic disc, or diskette, and read by a laser. Even as listeners were replacing all their LPs with CDs, new technologies were being developed that now make it possible to download music from the Internet onto a personal computer or portable device, such as an MP3 player.

The development of recordings irrevocably altered the way people listen to music. No longer did they have to get themselves to a concert hall or gather around a bandstand. They could now sit in their homes and order up a favorite singer or an entire orchestra at their convenience, listening to a single performance repeatedly, if it pleased them. The visual element of music making suddenly disappeared; listeners heard performers without seeing them, and musicians played in recording studios for invisible audiences. Listening to recordings often replaced amateur music making at home, with the paradoxical effect that people devoted less time and effort to engaging actively with music as participants. For many people, listening to music became largely a solitary pursuit rather than a communal activity. People also used recorded music as a background to other activities, rather than listening with focused concentration.

Along with performers and listeners, composers, too, have been influenced by the new technologies, being able to avail themselves of musical styles and ideas outside of their ordinary experience. Exotic musics from Africa, India, Asia, and elsewhere became available via recording without the hardships

Figure 22.9. Portrait by Abraham Archibald Anderson (1847–1940) of Thomas Alva Edison with his phonograph, ca. 1890. National Portrait Gallery, Smithsonian Institution, Washington, D.C.

or expense of travel, and the entire history of Western music, from the singing of plainchant by monks in a faraway monastery to the most recent pop tune, may be heard on a CD or through some other medium. Furthermore, composers since the 1940s have used recorded sounds to make music, allowing them to incorporate an unprecedented variety of sounds.

Figure 22.10. The "Trademark Model" of the phonograph by His Master's Voice, available beginning in 1898. The firm's name and the dog's pose implied that the device reproduced sound so faithfully that a dog would recognize a recording of its owner's voice.

Stravinsky avoids a Romantic orchestral sound and emphasizes what he called an "objective" rather than emotional sound palette by omitting violins, violas, and clarinets.

**Neotonality**

CD 11/31

In the first movement (NAWM 146), traditional elements are reinterpreted in new ways, and Stravinsky's personal idiom is much in evidence: changing meters, unexpected rests, and the alternation of contrasting sound blocks that are related through similar pitch collections. At the first vocal entrance (Example 22.5), the melody is restricted to two pitches, E and F, suggesting a simple Gregorian chant. It is accompanied by three layers of ostinatos sounding the full octatonic scale. The scoring for double reed instruments alone creates an unusual sound, evoking a Renaissance consort. Later, the opening E-minor triad returns in a diatonic rather than octatonic context. Although E is emphasized as a tonal center, it is established simply through assertion and repetition, both in harmonic and melodic contexts. Such assertion of a tonal center through reiteration is very different from Schoenberg's atonality. Yet this music cannot be described as tonal, since it does not follow the rules of traditional harmony. Such music, characterized by the composer's finding new ways to establish a single pitch as a tonal center, is called *neotonal*.

*Example 22.5: Igor Stravinsky,* Symphony of Psalms, *vocal entrance*

*Hear my prayer*

**Schoenberg and Stravinsky**

Partly because Stravinsky's music was based on tonal centers as well as on recognizable genres and styles, performers and audiences found his Neoclassical works easier to play and to follow than Schoenberg's twelve-tone compositions. Both composers attracted supporters, who argued about music's need to adhere to tradition versus the need to find new methods, echoing the Brahms-Wagner disputes of the nineteenth century. In recent decades, musicians and scholars have come to see how much in common the two composers had, especially in their music of the 1920s through the 1940s, when both sought to revivify traditional forms in an entirely new and personal musical language.

## Serial Period

After Schoenberg's death in 1951, the twelve-tone methods he had pioneered were as much a part of history as sonata form. They were also becoming popular with younger composers, who extended the serial principle to elements other than pitch, such as rhythm and timbre (see Chapter 24). Such music, no longer simply twelve-tone, became known as serial music, a term that has also been applied retrospectively to Schoenberg and his students.

In part to encompass yet another branch of the classical tradition and in part to keep up with the times, Stravinsky—already in his seventies—adapted serial techniques in his music from about 1953 on. His best-known serial works include the song cycle *In memoriam Dylan Thomas* (1954); *Threni* (1957–1958), for voices and orchestra on texts from the Lamentations of Jeremiah; and *Movements* (1958–1959), for piano and orchestra. All of them show his characteristic idiom of juxtaposed blocks, disrupted meter, and his other signature traits, although their pitch content is increasingly chromatic.

Stravinsky's particular genius lay in finding stylistic markers, derived from Russian sources yet distinctly his own, that proved so recognizable and adaptable that he could assimilate or allude to any style while putting his personal stamp on the music. By drawing on everything from early music to the serial music of his time, he claimed the entire tradition as his own.

Stravinsky's impact on other composers was in a league with that of Wagner and Debussy. Through Stravinsky, elements that had been nurtured in Russian music (ostinatos, construction by juxtaposing blocks of sound, discontinuity, lack of development) and traits he had introduced (such as frequent changes of meter, unpredictable accents and rests, and dry orchestration) became commonplaces of modern music, used by composers employing many different styles. Stravinsky popularized Neoclassicism, setting an example that many others imitated. His serial music was less well known, but his support for serialism helped it gain a strong following among composers and academics. His willingness to change styles encouraged others to do the same, though few if any matched his ability to project a single personality in any chosen style.

*Influence*

# Béla Bartók

Modernists other than Stravinsky found elements in their own national music that allowed them to create a distinctive voice while continuing the classical tradition. Two of the most significant—the Hungarian Béla Bartók and the American Charles Ives (the latter to be discussed in Chapter 23)—did so in part by paying attention to musical traditions and qualities that had been ignored or disdained.

Béla Bartók (1881–1945; see biography) created an individual modernist idiom by synthesizing elements of Hungarian, Romanian, Slovak, and Bulgarian peasant music with elements of the German and French classical tradition. He arrived at this synthesis only after thorough grounding in both traditions and exposure to several modern trends.

Born in the Austro-Hungarian Empire and trained as a pianist, Bartók started composing at a young age, progressing from short character pieces to longer works modeled on the music of Bach, Mozart, Beethoven, Brahms, and Liszt. Encounters with the tone poems of Richard Strauss in 1902, with Debussy's music over the following decade, and with the works of Schoenberg and Stravinsky in the 1910s and 1920s inspired Bartók to write music that emulated and ultimately absorbed their idioms.

*Classical and modern influences*

Peasant music

Bartók's search for an innately Hungarian music led him to collect and study peasant music, often in collaboration with fellow composer Zoltán Kodály (1882–1967). Bartók published nearly two thousand Hungarian, Romanian, Slovak, Croatian, Serbian, and Bulgarian song and dance tunes—only a small part of the music he had collected in expeditions ranging over central Europe, Turkey, and North Africa (see Figure 22.12). He used the new technology of audio recording, as shown in Figure 22.13, which preserved the unique and unfamiliar characteristics of each folksinger and style far better than the older method of transcribing music by ear into conventional notation. He then

## ✺ Béla Bartók (1881–1945)

A virtuoso pianist, educator, musicologist, and composer, Béla Bartók pursued multiple careers. He was also the outstanding nationalist composer of the twentieth century and left a body of work that matches or exceeds that of any nineteenth-century composer of a nationalist bent.

Bartók was born in the Austro-Hungarian Empire in a small Hungarian city now in Romania. His parents were teachers and amateur musicians, and he took piano lessons from age five and composed from age nine. He studied piano and composition at the Hungarian Royal Academy of Music in Budapest, returning there in 1907 to teach piano. As a virtuoso pianist, he performed all over Europe and edited the keyboard music of Bach, Scarlatti, Haydn, Mozart, Beethoven, and others.

In 1904, Bartók overheard the singing of a woman from Transylvania (a region then in Hun-

gary and now in Romania), which sparked a lifelong interest in the folk music of Hungary, Romania, and nearby lands. He collected thousands of songs and dances, edited them in collections, and wrote about folk music. He arranged many folk tunes, wrote pieces based on them, and borrowed elements from various folk traditions for use in his concert music.

In 1909, Bartók married his student Márta Ziegler, who assisted him in his work. Their son was born in 1910. In 1923, he divorced Márta and married Ditta Pásztory, with whom he had a second son the next year.

In 1934, Bartók left the Academy of Music and moved to a full-time position as ethnomusicologist at the Academy of Sciences, where he joined Zoltán Kodály and others in preparing a critical edition of Hungarian folk music. His compositions over the next five years, including the last two string quartets and *Music for Strings, Percussion and Celesta*, marked the high point of his career. When the rise of the Nazis in Germany and their 1938 takeover of Austria brought the threat of fascism to Hungary, Bartók arranged to send his manuscripts to the United States. He followed with his family in 1940, settling in New York, where his last years were difficult both financially and physically. Friends procured jobs and commissions for him, sometimes without his knowledge, but he was already suffering from leukemia, which took his life in 1945.

*Figure 22.11. Caricature by Aline Fruhauf of Béla Bartók at the piano (December 1927). The caption reads: "An impression of Béla Bartók, the mild-mannered Revolutionist who plays in New York this week." Presumably, it was the dissonant and angular style of his music that prompted the epithet "Revolutionist."*

**Major works:** *Bluebeard's Castle*, *The Miraculous Mandarin*, *Dance Suite*, Concerto for Orchestra, *Music for Strings, Percussion and Celesta*, 3 piano concertos, 2 violin concertos, 6 string quartets, 2 violin sonatas, 1 piano sonata, *Mikrokosmos*, numerous other works for piano, songs, choral works, and folk-song arrangements.

Figure 22.12. Europe
around the mid-1900s.

analyzed the collected specimens using techniques developed in the new discipline of ethnomusicology, and he edited collections and wrote books and articles that established him as the leading scholar of this music. Bartók argued that Hungarian peasant music represented the nation better than the urban popular music that had long been identified as "Hungarian." This position was politically radical at a time when Hungary was still ruled by an urban, German-speaking elite, but his views eventually prevailed.

Bartók first achieved a distinctive personal style around 1908, with compositions such as the First String Quartet and the one-act opera *Bluebeard's Castle*, composed in 1911 and premiered in 1918, which combines Hungarian folk elements with influences from Debussy's *Pelléas et Mélisande*. His *Allegro barbaro* (1911) and other piano works introduced a new approach to the piano, treating it more as a percussion instrument than as a medium for cantabile melodies and resonant accompaniments. In his compositions from the decade after World War I, he explored the limits of dissonance and tonal ambiguity, reaching the furthest point with his two violin sonatas of 1921 and 1922. Other works of this decade include the expressionist pantomime *The Miraculous Mandarin* and the Third and Fourth String Quartets. His later works, which seem in comparison more accessible to a broad audience, have become the most widely known, including the Fifth and Sixth Quartets, *Music for Strings, Percussion and Celesta* (1936), and the Concerto for Orchestra (1943). His *Mikrokosmos* (1929–1939)—153 piano pieces in six books of graded difficulty—is a work of great pedagogical value that also summarizes Bartók's own style and presents,

Stylistic evolution

*Figure 22.13. Béla Bartók in 1907, recording Slovakian folk songs on an acoustic cylinder machine in the Hungarian village of Zobordarázs. Ferenc Bónis Collection.*

in microcosm, the development of European music in the first third of the twentieth century.

In synthesizing peasant with classical music, Bartók emphasized what the traditions have in common and, at the same time, what is most distinctive about each. In both traditions, pieces typically have a single pitch center, use diatonic and other scales, and feature melodies built from motives that are repeated and varied. Then, from the classical tradition, Bartók retained certain contrapuntal and formal procedures, such as fugue and sonata form. From the peasant tradition, he drew rhythmic complexity and irregular meters, common especially in Bulgarian music; modal scales and mixed modes; and specific types of melodic structure and ornamentation, as will be seen in Example 22.6, below. By intensifying these distinctive qualities, Bartók wrote music that can be simultaneously more elaborate in its counterpoint than Bach's and more ornamented and rhythmically complex than his folk models. In addition, Bartók's use of dissonance, his harmony, and his love of symmetry result partly from mixing concepts and materials taken from the two traditions; for instance, his frequent use of seconds and fourths in chords derives both from their prominence in folk melodies and from the practice of his fellow modernists. His synthesis preserves the integrity of both traditions. While he used folk elements in a meaningful way rather than merely for color and never compromised their individuality for the sake of smoothness, his music always remains grounded in the classical tradition.

*Music for Strings, Percussion and Celesta* illustrates Bartók's synthesis and several characteristics of his personal style. The combination of peasant and classical elements to create a modernist idiom is seen in his use of neotonality. Each of the four movements establishes a tonal center by methods analogous to the modal melodies of folk song and to the chordal motion and tonic-dominant polarities of classical music, while avoiding common-practice harmony. The tonal center of the first and last movements is A, with an important secondary center at the tritone E♭/D♯, a post-tonal analogue to the conventional dominant E. The second movement is in C, with a similar tritone pole on F♯, those two tones being each a minor third on either side of A; the slow third movement (NAWM 147) has the opposite arrangement, centering on F♯ with C as the competing pole. Some of the principal themes of the four movements and all of the final cadences clearly bring out this tritone relationship, as shown in Example 22.6. In addition, the cadences evoke standard procedures in tonal music, from counterpoint in contrary motion (Example 22.6a) to a mock dominant-tonic cadence (Example 22.6c). There are also strong similarities to peasant melodies, which often rise from and return to a tonal center or circle around a central tone, as in the second movement theme (Example 22.6b); or descend to the tonal center from its upper octave, as in the finale (Example 22.6e). Here the synthesis of the two traditions to create a modernist idiom is rich in allusions to music in both traditions.

*Music for Strings, Percussion and Celesta*

CD 11/36    CD 6/19

The themes are created by varying small motives, a typical procedure both in classical music—from Bach and Haydn to Schoenberg and Stravinsky—and in the peasant music of central and southeastern Europe. Many Hungarian tunes use short phrases and repeated motives with slight variations, while Bulgarian dance tunes typically spin out a rhythmic-melodic motive, as in the finale's theme (Example 22.6e). The latter is diatonic, like many classical themes, but clearly in the Lydian mode, which is used in some peasant songs. Hungarian songs can mix modes, an effect Bartók borrows at the end of the second-movement theme (Example 22.6b), where the melodic rise and fall suggests Lydian, then Phrygian, modes.

*Example 22.6: Béla Bartók,* Music for Strings, Percussion and Celesta

*a. Final cadence of first movement*

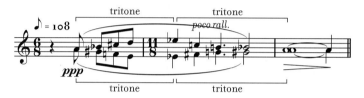

*b. Second-movement theme*

*c. Final cadence of second movement*

*d. Final cadence of third movement*

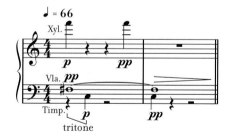

*e. Fourth-movement theme*

*f. Final cadence*

**Form and counterpoint**

The complex forms and contrapuntal procedures used by Bartók come strictly from the classical tradition. The first movement is an elaborate fugue, with entrances that successively rise and fall around the circle of fifths in both directions from A, meeting in a climax at the opposite pole of E♭. The second movement is a sonata form; the third movement a modified arch form (ABCB′A′) in which the phrases of the first-movement fugue theme are embedded; and the finale a rondo that includes a modified reprise of the fugue theme. Such thematic references to the first movement recall the cyclic symphonies of Berlioz, Franck, and Tchaikovsky, among others. Each movement includes canon and imitation, often in inversion. The palindromic form of the third movement is foreshadowed in the opening xylophone solo, shown in Example 22.7, which from the midpoint at the beginning of measure 3 is identical going in both directions. Bartók was very fond of such symmetries, as we can see in the mirror counterpoint at the end of the first movement (Example 22.6a).

*Example 22.7: Béla Bartók,* Music for Strings, *third movement, xylophone solo from opening*

**Peasant elements**

Elements from traditional peasant styles are also evident. Bulgarian dance meters feature long and short beats rather than strong and weak beats, with the longs half again as long as the short. In Western notation, this translates into irregular groupings of twos and threes as, for example, 2 + 3, 3 + 2 + 2, or 2 + 2 + 3. Bartók adopts this effect in the fourth movement theme (Example 22.6e),

*Example 22.8: Béla Bartók,* Music for Strings, *third movement, evocation of peasant ornamentation*

*a. Serbo-Croatian song*

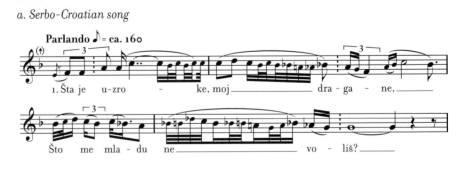

*b. Passage near beginning of third movement*

which exhibits the pattern $2 + 3 + 3$. The heavily ornamented, partly chromatic type of Serbo-Croatian song in Example 22.8a, which Bartók described as *parlando-rubato* ("speechlike-in free tempo"), is echoed near the beginning of the third movement, shown in Example 22.8b. Melodies over drones, as in this example, are also a feature of peasant music. String glissandi, snapped pizzicati, percussive chords laced with dissonant seconds, and other characteristics of Bartók's personal style do not derive directly from peasant music but can convey a rough, vibrant effect that suggests a source other than art music.

Like his fellow modernists, Bartók aspired to create masterpieces resembling those of the classical masters he took as models. He both emulated their music and sought new methods and materials in order to distinguish his music from that of other modern composers. The new elements he found were those of another tradition—the peasant music of his and other nations. Through his synthesis of both traditions, he created new works with a strong personal identity and a rich connection to the music of the past.

Bartók as modernist

# Germany

While Stravinsky in Paris and Bartók in Budapest were attempting to remain aloof from politics, composers in Germany under the Weimar Republic (1919–1933) found themselves in a hotbed of political contention, which echoed in the musical world. After the Nazis came to power in 1933, they attacked most modern music as decadent, banned the political Left and Jews from participating in public life, and persecuted Jews and other minorities. As a result, many leading musicians took refuge abroad.

## New Objectivity

In opposition to the emotional intensity of the late Romantics and the expressionism of Schoenberg and Berg, a new trend emerged in the 1920s under the slogan "Neue Sachlichkeit" (New Objectivity, or New Realism). The phrase was first used in art criticism and quickly adopted by musicians. As articulated by the composer Ernst Krenek (1900–1991) and others, the New Objectivity opposed complexity and promoted the use of familiar elements, borrowing from popular music and jazz or from Classical and Baroque procedures. In their view, music should be objective in its expression, as in the Baroque concept of the affections (see Chapter 9), rather than subjective or extreme. The notion of music as autonomous was rejected. Instead, it should be widely accessible, communicate clearly, and draw connections to the events and concerns of the time.

Krenek's *Jonny spielt auf* (Jonny Strikes Up), premiered in Leipzig in 1927, was the embodiment of these ideals, an opera set in the present time that used the interaction of a European composer and an African American jazz musician to examine dichotomies between contemplation and pleasure and between a seemingly exhausted and inward-looking European tradition and a new and energetic American one. The music drew on jazz and on a simplified harmonic language. The opera, an immediate success, was produced on more than seventy stages during the next three years, and established Krenek's reputation. But almost from the start it was vociferously attacked by the Nazis as "degenerate" for its use of African American elements. Krenek later adopted the twelve-tone method and emigrated to the United States after Nazi Germany absorbed his native Austria in 1938.

Ernst Krenek

## Kurt Weill

Kurt Weill (1900–1950), an opera composer in Berlin, was also an exponent of the New Objectivity. Sympathetic to the political Left, he sought to offer social commentary and to entertain everyday people rather than the intellectual elite.

*Mahagonny*

Weill collaborated with the playwright Bertolt Brecht on the allegorical opera *Aufstieg und Fall der Stadt Mahagonny* (Rise and Fall of the City of Mahagonny, premiered in 1930). In the opera, fugitives from justice build a town dedicated to pleasure, free of legal or moral taboos, but soon find that they have created a hell rather than a paradise on earth. Weill's score incorporates elements of popular music and jazz, and makes witty references to a variety of styles. The pit orchestra includes instruments typical of jazz bands—two saxophones, piano, banjo, and bass guitar—as well as winds and timpani, while three saxophones, zither, bandoneon (a kind of concertina), strings, and brass play in the stage orchestra. Through satire in both libretto and music, Brecht and Weill sought to expose what they regarded as the failures of capitalism, which the city of Mahagonny exemplified.

*The Threepenny Opera*

CD 7/12, 13

*Figure 22.14. Lotte Lenya as Jenny in the 1931 film version of Kurt Weill's* The Threepenny Opera.

The most famous collaboration between Weill and Brecht was *Die Dreigroschenoper* (The Threepenny Opera, premiered 1928). Brecht based the libretto on *The Beggar's Opera* by John Gay (see Chapter 14 and NAWM 95), although Weill borrowed only one air from the score. The cast included Lotte Lenya, shown in Figure 22.14, whom Weill had married in 1926; she became his favorite interpreter and, after his death, a champion of his work. The music parodied rather than imitated American hit songs, then the rage in Europe. Weill surreally juxtaposed the eighteenth-century ballad texts, European dance music, and American jazz. The original Berlin production ran for over two years, and within five years *The Threepenny Opera* enjoyed more than ten thousand performances in nineteen languages. The Nazis banned it in 1933, when Weill and Lenya left for Paris and then for the United States.

In New York, Weill began his second career as a composer for Broadway musicals. The most successful were *Knickerbocker Holiday* (1938), *Lady in the Dark* (1940), and the musical tragedy *Lost in the Stars* (1948), about apartheid in South Africa. The spirit of the New Objectivity lived on in these works, crafted by a classically trained modernist yet addressed to a broad musical public and meant to be immediately grasped by mind and heart.

## Hindemith

Paul Hindemith (1895–1963) was among the most prolific composers of the century. At the Berlin School of Music (1927–1937), Yale University (1940–1953), and the University of Zurich (1951–1957), he taught two generations of musicians (see Figure 22.15). He thought of himself as a practical musician, as witnessed by the title of his book *The Craft of Musical Composition*, which presents both a general system of composition and an analytical method. Since he performed professionally as violinist, violist, and conductor, and played many other instruments, the experience of performance became central to his music, whether it was intended for amateurs or professionals.

In the fragmented world of new music between the wars, Hindemith changed his approach several times. He began composing in a late Romantic style, then developed an individual expressionist language in works like the one-act opera *Murder, Hope of Women* (1919). Soon he adopted the aesthetic stance later dubbed the New Objectivity, which in his music was exemplified by an avoidance of

Figure 22.15. *Paul Hindemith teaching a composition class at the Yale University School of Music, 1953. Paul Hindemith Collection, Yale University Music Library, New Haven.*

Romantic expressivity and a focus on purely musical procedures, especially motivic development and a polyphony of independent lines. The seven works he entitled simply *Kammermusik* (Chamber Music, 1922–1927) include a piece for small orchestra and six concertos for solo instrument and chamber orchestra, which encompass a variety of movement types from neo-Baroque ritornello forms to military marches and dances. All his music is neotonal, establishing pitch centers through techniques from simple reiteration of a note to complex contrapuntal voice-leading.

By the late 1920s, Hindemith was disturbed by the widening gulf between modern composers and an increasingly passive public. In response, he began composing what was known as *Gebrauchsmusik*—"music for use," as distinguished from music for its own sake. His goal was to create for young or amateur performers works that were of high quality, modern in style, and challenging yet rewarding to perform.

*Gebrauchsmusik*

After the Nazis came to power, they attacked Hindemith in the press and banned much of his music as "cultural Bolshevism." He began to examine the role of the artist in relation to politics and power, and from his questioning emerged the opera *Mathis der Maler* (Matthias the Painter, 1934–1935; premiered 1938 in Zurich) and *Symphony "Mathis der Maler"* (1933–1934), his best-known work, composed while he was writing the libretto of the opera. The opera is based on the life of Matthias Grünewald, painter of the famous Isenheim Altarpiece shown in Figure 22.16. Mathis, the opera's main character, leaves his calling as a painter to join the peasants in their rebellion against the nobles during the Peasants' War of 1525. In despair after their defeat, he comes to realize that by abandoning his art he betrayed his gift and his true obligation to society, which is to paint. Yet Hindemith does not portray art as entirely autonomous since Mathis's experiences inform his moral vision. The opera can be read as an allegory for Hindemith's own career.

*Mathis der Maler*

For *Mathis* and his other works from the 1930s on, Hindemith developed a new, neo-Romantic style, with less dissonant linear counterpoint and more systematic tonal organization. He devised a new harmonic method that he called "harmonic fluctuation": fairly consonant chords progress toward combinations containing greater tension and dissonance, especially involving parallel fourths and seconds, which are then resolved either suddenly or by slowly moderating

"Harmonic fluctuation"

*Figure 22.16. Two panels from the Isenheim Altarpiece, painted by Matthias Grünewald between 1512 and 1516 for the chapel of a hospital and monastery. On the top right is the* Nativity, *with Mary holding the infant Jesus; on the left is the* Concert of Angels, *the inspiration for the first movement of Hindemith's* Symphony "Mathis der Maler." *The movement was reused in the opera* Mathis der Maler, *about Grünewald's life. Musée d'Unterlinden, Colmar.*

Later works

CD 11/64

the tension until consonance is again reached. A similar technique can be found in many of Hindemith's later works, such as his choral setting of Rilke's *Un Cygne* (A Swan, 1939; NAWM 153), part of a set of six pieces for a cappella chorus that exemplifies his music for amateur or school performers.

In 1936, the Nazi government forbade performances of Hindemith's music. *Mathis der Maler* had to be premiered in Switzerland, and Hindemith moved there in 1938. He emigrated to the United States in 1940 after the outbreak of World War II and stayed for over a decade, returning to Switzerland in 1953. Having found his mature style in *Mathis*, he applied it to a series of sonatas for almost every orchestral instrument (1935–1955). *Ludus tonalis* (Tonal Play, 1942) for piano evokes the model of Bach's *Well-Tempered Clavier* with twelve fugues, each centered on a different note in the chromatic scale, linked by modulating interludes and framed by a prelude (modulating from C to F♯) and postlude (F♯ to C). Other notable later works include *Symphonic Metamorphosis after Themes of Carl Maria von Weber* (1943) and the Symphony in B♭ for band (1951).

## Music under the Nazis

Krenek, Weill, and Hindemith all fled to the United States, but other composers stayed in Germany during the Nazi era. The Nazis established a Reich Chamber of Culture under Joseph Goebbels, which included a Reich Music Chamber to which all musicians had to belong. Richard Strauss, the grand old man of German music, was appointed its first president, but was soon forced to resign when he continued to collaborate on operas with a Jewish librettist, Stefan Zweig.

The Nazis' requirements for music were mostly expressed in negatives: music must not be dissonant, atonal, twelve-tone, "chaotic," intellectual, Jewish, jazz-influenced, or left wing, which excluded all modernist and most modern music. Composers had to cooperate with the regime in order to have their music performed, and most did. But many German composers continued to write in personal idioms influenced by Schoenberg, Stravinsky, Hindemith, or Weill, whose music the Nazis had attacked as decadent or banned outright. As a result, no coherent Nazi style of new music emerged. Rather, the government focused more on performance than on composition, exploiting the great German composers of the nineteenth century from Beethoven to Bruckner as symbols of the alleged superiority of the German people. They especially fostered a cult of Wagner, whose anti-Semitic views supported their own and whose *Ring* cycle embodied a German mythology they could embrace (see Chapter 19).

The one German composer who won an international reputation during the Nazi era was Carl Orff (1895–1982), who was far from sympathetic to the regime. His best-known work, *Carmina burana* (1936), for chorus and orchestra, set medieval poems akin to goliard songs (see Chapter 2) in an attractive, deceptively simple neo-modal idiom. Drawing on Stravinsky, folk songs, chant, and medieval secular song, Orff created a monumental pseudo-antique style based on drones, ostinatos, harmonic stasis, and strophic repetition. His *Carmina burana* is distinctive yet immediately comprehensible and has been much imitated, especially by composers for film and television. Orff also developed methods and materials for teaching music in schools, calling for movement, singing, and playing on percussion and other instruments, leading children in a natural way to experience a great variety of scales and rhythms and to arrive at a broadly based understanding of music.

Carl Orff

## The Soviet Union

In the Soviet Union, the government controlled the arts along with every other realm of life. The arts were seen as ways to indoctrinate the people in Marxist-Leninist ideology, enhance their patriotism, and venerate the leadership. Soon after the 1917 revolution, theaters, conservatories, concert halls, performing ensembles, publishers, and other musical institutions were all nationalized, and concert programming and the opera and ballet repertoires were strictly regulated.

Civil war in 1918–1920 and an economic crisis through the early 1920s preoccupied the government and forced some relaxation of state control over the arts. During this period of relative freedom, divergent tendencies emerged among composers and crystallized in two organizations founded in 1923. The Association for Contemporary Music sought to continue the modernist trends established by Scriabin and others before the war and promoted contacts with the West, sponsoring performances of music by Stravinsky, Schoenberg, Hindemith, and others. The Russian Association of Proletarian Musicians, on the other hand, considered such music elitist and instead encouraged simple tonal music with wide appeal, especially "mass songs" (songs for group unison singing) to socialist texts. After Joseph Stalin consolidated total power in 1929, dissent was quashed. The competing composers' groups were replaced in 1933 by a single new organization, the Union of Soviet Composers.

Composers' organizations

A 1934 writers' congress promulgated the movement socialist realism as the ideal for Soviet arts. In literature, drama, and painting, this doctrine called for using a realistic style (as opposed to abstraction or symbolism) in works that portrayed socialism in a positive light, showing signs of progress for the people under the Soviet state and celebrating revolutionary ideology and its heroes.

Socialist realism versus formalism

*Figure 22.17.  Sergey Prokofiev on the cover of* Time *magazine, November 19, 1945. The unflattering caption reads, "He keeps time with the Marxian metronome."*

*Figure 22.18.  A scene from a 2005 London performance of Prokofiev's ballet* Romeo and Juliet *by the Kirov Ballet Company. The work was first performed in Czechoslovakia in 1938.*

What this meant for music was the use of a relatively simple, accessible language, centered on melody, often drawing on folk or folklike styles, and promoting patriotic or inspirational subject matter. Interest in music for its own sake or in modernist styles was condemned as "formalism." But the definitions of socialist realism and formalism were so vague and arbitrary that composers, including Sergey Prokofiev and Dmitri Shostakovich, the two leading Soviet composers of the time, often ran afoul of the authorities.

## Sergey Prokofiev

Prokofiev (1891–1953), shown in Figure 22.17, made his initial reputation as a radical modernist, combining striking dissonance with motoric rhythms. He left Russia after the revolution and spent almost two decades residing and touring in North America and Western Europe, composing solo piano works and concertos for himself to play, and fulfilling commissions for larger compositions, among them an opera for Chicago, *The Love for Three Oranges* (1921), and ballets for Sergei Diaghilev's Ballets Russes in Paris.

His career at a low ebb, Prokofiev succumbed to promises from the Soviet regime of commissions and performances. He returned to Russia permanently in 1936, having already fulfilled Soviet commissions for the film *Lieutenant Kijé* (1934), later arranged as a concert suite, and for the ballet *Romeo and Juliet* (1935–1936). Both became favorites and entered the standard repertory (see Figure 22.18). So did his symphonic fairy tale for narrator and orchestra, *Peter and the Wolf* (1936)—one of many pieces he wrote in response to the Soviet demand for high-quality music for children—and a cantata drawn from music for the film *Alexander Nevsky* (1938). Prokofiev's pieces for state occasions, like his cantatas for the twentieth and thirtieth anniversaries of the Russian Revolution, were less successful and were ignored outside of the Soviet Union.

World War II again brought a relaxation of government control, and Prokofiev turned to absolute music in classical genres, notably the Piano Sonatas Nos. 6–8

(1939–1944) and the Fifth Symphony (1944). These works are largely tonal, with the unexpected harmonic juxtapositions and the alternation of acerbic dryness, lyricism, and motoric rhythms that had been features of his personal style since the 1910s. But after the war, the authorities again cracked down in a 1948 resolution that condemned the works of Prokofiev and other leading composers as "formalist." He tried to write more simply, but never recovered the balance between wit tempered by feeling and convention laced with surprise that marks his best music. He died in 1953—ironically, on the same day as Stalin, whose brutal regime had so circumscribed his freedom.

*Figure 22.19. Russian postage stamp commemorating the death of Dmitri Shostakovich in 1975.*

## Dmitri Shostakovich

Dmitri Shostakovich (1906–1975), shown in Figure 22.19, received his education and spent his entire career within the Soviet system. He studied at the Conservatory in Petrograd (later Leningrad, now Saint Petersburg), cultivating a combination of traditionalism with experimentation. In the 1920s, he was more aligned with the modernist than with the proletarian wing in Russia. The premiere of his First Symphony in 1926, when he was nineteen, and subsequent performances in the West rocketed him to international prominence.

Shostakovich's opera *Lady Macbeth of the Mtsensk District* was premiered in 1934 in both Leningrad (now Saint Petersburg) and Moscow, and scored a great success, with subsequent performances throughout the Soviet Union and abroad. But Stalin saw it in January 1936 and was angered by its discordant modernist music and surrealistic, often grotesque, portrayal of violence and sex (see Figure 22.20). Shortly thereafter, the newspaper *Pravda* printed an unsigned article attacking the opera as "chaos instead of music" (see vignette, page 591). In its wake, the production was closed down and the opera withdrawn. Shostakovich temporarily lost his favored status and may have feared for his life: the previous year, Stalin had begun a campaign of repression known as "the purges," during which many political figures, intellectuals, and artists were executed or banished to prison camps.

*Lady Macbeth of the Mtsensk District*

*Figure 22.20. Scene from Shostakovich's opera* Lady Macbeth of the Mtsensk District, *in a 1992 production by the English National Opera.*

## TIMELINE  Europe, 1900–1950

| MUSICAL EVENTS | HISTORICAL EVENTS |
|---|---|
| Bartók begins collecting peasant songs **1904** | |
| Schoenberg writes first atonal pieces **1908** | |
| Stravinsky, *The Firebird* **1910** | |
| Premiere of Stravinsky's *The Rite of Spring;* **1913** *The Art of Noises,* the futurist manifesto | **1914–1918** World War I |
| Satie, *Parade* **1917** Berg, *Wozzeck* **1917–1921** | **1917** Russian Revolution brings Bolsheviks to power |
| Stravinsky begins Neoclassical **1919–1920** period with *Pulcinella* Schoenberg writes first twelve-tone **1921–1923** work, Piano Suite Op. 25 | |
| | **1922** Fascists take over government in Italy |
| Milhaud, *La Création du monde* **1923** | |
| Krenek, *Jonny spielt auf* **1925–1926** | |
| Weill, *The Threepenny Opera* **1928** | |
| | **1929** New York stock market crash begins worldwide depression |
| Stravinsky, *Symphony of Psalms* **1930** | |
| Union of Soviet Composers founded; Schoenberg **1933** emigrates to the United States Hindemith, *Symphony "Mathis der Maler"* **1933–1934** | **1933** Hitler comes to power in Germany **1934** Doctrine of socialist realism adopted in Soviet Union |
| Prokofiev, *Romeo and Juliet* **1935–1936** Bartók, *Music for Strings, Percussion and Celesta;* **1936** Shostakovich's opera *Lady Macbeth* attacked in Soviet press; Orff, *Carmina burana* | **1936–1939** Spanish Civil War |
| Shostakovich, Fifth Symphony **1937** | |
| | **1938** Germany absorbs Austria **1939** Germany invades Poland, beginning World War II |
| Stravinsky and Bartók emigrate to the United States **1940** | |
| | **1945** World War II ends with defeat of Germany and Japan |
| Soviet Union cracks down on Prokofiev, Shostakovich, **1948** and "formalist" composers | |
| Stravinsky takes up serialism **1950s** | |

It is difficult not to see the Fifth Symphony, written and premiered to great acclaim in 1937, as Shostakovich's response to the criticism of his opera; indeed, he endorsed a description of the work as "a Soviet artist's reply to just criticism." The symphony embodies a new approach Shostakovich had been developing, inspired by close study of Mahler's symphonies, that encompassed a wide range of styles and moods—from lyricism to dynamism and from deep feeling and high tragedy to bombast and the grotesque. It is framed as a heroic symphony in the grand manner of Beethoven and Tchaikovsky and in the traditional four movements. A dynamic opening movement in sonata form, suggestive of struggle, is followed by a scherzo-like Allegretto (NAWM 154), an intensely sad slow movement, and a boisterous finale. The symphony outwardly conformed to the tenets of socialist realism, infusing the most prestigious nineteenth-century instrumental genre with an optimistic, populist outlook and adopting a clear, easily understood tonal language. For that reason, it provided the vehicle for Shostakovich's rehabilitation with the state. Yet it was also possible to hear in it messages of bitterness and mourning in the face of totalitarian repression. The Allegretto adopts the jarring contrasts of a Mahler scherzo, juxtaposing passages that evoke a variety of popular styles from waltz to fanfare. The sorrowful slow movement evokes traditional Russian funeral music; it prompted open tears at the premiere and has been seen by some as expressing sorrow at the purges. The triumphalism of the final movement could also be interpreted as false enthusiasm. Such double meanings do not suggest that Shostakovich was a dissident—there was no room for dissidence under Stalin—but that by composing multivalent music, he could at once please the party bosses and provide an outlet for emotions that had to remain unspoken.

All of Shostakovich's works were created in a politicized context, and the search for double meanings has been widespread in the West and in Russia after

Fifth Symphony

CD 11/66

---

**VIGNETTE**   Censuring Shostakovich

*After Shostakovich's opera* Lady Macbeth of the Mtsensk District *had been performed widely to great acclaim, Stalin's government singled it out for censure with a negative review in* Pravda (Truth), *the Communist Party newspaper. Through this attack on the nation's leading composer, it signaled a crackdown on composers' artistic freedoms.*

〜〜〜

From the first minute, the listener is shocked by deliberate dissonance, by a confused stream of sounds. Snatches of melody, the beginnings of a musical phrase, are drowned, emerge again, and disappear in a grinding and squealing roar. To follow this "music" is most difficult; to remember it, impossible.

Thus it goes practically throughout the entire opera. The singing on the stage is replaced by shrieks. If the composer chances to come on the path of a clear and simple melody, then immediately, as though frightened at this misfortune, he throws himself back into a wilderness of musical chaos—in places becoming cacophony. The expression which the listener demands is supplanted by wild rhythm. Passion is here supposed to be expressed by musical noise. All this is not due to lack of talent, or to lack of ability to depict simple and strong emotions in music. Here is music turned deliberately inside out in order that nothing will be reminiscent of classical opera, or have anything in common with symphonic music or with simple and popular musical language accessible to all. . . . The power of good music to infect the masses has been sacrificed to a petty-bourgeois, "formalist" attempt to create originality through cheap clowning. It is a game of clever ingenuity that may end very badly.

From "Chaos Instead of Music," as translated in Victor Seroff, *Dmitri Shostakovich: The Life and Background of a Soviet Composer* (New York: Knopf, 1943), pp. 204–205; repr. Oliver Strunk, ed., *Source Readings in Music History*, rev. ed. by Leo Treitler (New York: Norton, 1998), pp. 1397–1398.

Seventh Symphony

the fall of the Soviet Union. But the Seventh Symphony, which premiered in bombed-out Leningrad in 1941, at the peak of that city's siege by the Nazis, had a special significance for the people: it was broadcast across the USSR during the Soviets' darkest hour and both galvanized and comforted them during their resistance. The symphony, subtitled *Leningrad*, deals programmatically with the heroic defense of the city against Hitler's armies, although some hear in its depiction of the totalitarian invaders a complaint against Stalin's repression as well. It was performed in London and New York in 1942 and immediately became a symbol of the war against Nazi Germany, in which the United States, Britain, and the Soviet Union were allies.

Later works

In the 1948 crackdown, Shostakovich was denounced along with Prokofiev and others, and he had to write patriotic film scores and choral paeans to the regime to gain rehabilitation. He wrote some of his music "for the drawer"—with no expectation of performance until the political atmosphere changed. In an assertion of individuality, he musically signed the third movement of the Tenth Symphony (1953, the year of Stalin's death) with a motive drawn from the German spelling of his name, D–E♭–C–B, or, in German nomenclature, D–Es–C–H or D–S–C–H, from **D**mitri **SCH**ostakovich. He used the same motive in the Fifth and Eighth String Quartets (1952 and 1960) and the concertos for violin and for cello.

The ambivalence in Shostakovich's music reflects the accommodations he had to make to survive in a state where people could never say precisely what they felt, and thus where the arts—especially music—offered an outlet for what was otherwise inexpressible. The relative accessibility of his music combined with its impression of giving voice to inner feelings has won Shostakovitch many devoted listeners not only in Russia but also throughout the world.

# POSTLUDE

The works discussed in this chapter include some of the most widely performed art music of the twentieth century. By now, listeners and musicians have largely forgotten the political circumstances in which most of this music was created. Audiences enjoy Poulenc's sonatas, Orff's *Carmina burana*, Shostakovich's Seventh Symphony, and Stravinsky's ballets without regard to the politics or circumstances that shaped their creation. Indeed, the insistence on immediate wide appeal by authorities in totalitarian states seems to have helped the popularity of some works such as Prokofiev's *Romeo and Juliet* and *Peter and the Wolf*, which lack the dissonance and satire of his pieces composed in the West. Today Milhaud, Poulenc, and Weill are admired for their wit and clarity, Hindemith for his summation of the German tradition from Bach through Brahms in a novel musical language, Bartók for his artful synthesis of peasant and classical music, and Shostakovich and Prokofiev for their highly emotional and passionate symphonic styles—all with little thought to the ideologies that swirled around these composers and the constraints under which they labored. Yet politics still shapes the reception of some of this music—as shown, for example, by a continuing controversy in scholarly circles about whether Shostakovich meant his music to convey a dissident message.

The postwar depoliticizing of art music resulted in part from the idea that classical music is a thing apart, an idealized, autonomous art, a notion that continues today but has come under increasing scrutiny from historians and musicians. With historical distance comes a greater focus on the music itself and fading memories of the circumstances in which it was born. In the long run, what seems most important about classical music of the first half of the twentieth century, including that of the composers previously discussed in Chapters 20 and 21, is its great variety. Most composers still sought a place in the permanent repertoire and tried to secure it by combining elements from the classical tradition with individual and innovative traits that distinguished their music from that of their peers. The varied styles that emerged resulted in part from different views of what was valuable in the past classics and in part from composers' differing circumstances. They transformed their ways of thinking, from the political to the personal, into music of unprecedented diversity. Among their works are riches for every taste.

# Music in America

*Chapter Contents*

*Prelude*  594

A Backward Glance:
Music in the North
American Colonies  594

Diverging Trends in
Nineteenth- and Early
Twentieth-Century
America  596

The Classical Tradition
through Mid-
Century  605

Vernacular Styles  613

*Postlude*  628

## PRELUDE

The proliferation of traditions, styles, and genres makes it difficult to write a single coherent narrative of musical developments in the twentieth century. Yet one of the recurring themes is that very proliferation of styles, apparent in vernacular traditions as well as in the classical tradition. Nowhere is this more evident than in the United States, where varieties of popular music became better known and usually more lucrative than classical concert music, and where composers in the classical tradition struggled against a diverse European heritage to find their individual voices.

After briefly surveying some of the musical traditions in the North American colonies, we take note of the diverging trends in the American musical scene of the nineteenth century that gave rise to the burgeoning repertories of band music and other popular genres, to the musical influences of African Americans and other immigrant groups, and to such unique composers as Stephen Foster and Charles Ives. We then follow the development of the classical tradition in the Americas through the first half of the century, concentrating on those composers who collectively represent one of two strong currents of the time: ultramodernism and Americanism. Finally, we examine the growth of vernacular styles in the American twentieth century, from musical theater to film music and from blues to bebop, noting some of the prominent composers and performers in each genre as well as figures like George Gershwin and Duke Ellington, whose works embrace a variety of genres.

## A Backward Glance: Music in the North American Colonies

The music of contemporary Americans can be better understood if we look back to its roots, which the first colonists planted in lands inhabited by Native Americans. Coming from diverse traditions, the music of the settlers gave rise to the abundance of styles in the twenty-first-century United States. We know precious little about early Native American music, which was not recognized as something to be taken seriously until the turn of the twentieth century. The earliest American music about which we have any information grew out of the religious traditions of the settlers, who fled various forms of intolerance in Europe to find their own voices in the New World.

Church musicians in European settlements in the New World drew on their respective national styles: villancicos and other choral music throughout the Spanish colonies, the Catholic music of France in French Canada, English hymns and anthems in the Anglican churches of British North America. Two groups were especially notable for their music: the Puritans of New England and the Moravians of Pennsylvania and North Carolina.

Puritans

The Puritans who settled New England were Calvinists, and their worship music centered on metrical psalm singing. The original *Bay Psalm Book* (1640), the first book of any kind published in North America, contained no music, but the ninth edition of 1698 furnished thirteen melodies for singing the psalms. Eventually, singing schools established during the eighteenth century trained a core of amateurs to sing psalms and anthems in parts. The availability of such singers became an invitation for composers to write new music.

William Billings

William Billings (1746–1800), the most prominent of these composers, left a significant body of music and writings. His *New England Psalm Singer* (1770), shown in Figure 23.1, contained 108 psalms and hymn settings as well as 15 anthems and canons for chorus. He issued several more collections, including *The Continental Harmony* (1794), from which the fuging tune *Creation* provides a good example of Billings's rugged style (NAWM 97). Fuging tunes generally feature a passage in free imitation, framed by opening and closing sections in straightforward four-part harmony. But Billings declared his independence from the normal rules of counterpoint by using numerous parallel octaves and fifths as well as open chords without thirds, spiced with unconventional dissonances. Not only did these purposely austere sounds match Billings's colorful and eccentric personality, but they also led the way for a distinctive "yankee" idiom that stood apart from European styles.

CD 7/20

Moravians

In contrast, the Moravians cultivated the more sophisticated genres of the German-speaking Protestants from Moravia, Bohemia, and southern Germany. They embellished their church services with concerted arias and motets in current styles, whether imported from Europe or composed in America. Moravians

*Figure 23.1.  The frontispiece to William Billings's* New England Psalm Singer *(1770). Surrounding the singers at the table is a canon for six voices with a ground bass to be sung "by three or four deep voices." Engraving by Paul Revere. Germanisches National Museum, Nürnberg.*

also collected substantial libraries of music, both sacred and secular, and regularly performed chamber music and even symphonies by leading European composers.

# Diverging Trends in Nineteenth- and Early Twentieth-Century America

In the nineteenth century, a national cultural identity for the United States was complicated by the country's ethnic diversity and by the rapidly growing distinctions among classical, popular, and folk music. Among the many trends that emerged from the variety of musical traditions brought by settlers and immigrants to America, we will look at four: band music, which was strongly affected by a growing split between classical and popular music; popular song; music of African Americans, drawing on oral traditions but becoming a significant factor in both popular and classical music; and music in the classical tradition, culminating in the work of Charles Ives.

## Band Music

The earliest American bands were attached to military units, but in the nineteenth century, local bands became common everywhere as amateur bands were formed in communities across the country. They played indoors or outdoors, seated or on parade, in concerts but also at dances, holiday celebrations, fairs, picnics, parties, ball games, political rallies, store openings, sales events, weddings, funerals, and other public and private gatherings. The Civil War was called the most musical war in history because almost every regiment on both sides had its own band, which entertained the troops, led marches, performed in parades, and played during battles to hearten the soldiers. After the war,

*Figure 23.2. John Philip Sousa with the Sousa Band at a fashionable outdoor concert.*

community bands continued to proliferate, becoming such a fixture of American life that by the 1880s there were some ten thousand bands that performed at every opportunity.

The period between the Civil War and World War I was the heyday of professional bands. The most successful bandmaster was John Philip Sousa (1854–1932), whose years conducting the United States Marine Band (1880–1892) raised it to national prominence through tours and savvy promotion. In 1892, he organized his own band, shown in Figure 23.2, which made annual tours of the United States, several European tours, and a world tour.

John Philip Sousa

The repertory of nineteenth-century bands consisted of marches; quicksteps (fast marches); dances, including two-steps, waltzes, polkas, galops, and schottisches; arrangements of opera arias and songs, including medleys; transcriptions of pieces by classical composers from Rossini to Wagner; and virtuosic display pieces often featuring famous soloists. Sousa's programming was especially astute. After every selection listed on the program, the band played an encore, usually a light, quick piece guaranteed to please. Yet he also performed the European classics from Bach to Richard Strauss, introducing Wagner's music to more Americans than anyone else. The same variety is evident in the music that Sousa himself composed for band, which varies from programmatic fantasias to more than a hundred marches, including his most famous march, *The Stars and Stripes Forever* (1897; NAWM 135). Not limited to a single genre or medium, Sousa also wrote more than a dozen operettas and some seventy songs, but his ever-popular marches earned him the nickname "the March King."

Repertory

CD 10/38

Brass bands were one of the main training grounds for African American musicians, along with black churches and dance orchestras. During the late nineteenth and early twentieth centuries, black bands occupied an important place in both black and white social life in many big cities. These bands performed from notation and did relatively little improvising, but they played with a swinging and syncopated style that distinguished them from white bands. Among the bandleaders and composers who attracted national and international attention was James Reese Europe, whose band created a sensation in Paris during and after World War I, and whose sound the French Garde Républicaine tried in vain to imitate.

James Reese Europe

## Parlor and Popular Songs

While bands embraced a wide repertory from marches to classics, the world of song also reflected the diverging tastes and needs of the American public. During the first half of the nineteenth century, Schubert's lieder and parlor songs by American composers such as Stephen Foster (1826–1864) served similar purposes, intended primarily for home music making, as shown in Figure 23.3, and occasional performance in concerts.

Stephen Foster, the leading American song composer of the nineteenth century, grew up in Pittsburgh, where he heard German, Italian, and Irish music and taught himself to play several instruments, but had no formal training in composition. After his 1848 song *Oh! Susannah* achieved great success, he signed a contract with a New York publisher and became the first American to earn a living solely as a composer. One of his best-known "parlor songs," *Jeanie with the Light Brown Hair* (1853, NAWM 115)—with its diatonic, mostly stepwise melody, simple accompaniment, and clear, four-bar phrases—illustrates the features that made his music so appealing and memorable.

Stephen Foster

CD 8/75

Later in the century, we find a widening gulf between art song and popular song. While Foster's *Jeanie* had emulated Schubert's strophic, more folklike

Art song versus popular song

Figure 23.3. An American painter with impressionist leanings, Thomas Eakins (1844–1916) portrayed the parlor song in this work, entitled The Pathetic Song (1881). Corcoran Gallery of Art, Washington, D.C.

Tin Pan Alley

lieder, combined with elements from British and American ballad traditions, some art songs, such as those of Fauré and Wolf, had more elaborate, precisely notated piano parts, tended to be through-composed rather than strophic, were meant to engage listeners on a sophisticated plane, and required high professional standards of both pianist and singer. Composers of popular song sought instead to entertain their audience, accommodate amateur performers, and sell as many copies of the sheet music as possible. For this type of song, immediate appeal and a catchy quality that made for its easy recollection were the most important attributes.

Topics for popular songs included love, heartbreak, birth, death, racial and ethnic satire, new inventions like the bicycle and telephone, sentimental thoughts of mother and the old family home, and America's favorite pastime, baseball. This large variety of songs was pressed into service for every possible cause: abolition, the Civil War, temperance (the campaign against drunkenness), labor organizing, political campaigns, and evangelism, as in gospel songs such as *In the Sweet Bye and Bye*.

Popular art depends on the interplay of convention and novelty, and both are evident in the best popular songs. The standard form remained verse and refrain, with a four- or eight-measure introduction for the piano; an eight-, sixteen-, or thirty-two-measure verse; and a refrain of similar size. Often the refrain was scored in parts for chorus (or four solo singers), so that *chorus* came to be used as a term for refrain. Both verse and refrain typically had internal repetitions, falling into forms such as AABA; in some songs the verse and refrain shared material, and in others the chorus was wholly new, occasionally even in a different meter. The key to success was creating a catchy phrase, sometimes called the *hook*, that could grab the listener's attention and then be repeated and varied over the course of the song.

*Tin Pan Alley* was the jocular name for a district on West Twenty-eighth Street in New York City where, beginning in the 1880s, numerous publishers specializing in popular songs were located. A songwriter's typical strategy for promoting the song was to pay a singer to introduce the song in a show; and when it became a hit with audiences, people went out in droves to buy a copy of the sheet music. The link between success on stage and sales of printed music remained important even in the twentieth century.

## Music of African Americans

Africans were the one immigrant group that was brought to the United States unwillingly. Imported as slaves under inhuman conditions, they came from many ethnicities, each having a different language and customs. Mixed together on plantations or as domestic servants, they would have had a difficult time maintaining their original languages and cultures even if their owners had not actively worked to prevent this. But elements of their music were easier to preserve because they had been widely shared among African societies and because white slave owners did not consider singing a threat. Indeed, work songs were actively encouraged as a way to keep up the slaves' productivity and spirits.

Among the many traits of African American music that have been traced back to Africa are these:

- alternating short phrases between a leader and the group, called *call and response*
- improvisation, usually based on a simple formula that allows wide-ranging variation
- syncopation
- repetition of short rhythmic or melodic patterns
- multiple layers of rhythm, with beats in some instruments (or hand clapping or foot stomping) and offbeats in others
- bending pitches or sliding from one pitch to another
- moans, shouts, and other vocalizations
- instruments like the banjo, based on a west African stringed instrument

We will see these and other traits in ragtime, blues, jazz, and other twentieth-century genres based on African American traditions.

The African American form of music with the greatest impact in the nineteenth century was the spiritual, a religious song of southern slaves, passed down through oral tradition. The texts were usually based on images or stories from the Bible, but they often carried hidden meanings of the slaves' yearning for freedom. The first to appear in print was *Go Down, Moses*, which uses the story of Israel's deliverance from Egypt as a symbol for the liberation of the slaves. The song was published in 1861, during the first year of the Civil War, after a missionary heard it sung by refugee slaves.

The first publications of spirituals tried to document the songs as former slaves sang them, though the editors admitted that they could not notate the bent pitches and other aspects of performance. But soon dozens of spirituals were arranged as songs with piano accompaniments that anyone could play or in four-part harmony for choirs. The Fisk Jubilee Singers, depicted in Figure 23.4, popularized spirituals in the 1870s through polished performances in concert tours on both sides of the Atlantic. By the end of the nineteenth century, spirituals served simultaneously as folk music for those who had learned them from oral tradition, as popular songs for those who bought them in collections or as

*Figure 23.4. The original Fisk Jubilee Singers, photographed in 1873 in London during their European tour. Founded at Fisk University in Nashville, Tennessee, the group consisted of black student musicians who performed spirituals and other songs in four-part harmony.*

sheet music or heard them in popular venues, and as a source of melodic material for classical composers.

## The Classical Tradition

Louis Moreau Gottschalk

If song was the most popular medium of the nineteenth century, piano music ran a close second. The first American composer to achieve an international reputation was the globe-trotting Louis Moreau Gottschalk (1829–1869), a pianist in the Liszt tradition celebrated for his audacity and showmanship. Born in New Orleans, he completed his training in Paris, where Chopin heard him and predicted his fame. In addition to touring Europe, he performed throughout the United States, the Caribbean islands, and South America, playing largely his own compositions. The publication of pieces based on melodies and rhythms from his mother's West Indian heritage solidified his reputation as a composer. His *Souvenir de Porto Rico* (NAWM 120), which uses a theme derived from a Puerto Rican song, is a perfect example of nineteenth-century piano music designed to appeal to middle-class audiences.

CD 9/7

German immigration

Beginning in the 1840s, crop failures and the 1848 revolution spurred many Germans to emigrate to the United States, following others who had come during the previous century. Many of the immigrants were musicians and music teachers with a strong commitment to classical music, and they contributed to an extraordinary growth in performing institutions, music schools, and university departments of music in the second half of the nineteenth century. German musicians filled positions in orchestras, taught music at all levels, and—along with Americans who had studied in Germany—dominated the teaching of composition and music theory in conservatories and universities. The new immigrants and the institutions that they helped to found fostered an increasingly sharp divide between classical music and popular music. Not surprisingly, German tastes and styles dominated American music in the classical tradition until World War I.

German tradition

As classical music became well established, native-born composers were able to pursue careers that combined composition with performing and teaching, especially in the region from Boston to New York. Among them were John Knowles Paine (1839–1906), trained by a German immigrant, who became Harvard's first professor of music; George Whitefield Chadwick (1854–1931), who studied at the New England Conservatory in Boston and became its director; Chadwick's student Horatio Parker (1863–1919), who taught at Yale and was the first dean of its School of Music; and Edward MacDowell (1860–1908), a New Yorker who was the first professor of music at Columbia University in New York. All studied in Germany as well as the United States, and all pursued styles deeply rooted in the German tradition.

Nationalism

However, these composers had varying attitudes about nationalism. Parker believed American composers should simply write the best music they could; his Latin oratorio *Hora novissima* (1893), the piece that made his reputation, is in a universal style modeled on German and English oratorios. Chadwick, on the other hand, developed an idiom laced with American traits such as pentatonic melodies and characteristic rhythms from Protestant psalmody and African-Caribbean dances, used in his Symphony No. 2 in B♭ Major (1883–1885) and *Symphonic Sketches* (1895–1904). MacDowell opposed jingoistic nationalism, but like most Europeans he saw a national identity as an important aspect of any composer's claim to international attention. Among his overtly nationalist works is his Second (*Indian*) Suite for orchestra (1891–1895), based on American Indian melodies.

Another Boston composer, Amy Marcy Beach (1867–1944), shown in Figure 23.5, could not study or teach at the top universities because they excluded women. A child prodigy, she studied piano, harmony, and counterpoint privately, then taught herself to compose by analyzing and playing works of composers she admired. Married to a wealthy physician, she was freed of financial concerns and devoted herself to composition. At the time, women were considered incapable of composing in longer forms. As if to prove them wrong, she wrote large-scale works such as her Mass in E♭ (1890), *Gaelic* Symphony (1894–1896), Piano Concerto (1899), and Piano Quintet (1907), all of them well received. She also wrote about 120 songs and dozens of piano and choral pieces, many of them very popular. Beach was internationally recognized as one of America's leading composers, and she inspired many women in later generations.

Some of Beach's music has an ethnic flavor—for example, the *Gaelic* Symphony on Irish tunes and the String Quartet (1929) on American Indian melodies. But most of her works engage the traditions of the German classics. She based the themes of the first and third movements of her own Piano Quintet on a theme from Brahms's Piano Quintet Op. 34, which she had performed in 1900. Her individual voice emerges forcefully in the third and last movement (NAWM 134), going beyond the Brahmsian music of the first movement to embrace late nineteenth-century chromatic harmony, with unusual inversions, augmented triads, and colorful nonchordal tones.

*Figure 23.5. Amy Beach in about 1903.*

CD 10/31

## Charles Ives

Charles Ives (1874–1954; see biography), like Bartók in Europe, created a personal modernist idiom by synthesizing international and regional musical traditions. Ives was a fluent composer in four distinct spheres: American vernacular music, Protestant church music, European classical music, and experimental music, of which he was the first major exponent. In his mature music, he combined elements from all four, using the multiplicity of styles as a rhetorical device to convey rich musical meanings.

Ives grew up surrounded by American vernacular music, from parlor songs and minstrel show tunes to the marches and cornet solos his father performed as leader of the town band. In his teens, Ives wrote numerous marches and parlor songs in the styles of the day, and during his college years at Yale he composed part-songs for the glee club and stage music for fraternity shows. As a young church organist (1888–1902), he improvised organ preludes and postludes, and composed solo songs and sacred choral works representing all the styles then prominent in American Protestantism—from simple hymnody to the cultivated manner of his composition teacher at Yale, Horatio Parker. With Parker, he intensified his study of art music, writing exercises in counterpoint, fugue, and orchestration, and composing in genres from art song to symphony. His First Symphony, which he began in his last year in college, was directly modeled on Dvořák's *New World* Symphony, with elements from Schubert, Beethoven, and Tchaikovsky.

In his experimental music, Ives's typical approach was to preserve most of the traditional rules but change others to see what would happen. As a youth, he practiced drumming on the piano, devising dissonant chords that would suggest the sound of drums. He wrote several pieces in his teens that were polytonal,

Traditional influences

Experimental music

with the melody in one key and the accompaniment in another, or with four imitative voices, each in its own key. "If you can play a tune in one key," he asked, "why can't a feller, if he feels like [it], play one in two keys?" Polytonality was later developed independently by other composers, but Ives was the first to use it systematically. Like many of his experiments, his polytonal pieces introduced

## ✱ Charles Ives (1874–1954)

Like the archetypal artist in countless movies, Ives worked in obscurity for most of his career but lived to be recognized as one of the most significant classical-music composers of his generation.

Ives was born in Danbury, a small city in Connecticut where his father, George, was a bandmaster, church musician, and music teacher. Ives studied piano and organ, showing prodigious talent—at age fourteen he became the youngest professional church organist in the state. His father taught him theory and composition, and encouraged an experimental approach to sound.

At Yale, he took liberal-arts courses and studied music theory and composition with composer, teacher, and organist Horatio Parker. While in college, Ives wrote marches and songs for his fraternity brothers and church music for Centre Church in New Haven, where he was organist.

Figure 23.6. Charles Ives in an undated photograph.

After graduating in 1898, he settled in New York, where he worked as a church organist, got a job in the insurance business, and lived with fellow Yale graduates in an apartment they called "Poverty Flat." When his cantata The Celestial Country failed to garner strongly positive reviews, Ives quit his organist position and focused on insurance. His firm, Ives & Myrick, became one of the most successful agencies in the nation, as Ives pioneered the training of agents (his classes are one source for the modern business school) and the idea of estate planning.

His courtship with Harmony Twichell, whom he married in 1908, inspired a new confidence, and the next decade brought an outpouring of music, including most of the pieces that later made Ives's reputation. Composing evenings and weekends, he prepared finished copies of his less radical pieces, such as the first three symphonies and the violin sonatas, but published nothing and left many works in sketch or partial score.

After trying vainly for over a decade to interest performers and publishers in his music, Ives was spurred in 1918 by a health crisis to edit and self-publish *114 Songs* and his Second Piano Sonata (*Concord, Mass., 1840–60*), which was accompanied by a book, *Essays before a Sonata*. He devoted the 1920s to completing several large pieces. The remaining three decades of his life saw the premieres and publication of most of his major works. Although accused—despite his thorough musical training—of amateurism because he was a businessman, Ives won a number of advocates among younger composers, performers, and conductors, who promoted his music. By the time of his death at age seventy-nine, he was widely regarded as the first to create a distinctly American body of art music, and his reputation has continued to grow.

**Major works:** 4 symphonies, *Holidays Symphony*, *Three Places in New England*, *The Unanswered Question*, 2 string quartets, 4 violin sonatas, 2 piano sonatas, about 200 songs.

unprecedented levels of dissonance and rhythmic complexity, although they usually preserved the idea of a tonal center.

None of Ives's experimental pieces was published or performed in public until long after they were written; they were essentially ways of trying out ideas for purposes of expression or representation. But one experimental work became one of Ives's best-known pieces because his novel means fit the inspired program so perfectly: *The Unanswered Question* (1908). Slowly moving strings in G major represent "the silences of the Druids—who know, see and hear nothing," while over them a trumpet poses "the perennial question of existence" and four flutes attempt ever more energetic and dissonant answers until they give up in frustration, leaving the question to sound once more, unanswered. The trumpet and flute parts are atonal, making Ives one of the first composers to use atonality (roughly contemporary with Schoenberg but independent of him) and the first to combine tonal and atonal layers in the same piece.

*The Unanswered Question*

From 1902 on, Ives wrote only in classical genres, but he brought into his music the styles and sounds of the other traditions that he knew. Doing so was a radical act, for although classical audiences accepted folk melodies as sources for concert works, they tended to regard the hymn tunes and popular songs that Ives used as beneath notice and entirely out of place in the concert hall. Typically, he employed them to suggest extramusical meanings, whether in a character piece or programmatic work.

Syntheses

Ives's Third Symphony, four violin sonatas, and First Piano Sonata all feature movements based on American hymn tunes. In them, Ives uses procedures of thematic fragmentation and development from European sonata forms and symphonies but reverses the normal course of events so that the development happens first and the themes appear in their entirety only at the end. This procedure has been called *cumulative form*. While not overtly programmatic, these instrumental works suggest the coming together of individual voices and the fervent spirit of hymn singing at the camp-meeting revivals of the composer's youth. Thus, Ives is not only a musical nationalist in these works, but he is also asserting the universal value of his country's music by making a place for American melody within the European tradition (see vignette, page 604).

Many of Ives's later pieces are programmatic, celebrating aspects of American life. *Three Places in New England* presents successive orchestral pictures suggesting the first African American regiment in the Civil War, a band playing at a Fourth of July picnic, and the composer's walk by a river with his wife during their honeymoon. Other works are more philosophical, such as the Fourth Symphony, an extraordinary, complex work that poses and seeks to answer "the searching questions of What? and Why?" In all of these, Ives uses references to American tunes or musical styles, from Stephen Foster to ragtime (see below), to suggest the meanings that he wanted to convey. In some pieces, he uses multiple tunes, layered on top of each other in a musical collage or woven together like a patchwork quilt, to invoke the way experiences are recalled in memory. He also incorporates techniques developed in his experimental music, often to represent certain kinds of sounds or motions, such as exploding fireworks or mists over a river.

Programs

Collage

With such a wide range of styles at his command, Ives frequently mixed them—whether traditional or newly invented—within a single piece. This variety of styles provided a way for Ives to evoke a wide range of extramusical references and also to articulate the musical form, distinguishing each phrase, section, or passage from the next through stylistic contrast. He also used style, alongside timbre, rhythm, figuration, register, and other more traditional means, to differentiate layers heard simultaneously, as in *The Unanswered Question*.

Variety

Ives synthesized all four traditions his music encompassed in his song *General William Booth Enters into Heaven* (1914, NAWM 148), on a poem by Vachel

Lindsay that pictures the founder of the Salvation Army leading the poor and downtrodden into heaven. It is an art song, but the musical content is drawn primarily from American vernacular music, church music, and experimental music. At the opening, shown in Example 23.1, Ives evokes Booth's bass drum through the experimental technique of piano-drumming, using a standard rhythmic pattern of American drummers, and derives the vocal line from the hymn *There Is a Fountain Filled with Blood.* Each group of Booth's followers described in the poem receives a different musical characterization, using polytonality, novel chord structures, dissonant ostinatos, and other techniques that Ives first explored in his experimental works. Thus, Ives combines the art-song framework with the American vernacular tradition, church music (hymn tune), and experimental techniques to convey the experience of the poem.

Ives's place

Ives was isolated as a composer. Among his contemporaries, he was influenced by the music of Strauss, Debussy, and Scriabin, but he encountered that of Stravinsky only late in his career, after arriving independently at similar methods, and that of Schoenberg and other modernists only after he had ceased to compose. Nor did they know his music; except for some early vernacular and church works, most of his pieces were performed and published only long after he had written them. Thus, his direct influence was felt mostly after World War II,

---

**VIGNETTE**   Americanism in Music

*Dvořák had advised American composers to use African American or American Indian music as sources for a distinctively national music, and many did so. Charles Ives felt that for himself, as a white New Englander, a more appropriate source was the music regularly heard and sung by people in his own region, from hymns to popular song. No matter what sources are used, he argued, the composer must understand the music from the inside and know what it meant to the people who heard and performed it.*

If a man finds that the cadences of an Apache war-dance come nearest to his soul—provided he has taken pains to know enough other cadences, for eclecticism is part of his duty; sorting potatoes means a better crop next year—let him assimilate whatever he finds highest of the Indian ideal so that he can use it with the cadences, fervently, transcendentally, inevitably, furiously, in his symphonies, in his operas, in his whistlings on the way to work, so that he can paint his house with them, make them a part of his prayer-book—this is all possible and necessary, if he is confident that they have a part in his spiritual consciousness. With this assurance, his music will have everything it should of sincerity, nobility, strength, and beauty, no matter how it sounds; and if, with this, he is true to none but the highest of American ideals (that is, the ideals only that coincide with his spir-

itual consciousness), his music will be true to itself and incidentally American, and it will be so even after it is proved that all our Indians came from Asia.

The man "born down to Babbitt's Corners" may find a deep appeal in the simple but acute Gospel hymns of the New England "camp meetin'" of a generation or so ago. . . . If the Yankee can reflect the fervency with which "his gospels" were sung—the fervency of "Aunt Sarah," who scrubbed her life away for her brother's ten orphans, the fervency with which this woman, after a fourteen-hour work day on the farm, would hitch up and drive five miles through the mud and rain to "prayer meetin'," her one articulate outlet for the fullness of her unselfish soul—if he can reflect the fervency of such a spirit, he may find there a local color that will do all the world good. If his music can but catch that spirit by being a part with itself, it will come somewhere near his ideal—and it will be American too—perhaps nearer so than that of the devotee of Indian or negro melody. In other words, if local color, national color, any color, is a true pigment of the universal color, it is a divine quality, it is a part of substance in art—not of manner.

From Charles Ives, *Essays before a Sonata, The Majority, and Other Writings,* ed. Howard Boatwright (New York: Norton, 1970), pp. 79–81.

*Example 23.1: Charles Ives,* General Booth Enters into Heaven

when his departures from the conventional were taken as an example by post-war composers, encouraging them to experiment and providing models for some novel procedures. He can justifiably be called the founder of the experimental-music tradition in the United States and a modernist who, like Bartók, Stravinsky, and Berg, drew on his own nation's music to develop a distinctive idiom within the classical tradition. In all of these ways, his work has been of incalculable importance to younger generations of American musicians.

# The Classical Tradition through Mid-Century

The interwar period saw the emergence of North and South American composers who gained prominence in their own countries and recognition in Europe, placing their homelands on the international stage for the first time. Like composers in the "peripheral" nations of Europe, these composers of the Americas found that creating a distinctive national style was often the only way to gain attention from an international audience. Their nationalism was sometimes infused with national politics, but it was always linked to the cultural politics of securing for themselves and their countries a niche in the repertory of performed classics.

## North and South of the Border

Canada

Canada had a thriving musical life that developed along patterns similar to those in the United States. In both nations, performance of the European classical repertoire was far more central than playing music of homegrown composers in the classical tradition. Performing spaces, concert societies, bands, professional chamber ensembles, choral societies, and conservatories all emerged in Canada during the nineteenth century, and the twentieth century brought the founding of orchestras in most large cities, beginning with symphonies in Quebec (1903) and Toronto (1906).

The first Canadian composer to achieve an international reputation was Claude Champagne (1891–1965). He learned French-Canadian fiddle music and dance tunes in his youth, then as a young man was deeply influenced by Russian composers, from Musorgsky to Scriabin. During studies in Paris from 1921–1928, he encountered Renaissance polyphony, Fauré, and Debussy, and saw in their modal practice links to the folk tunes of Canada. He developed a distinctive nationalist style in his *Suite canadienne* (Canadian Suite, 1927) for chorus and orchestra, blending elements from French-Canadian folk music and polyphonic French chansons with the symphonic tradition. His best-known piece, *Danse villageoise* (Village Dance, 1929), evokes both French-Canadian and Irish folk styles, acknowledging another ethnic strain in Canada and in his own heritage.

The most important Brazilian composer was Heitor Villa-Lobos (1887–1959), who drew together traditional Brazilian elements with modernist techniques. He spent the years 1923 to 1930 mostly in Paris, where performances of his music won widespread praise and established him as the most prominent Latin American composer. He returned to Brazil in 1930 and, with government support, instituted a national effort to promote music in the schools and through choral singing. He was criticized for his collaboration with Brazil's nationalist dictatorship, akin to the totalitarian regimes of Europe at the time, but it is not clear whether he shared its ideology.

The series of fourteen pieces entitled *Chôros* (1920–1928), after a type of popular ensemble music that Villa-Lobos played in the streets of Rio de Janeiro in his youth, are among his most characteristic works. For various media, from solo guitar or piano to orchestra with chorus, each *Chôros* blends one or more vernacular styles of Brazil—typified by syncopated rhythms and unusual timbres—with modernist techniques such as ostinatos, polytonality, polyrhythms, and vivid orchestration to create a remarkably distinctive sound. Another series, the nine *Bachianas brasileiras* (1930–1945), pays tribute to Bach and thus to the Neoclassical trend of the times. Each is a suite of two to four movements combining elements of Baroque harmony, counterpoint, genres, and styles with Brazilian folk elements and long, lyrical melodic lines. This unique blend is exemplified in Villa-Lobos's most famous

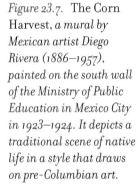

*Figure 23.7.* The Corn Harvest, *a mural by Mexican artist Diego Rivera (1886–1957), painted on the south wall of the Ministry of Public Education in Mexico City in 1923–1924. It depicts a traditional scene of native life in a style that draws on pre-Columbian art.*

*Figure 23.8. Brazilian Heitor Villa-Lobos (left) and Mexican Carlos Chávez in a caricature by John Minnion, with native musicians playing guitar and pipes in the background.*

work, *Bachianas brasileiras No. 5* (1938–1945) for solo soprano (mostly word-less) and eight or more cellos.

Beginning in 1921, the Mexican government began to support bringing the arts to a wide public and promoted a new nationalism that drew on native Indian cultures, especially from before the Spanish conquest. As part of this effort, Diego Rivera and other artists were commissioned to paint murals in public buildings that illustrated Mexican life, such as the fresco shown in Figure 23.7.

Mexico

The first composer associated with the new nationalism was Carlos Chávez (1899–1978; shown with Villa-Lobos in Figure 23.8), who also served as conductor of Mexico's first professional orchestra and director of the national conservatory. He wrote two ballets on Aztec scenarios, and his *Sinfonía india* (Indian Symphony, 1935–1936) uses Indian melodies in a modernist, primitivist idiom also apparent in his Piano Concerto (1938–1940). Other works, such as his *Sinfonía romántica* (Symphony No. 4, 1953), are not overtly nationalist.

Carlos Chávez

Silvestre Revueltas (1899–1940) studied in Mexico and then in the United States before returning to assume the post of assistant conductor under Chávez. His compositions do not use folk songs but combine melodies modeled on Mexican folk and popular music with a modernist idiom. Characteristic is his *Sensemayá* (1938, NAWM 155), a symphonic poem—really a song without words—based on a poem by Cuban poet Nicolás Guillén. The poetic text, though never sung, is rendered syllabically by strings and trombones in three sections of the work, framed by interludes. Both poem and piece tell of an African-Cuban magical rite in which a large figure representing a snake is carried by a dancer and ritualistically put to death. Borrowing methods and textures from Stravinsky's *Rite of Spring*, Revueltas builds up a layered fabric of ostinatos in irregular meters (mostly $\frac{7}{8}$) over which he juxtaposes melodies of contrasting characters and timbres as he slowly reaches the climax.

Silvestre Revueltas

CD 11/74  CD 6/41

## The United States

That American composers and performers developed new links with Europe between the wars was due in part to the immigration of many of Europe's leading composers for political or professional reasons. By the early 1940s, these refugees included Rachmaninov, Schoenberg, Stravinsky, Bartók, and others whom we will encounter in the next chapter. Americans had studied in Germany since the mid-nineteenth century, but World War I helped to foster a reorientation of American music away from Germany and toward France. Starting in the early 1920s, a steady stream of Americans went to France to study with Nadia Boulanger (1887–1979), renowned pedagogue and promoter of Fauré and Stravinsky, who taught classes in Paris and Fontainebleau until her death. Among those studying with her were Aaron Copland, Virgil Thomson, and Elliott Carter, all discussed below.

**Ultramodernists and Americanists**

The interwar period also saw several new currents among American composers. Two of the most salient were an experimentalist or ultramodernist trend, focused on developing new musical resources, and an Americanist trend, blending nationalism with a new populism inspired by the depression and by President Franklin Roosevelt's New Deal policies. The former group included the music of Edgard Varèse, Henry Cowell, and Ruth Crawford, and the latter encompassed that of Aaron Copland, William Grant Still, Cowell (his later works), and many others. Both currents asserted independence from Europe while still drawing on the European tradition. In order to secure performances for their music in a concert culture that focused on European masterworks, American composers formed their own organizations, including the International Composers Guild founded by Varèse and the League of Composers headed by Claire Reis; for similar reasons, Cowell established the print journal *New Music*.

**Edgard Varèse**

Among the experimentalists, the French-born Edgard Varèse (1883–1965) had a brief career in Paris and Berlin as a composer and as a conductor of early and contemporary music before moving to New York in 1915. Varèse celebrated his adopted country in his first major work, *Amériques* (1918–1921). Its fragmentary melodies and loose structure betray links to Debussy. He was also influenced by Schoenberg, notably in the use of strong dissonance and chromatic saturation, and by Stravinsky, especially in his avoidance of linear development.

**Spatial music and sound masses**

Next came a series of works that laid down a new agenda: *Offrandes* (1921), *Hyperprism* (1922–1923), *Octandre* (1923), *Intégrales* (1924–1925), *Ionisation* (for percussion only, 1929–1931), and *Ecuatorial* (1932–1934). In these works, Varèse aimed to liberate composition from conventional melody, harmony, meter, regular pulse, recurrent beat, and traditional orchestration. For Varèse, sounds as such were the essential structural components of music, which he defined as "organized sound," and he considered all sounds acceptable as raw material. He imagined music as spatial, akin to an aural ballet in which what he called *sound masses* moved through musical space, changing and interacting. A sound mass is a body of sounds characterized by a particular timbre, register, rhythm, and melodic gesture, which may be stable or gradually be transformed. In Varèse's compositions, these sound masses collide, intersect, speed up, slow down, combine, separate, diffuse, expand, and contract in range, volume, and timbre. A great variety of percussion instruments—some drawn from non-Western cultures and others (such as the siren) from city life—play key roles, acting independently as equals to the winds and strings. For Varèse, form was not the starting point but the result of working with the invented mate-

*Figure 23.9. Henry Cowell at the piano, playing clusters with his fist and forearm.*

rial; typically, his pieces are organized as a series of sections, each centered around a few sound masses, some of which may carry over to later sections. In Varèse's new conception of music, the listener must put aside expectations that music will be rhetorical or will develop organically, as in earlier styles, and must simply observe the interaction of "intelligent bodies of sound moving in space."

Since his music depended on sound itself, especially unusual ones, Varèse sought new instruments from the 1920s on. Only after World War II did the new resources of electronic sound generation and the tape recorder (discussed in Chapter 24) make possible the realization of the sounds he heard in his mind, in his *Déserts* (1950–1954) for winds, percussion, and tape and in the tape piece *Poème électronique* (1957–1958).

A contemporary of Varèse, California-born composer Henry Cowell (1897–1965) began composing as a teenager with little training in European music, and from the start he sought new resources for music. Many of his early pieces are experimental, designed to try out new techniques. *The Tides of Manaunaun* (ca. 1917) uses tone clusters—chords of diatonic or chromatic seconds produced by pressing the keys with the fist or forearm, as shown in Figure 23.9—to represent the tides moved by Manaunaun, the legendary Irish sea god. In *The Aeolian Harp* (1923), the player strums the piano strings while holding down three- and four-note chords on the keyboard, as if playing a grand autoharp. In *The Banshee* (1925), an assistant holds the damper pedal down so that the strings can resonate freely while the pianist strums the strings, plucks some, and rubs along the length of the lower, wire-wound strings with the fingertips to create an eerie, voice-like howl similar to that of a banshee, a spirit in Irish legend. Besides new playing techniques, Cowell also explored new textures and procedures, such as giving each voice a different subdivision of the meter. He summarized his new ideas in his book *New Musical Resources* (1930).

Throughout his career, Cowell was interested in non-Western musics. He took an eclectic approach to composition, trying out everything that interested him rather than developing a single identifiable style. During and after the 1930s, Cowell turned from experimentalism to a more accessible language, often incorporating American, Irish, or Asian elements. He wrote a series of works called *Hymn and Fuguing Tune* for band or for orchestra, modeled on the style of William Billings and his contemporaries, alongside symphonies and other traditional genres. In the years after World War II, several pieces show his interest in Asian music and incorporate instruments such as the Indian tabla and the Japanese koto.

Cowell promoted music by his contemporaries as well as his own through concerts and through the periodical *New Music*, in which he published scores by Ives and other modernist and ultra-modernist composers. His adventurous search for new resources and his interest in non-Western music had an enormous impact on younger composers, especially in the United States.

Among the composers whose works Cowell published was Ruth Crawford (1901–1953), shown in Figure 23.10, the first woman to win a Guggenheim Fellowship in music. She was most active as a composer in Chicago between 1924 and 1929 and in New York between 1929 and 1933. In New York, she studied composition with the composer and musicologist Charles Seeger, whom she married in 1932. Seeger had developed theories about dissonant counterpoint, rhythmic freedom between contrapuntal voices, and other modern techniques that Crawford helped to refine and then applied in her own music. In her New York period, she experimented with serial techniques, including their application to parameters

Henry Cowell

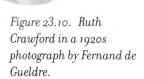

*Figure 23.10. Ruth Crawford in a 1920s photograph by Fernand de Gueldre.*

other than pitch. Influenced by the New Deal, she became convinced that preserving folk songs would be a greater contribution to the nation's musical life than writing modernist works that few would hear or appreciate. She collaborated with writer Carl Sandburg and folklorists John and Alan Lomax, editing American folk songs from field recordings. She also published many transcriptions and arrangements in which she sought to be faithful to the songs' native contexts. Crawford stands out for her advocacy in preserving American traditional music and for being one of the very few women in the ultramodernist group.

Crawford's best-known work is the String Quartet (1931), composed while in Europe on a Guggenheim Fellowship. Each movement is organized differently, embodying Crawford's constant search for new procedures. In the first movement, four thematic ideas unfold in dissonant counterpoint; rarely do two instruments attack a note at the same time, which creates a sense of great independence between the parts. The second movement develops a short motive through counterpoint and convergence, producing rapid changes of accent and implied meter. The third movement features "heterophony of dynamics": while all four instruments sustain long tones, one instrument at a time comes to the fore through a crescendo, and the dynamically prominent notes are heard as a composite melody that builds to an intense climax. The finale (NAWM 156) is laid out in two-part counterpoint, pitting the first violin against the three other instruments. Its unusual structure, described in detail in the NAWM commentary, involves a retrograde repetition of the first half of the musical fabric, which results in a nearly perfect palindrome. Thus, through four highly contrasting movements, Crawford simultaneously embraces the tradition of the string quartet and satisfies the ultramodernist desire for something truly new.

Aaron Copland (1900–1990), shown in Figure 23.11, moved from stringent dissonance in the 1920s to a streamlined style in the 1930s and 1940s that combined modernism with national American idioms. Copland's Jewish faith, his homosexuality, and his leftist politics made him something of an outsider, yet he became the most important and central American composer of his generation through his own compositions and his work for the cause of American music. He organized concert series and composer groups, and promoted works of his predecessors and contemporaries, including Ives, Chávez, and Thomson. Through encouragement, counsel, and by example, he influenced many younger American composers, among them Leonard Bernstein, Elliott Carter, and David Del Tredici.

Growing up in a Jewish immigrant family in Brooklyn, Copland was exposed to ragtime and popular music from a young age, while studying piano, theory, and composition in the European tradition. He was the first of many American composers to study in Paris with Nadia Boulanger, from whom he learned to write music that was clear, logical, and elegant. Jazz elements and strong dissonances figure prominently in his early works, such as *Music for the Theatre* (1925) and the Piano Concerto (1926).

Recognizing the growing number of radio and record listeners, Copland sought to appeal to a larger audience. At the same time, the depression had deepened his belief in socialism, and he turned to writing music in a language that the broad masses of people

CD 11/83    CD 6/50

Aaron Copland

*Figure 23.11. Aaron Copland in the 1930s, composing in his studio.*

could understand and on subjects that were relevant to their lives and concerns. He developed a new style that combined his modernist technique with simple textures and diatonic melodies and harmonies. He incorporated Mexican folk songs in the orchestral suite *El Salón México* (1932–1936) and cowboy songs in the ballets *Billy the Kid* (1938) and *Rodeo* (1942), which reflected the American frontier experience. His opera *The Second Hurricane* (1936)—written for schools—and his scores for a number of films including *Our Town* (1940) represent music composed specifically "for use."

Copland's Americanist idiom is exemplified in *Appalachian Spring* (1943–1944), first written as a ballet with an ensemble of thirteen instruments but better known in its arrangement as an orchestral suite (excerpt in NAWM 157). The work incorporates variations on the Shaker hymn *'Tis the Gift to Be Simple*. Example 23.2 shows two variations on the hymn's third phrase. The song is subtly transfigured and its essence is absorbed in music that simply and sincerely expresses the spirit of rural life in American terms. Copland's use of transparent, widely spaced sonorities, empty octaves and fifths, and diatonic dissonances creates a distinctive sound that has been frequently imitated and has become the quintessential musical emblem of America, especially in music for film and television.

*Appalachian Spring*

CD 11/86    CD 6/53

*Example 23.2: Aaron Copland,* Appalachian Spring, *passages showing two variations of the Shaker hymn's third phrase*

*a.*

*b.*

William Grant Still (1895–1978), shown in Figure 23.12, also incorporated specifically American idioms into art music. He drew on a diverse musical background, including composition studies with George Whitefield Chadwick (see above, page 600) and Edgard Varèse, and work as an arranger for W. C. Handy's dance band. Still's success as a composer, when blacks were still largely excluded from the field of classical music, earned him the sobriquet "Dean of Afro-American Composers." He broke numerous racial barriers and became the first African American to conduct a major symphony orchestra in the United States (the Los Angeles Philharmonic, 1936); the first to have an opera produced by a major company in the United States (*Troubled Island* at New York's

William Grant Still

Figure 23.12. William Grant Still in an undated photograph.

City Center, 1949); and the first to have an opera televised over a national network. His compositions, numbering over 150, include operas, ballets, symphonies, chamber works, choral pieces, and solo vocal works.

Afro-American Symphony

CD 12/1    CD 6/63

Still established his reputation with the *Afro-American Symphony* (1930), which encompasses African American musical elements within the traditional framework of a European four-movement symphony. The opening movement (NAWM 158) is in sonata form, with a first theme in twelve-bar blues structure and a second theme that suggests a spiritual. It also features numerous other traits from African American traditions: call and response, syncopation, varied repetition of short melodic or rhythmic ideas, jazz harmonies, dialogue between groups of instruments as in a jazz arrangement, and instrumental timbres common in jazz, such as trumpets and trombones played with mutes.

Virgil Thomson

Virgil Thomson (1896–1989) was a witty and caustic critic for the *New York Herald Tribune* (1940–1954) as well as a composer. During studies at Harvard and in Paris with Nadia Boulanger, he fell under the influence of Satie, whom he met in 1922. Thomson later described Satie as the only influential composer of the time "whose works can be enjoyed and appreciated without any knowledge of the history of music." Rejecting modernism's complexity, unfamiliarity, and obsession with the past classical tradition, Thomson adopted Satie's branch of avant-gardism and sought to write music that was simple, direct, playful, and focused on the present.

Figure 23.13. Caricature of collaborators Virgil Thomson and Gertrude Stein by Aline Fruhauf, ca. 1920.

Between 1925 and 1940, Thomson lived in Paris. There he found a kindred soul in another American expatriate, Gertrude Stein, with whom he collaborated on the opera *Four Saints in Three Acts* (1927–1928). The two appear in caricature in Figure 23.13. Stein's libretto on the life of Saint Teresa of Ávila (see Figure 9.11, page 200) seems absurdist—for example, there are four acts, not three, and many more than four saints. Yet the words are not without meaning: "Pigeons on the grass, alas" is about a visitation of the Holy Spirit, often shown as a dove. The libretto's use of simple words in complex arrangements is precisely reflected in Thomson's music, which mixes dance rhythms from waltz to tango, hymnlike melodies, simple diatonic chords and progressions, evocations of marches and patriotic tunes, and other familiar elements and styles, often in wild and surprising juxtapositions. Throughout, the setting of texts shows an uncanny facility for turning American speech into fluid musical lines.

Much of Thomson's other music is more overtly Americanist. He evoked the simplicity of nineteenth-century hymnody in his *Variations on Sunday School Tunes* (1926–1927) for organ and the *Symphony on a Hymn Tune* (1928). He wrote a series of "portraits" of friends and acquaintances, most for piano, some for chamber groups. His second opera, *The Mother of Us All* (1947), also a collaboration with Stein, is based on the life of the women's suffrage leader Susan B. Anthony. Its mix of hymnody, marches, and waltzes is direct and familiar but encompasses moments of deep sentiment. Like Copland, Thomson also wrote film scores, using American folk elements from cowboy songs to spirituals; indeed, he claimed that Copland had borrowed the Americanist style from him.

In addition to composers like Cowell and Copland, who forged new compositional paths using experimental techniques or American idioms, other Americans emerged to write in styles ranging from the Neoclassical to the Romantic. The astonishing variety of American idioms that emerged in the first half of the twentieth century illustrates the general point about modernist composers in the classical tradition, no matter what their stripe. Most sought a place in the crowded classical repertoire by writing music that was individual and distinctive yet drew on past traditions and genres. Meanwhile, each of the most radical composers—like Varèse, Cowell, and (in his own way) Thomson—forged a new concept of music. For them, the best solution to the problem of competing with the past was to ignore it and focus on creating something fundamentally new.

Americanist works

Diversity of styles

# Vernacular Styles

The impact of prosperity and technology on American music as well as the growing importance of African Americans are also apparent in the varied and vibrant musical traditions outside the classical concert hall and opera house. For example, we have already encountered the rise of band music in the nineteenth century, the increasing popularity of its repertory, which included marches and dances, and the proliferation of amateur as well as professional bands.

Among the dances played by both brass and concert bands were pieces in ragtime, a style popular from the 1890s through the 1910s that featured syncopated (or "ragged") rhythm against a regular, marchlike bass. This syncopation apparently derived from the patting (or pattin') juba of American blacks, a survival of African drumming and hand clapping. The emphasis on offbeats in one rhythmic layer against steady beats in another reflects the complex cross-rhythms common in African music.

The leading ragtime composer was Scott Joplin (1868–1917), shown in Figure 23.14. Son of a former slave, he studied music in his hometown of Texarkana, Texas, and worked in Sedalia and Saint Louis, Missouri, before moving to New York in 1907. His most ambitious work was the opera *Treemonisha*, completed in 1910 though not staged until 1972. But he was best known for his piano rags, especially

*Figure 23.14. Scott Joplin in a photograph printed on the cover of his rag* The Cascades *(1904).*

CD 10/43

*Maple Leaf Rag* (1899; NAWM 136a). Like most rags, it is in $\frac{2}{4}$ meter and follows the form of a march, with a series of sixteen-measure strains, each repeated. The second strain, excerpted in Example 23.3, shows several rhythmic features typical of ragtime. The left hand keeps up a steady pulse in eighth notes, alternating between bass notes and chords, while the right-hand figures syncopate both within and across the beat. The notes in octaves, which receive extra stress, occur every three sixteenth notes, momentarily creating the impression of $\frac{3}{16}$ meter in the right hand against $\frac{2}{4}$ in the left. Essentially the same rhythmic idea appears in each two-measure unit. Such repetition of a short rhythmic pattern, like syncopation and multiple rhythmic layers, is a characteristic of African American music that can be traced back to Africa. So while the form, left-hand pattern, harmony, and chromatic motion all ultimately derive from European sources, the rhythmic elements have African roots, and the resulting mixture is quintessentially African American.

*Example 23.3: Scott Joplin,* Maple Leaf Rag, *second strain*

## Popular Song and Stage Music

The period between the two world wars, and especially the 1920s, was a rich time for American popular music. Music for stage shows of all kinds enjoyed great popularity: vaudeville troupes (including singers and dancers) toured the Continent, and operettas, variety shows, and musicals attracted large audiences. Popular songs from Tin Pan Alley also proliferated. The period roughly from 1920 to 1955—before the advent of rock and roll and the demise of the sheet-music industry—is known as the "golden age" of Tin Pan Alley.

In the 1920s, as in the previous two decades, popular song and music for theater were inextricably linked. In large part, it was the attractiveness of the songs that drove the popularity of a musical and its composer. Many of the best-known songs, made familiar in hit shows, were then sold as sheet music, often with a picture of the performer who introduced the song on the cover. But changes in the popular-song industry began to occur as publishers and songwriters increasingly counted on recordings to spread their tunes. And with the arrival of sound technology for films in the late 1920s, the Hollywood musical was born, creating another important venue for songwriters. The most successful songwriters of this period—such as Irving Berlin (1888–1989), Jerome Kern (1885–1945), and George Gershwin (1898–1937)—were equally at home writing music for Tin Pan Alley, musical theater, and Hollywood musicals.

Musical comedy

A significant new genre, the musical comedy, or musical, featured songs and dance numbers in styles drawn from popular music in the context of a spoken play with a comic or romantic plot. George M. Cohan inaugurated a distinctive style of American musical with his *Little Johnny Jones* (1904), which brought together American subject matter and the vernacular sounds of vaudeville and Tin Pan Alley with the romantic plots and European styles of comic opera and operetta. That show included two of the most famous and enduring popular songs

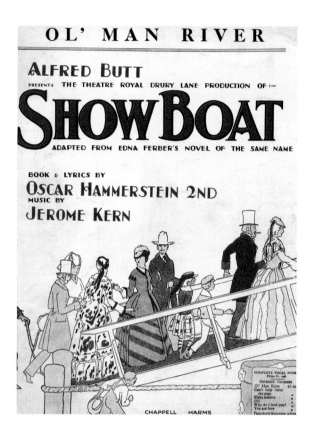

*Figure 23.15.  Sheet-music cover of the hit song* Ol' Man River *from Jerome Kern's musical* Show Boat *(1927).*

of the era, *Give My Regards to Broadway* and *The Yankee Doodle Boy* (whose chorus begins "I'm a Yankee Doodle Dandy"). From these roots would grow the musicals of Jerome Kern, Irving Berlin, George Gershwin, Rodgers and Hammerstein, and Andrew Lloyd Webber, among many others.

Characteristics

Like all forms of musical theater, musicals were complex collaborations, with different artists responsible for the music, lyrics (the texts set to music), book (the spoken words of the play), choreography, staging, lights, sets, costumes, and, often, orchestration. Some musicals were primarily vehicles for star entertainers, featuring new popular songs that were framed by a loose plot, a structure reminiscent of the singer-centered and aria-focused Italian opera of the Baroque stage. Others were more integrated shows in which the musical numbers are closely related to a story that is plot-driven rather than focused on the performers. Like reform opera of the late eighteenth century (see Chapter 14), such musicals were valued for their dramatic impact in addition to their appeal as entertaining spectacle.

Jerome Kern's masterpiece *Show Boat* (1927), with book and lyrics by Oscar Hammerstein II, best exemplifies this new, integrated approach. This musical brings together a number of traditions (opera, operetta, musical comedy, revues, vaudeville) and musical styles (ragtime, spirituals, sentimental ballads, marches), but the multiple styles all serve dramatic ends. The score is operatic in scope, with interwoven referential themes and motives, much like the operas of Richard Wagner (whose music dramas Kern greatly admired). Based on a novel by Edna Ferber, *Show Boat* dealt with serious social issues, such as racism and miscegenation, and captured recent historic events, such as the 1893 World's Columbian Exposition in Chicago. It was a tremendous success, toured the country after its Broadway run, enjoyed numerous revivals, and sold sheet-music arrangements of its hit songs, including *Ol' Man River*, in huge numbers (see Figure 23.15).

*Show Boat*

Figure 23.16. A publicity photo of the original cast of Rodgers and Hammerstein's Broadway musical Oklahoma! (1943).

Rodgers and Hammerstein produced some of Broadway's best-loved shows, including *Oklahoma!* (1943), *Carousel* (1945), *South Pacific* (1949), *The King and I* (1951), and *The Sound of Music* (1959). Their first collaboration, *Oklahoma!* not only enjoyed a record-breaking run of over 2,000 performances but also marked a pivotal moment in the development of the integrated musical. Set in the Oklahoma Territory around 1900, the story is richly textured, filled with both dramatic and comedic subplots. The characters, seen in Figure 23.16 as portrayed by the original cast, are developed not only through dialogue but also through song. Dance, choreographed by famed dancer Agnes de Mille, also played a crucial dramatic role. The story's emphasis on American folk history and the simple pleasures of rural life appealed greatly to Americans during wartime and the early postwar years.

Leonard Bernstein (1918–1990, shown in Figure 23.17) was a major presence both on Broadway and in classical music. Initially known as a classical composer, he became an overnight celebrity in 1944 after brilliantly conducting the New York Philharmonic as a last-minute replacement. That same year, his Broadway musical *On the Town* opened for a run of 463 performances. In addition to his career as a conductor and composer of symphonies and vocal music, Bernstein enjoyed enormous success with his musical *West Side Story* (1957), with lyrics by Stephen Sondheim (b. 1930) and book by Arthur Laurents. Set in gang-ridden New York City of the 1950s, *West Side Story* is a retelling of Shakespeare's *Romeo and Juliet*, substituting rival gangs for the warring families of the original. The setting provided Bernstein with rich opportunities for embracing a variety of musical styles, including Afro-Caribbean dance styles, jazz, and soaring melodies in Tin Pan Alley AABA formulas.

Figure 23.17. Leonard Bernstein conducting, 1975.

# Film Music

Sound in film

In the same way that recordings and radio fostered the explosive growth of popular song, new technologies transformed film music. In the late 1920s, methods were invented to synchronize recorded sound with film, opening up new possibilities for the use of music as part of a film, not merely as live accompaniment to it. The first "talking picture" (so called because it featured recorded dialogue) was *The Jazz Singer* (1927) starring Al Jolson, which included scenes of Jolson singing and other scenes in which music was used to accompany the action, as in earlier silent films. These two types of scene exemplify the two categories of music in film that have continued to the present:

1. music that is heard or performed by the characters themselves, known as *diegetic music* or *source music*
2. background music that conveys to the viewer a mood or other aspects of a scene or character, known as *nondiegetic music* or *underscoring*

Beginning in 1929, Hollywood studios produced numerous musicals composed for film. Sigmund Romberg (*Viennese Nights*), George Gershwin (*Delicious* and *Shall We Dance*), Irving Berlin (*Top Hat*), Jerome Kern (*Swing Time*), and Cole Porter (*Born to Dance*) all wrote music for movie musicals during the 1930s, considered the "golden age" of the Hollywood musical. The spectacular choreography of Busby Berkeley enlivened *Gold Diggers of 1933* and many other films, and the singing and dancing of Bing Crosby, Fred Astaire, and Ginger Rogers in many film musicals made them international stars. Movie musicals were enormously popular; they offered escape from the Great Depression, their level of talent was high, and they were inexpensive compared to Broadway shows. *The Wizard of Oz* (1939), with songs by Harold Arlen, introduced color photography to film musicals and launched the career of Judy Garland. A parallel development in Germany was the film operetta, including scores by Franz Lehár (*Where Is the Lady?*) and other prominent composers, but the rise of the Nazis in 1933 forced many of the leading figures to emigrate.

The Hollywood studios also fostered the rise of film scores that were fully integrated into the dramatic action, like the music for an opera—"opera without singing," in the memorable phrase of composer Erich Wolfgang Korngold. Many of the composers working in Hollywood were European immigrants, and they applied the language of Wagner, Strauss, and Debussy to music for film. Max Steiner (1888–1971), an immigrant from Vienna who had worked on Broadway for fifteen years as an arranger, orchestrator, and composer, established the model for the Hollywood film score with his music for *King Kong* (1933). The movie, whose poster is shown in Figure 23.18, centered on a giant gorilla discovered in Africa and brought to New York, where it threatens the city. Steiner's score is organized around leitmotives for characters and ideas, as in a Wagner opera, and coordinates the music with actions on screen, often marking particular movements with musical effects. The music conveys mood, character, and place through styles with strong associations, from primitivism for the African setting to orchestral Romanticism for dramatic moments, and it uses modernist techniques when appropriate, such as intense dissonance for fright and other extreme emotions. All of these traits became characteristic of film scoring.

*Figure 23.18. Poster for the original film* King Kong *(1933), whose score by Max Steiner established a high standard for Hollywood film music.*

*Figure 23.19. Bessie Smith (1894–1937), "Empress of the Blues," in the mid-1920s, when she was the most successful and prominent African American musician of the decade.*

W. C. Handy

CD 11/49

## The Jazz Age

Musicals and Tin Pan Alley songs continued traditions that had been imported from Europe or arose among Americans of European descent. But African American music and musicians played an increasingly influential role in American musical life, and in the 1920s two related traditions of African American origin gained wide currency: blues and jazz. Indeed, the 1920s became known as "the Jazz Age," and jazz became the emblematic music for that period when a new generation was cultivating a spirit of social liberation.

The origin of the blues is obscure, likely stemming from a combination of rural work songs and other African American oral traditions. The lyrics typically speak of disappointments, mistreatment, or other troubles that produce the state of mind known since the early nineteenth century as "the blues." Yet the words also convey defiance and a will to survive abandonment by a faithless lover, a lost job, oppression, or disaster. Often, touches of humor suggested the narrow separation between sorrow and laughter, tragedy and comedy. The music reflects the feelings implied by the words through melodic contours, freely syncopated rhythms, and distinctive vocal or instrumental effects (such as a slide, rasp, or growl) that evoke the sound of a person expressing pain, sorrow, or frustration. Blues often feature flatted or bent (slightly lowered or sliding) notes, sometimes called *blue notes*, on the third, fifth, and seventh scale degrees, which add to the emotional intensity. Yet the conventional framework of the blues allows the performers to display their artistry in a musical parallel to the defiance implied in the lyrics. Ultimately, the blues are not about *having* the blues, but about *conquering* them through a kind of catharsis embodied in the music.

The classic blues singers joined aspects of oral tradition with elements of popular song, thanks in part to W. C. Handy (1873–1958), known as the "Father of the Blues." Handy did not invent the blues, but, as a publisher, he introduced blues songs in sheet-music form as early as 1912, thus taking advantage of both the genre's new popularity and the booming sheet-music industry. With his publications, Handy solidified what we now think of as standard twelve-bar blues form. In this form, illustrated by Bessie Smith's *Back Water Blues* (1927, NAWM 149) in Example 23.4, each poetic stanza has three lines; the second line typically restates the first, and the third completes the thought. Each line of text is sung to four measures of music over a set harmonic pattern, in which the first four-measure phrase remains on the tonic chord; the second phrase begins on the subdominant and ends on the tonic; and the third phrase starts on the dominant and moves back to the tonic, as illustrated in the table below:

| Measure: | 1 | 2 | 3 | 4 | 5 | 6 | 7 | 8 | 9 | 10 | 11 | 12 |
|---|---|---|---|---|---|---|---|---|---|---|---|---|
| Harmony: | I | I(IV) | I | I | IV | IV | I | I | V | V(IV) | I | I |
| Poetic structure: | A | | | | A | | | | B | | | |

After a brief piano introduction, each of the seven stanzas of *Back Water Blues* follows the same form and general melodic outline. The form may be simple, but in Smith's recorded performance, the musical possibilities seem infinite. Known in the 1920s as "Empress of the Blues" (see Figure 23.19), she enlivens each stanza with unique timbres, phrasing, and melodic sensibility.

Jazz

Jazz, a mixture of ragtime and dance music combined with elements of the blues, was already established and growing in popularity during the late 1910s. The essence of 1920s jazz was syncopated rhythm combined with novel vocal

*Example 23.4: Bessie Smith,* Back Water Blues, *first stanza*

1. When it rains____ five days and the skies____ turn dark____ as night,____ when it rains____
Basic progression: I                    IV                        I              I

____ five  days____ and the skies____  turn dark____  as  night,____                    then
IV                         IV                          I              I

trou-ble's tak-in' place   in the low - lands____ at  night.____        2. I woke up____
V                          IV                       I              I

[1., 2., 3., 4., 5., 6.]

and instrumental sounds and an unbridled spirit that seemed to mock earlier social and musical properties. Improvisation was an important element of jazz, but often melodies in the style of an improvisation were worked out in rehearsals, played from memory, or written down and played from notation. Jazz was very much a player's art, so the rise of the recording industry and of radio played a key role in fostering its growth and dissemination.

Jazz differed from ragtime particularly in the way it was performed. Instead of playing the music "straight," observing the rhythms and textures of a fully notated piece, players extemporized arrangements that distinguished one performer or performance from another. A 1938 recording of early jazz pianist, composer, and New Orleans native Jelly Roll Morton (1890–1941) playing Joplin's *Maple Leaf Rag* (NAWM 136b) demonstrates the differences: the anticipations of beats, the swinging, uneven rendering of successions of equal note values, the grace notes, the enriched harmony, and the weaving of ragtime's brief motivic units into a more continuous line are all telling qualities of jazz.

Contrasted with ragtime

CD 10/47

*Figure 23.20. King Oliver's Creole Jazz Band in a 1923 publicity photo. King Oliver plays cornet in the center back; Louis Armstrong (kneeling), the slide trumpet; Lillian Hardin (later Armstrong's wife), piano.*

New Orleans jazz    The leading style of jazz in the period just after World War I is now known as *New Orleans jazz*. This style, named after the city where it originated, centers on group variation of a given tune, either actually improvised or in the same spontaneous style as improvisation. The result is a counterpoint of melodic lines, alternating with solos during which the rest of the ensemble provides a rhythmic and harmonic background. New Orleans jazz incorporates the African idiom of call and response, as well as the ecstatic outpourings of the African American Gospel tradition. The development of the style in New Orleans was enhanced by the healthy rivalry between musically literate Creoles and musically untutored African Americans, who possessed great improvisational skill. Leading musicians, including cornettist Joe "King" Oliver (1885–1938), trumpeter Louis Armstrong (1901–1971), and pianist Jelly Roll Morton, developed the style playing in clubs in Storyville, the city's red-light district. In the late 1910s, many New Orleans jazz performers left the city when professional opportunities elsewhere in the country beckoned, spreading the style to other regions.

---

**IN PERFORMANCE**   Jazz Improvisation

A crucial element of the musical language of jazz is improvisation over a given melody and/or set of chord "changes." This technique is illustrated in NAWM 150b (pages 994–1005), which presents a transcription of a recorded performance in 1928 by Louis Armstrong and His Hot Five in which the group varies an original tune by King Oliver. As the title suggests, *West End Blues* is built on a twelve-bar blues form. The published sheet music (NAWM 150a, pages 991–993) adapts the blues formula to Tin Pan Alley verse-refrain form. The blues progression (I–IV–I–V$_7$–I) appears once in its entirety in the verse, shown in Example 23.4, and twice more in the refrain. But the recorded performance dispenses with the piano introduction, the words, and their verse-refrain structure, and instead follows the conventions of jazz, presenting a series of improvised instrumental variations, or choruses (in this case, five), of the twelve-bar blues progression, in which members of the group take turns playing solos that are either spontaneously improvised or performed in the style of improvisation.

After a blazing trumpet solo by Armstrong that replaces the piano introduction of the original piece, the entire ensemble plays the first chorus together, with Armstrong taking the lead. He varies the published melody, as shown in Example 23.5 (which, unlike the NAWM score, is transposed to concert pitch), progressing from a fairly straight performance to increasingly fanciful acrobatics as he embellishes the tune both rhythmically, with triplet eighths and sixteenth notes, and melodically, with neighboring and chromatic passing tones. For example, in measure 7, he approaches every note of the E♭ triad from its upper neighbor. In the next measure, he uses six tones from the E♭ scale, omitting the A♭ until the beginning of measure 9, where the dominant harmony is introduced (A♭ being the seventh of the dominant chord). However, over the rest of the ensemble's dominant-seventh harmony (measures 9–10), Armstrong continues using the notes of the I chord, now inflecting them with chromatic passing tones. When the blues progression returns to the tonic chord at measure 11, he introduces a fanfare-like arpeggiation of F-minor⁷ (a passing ii chord) in the military-style marching-band tradition that Armstrong had heard in his native New Orleans.

In the second chorus, the trombonist plays off the first half of the published refrain and freely improvises over the rest. The third chorus features the clarinet alternating in call and response with Armstrong, who puts down his trumpet and sings in a novelty vocal style that he had made popular known as *scat*—that is, singing nonsense syllables to an improvised melody, making his voice sound like an instrument. The pianist takes the solo in the fourth chorus, alternating between elaborate figurations in the right hand and syncopated chordal decorations of the melody. The entire ensemble returns for the fifth and final chorus, with Armstrong once again assuming the lead.

Armstrong initially played in King Oliver's Creole Jazz Band (shown in Figure 23.20) but soon assembled his own group, calling it the Hot Five or Hot Seven, depending on the number of musicians. The recordings of both Oliver's and Armstrong's bands embody the classic New Orleans style. Armstrong's recording of Oliver's tune *West End Blues* (NAWM 150), recorded with the Hot Five in Chicago in 1928, exemplifies the conventions of that style. The ensemble is small and is divided into two groups: the "front line" of melodic instruments, including trumpet, clarinet, and trombone—and the rhythm section that keeps the beat and fills in the background—comprising drums, piano, and banjo. New Orleans jazz typically takes twelve-bar blues, a sixteen-measure strain from ragtime, or a thirty-two-bar popular song form (usually AABA) as a starting point. A tune is presented at the beginning over a particular harmonic progression; then that same progression repeats several times, while various soloists or combinations of instruments play over it. Each such repetition is called a *chorus* (not to be confused with the chorus in a song with verse and chorus). Typically, each chorus features different instruments and some new

King Oliver and
Louis Armstrong

CD 11/50

*Example 23.5: Verse of King Oliver's* West End Blues *with Louis Armstrong's variation*

Figure 23.21. Duke
Ellington's big band in
1943, with the composer/
arranger/band leader at
the piano.

Big bands

Swing

musical ideas, producing a kind of theme-and-variation form (see "In Performance," pages 620–621).

Although Armstrong's feats as a soloist inspired virtuosity in other jazz musicians, the main function of jazz was to accompany dancing. A fashion for larger
bands began in the 1920s, propelled partly by the availability of larger performance spaces for jazz, including supper clubs, ballrooms, auditoriums, and theaters. African American bandleaders such as Armstrong, Fletcher Henderson,
Duke Ellington (see below), and Count Basie, as well as white musicians—Paul
Whiteman and Benny Goodman, for example—organized what are called big
bands. By 1930, the typical dance band was divided into three sections: brass,
reeds, and a rhythm section consisting of piano, drums, guitar (replacing the
banjo), and double bass (see Figure 23.21). These sections interacted as units
and alternated with soloists, providing a great variety of sounds. Although solos
might still be improvised, the piece was written down by an arranger, who was
sometimes the leader (as in the case of Ellington) but more often a member of
the band or a skilled orchestrator. Successful arrangers captured in notation the
spontaneous spirit of improvised playing while making possible a wider variety
of planned effects. With the creation of fully or largely notated jazz pieces, jazz
composers who made their own arrangements came increasingly to resemble
their counterparts in the classical music world. They also borrowed sounds from
modern classical music, especially the four-note sonorities (such as seventh
chords and added sixth chords) and chromatic harmonies of Debussy and Ravel.

Much of the big-band repertory comprised popular songs in which the band
both accompanied a singer and elaborated on the song through clever, harmonically adventurous arrangements that highlighted one or another of the band's
sections. The combination of stylish, well-executed arrangements with hard-
driving jazz rhythms produced a music that became known as swing. Swing was
an immediate hit with the American public, igniting a dance craze across the

country. The number of swing bands exploded during the 1930s, boosted by new white bands entering the jazz world, especially those led by Tommy Dorsey and Glenn Miller.

## George Gershwin

Some American composers, such as George Gershwin, shown in Figure 23.22, were quick to recognize the potential of jazz and blues to add new dimensions to art music. Gershwin's most famous piece, *Rhapsody in Blue* (1924), billed as a "jazz concerto," had its premiere as the climactic number of an extravagant concert organized by bandleader Paul Whiteman as "An Experiment in Modern Music." Scored for solo piano and jazz ensemble, and influenced by popular song forms, blue notes, and other elements of jazz and blues, the *Rhapsody* met with immediate approval and pointed the way for other American composers to incorporate jazz into their art music. Gershwin himself continued to fuse the seemingly disparate traditions, producing compositions like the Piano Concerto in F (1925), the second movement of which is constructed over a twelve-bar blues harmonic pattern stretched to fit a sixteen-measure theme. Gershwin's *Porgy and Bess* (1935), which he called a folk opera, draws elements from both the operatic and Broadway traditions. The music is continuous and features recurring motives like those in Verdi or Wagner operas. Yet, in part because the characters are all African American, the musical style is heavily influenced by African American idioms such as spirituals, blues, and jazz. This blending of traditions is part of Gershwin's appeal, and it makes his music especially rich in reference and in meaning.

Gershwin was a writer of popular songs and musicals as well as a composer of jazz-influenced classical music. Like Irving Berlin, Gershwin got his start writing for revues (variety shows that included dances, songs, comedy, and other acts). And like Kern and Porter, Gershwin moved increasingly toward integrated musicals, even venturing into social commentary. *Of Thee I Sing* (1931), a

Musicals

*Figure 23.22. George Gershwin at the piano in 1937, during rehearsals for the film* Shall We Dance. *His brother, lyricist Ira Gershwin, is to his left. Seated, to his right, are the actors and dance team Fred Astaire and Ginger Rogers.*

satire of the American presidential election process, was the first musical to win the Pulitzer Prize for drama. From *Girl Crazy* (1930), the song *I Got Rhythm* (NAWM 151) became an instant hit and soon began a long career as a vehicle for jazz improvisation. The harmonic progression of the song's chorus (in jazz terminology, its "changes") was adopted for so many new jazz tunes that this progression itself came to be known as "rhythm changes."

CD 11/55 | CD 6/32

## Duke Ellington

Cotton Club years

One of the leading composers of the Jazz Age and after, and one of the most influential American composers ever, was Duke Ellington (see biography). Ellington developed his individual style and began to garner national attention from 1927 to 1931, when his group was house band at the Cotton Club in

### Duke Ellington (1899–1974)

Edward Kennedy ("Duke") Ellington, the most influential jazz composer of the twentieth century, was an innovator who expanded the boundaries of jazz and sought to break down barriers between it and art music. He admired the great jazz musicians, but his favorite composers were Debussy, Stravinsky, and Gershwin.

Born in Washington, D.C., Ellington was the son of a White House butler. He studied piano, including ragtime, from the age of seven and received a good education in music and other subjects. Known for his regal bearing and sartorial splendor, he earned the nickname "Duke" while still in high school. By the age of seventeen, Ellington was playing throughout the Washington area with his own group. In 1923, he moved to New York with his band, the Washingtonians, playing at clubs on Broadway and at the Cotton Club in Harlem and making recordings.

*Figure 23.23. Duke Ellington at the piano.*

During the 1930s and early 1940s, Ellington was the leading figure in jazz, and in later years he continued to play a prominent role, especially in efforts to have jazz recognized as a kind of art music, not merely as entertainment. He and his band made several international tours in the 1950s and 1960s, sponsored by the State Department and intended to create good will toward the United States. By the 1960s, he was regarded as a national treasure. He won thirteen Grammy awards, was awarded seventeen honorary degrees, was granted the Presidential Medal of Honor in 1969, and in the early 1970s was named a member of the National Institute of Arts and Letters and of the Swedish Royal Academy of Music, the first jazz musician to be so honored. He played and toured with his band until his death at age seventy-five, when his son, Mercer Ellington, took over the band and continued to tour.

**Major works:** *East St. Louis Toodle-oo; Black and Tan Fantasy; Mood Indigo; Creole Rhapsody; Concerto for Cootie; Ko-Ko; Cotton Tail; Black, Brown and Beige*; and more than 1,300 other compositions.

Harlem, the vibrant and famous African American area in New York. The Cotton Club period was crucial to the development of Ellington's sound. Because his was the house band, the personnel was relatively stable, they had time to rehearse, and Ellington could use the band as a workshop to try out new pieces and new effects, testing the unusual timbres and voicings that became his trademark. Picking up where Gershwin had left off, he started experimenting with longer jazz works, such as *Creole Rhapsody* and *Reminiscing in Tempo.* Rather than relying primarily on improvisation, the group moved more and more to arrangements worked out in advance that contrasted ensemble passages with solos, whether scored or improvised. He wrote specifically for, or in collaboration with, the players, emphasizing their individuality, as in *Black and Tan Fantasy* (1927), which featured his trumpeter, and *Mood Indigo* (1930) for his clarinet and saxophone player, giving each a little piece of the limelight.

The early 1940s is widely considered the peak of Ellington's creative abilities and of the performing rapport among the band members. Ellington took advantage of their talents, writing a number of new pieces to display their gifts and even using composer and arranger Billy Strayhorn's *Take the A Train* (1941) as one of the band's signature tunes. *Cotton Tail* (1940, NAWM 152) illustrates Ellington's music from this era. It follows the typical form for jazz performances, with a tune at the beginning followed by a series of choruses over the same progression. *Cotton Tail* might be called a *contrafact,* a new tune composed over a harmonic progression borrowed from a particular song—in this case, the chorus of Gershwin's *I Got Rhythm* (NAWM 151). Ellington's melody—fast, angular, highly syncopated, and full of unexpected twists—is nothing like Gershwin's, even though the harmonic progression is the same. The first two choruses featured solos by Ben Webster playing tenor saxophone, accompanied by the rhythm section with occasional punctuation from the rest of the band. Example 23.6 compares the opening measures of Ellington's tune with those of Webster's choruses. The solo plays off the same chord progression as the tune but does not vary or develop the tune; rather, the music at each chorus presents new ideas and may or may not use melodic or rhythmic motives from earlier in the piece. The remaining three choruses feature various combinations of instruments playing together or in call-and-response fashion, and the first eight bars of Ellington's tune return to bring the piece to a close.

The 1940s

CD 11/58    CD 6/35

CD 11/55    CD 6/32

*Example 23.6: Duke Ellington's* Cotton Tail *and Ben Webster's solo*

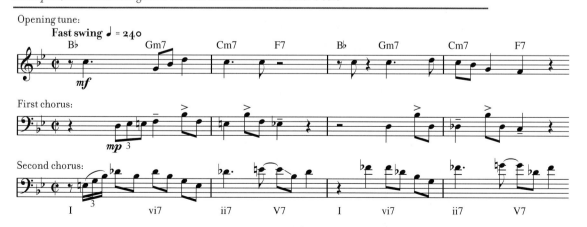

Throughout his career, Ellington rejected the label "jazz composer," preferring to consider his music (and all good music) "beyond category." He believed that jazz could serve not only as dance or entertainment music but also as art music, listened to for its own sake. He frequently pushed against the boundaries

"Beyond category"

of technology and convention, composing unconventionally long pieces that, before the introduction of long-playing records in the late 1940s, had to be recorded on multiple record sides, making them more difficult to market. Later in his career, he composed suites, such as *Black, Brown and Beige* (1943), *Harlem* (1950), and *Suite Thursday* (1960), and collaborated with Billy Strayhorn in rescoring for jazz band classical favorites such as Tchaikovsky's *Nutcracker Suite* and Grieg's *Peer Gynt Suite*. In asserting the value of jazz as an art music, he was declaring it worthy of attentive listening and of a permanent place in American culture. In both respects, his view has prevailed.

## Later Developments in Jazz

In the years immediately following the end of World War II, financial support for big bands declined sharply. More musicians now joined smaller groups, called *combos*. The styles they played differed from region to region and group to group. A new style of jazz built around virtuosic soloists fronting small combos, known as *bebop*, or *bop*, emerged in the early 1940s during the waning years of the swing craze.

Bebop    Bebop was rooted in standards from the swing era, in blues progressions, and in other popular sources for contrafacts, but it was newly infused with extreme virtuosity, harmonic ingenuity, unusual dissonances, chromaticism, complicated rhythms, and a focus on solo voices and improvisation. A typical bebop combo featured a rhythm section of piano, drums, bass, and one or more melody instruments, such as trumpet, alto or tenor saxophone, or trombone. In contrast to big-band music, bebop was meant not for dancing but for attentive listening. The focus was on the star performers and their prowess as improvisers. Performances in which one of the players was essentially the composer are preserved on recordings that have become classics, listened to over and over again, analyzed, and reviewed in critical essays.

*Figure 23.24. Alto saxophonist Charlie Parker and trumpeter Dizzy Gillespie on stage at Birdland, the legendary jazz club in New York City, ca. 1950.*

A characteristic example of bebop is *Anthropology* (NAWM 159), by alto saxo-phonist Charlie Parker (1920–1955, nicknamed "Bird") and trumpeter Dizzy Gillespie (1917–1993), who are shown in Figure 23.24. Like many other bebop standards, *Anthropology* is a contrafact on the "rhythm changes"—that is, it fea-tures a new melody over the chord progression for Gershwin's *I Got Rhythm* (see NAWM 151 and 152). A bebop performance normally begins with an introduction

| CD 12/8 | CD 6/70 |

| CD 11/55, 58 |

| CD 6/32, 35 |

---

**TIMELINE**  America, 1900–1950

---

| MUSICAL EVENTS | HISTORICAL EVENTS |
|---|---|
| Joplin, *Maple Leaf Rag* **1899** | **1899** Freud, *The Interpretation of Dreams* |
| | **1903** Wright brothers fly first successful airplane |
| Cohan, *Little Johnny Jones* **1904** | |
| | **1907** Braque and Picasso paint first cubist pictures |
| Ives, *The Unanswered Question* **1908** | **1908** Ford designs the Model T automobile |
| Ives, *General William Booth Enters into Heaven* **1914** | **1914–1918** World War I |
| | **1917** United States enters World War I; Russian Revolution brings Bolsheviks to power |
| | **1918–1919** Britain and United States give women right to vote |
| King Oliver forms the Creole Jazz Band **1920** | |
| Schoenberg writes first twelve-tone work, **1921–1923** Piano Suite Op. 25 | |
| | **1922** Eliot, *The Waste Land;* first sponsored radio broadcast in the United States; Fascists take over government in Italy |
| Gershwin, *Rhapsody in Blue* **1924** | |
| Electric microphones introduced **1925** | |
| Kern, *Showboat;* Smith, *Back Water Blues;* **1927** Champagne, *Suite canadienne* | |
| Duke Ellington's band at the Cotton Club **1927–1931** | |
| Armstrong and His Hot Five record *West End Blues* **1928** | |
| | **1929** New York stock market crash begins Great Depression |
| Still, *Afro-American Symphony;* Cowell establishes **1930** *New Musical Resources* | |
| Crawford, String Quartet **1931** | |
| Schoenberg emigrates to the United States; **1933** Steiner, film score for *King Kong* | **1933** Hitler comes to power in Germany |
| Gershwin, *Porgy and Bess* **1935** | |
| Revueltas, *Sensemayá* **1938** | **1938** Germany absorbs Austria |
| | **1939–1945** World War II |
| | **1939** Steinbeck, *The Grapes of Wrath* |
| Stravinsky and Bartók emigrate to the United States; **1940** Ellington, *Cotton Tail* | |
| Rodgers and Hammerstein, *Oklahoma!* **1943** | |
| Copland, *Appalachian Spring* **1943–1944** | |
| Parker and Gillespie, *Anthropology* **1945** | |
| Davis, *Birth of the Cool* **1949–1950** | |

and then the primary tune, known as the *head*, played in unison or octaves by the melody instruments. Players perform from an abbreviated score called a lead sheet (shown in NAWM 159a), which includes only the head, with chord symbols indicating the harmony. The tune for *Anthropology* is typical in consisting of short, rapid bursts of notes separated by surprising rests, creating a jagged, unpredictable melody. The head is followed by several choruses, solo improvisations over the harmony, and the piece ends with a final statement of the head. In the classic recording of *Anthropology*, Parker plays a sizzling solo of unusual length (transcribed in NAWM 159b), taking up three choruses and surrounding the chord changes with a flurry of chromatic alterations.

**After bebop**

Musicians like Parker, Gillespie, and Miles Davis (1926–1991) pioneered new jazz styles in the 1950s, seeking paths for individual expression by extending the methods and ideas of bebop. Some employed techniques borrowed from classical music: nonchordal dissonance, chromaticism, irregular phrase structures, modality, atonality, and unusual instrumental effects. Davis was behind a series of innovations, beginning with his album *Birth of the Cool* (1949–1950). Its softer timbres, more relaxed pace, and rhythmic subtleties inaugurated the trend that became known as *cool jazz*, soon taken up by the Modern Jazz Quartet, Dave Brubeck (b. 1920), and many others. Later, in *Kind of Blue* (1959), Davis explored yet another new style, *modal jazz*, which featured slowly unfolding melodies over stable, relatively static modal harmonies.

**Free jazz**

In the 1960s, Ornette Coleman (b. 1930) and his quartet introduced a more radically new jazz language called *free jazz*, named after their landmark album *Free Jazz* (1960). This experimental style moved away from jazz standards and familiar tunes, turning instead to a language built of melodic and harmonic gestures, innovative sounds, atonality, and free forms using improvisation that was carried on outside the strictures and structures of standard jazz forms. John Coltrane (1926–1967) developed a personal avant-garde style based on very fast playing, motivic development, new sonorities, and greater dissonance and density of sound. Like avant-garde composers in the classical tradition, creators of free jazz and other avant-garde jazz styles question some of the basic assumptions of the tradition yet clearly draw from it, wanting to say something new in a distinctive style that remains rooted in the tradition.

**Jazz as a classical music**

While some jazz performers were pursuing new alternatives, others maintained older styles, reviving ragtime and New Orleans jazz or continuing to play swing. In a striking parallel to the rise of the classical concert repertoire over a century earlier, by 1970 the jazz world had developed its own roster of classics that were treasured on recordings and kept alive in performance. A sense of history was inculcated by written histories and recorded anthologies of jazz. As younger listeners turned to the latest pop styles and other new trends, jazz increasingly became music for the well-informed listener. Jazz critics and historians began to describe jazz as a kind of classical music. Jazz ensembles were formed at many schools, colleges, and universities beginning in the 1950s and 1960s, and jazz history became part of the curriculum. Now respected as an art music, jazz nonetheless retains some of the aura of the rebellious popular music it had been half a century before.

## POSTLUDE

The twentieth century witnessed a reversal in the direction of musical influences between Europe and America: after absorbing European styles and trends through colonization and immigration during the preceding centuries, American popular music, jazz, and film music spread outward and made a huge impact on other countries. Jazz in particular spread quickly in the 1920s throughout North America, Latin America, and Europe, and became a frequent topic in European literature and arts. European musicians and music lovers encountered American jazz through imported recordings, sheet music, and traveling jazz ensembles. African American musician-soldiers serving in Europe during World War I, such as the band led by James Reese Europe, helped to introduce the new style. By the 1920s, jazz groups were forming in Europe, and a European jazz tradition was well established by the 1930s.

Through the new technologies of recordings, radio, and sound on film, American vernacular styles reached audiences throughout the Western world. Music could now be preserved and enjoyed year after year for decades to come. As a result, much of this music maintained its popularity, and within a generation or two many American works achieved the status of classics: widely known, heard and reheard, and highly valued. By the 1970s, canons of classics had developed for popular song, blues, jazz, and film music, parallel to the canon of classical music that had emerged in the nineteenth century. The central core of those canons—akin to Bach, Mozart, and Beethoven in the classical world—is in most cases formed by composers and performers whose music was popular between the world wars, including Berlin, Kern, Gershwin, Porter, Bessie Smith, King Oliver, Armstrong, Ellington, Steiner, and others. Today, in addition to recordings and movies, live ensembles perform Tin Pan Alley songs, Broadway musicals, blues, New Orleans jazz, swing, big-band jazz, and even movie scores from the 1920s and 1930s. This music is admired both for its original value as entertainment and because it is considered artful, worthy of attentive listening, and capable of offering musical experiences available nowhere else—the same reasons that music of earlier generations was preserved and revived in the nineteenth century.

In the classical tradition, while America was nurturing its own native composers such as Ives, Cowell, and Copland, it was also making room for new immigrants from the artistic communities fleeing Nazi Germany and war-torn Europe, including the composers Schoenberg, Stravinsky, Hindemith, Weill, and Bartók, who found jobs and made new lives for themselves in the United States. At the same time, a growing number of native composers throughout the Americas were winning international reputations with music that represented their nations on the world stage. Younger generations of native composers will be introduced in the next chapter, which surveys an increasingly global and amazingly varied world of art music after the war.

# 24

# The Changing World of Music since 1945

*Chapter Contents*

*Prelude* 630

Heirs to the Classical
Tradition 630

Serial and Nonserial
Complexity 636

New Sounds and
Textures 638

The Avant-Garde 646

The New Accessibility
and Other Trends 658

*Postlude* 666

## PRELUDE

The tradition of classical music performance became stronger than ever during the postwar years. Audiences grew, government support in many nations rose, schools of music expanded, and music education in primary and secondary schools increased in quantity and quality. But the living composers who saw themselves as participants in the tradition shared less and less common ground, with little consensus on style, aesthetic, or purpose. Some composers sought to preserve and extend particular aspects of the tradition, from audience appeal to modernist complexity, while others focused on the new. After two world wars, nationalism had come to seem a dangerous relic of the past and Neoclassicism an inadequate response to modernity. In every nation there was a diversity of styles and approaches, and ideas that began in one place were often imitated elsewhere. Thus, it makes sense to divide our survey not by nation, but by large trends, using individual composers as case studies. However, some composers (Babbitt, Cage, and Stockhausen, for example) participated in more than one trend, in which case their works are gathered together into individual discussions for convenience and brevity.

## Heirs to the Classical Tradition

Although critical discussion of twentieth-century music has often focused on new sounds and techniques, many postwar composers used traditional media. Like their forebears, they sought an individual voice within the classical tradition.

### Olivier Messiaen

Olivier Messiaen (1908–1992), shown in Figure 24.1, was the most important French composer born in the twentieth century. A native of Avignon in southern France, he studied organ and composition at the Paris Conservatoire, served as organist at Saint Trinité in Paris from 1931 on, and became professor of harmony at the Conservatoire in 1941. After the war, he taught many important composers of the younger generation, including his fellow Frenchman Pierre Boulez (b. 1925), the German Karlheinz Stockhausen (b. 1928), the Italian Luigi Nono (1924–1990), and the Netherlander Ton de Leeuw (1926–1996). It is a tribute to the quality and impartiality of Messiaen's teaching that each of these pupils went his own way.

A devout Catholic, Messiaen composed many pieces on religious subjects, such as the *Quatuor pour la fin du temps* (Quartet for the End of Time) for violin, clarinet, cello, and piano, written at a German military prison camp in 1941 for performance by the composer and three fellow prisoners; *Vingt regards sur l'Enfant-Jésus* (Twenty Looks at the Infant Jesus, 1944) for piano; his opera *Saint Francis of Assisi* (1975–1983); and numerous works for his own instrument, the organ. Other principal compositions include *Turangalîla-symphonie* (1946–1948) and *Catalogue d'oiseaux* (Catalogue of Birds, 1956–1958) for piano.

Messiaen sought to embody in music an aesthetic of ecstatic contemplation. His works typically present an experience of concentrated meditation on a few materials, like a musical mantra. Rather than develop themes, he juxtaposes static ideas, showing his heritage from Debussy and Stravinsky. Messiaen used several characteristic devices, described in his book *The Technique of My Musical Language* (1944), that helped him achieve his goal of writing meditative music. The opening movement of the *Quatuor pour la fin du temps*, entitled *Liturgie de cristal* (Crystal Liturgy, NAWM 160), illustrates several of them, as shown in Example 24.1. Both the violin and clarinet play figures that suggest birdcalls, which Messaien frequently used to convey a sense of contemplating the gifts of nature and the divine. The cello notes are all from a single whole-tone scale, in a repeating sequence of five notes (C–E–D–F♯–B♭), another device that makes Messiaen's music able to suggest contemplation and a negation of desire. Messiaen's harmony also avoids moving forward to a resolution. Rather, chord series are simply repeated to create a sense of stasis or meditation. In this

Music as
contemplation

CD 12/16    CD 6/75

Harmonic stasis

*Figure 24.1. Olivier Messiaen
playing the organ in the early 1950s.*

movement, the piano plays a succession of twenty-nine chords six times (the last incomplete); the second statement begins in measure 8.

Rhythmic stasis        Messiaen treats rhythm as a matter of duration, not meter. In Example 24.1 and throughout the movement, both piano and cello play a repeating series of

*Example 24.1: Olivier Messiaen,* Liturgie du cristal, *from* Quatuor pour la fin du temps

* Glissando bref; id. aux passages similaires.

durations that resemble the talea, or rhythmic pattern, of medieval isorhythm (see Chapter 4). The piano features a string of seventeen durations (numbered in the example) played ten times, of which the first two statements appear in the example. Because such repeating pitch and rhythmic series create cyclic repetition, and because they preserve their identity outside the propulsive force of regular meter, they seem to float in time, once again inviting contemplation.

Finally, Messiaen preferred beautiful timbres and colorful harmonies. Here, the cello plays in high harmonics (sounding two octaves above the notated pitches), creating an ethereal sound, augmented by the gentle birdcalls in the high violin and clarinet over soft dissonances in the piano. Messiaen invites us to meditate on these sonorous objects as they constantly recombine in new ways yet remain the same, like colorful shapes in a kaleidoscope.

*Ethereal sounds*

## Benjamin Britten

While Messiaen focused on music of contemplation, English composer Benjamin Britten (1913–1976) was concerned primarily with communication. After studying privately and at the Royal College of Music, Britten spent several years in the late 1930s writing music for films, an experience that shaped his style by teaching him to communicate by the simplest means. Like Copland, he tempered modernism with simplicity to achieve a clear and widely appealing idiom. Maturing in the 1930s, he was deeply influenced by humanitarian concerns and ideals of public service, manifest in his interest in writing music for children and amateurs, his allegorical pleas for tolerance, and his pacifism.

Most of Britten's choral music was written for the English choral tradition, nurtured in church and cathedral choirs, schools, and amateur choruses. Works such as *Hymn to St. Cecilia* (1941–1942), *A Ceremony of Carols* (1942), and *Missa brevis* (1959) were conceived for such groups and have become standards. His one-act opera *Noye's Fludde* (Noah's Flood, 1957–1958), on the text of a medieval miracle play, is intended for a mixture of professional performers with children of various ages and includes hymns that the audience is invited to sing. These and his other works for nonprofessionals are melodious, challenging pieces that suit their performers' abilities yet are not limited by them.

*Music for amateurs*

*Figure 24.2. Benjamin Britten (right) and Peter Pears, ca. 1944, when Britten was working on his opera* Peter Grimes.

Britten was a homosexual and was the life partner of the tenor Peter Pears (1910–1986). Shown in Figure 24.2, the two met in 1936 and lived together until Britten's death five decades later. Britten wrote most of his tenor roles for Pears, and the two collaborated as performers and as producers of the annual music festival at Aldeburgh in England. Several of Britten's operas have themes that relate to homosexuality, including *Billy Budd* (1950–1951) and *Death in Venice* (1971–1974).

*Peter Grimes* (1944–1945), which established Britten's reputation and became the first English opera since Purcell to enter the international repertory, centers on a fisherman who is disliked by the other residents of his village, pursued by mobs, and ultimately driven to suicide. The theme of the individual persecuted by the crowd can be read as an allegory for the condition of homosexuals in a hostile society (see Figure 24.3). Tellingly, Grimes is not a sympathetic character; we are meant to see ourselves not in him, but in the ugly crowd that unthinkingly persecutes outsiders on

*Figure 24.3. A scene from the 1995 production of* Peter Grimes *at the Royal Opera House in London, with Bryn Terfel (left) singing the title role.*

CD 12/17

the basis of suspicions and misinformation, forcing a poignant catharsis in the final tragedy. In the last scene (NAWM 161), as a search party pursues him calling his name, Grimes raves and mocks them in an unmeasured recitative, until his friend urges him to sail his boat out to sea and sink it. The opera ends with a stunning depiction of the uncaring sea and equally uncaring townsfolk in a most successful application of bitonality: strings, harp, and winds arpeggiate thirds that encompass all the notes of the C-major scale, depicting the shimmering sea, as the town's citizens go about their business, singing a slow hymn to the sea in A major. The entire scene displays the eloquent dramatic effects Britten creates out of simple means.

*War Requiem*

Britten's pacifism—his conscientious objection to war in any form—is expressed in his choral masterpiece, *War Requiem* (1961–1962). Commissioned for the consecration of the new cathedral at Coventry, a city destroyed in a German bombing raid during World War II, the work weaves together the Latin text of the Requiem Mass with verses by Wilfred Owen, an English soldier and poet killed in France in 1918 just days before the end of World War I. Britten's commitment—to pacifism, to tolerance, to including all ages and talents in music making—gives his music a quality of social engagement that has attracted many performers and listeners, and has inspired later composers.

## Tonal Traditionalism

Many twentieth-century composers developed individual styles without departing radically from the past. Tonality or neotonality often, though not necessarily, characterizes their music, along with identifiable themes, readily audible forms, and programmatic subjects or titles. (See also neo-Romanticism below.)

*Samuel Barber*

Of the American composers who remained committed to tonality, one of the most successful was Samuel Barber (1910–1981). His tonal romanticism is fully expressed in his best-known work, *Adagio for Strings* (arranged from the slow movement of his String Quartet, 1936), and in his Violin Concerto (1939) and Piano Concerto (1962). He often incorporated modernist resources into his tonal music—for example, his Piano Sonata (1949), which uses twelve-tone rows in a tonal framework. Barber was renowned for his vocal music, including

*Dover Beach* (1931) for voice and string quartet, *Knoxville: Summer of 1915* (1950) for voice and orchestra, and three operas. The songs in his cycle *Hermit Songs* (1952–1953), on texts by medieval Irish monks and hermits, are always tonally centered, yet each offers a novel blend of traditional tonality with modern resources. For instance, the eighth song, *The Monk and His Cat* (NAWM 162), shown in Example 24.2, is solidly in F major yet features almost no consonant harmonies. Barber uses open fifths in the bass line to suggest a medieval atmosphere and dissonant augmented unisons (B♭–B♮ and E–E♭) in the piano to suggest the cat. Against the steady rhythm of the piano, the vocal melody projects the natural text accentuation in a syncopated, flexible line. This song shows Barber's ability to write music that sounds fresh, like no other music, while using only traditional resources.

CD 12/23    CD 6/76

*Example 24.2: Samuel Barber,* The Monk and His Cat, *from* Hermit Songs

*Notes marked (–) in these two measures should be slightly longer, pochissimo rubato.

## Stylistic Mixtures

The wide dissemination of music from all over the world encouraged composers to mix styles and traditions. Some blended their own national or regional traditions with international ones, while other composers incorporated elements from distant lands.

Alberto Ginastera (1916–1983) of Argentina, the most prominent Latin American composer after Villa-Lobos, drew on both nationalism and international sources. He divided his own career into three periods. His "objective nationalism" (to 1947), typified in *Danzas argentinas* for piano (1937), is characterized by tonal music infused with traditional Argentine folk elements. In the second period, "subjective nationalism" (1947–1957), he forged an original style through a Bartóklike synthesis of native and international elements, as

Latin America: Alberto Ginastera

in *Pampeanas No. 1* for violin and piano (1947) and *No. 2* for cello and piano (1950). His "neo-expressionism" (after 1957) combines earlier traits with twelve-tone and avant-garde techniques, as in his operas *Don Rodrigo* (1963–1964), *Bomarzo* (1966–1967), and *Beatrix Cenci* (1971). Ginastera's turn from nationalism to a more abstract style is typical of the postwar era.

Third stream

In the 1950s and 1960s, as jazz was being taken more and more seriously, some American composers who were conversant with both jazz and classical music sought consciously to merge the two. One of the most successful of these, Gunther Schuller (b. 1925), called this combination "third stream." In his *Transformation* (1957), a pointillistic twelve-tone context with elements of Schoenberg's *Klangfarbenmelodie* is transformed into a full-blown modern jazz piece.

Michael Tippett

Englishman Michael Tippett (1905–1998) represents a different kind of synthesis, remarkably open to historical, ethnic, and non-Western styles and materials. The rhythmic and metrical independence that Tippett assigned to instrumental parts derived partly from English Renaissance music. The Piano Concerto (1953–1955) and the Triple Concerto for violin, viola, and cello (1979) reveal Tippett's admiration for Javanese gamelan music, the former work in its textures and instrumental combinations, the latter in its use of a Javanese melody with rippling figuration and sounds such as gongs in the accompaniment of the slow movement. As we will see below, many other composers drew on Asian music as part of their exploration of new sounds and textures.

## Serial and Nonserial Complexity

After World War II, young composers in Germany and elsewhere embraced music that the Nazi regime had condemned, especially that of Schoenberg and Webern. By the early 1950s, many composers had adopted twelve-tone methods, adapting them to their own purposes. We have seen that established composers like Stravinsky and Ginastera took up serialism, but it had its most profound impact on the generation of composers who were just beginning their careers at the end of the war. Their interest was partly musical, reflecting enthusiasm for new possibilities, and partly political, expressing a rejection of the Nazi and communist ideologies that had opposed such dissonant and esoteric music.

Politics and institutional support

The new developments were encouraged by government-sponsored musical institutions, such as the courses for new music held in Darmstadt, West Germany, each summer beginning in 1946 (with the secret assistance of the United States' occupying forces). At a memorial concert of his works at Darmstadt in 1953, Webern was hailed as the father of a new movement. In the United States, serialism was adopted by many university composers and others, even Copland, as a way to achieve a music free of nationalist, fascist, or leftist ideology and thus escape the taint of politics many styles had acquired during the 1930s and early 1940s. Government and university support was crucial since there was never a large or enthusiastic audience for serial music. Some saw that as a virtue, allowing music to advance in its own terms, like physics, without having to please the untutored listener (see vignette, page 643).

The ideas fostered at Darmstadt and other centers for new music inspired experiments by composers in many countries. But every composer worked independently, striking out in new directions, cultivating a personal language and style. Pierre Boulez of Paris and Karlheinz Stockhausen (see page 640) of Cologne, both pupils of Messiaen, became the two principal composers of the

Darmstadt group, and Milton Babbitt (b. 1916; see Figure 24.7 below, and page 642) became the leading serial composer and theorist in the United States.

## Extensions of Serialism

Beginning in the late 1940s, composers applied the principle of Schoenberg's tone rows to musical parameters other than pitch, giving rise to what has been called *total serialism*. If the twelve notes of the chromatic scale could be serialized, so could durations, intensities, timbres, and other elements, although typically only some nonpitch elements are treated serially, and the rest are used to highlight the serial structure.

Pierre Boulez (see Figure 24.4) was inspired by some of the methods of his teacher, Messiaen, to write the first European work of total serialism, *Structures* (1952) for two pianos, in which pitches and durations are both serial while dynamics and articulation are used to distinguish rows from one another. Boulez soon relaxed the rigidity of total serialism. In *Le Marteau sans maître* (The Hammer without a Master, 1954, revised 1957), he fused the pointillist style—featuring a very spare texture with only a few notes at once—and the serial method with sensitive musical realization of the text. This work, in nine short movements, is a setting of verses from a cycle of surrealist poems by René Char, interspersed with instrumental "commentaries." The ensemble—a different combination in each movement, as in Schoenberg's *Pierrot lunaire*—comprises alto flute, xylorimba, vibraphone, guitar, viola, and a variety of soft percussion instruments. The ensemble produces a translucent scrim of sound, all in the middle and high registers, with effects often suggestive of Balinese gamelan music. The contralto vocal line is characterized by wide melodic intervals, glissandos, and occasional *Sprechstimme*.

*Figure 24.4. Pierre Boulez conducting in the 1970s.*

**The listener**

A totally serial composition may give a listener an impression of randomness because music based on these principles typically lacks readily perceived themes, a distinct rhythmic pulse, and a sense of progression toward points of climax. Instead, the listener hears only unrepeated and unpredictable musical events. To be sure, the totality of these events in a well-constructed work does form a logical pattern, but it will inevitably be unique, likely resembling nothing the listener has heard before, and, therefore, difficult to perceive. As a result, postwar serial music has enjoyed an enduring unpopularity, appealing principally to a small set of enthusiasts.

**Virtuosity**

The music of total serialism was extraordinarily difficult to perform. For the structure to be clear, not only must the pitches and rhythms be absolutely accurate, but the dynamics must be exact—every *ff* exactly that and not *f* or *fff*. In the postwar years, a new generation of technically proficient performers emerged who were capable of playing such works and who made careers as champions of the newest music. Their presence encouraged composers to write pieces to challenge the skills of these new virtuosos. Much of this new music was not serial, but drew on sounds and textures like those explored in serial music.

**Luciano Berio**

The new virtuosity is well represented by the series of works by Italian composer Luciano Berio (1925–2003) entitled *Sequenza*, each for an unaccompanied solo instrument from flute (1958) to accordion (1995–1996) and each composed for a specific performer. The excerpt from *Sequenza IV* for piano (1965–1966) in Example 24.3 shows the rapid gestures and sudden changes of register and dynamic level that are typical of the work. The atonal language, figuration, and textures that Berio uses here resemble those of his earlier serial music. Throughout, he uses the sustain pedal (which holds the dampers off the strings for notes that are being held when the pedal is pressed) to allow open strings to continue sounding or to catch harmonics from other notes, creating an unusual effect.

*Example 24.3: Luciano Berio, passage from* Sequenza IV *for piano*

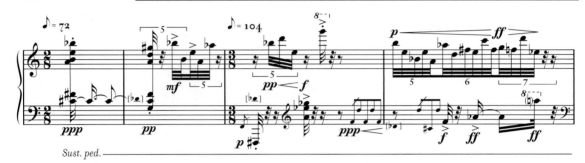

**Elliott Carter**

The American composer Elliott Carter (b. 1908) also wrote for virtuoso performers, using a complex, nonserial style characterized by innovations in rhythm and form. Beginning with his Cello Sonata (1948), Carter developed what he called "metric modulation," in which a transition is made from one tempo and meter to another through an intermediary stage that shares aspects of both, resulting in a precise proportional change in the value of a durational unit. In his String Quartet No. 2 (1959), each instrumental part takes on a distinctive personality that interacts with the others as if in a dramatic work. The instruments are differentiated by their most prominent intervals as well as by their individual rhythmic profiles. For example, the first violin dwells on minor thirds and perfect fifths and plays rapid, even notes, whereas the viola part is characterized by tritones and ninths with a triplet rhythmic pattern. The result is a counterpoint of sharply differentiated lines, inspired in part by the multi-layered textures in the music of Ives, whom Carter knew in his youth.

The difficulties of performing works like these have meant that they are seldom played and are known mainly through recordings. Yet, like nineteenth-century virtuoso showpieces, the best of these pieces attract some of the top performers and are likely to endure.

## New Sounds and Textures

One prominent strand in twentieth-century music was the exploration of new musical resources, including new sounds and new conceptions of music. In the postwar period, the search for new resources intensified. Among all the variety, at least four overlapping trends can be identified: the use of new instruments, sounds, and scales; incorporation of non-Western sounds and instruments; electronic music; and music of texture and process.

### New Instruments, Sounds, and Scales

In their effort to offer something new and distinctive in art music, many composers sought out new sounds, sometimes building new instruments or reconfiguring traditional ones, and some explored scales featuring intervals smaller than a semitone.

One composer who combined the exploration of new instrumental sounds with a new approach to pitch was Harry Partch (1901–1974), who undertook an individualistic, single-minded search for new sonic media. He repudiated equal temperament and Western harmony and counterpoint to seek a wholly new system inspired partly by Chinese, Native American, Jewish, Christian, African, and rural American music. His writings speak of a "monophonic" musical ideal, harking back to the ancient Greeks. Partch devised a new scale with forty-three notes to the octave based on just intonation, in which notes relate to each other through pure intervals from the harmonic series. He then built new instruments that could play in this scale, including modified guitars, marimbas, tuned cloud-chamber bowls (large glass containers used in early particle physics), a large string instrument like the ancient Greek kithara, and the gourd tree, shown in Figure 24.5. In his multimedia works of the 1950s and 1960s, these instruments accompany speaking and chanting voices and dancing by singer-actor-dancers. In much of his work, in particular *Oedipus—a Music-Dance Drama* (1951) and *Revelation in the Courthouse Park* (1962), based on Euripides' *The Bacchae*, Partch aspired to the ideal of Greek tragedy.

Figure 24.5.  *Harry Partch playing the gourd tree, one of the instruments he invented to realize his music based on a forty-three-note untempered scale. Beside him are two cone gongs.*

CD 12/26, 27

Taking a path similar to Partch, George Crumb (b. 1929) has been most imaginative in coaxing new sounds out of ordinary instruments and objects. In *Ancient Voices of Children* (1970), a cycle of four songs on poems by Federico García Lorca with two instrumental interludes, his unconventional sound sources include toy piano, musical saw, harmonica, mandolin, Tibetan prayer stones, Japanese temple bells, and electric piano. He obtained special effects also from conventional instruments: for example, players must bend the pitch of the piano by applying a chisel to the strings, thread paper through the harp strings, and tune the mandolin a quarter tone flat. In *Black Angels* (1970, NAWM 163), a string quartet is electronically amplified to produce surrealistic, dreamlike juxtapositions. The composer explored unusual means of bowing, such as striking the strings near the pegs with the bow and bowing between the left-hand fingers and the pegs. The new and unusual effects in Crumb's music always have a musical purpose, providing material for juxtaposition and variation; they usually evoke extramusical associations as well. Here, they help to express his reactions to the Vietnam conflict, the social unrest in the United States, and the horrors of war. Crumb's works also often reflect on music of the past; in this case, *Black Angels* quotes the chant *Dies irae* and Schubert's *Death and the Maiden* Quartet for their affective associations.

## Non-Western Styles and Instruments

Growing sensitivity to the perspectives of other cultures led to an exploration of their music with respect for its uniqueness, rather than invoking the "foreign" for its sheer otherness, as in nineteenth-century exoticism. Several Western composers became fascinated with Asian instruments, sounds, and textures. While Tippett and Partch drew on ideas from Asian music, Canadian American composer Colin McPhee (1900–1964) studied music in Bali in the 1930s, transcribed gamelan music for Western instruments, and composed *Tabuh-tabuhan* (1936) for orchestra and many other pieces that drew on Balinese materials.

Colin McPhee

Henry Cowell

Henry Cowell's lifelong interest in Asian music (see Chapter 23) grew after World War II, and travels to Iran, India, and Japan led to several works that blended Asian and Western elements, including *Persian Set* (1957) for chamber orchestra, Symphony No. 13 (*Madras*) (1956–1958), *Ongaku* (1957) for orchestra, and two concertos for the Japanese koto (a plucked string instrument) and orchestra (1961–1962 and 1965). Cowell's student and friend Lou Harrison (1917–2003) combined his interest in just intonation and his penchant for inventing new instruments—inspired by Partch—with enthusiasm for the music of Asia. After visiting Korea and Taiwan in 1961–1962, Harrison wrote several works that combine Western and Asian instruments, including *Pacifika Rondo* (1963) and *La Koro Sutro* (1972), and beginning in the 1970s he composed dozens of pieces for traditional Javanese gamelan.

Lou Harrison

## Electronic Music

As new technologies developed, musicians explored their potential for new sounds and compositional techniques. No technology promised more far-reaching changes for music than the electronic recording, production, and transformation of sounds. These technologies were first exploited in art music but ultimately became more significant for popular music, especially after 1970.

*Musique concrète*

One approach was to work with recorded sounds, taking the entire world of sound as potential material for music, manipulating the chosen sounds through mechanical and electronic means, and assembling them into collages. Pierre Schaeffer (1910–1995), who pioneered music of this type at Radiodiffusion Française (French Radio) in Paris in the 1940s, named it *musique concrète* because the composer worked concretely with sound itself rather than with music notation. He and his collaborator, Pierre Henry, created the first major work of musique concrète, *Symphonie pour un homme seul* (Symphony for One Man), premiered in a 1950 radio broadcast. Tape recorders, which became widely available around that year, made it possible to record, amplify, and transform sounds, then superimpose, juxtapose, fragment, and arrange them as desired to produce pieces of music.

Another source for new sounds was to produce them electronically. Most electronic sounds are created by oscillators, invented in 1915. The first successful electronic instrument was the theremin, invented around 1920 by Lev Termen, which changed pitch according to the distance between the instrument's antenna and the performer's hand. The ondes martenot, invented in 1928 by Maurice Martenot, was controlled by a wire, ribbon, or keyboard. Both instruments produced only one note at a time, were capable of glissandos along the entire pitch continuum, and projected a haunting, almost voice-like sound. Featured in some orchestral works, they became common in film scores like Hitchcock's *Spellbound*, where they lent an eerie or futuristic effect, but they were not used in electronic music itself.

Electronic music studios

Between 1951 and 1953, studios to create electronic music were founded at Columbia University in New York and at radio stations in Cologne (Germany), Milan (Italy), and Tokyo (Japan), followed by many others across Europe and the Americas. At most studios, composers focused on producing sounds electronically and manipulating them through electronic devices and on tape. A new realm of possible sounds became available, including sounds not producible by any "natural" means.

Karlheinz Stockhausen

Karlheinz Stockhausen (b. 1928) was one of the pioneers of electronic music composition. He and others often used recorded sounds alongside electronic ones, as in his *Gesang der Jünglinge* (Song of the Youths, 1955–1956), which incorporated a boy's voice. This was the first major electronic piece to use multiple tracks, played in concert through several loudspeakers placed in various positions relative to the audience, thereby creating a sense of the music coming from numerous directions and moving through space. At the same time, Stockhausen maintained his links with the past and with his teacher, Messaien, by using borrowed material in several works, notably *Gesang der Jünglinge, Telemusik* (1966), *Hymnen* (1967), and *Opus 1970* (1970). Hymnen (Hymns) incorporates words and melodies of many different national anthems—a technique noted below as "quotation and collage" (see page 660—in a performance combining electronic sounds with voices and instruments. The intention, Stockhausen claimed, was "not to interpret, but to hear familiar, old, preformed musical material with new ears, to penetrate and transform it with a musical consciousness of today." This aim represents a new way of relating music of the present to that of the past.

Edgard Varèse (see Chapter 23) combined electric sounds with recorded ones. His *Poème électronique* (Electronic Poem, 1957–1958), incorporating recorded sounds—noises, a singer—represented a pinnacle of his concept of spatial music. Commissioned by the Philips Radio Corporation for the Brussels World's Fair in 1958, the eight-minute piece was projected by 425 loudspeakers arranged all about the interior space of the pavilion (designed by Le Corbusier and shown in Figure 24.6), and was accompanied by moving colored lights and projected images. Fifteen thousand people a day experienced this multimedia piece over a six-month period, so it was probably heard "live" by more people than any other serious work of electronic music.

Electronic music was at first produced by combining, modifying, and controlling in various ways the output of oscillators, then recording these sounds on tape. The composer had to splice the tapes and mix their output, sometimes in combination with recorded sounds of physical objects in motion or of musicians, speakers, or singers. Electronic sound synthesizers were developed to make the process much easier. The composer could call on pitches from a music keyboard and, with switches and knobs, control harmonics, waveform (which determines timbre), resonance, and location of the sound sources. The RCA Mark II Electronic Music Synthesizer, shown in Figure 24.7, was developed at the joint Columbia-Princeton Electronic Music Center in the late 1950s and used by many composers from the United States and abroad.

In the mid-1960s, Robert Moog and Donald Buchla each developed far simpler and more compact synthesizers based on voltage-controlled oscillators. When these became commercially available in 1966, they were adopted by electronic music studios and individual composers around the world. One of the early works created on the Buchla synthesizer was *Silver Apples of the Moon* (1967) by Morton Subotnick (b. 1933), the first electronic piece to be commissioned by a record company, designed to fill two sides of an LP and to be played at home rather than in concert. The new synthesizers were also adopted by popular artists such as the Beatles, and electronic synthesizers soon became a familiar sound in pop music.

The electronic medium gave composers complete, unmediated control over their compositions. Much of the new music already demanded complex rhythms and minute shadings of pitch, intensity, and timbre that could barely be realized by human performers, but in the electronic studio, every detail could be

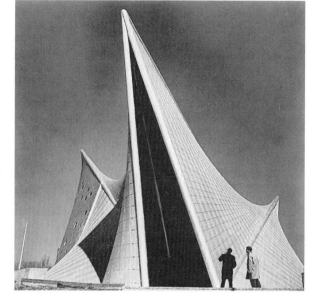

*Figure 24.6. The Philips Pavilion at the 1958 World's Fair in Brussels, Belgium. Edgard Varèse collaborated with the architect Le Corbusier to fill this building with the sound of his* Poème électronique.

Synthesizers

Role of performers

Figure 24.7. *American composer Milton Babbitt at the console of the RCA Mark II Electronic Music Synthesizer at the Columbia-Princeton Electronic Music Center in New York, ca. 1960.*

Milton Babbitt

CD 12/28    CD 6/79

accurately calculated and recorded. Yet the absence of performers hindered the acceptance of purely electronic music since audiences expect to have performers they watch and respond to. Furthermore, performers' lack of involvement was detrimental on another level because performers are the main promoters and advocates for new music. Recognizing these factors, composers soon began to create works that combined prerecorded tape with live performers.

One of the most moving early examples was Milton Babbitt's *Philomel* (1964, first section in NAWM 164), for soprano soloist with a tape that includes a kind of distorted echo of her own voice together with electronic sounds. The live voice and the voice on tape engage in dialogue, accompanied by synthesized sounds, all worked out according to Babbitt's usual serial procedures, discussed below. The poem is based on a story from Ovid's *Metamorphoses* involving betrayal, pain, revenge, and lament. After Philomel is violated by her brother-in-law, her tongue is cut out to prevent her from disclosing the crime. Only after being transformed into a nightingale does Philomel regain her voice, at which point the sung text begins. In fear and confusion, she runs through the forest seeking counsel from a thrush, a hawk, an owl, and a gull, all represented on the tape by recorded birdsong. (A detailed discussion appears in NAWM 164.)

Babbitt (shown with the synthesizer in Figure 24.7) was the first American composer to expand the serial techniques of Schoenberg and Webern into new dimensions. In his Three Compositions for Piano (1947), he subjected both pitch and duration to serial control for the first time, anticipating similar experiments by Boulez and Stockhausen. Babbitt went beyond the practices of Schoenberg and his circle to realize new potentials of the twelve-tone system. At the same time, he became an outspoken proponent of the composer's right to be indifferent to the public's likes and dislikes. He expressed this attitude in a 1958 essay entitled by a magazine editor "Who Cares If You Listen?" (see vignette, page 643).

## Music of Texture and Process

Varèse's conception of music as spatial, with sound masses moving through musical space and interacting with each other like an abstract ballet in sound, opened the door to music that centered not on melody, harmony, or counterpoint, but on sound itself. Moreover, the exploration of electronic sounds stimulated the invention of new sound effects obtainable from conventional instruments and voices, often imitating electronic music. Composers now wrote pieces whose material consists primarily of striking sound combinations that create interesting and novel textures, organized by gradual or sudden processes of change.

One of the first to write such music for acoustic instruments was Iannis Xenakis (1922–2001). A Greek who spent most of his career in France, Xenakis was an engineer and architect as well as a composer. Like the ancient Greeks, he saw mathematics as fundamental to both music and architecture, so he based his music on mathematical concepts. In *Metastaseis* (1953–1954), he gave each string player in the orchestra a unique part to play. In many sections of the work, each player has a glissando, moving slowly or quickly in comparison to the other parts. In Figure 24.8, Xenakis plotted out the glissandos as straight lines

Iannis Xenakis

---

**VIGNETTE    Composition as Research**

*Milton Babbitt, professor of music and of mathematics at Princeton University, argued that composers, like scientists, engage in research that advances knowledge and should be supported for that work, even if it lies beyond most people's comprehension. His view extends in new terms the nineteenth-century view of music as an autonomous art to be pursued for its own sake. This excerpt is from an essay he wrote under the title "The Composer as Specialist," changed by an editor at the magazine where it first appeared to the more provocative "Who Cares If You Listen?"*

Why should the layman be other than bored and puzzled by what he is unable to understand, music or anything else? It is only the translation of this boredom and puzzlement into resentment and denunciation that seems to me indefensible. After all, the public does have its own music, its ubiquitous music: music to eat by, to read by, to dance by, and to be impressed by. Why refuse to recognize the possibility that contemporary music has reached a stage long since attained by other forms of activity? The time has passed when the normally well-educated man without special preparation can understand the most advanced work in, for example, mathematics, philosophy, and physics. Advanced music, to the extent that it reflects the knowledge and originality of the informed composer, scarcely can be expected to appear more intelligible than these arts and sciences to the person whose musical education usually has been even less extensive than his background in other fields. But to this, a double standard is invoked,

with the words "music is music," implying also that "music is just music." Why not, then, equate the activities of the radio repairman with those of the theoretical physicist, on the basis of the dictum that "physics is physics"? . . .

I dare suggest that the composer would do himself and his music an immediate and eventual service by total, resolute, and voluntary withdrawal from this public world to one of private performance and electronic media, with its very real possibility of complete elimination of the public and social aspects of musical composition. By so doing, the separation between the domains would be defined beyond any possibility of confusion of categories, and the composer would be free to pursue a private life of professional achievement, as opposed to a public life of unprofessional compromise and exhibitionism.

But how, it may be asked, will this serve to secure the means of survival for the composer and his music? One answer is that after all such a private life is what the university provides the scholar and the scientist. It is only proper that the university, which—significantly—has provided so many contemporary composers with their professional training and general education, should provide a home for the "complex," "difficult," and "problematical" in music.

From Milton Babbitt, "Who Cares If You Listen?" *High Fidelity* 8, no. 2 (February 1958): 39–40; repr. in Oliver Strunk, ed., *Source Readings in Music History*, rev. ed. by Leo Treitler (New York: Norton, 1998), pp. 1308–1310.

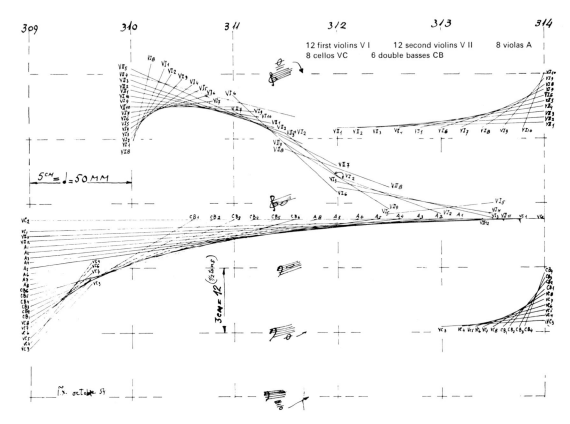

*Figure 24.8. Iannis Xenakis's graph for a passage in* Metastaseis, *with pitch as the vertical axis and time as the horizontal axis. The lower half of the graph represents the lower strings attacking a chromatic cluster together, then curving upward as the lowest pitches in the cluster rise in rapid glissandi and the higher ones move progressively more slowly. Toward the end of the passage, groups of strings enter on the same note one after another, each successively rising in a faster glissando until all end together in a chromatic cluster.*

on a graph that add up to create an effect of curves in musical space. He then transferred the lines to standard musical notation. The resulting motions—of a chromatic cluster gradually closing to a unison or a unison expanding to a cluster—resemble changes achievable in electronic music through the use of pitch filters. The overall effect is very strongly visual, although the materials are musical. Indeed, Xenakis later applied the same idea of straight lines creating a curving effect in the design for the Philips Pavilion (see Figure 24.6), on which he worked with Le Corbusier.

**Krzysztof Penderecki**

CD 12/33

One of the best-known pieces based on texture and process is *Threnody: To the Victims of Hiroshima* (1960, NAWM 165) for fifty-two string instruments by Polish composer Krzysztof Penderecki (b. 1933; see also neo-Romanticism and below, page 662). The score gives few definite pulses or note values, instead measuring time by seconds. Again, each instrument has a unique part to play. Each section focuses on a particular kind of sound, using newly invented notation that shows the effect graphically but not imprecisely. At the beginning, four to six instruments enter at a time, each playing its highest possible note, like a scream of very high clusters. This gradually gives way to a section in which each player rapidly repeats a series of sound effects—such as bowing or arpeggiating behind the bridge (producing high pitches), striking the soundboard, or bowing or plucking the highest possible note. The players may choose one of four patterns, they may move at different speeds (each as fast as possible), and the exact sounds each produces are indeterminate, but the overall effect is essentially the same in each performance, creating a prickly, interesting texture. Next is a section based on sustained tones, quarter-tone clusters, and glissandos between them, shown graphically in the score in Example 24.4 and notated precisely in the parts. The entire pitched and unpitched world, animate and inanimate, wailing and weeping at once, often in polychoral and antiphonal calls and responses, seems to mourn in this dirge. Remarkably, Penderecki originally conceived the work as a purely abstract play of sound and called it *8′37″* (its timing); the evocative final title has won it a

*Example 24.4: Krzysztof Penderecki,* Threnody: To the Victims of Hiroshima

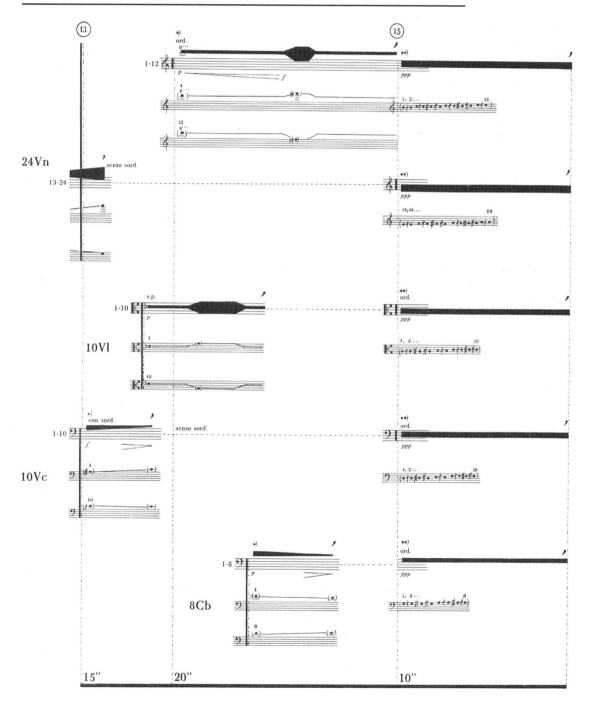

much larger audience than it would otherwise have had, by connecting the new musical resources it uses to the tradition of expressive instrumental music extending back to the eighteenth century.

Penderecki used similar techniques in many other pieces, including the *St. Luke Passion* (1963–1966) and his opera *The Devils of Loudon* (1968), which show how the new resources can be used dramatically. But in these works he already began to incorporate elements of more traditional styles, and in the mid-1970s he turned to a personal style of neo-Romanticism (see below).

György Ligeti

The music of Hungarian composer György Ligeti (1923–2006) achieved world renown through Stanley Kubrick's science fiction film *2001: A Space Odyssey*, which uses excerpts from three of his works: *Atmosphères* (1961), *Requiem* (1963–1965), and *Lux aeterna* (1966). This music is in constant motion yet static both harmonically and melodically. *Atmosphères* begins with fifty-six muted strings, together with a selection of woodwinds and horns, playing simultaneously all the chromatic notes through a five-octave range. Instruments imperceptibly drop out until only the violas and cellos remain. An orchestral tutti follows with a similar panchromatic layout, but out of it emerge two clusters: one, in the strings, made up of the seven notes of a diatonic scale, contrasts with the other, a pentatonic cluster of the remaining five notes of the chromatic scale, in the woodwinds and horns. While one group grows louder, the other becomes softer; then the two reverse, creating changing sonorities that suggest the play of light and shadow on clouds.

New thinking

Whether using new instruments, traditional instruments, modified instruments (such as a prepared piano or an amplified string quartet), non-Western instruments, electronic instruments, or tape, composers using new sounds had to hope that listeners would forgo traditional expectations for melody, harmony, and form, and engage each work instead as an experience of sound itself. These pieces demand new thinking about music from their listeners as much as from their composers, and the questions and new insights they stimulate are part of what many have valued in these works.

# The Avant-Garde

In some discussions of twentieth-century music, total serialism, the new virtuosity, the exploration of new sounds, electronic music, music of texture and process, and other postwar developments are all lumped together as manifestations of the avant-garde. But this obscures an important distinction. Many of the composers discussed here intended their music (or at least some of it) to find a place in the permanent classical repertoire alongside the masterpieces of the past, and they designed their works to function in the same way as the established classics, drawing on the art-music tradition, proclaiming a distinctive musical personality, and rewarding rehearings. Even as they introduced radical new methods, as Babbitt, Carter, and Crumb did, these composers continued the goals of modernism. Other works were experimental, intended to try out new methods for their own sake.

Modernist, experimentalist, avant-garde

As noted in our discussion of Satie and futurism in Chapter 22, avant-garde composers have quite different motivations: they challenge accepted aesthetics, even the very concept of permanent classics, and invite listeners to focus on what is happening in the present. The distinction does not lie in what techniques are used, but in the music's purpose. It is sometimes hard to discern a composer's motivations: did Penderecki intend his *Threnody* as an experiment in new musical sounds and resources, as a challenge to the basic concepts of concert music, or as a piece to be heard repeatedly, admired, and played alongside the classics? That it has been performed and recorded many times suggests the last, but the very question shows how entangled the three streams have become in postwar music.

## John Cage

The leading composer and philosopher of the postwar avant-garde was John Cage (1912–1992), shown in Figure 24.9. Over the course of a long and influential career, Cage sought to bring into music sounds, approaches, and ideas that previously had been excluded, repeatedly challenging the core concepts of music itself. Building on the work of his teacher Henry Cowell, Cage focused on the use of novel sounds in his music of the late 1930s and 1940s. He wrote numerous works for percussion ensemble, using both traditional instruments and untraditional ones, such as tin cans of varying size and pitch in *Third Construction in Metal* (1941) and an electric buzzer and electronically amplified noises in *Imaginary Landscape No. 3* (1942).

*Figure 24.9. Avant-garde composer John Cage in a photograph taken in 1987.*

Cage's experimentation with timbre culminated in his invention of the prepared piano, in which various objects—such as pennies, bolts, screws, pieces of wood, rubber, plastic, weather stripping, or slit bamboo—are inserted between the strings, resulting in delicate, complex percussive sounds when the piano is played from the keyboard. Essentially, the prepared piano is a one-person percussion ensemble, with sounds that resemble drums, woodblocks, gongs, and other standard or unusual instruments. Cage's *Sonatas and Interludes* (1946–1948) is his best-known work for prepared piano, consisting of twenty-six "sonatas"—movements in two repeated parts, as in a Scarlatti sonata, but without thematic returns—and four interludes. The pianist prepares the piano in advance, following detailed instructions concerning what objects to place between the strings and where to put them, and each movement explores a different set of timbres and figurations.

Drawing on his earlier experimentation with percussion music and the prepared piano, Cage turned in the 1950s and 1960s to ever more radical reconceptions of music. In his writings, he strongly opposed the museumlike preservation of music from the past and argued for music that focused the listener's attention on the present moment. He did not seek to write works that expressed emotions, conveyed images, developed material, revealed a coherent structure, or unfolded a logical series of events, as music had done for centuries. Instead, influenced by Zen Buddhism, he created opportunities for experiencing sounds as themselves, not as vehicles for the composer's intentions (see vignette, page 650). His three main strategies for accomplishing this were chance, indeterminacy, and the blurring of boundaries between music, art, and life.

By leaving some of the decisions normally made by a composer to chance, Cage created pieces in which the sounds did not convey his intentions, but simply existed. His approach varied from piece to piece but typically involved choosing a gamut of elements to be included, planning how they were to be selected, and then using chance operations to do the selection. *Music of Changes* for piano (1951, Book I in NAWM 166) took its name from the ancient Chinese book of prophecy *I-Ching* (Book of Changes), which offers a method of divination by tossing coins six times to determine the answer from a list of sixty-four possibilities. For *Music of Changes*, Cage devised charts of possible sounds (half were

Chance

CD 12/40    CD 6/84

## IN PERFORMANCE    John Cage and Musical Notation

Although Cage constructed his *Music of Changes* (NAWM 166) according to principles governed by chance operations, nothing about its performance is left to chance. Example 24.5 shows an excerpt from *Music of Changes* in Cage's distinctive and very precise notation on the piano's grand staff. The "beat" equals the quarter note, or one-fourth of a measure, shown by a horizontal line above the staff that is 2.5 centimeters in the original score (here reduced). Thus, every measure is 2.5 × 4 or 10 centimeters wide and contains the same amount of space no matter how many or few notes appear in it. The beats are set to a particular tempo—in this case, 58 beats per minute, as shown above the first measure of the excerpt (measure 31). The rhythmic values are arranged proportionally, so that every note's place in time is indicated precisely by its position in the measure, reading the length of the measure as an exact timeline, while the fractions above and below the staff evidently have more to do with the composing process than with the performance. The pitches are displayed normally, although they are subject to a staggering array of dynamic marks, ranging from *pppp* (in measure 32) to *ffff* (elsewhere in the piece), and to other timbral variations that require the pianist's utmost control.

For example, Cage uses three different types of pedal markings, sometimes singly, as shown, but sometimes in combination with one another. A solid line under the staff requires the use of the damper pedal; a dashed line, as in measures 33–34, indicates the "soft," or *una corda*, pedal, which shifts the hammers to strike one instead of three strings for each note; and a line comprising dashes and dots, as in measure 32, calls for the sostenuto or sustain pedal, which holds only the dampers of selected notes (indicated by diamond-shaped note heads, such as the tied G below middle C in measure 32) off their strings. The notes selected to be sustained in this way are initially depressed silently but resonate in sympathy with the vibrations of other pitches related to their harmonic series of overtones. Furthermore, a plus sign above or below a note, as in measure 33, instructs the performer to release a key that was previously struck in order to stop its sounding tone.

While the myriad details described here make the piece difficult to play, the performer can take comfort from Cage's comment about this and other pieces generated by chance: "A 'mistake' is beside the point, for once anything happens it authentically is."

*Example 24.5: John Cage,* Music of Changes

silences), dynamics, durations, and tempos, and used the method from the *I-Ching* to select which were to be used, filling in a formal structure based on units of time. The result is a piece in which sounds occur (and may recur) randomly and at random volumes, durations, and speeds. (See "In Performance.")

Chance is a way to determine certain aspects of the music without recourse to the composer's intentions. Another approach Cage pioneered is what he called *indeterminacy*, in which the composer leaves certain aspects of the music unspecified and indicates other aspects only in the most general way, using graphic notation, leaving the details to the performer or even to the ambience. Cage's *Concert* for piano and orchestra (1957–1958) is intended to be realized by the players according to instructions in the score; the exact sounds produced vary considerably from one performance to another. Cage's most extreme indeterminate work—and his most famous piece—was *4′33″* (Four Minutes Thirty-three Seconds, 1952), in which the performer or performers sit silently at or with their instruments of choice for a span of time specified in the title (subdivided into three "movements"; see Figure 24.10), while whatever noises that can be heard in the concert hall or from outside constitute the music. The piece implies that silence is simply openness to ambient sound and that there are always environmental sounds worth contemplating.

In chance music, some elements are determined by chance; in indeterminate music, some elements are left unspecified by the composer. In both, Cage invites the listener simply to hear sounds as sounds, whether notated in the music or not, whether generated by the performers or occurring as part of the ambient sounds, experiencing each sound as it comes along, not trying to connect it to what precedes or follows it, not expecting the music to communicate feelings or meanings of any kind, but listening as intently as we would listen to any art music. Thus, as we learn to extend our attention beyond music to the world itself, value judgments become irrelevant (see vignette, page 650).

Beginning in the late 1950s, Cage moved toward complete openness in every aspect of composition and performance. *Variations IV* (1963), for instance, uses both indeterminacy and chance (pages of transparent plastic with lines, dots, and other symbols are superimposed randomly and then read as graphic notation) to create a piece "for any number of players, any sounds or combinations of sounds produced by any means, with or without other activities." The "other activities" might include speech, theater, dance, and activities of daily life. Accordingly, these "musical" works blurred the boundaries between music, other arts, and the rest of life. *Musicircus* (1967) is an open-ended "happening," consisting of any number of musicians and ensembles, each performing different music, all playing at once in a large space while the audience wanders freely. Through such events, Cage sought to focus our attention on whatever is happening in the present, experiencing it without prejudice.

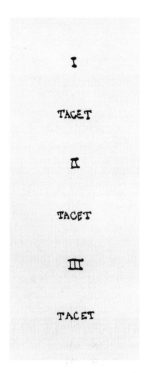

*Figure 24.10. The score of Cage's three-movement work 4′33″, published by Edition Peters. "Tacet" means "Be silent."*

Blurring the boundaries

## Indeterminacy in Works of Other Composers

Earle Brown

Many composers adopted indeterminacy in some form under Cage's influence. Inspired by the mobiles of Alexander Calder, Earle Brown (1926–2002) wrote *Available Forms I* (1961) for eighteen players and *Available Forms II* (1962) for large orchestra, in which the musicians play completely scored fragments—with some leeway in the choice of pitches—in the order and tempos determined by the conductor. In contrast, some composers, like John Cage, relied on graphic notation to transmit entire sections of their compositions. As we have seen, Penderecki used indeterminate graphic notation in sections of *Threnody*, although the effect is similar in each performance.

Witold Lutosławski

The Polish composer Witold Lutosławski (1913–1994) made selective use of indeterminacy, while insisting on his authorship of the entire composition—a stance quite at odds with Cage's, suggesting an orientation more modernist than avant-garde. In his String Quartet (1964), pitches and rhythms are specified but not the coordination of parts; the players begin a section together, but each plays independently, changing tempo as desired, until the next checkpoint is reached, when at a signal from one of the players they begin together again. Symphony No. 3 (1983) applies this method with great subtlety. Some sections invite individual players to dwell upon a figure in the manner of a soloist playing a cadenza; at other times, eight stands of violins, guided by prescribed pitches but only approximate durations, go their own ways like tendrils of a vine. These passages achieve a freedom and eloquence hardly possible through precise notation and show the power of limited indeterminacy within a traditional genre.

Significance of indeterminacy

One by-product of indeterminacy is the variety of new kinds of notation. Scores range all the way from fragments of conventional staff notes through purely graphic suggestions of melodic curves, dynamic ranges, rhythms, and the

---

**VIGNETTE** Music in the Present Moment

*John Cage articulated his views about music in a series of lectures given at Darmstadt, Germany, in 1958 and published in his first book of writings,* Silence *(1961). The lecture "Changes," from which the following is excerpted, was interleaved in its presentation with excerpts from Cage's* Music of Changes.

[In my recent works,] the view taken is not of an activity the purpose of which is to integrate the opposites, but rather of an activity characterized by process and essentially purposeless. The mind, though stripped of its right to control, is still present. What does it do, having nothing to do? And what happens to a piece of music when it is purposelessly made?

What happens, for instance, to silence? That is, how does the mind's perception of it change? Formerly, silence was the time lapse between sounds, useful towards a variety of ends, among them that of tasteful arrangement, where by separating two sounds or two groups of sounds their differences or relationships might receive emphasis; or that of expressivity, where silences in a musical discourse might provide pause or punctuation; or again, that of architecture, where the introduction or interruption of silence might give definition either to a predetermined structure or to an organically developing one. Where none of these or other goals is present, silence becomes something else—not silence at all, but sounds, the ambient sounds. The nature of these is unpredictable and changing. These sounds (which are called silence only be-

cause they do not form part of a musical intention) may be depended upon to exist. The world teems with them, and is, in fact, at no point free of them. He who has entered an anechoic chamber, a room made as silent as technologically possible, has heard there two sounds, one high, one low—the high the listener's nervous system in operation, the low his blood circulation. There are, demonstrably, sounds to be heard and forever, given ears to hear. Where these ears are in connection with a mind that has nothing to do, that mind is free to enter into the act of listening, hearing each sound just as it is, not as a phenomenon more or less approximating a preconception. . . .

The early works have beginnings, middles, and endings. The later ones do not. They begin anywhere, last any length of time, and involve more or fewer instruments and players. They are therefore not preconceived objects, and to approach them as objects is to utterly miss the point. They are occasions for experience. . . . The mind may be used either to ignore ambient sounds, pitches other than the eighty-eight [keys on a piano], durations which are not counted, timbres which are unmusical or distasteful, and in general to control and understand an available experience. Or the mind may give up its desire to improve on creation and function as a faithful receiver of experience.

From John Cage, "Changes," in *Silence: Lectures and Writings* (Middletown, Conn.: Wesleyan University Press, 1961), pp. 22–23 and 31–32.

like to even more slippery and meager directives. Another consequence of indeterminacy is that no two performances of a piece are identical. In effect, a composition does not exist as such, but only as a performance, or as the sum of possible performances. Through the reconsideration of "the musical work" that indeterminacy and related notions stimulated, musicians in the late twentieth century became increasingly aware of the openness of early music as well, coming to understand that a medieval song or an early Baroque aria is also a platform for performance open to a variety of choices within a stylistically appropriate range, not a rigidly defined, unchanging work.

## Digital Technologies

Since the 1970s, new technologies have once again altered the ways musicians work with music and listeners consume it. Among the most important new inventions are the digital synthesis, recording, and reproduction of sound, which have given creators of music new tools and listeners new flexibility (see "A Closer Look," page 652).

One significant technique, called *sampling*, is a process of creating new compositions by patching together digital chunks of previously recorded music. Although sampling raises copyright concerns, it has been used extensively in various types of pop music as well as in experimental, avant-garde, and classical concert music.

Sampling

Advances in computing and the miniaturization of the computer have offered many new possibilities, explored by composers whose music is part experimentation with technology and part sound sculpture. One of the pioneers of computer music is Charles Dodge (b. 1942), whose *Speech Songs* (1972) features computer-synthesized vocal sounds, mixing life-like imitations of speech with transformations that change vowels into noise or natural inflections into melodies to create a word-based music well suited to the surrealistic poetry he uses as a text. Paul Lansky (b. 1944) developed his own software to create computer works. He manipulates recorded sounds, such as speech in *Six Fantasies on a Poem by Thomas Campion* (1979) and *Smalltalk* (1988) or highway traffic noises in *Night Traffic* (1990), transforming them beyond immediate recognition and using them as a kind of pitched percussion. Despite the unusual sound sources, his music draws on pop traditions, with tonal harmonies, regular meter, propulsive beat, and layered syncopated rhythms. A very different aesthetic is pursued at the Institut de Recherche et Coordination Acoustique/ Musique (Institute for Acoustic and Musical Research and Coordination, usually referred to by its French acronym, IRCAM) in Paris, founded by Pierre Boulez, one of the premier centers for computer music in Europe. In *Inharmonique* (1977) and other works written during his time as director of the IRCAM computer music department, Jean-Claude Risset (b. 1938) has used the computer to mediate between live voices or acoustic instruments and synthesized or electronically processed sound. He has continued to design new sounds, exploring the interaction of sound waves, harmonics, timbre, and other basic elements of sound. The work of these three composers only begins to illustrate the potential of computer music.

Computer music

## Minimalism and Postminimalism

One of the most prominent new trends since the 1960s is labeled *minimalism*, in which materials are reduced to a minimum and procedures simplified so that what is going on in the music is immediately apparent. Minimalism began as an avant-garde aesthetic focused on the musical processes themselves but over time became a widely used, popular technique, capable of a wide range of expressive content. Composers of minimalist works absorbed influences from rock, African music, Asian music, tonality, and finally Romanticism to create what has been called the leading musical style of the late twentieth century.

---

**A CLOSER LOOK** Digital Technologies

In the 1970s and early 1980s, music joined the digital revolution. Inventors devised a method for translating sound into a coded series of on-off pulses, or ones and zeros, in the same way that computers stored and transmitted data. Soon digital processes were replacing older ones, known as *analog* because they rely on creating an analogue of the sound waves, such as the undulations in the groove of a record.

By the 1980s, musicians were using digital synthesizers, as in Figure 24.11, instead of the older analog devices that produced sounds generated from or processed by electrical circuits. Because digital processes produced and recorded sounds as streams of numbers, musical sounds could be reproduced and controlled precisely. Electronic keyboards combined with computers made synthesized music accessible to musicians everywhere. Through computers, composers could control all the parameters of pitch, timbre, dynamics, and rhythm, and the characteristics thus digitally encoded could be translated directly into music through MIDI (musical instrument digital interface).

*Figure 24.11. Keyboard console of the Synclavier II digital synthesizer from 1981.*

Some musicians combined live performers with synthesized or computer-generated music into a performance medium that is now commonplace. Using software programs that respond to music, the composer devises formulas that are then played on a synthesizer, digital piano, or acoustic instrument. In this way, a musician can generate imitative or nonimitative polyphony, rhythmic or melodic ostinatos, heterophony, and a variety of other textures by playing on a synthesizer keyboard in "real time"—that is, as actually played and heard, rather than laboriously prepared in advance and tape-recorded.

Vinyl records, the primary means of distribution for decades, gave way in the 1980s to compact discs (CDs), which were smaller, more durable, and able to reproduce music digitally, offering greater fidelity. Thousands of recordings first released on 78- or 33⅓-rpm records were reissued on CDs, making an entire century of recorded sound more widely accessible than ever before. Portable playback devices with headphones or earbuds have made it possible to carry music of one's own choice everywhere. By the twenty-first century, CDs were themselves rivaled by newer digital technologies. Using MP3 files, computers and portable players can store and play thousands of songs. Individual consumers swap digital music files on peer-to-peer file-sharing Internet sites, some of which have been shut down because of copyright-infringement lawsuits. More recently, various Web sites have begun to offer legal downloads, as recording companies have begun to find ways to make money through the Internet. Many musicians use their own Web sites to gain exposure, offering free downloads of excerpts or entire works. Thousands of radio stations are now also available via the Internet. The way we interact with music is being transformed by digital technology, bringing changes that are hard to describe and harder to predict.

Art critic Richard Wollheim coined *minimal art* in 1965 as a term for art that reduced materials and form to fundamentals and was not intended to express feelings or convey the artist's state of mind. Minimalist works of art often feature a repetitive pattern of simple elements. For example, Carl Andre's *64 Copper Squares* (1969) consists of sixty-four square copper plates laid on the floor in a square, and Frank Stella's painting *Hyena Stomp* (1962), shown in Figure 24.12, forms a spiral pattern from straight lines and bands of bright color. Such art focused on its materials, making it part of the avant-garde concept of art of the 1960s.

A parallel movement was nurtured among musicians in New York City and in the California counterculture. One of the pioneers of musical minimalism was La Monte Young (b. 1935), whose *The Tortoise: His Dreams and Journeys* (1964) is an improvisation in which instrumentalists and singers come in and out on various harmonics over a fundamental played as a drone by a synthesizer. Terry Riley (b. 1935), who once performed in Young's ensemble, experimented with tape loops, short segments of magnetic tape spliced into loops that, when fed through a tape recorder, play the same recorded sounds again and again. His tape piece *Mescalin Mix* (1962–1963) piled up many such loops, each repeating a short phrase, over a regular pulse. His most famous work, *In C* (1964), uses a similar procedure with live instruments. It can be performed by any number of instruments, each playing the same series of brief repeated figures over a quickly pulsing octave C, with the number of repetitions in each part and the coordination of parts left indeterminate. The resulting sound combines a steady pulsation with a process of slow change from consonance to diatonic dissonance and back. The concept and materials are simple and the process immediately audible, but the multilayered texture is complex and like nothing ever heard before.

*Figure 24.12.* Hyena Stomp *(1962) by Frank Stella (b. 1936). Stella reduced painting to its fundamentals, intending his work to be understood as only a play of form and color, not as an expression of feelings. The title, from a jazz piece by Jelly Roll Morton, reflects Stella's interest in translating syncopation into visual form in this painting. Tate Gallery, London.*

## From Avant-Garde to Widespread Appeal

While Young remained an avant-garde experimentalist and Riley moved toward rock music, three other Americans brought minimalist procedures into art music intended for a broad audience.

Steve Reich (b. 1936), shown in Figure 24.13, developed a quasi-canonic procedure in which musicans play the same material out of phase with each other. Like Riley, he began in the electronic studio, superimposing tape loops of the same spoken phrase in such a way that one loop was slightly shorter and thus gradually moved ahead of the other, an effect called *phasing*. In *Piano Phase* (1967), shown in Example 24.6, Reich applied a similar idea to a work for two pianos. Both pianists repeat the same figure in unison several times, then one gradually pulls ahead until the two are exactly one eighth-note apart, and they repeat the figure several times in rhythmic synchronization but melodically out of phase. This process is repeated twelve times, producing a different series of harmonic combinations each time the parts slip into synchrony, until the two parts are again in melodic unison; then the same process is used for a figure of

Steve Reich

*Figure 24.13. Steve Reich, one of the pioneers of minimalism, playing the xylophone at his home studio in New York in 1997.*

eight notes and then one of four notes. The fascination with music like this lies in observing gradual changes and the many possible permutations of very simple ideas. The processes that underlie the composition are revealed for every listener to hear and experience.

*Example 24.6: Steve Reich,* Piano Phase, *opening*

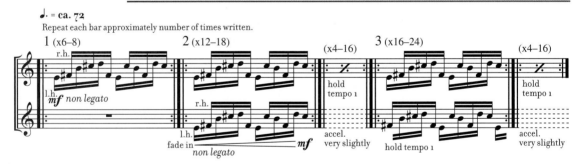

Reich formed his own ensemble and was able to make a living by performing, touring, and recording his works. Much of his music in the 1970s was percussive, superimposing layers of figuration in ways that parallel African drumming, one source of his inspiration. He attracted a wide range of listeners, drawing audiences accustomed to jazz, rock, and pop music as well as classical, as the diatonic material and rapid pulsation gave his music wide appeal. By the 1980s, he no longer subscribed to a minimalist aesthetic, instead using minimalist techniques to create large-scale works with significant emotional content, often drawing on his Jewish heritage. *Tehillim* (Psalms; 1981) is a setting of psalm texts in the original Hebrew for four singers and orchestra, using rhythmic and melodic canons at the unison. The texture in each section gradually becomes more complex, with all four soloists singing the same melody in close succession. As it becomes harder to follow a single part, we can shift our focus to hear the salient points of each. A piece as rich and complex as this can hardly be called minimalist, but it shows the application of minimalist techniques to a broad range of art music.

Philip Glass (b. 1937), shown in Figure 24.14, had published twenty works by the time he completed degrees at the University of Chicago and the Juilliard School and finished studies with Nadia Boulanger, but withdrew all of them after working with the Indian sitarist Ravi Shankar in Paris. Glass's works since the mid-1960s have been deeply influenced by the rhythmic organization of Indian music. They emphasize melodiousness, consonance, and rock music's simple harmonic progressions and abundant amplification, and have won Glass a large and diverse following from rock enthusiasts to classical listeners. Like Reich, he initially wrote mainly for his own ensemble, but he has secured his reputation with a series of major works, including symphonies, concertos, and operas.

Glass's one-act, four-and-a-half-hour opera *Einstein on the Beach*, which premiered at the Metropolitan Opera House in 1976, was a collaboration with avant-garde director Robert Wilson, who wrote the scenario. The opera avoids narrative, has no sung text other than solfège syllables, and involves mostly nonsensical stage action. The music consists primarily of repeated figures, mostly arpeggiated triads, performed by an orchestra of electronic keyboard instruments, woodwinds, and a solo violinist. Other operas followed, including *Satyagraha* (1980), about Gandhi's nonviolent struggle for Indian independence, and *Akhnaten* (1984), about an Egyptian pharoah martyred for his monotheistic worship of the sun god. *The Voyage* (1992), commissioned by the Metropolitan Opera to commemorate the five-hundredth anniversary of Columbus's voyage to the New World, blends Glass's signature style of multilayered ostinatos, rapid pulse, and slowly changing tonal or modal harmonies with the standard orchestra, recitatives, and arias of the operatic tradition.

John Adams (b. 1947), shown in Figure 24.15, has traced a path from minimalism to a personal style that blends minimalist techniques with a variety of other approaches. His *Phrygian Gates* for piano (1977–1978; opening excerpt in NAWM 168) is representative of the period when minimalism was moving beyond its avant-garde origins to become a style rather than an aesthetic. Except

*Figure 24.14. Composer Philip Glass biting his eyeglass frames as he rehearses at the synthesizer with the Philip Glass Ensemble in 1993 amid a tangle of electric wires.*

*Figure 24.15. American composer and conductor John Adams conducting the BBC Symphony Orchestra in London, five days before the 9/11 attack on the World Trade Center in New York.*

for a middle section of shifting sustained chords, this twenty-four-minute piece relies almost entirely on quick repetitive figurations, primarily in diatonic modes. The music goes through what Adams calls "gates," changing from one set of notes to another: from the Lydian scale on A to the Phrygian scale on A, as shown in Example 24.7, then the Lydian and Phrygian scales on E, and so on. These changes give the work its title, and they convey the sense of a journey through a gradually changing environment.

*Example 24.7: John Adams,* Phrygian Gates, *a gate change*

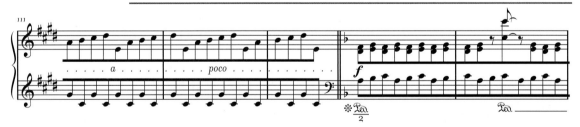

Adams continued to use minimalist techniques in his later works, but also embraced elements from popular and classical music. *Harmonielehre* (Theory of Harmony; 1985), a symphonic poem that draws on Romantic and modernist styles, was greeted by one news magazine with the enthusiastic headline "The Heart Is Back in the Game." The first movement begins with loud, repeated E-minor chords, then moves through a minimalist landscape to arrive at a middle section with a tragic, almost expressionist melody that recalls late Mahler or Berg. Adams's opera *Nixon in China* (1987), on Nixon's 1972 trip to China to open relations with the communist regime (see Figure 24.16), treats its up-to-date subject with the formality of a Baroque historical opera while applying minimalist techniques. Short, driving, pulsating ideas, insistently repeated, constantly evolve, using an orchestra dominated by brass, winds, and percussion. Over time, Adams has relied less on minimalist techniques and more on traditional harmonic and contrapuntal means. He has embraced a wide range of topics, from celebrating Jesus' Nativity, in the oratorio *El Niño* (1999–2000), to

*Figure 24.16.  A scene from John Adams's opera* Nixon in China, *from the English National Opera production.*

mourning the deaths in the terrorist attacks of September 11, 2001, in *On the Transmigration of Souls* (2002).

## Interactions with Non-Western Musics

Minimalism was only one of many currents in Western music to be inspired by the musics of Asia and Africa. Some composers drew directly on Asian musics. Bright Sheng (b. 1955), born and trained in China, moved to New York in 1982 for further study and has made his career in the United States (see Figure 24.17). He seeks to integrate elements of Asian and Western music while respecting the integrity of each, inspired by the attempts of Bartók to do the same

*Figure 24.17.  Chinese-born composer Bright Sheng in a photograph taken in Los Angeles in 1998.*

CD 12/75   CD 6/87

with Eastern European folk and Western classical music. In the solo cello suite *Seven Tunes Heard in China* (1995; No. 1 in NAWM 172), Sheng joins the European tradition of the Bach cello suites—with sequences, double stops, and implied polyphony—to the playing style of Chinese bowed string instruments, marked by grace notes, glissandos, sudden dynamic changes, and flexible rhythm. The mostly pentatonic Chinese tune used as a source is fragmented and spun out using both Baroque and modernist methods, including polytonality. The result blends together fundamental aspects of Chinese, Western classical, and modern music.

In the final analysis, all the works described in this section are quintessentially Western, representing new instances of the centuries-old capacity of European music to absorb foreign elements and arrive at a new synthesis, as in the merging of French, Italian, and English traditions into an international language in the fifteenth century (see Chapter 5) or of various styles and habits into the cosmopolitan idiom of the Classical era (see Chapters 14–16). But these recent works go beyond nineteenth-century exoticism in the respect they show for the intrinsic value of the non-Western traditions on which they draw.

## The New Accessibility and Other Trends

In the late twentieth century, composers in the classical tradition faced a new reality. While they were able to make a living teaching at universities or conservatories, obtaining performances for their music was increasingly difficult. It was often easier to win a commission for a new piece than to secure a second or third performance of an existing work. Few compositions entered the repertory, and few listeners heard a piece more than once. In some respects, the situation was like that of the eighteenth century, when a concerto or symphony was seldom heard twice by the same listeners. Moreover, at a time when music was growing more plentiful and easy to access, the audience for classical music seemed to be shrinking.

Some composers took this situation as the price of artistic freedom and continued writing as they had before. Others sought to attract wider interest by writing music that could be understood on first hearing. Composers like Reich, Glass, and Adams found one solution in minimalism. Other composers used a variety of approaches, often in tandem: modifying their modernist idiom to make it more accessible; radically simplifying their material and procedures; quoting from and alluding to past styles; resurrecting nineteenth-century tonal Romanticism; and invoking extramusical meanings and imagery.

### Accessible Modernism and Radical Simplification

Some composers writing in a modernist idiom have made their music accessible by keeping the ideas and procedures relatively simple and easy to grasp.

Ellen Taaffe Zwilich

Ellen Taaffe Zwilich (b. 1939), shown in Figure 24.18, joins continuous variation with older formal devices of recurrence and contrast. Like Schoenberg, she presents the main idea at the outset, then elaborates it through developing variation in which everything grows logically from the initial seed. Yet the basic idea is usually simple, and the textures are clear, making her music much easier to follow than Schoenberg's. A prime example is her Symphony No. 1 (1982), which won the first Pulitzer Prize in Music awarded to a woman. In the first

*Figure 24.18. Pulitzer Prize–winning American composer Ellen Taaffe Zwilich, ca. 2003.*

CD 12/59

movement (NAWM 169), all the melodic material derives through variation from the initial interval of a rising minor third, and the harmonies combine thirds to produce dissonant sonorities. The soft opening gesture, a threefold rising third with an accelerando, serves as a motto that generates a gradual increase in tempo, dynamics, and density to a central Allegro, then toward the end the music slows and thins to a quiet close. The gradual process of development is easy to hear, and the experience of listening is satisfying, both intellectually and emotionally.

Arvo Pärt

Estonian composer Arvo Pärt (b. 1935) forged a highly individual, instantly recognizable style using the simplest materials. Following early Neoclassical and serial works and others that contrasted modernist with Baroque styles, he turned to a study of Gregorian chant and early polyphony. In the 1970s, he devised a method he called "tintinnabuli," after the bell-like sonorities it produced. Its essence lies in counterpoint between a pitch-centered, mostly stepwise diatonic melody and one or more other voices that sound only notes of the tonic triad, with the placement of each note determined by a preset system. The technique is exemplified in Pärt's *Seven Magnificat Antiphons* (1988, rev. 1991, excerpts in NAWM 170) and illustrated in Example 24.8, which shows the opening of No. 6, *O König aller Völker*. The second tenor (the lower part on the

CD 12/65, 66

*Example 24.8: Arvo Pärt*, Magnificat Antiphons, *No. 6*, O König aller Völker

*O king of all peoples, their expectation [and hope]*

tenor staff) presents a plain modal tune that is centered on A and that moves no more than a fourth away in either direction. Its rhythm is restricted to quarter and half notes, and measures change length to fit the text accentuation. The tenor melody is echoed by the second soprano to form an augmentation canon. The altos recite the text, phrase by phrase, on D. The other parts sound notes of the D-minor triad, following strict but simple rules reminiscent of early polyphony (see Chapter 3). The resulting texture alternates between consonance and diatonic dissonance, allowing for variety and dramatic climaxes within a stripped-down, pitch-centered style.

## Quotation, Collage, and Polystylism

A resource used by many composers of varying orientations was the "quotation" of existing music, including a "collage" of multiple quotations. The reworking of borrowed material by earlier composers from Bach and Handel to modernists like Schoenberg, Ives, and Stravinsky served as inspiration, as did quotations in modern poetry and collage in modern art. But postwar composers turned borrowing to new purposes, using evocations of older music to carry meanings that were not available by other means.

English composer Peter Maxwell Davies (b. 1934) drew on chant and English Renaissance music for many works, emphasizing the gulf between modern times and the distant past by distorting the source material or transforming it through modern procedures. His opera *Taverner* (1962–1970), on the life of Renaissance composer John Taverner, reworks the latter's *In Nomine* in a variety of ways before finally presenting it in recognizable form at the end, recalling Ives's cumulative form.

American composer George Rochberg (1918–2005; see also neo-Romanticism, below, page 662), who had written mostly serial music, found it inadequate to express his feelings on the death of his son in 1964 and turned the next year to works based on borrowed material. *Contra mortem et tempus* (Against Death and Time) quotes passages from Boulez, Berio, Varèse, and Ives, and *Music for a Magic Theater* incorporates music of Mozart, Beethoven, Mahler, Webern, Varèse, Stockhausen, and his own earlier works, seeking in both pieces to evoke "the many-layered density of human existence." *Nach Bach* (After Bach, 1966) for harpsichord is a "commentary" on Bach's Keyboard Partita No. 6 in E Minor, BWV 830, in which fragments of the Bach, altered to varying degrees, emerge from Rochberg's own atonal music to create a dialogue between composers and styles.

Another approach was to extend quotation and collage to include combining past and present styles. Such blending of styles in music has been compared to the architecture of Philip Johnson, Robert Venturi, César Pelli, and others, who left behind the bare glass façades of mid-twentieth-century modernism by incorporating elements of earlier styles into essentially modern designs, as in Figure 24.19, a mixture that came to be called *postmodernism*. A central aspect of postmodernism is a turning away from the belief, crucial to modernist thought, that

*Figure 24.19. The AT&T Building in New York City, renamed the Sony Building. The architect, Philip Johnson, blends elements from the past, such as columns and arches, with modern elements of glass and concrete in his design. The resulting composite style, sometimes called postmodernism, rejects the stark glass walls and undecorated façades of many mid-twentieth-century buildings.*

history progresses irreversibly in one direction. In music, this idea means abandoning the notion that musical idioms develop continuously, as if according to a plan or some inner necessity. To the postmodernist, history gives the artist more freedom than that; the styles of all epochs and cultures are equally available as musical material, to be employed as the composer sees fit.

A composer who quoted from and borrowed past styles effectively was Alfred Schnittke (1934–1998). He worked in the Soviet Union, where he was known chiefly for his film music, before moving to Germany in 1990. The Soviet government began to relax its control over culture in the 1960s under Nikita Khrushchev, exposing Schnittke and other young composers to Western trends such as serial, chance, and electronic music. After writing several works based on serialism, indeterminacy, and new instrumental sounds, Schnittke turned to what he called "polystylism," a combination of new and older styles created through quotation or stylistic allusion. His Symphony No. 1 (1969–1972) incorporates passages from works by Haydn, Beethoven, Chopin, Tchaikovsky, Grieg, Johann Strauss (the "Waltz King"), and Schnittke himself. For listeners familiar with works of these composers, such music embodies a contrast not only of styles, but of historical periods. Schnittke's later works—including eight more symphonies, numerous concertos, and chamber music—depend less on stark juxtapositions than on integrating a small number of ideas borrowed from or modeled on earlier music.

Like Schnittke, the American composer John Corigliano (b. 1938) frequently juxtaposes styles to convey meanings, drawing on a stylistic continuum from Baroque and Classical to avant-garde. His opera *The Ghosts of Versailles* (1987) centers around ghosts in the French royal palace, including Marie Antoinette and others slain during the Revolution, and a play staged for their entertainment; the ghosts are rendered with modern serial music and timbral effects, while the play is set in a style based on Mozart operas. Corigliano's Symphony No. 1 (1989), a memorial to friends who died of AIDS, incorporates quotations from some of their favorite pieces framed by deeply expressive, often angry or tragic music drawing on a variety of modern techniques.

The wittiest and most popular composer to use quotation and stylistic allusion is Peter Schickele (b. 1935). His works, such as his five string quartets (1983–1998), are mostly tonal. They draw on a wide variety of styles, from Stravinsky to jazz and rock, and create form and expression through contrasts of style, mood, texture, figuration, timbre, dynamics, and other factors, sometimes using quotation for humorous effect. He is best known for his music under the guise of "P. D. Q. Bach," the supposed youngest son of J. S. Bach who inherited none of his father's talent. This persona allows Schickele to spoof old music, its performing practice, and musicologists. Performing conventions go awry, as in the long-winded continuo accompaniment in the cantata *Iphigenia in Brooklyn* (1964); bizarre instruments are featured, like the double-reed slide music stand, parodying the unfamiliar instruments called for in early music; and every stylistic expectation is violated, with hilarious results. For example, in the *"Howdy"* Symphony (1982)—a response to Haydn's *Farewell* Symphony—the first movement Allegro uses contrasts of style to delineate form, as in Classical-era music (see Chapter 15), but here the styles range from Classical to vaudeville, big-band jazz, and modernist dissonance; the witty incongruities and surprises typical of Haydn become burlesque.

Music based on quotation can carry many meanings, but often it gives the audience something familiar to grasp—either the quoted piece itself or the style or type of piece it represents—and provides a new experience drawing on what the listener already knows. As a result, many listeners find it much more approachable than the unfamiliar sounds of serialism, electronic music, the avant-garde,

Alfred Schnittke

John Corigliano

Peter Schickele and "P. D. Q. Bach"

and other postwar trends. For some composers, using borrowed material has been a way to rediscover styles and methods of the past, including tonality. This is one origin for the recent trend of neo-Romanticism.

## Neo-Romanticism

The familiar tonal idiom of nineteenth-century Romanticism attracted some composers in search of expressive tools that connect directly with listeners.

*Krzysztof Penderecki*

For example, after making his reputation with pieces based on texture and process (see above), Krzysztof Penderecki, shown in Figure 24.20, focused increasingly on melody and drew on past styles, genres, and harmonic practice in neo-Romantic works of the mid-1970s and beyond, such as the Violin Concerto No. 1 (1976–1977) and the opera *Paradise Lost* (1975–1978). The struggles of the trade union Solidarity to achieve democracy in Poland inspired the *Polish Requiem* (1980–1984), in which Penderecki combined neo-Romanticism, elements from Renaissance and Baroque styles, and his signature textures from the 1960s in a new synthesis of styles.

*George Rochberg*

Having turned from serialism to quotation in the 1960s (see above), George Rochberg moved on in the 1970s to use Romantic and early modernist styles for their expressive potential. His String Quartet No. 5 (1978) is neo-Romantic in three of its five movements. Each movement is written in a consistent style, but the styles differ considerably between movements. The first movement is a sprightly sonata form in A major reminiscent of late Beethoven or Schubert; the second, a sad E♭-minor slow movement whose canons and loosely dissonant harmonies recall early Bartók; the third, a Beethovenian scherzo in A minor with a Mahlerian trio; the fourth, an atonal serenade that resembles works of Schoenberg or Berg; and the finale, an energetic, constantly developing, rapidly modulating yet tonal rondo in late Romantic style, akin to Schoenberg's First Quartet. The mixture of idioms challenged the traditional expectation that music be stylistically uniform; but even more radical was Rochberg's choice to reclaim styles of the past and use them in a wholehearted effort to make their

*Figure 24.20. Krzysztof Penderecki, Polish composer and conductor, leads the Warsaw Symphony Orchestra in a concert on December 2, 2001, in memory of the victims of the 9/11 terrorist attack on the World Trade Center in New York.*

resources his own without the distancing effects notable in Stravinsky's Neo-classicism (see Chapter 23) or Schnittke's polystylism.

David Del Tredici (b. 1937) embraced neo-Romanticism for a different reason. After using atonal and serial methods in the 1960s, he changed his style radically when he started to set excerpts from Lewis Carroll's stories for children, feeling that their whimsy called for a direct, comprehensible presentation. *Final Alice* (1975), to a text from the final chapters of Carroll's *Alice's Adventures in Wonderland*, is scored for amplified soprano and orchestra, with a "folk group" of banjo, mandolin, accordion, and two soprano saxophones. The soprano narrates, plays all the parts, and sings a series of arias. The central motive of the piece, a rising major sixth introduced by the saxophones, is taken up by other instruments and becomes the fundamental interval of "The Accusation," sung by the White Rabbit, and shown in Example 24.9; a greater concentration of rising sixths in a melody is hard to imagine. Through this and other arias, the orchestra and folk group accompany in a kind of nonsense tonality, with slightly off-kilter dance rhythms and multiple layers in differing tempos. Most of the music is tonal, ranging from folklike episodes to an idiom reminiscent of Richard Strauss. But when Alice begins to grow larger, Del Tredici suggests the strange occurrence with atonal music, a twelve-tone motive, and the electronic sounds of the theremin. By using tonal and atonal styles side by side for their expressive effect, Del Tredici renounced the modernist ideology of progress. In its place, he returned to eighteenth- and nineteenth-century ideals of music, mixing diverse styles in a coherent whole that is comprehensible on first hearing to an untrained listener yet holds hidden delights for the connoisseur (see the vignette, page 664).

David Del Tredici

*Example 24.9: David Del Tredici,* The Accusation, *from* Final Alice

## Extramusical Imagery and Meanings

Composers using various styles invoked extramusical meanings and imagery, hoping that listeners would accept unusual sounds if their meanings were clear. Spirituality was a frequent theme, continuing music's long association with religion and the transcendent.

Despite the official atheism of her native Soviet Union, almost all the works of Sofia Gubaidulina (b. 1931), shown in Figure 24.21, have a spiritual dimension, often suggested in the title. The five movements of her sonata for violin and cello, *Rejoice!* (1981), were inspired by eighteenth-century devotional texts. According to the composer, the sonata expresses the transcendence from ordinary reality to a state of joy and relies particularly on the passage from a fundamental note to its harmonics to embody this journey of consciousness. The fifth movement (NAWM 171), inscribed with the text "Listen to the still small voice within," is a study in chromatics, tremolos, and harmonics, particularly glissandos from low fundamental notes in the cello to their higher harmonics.

Sofia Gubaidulina

CD 12/67

*Figure 24.21. Russian composer Sofia Gubaidulina, seated at the piano, playing an African drum in Moscow.*

**R. Murray Schafer**

R. Murray Schafer (b. 1933), the leading Canadian composer of the era, traversed a wide variety of styles from Neoclassical to avant-garde, yet most of his pieces are based on extramusical inspirations. His orchestral works *Dream Rainbow Dream Thunder* (1986) and *Manitou* (1995), for example, reflect ideas from the culture of the Inuits, natives of Canada. His most striking innovation is what he calls "environmental music," pieces that break out of the concert hall and require more than passive attention from listeners. *Music for Wilderness Lake* (1979)

---

**VIGNETTE   On Reaching an Audience**

*David Del Tredici's* Final Alice *won immediate praise from listeners, as noted in the reviews of its premiere in October 1976.*

When the last stroke of *Final Alice* died away at the Chicago Symphony concert, the audience broke into sustained applause which quickly grew into a standing ovation. Cheers and bravos mingled with the handclaps. . . . It was the most enthusiastic reception of a new work that I have ever heard at a symphony concert.

Thomas Willis, *Chicago Tribune*, October 9, 1976.

*But some of his fellow composers viewed the piece as a betrayal of the tenets of modernism, and Del Tredici found himself having to defend his success.*

About halfway through [composing] the piece, I thought, "Oh my God, if I just leave it like this, my colleagues will think I'm crazy." But then I thought, "What else can I do? If nothing else occurs to me I can't go against my instincts." But I was terrified my colleagues would think I was an idiot. . . . People think now that I wanted to be tonal and have a big audience. But that was just not true. I didn't want to be tonal. My world was my colleagues—my composing friends. . . . The success of *Final Alice* was very defining as to who my real friends were. I think many composers regard success as a kind of threat. It's really better, they think, if nobody has any success, to be all in one boat. Composers now are beginning to realize that if a piece excites an audience, that doesn't mean it's terrible. For my generation, it is considered vulgar to have an audience really, really like a piece on a first hearing. But why are we writing music except to move people and to be expressive? To have what has moved us move somebody else?

Right now, audiences just reject contemporary music. But if they start to like one thing, then they begin to have perspective. That will make a difference, it always has in the past. The sleeping giant is the audience.

From John Rockwell's interview with David Del Tredici, *New York Times*, October 26, 1980, sect. D, pp. 23, 28.

## TIMELINE  The End of the Millennium

| MUSICAL EVENTS | | HISTORICAL EVENTS |
|---|---|---|
| | | **1939** Germany invades Poland, beginning World War II |
| Stravinsky and Bartók emigrate to the United States; Ellington, *Cotton Tail* | **1940** | |
| Messiaen, *Quartet for the End of Time* | **1941** | |
| Copland, *Appalachian Spring* | **1943–1944** | |
| Britten, *Peter Grimes* | **1944–1945** | |
| | | **1945** World War II ends with defeat of Germany and Japan |
| Soviet Union cracks down on Shostakovich and other "formalist" composers | **1948** | |
| First piece of *musique concrète* | **1950** | **1950–1953** Korean War |
| Cage, *Music of Changes* | **1951** | |
| Barber, *Hermit Songs* | **1952–1953** | |
| Penderecki, *Threnody: To the Victims of Hiroshima* | **1960** | |
| | | **1962** Stella, *Hyena Stomp* |
| | | **1963** President Kennedy assassinated |
| Babbitt, *Philomel* | **1964** | **1964–1975** Vietnam conflict |
| Moog and Buchla synthesizers introduced | **1966** | |
| | | **1968** Students riot in Paris, antiwar protests in the United States |
| | | **1969** First humans set foot on the moon |
| Crumb, *Black Angels* | **1970** | |
| | | **1972** President Nixon visits China |
| | | **1973** OPEC embargo forces oil prices to rise |
| | | **1974** Resignation of President Nixon following Watergate scandal |
| Del Tredici, *Final Alice* | **1975** | |
| Adams, *Phrygian Gates* | **1977–1978** | |
| | | **1978** Election of Pope John Paul II, first Polish pope |
| Sondheim, *Sweeney Todd* | **1979** | |
| | | **1980** Solidarity strikes in Poland |
| Gubaidulina, *Rejoice!* | **1981** | |
| | | **1982** New disease described, later called AIDS |
| Zwilich, Symphony No. 1 | **1983** | |
| Pärt, *Seven Magnificat Antiphons* | **1988** | |
| | | **1989** Berlin Wall torn down |
| | | **1991** Soviet Union dissolves, ending Cold War |
| Sheng, *Seven Tunes Heard in China* | **1995** | |
| | | **2000** New millennium celebrated worldwide |
| | | **2001** Terrorist attacks on World Trade Center (New York) and Pentagon |
| | | **2002** Euro introduced as new currency in European Union |
| Jazz at Lincoln Center opens its own performance space in New York | **2004** | |

is to be performed at sunrise and sunset at a small lake away from human settlements, with twelve trombonists positioned around its shores playing meditative melodies to one another across the water, cued by a conductor in a raft, and joined by animal sounds. Ideally, listeners would participate in the event by experiencing the lake, its stillness, its sounds, and its surrounding wilderness as the music is performed; in fact, most can only watch the event on film.

Joan Tower

Many works by American composer Joan Tower (b. 1938) are based on images. *Silver Ladders* (1986) for orchestra features rising lines (the "ladders" of the title), either stepwise or leaping by fourths, moving at different speeds amid a variety of textures. The "silver" in the title is meant to evoke the metal in both its solid state, embodied in the dense orchestral sections, and its molten state, represented through freely flowing solos for clarinet, oboe, marimba, and trumpet. The piece offers an abstract play of musical ideas, but the imagery offers the listener a welcome hook that makes the work easier to follow.

Direct communication

The pieces discussed here represent only a few of the many strategies composers have used to communicate directly with listeners. By the 1990s, most composers sought to write music that nonspecialist audiences could grasp, by employing familiar idioms, gestures, and other elements drawn from the entire range of music history, popular styles, and musics of the world. These familiar elements were often juxtaposed or blended in unprecedented ways in order to provide a new experience and achieve a distinctive profile. Thus, composers sought to uphold the high value placed on individuality since the nineteenth century while seeking to reclaim the immediate appeal that, many felt, had been lost in the modernist era.

# POSTLUDE

It is too early to know what music from the late twentieth or early twenty-first century will be remembered, performed, and listened to in the future or will influence later music. Trends change too quickly to give a balanced or complete overview of recent music. But it seems clear that there is a continuing tension in all types of music between finding a niche of committed listeners whose support will endure and finding a wide audience. Other, perhaps, than *Happy Birthday*, there are few pieces that everyone knows; perhaps national anthems and film music come closest to providing the shared musical experiences that seem to have been more common in the past. The immediate success and enduring place enjoyed by Beethoven in orchestral music, Verdi in opera, or Duke Ellington in jazz no longer seem possible for musicians of today because the audience is so divided that such unanimity of opinion is unlikely to be achieved.

Yet, the relative lack of dominant figures may be a good thing. Music of the past and of the entire world is more available now than ever. Thanks to radio, recordings, and marketing, most of the music we have studied is heard by more people each year today than it was during the composer's lifetime. There is no need to focus our interest on a few great composers when there is so much variety to enjoy. The choices we have for music to hear and perform have become almost limitless. So, too, are the possibilities for new music. With new computer software and the collage approach found in both classical and rap music, it is now possible for all of us with access to technology to make our own music, without performance training. In some respects, we are surrounded by more music than we can ever consume. But perhaps we are also returning to something akin to the condition of music long ago, when every singer sang his or her own song.

# FURTHER READING

## Part One: The Ancient and Medieval Worlds

Aubrey, Elizabeth. *The Music of the Troubadours.* Bloomington: Indiana University Press, 1996.

Hiley, David. *Western Plainchant: A Handbook.* New York: Oxford University Press, 1993.

Hoppin, Richard H. *Medieval Music.* New York: Norton, 1978.

Levy, Kenneth. *Gregorian Chant and the Carolingians.* Princeton, N.J.: Princeton University Press, 1998.

Long, Michael. "Trecento Italy." In *Antiquity and the Middle Ages.* Ed. James W. McKinnon. Englewood Cliffs, N.J.: Prentice Hall, 1991.

McKinnon, James, ed. *Antiquity and the Middle Ages.* Englewood Cliffs, N.J.: Prentice Hall, 1991.

———, ed. *Music in Early Christian Literature.* New York: Cambridge University Press, 1987.

Mathiesen, Thomas J. *Apollo's Lyre: Greek Music and Music Theory in Antiquity and the Early Middle Ages.* Lincoln: University of Nebraska Press, 1999.

Page, Christopher. *Voices and Instruments of the Middle Ages: Instrumental Practice and Songs in France, 1100–1300.* Berkeley: University of California Press, 1986.

Robertson, Anne Walters. *Guillaume de Machaut and Reims: Context and Meaning in His Musical Works.* New York: Cambridge University Press, 2002.

Rosenberg, Samuel N., Margaret Switten, and Gerard Le Vot, eds. *Songs of the Troubadours and Trouvères: An Anthology of Poems and Melodies.* New York: Garland, 1998.

Strunk, Oliver, ed. *Source Readings in Music History.* Rev. ed. Leo Treitler. Vol. 1: *Greek Views of Music.* Ed. Thomas J. Mathiesen. New York: Norton, 1998.

Treitler, Leo. *With Voice and Pen: Coming to Know Medieval Song and How It Was Made.* New York: Oxford University Press, 2003.

Wright, Craig. *Music and Ceremony at Nôtre Dame of Paris: 500–1500.* New York: Cambridge University Press, 1989.

## Part Two: The Age of the Renaissance

Atlas, Allan. *Renaissance Music: Music in Western Europe, 1400–1600.* New York: Norton, 1998.

Blume, Friedrich. *Protestant Church Music: A History.* New York: Norton, 1974.

Brown, Howard M., and Louise Stein. *Music in the Renaissance*. Rev. ed. Upper Saddle River, N.J.: Prentice Hall, 1999.

Cumming, Julie E. *The Motet in the Age of Du Fay*. New York: Cambridge University Press, 1999.

Fenlon, Iain. *Music and Culture in Late Renaissance Italy*. New York: Oxford University Press, 2002.

*The Josquin Companion*. Ed. Richard Sherr. New York: Oxford University Press, 2000.

*Keyboard Music before 1700*. 2nd ed. Ed. Alexander Silbiger. New York: Routledge, 2004.

LeHuray, Peter. *Music and the Reformation in England, 1549–1660*. New York: Cambridge University Press, 1967, 1978.

*A Performer's Guide to Renaissance Music*. Ed. Jeffery T. Kite-Powell. New York: Schirmer, 1994.

Perkins, Leeman. *Music in the Age of the Renaissance*. New York: Norton, 1998.

Roche, Jerome. *The Madrigal*. 2nd ed. New York: Oxford University Press, 1990.

Sparks, Edgar H. *Cantus Firmus in Mass and Motet, 1420–1520*. Berkeley: University of California Press, 1963.

Strohm, Reinhard. *The Rise of European Music, 1380–1500*. New York: Cambridge University Press, 1993.

Wright, Craig. *Music at the Court of Burgundy, 1364–1419: A Documentary History*. Henryville, Pa.: Institute of Medieval Music, 1979.

## Part Three: The Seventeenth Century

Anthony, James R. *French Baroque Music from Beaujoyeaulx to Rameau*. Rev. ed. Portland, Ore.: Amadeus Press, 1997.

Arnold, Denis, et al. *The New Grove Italian Baroque Masters: Monteverdi, Frescobaldi, Cavalli, Corelli, A. Scarlatti, Vivaldi, D. Scarlatti*. New York: Norton, 1984.

*The Cambridge History of Seventeenth-Century Music*. Ed. Tim Carter and John Butt. New York: Cambridge University Press, 2005.

Carter, Tim. *Music in Late Renaissance and Early Baroque Italy*. Portland, Ore.: Amadeus Press, 1992.

Grout, Donald J., and Hermine Weigel Williams. *A Short History of Opera*. 4th ed. New York: Columbia University Press, 2003.

Hill, John Walter. *Baroque Music: Music in Western Europe, 1580–1750*. New York: Norton, 2005.

*History of Opera*. Ed. Stanley Sadie. New York: Norton, 1990.

Palisca, Claude V. *Baroque Music*. 3rd ed. Englewood Ciffs, N.J.: Prentice Hall, 1991.

*A Performer's Guide to Seventeenth-Century Music*. Ed. Stewart Carter. New York: Schirmer, 1997.

Rifkin, Joshua, et al. *The New Grove North European Masters: Schütz, Froberger, Buxtehude, Purcell, Telemann*. New York: Norton, 1985.

Spitzer, John, and Neal Zaslaw. *The Birth of the Orchestra: History of an Institution, 1650–1815*. New York: Oxford University Press, 2004.

## Part Four: The Eighteenth Century

### THE LATE BAROQUE

Burrows, Donald. *Handel*. New York: Oxford University Press, 1996.

Christensen, Thomas. *Rameau and Musical Thought in the Enlightenment*. New York: Cambridge University Press, 1993.

David, Hans T., and Arthur Mendel. *The New Bach Reader: A Life of Johann Sebastian Bach in Letters and Documents*. Rev. and enl. by Christoph Wolff. New York: Norton, 1998.

Dill, Charles William. *Monstrous Opera: Rameau and the Tragic Tradition*. Princeton, N.J.: Princeton University Press, 1998.

Marshall, Robert L. *The Music of Johann Sebastian Bach: The Sources, the Style, the Significance*. New York: Schirmer, 1989.

Robbins Landon, H. C. *Handel and His World.* London: Weidenfeld & Nicolson, 1984.
——. *Vivaldi: Voice of the Baroque.* New York: Thames and Hudson, 1993.
Smith, Ruth. *Handel's Oratorios and Eighteenth-Century Thought.* New York: Cambridge University Press, 1995.
Strohm, Reinhard. *Essays on Handel and Italian Opera.* New York: Cambridge University Press, 1985.
Talbot, Michael. *Vivaldi.* New York: Oxford University Press, 2000.
Tunley, David. *François Couperin and the "Perfection of Music."* Aldershot, Eng.: Ashgate, 2003.
Wolff, Christoph. *Johann Sebastian Bach: The Learned Musician.* New York: Norton, 2000.
——, et al. *The New Grove Bach Family.* New York: Norton, 1983.

## THE CLASSICAL PERIOD

Brown, Clive. *Classical and Romantic Performance Practice 1750–1900.* New York: Oxford University Press, 1999.
Burnham, Scott, and Michael P. Steinberg, eds. *Beethoven and His World.* Princeton: Princeton University Press, 2000.
*The Cambridge Companion to Beethoven.* Ed. Glenn Stanley. New York: Cambridge University Press, 2000.
Cuyler, Louise. *The Symphony.* 2nd ed. Warren, Mich.: Harmonie Park Press, 1995.
Downs, Philip G. *Classical Music: The Era of Haydn, Mozart, and Beethoven.* New York: Norton, 1992.
Geiringer, Karl. *Haydn: A Creative Life in Music.* 3rd rev. and enl. ed. Berkeley: University of California Press, 1982.
Gutman, Robert W. *Mozart: A Cultural Biography.* New York: Harcourt Brace, 1999.
*Haydn and His World.* Ed. Elaine Sisman. Princeton, N.J.: Princeton University Press, 1997.
Heartz, Daniel. *Music in European Capitals: The Galant Style, 1720–1780.* New York: Norton, 2003.
Robbins Landon, H. C. *Essays on the Viennese Classical Style: Gluck, Haydn, Mozart, Beethoven.* New York: Macmilllan, 1970.
——, ed. *The Mozart Compendium: A Guide to Mozart's Life and Music* London: Thames & Hudson, 1999.
Rosen, Charles. *The Classical Style: Haydn, Mozart, Beethoven.* Expanded ed. New York: Norton, 1997.
——. *Sonata Forms.* Rev. ed. New York: Norton, 1988.
Solomon, Maynard. *Beethoven.* 2nd rev. ed. New York: Schirmer, 1998.
Webster, James, and Georg Feder. *The New Grove Haydn.* New York: Palgrave, 2002.
Zaslaw, Neal, ed. *The Classical Era: From the 1740s to the End of the Eighteenth Century.* Englewood Cliffs, N.J.: Prentice Hall, 1989.
——, with William Cowdery. *The Compleat Mozart: A Guide to the Musical Works of Wolfgang Amadeus Mozart.* New York: Norton, 1990.

## Part Five: The Nineteenth Century

Abraham, Gerald, and David Brown, et al. *The New Grove Russian Masters.* 2 vols. New York: Norton, 1986.
*A Brahms Reader.* Ed. Michael Musgrave. New Haven, Conn.: Yale University Press, 2000.
*The Cambridge Companion to Grand Opera.* Ed. David Charlton. New York: Cambridge University Press, 2003.
Cooper, Martin. *French Music from the Death of Berlioz to the Death of Fauré.* New York: Oxford University Press, 1951.
Dahlaus, Carl. *Nineteenth-Century Music.* Trans. J. Bradford Robinson. Berkeley: University of California Press, 1989.
——. *Realism in Nineteenth-Century Music.* Trans. Mary Whittall. New York: Cambridge University Press, 1985.
Daverio, John. *Nineteenth-Century Music and the German Romantic Ideology.* New York: Schirmer, 1993.

——. *Crossing Paths: Schubert, Schumann, and Brahms.* New York: Oxford University Press, 2002.

Dent, Edward J. *The Rise of Romantic Opera.* Ed. Winton Dean. New York: Cambridge University Press, 1976.

*Dvořák and His World.* Ed. Michael Beckerman. Princeton, N.J.: Princeton University Press, 1993.

Garden, Edward. *Tchaikovsky.* New York: Oxford University Press, 2000.

Gooley, Dana. *The Virtuoso Liszt.* New York: Cambridge University Press, 2004.

Kramer, Richard. *Distant Cycles: Schubert and the Conceiving of Song.* Chicago: University of Chicago Press, 1994.

*Liszt and the Birth of Modern Europe: Music as a Mirror of Religious, Political, Cultural and Aesthetic Transformation.* Ed. Michael Saffle and Rossana Dalmonte. Hillsdale, N.Y.: Pendragon Press, 2003.

Millington, Barry, ed. *The New Grove Wagner.* New York: Grove, 2002.

Pistone, Danièle. *Nineteenth-Century Italian Opera from Rossini to Puccini.* Trans. E. Thomas Glasow. Portland, Ore.: Amadeus Press, 1995.

Plantinga, Leon. *Romantic Music.* New York: Norton, 1984.

Reich, Nancy B. *Clara Schumann: The Artist and the Woman.* Rev. ed. Ithaca, N.Y.: Cornell University Press, 2001.

*Richard Strauss and His World.* Ed. Bryan Gilliam. Princeton, N.J.: Princeton University Press, 1992.

Rosen, Charles. *Romantic Poets, Critics, and Other Madmen.* Cambridge, Mass.: Harvard University Press, 1998.

——. *The Romantic Generation.* Cambridge, Mass.: Harvard University Press, 1995.

Rosselli, John. *The Life of Verdi.* New York: Cambridge University Press, 2000.

Samson, Jim. *Chopin.* New York: Oxford University Press, 1996.

Todd, R. Larry. *Mendelssohn: A Life in Music.* New York: Oxford University Press, 2003.

Tyrell, John, et al. *The New Grove Turn of the Century Masters: Janáček, Mahler, Strauss, Sibelius.* New York: Norton, 1985.

*The Verdi Companion.* Ed. William Weaver and Martin Chusid. New York: Norton, 1979.

*Wagner and His Operas.* Ed. Stanley Sadie. New York: St. Martin's, 2000.

## Part Six: The Twentieth Century and Today

*The Cambridge Companion to Bartók.* Ed. Amanda Bayley. New York: Cambridge University Press, 2001.

*The Cambridge Companion to Stravinsky.* Ed. Jonathan Cross. New York: Cambridge University Press, 2003.

*The Cambridge History of Twentieth-Century Music.* Ed. Nicholas Cook and Anthony Pople. New York: Cambridge University Press, 2004.

Crawford, Richard. *An Introduction to America's Music.* New York: Norton, 2001.

Hamm, Charles. *Music in the New World.* New York: Norton, 1983.

Hitchcock, H. Wiley. *Music in the United States: A Historical Introduction.* 3rd ed. Englewood Cliffs, N.J.: Prentice Hall, 1988.

Horowitz, Joseph. *Classical Music in America: A History of Its Rise and Fall.* New York: Norton, 2005.

Lampert, Vera, et al. *The New Grove Modern Masters: Bartók, Stravinsky, Hindemith.* New York: Norton, 1984.

McVeagh, Diana, et al. *The New Grove Twentieth-Century English Masters: Elgar, Delius, Vaughan Williams, Holst, Walton, Tippett, Britten.* New York: Norton, 1986.

*Modern Times: From World War I to the Present.* Ed. Robert P. Morgan. Englewood Cliffs, N.J.: Prentice Hall, 1993.

*Modernism and Music: An Anthology of Sources.* Ed. Daniel Albright. Chicago: University of Chicago Press, 2004.

Morgan, Robert P. *Twentieth-Century Music: A History of Musical Style in Modern Europe and America.* New York: Norton, 1991.

Nectoux, Jean-Michel, et al. *The New Grove Twentieth-Century French Masters: Fauré, Debussy, Satie, Ravel, Poulenc, Messiaen, Boulez.* New York: Norton, 1986.

Reich, Willi. *Schoenberg: A Critical Biography.* Trans. Leo Black. 1971; repr. New York: Da Capo, 1981.

Salzman, Eric. *Twentieth-Century Music: An Introduction.* 3rd ed. Englewood Cliffs, N.J.: Prentice Hall, 1988.

*Schoenberg, Berg, and Webern: A Companion to the Second Viennese School.* Ed. Bryan R. Simms. Westport, Conn.: Greenwood Press, 1999.

Schwarz, Boris. *Music and Musical Life in Soviet Russia, Enlarged Edition, 1917–1981.* Bloomington: Indiana University Press, 1983.

Simms, Bryan R. *Music of the Twentieth Century: Style and Structure.* 2nd ed. New York: Schirmer, 1996.

Smith, Joan A. *Schoenberg and His Circle: A Viennese Portrait.* New York: Schirmer, 1986.

Straus, Joseph N. *Remaking the Past: Musical Modernism and the Influence of the Tonal Tradition.* Cambridge, Mass.: Harvard University Press, 1990.

Swafford, Jan. *Charles Ives: A Life with Music.* New York: Norton. 1996.

Taruskin, Richard. *Stravinsky and the Russian Traditions: A Biography of the Works through Mavra.* Berkeley: University of California Press, 1996.

Tawa, Nicholas E. *The Coming of Age of American Art Music: New England's Classical Romanticists.* New York: Greenwood Press, 1991.

Tirro, Frank. *Jazz: A History.* 2nd ed. New York: Norton, 1993.

Watkins, Glenn. *Soundings: Music in the Twentieth Century.* New York: Schirmer, 1988.

——. *Pyramids at the Louvre: Music, Culture, and Collage from Stravinsky to the Postmodernists.* Cambridge, Mass.: Harvard University Press, 1994.

# GLOSSARY

Within a definition, terms that are themselves defined in this glossary are printed in SMALL CAPITALS. Terms defined in general dictionaries are not included here. Pronunciation of foreign words is approximate and is given only when the spelling makes mispronunciation likely; "nh" stands for a final "n" in French, which nasalizes the preceding vowel (as in "chanson," rendered here as "shanh-SONH").

**Abgesang** (pronounced AHP-ge-zong)   See BAR FORM.

**absolute music**   Music that is independent of words, drama, visual images, or any kind of representational aspects.

**a cappella** (Italian, "in chapel style")   Manner of choral singing without instrumental accompaniment.

**accidental**   Sign that calls for altering the pitch of a NOTE: a sharp (♯) raises the pitch a semitone, a flat (♭) lowers it a semitone, and a natural (♮) cancels a previous accidental.

**accompanied recitative**   RECITATIVE that uses ORCHESTRAL accompaniment to dramatize the text.

**act**   Main division of an OPERA. Most operas have two to five acts, although some have only one.

**affections**   Objectified or archetypal emotions or states of mind, such as sadness, joy, fear, or wonder; one goal of much BAROQUE music was to arouse the affections.

**Agnus Dei** (Latin, "Lamb of God")   Fifth of the five major musical items in the MASS ORDINARY, based on a litany.

**agrément** (French, "charm"; pronounced ah-gray-MANH)   ORNAMENT in French music, usually indicated by a sign.

**air**   English or French song for solo voice with instrumental accompaniment, setting rhymed poetry, often STROPHIC, and usually in the METER of a dance.

**air de cour** (French, "court air")   Type of song for voice and accompaniment, prominent in France from about 1580 through the seventeenth century.

**Alberti bass**   Broken-CHORD accompaniment common in the second half of the eighteenth century and named after Domenico Alberti, who used the FIGURATION frequently.

**Alleluia**   Item from the MASS PROPER, sung just before the Gospel reading, comprising a RESPOND to the text "Alleluia," a verse, and a repetition of the respond. CHANT alleluias are normally MELISMATIC in style and sung in a RESPONSORIAL manner, one or more soloists alternating with the CHOIR.

**allemande** (French for "German")   Highly stylized DANCE in BINARY FORM, in moderately fast quadruple METER with almost continuous movement, beginning with an upbeat. Popular during the RENAISSANCE and BAROQUE; appearing often as the first dance in a SUITE.

**alto** (from ALTUS)   (1) Relatively low female voice, or high male voice. (2) Part for such a voice in an ENSEMBLE work.

**altus** (Latin, "high")   In fifteenth- and sixteenth-century POLYPHONY, a part in a range between the TENOR and the SUPERIUS; originally CONTRATENOR ALTUS.

**Ambrosian chant**   A repertory of ecclesiastical CHANT used in Milan.

**answer**   In the EXPOSITION of a FUGUE, the second entry of the SUBJECT, normally on the DOMINANT if the subject was on the TONIC, and vice versa. Also refers to subsequent answers to the subject.

**anthem**   A POLYPHONIC sacred work in English for Anglican religious services.

**antiphon**   (1) A LITURGICAL CHANT that precedes and follows a PSALM or CANTICLE in the OFFICE. (2) In the MASS, a chant originally associated with ANTIPHONAL PSALMODY; specifically, the COMMUNION and the first and final portion of the INTROIT.

**antiphonal**  Adjective describing a manner of performance in which two or more groups alternate.

**Aquitanian polyphony**  Style of POLYPHONY from the twelfth century, encompassing both DISCANT and FLORID ORGANUM.

**aria** (Italian, "air")  (1) In the late sixteenth and early seventeenth centuries, any section of an Italian STROPHIC poem for a solo singer. (2) Lyrical monologue in an OPERA or other vocal work such as CANTATA and ORATORIO.

**arioso**  (1) RECITATIVO ARIOSO. (2) Short, ARIA-like passage. (3) Style of vocal writing that approaches the lyricism of an ARIA but is freer in form.

**arpeggio** (from Italian *arpa*, "harp")  Broken-CHORD figure.

**Ars nova** (Latin, "new art")  Style of POLYPHONY from fourteenth-century France, distinguished from earlier styles by a new system of rhythmic NOTATION that allowed duple or triple division of NOTE values, SYNCOPATION, and great rhythmic flexibility.

**Ars subtilior** (Latin, "the subtler art")  Style of POLYPHONY from the late fourteenth or very early fifteenth centuries in southern France and northern Italy, distinguished by extreme complexity in rhythm and NOTATION.

**art music**  Music that is (or is meant to be) listened to with rapt attention, for its own sake. Compare POPULAR MUSIC.

**art song**  A song intended to be appreciated as an artistic statement rather than as entertainment, featuring precisely notated music, usually THROUGH-COMPOSED, and requiring professional standards of performance. Compare POPULAR SONG.

**atonal, atonality**  Terms for music that avoids establishing a central pitch or tonal center (such as the TONIC in TONAL music).

**aulos**  Ancient Greek reed instrument, usually played in pairs.

**authentic mode**  A MODE (2) in which the RANGE normally extends from a STEP below the FINAL to an octave above it. See also PLAGAL MODE.

**avant-garde**  Term for music (and art) that is iconoclastic, irreverent, antagonistic, and nihilistic, seeking to overthrow established aesthetics.

**ballad**  (1) Long narrative poem, or musical setting of such a poem. (2) Late-eighteenth-century German poetic form that imitated the folk ballad of England and Scotland and was set to music by German composers. The ballad expanded the LIED in both FORM and emotional content.

**ballad opera**  GENRE of eighteenth-century English comic play featuring songs in which new words are set to borrowed tunes.

**ballade**  (a) French FORME FIXE, normally in three stanzas, in which each stanza has the musical FORM aab and ends with a REFRAIN. (2) Instrumental piece inspired by the GENRE of narrative poetry.

**ballata** (from Italian *ballare*, "to dance"; pl. *ballate*)  Fourteenth-century Italian song GENRE with the FORM AbbaA, in which A is the *ripresa* or REFRAIN, and the single stanza consists of two *piedi* (bb) and a *volta* (a) sung to the music of the ripresa.

**ballet**  In sixteenth- and seventeenth-century France, an entertainment in which both professionals and guests danced; later, a stage work danced by professionals.

**balletto, ballett** (Italian, "little dance")  Sixteenth-century Italian (and later English) song GENRE in a simple, dancelike, HOMOPHONIC style with repeated sections and "fa-la-la" refrains.

**band**  Large ENSEMBLE of winds, brass, and percussion instruments, or of brass and percussion instruments without winds.

**bar form**  Song FORM in which the first section of MELODY is sung twice with different texts (the two STOLLEN) and the remainder (the ABGESANG) is sung once.

**bard**  Medieval poet-singer, especially of epics.

**Baroque** (from Portuguese *barroco*, "a misshapen pearl")  PERIOD of music history from about 1600 to about 1750, overlapping the late RENAISSANCE and early CLASSICAL periods.

**bas** (French, "low"; pronounced BAH)  In the fourteenth through sixteenth centuries, term for soft instruments such as VIELLES and HARPS. See HAUT.

**bass** (from BASSUS)  (1) The lowest part in an ENSEMBLE work. (2) Low male voice. (3) Low instrument, especially the string bass or bass VIOL.

*basse danse* (French, "low dance")  Type of stately couple DANCE of the fifteenth and early sixteenth centuries.

**basso continuo** (Italian, "continuous bass")  (1) System of NOTATION and performance practice, used in the BAROQUE PERIOD, in which an instrumental BASS line is written out and one or more players of keyboard, LUTE, or similar instruments fill in the HARMONY with appropriate CHORDS or IMPROVISED MELODIC lines. (2) The bass line itself.

**basso ostinato** (Italian, "persistent bass") or **ground bass**  A pattern in the BASS that repeats while the MELODY above it changes.

**bassus** (Latin, "low")  In fifteenth- and sixteenth-century POLYPHONY, the lowest part; originally CONTRATENOR BASSUS.

**bebop** (or **bop**)  A style of JAZZ developed in New York in the 1940s that had a diversified rhythmic texture, enriched HARMONIC vocabulary, and an emphasis on IMPROVISATION with rapid MELODIES and asymmetrical PHRASES.

**bel canto** (Italian, "beautiful singing")  Elegant Italian vocal style of the early nineteenth century marked by lyrical, embellished, and florid melodies that show off the beauty, agility, and fluency of the singer's voice.

**big band**  Type of large JAZZ ENSEMBLE popular between the world wars, featuring brass, reeds, and RHYTHM SECTIONS, and playing prepared arrangements that included rhythmic unisons and coordinated dialogue between sections and soloists.

**binary form**  A FORM comprised of two complementary sections, each of which is repeated. The first section usually ends on the DOMINANT or the relative major, although it many end of the TONIC or other KEY; the second section returns to the tonic.

**blue note**  Slight drop or slide in pitch on the third, fifth, or seventh degree of a MAJOR SCALE, common in BLUES and JAZZ.

**blues** (1) African-American vocal GENRE that is based on a simple repetitive formula and characterized by a distinctive style of performance. (2) TWELVE-BAR BLUES.

**bop** See BEBOP.

**branle gay** RENAISSANCE DANCE in a lively triple METER based on a sideways swaying step.

**breve** (from Latin *brevis*, "short") In medieval and RENAISSANCE systems of RHYTHMIC NOTATION, a NOTE that is normally equal to half or a third of a LONG.

**bull lyre** Sumerian LYRE with a bull's head at one end of the soundbox.

**burden** (1) In English medieval POLYPHONY, the lowest voice. (2) In the English CAROL, the REFRAIN.

**Byzantine chant** The repertory of ecclesiastical CHANT used in the Byzantine RITE and in the modern Greek Orthodox Church.

**cabaletta** In the operatic scene structure developed by Gioachino Rossini in the early nineteenth century, the last part of an ARIA or ENSEMBLE, which was lively and brilliant and expressed active feelings, such as joy or despair. See also CANTABILE and TEMPO DI MEZZO.

**cabaret** Type of nightclub, first introduced in nineteenth-century Paris, that offered serious or comic sketches, dances, songs, and poetry.

**caccia** (Italian, "hunt"; pronouced CAH-cha; pl. *cacce*) Fourteenth-century Italian FORM featuring two voices in CANON over a free untexted TENOR.

**cadence** MELODIC or HARMONIC succession that closes a musical PHRASE, PERIOD, section, or COMPOSITION.

**cadenza** (Italian, "cadence") Highly embellished passage, often IMPROVISED, at an important CADENCE, usually occurring just before the end of a piece or section.

**café-concert** Type of dining establishment, prominent in late-nineteenth- and early-twentieth-century Pans, that combined the food and drink of a café with musical entertainment, usually songs on sentimental, comic, or political topics.

**call and response** Alternation of short PHRASES between a leader and a group; used especially for music in the African-American tradition.

**cambiata** (Italian, "changed") Figure in sixteenth-century POLYPHONY in which a voice skips down from a DISSONANCE to a CONSONANCE instead of resolving by STEP, then moves to the expected NOTE of resolution.

**Camerata** (Italian, "circle" or "association") Circle of intellectuals and amateurs of the arts that met in Florence, Italy, in the 1570s and 1580s.

**canon** (Latin, "rule") (1) Rule for performing music, particularly for deriving more than one voice from a single line of notated music, as when several voices sing the same MELODY, entering at certain intervals of time or singing at different speeds simultaneously. (2) COMPOSITION in which the voices enter successively at determined pitch and time intervals, all performing the same MELODY.

**cantabile** (Italian, "songlike") (1) Songful, lyrical, in a songlike style. (2) In the operatic scene structure developed by Gioachino Rossini in the early nineteenth century, the first section of an ARIA or ENSEMBLE, some-

what slow and expressing a relatively calm mood. See also CABALETTA and TEMPO DI MEZZO.

**cantata** (Italian, "to be sung") (1) In the seventeenth and eighteenth centuries, a vocal chamber work with CONTINUO, usually for solo voice, consisting of several sections or MOVEMENTS that include RECITATIVES and ARIAS and setting a lyrical or quasi-dramatic text. (2) Form of Lutheran church music in the eighteenth century, combining poetic texts with texts drawn from CHORALES or the Bible, and including RECITATIVES, ARIAS, chorale settings, and usually one or more CHORUSES. (3) In later eras, a work for soloists, CHORUS, and ORCHESTRA in several MOVEMENTS but smaller than an ORATORIO.

**canticle** HYMN-like or PSALM-like passage from a part of the Bible other than the Book of Psalms.

**cantiga** Medieval MONOPHONIC song in Spanish or Portuguese.

**cantilena** (Latin, "song") POLYPHONIC song not based on a CANTUS FIRMUS; used especially for polyphonic songs by English composers of the late thirteenth through early fifteenth centuries.

**cantillation** Chanting of a sacred text by a solo singer, particularly in the Jewish synagogue.

**cantional style** (from Latin *cantionale*, "songbook") Manner of setting CHORALES in CHORDAL HOMOPHONY with the MELODY in the highest voice.

**cantor** In Jewish synagogue music, the main solo singer. In the medieval Christian church, the leader of the CHOIR.

**cantus** (Latin, "melody") In POLYPHONY of the fourteenth through sixteenth centuries, the highest voice, especially the texted voice in a polyphonic song.

**cantus firmus** (Latin, "fixed melody") An existing MELODY, often taken from a GREGORIAN CHANT, on which a new POLYPHONIC work is based; used especially for MELODIES presented in long NOTES.

**cantus-firmus Mass** POLYPHONIC MASS in which the same CANTUS FIRMUS is used in each MOVEMENT, normally in the TENOR.

**cantus-firmus/imitation Mass** POLYPHONIC MASS in which each MOVEMENT is based on the same polyphonic work, using that work's TENOR (sometimes the SUPERIUS) as a CANTUS FIRMUS, normally in the tenor, and borrowing some elements from the other voices of the model to use in the other voices of the MASS.

**cantus-firmus variations** Instrumental GENRE of the late 1500s and early 1600s, comprising a set of VARIATIONS in which the MELODY repeats with little change but is surrounded by different CONTRAPUNTAL material in each variation.

**canzona (canzon)** (Italian, "song") (1) Sixteenth-century Italian GENRE, an instrmental work adapted from a CHANSON or composed in a similar style. (2) In the late sixteenth and early seventeenth centuries, an instrumental work in several contrasting sections, of which the first and some of the others are in IMITATIVE COUNTERPOINT.

**canzonetta, canzonet** (Italian, "little song") Sixteenth-century Italian (and later English) song GENRE in a simple, mostly HOMOPHONIC style. Diminutive of CANZONA.

capriccio (Italian, "whim")    (1) In the BAROQUE PERIOD, a FUGAL piece in continuous IMITATIVE COUNTERPOINT. (2) In the nineteenth century, a short COMPOSITION in free FORM, usually for PIANO.

carol    English song, usually on a religious subject, with several stanzas and a BURDEN, or REFRAIN. From the fifteenth century on, most carols are POLYPHONIC.

carole    Medieval circle or line dance, or the MONOPHONIC song that accompanied it.

castrati (sing. castrato)    Male singers who were castrated before puberty to preserve their high vocal RANGE, prominent in the seventeenth and early eighteenth centuries, especially in OPERA.

catch    English GENRE of CANON, usually with a humorous or ribald text.

cauda (Latin, "tail"; pl. caudae)    MELISMATIC passage in a POLYPHONIC CONDUCTUS.

centonization (from Latin cento, "patchwork")    A process of composing a new MELODY by combining standard MOTIVES and formulas, used in BYZANTINE CHANT.

chacona (Italian, ciaccona)    A vivacious dance-song imported from Latin America into Spain and then into Italy, popular during the seventeenth century

chaconne (or ciaccona)    BAROQUE GENRE derived from the CHACONA, consisting of VARIATIONS over a BASSO CONTINUO.

chamber sonata    See SONATA DA CAMERA.

chance    Approach to composing music pioneered by John Cage, in which some of the decisions normally made by the composer are instead determined through random procedures, such as tossing coins. Chance differs from INDETERMINACY but shares with it the result that the sounds in the music do not convey an intention and are therefore to be experienced only as pure sound.

chanson (French, "song"; pronounced shanh-SONH)    Secular song with French words; used especially for POLYPHONIC songs of the fourteenth through sixteenth centuries.

chanson de geste (French, "song of deeds")    Type of medieval French epic recounting the deeds of national heros, sung to MELODIC formulas.

chansonnier (French, "songbook")    Manuscript collection of secular songs with French words; used both for collections of MONOPHONIC TROUBADOUR and TROUVÈRE songs and for collections of POLYPHONIC songs.

chant    (1) Unison unaccompanied song, particularly that of the Latin LITURGY (also called PLAINCHANT). (2) The repertory of unaccompanied liturgical songs of a particular RITE.

chant dialect    One of the repertories of ecclesiastical CHANT, including GREGORIAN, BYZANTINE, AMBROSIAN, and OLD ROMAN CHANT.

chapel    A group of salaried musicians and clerics employed by a ruler, nobleman, church official, or other patron, who officiate at and furnish music for religious services.

character piece    A piece of CHARACTERISTIC MUSIC, especially one for PIANO.

characteristic (or descriptive) music    Instrumental music that depicts or suggests a mood, personality, or scene, usually indicated in its title.

charts    In postwar POPULAR MUSIC, weekly rankings of songs by sales or other measures of popularity.

choir    A group of singers who perform together, singing either in unison or in parts. Used especially for the group that sings in a religious service.

choral society    Amateur CHORUS whose members sing for their own enjoyment and may pay dues to purchase music, pay the CONDUCTOR, and meet other expenses.

chorale (pronounced ko-RAL)    STROPHIC HYMN in the Lutheran tradition, intended to be sung by the congregation.

chorale motet    CHORALE setting in the style of a sixteenth-century MOTET.

chorale prelude    Relatively short setting for organ of a CHORALE MELODY, used as an introduction for congregational singing or as an interlude in a Lutheran church service.

chorale variations    A set of VARIATIONS on a CHORALE MELODY.

chord    Three or more simultaneous NOTES heard as a single entity. In TONAL music, three or more notes that can be arranged as a succession of thirds, such as a TRIAD.

chorus    (1) Group of singers who perform together, usually with several singers on each part. (2) A MOVEMENT or passage for such a group in an ORATORIO, OPERA, or other multimovement work. (3) The REFRAIN of a POPULAR SONG. (4) In JAZZ, a statement of the HARMONIC PROGRESSION of the opening tune, over which one or more instruments play variants or new musical ideas.

chromatic (from Greek chroma, "color")    (1) In ancient Greek music, adjective describing a TETRACHORD comprising a minor third and two SEMITONES, or a MELODY that uses such tetrachords. (2) Adjective describing a melody that uses two or more successive semitones in the same direction, a SCALE consisting exclusively of semitones, an INTERVAL or CHORD that draws NOTES from more than one DIATONIC scale, or music that uses many such melodies or chords.

chromatic saturation    The appearance of all twelve PITCH-CLASSES within a segment of music.

chromaticism    The use of many NOTES from the CHROMATIC SCALE in a passage or piece.

church calendar    In a Christian RITE, the schedule of days commemorating special events, individuals, or times of year.

church sonata    See SONATA DA CHIESA.

ciaccona    See CHACONA.

Classical period    In music history, the era from about 1730 to about 1815, between and overlapping the BAROQUE and ROMANTIC PERIODS.

classical music    (1) Common term for ART MUSIC of all PERIODS, as distinct from POPULAR MUSIC OR FOLK MUSIC. (2) Music in the tradition of the repertoire of musical masterworks that formed in the nineteenth century, including lesser works in the same GENRES (such as OPERA, ORATORIO, SYMPHONY, SONATA, STRING QUARTET, and ART SONG) or for the same performing forces and newly composed works intended as part of the same tradition. (3) Music in the CLASSICAL PERIOD.

**Classical style**  Musical idiom of the eighteenth century, generally characterized by an emphasis on MELODY over relatively light accompaniment; simple, clearly articulated harmonic plans; PERIODIC phrasing; clearly delineated FORMS based on contrast between THEMES, between KEYS, between stable and unstable passages, and between sections with different functions; and contrasts of mood, style, and figuration within MOVEMENTS as well as between them.

**clausula** (Latin, "clause," pl. *clausulae*)  In NOTRE DAME POLYPHONY, a self-contained section of an ORGANUM that closes with a CADENCE.

**clavecin**  French term for HARPSICHORD. A person who performs on or composes works for the clavecin is known as a **clavecinist**.

**clavichord**  Keyboard instrument popular between the fifteenth and eighteenth centuries. The loudness, which depends on the force with which a brass blade strikes the strings, is under the direct control of the player.

**clos**  See OPEN AND CLOSED ENDINGS.

**coda** (Italian, "tail")  A supplementary ending to a COMPOSITION or MOVEMENT; a concluding section that lies outside the FORM as usually described.

**collage**  Work or passage that uses multiple QUOTATIONS without following a standard procedure for doing so, such as QUODLIBET or medley.

**collegium musicum**  An association of amateurs, popular during the BAROQUE PERIOD, who gathered to play and sing together for their own pleasure. Today, an ensemble of university students that performs early music.

**color** (Latin rhetorical term for ornament, particularly repetition, pronounced KOH-lor)  In an ISORHYTHMIC COMPOSITION, a repeated MELODIC pattern, as opposed to the repeating rhythmic pattern (the TALEA).

**coloratura**  Florid vocal ORNAMENTATION.

**Communion**  Item in the MASS PROPER, originally sung during communion, comprising an ANTIPHON without verses.

**composition**  The act or process of creating new pieces of music, or a piece that results from this process and is substantially similar each time it is performed; usually distinguished from IMPROVISATION and performance.

**concert band**  Large ENSEMBLE of winds, brass, and percussion instruments that performs seated in concert halls, like an ORCHESTRA.

**concert étude**  See ÉTUDE

**concertato medium** (from Italian *concertare*, "to reach agreement")  In seventeenth-century music, the combination of voices with one or more instruments, where the instruments do not simply double the voices but play independent parts.

**concerted madrigal**  Early-seventeenth-century type of MADRIGAL for one or more voices accompanied by BASSO CONTINUO and in some cases by other instruments.

**concerto** (from Italian *concertare*, "to reach agreement")  (1) In the seventeenth century, ENSEMBLE of instruments or of voices with one or more instruments, or a work for such an ensemble. (2) COMPOSITION in which one or more solo instruments (or instrumental group) contrasts with an ORCHESTRAL ENSEMBLE. See also SOLO CONCERTO, CONCERTO GROSS, and ORCHESTRAL CONCERTO.

**concerto grosso**  Instrumental work that exploits the contrast in sonority between a small ENSEMBLE of solo instruments (*concertino*), usually the same forces that appeared in the TRIO SONATA, and a large ENSEMBLE (RIPIENO or *concerto grosso*).

**concitato**  See STILE CONCITATO.

**conductor**  A person who leads a performance, especially for an ORCHESTRA, BAND, CHORUS, or other large ENSEMBLE, by means of gestures.

**conductus**  A serious medieval song, MONOPHONIC or POLYPHONIC, setting a rhymed, rhythmic Latin poem.

**conjunct**  (1) In ancient Greek music, adjective used to describe the relationship between two TETRACHORDS when the bottom NOTE of one is the same as the top note of the other. (2) Of a MELODY, consisting mostly of STEPS.

**conservatory**  School that specializes in teaching music.

**consonance**  INTERVAL or CHORD that has a stable, harmonious sound. Compare DISSONANCE.

**consort**  English name (current ca. 1575–1700) for a group of instruments, either all of one type (called a *full consort*), such as a consort of VIOLS, or of different types (called a *broken consort*).

**consort song**  RENAISSANCE English GENRE of song for voice accompanied by a CONSORT of VIOLS.

*contenance angloise* (French, "English guise")  Characteristic quality of early-fifteenth-century English music, marked by pervasive CONSONANCE with frequent use of HARMONIC thirds and sixths, often in parallel motion.

**continuo**  BASSO CONTINUO.

**continuo instruments**  Instruments used to REALIZE a BASSO CONTINUO, such as HARPSICHORD, organ, LUTE, or THEORBO.

**contrafact**  In JAZZ, a new MELODY composed over a HARMONIC PROGRESSION borrowed from another song.

**contrafactum** (Latin, "counterfeit"; pl. *contrafacta*)  The practice of replacing the text of a vocal work with a new text while the music remains essentially the same; or the resulting piece.

**contrapuntal**  Employing COUNTERPOINT, or two or more simultaneous MELODIC lines.

**contratenor** (Latin, "against the tenor")  In fourteenth- and fifteenth-century POLYPHONY, voice composed after or in conjunction with the TENOR and in about the same RANGE, helping to form the HARMONIC foundation.

**contratenor altus, contratenor bassus** (Latin)  In fifteenth-century POLYPHONY, CONTRATENOR parts that lie relatively high (ALTUS) or low (BASSUS) in comparison to the TENOR. Often simply written as "altus" or "bassus," these are the ancestors of the vocal ranges ALTO and BASS.

**cornett**  Wind instrument of hollowed-out wood or ivory, with finger holes and a cup mouthpiece, blown like a brass instrument.

**counterpoint**  The combination of two or more simultaneous MELODIC lines according to a set of rules.

**country music** (also known as *country-and-western*)  A type of POPULAR MUSIC associated primarily with white southerners, that blends elements of FOLK MUSIC, POPU-LAR SONG, and other traditions.

**couplet**  In a RONDO or seventeenth- or eighteenth-century RONDEAU, one of several PERIODS or passages that alternate with the REFRAIN.

**courante**  A DANCE in BINARY FORM, in triple METER at a moderate tempo and with an upbeat, featured as a standard MOVEMENT of the Baroque dance SUITE.

**court ballet**  Seventeenth-century French GENRE, an extensive musical-dramatic work with costumes, scenery, poetry, and dance that featured members of the court as well as professional dancers.

**courtly love**  See FINE AMOUR.

**Credo** (Latin, "I believe")  Third of the five major musical items in the MASS ORDINARY, a creed or statement of faith.

**cumulative form**  FORM used by Charles Ives and others in which the principal THEME appears in its entirety only at the end of a work, preceded by its DEVELOPMENT.

**cycle**  A group of related works, comprising MOVEMENTS of a single larger entity. Examples include cycles of CHANTS for the MASS ORDINARY, consisting of one setting each of the KYRIE, GLORIA, SANCTUS, and AGNUS DEI (and sometimes also *Ite, missa est*); the POLYPHONIC MASS cycle of the fifteenth through seventeenth centuries; and the SONG CYCLE of the nineteenth century.

**da capo aria**  ARIA FORM with two sections. The first section is repeated after the second section's close, which carries the instruction *da capo* (Italian, "from the head"), creating an ABA FORM.

**dances**  Pieces in stylized dance rhythms, whether independent, paired, or linked together in a SUITE.

**descriptive music**  See CHARACTERISTIC MUSIC.

**developing variation**  Term coined by Arnold Schoenberg for the process of deriving new THEMES, accompaniments, and other ideas throughout a piece through variations of a germinal idea.

**development**  (1) The process of reworking, recombining, fragmenting, and varying given THEMES or other material. (2) In SONATA FORM, the section after the EXPOSITION, which MODULATES through a variety of KEYS and in which THEMES from the exposition are presented in new ways.

**diastematic**  Having to do with INTERVALS. In diastematic motion, the voice moves between sustained pitches separated by discrete intervals; in diastematic NOTATION, the approximate intervals are indicated by relative height (see HEIGHTED NEUMES).

**diatonic**  (1) In ancient Greek music, adjective describing a TETRACHORD with two WHOLE TONES and one SEMITONE. (2) Name for a SCALE that includes five whole tones and two semitones, where the semitones are separated by two or three whole tones. (3) Adjective describing a MELODY, CHORD, or passage based exclusively on a single diatonic scale.

**diegetic music or source music**  In film, music that is heard or performed by the characters themselves.

**digital**  Relating to methods for producing or recording musical sounds by translating them into a coded series of on-off pulses, or 1s and 0s, in the same way that computers store and transmit data.

**diminution**  (1) Uniform reduction of NOTE values in a MELODY or PHRASE. (2) Type of IMPROVISED ORNAMENTATION in the sixteenth and seventeenth centuries, in which relatively long notes are replaced with SCALES or other FIGURES composed of short notes.

**direct**  Pertaining to a manner of performing CHANT without alternation between groups (see ANTIPHONAL) or between soloist and group (see RESPONSORIAL).

**discant** (Latin, "singing apart")  (1) Twelfth-century style of POLYPHONY in which the upper voice or voices have about one to three NOTES for each note of the lower voice. (2) TREBLE part.

**disjunct**  (1) In ancient Greek music, adjective used to describe the relationship between two TETRACHORDS when the bottom NOTE of one is a whole tone above the top note of the other. (2) Of a MELODY, consisting mostly of skips (third) and leaps (larger INTERVALS) rather than STEPS.

**dissonance**  (1) Two or more NOTES sounding together to produce a discord, or a sound that needs to be resolved to a CONSONANCE. (2) A NOTE that does not belong to the CHORD that sounds simultaneously with it; a nonchord TONE.

**diva**  A leading and successful female OPERA singer. See also PRIMA DONNA.

**divertissement**  In *TRAGÉDIE EN MUSIQUE*, a long interlude of BALLET, solo AIRS, choral singing, and spectacle, intended as entertainment.

**division**  See DIMINUTION (2).

**dominant**  In TONAL music, the NOTE and CHORD a perfect fifth above the TONIC.

**double leading-tone cadence**  CADENCE popular in the fourteenth and fifteenth centuries, in which the bottom voice moves down a WHOLE TONE and the upper voices move up a SEMITONE, forming a major third and major sixth expanding to an open fifth and octave.

**double motet**  Thirteenth-century MOTET in three voices, with different texts in the DUPLUM and TRIPLUM.

**Doxology**  A formula of praise to the Trinity. Two FORMS are used in GREGORIAN CHANT: the Greater Doxology, or GLORIA, and the Lesser Doxology, used with PSALMS, INTROITS, and other chants.

**dramatic opera**  Seventeenth-century English mixed GENRE of musical theater, a spoken play with an OVERTURE and four or more MASQUES or long musical interludes. Today often called SEMI-OPERA.

**drone**  NOTE or notes sustained throughout an entire piece or section.

**duplum** (from Latin *duplus*, "double")  In POLYPHONY of the late twelfth through fourteenth centuries, second voice from the bottom in a four-voice TEXTURE, above the TENOR.

**dynamics**  Level of loudness or softness, or intensity.

**echos** (Greek; pl. *echoi*)  One of the eight MODES associated with BYZANTINE CHANT.

**electronic music**  Music based on sounds that are produced or modified through electronic means.

*empfindsamer* **style** (German, "sensitive style" or "sentimental style")   Close relative of the GALANT style, featuring surprising turns of HARMONY, CHROMATICISM, nervous RHYTHMS, and speechlike MELODIES.

**enharmonic**   (1) In ancient Greek music, adjective describing a TETRACHORD comprising a major third and two quartertones, or a MELODY that uses such tetrachords. (2) Adjective describing the relationship between two pitches that are notated differently but sound alike when played, such as G♯ and A♭.

**ensemble**   (1) A group of singers or instrumentalists who perform together. (2) In an OPERA, a passage or piece for more than one singer.

**episode**   (1) In a FUGUE, a passage of COUNTERPOINT between statements of the SUBJECT. (2) In RONDO FORM, a section between two statements of the main THEME. (3) A subsidary passage between presentations of the main thematic material.

**equal temperament**   A TEMPERAMENT in which the octave is divided into twelve equal SEMITONES. This is the most commonly used tuning for Western music today.

**estampie**   Medieval instrumental DANCE that features a series of sections, each played twice with two different endings, OUVERT and CLOS.

**ethos** (Greek, "custom")   (1) Moral and ethical character or way of being or behaving. (2) Character, mood, or emotional effect of a certain TONOS, MODE, METER, or MELODY.

**étude** (French, "study")   An instrumental piece designed to develop a particular skill or performing technique. Certain nineteenth-century études that contained significant artistic content and were played in concert were called CONCERT ÉTUDES.

**exoticism**   Nineteenth-century trend in which composers wrote music that evoked feelings and settings of distant lands or foreign cultures.

**experimental music**   A trend in twentieth-century music that focused on the exploration of new musical sounds, techniques, and resources.

**exposition**   (1) In a FUGUE, a set of entries of the SUBJECT. (2) In SONATA FORM, the first part of the MOVEMENT, in which the main THEMES are stated, beginning in the TONIC and usually closing in the DOMINANT (or relative major).

**expressionism**   Early-twentieth-century term derived from art, in which music avoids all traditional forms of "beauty" in order to express deep personal feelings through exaggerated gestures, angular MELODIES, and extreme DISSONANCE.

**faburden**   English style of IMPROVISED POLYPHONY from the late Middle Ages and RENAISSANCE, in which a CHANT in the middle voice is joined by an upper voice moving in parallel a perfect fourth above it and a lower voice that follows below the chant mostly in parallel thirds, moving to a fifth below to mark the beginning and end of phrases and the ends of most words.

**fantasia** (Italian, "fantasy"), **fantasy**   (1) Instrumental COMPOSITION that resembles an IMPROVISATION or lacks a strict FORM. (2) IMITATIVE instrumental piece on a single subject.

**fauxbourdon** (pronounced FOH-boor-donh)   Continental style of POLYPHONY in the early RENAISSANCE, in which two voices are written, moving mostly in parallel sixths and ending each PHRASE on an octave, while a third unwritten voice is sung in parallel perfect fourths below the upper voice.

**figuration, figure**   MELODIC pattern made of commonplace materials such as SCALES or ARPEGGIOS, usually not distinctive enough to be considered a MOTIVE or THEME.

**figured bass**   A form of BASSO CONTINUO in which the BASS line is supplied with numbers or flat or sharp signs to indicate the appropriate CHORDS to be played.

**final**   The main NOTE in a MODE; the normal closing note of a CHANT in that mode.

**finale**   Last MOVEMENT of a work in three or more movements, or the closing portion of an ACT in an OPERA.

*fine amour* (French, "refined love"; pronounced FEEN ah-MOOR; *fin' amors* in Occitan; also called **courtly love**)   An idealized love for an unattainable woman who is admired from a distance. Chief subject of the TROUBADOURS and TROUVÈRES.

**first practice**   See *PRIMA PRATICA*.

**florid organum**   Twelfth-century style of two-voice POLYPHONY in which the lower voice sustains relatively long NOTES while the upper voice sings note-groups of varying length above each note of the lower voice.

**folk music**   (1) Music of unknown authorship from a particular region or people, passed down through oral tradition. (2) In the decades after World War II, a type of POPULAR MUSIC that drew on folk traditions, which included both genuine FOLK SONGS and POPULAR SONGS.

**folk song**   Song of unknown authorship from a particular region or people, passed down through oral tradition.

**form**   The shape or structure of a COMPOSITION or MOVEMENT.

*formes fixes* (French, "fixed forms"; pronounced form FEEX)   Schemes of poetic and musical repetition, each featuring a REFRAIN, used in late medieval and fifteenth-century French CHANSONS; in particular, the BALLADE, RONDEAU, and VIRELAI.

**Franconian notation**   System of NOTATION described by Franco of Cologne around 1280, using noteshapes to indicate durations.

**free jazz**   An experimental JAZZ style introduced in the 1960s by Ornette Coleman, using IMPROVISATION that disregards the standard forms and conventions of jazz.

**free organum**   Style of ORGANUM in which the ORGANAL voice moves in a free mixture of contrary, oblique, parallel, and similar motion against the CHANT (and usually above it).

**French overture**   Type of OVERTURE used in TRAGÉDIE EN MUSIQUE and other GENRES, that opens with a slow, HOMOPHONIC, and majestic section, followed by a faster second section that begins with IMITATION.

**frottola** (pl. *frottole*)   Sixteenth-century GENRE of Italian POLYPHONIC song in mock-popular style, typically

SYLLABIC, HOMOPHONIC, and DIATONIC, with the MELODY in the upper voice and marked rhythmic patterns.

**fugal**    Resembling a FUGUE; featuring fugue-like IMITATION.

**fuging tune**    Eighteenth-century American type of PSALM or HYMN tune that features a passage in free IMITATION, usually preceded and followed by HOMOPHONIC sections.

**fugue** (from Italian *fuga*, "flight")    COMPOSITION or section of a composition in IMITATIVE TEXTURE that is based on a single SUBJECT and begins with successive statements of the subject in voices.

**full anthem**    ANTHEM for unaccompanied CHOIR in CONTRAPUNTAL style.

**fundamental bass**    Term coined by Jean-Philippe Rameau to indicate the succession of the roots or fundamental tones in a series of CHORDS.

**futurism, futurists**    Twentieth-century movement that created music based on noise.

**galant** (French, "elegant")    Eighteenth-century musical style that featured songlike MELODIES, short PHRASES, frequent CADENCES, and light accompaniment.

**galliard**    Sixteenth-century dance in fast triple METER, often paired with the PAVANE and in the same FORM (AABBCC).

**gamut**    The entire range of pitches normally written in the Middle Ages.

**gavotte**    BAROQUE duple-time dance in BINARY FORM, with a half-measure upbeat and a characteristic rhythm of short-short-*long*.

*Gebrauchsmusik* (German "utilitarian music" or "music for use")    Term from the 1920s to describe music that was socially relevant and useful, especially music for amateurs, children, or workers to play or sing.

**genre**    Type or category of musical COMPOSITION, such as SONATA or SYMPHONY.

**genus** (Latin, "class"; pronounced GHEH-noos; pl. *genera*)    In ancient Greek music, one of three forms of TETRACHORD: DIATONIC, CHROMATIC, and ENHARMONIC.

*Gesamtkunstwerk* (German, "total artwork" or "collective artwork")    Term coined by Richard Wagner for a dramatic work in which poetry, scenic design, staging, action, and music all work together toward one artistic expression.

**gigue** (French for "jig")    Stylized DANCE movement of a standard BAROQUE SUITE, in BINARY FORM, marked by fast compound METER such as $\frac{6}{4}$ or $\frac{12}{8}$ with wide MELODIC leaps and continuous triplets. The two sections usually both begin with IMITATION.

**Gloria** (Latin, "Glory")    Second of the five major musical items in the MASS ORDINARY, a praise formula also known as the Greater DOXOLOGY.

**goliard songs**    Medieval Latin songs associated with the goliards, who were wandering students and clerics.

**Gradual** (from Latin *gradus*, "stairstep")    Item in the MASS PROPER, sung after the Epistle reading, comprising a RESPOND and VERSE. CHANT graduals are normally MELISMATIC in style and sung in a RESPONSORIAL manner, one or more soloists alternating with the CHOIR.

**grand motet**    French version of the large-scale SACRED CONCERTO, for soloists, double CHORUS, and ORCHESTRA.

**grand opera**    A serious form of OPERA popular during the ROMANTIC era, that was sung throughout and included BALLETS, CHORUSES and spectacular staging.

**Greater Perfect System**    In ancient Greek music, a system of TETRACHORDS spanning two octaves.

**Gregorian chant**    The repertory of ecclesiastical CHANT used in the Roman Catholic Church.

**ground bass**    BASSO OSTINATO.

**half step** (or *semitone*)    The smallest INTERVAL normally used in Western music, equivalent to the interval between any two successive NOTES on the PIANO keyboard; half the size of a WHOLE STEP.

**harmonia** (pl. *harmoniai*)    Ancient Greek term with multiple meanings: (1) the union of parts in an orderly whole; (2) INTERVAL; (3) SCALE type; (4) style of MELODY.

**harmonic progression**    A logical succession of CHORDS with a sense of direction; especially, the succession of chords used to accompany a MELODY or used as the basis for VARIATIONS.

**harmony**    Aspect of music that pertains to simultaneous combinations of NOTES, the INTERVALS and CHORDS that result, and the correct succession of chords.

**harp**    Plucked string instrument with a resonating soundbox, neck, and strings in roughly triangular shape. The strings rise perpendicular from the soundboard to the neck.

**harpsichord**    Keyboard instrument in use between the fifteenth and eighteenth centuries. It was distinguished from the CLAVICHORD and the PIANO by the fact that its strings were plucked, not struck.

**haut** (French, "high"; pronounced OH)    In the fourteenth through sixteenth centuries, term for loud instruments such as CORNETTS and SACKBUTS. See BAS.

**head-motive**    Initial passage or MOTIVE of a piece or MOVEMENT; used especially for a motive or PHRASE that appears at the beginning of each movement of a MOTTO MASS or CANTUS-FIRMUS MASS.

**heighted neumes**    In an early form of NOTATION, NEUMES arranged so that their relative height indicated higher or lower pitch. Also called DIASTEMATIC neumes.

**hemiola** (from Greek *hemiolios*, "one and a half")    A metrical effect in which three duple units substitute for two triple ones, such as three successive quarter NOTES within a MEASURE of $\frac{6}{8}$, or three two-beat groupings in two measures of triple METER. Hemiola may occur between voices or successive measures.

**heterophony**    Music or musical TEXTURE in which a MELODY is performed by two or more parts simultaneously in more than one way, for example, one voice performing it simply, and the other with embellishments.

**hexachord** (from Greek, "six strings")    (1) A set of six pitches. (2) In medieval and RENAISSANCE SOLMIZATION, the six NOTES represented by the syllables *ut, re, mi, fa, sol, la*, which could be transposed to three positions: the "natural" hexachord, C-D-E-F-G-A; the "hard" hexachord, G-A-B-C-D-E; and the "soft" hexachord, F-G-A-B♭-C-D. (3) In TWELVE-TONE theory, the first six or last six notes in the ROW.

**historia** In Lutheran music of the sixteenth to eighteenth centuries, a musical setting based on a biblical narrative. See PASSION.

**hocket** (French *hoquet*, "hiccup") In thirteenth- and fourteenth-century POLYPHONY, the device of alternating rapidly between two voices, each resting while the other sings, as if a single MELODY is split between them; or, a COMPOSITION based on this device.

**homophony** Musical TEXTURE in which all voices move together in essentially the same RHYTHM, as distinct from POLYPHONY and HETEROPHONY. See also MELODY AND ACCOMPANIMENT.

**homorhythmic** Having the same RHYTHM, as when several voices or parts move together.

**humanism** Movement in the RENAISSANCE to revive ancient Greek and Roman culture and to study things pertaining to human knowledge and experience.

**hurdy-gurdy** An instrument with MELODY and DRONE strings, bowed by a rotating wheel turned with a crank, with levers worked by a keyboard to change the pitch on the melody string(s).

**hymn** Song to or in honor of a god. In the Christian tradition, song of praise sung to God.

**idée fixe** (French, "fixed idea") term coined by Hector Berlioz for a MELODY that is used throughout a piece to represent a person, thing, or idea, transforming it to suit the mood and situation.

**imitate** (1) To repeat or slightly vary in one voice or part a segment of MELODY just heard in another, at pitch or transposed. (2) To follow the example of an existing piece or style in composing a new piece.

**imitation** (1) In POLYPHONIC music, the device of repeating (imitating) a MELODY or MOTIVE announced in one part in one or more other parts, often at a different pitch level and sometimes with minor MELODIC or rhythmic alterations. Usually the voices enter with the element that is imitated, although sometimes imitation happens within the middle of a segment of melody. (2) The act of patterning a new work after an existing work or style; especially, to borrow much of the existing work's material.

**imitative counterpoint** CONTRAPUNTAL TEXTURE marked by IMITATION between voices.

**imperfect (or minor) division** In medieval and RENAISSANCE NOTATION, a division of a NOTE value into two of the next smaller units (rather than three). See MODE, TIME, and PROLATION.

**impressionism** Late-nineteenth-century term derived from art, used for music that evokes moods and visual imagery through colorful HARMONY and instrumental TIMBRE.

**impresario** During the BAROQUE PERIOD, a businessman who managed and oversaw the production of OPERAS; today, someone who books and stages operas and other musical events.

**improvisation, improvising** Spontaneous invention of music while performing, including devising VARIATIONS, embellishments, or accompaniments for existing music.

**indeterminacy** An approach to composition, pioneered by John Cage, in which the composer leaves certain aspects of the music unspecified. Should not be confused with CHANCE.

**instrumental family** Set of instruments, all of the same type but of different sizes and RANGES, such as a VIOL CONSORT.

**intabulation** Arrangement of a vocal piece for LUTE or keyboard, typically written in TABLATURE.

**intermedio** Musical interlude on a pastoral, allegorical, or mythological subject performed before, between, or after the acts of a spoken comedy or tragedy.

**intermezzo** Eighteenth-century GENRE of Italian comic OPERA, performed between acts of a serious OPERA or play.

**interval** Distance in pitch between two NOTES.

**intonation** The first NOTES of a CHANT, sung by a soloist to establish the pitch for the CHOIR, which joins the soloist to continue the chant.

**Introit** (from Latin *introitus*, "entrance") First item in the MASS PROPER, originally sung for the entrance procession, comprising an ANTIPHON, PSALM verse, Lesser DOXOLOGY, and reprise of the ANTIPHON.

**inversion** (1) In a MELODY or TWELVE-TONE ROW, reversing the upward or downward direction of each INTERVAL while maintaining its size; or the new melody or row form that results. (2) In HARMONY, a distribution of the NOTES in a CHORD so that a note other than the ROOT is the lowest note. (3) In COUNTERPOINT, reversing the relative position of two melodies, so that the one that had been lower is now above the other.

**isorhythm** (from Greek *iso-*, "equal," and *rhythm*) Repetition in a voice part (usually the TENOR) of an extended pattern of durations throughout a section or an entire COMPOSITION.

**jazz** A type of music developed mostly by African Americans in the early part of the twentieth century that combined elements of African, popular, and European music, and that has evolved into a broad tradition encompassing many styles.

**jongleur** (French) Itinerant medieval musician or street entertainer.

**jubilus** (Latin) In CHANT, an effusive MELISMA, particularly the melisma on "-ia" in an ALLELUIA.

**just intonation** A system of tuning NOTES in the SCALE, common in the RENAISSANCE, in which most (but not all) thirds, sixths, perfect fourths, and perfect fifths are in perfect tune.

**key** In TONAL music, the hierarchy of NOTES, CHORDS, and other pitch elements around a central note, the TONIC. There are two kinds of keys, major and minor.

**kithara** Ancient Greek instrument, a large LYRE.

*Klangfarbenmelodie* (German, "tone-color melody") Term coined by Arnold Schoenberg to describe a succession of tone colors that is perceived as analogous to the changing pitches in a MELODY.

**krummhorn** RENAISSANCE wind instrument, with a double reed enclosed in a cap so the player's lips do not touch the reed.

**Kyrie** (Greek, "Lord")  One of the five major musical items in the MASS ORDINARY, based on a BYZANTINE litany.

**lauda** (from Latin *laudare*, "to praise")  Italian devotional song.

**leitmotive** (German, "leading motive")  In an OPERA or MUSIC DRAMA, a MOTIVE, THEME, or musical idea associated with a person, thing, mood, or idea, which returns in original or altered form throughout.

**Lesser Doxology**  See DOXOLOGY.

**libretto** (Italian, "little book")  Literary text for an OPERA or other musical stage work.

**lied** (German, "song"; pl. *lieder*)  Song with German words, whether MONOPHONIC, POLYPHONIC, or for voice with accompaniment; used especially for polyphonic songs in the RENAISSANCE and songs for voice and PIANO in the eighteenth and nineteenth centuries.

**ligature**  NEUME-like noteshape used to indicate a short RHYTHMIC pattern in twelfth- to sixteenth-century NOTATION.

**liturgical drama**  Dialogue on a sacred subject, set to music and usually performed with action, and linked to the LITURGY.

**liturgy**  The prescribed body of texts to be spoken or sung and ritual actions to be performed in a religious service.

**long**  In medieval and RENAISSANCE systems of RHYTHMIC NOTATION, a NOTE equal to two or three BREVES.

**lute**  Plucked string instrument popular from the late Middle Ages through the BAROQUE PERIOD, typically pear- or almond-shaped with a rounded back, flat fingerboard, frets, and one single and five double strings.

**lute song**  English GENRE of solo song with LUTE accompaniment.

**lyre**  Plucked string instrument with a resonating sound box, two arms, crossbar, and strings that run parallel to the soundboard and attach to the crossbar.

**lyric opera**  ROMANTIC OPERA that lies somewhere between light OPÉRA COMIQUE and GRAND OPERA.

**madrigal** (Italian *madrigale*, "song in the mother tongue")  (1) Fourteenth-century Italian poetic form and its musical setting having two or three stanzas followed by a RITORNELLO. (2) Sixteenth-century Italian poem having any number of lines, each of seven or eleven syllables. (3) POLYPHONIC or CONCERTATO setting of such a poem or of a sonnet or other nonrepetitive VERSE form. (4) English polyphonic work imitating the Italian GENRE.

**madrigal comedy, madrigal cycle**  In the late sixteenth and early seventeenth centuries, a series of MADRIGALS that represents a succession of scenes or a simple plot.

**madrigalism**  A particularly evocative—or, if used in a disparaging sense, a thoroughly conventional—instance of TEXT DEPICTION or WORD PAINTING; so called because of the prominent role of word-painting in MADRIGALS.

**major scale**  DIATONIC succession of NOTES with a major third and major seventh above the TONIC.

**march**  A piece in duple or $\frac{6}{8}$ METER comprising an introduction and several STRAINS, each repeated. Typically, there are two strains in the initial key followed by a TRIO in a key a fourth higher; the opening strains may or may not repeat after the trio.

**masque**  Seventeenth-century English entertainment involving poetry, music, DANCE, costumes, CHORUSES, and elaborate sets, akin to the French COURT BALLET.

**Mass** (from Latin *missa*, "dismissed")  (1) The most important service in the Roman Church. (2) A musical work setting the texts of the ORDINARY of the Mass, typically KYRIE, GLORIA, CREDO, SANCTUS, and AGNUS DEI.

**mazurka**  A type of Polish folk dance (and later ballroom dance) in triple METER, characterized by accents on the second or third beat and often by dotted figures on the first beat, or a stylized PIANO piece based on such a DANCE.

**mean-tone temperament**  A type of TEMPERAMENT in which the fifths are tuned small so that the major thirds sound well; frequently used for keyboard instruments from the RENAISSANCE through the eighteenth century.

**measure**  (1) A unit of musical time consisting of a given number of beats; the basic unit of METER. (2) Metrical unit set off by bar lines.

**mediant**  In a PSALM TONE, the CADENCE that marks the middle of the PSALM verse.

**Meistersinger** (German, "master singer")  Type of German amateur singer and poet-composer of the fourteenth through seventeenth centuries, who was a member of a guild that cultivated a style of MONOPHONIC song derived from MINNELIEDER.

**melisma**  A long MELODIC passage sung to a single syllable of text.

**melismatic**  Of a MELODY, having many MELISMAS.

**melodrama**  A genre of musical theater that combined spoken dialogue with background music.

**melody**  (1) Succession of tones perceived as a coherent line. (2) Tune. (3) Principal part accompanied by other parts or CHORDS.

**melody and accompaniment**  A kind of HOMOPHONIC TEXTURE in which there is one main MELODY, which is accompanied by CHORDS or other FIGURATION.

**mensuration canon**  A CANON in which voices move at different rates of speed by using different MENSURATION SIGNS.

**mensuration signs**  In ARS NOVA and RENAISSANCE systems of rhythmic NOTATION, signs that indicate which combination of time and prolation to use (see MODE, TIME, AND PROLATION). The predecessors of TIME SIGNATURES.

**meter**  Recurring patterns of strong and weak beats, dividing musical time into regularly recurring units of equal duration.

**metrical psalm**  Metric, rhymed, and STROPHIC vernacular translation of a PSALM, sung to a relatively simple MELODY that repeats for each strophe.

**minim**  In ARS NOVA and RENAISSANCE systems of rhythmic NOTATION, a NOTE that is equal to half or a third of a SEMIBREVE.

**minimalism**  One of the leading musical styles of the late twentieth century, in which materials are reduced to a minimum and procedures simplified so that what is going on in the music is immediately apparent. Often characterized by a constant pulse and many repetitions of simple RHYTHMIC, MELODIC, or HARMONIC patterns.

**Minnelieder** (German, "love songs") Songs of the MINNESINGER.

**Minnesinger** (German, "singer of love"; also pl.) A poet-composer of medieval Germany who wrote MONOPHONIC songs, particularly about love, in Middle High German.

**minor scale** DIATONIC SCALE that begins with a WHOLE STEP and HALF STEP, forming a minor third above the TONIC. The sixth and seventh above the tonic are also minor in the natural minor scale but one or both may be raised.

**minstrel** (from Latin *minister*, "servant") Thirteenth-century traveling musician, some of whom were also employed at a court or city.

**minstrelsy** Popular form of musical theater in the United States during the mid-nineteenth century, in which white performers blackened their faces and impersonated African Americans in jokes, skits, songs, and dances.

**minuet** DANCE in moderate triple METER, two-measure units, and BINARY FORM.

**minuet and trio form** FORM that joins two BINARY-FORM MINUETS to create an ABA pattern, where A is the minuet and B the TRIO.

**mixed media** Trend of the late twentieth century that combines two or more of the arts, including music, to create a new kind of PERFORMANCE ART or musical theater.

**mixed parallel and oblique organum** Early form of ORGANUM that combines parallel motion with oblique motion (in which the ORGANAL VOICE remains on the same NOTE while the PRINCIPAL VOICE moves) in order to avoid TRITONES.

**modal** Making use of a MODE. Compare TONAL.

**mode** (1) A SCALE or MELODY type, identified by the particular INTERVALLIC relationships among the NOTES in the mode. (2) In particular, one of the eight scale or melody types recognized by church musicians and theorists beginning in the Middle Ages, distinguished from one another by the arrangement of WHOLE TONES and SEMITONES around the FINAL, by the RANGE relative to the final, and by the position of the TENOR or RECITING TONE. (3) RHYTHMIC MODE. See also MODE, TIME, AND PROLATION.

**mode, time, and prolation** (Latin *modus, tempus, prolatio*) The three levels of rhythmic DIVISION in ARS NOVA NOTATION. Mode is the division of LONGS into BREVES; time the division of breves into SEMIBREVES; and prolation the division of semibreves into MINIMS.

**modernists** Twentieth-century composers who made a radical break from the musical language of their predecessors and contemporaries while maintaining strong links to the tradition.

**modified strophic form** Variant of STROPHIC FORM in which the music for the first stanza is varied for later stanzas, or in which there is a change of KEY, RHYTHM, character, or material.

**modulation** The TONAL music, a gradual change from one KEY to another within a section of a MOVEMENT.

**monody** (1) An accompanied solo song. (2) The musical TEXTURE of solo singing accompanied by one or more instruments.

**monophonic** Consisting of a single unaccompanied MELODIC line.

**monophony** Music or musical TEXTURE consisting of unaccompanied MELODY.

**motet** (from French *mot*, "word") POLYPHONIC vocal COMPOSITION; the specific meaning changes over time. The earliest motets add a text to an existing DISCANT CLAUSULA. Thirteenth-century motets feature one or more voices, each with its own sacred or secular text in Latin or French, above a TENOR drawn from CHANT or other MELODY. Most fourteenth- and some fifteenth-century motets feature ISORHYTHM and may include a CONTRATENOR. From the fifteenth century on, any polyphonic setting of a Latin text (other than a MASS) could be called a motet; from the sixteenth century on, the term was also applied to sacred compositions in other languages.

**motive** Short MELODIC or RHYTHMIC idea that recurs in the same or altered form.

**motto mass** POLYPHONIC MASS in which the MOVEMENTS are linked primarily by sharing the same opening MOTIVE or PHRASE.

**movement** Self-contained unit of music, complete in itself, that can stand alone or be joined with others in a larger work. Some types of COMPOSITION typically consist of several movements (such as the four movements common in the SYMPHONY).

**music drama** Nineteenth-century GENRE created by Richard Wagner in which drama and music become organically connected to express a kind of absolute oneness. See also *GESAMTKUNSTWERK*.

**music video** Type of short film popularized in the early 1980s that provides a visual accompaniment to a POP SONG.

**musica ficta** (Latin, "feigned music") (1) In early music, NOTES outside the standard GAMUT, which excluded all flatted and sharped notes except B♭. (2). In POLYPHONY of the fourteenth through sixteenth centuries, the practice of raising or lowering by a SEMITONE the pitch of a written note, particularly at a CADENCE, for the sake of smoother HARMONY or motion of the parts.

*musica mundana, musica humana, musica instrumentalis* (Latin, "music of the universe," "human music," and "instrumental music") Three kinds of music identified by Boethius (ca. 480–524), respectively the "music" or numerical relationships governing the movement of stars, planets, and the seasons; the "music" that harmonizes the human body and soul and their parts; and audible music produced by voices or instruments.

**musical** GENRE of musical theater that features songs and dance numbers in styles drawn from POPULAR MUSIC in the context of a spoken play with a comic or romantic plot.

**musical figure** In BAROQUE music, a MELODIC pattern or CONTRAPUNTAL effect conventionally employed to convey the meaning of a text.

**musique concrète** (French, "concrete music") Term coined by composers working in Paris in the 1940s for music composed by assembling and manipulating recorded sounds, working "concretely" with sound itself rather than with music NOTATION.

**musique mesurée** (French, "measured music") Late-sixteenth-century French style of text-setting, especially in CHANSONS, in which stressed syllables are given longer NOTES than unstressed syllables (usually twice as long).

**mutation** In SOLMIZATION, the process of changing from one HEXACHORD to another.

**nationalism** (1) In politics and culture, an attempt to unify or represent a particular group of people by creating a national identity through characteristics such as common language, shared culture, historical traditions, and national institutions and rituals. (2) Nineteenth- and twentieth-century trend in music in which composers were eager to embrace elements in their music that claimed a national identity.

**neoclassicism** Trend in music from the 1910s to the 1950s in which composers revived, imitated, or evoked the styles, GENRES, and FORMS of pre-ROMANTIC music, especially those of the eighteenth century.

**neo-Romanticism** A trend of the late twentieth century in which composers adopted the familiar tonal idiom of nineteenth-century ROMANTIC music and incorporated its sounds and gestures.

**neotonal** Term for music since the early 1900s that establishes a single pitch as a tonal center, but does not follow the traditional rules of TONALITY.

**neumatic** In CHANT, having about one to six NOTES (or one NEUME) sung to each syllable of text.

**neume** A sign used in NOTATION of CHANT to indicate a certain number of NOTES and general MELODIC direction (in early forms of notation) or particular pitches (in later forms).

**New Objectivity** Term coined in the 1920s to describe a kind of new realism in music, in reaction to the emotional intensity of the late ROMANTICS and the EXPRESSIONISM of Schoenberg and Berg.

**New Orleans jazz** Leading style of JAZZ just after World War I, which centers on group VARIATION of a given tune, either IMPROVISED or in the style of improvisation.

**nocturne** Type of short PIANO piece popular during the ROMANTIC PERIOD, marked by highly embellished MELODY, sonorous accompaniments, and a contemplative mood.

**nondiegetic music** or **underscoring** In film, background music that conveys to the viewer a mood or other aspect of a scene or character but is not heard by the characters themselves. Compare DIEGETIC MUSIC.

**notation** A system for writing down musical sounds, or the process of writing down music. The principal notation systems of European music use a staff of lines and signs that define the pitch, duration, and other qualities of sound.

**note** (1) A musical TONE. (2) A symbol denoting a musical tone.

*notes inégales* (French, "unequal notes"; pronounced NOTS an-ay-GALL) Seventeenth-century convention of performing French music in which passages notated in short, even durations, such as a succession of eighth notes, are performed by alternating longer notes on the beat with shorter offbeats to produce a lilting rhythm.

**Notre Dame polyphony** Style of POLYPHONY from the late twelfth and thirteenth centuries, associated with the Cathedral of Notre Dame in Paris.

**octatonic scale** (or *octatonic collection*) A SCALE that alternates WHOLE and HALF STEPS.

**Offertory** Item in the MASS PROPER, sung while the COMMUNION is prepared, comprising a RESPOND without VERSES.

**Office** (from Latin *officium*, "obligation" or "ceremony") A series of eight prayer services of the Roman Church, celebrated daily at specified times, especially in monasteries and convents; also, any one of those services.

**Old Roman chant** A repertory of ecclesiastical CHANT preserved in eleventh- and twelfth-century manuscripts from Rome representing a local tradition; a near relative of GREGORIAN CHANT.

**open and closed endings** (French, *ouvert* and *clos*) In an ESTAMPIE, BALLADE, or other medieval form, two different endings for a repeated section. The first ("open") closes on a pitch other than the FINAL, and the second ("closed") ends with a full CADENCE on the final.

**opera** (Italian, "work") Drama with continuous or nearly continuous music, staged with scenery, costumes, and action.

**opéra bouffe** ROMANTIC operatic GENRE in France that emphasized the smart, witty, and satirical elements of OPÉRA COMIQUE.

**opera buffa** (Italian, "comic opera") Eighteenth-century GENRE of Italian comic OPERA, sung throughout.

**opéra comique** (French, "comic opera") (1) In the eighteenth century, light French comic OPERA, which used spoken dialogue instead of RECITATIVES. (2) In nineteenth-century France, opera with spoken dialogue, whether comic or tragic.

**opera seria** (Italian, "serious opera") Eighteenth-century GENRE of Italian OPERA, on a serious subject but normally with a happy ending, usually without comic characters and scenes.

**operetta** Nineteenth-century kind of light OPERA with spoken dialogue, originating in OPÉRA BOUFFE.

**opus** (Latin, "work") Work or collection of works in the same GENRE, issued as a publication.

**oratorio** GENRE of dramatic music that originated in the seventeenth century, combining narrative, dialogue, and commentary through ARIAS, RECITATIVES, ENSEMBLES, CHORUSES, and instrumental music, like an unstaged OPERA. Usually on a religious or biblical subject.

**orchestra** ENSEMBLE whose core consists of strings with more than one player on a part, usually joined by woodwinds, brass, and percussion instruments.

**orchestral concerto** Orchestral GENRE in several MOVEMENTS, originating in the late seventeenth century, that emphasized the first VIOLIN part and the BASS, avoiding the more CONTRAPUNTAL TEXTURE of the SONATA.

**orchestral suite**   Late-seventeenth-century German SUITE for ORCHESTRA patterned after the groups of DANCES in French BALLETS and OPERA.

**Ordinary** (from Latin *ordinarium*, "usual")   Texts of the MASS that remain the same on most or all days of the CHURCH CALENDAR, although the tunes may change.

**organ Mass**   Setting for organ of all sections of the MASS for which the organ would play, including ORGAN VERSES and other pieces.

**organ verse**   Setting for an organ of an existing MELODY from the Roman Catholic LITURGY.

**organal voice** (Latin, *vox organalis*)   In an ORGANUM, the voice that is added above or below the original CHANT MELODY.

**organum** (Latin; pronounced OR-guh-num)   (1) One of several styles of early POLYPHONY from the ninth through thirteenth centuries, involving the addition of one or more voices to an existing CHANT. (2) A piece, whether IMPROVISED or written, in one of those styles, in which one voice is drawn from a CHANT. The plural is *organa*.

**organum duplum**   In NOTRE DAME POLYPHONY, an ORGANUM in two voices.

**ornament**   A brief, conventional formula, such as a TRILL or turn, written or IMPROVISED, that adds expression or charm to a MELODIC line.

**ornamentation**   The addition of embellishments to a given MELODY, either during performance or as part of the act of COMPOSITION.

**ostinato** (Italian, "obstinate")   Short musical pattern that is repeated persistently throughout a piece or section. See BASSO OSTINATO.

**ouvert**   See OPEN AND CLOSED ENDINGS.

**ouverture** (French, "opening")   (1) OVERTURE, especially FRENCH OVERTURE. (2) SUITE for ORCHESTRA, beginning with an OVERTURE.

**overdotting**   Performing practice in French BAROQUE music in which a dotted NOTE is held longer than written, while the following short note is shortened.

**overture**   (1) An ORCHESTRAL piece introducing an OPERA or other long work. (2) Independent ORCHESTRAL WORK in one movement, usually descriptive.

**parallel organum**   Type of POLYPHONY in which an added voice moves in exact parallel to a CHANT, normally a perfect fifth below it. Either voice may be doubled at the octave.

**paraphrase**   Technique in which a CHANT or other MELODY is reworked, often by altering rhythms and adding NOTES, and placed in a POLYPHONIC setting.

**paraphrase Mass**   POLYPHONIC MASS in which each MOVEMENT is based on the same MONOPHONIC MELODY, normally a CHANT, which is PARAPHRASED in most or all voices rather than being used as a CANTUS FIRMUS in one voice.

**parlor song**   Song for home music-making, sometimes performed in public concerts as well.

**parody Mass**   POLYPHONIC MASS in which each MOVEMENT is based on the same polyphonic model, normally a CHANSON or MOTET, and all voices of the model are used in the Mass, but none is used as a CANTUS FIRMUS.

**partbook**   A manuscript or printed book containing the music for one voice or instrumental part of a POLYPHONIC COMPOSITION (most often, an anthology of pieces); to perform any piece, a complete set of partbooks is needed, so that all the parts are represented.

**partita**   BAROQUE term for a set of VARIATIONS on a MELODY or BASS line.

**part-song**   (1) A song for more than one voice. (2) In the nineteenth century, a song for CHORUS, parallel in function and style to the LIED or PARLOR SONG.

**passacaglia**   BAROQUE GENRE of VARIATIONS over a repeated BASS line or HARMONIC PROGRESSION in triple METER.

**Passion**   A musical setting of one of the biblical accounts of Jesus' crucifixion, the most common type of HISTORIA.

**pastoral drama**   Play in verse with incidental music and songs, normally set in idealized rural surroundings, often in ancient times; a source for the earliest OPERA LIBRETTOS.

**pavane**   Sixteenth-century dance in slow duple METER with three repeated sections (AABBCC). Often followed by a GALLIARD.

**perfect (or major) division**   In medieval and RENAISSANCE NOTATION, a division of a note value into three (rather than two) of the next smaller unit. See MODE, TIME, AND PROLATION.

**perfection**   (1) What we all strive for. (2) In medieval systems of NOTATION, a unit of duration equal to three TEMPORA, akin to a MEASURE of three beats.

**performance art**   A type of art that first came to prominence in the 1960s, based on the idea that performing a prescribed action in a public place constitutes a work of art.

**period**   (1) In music history, an era whose music is understood to have common attributes of style, conventions, approach, and function, in contrast to the previous and following eras. (2) In musical FORM, especially since the eighteenth century, a complete musical thought concluded by a CADENCE and normally containing at least two PHRASES.

**periodic**   Organized in discrete PHRASES or PERIODS.

**periodicity**   The quality of being PERIODIC, especially when this is emphasized through frequent resting points and articulations between PHRASES and PERIODS.

*petit motet* (French, "little motet")   French version of the SMALL SACRED CONCERTO for one, two, or three voices and CONTINUO.

**phrase**   A unit of MELODY or of an entire musical TEXTURE that has a distinct beginning and ending and is followed by a pause or other articulation but does not express a complete musical thought. See PERIOD (2).

**Phrygian cadence**   CADENCE in which the bottom voice moves down a semitone and upper voices move up a whole tone to form a fifth and octave over the cadential NOTE.

**piano** or **pianoforte**   A keyboard instrument invented in 1700 that uses a mechanism in which the strings are struck, rather than plucked as the HARPSICHORD was, and which allowed for crescendos, dimuendos, and other effects.

**pipe and tabor**   Two instruments played by one player, respectively a high whistle fingered with one hand and a small drum beaten with a stick or mallet.

**pitch-class** Any one of the twelve NOTES of the CHROMATIC SCALE, including its ENHARMONIC equivalents, in any octave.

**pitch-class set (or set)** A collection of PITCH-CLASSES that preserves its identity when transposed, inverted, or re-ordered and used MELODICALLY or HARMONICALLY.

**plagal mode** A MODE (2) in a which the RANGE normally extends from a fourth (or fifth) below the FINAL to a fifth or sixth above it. See also AUTHENTIC MODE.

**plainchant, plainsong** A unison unaccompanied song, particularly a LITURGICAL song to a Latin text.

**plainsong Mass** A MASS in which each MOVEMENT is based on a CHANT to the same text (the KYRIE is based on a chant Kyrie, the GLORIA on a chant Gloria, and so on).

**point of imitation** Passage in a POLYPHONIC work in which two or more parts enter in IMITATION.

**polonaise** A stately Polish processional DANCE in triple METER, or a stylized piece in the style of such a dance.

**polychoral** For more than one CHOIR.

**polychoral motet** MOTET for two or more choirs.

**polyphony** Music or musical TEXTURE consisting of two or more simultaneous lines of independent MELODY. See also COUNTERPOINT.

**polystylism** Term coined by Alfred Schnittke for a combination of newer and older musical styles created through QUOTATION or stylistic allusion.

**polytonality** The simultaneous use of two or more KEYS, each in a different layer of the music (such as MELODY and accompaniment).

**pop music** Term coined in the 1950s for music that reflected the tastes and styles popular with the teen and young-adult market.

**popular music** Music, primarily intended as entertainment, that is sold in printed or recorded form. It is distinguished from FOLK MUSIC by being written down and marketed as a commodity, and from CLASSICAL MUSIC by being centered on the performer and the performance, allowing great latitude in rearranging the notated music.

**popular song** Song that is intended primarily to entertain an audience, accommodate amateur performers, and sell as many copies as possible. Compare ART SONG.

**portative organ** Medieval or RENAISSANCE organ small enough to be carried, played by one hand while the other worked the bellows.

**positive organ** Organ from the medieval through BAROQUE PERIODS that was small enough to be moved, usually placed on a table.

**postmodernism** Trend in the late twentieth century that blurs the boundaries between high and popular art, and in which styles of all epochs and cultures are equally available for creating music.

**post-tonal** General term for music after 1900 that does not adhere to TONALITY but instead uses any of the new ways that composers found to organize pitch, from ATONALITY to NEOTONALITY.

**prelude** Introductory piece for solo instrument, often in the style of an IMPROVISATION, or introductory MOVEMENT in a multimovement work such as an OPERA or SUITE.

**prepared piano** An invention of John Cage in which various objects—such as pennies, bolts, screws, or pieces of wood, rubber, plastic, or slit bamboo—are inserted between the strings of a PIANO, resulting in complex percussive sounds when the piano is played from the keyboard.

**prima donna** (Italian, "first lady") A soprano singing the leading female role in an OPERA. See also DIVA.

*prima pratica* (Italian, "first practice") Claudio Monteverdi's term for the style and practice of sixteenth-century POLYPHONY, in contradistinction to the *SECONDA PRATICA*.

**prime** In TWELVE-TONE music based on a particular ROW, the original form of the row, transposed or untransposed, as opposed to the INVERSION, RETROGRADE, or RETROGRADE INVERSION.

**principal voice** (Latin, *vox principalis*) In an ORGANUM, the original CHANT MELODY.

**program** Text to accompany an instrumental work of PROGRAM MUSIC, describing the sequence of events depicted in the music.

**program music** Instrumental music that tells a story or follows a narrative or other sequence of events, often spelled out in an accompanying text called a PROGRAM.

**prolation** See MODE, TIME, AND PROLATION.

**Proper** (from Latin *proprium*, "particular" or "appropriate") Texts of the MASS that are assigned to a particular day in the CHURCH CALENDAR.

**psalm** A poem of praise to God, one of 150 in the Book of Psalms in the Hebrew Scriptures (the Christian Old Testament). Singing psalms was a central part of Jewish, Christian, Catholic, and Protestant worship.

**psalm tone** A MELODIC formula for singing PSALMS in the OFFICE. There is one psalm tone for each MODE.

**psalmody** The singing of PSALMS.

**psalter** A published collection of METRICAL PSALMS.

**psaltery** A plucked string instrument whose strings are attached to a frame over a wooden sounding board.

**Pythagorean intonation** A system of tuning NOTES in the SCALE, common in the Middle Ages, in which all perfect fourths and fifths are in perfect tune.

**quadruplum** (Latin, "quadruple") (1) In POLYPHONY of the late twelfth through fourteenth centuries, fourth voice from the bottom in a four-voice TEXTURE, added to a TENOR, DUPLUM, and TRIPLUM. (2) In NOTRE DAME POLYPHONY, an ORGANUM in four voices.

**quodlibet** (Latin, "whatever you please") COMPOSITION or passage in which two or more existing MELODIES, or parts of melodies, are combined in COUNTERPOINT.

**quotation** Direct borrowing of one work in another, especially when the borrowed material is not reworked using a standard musical procedure (such as VARIATIONS, PARAPHRASE, or PARODY MASS) but is set off as a foreign element.

**rag** Instrumental work in RAGTIME style, usually in the FORM of a MARCH.

**ragtime** Musical style that features SYNCOPATED rhythm against a regular, marchlike BASS.

**range** A span of NOTES, as in the range of a MELODY or of a MODE.

**realization**   Performing (or creating a performable edition of) music whose NOTATION is incomplete, as in playing a BASSO CONTINUO or completing a piece left unfinished by its composer.

**recapitulation**   In SONATA FORM, the third main section, which restates the material from the EXPOSITION, normally all in the TONIC.

**recital**   Term popularized by Franz Liszt for his solo piano performances and used today for any presentation given by a single performer or a small group.

*récitatif mesuré* (French, "measured recitative")   In French BAROQUE OPERA, RECITATIVE in a songlike, measured style, in a uniform METER, and with relatively steady motion in the accompaniment.

*récitatif simple* (French, "simple recitative")   In French BAROQUE OPERA, RECITATIVE that shifts frequently between duple and triple METER to allow the natural speechlike declamation of the words.

**recitation formula**   In CHANT, a simple outline MELODY used for a variety of texts.

**recitative**   A passage or section in an OPERA, ORATORIO, CANTATA, or other vocal work in RECITATIVE STYLE.

**recitative style** (from Italian *stile recitativo*, "recitational style")   A type of vocal singing that approaches speech and follows the natural rhythms of the text.

*recitativo arioso*   A passage or selection in an OPERA or other vocal work in a style that lies somewhere between RECITATIVE STYLE and ARIA style.

**reciting tone** (also called TENOR)   The second most important NOTE in a MODE (after the FINAL), often emphasized in CHANT and used for reciting text in a PSALM TONE.

**recorder**   End-blown wind instrument with a whistle mouthpiece, usually made of wood.

**refrain**   In a song, a recurring line (or lines) of text, usually set to a recurring MELODY.

**reminiscence motive**   In an OPERA, a MOTIVE, THEME, or MELODY that recurs in a later scene, in order to recall the events and feelings with which it was first associated. Compare LEITMOTIVE.

**Renaissance** (French, "rebirth")   PERIOD of art, cultural, and music history between the Middle Ages and the BAROQUE PERIOD, marked by HUMANISM, a revival of ancient culture and ideas, and a new focus on the individual, the world, and the senses.

**respond**   The first part of a RESPONSORIAL CHANT, appearing before and sometimes repeated after the PSALM verse.

**responsorial**   Pertaining to a manner of performing CHANT in which a soloist alternates with a group.

**responsory**   RESPONSORIAL CHANT used in the OFFICE. Matins includes nine Great Responsories, and several other office services include a Short Responsory.

**retrograde**   Backward statement of a previously heard MELODY, passage, or TWELVE-TONE ROW.

**retrograde inversion**   Upside-down and backward statement of a MELODY or TWELVE-TONE ROW.

**revue**   Type of musical theater that includes a variety of dances, songs, comedy, and other acts, often united by a common theme.

**rhythm**   (1) The pattern of music's movement in time. (2) A particular pattern of short and long durations.

**rhythm section**   In a JAZZ ENSEMBLE, the group of instruments that keeps the beat and fills in the background.

**rhythm-and-blues**   African American style of POPULAR MUSIC, originating in the 1940s, that featured a vocalist or vocal quartet, PIANO or organ, electric guitar, bass, and drums, and songs built on TWELVE-BAR BLUES or POPULAR SONG formulas.

**rhythmic modes**   System of six durational patterns (for example, mode 1, long-short) used in POLYPHONY of the late twelfth and thirteenth centuries, used as the basis of the rhythmic NOTATION of the Notre Dame composers.

**ricercare (ricercar)** (Italian, "to seek out" or "to attempt")   (1) In the early to mid-sixteenth century, a PRELUDE in the style of an IMPROVISATION. (2) From the late sixteenth century on, an instrumental piece that treats one or more SUBJECTS in IMITATION.

**ripieno** (Italian, "full")   In a SOLO CONCERTO or CONCERTO GROSSO, designates the full ORCHESTRA. All called TUTTI.

**rite**   The set of practices that defines a particular Christian tradition, including a CHURCH CALENDAR, a LITURGY, and a repertory of CHANT.

**ritornello** (Italian, "refrain")   (1) In a fourteenth-century MADRIGAL, the closing section, in a different METER from the preceding verses. (2) In sixteenth- and seventeenth-century vocal music, instrumental introduction or interlude between sung stanzas. (3) In an ARIA or similar piece, an instrumental passage that recurs several times, like a refrain. Typically, it is played at the beginning, as interludes (often in modified form), and again at the end, and it states the main THEME. (4) In a fast MOVEMENT of a CONCERTO, the recurring thematic material played at the beginning by the full orchestra and repeated, usually in varied form, throughout the movement and at the end.

**ritornello form**   Standard FORM for fast MOVEMENTS in CONCERTOS of the first half of the eighteenth century, featuring a RITORNELLO (4) for full ORCHESTRA that alternates with EPISODES characterized by virtuosic material played by one or more soloists.

**rock and roll** (or **rock**)   A musical style that emerged in the United States in the mid-1950s as a blend of black and white traditions of POPULAR MUSIC, primarily RHYTHM-AND-BLUES, COUNTRY MUSIC, POP MUSIC, and TIN PAN ALLEY.

**Romantic**   Term applied to music of the nineteenth century. Romantic music had looser and more extended FORMS, greater experimentation with HARMONY and TEXTURE, richly expressive and memorable MELODIES, improved musical instruments, an interest in musical NATIONALISM, and a view of music as a moral force, in which there was a link between the artists' inner lives and the world around them.

**rondeau** (pl. *rondeaux*)   (1) French FORME FIXE with a single stanza and the musical FORM ABaAabAB, with capital letters indicating lines of REFRAIN and lowercase letters indicating new text set to music from the refrain. (2) FORM in seventeenth- and eighteenth-century instrumental music in which a repeated STRAIN alternates with other strains, as in the pattern AABACA.

**rondellus**   Technique in medieval English POLYPHONY in which two or three PHRASES of music, first heard simultaneously in different voices, are each sung in turn by each of the voices.

**rondo**   Piece or MOVEMENT in RONDO FORM.

**rondo form**   Musical FORM in which the first or main section recurs, usually in the TONIC, between subsidiary sections or EPISODES.

**root**   The lowest NOTE in a CHORD when it is arranged as a succession of thirds.

**rota**   FORM of medieval English POLYPHONY in which two or more voices sing the same MELODY, entering at different times and repeating the melody until all stop together. See CANON.

**rounded binary form**   BINARY FORM in which the latter part of the first section returns at the end of the second section, but in the TONIC.

**row**   In TWELVE-TONE MUSIC, an ordering of all twelve PITCH-CLASSES that is used to generate the musical content.

**rubato** (from Italian *tempo rubato*, "stolen time")   Technique common in ROMANTIC music in which the performer holds back or hurries the written NOTE values.

**sackbut**   RENAISSANCE brass instrument, an early form of the trombone.

**sacred concerto**   In the seventeenth century, a COMPOSITION on a sacred text for one or more singers and instrumental accompaniment.

**salsa**   A type of dance music that emerged in the 1960s combining elements of Cuban dance styles with JAZZ, ROCK, and Puerto Rican music.

**sampling**   A process of creating new COMPOSITIONS by patching together snippets of previously recorded music.

**Sanctus** (Latin, "Holy")   One of the five major musical items in the MASS ORDINARY, based in part on Isaiah 6:3.

**saraband**   (1) Originally a quick dance-song from Latin America. (2) In French BAROQUE music, a slow DANCE in BINARY FORM and in triple METER, often emphasizing the second beat; a standard MOVEMENT of a SUITE.

**scale**   A series of three or more different pitches in ascending or descending order and arranged in a specific pattern.

**scat singing**   Technique in JAZZ in which the performer sings nonsense syllables to an IMPROVISED or composed MELODY.

**scherzo** (Italian, "joke")   A joking or particularly fast MOVEMENT in MINUET AND TRIO FORM.

**score notation**   A type of NOTATION in which the different voices or parts are aligned vertically to show how they are coordinated with each other.

*seconda pratica* or **second practice**   Monteverdi's term for a practice of COUNTERPOINT and COMPOSITION that allows the rules of sixteenth-century counterpoint (the PRIMA PRATICA) to be broken in order to express the feelings of a text. Also called *stile moderno*.

**semibreve**   In medieval and RENAISSANCE systems of rhythmic NOTATION, a NOTE that is normally equal to half or a third of a BREVE.

**semiminim**   In ARS NOVA and RENAISSANCE systems of rhythmic NOTATION, a NOTE that is equal to half of a MINIM.

**semi-opera**   Modern term for DRAMATIC OPERA.

**semitone** (or **half step**)   The smallest INTERVAL normally used in Western music; half of a TONE.

**sequence** (from Latin *sequentia*, "something that follows")   (1) A category of Latin CHANT that follows the ALLELUIA in some MASSES. (2) Restatement of a pattern, either MELODIC or HARMONIC, on successive or different pitch levels.

**serenata** (Italian, "serenade")   A semidramatic piece for several singers and small ORCHESTRA, usually written for a special occasion.

**serial music**   Music that uses the TWELVE-TONE METHOD; used especially for music that extends the same general approach to SERIES in parameters other than pitch.

**series**   (1) A ROW. (2) An ordering of specific durations, dynamic levels, or other non-pitch elements, used in SERIAL MUSIC.

**service**   A setting of Anglican service music, encompassing specific portions of Matins, Holy Communion, and Evensong. A *Great Service* is a MELISMATIC, CONTRAPUNTAL setting of these texts; a *Short Service* sets the same text in SYLLABIC, CHORDAL style.

**set**   PITCH-CLASS SET.

**shape-note singing**   A tradition of group singing that arose in nineteenth-century America, named after the NOTATION used in song collections in which the shape of the noteheads indicates the SOLMIZATION syllables, allowing for easy sight-reading in parts.

**shawm**   Double-reed instrument, similar to the oboe, used in the medieval, RENAISSANCE, and BAROQUE PERIODS.

**sinfonia**   (1) Generic term used throughout the seventeenth century for an abstract ENSEMBLE piece, especially one that serves as an introduction to a vocal work. (2) Italian OPERA OVERTURE in the early eighteenth century. (3) Early SYMPHONY.

**simple recitative**   Style of RECITATIVE scored for solo voice and BASSO CONTINUO, used for setting dialogue or monologue in as speechlike a fashion as possible, without dramatization.

**singspiel** (German, "singing play")   German GENRE of OPERA, featuring spoken dialogue interspersed with songs, CHORUSES, and instrumental music.

**sketch**   General term for a compositional idea jotted down in a notebook, or an early draft of a work.

**slow-movement sonata form**   Classical-era variant of SONATA FORM that omits the DEVELOPMENT.

**small sacred concerto**   Seventeenth-century GENRE of sacred vocal music featuring one or more soloists accompanied by organ CONTINUO (or modest instrumental ENSEMBLE).

**socialist realism**   A doctrine of the Soviet Union, begun in the 1930s, in which all the arts were required to use a realistic approach (as opposed to an abstract or symbolic one) that portrayed socialism in a positive light. In music this meant use of simple, accessible language, centered on MELODY, and patriotic subject matter.

**solmization**   A method of assigning syllables to STEPS in a SCALE, used to make it easier to identify and sing the WHOLE TONES and SEMITONES in a MELODY.

**solo concerto**   CONCERTO in which a single instrument, such as a VIOLIN, contrasts with an ORCHESTRA.

**solo madrigal**    In the late sixteenth and early seventeenth centuries, a THROUGH-COMPOSED setting of a nonstrophic poem for solo voice with accompaniment, distinguished from an ARIA and from a MADRIGAL for several voices.

**sonata** (Italian, "sounded")    (1) A piece to be played on one or more instruments. (2) BAROQUE instrumental piece with contrasting sections or MOVEMENTS, often with IMITATIVE COUNTERPOINT. (3) GENRE in several movements for one or two solo instruments.

**sonata da camera** or **chamber sonata**    BAROQUE SONATA, usually a SUITE of stylized DANCES, scored for one or more TREBLE instruments and CONTINUO.

**sonata da chiesa** or **church sonata**    BAROQUE instrumental work intended for performance in church; usually in four MOVEMENTS—slow-fast-slow-fast—and scored for one or more TREBLE instruments and CONTINUO.

**sonata form**    FORM typically used in first MOVEMENTS of SONATAS, instrumental chamber works, and SYMPHONIES during the CLASSICAL and ROMANTIC PERIODS. An expansion of ROUNDED BINARY FORM, it was described in the nineteenth century as consisting of an EXPOSITION, DEVELOPMENT, and RECAPITULATION based on a limited number of THEMES.

**sonata-rondo**    A FORM that blends characteristics of SONATA FORM and RONDO FORM. One frequent structure is ABACABA, in which A and B correspond to the first and second THEMES of SONATA FORM and B appears first in the DOMINANT and returns in the TONIC.

**song cycle**    A group of songs performed in succession that tells or suggests a story.

**soprano** (from SUPERIUS)    (1) High female voice. (2) Part for such a voice in an ENSEMBLE work.

**soul**    The leading African American tradition of POPULAR MUSIC in the 1960s that combined elements of RHYTHM-AND-BLUES and gospel singing in songs on love, sex, and other secular subjects.

**sound mass**    Term coined by Edgard Varèse for a body of sounds characterized by a particular TIMBRE, register, RHYTHM, or MELODIC gesture, which may remain stable or may be transformed as it recurs.

**source music**    See DIEGETIC MUSIC.

**spatial**    Pertaining to a conception of music as sounds moving through musical space, rather than as the presentation and VARIATION of THEMES or MOTIVES.

**species**    The particular ordering of WHOLE TONES and SEMITONES within a perfect fourth, fifth, or octave.

**spiritual**    African American type of religious song that originated among southern slaves and was passed down through oral tradition, with texts often based on stories or images from the Bible.

*Sprechstimme* (German, "speaking voice")    A vocal style developed by Arnold Schoenberg in which the performer approximates the written pitches in the gliding tones of speech, while following the notated rhythm.

*Stadtpfeifer* (German, "town pipers")    Professional town musicians who had the exclusive right to provide music within city limits.

**step**    INTERVAL between two adjacent pitches in a DIATONIC, CHROMATIC, OCTATONIC, or WHOLE-TONE SCALE; WHOLE STEP or HALF STEP.

*stile antico* (Italian, "old style")    Style used in music written after 1600 in imitation of the old contrapuntal style of Palestrina, used especially for church music.

*stile concitato* (Italian, "excited style")    Style devised by Claudio Monteverdi to portray anger and warlike actions, characterized by rapid reiteration of a single NOTE, whether on quickly spoken syllables or in a measured string tremolo.

*stile moderno* (Italian, "modern style")    Seventeenth-century style that used BASSO CONTINUO and applied the rules of COUNTERPOINT freely. See *SECONDA PRATICA*.

**Stollen**    See BAR FORM.

**stop**    (1) Mechanism on an organ to turn on or off the sounding of certain sets of pipes. (2) The particular set of pipes controlled by such a mechanism.

**string quartet**    (1) Standard chamber ENSEMBLE consisting of two VIOLINS, viola, and cello. (2) Multimovement COMPOSITION for this ENSEMBLE.

**strain**    In a MARCH or RAG, a PERIOD, usually of sixteen or thirty-two measures.

**strophic**    Of a poem, consisting of two or more stanzas that are equivalent in form and can each be sung to the same MELODY; of a vocal work, consisting of a strophic poem set to the same music for each stanza.

**strophic variation**    Early seventeenth-century vocal GENRE, a setting of a STROPHIC poem, in which the MELODY of the first stanza is varied but the HARMONIC plan remains essentially the same, although the duration of harmonies may change to reflect the accentuation and meaning of the text.

**style luthé** (French, "lute style") or **style brisé** (French, "broken style")    Broken or ARPEGGIATED TEXTURE in keyboard and LUTE music from seventeenth-century France. The technique originated with the lute, and the FIGURATION was transferred to the HARPSICHORD.

**subdominant**    In TONAL music, the NOTE and CHORD a fifth below the TONIC.

**subject**    THEME, used especially for the main MELODY used in a RICERCARE, FUGUE, or other IMITATIVE work.

**substitute clausula**    In NOTRE DAME POLYPHONY, a new CLAUSULA (usually in DISCANT style) designed to replace the original polyphonic setting of a particular segment of a CHANT.

**suite**    A set of pieces that are linked together into a single work. During the BAROQUE, a suite usually referred to a set of stylized DANCE pieces.

**superius** (Latin, "highest")    In fifteenth- and sixteenth-century POLYPHONY, the highest part (compare CANTUS).

**suspension**    DISSONANCE created when a NOTE is sustained while another voice moves to form a dissonance with it; the sustained voice descends a STEP to resolve the dissonance.

**syllabic**    Having (or tending to have) one NOTE sung to each syllable of text.

**symphonic poem** (or **tone poem**)    Term coined by Franz Liszt for a one-movement work of PROGRAM MUSIC for orchestra that conveys a poetic idea, story, scene, or succession of moods by presenting THEMES that are repeated, varied, or transformed.

**symphonie concertante**    A CONCERTO-like GENRE of the late eighteenth and early nineteenth centuries for two or more solo instruments and ORCHESTRA, characterized by its lightheartedness and MELODIC variety.

**symphony**    Large work for ORCHESTRA, usually in four MOVEMENTS.

**swing**    A style of JAZZ originating in the 1930s that was characterized by large ENSEMBLEs and hard-driving jazz rhythms.

**syncopation**    Temporary disruption of METER by beginning a long NOTE on an offbeat and sustaining it through the beginning of the next beat.

**synthesizer**    Electronic instrument that generates and processes a wide variety of sounds.

**tablature**    A system of NOTATION used for LUTE or other plucked string instrument that tells the player which strings to pluck and where to place the fingers on the strings, rather than indicating which NOTES will result. Tablatures were also used for keyboard instruments until the seventeenth century.

**tabor**    See PIPE AND TABOR.

**talea** (Latin, "cutting"; pronounced TAH-lay-ah)    In an ISORHYTHMIC COMPOSITION, an extended rhythmic pattern repeated one or more times, usually in the TENOR. Compare COLOR.

**temperament**    Any system of tuning NOTES in the SCALE in which pitches are adjusted to make most or all INTERVALS sound well, though perhaps not in perfect tune.

**tempo** (Italian, "time")    Speed of performance, or relative pace of the music.

**tempo di mezzo** (Italian, "middle movement")    The operatic scene structure developed by Gioachino Rossini in the early nineteenth century, the middle section of an ARIA or ENSEMBLE, usually an interruption or a TRANSITION, that falls between the CANTABILE and the CABALETTA.

**tempus** (Latin, "time"; pl. *tempora*)    In medieval systems of NOTATION, the basic time unit. See also MODE, TIME, AND PROLATION.

**tenor** (from Latin *tenere*, "to hold")    (1) In a MODE or CHANT, the RECITING TONE. (2) In POLYPHONY of the twelfth and thirteenth centuries, the voice part that has the chant or other borrowed MELODY, often in long-held NOTES. (3) Male voice of a relatively high range.

**tenor Mass**    CANTUS FIRMUS MASS.

**termination**    In a PSALM TONE, the CADENCE that marks the end of the PSALM VERSE.

**ternary form**    A FORM in three main sections, in which the first and third are identical or closely related and the middle section is contrasting, creating an ABA pattern.

**tetrachord** (from Greek, "four strings")    (1) In Greek and medieval theory, a SCALE of four NOTES spanning a perfect fourth. (2) In modern theory, a SET of four pitches or PITCH-CLASSES. (3) In TWELVE-TONE theory, the first four, middle four, or last four notes in the ROW.

**text depiction**    Using musical gestures to reinforce or suggest images in a text, such as rising on the word "ascend."

**text expression**    Conveying or suggesting through musical means the emotions expressed in a text.

**texture**    The combination of elements in a piece or passage, such as the number and relationship of independent parts (as in MONOPHONY, HETEROPHONY, POLYPHONY, or HOMOPHONY), GROUPS (as in POLYCHORAL MUSIC), OR MUSICAL EVENTS (as in relatively dense or transparent sonorities).

**theme**    Musical subject of a COMPOSITION or section, or of a set of VARIATIONS.

**thematic transformation**    A method devised by Franz Liszt to provide unity, variety, and a narrative-like logic to a composition by transforming the thematic material into new THEMES or other elements, in order to reflect the diverse moods needed to portray a PROGRAMMATIC subject.

**theorbo**    Large LUTE with extra BASS strings, used especially in the seventeenth century for performing BASSO CONTINUO as accompaniment to singers or instruments.

**thoroughbass**    BASSO CONTINUO.

**through-composed**    Composed throughout, as when each stanza or other unit of a poem is set to new music rather than in a STROPHIC manner to a single MELODY.

**tiento**    Spanish IMPROVISATORY-style instrumental piece that features IMITATION, akin to the sixteenth-century FANTASIA.

**timbre** or **tone color**    Characteristic color or sound of an instrument or voice.

**time signature**    Sign or numerical proportion, such as $\frac{3}{4}$, placed at the beginning of a piece, section, or MEASURE to indicated the METER.

**Tin Pan Alley**    (1) Jocular name for a district in New York where numerous publishers specializing in POPULAR SONGS were located from the 1880s through the 1950s. (2) Styles of American popular song from that era.

**toccata** (Italian, "touched")    Piece for keyboard instrument or LUTE resembling an IMPROVISATION that may include IMITATIVE sections or may serve as a PRELUDE to an independent FUGUE.

**tonal**    Operating within the system of TONALITY.

**tonality**    The system, common since the late seventeenth century, by which a piece of music is organized around a TONIC NOTE, CHORD, and KEY, to which all the other notes and keys in the piece are subordinate.

**tone**    (1) A sound of definite pitch. (2) See WHOLE STEP.

**tone cluster**    Term coined by Henry Cowell for a CHORD of DIATONIC or CHROMATIC seconds.

**tone color**    See TIMBRE.

**tone poem**    SYMPHONIC POEM, or a similar work for a medium other than ORCHESTRA.

**tonic**    (1) The first and central NOTE of a MAJOR or MINOR SCALE. (2) The main KEY of a piece or MOVEMENT, in which the piece or movement begins and ends and to which all other keys are subordinate.

**tonos** (pl. *tonoi*)    Ancient Greek term used with different meanings by various writers; one meaning is a particular set of pitches within a certain RANGE or region of the voice.

**topics**    Term for the different and contrasting styles in Classical-era music that serve as subjects for musical discourse.

**total serialism**    The application of the principles of the TWELVE-TONE METHOD to musical parameters other than pitch, including duration, intensities, and TIMBRES. See SERIAL MUSIC.

**Tract** (from Latin *tractus*, "drawn out") Item in the MASS PROPER that replaces the ALLELUIA on certain days in Lent, comprising a series of PSALM VERSES.

*tragédie en musique* (French, "tragedy in music"; later *tragédie lyrique*, "lyric tragedy") French seventeenth- and eighteenth-century form of OPERA, pioneered by Jean-Baptiste Lully, that combined the French classic drama and BALLET traditions with music, DANCES, and spectacles.

**transcription** Arrangement of a piece for an instrumental medium different from the original, such as a reduction of an ORCHESTRAL score for PIANO.

**transition** (1) In the EXPOSITION of a MOVEMENT in SONATA FORM, the passage between the first and second THEMES that effects the MODULATION to a new KEY. (2) More generally, a passage between two MOVEMENTS or SECTIONS of a work.

**transverse flute** Flute blown across a hole in the side of the pipe and held to one side of the player; used for medieval, RENAISSANCE, and BAROQUE forms of the flute to distinguish it from the RECORDER, which is blown in one end and held in front.

**treble** (French, "triple") (1) A high voice or a part written for high voice, especially the highest part in three-part POLYPHONY of the fourteenth and fifteenth centuries. (2) Pertaining to the highest voice.

**treble-dominated style** Style common in the fourteenth and fifteenth centuries, in which the main MELODY is in the CANTUS, the upper voice carrying the text, supported by a slower-moving TENOR and CONTRATENOR.

**trecento** (Italian, short for *mille trecento*, "one thousand three hundred"; pronounced treh-CHEN-toh) The 1300s (the fourteenth century), particularly with reference to Italian art, literature, and music of the time.

**triad** CHORD consisting of two successive thirds (for instance, C–E–G), or any INVERSION of such a chord.

**trill** Rapid alternation between a NOTE and another HALF STEP or WHOLE STEP above.

**trio** (1) Piece for three players or singers. (2) The second of two alternating DANCES, in the Classical-era MINUET AND TRIO FORM. (3) The second main section of a MARCH.

**trio sonata** Common instrumental GENRE during the BAROQUE PERIOD, a SONATA for two TREBLE instruments (usually VIOLINS) above a BASSO CONTINUO. A performance featured four or more players if more than one was used for the continuo part.

**triple motet** Thirteenth-century MOTET in four voices, with a different text in each voice above the TENOR.

**triplum** (from Latin *triplus*, "triple") (1) In POLYPHONY of the late twelfth through fourteenth centuries, third voice from the bottom in a three- or four-voice TEXTURE, added to a TENOR and DUPLUM. (2) In NOTRE DAME POLYPHONY, an ORGANUM in three voices.

**tritone** INTERVAL spanning three WHOLE TONES or six SEMITONES, such as F to B.

**trobairitz** (from Occitan *trobar*, "to compose a song") A female TROUBADOUR.

**trope** Addition to an existing CHANT, consisting of (1) words and MELODY; (2) a MELISMA; or (3) words only, set to an existing melisma or other melody.

**troubadour** (from Occitan *trobar*, "to compose a song") A poet-composer of southern France who wrote MONOPHONIC songs in Occitan (*langue d'oc*) in the twelfth or thirteenth century.

**trouvère** (from Old French *trover*, "to compose a song") A poet-composer of northern France who wrote MONOPHONIC songs in Old French (*langue d'oïl*) in the twelfth or thirteenth century.

**tutti** (Italian, "all") (1) In both the SOLO CONCERTO and the CONCERTO GROSSO, designates the full ORCHESTRA. Also called RIPIENO (Italian, "full"). (2) Instruction to an ENSEMBLE that all should play.

**twelve-bar blues** Standard formula for the BLUES, with a HARMONIC PROGRESSION in which the first four-measure PHRASE is on the TONIC, the second phrase begins on the SUBDOMINANT and ends on the tonic, and the third phrase starts on the DOMINANT and returns to the tonic.

**twelve-tone method** A form of ATONALITY based on the systematic ordering of the twelve notes of the CHROMATIC scale into a ROW that may be manipulated according to certain rules.

**unmeasured prelude** A French BAROQUE keyboard GENRE, usually the first MOVEMENT in a SUITE, whose nonmetric NOTATION gives a feeling of IMPROVISATION.

**underscoring** See NONDIEGETIC MUSIC.

**variation** The process of reworking a given MELODY, song, THEME, or other musical idea, or the resulting varied FORM of it.

**variations (variations form)** FORM that presents an uninterrupted series of variants (each called a VARIATION) on a THEME; the theme may be a MELODY, a BASS line, a HARMONIC plan, or other musical subject.

**vaudeville** In late-nineteenth- and early-twentieth-century America, a type of variety show including musical numbers, but without the common theme of a REVUE.

**verismo** (Italian, "realism") Nineteenth-century operatic MOVEMENT that presents everyday people in familiar situations, often depicting sordid or brutal events.

**verse** (1) Line of poetry. (2) Stanza of a HYMN or STROPHIC song. (3) Sentence of a PSALM. (4) In GREGORIAN CHANT, a setting of a psalm verse or similar text, such as the verses that are part of the INTROIT, GRADUAL, and ALLELUIA.

**verse anthem** ANTHEM in which passages for solo voice(s) with accompaniment alternate with passages for full CHOIR doubled by instruments.

**verse-refrain form** A FORM in vocal music in which two or more stanzas of poetry are each sung to the same music (the VERSE) and each is followed by the same REFRAIN.

**versus** (Latin, "verse") A type of Latin sacred song, either MONOPHONIC or POLYPHONIC, setting a rhymed, rhythmic poem.

**vielle** Medieval bowed string instrument, early form of the fiddle and predecessor of the VIOLIN and VIOL.

vihuela    Spanish relative of the LUTE with a flat back and guitar-shaped body.

villancico (from Spanish *villano*, "peasant"; pronounced vee-yan-THEE-co)    Type of POLYPHONIC song in Spanish, with several stanzas framed by a REFRAIN; originally secular, the FORM was later used for sacred works, especially associated with Christmas or other important holy days.

villanella    Type of sixteenth-century Italian song, generally for three voices, in a rustic HOMOPHONIC style.

viol (viola da gamba)    Bowed, fretted string instrument popular from the mid-fifteenth to the early eighteenth centuries, held between the legs.

violin    Bowed, fretless string instrument tuned in fifths ($g$-$d'$-$a'$-$e''$).

virelai    French FORME FIXE in the pattern A bba A bba A bba A, in which a REFRAIN (A) alternates with stanzas with the musical FORM bba, the a using the same music as the refrain.

virginal    (1) English name for HARPSICHORD, used for all types until the seventeenth century. (2) Type of HARPSICHORD that is small enough to place on a table, with a single keyboard and strings running at right angles to the keys rather than parallel with them as in larger harpsichords.

virtuoso    Performer who specializes in one instrument and dazzles audiences with his or her technical prowess.

voice exchange    In POLYPHONY, technique in which voices trade segments of music, so that the same combination of lines is heard twice or more, but with different voices singing each line.

walking bass    BASS line in BAROQUE music—and later in JAZZ—that moves steadily and continuously.

waltz    Type of couple dance in triple meter, popular in the late eighteenth and nineteenth centuries, or a short, stylized work for the PIANO in the style of such a dance.

whole step (or whole tone)    An interval equivalent to two SEMITONES.

whole-tone scale (or *whole-tone collection*)    A SCALE consisting of only WHOLE STEPS.

wind ensemble    Large ENSEMBLE of winds, brass, and percussion instruments, mostly with one player per part, dedicated solely to serious music, rather than to the mix of MARCHES and other fare typically played by BANDS.

word painting    TEXT DEPICTION.

zarzuela    Spanish GENRE of musical theater, a light, mythological play in a pastoral setting that alternates between sung and spoken dialogue and various types of ENSEMBLE and solo song.

# CREDITS

Pages 2–3: Museo di San Marco dell'Angelico, Florence, Italy. Photo: Bridgeman Art Library; p. 5: (top) The Metropolitan Museum of Art, Fletcher Fund, 1056 (56.171.38) All Rights Reserved; p. 5: (middle) Bibliothèque Nationale, Paris; p. 5: (bottom) Chartres Cathedral, Chartres, France. Photo: Erich Lessing/Art Resource, NY; p. 6: (left) British Museum; p. 6: (right) British Museum; p. 8: Bibliothèque de l'Arsenal, Paris. Photo: Scala/Art Resource, NY; p. 10: Biblioteca Capitolare, Padua, Italy. Photo: Giraudon/Art Resource, NY; p. 11: Royal Library of Belgium; p. 12: (top) Photo: Scala/Art Resource, NY; p. 12: (bottom) Photo: Vanni/Art Resource, NY; p. 13: Centre Jeanne d'Arc, Orleans, France. Photo: Erich Lessing/Art Resource, NY; p. 16: (top left) Museo dell'Opera Metropolitana, Siena, Italy. Photo: Foto LENSINI, Siena; p. 16: (top right) Scrovegni Chapel, Padua, Italy. Photo: Cameraphoto/Art Resource, NY; p. 16: (bottom) Sandro Vannini/Corbis; p. 20: (top) The Metropolitan Museum of Art, Fletcher Fund, 1056. [56.171.38] All Rights Reserved; p. 20: (bottom) Archivo Fotografica, Museo Arquelogico Nacional, Madrid; p. 21: National Museum, Copenhagen, Department of Classical and Near Eastern Antiquities, Inventory No. 14897; p. 24: By permission of the Syndics of Cambridge University Library, England; p. 26: From *Liber Astrologiae.* Courtesy The British Library, Sloane 3983, f. 42v; p. 32: Corbis; p. 34: Gilles Mermet/Art Resource, NY; p. 36: (top) Biblioteca Nacional, Madrid, Spain; p. 37: Bridgeman Art Library; p. 40: British Library, London; p. 42: Bibliothèque Nationale, Paris, MS 118, fol. 8v; p. 43: Art Resource, NY; p. 47: Societé Civile Immobiliere; p. 49: Bibliothèque Nationale, Paris; p. 52: (top) Bibliothèque Nationale, Paris; p. 52: (middle) Universitätsbibliothek, Heidelberg; p. 52: (bottom) Oronoz, Madrid; p. 55: Photo: Erich Lessing/Art Resource, NY; p. 57: Santiago de Compostela, Spain. Photo: Giraudon/Art Resource, NY; p. 58: Photograph Bibliothèque Nationale, Paris, fonds Latin, MS 1139, fol. 41; p. 59: Royalty Free/Corbis; p. 61: Scala/Art Resource, NY; p. 62: British Library; p. 63: Biblioteca Medicea-Laurenziana; p. 65: (top right and left) Bridgeman Art Library; 65: (bottom) Alinari/Art Resource, NY; p. 68: Photo: Anthony Scibilia/Art Resource, NY; p. 72: Art Resource, NY; p. 73: Bibliothèque Nationale,

Paris, MS Fr. 146; p. 76: Bibliothèque Nationale, Paris; p. 78: SEF/Art Resource, NY; p. 79: Bilbiothèque Nationale, Paris; p. 80: Biblioteca Medicea-Laurenziana; p. 84: Art Resource, NY; p. 85: (top) Musée Conde, MS 564; p. 85: (bottom) Lebrecht Music & Arts Photo Library; p. 86: Art Resource, NY; pp. 88–9: Museo di Castelvecchio, Verona, Italy. Photo: Scala/Art Resource, NY; p. 90: (top) Hamburger Kunsthalle, Hamburg, Germany. Photo: Bildarchiv Preussischer Kulturbesitz/Art Resource, NY; p. 90: (middle) Palazzo Ducale, Urbino, Italy. Photo: Bridgeman Art Library; p. 90: (bottom) National Gallery, London. Photo: Bridgeman Art Library; p. 92: Museo Nazionale del Bargello, Florence, Italy. Photo: Nimatallah/Art Resource, NY; p. 93: (top) Galleria delle Marche, Urbino, Italy. Photo: Erich Lessing/Art Resource, NY; p. 93: (bottom) Scala/Art Resource, NY; p. 96: (top) Royal Library of Belgium; p. 97: Uffizi Gallery, Florence, Italy. Photo: Scala/Art Resource, NY; p. 100: Réunion des Musées Nationaux/Art Resource, NY; p. 102: Altarpiece, Church of St. Bavo, Ghent. Photo: Scala/Art Resource, NY; p. 103: (bottom) Bibliothèque Nationale, Paris, MS fr. 12476, f. 98r; p. 104: Royal Library of Belgium, Robert Waggermee, *Flemish Music and Society in the Fifteenth and Sixteenth Centuries,* © 1968 Frederick A. Praeger, Publishers; p. 105: Art Resource, NY; p. 106: Art Resource, NY; p. 107: Portraitgalerie, Schloss Ambras, Innsbruck, Austria. Photo: Erich Lessing/Art Resource, NY; p. 114: National Gallery, London. Photo: Bridgeman Art Library; p. 117: (top) Österreichische Nationalbibliothek; p. 117: (bottom) Musée de l'Hotel Lallemant a Bourges/Art Resource, NY; p. 119: Private collection; p. 121: Bibliothèque Nationale, Paris, MS F.1587, fol. 58v; p. 122: Kimball Art Museum; p. 124: Corbis; p. 126: Royal Library of Belgium, Robert Waggermee, *Flemish Music and Society in the Fifteenth and Sixteenth Centuries,* © 1968 Frederick A. Praeger, Publishers; p. 130: Metropolitan Museum of Art; p. 131: Kunsthistorisches Museum, Vienna; p. 135: Lebrecht Music & Arts Photo Library; p. 138: The Harris Collection, Schloss Rohrau, Vienna/Art Resource, NY; p. 139: National Portrait Gallery; p. 140: British Library; p. 141: Wallrof-Richartz Museum, Cologne. Photo: Lebrecht Music & Arts Photo Library; p. 142: Private Collection. Photo Courtesy of The Metropolitan Museum of Art, NY. Photo:

# INDEX

Page numbers in *italics* refer to illustrations and also to musical examples that are on a different page from where they are discussed.

Abel, Carl Friedrich, 358, 362n
Abendmusiken concerts, 242, 245
Abgesang, 51
absolute music, 408, 439
abstract art, 528
Académie Royale de Musique, 231–32, 288
academies, 131, 166, 184–85, 239, 261, 280
Academy of Ancient Music, 358
a cappella, 142
Accademia degli Alterati, 187
accessibility, goal of, 529, 561, 579, 588, 592, 610–11, 633–34, 658–59, 661–62, 664, 666
accidentals, 133, 242, 329. *See also* musica ficta
  in chant, 46
  figured bass indications, 180–81
*A chantar* (Beatriz de Día), 49
*Adagio for Strings* (Barber), 634
Adam de la Halle, 66, 67
Adams, John, 655–57, 656, 658
Adler, Guido, 557
*Admeto* (Handel), 306, 307
*L'Adone* (Marino), 170
*Adoration of the Magi* (Botticelli), 97
*Ad organum faciendum*, 56
*Advancement of Learning and New Instruments, The* (Bacon), 170
Advent season, 32
*Aeneid* (Virgil), 421, 468
*Aeolian Harp, The* (Cowell), 609
Aeschylus, 20
affections doctrine, 168–69, 172, 179, 196–97, 206, 210, 229, 254, 316, 318
*affetti*, 219
*L'Africaine* (Meyerbeer), 467

African American music, 594, 598–600. *See also* blues; jazz; ragtime
  Dvořák's use of, 459, 604
  Krenek's use of, 583
African Americans, 522, 525, 531, 597, 611–14, 618–28
African music, 652, 654
*Afro-American Symphony* (Still), 612
Agazzari, Agostino, 182
Age of Reason. See Enlightenment
Agincourt, Battle of, 98
Agnus Dei, 33, 35, 36, 42
agréments, 248, 251, 258, 265
agriculture, 11, 15, 34, 269, 400
*Agrippina* (Handel), 304, 306
*Ah, vous dirais-je maman* (Mozart), 355–56
*Aida* (Verdi), 467, 477, 478, 492
airs
  English, 140–41
  French, 233, 289
*Akhnaten* (Glass), 655
alba, 48, 51
Albania, 523
Alberti, Domenico, 317, 331
Alberti bass, 317
Albinoni, Tomaso, 262
Albrecht IV, Duke, 211
Albrecht V, Duke, 217
*Album für die Jugend* (Schumann), 429
*Alceste* (Gluck), 327, 328
*Alcina* (Handel), 325
Alcuin of York, 34–35
d'Alembert, Jean le Rond, 271
*Alessandro nell'Indie* (Metastasio), 323
Alexander II, czar of Russia, 506
*Alexander Nevsky* (Prokofiev), 588
Alfonso el Sabio, king of Castile and León, 52

*Alice's Adventures in Wonderland* (Carroll), 663
*Allegro barbaro* (Debussy), 579
Alleluia, 33, 35, 41, 56, 59
*Alleluia Justus ut palma*, 56
allemandes, 175, 210, 251, 286, 296
*Allgemeine musikalische Zeitung* (periodical), 303, 442
*Almira* (Handel), 304, 305
*Also sprach Zarathustra* (Strauss), 500, 502
*Amalfi in May 1831* (Mendelssohn), 424
amateur music and musicians
  Baroque, 165, 194, 206, 216, 221, 239, 286
  eighteenth-century, 277–78, 280, 286, 318–19, 334, 375–76
  nineteenth-century, 318, 384, 402, 416, 419, 596, 597, 598
  Renaissance, 91, 118, 119, 128–29, 131, 136, 137, 140
  twentieth-century, 543–44, 561, 575, 585, 633
Amati, Nicolò, 245, 255
Ambrose, Saint, 23
Ambrosian chant, 28
*American* Quartet (Dvořák), 458, 459
American Revolution, 271, 374
Americas, colonies in, 91, 164, 594–96
*Amériques* (Varèse), 608
*Am Meer* (Schubert), 412, 413
*Amor brujo, El* (Falla), 543
analog, 652
*Ancient Voices of Children* (Crumb), 639
Anderson, Abraham Archibald, 575
Andre, Carl, 653
Anglican Church. *See* Church of England
Anglican church music. *See* church music, Anglican

*Anna Bolena* (Donizetti), 474
*Anna Karenina* (Tolstoy), 407
Anne, queen of England, 305
Anselm, Saint, 55
anthems, 152, 239, 595
*Anthropology* (Parker/Gillespie), 627–28
*L'antica musica ridotta alla moderna prattica* (Vicentino), 135
antimasques, 175, 235
antiphonal music, 199, 217–18. *See also* polychoral music
antiphonal performance of chant, 35, 40–41, 42
antiphons, *38, 39,* 55, 150, 659–60. *See also* Marian antiphons
  Marian, 42
  Mass, 40–41
  Office, 32, 39–40
  three-voice, 101–2
anti-Semitism, 489, 522, 583, 587
*Antony and Cleopatra* (Barber), 465
Antwerp, 95, 119
Apollo, 20
*Apollo and the Muses* (de Vos), 207
*Apotheosis of Lully, The* (Couperin), 286
*Appalachian Spring* (Copland), 611
*Appassionata* Sonata (Beethoven), 387–88
appoggiaturas, 258, 326, 334, 431, 435, 495
apprentice system, 96
Aquitanian organum, 57, 58
Arab world, medieval, 9–10, 11, 34, 47, 55, 211–12
Arbeau, Thoinot, 208
Arcadelt, Jacques, 96, 132, 142
archaeological evidence, 4, 18
architecture
  Baroque, 352
  medieval, 12, 15, 55–56, 67, 68
  Renaissance, 92–94, 105
  rococo, 268, *268*
  seventeenth-century, 166, 168, 171, 175, *176*
  twentieth-century, 641, *641,* 644, 660, *660*
arcicembalo, 135
arciorgano, 135
Arco, Livia d', 131
*L'Arianna* (Monteverdi), 190
arias
  cavatina, 471–72
  da capo, 223, 226–27, 230, 262, 300, 307, 309, 320, 323–25, 326, 337
  double, 471–72, 479
  ground-bass, 223, 236–37
  of Handel, 306, 307–8
  of Haydn, 352
  in instrumental music, 206
  in opera buffa, 320
  in opera seria, 323–26
  in oratorios, 201
  in Passions, 302
  patter, 471, *472*
  of Puccini, 517

  of Rossini, 471, 479
  seventeenth-century, 169, 172, 175, 186, 192, 194, 201, 222, 223, 226, 236–37, 240
  strophic, 197
  types of, 223
ariettes, 321
arioso, 193, 302, 495
Ariosto, Ludovico, 94, 130, 192, *192*
Aristides Quintilianus, 22, 114
Aristotle, 6, 7, 13, 14, 19, 20, 21–22, 114, 561
Aristoxenus, 22
Arlen, Harold, 617
*Armida* (Haydn), 351–52
*Armide* (Gluck), 328
*Armide* (Lully), *232, 233, 234*
Armstrong, Louis, *619,* 620–22
Arnstadt, 291, 292–93
arrangements
  of American folk music, 610
  band, 597
  big band, 625, 626
  by Liszt, 441–42
  of Renaissance vocal music, 137, 142, 144
*Ars antiqua,* 70, 74
*Ars combinatoria,* 364
*Ars nova,* 70, 72–80
*Ars nova* (Philippe de Vitry), 72
*Ars subtilior,* 84–85, 103
art
  eighteenth-century, 268, 269, 275, 276, 318
  medieval, 15–16, 72
  nineteenth-century, 318, 403–5, 407, 510
  Renaissance, 91, 92–95
  seventeenth-century, 150, 166, 168, 169, 171, 173, *174*
  twentieth-century, 527–29, 533, 550, 649, 653
*Art de toucher le clavecin, L'* (Couperin), 258, 259, 286
*Art of Fugue, The* (Bach). *See Kunst der Fuge, Die*
*Art of Noises, The: Futurist Manifesto* (Russolo), 563, *564*
*Art of Playing on the Violin, The* (Geminiani), 258–59
art songs, 31. *See also* lieder; songs
Artusi, Giovanni Maria, 178, 180
*Artusi overo Delle imperfettioni della moderna musica, L',* 180
*Artwork of the Future* (Wagner), 483, 484
Asians and Asian music, 531, 538, 609, 636, 639–40, 652, 655, 657–58
Association for Contemporary Music, 587
Astaire, Fred, 617, *623*
astrology and music, 26
astronomy and music, 26, 164, 170
*As Vesta was* (Weelkes), 139–40
*Atlas, Der* (Schubert), 412, 414
*Atmosphères* (Ligeti), 646

atonality, 547, 549, 551, 554–56, 603, 628, 637–38. *See also* serial music
Attaingnant, Pierre, 118–19, 137, 207, 209
*Attilio Regolo* (Hasse), 324
Auber, Daniel-François, 468
audiences
  eighteenth-century, 280, *306,* 346, 347, 359, 365–66
  nineteenth-century, 410, 419, 423, 438, 447, 462, 463, 464, 476–77, 600
  seventeenth-century, 193, 223, 232, 235, 236, 239–40
  sixteenth-century, 131
  twentieth-century, 532–33, 534, 545–46, 559, 561, 569, 571, 592, 610–11, 630, 636, 637, 642, 643, 654, 658, 661–62, 664, 666
*Auf dem Wasser zu singen* (Schubert), 414
*Aufenthalt* (Schubert), 412
*Aufstieg und Fall der Stadt Mahagonny* (Weill), 584
augmentation, 247, 296
augmented triads, 442, 444, 601
Augustine, Saint, 14, 23, 24, 26, 60
aulos, 20, *20*
Auric, Georges, 565, *565*
Austen, Jane, 275, 277, 318
Austrian music. *See* German music
Austro-Hungarian Empire, 269
authentic modes, 45
*Automatic Descriptions* (Satie), 562
*Available Forms* (Brown), 649
avant-garde music, 562–63, 628, 646–58
*Avant que tu ne t'en ailles* (Fauré), *514,* 515
*Ave Maria . . . virgo serena* (Josquin des Prez), 124–25
*Ave virgo virginum,* 67, 69
Avignon, papal court in, 14, 17, 71, 84

Babbitt, Milton, 637, 642, *642,* 643, 646
Babylonia, 4
*Bacchae, The* (Euripides), 639
Bach, Carl Philipp Emanuel, 277, 302, *332, 333*
  sonatas of, 268, 278
  symphonies of, 333
  works edition edited by Brahms, 448
Bach, Gottlieb Friedrich, *333*
Bach, Johann Christian, 302, 318, *335,* 335–37, 355, 358, 366
Bach, Johann Christoph, 291
Bach, Johann Sebastian, 146, 160, 267, 268, 290–303, *291, 302*
  biography of, 291
  Buxtehude's influence on, 242, 245
  complete works edition of, 438
  Corelli's influence on, 259
  harpsichord music of, 294, 296–97, 660
  influence of, 305, 314, 361, 391–92, 429, 432–33, 453, 543, 547, 586, 606
  melodies of, 316
  organ music of, 148, 278, 292–94
  reception history of, 302–3, 425

solo and ensemble music of, 265, 297–98
Telemann and, 240
Vivaldi's influence on, 293, 314
vocal music of, 298–302, 557
"Bach, P. D. Q.," 661–62
Bach, Wilhelm Friedemann, 333
Bach-Gesellschaft, 303
*Bachianas brasileiras* (Villa-Lobos), 606–7
Bach Society, 437
*Back Water Blues* (Smith), 618, *619*
Bacon, Francis, 164, 170
Bacon, Roger, 13, 14
Balakirev, Mily, 506, 538
Balanchine, George, 567
ballades (instrumental), 433, 435
ballades (medieval), 78–80, 84, 104, 121
ballad operas, 309, 321–22
ballads
    eighteenth-century, 411
    nineteenth-century, 411, 414, 598
ballata, 81, 82–83, 84, 102
ballets
    of Copland, 611
    of Debussy, 532, 540, 572
    eighteenth-century, 360
    of Falla, 543
    of Milhaud, 565
    nineteenth-century, 464, 465
    of Prokofiev, 588
    of Ravel, 542
    of Satie, *562, 563, 563*
    seventeenth-century, 191, 222, 223, 230,
        233, 236
    of Stravinsky, 567, 568–73, 592
    of Tchaikovsky, 454–55
Ballets Russes, 567, 568, 571, 572, 588
ballett, 139, 140
balletto, 130
*balli*, 195
*ballo in maschera, Un* (Verdi), 478
*Banchetto musicale* (Schein), 210
band music, 574, 586, 596–97, 601, 613–14
bandoneon, 584
Banister, John, 239
banjo, 599
*Banshee, The* (Cowell), 609
Barber, Samuel, 465, 634–35
*Barber of Seville*, The (Beaumarchais),
    272–73, 274
*barbiere di Siviglia, Il* (Rossini), 469–73,
    474
barcarolles, 514, 551
Bardi, Giovanni de', 184–85
Bardua, Caroline, *480*
bar form, 50–51
bar lines, 75, 180
Baroque
    affections doctrine in, 168–69, 172, 179,
        254
    boundary dates for, 177
    ceremonial music in, 238–39
    church music in, 235, 241–42, 245–48,
        293–94, 298–302, 595

cultural-historical context, 163–76
defined, 163
English music in, 175–76, 213, 216,
    235–40, 305–13
French music in, 230–35, 248–53,
    285–90
French vs. Italian styles in, 286
general characteristics of music in,
    178–82
German music in, 202, 204–5, 240–42,
    245–48, 263–64, 290–303
instrumental music in, 206–21, 244–65,
    292–98, 311–13
Italian music in, 177, 186–94, 199–201,
    214–16, 217–19, 222–30, 253–62,
    279–85
late, 267, 268, 278, 279–314
musical theater in, 235–38
opera in, 222–26, 230–35, 240, 288–90,
    304
oratorios in, 310–11
seventeenth-century, 163–265
vocal chamber music in, 226–30, 239
Bartók, Béla, 577–83, *578, 580,* 607
    biography of, 578
    Debussy's influence on, 541
    influence of, 635–36, 657–58
    reception of, 592
Bartoli, Cosimo, 113, 117
Bartolozzi, Therese Jansen, 351
baryton, 341, *342*
Basie, Count, 622
Basil, Saint, 23, 35
basilicas, *32,* 218
*basse danse,* 209
*basse fondamentale,* 289
basso continuo, 177, 180–81, 182, 185–86,
    194, 199, 201, 206, 210, 211, 218,
    219, 228, 233, 254, 262, 306
bassoon, 180
basso ostinato, 173, 175, 194, 195–96, 214,
    453
bass viol, *210*
Bastille, fall of, 272, 273
Baude Cordier, 75, *85*
Baudelaire, Charles, 540
Bayeux tapestry, *70*
*Bay Psalm Book,* 595
Bayreuth Festival Theater, 485, *488*
BBC Symphony Orchestra, 531
Beach Amy Marcy, 601, *601*
Beatles, the, 641
*Béatrice et Bénédict* (Berlioz), 421, 468
*Beatrix Cenci* (Ginastera), 636
Beatriz de Día, 49
Beaumarchais, 272–73, 274, 471
bebop, 594, 626–28
Becket, Saint Thomas, 15–16
Bedford, duke of, 100
Beethoven, Caspar van, 377
Beethoven, Karl van, 377
Beethoven, Ludwig van, 276, 374–95, 377,
    *389, 391*

appearance of, 389
Bach's influence on, 391–92
biography of, 376–77
birthplace of, 360, *378*
church music of, 389, 391, 393–94
concertos of, 388
deafness of, 376, 380, 388, 394
first period of, 375–79
Gypsy influences on, 467
Haydn's influence on, 373
Heiligenstadt Testament of, 376, 378,
    379
Immortal Beloved and, 390
influence of, 391, 395, 410, 415–16, 438,
    447, 453, 457, 459–61, 478, 483,
    494, 547, 601
Mozart's influence on, 373
nineteenth-century views of, 398
opera of, 382–83
orchestral instrumentation of, 423
second period of, 379–88
signature of, *395*
sketchbooks of, 374, 379–80
sonatas of, 376–77, 387
string quartets of, 375, 377–78, 383, 389,
    391–92, 559
style of, 267
symphonies of, 272, 378–79, 380–82,
    383–86, 389, 391, 394–95, 423,
    451, 460–61, 483, 494, 497, 574
tempo of, 384–85
third period of, 388–89, 391–95
Beethoven-Haus, *378*
*Beggar's Opera, The* (Gay), 309, 321–22, *322,*
    584
*Being and Nothingness* (Sartre), 533
*bel canto,* 471
*Belle, bonne, sage* (Cordier), *85*
Bellini, Gentile, 202, 463, 465, 478
Bellini, Vincenzo, 473–74
bells, 4
*Bells, The* (Rachmaninov), 545
Benedictine, Saint, 14
Benedictine order, 8, 14, 43
Beneventan chant, 28
Benton, Thomas Hart, 529, *530,* 533
*Benvenuto Cellini* (Berlioz), 468
Bérain, Jean, *232*
Berg, Alban, 550, 554–57, *558*
    Debussy's influence on, 541
    Schoenberg and, 548
Berio, Luciano, 637–38
Berkeley, Busby, 617
Berlin, 290, 332, 333–35
    Mendelssohn in, 425
    public concerts in, 359, 410
Berlin, Irving, 614, 615, 617, 623
Berliner, Emile, 574
Berlin Philharmonic, 574
Berlioz, Hector, 381, 420–22, *421,* 424, 433,
    *461*
    Beethoven's influence on, 460
    biography of, 421

Berlioz (*continued*)
    church music of, 489–91
    as conductor, 410
    Gluck's influence on, 328
    influence of, 424, 439, 506, 582
    operas of, 404, 421, 468–69
    orchestral music of, 404, 408, 420–24,
        460, 500
    writings of, 408
Bernart de Ventadorn, 49, 50
Bernini, Gian Lorenzo, 166, *166*, 168, *169*,
        171, 172, 176, 199, 200
Bernstein, Leonard, 610, 616, *616*
*bianco e dolce cigno, Il* (Arcadelt), 132
biblical references to music, 19
big bands, 622, 624
Billings, William, 595, 609
*Billy Budd* (Britten), 633
*Billy the Kid* (Copland), 611
binary form, 209, 250, 257, 286, 329, 331
Binchois, Gilles, 100, 101, 102–4, *103*, *104*,
        108, 117, 120
biographies
    of Bach, 291
    of Bartók, 578
    of Beethoven, 376–77
    of Berlioz, 421
    of Bordoni, 324
    of Brahms, 448
    of Chopin, 433
    of Corelli, 256
    of Debussy, 537
    of Du Fay, 105
    of Dvořák, 458
    of Ellington, 624
    of Frescobaldi, 215
    of Gabrieli, 217
    of Handel, 304
    of Haydn, 340
    of Hildegard of Bingen, 43
    of Ives, 602
    of Jacquet de La Guerre, 249
    of Josquin des Prez, 124
    of Landini, 84
    of Léonin, 62
    of Liszt, 440
    of Lully, 231
    of Machaut, 76
    of Mahler, 496
    of Mendelssohn, 425
    of Monteverdi, 190
    of Mozart, 354
    of Ockeghem, 117
    of Palestrina, 153
    of Pérotin, 62
    of Purcell, 236
    of Rameau, 287
    of Rossini, 470
    of Schoenberg, 548
    of Schubert, 413
    of C. Schumann, 445
    of R. Schumann, 430
    of Schütz, 204

    of Strauss, 501
    of Stravinsky, 567
    of Strozzi, 198
    of Tchaikovsky, 454
    of Verdi, 476–77
    of Vivaldi, 281
    of Wagner, 484–85
bird calls, 137–38, 385–86, 631
Birdland (New York club), *626*
*Birth of the Cool* (Davis album), 628
*Birth of Tragedy, The* (Nietzsche), 406
Bischoff, Hans, *296*
Bismarck, Otto von, 507
bitonality, 634
Bizet, Georges, 467, 469
*Black, Brown and Beige* (Ellington), 626
*Black and Tan Fantasy* (Ellington), 625
*Black Angels* (Crumb), 639
Black Death, 15, 71, 80
black music. *See* African-American music
Blanche, Jacques-Émile, *537, 565*
*Bleak House* (Dickens), 407
Blow, John, 236, 239
*Bluebeard's Castle* (Bartók), 579
*Blue Boy, The* (Gainsborough), 275, *318*
blue notes, 618
blues, 594, 599, 618, 620, 623
    Milhaud's use of, 565
    Ravel's use of, 565
Boccaccio, Giovanni, 15, 72, 80, 81, 82
Boehm, Theobald, 419, *419*
Boethius, 8, 24, *24*, 31, 44, 60, 114
*Boeuf sur le toit, Le* (Milhaud), 565
*Bohème, La* (Puccini), 461, 516, 517
Bohemia, nationalism in, 400
Bohemian music. *See* Czech music
Böhler, Otto, *460*
Böhm, Georg, 291
Boito, Arrigo, 479
Boldoni, Giovanni, *476*
*Bolero* (Ravel), 542, 565
Bologna, 260
Bologna, University of, 12, 55
Bolshevik Revolution, 573
*Bomarzo* (Ginastera), 636
Bonaparte, Napoleon, 273, *273*–74, 275,
        276, 381, 386, 398, 462
*bonne chanson, La* (Fauré), 515
Bononcini, Giovanni, 306
Book of Common Prayer, 152
*Book of the Courtier, The* (Castiglione), 95,
        128, 129
*Book of the Hanging Gardens, The*
        (Schoenberg), 549, 551
bop. *See* bebop
Bordoni, Faustina, 306, 309, *324*, 325
    biography of, 324
*Boris Godunov* (Musorgsky), 508–9
*Born to Dance* (film), 617
Borodin, Aleksander, 506
Borromini, Francesco, 175, *176*
borrowing. *See also* collage technique
    in Baroque music, 300, 311

    in medieval music, 64–67
    in nineteenth-century music, 417
    in Renaissance music, 101, 106–8, 120,
        122, 125–26, 154
    in twentieth-century music, 568, 578,
        660–62
Botticelli, Sandro, 94, 96, 97
Boulanger, Nadia, 513, 608, 610, 612, 655
Boulez, Pierre, 541, 631, 636–67, *637*, 651
Bourgeois, Loys, 149
Brahms, Johannes, 439, 447–53, *448*, 460
    Beethoven's influence on, 391, 438, 447,
        453, 460
    biography of, 448
    chamber music of, 411, 449–50, 601
    influence of, 457, 458, 512, 547
    piano music of, 411, 447–49
    Requiem of, 490–91
    Schumann's advocacy of, 430
    symphonies of, 451–53, 460, 479
*Brandenburg Concertos* (Bach), 297–98
branles, 208
Braque, Georges, 528, 533
brass instrument construction, 419
Brazilian music, 565–66, 606–7
Brecht, Bertolt, 529, 584
Breitkopf & Härtel, 362n, 381
Brennglas, Adolph, *442*
Brentano, Antonie, 390, *390*
Brentano, Franz, 390
breves, 74, 127
Britten, Benjamin, *633*, 633–34
Broadwood & Sons, 418
broken consorts, 210
Brontë, Charlotte, 407
Brontë, Emily, 407
Bronzino, 130
Broschi, Carlo. *See* Farinelli
Brosses, Charles de, 282
Brown, Earle, 649
Brubeck, Dave, 628
Bruckner, Anton, 490, 494, *494*
Brückwald, Otto, *488*
Bruges, 95
Brunelleschi, Filippo, 105
Buchla, Donald, 641
Büchner, Georg, 554
Bulgarian Women's Choir, 531
bull lyre, 6
Bülow, Hans von, 451, 460, 485, 501
Buonarroti, Michelangelo. *See*
        Michelangelo
Buontalenti, Bernardo, *184, 186*
Burgtheater (Vienna), *368*
Burgundian music, 99–100, 102–10
    court chapel, 99–100, 102
Burgundy, duchy of, 98–99, 99
Burleigh, Harry T., 459
Burne-Jones, Edward, 403, *404*, 407
Burney, Charles, 278, 308, 324, 325, 340
Busnoys, Antoine, 117, 121
Buxtehude, Dietrich, 216, *246*
    influence of, 293

organ music of, 245, 453
sacred concertos of, 242
Byrd, William, 152, 157, 160–61, 212, 213
Byron, George Gordon, Lord, 403, 406, 422, 461
Byzantine Empire, 9–10, 27, 91
Byzantine processional litany, 34–35
Byzantium, 27

cabaletta, 472, 479
cable television, 531
caccia, 81, 82
Caccini, Francesca, 191–92, 192
Caccini, Giulio, 142, 182, 183, 185–86, 187–89, 192, 229
Caccini, Margherita, 192
Caccini, Settimia, 192
cadences
  in Baroque music, 316
  of Beethoven, 391
  Burgundian, 103, 107
  in chant, 41
  chromatically altered, 87
  double-leading-tone, 102
  in eighteenth-century music, 317, 329, 344, 364
  in fifteenth-century music, 116
  in Franco-Flemish music, 125
  Landini, 82–83, 103
  in sixteenth-century music, 136, 155
  in toccatas, 215
  in twentieth-century music, 580, 581
cadenzas, 229, 257, 324, 337, 367
Cage, John, 541, 563, 647, 647–49, 650
Calder, Alexander, 649
call and response, 599
Calvin, Jean, and Calvinism, 95, 146, 148, 149, 150
Calzabigi, Raniero de, 327, 360
cambiata, 157
Cambrai, 95, 105
Camerata, Florentine, 184–86
Campanella, La (Paganini), 441
Campion, Thomas, 140
Camuccini, Vincenzo, 470
Camus, Albert, 522
Canada and Canadian music, 522, 606, 639, 664, 666
Canavesio, 34
Candide (Voltaire), 274
Canonical Hours. See Office
canons
  Ars nova, 82
  Ars subtilior, 84
  of Bach, 296, 297, 298
  of Beethoven, 391
  of Billings, 595
  cancrizans ("crab"), 121
  in Masses, 154
  medieval, 69–70, 100
  mensuration, 121
  in twentieth-century music, 558–59, 582, 654–56

canso, 48, 49
cantabile, 285, 471–72
cantatas
  of Bach, 292, 299–302, 453
  of Ives, 602
  of Prokofiev, 588
  of Schoenberg, 548
  seventeenth-century, 197–98, 226–30
Canterbury Tales (Chaucer), 15–16, 72
canticles, 32
Canticum sacrum (Stravinsky), 567
cantigas, 52
Cantigas de Santa María, 52, 52
cantor, 40
cantus durus, 181
cantus firmus, 64, 67, 76, 101, 121
  in chorales, 300, 301
  in Masses, 106–8, 109, 120, 125–26, 154–56
cantus mollis, 181
Can vei la lauzeta mover (Bernart de Ventadorn), 49
canzonas, 217–18, 219, 257
canzonets, 139, 140, 190
canzonettas, 130, 195
canzon villanesca, 130
capitalism, 164–65, 406
capriccios, 294, 449
Caproli, Carlo, 224
Caravaggio, Michelangelo Merisi da, 142, 142
Carissimi, Giacomo, 197, 201
Carmen (Bizet), 467, 467, 469, 478, 492
Carmina burana (Orff), 587, 592
Carnaval (Schumann), 429
Carnegie Hall (New York), 454
carnival, 193
carols, 100
Carousel (Rodgers), 616
Carracci, Annibale, 217
Carrogis de Carmontelle, Louis, 357
Carroll, Lewis, 663
Carter, Elliott, 608, 610, 638, 646
Caruso, Enrico, 574
Casanova, Giovanni Giacomo, 288
cassette tapes, 575
Castiglione, Baldassare, 95, 128, 129
Castor et Pollux (Rameau), 288
castrati, 192–93, 308–9, 324, 326
Catalogue d'oiseaux (Messiaen), 631
catches, 239
cathedrals and abbeys, 11–12, 12, 34, 68
Catherine the Great, empress of Russia, 271
caudae, 69
Cavalleria rusticana (Mascagni), 515
Cavalli, Pier Francesco, 193–94, 198
cavatina, 471–72
Cecilia, Saint, 213, 252, 490
Cecilian movement, 490, 492
Celestial Country, The (Ives), 602
Cellini, Benvenuto, 421
cello. See violoncello
Cento concerti ecclesiastici (Viadana), 201

ceremonial music, 238–39, 264
Ceremony of Carols, A (Britten), 633
Cervantes, Miguel de, 166, 170, 502
Cesti, Antonio, 193, 194
cetra, La (Vivaldi), 285
Cézanne, Paul, 527, 528, 533
Chabrier, Emmanuel, 538
chace, 82
chaconnes, 214, 453. See also passacaglia
Chadwick, George Whitefield, 600, 611
Chaliapin, Boris, 545
chamber music. See also instrumental music; specific genres and composers
  Baroque, 165, 194–98, 222, 286
  of Bartók, 579
  of Beethoven, 375, 377–78, 383, 389, 391
  of Brahms, 449–50
  of Dvořák, 459
  eighteenth-century, 278, 286, 334
  of Fauré, 514
  of Franck, 513–14
  of Ginastera, 635–36
  of Haydn, 347–50, 361
  of Mozart, 361–62
  nineteenth-century, 402, 409, 411
  of Ravel, 542
  of Schoenberg, 551
  of Schubert, 416–17, 420, 467
  of R. Schumann, 430, 432
  of C. Schumann, 445–46
  of Webern, 558
chamber sonatas. See sonata da camera
Chambonnières, Jacques Champion de, 248
Champagne, Claude, 606
Champion des dames, Le (Le Franc), 101, 102, 103
chance music, 647, 649
chansonniers, 47, 104
chansons
  Ars nova, 78–80, 82, 102
  Ars subtilior, 84–85
  Burgundian, 103, 104, 108, 120
  Franco-Flemish, 121, 122–23
  French sixteenth-century, 129, 134, 137, 142, 144
  Odhecaton anthology, 122
  twentieth-century, 566
chansons de geste, 47
chant. See also Gregorian chant
  church leaders' attitudes toward, 4
  dialects of, 27–28
  written transmission of, 28
Chant d'amour, Le (Burne-Jones), 404
Chant des oiseaux, Le (Janequin), 138
Char, René, 637
character pieces, 429, 431, 447, 510, 539
Chardin, Jean-Baptiste-Siméon, 287
charivari, 73
Charlemagne, Emperor, 8, 8–10, 33, 34–35
Charles I, duke of Bourbon, 117
Charles I, king of England, 164, 222
Charles II, king of England, 164, 236, 239

Charles the Bold, duke of Burgundy, 100
Charles the Good, duke of Burgundy, 106
Charles VI, Holy Roman emperor, 327
Charles VII, king of France, *13*
Charpentier, Marc-Antoine, 235
Chartres, cathedral of, *12*
Chaucer, Geoffrey, 15–16, 72
Chávez, Carlos, 607, *607*, 610
Cherubini, Luigi, 328
Childe, Warren, *425*
*Childe Harold* (Byron), 406, 422
*Children's Corner* (Debussy), 539
China, 523, 525
chitarrone, 180, *180*
Chodowiecki, Daniel Nikolaus, *334*
choirbooks, 119, *121*
choir schools, 95–96, 105, 141
Chopin, Fryderyk, 402, 405, 432–35, *433*
    biography of, 433
    influence of, 441, 447, 469, 506, 512,
        546, 600
    piano music of, 411, 416, 432–35, *433*
    Sand and, 433, 436
    Schumann's advocacy of, 430
chorale cantatas, 300–302
chorale fantasias, 148, 247
chorale motets, 148, 204
chorale partitas, 247
chorale preludes, 148, 247–48, 293–94
chorales, 146, 147–48, 149, 204, 241–42
    Berg's quotation of, 557
    Meyerbeer's quotation of, 465
    polyphonic settings, 148, 293–94
chorale variations, 247
choral music. *See specific composers and
        genres*
choreography, 208, 616, 617
*Chôros* (Villa-Lobos), 606
chorus (in jazz), 620, 621–22, 625
chorus (in popular song), 598
Christian church, early. *See* church music,
        early Christian
Christian IV, king of Denmark, *210*
Christian Ludwig, margrave of
        Brandenburg, 297–98
Christina, queen of Sweden, 201, 225, 256,
        261, *261*
*Christ lag in Todesbanden* (Luther), 147
Christmas, 32, 42–43, 44, 59, 66
*Christmas Carol, A* (Dickens), 407
*Christophe Colomb* (Milhaud), 465, 565
chromaticism
    in Baroque music, 181, 193, 216
    in Counter-Reformation music, 155
    in eighteenth-century music, 349
    in nineteenth-century music, 444, 469,
        480, 482, 488–89, 492, 499, 515,
        601
    in sixteenth-century music, 133, 135–36
    in twentieth-century music, 499–500,
        504, 546, 549, 608, 626
chromatic saturation, 549, 551

church calendar, 32, 42
Church Fathers, 18, 22, 23–24, 27, 60
church music, Anglican, 146–47, 150–51,
        152, 157, 239, 595, 633
church music, Baroque, 222
    in American colonies, 595
    Anglican, 239
    Catholic, 177–78, 199, 201, 235
    Lutheran, 178, 202, 204–5, 241–42,
        245–48, 290, 292, 293–94, 299–302
church music, early Christian, 4, 8–9,
        18–19, 23–25, 27–28, 30–31, 34, 40
church music, eighteenth-century, 268,
        298–302, 352, 372, 595–96
church music, Lutheran
    Baroque, 178, 202, 204–5, 241–42,
        245–48, 290, 292, 293–94,
        299–302
    sixteenth century, 146
church music, nineteenth-century, 389,
        391, 393–94, 464, 489–91, 492,
        494, 602
church music, Reformation, 146–51
    Anglican, 146, 150–51, 152, 157, 595
    Calvinist, 146, 149, 595
    Lutheran, 146, 147–48, 425
church music, Roman Catholic
    Baroque, 177, 199, 201, 235, 595
    eighteenth century, 352, 372
    nineteenth century, 389, 391, 393–94,
        490, 494
    Renaissance, 144, 147, 150, 151, 153–61
    twentieth century, 631
church music, twentieth-century, 631, 633
Church of England, 146–47, 152
church sonatas. *See* sonata da chiesa
*ciacona. See* chaconne
Cicero, 92
Ciconia, Johannes, *85*
*cimento dell'armonia e dell'inventione, Il*
        (Vivaldi), 285
circle of fifths, 258–59, 293, 356, 433
Cirillo, Bernardino, 112, 115
cities, growth of, 11, 55, 91, 521
citole, *81*
cittern, 26, *81*
*Civilization and Its Discontents* (Freud), 532
civil rights movement, 525
Civil War, American, 596, 599
Claeszoon, Pieter, 150, *150*
clarinet, 419
clarinet music, 449–50
Clarinet Quintet (Mozart), 362
Classical style, 267–68, 274–77, 315–19,
        339, 360, 373, 397. *See also*
        eighteenth-century music; *specific
        composers*
Classic style, eighteenth-century. *See*
        eighteenth-century music
clausula, *60*, 61–63
    motet and, 64, 65, 73
    substitute, 61–63, *63*, 64

clavecin. *See* harpsichord
clavicembalo, 351
clavichord, 295, *295*, 333, 350
clavicytherium, *295*
clavier, 295
Clement IX, Pope, 192
Clement of Alexandria, 23
*clemenza di Tito, La* (Metastasio), 323
Cleonides, 22, 114
*Clock* Symphony (Haydn), 347
*Clori vezzosa, e bella* (Scarlatti), 226–27
Closterman, John, *236*
Cocteau, Jean, 563, 565, *565*
codas, 379
Codde, Pieter, *208*
Cohan, George M., 614–15
Colbran, Isabella, 470, *470*
Cold War, 523, 525
Coleman, Ornette, 628
collage technique, 603, 641, 660–62
Collect, 33, 35
collegia musica, 263, *265*, 297, 298
colonialism, 91, 164
color, 73
coloratura, 307
Coltrane, John, 628
Columbia-Princeton Electronic Music
        Center, 641, *642*
Columbia Records, 575
Columbia University, 600, 640
*Combattimento di Tancredi e Clorinda*
        (Monteverdi), 195
combos, 626
*comédies-ballets,* 231
comic opera. *See* opera buffa; *opera buffa;
        opera comique; opéra comique*
commedia dell'arte, 320
communications satellites, 531
Communion, 32, 33, 35, 40–41, 152
communism, 522–23, 525
compact discs (CDs), 575, 652
Compère, Loyset, *118*
composers' organizations, 587, 608, 610
composition, concept of, 41, 54
computer music, 651
*Concert* (Cage), 649
*concert, Le* (Tournier), *195*
concertato medium, 181, 194–98, 199, 210,
        *307*
*Concert champêtre* (Poulenc), 566
concerti grossi, 260–62, 298, 312
concertino, 309
*concerto delle donne,* 131, 142, 192
concerto form, 282–83, 366–67
Concerto for Orchestra (Bartók), 579
concertos. *See also* piano concertos; violin
        concertos
    of J. C. Bach, 335–37, 366
    of J. S. Bach, 294, 297–98
    Baroque, 244, 260–62
    of Beethoven, 388

of Falla, 543
of Handel, 312
of Mozart, 336, 337, 357, 365–67
nineteenth-century, 388
types of, 260
of Vivaldi, 281–85
concerts, public
eighteenth century, 278, 286, 298,
318–19, 345, 353, 357, 358–59,
378–79
nineteenth century, 410, 441, 596–97
seventeenth century, 165, 166, 239–40,
242, 245
twentieth century, 534, 609
*Concerts royaux* (Couperin), 286
Concerts spirituels (Paris), 278, 286, 345,
358, *359*
*concitato genere*, 173, 195
*Conditioned Reflexes* (Pavlov), 532
*Conditor alme siderum* (Du Fay), 104
conductors and conducting, 231, 233, 394,
410, 423, *423*, 425, 440, 460, 496,
534, 611, 616
conductus, polyphonic, 67, 69
*Confessions* (Saint Augustine), 14, 23, 24
confraternities, 217
congregational singing, 146, 148, 149
Congress of Vienna, 274, 400
consonance and dissonance. *See also*
chromaticism; harmony
in ancient Greek music, 22
in early polyphony, 56, 57
in English polyphony, 69–70, 98, 100
in fifteenth-century music, 91, 109,
114–15
in seventeenth-century music, 174–75,
178, 179–80, 181, 188, 191, 193,
196–97, 205, 237
in sixteenth-century music, 133, 134,
136–37, 155, 157
in trecento music, 83
in twentieth-century music, 503–4, 549,
566, 571, 579, 601, 603, 608, 655,
660
consorts, *209*, 209–10, 216
consort song, 152
Constable, John, 403
*contenance angloise*, 98, 101, 102
*Continental Harmony, The* (Billings), 595
contrafacta, 146, 147, 625, 627–28
*Contra mortem et tempus* (Rochberg), 660
contratenor, 76
convents, 32, 43, 44, 55, 96
cool jazz, 628
Copernicus, Nicolaus, 94
Copland, Aaron, 534, 608, *610*, 610–11, 633
Coprario, John, 216
copyright issues, 476, 652
Corelli, Arcangelo, 175, 181, *256*
biography of, 256
concertos of, 260–61, 312
French music influenced by, 286, 290

influence of, 259–60, 304, 314
sonatas of, 256–60, 285
Corigliano, John, 465, 661
Corinth, Louis, *504*
*Coriolan Overture* (Beethoven), 386–87
*cori spezzati*, 199, 217, *218*
Cornaro Chapel (Bernini), *200*
Corneille, Pierre, 230
cornett, *207*, *209*, 218
*Corn Harvest, The* (Rivera), *606*
Corsi, Jacopo, 187
*Così fan tutte* (Mozart), 368–69, 371
Cöthen, 291, 292, 294, 297–98
Cotton Club (Harlem), 624–25
*Cotton Tail* (Ellington), 625
Council of Trent, 43, 151, 153, 154, 156, 201
counterpoint
in Baroque music, 296, 298, 300, 302,
315
of Beethoven, 391–92
of Billings, 595
dissonant, 609–10
in eighteenth-century music, 344, 364
in fifteenth-century music, 115, 117,
120–21
fugal, 216
imitative, 91, 121, 122, 124, 126, 135,
215–16, 232–33, 245, 257, 300, *301*,
391–92, 601
in jazz, 620
monody and, 185
of Palestrina, 157, 159, 174
prehistory of, 54
in twentieth-century music, 580, 582,
585
Counter-Reformation, 147, 151, 153–61
Couperin, François, 268, 279
chamber music of, 286
harpsichord music of, 248, 314
harpsichord treatise of, 258, 259, 286
influence of, 565
works edition edited by Brahms, 448
courante, 175, 210, 251–52, 296
court chapels, 91–92, 95
Burgundy, 99–100, 102
England, 160, 236
France, 235, 262
Germany, 204–5
courtly love, concept of, 13, 17, 48–49, 103
Courtois, Antoine, *419*
cowboy songs, 611, 613
Cowell, Henry, 608, *608*, 609, 613, 640,
647
Coyzevox, Antoine, *231*
Craft, Robert, 567
*Craft of Musical Composition, The*
(Hindemith), 584
Crawford, Ruth, 608, *609*, 609–10
*Creation* (Billings), 595
*Creation, The* (Haydn), 352–53, *353*, 384
*Création du monde, Le* (Milhaud), 565
Credo, 33, 35, 41

Cremona, 245, 255
Creole Jazz Band, *619*, 621
*Creole Rhapsody* (Ellington), 625
criticism, music, 278, 303, 417, 421, 430,
442, 451, 628
*Critique of Pure Reason* (Kant), 274
Cromwell, Oliver, 164, 236
Crosby, Bing, 617
cross relations, 452
*Crouching Tiger, Hidden Dragon* (film), 531
*Cruda Amarilli* (Monteverdi), 137, 178,
179–80, 184
Crüger, Johann, 242
Crumb, George, 639, 646
Crusades, *10*, 11, 51, 55, 106, 107
Cuban missile crisis, 523
cubism, 528, 531, 533, 568
Cui, César, 506
cumulative form, 603, 660
*Cunning Little Vixen, The* (Janáček), 544
Cuzzoni, Francesca, 306, 309, 324
*Cygne, Un* (Hindemith), 586
cymbals, 4
Czech music, 457–59, 507, 512, 544,
595–96
Czechoslovakia, 522, 523
Czerny, Carl, *296*, 381, 440

da capo arias, 262
in cantatas, 226–27, 300
embellishment of, 226, 230
form of, 223, 227
instrumental cadenzas developed from,
337, 367
in opera buffa, 320
in opera seria, 307, 309, 323–25, 326
*Dafne* (Rinuccini), 187
d'Agoult, Marie, 440, *461*, 485
*Da le belle contrade d'oriente* (Rore), 132–33
Dalí, Salvador, 528
dal segno, 323
*Dame aux camélias, La* (Dumas), 478
*Damnation of Faust, The* (Berlioz), 421, 424
damper pedal, 418, 434, 609
dance, social, 208
dance bands, 531, 611
dance music. *See also* ballets; suites,
Baroque
Baroque, 180, 207–10, 249–53, 288, 384
medieval, 47, 52, 80, 82
nineteenth-century, 597
sixteenth-century, 130
twentieth-century, 561, 613–14, 616,
618, 622–23
dance suites, 175, 180, 210, 250–53, 286,
296–97, 311–12, 542
*Dancing Party* (Codde), 208
D'Anglebert, Jean-Henry, 248, *250*, 258
Danhauser, Josef Franz, 461, *461*
D'Annunzio, Gabriele, 540
*Danseries à 4 parties* (anthology), 209–10
*Danse villageoise* (Champagne), *606*

Dante Alighieri, 26, 72, 81
*Danzas argentines* (Ginastera), 635
*Daphnis et Chloé* (Ravel), 542
Da Ponte, Lorenzo, 274, *368*, 368–69
Darmstadt, 636
Darwin, Charles, 401, 406
*David* (Bernini), 168, *169*
*David* (Donatello), 92, *92*, 93
*David* (Michelangelo), 94, 168, *169*
David, Jacques-Louis, *273*, *275*, 276, *276*, *404*, *405*, 468
*David Copperfield* (Dickens), 407
*Davidsbundlertänze* (Schumann), 429
Davies, Peter Maxwell, 660
Davis, Miles, 628
"Death and the Maiden" Quartet (Schubert), 417, 639
*Death in Venice* (Britten), 633
*Death of Sardanapalus, The* (Delacroix), *403*, 405, *409*
Debussy, Claude, 519, 532, *537*, 537–41, 547
    Berlioz's influence on, 424
    biography of, 537
    block construction of, 538–39, 544, 546
    influence of, 541, 543, 577, 604, 608, 617, 622, 624, 631
    orchestral music of, 539–40, 572
    piano music of, 538–39
    reception of, 559
    Satie's influence on, 562
    songs and stage music of, 540–41
decadence, 503
*Decameron* (Boccaccio), 15, 72, 80, 82
declamation, 288
Declaration of Independence, 271
Degas, Edgar, *423*
*De institutione musica* (Boethius), 24, 25, 60
Delacroix, Eugène, 403, *405*, 407, *409*, 433
Delafosse, Jean-Baptiste, *357*
de Leeuw, Ton, 631
*Delicious* (film), 617
della Croce, J. N., *370*
*Del sonare sopra il basso* (Agazzari), 182
Del Tredici, David, 610, 663, 664
*De ma dame vient/Dieus, comment porroie/Omnes* (Adam de la Halle), 66, *67*
de Mille, Agnes, 616
*De musica* (Augustine), 60
Denmark, 164
depictive music, 424–26. *See also* program music
    eighteenth-century, 288, 289–90, 300, 310, 353
    nineteenth-century, 414, 460
    seventeenth-century, 195, 226, 238
    sixteenth-century, 137–38
    twentieth-century, 663–64, 666
*De plus en plus* (Binchois), 103, *104*, 108, 120
descant, 83
Descartes, René, 164, 168, 170, 174, 261, *261*, 290
*Déserts* (Varèse), 609

des Prez, Josquin. *See* Josquin des Prez
*Dessicated Embryos* (Satie), 563
détente, 525
Deutsch, Otto Erich, 416n
*deutsches Requiem, Ein* (Brahms), 490–91
developing variation, 450, 453, 548–49, 555, 658–59
development, 332, 333, 344, 348, 494
*Devils of Loudon, The* (Penderecki), 646
*Devin du village, Le* (Rousseau), 321
*Diabelli Variations* (Beethoven), 389, 391, 448
Diaghilev, Sergei, 567, 571, 572, 573, 588
*Dialogo della musica antica et della moderna* (Galilei), 185
*Dialogue on the Great World Systems* (Galileo), 170
dialogues, 44
*Dialogues of the Carmelites* (Poulenc), 566
diatonic scales, 4
*Dichterliebe* (Schumann), 431, 436
Dickens, Charles, 397, 407
Diderot, Denis, 271, 274, 277
*Dido and Aeneas* (Purcell), 176, 236–38
*Didone abbandonata* (Metastasio), 322
diegetic music, 617
*Dies irae*, 43, 422, 490, 639
*diferencias*, 212
digital technologies, 651, 652
Dijon, 95
diminution, 229
Dionysius, 20
direct performance of chant, 35
discant, 57, 58, 59–63, 76, 100
disc jockeys, 531
*Discorso sopra la musica de' suoi tempi* (Giustiniani), 135
*Discourse on Method* (Descartes), 170
*Discourses on Art* (Reynolds), 275
dissemination
    of ancient Greek culture, 6, 8, 13, 18, 22–23
    of chant melodies, 30–31, 33–34
    of Christianity, 8, 30, *31*, 34
    printing and, 116
dissonance. *See* consonance and dissonance
divas, 224–25, 324
divertimenti, 357
divertissements, 232, 233, 288, 289
*Divine Comedy* (Dante), 72
division, 229
*Dixit Dominus*, 40
*Dmitrij* (Dvořák), 459
*Dodekachordon* (Glarean), 114
Dodge, Charles, 651
dominant, 289
Donatello, 92, *92*, 93, 94, 96
*Don Carlos* (Verdi), 478
*Don Giovanni* (Mozart), 368–69, *371*
Donizetti, Gaetano, 462, 463, 474, 478
*Don Juan* (Strauss), 500
Donne, John, 166, 170

*Don Pasquale* (Donizetti), 474
*Don Quixote* (Cervantes), 166, 170, *502*, 543
*Don Quixote* (Strauss), 500, 502
*Don Rodrigo* (Ginastera), 636
Dorsey, Tommy, 623
*double*, 297
*Dover Beach* (Barber), 635
Dowland, John, *140*, 140–41, 213
downloading technologies, 575, 652
*Dream of Gerontius, The* (Elgar), 512–13
*Dream Rainbow Dream Thunder* (Schafer), 664
*Dreigroschenoper, Die* (Weill), 584
Dresden, 204–5, 324, 325
drones, 57, 512, 583, 587, 653
drums, 4, *211*
*Duet, The* (Kilburne), *418*
Du Fay, Guillaume, 95, 100, 102, *103*, 104–10
    biography of, 105
    chansons of, 79, 104
    Le Franc's tribute to, 101
    Masses of, 105–10
    motets of, 105
    Ockeghem and, 117
Dumas, Alexandre, the Elder, *461*
Dumas, Alexandre, the Younger, 478
Dumesnil, Pierre, *261*
Dunstable, John, 100–102, 115
Duplessis, Joseph-Siffred, *327*
duplum, 63, 64, 65, 78
Durazzo, Giacomo, 327, 360
*Durch Adams Fall* (Bach), 294
Dürer, Albrecht, 94, *141*
Durey, Louis, 565
Dvořák, Antonín, 439, 453, 457–59, *458*, 512
    biography of, 458
    nationalism viewed by, 507, 604
    operas of, 459
    symphonies of, 459, 601
dynamics, 218
    in eighteenth-century music, 333, 334, 345, 347, 350–51, 379
    in nineteenth-century music, 473
    on piano, 411
    in twentieth-century music, 558, 637, 648

Eakins, Thomas, *598*
Easter, 32, 43, 44, 147
*Ebony Concerto* (Stravinsky), 567
economy
    in eighteenth century, 269, 272–73
    in Middle Ages, 11, 55, 71
    in nineteenth century, 374, 400–401, 418–19, 437, 438, 461
    in Renaissance, 91, 116, 119, 128
    in seventeenth century, 164–65
    in twentieth century, 521–23, 525–26, 529, 530, 534
*Ecstasy of Saint Teresa, The* (Bernini), 199, 200

*Ecuatorial* (Varèse), 608
Edict of Nantes, 164
Edison, Thomas Alva, 401, 406, 574, *575*
education, music
   ancient Greece, 6, 7, 20, 21–22
   eighteenth century, 269, 271, 280–82, 294, 296, 298–99, 595
   Middle Ages, 9, 10, 11–13, 24, 31, 34–35, 44, 46, 55, 60, 141
   nineteenth century, 506, 600
   Renaissance, 95–96, 141
   Roman Empire, 6
   twentieth century, 579, 584, 587
Edward VI, king of England, 151
*Effects of Good and Bad Government . . . , The* (Lorenzetti), 93
*Egmont* Overture (Beethoven), 387
*Ego and the Id, The* (Freud), 532
Egypt, ancient, 4
Eichendorff, Joseph Freiherr von, 494
Eichhorn, Albert, *448*
eighteenth-century culture and politics, 267–78
eighteenth-century music, 277–395. *See also* Baroque; Haydn, Franz Joseph; Mozart, Wolfgang Amadeus
   church music, 298–302, 352, 372, 595–96
   French, 285–90
   German, 290–303, 339–73, 375–79
   instrumental, 279–86, 292–98, 311–13, 329–37, 342–51, 355–57, 361–67, 375–79
   Italian, 279–85
   in North America, 595–96
   operas, 288–90, 305–9, 319–28, 351–52, 355, 357, 367–69, 371
   oratorios, 310–11, 352–53
*Eine kleine Nachtmusik* (Mozart), 357
*Ein' feste Burg ist unser Gott* (Luther), 147, *148*, 465
*Einstein on the Beach* (Glass), 655
Eleanor of Aquitaine, 49, 50
*Electric Power, Motor-Cars, Steel* (Benton), *530*
electronic keyboards, 652
electronic music, 531, 563, 609, 640–42, 651, 653–54
*Elektra* (Sophocles), 503
*Elektra* (Strauss), 501, 503–4
Elgar, Edward, 512–13
*Elijah* (Mendelssohn), 425, 427
Eliot, T. S., 529, 533
*L'elisir d'amore* (Donizetti), 474
Elizabeth I, queen of England, *139*, 151, 152
Ellington, Duke, 594, 622, *622*, 624, 624–26
   biography of, 624
Ellington, Mercer, 624
emotions and music. *See also* ethos
   eighteenth-century concepts, 268, 276–77, 318–19, 333–35
   nineteenth-century concepts, 408, 410–11

seventeenth-century concepts, 168–69, 172, 178–79, 181, 200
*Emperor* Concerto (Beethoven), 388
*empfindsamer* style, 268, 277, 333–35
Encina, Juan del, 141
*Encyclopédie*, 271, 274, 276–77
Engelbrecht, Martin, *247*
Engels, Friedrich, 406
England
   Calvinism in, 149
   colonies of, 164
   eighteenth-century, 268–69
   industrial revolution in, 400
   medieval, 11, 14
   music and social custom in, 318–19
   Norman Conquest of, 11, 55, 69
   seventeenth-century, 164, 166, 222
English Civil War, 164, 236
*English Hymnal*, 543, 544
English music
   Baroque, 213, 216, 235–40, 305–13
   eighteenth-century, 321–22, 335–37
   fifteenth-century, 98, 100–102, 103
   medieval, 69–70, 83
   nineteenth-century, 512–13
   in North America, 595
   Renaissance, 138–41, 146–47, 149–51, 160–61
   seventeenth-century, 175–76
   twentieth-century, 543–44, 633–34, 636, 660
"English" suites (Bach), 296–97
*Enigma Variations* (Elgar), 513
Enlightenment, 267, 271, 273, 274–75, 315, 339, 403. *See also* eighteenth-century music
ensemble music. *See also* chamber music; *specific composers and genres*
   seventeenth-century, *195*, 209, 216–19, 229, 244, 253–65
   sixteenth-century, 119, 131, 140, 142, *160*
*Entführung aus dem Serail, Die* (Mozart), 354, 357, 367–68, 369, 466
environmental music, 664, 666
Episcopal Church, 152
episodes, 247, 283–84, 298, 337
Epistle, 33, 35
*Epitaph of Seikilos*, 19, *21*
Érard, Sébastien, 419
*Erlkönig* (Schubert), 414
*Eroica* Symphony (Beethoven), 380–82, 453
*Erwartung* (Schoenberg), 550, 551
*Es ist genug!* (Bach), 557
*Essay on a Method for Playing the Transverse Flute* (Quantz), 316
*Essays Before a Sonata* (Ives), 602, 604
*Estampes* (Debussy), 539
Este family, 96, 97, 116, 124–25, 131, 136
Esterházy, Nikolaus, II, 340, *342*, 440
Esterházy, Paul Anton, 340, 341, 343, 345–46

*Esther* (Handel), 310
Estonia and Estonian music, 522, 659–60
*L'estro armonico* (Vivaldi), 285
Eszterháza Palace, *341*, 341–42, 351–52
ethnomusicology, 578–79, 610
ethos, 3–4, 7, 21, 23, 114, 115
études, 296, 435, 539, 546
*Études d'exécution transcendante d'après Paganini* (Liszt), 441
*Études-Tableaux* (Rachmaninov), 545
Eucharist, 32, 33, 34
Euclid, 114
Eugene IV, Pope, 105
*Eugene Onegin* (Tchaikovsky), 456
*L'Euridice* (Peri and Caccini), 187–89, 190–91
Euripides, 20, 183, 639
Europe
   ca. 1500, *113*
   ca. 1610, *165*
   early medieval, 8–13
   eighteenth-century, 268–78
   eleventh- to thirteenth-century, 54–56
   fourteenth-century, 13–17
   nineteenth-century, 398–403
   Renaissance, 91–92, 98–99
   seventeenth-century, 164–66
Europe, James Reese, 597, 629
evolution, theory of, 401
existentialism, 522, 533
exoticism, *307*, 367–68, 403, 466–67, 469, 505, 511, 543, 546, 568, 658. *See also* non-Western musics
experimental music, 601–3, 605, 608–9, 613, 646–49, 653
exposition, 247, 331–32, 337, 344, 348, 366–67, 416
expressionism, 503, 528–29, 531, 533, 548, 550, 551, 554–56, 579, 584
Eyck, Jan van, *102*

*Factum est salutare/Dominus*, 64, 67
Facundus, *36*
*Fairy Queen, The* (Purcell), 238
Falla, Manuel de, 541, 543, 547
*Falstaff* (Verdi), 477, 480
*Family Concert in Basle* (Gutzwiller), *401*
fancy, 216
*Fantasia on a Theme of Thomas Tallis* (Vaughan Williams), 544
fantasias
   Baroque, 214, 216, 293, 294
   of Mozart, 361
*Fantasiestücke* (Schumann), 429, 431
*Farewell* Symphony (Haydn), 345–46, 661
Farinelli, 308–9, *309*
Fauré, Gabriel, 513, *514*, 514–15, 598, 608
*Faust* (Goethe), 406, 414, 420
*Faust* (Gounod), 468, 492
*Faust* Symphony (Liszt), 444
Feast of the Oath of the Pheasant, 100, 107
*Fenice fù* (Jacopo da Bologna), 81–82
Ferber, Edna, 615

Ferdinand, king of Aragon, 141
Ferrabosco, Alfonso, the Younger, 216
Ferrara, 96, 116, 122, 124–25, 129, 135–36, 142
festivals, music
  in ancient Greece, 20
  Darmstadt, 636
  Roman, 23
  in Venice, 280
*fête galante*, 269, *269*, 275
feudalism, 11
fiddles, 26, *207*, *211*
*Fidelio* (Beethoven), 382–83
Field, John, 432
Fielding, Henry, 272
figuration
  in eighteenth-century music, 284–85, 293
  in nineteenth-century music, 428, 431, 441
  in seventeenth-century music, 229, 245
  in twentieth-century music, 546, 637, 654–56
figured bass, 180–81, 182, 242. *See also* basso continuo
*Fille du régiment, La* (Donizetti), 474
films and film music, 489, 522, 530, 531, 534, 561, 587, 588, 592, 594, 611, 613, 617, 640, 646, 661
final, 45, 49
*Final Alice* (Del Tredici), 663, 664
*fine amour*, 48, 103
*Fingal's Cave* Overture (Mendelssohn), 426
Finland and Finnish music, 522, 544–45
*Finlandia* (Sibelius), 545
*Finnegans Wake* (Joyce), 532
*Fiori musicali* (Frescobaldi), 215, 216
*Firebird, The* (Stravinsky), 567, 568
Fisk Jubilee Singers, 599, *599*
Five Orchestral Pieces (Schoenberg), 551
Five Pieces for Orchestra (Webern), 558
*Five Senses, The* (Rombouts), *180*
*Five Variants of "Dives and Lazarus"* (Vaughan Williams), 543
Fleming, Alexander, 532
*fliegende Holländer, Der* (Wagner), 484
Florence, 81
  Baroque, 166, 177, 184–89, 191–92
  Camerata in, 184–86
  cathedral in, 105, *106*
  medieval, 11
  plague in, 15
  Renaissance, 96, 116, 122, 131
  theatrical productions in, 183–86
florid organum, 57
*Florilegium* (Muffat), 264
*Flow, my tears* (Dowland), 140–41, 213
flute music, 297
flutes, transverse, *52*, *138*, *210*, 264, 419, *419*
Fokine, Mikhail, 567
*Fole acostumance/Dominus*, 65–66, *67*
folk music. *See also* non-Western musics
  American, 610, 612, 613

eastern European, 578–79, 580, 581, 582–83
English, 543, 544
Haydn's use of, 347
medieval, 100
Mendelssohn's use of, 426
nationalism and, 505, 507
Norwegian, 512
Russian, 505, 507, 508, 511, 568, 569, 588
singspiel tunes, 322
Tchaikovsky's use of, 455
Ford, Henry, 530, 532
*Forelle, Die* (Schubert), 416
Forkel, Johann Nikolaus, 303, 317, 331
form. *See also* ritornello form; sonata form; strophic form
  ballade, 79
  ballata, 82
  ballett, 139
  bar, 50–51
  in Beethoven's late works, 392, 394–95
  binary, 209, 250, 257, 286, 329, 331
  block construction, 509, 538, 544, 546, 566, 568, 570–71, 576, 577
  in Burgundian Masses, 106
  in chant repertory, 38, 42
  concerto, 282–83, 366–67
  cumulative, 603, 660
  cyclic, 106, 120, 456, 513–14, 582
  da capo aria, 223, 226, 227, 283, 323
  in dance suites, 175, 209
  double aria, 471–72
  of eighteenth-century symphonies, 343–45
  ground-bass aria, 223
  minuet and trio, 345
  pavane, 140–41, 210, 213
  ritornello, 262, 283–84
  rondeau, 79
  rondo, 345
  in Schubert's lieder, 414
  in seventeenth-century music, 175
  sonata, 331–32, 336–37
  sonata-rondo, 347
  thematic transformation as unifying strategy, 442
  through-composed, 49, 130, 186, 195, 285, 414, 598
  trecento madrigal, 82
  troubadour and trouvère songs, 47–48
  twelve-bar blues, 618
  verse-refrain, 598, 620
  virelai, 79
"formalism," 587–88, 589
*formes fixes*, 78–80, 84, 121
fortepiano, 333, 350–51
*forza del destino, La* (Verdi), 478
Foster, Stephen, 594, 597–98, 603
*4'33"* (Cage), 649
*Four Saints in Three Acts* (Thomson), 612–13
*Four Seasons, The* (Vivaldi), 285
*Fra Diavolo* (Auber), 468

Francart, François, 224
France
  Bourbon restoration in, 462–63
  Calvinism in, 146, 149
  early chant repertories in, 27–28
  eighteenth-century, 268, 271, 272, 276
  linguistic boundaries in, 47, *48*
  medieval, 8–13, 14, 17
  seventeenth-century, 164, 166
*Francesca da Rimini* (Tchaikovsky), 444
Franciscan order, 14
Francis I, Holy Roman emperor, 360
Francis I, king of France, 137
Francis II, Holy Roman emperor, 375
Franck, César, 444, 513–14, 582
Franco, Francisco, 522
Franco-Flemish music, 95, 98, 112, 117–27, 132–34, 147, 151, 158–60
Franconian motet, 66–67
Franco of Cologne, 66
Frankish Empire, 8–10, 33–35, 41
*Frauenliebe und -leben* (Schumann), 431
Frederick the Great, king of Prussia, 269, 271, 290, 298, 326, *332*, 333
free jazz, 628
Freemasonry, 271–72, 371
free organum, 56, *58*
*Freischütz, Der* (Weber), 480, 482, *482*
French music. *See also* Burgundian music; Franco-Flemish music
  in Canada, 595, 606
  eighteenth-century, 285–90, 321, 327–28
  medieval, 47–49, 54, 55, 57–69, 72–80, 83
  nineteenth-century, 420–22, 424, 462, 463, 464–65, 468–69, 489, 492, 513–15
  Renaissance, 117, 146
  seventeenth-century, 222, 230–35, 245, 248–53, 260
  sixteenth-century, 137–38
  twentieth-century, 489, 537–42, 562–66, 573, 576, 630–33, 636–37, 640, 641, 651
French overtures, 229, 232–33, 257, 264, 286, 364
French Revolution, 269, 271, 273, 276, 339, 358, 374, 382, 398, 403, 566
"French" suites (Bach), 296
Frescobaldi, Girolamo, 214–15, *215*
  biography of, 215
Freud, Sigmund, 526, 528, 532, 550
Froberger, Johann Jacob, 215–16
*From the House of the Dead* (Janáček), 544
front line, 621
frottola, 129, 137, 142
Fruhauf, Aline, *578*
Füger, Friedrich Heinrich, 271
fuging tunes, 595, 609
fugues
  of Bach, 293, 294–95, 298, 303
  Baroque, 175, 215–16, 246–47

of Bartók, 582
of Beethoven, 391–92
of Haydn, 348
of Hindemith, 586
of Mozart, 364
of Stravinsky, 573
Fuseli, Henry, *402, 403, 407*
futurism, 563, 564, 646
Fux, Johann Joseph, 199, 340

Gabbiani, Antonio Domenico, *254*
Gabrieli, Andrea, 217
Gabrieli, Giovanni, *217*
    biography of, 217
    French music influenced by, 235
    polychoral music of, 199, 205, 217–18
    Schütz and, 202, 204
*Gaelic* Symphony (Beach), 601
Gaffurio, Franchino, 114
*gagliarda. See* galliard
Gainsborough, Thomas, 275, 318–19, *319,
    335*
galant style, 268, 279, 303, 315, 316–17,
    344, 348
Galilei, Vincenzo, 170, 184–85, 189
Galileo, Galilei, 164, 170, 172, 178
galliard, 208, 210, *211*
Gallican chant, 28
galops, 597
gamelan music, 636, 639–40
Ganassi, Silvestro, *209*
Gandhi, Mohandas, 525
García Lorca, Federico, 639
Garibaldi, Giuseppe, 507
Garland, Judy, 617
Garnier, Charles, *464*
*Gaspard de la nuit* (Ravel), 542
Gassmann, Florian, 360
Gastoldi, Giovanni Giacomo, 139
Gauci, Massimo, *272*
Gaultier, Denis, 248
Gause, Wilhelm, *455*
gavotte, *251,* 253, 384
Gay, John, 309, 321–22, 584
gay liberation movement, 525
Geminiani, Francesco, 258–59
*General History of Music* (Forkel), 317
*General History of Music, A* (Burney), 278
*General William Booth Enters into Heaven*
    (Ives), 603–4, *605*
Gentileschi, Artemisia, 171, 172, *172*
*George, Earl of Cowper, with the Family of
    Charles Gore* (Zoffany), *351*
George, Stefan, 527, 549
George I, king of England, 305
Géricault, Théodore, 404–5, 407, *408*
German music
    Baroque, 178, 202, 204–5, 240–42,
        245–48, 263–64, 290–303, 316
    eighteenth-century, 322, 332–35,
        339–73, 354, 357, 374–79
    late nineteenth- to early twentieth-
        century, 494–504

medieval, 50–51
nineteenth-century, 379–95, 412–17,
    420, 424–32, 444–53, 462, 480,
    482–89, 492
in North America, 595–96, 600
operas, 464
Renaissance, 146, 147–48
twentieth-century, 583–87, 617, 636,
    640–41
Germany and German-speaking lands
    Brahms-Wagner debates, 439
    early chant repertories in, 27
    eighteenth-century, 269, 271, 273,
        290–91
    medieval, 11, 50–51
    musicology in, 438
    nationalism in, 400, 438, 493, 507
    Romanticism in, 397
    seventeenth-century, 164, 166
    twentieth-century, 522, 523, 583, 584,
        586–87, 617, 638
Gershwin, George, 594, 614, 615, 617, *623,*
    623–24
Gershwin, Ira, *623*
Gerstl, Richard, 550,*550*
*Gesamtkunstwerk,* 461, 483, 484, 489, 492,
    494–95
*Gesang der Jünglinge* (Stockhausen),
    640–41
Gesellschaft der Musikfreunde, 448
Gesualdo, Carlo, *135,* 135–36
Gewandhaus Orchestra, 359, 417, 425
*Ghent Altarpiece* (van Eyck), *102*
Ghezzi, P. L., *285*
Ghirardello da Firenze, 82
*Ghosts of Versailles, The* (Corigliano), 465,
    661
*Giasone* (Cavalli), 193–94
Gibbon, Edward, 274
Gibbons, Orlando, 152
Giere, F., *445*
*Gierusalemme liberata* (Tasso), 195, *196*
giga, 253
gigue, *251,* 253, 257, 286, 297, 331
Gillespie, Dizzy, *626,* 627–28
Ginastera, Alberto, 635–36, 638
Giotto, 15, 16, *16, 72, 72,* 92
Giovanni da Prato, 84
Giovanni Pisano. *See* Pisano, Giovanni
Giraud, Albert, 551
*Girl Crazy* (Gershwin), 624
*Girl with a Dead Canary* (Greuze), 277, *277*
Girò, Anna, 281
*Giulio Cesare* (Handel), 306, 307, 308–9,
    466
Giustiniani, Vincenzo, 135, 142
*Give My Regards to Broadway* (Cohan), 615
Glarean, Heinrich, 114
glasnost, 525
Glass, Philip, 655, *655,* 658
Glazunov, Aleksander, 511
Glinka, Mikhail, 505–6, 511, 571
global culture, 531

Gloria, 33, 35, 41, 56
Gluck, Christoph Willibald, 240, 308, 315,
    321, 327, 327–28, 355, 360, 373, 513
*Go Down, Moses,* 599
Godunov, Boris, czar of Russia, *508*
Goebbels, Joseph, 586
Goethe, Johann Wolfgang von, 403–4
    Beethoven's Fifth Symphony viewed by,
        459
    as Mason, 272
    settings or adaptations of works by, 406,
        414, 420, 421, 444, 468, 494
*Goldberg Variations* (Bach), 297, 448
*Gold Diggers of 1933* (film), 617
*Golden Cockerel, The* (Rimsky-Korsakov),
    511
goliard songs, 46–47, 587
Goltzius, Hendrik, *213*
gondolier songs, 280
Gonzaga, Margherita, 131
Gonzaga family, 116, 131, 190
Goodman, Benny, 531, 622
Gorbachev, Mikhail, 525
Gospel, 35
gospel songs, 598
Gothic architecture, 12, *12,* 55–56, 67, 68,
    78, 93
*Götterdämmerung* (Wagner), 486
*Gott erhalte Franz den Kaiser* (Haydn), 350
Gottschalk, Louis Moreau, 600
Goudimel, Claude, 149
Gounod, Charles, 468, 514
*Goûts-réunis, Les* (Couperin), 286
Goya, Francisco, 403, *403,* 407
Gradual, 33, 35, 41, 56, 59–63
*Gradus ad Parnassum* (Fux), 199, 340
*Grande Messe des morts* (Berlioz), 421,
    489–90
Grandi, Alessandro, 201, 202
*grand motet,* 235
grand opera, 463, 464–65, 467, 470, 478,
    492
*Grand Turk Giving a Concert for His Consort,
    The* (Van Loo), *307, 466,* 467
*Grapes of Wrath, The* (Steinbeck), 529, 533
Graun, Johann Gottlieb, 333
*Great Expectations* (Dickens), 407
Great Schism, 14
"Great" Symphony in C Major (Schubert),
    415–16, 417, 431, 467
Greco, El, 95, *158*
Greek music, ancient, 18, 19–22
    Aristotle on, 7
    Baroque music influenced by, 183–84,
        187, 189
    eighteenth-century music influenced
        by, 267, 276
    extant, 18, 19
    instruments in, 20
    medieval music influenced by, 8, 25, 27,
        31, 45
    modes in, 7
    powers of, 6, 7, 19, 21–22

Greek music, ancient (*continued*)
  Renaissance music influenced by, 91,
    112, 114, 133
  transmission of, 10
  vocal, 3–4
Greek music, twentieth-century, 643–44
Gregorian chant and liturgy, 8, 9, 19, 22.
    *See also* chant
  as chorale source, 146
  classification of, 35, 37
  Frankish influence on, 35
  genres and forms of, 35–44
  liturgical drama, 44
  liturgy and, 31–35
  for Mass, 40–42
  for Office, 39–40
  polyphonic settings of, 54
  standardization of, 33–44
  text setting of, 38
  transmission of, 28
  tropes, 42–43
Gregory, Saint, 33, *37*
*Gretchen am Spinnrade* (Schubert), 414
Grétry, André-Ernest-Modeste, 321
Greuze, Jean-Baptiste, 275, 277, *277*
Grieg, Edvard, 507, 512
*Grosse Fuge* (Beethoven), 392
ground bass. *See* basso ostinato
ground-bass arias, 223, 236–37, 551
Grünewald, Matthias, 585, *586*
*Gruppe aus dem Tartarus* (Schubert), 413
*Guárdame las vacas*, 196, 212
Guardi, Francesco, *280*
Guarini, Anna, 131
Guarini, Giovanni Battista, 130, 170, 184
Guarneri, Bartolomeo Giuseppe, 245
Guarneri family, 255
Gubaidulina, Sofia, 663, *664*
Gueldre, Fernand de, *609*
*Guernica* (Picasso), 529
*Guerre, La* (Janequin), 137–38
*Guerre des bouffons. See Querelle des bouffons*
Guidonian hand, 46, *46*
Guido of Arezzo, 45–46
guilds, musicians', 47, 96
Guillaume de Machaut. *See* Machaut,
    Guillaume de
Guillaume de Poitiers, 49
*Guillaume Tell* (Rossini), 465, 470, 471
Guillén, Nicolás, 607
guitar music, 331
*Gurrelieder* (Schoenberg), 548
Gutenberg, Johannes, 118
Gutzwiller, Sebastian, *401*
*Gymnopédies* (Satie), 562
Gypsy music, 467, 469, 542, 565

habanera, 469
*Haffner* Symphony (Mozart), 363–64
Hamburg, 165, 292
  opera in, 240, 304, 305
*Hamlet* (Liszt), 443
Hammerstein, Oscar, II, 615, 616

Handel, George Frideric, 240, 267, 268, 279,
    290, *304*, 304–13, 311, 318
  biography of, 304
  Corelli's influence on, 259
  as impresario, 309, 322
  influence of, 314, 352, 361, 391, 438, 543
  instrumental music of, 311–13
  international style of, 493
  operas of, 305–9, 324, 325, 466
  oratorios of, 278, 310–11, 352
  Purcell's influence on, 239
  reputation of, 312–13
Handy, W. C., 611, 618
Hanslick, Eduard, 439, 451
Hapsburg Empire, 360
Hardin, Lillian, *619*
Hardy, Thomas, *340*
*Harlem* (Ellington), 626
*harmonia*, 22
*Harmonic Elements* (Aristoxenus), 22
*Harmonice musices odhecaton* collections,
    118, 122
"harmonic fluctuation," 585–86
*Harmonics* (Ptolemy), 25
harmonics, Greek discipline of, 22
*Harmonielehre* (Adams), 656
harmony
  in Baroque music, 180–81, 181–82,
    190–91, 199, 214, 242, 258–59,
    288, 289
  in eighteenth-century music, 317, 346,
    349, 353
  in Franco-Flemish music, 127
  in nineteenth-century music, 402, 413,
    442, 444, 473, 488–89, 492, 499,
    508–9, 511, 515, 537, 539
  in sixteenth-century music, 100, 103–4,
    133, 134, 137
  in twentieth-century music, 499–500,
    503–4, 538, 539, 542, 546, 547,
    549, 551, 552–53, 557, 562, 580,
    589, 626, 631–32, 633, 655
*Harmony of the Worlds* (Kepler), 170
*Harold en Italie* (Berlioz), 422, 424, 439
harps, 4, *81*, *102*, *210*, *418*
harpsichord music
  of Bach, 294, 296–97
  of Falla, 543
  French, 248–53, 286
  of Handel, 311–12
  of Haydn, 350–51
  Italian, 215, 216
  of Scarlatti, 329–31
harpsichords, *246*, *252*, *254*, 297
  as continuo instrument, 180, 282
  double-manual, 244, *245*, *248*
  paintings on, *207*
Harrison, Lou, 640
Hartmann, Viktor, 510, *510*
Harvard University, 600
Hasse, Johann Adolf, 240, 278, 303, 324,
    325, *325*, 325–26, 360
Haussmann, Elias Gottlob, *302*

Haydn, (Franz) Joseph, 290, 339, *340*,
    341–53
  Bach's influence on, 303
  biography of, 340
  birthplace of, 360
  contract of, 343
  humor of, 347, 349
  influence of, 361, 376, 391, 432, 470
  international style of, 493
  Janissary music imitated by, 466
  as Mason, 272
  Masses of, 352
  Mozart's friendship with, 340, 355
  nineteenth-century views of, 397
  operas of, 351–52
  oratorios of, 352–53, 384
  orchestral instrumentation of, 423
  significance of, 372–73
  sonatas of, 350–51
  *Stabat Mater* of, 351
  string quartets of, 347–50, 361, 416
  style of, 267
  symphonies of, 272, 277, 342–47, 358,
    363, 661
Haydn, Michael, 362n
*Haydn* Quartets (Mozart), 361–62
head, 628
healing through music, 6
*Hebrides* Overture (Mendelssohn), 426
*Heidenröslein* (Schubert), 412, 414
Heiligenstadt Testament, 376, 378, 379,
    380
*Heimweh, Das* (Schubert), 413
Heine, Heinrich, 406, 414, 431
*Heldenleben, Ein* (Strauss), 500
hemiola rhythm, 190
Henderson, Fletcher, 622
Henry, Pierre, 640
Henry II, king of England, 50
*Henry IV* (Shakespeare), 480
Henry IV, king of France, 164
Henry VII, king of England, 149
Henry VIII, king of England, 146, 149, 151,
    *152*
Herculaneum, 275
Herman, Woody, 567
*Hermit Songs* (Barber), 635
heterophony (texture), 19, 610
hexachords, 45–46
Hildegard of Bingen, *43*, 44
  biography of, 43
Hiller, Johann Adam, 322, 359
Hindemith, Paul, 534, 584–86, *585*, 592
*Hippolyte et Aricie* (Rameau), 287, 288,
    289–90, 327
His Master's Voice, 574, *575*
*Histoire de France* (Michelet), 89
*Histoire du soldat, L'* (Stravinsky), 572
*Histoires naturelles* (Ravel), 542
*History of Ancient Art, The* (Winckelmann),
    274
*History of the Decline and Fall of the Roman
    Empire, The* (Gibbon), 274

Hitchcock, Alfred, 640
Hitler, Adolf, 522
hocket, 74–75
Hoffmann, E. T. A., 395, 406, 408
Hoffmann, Felicitas, *325*
Hofmannsthal, Hugo von, 503
Hogarth, William, 269, 275, *310*, 322
Hohenstein, Adolfo, *516*
Holbein, Hans, the Younger, *152*
Holdermann, Carl Wilhelm, *482*
Holst, Gustav, 543
Holy Roman Empire, 11, 164, 166, 273, 290
    maps of, *36*
Homer, 20
*L'Homme armé* tune, 106, 125–26, 154
homophony, 91, 100, 122, 129, 132, 180,
    315. *See also* texture
homosexuality, 304, 413, 454, 525, 610,
    633–34
Honegger, Arthur, 565, *565*
hook, 598
*Hora novissima* (Parker), 600
Hot Five (or Hot Seven), 621
Hotteterre, Jean, 264
Howard, Hugh, 256
"Howdy" Symphony (Schickele), 661
Huber, A., 494
Hugo, Victor, 397, 407, 478
*Huguenots, Les* (Meyerbeer), 464–65, *465*
humanism, 22, 92, 93, 94, 97, 114, 115–16,
    129, 133, 151, 153, 189
humanitarianism, 271–72
Hundred Years' War, 14, 71, 91–92, 98
Hungarian music, 439–44, 448, 467,
    577–83, 646
*Hungarian Rhapsodies* (Liszt), 442
Hungary, 400, 522, 523
*Hunnenschlacht* (Liszt), 443
Hus, Jan, 512
*Hyena Stomp* (Stella), 653, *653*
*Hymn and Fuguing Tune* (Cowell), 609
*Hymnen* (Stockhausen), 641
hymns, 55, 126, 425
    American, 164, 595, 603–4, 611, 613
    English, 543
    Greek, 18
    Office, 32
    sixteenth-century, 144, 148, 151
    strophic form in, 38
*Hymn to St. Cecilia* (Britten), 633
*Hyperprism* (Varèse), 608

*Ich grolle nicht* (Schumann), 431
*I-Ching*, 647, 649
*Idealized View of the City* (Piero della
    Francesca), *93*
idée fixe, 420, 422, 444, 460
*Idomeneo* (Mozart), 355
*I Got Rhythm* (Gershwin), 624, 625, 627
*Iliad* (Homer), 20
*Images* (Debussy), 539
*Imaginary Landscape No. 3* (Cage), 647
imitation, theory of, 7, 21–22

imitative counterpoint. *See under*
    counterpoint
Immortal Beloved, 390
*Immortal Beloved* (film), 390n
impresarios, 223, 224–25, 240, 280, 309,
    335
*Impression: Soleil levant* (Monet), *526*,
    527–28, 533
impressionism, 513, 527–28, 531, 533,
    538–39
impromptus, 416, 432, 514
improvisation
    in African American music, 599
    in ancient cultures, 4, 19
    in Baroque music, 181, 182, 196, 207,
        214, 229
    of Beethoven, 378–79, 391
    of cadenzas, 337, 367
    in jazz, 620, 624
    in medieval music, 30, 54, 55, 80–81, 141
    of Mozart, 356
    in Renaissance music, 142, 148, 185
*Im wunderschönen Monat Mai* (Schumann),
    431
*In C* (Riley), 653
incidental music
    ancient Greek, 20
    of Beethoven, 387
    of Debussy, 540
    of Mendelssohn, 425, 426
    pastoral dramas, 183–84
    of Purcell, 238
*incoronazione di Poppea, L'* (Monteverdi),
    193, 225
*Indes galantes, Les* (Rameau), 288, 466
indeterminacy, 649–51, 653
*Indian* Suite (MacDowell), 600
industrial revolution, 374, 400–401,
    418–19, 437, 438
*Inharmonique* (Risset), 651
*In memoriam Dylan Thomas* (Stravinsky),
    577
Innocent XI, Pope, 261
*In Nomine* (Davies), 660
Innsbruck, 225
*Innsbruck, ich muss dich lassen* (Isaac), 122,
    147
Institut de Recherche et Coordination
    Acoustique/Musique (IRCAM), 651
instrumental music. *See also* keyboard
    music; *specific composers,
    instruments, and genres*
    ancient Greek, 20
    Baroque, 165, 175, 180, 182, 206–21,
        229, 244–65, 292–98, 311–13
    eighteenth-century, 279–86, 292–98,
        311–13, 329–37, 342–51, 375–79
    medieval, 30, 86–87
    nineteenth-century, 380–95, 411,
        415–20, 422–29, 431–35, 439–61,
        494, 495–502, 505–7, 510–15,
        596–97, 600–602
    Renaissance, 91, 100, 107, 129, 141–44

twentieth-century, 538–93, 601–66
    types of, 207
instrumentation and orchestration
    Baroque ensemble music, 233, 260, 262,
        264, 282
    of Beethoven, 384
    of Berlioz, 422, 424, 489–90
    Berlioz's treatise on, 421
    of dance bands, 622
    eighteenth-century orchestra, 423
    exoticism and, 466, 467
    of Gabrieli, 218
    of jazz ensembles, 621
    of Mahler, 498–99
    of Mozart, 368–69
    nineteenth-century orchestra, 423,
        489–90
    of Rameau, 288
    Rimsky-Korsakov's treatise on, 511
    of Rossini, 472–73
    of Strauss, 500
    of Stravinsky, 571–72, 577
    of Tchaikovsky, 456
    of Villa-Lobos, 606
instruments. *See also specific instruments*
    ancient Greek, 20
    archaeological finds, 4, 6
    Asian, 609, 636, 640
    Baroque, 206, 244, 255
    basso continuo, 180, 182, 282
    digital, 652
    "haut" and "bas" categories, 87, *102*
    medieval, 52, *57*, *61*, *65*, *72*, *81*, 86–87
    nineteenth-century mass production of,
        401, 418–19, 423
    percussion, 608–9
    Renaissance, 135
    twentieth-century inventions, 563,
        638–39, 640, 641, 661
*Intégrales* (Varèse), 608
intermedi, 183, *184*, *186*, 191
intermezzi, 320, *320*, 328, 449
International Composers Guild, 608
international musical styles
    in eighteenth century, 278, 286, 294,
        296–97, 305–6, 315, 493
    in fifteenth century, 87, 91, 97, 98–111,
        100
    in Renaissance, 122, 157, 177
Internet, 531
*Interpretation of Dreams, The* (Freud), 532,
    550
intervals
    in ancient Greek music, 22
    tuning systems and, 114
*In the Sweet Bye and Bye*, 598
intonation (for psalm tone), 39, 41
Introit, 33, 34, 40–41, 42–43, 44
*intuonarumori*, 563
Inuit culture, 664
inventions, 555
inversion, 296, 552–53, 558–59
*Ionisation* (Varèse), 608

*"Io parto" e non più dissi* (Gesualdo), 136
*Iphigenia in Brooklyn* (Schickele), 661
*Iphigénie en Aulide* (Gluck), 328
*Iphigénie en Tauride* (Gluck), 328
*Ippolito ed Aricia* (Traetta), 327
Ireland, 34
Isaac, Henricus (Heinrich), 96, 121–22, 124, 147, 558
Isabella, queen of Castille and Aragon, 141
Isenheim Altarpiece (Grünewald), *586*
Islam, 9, 14
*Isle joyeuse, L'* (Debussy), 538–39, 542, 547
*Isle of the Dead, The* (Rachmaninov), 545
isorhythm, 72, 73, 74–75, 76, 78, 100–101, 102, 105, 108
*Israel in Egypt* (Handel), 311
*istitutioni harmoniche, Le* (Zarlino), 115, 133, 134, 157
*Italiana in Algeri, L'* (Rossini), 466–67
Italian music. *See also* Italian opera
  eighteenth-century, 279–85, 331
  seventeenth-century, 177, 195–96, 199–201, 217–19, 222–27, 245, 253–62
  sixteenth-century, 4, 129–37, 151, 153–56
  trecento, 80–84
  twentieth-century, 563, 564, 637–38
Italian opera
  eighteenth-century, 281, 304, 305–9, 319–28, 324, 325, 351–52, 355
  in England, 304
  ensemble scenes in, 473
  forerunners of, 183–86
  in Germany, 240
  nineteenth-century, 462, 463, 469–80, 492, 515–17
  opera buffa, 319–21, 328, 368–69, 371, 471, 480
  opera seria, 322–25, 351–52, 355, 369, 371
  reform of, 325, 327–28
  scene structure in, 471–72, 479, 517
  seventeenth-century, 186–94, 222–26
  verismo, 515–16
*Italian* Symphony (Mendelssohn), 424–26, 436
Italy
  early chant repertories in, 27–28
  eighteenth-century, 273
  medieval, 11, 17, 80
  nationalism in, 400, 493, 507
  Renaissance, 91–93, 116
  seventeenth-century, 164, 165–66, 168, 177
Ite, missa est, 33, 35
Ives, Charles, 594, 601–5, *602*
  biography of, 602
  Copland's championship of, 610
  Debussy's influence on, 541
  experimental music of, 601–3, 605
  influence of, 638
Ives, George, 601, 602

Jabach Altarpiece (Dürer), *141*
Jacopo da Bologna, 81–82
Jacques de Liège, 77
Jacquet de La Guerre, Élisabeth-Claude, 248, 249, 250–53
  biography of, 249
Janáček, Leoš, 541, 544, 547
*Jane Eyre* (Brontë), 407
Janequin, Clément, 137–38
Janissary music, 357, 466–67
*Ja nus hons pris* (Richard I), 50
Jaufré Rudel, 52
jazz, 522, 534, 599
  Debussy's influence on, 541
  Krenek's use of, 583
  Milhaud's use of, 565
  post–World War II, 626–28
  pre–World War II, 618–23
  Ravel's use of, 565
  Satie's use of, 563
  Stravinsky's use of, 567
  "swing" effect in, 229
  third-stream, 636
  Weill's use of, 584
*Jazz Singer, The* (film), 617
*Jeanie with the Light Brown Hair* (Foster), 597–98
Jenner, Edward, 401
*Jenůfa* (Janáček), 544
*Jephte* (Carissimi), 201
Jerome, Saint, 23
Jesus of Nazareth, 27
*Jeux* (Debussy), 540
*Jeux d'eau* (Ravel), 541–42
Jewish music, 27, 565
Joachim, Joseph, *447*
Joan of Arc, *13*, 14, 94, 100
John Chrysostom, Saint, 23
John of Luxembourg, king of Bohemia, 76
Johnson, Philip, 660, *660*
Johnson, Samuel, 322, *358*
Jolson, Al, 617
Jommelli, Nicolò, 325, 327
jongleurs, 47, *47*
*Jonny spielt auf* (Krene), 583
Jonson, Ben, 175
Joplin, Scott, 613–14, 619
Joseph II, Holy Roman emperor, 271, 339
*Joshua* (Handel), 311
Josquin des Prez, 95, 96, 113, 117, 121–26, *124*, 147
  biography of, 124
  chansons of, 122–23
  influence of, 123
  Masses of, 119, 125–26, *127*
  motets of, 123–25
Joyce, James, 527, 529, 532
*Joyssance vous donneray* (Sermisy), *138*
juba, 613
*Jubilemus, exultemus*, 57, *58*
jubilus, 41
Judaism, 27, 30, 425
*Judas Maccabaeus* (Handel), 311

*Judentum in der Musik, Das* (Wagner), 489
*Judith Slaying Holofernes*, *172, 172*
Julius III, Pope, 153, *154*
Junker, Carl Ludwig, 379
*Jupiter* Symphony (Mozart), 363–64
just intonation, 639
Justus of Ghent, *114*

*Kalevala* epic, 545
*Kammermusik* (Hindemith), 585
Kant, Immanuel, 271, 274
*Kát'a Kabanová* (Janáček), 544
Keats, John, 403
Keiser, Reinhard, 240, 305
Kennedy, Robert F., 525
Kepler, Johannes, 164, 170
Kern, Jerome, 614, 615, 617, 623
kettledrums, *211*, 265
keyboard music. *See also* harpsichord music; organ music
  of C. P. E. Bach, 333
  of J. S. Bach, 292, 294–97
  eighteenth-century, 278
  of Handel, 311–12
  of Haydn, 350–51
  of Scarlatti, 329–31
  seventeenth-century, 209–10, *210*, 213–16, 244–53
  sixteenth-century, 144
*Khovanshchina* (Musorgsky), 508
Kilburne, George Goodwin, *418*
*Kinderscenen* (Schumann), 429
*Kindertotenlieder* (Mahler), 499–500
*Kind of Blue* (Davis album), 628
King, Martin Luther, Jr., 525
*King and I, The* (Rodgers), 616
*King Kong* (film), 617
Kinsky, Ferdinand Johann Nepomuk, 375
Kirchenlied. *See* chorales
Kirchner, Ernst Ludwig, 550
kithara, 20, *20*, 207, 497
kitharode, 20
*Klangfarbenmelodie*, 559, 636
*Kleine geistliche Konzerte* (Schütz), 204
Klimt, Gustav, 497, 498
Klöber, August von, *391*
*Knaben Wunderhorn, Des* (Mahler), 498
*Knickerbocker Holiday* (Weill), 584
oxville: Summer of 1915 (Barber), 635
Koch, Heinrich Christoph, 366
Köchel, Ludwig von, 354
Korean War, 523
Korngold, Erich Wolfgang, 617
*Koro Sutro, La* (Harrison), 640
koto, 609, 640
Krenek, Ernst, 583, 586
Krushchev, Nikita, 661
Kubrick, Stanley, 646
*Kullervo* (Sibelius), 545
*Kunst der Fuge, Die* (Bach), 298, 302, 303, 361
Kyrie, 33, 34–35, 38, 41–42, 56

La Cave, François Morellon, *281*
*Lady in the Dark* (Weill), 584
*Lady Macbeth of the Mtsensk District*
    (Shostakovich), 589, 591
*Lagrime mie* (Strozzi), 197–98, 226
lai, 78
Lalande, Michel-Richard de, 235
Lamartine, Alphonse-Marie-Louis de, 443
Lambert, Michel, 231
Lamentations, 151
*Lamento della ninfa* (Monteverdi), 196–97
Landi, Stefano, 192
Landini, Francesco, 72, 81, *81*, 82–84, *84*
    biography of, 84
Lange, Joseph, *354*
*langue d'oc*, 47
*langue d'oïl*, 47
Lansky, Paul, 651
la Pouplinière, Alexandre-Jean-Joseph le
        Riche de, 287, 288
Laprade, Pierre, *505*
La Scala (Milan), *475*, 476
Lasso, Orlando di, 134, 148, 156, 158–60,
        *160*, 217, 438
Last Supper, 27, 32, *34*, 65
Latin American music, 214, 252, 606–7,
        635–36
*Laudate Dominum* (Manchicourt), *119*
laude, 81, 129
Laurents, Arthur, 616
Lawes, William, 235
*Laws* (Plato), 14
lead sheet, 628
League of Composers, 608
*Lebe wohl!* (Wolf), 495
Le Brun, Charles, 169, *169*
Le Corbusier, 641, 644
Le Franc, Martin, 100, 101, 102, *103*
Lehár, Franz, 617
Lehmann, Henri Charles, *440*
Leipzig
    Bach in, 290, 291, 294, 298–302
    printing in, 402
    public concerts in, 359, 417, 425
leitmotives, 484–85, 487–88, 489,
        500–501, 504, 512–13, 516, 555
Le Jeune, Claude, 149
Lenbach, Franz von, *485*
Lenten season, 32
Lenya, Lotte, 584, *584*
Leo III, Pope, *8*
Leonardo da Vinci, 94, 96, 185
Leoncavallo, Ruggero, 515
Léonin, 57, 58–61
    biography of, 62
*Leonore* (Beethoven), 382–83
*Leonore* Overtures (Beethoven), 386
Lesser Doxology, 39, 41
lessons (Bible readings), 32
liberal arts, 25, 26
*Liber astrologiae*, 26
*liberazione di Ruggiero dall'isola d'Alcina, La*
        (Caccini), 191, *192*

*Liber de arte contrapuncti* (Tinctoris), 115
*Liber decimus quartus XIX . . .* collection, *119*
librettos
    American, 612–13
    concerns of nineteenth-century, 462
    French, 232, 328, 464
    German, 322, 382, 480, 483, 485, 503–4
    Italian, 189–90, 192, 274, 322–23, 325,
        327, 368–69, 475, 479
    opera seria, 322–23, 325
    oratorio, 201, 310–11
    Russian, 505
    vernacular comic opera, 321
Lichnowsky, Karl von, 375
lieder
    of Mahler, 497–500
    nineteenth-century, 408, 409, 410–11
    Renaissance, 134, 147, 148
    of Schoenberg, 549
    of Schubert, 412–15, 597
    of Schumann, 430, 431
    of Webern, 558
    of Wolf, 494–95, 549, 598
*Lieder eines fahrenden Gesellen* (Mahler),
        497–98
*Lieder ohne Worte* (Mendelssohn), 427–29
*Lied von der Erde, Das* (Mahler), 500
*Lieutenant Kijé* (Prokofiev), 588
*Life for the Czar, A* (Glinka), 505
Ligeti, György, 646
*Lindenbaum, Der* (Schubert), 412, 414
Lindsay, Vachel, 603–4
Linley, Thomas, 318–19
Linley sisters, 318, *319*
*Linz* Symphony (Mozart), 363
lira viol, 185
Liszt, Franz, 433, 439–44, *440*, *442*
    Beethoven's Gypsy influence viewed by,
        467
    Beethoven's influence on, 438–39
    biography of, 440
    church music of, 490
    as conductor, 440, 460
    influence of, 444, 469, 502, 506, 513,
        542, 546, 549
    orchestral music of, 408, 442–44, 500
    as pianist, 402, 434, 435–36, 439–41
    piano music of, 411, 441–42
    program music viewed by, 439
    style of, 439, 441
    Wagner and, 485
literature
    ancient Greek, 20
    eighteenth-century, 268, 271, 272,
        274–75, 275, 318, 335
    Greek, 92, 183–84
    medieval, 13, 15–16, 72, 80
    nineteenth-century, 318, 397, 403–5,
        406–7
    Renaissance, 91, 95, 183–84
    seventeenth-century, 166, 170–71, 230
    twentieth-century, 522, 527, 529,
        532–33, 541

*Little Johnny Jones* (Cohan), 614–15
liturgical dramas, 35, 43, 44, 183
liturgy, 27–28, 30, 32. *See also* Gregorian
        chant and liturgy
    Anglican, 152
    Mass, 33–35, 147
    Office, 32, 33
    standardization of, 19
Liturgy of the Eucharist, 33, 35
Liturgy of the Word, 33, 35
Lloyd Webber, Andrew, 615
*Lob der Thränen* (Schubert), 413
Lobkowitz, Joseph Franz Maximilian, 375
*Lohengrin* (Wagner), 440
Lomax, John and Alan, 610
London. *See also* English music
    J. C. Bach in, 335–37, 355
    Handel in, 304, 305–13
    Haydn in, 340, 342, 346–47
    medieval, 11
    opera houses in, 165, 306, 324
    printing in, 119, 402
    public concerts in, 239–40, 358
    royal chapel in, 160
*London* Symphonies (Haydn), 342, 344,
        346–47, 363
Longfellow, Henry Wadsworth, 459
Longhi, Antonio, *306*
*Lord Nelson Mass* (Haydn), 352
Lord's Supper. *See* Eucharist
Lorenzetti, Ambrogio, *93*
*Lost in the Stars* (Weill), 584
Louis I the Pious, Emperor, 10
Louis VII, king of France, 50
Louis XIV, king of France, 164, 166, 222,
        230, *230*, 235, 248, 249, 264, 268
Louis XV, king of France, 268, 286
Louis XVI, king of France, 273
Louvain, 119
*Love for Three Oranges, The* (Prokofiev), 588
*Loves of Paris and Helen, The* (David), 404,
        *405*
love songs
    fourteenth-century, 72, 78
    Minnesinger, 50
    troubadour and trouvère, 47–49, 55
Low Countries, 112–27
    Calvinism in, 149
Lübeck, 242, 245, 293
*Lucia di Lammermoor* (Donizetti), 474
*Ludus tonalis* (Hindemith), 586
Ludwig, King of Bavaria, 484
*Luisa Miller* (Verdi), 478
Lully, Jean-Baptiste, 181, *231*, 335
    biography of, 231
    Couperin's tribute to, 286
    influence of, 288
    motets of, 235
    operas of, 230–35, 264, 328
    overtures of, 229, 232–33
*Lulu* (Berg), 556
lute music, 137, 209–10, 211–12, 248–49
*Lute Player, The* (Caravaggio), 142, *142*

lutes, 4, *81*, *142*, 144, 180, *208*, *209*, *210*, 211, 246
lute songs, 129, 140–41
Luther, Martin, 95, 113, 146, 147, 150, 300, 425
Lutheran Church, 146, 147
Lutheran church music. *See* church music, Lutheran
Lutosławski, Witold, 650
*Lux aeterna* (Ligeti), 646
Luzzaschi, Luzzasco, 135
Lyon, 95, 119, *148*
lyres, 4, 6, 20
*Lyrical Intermezzo* (Heine), 431
lyric opera, 468
*Lyric Suite* (Berg), 556

*Macbeth* (Strauss), 500
MacDowell, Edward, 600
Machaut, Guillaume de, 72, 74–80, *76*, *80*, 86
    biography of, 76
    Mass of, 73, 75–78, 105–6
    motets of, 74–75, 103
*Madama Butterfly* (Puccini), 467, 516
*Madras* Symphony (Cowell), 640
*Madrigali guerrieri et amorosi* (Monteverdi), 195–97
madrigalisms, 134–35
*madrigali spirituali*, 134
madrigals
    concerted, 194–97
    seventeenth-century Italian, 168, 174–75, 178, 179–80, 181, 184, 1862, 190, 194–97
    sixteenth-century English, 129, 138–39
    sixteenth-century Italian, 129, 130–37, 142, 144, 153
trecento, 81–82
Maelzel, Johann Nepomuk, 384
Maeterlinck, Maurice, 541
*Magic Flute, The. See Zauberflöte, Die*
Magnificat, 150–51, 299
*Magnus liber organi*, 59, 61, 62
Magritte, René, 528
Mahler, Gustav, 495–500, 536
    biography of, 496
    as conductor, 496
    influence of, 495, 547, 551, 554
    lieder of, 497–500
    reception of, 559
    Schoenberg and, 548
    Shostakovich's quote of, 591
    symphonies of, 495, 497–99, 521
Mähler, Willibrord Joseph, *377*
*Makropulos Affair, The* (Janáček), 544
*Malade imaginaire, Le* (Molière), 232
Malfatti family, *383*
Mallarmé, Stéphane, 527, 532, 539, 542
*Mamelles de Tirésias, Les* (Poulenc), 566
Manchicourt, Pierre de, *119*
mandolin, *254*
*Manifesto of the Communist Party* (Marx), 406
*Manitou* (Schafer), 664

Mannheim, 332–33, 410
*Manon Lescaut* (Puccini), 516
Mantua, 114, 116, 129, 131, 135, 166, 190
manuscript production, medieval, 37
Manzoni, Alessandro, 406, 490
*Maple Leaf Rag* (Joplin), 613–14, 619
maps
    ancient Near East, *4*
    Bach cities, *292*
    Burgundian possessions, *99*
    diffusion of Christianity, *31*
    Europe, 1815–1848, *398*
    Europe, mid-1900s, *579*
    Europe, mid-fourteenth century, *9*
    European opera houses, nineteenth-century, *463*
    Europe ca. 1610, *165*
    Europe during the Cold War, *523*
    Holy Roman Empire, *36*
    Italian violin centers, *253*
    Mozart cities, *356*
    Occitan/French medieval linguistic boundary, *48*
    Renaissance music training centers, *96*
    Roman Empire, *7*
    Vienna as cultural center, *360*
    Western Europe ca. 1500, *113*
Marcello, Benedetto, 324
marches, 597, 601, 602
Marenzio, Luca, 134–35, 174
Marian antiphons, 42, 108, 150
Marian veneration, 52, 69, 75
Maria Theresa, Holy Roman empress, 269, 271, 324
Marie Antoinette, queen of France, 273, 327, 346, 419
Marini, Biagio, 219, 254
Marino, Giambattista, 166, 170, 172, 192
*Marriage of Figaro, The* (Beaumarchais), 272–73, 274
*Marriage of Figaro, The* (Mozart). *See nozze di Figaro, Le*
*Marriage of Mercury and Philology, The* (Martianus Capella), 25
*Marteau sans maître* (Boulez), 637
Martenot, Maurice, 640
Martianus Capella, 25
Martin, Jean-Baptiste, 264
Martini, Giovanni Battista, 335, 355
*Martyrdom of Saint Sebastian, The* (Debussy), 540
Marx, Karl, 406
Marxism, 400
Mary I, queen of England, 151, 152
Mascagni, Pietro, 515
Masons. *See* Freemasonry
masques, 175, 191, 235
Mass
    experience of, 34–35
    Jewish liturgical influences on, 27
    liturgy of, 32–35
    Ordinary of, 33, 35, 41–42, 56, 75–76
    organ played during, 144

Proper of, 33, 35, 40–41, 56
recitation formulas for, 37–38
structure of, 35
Masses. *See also entries under Messe and Missa;* Requiem Masses
    of Bach, 302, 303
    of Beach, 601
    of Beethoven, 389
    of Bruckner, 490
    Burgundian, 103, 105–10
    cantus firmus or tenor, 106–8, 120, 154
    cyclic, 75–76, 120, 126
    of Dunstable, 100–101
    English, 150–51, 160
    fifteenth-century, 98
    Franco-Flemish, 117, 119, 120–21, 125–26
    German, 147
    of Haydn, 352
    of Liszt, 490
    of Machaut, 73, 105–6
    motto, 106
    naming, 120–21
    organ, 215
    of Palestrina, 153, 154–56
    paraphrase, 126, 154
    parody, 126, 151, 154
    of Poulenc, 566
    sixteenth-century, 151, 158
    trecento, 83
Massine, Léonide, 563
mass media, 531, 534
mass songs, 587
Master of the Female Half-Lengths, *138*
Master of the Platerias Portal, *57*
mathematics and music, 21, 22, 24, 25, 26, 44, 170, 364
*Mathis der Maler* (Hindemith), 585, 586
Matins, 32, 152
Mattheson, Johann, 311
*á vlast* (Smetana), 444, 512
Mayer, Marcelle, *565*
*Mazeppa* (Liszt), 443
mazurkas, 432, 434, 507, 546
McPhee, Colin, 639
Meck, Nadezhda von, 454
Medici family, 92, 96, 97, 116, 122, 131, 183, 187, 254, 304
medieval drama. *See* liturgical drama; musical theater
meditative music, 631
*Meerestille und glückliche Fahrt* (Mendelssohn), 426
Mei, Girolamo, 184–85
*Meistersinger, Die* (Wagner), 484
melismas, 37, 38, 41, 42, 43, 56, 57, 59, 78, 82, 104, 151
Mellan, Claude, *215*
melody
    in ancient Greek music, 19
    in chant, 32, 33, 37–38, 39, 40, 41, 56, 59, 61
    in chorales, 146

in Counter-Reformation music, 154–55
in eighteenth-century music, 278, 285, 288, 305–6, 316, 325, 347
in Franco-Flemish music, 127
in Minnelieder, 50
in monody, 185
in nineteenth-century music, 402, 412, 415, 426, 441, 472–74, 477, 480, 488, 508, 515
in seventeenth-century opera, 191
in sixteenth-century chansons, 137
in sixteenth-century English music, 151
in troubadour and trouvère songs, 49
in twentieth-century music, 517, 545–46, 549, 552–53, 580, 581, 589, 628, 654, 655
*melos*, 19
memory, performing from, 4, 30, 33, 41, 43, 54, 60, 81, 141, 206, 207
Mendelssohn, Fanny, 425, *428*
Mendelssohn, Felix, 424–29, *425*
   Bach Passion revived by, 303
   biography of, 425
   chamber music of, 411
   as conductor, 410, 417, 425, 460
   oratorios of, 490–91
   orchestral music of, 424–27, 432
   piano music of, 411, 427–29
   watercolor by, *424*
Mendelssohn, Moses, 425
mensuration, 74–75
*Menuet antique* (Ravel), 542
Menzel, Adolph von, *332, 447*
*Mer, La* (Debussy), 539–40
Mercier, Philippe, *304*
*Merry Wives of Windsor, The* (Shakespeare), 480
*Mescalin Mix* (Riley), 653
Mesopotamia, 4
*Messe de Nostre Dame* (Machaut), 75–76, 77, 78
Messiaen, Olivier, 541, 630–33, *631,* 636, 641
*Messiah* (Handel), 310–11, 352
*Metamorphoses* (Ovid), 642
*Metastaseis* (Xenakis), 643–44
Metastasio (Pietro Trapassi), 322–23, 325, 360
metric modulation, 638
metronome, 384–85, *385*
Mexican art, 529, 533, *606, 607*
Mexican music, 607, 611
Meyerbeer, Giacomo
   operas of, 462, 464, 467, 478
   Wagner's attack on, 489
Michelangelo Buonarroti, 94, 96, 113, 168, *169*
Michelet, Jules, 89
microtonal music, 563
Middle Ages, 30–87. *See also specific composers and topics*
   Ars nova in, 72–80
   astrology in, 26

chant in, 4, 27–28, 31–44
cultural-historical context, 8–17, 71–72
defined, 8
early Christian Church, 23–28
education in, 11–13
music theory and practice in, 44–46
non-extant music from, 28–29
polyphony in, 54–70
secular song in, 46–52
timeline for, 51
trecento music in, 80–84
middle classes
   eighteenth century, 269, 272, 277–78, 311, 358
   nineteenth century, 400, 401, 402, 410, 418, 463, 464, 600
   seventeenth century, 165, 239–40
   twentieth century, 523, 525
MIDI, 652
*Midsummer Night's Dream, A* (Shakespeare), 238, 425
*Midsummer Night's Dream* Overture (Mendelssohn), 426, 435
Mielich, Hans, *160*
Mighty Handful, the, 506–12
*Mikrokosmos* (Bartók), 579
Milan
   medieval, 11
   opera in, *475,* 476
   orchestras in, 260
   Renaissance, 96, 116, 124
Milhaud, Darius, 465, 534, 563, 565, 565–66, 592
*Military* Symphony (Haydn), 347
Miller, Glenn, 623
*Mille regretz* (Josquin des Prez?), 122–23
Mills College, 534
Milton, John, 26, 166, 171, 352
minimal art, 653
minimalism, 651–53
minims, 74
Minnesingers, 50
Minnion, John, *546, 607*
minstrels, 47, 100
minstrel shows, 601
minuet and trio form, 345, 347
minuets, *251,* 253, 331, 384
*Miraculous Mandarin, The* (Bartók), 579
*Miroirs* (Ravel), 542
*Misérables, Les* (Hugo), 407
*Missa Ave maris stella* (Josquin des Prez), *127*
*Missa Ave regina caelorum* (Du Fay), 108
*Missa brevis* (Britten), 633
*Missa cuiusvis toni* (Ockeghem), 121
*Missa De plus en plus* (Ockeghem), 120
*Missa Hercules dux Ferrariae* (Josquin des Prez), 126
*Missa in angustiis* (Haydn), 352
*Missa in tempore belli* (Haydn), 352
*Missa L'homme armé super voces musicales* (Josquin des Prez), 125–26
*Missa Malheur me bat* (Josquin des Prez), 126

*Missa mi-mi* (Ockeghem), 121
*Missa Pange lingua* (Josquin des Prez), 126
*Missa Papae Marcelli* (Palestrina), 154–56
*Missa prolationum* (Ockeghem), 121
*Missa Se la face ay pale* (Du Fay), 106, 108–10, 120
*Missa sine nomine*, 121
*Missa solemnis* (Beethoven), 389, 391, 393–94, 464
missionaries, 8, 27, 33, 34
modal jazz, 628
modal music, 512, 581, 656
modernism, 531–34
Modern Jazz Quartet, 628
modes, Byzantine, 27
modes, church, 27, 31, 45, 50, 114, 120–21, 181
modes, Greek, 7, 21–22, 45, 114, 115
modes, rhythmic, 58, 60–61, 62, 70
modulation, 289
Molière (Jean-Baptiste Poquelin), 170, 231, *232*
*Moments musicaux* (Schubert), 416
monasticism, 8, 14, 27, 28, 32, 37, 43, 55
Monet, Claude, *526,* 527–28, 533
Monn, Matthias, 333
monochord, 24
monody, 30, 31, 142, 177, 185, 189, 199, 201, 219
monophony (texture). *See also* Gregorian chant; texture
   in ancient Greek music, 19
   in medieval music, 30, 54–55, 73, 78, 81
Monte, Philippe de, 134
Monteverdi, Claudio, 132, *190*
   biography of, 190
   church music of, 202
   *concitato genere* of, 173, 195
   madrigals of, 136–37, 168, 174–75, 178, 179–80, 184, 185, 194–97
   operas of, 176, 189–91, 193, 225, 228, 229
   Schütz influenced by, 204, 205
   Vespers of, 201
   Wert's influence on, 134
Monteverdi, Giulio Cesare, 178
*Mont Sainte-Victoire* (Cézanne), 527, 528, 533
*Mood Indigo* (Ellington), 625
Moog, Robert, 641
*Moonlight* Sonata (Beethoven), 387
morals and music, 4, 20, 21–22, 23, 24, 27, 323
*Moravian Folk Songs* (Janáček), *544*
Moravians, 595–96
mordents, 258, 326, 512
More, Thomas, 95
Mörike, Eduard, 494–95
Moritz, landgrave of Hesse, 204
Morley, Thomas, 139–41
Morton, Jelly Roll, 619, 620
Morzin, Karl Joseph Franz, Count, 340
Moscow Conservatory, 506, 545

motets. *See also* motets, thirteenth-century
  Ars nova, 71, 72, 73–75
  of Bruckner, 490
  Burgundian, 104
  changing meanings of, 102, 103
  chorale, 148, 204
  fifteenth-century, 98, 101–2
  Franco-Flemish, 123–25
  French, 235
  isorhythmic, 73, 74–75, 100, 102, 105
  of Machaut, 74–75
  of Poulenc, 566
  seventeenth-century, 178, 201, 202, 204
  sixteenth-century, 151, 158–60
motets, thirteenth-century, 55, 64–69
*other of Us All, The* (Thomson), 613
motto Masses, 106
*Motu proprio* (Pius X), 490
*Movements* (Stravinsky), 577
Mozarabic chant, 28
Mozart, Constanze Weber, 354, 370
Mozart, Leopold, 354, 355, 357, 362n, 370, 370, 372
Mozart, Nannerl, 354, 355, 357, 370
Mozart, Wolfgang Amadeus, 290, 339, 354, 354–73, 357, 370
  J. C. Bach's influence on, 335–36, 355
  J. S. Bach's influence on, 303, 361
  Beethoven influenced by, 376
  biography of, 354
  birthplace of, 360
  church music of, 372
  father and, 370
  Handel's influence on, 361
  Haydn's influence on, 340, 355, 361
  influence of, 391, 432, 438, 470, 498, 547
  international style of, 493
  Janissary music imitated by, 466
  as Mason, 272, 371
  nineteenth-century views of, 397
  operas of, 272, 274, 355, 357, 367–69, 371, 462, 464, 471, 503
  orchestral instrumentation of, 423
  Salzburg years, 355–57
  serenades and divertimenti of, 357
  significance of, 372–73
  sonatas of, 331, 355–57, 361, 466
  string quartets of, 349, 361–62, 416
  style of, 267, 278
  symphonies of, 362–65
  teachers of, 355
  Vienna years of, 357, 361–72
  Wagenseil's influence on, 333
MP3 players, 575, 652
*Much Ado about Nothing* (Shakespeare), 421, 468
*Muette de Portici, La* (Auber), 465
Muffat, Georg, 264
Muhammad, 9, 14
Mühlhausen, 291, 292–93
Müller, Wilhelm, 414
Munch, Edvard, 528, 529, 533

Munich, 204, 324
*Murder, Hope of Women* (Hindemith), 584
*Music* (Klimt), 497, 498
*Musica enchiriadis*, 54, 56
musica ficta, 86–87, 155
*musica humana*, 24, 26
*musica instrumentalis*, 24
*Musical Offering, A* (Bach). *See Musikalisches Opfer*
musical theater
  Greek, 183–84
  medieval drama, 31, 35, 43, 44, 183
  Renaissance, 107, 183
  twentieth-century, 407, 584, 594, 614–16, 617, 623–24, 639
*musica mundana*, 24, 26. *See also* "music of the spheres"
*Musica transalpine* anthology, 118, 138–39
music drama. *See under* Wagner, Richard
*Music for Strings, Percussion and Celesta* (Bartók), 578, 579, 580–83
*Music for the Magic Theater* (Rochberg), 660
*Music for the Royal Fireworks* (Handel), 304, 305, 312
*Music for the Theatre* (Copland), 610
*Music for Wilderness Lake* (Schafer), 664, 666
*Musicians* (Timm), 210
*Musicians in the Orchestra* (Degas), 423
*Musicircus* (Cage), 649
*Music Lesson, The* (Vermeer), 252
*Music of Changes* (Cage), 647–48, 650
Music of La Grande Écurie, 262, 264
"music of the spheres," 22, 26
musicology, 438, 448, 557, 561
*Music Party, The* (Watteau), 269
music theory. *See* theory, music
*Musikalische Exequien* (Schütz), 204
*Musikalisches Opfer* (Bach), 298, 302
musique concrète, 640–41
Musorgsky, Modest, 506, 508–10, 509
  block construction of, 509, 544, 546
  influence of, 538, 540, 606
  instrumental music of, 510
  operas of, 508–9
Mussolini, Benito, 522
*My bonny lass she smileth* (Morley), 139

*Nabucco* (Verdi), 475, 476
*Nach Bach* (Rochberg), 660
*Nachtstücke* (Schumann), 429
Nádherný, V. E., 458
Naples, 177, 470
Napoleon. *See* Bonaparte, Napoleon
Napoleon III, emperor of France, 468
*Napoleon's Consecration* (David), 273
Narváez, Luys de, 212
nationalism and national styles
  in eighteenth-century music, 278
  in nineteenth-century music, 398, 400, 402–3, 432, 438, 442, 457–59, 474–75, 480, 493, 504–13, 600, 605
  in seventeenth-century music, 222

  in twentieth-century music, 543, 544–45, 568, 577–83, 606–7, 611–12, 630, 635–36, 658
*Nations, Les* (Couperin), 286
Native American music, 594
  Beach's use of, 601
  Chávez's use of, 607
  Dvořák's use of, 459, 604
  MacDowell's use of, 600
  Rameau's impressions of, 466
Nazari, Bartolommeo, 309
Nazism, 489, 522, 578, 583, 584, 586–87, 617, 638
NBC Symphony Orchestra, 531
Near East, ancient, 4, 6, 18
  map of, 4
Neefe, Christian Gottlob, 376
neo-Baroque music, 573, 585, 606
Neoclassicism (in art), 404, 468
Neoclassicism (in music), 564–65, 566, 567, 573, 576, 606, 630, 663
neo-Romanticism, 585–86, 646, 652, 660, 662–63
neotonal music, 576, 585
Nero, Roman emperor, 18
Netherlandish music. *See* Franco-Flemish music
Netherlands, the
  medieval, 11
  seventeenth-century, 164
*Neue Sachlichkeit. See* New Objectivity
*Neue Zeitschrift für Musik*, 430
neumes, 46. *See also* notation
New England Conservatory, 600
*New England Psalm Singer*, 595
Newman, John Henry, 513
*New Music* (journal), 608, 609
*New Musical Resources* (Cowell), 609
New Objectivity, 583–85
New Orleans jazz, 620–22, 628
Newton, Isaac, 164, 170, 178, 290
New World. *See* Americas, colonies in; *specific countries*
*New World* Symphony (Dvořák), 458, 459, 601
New York
  Broadway musicals in, 584, 614–16
  Dvořák in, 458, 507
  Tchaikovsky in, 454
  Tin Pan Alley in, 598
New York Philharmonic, 616
Nicomachus, 24, 25
Nietzsche, Friedrich, 397, 406, 502
*Nightmare, The* (Fuseli), 402
*Night on Bald Mountain* (Musorgsky), 510
*Night Traffic* (Lansky), 651
Nijinsky, Vaslav, 532, 567, 571, 572
nineteenth-century culture and politics, 398–403
nineteenth-century music, 397–519
  American, 596–602
  art songs and lieder, 410–11, 412–15, 431, 494–95, 497–500, 514–15

church music, 393–94, 464, 489–91, 492, 494
  general trends, 408–9
  instrumental, 380–82, 383–89, 391–93, 394–95, 411, 415–36, 439–61, 494, 495–502, 505–7, 510–15
  opera, 382–83, 455–56, 459, 462–89, 501, 503–4, 505–6, 508–9, 511, 515–17
  oratorios, 427, 490–91, 512–13
*Niño, El* (Adams), 656
Nixon, Richard, 525
*Nixon in China* (Adams), 656, 657
nocturnes, 432, 514, 546
*Nocturnes* (Debussy), 539, 540
noise, 563
*Non avrà ma' pieta* (Landini), 82–83
nondiegetic music, 617
Nono, Luigi, 631
*Non sofre Santa María*, 52
non-Western musics, 525, 531, 575, 609, 639–40
*Norfolk Rhapsodies* (Vaughan Williams), 543
*Norma* (Bellini), 473
Norman Conquest, 11, 55, 69
North, Roger, 239
North Atlantic Treaty Organization (NATO), 523
Norwegian music, 507, 512
notation
  Babylonian, 4
  bar lines, 180
  of big band music, 622
  chant, 28, 30, 33–34
  colored, 75, 84, *85*
  figured bass, 180–81, 182
  graphic, 644–45, 649
  indeterminacy and, 650–51
  medieval, 9, 30, 46–47, 49, 54, 57–58, 60, 72, 74–75, 84, 85, 128
  of ornaments, 229
  proportional, 648
  of recitatives, 288
  score, 180
  tablature, 140, 212, 216
  of unmeasured preludes, 251
  white, *118*
*notes inégales*, 229
Notker Balbulus, 43
*Notre-Dame de Paris* (Hugo), 407
Notre Dame polyphony, 12, 54, 55, 58–66, 67, 69, 73, 74
*Noye's Fludde* (Britten), 633
*nozze di Figaro, Le* (Mozart), 368–69, 471
*Nuages gris* (Liszt), 442
*Nuits d'été, Les* (Berlioz), 421
*Nun komm, der Heiden Heiland* (Bach), 300, *301*, 302
*Nun komm, der Heiden Heiland* (Luther), 300
*nuove musiche, Le* (Caccini), 185–86, 189, 194

Nuremberg, 119
*Nutcracker, The* (Tchaikovsky), 454–55, 626

oblique organum, 56
oboe, 264
Obrecht, Jacob, 96, 121–22, *122*
*Observations on the Florid Song* (Tosi), 326
occasional music. *See* ceremonial music
Ockeghem, Jean de, 95, 103, 108, *117*, 121
  biography of, 117
  chansons of, 121
  Masses of, 117, 120–21
  pupils of, 121–22
*Octandre* (Varèse), 608
octatonic scales, 511, 538, 546, 566, 568, 571, 576
*Ode for St. Cecilia's Day* (Purcell), 239, 394
*Ode to Joy* (Schiller), 272, 394
*Odhecaton. See Harmonice musices odhecaton*
*Odyssey* (Homer), 20
*Oedipus—a Music-Dance Drama* (Partch), 639
Offenbach, Jacques, 468
Offertory, 33, 35, 41
Office, 32, *33*
  chants for, 39–40
  polyphonic settings of, 56, 59, 104
  recitation formulas for, 37–38
*Offrandes* (Varèse), 608
*Of Thee I Sing* (Gershwin), 623–24
*Oh! Susannah* (Foster), 597
*Oklahoma!* (Rodgers), 616
Oklahoma City bombing, 525
"Old Hundredth," 149
Old Roman chant, 28
*O lieber Herre Gott* (Schütz), 204
Oliver, Joe "King," *619*, 620, 621
*Ol' Man River* (Kern), 615
*O magnum mysterium* (Victoria), 158
ondes martenot, 640
*114 Songs* (Ives), 602
*Ongaku* (Cowell), 640
*On the Beautiful in Music* (Hanslick), 439
*On the Origin of Species* (Darwin), 406
*On the Town* (Bernstein), 616
*On the Transmigration of Souls* (Adams), 657
opéra bouffe, 468
opera buffa, 278, 319–21, 328, 368–69, 371, 471, 480
opéra comique, 321, 360, 465, 468, 474
opera houses. *See* theaters and opera houses, public
*Opera intitulata Fontegara* (Ganassi), *209*
Opera of the Nobility, 309
operas. *See also* Italian opera; *specific composers and operas*
  American, 611–13, *613*, 623, 655, 656, 661
  Argentine, 636
  choruses in, 236, 289, 328, 464, 475
  Czech, 459, 544
  eighteenth-century, 268, 278, 280, 281, 287, 288–90, 304, 305–9, 319–28

eighteenth-century reforms, 278, 325, 327–28
  English, 236–38, 567, 633–34, 660
  French, 230–35, 262, 287, 288–90, 328, 404, 421, 463, 464–65, 468–69, 540–41, 566, 631
  German, 222, 240, 371, 382–83, 464, 480, 482–89, 501, 503–4, 551, 554–56, 583–85
  Hungarian, 579
  Italian (*See* Italian opera)
  nineteenth-century, 404, 421, 455–56, 459, 462–89, 501, 503–4, 505–6, 508–9, 511
  overtures to, 236, 262, 288, 327, 331, 383 (*See also* French overture; sinfonia)
  permanent repertory of, 462
  Polish, 646, 662
  "rescue" genre, 367–68
  Russian, 455–56, 508–9, 511, 588, 589, 591
operas
  scene complexes, 308
  seventeenth-century, early, 166, 172, 176, 177, 183–94
  seventeenth-century, late, 222–26, 230–35, 236–38, 240, 262
  Spanish, 543
  twentieth-century, 540–41, 543, 544, 550, 551, 554–56, 566, 567, 579, 583–85, 588, 589, 591, 611–13, 623, 631, 633–34, 636, 646, 655, 656, 660, 661, 662
opera seria, 320, 322–25, 351–52, 355, 369, 371
operettas, 597, 614, 617
*Oper und Drama* (Wagner), 484
*Opus maius* (Bacon), 14
*Opus 1970* (Stockhausen), 641
*O quam tu pulchra es* (Grandi), 201
oral transmission, 30, 33, 46, 57, 196, 599, 618
oratorios
  of Adams, 656
  choruses in, 310
  of Elgar, 512–13
  of Handel, 239, 304, 310–11
  of Haydn, 352–53
  of Honegger, 565
  of Mendelssohn, 425, 427
  of Milhaud, 565
  nineteenth-century, 490–91
  of Parker, 600
  seventeenth-century, 177–78, 201, 235
oratory and music, 317
Orcagna, Andrea, *16*
*Orchésographie* (Arbeau), 208
orchestra. *See also* instrumentation and orchestration
  eighteenth-century, 335
  French Baroque, 231, 233, 235, 260, 262, 264
  of Haydn, 341, 342

orchestra (*continued*)
  Italian Baroque, 260–61, 262, 282
  Mannheim, 332–33
  nineteenth-century, 409, 410–11, 423,
      489–90
orchestral music. *See specific composers and*
      *genres*
orchestral music, Baroque, 233, 235,
      260–65, 288, 298, 304. *See also*
      *specific composers and genres*
Order of the Golden Fleece, 106, 107
Ordinary of the Mass, 33, 35, 41–42, 56,
      75–76
*Ordo virtutum* (Hildegard of Bingen), 43, 44
*ordres*, 286
*Orfeo, L'* (Monteverdi), 189–91, 228, 229
*Orfeo ed Euridice* (Gluck), 327, 328, 443
Orff, Carl, 587, 592
organ chorales, 245, 247, 293–94. *See also*
      chorale preludes
organ Masses, 215
organ music
  of Bach, 291, 292–94
  of Ives, 601
  of Messiaen, 631
  seventeenth-century, 215, 216, 242,
      245–48
  sixteenth-century, 144, 148
organs, 213, 214, 244–45, 245
  as continuo instrument, 180, 199, 201,
      282
  portative, 81, 84, 87, 103
  positive, 86, 102, 247
organum
  Aquitanian, 57, 58
  Debussy influenced by, 538
  early, 55, 56–58
  eleventh-century, 56
  florid, 57
  free, 56
  Notre Dame, 58–63
  twelfth-century, 57
*Orgelbüchlein* (Bach), 293–94
Origen, 23
*Orlando* (Woolf), 532
*Orlando furioso* (Ariosto), 94, 192
ornamentation
  in chant, 43
  in eighteenth-century music, 268, 285,
      307, 324, 326
  in nineteenth-century music, 479
  in seventeenth-century music, 186, 195,
      209, 219, 224, 226, 228–29, 230,
      248–49, 257, 258–59
  in sixteenth-century music, 137, 142
  in troubadour songs, 49
  in twentieth-century music, 580
*Orontea* (Cesti), 194
*Orphée aux enfers* (Offenbach), 468
*Orpheus* (Liszt), 443
Orpheus myth, 6, 172, 187–91
Orthodox Eastern churches, 27
*Os justi* (Bruckner), 490

ostinatos, 570, 573, 576, 577, 587, 606, 607,
      655. *See also* basso ostinato
*Otello* (Rossini), 471
*Otello* (Verdi), 477, 480, 481, 492
*Othello* (Shakespeare), 478, 480
Ottoman Empire, 91
*Ottone* (Handel), 306
*Our Town* (film), 611
*ouverture*. *See* French overture
overdotting, 229, 232–33, 364
overtures. *See also* French overture;
      sinfonias
  of Beethoven, 386–87
  of Berlioz, 421
  of Liszt, 443
  of Mendelssohn, 426
  opera, 236, 262, 288, 327, 331, 383
Ovid, 642
*O Welt, ich muss dich lassen*, 147
Owen, Wilfred, 634
*Oxford* Symphony (Haydn), 343–45, 345
Oxford University, 12, 15, 55
*Oy comamos y bebamos* (Encina), 141
Ozawa, Seiji, 531

Pachelbel, Johann, 242
*Pacific 231* (Honegger), 565
*Pacifika Rondo* (Harrison), 640
*paduana*. *See* pavane
Paganini, Niccolò, 402, 422, 436, 441, 441,
      461
paganism, 34
*pagliacci, I* (Leoncavallo), 515
Paine, John Knowles, 600
Palais Garnier (Paris), 463, 464
*Palästinalied* (Walther von der Vogelweide),
      51
Palestrina, Giovanni Pierluigi da, 147, 153,
      153–56, 154
  biography of, 153
  complete works edition of, 438
  contemporaries of, 156–61
  counterpoint of, 157, 199
  Masses of, 154–56
*Pamela* (Richardson), 272
*Pampeanas* (Ginastera), 636
*Pange lingua gloriosi*, 126
papacy
  Great Schism, 14, 71, 83, 84
  as patron, 96–97, 166
  rise in importance, 8, 11, 19, 24
*Papillons* (Schumann), 429
*arade* (Satie), 563
*Paradise Lost* (Milton), 166, 171, 352
*Paradise Lost* (Penderecki), 662
*Paradiso degli Alberti* (Giovanni da Prato), 84
parallel organum, 56, 538
paraphrase Mass. *See under* Masses
Parigi, Giulio, 192
Paris
  Americans studying in, 608, 610, 612,
      655
  Ballets Russes in, 567, 568, 571, 572, 588

  chanson composition in, 137
  choir schools in, 95
  Chopin and Sand in, 433, 436, 507
  eighteenth-century, 285–86, 288
  harp industry in, 419
  Liszt in, 441
  medieval, 11
  Notre Dame cathedral in, 12, 54, 55,
      58–63, 59, 273
  opera in, 462–63, 464, 470
  printing in, 118–19, 402
  public concerts in, 240, 278, 286, 342,
      346, 358, 513
  *querelle des bouffons* in, 328
Paris, University of, 12–13, 14, 15, 55, 58,
      60, 62
Paris Conservatoire, 513, 514, 631
*Paris* Symphonies (Haydn), 342, 346, 358
*Paris* Symphony (Mozart), 358–59
Parker, Charlie, 626, 627–28
Parker, Horatio, 600, 601, 602
*parlando-rubato*, 583
parlor songs, 597–98, 601
*Parnassus: or, The Apotheosis of Corelli*
      (Couperin), 286
parody Mass. *See under* Masses
*Parsifal* (Wagner), 485, 513, 537
Pärt, Arvo, 659–60
partbooks, 119, 128, 140, 207, 209
Partch, Harry, 639, 639
*Parthenia* (Byrd), 212, 213
partitas, 213, 247, 296, 297, 660
passacaglias, 214, 551, 555. *See also*
      chaconnes
passacalle, 214
*passaggi*, 229
passamezzo, 210, 250
Passions
  of Bach, 299, 302, 303, 425, 435
  of Penderecki, 646
*Passions of the Soul, The* (Descartes), 168,
      170, 174
Pasteur, Louis, 401, 406
pastoral dramas, 183–84
*Pastoral Symphony* (Beethoven), 385–86, 460
*pastor fido, Il* (Guarini), 170, 184
*Pathetic Song, The* (Eakins), 598
*Pathétique* Symphony (Tchaikovsky), 456
*Path to the New Music, The* (Webern), 557
patronage
  Arab rulers, 10
  Baroque, 165–66, 186–87, 193, 198,
      230–32, 235, 236, 238–39, 249,
      260, 261
  of Beethoven, 375–76
  eighteenth-century, 271, 278, 286, 287,
      288, 290, 297–98, 304, 305, 327,
      341–42, 358
  of instrumental music, 206
  medieval, 10, 11, 14, 17, 49, 50, 71, 76,
      81, 84
  nineteenth-century, 401–2, 454,
      484–85

Renaissance, 91–92, 93, 95, 96, 106, 116, 122, 131, 186–87
Roman, 18
twentieth-century, 534, 561, 630, 638
Patti, Adelina, *471*
*Pavana Lahrymae* (Byrd), 213
*Pavane pour une infante défunte* (Ravel), 542
pavanes, 140–41, 208, 210, 211, *211*, 213, 250
Pavlov, Ivan, 526, 532
Pears, Peter, 633, *633*
pedagogy. *See* education, music
pedal points, 247, 450, 545
*Peer Gynt* suites (Grieg), 512, 626
*Pelléas et Mélisande* (Debussy), 540–41, 579
*Pelleas und Melisande* (Schoenberg), 548
Pelli, César, 660
Penderecki, Krzysztof, 644–47, 649, 662, *662*
pentatonic scales, 426, 538, 600, 658
percussion music, 608–9, 647
*perestroika*, 525
performance practices
of Baroque music, 180–81, 182, 286, 293, 299, 307–8, 311
of Baroque ornaments, 228–29, 258–59
of cadenzas, 367
chance music, 648
of chant, 37–38, 40, 41
of early motets, 64
of *formes fixes*, 80
jazz improvisation, 620
of liturgical dramas, 44
musica ficta, 86–87
of nineteenth-century opera, 479
of opera seria, 324
of organum, 56–58
of sixteenth-century songs, 142
tempo and metronome markings, 384–85
*tempo rubato*, 434
of troubadour and trouvère songs, 49
vocal embellishments, 326
performers, professional. *See also* specific names
Baroque, 262–64
eighteenth-century, 357, 361, 365–66
medieval, 47–51, 56
nineteenth-century, 402
opera buffa troupes, 321
opera singers, 192–93, 223, 224–25, 280, 306, 307–9, 324, 326, 462, 470, 476–77
Renaissance, 95–96, 99–100, 131
twentieth-century, 641–42
Pergolesi, Giovanni Battista, 278, 320, *321*, 325, 328, 471, *573*
Peri, Jacopo, *186*, 187, 190–91, 233
periodicity, musical, 316–17, 344
Pérotin, 57, 58, 61–63, 64
biography of, 62
*Persian Set* (Cowell), 640
perspective, 92–93

*Peter and the Wolf* (Prokofiev), 588, 592
*Peter Grimes* (Britten), 633–34
Peter the Venerable, 37n
*petit motet*, 235
Petits Violons, 231, 233, 235
Petrarch, 14, 15, 130, 132–33, 134
Petrucci, Ottaviano, 118, 122, 123, 129, 142, 207
*Petrushka* (Stravinsky), 567, 568–69
Peverara, Laura, 131
phasing, 653–55
Philidor, Anne Danican, 358
Philip II, king of Spain, 134
Philip IV, king of France, 71
Philippe de Vitry, 72, 73
Philips Pavilion (Brussels), *641*, 644
Philip the Good, duke of Burgundy, 95, 96, 100, 102, 105, 107, *107*
*Philomel* (Babbitt), 642
philosophes, 271, 274
philosophy. *See also* Scholasticism
early Christian, 24, 26
Enlightenment, 271, 274, 318
existentialist, 522
Greek, 10, 13, 14, 19, 21–22, 24, 92, 189
medieval, 71–72
nineteenth-century, 400, 406, 483
Renaissance, 92
seventeenth-century, 168–69
*Phrygian Gates* (Adams), 655–56
piano concertos
of Barber, 634
of Beach, 601
of Beethoven, 388
of Chávez, 607
of Gershwin, 623
of Grieg, 512
of Liszt, 444
of Mozart, 357, 365–67
nineteenth-century, 411
of Rachmaninov, 545
of Ravel, 542, 565
of Schoenberg, 553
of Tailleferre, 565
of Tippett, 636
piano music
of Bartók, 579–80
of Beach, 601
of Brahms, 447–49
of Cage, 647
of Chopin, 432–35, *433*
of Cowell, 609
of Debussy, 538–39
of Fauré, 514
of Franck, 513
of Ginastera, 635
of Gottschalk, 600
of Joplin, 613–14
of Liszt, 441–42
of Mendelssohn, 427–29
of Musorgsky, 510
nineteenth-century, 409, 411
of Rachmaninov, 545

of Ravel, 541–42
of Reich, 653–54
of Satie, 562–63
of Schoenberg, 548, 551, 552–53
of Schubert, 416
of Schumann, 429–31
of Scriabin, 546
of Thomson, 613
*Piano Phase* (Reich), 653–54
piano quintets, 416, 432, 449–50, 513–14, 601
pianos
damper pedal on, 418, 434, 609
fortepiano, 333, 350–51
nineteenth-century improvements to, 411, 418–19
square, *351*, *401*, 418, *418*, 428
sustain pedal on, 638, 648
piano sonatas
of Barber, 634
of Beethoven, 361, 376–77, 387, 391
of Haydn, 350–51
of Ives, 602, 603
of Liszt, 442, 549
of Mozart, 355–57, 361, 466
of Prokofiev, 588–89
of Schubert, 361, 416
of Scriabin, 546
Piano Suite (Schoenberg), 548, 552–53
piano trios, 432, 445–46
Picasso, Pablo, 528, *528*, 529, 533, 563, *563*, 567, 568, *573*
Piccinni, Niccolò, 328
*Pictures at an Exhibition* (Musorgsky), 510
*Pièces de clavecin* (D'Anglebert), 248, *250*, 258
*Pièces de clavecin* (Jacquet de La Guerre), 250–53
Piero della Francesca (school of), 93
*Pierrot lunaire* (Schoenberg), 551, 637
Pietism, 241–42
Pilgrims, 149
Pio Ospedale della Pietà, 280, *280*–82
pipes, 4, *52*, *211*
Pisano, Giovanni, 15, 16, *16*
pitch-class sets, 549, 555
Pius X, Pope, 490
*pizzicato*, 282, 391
plagal modes, 45
plague. *See* Black Death
plainchant, 30, 32. *See also* chant; Gregorian chant
*Platée* (Rameau), 288
Plato, 6, 14, 19, 21–22, 24, *24*, 92, 114, 561
*Play of Daniel, The*, 44
*Play of Herod, The*, 44
plays. *See* literature
pleasure gardens, 358
Pleyel, Ignaz, 347
*Poème électronique* (Varèse), 609, 641
*Poem of Ecstasy* (Scriabin), 546
*Poetics* (Aristotle), 14

poetry. *See also* text setting
  ancient Greek, 19, 20, 22
  chanson, 103
  of Machaut, 76
  madrigal, 130, 168
  Minnesinger, 50
  nineteenth-century, 397, 403, 406, 414, 494–95
  pastoral, 130, 170, 184
  Petrarchan movement, 14, 15, 130, 132–33
  seventeenth-century, 170, 172
  Symbolist, 527, 532, 538, 539, 540, 542, 549, 551
  troubadour and trouvère, 13, 31, 49
  twentieth-century, 532–33
Poitiers, church of Notre-Dame-la-Grande, 12
Poland, 269, 400, 522, 523
Polish music, 432–35, 507, 644–46, 650, 662
*Polish Requiem* (Penderecki), 662
*Politics* (Aristotle), 7, 14, 21
politics and music
  in eighteenth century, 268–69, 271, 272–74, 339, 360, 374
  fourteenth-century Europe, 13–15, 71, 72–73, 80
  in Middle Ages, 9, 11, 33–35, 55
  in nineteenth century, 381, 397, 400, 401, 403, 437, 461, 462–63, 465, 475, 477, 493, 505, 507
  in Renaissance, 91–92, 98–99, 106, 116, 146, 151
  in seventeenth century, 164, 222, 236
  in twentieth century, 489, 521–23, 525–26, 561–62, 583, 584, 586, 587–88, 589, 591–93, 608, 610–11, 636
polkas, 597
polonaises, 432
polychoral music, 199, 205, 217–18
polyphony. *See also* texture; *specific genres*
  art song, 72
  in choral settings, 148
  conductus, 67, 69
  early, 43, 54, 55–58
  early English, 69–70
  fifteenth-century, 91, 105–10
  fourteenth-century, 17
  Franconian motet, 66–67
  Notre Dame, 12, 54, 55, 58–66
  Renaissance, 94, 150–51, 154–61, 558
  seventeenth-century, 199
polystylism, 661, 663
polytonality, 566, 601–3, 606, 658
Pompeii, 275, 276
*Pope Marcellus Mass* (Palestrina). *See Missa Papae Marcelli*
Pöppelmann, Matthäus Daniel, 268
popular music, 534, 594
  Debussy's influence on, 541
  French chansons, 566

  Krenek's use of, 583
  songs, 521, 584, 597–98, 601, 603, 614–16
  synthesizers in, 641
  technology and, 530–31, 574
  Weill's parodies of, 584
*Porgy and Bess* (Gershwin), 623
Porpora, Nicola, 309, 340
Porporino, 326
portative organ, *1, 84, 87, 103*
Porter, Cole, 617, 623
positive organ, *86, 102, 247*
postminimalism, 654
postmodernism, 660–61
post-tonal music, 547
Poulenc, Francis, 563, 565, *565,* 566, 592
*Pour le piano* (Debussy), 539
Poussin, Nicolas, 171, 174, *174,* 252
power of music
  in ancient Greece, 6, 7, 19, 21–22
  in early Christian church, 23–24
  in Hebrew scriptures, 19
praeludium. *See* preludes; toccatas
Praeludium in E Major (Buxtehude), 245–46
Praetorius, Michael, *295*
Prague, 204
*Prague* Symphony (Mozart), 363
*Pravda* (newspaper), 589, 591
*Praxis pietatis melica* (Crüger), 242
prayers, 32, 33, 34–35
*Prelude, Chorale, and Fugue* (Franck), 513
*Prélude à "L'Après-midi d'un faune"* (Debussy), 532, 539, 572
preludes. *See also* chorale preludes
  of Bach, 293, 294–96, 297, 303
  Baroque, 175, 214, 245–46, 251
  of Chopin, 432–33, *433*
  of Debussy, 539
  of Fauré, 514
  of Ives, 601
  in oratorios, 201
  of Rachmaninov, 545–46, 546
  rhythm in, 180
  of Scriabin, 546
*Préludes, Les* (Liszt), 443, 500
preluding, 293
prepared piano, 647
Pre-Raphaelite movement, 407
*Pride and Prejudice* (Austen), 318
prima donna, 225, 307
*prima pratica,* 174–75, 178
prime order, 552–53
*Principia mathematica* (Newton), 170
printing and publishing
  development of, 118–19
  early Renaissance, 91, 116, 122, 123, 128
  eighteenth century, 258, 278, 285, 311, 347
  nineteenth century, 379, 402, 598
  seventeenth century, 165, 198, 207
  sixteenth century, 131
  twentieth century, 530, 598, 618

*Procession in Piazza San Marco* (Gentile Bellini), 202
program music, 385–86, 387, 420–22, 424, 432. *See also* affections; depictive music; rhetoric; text setting
  aesthetic debates over, 439
  Beethoven's influence on, 460, 497
  concept of, 408
  of Ives, 603–4
  Liszt's views on, 439
  Mahler's hidden, 497, 498
  Satie's satires of, 562–63
  symphonic poems and suites, 442–44, 488, 500–503, 511, 512, 539–40, 545, 565, 588
progress, idea of, 438, 459, 663
Prokofiev, Sergey, *588,* 588–89
prolation, 74
*promessi sposi, I* (Manzoni), 406, 490
*Prometheus* (Liszt), 443
*Prometheus* (Scriabin), 546
Proper of the Mass, 33, 35, 40–41, 56
Protestantism. *See* Reformation
Proust, Marcel, 527, 529, 532
Prussia, 269
*Prussian* Sonatas (C.P.E. Bach), 333
*Psalmen Davids* (Schütz), 202, 204
psalmody, 39–40
psalms, 32, 34
  antiphonal performance of, 199
  early Christian, 27
  in Jewish services, 27
  Reformation settings, 146, 149, 164, 595
psalm tones, 38, 39–40, 41, 45, 201
Psalters, 146, 149
psaltery, *26, 81*
*Psyché* (Franck), 444
psychoanalysis, 526, 532, 550
Ptolemy, Claudius, 25, 26, 114
publishing. *See* printing and publishing
Puccini, Giacomo, *515*
  Debussy's influence on, 541
  operas of, 461, 465, 467, 516, *516–17*
*Puer nobis* (Tallis), 151
*Pulcinella* (Stravinsky), 573
Purcell, Henry, *236,* 543
  biography of, 236
  ceremonial music of, 239
  Corelli's influence on, 259
  domestic music of, 239
  incidental music of, 238
  operas of, 175–76, 236–38
  verse anthems of, 239
*Puritani, I* (Bellini), 473
Puritanism, 236
Puritans, 149, 164, 595
Pushkin, Alexander, 407, 455–56, 505, 508
Pythagoras, 21, 22, 24, 26, 114

quadrivium, 25, 26, 60
quadruplum, 62, 63, 64
*Quam pulchra es* (Dunstable), 101–2
Quantz, Johann Joachim, 315, 316

Index    A53

quarter tones, 135
*Quartettsatz* (Schubert), 416
*Quatuor pour la fin du temps* (Messiaen), 631–33
*Queen of Spades, The* (Tchaikovsky), 456
*Quem queritis in presepe*, 42, 43, 44
*Quem queritis in sepulchro*, 44
*querelle des bouffons*, 320, 328
quicksteps, 597
Quinault, Jean-Philippe, 232, 328
Quintilian, 92
quodlibets, 297
quotation. *See* borrowing; collage technique
Quran, 14

Rachmaninov, Sergei, *545*, 545–46, 547, 559, 607
Racine, Jean, 166, 171, 230, 328
*Radamisto* (Handel), 306
radio, 530–31, 534, 561, 610–11, 629, 640
*Raft of the "Medusa," The* (Géricault), 404–5, 407, *408*
ragtime, 599, 603, 613–14, 618–19, 628
Milhaud's use of, 565
*Ragtime* (Stravinsky), 572, *573*
*Rain, Steam and Speed: The Great Western Railway* (Turner), *400*
*Rake's Progress, The* (Stravinsky), 567
Rambaud d'Orange, 49
Rameau, Jean-Philippe, 181, 268, 279, 287, *287*–90, 335
biography of, 287
influence of, 305, 565, 566
instrumental music of, 288
operas of, 288, 289–90, 327, 328, 466
revival of, 513
theories of, 289, 421
rap, 31
*Rape of the Sabine Women, The* (Poussin), *174*
*Rape of the Sabine Women, The* (Rubens), *175*
*rappresentazione*, 166
*Rapsodie espagnole* (Ravel), 542
Rastell, John, 118
Rasumovsky, Andreas, 383
*Rasumovsky Quartets* (Beethoven), 383
rattles, 4
Ravel, Maurice, 510, 541–42, 546, 564–65
influence of, 543, 622
orchestral music of, 542
reception of, 559
Satie's influence on, 562
songs of, 542
realism, 469, 508, 509
rebec, *57, 61*
recapitulation, 332, 344, 348
*récitatif mesuré*, 233, *234*
*récitatif simple*, 233, *234*
recitation formulas, 37–38
recitatives, 137. *See also specific types*
in cantatas, 226, 300
English, 238

French, 233, 288, 290
German, 240
of Handel, 306–7, 310
in instrumental music, 206
in opera buffa, 320
in opera seria, 323, 355
in oratorios, 201
in Passions, 302
quasi-, 472
seventeenth-century, 175, 177, 180, 187–89, 192, 194, 201, 222
*recitativo accompagnato*, 307, 352, 355
*recitativo obbligato*, 307, 320, 327
*recitativo secco*, 307, 479
*recitativo semplice*, 306–7, 310
reciting tone, 39, 45
recorders, *81*, 209
Reformation, 24, 91, 146–51, 164, 464. *See also* church music, Reformation
*Reformation* Symphony (Mendelssohn), 425
refrains. *See also* ritornello
in arias, 223
in ballatas, 82, 83
in cantigas, 52
in carols, 100
in fourteenth-century chansons, 78–79
in popular songs, 598
in sixteenth-century songs, 129, 130, 139
in trouvère songs, 47–48, 72
in twentieth-century music, 551
Reger, Max, 547
Reich, Steve, 653–55, *654*, 658
Reims Cathedral, 75, 76, *78*, 93
Reis, Claire, 608
*Rejoice!* (Gubaidulina), 663
*Relâche* (Satie), 563
Rembrandt van Rijn, 171, *173*
*Remembrance of Things Past* (Proust), 529, 532
reminiscence motives, 478, 488
*Reminiscing in Tempo* (Ellington), 625
Renaissance, 89–161
beginning of, 90–91, 116
Burgundian music in, 102–10
cultural-historical context, 89–97, 112
defined, 89
English music in, 100–102, 138–41, 149–51, 160–61
Franco-Flemish music in, 117–27, 151, 158–60
French music in, 137–38, 149
German music in, 147–48
instrumental music, 141–44
Italian music in, 4, 129–37, 151, 153–56
legacy of, 97
musical culture of, 114–16
Reformation in, 146–51
Spanish music in, 141, 156–58
René, duke of Anjou, 124
Renzi, Anna, 224–25, *225*
Repin, Ilya, 508, *509*

*Republic* (Plato), 6, 14, 21, 26
*Requiem* (Ligeti), 646
Requiem Masses, 43
of Berlioz, 421, 489–90
of Brahms, 490–91
of Britten, 634
of Mozart, 372
of Penderecki, 662
of Stravinsky, 567
of Verdi, 478, 490
"rescue" operas, 367–68
respond, 41
responsorial performance of chant, 35, 40–41, 59–63
responsories, 32, 56, 59, 151
Restoration, 236
*Resvellies vous* (Du Fay), 79, 104
*Retablo de maese Pedro, El* (Falla), 543
retrograde, 552–53, 558–59, 610
retrograde inversion, 552–53
*Revelation in the Courthouse Park* (Partch), 639
Revere, Paul, 595
Revueltas, Silvestre, 607
Reynolds, Joshua, 275, 276
rhapsodies, 449
*Rhapsody in Blue* (Gershwin), 623
*Rhapsody on a Theme of Paganini* (Rachmaninov), 545
*Rheingold, Das* (Wagner), 484, 486
*Rhenish* Symphony (Schumann), 432
rhetoric, 92
rhythm and meter
in African American music, 599
in ancient Greek music, 19, 22
in Ars nova music, 72
in Ars subtilior, 84
in Baroque music, 180, 193, 209
in Bulgarian music, 580, 581, 582
in chant, 40, 60
in conductus, 69
in early organum, 56, 57–58, 74
in eighteenth-century music, 317, 334
in Franco-Flemish music, 122–23, 127
in French overtures, 232, 257
hemiola, 190
in Indian music, 655
in isorhythmic motets, 73, 76, 78
in jazz, 618–19
in Minnelieder, 50
in motet, 68
in nineteenth-century music, 452, 472–73, 512
notating, 74–75
*notes inégales*, 229
in poetry, 60
in polyphonic chansons, 78
in ragtime, 613–14
in troubadour and trouvère songs, 49
in twentieth-century music, 555, 566, 570, 577, 580, 582–83, 589, 603, 606, 607, 626, 632–33, 638, 654
in villancico, 141

"rhythm changes," 624, 625, 627
rhythmic modes, 58, 60–61, 62, 70
rhythm section, 622
ricercare, 214, 216, 296
Richard, Michel, 248
*Richard Coeur-de-Lion* (Grétry), 321
Richard I ("Lion Heart"), king of England, 50
Richardson, Samuel, 272
Ricordi, Giulio, 477, 478–79
Rieder, Wilhelm August, *413*
*Rienzi* (Wagner), 484
Ries, Ferdinand, 381
Rigaud, Hyacinthe, *230*
*Rigoletto* (Verdi), 476, 478, 492
Riley, Terry, 653
Rilke, Rainer Maria, 586
*Rime sparse* (Petrarch), 15
Rimsky-Korsakov, Nikolay, 506, 510–12
    influence of, 538, 546, 567, 568, 571
*Rinaldo* (Handel), 306
*Ring des Nibelungen, Der* (Wagner), 479, 484, 485, 486, 587
Rinuccini, Ottavio, 187, 189
ripieno, 260
Risorgimento, 475, 477, 493, 507
Risset, Jean-Claude, 651
*Rite of Spring, The* (Stravinsky), 567, 568, 569–71, 607
ritornello form, 262, 283–85, 336–37, 366–67, 585
ritornellos, 190, 193, 194, 201, 214, 227, 262, 293, 298, 300, 323
*ritorno d'Ulisse, Il* (Monteverdi), 193
Rivera, Diego, 529, 533, *606*, 607
*Robert le diable* (Meyerbeer), 464
Rochberg, George, 660, 662–63
rock, 652, 653, 655
rococo style, 268, *268*, 275
*Rodelinda* (Handel), 306
*Rodeo* (Copland), 611
Rodgers, Richard, 615, 616
*Rodrigo* (Handel), 304
Roerich, Nicholas, 569, 572, *572*
Roger, Estienne, 258, *259*
Rogers, Ginger, 617, *623*
Rogier van der Weyden, *107*
*Roi s'amuse, Le* (Hugo), 478
*Roman Carnival* overture (Berlioz), 421
Roman Catholic Church, 27, 28, 71–72, 92
    in eighteenth century, 271
    as patron, 96–97
    in seventeenth century, 164
    in sixteenth century, 146–47
romances, medieval, 397
*Roman de Fauvel*, 72–73, *73*
Roman Empire, 6, 8, 18, 22–23, 30, 92, 275
    map of, *7*
romanesca, 196, 212
Romanesque architecture, 12, *12*, 55, *55*, 61
Romanticism, 277, 375. *See also* nineteenth-century music; *specific composers, genres, and topics*

in art and literature, 403–5, 439
Beethoven's influence on, 459–61
composite art forms in, 463–64, 483, 489
concept of, 397–98
early, 410–37
in music, 405, 408–9
tenets of, 410
twentieth-century challenges to, 526–27, 550, 573
Romberg, Sigmund, 617
Rombouts, Theodoor, *180*
Rome
    Baroque, 166, 177, 256
    Baroque art and architecture in, 168, 171, 175, *176*, 200
    cantatas in, 197, 226
    choir schools in, 95
    Christina of Sweden in, 261
    Counter-Reformation in, 147
    opera in, 192–93
    oratorios in, 201
    orchestras in, 260–61
    papal court in, 14, 153
    printing in, 119
    Saint Peter's Square and Basilica, *166*, 168
    San Clemente basilica in, 32
*Romeo and Juliet* (Prokofiev), 588, 592
*Romeo and Juliet* (Shakespeare), 377, 616
*Roméo et Juliette* (Berlioz), 421, 422, 424
rondeau, 78–80, 84, 85, 103, 121
"*Rondo alla turca*" (Mozart), 357, 466
rondo form, 345, 347, 349, 367, 502, 555
*Room of One's Own, A* (Woolf), 532
Roosevelt, Franklin D., 608
Rore, Cipriano de, *131*, 132–33, 151, 174
*Rose, liz, printemps, verdure* (Machaut), 78, 79
*Rosenkavalier, Der* (Strauss), 504, 505
Rospigliosi, Giulio. *See* Clement IX, Pope
Rossi, Luigi, 197
Rossini, Gioachino, 433, 461, 469–73, *470*
    biography of, 470
    church music of, 490
    operas of, 274, 462, 463, 466–67, 469–73
    scene structure of, 471, 478, 479
    style of, 472–73
rota, 70
Roubiliac, Louis-François, *311*
*Rouet d'Omphale, Le* (Saint-Saëns), 444
Rousseau, Jean-Jacques, 271, 274, 276–77, 288, 321, 328
row, 552–53
Rowlandson, Thomas, *358*
Royal Academy (London), 276
Royal Academy of Music, 306, 309
*Royne de ciel* (Compère), *118*
rubato, 434
Rubens, Peter Paul, 171, 174, *175*
Rubinstein, Anton, 454, 506
Rubinstein, Nikolay, 506
Ruckers firm, 245

Rückert, Friedrich, 499
Rudel, Jaufré, *52*
Rudolph, Archduke, 375
Ruggiero, 196, 212
Rule of Saint Benedict, 8, 14, 32
*Rusalka* (Dvořák), 459
*Ruslan and Lyudmila* (Glinka), 505
Russia, 522. *See also* Soviet Union
Russian Association of Proletarian Musicians, 587
Russian music
    nineteenth-century, 453–56, 505–11, 538
    twentieth-century, 511–12, 545–46, 566–73, 576–77, 587–92, 661, 663
Russolo, Luigi, 563

Sacchi, Andrea, *238*
sackbut, 218
*Sacrae symphoniae* (Gabrieli), 217–18
Sacrati, Francesco, 225
sacred concertos, 177–78, 181, 199, 201, 204–5, 235, 242
*Sacred Service* (Milhaud), 565
*Sacre du printemps, Le. See Rite of Spring, The* (Stravinsky)
*St. Luke Passion* (Penderecki), 646
*Saint Francis of Assisi* (Messiaen), 631
Saint Gall monastery, 35, 43
*Saint John Passion* (Bach), 302
Saint Mark's Church. *See* Venice
*Saint Matthew Passion* (Bach), 302, 303, 425, 435
*Saint Paul* (Mendelssohn), 427
Saint Petersburg Conservatory, 506, 510
Saint-Saëns, Camille, 444, 514
Saint Thomas School (Leipzig), 291, 292, 298–99
Salieri, Antonio, 360, 373, 413, 440
*Salome* (Strauss), 501, 503
Salomon, Johann Peter, 342, 346
*Salón México, El* (Copland), 611
salons, 267, 269, 288, 416, 433
saltarello, 210
*Salve Regina*, 38, *39*, 42
Salzburg, 204, 355–57, 372
Sammartini, Giovanni Battista, 327, 331, 335, 355
sampling, 651
Sanctus, 33, 35, 41–42
Sand, George, 433, 436, *436*, 461
Sandburg, Carl, 610
*Sant'Alessio, Il* (Landi), 192
sarabande, *251*, 252, 296, 297
Sargent, John Singer, *514*
Sartre, Jean-Paul, 522, 533
Satie, Erik, 562–63, 565, 612, 646
*Satyagraha* (Glass), 655
*Saudades do Brasil* (Milhaud), 565–66
*Saul* (Handel), 310, *311*
*Saul, was verfolgst du mich* (Schütz), 204–5
Sax, Adolphe, 419
saxophone, 419

scales. *See also* diatonic scales; octatonic scales; pentatonic scales; whole-tone scales
  in ancient Greek music, 22
  Babylonian, 4
Scarlatti, Alessandro, *226*, 226–27, 261, 304, 305
Scarlatti, Domenico, *329*, 329–31, 566
scat, 620
*scena*, 479
scenography
  nineteenth-century, 462, 464, 486
  seventeenth-century, 191, 192, 194, 224
  twentieth-century, 489
Schaeffer, Pierre, 640
Schafer, R. Murray, 664, 666
Scheibe, Johann Adolph, 303
Scheidt, Samuel, 216
Schein, Johann Hermann, 210
scherzo, 347, 349
*Scherzo fantastique* (Stravinsky), 567
scherzos, 433, 435
Schickele, Peter, 661
Schiller, Johann von, 272, 394
Schindler, Alma, 496
Schliessmann, Hans, *496*
Schmieder, Wolfgang, 291
Schmitt, Florent, 571
Schnittke, Alfred, 661, 663
Schobert, Johann, 355, 356
Schoenberg, Arnold, 528, 534, 547–54, 607
  atonal music of, 549, 551
  biography of, 548
  Brahms's influence on, 453
  influence of, 554, 557, 567, 577, 608, 636, 658
  Ives and, 604
  musical tradition viewed by, 547
  paintings of, *529*, *548*, *550*
  tonal works of, 547–48
  twelve-tone music of, 551–54, *573*, 576
Scholasticism, 13, 14–15, 55, 60, 62, 92
*schöne Müllerin, Die* (Schubert), 414, 435
Schopenhauer, Arthur, 400, 406, 408, 483
schottisches, 597
Schubert, Franz, 412–17, *413*, *415*, 420
  art songs of, 408
  biography of, 413
  chamber music of, 411, 416–17, 420, 467, 639
  influence of, 547, 601
  lieder of, 410–11, 412–15, 431
  operas of, 482
  orchestral music of, 415–16, 417
  piano music of, 411, 416
  sonatas of, 361
  symphonies of, 431, 460
Schuller, Gunther, 636
Schumann, Clara Wieck, *430*, 436, 439, 444–46, *445*, 447
  biography of, 445
  Brahms and, 448, 450
  piano music of, 460

Schumann, Robert, 425, 429–32, *430*, 444–45
  Bach-Gesellschaft founded by, 303
  Beethoven's influence on, 391
  biography of, 430
  Brahms and, 448
  chamber music of, 411
  as conductor, 410
  influence of, 506
  lieder of, 408, 431
  piano music of, 411, 429–31, 460
  Schubert C-Major Symphony viewed by, 415, 417
  symphonies of, 431–32
  writings of, 408
Schütz, Heinrich, 160, *204*
  biography of, 204
  complete works edition of, 438
  legacy of, 205
  sacred music of, 178, 199, 202, 204–5, 235, 242, 302
*Schwanengesang* (Schubert), 414
Schwind, Moritz von, *415*
science and technology. *See also* electronic music
  digital technologies, 651, 652
  eighteenth-century, 271, 290, 374
  Middle Ages, 10, 13, 14, 15, 72
  nineteenth-century, 400, 406, 418–19, 438
  seventeenth-century, 164, 170, 172
  sound recording and reproduction, 530, 534, 574–75, 629
  twentieth-century, 521, 523, 530–31, 532
  violin making, 255
*Scivias* (Hildegard of Bingen), 43
Scotch snaps, 334, 426
Scotland, 34
*Scottish* Symphony (Mendelssohn), 424–25, 426, 427, 432
*Scream, The* (Munch), *529*, 533
Scriabin, Alexander, 541, 546, *546*, 547
  influence of, 604, 606
Scribe, Eugène, 464
scriptorium, 37
Scrovegni Chapel, 72
*Seasons, The* (Haydn), 352
Secessionist art, 497
*seconda pratica*, 174–75, 178, 179–80, 185
*Second Hurricane, The* (Copland), 611
Second Viennese school, 554
Seeger, Charles, 529, 609
Seeger, Ruth Crawford, 528–29
seguidilla, 469
Seikilos, epitaph of, 19, *21*
*Se la face ay pale* (Du Fay), 104, 108
*Self-Portrait* (Schoenberg), *529*, *548*
semibreves, 74, *118*
semiminims, *118*
semi-operas, 238
Senesino, 306, 309
*Sense and Sensibility* (Austen), 277
*Sensemayá* (Revueltas), 607

September 11, 2001, terrorist attacks, 525, 657
Sequence, 35, 56
sequences, liturgical, 35, 43, 55, 147, 422. *See also* Dies irae; Stabat Mater
sequences, structural, 258–59, 316
*Sequenza IV* (Berio), 637–38
serenades, 357, 551
serialism, 576–77, 609–10, 636–38
series, 552–53
Sermisy, Claudin de, 137, *138*
*Serse* (Handel), 325
*serva padrona, La* (Pergolesi), 320, *321*, 328, 471
service, Anglican, 151, 152, 239
*Seven Magnificat Antiphons* (Pärt), 659–60
*Seven Tunes Heard in China* (Sheng), 658
Seven Years' War, 269
*seys libros del Delphin, Los* (Narváez), 212
Sforza family, 96, 97, 116, 124
Shakespeare, William, 26, 166
  Berlioz inspired by, 377, 421, 468
  incidental music or overtures to works by, 238, 425, 443
  Italian subjects of, 138
  musical adaptations of, 616
  Verdi's adaptations of, 477, 480
*Shall We Dance* (film), 617, *623*
Shankar, Ravi, 655
Sharp, Cecil, 543
*Sharp Family's Boating Party on the Thames* (Zoffany), *312*
shawms, *52*, 81, 87, 141, 264
sheet music, 530, 598, 618, 620
*Sheherazade* (Rimsky-Korsakov), 511
Sheldonian Theatre (Oxford), *277*
Shelley, Percy Bysshe, 403
Sheng, Bright, 657, *657*–58
Sheridan, Richard Brinsley, 318
Shostakovich, Dmitri, 588, 589, *589*, 591–92
*Show Boat* (Kern), 615
Sibelius, Jean, 544–45, 559, 560
Siena, cathedral of, 15
sightsinging, 31, 45–46
Signol, Émile, *421*
*Silence* (Cage), 650
*Silver Apples of the Moon* (Subotnick), 641
*Silver Ladders* (Tower), 666
Silvestre, Israel, *224*
*Sinfonía India* (Chávez), 607
*Sinfonía romántica* (Chávez), 607
sinfonias, 254, 285, 331
*Sinfonietta* (Janáček), 544
singing
  attitudes toward, 3–4, 6, 27, 185
  bel canto, 471
  teachers of, 221
singing schools, 595
*Sing joy fully unto God* (Byrd), 152
singspiels, 322, 354, 357, 367–68, 369, 371, 464, 466
Six, Les, 565–66

Six Bagatelles (Webern), 558
*Six Fantasies on a Poem by Thomas Campion* (Lansky), 651
*64 Copper Squares* (Andre), 653
*Slåtter* (Grieg), 512
slavery, 164
*Sleeping Beauty, The* (Tchaikovsky), 454–55
*Smalltalk* (Lansky), 651
Smetana, Bedřich, 444, 458, 512
Smith, Bessie, 618, *618, 619*
Smithson, Harriet, 421, *421*
*Social Contract, The* (Rousseau), 274
socialism, 400, 610–11
socialist realism, 587–88, 591
Société Nationale de Musique, 513
Soler, Antonio, 331
Solidarity movement, 525
solmization, 45–46
*Solo e pensoso* (Marenzio), 134
Solomon, Maynard, 390
*Sombrero de tres picos, El* (Falla), 543
sonata da camera, 254
sonata da chiesa, 254, 256–57, 261, 286, 297, 312, 343
sonata form, 331–32, 336–37, 347–48, 366–67, 426, 447, 494, 582
*Sonata IV per il violino per sonar con due corde* (Marini), 219
*Sonata pian' e forte* (Gabrieli), 218
sonata-rondo form, 347, 367
sonatas. *See also* piano sonatas; trio sonatas; violin sonatas; violoncello sonatas
    Baroque, 218–19, 254–60, 294, 297, 312
    of Beethoven, 387, 391
    dance movements in, 210
    development of, 254
    eighteenth-century, 329–31, 333–35, 350–51
    ensemble, 255, 263
    of Hindemith, 586
    of Poulenc, 592
    trio, 254–55, 256–57, 259–60, 261
    *Turmsonaten*, 263
*Sonatas and Interludes* (Cage), 647
*Sonatas for Connoisseurs and Amateurs* (C. P. E. Bach), 278
*Sonate pathétique* (Beethoven), 361, 376–77
Sondheim, Stephen, 616
song cycles, 411, 421, 499–500, 510, 515, 551, 577, 635, 639
*Song of Hiawatha, The* (Longfellow), 459
Song of Songs, 102, 201
songs. *See also* lieder; *specific genres*
    American, 601, 602, 603–5, 635
    ancient Greek, 18, 19
    French, 47–49, 78–80, 514–15, 538, 540–41, 542, 566, 598
    Italian, 81
    mass, 587
    medieval Latin, 46–47
    medieval vernacular, 13, 17, 30, 31, 47–52, 78–80, 587

Renaissance vernacular, 91, 97, 101, 128–45, 149–50, 185–86
    Roman, 23
    spirituals, 599–600
*Songs without Words. See Lieder ohne Worte*
*Sonnambula, La* (Bellini), 473
sonority. *See* texture
Sophocles, 20, 183, 503
*Sound of Music, the* (Rodgers), 616
sound recordings, 530–31, 534, 574–75, 578, *580*, 610–11, 626, 629
source music, 617
Sousa, John Philip, 574, *596*, 597
*South Pacific* (Rodgers), 616
*Souvenir de Porto Rico* (Gottschalk), 600
Soviet Union, 522–23, 525, 573, 587–89, 591–92, 661
Spain
    colonies of, 164
    early chant repertories in, 28
    eighteenth-century, 273
    medieval, 11, 47, 52, 55
    Muslim conquest of, 34, *36*
    seventeenth-century, 164, 166, 171
Spanish Civil War, 522, 529
Spanish music
    colonial, 595
    eighteenth-century, 329–31
    French evocations of, 469, 542, 565
    Renaissance, 141, 156–58
    seventeenth-century, 195–96, 212
    twentieth-century, 543
spatial music, 44, 199, 608–9
Spaun, Joseph von, *415*
*Speculum musicae* (Jacques de Liège), 77
*Speech Songs* (Dodge), 651
*Spellbound* (film), 640
Spetner, Christoph, *204*
spinet, *207*
spirituals, 459, 599–600, 613, 623
*Sprechstimme*, 551, 554, 637
*sprezzatura*, 95, *130*
*Spring* Symphony (Schumann), 432
Squarcialupi, Antonio, 81, 105
Squarcialupi Codex, 81, *81*
*Stabat Mater* (Haydn), 351
*Stabat Mater* (Rossini), 490
*Stadtpfeifer*, 263
staff, musical, 46
Stalin, Joseph, 587, 589, 591
Stalmann, Johann Joseph, *342*
Stamitz, Johann, 332–33
*Ständchen* (Schubert), 414
*Stars and Stripes Forever, The* (Sousa), 597
Stein, Gertrude, *612*, 612–13
Steinbeck, John, 529, 533
Steiner, Max, 617
Stella, Frank, 653, *653*
*stile antico*, 199, 302
*stile concertato. See* concertato medium
*stile moderno*, 199, 204
Still, William Grant, 608, 611–12, *612*
Stockhausen, Karlheinz, 631, 636, 640–41

Stollen, 51
Stradivari, Antonio, 245, 255
Strassburg, Gottfried von, 485
Strauss, Richard, 495, 500–504, *501*, 519, 536, 546
    biography of, 501
    Debussy's influence on, 541
    influence of, 547, 549, 554, 577, 604, 617, 663
    Nazis and, 586
    operas of, 501, 503–4
    reception of, 559, 560
    Schoenberg and, 548
    tone poems of, 406, 424
*stravaganza, La* (Vivaldi), 285
Stravinsky, Igor, 534, 566–73, *567*, 576–77, 607
    biography of, 567
    block construction of, 566, 568, 570–71, 576, 577
    Boulanger and, 608
    Debussy's influence on, 541
    influence of, 577, 587, 607, 624, 631
    Ives and, 604
    Neoclassical works of, 567, 573, 663
    reception of, 592
    Rimsky-Korsakov's influence on, 511
    Russian period of, 568–72
    serial music of, 576–77, 638
Strayhorn, Billy, 625, 626
stream of consciousness, 529, 532
street cries, 137
Strepponi, Giuseppina, 476–77, *477*
stretto, 247
Striggio, Alessandro, 189–90
string quartets
    of Bartók, 579
    of Beach, 601
    of Beethoven, 375, 377–78, 383, 389, 391–92, 559
    of Berg, 556
    of Brahms, 449
    of Carter, 638
    of Crawford, 610
    of Dvořák, 459
    of Franck, 513–14
    of Haydn, 347–50, 361
    of Janáček, 544
    of Lutosławski, 650
    of Mozart, 361–62
    of Ravel, 542
    of Rochberg, 662–63
    of Schickele, 661, *554*, 662
    of Schubert, 420
    of Schumann, 432
    of Smetana, 512
    of Webern, 558
string quartet table, *350*
string quintets, 362, 417, 420
string sextets, 548
strophic form
    in arias, 186, 192, 194, 197, 223, 240
    in carols, 100

in *formes fixes*, 78
in hymns, 38
in lieder, 414
in medieval secular songs, 49, 50
in parlor songs, 597–98
in sixteenth-century hymns, 146
in sixteenth-century songs, 129, 137, 139, 141
strophic variations, 194, 195
Strozzi, Barbara, 197–98, *198*, 226
biography of, 198
Strozzi, Bernardo, *190*, 198
Strozzi, Giulio, 168, 198, 225
*Structures* (Boulez), 637
*Sturm und Drang*, 334–35, 345–46, 348
style brisé, 248–49, 251
style galant. *See* galant style
subdominant, 289
Subotnick, Morton, 641
substitute clausulae, 61–63, *63*, 64
*Suite bergamasque* (Debussy), 539
*Suite canadienne* (Champagne), 606
suites, Baroque, 210, 250–53, 263, 264–65, 286, 296–97, 298, 305, 311–12, 552, 553, 555, 658
*Suite Thursday* (Ellington), 626
Sullivan, Arthur, 318
*sul ponticello*, 391
Sumer, 6
*Sumer is icumen in*, 69–70, 100
*Summa theological* (Thomas Aquinas), 15
*Super te Ierusalem/Sed fulsit virginitas/Dominus*, 65–66, 67
*Surprise* Symphony (Haydn), 347
surrealism, 528, 637
suspensions
in Baroque music, 180, 205, 245, 257
chains of, 256, 258–59
in Renaissance music, 101, 115, 157, 160
Süssmayr, Franz Xaver, 372
sustain pedal, 638, 648
*Sus une fontayne* (Ciconia), 85
Svolinský, Karel, *544*
*Swan Lake* (Tchaikovsky), 454–55
*Swan of Tuonela, The* (Sibelius), 545
Sweden, 164
Sweelinck, Jan Pieterszoon, 149, 216, 245
Swieten, Gottfried van, 352, 361
swing, 622–23
*Swing Time* (film), 617
Switzerland, 273
Calvinism in, 149
Symbolism, 527, 531, 532, 538, 539, 540, 541, 542, 549, 551
*Symphoniae sacrae* (Schütz), 202, 204–5
*Symphonic Études* (Schumann), 391
*Symphonic Metamorphosis after Themes of Carl Maria von Weber* (Hindemith), 586
symphonic poems, 444
of Adams, 656
of Debussy, 539–40
of Honegger, 565

of Liszt, 442–44, 488
of Rachmaninov, 545
of Ravel, 542
of Schoenberg, 548
of Scriabin, 546
of Sibelius, 545
of Smetana, 512
of Strauss, 500–503, 577
*Symphonic Sketches* (Berlioz), *404, 408, 420–22, 423, 424, 430, 435, 460, 500*
*Symphonie pour un homme seul* (Henry), 640
symphonies. *See also specific composers*
of Beach, 601
of Beethoven, 272, 378–79, 380–82, 383–86, 389, 391, 394–95, 423, 435, 451, 453, 483, 494, 497
of Berlioz, 420–24
of Brahms, 451–53, 460
of Bruckner, 490, 494
of Chadwick, 600
of Corigliano, 661
of Cowell, 640
of Dvořák, 459
eighteenth-century, 331–33, 335
of Franck, 514
of Haydn, 272, 277, 342–47, 358
of Hindemith, 586
of Ives, 601, 603
of Liszt, 444
of Lutosławski, 650
of Mahler, 495, 497–99, 521
of Mendelssohn, 424–27
of Mozart, 358–59, 362–65
nineteenth-century, 410
of Prokofiev, 589
of Rachmaninov, 545
of Schnittke, 661
of Schubert, 415–16, 417, 460
of Schumann, 430, 431–32
of Shostakovich, 591–92
of Sibelius, 545
of Still, 612
of Tchaikovsky, 456
of Vaughan Williams, 543
of Webern, 558–59
of Zwilich, 658–59
*Symphonies of Wind Instruments* (Stravinsky), 573
Symphony in G Minor (Mozart), 363, 364
*Symphony "Mathis der Maler"* (Hindemith), 585
*Symphony of Psalms* (Stravinsky), 573, 576
*Symphony on a Hymn Tune* (Thomson), 613
Synclavier II, 653
syncopation, 84
in African American music, 597, 599
in jazz, 618–19, 625
in medieval music, 74–75, 76, 78
in ragtime, 613–14
in Renaissance music, 104
in seventeenth-century music, 191
in twentieth-century music, *651*

*Syntagma musicum* (Praetorius), 295
synthesizers, 641–42
Syria, 27, 34, 40

tabla, 609
*Tablatura nova* (Scheidt), 216
tablature, 140, 212, 216
tabors, 52
*Tabuh-tabuhan* (McPhee), 639
Tailleferre, Germaine, 565, *565*
*Take the A Train* (Strayhorn), 625
talea, 73, 76
*Tale of Two Cities, A* (Dickens), 407
Tallis, Thomas, 151, 152, 160, 543
tambourine, 207
Tan Dun, 531
*Tant que vivray* (Sermisy), 137, *138*
tape recorders, 531, 609, 640
Tasso, Torquato, 130, 192, 195, *196*
*Taverner* (Davies), 660
Taverner, John, 660
Tavernier, Jean le, *96*
Tchaikovsky, Piotr Il'yich, 439, 444, 453–56, 460, 511
ballets of, 454–55
biography of, 454
Dvořák and, 458
influence of, 582, 601
operas of, 455–56
symphonies of, 456
*teatro alla moda, Il* (Marcello), 324
*Technique of My Musical Language, The* (Messiaen), 631
technology. *See* science and technology
*Tecum principium*, 40
*Te Deum* (Berlioz), 489
*Tehillim* (Reich), 654
Telemann, Georg Philipp, 240, 290, 298
overture suites of, 265
Telemann, Paul, *467*
*Telemusik* (Stockhausen), 641
television, 531
temperament. *See* tuning and temperament
tempo
metric modulation and, 638
metronome markings and, 384–85
rubato, 434
*tempo d'attacco*, 478, 479
*tempo di mezzo*, 478, 479
tenors, 45
cantus firmus, 64, 67, 101
conductus, 69
in Masses, 106–8, 120
motet, 64–65, 68, 70, 73, 74–75, 76
in organum, 57, 62
tenson, 48
Teresa of Ávila, Saint, 200
Termen, Lev, 640
terrorism, 525, 657
tetrachords, 22, 133
descending, 173, 196–97, 201, 237
in twelve-tone music, 553

text declamation, 91, 97
  of Dunstable, 102
  of Landini, 82
  of Palestrina, 156
text setting
  ancient Greek, 19
  of Bach, 300
  of chant, 35, 37, 38
  in conductus, 69
  of Debussy, 538
  in fifteenth-century music, 116
  in Franco-Flemish music, 123, 124
  of Handel, 310
  of Machaut, 76, 78
  melismatic, 37, 38, 41, 43, 49, 56, 78, 82, 151
  in motets, 64, 65–66
  of Musorgsky, 508
  neumatic, 37
  in Notre Dame polyphony, 59, 61, 63
  in organum, 57
  of Puccini, 517
  of Schoenberg, 551
  of Schubert, 414
  of Schumann, 431
  in seventeenth-century French opera, 233
  in seventeenth-century Italian opera, 188, 189, 191
  in seventeenth-century music, 174–75, 186
  in sixteenth-century music, 130, 132–33, 134–35, 137, 139–40, 140, 153, 156, 159–60
  syllabic, 35, 37, 38, 41, 49, 69, 124, 129, 137
  in trecento madrigal, 82
  of Wolf, 495
texture. See also heterophony; homophony; monophony; polyphony
  in Anglican music, 151
  in Baroque music, 180, 181, 199, 210, 260, 310
  in Burgundian music, 102
  in eighteenth-century music, 317, 347–48
  four-voice, 108, 121
  in Franco-Flemish music, 122–23, 124–25
  in French chanson, 78, 86
  layered, 108, 566, 570–71, 576, 638, 653, 654
  in nineteenth-century music, 391, 472–73, 482
  in Renaissance music, 180
  in sixteenth-century madrigals, 129, 130, 132, 136–37, 139
  sound masses, 608–9, 642–43
  in trecento madrigals, 81–82
  of trio sonata, 254–55
Theater an der Wien (Vienna), 386
theaters and opera houses, public, 165,
166, 193, 193–94, 280, 306, 309, 368, 462, 463, 464, 485
thematic transformation, 442, 443–44, 502, 503, 513
theme and variations. See variations
theorbo, 180, 180, 466
theory, music
  ancient Greek, 6, 18, 19, 22, 24–25, 26, 55, 114, 115, 133
  eighteenth-century, 268, 287, 289, 290, 316–17, 364, 366
  medieval, 24–25, 31, 44–46, 54, 72, 73
  Renaissance, 114, 133
There Is a Fountain Filled with Blood (hymn), 604
theremin, 640, 663
Third Construction in Metal (Cage), 647
Third of May, The (Goya), 403
third-stream jazz, 636
Thirty Years' War, 164, 166, 204
Thomas Aquinas, Saint, 13, 14–15, 26, 55
Thomson, James, 352
Thomson, Virgil, 563, 608, 610, 612, 612–13
thorough bass. See basso continuo
Three Compositions for Piano (Babbitt), 642
Three Little Pieces for Cello and Piano, 558
Three Musicians (Master of the Female Half-Lengths), 138
Three Musicians (Velázquez), 173
Three Pieces in the Form of a Pear (Satie), 562
Three Places in New England (Ives), 603
Threni (Stravinsky), 577
Threnody: To the Victims of Hiroshima (Penderecki), 644–47, 649
through-composed form, 49, 130, 186, 195, 285, 414, 598
Thus Spake Zarathustra (Nietzsche), 406
Tides of Manaunaum, The (Cowell), 609
Till Eulenspiegels lustige Streiche (Strauss), 500–502
Timaeus (Plato), 14
timbre
  Cage's use of, 647
  Crumb's use of, 639
  Debussy's use of, 538, 539, 540
  Ellington's use of, 625
  Messiaen's use of, 633
  serialization of, 577
  Sibelius's use of, 545
  Stravinsky's use of, 566, 571–72
  twentieth-century explorations of, 563
  Webern's use of, 559
time (division of breve), 74
timelines
  America, 1900–1950, 627
  ancient and medieval worlds, 5
  Beethoven years, 393
  early Baroque period, 203
  early Classical period, 336
  early eighteenth century, 313
eighteenth century, 270
  end of the millennium, 665
  Europe, 1900–1950, 590
  European mainstream in early twentieth century, 556
  fifteenth-century England and Burgundy, 110
  fourteenth-century France and Italy, 86
  Greece and Rome, 25
  late eighteenth century, 372
  late Romanticism, 518
  Middle Ages, 51
  nineteenth century, 399
  nineteenth-century opera, 491
  ninth through thirteenth centuries, 69
  Reformation Era, 156
  Renaissance, 90, 123
  Romantic century, 457
  secular song in the Renaissance, 143
  seventeenth century, 167, 220, 241, 263
  twentieth century and today, 524
time signatures, 74
Timm, Reinhold, 210
Timotheus, 6
timpani, 419
Tinctoris, Johannes, 115
Tin Pan Alley, 598, 614
tintinnabuli, 659–60
Tippett, Michael, 636
'Tis the Gift to Be Simple (Shaker hymn), 611
toccatas, 175, 214–16, 245–46
  of Bach, 293, 294, 296
  rhythm in, 180
Tod und das Mädchen, Der (Schubert), 417
Tod und Verklärung (Strauss), 500
Tolstoy, Leo, 407
Tombeau de Couperin, Le (Ravel), 542
Tom Jones (Fielding), 272
Tomkins, Thomas, 152
tonality, major-minor, 181–82, 258–59, 546–47
tone clusters, 609, 644–46
tone poems. See symphonic poems
tonic, 289
tonus peregrinus, 39
Top Hat (film), 617
Torelli, Giuseppe, 224, 262, 283, 285
Tortoise, The: His Dreams and Journeys (Young), 653
Tosca (Puccini), 516, 516
Tosi, Pier Francesco, 326
total serialism, 637
To the Lighthouse (Woolf), 532
Tournier, Nicholas, 195
Tower, Joan, 666
Tracts, 56
traditional music. See folk music
Traetta, Tommaso, 325, 327
tragédie lyrique, 231, 327, 328, 355
Traité de l'harmonie (Rameau), 181, 287, 290, 421

transcriptions
    of American folk music, 610
    band, 597
    piano, 441–42
*Transformation* (Schuller), 636
*traviata, La* (Verdi), 476, 478, 479
*Treble Clef, The* (Picasso), 528
*Treemonisha* (Joplin), 613
*trionfo di Dori, Il* (anthology), 139
trio sonatas, 254–55, 256–57, 259–60, 261,
    296, 297, 312
tripla, 210
Triple Concerto (Tippett), 636
triplum, 62, 63, 64, 78
*Tristan und Isolde* (Wagner), 483, 484, 485,
    487–89, 492, 495, 537, 540–41,
    546, 548
*Tristis est anima mea* (Lasso), 159–60
*Triumphes of Oriana, The* (anthology), 139
*Triumph of Peace, The* (Lawes), 235
trivium, 25
trobairitz, 47–49
*Troilus and Criseyde* (Chaucer), 15
*Trois études de concert* (Liszt), 441
trombones, 87
tropes, 35, 42–43, 44, 54, 56
troubadours, 11, 31, 47–49, 50, 52, 55
*Troubled Island* (Still), 611–12
trouvères, 11, 31, 47–49, 50, 55, 78, 79
*trovatore, Il* (Verdi), 476, 478
trovatori, 81
Troy, François de, 249
*Troyens, Les* (Berlioz), 404, 421, 468–69
trumpet music, 262
trumpets, 52, 87, 207, 211, 265, 419
tuba, 419
tuning and temperament
    equal temperament, 294–96
    just intonation, 639
    Renaissance, 114
Tuotilo, 43
*Turandot* (Puccini), 465, 467, 516
*Turangalila-symphonie* (Messiaen), 631
Turin, Pierre, *117*
"Turkish" music, *307*, 347, 357, 367–68,
    394, 466–67
*Turmsonaten*, 263
Turner, J. M. W., *400*, 403, 407
tutti, 260
Tuvan throat-singing, 531
twelve-bar blues form, 618, 620, 623
twelve-tone music, 551–54, 556–59, 567,
    573, 576, 634, 636, 642. *See also*
    serialism; serial music
twentieth-century culture and politics,
    521–35
twentieth-century music, 531–666. *See also*
    serial music; *specific composers and*
    *genres*
    avant-garde, 572–73
    Chinese composers, 657–58

early-twentieth-century mainstream,
    536–60
English composers, 633–34, 636, 660
Estonian composers, 659–60
ethnic contexts, 577–83
French composers, 564–66, 630–33,
    636–37, 640, 641, 651
German composers, 583, 636, 640–41
Greek composers, 643–44
Italian composers, 637–38
Latin American composers, 606–7,
    635–36
North American composers, 602–6,
    607–13, 634–35, 636, 638–40,
    641–42, 647–66
Polish composers, 644–46
post-World War II, 630–66
Russian composers, 511–12, 545–46,
    566–73, 576–77, 587–92, 661, 663
stylistic diversification in, 534, 613
vernacular, 613–28, 652
twenty-first century, 525–26, 666
two-steps, 597
*2001: A Space Odyssey* (film), 502, 646
*Tzigane* (Ravel), 542, 565

*'ud*, 211–12
*Ulysses* (Joyce), 529, 532
*Unanswered Question, The* (Ives), 603
*Una voce poco fa* (Rossini), 471, 479
underscoring, 617
*Unfinished Symphony* (Schubert), 415
United Nations, 523
United States, 594–629
    colonial music of, 149, 594–96
    Dvořák in, 458, 507
    emergence as world power, 522, 523, 525
    Enlightenment thought and, 271
    folk music in, 610
    Italian opera in, 463
    jazz in, 534
    nineteenth-century immigrants to, 437,
      600
    nineteenth-century music in, 596–602
    twentieth-century immigrants to, 522,
      534, 567, 578, 583, 584, 586, 607,
      617, 629
    twentieth-century music in, 602–5,
      602–6, 607–13, 634–35, 636,
      638–40, 641–42, 647–66
    vernacular music in, 613–28, 652
United States Marine Band, 597
universities
    American, 600
    as patron, 636
    rise of, 12–13, 55
University of California at Los Angeles, 534
Ur, 6
*Utopia* (More), 95

Valéry, Paul, 527
*Valse, La* (Ravel), 542, 565

*Vanitas: Still Life with a Violin* (Claeszoon),
    150, *150*
*vanitas* paintings, 150
Van Loo, Charles-André (Carle), 288, *307*,
    *466*, 467
Varèse, Edgard, 541, 608–9, 611, 613, 641
variations. *See also* chorale variations;
    *romanesca*
    in Baroque music, 210–14, 294, 297
    of Beethoven, 389, 391
    in eighteenth-century music, 345,
      346–47, 350, 355–57
    in jazz, 621, 622
    nineteenth-century, 391, 447–48
    strophic, 194, 195
*Variations and Fugue on a Theme of Handel*
    (Brahms), 447–48
Variations for Orchestra (Schoenberg), 553
*Variations IV* (Cage), 649
*Variations on a Theme of Handel* (Brahms),
    391
*Variations on a Theme of Paganini* (Brahms),
    448
*Variations on Sunday School Tunes*
    (Thomson), 613
vaudeville (American), 614
vaudevilles (French), 321
Vaughan Williams, Ralph, 543–44, 546
Vauxhall Pleasure Gardens, 358, *358*
*Vedrò 'l mio sol* (Caccini), 182, *183*
Velasco, Domingo Antonio de, *329*
Velázquez, Diego, 171, *173*
Venice
    choir schools in, 95
    eighteenth-century, 279–85
    medieval, 11
    orchestras in, 260
    printing in, 118, 119
    public opera houses in, 166, 177, 193,
      193–94, 222, 223, 224–25, 280
    Saint Mark's church in, 132, 151, 177,
      190, 193, 199, 201, 202, 202, 217,
      *218*, 219, 280
Venturi, Robert, 660
*Venus and Adonis* (Blow), 236
*Vêpres siciliennes, Les* (Verdi), 477, 478
Verdi, Giuseppe, 402, *476*
    biography of, 476–77
    compositional approach of, 475–77
    French grand opera's influence on, 465
    nationalism and, 507
    operas of, 407, 462, 463, 467, 474–80,
      481, 484
    Requiem of, 478, 490
    style of, 477–78
verismo, 515–16
*Verklärte Nacht* (Schoenberg), 548
Verlaine, Paul, 527, 540
Vermeer, Jan, 171, 173, 252
Versailles, palace of, 175, *176*, 264
verse anthems, 152, 239
verse-refrain form, 598, 620

*Vers la flame* (Scriabin), 546, 547
Vespers, 32, 152, 299
*Vespers* (Monteverdi), 201
Viadana, Lodovico, 201
Vicentino, Nicola, 135, 151
*Victimae paschali laudes*, 43, 147
Victor Emmanuel II, king of Italy, 507
Victoria, queen of England, 425, 428
Victoria, Tomás Luis de, 156, 157–58
*vida*, 49
*Vida breve, La* (Falla), 543
*Viderunt omnes* (Gradual), 59, 66
*Viderunt omnes* (Léonin), 59–63
*Viderunt omnes* (Pérotin), 63
Vidman, Giovanni Paolo, 198
vielle, *72, 81,* 102
Vienna, 204, 269, 290, 339
    as cosmopolitan cultural center, 360,
        374, 493
    Italian opera in, 322, 324
    Mozart in, 357, 361–72
    oratorios in, 352–53
    public concerts in, 359, 410
    Saint Michael's Square in, 368
    symphonic composition in, 332–33
Vienna Philharmonic, 423
*Viennese Ball, The* (Gause), *455*
*Viennese Nights* (film), 617
Vietnam War, 523, 525
vihuela, 212
Villa-Lobos, Heitor, 606–7, *607*
villancicos, 129, 137, 141, 164, 595
villanellas, 130
Villon, François, 540
*Vingt-cinquième ordre* (Couperin), 286
Vingt-quatre Violons du Roi, 231, 233, 264
*Vingt regards sur l'Enfant-Jésus* (Messiaen),
    631
viola, 254
viola da gamba, 180, *198, 246*
viola da gamba music, 297
violin, 244, *254. 255*
violin concertos
    of Barber, 634
    of Beethoven, 388
    of Berg, 556–57
    of Mendelssohn, 426–27
    of Mozart, 357
    of Penderecki, 662
    of Schoenberg, 553
    of Sibelius, 545
    of Vivaldi, 283–84
violin music, 206
    Baroque, 219, 221, 254–60, 262
    idiomatic writing in, 257
violin sonatas
    of Bach, 297
    of Bartók, 579
    of Franck, 513–14
    of Ives, 603
    of Ravel, 542, 565
violoncello, *254*
    as continuo instrument, 180, 254

violoncello sonatas, 297, 638
viols, 140, *209, 211,* 216
virelai, 78–80, 82, 84, 85, 121
*Virga Jesse* (Bruckner), 490
Virgil, 421, 468
virginal, *160, 207, 213,* 252
virginalists, 213
*Vi ricorda, o boschi ombrosi* (Monteverdi),
    190
virtuosity
    in ancient Greek music, 6, 20
    Baroque, 206, 215, 221, 224, 245, 282,
        283, 293, 308–9
    in eighteenth-century music, 332–33,
        379
    in nineteenth-century music, 402, 434,
        435–36, 439–41, 444–46, 447,
        460, 479, 597, 600
    Renaissance, 131, 134, 139
    in Roman music, 23
    in twentieth-century music, 545, 578,
        626–28, 637–38
Visigothic chant, 28
Vitry, Philippe de. *See* Philippe de Vitry
Vivaldi, Antonio, 268, *281,* 281–85, *285*
    Bach influenced by, 293, 298
    biography of, 281
    concertos of, 262
    Corelli's influence on, 259
    influence of, 305, 313–14
vocal music. *See specific composers, genres,*
    *and types*
vocal ranges
    of Burgundian chansons, 102
    of chant melodies, 40
    of church modes, 45
    in Ockeghem's Masses, 117
    of Russian folk songs, 508
    of troubadour and trouvère songs, 49
Vogler, Georg Joseph, 379
Voltaire, 271, 274, 288
Voorhout, Johannes, *246*
Vos, Maerten de, *207*
*vox organalis,* 56
*vox principalis,* 56
*Voyage, The* (Glass), 655
*Voyager* spacecrafts, 303

*Wachet auf* (Buxtehude), 242
Wagenseil, Georg Christoph, 333
Wagner, Cosima Liszt, 440, 485
Wagner, Richard, *485*
    anti-Semitic remarks of, 489
    band transcriptions of music by, 597
    Beethoven's influence on, 438–39,
        460–61
    Beethoven viewed by, 483
    biography of, 484–85
    French grand opera's influence on, 465
    goals of, 482–83
    influence of, 459, 488–89, 492, 494,
        495, 512, 513, 537, 546, 547, 548,
        615, 617

    leitmotives of, 484–85, 487–88
    Liszt's influence on, 444
    music dramas of, 403, 462, 464, 479,
        482–89, 540–41
    Nazi cult of, 587
Wakeling, Donald R., 416n
waldhorn, 449
*Waldstein* Sonata (Beethoven), 387
Walker, Thomas, 322
Walsh, John, 306, 311
Walter, Johann, 148
Walther, Johann Jakob, 52
Walther von der Vogelweide, 51
waltzes, 432, 454, 456, 504, 551, 564–65, 597
*Wanderer, Der* (Schubert), 412, 414, 416
*Wanderer Fantasie* (Schubert), 416
*Wandern, Das* (Schubert), 414
*War and Peace* (Tolstoy), 407
*War Requiem* (Britten), 634
Washington, George, 272
*Waste Land, The* (Eliot), 529, 533
Waterloo, Battle of, 274
*Water Music* (Handel), 304, 312
Watteau, Antoine, 269, *269, 275,* 314
wax cylinders, 574
Webb, Daniel, 318
Weber, Carl Maria von, 389, *480*
    operas of, 462, 480, 482, 488
Webern, Anton von, 557–59, *558*
    influence of, 567, 636
    Schoenberg and, 548, 554
Webster, Ben, 625
*Wedding March* (Mendelssohn), 426
Weelkes, Thomas, 139–40, 152
Weill, Kurt, 584, 586, 592
Weimar, 291, 293–94
Weimar Republic, 522, 583
*Wellington's Victory* (Beethoven), 386
*Well-Tempered Clavier, The* (Bach). *See*
    *wohltemperirte Clavier, Das*
Wert, Giaches de, 134
Wesendonck, Mathilde, 485
*West End Blues* (Oliver), 620, 621
*West Side Story* (Bernstein), 616
*What if I never speede* (Dowland), *140*
*Where Is the Lady?* (film), 617
Whiteman, Paul, 622, 623
whole-tone scales, 511, 538, 631
Wieck, Clara. *see* Schumann, Clara Wieck
Wieck, Friedrich, 430, 445
Wiener, Jean, *565*
Wigand, Balthasar, *353*
Willaert, Adrian, 132, *151, 151,* 153, 157, 199
William IX, ninth duke of Aquitaine, 50
Willis, Thomas, 664
Wilson, Robert, 655
Wilson, Woodrow, 522
Winckelmann, Johann Joachim, 274, 275,
    276
wind instruments
    Baroque, 244, 264
    nineteenth-century improvements to,
        419

*Winterreise* (Schubert), 414–15, 435

Wittgenstein, Paul, 542

*Wizard of Oz, The* (film), 617

*Wohin?* (Schubert), 414

*wohltemperirte Clavier, Das* (Bach), 294–96, 302, 303, 361, 429, 432–33, 586

Wolf, Hugo, 494–95, 549, 598

Wollheim, Richard, 653

Wollner, Johann Anton, *430*

women musicians. *See also specific names*
    Baroque, 191–92, 194, 197–98, 226
    in convents, 43, 44
    eighteenth-century, 280–82, 306, 309, 324, 325
    nineteenth-century, 425, 436, 439, 444–46, 470, 476–77, 601
    Renaissance, 95–96, 131, 135
    twentieth-century, 496, 601, 609–10, 618, 658–59, 663–64, 666

women's liberation movement, 525

women's vocal ensembles, 131, 135, 191–92

Woolf, Virginia, 529, 532

word painting. *See* depictive music; text setting

work songs, 598

*World as Will and Representation, The* (Schopenhauer), 406, 483

World War I, 522, 607–8

World War II, 522

*Wozzeck* (Berg), 550

Wren, Christopher, *277*

Wright, Wilbur and Orville, 530, 532

*Württemberg* Sonatas (C. P. E. Bach), 333

*Wuthering Heights* (Brontë), 407


Xenakis, Iannis, 643–44


Yale University, 534, 600, 601, 602

*Yankee Doodle Boy, The* (Cohan), 615

Yonge, Nicholas, 118, 138–39

Young, La Monte, 653

Yugoslavia, 523

Zachow, Friedrich Wilhelm, 304

Zarlino, Gioseffo, 115, 133, 134, 151, 157, 174, 178

*Zauberflöte, Die* (Mozart), 272, 371, 464

Zelter, Carl Friedrich, 303

Zemlinsky, Alexander von, 548

Zen Buddhism, 647

Zoffany, Johann, *312, 351*

*Zoroastre* (Rameau), 288

Zweig, Stefan, 586

Zwilich, Ellen Taaffe, 658–59, *659*

Zwinger Palace (Dresden), *268*